Toward Benevolent Neutrality: Church, State, and the Supreme Court

(Third Edition)

by

Robert T. Miller
Baylor University

and

Ronald B. Flowers
Texas Christian University

MARKHAM PRESS FUND
Waco, Texas

TABLE OF CONTENTS

PREFACE TO THE THIRD EDITION

Religious freedom and separation of church and state have been embodied within the Constitution of the United States of America since the early days of the Republic. Although taken for granted by most twentieth-century Americans, these important constitutional guarantees were uncommon in the world of the late eighteenth century and are far from universal even today. The interpretation of the First Amendment's Free Exercise and Establishment Clauses is primarily a function of the judiciary, and the final word on First Amendment issues comes from the United States Supreme Court. The process of explaining the meanings and marking the boundaries of these constitutional provisions has been described and summarized by Chief Justice Burger in *Walz* v. *Tax Commission*:

> The general principle deducible from the First Amendment and all that has been said by the Court is this: that we will not tolerate either governmentally established religion or governmental interference with religion. Short of those expressly proscribed governmental acts there is room for play in the joints productive of a benevolent neutrality which will permit religious exercise to exist without sponsorship and without interference. (397 U.S. 664, 669)

As it has worked toward "benevolent neutrality," the Court has produced a body of fascinating literature that is of great value to those who seek to understand this important facet of American constitutional development. Although most Americans have strong sentiments about the Supreme Court, only a few persons have read many of its opinions. This volume presents virtually every Supreme Court decision concerning religious freedom and separation of church and state. It also features essays designed to assist readers in understanding the historical background and legal issues involved in each case. It is hoped that this book will meet a wide range of needs: those of members of the university community pursuing studies in political science, religion, history, or law; ministers, priests, rabbis, and other professionals in the field of religion; lawyers and judges; politicians and public administrators; writers and editors engaged in diverse areas of publication; and everyone who seeks deeper understanding of the Court's thinking on church-state issues affecting the lives of all Americans. Realizing that legal

specialists will have access to law libraries, cases have been edited in order to remove technical material. In this revised edition the cases are supplied with cross references to the appropriate page number in *United States Reports,* the official reporting service of the Federal Government for Supreme Court opinions. The points where page breaks occur are marked with the symbol ⊥ and the *United States Reports* page numbers appear in the margin. Obviously, recent cases not yet published in *United States Reports*, i.e. those which have a citation from the *Supreme Court Reporter* (such as 106 S.Ct. 1234) will not have cross references.

An introductory essay deals in historical fashion with the principal events leading to adoption of the First Amendment. Other parts of the volume are arranged topically. Two major sections deal with the Free Exercise Clause and the Establishment Clause. An essay precedes each of these sections and gives an historical overview describing legal principles employed in the interpretation of each clause and explaining how these principles developed. Other essays are designed to assist the reader by describing how the Court has dealt with constitutional issues and by outlining the chronological sequence in which cases arose and were decided.

Included in the final pages of the book are various aids to facilitate study of the case literature on American church-state relationships. First, Appendices A and B provide the texts of Thomas Jefferson's "A Bill for Establishing Religious Freedom" and James Madison's "Memorial and Remonstrance Against Religious Assessments." These historic documents figure prominently in the development of religious freedom in this country, and both are referred to repeatedly by the Court in its opinions.

Second, there is a glossary of legal terms. Although neither extensive nor comprehensive, the glossary does contain all technical legal terms appearing in this collection of cases.

Third, a bibliography lists many important books and articles that form part of the vast literature on church-state relations.

Fourth, the reader is provided with an alphabetical listing of cases that immediately relate to church-state issues cited in the opinions of the Court. Also included is a listing of cases decided at lower court levels. All the cases referred to in the introductory essays are included in the tables as well. Because many of the leading cases are frequently cited both in opinions and essays, full citations are given only at the end of the volume in order to conserve space and to provide a minimum of distraction for the reader. In introductory essays and in listings of cases, titles for opinions published in this volume are printed in CAPITAL LETTERS while other case titles are printed in *italics*.

Fifth, a table identifies opinions written by each of the Supreme Court justices in the sixty-nine cases edited and reprinted in this book. This tabulation is designed to facilitate tracing the church-state thought of each jurist without scanning the entire collection of opinions.

We acknowledge gratefully the assistance of several persons who have helped in producing this volume. Mrs. Patricia Bibb and Mrs. Nancy Stone, secretaries in the Department of Political Science at Baylor University gave of their typing skills while continuing to perform regular departmental duties with efficiency and good humor. Ms. Susan Kendrick, Assistant Law Librarian at the Baylor University School of Law, assisted us in our legal research with efficiency and unfailing patience. Mrs. Melanie McQuere and Mrs. Janet Burton, successive Academic Publications Coordinators for Baylor University Press, skillfully guided us through the technology used in the preparation of this edition and unfailingly provided encouragement and administrative assistance. Miss Kristie Harlson and Miss Kim Cornish, student assistants in the

Department of Religion-Studies at Texas Christian University, and Miss Cyndi Eggebrecht, editorial assistant at the Baylor University Press, rendered invaluable aid in typing, compiling the various tables, and proofreading. Finally, but far from least, wives and other family members provided needed encouragement and sacrificed "family times" so that the book could be completed on schedule. In scholarship, as in so many other areas of life, no one stands alone; thus, we express our appreciation to these persons who have helped in so many ways.

Ronald B. Flowers
Professor of Religion-Studies
Texas Christian University

Robert T. Miller
Professor of Political Science
Baylor University

This work is the nineteenth volume published by the Markham Press Fund of Baylor University Press, established in memory of Dr. L. N. and Princess Finch Markham of Longview, Texas, by their daughters, Mrs. R. Matt Dawson of Waco, Texas and Mrs. B. Reid Clanton of Longview, Texas.

Rufus B. Spain
Chairman, Markham Press Fund
of Baylor University Press

1 INTRODUCTION

The broad religious freedom that is today enjoyed and largely taken for granted in the United States is not part of our European heritage. This freedom is primarily native to these shores and is the evolutionary outcome of a distinctly American experience. In his classic treatise on the development of religious freedom in America, Sanford H. Cobb asserted that

> this revolutionary principle, declarative of the complete separation of Church from State, so startlingly in contrast with the principles which had dominated in the past—this pure Religious Liberty—may be confidently reckoned as of distinctly American origin. . . . Here, among all the benefits to mankind to which this soil has given rise, this pure religious liberty may be justly rated as the great gift of America to civilization and the world. . . . [1]

Although there were scattered advocates of religious toleration and even a few bold thinkers who argued for the inherent right of the individual to worship freely according to the dictates of conscience, the prevailing pattern in the Europe from which the early American colonists came was one of close cooperation between state and church in the maintenance of religious as well as political orthodoxy. Establishment was the order of the day: the state was the defender and sponsor of the church, and the church was a bulwark of the existing political order. Persecution of domestic dissenters and bloody foreign wars in the name of religion were frequent in the sixteenth and seventeenth centuries.

The exact part played by religion in the settlement of the English colonies in America is impossible to determine. In times past its role has perhaps been exaggerated. Undoubtedly there were a number of motives, and these were mixed. However, many individuals and congregations—Puritans, Quakers, Mennonites, Roman Catholics, Brethren (Dunkers)—did come in search of a "Zion in the wilderness" where they could practice their religious beliefs without fear of the persecution to which they had been subjected.

The missionary spirit also impelled some to make the hazardous voyage. Even those colonies not ordinarily associated with religion paid at least lip service to this objective. The royal charter of 1606, granted to the commercial corporation that colonized Virginia, emphasized a commitment to the propagation of the Christian faith to the aborigines "who yet live in Darkness and miserable Ignorance of the true Knowledge and Worship of God," and expressed the hope that in time those who went might "bring the Infidels and Savages, living in those parts, to human Civility, and to a settled and quiet government." [2]

While economic considerations may well have lurked behind the rhetoric, it is still significant that in practically every statement of purpose, appeal for settlers, and charter issued, missionary and other religious purposes were given a prominent position.

One should not assume, however, that all of those who appealed for religious tolerance and Christian love while undergoing persecution in their homeland became practitioners of those virtues when they came into authority in the new land. Too often their concept of religious freedom

---

[1] *The Rise of Religious Liberty in America: A History* (New York: Macmillan Co., 1902), p. 2. Despite its date of publication, this is still perhaps the most thorough and frequently cited single work on the history of the development of religious freedom from the early colonial period to the adoption of the first state constitutions. Another valuable study of the period is William W. Sweet, *Religion in Colonial America* (New York: Charles Scribner's Sons, 1942).

[2] Benjamin P. Poore, ed., *The Federal and State Constitutions, Colonial Charters, and Other Organic Laws of the United States*, 2 vols. (Washington, D.C.: Government Printing Office, 1878), 2:1888.

proved to mean freedom for their own particular beliefs and practices only, and they set out to reproduce the European model of establishment and oppression. The scene shifted but the scenario remained largely the same.

In Massachusetts Bay, Plymouth, Connecticut, and New Hampshire, Congregationalism was the established church. In North and South Carolina, as well as Virginia, the Church of England was the official church just as in the England from which most of the settlers came. New York, Maryland, and Georgia passed through various stages of establishment and disestablishment during the colonial period. The status of New Jersey is subject to considerable debate as to whether there was ever a formal establishment or whether it was simply an informal arrangement without benefit of legislative enactment. Only in William Penn's Pennsylvania and Delaware and in Roger Williams's Rhode Island was there never an established church.

The fate of dissenters in most of the early colonies was little different from what it would have been in England, except perhaps even more unpleasant. Such fellow Congregationalists as Roger Williams, Anne Hutchinson, and John Wheelwright were banished from Massachusetts because of their failure to conform to the prescribed orthodoxy of the dominant church leadership. Roman Catholics were forbidden to enter the colony under threat of death. Baptists and Quakers were frequently fined, imprisoned, whipped, and banished; at least four Quakers were executed. Settlement of Rhode Island, Connecticut, and New Hampshire can be attributed primarily to the intolerant actions of Massachusetts authorities. One of the supreme ironies of the entire colonial period occurred when in 1662 Charles II wrote the legislature of the Bay Colony criticizing that colony's officials for excessive acts of persecution against religious dissenters and demanding that Church of England worship be permitted. [3]

Though physical persecution was never as prevalent outside Massachusetts, the spirit of intolerance was likely just as strong in most other colonies as is evidenced by the repressive legislative acts and executive proclamations which sprinkle the early colonial records. Even the more secular southern colonies had repressive laws that were not infrequently enforced. For example, a considerable number of Quakers were arrested, fined, and ordered to leave Virginia under a law passed by that colony's legislature in 1663. A strange repetition of this repression occurred a hundred years later on the very eve of the Revolution.

During the years from 1768 to 1770, Baptists bore the brunt of this belated persecution for their refusal to comply with a requirement of licenses for meeting houses and for their outspoken criticism of the established church. At one point some thirty Baptist ministers were imprisoned, to the great anger of Patrick Henry, who rode fifty miles on horseback to make a successful, dramatic appearance on behalf of three defendants in a Spotsylvania County trial.

The colonies of Roger Williams and William Penn—and Maryland in its early years—were striking exceptions in a society that demanded religious conformity. These soon became havens for the religiously harassed of both the Old and New worlds. Penn and the Baltimores are rightly commended for their practice of toleration. Roger Williams, however, argued, not for mere toleration, but rather for complete religious freedom and disestablishment based on the natural rights of man as well as biblical authority.

Though Williams's concept of religious rights was far ahead of his day, the success of his "livelie experiment" inevitably had an effect outside Rhode Island. As persecution gradually subsided in all the colonies, a great variety of sects began to appear, spelling the eventual doom of any single established church. There was also a steadily growing number of persons without church affiliation who obviously had no taste for either persecution or establishment: William Warren Sweet has estimated that even in stern New England only one in eight persons was a church member by the end of the colonial era. [4]

In addition, many Deists began to come to positions of prominence and added their influence to that of Baptists, Presbyterians, Quakers, and other opponents of establishment and oppression.

By the time of the Revolution, conditions were ripe for enunciation of religious liberty and separation of church and state. Each colony had its own specific experiences, but there was now a common and growing feeling as to the desirability of incorporating in the new fundamental laws to be framed as states the more tolerant attitude which existed in the minds of the people, notwithstanding the severity of the codes under which they lived. The religious movement known as the Great Awakening, which swept the country just prior to the Revolution, resulted in new alignments. It placed great emphasis on individual conversion and thus tended to make church membership more a matter of personal decision and less a matter of family inheritance. It also produced church leaders who subsequently urged disestablishment and advocated religious freedom.

The war itself had a liberalizing and unifying effect on the country; it tended to submerge internal differences. Ideologically, thinking persons could not fail to see the inconsistency of the natural rights philosophy proclaimed on all sides and the practices of religious discrimination. More important, perhaps, was the necessity of making concessions to dissenting church members and the unchurched to ensure their cooperation in the war effort.

Between 1776 and 1780 all of the states except Rhode Island and Connecticut adopted new written constitutions. Seven of these Revolutionary state constitutions contained separate bills of rights, while the remainder had within them various sections guaranteeing individual liberties. The provisions that relate to religion point up both the advances made toward the achievement of complete freedom and the restrictions still present. Most of the documents expressed support for religious liberty;

---

[3] Cobb, *The Rise of Religious Liberty in America*, p. 224.

[4] Sweet, *Religion in Colonial America*, p. 229. Other scholars question the seeming significance of Sweet's statement on the ground that church membership in the colonial period was very strict and the aggregate of sympathizers and attenders of any given church was likely much more numerous than the actual membership.

half provided for separation of church and state. However, the liberty proclaimed, while broader than anywhere else in the world at that time, fell short of granting complete freedom and equality to all beliefs. For example, the Pennsylvania Constitution, though it declared the "unalienable right" of all to worship God "according to the dictates of their own consciences and understanding," required members of the State Assembly to profess belief in God and the divine inspiration of both the Old and New Testaments.

Though religious liberty, at least for Protestants, was guaranteed in these first state constitutions, the struggle for disestablishment proved long and bitter. The last vestiges of official establishment did not disappear until 1833, when Massachusetts finally adopted an amendment providing for separation. Even in Virginia, whose 1776 Declaration of Rights contained a stirring and comprehensive statement of religious freedom, supporters of the Episcopal Church fiercely resisted the combined efforts of Thomas Jefferson and James Madison to disestablish that church. Indeed, Jefferson was to record the struggle as the most severe contest in which he had ever been engaged.

In December 1776 the legislature passed a bill that exempted dissenters from supporting the established church. In June 1779, Jefferson presented his Bill for Establishing Religious Freedom (See Appendix A), but Virginia was not yet ready to take the final step. Session after session of the legislature passed without action, and in 1784 the forces of establishment counterattacked by introducing a bill providing for a general assessment for the teaching of religion. Madison, who assumed the primary role of leadership on Jefferson's departure to France, finally brought about the narrow defeat of the Assessment Bill by circulating his celebrated "Memorial and Remonstrance Against Religious Assessment" (See Appendix B). He then reintroduced Jefferson's bill for religious liberty; it became law in January 1786, the year before the Philadelphia Convention, at which Madison would come to be known as the "Father of the Constitution."

In view of all that had gone before, one might assume that those who in 1787 framed the federal Constitution would have devoted substantial time and attention to the issue of religion. Actually, there was remarkably little discussion of the question. A few days after the sessions began, Charles C. Pinckney submitted his draft of a proposed constitution providing that "the Legislature of the United States shall pass no law on the subject of religion. . . ." This draft was not accepted, but toward the end of the convention he submitted another more limited proposal which passed on 30 August. Ultimately, Pinckney's proposal became the last clause of Article VI, which provides that, while all state and national officers are bound by oath or affirmation to support the U.S. Constitution, "no religious test shall ever be required as a qualification to any office or public trust under the United States." Only Roger Sherman of Connecticut spoke against this single reference to religion in the original Constitution. He thought it unnecessary, "the prevailing liberality being a sufficient security against such tests."

In the state ratifying conventions there was some complaint because of the omission of any reference to God,

and in at least two conventions fear was expressed at the inclusion of Pinckney's "no test oath" clause. In Massachusetts, Major T. Lusk said balefully that he "shuddered at the idea that Roman Catholics, Papists, and Pagans might be introduced into office, and that Popery and the Inquisition may be established in America." [5]

The strongest and most persistent criticism of the Constitution during the entire ratification struggle, however, concerned the absence of a bill of rights containing a specific guarantee of religious liberty as well as other fundamental rights. From his diplomatic post in France, Jefferson wrote his friend Madison, "I will now add what I do not like. First the omission of a bill of rights providing clearly and without the aid of sophisms for freedom of religion. . . ." [6]

Supporters of the Constitution responded to the criticism by contending that the inclusion of a bill of rights was not only unnecessary but that, if included, it might prove dangerous to the rights of the people. The national government, they reasoned, was one of delegated authority only: it possessed no powers except those given it in the Constitution, and no such grant of power to impinge on the rights of individuals had been made. The danger of inclusion of a bill of rights lay in the fact that no listing of such rights could possibly be all-inclusive, and the inadvertent failure to include a particular right could be taken to mean that it had been intentionally omitted. As Alexander Hamilton warned in *Federalist* 84, such a bill of rights "would contain various exceptions to powers not granted; and on this very account, would afford a colorable pretext to claim more than was granted. For why declare that things shall not be done which there is no power to do?"

Notwithstanding the assurances that they gave, advocates of the Constitution respected the apprehensions of the people and committed themselves at various state conventions to work for adoption of a bill of rights by amendment when the new government was established. In his inaugural address, President Washington called for congressional response to the commitments made; and on 8 June 1789 Madison, now a congressman from Virginia, submitted a series of amendments prepared largely from those suggested by the ratifying conventions of his own and other states. Debate on the proposals was lengthy in both houses of Congress. Action was finally completed by the Senate on 25 September, and twelve amendments were submitted to the states for ratification. During the next two years, ten of the twelve proposals received requisite state legislative approval and were added to the Constitution by proclamation on 15 December 1791. Significantly, the First Amendment begins with restrictions concerning religion: "Congress shall make no law respecting an establishment of religion, or prohibiting the free exercise thereof. . . ." In this brief but emphatic statement the long and bitter struggle toward the goal of constitutionally protected freedom of religion was brought to fruition. Of these clauses, Justice Wiley Rutledge wrote

[5] Jonathan Elliot, ed., *The Debates in the Several State Conventions on the Adoption of the Federal Constitution,* 2d ed., 5 vols. (Philadelphia: J. P. Lippincott Company, 1891), 2:148.

[6] Julian P. Boyd, ed., *The Papers of Thomas Jefferson* (Princeton, N.J.: Princeton University Press, 1950-   ), 12:440.

in 1947 (EVERSON v. BOARD OF EDUCATION) (p. 461): "No provision of the Constitution is more closely tied to or given content by its generating history than the religious clause of the First Amendment. It is at once the refined product and the terse summation of that history." (330 U.S. 1, 33)

Important as the religious guarantee of the First Amendment was, however, the circle of protection drawn around the individual was not yet complete. Although the national government was thus denied any power to interfere with the free exercise of religion or to establish religion, such actions on the part of the states were not prohibited by the terms of the amendment.

By this time, to be sure, all of the states had either bills of rights or other specific constitutional provisions assuring religious freedom. These were strengthened as the states amended their original constitutions or adopted new ones. As has been noted, the last establishment provision was taken from a state constitution in 1833; and as new states applied for admission to the Union, Congress insisted on adequate constitutional guarantees of freedom of religion and separation. However, state judges sometimes failed to apply vigorously the protective guarantees of the state constitutions; and, because no federal question was involved, there was no recourse to the U.S. Supreme Court from their decisions.

In 1810 Chief Justice John Marshall suggested that the Court might be ready to extend the prohibitions of the federal Bill of Rights to the states when he said, "The Constitution of the United States contains what may be deemed a Bill of Rights for the people of each state." (*Fletcher* v. *Peck*, 6 Cranch 87, 138). But in 1833 the great chief justice removed any question as to the applicability of the Bill of Rights when he wrote: "These amendments contain no expression indicating an intention to apply them to the State governments. This Court cannot so apply them." (*Barron* v. *Baltimore*, 7 Peters 243, 250).

Eleven years later (*Permoli* v. *First Municipality of New Orleans*) the Court again rejected an opportunity to expand its jurisdiction when it held specifically with respect to the free exercise clause of the First Amendment: "The Constitution makes no provision for protecting the citizens of the respective States in their religious liberties; this is left to the State constitutions and laws; nor is there any inhibition imposed by the Constitution of the United States in this respect on the States." (3 How. 589, 609)

Here the question rested until 1868 when the Fourteenth Amendment, which did unquestionably apply to the states, was adopted. This amendment forbids the states to "make or enforce any law which shall abridge the privileges or immunities of citizens of the United States" or to "deprive any person of life, liberty, or property without due process of law." Almost from the time of its adoption there were persons, sometimes members of the Court itself, who contended that the purpose, or at least the effect, of the amendment was to "incorporate," "absorb," or "nationalize" the federal Constitution's Bill of Rights, thus making its guarantees applicable to the states.

Historical evidence supporting this contention gives it some credence. However, the Court consistently rejected the argument in case after case until 1925. Then, in a landmark decision (*Gitlow* v. *New York*) involving questions of free speech and press, Justice Sanford opened the door to "selective incorporation" when he wrote, "for present purposes we may and do assume that freedom of speech and press—which are protected by the First Amendment from abridgement by Congress—are among the fundamental personal rights and 'liberties' protected by the due process clause of the Fourteenth Amendment from impairment by the states." (268 U.S. 666)

This assumption heralded what has become one of the most significant movements in American constitutional law. Although even today the argument made with great force by such justices as Black and Douglas for *in toto* "incorporation" has not been accepted by a majority of the Court, virtually all provisions of the Bill of Rights have been brought to bear against the states. In 1940 the free exercise clause of the First Amendment was specifically incorporated in one of the leading Jehovah's Witnesses cases, CANTWELL v. CONNECTICUT (p. 60). [7]

In EVERSON v. BOARD OF EDUCATION (p. 461), the 1947 New Jersey "Bus Case," the establishment clause was similarly applied to the states.

Thus the protective circle thrown around the rights of the individual by constitutional mandate was completed. Insofar as formal documents can guarantee religious liberty, it is secure. But as Anson Phelps Stokes has warned, "It is one thing to secure 'rights,' a very different thing to see that they are preserved inviolate." [8]

In a democracy, it is incumbent upon the people themselves and all agencies of government to see that these constitutional provisions are respected and implemented. Perhaps oddly, for a country which rightfully boasts of its democratic institutions, the United States has most often ultimately imposed this awesome, and generally onerous, burden upon its least "democratic" institution—the non-elective, life-tenured Supreme Court. As in no other country, the judiciary has been called upon to interpret and defend the constitutional pronouncements.

Constitutional clauses such as "free exercise" of religion and "establishment of religion" are obviously not self-defining. They are emotion-laden and susceptible to varied and contradictory definitions. The conflicts which result must sooner or later be submitted to a recognized arbiter if they are to be resolved peacefully. In large part because of its power to pass on the constitutionality of the action of other governmental agencies, this role of arbiter has fallen to the Supreme Court. Because the arbiter

---

[7] It is contended by some authorities, such as Henry J. Abraham, that the religious exercise guarantee was incorporated in 1934 in *Hamilton* v. *Regents of the University of California* (p. 118). In that case, Justice Cardozo said in a concurring opinion: "I assume for present purposes that the religious liberty protected by the First Amendment against invasion by the nation is protected by the Fourteenth Amendment against invasion by the states." (293 U.S. 245, 265) An excellent discussion of the entire incorporation movement is found in Chapter 3 of Abraham's *Freedom and the Court: Civil Rights and Liberties in the United States,* 4th ed. (New York: Oxford University Press, 1982). Chapter 6 is devoted in its entirety to the Court's interpretation of the religion clauses.

[8] *Church and State in the United States,* 3 vols. (New York: Harper & Brothers, Publishers, 1950), 1:593. This is the most definitive work on the entire topic of church and state in this country. A revised one-volume edition has been prepared by Leo Pfeffer: Anson Phelps Stokes and Leo Pfeffer, *Church and State in the United States* (New York: Harper & Row, 1964).

must defend as well as interpret constitutional guarantees of fundamental religious rights, it is fortunate that the Court has assumed the role. Though the idea is now generally accepted that the Court is a political as well as judicial institution, its more insulated position often permits members to make necessary but unpopular decisions that their more politically vulnerable associates in the other branches cannot, or think they cannot, afford.

Many of the decisions have been subjected to heavy criticism. Presidents have called for corrective actions; literally hundreds of constitutional amendments designed to modify the rulings have been introduced by incensed members of Congress. Still, compliance—though grudging—has eventually been forthcoming, likely because, as Justice Robert Jackson wrote in 1954: "The people have seemed to feel that the Supreme Court, whatever its defects, is still the most detached, dispassionate, and trustworthy custodian that our system affords for the translation of abstract into constitutional commands." [9]

More than their counterparts in the elective branches, the judges are expected to spell out and to justify their decisions in understandable written opinions not only for the benefit of the parties to the immediate litigation but also for the enlightenment and guidance of other judges, lawyers, and laymen of this and subsequent generations. Even those judges whose arguments do not at the moment prevail frequently feel an obligation to offer alternatives for the future in the form of dissenting and concurring opinions. These, too, make up the subject matter for the continuing national constitutional seminar that the educational function of the Court requires it to conduct. Speaking to the difficult problems inevitably involved in determining the proper relationship of religion and the state, these opinions (majority, dissenting, and concurring) form the substance of this volume.

---

[9] *The Supreme Court in the American System of Government* (Cambridge, Mass.: Harvard University Press, 1955), p. 23.

2 GOVERNMENT INTERVENTION IN CHURCH CONTROVERSIES

Clearly, the purpose of the First Amendment is to prevent domination of the state by the church or domination of the church by the state. Their co-existence, however, makes inevitable some degree of involvement in the internal affairs of each on the part of the other. One area in which the state has been drawn into church affairs—either by its own volition or at the invitation of church members—is that of disputes within churches.

While state courts have always disclaimed the right or intent to deal with purely ecclesiastical disputes, they have frequently accepted jurisdiction of cases involving church conflicts and schisms, particularly where property rights are involved. In the adjudication of property disputes, doctrinal issues cannot be completely avoided because they are often the cause of division.

In order to keep the doctrinal involvement to a minimum, the courts generally follow a rule which places churches in two categories: "congregational" and "hierarchical." For example, in disputes between factions of a local Congregational or Baptist church, majority decision of the autonomous congregation will ordinarily be accepted by the courts. The church polity of the Roman Catholic, Episcopal, and Presbyterian churches is such, however, that the members of a local church are under the control of a larger hierarchical church body with respect to doctrine and procedure. There, the courts will follow the decision of the proper institutional authority in the hierarchical structure. [1]

State courts have not, however, always been content to apply this self-restraining rule. Particularly in cases involving congregationally governed churches, they have sometimes felt that the momentary majority faction within the church has departed from the fundamental doctrines on which the church was founded to the extent that the minority group has greater entitlement to the property. Obviously, the ascertainment of the original doctrines and the nature and extent of the departure from those beliefs represents a substantial state intervention into doctrinal issues. [2]

The United States Supreme Court was confronted with an internal church dispute for the first time in 1872 in WATSON v. JONES (p.10). This litigation arose when the Walnut Street Presbyterian Church of Louisville, Kentucky, suffered a split in 1866 after the General Assembly of the Presbyterian Church in the U.S.A. issued instructions that persons who had voluntarily aided the rebellion or believed in slavery as a divine institution could not be received as church members until they agreed "to repent and forsake these sins." Although the General Assembly held the loyal faction to be the "true" Walnut Street Church, the Kentucky Supreme Court found in favor of the nonloyal group. Because members of the church lived in Indiana as well as Kentucky, the United States Circuit Court accepted jurisdiction on grounds of diverse citizenship and decided in favor of the loyal group. The case eventually reached the Supreme Court.

Justice Miller, speaking for the Court, rejected the use of the "departure-from-doctrine" guideline for federal courts. Because the Presbyterian Church had a hierarchical policy, and because the General Assembly was the highest church body, he held that it was binding on the Court to accept as final the findings of the assembly.

---

[1] Judges have found, however, that it is often not a simple task to determine the polity of a church body. Church organizations do not necessarily fit neatly into either designation, and a limited amount of judicial intervention cannot be avoided in seeking to ascertain the proper category. In 1983 the Fourth District Court of Illinois found that there was such conflicting evidence as to the polity of the Lutheran Church-Missouri Synod that it could not constitutionally make the detailed inquiry that was necessary to determine the polity of the synod because such an investigation would in itself be an unconstitutional inquiry. (*Grace Evangelical Lutheran Church of River Forest* v. *Lutheran Church-Missouri Synod*)[1983]. The U.S. Supreme Court denied certiorari the next year.

[2] An explanation of the "departure from doctrine" standard is found in Paul G. Kauper's "Church Autonomy and the First Amendment: the Presbyterian Church Case," in *Church and State: The Supreme Court and the First Amendment*, ed. Philip B. Kurland (Chicago: University of Chicago Press, 1975), pp. 69-76.

Miller expressed the opinion that ecclesiastical agencies are more competent than civil court judges in an area such as this. Further and more importantly, he declared that federal courts must refrain from consideration of religious doctrine and practice because "[t]he law knows no heresy, and is committed to the support of no dogma, the establishment of no sect." Although the *Watson* decision, as a rule of federal common law, was not binding on state courts, Justice Brennan was to say in 1969 that its language had a "clear constitutional ring." Its words, taken at face value, left no role for federal courts to review the determination of the appropriate church body.

Not until 1929 did the Court have occasion to return to the issue. In that year in *Gonzales* v. *Archbishop* the Court forcefully reiterated the *Watson* ruling as it accepted without question a decision of the Roman Catholic archbishop of the Philippines concerning a chaplain's appointment. However, Justice Brandeis in the majority opinion weakened the doctrine when he suggested that civil courts might give "marginal" review to decisions of church authorities to ascertain if there had been "fraud, collusion, or arbitrariness" on the part of the ecclesiastical agency.

In 1952 in KEDROFF v. SAINT NICHOLAS CATHEDRAL (p. 20), the Court converted its decision in *Watson*, as now qualified by Brandeis' suggestion in *Gonzales*, into a constitutional rule of law. Because by that time both religion clauses of the First Amendment had been applied to the states by incorporation, the case had particular significance for state courts. In *Kedroff*, the Court invalidated a New York statute designed to free the Russian Orthodox Church in America from Moscow's control and to give it title to Saint Nicholas Cathedral and other assets of the church in the United States. The Court held that the First Amendment prevented the legislature from determining which group was to control the cathedral. The decision of the Patriarch of Moscow, the appropriate hierarchical authority, was entitled to enforcement.

Because the New York Court of Appeals had earlier upheld the legislative act, the Supreme Court remanded the case for appropriate action. When the Court of Appeals undertook to reassert its original support of the independent churches, the Supreme Court reversed this judicial action in *Kreshik* v. *Saint Nicholas Cathedral* (1960), thus refusing to permit the judiciary to do what the legislature could not.

Notwithstanding Supreme Court decisions warning against judicial interpretation of religious doctrines in property disputes, state courts continued to resort to the "departure-from-doctrine" standard. Such had been the situation in PRESBYTERIAN CHURCH IN THE UNITED STATES v. MARY ELIZABETH BLUE HULL MEMORIAL PRESBYTERIAN CHURCH(1969) (p. 26). Here the dispute, which had caused two Georgia congregations to withdraw from the general church, was social and political as well as religious. The local congregations contended that they were entitled to keep the church property after the break. The General Assembly, they contended, had departed from doctrine and practice not only by the ordination of women and the use of literature which taught alien "neo-orthodoxy" but also by membership in the National Council of Churches of Christ and by the issuance of pronouncements on the Vietnam conflict. A jury decided that the General Assembly had indeed substantially departed from doctrine and could not therefore deprive the local churches of their property. The Supreme Court of Georgia affirmed this verdict, and the United States Supreme Court agreed to review on First Amendment grounds.

Written by Justice Brennan, the majority opinion reversed the Georgia court and categorically ruled out further use of the departure-from-doctrine standard in subsequent state court proceedings. The majority opinion agreed that a civil court is a proper forum for the settlement of property disputes, but held that the *Watson* rules means that courts may not interpret and weigh church doctrine as they resolve the disputes. Interpretation of religious tenets is reserved to the appropriate church authority. The Court further suggested that certain recognized "neutral principles of law" developed for settlement of secular property disputes could be applied to church disputes. The "neutral principles of law" concept was affirmed and further delineated the following year in *Mary and Virginia Eldership of the Churches of God* v. *The Church of God at Sharpsburg*(1970). Here, a *per curiam* opinion of the Court upheld the procedure followed by the Maryland Court of Appeals in settling a church property dispute by reliance upon such neutral principles as provisions of state laws governing the holding of property by religious corporations, language in deeds conveying the property to the local churches, the charters of the religious corporations, and appropriate provisions of the constitution of the General Eldership.

Justice Brennan, joined by Douglas and Marshall, wrote a concurring opinion in which he summed up three approaches that states might use in resolving church property disputes: the *Watson* hierarchical-congregational policy approach; the "neutral principles of law" doctrine; and the passage of special laws governing church property arrangements "in a manner that precludes state interference in doctrine."

In spite of the clear mandate against judicial interpretation of religious dogma, the qualification found in the *Gonzales* case (i.e., permitting marginal review of the decision of the ecclesiastical authority as to "fraud, collusion, and arbitrariness") survived even the Presbyterian Church case. It was to the *Gonzales* qualification of *Watson* that the Supreme Court addressed itself in 1976 in SERBIAN EASTERN ORTHODOX DIOCESE FOR THE UNITED STATES AND CANADA v. MILIVOJEVICH (p. 28). Here, by a seven-to-two vote, the Court overturned a ruling by the Illinois Supreme Court that the decision of the Mother Church of the Serbian Orthodox Church in Belgrade, Yugoslavia, had been "arbitrary" when thirteen years earlier it had suspended and defrocked Bishop Milivojevich. The Illinois court had ordered the bishop's reinstatement after a review of the action of the Mother Church had convinced the court that the prescribed church procedure had not been followed. Justice Brennan, for the majority, asserted that this detailed review, "under the umbrella of arbitrariness," had far exceeded the "minimal" review allowed civil courts. By substituting its interpretation of doctrine for that of the appropriate church authority, the Illinois court had violated the First and Fourteenth Amendments despite its contention that it had applied neutral principles of law. This narrowing of the "arbitrariness" rule further evidenced the increasing unwillingness of the Supreme Court to sustain encroachments of civil authorities upon matters of ecclesiastical custom or law.

However, to some who read the majority opinion, the Court seemed to be negating or severely restricting the neutral principles approach. In conflicting state court decisions that followed, some judges apparently were convinced that they must inevitably defer to the findings of the highest church tribunal of the church polity. Others believed that the church tribunal was the final authority only if the dispute could not be resolved through neutral principles of law relying on "objective, well-established concepts of trust and property law" such as the examination of state statutes, deeds, and local church charters, as well as the provisions of the general church constitution.

In 1979, in JONES v. WOLF, (1979) (p. 38), the Court was again confronted with a dispute over ownership of church property in a hierarchical structure after a schism had occurred in the Vineville Presbyterian Church in Macon, Georgia. Making an apparent effort to give guidance to civil courts and also to allow them greater latitude in resolving church property controversies, Justice Blackman, writing for the Court, expressly approved the neutral principles approach. He wrote:

> The primary advantages of the neutral-principles approach are that it is completely secular in operation, and yet flexible enough to accommodate all forms of religious organization and polity. The method relies exclusively on objective, well-established concepts of trust and property law familiar to lawyers and judges. It thereby promises to free civil courts completely from entanglement in questions of religious doctrine, polity, and practice. (443 U.S. 595, 603)

He admitted that this approach is not free of difficulty, and accepted the doctrine of judicial deference to the highest internal authority of a hierarchical polity as an acceptable alternative. Sternly warning against judicial inquiry into religious doctrine and practice, Blackmun emphasized once again the limited role of civil courts in church disputes. [3]

Joined by Chief Justice Burger and Justices Stewart and White, Justice Powell dissented. He argued for the rule of compulsory deference to the "authoritative resolution of the dispute within the church itself." [4]

Although disappointed litigants in intrachurch disputes have continued to appeal to the Supreme Court for redress

from lower court decisions, that body has not since Wolf accepted a case for oral hearing and decision. In 1984, in addition to the Grace Evangelical Lutheran Church case commented on earlier (p.7), the Court refused certiorari in an Ohio property dispute between a local A.M.E. congregation and the Mother Church. (Board of Trustees of the Allen Chapel A.M.E. Church v. Grogans).

During its 1985-1986 session, the Court refused to hear appeals from decisions involving disputes within a Church of Christ congregation in Florida and a Baptist church in Chesapeake, Virginia. [5]

However, in the Virginia case, which concerned removal of a pastor, Justice Marshall, joined by Justice Brennan, dissented from the denial of certiorari maintaining that the excessive involvement of the trial court in settling the dispute warranted review by the Court. The lower court had, Marshall complained, "imposed its own view of proper procedures on the congregation's decision-making," and had engaged in action which "threatens to erode the First Amendment's prohibitions against entanglement between religious and secular authority . . . " (106 S.Ct. 1802, 1803)

Controversy resulting from rulings of President Charles Stanley of the Southern Baptist Convention when serving as chair of the June 1985 annual convention in Dallas resulted in the filing of a suit against the convention and its executive committee by three "messengers" to that meeting in the United States District Court for the Northern District of Georgia. They contended that certain rulings by the chair had violated the bylaws of the Southern Baptist Convention. A parallel suit was filed in the Supreme Court of Fulton County, Georgia. In May 1986, U.S. District Judge Robert H. Hall held that the issue was a question of church governance and that for him to decide on the validity of the president's rulings would unconstitutionally involve the court in the internal affairs of the convention which would be "clearly impermissible." (Crowder v. Southern Baptist Convention and Executive Committee of the Southern Baptist Convention).

Another area in which the Court has encountered great difficulty is that of "defining" religion, and in recent years it has evidenced a strong desire to abandon the effort altogether. The Court's first and classic definition of religion was that undertaken by Justice Field in DAVIS v. BEASON (1890) (p. 52). Broad as it was, Field's definition was not extensive enough to encompass the practice of polygamy as a religious tenet.

State and federal courts have since been required to define religion in connection with such varied issues as conscientious objection to war, [6] tax exemption for reli-

---

[3] A similar suggestion was made by the Supreme Court in what was actually the first church-state case to come before it, Terrett v. Taylor (1815). The Virginia Legislature in 1801 had rescinded a 1776 statute that had confirmed to the Episcopal Church the property it held. Relying on the "maxims of eternal justice", rather than any specific provision of the Constitution, the Court voided the rescinding act. Church property, Justice Story held for the Court, enjoys the same protection as property of non-religious corporations.

[4] An excellent discussion of Jones v. Wolf and the entire problem of civil adjudication of church property disputes is found in Arlin M. Adams and William R. Hanlon, "Jones v. Wolf: Church Autonomy and the Religion Clauses of the First Amendment," University of Pennsylvania Law Review 128 (June 1980): 1291-1339.

---

[5] Black v. Wyche (1986) and Little v. First Baptist Church, Crestwood (1986).

[6] In the area of conscientious objection to war, the definition of religion, or "religious training and belief," came to be particularly important. See the discussion of such cases as UNITED STATES v. SEEGER (1965) and WELSH v. UNITED STATES (1970) at a later point (p. 104). Two helpful articles which specifically deal with the definition of religion in American constitutional law are, Timothy L. Hall, "The Sacred and the Profane: A First Amendment Definition of Religion," Texas Law Review 61(August 1982): 139-73; and Terry L. Slye, "Rendering Unto Caesar: Defining 'Religion' for Purposes of Administering Religion-Based Tax Exemptions," Harvard Journal of Law and Public Policy 6 (Summer 1983): 219-94.

gious organizations, the alleged use of religious claims to defraud, and the religious rights to be accorded Black Muslims, Buddhists, and members of the Church of the New Song when they are in prison.

Undoubtedly, one of the most unusual cases ever to reach the Supreme Court was UNITED STATES v. BALLARD(1944) (p. 15). This case involved the ''I Am'' movement, founded by Guy and Edna Ballard and their son Donald. The organizers of the movements were charged in a federal district court with having used the mails to defraud by representing that they could by virtue of supernatural powers, heal diseases and other ailments or injuries. All together, eighteen misrepresentations were listed in the twelve counts against them. The trial judge instructed members of the jury that they should not decide whether the religious claims made by the defendants were actually true but only whether the Ballards *believed* them to be true.

Justice Douglas, for the majority, upheld the action of the judge of the lower court. Determination of the truth of religious allegations, Douglas said, was beyond the power of any agency of the secular state even though those beliefs ''might seem incredible, if not preposterous, to most people.'' He quoted with approval the Court's words in *Watson* v. *Jones*: ''The law knows no heresy, and is committed to the support of no dogma, the establishment of no sect.'' Thus, the only issue for secular courts to determine was whether asserted religious belief was sincerely held.

Justice Jackson, in dissent, would have gone even further by also withholding from the jury the question of whether the Ballards believed their religious claims to be true; he would have dismissed the charges completely and ''have done with this business of judicially examining other people's faiths.'' The Court majority was not at the time willing to support it, but the Jackson position has been reflected in the Court's later reluctance to define religion, its refusal to insist on traditional definitions, and its greater tolerance toward ''self definition,'' if the beliefs of a group are ''sincere and meaningful'' to them. In 1953 Justice Douglas said for the majority in *Fowler* v. *Rhode Island*: ''it is no business of courts to say that what is a religious practice or activity for one group is not religion under the protection of the First Amendment.'' (345 U.S. 67,70)

Almost two decades later Chief Justice Burger in WISCONSIN v. YODER (p. 200) cautioned in less libertarian and conceivably ominous words that ''the very concept of ordered liberty precludes allowing every person to make his own standards on matters of conduct in which society as a whole has important interests.'' (406 U.S. 205, 215-216) Again, in THOMAS v. REVIEW BOARD OF INDIANA EMPLOYMENT SECURITY DIVISION, he observed that ''Only beliefs rooted in religion are protected by the Free Exercise Clause,'' and speculated that ''One can, of course, imagine an asserted claim so bizarre, so clearly nonreligious in motivation, as not to be entitled to protection under the Free Exercise Clause . . .'' (450 U.S. 707,714,715) Yet in that same 1981 case the Chief Justice essentially restated the philosophy expressed in *Ballard* when he said, ''religious beliefs need not be acceptable, logical, consistent, or comprehensible to others in order to merit First Amendment protection.''

WATSON v. JONES

13 Wallace 679
⊥ON APPEAL FROM THE CIRCUIT COURT ⌊680
OF THE UNITED STATES
FOR THE DISTRICT OF KENTUCKY
Argued March 10, 1871 — Decided April 15, 1872

[Editor's note: The following is a condensation of the facts of the case, as given in 13 Wallace.]⊥From ⌊690 the commencement of the late war of insurrection to its close, the General Assembly of the Presbyterian Church at its annual meetings expressed, in declaratory statements⊥ or resolutions, its sense of the ob- ⌊691 ligation of all good citizens to support the Federal Government in that struggle; and when, by the Proclamation of President Lincoln, emancipation of the slaves of the States in insurrection was announced, that body also expressed views favorable to emancipation, and adverse to the institution of slavery. At its meeting in Pittsburg, in May, 1865, instructions were given to the Presbyteries, the Board of Missions, and to the sessions of the Churches, that when any persons from the Southern States should make application for employment as missionaries, or for admission as members or ministers of churches, inquiry should be made as to their sentiments in regard to loyalty to the government, and on the subject of slavery; and if it was found that they had been guilty of voluntarily aiding the war of the rebellion, or held the doctrine announced by the large body of the churches in the insurrectionary States, which had organized a new General Assembly, that ''the system of negro slavery in the South is a divine institution, and that it is the peculiar mission of the Southern Church to conserve that institution'' they should be required to repent and forsake these sins before they could be received.

In the month of September, thereafter, the Presbytery of Louisville, under whose immediate jurisdiction was the Walnut Street Church, adopted and published in pamphlet form, what is called''a declaration and testimony against the erroneous and heretical doctrines and practices which have obtained and been propagated in the Presbyterian Church of the United States during the last five years.'' This declaration denounced, in the severest terms, the action of the General Assembly in the matters we have just mentioned, declared their intention to refuse to be governed by that action, and invited the co-operation of all the members of the Presbyterian Church who shared these sentiments of the declaration, in a conceded resistance to what they called the usurpation of authority by the Assembly.

The General Assembly of 1866 denounced the declaration and testimony, and declared that every Pres⊥bytery which refused to obey its order should ⌊692 be *ipso facto* dissolved and called to answer before the next General Assembly, giving the Louisville Presbytery an opportunity for repentance and conformity. The Louisville Presbytery divided, and the adherence of the declaration and testimony sought and obtained admission in 1868, into "The Presbyterian Church of the Confederate States" of which we have already spoken, as having several years previously withdrawn from the General Assembly of the United States, and set up a new organization.

In January, 1866, the congregation of the Walnut Street Church became divided, . . . each claiming to constitute the Church, although the issue as to membership was not distinctly made in the chancery suit of *Avery* v. *Watson*. Both parties at this time recognized the same superior church judicatories.

On the 19th June, 1866, the Synod of Kentucky became divided, the opposing parties in each claiming to constitute respectively the true Presbytery and the true Synod; each meanwhile recognizing and claiming to adhere to the same General Assembly. Of these contesting bodies, the appellants adhered to one; the appellees to another.

On the 1st of June, 1867, the Presbytery and Synod recognized by the appellants, were declared by the General Assembly to be "in no sense the true and lawful Synod and Presbytery, in connection with and under the care and authority of the General Assembly of the Presbyterian Church in the United States of America;" and were permanently excluded from connection with or representation in the Assembly; by the same resolution the Synod and Presbytery adhered to by appellees were declared to be the true and lawful Presbytery of Louisville, and Synod of Kentucky.

⊥693   ⊥ The Synod of Kentucky thus excluded by a resolution adopted the 28th June, 1867, declared "That, in its future action, it will be governed by this recognized sundering of all its relation to the aforesaid revolutionary body (the General Assembly) by the acts of that body itself." The Presbytery took substantially the same action.

In this final severance of Presbytery and Synod from the General Assembly, the appellants and appellees continued to adhere to both bodies at first recognized by them respectively. . . . The reader will now readily perceive, if he have not done so before, how in the earliest stages of this controversy it was found that a majority of the members of the Walnut Street Church concurred with the action of the General Assembly, while Watson and Gault, as ruling elders, and Fulton and Farley as trustees, constituting in each case a majority of the Session and of the trustees, with Mr. McElroy, the pastor, sympathized with the party of the declaration and testimony of the Louisville Presbytery. And how this led to efforts by each party to exclude the other from participation in the session of the Church and the use of the property ⊥ . . .

⊥694   The division and separation finally extended to the Presbytery of Louisville and the Synod of Kentucky. It is now complete and apparently irrecon-

cilable, and we are called upon to declare the beneficial uses of the church property in this condition of total separation between the members of what was once a united and harmonious congregation of the Presbyterian Church. . . .

⊥ *Mr. Justice MILLER* now delivered the opinion   ⊥713
of the court:

This case belongs to a class, happily rare in our courts, in which one of the parties to a controversy, essentially ecclesiastical, resorts to the judicial tribunals of the State for the maintenance of rights which the Church has refused to acknowledge, or found itself unable to protect. Much as such dissensions among the members of a religious society should ⊥ be regretted, a regret which is increased when passing from the control of the judicial and legislative bodies of the entire organization to which the society belongs, an appeal is made to the secular authority; the courts when so called on must perform their functions as in other cases.

Religious organizations come before us in the same attitude as other voluntary associations for benevolent or charitable purposes, and their rights of property, or of contract, are equally under the protection of the law, and the actions of their members subject to its restraints. Conscious as we may be of the excited feeling engendered by this controversy, and of the extent to which it has agitated the intelligent and pious body of Christians in whose bosom it originated, we enter upon its consideration with the satisfaction of knowing that the principles on which we are to decide so much of it as is proper for our decision, are those applicable alike to all of its class, and that our duty is the simple one of applying those principles to the facts before us. . . .

⊥ The questions which have come before the civil   ⊥722
courts concerning the rights to property held by ecclesiastical bodies, may, so far as we have been able to examine them, be profitably classified under three general heads, which of course do not include cases governed by considerations applicable to a church established and supported by law as the religion of the State.

1. The first of these is when the property which is the subject of controversy has been, by the deed or will of the donor, or other instrument by which the property is held, by the express terms of the instrument devoted to the teaching, support or spread of some specific form of religious doctrine or belief.

2. The second is when the property is held by a religious congregation which, by the nature of its organization, is strictly independent of other ecclesiastical associations, and so far as church government is concerned, owes no fealty or obligation to any higher authority.

3. The third is where the religious congregation or ecclesiastical body holding the property is but a subordinate member of some general church organization in which there are superior ecclesiastical

⌐723 tribunals with a general and ultimate power of control more or less complete in some su⊥preme judiciary over the whole membership of that general organization.

In regard to the first of these classes it seems hardly to admit of a rational doubt that an individual or an association of individuals may dedicate property by way of trust to the purpose of sustaining, supporting and propagating definite religious doctrines or principles, providing that in doing so they violate no law of morality, and give to the instrument by which their purpose is evidenced, the formalities which the laws require. And it would seem also to be the obvious duty of the court, in a case properly made, to see that the property so dedicated is not diverted from the trust which is thus attached to its use. So long as there are persons qualified within the meaning of the original dedication, and who are also willing to teach the doctrines or principles prescribed in the act of dedication, and so long as there is any one so interested in the execution of the trust as to have a standing in court, it must be that they can prevent the diversion of the property or fund to other and different uses. This is the general doctrine of courts of equity as to charities, and it seems equally applicable to ecclesiastical matters.

In such case, if the trust is confided to a religious congregation of the independent or congregational form of church government, it is not in the power of the majority of that congregation, however preponderant, by reason of a change of views on religious subjects, to carry the property so confided to them to the support of new and conflicting doctrine. A pious man building and dedicating a house of worship to the sole and exclusive use of those who believe in the doctrine of the Holy Trinity, and placing it under the control of a congregation which at the time holds the same belief, has a right to expect that the law will prevent that property from being used as a means of support and dissemination of the Unitarian doctrine, and as a place of Unitarian worship. Nor is the principle varied when the organization to which the trust is confided is of the second or associated form of church government. The protection which ⌐724 the law ⊥ throws around the trust is the same. And though the task may be a delicate one and a difficult one, it will be the duty of the court in such cases, when the doctrine to be taught or the form of worship to be used is definitely and clearly laid down, to inquire whether the party accused of violating the trust is holding or teaching a different doctrine, or using a form of worship which is so far variant as to defeat the declared objects of the trust. In the leading case on this subject, in the English courts, of the *Attorney-General* v. *Pearson*, Lord Eldon said: "I agree with the defendants that the religious belief of the parties is irrelevant to the matters in dispute, except so far as the King's Court is called upon to execute the trust." That was a case in which the trust deed declared the house which was erected under it, was for the worship and service of God. And though we may not be satisfied with the very artificial and elaborate argument by which the *Chancellor* arrives at the conclusion, that because any other view of the nature of the Godhead than the Trinitarian view was heresy by the laws of England, and any one giving expression to the Unitarian view was liable to be severely punished for heresy by the secular courts, at the time the deed was made, that the trust was, therefore, for Trinitarian worship, we may still accept the statement that the court has the right to enforce a trust clearly defined on such a subject. . . .

The second class of cases which we have described has reference to the case of a church of a strictly congregational or independent organization, governed solely within itself, either by a majority of its members or by such other local organism as it may have instituted for the purpose of ecclesiastical government; and to property held by such a church, either by way of purchase or donation, with no other specific ⊥ trust attached to it in the hands of the ⌐725 church than that it is for the use of that congregation as a religious society.

In such cases, where there is a schism which leads to a separation into distinct and conflicting bodies, the rights of such bodies to the use of the property must be determined by the ordinary principles which govern voluntary associations. If the principle of government in such cases is that the majority rules, then the numerical majority of members must control the right to the use of the property. If there be within the congregation officers in whom are vested the powers of such control, then those who adhere to the acknowledged organism by which the body is governed are entitled to the use of the property. The minority in choosing to separate themselves into a distinct body, and refusing to recognize the authority of the governing body, can claim no rights in the property from the fact that they had once been members of the Church or congregation. This ruling admits of no inquiry into the existing religious opinions of those who comprise the legal or regular organization; for, if such was permitted, a very small minority, without any officers of the church among them, might be found to be the only faithful supporters of the religious dogmas of the founders of the Church. There being no such trust imposed upon the property when purchased or given, the court will not imply one for the purpose of expelling from its use those who by regular succession and order constitute the Church, because they may have changed in some respect their views of religious truth. . . .

The case of *Smith* v. *Nelson* asserts this doctrine in a case where a legacy was left to the Associate Congregation of Ryegate, the interest whereof was to be annually paid to their minister forever. In that case, though the Ryegate ⊥ congregation was one of ⌐726 a number of Presbyterian churches connected with the general Presbyterian body at large, the court held that the only inquiry was whether the society still exists, and whether they have a minister chosen and appointed by the majority and regularly ordained over the society, agreeably to the usage of that denomination. And though we may be of opinion that the doctrine of that case needs modification, so far as it discusses the relation of the Ryegate congregation to the other judicatories of the body to which it belongs, it certainly lays down the principle correctly if that congregation was to be treated as an independent one.

But the third of these classes of cases is the one which is oftenest found in the courts, and which, with reference to the number and difficulty of the questions involved, and to other considerations, is every way the most important.

It is the case of property acquired in any of the usual modes for the general use of a religious congregation which is itself part of a large and general organization of some religous denomination, with which it is more or less intimately connected by religious views and ecclesiastical government.

The case before us is one of this class, growing out of a schism which has divided the congregation and its officers, and the presbytery and synod, and which appeals to the courts to determine the right to the use of the property so acquired. Here is no case of property devoted forever by the instrument which conveyed it, or by any specific declaration of its owner, to the support of any special religious dogmas, or any peculiar form of worship, but of property purchased for the use of a religious congregation, and so long as any existing religious congregation can be ascertained to be that congregation, or its regular and legitimate successor, it is entitled to the use of the property. In the case of an independent congregation we have pointed out how this identity, or succession, is to be ascertained but in cases of this character we are bound to look at the fact that the ⎿727 local congregation is itself but a member of a much ⊥ larger and more important religious organization, and is under its government and control, and is bound by its orders and judgments. There are in the Presbyterian system of ecclesiastical government, in regular succession, the Presbytery over the session or local church, the Synod over the Presbytery, and the General Assembly over all. These are called, in the language of the church organs, "judicatories," and they entertain appeals from the decisions of those below, and prescribe corrective measures in other cases.

In this class of cases we think the rule of action which should govern the civil courts, founded in a broad and sound view of the relations of church and state under our system of laws, and supported by a preponderating weight of judicial authority is, that, whenever the questions of discipline or of faith or ecclesiastical rule, custom or law have been decided by the highest of these church judicatories to which the matter has been carried, the legal tribunals must accept such decisions as final, and as binding on them, in their application to the case before them.

We concede at the outset that the doctrine of the English courts is otherwise. In the case of *The Attorney-General* v. *Pearson*, the proposition is laid down by Lord Eldon, and sustained by the peers, that it is the duty of the court in such cases to inquire and decide for itself, not only what was the nature and power of these church judicatories, but what is the true standard of faith in the church organization, and which of the contending parties before the court holds to this standard. And in the subsequent case of *Craigdallie* v. *Aikman* the same learned judge expresses in strong terms his chagrin that the Court of Sessions of Scotland, from which the case had been appealed, had failed to find on this latter subject, so that he could rest the case on religious belief, but had declared that in this matter there was no difference between the parties. And we can very well understand how the Lord Chancellor of England, who is, in his office, in a large sense, the head and representative of ⊥ the Established ⎿728 Church, who controls very largely the church patronage, and whose judicial decision may be, and not unfrequently is, invoked in cases of heresy and ecclesiastical contumacy, should feel, even in dealing with a dissenting church, but little delicacy in grappling with the most abstruse problems of theological controversy, or in construing the instruments which those churches have adopted as their rules of government, or inquiring into their customs and usages. The dissenting church in England is not a free church in the sense in which we apply the term in this country, and it was much less free in Lord Eldon's time than now. Laws then existed upon the statute book hampering the free exercise of religious belief and worship in many most oppressive forms, and although Protestant dissenters were less burdened than Catholics and Jews, there did not exist that full, entire and practical freedom for all forms of religious belief and practice which lies at the foundation of our political principles. . . .

In this country the full and free right to entertain any religious belief, to practice any religious principle, and to teach any religious doctrine which does not violate the laws of morality and property, and which does not infringe personal rights, is conceded to all. The law knows no heresy, and is committed to the support of no dogma, the establishment of no sect. The right to organize voluntary religious associations to assist in the expression and dissemination of ⊥ any religious doctrine, and to create tri- ⎿729 bunals for the decision of controverted questions of faith within the association, and for the ecclesiastical government of all the individual members, congregations and officers within the general association, is unquestioned. All who unite themselves to such a body do so with an implied consent to this government, and are bound to submit to it. But it would be a vain consent and would lead to the total subversion of such religious bodies, if any one aggrieved by one of their decisions could appeal to the secular courts and have them reversed. It is of the essence of these religious unions, and of their right to establish tribunals for the decision of questions arising among themselves, that those decisions should be binding in all cases of ecclesiastical cognizance, subject only to such appeals as the organism itself provides for.

Nor do we see that justice would be likely to be promoted by submitting those decisions to review in the ordinary judicial tribunals. Each of these large and influential bodies (to mention no others, let reference be had to the Protestant Episcopal, the Methodist Episcopal, and the Presbyterian churches) has a body of constitutional and ecclesiastical law of its own, to be found in their written organic laws, their books of discipline, in their collections of precedents, in their usage and customs, which as to each constitute a system of ecclesiastical law and religious faith that tasks the ablest minds to become familiar with. It is not to be supposed that the judges of the civil courts can be as competent in the ecclesiastical law and religious faith of all these bodies as the ablest men in each are in reference to their own. It would therefore be an appeal from the more learned tribunal in the law which should decide the case, to one which is less so.

We have said that these views are supported by the preponderant weight of authority in this country, and for the reasons which we have given, we do not think the doctrines of the English Chancery Court on this subject should have with us the influence which we would cheerfully accord to it on others. . . .

⊥730   ⊥ One of the most careful and well considered judgments on the subject is that of the Court of Appeals of South Carolina, delivered by *Chancellor* Johnson in the case of *Harmon* v. *Dreher.* The case turned upon certain rights in the use of the church property claimed by the minister notwithstanding his expulsion from the synod as one of its members. "He stands," says the Chancellor, "convicted of the offenses alleged against him, by the sentence of the spiritual body of which he was a voluntary member, and whose proceedings he had bound himself to abide. It belongs not to the civil power to enter into or review the proceedings of a spiritual court. The structure of our government has, for the preservation of civil liberty, rescued the temporal institutions from religious interference. On the other hand, it has secured religious liberty from the invasion of the

⊥731   civil authority. The judgments, therefore, of ⊥ religious associations, bearing on their own members, are not examinable here, and I am not to inquire whether the doctrines attributed to Mr. Dreher were held by him, or whether if held were anti-

Lutheran; or whether his conduct was or was not in accordance with the duty he owed to the synod or to his denomination. . . . When a civil right depends upon an ecclesiastical matter, it is the civil court and not the ecclesiastical which is to decide. But the civil tribunal tries the civil right, and no more, taking the ecclesiastical decisions out of which the civil right arises, as it finds them." The principle is re-affirmed by the same court in the *John's Island Church* case. . . .

⊥ In the case of *Watson* v. *Farris,* which was a   ⊥732 case growing out of the schism in the Presbyterian Church in Missouri in regard to this same declaration and testimony and the action of the General Assembly, that court held that whether a case was regularly or irregularly before the Assembly was a question which the Assembly had the right to determine for itself, and no civil court could reverse, modify, or impair its action in a matter of merely ecclesiastic concern.

We cannot better close this review of the authorities than in the language of the Supreme Court of Pennsylvania, in the case of *The German Reformed Church* v. *Seibert:* "The decisions of ecclesiastical courts, like every other judicial tribunal, are final, as they are the best judges of what constitutes an offense against the word of God and the discipline of the Church. Any other than those courts must be incompetent judges of matters of faith, discipline and doctrine; and civil courts, if they should be so unwise as to attempt to supervise their judgments on matters which come within their jurisdiction, would only involve themselves in a sea of uncertainty and doubt which would do anything but improve either religion or good morals."

In the subsequent case of *McGinnis* v. *Watson,* this principle is again applied and supported by a more elaborate argument.

The Court of Appeals of Kentucky, in the case of *Watson* v. *Avery* before referred to, while admitting the general principle here laid down, maintains that when a decision of an ecclesiastical tribunal is set up in the civil courts, it is always open to inquiry whether the tribunal acted within its jurisdiction, and if it did not, its decision could not be conclusive.

There is, perhaps, no word in legal terminology so frequently used as the word "jurisdiction," so capable of use in a general and vague sense, and which is used so often by men learned in the law without a due regard to precision in its application. As regards its use in the matters we have ⊥ been discussing, it may very well be conceded that if the General Assembly of the Presbyterian Church should undertake to try one of its members for murder, and punish him with death or imprisonment, its sentence would be of no validity in a civil court or anywhere else. Or if it should at the instance of one of its members entertain jurisdiction as between him and another member as to their individual right to property, real or personal, the right in no sense de-   ⊥733 pending on ecclesiaslical questions, its decision would be utterly disregarded by any civil court where it might be set up. And it might be said in a certain general sense very justly, that it was because the General Assembly had no jurisdiction of the case. Illustrations of this character could be multiplied in which the proposition of the Kentucky court would be strictly applicable.

But it is a very different thing where a subject-matter of dispute, strictly and purely ecclesiastical in its character,—a matter over which the civil courts exercise no jurisdiction,—a matter which concerns theological controversy, church discipline, ecclesiastical government, or the conformity of the members of the church to the standard of morals required of them,—becomes the subject of its action. It may be said here, also, that no jurisdiction has been conferred on the tribunal to try the particular case before it, or that, in its judgment, it exceeds the powers conferred upon it, or that the laws of the church do not authorize the particular form of proceeding adopted; and, in a sense often used in the courts, all of those may be said to be questions of jurisdiction. But it is easy to see that if the civil courts are to inquire into all these matters, the whole subject of the doctrinal theology, the usages and customs, the written laws, and fundamental organization of every religious denomination may, and must, be examined into with minuteness and care, for they would become, in almost every case, the *criteria* by which the validity of the ecclesiastical decree would be determined in the civil court. This principle would deprive these bodies of the right of construing their own church laws, would open the way to all the evils which we ⊥ have depicted as attendant upon the doctrine of Lord Eldon, and would, in effect, transfer to the civil courts where property rights were concerned the decision of all ecclesiastical questions.

⊥734

And this is precisely what the Court of Appeals of Kentucky did in the case of *Watson* v. *Avery*. Under cover of inquiries into the jurisdiction of the synod and presbytery over the congregation, and of the General Assembly over all, it went into an elaborate examination of the principles of Presbyterian church government, and ended by overruling the decision of the highest judicatory of that church in the United States, both on the jurisdiction and the merits; and, substituting its own judgment for that of the ecclesiastical court, decided that ruling elders, declared to be such by that tribunal, are not such, and must not be recognized by the congregation, though four-fifths of its members believe in the judgment of the Assembly and desired to conform to its decree.

But we need pursue this subject no further. Whatever may have been the case before the Kentucky court, the appellants in the case presented to us have separated themselves wholly from the church organization to which they belonged when this controversy commenced. They now deny its authority, denounce its action, and refuse to abide by its judgments. They have first erected themselves into a new organization, and have since joined themselves to another totally different, if not hostile, to the one to which they belonged when the difficulty first began. Under any of the decisions which we have examined, the appellants, in their present position, have no right to the property, or to the use of it, which is the subject of this suit.

The novelty of the questions presented to this court for the first time, their intrinsic importance and far-reaching influence, and the knowledge that the schism in which the case originated has divided the Presbyterian churches throughout Kentucky and Missouri, have seemed to us to justify the careful and laborious examination and discussion which we ⊥ have made of the principles which should govern the case. For the same reasons we have held it under advisement for a year; not uninfluenced by the hope, that since the civil commotion, which evidently lay at the foundation of the trouble, has passed away, that charity, which is so large an element in the faith of both parties, and which, by one of the apostles of that religion, is said to be the greatest of all the Christian virtues, would have brought about a reconciliation. But we have been disappointed. It is not for us to determine or apportion the moral responsibility which attaches to the parties of this result. We can only pronounce the judgment of the law as applicable to the case presented to us, and that requires us to affirm the decree of the Circuit Court as it stands.

⊥735

DECREE AFFIRMED.

UNITED STATES v. BALLARD

322 U.S. 78
ON WRIT OF CERTIORARI TO THE UNITED STATES
CIRCUIT COURT OF APPEALS FOR THE
NINTH CIRCUIT
Argued March 3 and 6, 1944 — Decided April 24, 1944

⊥ *Mr. Justice DOUGLAS* delivered the opinion of the Court:

⊥79

Respondents were indicted and convicted for using, and conspiring to use, the mails to defraud. The indictment was in twelve counts. It charged a scheme to defraud by organizing and promoting the I Am movement through the use of the mails. The charge was that certain designated corporations were formed, literature distributed and sold, funds solicited, and memberships in the I Am movement sought "by means of false and fraudulent representations, pretenses and promises." The false representations charged were eighteen in number. It is sufficient at this point to say that they covered respondents' alleged religious doctrines or beliefs. They were all set forth in the first count. The following are representative:

that Guy W. Ballard, now deceased, alias Saint Germain, Jesus, George Washington, and Godfre Ray King, had been selected and thereby designated by the alleged "ascertained masters," Saint Germain, as a divine messenger; and that the words of "ascended masters" and the words of the alleged divine entity, Saint Germain, would be transmitted to mankind through the medium of the said Guy W. Ballard;

that Guy W. Ballard, during his lifetime, and Edna W. Ballard, and Donald Ballard, by reason of their alleged high spiritual attainments and righteous conduct, had been selected as divine messengers through which the words of the alleged "ascended masters," ⌐80 in⊥cluding the alleged Saint Germain, would be communicated to mankind under the teachings commonly known as the "I Am" movement;

that Guy W. Ballard, during his lifetime, and Edna W. Ballard and Donald Ballard had, by reason of supernatural attainments, the power to heal persons of ailments and diseases and to make well persons afflicted with any diseases, injuries, or ailments, and did falsely represent to persons intended to be defrauded that the three designated persons had the ability and power to cure persons of those diseases normally classified as curable and also of diseases which are ordinarily classified by the medical profession as being incurable diseases; and did further represent that the three designated persons had in fact cured either by the activity of one, either, or all of said persons, hundreds of persons afflicted with diseases and ailments;

Each of the representations enumerated in the indictment was followed by the charge that respondents "well knew" it was false. After enumerating the eighteen misrepresentations the indictment also alleged:

At the time of making all of the afore-alleged representations by the defendants, and each of them, the defendants, and each of them, well knew that all of said aforementioned representations were false and untrue and were made with the intention on the part of the defendants, and each of them, to cheat, wrong, and defraud persons intended to be defrauded, and to obtain from persons intended to be defrauded by the defendants, money, property, and other things of value and to convert the same to the use and the benefit of the defendants, and each of them;

The indictment contained twelve counts, one of which charged a conspiracy to defraud. The first count set forth all of the eighteen representations, as we have said. Each of the other counts incorporated and realleged all of them and added no additional ones. There was a demurrer and a motion to quash each of which asserted among other things that the ⌐81 indictment attacked the religious beliefs ⊥of respondents and sought to restrict the free exercise of

their religion in violation of the Constitution of the United States. These motions were denied by the District Court. Early in the trial, however, objections were raised to the admission of certain evidence concerning respondents' religious beliefs. The court conferred with counsel in absence of the jury and with the acquiescence of counsel for the United States and for respondents confined the issues on this phase of the case to the question of the good faith of respondents. At the request of counsel for both sides the court advised the jury of that action in the following language:

Now gentlemen, here is the issue in this case:

First, the defendants in this case made certain representations of belief in a divinity and in a supernatural power. Some of the teachings of the defendants, representations, might seem extremely improbable to a great many people. For instance, the appearance of Jesus to dictate some of the works that we have had introduced in evidence, as testified to here at the opening transcription, or shaking hands with Jesus, to some people that might seem highly improbable. I point that out as one of the many statements.

Whether that is true or not is not the concern of this Court and is not the concern of the jury—and they are going to be told so in their instructions. As far as this Court sees the issue, it is immaterial what these defendants preached or wrote or taught in their classes. They are not going to be permitted to speculate on the actuality of the happening of those incidents. Now, I think I have made that as clear as I can. Therefore, the religious beliefs of these defendants cannot be an issue in this court.

The issue is: Did these defendants honestly and in good faith believe those things? If they did, they should be acquitted. I cannot make it any clearer than that.

If these defendants did not believe those things, they did not believe that Jesus came down and dic-
⊥tated, or that Saint Germain came down and dic-   ⌐82
tated, did not believe the things that they wrote, the things that they preached, but used the mail for the purpose of getting money, the jury should find them guilty. Therefore, gentlemen, religion cannot come into this case.

The District Court reiterated that admonition in the charge to the jury and made it abundantly clear. The following portion of the charge is typical:

The question of the defendants' good faith is the cardinal question in this case. You are not to be concerned with the religious belief of the defendants, or any of them. The jury will be called upon to pass on the question of whether or not the defendants honestly and in good faith believed the representations which are set forth in the indictment, and honestly and in good faith believed that the benefits which they represented would flow from their belief to those who embraced and followed their teachings, or whether these representations were mere pretenses without honest belief on the part of the defendants or any of them, and, were the representations made for the purpose of procuring money, and were the mails used for this purpose.

As we have said, counsel for the defense acquiesced in this treatment of the matter, made no objection to it during the trial, and indeed treated it without protest as the law of the case throughout the proceedings prior to the verdict. Respondents did not change their position before the District Court after verdict and contend that the truth or verity of their religious doctrines or beliefs should have been submitted to the jury. In their motion for new trial they did contend, however, that the withdrawal of these issues from the jury was error because it was in effect an amendment of the indictment. That was also one of their specifications of errors on appeal. And other errors urged on appeal included the overruling of the demurrer to the indictment and the motion to quash, and the⊥ disallowance of proof of the truth of respondents' religious doctrines or beliefs.

⌊83

The Circuit Court of Appeals reversed the judgment of conviction and granted a new trial, one judge dissenting. In its view the restriction of the issue in question to that of good faith was error. Its reason was that the scheme to defraud alleged in the indictment was that respondents made the eighteen alleged false representations; and that to prove that defendants devised the scheme described in the indictment "it was necessary to prove that they schemed to make some, at least, of the [eighteen] representations... and that some, at least, of the representations which they schemed to make were false." One judge thought that the ruling of the District Court was also error because it was "as prejudicial to the issue of honest belief as to the issue of purposeful misrepresentation."

The case is here on a petition for a writ of certiorari which we granted because of the importance of the question presented.

The United States contends that the District Court withdrew from the jury's consideration only the truth or falsity of those representations which related to religious concepts or beliefs and that there were representations charged in the indictment which fell within a different category. The argument is that this latter group of⊥ representations was submitted to the jury, that they were adequate to constitute an offense under the Act, and that they were supported by the requisite evidence. . . .

⌊84

A careful reading of the whole charge leads us to agree with the Circuit Court of Appeals on this phase of the case that the only issue submitted to the jury was the question as stated by the District Court, of respondents' "belief in their representations and promises."

The United States contends that respondents acquiesced in the withdrawal from the jury of the truth of their reli⊥gious doctrines or beliefs and that their

⌊85

consent bars them from insisting on a different course once that one turned out to be unsuccessful. Reliance for that position is sought in *Johnson* v. *United States*. That case stands for the proposition that, apart from situations involving an unfair trial, an appellate court will not grant a new trial to a defendant on the ground of improper introduction of evidence or improper comment by the prosecutor, where the defendant acquiesced in that course and made no objection to it. In fairness to respondents that principle cannot be applied here. The real objection of respondents is not that the truth of their religious doctrines or beliefs should have been submitted to the jury. Their demurrer and motion to quash made clear their position that that issue should be withheld from the jury on the basis of the First Amendment. Moreover, their position at all times was and still is that the court should have gone the whole way and withheld from the jury both that issue and the issue of their good faith. Their demurrer and motion to quash asked for dismissal of the entire indictment. Their argument that the truth of their religious doctrines or beliefs should have gone to the jury when the question of their good faith was submitted was and is merely an alternative argument. They never forsook their position that the indictment should have been dismissed and that none of it was good. Moreover, respondents' motion for new trial challenged the propriety of the action of the District Court in withdrawing from the jury the issue of the truth of their religious doctrines or beliefs without also withdrawing the question of their good faith. So we conclude that the rule of *Johnson* v. *United States*, supra, does not prevent respondents from reasserting now that no part of the indictment should have been submitted to the jury.

As we have noted, the Circuit Court of Appeals held that the question of the truth of the representations concerning⊥ respondents' religious doctrines or beliefs should have been submitted to the jury. And it remanded the case for a new trial. It may be that the Circuit Court of Appeals took that action because it did not think that the indictment could be properly construed as charging a scheme to defraud by means other than misrepresentations of respondents' religious doctrines or beliefs. Or that court may have concluded that the withdrawal of the issue of the truth of those religious doctrines or beliefs was unwarranted because it resulted in a substantial change in the character of the crime charged. But on whichever basis that court rested its actions, we do not agree that the truth or verity of respondents' religious doctrines or beliefs should have been submitted to the jury. Whatever this particular indictment might require, the First Amendment precludes such a course, as the United States seem to concede. "The law knows no heresy, and is committed to the support of no dogma, the establishment of no sect." *Watson* v. *Jones*. The

⌊86

First Amendment has a dual aspect. It not only "forestalls compulsion by law of the acceptance of any creed or the practice of any form of worship" but also "safeguards the free exercise of the chosen form of religion." *Cantwell* v. *Connecticut.* "Thus the Amendment embraces two concepts,—freedom to believe and freedom to act. The first is absolute but, in the nature of things, the second cannot be." Freedom of thought, which includes freedom of religious belief, is basic in a society of free men. *West Virginia State Bd. of Edu.* v. *Barnette.* It embraces the right to maintain theories of life and of death and of the hereafter which are rank heresy to followers of the orthodox faiths. Heresy trials are foreign to our Constitution. Men may believe what they cannot prove. They may not be put to the proof of their religious doctrines or beliefs. Religious experiences which are as real as life to some may be ⊥187⊥ incomprehensible to others. ⊥ Yet the fact that they may be beyond the ken of mortals does not mean that they can be made suspect before the law. Many take their gospel from the New Testament. But it would hardly be supposed that they could be tried before a jury charged with the duty of determining whether those teachings contained false representations. The miracles of the New Testament, the Divinity of Christ, life after death, the power of prayer are deep in the religious convictions of many. If one could be sent to jail because a jury in a hostile environment found those teachings false, little indeed would be left of religious freedom. The Fathers of the Constitution were not unaware of the varied and extreme views of religious sects, of the violence of disagreement among them, and of the lack of any one religious creed on which all men would agree. They fashioned a charter of government which envisaged the widest possible toleration of conflicting views. Man's relation to his God was made no concern of the state. He was granted the right to worship as he pleased and to answer to no man for the verity of his religious views. The religious views espoused by respondents might seem incredible, if not preposterous, to most people. But if those doctrines are subject to trial before a jury charged with finding their truth or falsity, then the same can be done with the religious beliefs of any sect. When the triers of fact undertake that task, they enter a forbidden domain. The First Amendment does not select any one group or any one type of religion for preferred treatment. It puts them all in that position. "With man's relations to his Maker and the obligations he may think they impose, and the manner in which an expression shall be made by him of his belief on those subjects, no interference can be permitted, provided always the laws of society, designed to secure its peace and prosperity, and the morals of its ⊥188⊥ people, are not interfered with." ⊥ So we conclude that the District Court ruled properly when it withheld from the jury all questions concerning the truth or falsity of the religious beliefs or doctrines of respondents. . . .

The judgment is reversed and the cause is remanded to the Circuit Court of Appeals for further proceedings in conformity to this opinion.

Reversed.

Mr. Chief Justice Stone, dissenting:

I am not prepared to say that the constitutional guaranty of freedom of religion affords immunity from criminal prosecution for the fraudulent procurement of money by false statements as to one's religious experiences, ⊥ more than it renders polyga- ⊥189⊥ my or libel immune from criminal prosecution. I cannot say that freedom of thought and worship includes freedom to procure money by making knowingly false statements about one's religious experiences. To go no further, if it were shown that a defendant in this case had asserted as a part of the alleged fraudulent scheme, that he had physically shaken hands with St. Germain in San Francisco on a day named, or that, as the indictment here alleges, by the exertion of his spiritual power he "had in fact cured . . . hundreds of persons afflicted with diseases and ailments," I should not doubt that it would be open to the Government to submit to the jury proof that he had never been in San Francisco and that no such cures had ever been effected. In any event I see no occasion for making any pronouncement on this subject in the present case.

The indictment charges respondents' use of the mails to defraud and a conspiracy to commit that offense by false statements of their religious experiences which had not in fact occurred. But it also charged that representations were "falsely and fraudulently" made, that respondents "well knew" that these representations were untrue, and that they were made by respondents with the intent to cheat and defraud those to whom they were made. With the assent of the prosecution and the defense the trial judge withdrew from the consideration of the jury the question whether the alleged religious experiences had in fact occurred, but submitted to the jury the single issue whether petitioners honestly believed that they had occurred, with the instruction that if the jury did not so find, then it should return a verdict of guilty. On this ⊥ issue the jury, on ample ⊥190⊥ evidence that respondents were without belief in the statements which they had made to their victims, found a verdict of guilty. The state of one's mind is a fact as capable of fraudulent misrepresentation as is one's physical condition or the state of his bodily health. There are no exceptions to the charge and no contention that the trial court rejected any relevant evidence which petitioners sought to offer. Since the indictment and the evidence support the conviction, it is irrelevant whether the religious experiences alleged did or did not in fact occur or whether that issue could or could not, for constitutional reasons, have been rightly submitted to the jury. Certainly none of respondents' constitutional rights are violated if they are prosecuted for the fraudulent procurement of money by false representations as to their beliefs, religious or otherwise.

Obviously if the question whether the religious experiences in fact occurred could not constitutionally have been submitted to the jury the court rightly withdrew it. If it could have been submitted I know of no reason why the parties could not, with the advice of counsel, assent to its withdrawal from the jury. And where, as here, the indictment charges two sets of false statements, each independently sufficient to sustain the conviction, I cannot accept respondents' contention that the withdrawal of one set and the submission of the other to the jury amounted to an amendment of the indictment. . . . ⊥

⌊92

On the issue submitted to the jury in this case it properly rendered a verdict of guilty. As no legally sufficient reason for disturbing it appears, I think the judgment below should be reversed and that of the District Court reinstated.

Mr. Justice ROBERTS and *Mr. Justice FRANK-FURTER* join in this opinion.

Mr. Justice JACKSON, dissenting:

I should say the defendants have done just that for which they are indicted. If I might agree to their conviction without creating a precedent, I cheerfully would do so. I can see in their teachings nothing but humbug, untainted by any trace of truth. But that does not dispose of the constitutional question whether misrepresentation of religious experience or belief is prosecutable; it rather emphasizes the danger of such prosecutions.

The Ballard family claimed miraculous communication with the spirit world and supernatural power to heal the sick. They were brought to trial for mail fraud on an indictment which charged that their representations were false and that they "well knew" they were false. The trial judge, obviously troubled, ruled that the court could not try whether the statements were untrue, but could inquire whether the defendants knew them to be untrue; and, if so, they could be convicted.

I find it difficult to reconcile this conclusion with our traditional religious freedoms.

In the first place, as a matter of either practice or philosophy I do not see how we can separate an issue as to what is believed from considerations as to what is believable. The most convincing proof that one believes his statements is to show that they have been ⌊93 true in his expe⊥rience. Likewise, that one knowingly falsified is best proved by showing that what he said happened never did happen. How can the Gov-

ernment prove these persons knew something to be false which it cannot prove to be false? If we try religious sincerity severed from religious verity, we isolate the dispute from the very considerations which in common experience provide its most reliable answer.

In the second place, any inquiry into intellectual honesty in religion raises profound psychological problems. William James, who wrote on these matters as a scientist, reminds us that it is not theology and ceremonies which keep religion going. Its vitality is in the religious experiences of many people. "If you ask what these experiences are, they are conversations with the unseen, voices and visions, responses to prayer, changes of heart, deliverances from fear, inflowings of help, assurances of support, whenever certain persons set their own internal attitude in certain appropriate ways." If religious liberty includes, as it must, the right to communicate such experiences to others, it seems to me an impossible task for juries to separate fancied ones from real ones, dreams from happenings, and hallucinations from true clairvoyance, Such experiences, like some tones and colors, have existence for one, but none at all for another. They cannot be verified to the minds of those whose field of consciousness does not include religious insight. When one comes to trial which turns on any aspect of religious belief or representation, unbelievers among his judges are likely not to understand and are almost certain not to believe him.

And then I do not know what degree of skepticism or disbelief in a religious representation amounts to actionable fraud. James points out that "Faith means belief⊥ in something concerning which doubt is still theoretically possible." Belief in what one may demonstrate to the senses is not faith. All schools of religious thought make enormous assumptions, generally on the basis of revelations authenticated by some sign or miracle. The appeal in such matters is to a very different plane of credulity than is invoked by representations of secular fact in commerce. Some who profess belief in the Bible read literally what others read as allegory or metaphor, as they read Aesop's fables. Religious symbolism is even used by some with the same mental reservations one has in teaching of Santa Claus or Uncle Sam or Easter bunnies or dispassionate judges. It is hard in matters so mystical to say how literally one is bound to believe the doctrine he teaches and even more difficult to say how far it is reliance upon a teacher's literal belief which induces followers to give him money.

⌊94

There appear to be persons—let us hope not many—who find refreshment and courage in the teachings of the "I Am" cult. If the members of the sect get comfort from the celestial guidance of their "Saint Germain," however doubtful it seems to me, it is hard to say that they do not get what they pay for. Scores of sects flourish in this country by teaching what to me are queer notions. It is plain that there is wide variety in American religious taste. The Ballards are not alone in catering to it with a pretty dubious product.

The chief wrong which false prophets do to their following is not financial. The collections aggregate a tempting total, but individual payments are not ruinous. I doubt if the vigilance of the law is equal to making money stick by overcredulous people. But the real harm is on the mental and spiritual plane. There are those who hunger and thirst after higher ⌞95 values which they feel wanting in⊥ their humdrum lives. They live in mental confusion or moral anarchy and seek vaguely for truth and beauty and moral support. When they are deluded and then disillusioned, cynicism and confusion follow. The wrong of these things, as I see it, is not in the money the victims part with half so much as in the mental and spiritual poison they get. But that is precisely the thing the Constitution put beyond the reach of the prosecutor, for the price of freedom of religion or of speech or of the press is that we must put up with, and even pay for, a good deal of rubbish.

Prosecutions of this character easily could degenerate into religious persecution. I do not doubt that religious leaders may be convicted of fraud for making false representations on matters other than faith or experience, as for example if one represents that funds are being used to construct a church when in fact they are being used for personal purposes. But that is not this case, which reaches into wholly dangerous ground. When does less than full belief in a professed credo become actionable fraud if one is soliciting gifts or legacies? Such inquiries may discomfort orthodox as well as unconventional religious teachers, for even the most regular of them are sometimes accused of taking their orthodoxy with a grain of salt.

I would dismiss the indictment and have done with this business of judicially examining other people's faiths.

KEDROFF v. SAINT NICHOLAS CATHEDRAL

344 U.S. 94
ON APPEAL FROM THE COURT OF APPEALS
OF NEW YORK
Argued February 1, 1952 — Reargued October 14, 1952
Decided November 24, 1952

⌞95   ⊥Mr. Justice REED delivered the opinion of the Court.

The right to the use and occupancy of a church in the city of New York is in dispute.

The right to such use is claimed by appellee, a corporation created in 1925 by an act of the Legislature of New York for the purpose of acquiring a cathedral for the Russian Orthodox Church in North America as a central place of worship and residence of the ruling archbishop "in accordance with the doctrine, discipline and worship of the Holy Apostolic Catholic Church of Eastern Confession as taught by the holy scriptures, holy tradition, seven ecumenical councils and holy fathers of that church."

The corporate right is sought to be enforced so that the head of the American churches, religiously affiliated with the Russian Orthodox Church, may occupy the ⊥Cathedral. At the present time that ⌞96 head is the Metropolitan of All America and Canada, the Archbishop of New York, Leonty, who like his predecessors was elected to his ecclesiastical office by a sobor of the American churches.

That claimed right of the corporation to use and occupancy for the archbishop chosen by the American churches is opposed by appellants who are in possession. Benjamin Fedchenkoff bases his right on an appointment in 1934 by the Supreme Church Authority of the Russian Orthodox Church, to wit, the Patriarch locum tenens of Moscow and all Russia and its Holy Synod, as Archbishop of the Archdiocese of North America and the Aleutian Islands. The other defendant-appellant is a priest of the Russian Orthodox Church, also acknowledging the spiritual and administrative control of the Moscow hierarchy.

Determination of the right to use and occupy Saint Nicholas depends upon whether the appointment of Ben⊥jamin by the Patriarch or the election ⌞97 of the Archbishop for North America by the convention of the American churches validly selects the ruling hierarch for the American churches. The Court of Appeals of New York, reversing the lower court, determined that the prelate appointed by the Moscow ecclesiastical authorities was not entitled to the Cathedral and directed the entry of a judgment that appellee corporation be reinvested with the possession and administration of the temporalities of St. Nicholas Cathedral. This determination was made on the authority of Article 5-C of the Religious Corporations Law of New York against appellants' contention that this New York statute, as construed, violated the Fourteenth Amendment to the Constitution of the United States.

Because of the constitutional questions thus generally involved, we noted probable jurisdiction, and, after argument and submission of the case last term, ordered reargument and requested counsel to include a discussion of whether the judgment might be sustained on state grounds. . . .

Article 5-C was added to the Religious Corporations Law of New York in 1945 and provided both for the incorporation and administration of Russian Orthodox churches. Clarifying amendments were added in 1948.⊥ The purpose of the article was to ⌞98 bring all the New York churches, formerly subject to the administrative jurisdiction of the Most Sacred Governing Synod in Moscow or the Patriarch of Moscow, into an administratively autonomous metropolitan district. That district was North American in area, created pursuant to resolutions adopted at a sobor held at Detroit in 1924. This declared autonomy was made effective by a further legislative requirement that all the churches formerly administratively subject to the Moscow synod and patri⊥archate should for the future be governed by the ecclesiastical body and hierarchy of the American metropolitan district. The foregoing analysis follows the interpretation of this article by the Court of Appeals of New York, an interpretation binding upon us.⊥

Article 5-C is challenged as invalid under the constitutional prohibition against interference with the exercise of religion. The appellants' contention, of course, is based on the theory that the principles of the First Amendment are made applicable to the states by the Fourteenth.

The Russian Orthodox Church is an autocephalous member of the Eastern Orthodox Greek Catholic Church. It sprang from the Church of Constantinople in the Tenth Century. The schism of 1054 A.D. split the Universal Church into those of the East and the West. Gradually self-government was assumed by the Russian Church until in the Sixteenth Century its autonomy was recognized and a Patriarch of Moscow appeared. For the next one hun⊥dred years the development of the church kept pace with the growth of power of the Czars but it increasingly became a part of the civil government—a state church. Throughout that period it also remained a hierarchical church with a Patriarch at its head, governed by the conventions or sobors called by him. However, from the time of Peter the Great until 1917 no sobor was held. No patriarch ruled or was chosen. During that time the church was governed by a Holy Synod, a group of ecclesiastics with a Chief Procurator representative of the government as a member.

Late in the Eighteenth Century the Russian Church entered the missionary field in the Aleutian Islands and Alaska. From there churches spread slowly down the Pacific Coast and later, with the Slavic immigration, to our eastern cities, particularly to Detroit, Cleveland, Chicago, Pittsburgh and New York. The character of the administrative unit changed with the years as is indicated by the changes in its name. In 1904 when a diocese of North America was created its first archbishop, Tikhon, shortly thereafter established himself in his seat at Saint Nicholas Cathedral. His appointment came from the Holy Synod of Russia as did those of his successors in order Platon and Evdokim. Under those appointments the successive archbishops occupied the Cathedral and residence of Saint Nicholas under the administrative authority of the Holy Synod.

In 1917 Archbishop Evdokim returned to Russia permanently. Early that year an All Russian Sobor

was held, the first since Peter the Great. It occurred during the interlude of political freedom following the fall of the Czar. A patriarch was elected and installed—Tikhon who had been the first American Archbishop. Uncertainties as to the succession to and administration of the American archbishopric made their appearance following this sobor and were largely induced ⊥by the almost contemporaneous political disturbances which culminated swiftly in the Bolshevik Revolution of 1917. The Russian Orthodox Church was drawn into this maelstrom. After a few years the Patriarch was imprisoned. There were suggestions of his counterrevolutionary activity. Church power was transferred, partly through a sobor considered by many as non-canonical to a Supreme Church Council. The declared reforms were said to have resulted in a "Living Church" or sometimes in a "Renovated Church." Circumstances and pressures changed. Patriarch Tikhon was released from prison and died in 1925. He named three bishops as locum tenens for the patriarchal throne. It was one of these, Sergius, who in 1933 appointed the appellant Benjamin as Archbishop. The Church was registered as a religious organization under Soviet law in 1927. Thereafter the Russian Church and the Russian State approached if not a reconciliation at least an adjustment which eventuated by 1943 in the election of Sergius, one of the bishops named as locum tenens by Tikhon, to the Patriarchate. The Living or Renovated Church, whether deemed a reformed, a schismatic or a new church, apparently withered away. After Sergius' death a new patriarch of the Russian Orthodox Church, Alexi, was chosen Patriarch in 1945 at Moscow at a sobor recognized by all parties to this litigation as a true sobor held in accordance with the church canons.

The Russian upheaval caused repercussions in the North American Diocese. That Diocese at the time of the Soviet Revolution recognized the spiritual and ad⊥ministrative control of Moscow. White Russians, both lay and clerical, found asylum in America from the revolutionary conflicts, strengthening the feeling of abhorrence of the secular attitude of the new Russian Government. The church members already here, immigrants and native-born, while habituated to look to Moscow for religious direction, were accustomed to our theory of separation between church and state. The Russian turmoil, the restraints on religious activities and the evolution of a new ecclesiastical hierarchy in the form of the "Living Church," deemed noncanonical or schismatic by most churchmen, made very difficult Russian administration of the American diocese. Furthermore, Patriarch Tikhon, on November 20, 1920, issued Decision No. 362 relating to church administration for troublesome times. This granted a large measure of autonomy, when the Russian ruling authority was unable to function, subject to "confirmation later to the Central Church Authority when it is reestablished." Naturally the growing number of American-born members of the Russian Church did not cling to a hierarchy identified with their country of remote origin with the same national feeling that moved their immigrant ancestors. These facts and forces generated in America a separatist movement.

That movement brought about the arrangements at the Detroit Sobor of 1924 for a temporary American administration of the church on account of the disturbances in Russia. This was followed by the declarations of autonomy of the successive sobors ⌐104 since that date, a spate⊥ of litigation concerning control of the various churches and occupancy of ecclesiastical positions, the New York legislation and this controversy. . . .

From those circumstances it seems clear that the Russian Orthodox Church was, until the Russian Revolution, an hierarchical church with unquestioned paramount jurisdiction in the governing body in Russia over the American Metropolitanate. Nothing indicates that either the Sacred Synod or the ⌐106 succeeding Patriarchs⊥ relinquished that authority or recognized the autonomy of the American church. The Court of Appeals decision proceeds, we understand, upon the same assumption. That court did consider "whether there exists in Moscow at the present time a true central organization of the Russian Orthodox Church capable of functioning as the head of a free international religious body." It concluded that this aspect of the controversy had not been sufficiently developed to justify a judgment upon that ground.

The Religious Corporations Law.—The New York Court of Appeals depended for its judgment, refusing recognition to Archbishop Benjamin, the appointee of the Moscow Hierarchy of the Russian Orthodox Church, upon Article 5-C of the Religious Corpora- ⌐107 tions Law. Certainly a legislature is⊥ free to act upon such information as it may have as to the necessity for legislation. But an enactment by a legislature cannot validate action which the Constitution prohibits, and we think that the statute here in question passes the constitutional limits. We conclude that Article 5-C undertook by its terms to transfer the control of the New York churches of the Russian Orthodox religion from the central governing hierarchy of the Russian Orthodox Church, the Patriarch of Moscow and the Holy Synod, to the governing authorities of the Russian Church in America, a church organization limited to the diocese of North America and the Aleutian Islands. This transfer takes place by virtue of the statute. Such a law violates the Fourteenth Amendment. It prohibits in this country the free exercise of religion. Legislation that regulates church administration, the operation of the churches, the appointment of clergy, by requiring conformity to church statutes "adopted at a general ⌐108 conven⊥tion (sobor) held in the City of New York on or about or between October fifth to eighth, nine-

teen hundred thirty-seven, and any amendments thereto," prohibits the free exercise of religion. Although this statute requires the New York churches to "in all other respects conform to, maintain and follow the faith, doctrine, ritual, communion, discipline, canon law, traditions and usages of the Eastern Confession (Eastern Orthodox or Greek Catholic Church)," their conformity is by legislative fiat and subject to legislative will. Should the state assert power to change the statute requiring comformity to ancient faith and doctrine to one establishing a different doctrine, the invalidity would be unmistakable.

Although § 5 of the Religious Corporations Law had long controlled religious corporations, the Court of Appeals held that its rule was not based on any constitutional requirement or prohibition. Since certain events of which the Court took judicial notice indicated to it that the Russian Government ex- ⌐109 ercised control over the cen⊥tral church authorities and that the American church acted to protect its pulpits and faith from such influences, the Court of Appeals felt that the Legislature's reasonable belief in such conditions justified the State in enacting a law to free the American group from infiltration of such atheistic or subversive influences.

This legislation, Art 5-C, in the view of the Court of Appeals, gave the use of the churches to the Russian Church in America on the theory that this church would most faithfully carry out the purposes of the religious trust. Thus dangers of political use of church pulpits would be minimized. Legislative power to punish subversive action cannot be doubted. If such action should be actually attempted by a cleric, neither his robe nor his pulpit would be a defense. But in this case no problem⊥ of punishment for the ⌐110 violation of law arises. There is no charge of subversive or hostile action by any ecclesiastic. Here there is a transfer by statute of control over churches. This violates our rule of separation between church and state. That conclusion results from the purpose, meaning and effect of the New York legislation stated above, considered in the light of the history and decisions considered below.

Hierarchical churches may be defined as those organized as a body with other churches having similar faith and doctrine with a common ruling convocation or ecclesiastical head. . . .

⊥ This controversy concerning the right to use St. ⌐115 Nicholas Cathedral is strictly a matter of ecclesiastical government, the power of the Supreme Church Authority of the Russian Orthodox Church to appoint the ruling hierarch of the archdiocese of North America. No one disputes that such power did lie in that Authority prior to the Russian Revolution.

Watson v. *Jones*, although it contains a reference to the relations of church and state under our system of laws, was decided without depending upon prohibition of state interference with the free exercise of religion. It was decided in 1871, before judicial recognition of the coercive power of the Fourteenth Amendment to protect the limitations of the First ⌐116 Amendment against state action. . . . ⌐ The opinion radiates, however, a spirit of freedom for religious organizations, an independence from secular control or manipulation, in short, power to decide for themselves, free from state interference, matters of church government as well as those of faith and doctrine. Freedom to select the clergy, where no improper methods of choice are proven, we think, must now be said to have federal constitutional protection as a part of the free exercise of religion against state ⌐117 interference. ⌐

Legislative Power.—The Court of Appeals of New York recognized, generally, the soundness of the philosophy of ecclesiastical control of church administration and polity but concluded that the exercise of that control was not free from legislative interference. That Court presented forcefully the argument supporting legislative power to act on its own knowledge of "the Soviet attitude toward things religious." It was said: "The Legislature realized that the North American church, in order to be free of Soviet interference in its affairs, had declared its temporary administrative autonomy in 1924, pursuant to the ukase of 1920, while retaining full *spiritual* communion with the patriarchate, and that there was a real danger that those properties and temporalities long enjoyed and used by the Russian Orthodox Church worshippers in this State would be taken from them by the representatives of the pa-⌐119 triarchate. . . ." ⌐

In upholding the validity of Article 5-C, the New York Court of Appeals apparently assumes Article 5-C does nothing more than permit the trustees of the Cathedral to use it for services consistent with the desires of the members of the Russian Church in America. Its reach goes far beyond that point. By fiat it displaces one church administrator with another. It passes the control of matters strictly ecclesiastical from one church authority to another. It thus intrudes for the benefit of one segment of a church the power of the state into the forbidden area of religious freedom contrary to the principles of the First Amendment. . . . New York's Article 5-C directly prohibits the free exercise of an ecclesiastical ⌐120 right, the Church's choice of its hierarchy. . . . ⌐

The record before us shows no schism over faith or doctrine between the Russian Church in America and the Russian Orthodox Church. It shows administrative control of the North American Diocese by the Supreme Church Authority of the Russian Orthodox Church, including the appointment of the ruling hierarch in North America from the foundation of the diocese until the Russian Revolution. We find nothing that indicates a relinquishment of this power by the Russian Orthodox Church.

Ours is a government which by the law of its being allows no statute, state or national, that prohibits the free exercise of religion. There are occasions when civil courts must draw lines between the responsibilities of church and state for the disposition or use of property. Even in those cases when the property right follows as an incident from decisions of the church custom or law on ecclesiastical⌐ is-   ⌐121 sues, the church rule controls. This under our Constitution necessarily follows in order that there may be free exercise of religion.

The decree of the Court of Appeals of New York must be reversed, and the case remanded to that court for such further action as it deems proper and not in contravention of this opinion.

It is so ordered.

Mr. Justice *FRANKFURTER*, concurring.

Let me put to one side the question whether in our day a legislature could, consistently with due process, displace the judicial process and decide a particular controversy affecting property so as to decree that A not B owns it or is entitled to its possession. Obviously a legislature would not have that power merely because the property belongs to a church.

In any event, this proceeding rests on a claim which cannot be determined without intervention by the State in a religious conflict. St. Nicholas Cathedral is not just a piece of real estate. It is no more that than is St. Patrick's Cathedral or the Cathedral of St. John the Divine. A cathedral is the seat and center of ecclesiastical authority. St. Nicholas Cathedral is an archiepiscopal see of one of the great religious organizations. What is at stake here is the power to exercise religious authority. That is the essence of this controversy. It is that even though the religious authority becomes manifest and is exerted through authority over the Cathedral as the outward symbol of a religious faith. ⌐   ⌐122

The judiciary has heeded, naturally enough, the menace to a society like ours of attempting to settle such religious struggles by state action. And so, when courts are called upon to adjudicate disputes which, though generated by conflicts of faith, may fairly be isolated as controversies over property and therefore within judicial competence, the authority of courts is in strict subordination to the ecclesiastical law of a particular church prior to a schism. This very limited right of resort to courts for determination of claims, civil in their nature, between rival parties among the communicants of a religious faith is merely one aspect of the duty of courts to enforce the rights of members in an association, temporal or religious, according to the laws of that association.

Legislatures have no such obligation to adjudicate and no such power. Assuredly they have none to settle conflicts of religious authority and none to define religious obedience. These aspects of spiritual differences constitute the heart of this controversy. The New York legislature decreed that one party to the dispute and not the other should control the common center of devotion. In doing so the legislature effectively authorized one party to give religious direction not only to its adherents but also to its opponents.

The arguments by which New York seeks to justify this inroad into the realm of faith are echoes of past attempts at secular intervention in religious conflicts. It is said that an impressive majority both of the laity and of the priesthood of the old local church now adhere to the party whose candidate New York enthroned, as it were, as Archbishop. Be that as it may, it is not a function of civil government under our constitutional system to assure rule to any religious body by a counting of heads.⊥ Our ⌐123 Constitution does assure that anyone is free to worship according to his conscience. A legislature is not free to vest in a schismatic head the means of acting under the authority of his old church, by affording him the religious power which the use and occupancy of St. Nicholas Cathedral make possible.

Again, it is argued that New York may protect itself from dangers attributed to submission by the mother church in Moscow to political authority. To reject this claim one does not have to indulge in the tendency of lawyers to carry arguments to the extreme of empty formal logic. Scattered throughout the country there are religious bodies with ties to various countries of a world in tension—tension due in part to shifting political affiliation and orientation. The consideration which permeates the court's opinion below would give each State the right to assess the circumstances in the foreign political entanglements of its religious bodies that make for danger to the State, and the power, resting on plausible legislative findings, to divest such bodies of spiritual authority and of the temporal property which symbolizes it.

Memory is short but it cannot be forgotten that in the State of New York there was strong feeling against the Tsarist regime at a time when the Russian Church was governed by a Procurator of the Tsar. And when Mussolini exacted the Lateran Agreement, argument was not wanting by those friendly to her claims that the Church of Rome was subjecting herself to political authority. The fear, perhaps not wholly groundless, that the loyalty of its ⌐124 citizens might be diluted by their adherence to a⊥ church entangled in antagonistic political interests, reappears in history as the ground for interference by civil government with religious attachments. Such fear readily leads to persecution of religious beliefs deemed dangerous to ruling political authority. It was on this basis, after all, that Bismarck sought to detach German Catholics from Rome by a series of laws not too different in purport from that before us today. The long, unedifying history of the contest between the secular state and the church is replete

with instances of attempts by civil gov⊥ernment to   ⌐125 exert pressure upon religious authority. Religious leaders have often made gestures of accommodation to such pressures. History also indicates that the vitality of great world religions survived such efforts. In any event, under our Constitution it is not open to the governments of this Union to reinforce the loyalty of their citizens by deciding who is the true exponent of their religion.

Finally, we are told that the present Moscow Patriarchate is not the true superior church of the American communicants. The vicissitudes of war and revolution which have beset the Moscow Patriarchate since 1917 are said to have resulted in a discontinuity which divests the present Patriarch of his authority over the American church. Both parties to the present controversy agree that the present Patriarch is the legitimately chosen holder of his office, and the account of the proceedings and pronouncements of the American schismatic group so indicate. Even were there doubt about this it is hard to see by what warrant the New York Legislature is free to substitute its own judgment as to the validity of Patriarch Alexi's claim and to disregard acknowledgment of the present Patriarch by his coequals in the Eastern Confession, the Patriarchs of Constantinople, Alexandria, Antioch, and Jerusalem, and by religious leaders throughout the world, including the present Archbishop of York.⊥   ⌐126

These considerations undermine the validity of the New York legislation in that it enters the domain of religious control barred to the States by the Fourteenth Amendment.

Mr. Justice BLACK agrees with this opinion on the basis of his view that the Fourteenth Amendment makes the First Amendment applicable to the States.

Mr. Justice DOUGLAS, while concurring in the opinion of the Court, also joins this opinion.

Mr. Justice JACKSON, dissenting . . .⊥   ⌐127

I greatly oversimplify the history of this controversy to indicate its nature rather than to prove its merits. This Cathedral was incorporated and built in the era of the Czar, under the regime of a state-ridden church in a church-ridden state. The Bolshevik Revolution may have freed the state from the grip of the church, but it did not free the church from the grip of the state. It only brought to the top a new master for a captive and submissive ecclesiastical establishment. By 1945, the Moscow patriarchy had been reformed and manned under the Soviet regime and it sought to re-establish in other countries its prerevolutionary control of church property and its sway over the minds of the religious.

As the Court's opinion points out, it demanded of the Russian Church in America, among other things, that it abstain "from political activities against the U.S.S.R." The American Cathedral group, along with others, refused submission to the representative of the Moscow Patriarch, whom it regarded as an arm of the Soviet Government. Thus, we have an ostensible religious schism with decided political overtones.

If the Fourteenth Amendment is to be interpreted to leave anything to the courts of a state to decide without our interference, I should suppose it would be claims to ownership or possession of real estate within its borders and the vexing technical questions pertaining to the creation, interpretation, termination, and enforcement of uses and trusts, even though they are for religious and charitable purposes. This controversy, I believe, is a matter for settlement by state law and not within the proper province of this Court. . . .⊥

⌐128

I

Nothing in New York law required this denomination to incorporate its Cathedral. The Religious Corporations Law of the State expressly recognizes unincorporated churches and undertakes no regulation of them or their affairs. But this denomination wanted the advantages of a corporate charter for its Cathedral, to obtain immunity from personal liability and other benefits. This statute does not interfere with religious freedom but furthers it. If they elect to come under it, the statute makes separate provision for each of many denominations with corporate controls appropriate to its own ecclesiastical order. When it sought the privilege of incorporation under the New York law applicable to its denomination, it seems to me that this Cathedral and all connected with its temporal affairs were submitted to New York law. . . .⊥

⌐129

What has been done here, as I see it, is to exercise this reserved power which permits the State to alter corporate controls in response to the lessons of experience. Of course, the power is not unlimited and could be so exercised as to deprive one of property without due process of law. But, I do not think we can say that a legislative application of a principle so well established in our common law as the *cy-pres* doctrine is beyond the powers reserved by the New York Constitution.

II

The Court holds, however, that the State cannot exercise its reserved power to control this property without invading religious freedom, because it is a Cathedral and devoted to religious uses. I forbear discussion of the extent to which restraints imposed upon Congress by the First Amendment are transferred against the State by the Fourteenth Amendment beyond saying that I consider that the same

differences which apply to freedom of speech and press are applicable to questions of freedom of religion and of separation of church and state.

It is important to observe what New York has not done in this case. It has not held that Benjamin may not act as Archbishop or be revered as such by all who will follow him. It has not held that he may not have a Cathedral. ⊥ Indeed, I think New York would agree that no one is more in need of spiritual guidance than the Soviet faction. It has only held that this cleric may not have a particular Cathedral which, under New York law, belongs to others. It has not interfered with his or anyone's exercise of his religion. New York has not outlawed the Soviet-controlled sect nor forbidden it to exercise its authority or teach its dogma in any place whatsoever except on this piece of property owned and rightfully possessed by the Cathedral Corporation.

⌐130

The fact that property is dedicated to a religious use cannot, in my opinion, justify the Court in sublimating an issue over property rights into one of deprivation of religious liberty which alone would bring in the religious guaranties of the First Amendment. I assume no one would pretend that the State cannot decide a claim of trespass, larceny, conversion, bailment or contract, where the property involved is that of a religious corporation or is put to religious use, without invading the principle of religious liberty.

Of course, possession of the property will help either side that obtains it to maintain its prestige and to continue or extend its sway over the minds and souls of the devout. So would possession of a bank account, an income-producing office building, or any other valuable property. But if both claimants are religious corporations or personalities, can not the State decide the issues that arise over ownership and possession without invading the religious freedom of one or the other of the parties?

Thus, if the American group, which owns the title to the Cathedral, had by force barred Benjamin from entering it physically, would the Court say it was an interference with religious freedom to entertain and decide his ejectment action? If state courts are to decide such controversies at all instead of leaving them to be settled by a show of force, is it constitutional to decide for only ⊥ one side of the controversy and unconstitutional to decide for the other? In either case, the religious freedom of one side or the other is impaired if the temporal goods they need are withheld or taken from them.

⌐131

As I have earlier pointed out, the Soviet Ecclesiast's claim, denial of which is said to be constitutional error, is not that this New York property is impressed with a trust by virtue of New York law. The claim is that it is impressed with a trust by virtue of the rules of the Russian Orthodox Church. This Court so holds.

I shall not undertake to wallow through the complex, obscure and fragmentary details of secular and ecclesiastical history, theology, and canon law in which this case is smothered. To me, whatever the canon law is found to be and whoever is the rightful head of the Moscow patriarchate, I do not think New York law must yield to the authority of a foreign and unfriendly state masquerading as a spiritual institution.

I have supposed that a State of this Union was entirely free to make its own law, independently of any foreign-made law, except as the Full Faith and Credit Clause of the Constitution might require deference to the law of a sister state or the Supremacy Clause require submission to federal law. I do not see how one can spell out of the principles of separation of church and state a doctrine that a state submit property rights to settlement by canon law. If there is any relevant inference to be drawn, I should think it would be to the contrary, though I see no obstacle to the state allowing ecclesiastical law to govern in such a situation if it sees fit. . . .

PRESBYTERIAN CHURCH IN THE UNITED STATES
v.
MARY ELIZABETH BLUE HULL MEMORIAL PRESBYTERIAN CHURCH

393 U.S. 440
ON WRIT OF CERTIORARI TO THE SUPREME COURT OF GEORGIA
Argued December 9 and 10, 1968 — Decided January 27, 1969

⌐441   ⌐*Mr. Justice BRENNAN* delivered the opinion of the Court.

This is a church property dispute which arose when two local churches withdrew from a hierarchical general church organization. Under Georgia law the right to the property previously used by the local churches was made to turn on a civil court jury decision as to whether the general church abandoned or departed from the tenets of faith and practice it held at the time the local churches affiliated with it. The question presented is whether the restraints of the First Amendment, as applied to the States through the Fourteenth Amendment, permit a civil court to award church property on the basis of the interpretation and significance the civil court assigns to aspects of church doctrine.

Petitioner, Presbyterian Church in the United States, is an association of local Presbyterian
⌐442   churches governed ⌐ by a hierarchical structure of tribunals which consists of, in ascending order, (1) the Church Session, composed of the Elders of the local church; (2) the Presbytery, composed of several

churches in a geographical area; (3) the Synod, generally composed of all Presbyteries within a State; and (4) the General Assembly, the highest governing body.

A dispute arose between petitioner, the general church, and two local churches in Savannah, Georgia—the respondents, Hull Memorial Presbyterian Church and Eastern Heights Presbyterian Church—over control of the properties used until then by the local churches. In 1966, the membership of the local churches, in the belief that certain actions and pronouncements of the general church were violations of that organization's constitution and departures from the doctrine and practice in force at the time of affiliation, voted to withdraw from the general church and to reconstitute the local churches as an autonomous Presbyterian organization. The ministers of the two churches renounced the general church's ⌐ jurisdiction and authority   ⌐443 over them, as did all but two of the ruling elders. In response, the general church, through the Presbytery of Savannah, established an Administrative Commission to seek a conciliation. The dissident local churchmen remained steadfast; consequently, the Commission acknowledged the withdrawal of the local leadership and proceeded to take over the local churches' property on behalf of the general church until new local leadership could be appointed.

The local churchmen made no effort to appeal the Commission's action to higher church tribunals—the Synod of Georgia or the General Assembly. Instead, the churches filed separate suits in the Superior Court of Chatham County to enjoin the general church from trespassing on the disputed property, title to which was in the local churches. The cases were consolidated for trial. The general church moved to dismiss the actions and cross-claimed for injunctive relief in its own behalf on the ground that civil courts were without power to determine whether the general church had departed from its tenets of faith and practice. The motion to dismiss was denied, and the case was submitted to the jury on the theory that Georgia law implies a trust of local church property for the benefit of the general church on the sole condition that the general church adhere to its tenets of faith and practice existing at the time of affiliation by the local churches. Thus, the jury was instructed to determine whether the actions of the general church "amount to a fundamental or substantial abandonment of the original tenets and doctrines of the [general ⌐ church], so that the new   ⌐444 tenets and doctrines are utterly variant from the purposes for which the [general church] was founded." The jury returned a verdict for the local churches, and the trial judge thereupon declared that the implied trust had terminated and enjoined the general church from interfering with the use of the property in question. The Supreme Court of Georgia affirmed. We granted certiorari to consider the First Amendment questions raised. *

⌊445   We reverse.⊥

It is of course true that the State has a legitimate interest in resolving property disputes, and that a civil court is a proper forum for that resolution. Special problems arise, however, when these disputes implicate controversies over church doctrine and practice. The approach of this Court in such cases was originally developed in *Watson* v. *Jones*, a pre-*Erie* v. *Thompkins* diversity decision decided before the application of the First Amendment to the States but nonetheless informed by First Amendment considerations. There, as here, civil courts were asked to resolve a property dispute between a national Presbyterian organization and local churches of that organization. There, as here, the disputes arose out of a controversy over church doctrine. There, as here, the Court was asked to decree the termination of an implied trust because of departures from doctrine by the national organization. The *Watson* Court refused, pointing out that it was wholly inconsistent with the American concept of

⌊446   the re⊥lationship between church and state to permit civil courts to determine ecclesiastical ques-

⌊447   tions. . . .⊥ The logic of this language leaves the civil courts *no* role in determining ecclesiastical questions in the process of resolving property disputes.

Later cases, however, also decided on nonconstitutional grounds, recognized that there might be some circumstances in which marginal civil court review of ecclesiastical determinations would be appropriate. The scope of this review was delineated in *Gonzalez* v. *Archbishop*. There, Gonzalez claimed the right to be appointed to a chaplaincy in the Roman Catholic Church under a will which provided that a member of his family receive that appointment. The Roman Catholic Archbishop of Manila, Philippine Islands, refused to appoint Gonzalez on the ground that he did not satisfy the qualifications established by Canon Law for that office. Gonzalez brought suit

---

* We reject the contention of respondent local churches that no First Amendment issues were raised or decided in the state courts. Petitioner's answer and cross-claim in each case included an express allegation that the action of respondents in appropriating the church property to their use was "in violation of the laws of Georgia, the United States of America, and the Southern Presbyterian Church." (Italics supplied.) At trial, petitioner's counsel objected to the admission of all testimony "pertaining to [the] alleged deviation from the faith and practice of the Presbyterian Church in the United States" because that question was "exclusively within the right of the Presbyterian Church in the United States through its proper judicial body to determine." On appeal, petitioner again contended "that questions of an ecclesiastical nature concerning whether or not a church has abandoned its tenets [sic] and doctrines, or some of them, are exclusively within the jurisdiction of the church courts and should not be submitted to a jury for determination as this would destroy the doctrine of separation of church and state." Petitioner thus clearly raised claims under the First Amendment as applied to the States by the fourteenth Amendment. Kedroff v. St. Nicholas Cathedral. . . .

in the Court of First Instance of Manila for a judgment directing the Archbishop, among other things, to appoint him chaplain. The trial court entered such an order, but the Supreme Court of the Philippine Islands reversed and "absolved the Archbishop from the complaint." This Court affirmed. Mr. Justice Brandeis, speaking for the Court, defined the civil court role in the following words: "In the absence of fraud, collusion, or arbitrariness, the decisions of the proper church tribunals on matters purely ecclesiastical, although affecting civil rights, are accepted in litigation before the secular courts as conclusive, because the parties in interest made them so by contract or otherwise."

In *Kedroff* v. *St. Nicholas Cathedral*, the Court converted the principle of *Watson* as qualified by *Gonzalez* into a Constitutional rule. . . .⊥   ⌊449

Thus, the First Amendment severely circumscribes the role that civil courts may play in resolving church property disputes. It is obvious, however, that not every civil court decision as to property claimed by a religious organization jeopardizes values protected by the First Amendment. Civil courts do not inhibit free exercise of religion merely by opening their doors to disputes involving church property. And there are neutral principles of law, developed for use in all property disputes, which can be applied without "establishing" churches to which property is awarded. But First Amendment values are plainly jeopardized when church property litigation is made to turn on the resolution by civil courts of controversies over religious doctrine and practice. If civil courts undertake to resolve such controversies in order to adjudicate the property dispute, the hazards are ever present of inhibiting the free development of religious doctrine and of implicating secular interests in matters of purely ecclesiastical concern. Because of these hazards, the First Amendment enjoins the employment of organs of government for essentially religious purposes, *Abington* v. *Schempp*; the Amendment therefore commands civil courts to decide church property disputes without resolving underlying controversies over religious doctrine. Hence, States, religious organizations and individuals must structure relationships involving church property so as not to require the civil courts to resolve ecclesiastical questions.

The Georgia courts have violated the command of the First Amendment. The departure-from-doctrine element of the implied trust theory which they applied ⊥ requires the civil judiciary to determine   ⌊450 whether actions of the general church constitute such a "substantial departure" from the tenets of faith and practice existing at the time of the local churches' affiliation that the trust in favor of the general church must be declared to have terminated. This determination has two parts. The civil court must first decide whether the challenged actions of the general church depart substantially from prior doctrine. In reaching such a decision, the court must of necessity make its own interpretation of the meaning of church doctrines. If the court should decide that a substantial departure has occurred, it must then go on to determine whether the issue on which the general church has departed holds a place of such importance in the traditional theology as to require that the trust be terminated. A civil court can make this determination only after assessing the relative significance to the religion of the tenets from which departure was found. Thus, the departure-from-doctrine element of the Georgia implied trust theory requires the civil court to determine matters at the very core of a religion—the interpretation of particular church doctrines and the importance of those doctrines to the religion. Plainly, the First Amendment forbids civil courts from playing such a role.

Since the Georgia courts on remand may undertake to determine whether petitioner is entitled to relief on its cross-claims, we find it appropriate to remark that the departure-from-doctrine element of Georgia's implied trust theory can play *no* role in any future judicial proceedings. The departure-from-doctrine approach is not susceptible of the marginal judicial involvement contemplated in *Gon-* ⌐451 *zalez.* In *Gonzalez,* Gonzalez' rights under a will ⊥ turned on a church decision, the Archbishop's, as to church law, the qualifications for the chaplaincy. It was the archbishopric, not the civil courts, which had the task of analyzing and interpreting church law in order to determine the validity of Gonzalez' claim to a chaplaincy. Thus, the civil courts could adjudicate the rights under the will without interpreting or weighing church doctrine but simply by engaging in the narrowest kind of review of a specific church decision—*i.e.,* whether that decision resulted from fraud, collusion, or arbitrariness. Such review does not inject the civil courts into substantive ecclesiastical matters. In contrast, under Georgia's departure-from-doctrine approach, it is not possible for the civil courts to play so limited a role. Under this approach, property rights do not turn on a church decision as to church doctrine. The standard of departure-from-doctrine, though it calls for resolution of ecclesiastical questions, is a creation of state not church law. Nothing in the record suggests that this state standard has been interpreted and applied in a decision of the general church. Any decisions which have been made by the general church about the local churches' withdrawal have at most a tangential relationship to the state-fashioned departure-from-doctrine standard. A determination whether such decisions are fraudulent, collusive, or arbitrary would therefore not answer the questions posed by the state standard. To reach those questions would require the civil courts to engage in the forbidden process of interpreting and weighing church doctrine. Even if the general church had attempted to apply the state standard, the civil courts could not review and enforce the church decision without violating the Constitution. The First Amendment prohibits a State from employing religious organizations as an arm of the civil judiciary to perform the function of interpreting and applying state standards.⊥   ⌐452 Thus, a civil court may no more review a church decision applying a state departure-from-doctrine standard than it may apply that standard itself.

The judgment of the Supreme Court of Georgia is reversed, and the case is remanded for further proceedings not inconsistent with this opinion.

It is so ordered.

SERBIAN EASTERN ORTHODOX DIOCESE FOR THE UNITED STATES OF AMERICA AND CANADA v. MILIVOJEVICH

426 U.S. 696

ON WRIT OF CERTIORARI TO THE SUPREME COURT OF ILLINOIS

Argued March 22, 1976 — Decided June 21, 1976

⊥ *Mr. Justice BRENNAN* delivered the opinion of   ⌐697 the Court.

In 1963, the Holy Assembly of Bishops and the Holy Synod of the Serbian Orthodox Church (Mother Church) ⊥ suspended and ultimately removed re-   ⌐698 spondent Dionisije Milivojevich (Dionisije) as Bishop of the American-Canadian Diocese of that Church, and appointed petitioner Bishop Firmilian Ocokoljich (Firmilian) as Administrator of the Diocese, which the Mother Church then reorganized into three Dioceses. In 1964 the Holy Assembly and Holy Synod defrocked Dionisije as a Bishop and cleric of the Mother Church. In this civil action brought by Dionisije and the other respondents in Illinois Circuit Court, the Supreme Court of Illinois held that the proceedings of the Mother Church respecting Dionisije were procedurally and substantively defective under the internal regulations of the Mother Church and were therefore arbitrary and invalid. The State Supreme Court also invalidated the Diocesan reorganization into three Dioceses. We granted certiorari to determine whether the actions of the Illinois Supreme Court constituted improper judicial interference with decisions of the highest authorities of a hierarchial church in violation of the First and Fourteenth Amendments. We hold that the inquiries made by the Illinois Supreme Court into matters of ecclesiastical cognizance and polity and the court's actions pursuant thereto contravened the First and Fourteenth Amendments. We therefore reverse.

I

The basic dispute is over control of the Serbian Eastern Orthodox Diocese for the United States of America and Canada (American-Canadian Diocese), its property and assets. Petitioners are Bishops Firmilian Ocokoljich, Gregory Udicki, and Sava Vukovich, and the Serbian Eastern ⊥ Orthodox Diocese for the United States of America and Canada (the religious body in this country). Respondents are Bishop Dionisije Milivojevich, the Serbian Orthodox Monastery of St. Sava, and the Serbian Eastern Orthodox Diocese for the United States of America and Canada, an Illinois religious corporation. A proper perspective of the relationship of these parties and the nature of this dispute requires some background discussion.

The Serbian Orthodox Church, one of the 14 autocephalous, hierarchical churches which came into existence following the schism of the universal Christian church in 1054, is an episcopal church whose Seat is the Patriarchate in Belgrade, Yugoslavia. Its highest legislative, judicial, ecclesiastical, and administrative authority resides in the Holy Assembly of Bishops, a body composed of all Diocesan Bishops presided over by a Bishop designated by the Assembly to be Patriarch. The Church's highest executive body, the Holy Synod of Bishops, is composed of the patriarch and four Diocesan Bishops selected by the Holy Assembly. The Holy Synod and the Holy Assembly have the exclusive power to remove, suspend, defrock, or appoint Diocesan Bishops. The Mother Church is governed according to the Holy Scriptures, Holy Tradition, Rules of the Ecumenical Councils, the Holy Apostles, the Holy Faiths of the Church, the Mother Church Constitution adopted in 1931, and a "penal code" adopted in 1962. These sources of law are sometimes ambiguous and seemingly inconsistent. Pertinent provisions of the Mother Church Constitution provide that the Church's "main administrative division is composed of dioceses, both in regard to church hierarchial and church administrative aspect," Art. 12, and that "[d]ecisions of establishing, naming liquidating, reorganizing, and the seat of the dioceses, and establishing or eliminating of position of vicar bish⊥ops, is decided upon by the [Holy Assembly], in agreement with the patriarchal Council," Art. 16.

During the late 19th century, migrants to North America of Serbian descent formed autonomous religious congregations throughout this country and Canada. These congregations were then under the jurisdiction of the Russian Orthodox Church, but that Church was unable to care for their needs and the congregations sought permission to bring themselves under the jurisdiction of the Serbian Orthodox Church.

In 1913 and 1916, Serbian priests and laymen organized a Serbian Orthodox Church in North America. The 32 Serbian Orthodox congregations were divided into 4 presbyteries, each presided over by a Bishop's Aide, and constitutions were adopted. In 1917, the Russian Orthodox Church commissioned a Serbian priest, Father Mardary, to organize

an independent Serbian Diocese in America. Four years later, as a result of Father Mardary's efforts, the Holy Assembly of Bishops of the Mother Church created the Eastern Orthodox Diocese for the United States of America and Canada and designated a Serbian Bishop to complete the formal organization of a diocese. From that time until 1963, each bishop who governed the American-Canadian Diocese was a Yugoslav citizen appointed by the Mother Church without consultation with Diocesan officials.

In 1927, Father Mardary called a Church National Assembly embracing all of the known Serbian Orthodox congregations in the United States. The assembly drafted and adopted the constitution of the Serbian Orthodox Diocese for the United States of America and Canada, and submitted the constitution to the Mother Church for approval. The Holy Assembly made changes to provide for appointment of the Diocesan Bishop by the Holy Assembly and to require Holy As⊥sembly approval for any amendments to the constitution, and with these changes approved the constitution. The American-Canadian Diocese was the only diocese of the Mother Church with its own constitution.

Article 1 of the constitution provides that the American-Canadian Diocese "is considered ecclesiastically-judicially as an organic part of the Serbian Patriarchate in the Kingdom of Yugoslavia," and Art. 2 provides that all "statutes and rules which regulate the ecclesiastical-canonical authority and position of the Serbian Orthodox Church in the Kingdom of Yugoslavia are also compulsory for the" American-Canadian Diocese. Article 3 states that the "jurisdiction of the . . . Diocese . . . includes the entire political territory of the United States of America and Canada, which as such by its geographical location enjoys full administrative freedom and accordingly, it can independently regulate and rule the activities of its church, school and other diocesan institutions and all funds and beneficiencies, through its organs. . . ." Article 9 provides that the Bishop of the Diocese "is appointed by the Holy Assembly of Bishops of the Serbian Patriarchate"; various provisions of the constitution accord that Bishop extensive powers both over religious matters and with respect to control of Diocesan property. The constitution also provides for such Diocesan organs as a Diocesan National Assembly, which exercises considerable legislative and administrative authority within the Diocese.

In 1927, Father Mardary also organized a not-for-profit corporation, the Serbian Eastern Orthodox Council for the United States and Canada, under the laws of Illinois. The corporation was to hold title to 30 acres of land in Libertyville, Ill., that Father Mardary had personally purchased in 1924. The charter of that corporation was allowed to lapse, and Father Mardary organized ⊥ another Illinois not-for-profit corporation, respondent Serbian Eastern

Orthodox Diocese for the United States and Canada, under Illinois laws governing incorporation of hierarchial religious organizations. In 1945, respondent not-for-profit monastery corporation, the Monastery of St. Sava, was organized under these same Illinois laws, and title to the Libertyville property was transferred to it. Similar secular property-holding corporations were subsequently organized in New York, California, and Pennsylvania.

Respondent Bishop Dionisije Milivojevich was elected Bishop of the American-Canadian Diocese by the Holy Assembly of Bishops in 1931. He became a controversial figure; during the years before 1963, the Holy Assembly received numerous complaints challenging his fitness to serve as Bishop and his administration of the Diocese.

During his tenure, however, the Diocese grew so substantially that Dionisije requested that the Patriarch and Holy Assembly appoint bishops to assist him but to serve under his supervision. Eventually, the Diocese sought its elevation by the Holy Assembly to the rank of Metropola, that South America be added to the Diocese, and that several assistant bishops be appointed under Dionisije. Dionisije specifically recommended that petitioners Firmilian Ocokoljich and Gregory Udicki, and one Stefan Lastavica be named assistant bishops. A delegation from the Diocese was sent to the May 1962 meeting of the Holy Assembly in Belgrade to urge adoption of these reorganization proposals, and on June 12, 1962, the Holy Synod appointed a delegation to visit the United States and study the proposals. The delegation was also directed to confer with Dionisije concerning the complaints made against him and his administration over the years.

⌐703 The delegation remained in the United States for three ⊥ months, visiting parishes throughout the Diocese and discussing both the reorganization proposals and the complaints against Dionisije. After completion of its survey, the delegation suggested to the Holy Synod the assignment of vicar bishops to the Diocese and recommended that a commission be appointed to conduct a thorough investigation into the complaints against Dionisije. However, the Holy Assembly on May 10, 1963, instead recommended that the Holy Synod institute disciplinary proceedings against Dionisije. The Holy Synod thereupon met immediately and suspended Dionisije pending investigation and disposition of the complaints. The Holy Synod appointed petitioner Firmilian, Dionisije's chief episcopal deputy since 1955 and one of Dionisije's candidates for assistant bishop, as Administrator of the Diocese pending completion of the proceedings.

The Holy Assembly thereafter reconvened and, acting under Art. 16 of the constitution of the Mother Church, reorganized the American-Canadian Diocese into three new dioceses—the Middle Western, the Western, and the Eastern—whose boundaries were roughly those of the episcopal districts pre-

viously created by Dionisije. The final fixing of boundaries for the new dioceses and all other organizational and administrative matters were left to be determined by the officials of the old American-Canadian Diocese. Dionisije was appointed Bishop of the Middle Western Diocese and, seven days later, petitioners Achimandrites Firmilian and Gregory, and Reverend Stefan were appointed temporary administrators for the new dioceses.

⊥ Dionisije's immediate reaction to these decisions of the Mother Church was to refuse to accept the reorganization on the ground that it contravened the administrative autonomy of the Diocese guaranteed by the Diocesan constitution, and to refuse to accept his suspension on the ground that it was not effectuated in compliance with the constitution and laws of the Mother Church. On May 25, 1963, he prepared and mailed a circular to all American-Canadian parishes stating his refusal to recognize these actions, and on May 27 he issued a press release stating his refusal to recognize his suspension and his intent to litigate it in the civil courts. This refusal to recognize the diocesan reorganization and his suspension as Bishop was again stated by Dionisije in a circular issued on June 3 and addressed to the Patriarch, the Holy Assembly, the Holy Synod, all clergy, congregations, Diocesan committees, and all Serbians in North America. He also continued to officiate as Bishop, refusing to turn administration of the Diocese over to Firmilian; in a May 30 letter to Firmilian, Dionisije repeated this refusal, asserted that he no longer recognized the decisions of the Holy Assembly and Holy Synod, and charged those bodies with being "communistic."

The Diocesan Council met on June 6, and Dionisije reaffirmed his refusal to turn over administration of the Diocese to Firmilian; he also announced that he had discharged two of his vicars general because of their loyalty to the Mother Church. The Council resolved at the meeting to advise the Holy Synod that the proposal to reorganize the Diocese into three dioceses would be submitted to the Diocesan National Assembly in August for acceptance or rejection. The Council also requested that the Holy Assembly promptly send a committee to investigate the complaints against Dionisije.

On June 13, the Holy Synod appointed such a commis⊥sion, composed of two Bishops and the Secretary of the Holy Synod. On July 5, the commission met with Dionisije, who reiterated his refusal to recognize his suspension or the diocesan reorganization, and who demanded all accusations in writing. The commission refused to give Dionisije the written accusations on the ground that defiance of decisions of higher church authorities itself established wrongful conduct, and advised him that the Holy Synod would appoint a Bishop as court prosecutor to prepare an indictment against him.

On the basis of the commission's report and recommendations, which recited Dionisije's refusal to accept the decisions of the Holy Synod and Holy Assembly and his refusal to recognize the court of the Holy Synod or its competence to try him, the Holy Assembly met on July 27, 1963, and voted to remove Dionisije as Bishop. The minutes of the Holy Assembly meeting and the Patriarch's letter to Dionisije informing him of the Holy Assembly's actions made clear that the removal was based solely on his acts of defiance subsequent to his May 10, 1963, suspension, and his violation of his oath and loss of certain qualifications for Bishop under Art. 104 of the constitution of the Mother Church.

The Diocesan National Assembly, with Dionisije presiding despite his removal, met in August 1963 and issued a resolution repudiating the division of the Diocese into three dioceses and demanding a revocation by the Mother Church of the decisions concerning that division. When the Holy Assembly refused to reconsider, the Diocesan National Assembly in November 1963 declared the Diocese completely autonomous and reinstated the provisions of the diocesan constitution that provided for election of the Bishop of the Diocese itself and for amendments without the approval of the Holy Assembly.

Meanwhile, the Holy Synod in October 1963 for⌐706 ⊥warded to Dionisije a formal written indictment based on the charges of canonical misconduct. In November 1963, Dionisje responded with a demand for the verified reports and complaints referred to in the indictment and for a six-month extension to answer the indictment. The Holy Assembly granted a 30-day extension in which to answer, but declined to furnish verified charges on the grounds that they were described in the indictment that additional details would be evidentiary in nature, and that there was no legal or canonical basis for forwarding such material to an accused Bishop.

Dionisije returned the indictment in January, refusing to answer without the verified charges, denouncing the Holy Assembly and Holy Synod as schismatic and pro-Communist, and asserting that the Mother Church was proceeding in violation of its penal code and constitution.

The Holy Synod, on February 25, 1964, declared that it could not proceed further without Dionisije and referred the matter to the Holy Assembly, which tried Dionisije as a default case on March 5, 1964, because of his refusal to participate. The indictment was also amended at that time to include charges based on Dionisije's acts of rebellion such as those committed at the November meeting of the National Assembly which had declared the Diocese separate from the Mother Church. Considering the original and amended indictments, the Holy Assembly unanimously found Dionisije guilty of all charges and divested him of his episcopal and monastic ranks.

Even before the Holy Assembly had removed Dionisije as Bishop, he had commenced what eventually became his protracted litigation, now carried on for almost 13 years. Acting upon the threat contained in his May 27, 1963, press release, Dionisije filed suit in ⊥ the Circuit Court of Lake County, ⌐707 Ill., on July 26, 1963, seeking to enjoin petitioners from interfering with the assets of respondent corporations and to have himself declared the true Diocesan Bishop. Petitioners countered with a separate complaint, which was consolidated with the original action, seeking declaratory relief that Dionisije had been removed as Bishop of the Diocese and that the Diocese had been properly reorganized into three dioceses, and injunctive relief granting petitioner Bishops control of the reorganized dioceses and their property. After the trial court granted summary judgment for respondents and dismissed petitioners, counter-complaint, the Illinois Appellate Court reversed and remanded for a hearing on the merits.

Following a lengthy trial, the trial court filed an unreported Memorandum Opinion and entered a Final Decree which concluded that "no substantial evidence was produced . . . that fraud, collusion or arbitrariness existed in any of the actions or decisions preliminary to or during the final proceedings of the decision to defrock Bishop Dionisije made by the highest Hierarchical bodies of the Mother Church;" that the property held by respondent corporations is held in trust for all members of the American-Canadian Diocese; that it was "improper and beyond the power of the Mother Church to take its action in dividing the whole American Diocese into three new Dioceses, changing its boundaries, and in appointing new bishops for ⊥ said so-called ⌐708 new Dioceses;" and that "Firmilian was validly appointed by the Holy Episcopal Synod as temporary Administrator of the whole American-Canadian Diocese in place of the defrocked Bishop Dionisije."

On appeal, the Supreme Court of Illinois affirmed in part and reversed in part, essentially holding that Dionisije's removal and defrockment must be set aside as "arbitrary" because the proceedings resulting in those actions were not conducted according to the Illinois Supreme Court's interpretation of the Church's constitution and penal code, and that the diocesan reorganization was invalid because it was beyond the scope of the Mother Church's authority to effectuate such changes without Diocesan approval. Although the court denied rehearing, it amended its original opinion to hold that, although Dionisije had been properly suspended, that suspension terminated by operation of church law when he was not validly tried within one year to his indictment. Thus, the court purported in effect to reinstate Dionisije as Diocesan Bishop.

II

The fallacy fatal to the judgment of the Illinois Supreme Court is that it rests upon an impermissible rejection of the decisions of the highest ecclesiastical tribunals of this hierarchial church upon the issues in dispute, and impermissibly substitutes its own inquiry into church polity and resolutions based thereon of those disputes. Consistently with the First and Fourteenth Amendments "[c]ivil courts do not inquire whether the relevant [hierarchial] church governing body has power under religious law . . . [to decide such disputes]. . . . Such a determination . . . frequently necessitates the interpretation of ambiguous religious law and usage. ⊥ To permit civil courts to probe deeply enough into the allocation of power within a [hierarchial] church so as to decide . . . religious law . . . [governing church polity] . . . would violate the First Amendment in much the same manner as civil determination of religious doctrine." *Md. and Va. Churches* v. *Sharpsburg Church.* For where resolution of the disputes cannot be made without extensive inquiry by civil courts into religious law and polity, the First and Fourteenth Amendments mandate that civil courts shall not disturb the decisions of the highest ecclesiastical tribunal within a church of hierarchial polity, but must accept such decisions as binding on them, in their application to the religious issues of doctrine or polity before them.

⌋709

Resolution of the religious disputes at issue here affects the control of church property in addition to the structure and administration of the American-Canadian Diocese. This is because the Diocesan Bishop controls respondent Monastery of St. Sava and is the principal officer of respondent property holding corporations. Resolution of the religious dispute over Dionisije's defrockment therefore determines control of the property. Thus, this case essentially involves not a church property dispute but a religious dispute the resolution of which under our cases is for ecclesiastical and not civil tribunals. Even when rival church factions seek resolution of a church property dispute in the civil courts there is substantial danger that the State will become entangled in essentially religious controversies or intervene on behalf of groups espousing particular doctrinal beliefs. Because of this danger, "the First Amendment severely circumscribes the role that civil courts may play in resolving church property disputes." *Presbyterian Church* v. *Hull Church.* "First Amend ⊥ ment values are plainly jeopardized when church property litigation is made to turn on the resolution by civil courts of controversies over religious doctrine and practice. If civil courts undertake to resolve such controversies in order to adjudicate the property dispute, the hazards are ever present in inhibiting the free development of religious doctrine and of implicating secular interests in matters of purely ecclesiastical concern. . . . [T]he [First] Amendment therefore commands civil courts to decide church property disputes without resolving underlying controversies over religious doctrine." This principle applies with equal force to church disputes over church polity and church administration.

⌋710

The principles limiting the role of civil courts in the resolution of religious controversies that incidentally affect civil rights were initially fashioned in *Watson* v. *Jones,* a diversity case decided before the First Amendment had been rendered applicable to the States through the Fourteenth Amendment. With respect to hierarchical churches, *Watson* held that "the rule of action which should govern the civil courts . . . is, that, whenever the questions of discipline, or of faith, or ecclesiastical rule, custom, or law have been decided by the highest of these church judicatories to which the matter has been carried, the legal tribunals must accept such decisions as final, and as binding on them, in their application to the case before them."

In language having "a clear constitutional ring," *Presbyterian Church* v. *Hull Church, Watson* reasoned:

"The law knows no heresy, and is committed to the ⊥ support of no dogma, the establishment of no sect. The right to organize voluntary religious associations to assist in the expression and dissemination of any religious doctrine, and to create tribunals for the decision of controverted questions of faith within the association, and for the ecclesiastical government of all the individual members, congregations, and officers within the general association, is unquestioned. All who unite themselves to such a body do so with an implied consent to this government, and are bound to submit to it. But it would be a vain consent and would lead to the total subversion of such religious bodies, if any one aggrieved by one of their decisions could appeal to the secular courts and have them reversed. *It is of the essence of these religious groups, and of their right to establish tribunals for the decision of questions arising among themselves, that those decisions should be binding in all cases of ecclesiastical cognizance, subject only to such appeals as the organism itself provides for*" (emphasis supplied).

⌋711

Gonzalez v. *Archbishop* applied this principle in a case involving dispute over entitlement to certain income under a will that turned upon an ecclesiastical determination as to whether an individual would be appointed to a chaplaincy in the Roman Catholic Church. The Court, speaking through Mr. Justice Brandeis, observed:

"Because the appointment [to the chaplaincy] is a canonical act, it is the function of the church authorities to determine what the essential qualifications of a chaplain are and whether the candidate possesses them. In the absence of fraud, collusion, or arbitrariness, the decisions of the proper church ⊥ tribunals on matters purely ecclesiastical, although affecting civil rights, are accepted in litigation before the secular courts as conclusive, because the parties in interest made them so by contract or otherwise.

⌋712

Thus, although *Watson* had left civil courts no role to play in reviewing ecclesiastical decisions during the course of resolving church property disputes,

Gonzalez first adverted to the possibility of "marginal civil court review," *Presbyterian Church* v. *Hull Church*, in cases challenging decisions of ecclesiastical tribunals as products of "fraud, collusion, or arbitrariness." However, since there was "not even a suggestion that [the Archbishop] exercised his authority [in making the chaplaincy decision] arbitrarily," the suggested "fraud, collusion, or arbitrariness" exception to the *Watson* rule was dictum only. And although references to the suggested exception appear in opinions in cases decided since the *Watson* rule has been held to be mandated by the First Amendment, no decision of this Court has given concrete content to or applied the "exception." However, it was the predicate for the Illinois Supreme Court's decision in this case, and we therefore turn to the question whether reliance upon it in the circumstances of this case was consistent with the prohibition of the First and Fourteenth Amendments against rejection of the decisions of the Mother Church upon the religious disputes in issue.

⌐713 The conclusion of the Illinois Supreme Court that the decisions of the Mother Church were "arbitrary" was grounded upon an inquiry that persuaded the Illinois Su⊥preme Court that the Mother Church had not followed its own laws and procedures in arriving at those decisions. We have concluded that whether or not there is room for "marginal civil court review" under the narrow rubrics of "fraud" or "collusion" when church tribunals act in bad faith for secular purposes, no "arbitrariness" exception—in the sense of an inquiry whether the decisions of the highest ecclesiastical tribunal of a hierarchical church complied with church laws and regulations—is consistent with the constitutional mandate that civil courts are bound to accept the decisions of the highest judicatories of a religious organization of hierarchical polity on matters of discipline, faith, internal organization, or ecclesiastical rule, custom or law. For civil courts to analyze whether the ecclesiastical actions of a church judicatory are in that sense "arbitrary" must inherently entail inquiry into the procedures that canon or ecclesiastical law supposedly require the church adjudicatory to follow, or else into the substantive criteria by which they are supposedly to decide the ecclesiastical question. But this is exactly the inquiry that the First Amendment prohibits; recognition of such an exception would undermine the general rule that religious controversies are not the proper subject of civil court inquiry, and that a civil court must accept the ecclesiastical decisions of church tribunals as it finds them. *Watson* itself requires our conclusion in its rejection of the analogous argument that ecclesiastical decisions of the highest church judicatories need only be accepted if the subject matter of the dispute is within their "jurisdiction."

"But it is a very different thing where a subject-matter of dispute, strictly and purely ecclesiastical in its character,—a matter over which the civil courts ⊥ exercise no jurisdiction,—*a matter which concerns theological controversy, church discipline, ecclesiastical government, or the conformity of the members of the church to the standard of morals required of them,*— becomes the subject of its action. It may be said here, also, that no jurisdiction has been conferred on the tribunal to try the particular case before it, or that, in its judgment, it exceeds the powers conferred upon it, or that the laws of the church do not authorize the particular form of proceeding adopted; and, in a sense often used in the courts, all of those may be said to be quotations of jurisdiction. But is is easy to see that *if the civil courts are to inquire into all these matters, the whole subject of the doctrinal theology, the usages and customs, the written laws, and fundamental organization of every religious denomination may, and must, be examined into with minuteness and care, for they would become, in almost every case, the* criteria *by which the validity of the ecclesiastical decree would be determined in the civil court. This principle would deprive these bodies of the right of construing their own church laws,* would open the way to all the evils which we have depicted as attendant upon the doctrine of Lord Eldon, *and would, in effect, transfer to the civil courts where property rights were concerned the decision of all ecclesiastical questions."* (Emphasis supplied.)

Indeed, it is the essence of religious faith that ecclesiastical decisions are reached and are to be accepted as matters of faith whether or not rational or measurable by ⊥ objective criteria. Constitutional ⌐715 concepts of due process, involving secular notions of "fundamental fairness" or impermissible objectives, are therefore hardly relevant to such matters of ecclesiastical cognizance.

The constitutional evils that attend upon any "arbitrariness" exception in the sense applied by the Illinois Supreme Court to justify civil court review of ecclesiastical decisions of final church tribunals are manifest in the instant case. The Supreme Court of Illinois recognized that all parties agree that the Serbian Orthodox Church is a hierarchical church, and that the sole power to appoint and remove Bishops of the Church resides in its highest ranking organs, the Holy Assembly and the Holy Synod. Indeed, final authority with respect to the ⊥ promulgation ⌐716 and interpretation of *all* matters of church discipline and internal organization rests with the Holy Assembly ⊥ . . . . Nor is there any dispute that questions ⌐717 of church discipline and the composition of the church hierarchy are at the core of ecclesiastical concern; the Bishop of a church is clearly one of the central figures in such a hierarchy and the embodiment of the church within his diocese, and the Mother Church constitution states that [h]e is, according to the church canonical regulations, chief

⌐714 (margin)

representative and guiding leader of all spiritual life and church order in the diocese." Article 13.

⌞718 Yet having recognized that the Serbian Eastern Church is hierarchical and that the decisions to suspend and ⊥ defrock respondent Dionisije were made by the religious bodies in whose sole discretion the authority to make those ecclesiastical decisions was vested, the Supreme Court of Illinois nevertheless invalidated the decision to defrock Dionisije on the ground that it was "arbitrary" because a "detailed review of the evidence discloses that the proceedings resulting in Bishop Dionisije's removal and defrockment were not in accordance with the prescribed procedure of the constitution and the penal code of the Serbian Orthodox Church." Not only was this "detailed review" impermissible under the First and Fourteenth Amendments, but in reaching this conclusion, the court evaluated conflicting testimony concerning internal church procedures and rejected the interpretations of relevant procedural provisions by the Mother Church's highest tribunals. The court also failed to take cognizance of the fact that the church judicatories were also guided by other sources of law, such as canon law, which are admittedly not always consistent, and it rejected the testimony of petitioners five expert witnesses that church procedures were properly followed, denigrating the testimony of one witness as contradictory and discounting that of another on the ground that it was "premised upon an assumption which did not consider the penal code," even though there was some question whether that code even applied to dis-
⌞719 cipline of Bishops. The court ⊥ accepted, on the other hand, the testimony of respondents sole expert witness that the Church's procedures had been contravened in various specifics. We need not, and under the First Amendment cannot, demonstrate the propriety or impropriety of each of Dionisije's procedural claims, but we can note that the state court even rejected petitioners' contention that Dionisije's failure to participate in the proceedings undermined all procedural contentions because Arts. 66 and 70 of the penal code specify that if a person charged with a violation fails to participate or answer the indictment, the allegations are admitted and due process will be concluded without his participation; the court merely asserted that "application of this provision . . . must be viewed from the perspective that Bishop Dionisije refused to participate because he maintained that the proceedings against him were in violation of the constitution and the penal code of the Serbian Orthodox Church." The court found no support in any church dogma for this judicial rewriting of church law, and compounded further the error of this intrusion into a religious thicket by declaring that although Dionisije had, even under the court's analysis, been properly suspended and replaced by Firmilian as temporary administrator, he must be reinstated as Bishop because church law mandated a trial on ecclesiastical charges within one

year of the indictment. Yet the only reason more time than that had expired was due to Dionisije's decision to resort to the civil courts for redress without attempting to vindicate himself by pursuing available ⊥ remedies within the church. Indeed, the ⌞720 Illinois Supreme Court overlooked the clear substantive canonical violations for which the church disciplined Dionisije, violations based on Dionisije's conceded open defiance and rebellion against the church hierarchy immediately after the Holy Assembly's decision to suspend him (a decision which even the Illinois courts deemed to be proper) and Dionisije's decision to litigate the Mother Church's authority in the civil courts rather than participate in the disciplinary proceedings before the Holy Synod and the Holy Assembly. Instead, the Illinois Supreme Court would sanction this circumvention of the tribunals set up to resolve internal church disputes and has ordered the Mother Church to reinstate as Bishop one who espoused views regarded by the church hierarchy to be schismatic and which the proper church tribunals have already determined merit severe sanctions. In short, under the guise of "minimal" review under the umbrella of "arbitrariness," the Illinois Supreme Court has unconstitutionally undertaken the resolution of quintessentially religious controversies whose resolution the First Amendment commits exclusively to the highest ecclesiastical tribunals of this hierarchical church. And although the Diocesan Bishop controls respondent Monastery of St. Sava and is the principal officer of respondent property-holding corporations, the civil courts must accept that consequence as the incidental effect of an ecclesiastical determination that is not subject to judicial abrogation, having been reached by the final church judicatory in which authority to make the decision resides.

III

Similar considerations inform our resolution of the second question we must address—the constitutionality of the Supreme Court of Illinois' holding that the Mother Church's reorganization of the American-Canadian Dio⊥cese into three Dioceses   ⌞721 was invalid because it was "in clear and palpable excess of its own jurisdiction." Essentially, the court premised this determination on its view that the early history of the Diocese "manifested a clear intention to retain independence and autonomy in its administrative affairs while at the same time becoming ecclesiastically and judicially an organic part of the Serbian Orthodox Church," and its interpretation of the constitution of the American-Canadian Diocese as confirming this intention. It also interpreted the constitution of the Serbian Orthodox Church, which was adopted after the Diocesan constitution, in a manner consistent with this conclusion.

This conclusion was not, however, explicitly based on the "fraud, collusion, or arbitrariness" exception.

Rather the Illinois Supreme Court relied on purported "neutral principles" for resolving property disputes which would "not entangle this court in the determination of theological or doctrinal matters." Nevertheless the Supreme Court of Illinois substituted its interpretation of the Diocesan and Mother Church constitutions for that of the highest ecclesiastical tribunals in which church law vests authority to make that interpretation. This the First and Fourteenth Amendments forbid.

We will not delve into the various church constitutional provisions relevant to this conclusion, for that would repeat the error of the Illinois Supreme Court. It suffices to note that the reorganization of the Diocese involves a matter of internal church government, an issue at the core of ecclesiastical affairs; Arts. 57 and 64 of the Mother Church constitution commit such questions of church polity to the final province of the Holy Assembly. *Kedroff* v. *St. Nicholas Cathedral* stated that religious freedom encompasses the ⊥ "power [of religious bodies] to decide for themselves, free from state interference, matters of church government as well as those of faith and doctrine." The subordination of the Diocese to the Mother Church in such matters, which are not only "administrative, " but also "hierarchical," was provided, and the power of the Holy Assembly to reorganize the Diocese is expressed in the Mother Church constitution. Contrary to the interpretation of the Illinois court, the church judicatories interpreted the provisions of the Diocesan constitution not to interdict or govern this action, but only to relate to the day-to-day administration of Diocesan property. ⊥ The constitutional provisions of the American-Canadian Diocese were not so express that the civil courts could enforce them without engaging in a searching and therefore impermissible inquiry into church polity. See *Md. and Va. Churches* v. *Sharpsburg Church.*

The control of Diocesan property may be little affected by the changes; respondents' allegation that the reorganization was a fraudulent subterfuge to divert Diocesan property from its intended beneficiaries has been rejected by the Illinois courts. Formal title to the property remains in respondent property-holding corporations, to be held in trust for all members of the new Dioceses. The boundaries of the reorganized Dioceses generally conform to the episcopal districts which the American-Canadian Diocese had already employed for its internal government, and the appointed administrators of the new Dioceses were the same individuals nominated by Dionisije as assistant bishops to govern similar divisions under him. Indeed, even the Illinois courts' rationale that the reorganization would effectuate an abrogation of the Diocesan constitution has no support in the record, which establishes rather that the details of the reorganization and any decisions pertaining to a distribution of ⊥ the property among

the three Dioceses were expressly left for the Diocesan National Assembly to determine. In response to inquiries from the Diocese, the Holy Assembly assured Bishop Firmilian:

"1. That all the rights of the former American-Canadian Diocese, as they relate to the autonomy in the administrative sense, remain unchanged. The only exception is the forming of three dioceses and

"2. That the Constitution of the former American-Canadian Diocese remains the same and that the Dioceses in America and Canada will not, in an administrative sense, the management *(or direction)* of the properties be managed *(or directed)* in the same manner as those in Yugoslavia."

As a practical matter the effect of the reorganization is a tripling of the Diocesan representational strength in the Holy Assembly and a decentralization of hierarchical authority to permit closer attention to the needs of individual congregations within each of the new Dioceses, a result which Dionisije and Diocesan representatives had already concluded was necessary. Whether corporate bylaws or other documents governing the individual property-holding corporations may affect any desired disposition of the Diocesan property is a question not before us.

IV

In short, the First and Fourteenth Amendments permit hierarchical religious organizations to establish their own rules and regulations for internal discipline and government, and to create tribunals for adjudicating disputes over these matters. When this choice is exercised and ecclesiastical tribunals are created to decide disputes over ⊥ the government and direction of subordinate bodies, the Constitution requires that civil courts accept their decisions as binding upon them.

Reversed.

The CHIEF JUSTICE concurs in the judgment.

Mr. Justice WHITE, concurring.

Major predicates for the Court's opinion are that the Serbian Orthodox Church is a hierarchical church and the American and Canadian diocese, involved here, is part of that church. These basic issues are for the courts' ultimate decision, and the fact that church authorities may render their opinions on them does not foreclose the courts from coming to their independent judgment. I do not understand the Court's opinion to suggest otherwise and join the views expressed therein.

Mr. Justice REHNQUIST, with whom *Mr. Justice STEVENS* joins, dissenting.

The Court's opinion, while long on the ecclesiastical history of the Serbian Orthodox Church, is somewhat short on the procedural history of this case. A casual reader of some of the passages in the Court's opinion could easily gain the impression that the State of Illinois had commenced a proceeding designed to brand Bishop Firmilian as a heretic, with appropriate pains and penalties. But the state trial judge in the Circuit Court of Lake County was not the Bishop of Beauvais, trying Joan of Arc for heresy; the jurisdiction of his court was invoked by petitioners themselves, who sought an injunction establishing their control over property of the American-Canadian Diocese of the church located in Lake County.

|726   The jurisdiction of that court having been invoked ⊥ for such a purpose by both petitioners and respondents, contesting claimants to diocesan authority, it was entitled to ask if the real bishop of the American-Canadian diocese would please stand up. The protracted proceedings in the Illinois courts were devoted to the ascertainment of who that individual was, a question which the Illinois courts sought to answer by application of the canon law of the church, just as they would have attempted to decide a similar dispute among the members of any other voluntary association. The Illinois courts did not in the remotest sense inject their doctrinal preference into the dispute. They were forced to decide between two competing sets of claimants to church office in order that they might resolve a dispute over real property located within the State. Each of the claimants had requested them to decide the issue. Unless the First Amendment requires control of disputed church property to be awarded solely on the basis of ecclesiastical paper title, I can find no constitutional infirmity in the judgment of the Supreme Court of Illinois.

Unless civil courts are to be wholly divested of authority to resolve conflicting claims to real property owned by a hierarchical church, and such claims are to be resolved by brute force, civil courts must of necessity make some factual inquiry even under the rules the Court purports to apply in this case. We are told that "a civil court must accept the ecclesiastical decisions of church tribunals as it finds them." But even this rule requires that proof be made as to what these decisions are, and if proofs on that issue conflict the civil court will inevitably have to choose one over the other. In so choosing, if the choice is to be a rational one, reasons must be adduced as to why one proffered decision is to prevail over another. Such |727   reasons will ⊥ obviously be based on the canon law by which the disputants have agreed to bind themselves, but they must also represent a preference for one view of that law over another.

If civil courts, consistently with the First Amendment may do that much, the question arises why they may not do what the Illinois courts did here regarding the defrockment of Bishop Dionisije, and

conclude, on the basis of testimony from experts on the canon law at issue, that the decision of the religious tribunal involved was rendered in violation of its own stated rules of procedure. Suppose the Holy Assembly in this case had a membership of 100; its rules provided that a bishop could be defrocked by a majority vote of any session at which a quorum was present, and also provided that a quorum was not to be less than 40. Would a decision of the Holy Assembly attended by 30 members, 16 of whom voted to defrock Bishop Dionisije, be binding on civil courts in a dispute such as this? The hypothetical example is a clearer case than the one involved here, but the principle is the same. If the civil courts are to be bound by any sheet of parchment bearing the ecclesiastical seal and purporting to be a decree of a church court, they can easily be converted into handmaidens of arbitrary lawlessness.

The cases upon which the Court relies are not a uniform line of authorities leading inexorably to reversal of the Illinois judgment. On the contrary, they embody two distinct doctrines which have quite separate origins. The first is a common-law doctrine regarding the appropriate roles for civil courts called upon to adjudicate church property disputes—a doctrine which found general application in federal courts prior to *Erie R. Co.* v. *Tompkins*, but which has never had any application to our review of a state-court ⊥ decision. The other is derived from |728 the First Amendment to the Federal Constitution, and is of course applicable to this case; it, however, lends no more support to the Court's decision than does the common-law doctrine.

The first decision of this Court regarding the role of civil courts in adjudicating church property disputes was *Watson* v. *Jones*. There the Court canvassed the American authorities and concluded that where people had chosen to organize themselves into voluntary religious associations, and had agreed to be bound by the decisions of the hierarchy created to govern such associations, the civil courts could not be availed of to hear appeals from otherwise final decisions of such hierarchical authorities. The bases from which this principle was derived clearly had no constitutional dimension; there was not the slightest suggestion that the First Amendment or any other provision of the Constitution was relevant to the decision in that case. Instead the Court was merely recognizing and applying general rules as to the limited role which civil courts must have in settling private intraorganizational disputes. While those rules, and the reasons behind them, may seem especially relevant to intrachurch disputes, adherence or nonadherence to such principles was certainly not thought to present any First Amendment issues. For as the Court in *Watson* observed:

"Religious organizations come before us in the same attitude as other voluntary associations for benevolent or charitable purposes, and their rights of property, or of contract, are equally under the protection of the law, and the actions of their members subject to its restraints."

The Court's equation of religious bodies with other private voluntary associations makes it clear that the prin⊥ciples discussed in that case were not dependent upon those embodied in the First Amendment.

|729

A year later *Watson*'s observations about the roles of civil courts were followed in *Bouldin* v. *Alexander*, where the Court held that the appointed trustees of the property of a congregational church "cannot be removed from their trusteeship by a minority of the church society or meeting, without warning, and acting without charges, without citation or trial, and in direct contravention of the church rules."

Again, there was nothing to suggest that this was based upon anything but commonsense rules for deciding an intraorganizational dispute; in an organization which provided for majority rule through certain procedures, a minority's attempt to usurp that rule and those procedures need be given no effect by civil courts.

In *Gonzalez* v. *Archbishop*, the Court again recognized the principles underlying *Watson* in upholding a decision of the Supreme Court of the Phillipine Islands that the petitioner was not entitled to the chaplaincy which he claimed because the decision as to whether he possessed the necessary qualifications for that post was one committed to the appropriate church authorities. In dicta which the Court today conveniently truncates, Mr. Justice Brandeis observed:

"In the absence of fraud, collusion, or arbitrariness, the decisions of the proper church tribunals on matters purely ecclesiastical, although affecting civil rights, are accepted in litigation before the secular courts as conclusive, *because the parties in interest made them so by contract or otherwise. Under like circumstances, effect is given in the courts to the determinations of the judicatory bodies estab*

|730

⊥*lished by clubs and civil associations.*" (emphasis supplied).

Gonzalez clearly has no more relevance to the meaning of the First Amendment than do its two predecessors.

1952 was the first occasion on which this Court examined what limits the First and Fourth Amendments might place upon the ability of the States to entertain and resolve disputes over church property. In *Kedroff* v. *St. Nicholas Cathedral*, the Court reversed a decision of the New York Court of Appeals which had upheld a statute awarding control of the New York property of the Russian Orthodox Church to an American group seeking to terminate its relationships with the hierarchical Mother Church in Russia. The New York Legislature had concluded that the communist government of Russia was actually in control of the Mother Church and that "the Moscow patriarchate was no longer capable of functioning as a true religious body, but had become a

tool of the Soviet Government primarily designed to implement its foreign policy," and the New York Court of Appeals sustained the statute against the constitutional attack. This Court, however, held the statute was a violation of the Free Exercise Clause, noting that it [b]y fiat . . . displaces one church administrator with another. It passes the control of matters strictly ecclesiastical from one church authority to another. It thus intrudes for the benefit of one segment of a church the power of the state into the forbidden area of religious freedom contrary to the principles of the First Amendment."

On remand from the decision in *Kedroff*, the New York Court of Appeals again held that the American ⊥ group was entitled to the church property at issue. This time relying upon the common law of the State, the Court of Appeals ruled that the Moscow Patriarchate was so dominated by the secular government of Russia that his appointee could not validly occupy the Church's property. On appeal, this Court reversed summarily, noting in its *per curiam* that "the decision now under review rests on the same premises which were found to have underlain the enactment of the statute struck down in *Kedroff*".

|731

Nine years later, in *Presbyterian Church in the United States* v. *Mary Elizabeth Blue Hull Memorial Presbyterian Church*, the Court held that Georgia's common law, which implied a trust upon local church property for the benefit of the general church only on the condition that the general church adhere to its tenets of faith and practice existing at the time of affiliation by the local churches, was inconsistent with the First and Fourteenth Amendments and therefore could not be utilized to resolve church property disputes. The Georgia law was held impermissible because "[u]nder [the Georgia] approach, property rights do not turn on a church decision as to church doctrine. The standard of departure-from-doctrine, though it calls for resolution of ecclesiastical questions, is a creation of state, not church, law."

Finally, in *Maryland & Virginia Eldership of the Churches of God* v. *Church of God at Sharpsburg, Inc.*, the Court Considered an appeal from a judgment of the Court of Appeals of Maryland upholding the dismissal of two actions brought by the Eldership seeking to prevent two of its local churches from withdrawing from that general religious association. The Eldership had also claimed the rights to select the ⊥ clergy and to control the property of the two local churches, but the Maryland courts, relying "upon provisions of the state statutory law governing the holding of property by religious corporations, upon language in the deeds conveying the properties in question to the local church corporations, upon the terms of the charters of the corporations, *and upon provisions in the constitution of the General Eldership pertinent to the ownership and control of church property,*" (emphasis sup-

|732

plied), concluded that the Eldership had no right to invoke the State's authority to compel their local churches to remain within the fold or to succeed to control of their property. This Court dismissed the Eldership's contention that this judgment violated the First Amendment for want of a substantial federal question.

Despite the Court's failure to do so, it does not seem very difficult to derive the operative constitutional principle from this line of decisions. As should be clear from even this cursory study, *Watson, Bouldin,* and *Gonzalez* have no direct relevance to ⌐733 the question before us today: ⊥ whether the First Amendment, as made applicable to the States by the Fourteenth, prohibits Illinois from permitting its civil courts to settle religious property disputes in the manner presented to us on this record. I think it equally clear that the only cases which *are* relevant to that question— *Kedroff, Kreshik, Blue Hull,* and *Md. & Va. Churches*—require that this question be answered in the negative. The rule of those cases, one which seems fairly implicit in the history of our First Amendment, is that the government may not displace the free religious choices of its citizens by placing its weight behind a particular religious belief, tenet, or sect. That is what New York attempted to do in *Kedroff* and *Kreshik,* albeit perhaps for non-religious reasons, and the Court refused to permit it. In *Blue Hull,* the State transgressed the line drawn by the First Amendment when it applied a state-created rule of law based upon "departure from doctrine" to prevent the national hierarchy of the Presbyterian Church in the United States from seeking to reclaim possession and use of two local churches. When the Georgia courts themselves required an examination into whether there had been a departure from the doctrine of the church in order to apply this state-created rule, they went beyond mere application of neutral principles of law to such a dispute.

There is nothing in this record to indicate that the Illinois courts have been instruments of any such impermissible intrusion by the State on one side or the other of a religious dispute. There is nothing in the Supreme Court of Illinois' opinion indicating that it placed its thumb on the scale in favor of the respondents. Instead that opinion appears to be pre-⌐734 cisely what it pur⊥ports to be: an application of neutral principles of law consistent with the decisions of this Court. Indeed, petitioners make absolutely no claim to the contrary. They agree that the Illinois courts *should* have decided the issues which *they* presented; but they contend that in doing so those courts should have deferred entirely to the representations of the announced representatives of the Mother Church. Such blind deference, however, is counselled neither by logic nor by the First Amendment. To make available the coercive powers of civil courts to rubber-stamp ecclesiastical decisions of hierarchical religious associations, when such deference is not accorded similar acts of secular

voluntary associations, would, in avoiding the Free Exercise problems petitioners envision, itself create far more serious problems under the Establishment Clause.

In any event the Court's decision in *Md. & Va. Churches* demonstrates that petitioners' position in this regard is untenable. And as I read that decision, it seems to me to compel affirmance of at least that portion of the Illinois court's decision which denied petitioners' request for the aid of the civil courts in enforcing its desire to divide the American-Canadian diocese. I see no distinction between the Illinois courts' refusal to place their weight behind the representatives of the Serbian Mother Church who sought to prevent portions of their American congregation from splitting off from that body and the Maryland courts' refusal to do the same thing for the Eldership of the Church of God. The Court today expressly eschews any explanation for its failure to follow *Md. & Va. Churches,* contenting itself with this conclusory statement:

"The constitutional provisions of the American-Canadian Diocese were not so express that the civil ⊥ courts could enforce them without engaging in a ⌐735 searching and therefore impermissible inquiry into church polity."

But comparison of the relevant discussions by the state tribunals regarding their consideration of church documents makes this claimed distinction seem quite specious.

In conclusion, while there may be a number of good arguments that civil courts of a State should, as a matter of the wisest use of their authority, avoid adjudicating religious disputes to the maximum extent possible, they obviously cannot avoid all such adjudications. And while common-law principles like those discussed in *Watson, Bouldin,* and *Gonzalez* may offer some sound principles for those occasions when such adjudications are required, they are certainly not rules to which state courts are required to adhere by virtue of the Fourteenth Amendment. The principles which that Amendment, through its incorporation of the First, *does* enjoin upon the state courts—that they remain neutral on matters of religious doctrine—have not been transgressed by the Supreme Court of Illinois.

JONES v. WOLF

443 U.S. 595
ON WRIT OF CERTIORARI TO THE SUPREME COURT
OF THE STATE OF GEORGIA
Argued January 16, 1979 — Decided July 2, 1979
⊥ *Mr. Justice BLACKMUN* delivered the opinion ⌐597 of the Court.

This case involves a dispute over the ownership of church property following a schism in a local church affiliated with a hierarchical church organization. The question for decision is whether civil courts, consistent with the First and Fourteenth Amendments to the Constitution, may resolve the dispute on the basis of "neutral principles of law," or whether they must defer to the resolution of an authoritative tribunal of the hierarchical church.

I

The Vineville Presbyterian Church of Macon, Ga., was organized in 1904, and first incorporated in 1915. Its corporate charter lapsed in 1935, but was revived and renewed in 1939, and continues in effect at the present time.

The property at issue and on which the church is located was acquired in three transactions, and is evidenced by conveyances to the "Trustees of [or "for"] Vineville Presbyterian Church and their successors in office," or simply to the "Vineville Presbyterian Church." The funds used to acquire the property were contributed entirely by local church members. Pursuant to resolutions adopted by the congregation, the church repeatedly has borrowed money on the property. This indebtedness is evidenced by security deeds variously issued in the name of the "Trustees of the Vineville Presbyterian Church."

In the same year it was organized, the Vineville church was established as a member church of the Augusta-Macon Presbytery of the Presbyterian Church in the United States (PCUS). The PCUS _|598 has a generally hierarchical or connec⊥tional form of government, as contrasted with a congregational form. Under the polity of the PCUS, the government of the local church is committed to its Session in the first instance, but the actions of this assembly or "court" are subject to the review and control of the higher church courts, the Presbytery, Synod, and General Assembly, respectively. The powers and duties of each level of the hierarchy are set forth in the constitution of the PCUS, the Book of Church Order, which is part of the record in the present case.

On May 27, 1973, at a congregational meeting of the Vineville church attended by a quorum of its duly enrolled members, 164 of them, including the pastor, voted to separate from the PCUS. Ninety-four members opposed the resolution. The majority immediately informed the PCUS of the action, and then united with another denomination, the presbyterian Church in America. Although the minority remained on the church rolls for three years, they ceased to participate in the affairs of the Vineville church and conducted their religious activities elsewhere.

In response to the schism within the Vineville congregation, the Augusta-Macon Presbytery appointed a commission to investigate the dispute and, if possible, to resolve it. The commission eventually issued a written ruling declaring that the minority faction constituted "the true congregation of Vineville Presbyterian Church," and withdrawing from the majority faction "all authority to exercise office derived from the [PCUS]." The majority took no part in the commission's inquiry, and did not appeal its ruling to a higher PCUS tribunal.

Representatives of the minority faction sought relief in federal court, but their complaint was dismissed for want of jurisdiction. *Lucas* v. *Hope*, cert. denied. They then brought this class action in state court, seeking declaratory and injunctive orders establishing their right to exclusive possession and use of the ⊥ Vineville church property as a member   _|599 congregation of the PCUS. The trial court, purporting to apply Georgia's "neutral principles of law" approach to church property disputes, granted judgment for the majority. The Supreme Court of Georgia, holding that the trial court had correctly stated and applied Georgia law, and rejecting the minority's challenge based on the First and Fourteenth Amendment, affirmed. We granted a writ of certiorari.

II

Georgia's approach to church property litigation has evolved in response to *Presbyterian Church* v. *Hull Church (Presbyterian Church I)*, rev'g *Presbyterian Church* v. *Eastern Heights Church*. That case was a property dispute between the PCUS and two local Georgia churches that had withdrawn from the PCUS. The Georgia Supreme Court resolved the controversy by applying a theory of implied trust, whereby the property of a local church affiliated with a hierarchical church organization was deemed to be held in trust for the general church, provided the general church had not "substantially abandoned" the tenets of faith and practice as they existed at the time of affiliation. This Court reversed, holding that Georgia would have to find some other way of resolving church property disputes that did not draw the state courts into religious controversies. The Court did not specify what that method should be, although it noted in passing that "there are neutral principles of law, developed for use in all property disputes, which can be applied without 'establishing' churches to which property is awarded." 393 U.S., at 449.

⊥ On remand, the Georgia Supreme Court concluded that, without the departure-from-doctrine   _|600 element, the implied trust theory would have to be abandoned in its entirety. *Presbyterian Church* v. *Eastern Heights Church (Presbyterian Church II)*. In its place, the court adopted what is now known as the "neutral principles of law" method for resolving church property disputes. The court examined the deeds to the properties, the state statutes dealing with implied trusts, Ga. Code §§ 108-106, 108-107, and the Book of Church Order, to determine whether there was any basis for a trust in favor of the general church. Finding nothing that would give rise to a trust in any of these documents, the court awarded the property on the basis of the legal title, which was in the local church, or in the names of trustees for the local church. Review was again sought in this Court, but was denied.

The neutral principles analysis was further refined by the Georgia Supreme Court in *Carnes* v. *Smith.* That case concerned a property dispute between The United Methodist Church and a local congregation that had withdrawn from that church. As in *Presbyterian Church II*, the court found no basis for a trust in favor of the general church in the deeds, the corporate charter, or the state statutes dealing with implied trusts. The court observed, however, that the constitution of The United Methodist Church, its Book of Discipline, contained an express trust provision in favor of the general church. On this basis, the |601 church property was⊥ awarded to the denominational church.

In the present case, the Georgia courts sought to apply the neutral principles analysis of *Presbyterian Church II* and *Carnes* to the facts presented by the Vineville church controversy. Here, as in those two earlier cases, the deeds conveyed the property to the local church. Here, as in the earlier cases, neither the state statutes dealing with implied trusts, nor the corporate charter of the Vineville church, indicated that the general church had any interest in the property. And here, as in *Presbyterian Church II*, but in contrast to *Carnes*, the provisions of the constitution of the general church, the Book of Church Order, concerning the ownership and control of property failed to reveal any language of trust in favor of the general church. The courts accordingly held that legal title to the property of the Vineville church was vested in the local congregation. Without further analysis or elaboration, they further decreed that the local congregation was represented by the majority faction, respondents herein.

|602   ⊥ III

The only question presented by this case is which faction of the formerly united Vineville congregation is entitled to possess and enjoy the property located at 2193 Vineville Avenue in Macon, Ga. There can be little doubt about the general authority of civil courts to resolve this question. The State has an obvious and legitimate interest in the peaceful resolution of property disputes, and in providing a civil forum where the ownership of church property can be determined conclusively.

It is also clear, however, that "the First Amendment severely circumscribes the role that civil courts may play in resolving church property disputes." Most importantly, the First Amendment prohibits civil courts from resolving church property disputes on the basis of religious doctrine and practice. *Serbian Orthodox Diocese* v. *Milivojevich; Md. & Va. Churches* v. *Sharpsburg Church; Presbyterian Church I.* As a corollary to this commandment, the Amendment requires that civil courts defer to the resolution of issues of religious doctrine or polity by the highest court of a hierarchical church organization. *Serbian Orthodox Diocese,* cf. *Watson* v. *Jones.* Subject to these limitations, however, the First Amendment does not dictate that a State must follow a particular method of resolving church property disputes. Indeed, "a State may adopt *any* one of various approaches for settling church property disputes so long as it involves no consideration of doctrinal matters, whether the ritual and liturgy of worship or the tenets of faith." *Md. & Va. Churches* (Brennan, J., concurring) (emphasis in original).

At least in general outline, we think the "neutral principles of law" approach is consistent with the foregoing constitutional principles. The neutral principles approach was ap⊥proved in *Md. & Va.* |603 *Churches,* an appeal from a judgment of the Court of Appeals of Maryland settling a local church property dispute on the basis of the language of the deeds, the terms of the local church charters, the state statutes governing the holding of church property, and the provisions in the constitution of the general church concerning the ownership and control of church property. Finding that this analysis entailed "no inquiry into religious doctrine," the Court dismissed the appeal for want of a substantial federal question. "Neutral principles of law" also received approving reference in *Presbyterian Church I*; in Mr. Justice Brennan's concurrence in *Md. & Va. Churches*; and in *Serbian Orthodox Diocese.*

The primary advantages of the neutral principles approach are that it is completely secular in operation, and yet flexible enough to accommodate all forms of religious organization and polity. The method relies exclusively on objective, well-established concepts of trust and property law familiar to lawyers and judges. It thereby promises to free civil courts completely from entanglement in questions of religious doctrine, polity, and practice. Furthermore, the neutral principles analysis shares the peculiar genius of private-law systems in general—flexibility in ordering private rights and obligations to reflect the intentions of the parties. Through appropriate reversionary clauses and trust provisions, religious societies can specify what is to happen to church property in the event of a particular contingency, or what religious body will determine the ownership in the event of a schism or doctrinal controversy. In this manner, a religious organization⊥ can ensure |604 that a dispute over the ownership of church property will be resolved in accord with the desires of the members.

This is not to say that the application of the neutral principles approach is wholly free of difficulty. The neutral principles method, at least as it has evolved in Georgia, requires a civil court to examine certain religious documents, such as a church constitution, for language of trust in favor of the general church. In undertaking such an examination, a civil court must take special care to scrutinize the document in purely secular terms, and not to rely on religious precepts in determining whether the document indicates that the parties have intended to create a trust. In addition, there may be cases where the deed, the corporate charter, or the constitution of the general church incorporates religious concepts in the provisions relating to the ownership of property. If in such a case the interpretation of the instruments of ownership would require the civil court to resolve a religious controversy, then the court must defer to the resolution of the doctrinal issue by the authoritative ecclesiastical body. *Serbian Orthodox Diocese.*

On balance, however, the promise of nonentanglement and neutrality inherent in the neutral principles approach more than compensates for what will be occasional problems in application. These problems, in addition, should be gradually eliminated as recognition is given to the obligation of "States, religious organizations, and individuals [to] structure relationships involving church property so as not to require the civil courts to resolve ecclesiastical questions." *Presbyterian Church I.* We therefore hold that a State is constitutionally entitled to adopt neutral principles of law as a means of adjudicating a church property dispute.

The dissent would require the States to abandon the neutral principles method, and instead would insist as a matter of constitutional law that whenever a dispute arises over the⊥ ownership of church property, civil courts must defer to the "authoritative resolution of the dispute within the church itself." It would require, first, that civil courts review ecclesiastical doctrine and polity to determine where the church has "placed ultimate authority over the use of the church property." After answering this question, the courts would be required to "determine whether the dispute has been resolved within that structure of government and, if so, what decision has been made." They would then be required to enforce that decision. We cannot agree, however, that the First Amendment requires the States to adopt a rule of compulsory deference to religious authority in resolving church property disputes, even where no issue of doctrinal controversy is involved.

The dissent suggests that a rule of compulsory deference would somehow involve less entanglement of civil courts in matters of religious doctrine, practice, and administration. Under its approach, however, civil courts would always be required to examine the polity and administration of a church to determine which unit of government has ultimate control over church property. In some cases, this task would not prove to be difficult. But in others, the locus of control would be ambiguous, and "A careful examination of the constitutions of the general and local church, as well as other relevant documents, [would] be necessary to ascertain the form of governance adopted by the members of the religious association." In such cases, the suggested rule would appear to require "a

⌊605

searching and therefore impermissible inquiry into church polity." *Serbian Orthodox Diocese.* The neutral principles approach, in contrast, obviates entirely the need for an analysis or examination of ecclesiastical polity or doctrine in settling church property disputes.

The dissent also argues that a rule of compulsory deference is necessary in order to protect the free exercise rights "of⊥ those who have formed the association and submitted themselves to its authority." This argument assumes that the neutral principles method would somehow frustrate the free exercise rights of the members of a religious association. Nothing could be further from the truth. The neutral principles approach cannot be said to "inhibit" the free exercise of religion, any more than do other neutral provisions of state law governing the manner in which churches own property, hire employees, or purchase goods. Under the neutral principles approach, the outcome of a church property dispute is not foreordained. At any time before the dispute erupts, the parties can ensure, if they so desire, that the faction loyal to the hierarchical church will retain the church property. They can modify the deeds or the corporate charter to include a right of reversion or trust in favor of the general church. Alternatively, the constitution of the general church can be made to recite an express trust in favor of the denominational church. The burden involved in taking such steps will be minimal. And the civil courts will be bound to give effect to the result indicated by the parties, provided it is embodied in some legally cognizable form.

⌊606

IV

It remains to be determined whether the Georgia neutral principles analysis was constitutionally applied on the facts of this case. Although both the trial court and the Supreme Court of Georgia viewed the case as involving nothing more than an application of the principles developed in *Presbyterian Church II* and in *Carnes*, the present case contains a significant complicating factor absent in each of those earlier cases. *Presbyterian Church II* and *Carnes* each involved a⊥ church property dispute between the general church and the entire local congregation. Here, the local congregation was itself divided between a majority of 164 members who sought to withdraw from the PCUS, and a minority of 94 members who wished to maintain the affiliation. Neither of the state courts alluded to this problem, however; each concluded without discussion or analysis that the title to the property was in the local church and that the local church was represented by the majority rather than the minority.

Petitioners earnestly submit that the question of which faction is the true representative of the Vineville church is an ecclesiastical question that cannot be answered by a civil court. At least, it is said, it

⌊607

cannot be answered by a civil court in a case involving a hierarchical church, like the PCUS, where a duly appointed church commission has determined which of the two factions represents the "true congregation." Respondents, in opposition, argue in effect that the Georgia courts did no more than apply the ordinary presumption that, absent some indication to the contrary, a voluntary religious association is represented by a majority of its members.

If in fact Georgia has adopted a presumptive rule of majority representation, defeasible upon a showing that the identity of the local church is to be determined by some other means, we think this would be consistent with both the neutral principles analysis and the First Amendment. Majority rule is generally employed in the governance of religious societies. See *Bouldin* v. *Alexander.* Furthermore, the majority faction generally can be identified without resolving any question of religious doctrine or polity. Certainly, there was no dispute in the present case about the identity of the duly enrolled members of the Vineville church when the dispute arose, or about the fact that a quorum was present, or about the final vote. Most importantly, any rule of majority representation can always be overcome, under the neutral principles approach, either by providing, in ⌐608 the corporate⊥ charter or the constitution of the general church, that the identity of the local church is to be established in some other way, or by providing that the church property is held in trust for the general church and those who remain loyal to it. Indeed, the State may adopt any method of overcoming the majoritarian presumption, so long as the use of that method does not impair free exercise rights or entangle the civil courts in matters of religious controversy.

Neither the trial court nor the Supreme Court of Georgia, however, explicitly stated that it was adopting a presumptive rule of majority representation. Moreover, there are at least some indications that under Georgia law the process of identifying the faction that represents the Vineville church involves considerations of religious doctrine and polity. Georgia law requires that "church property be held according to the terms of the church government," and provides that a local church affiliated with a hierarchical religious association "is part of the whole body of the general church and is subject to the higher authority of the organization and its law and ⌐609 regulations." *Carnes* v. *Smith;*⊥ see Ga. Code §§ 22-5507, 22-5508. All this may suggest that the identity of the "Vineville Presbyterian Church" named in the deeds must be determined according to terms of the Book of Church Order, which sets out the laws and regulations of churches affiliated with the PCUS. Such a determination, however, would appear to require a civil court to pass on questions of religious doctrine, and to usurp the function of the commission appointed by the Presbytery, which already has determined that petitioners represent the "true

congregation" of the Vineville church. Therefore, if Georgia law provides that the identity of the Vineville church is to be determined according to the "laws and regulations" of the PCUS, then the First Amendment requires that the Georgia courts give deference to the presbyterial commission's determination of that church's identity.

This Court, of course, does not declare what the law of Georgia is. Since the grounds for the decision that respond⊥ents represent the Vineville church ⌐610 remain unarticulated, the judgment of the Supreme Court of Georgia is vacated and the case is remanded for further proceedings not inconsistent with this opinion.

It is so ordered.

Mr. Justice POWELL, with whom *The CHIEF JUSTICE, Mr. Justice STEWART*, and *Mr. Justice WHITE* join, dissenting.

This case presents again a dispute among church members over the control of a local church's property. Although the Court appears to accept established principles that I have thought would resolve this case, it superimposes on these principles a new structure of rules that will make the decision of these cases by civil courts more difficult. The new analysis also is more likely to invite intrusion into church polity forbidden by the First Amendment.

I

The Court begins by stating that "[t]his case involves a dispute over the ownership of church property," suggesting that the concern is with legal or equitable ownership in the real property sense. But the ownership of the property of the Vineville church is not at issue. The deeds place title in the Vineville Presbyterian Church, or in trustees of that church, and none of the parties has questioned the validity of those deeds. The question actually presented is which of the factions within the local congregation has the right to control the actions of the titleholder, and thereby to control the use of the property, as the Court later acknowledges.

Since 1872 disputes over control of church property usually have been resolved under principles established by *Watson* v. *Jones*. Under the new and complex, two-stage analysis approved today, a court instead first must apply newly defined "neutral principles of law" to determine⊥ whether property titled ⌐611 to the local church is held in trust for the general church organization with which the local church is affiliated. If it is, then the court will grant control of the property to the councils of the general church. If not, then control by the local congregation will be recognized. In the latter situation, if there is a schism in the local congregation, as in this case, the second stage of the new analysis becomes applicable. Again, the Court fragments the analysis into two substeps for the purpose of determining which of the factions should control the property.

As this new approach inevitably will increase the involvement of civil courts in church controversies, and as it departs from long-established precedents, I dissent.

A

The first stage in the "neutral principles of law" approach operates as a restrictive rule of evidence. A court is required to examine the deeds to the church property, the charter of the local church (if there is one), the book of order or discipline of the general church organization, and the state statutes governing the holding of church property. The object of the inquiry, where the title to the property is in the local church, is "to determine whether there [is] any basis for a trust in favor of the general church." The court's investigation is to be "completely secular," "rel[ying] exclusively on objective, well-established concepts of trust and property law familiar to lawyers and judges." Thus, where religious documents such as church constitutions or books of order must be examined "for language of trust in favor of the general church," "a civil court must take special care to scrutinize the documents in purely secular terms, and not to rely on religious precepts in determining whether the document indicates that the parties have intended to create a trust." It follows that the civil courts using this analysis may consider the form ⌐612 of religious govern⊥ment adopted by the church members for the resolution of intrachurch disputes *only* if that policy has been stated, in express relation to church property, in the language of trust and property law.

One effect of the Court's evidentiary rule is to deny to the courts relevant evidence as to the religious polity—that is, the form of governance—adopted by the church members. The constitutional documents of churches tend to be drawn in terms of religious precepts. Attempting to read them "in purely secular terms" is more likely to promote confusion than understanding. Moreover, whenever religious polity has not been expressed in specific ⌐613 statements referring to the property⊥ of a church, there will be no evidence of that polity cognizable under the neutral-principles rule. Lacking such evidence, presumably a court will impose some rule of church government derived from state law. In the present case, for example, the general and unqualified authority of the Presbytery over the actions of the Vineville church had not been expressed in secular terms of control of its property. As a consequence, the Georgia courts could find no acceptable evidence of this authoritative relationship, and they imposed instead a congregational form of government determined from state law.

This limiting of the evidence relative to religious government cannot be justified on the ground that it "free[s] civil courts completely from entanglement in questions of religious doctrine, polity, and practice." For unless the body identified as authoritative under state law resolves the underlying dispute in accord with the decision of the church's own authority, the state court effectively will have reversed the decisions of doctrine and practice made in accordance with church law. The schism in the Vineville church, for example, resulted from disagreements among the church members over questions of doctrine and practice. Under the Book of Church Order, these questions were resolved authoritatively by the higher church courts, which then gave control of the local church to the faction loyal to that resolution. The Georgia courts, as a matter of state law, granted control to the schismatic faction, and thereby effectively reversed the doctrinal decision of the church courts. This indirect interference by the civil courts with the resolution of religious disputes within the church is no less proscribed by the First Amendment than is the direct decision of questions of doctrine and practice.

⊥ When civil courts step in to resolve intrachurch   ⌐614 disputes over control of church property, they will either support or overturn the authoritative resolution of the dispute within the church itself. The new analysis, under the attractive banner of "neutral principles," actually invites the civil courts to do the latter. The proper rule of decision, that I thought had been settled until today, requires a court to give effect in all cases to the decisions of the church government agreed upon by the members before the dispute arose.

B

The Court's basic neutral-principles approach, as a means of isolating decisions concerning church property from other decisions made within the church, relies on the concept of a trust of local church property in favor of the general church. Because of this central premise, the neutral-principles rule suffices to settle only disputes between the central councils of a church organization and a unanimous local congregation. Where, as here, the neutral-principles inquiry reveals no trust in favor of the general church, and the local congregation is split into factions, the basic question remains unresolved: which faction should have control of the local church?

⊥ The Court acknowledges that the church law of   ⌐615 the Presbyterian Church in the United States (PCUS), of which the Vineville church is a part, provides for the authoritative resolution of this question by the Presbytery. Indeed, the Court indicates that Georgia, consistently with the First Amendment, may adopt the *Watson* v. *Jones* rule of adherence to the resolution of the dispute according to church law—a rule that would necessitate reversal of the judgment for the respondents. But instead of requiring the state courts to take this approach, the

Court approves as well an alternative rule of state law: the Georgia courts are said to be free to "adop[t] a presumptive rule of majority representation, defeasible upon a showing that the identity of the local church is to be determined by some other means." This showing may be made by proving that the church has provid[ed], in the corporate charter or the constitution of the general church, that the identity of the local church is to be established in some other way."

On its face, this rebuttable presumption also requires reversal of the state court's judgment in favor of the schismatic faction. The polity of the PCUS commits to the Presbytery the resolution of the dispute within the local church. Having shown this structure of church government for the determination of the identity of the local congregation, the petitioners have rebutted any presumption that this question has been left to a majority vote of the local congregation.

The Court nevertheless declines to order reversal. Rather than decide the case here in accordance with established First Amendment principles, the Court leaves open the possibility that the state courts might adopt some restrictive evidentiary rule that would render the petitioners' evidence inadequate to overcome the presumption of majority control. But, aside from a passing reference to the use of the neutral-principles approach developed earlier in its⊥ opinion, the Court affords no guidance as to the constitutional limitations on such an evidentiary rule; the state courts, it says, are free to adopt any rule that is constitutional.

⌐616

"Indeed, the state may adopt any method of overcoming the majoritarian presumption, so long as the use of that method does not impair free exercise rights or entangle the civil courts in matters of religious controversy."

In essence, the Court's instructions on remand therefore allow the state courts the choice of following the long-settled rule of *Watson* v. *Jones* or of adopting some other rule—unspecified by the Court—that the state courts view as consistent with the First Amendment. Not only questions of state law but also important issues of federal constitutional law thus are left to the state courts for their decision, and if they depart from *Watson* v. *Jones*, they will travel a course left totally uncharted by this Court.

II

Disputes among church members over the control of church property arise almost invariably out of disagreements regarding doctrine and practice. Because of the religious nature of these disputes, civil courts should decide them according to principles that do not interfere with the free exercise of religion in accordance with church polity and doctrine. *Serbian*⊥ *Orthodox Diocese* v. *Milivojevich; Presbyterian Church* v. *Hull Church; Kedroff* v. *Saint Nicholas*

⌐617

Cathedral; (Frankfurter, J., concurring). See also *Kreshik* v. *Saint Nicholas Cathedral; Maryland & Va. Eldership* v. *Sharpsburg Church*, appeal dismissed for want of a substantial federal question. The only course that achieves this constitutional requirement is acceptance by civil courts of the decisions reached within the polity chosen by the church members themselves. The classic statement of this view is found in *Watson* v. *Jones.*

"The right to organize voluntary religious associations to assist in the expression and dissemination of any religious doctrine, and to create tribunals for the decision of controverted questions of faith, within the association, and for the ecclesiastical government of all the individual members, congregations, and officers within the general association, is unquestioned. All who unite themselves to such a body do so with an implied consent to this government, and are bound to submit to it. But it would be a vain consent and would lead to the total subversion of such religious bodies, if any one aggrieved by one of their decisions could appeal to the secular courts and have them reversed. It is of the essence of these religious⊥ unions, and of their right to establish tribunals for the decision of questions arising among themselves, that those decisions should be binding in all cases of ecclesiastical cognizance, subject only to such appeals as the organism itself provides for."

618⌐

Accordingly, in each case involving an intrachurch dispute—including disputes over church property—the civil court must focus directly on ascertaining, and then following, the decision made within the structure of church governance. By doing so, the court avoids two equally unacceptable departures from the genuine neutrality mandated by the First Amendment. First, it refrains from direct review and revision of decisions of the church on matters of religious doctrine and practice that underlie the church's determination of intrachurch controversies, including those that relate to control of church property. Equally important, by recognizing the authoritative resolution reached with the religious association, the civil court avoids interfering indirectly with the religious governance of those who have formed the association and submitted themselves to its authority. See *Watson* v. *Jones; Kedroff* v. *Saint Nicholas Cathedral.*

III

Until today, and under the foregoing authorities, the first question presented in a case involving an intrachurch dispute over church property was where within the religious associa⊥tion the rules of polity, accepted by its members before the schism, had placed ultimate authority over the use of the church property. The courts, in answering this question have recognized two broad categories of church government. One is congregational, in which authority over questions of church doctrine, practice, and administration rests entirely in the local congregation

619⌐

or some body within it. In disputes over the control and use of the property of such a church, the civil courts enforce the authoritative resolution of the controversy within the local church itself. *Watson* v. *Jones*. The second is hierarchical, in which the local church is but an integral and subordinate part of a larger church and is under the authority of the general church. Since the decisions of the local congregation are subject to review by the tribunals of the church hierarchy, this Court has held that the civil courts must give effect to the duly made decisions of the highest body within the hierarchy that has considered the dispute. As we stated in *Serbian Orthodox Diocese* v. *Milivojevich*,

"[T]he First and Fourteenth Amendments permit hierarchical religious organizations to establish their own rules and regulations for internal discipline and government, and to create tribunals for adjudicating disputes over these matters. When this choice is exercised and ecclesiastical tribunals are created to decide disputes over the government and direction of subordinate bodies, the Constitution *requires* that civil courts accept their decisions as binding upon them."

⌐620 A careful examination of the constitutions of the general⊥ and local church, as well as other relevant documents, may be necessary to ascertain the form of governance adopted by the members of the religious association. But there is no reason to restrict the courts to statements of polity related directly to church property. For the constitutionally necessary limitations are imposed not on the evidence to be considered but instead on the object of the inquiry, which is both limited and clear: the civil court must determine whether the local church remains autonomous, so that its members have unreviewable authority to withdraw it (and its property) from the general church, or whether the local church is inseparably integrated into and subordinate to the general church.

IV

The principles developed in prior decisions thus afford clear guidance in the case before us. The Vineville church is presbyterian, a part of the PCUS. The presbyterian form of church government, adopted by the PCUS, is "a hierarchical structure of tribunals which consists of, in ascending order, (1) the Church Session, composed of the leaders of the local church; (2) the Presbytery, composed of several churches in a geographical area; (3) the Synod, generally composed of all Presbyteries within a State; and (4) the General Assembly, the highest governing body." *Pres-*
⌐621 *byterian Church* v. *Hull*⊥ *Church*. The Book of Church Order subjects the Session to "review and control" by the Presbytery in all matters, even authorizing the Presbytery to replace the leadership of the local congregation, to winnow its membership, and to take control of it. No provision of the Book of

Church Order gives the Session the authority to withdraw the local church from the PCUS; similarly, no section exempts such a decision by the local church from review by the Presbytery. Thus, while many matters, including the management of the church property, are committed in the first instance to the Session and congregation of the local church, their actions are subject to review by the Presbytery. Here, the Presbytery exercised its authority over the local church, removing the dissidents from church office, asserting direct control over the government of the church, and recognizing the petitioners as the legitimate congregation and Session of the church. It is undisputed that under the established government of the Presbyterian church—accepted by the members of the church before the schism—the use and control of the church property have been determined authoritatively to be in the petitioners. Accordingly, under the principles I have thought were settled, there is no occasion for the further examination of the law of Georgia that the Court directs. On remand, the Georgia courts should be directed to enter judgment for the petitioners.

3 THE FREE EXERCISE OF RELIGION

The Mormon Cases

Both because of specific guarantees of the basic documents of national and state governments and the general spirit of liberality that has ordinarily prevailed in this country, the American people enjoy a great degree of religious freedom. At least 1200 religious bodies exist in the United States [1] and quite remarkable, sometimes even bizarre, activities have been countenanced as legitimate exercises of religion.

Broad though it is, however, religious freedom is not without limits. No freedom is absolute, and liberty can never be equated with license. The cherished right of the individual to free exercise of religion often conflicts with equally valued rights of other individuals and the interests of society. It is difficult, at best, to apply general constitutional principles to concrete problem situations; when these principles collide with one another, the difficulty is increased.

One of the primary functions and traditional powers of government is its authority to protect the health, safety, morals, and welfare of society. Exercise of this "police power" has frequently created conflict between governmental authority and avowed religious rights of individuals and groups. Examples are not difficult to find. Compulsory vaccination of school children is required though opposed by some on religious grounds. Physical examinations before marriage or before admission to state universities are demanded even of those whose religion forbids such examination. Practice of medicine for a fee by an unlicensed physician is illegal though the practitioner claims to heal through prayer. Sabbatarians are often subjected to Sunday observance laws that result in economic loss as well as religious distress. Handling of poisonous snakes in a public place without reasonable care, even as a religious ritual, is forbidden. [2] Churches must comply with zoning ordinances and building codes thought necessary to protect the public.

Violations of statutory provisions in these and innumerable other areas result in prosecution of those who, on religious grounds, fail to comply with the law. Courts, as constitutional arbiters, are then called on to undertake the difficult, if not impossible, task of resolving the resulting conflict between religious claims and asserted societal interests. Members of recognized mainline churches seldom find it necessary to call on courts to protect their First Amendment rights. Members of "cults" and other new or unorthodox movements that have not yet gained public acceptance often feel that need acutely. Their doctrines and methods are viewed as "strange" by the public, and they are regarded with great distrust. They are too often subjected to discriminatory action by government as well as individuals. [3]

From their earliest creation, state courts have dealt with the issue of religious liberty in cases brought before them. But, because Congress enacted no such legislation

---

[1] J. Gordon Melton gives this figure in his extensive study of the various religious groups in the United States, *The Encyclopedia of American Religions*, 2 vols. (Wilmington, N.C.: McGrath Publishing Company, 1978).

[2] As late as 1976, through denial of a petition for a writ of certiorari, in *Pack* v. *Tennessee ex rel. Swan*, the Supreme Court let stand action of the State of Tennessee in permanently enjoining a religious group, the Holiness Church of God in Jesus Name, of Newport, Tennessee, from handling or displaying dangerous and poisonous snakes or consuming strychnine or other similarly poisonous substances.

[3] Although the Supreme Court has rather consistently refused to hear appeals, members of such new and unorthodox religions as the Founding Church of Scientology, the Worldwide Church of God, the Unification Church, the International Society for Krishna Consciousness, and Children of God have in recent years been heavily involved in litigation in lower courts. An excellent discussion of the tribulations of unpopular new religions is found in Chapter 7 of Leo Pfeffer's *Religion, State and the Supreme Court* (New York: Prometheus Books, 1984), pp. 201-34.

and the states were long held not to be subject to the inhibitions of the First Amendment, no such cases reached the Supreme Court of the United States during its first hundred years, and only a few were heard by the Court until 1940. Since that time, however, a substantial body of federal constitutional law relating to freedom of religion has been developed. There has been an ever increasing opportunity for both federal and state courts to add to and refine this case law in recent years. In 1983, Frank Way and Barbara J. Burt reported that from 1946 to 1956 there were sixty-six state and federal cases in which free exercise claims were raised. In the ten years from 1970 to 1980 there were 384 such cases. [4]

Adherents of the Church of Jesus Christ of Latter Day Saints, better known as Mormans, [5] gave the Supreme Court its first opportunity to speak directly to the issue of religious liberty in litigation involving claims of its violation. The Mormons were subjected to both private and governmental harassment almost from the founding of their denomination by Joseph Smith in 1830. Most of Smith's followers migrated within a short time to the Midwest. After a few years in Ohio, they moved on to Jackson County, Missouri. There they were regarded with great suspicion by the other inhabitants of the area. This distrust stemmed in part from accounts of the eccentric religious beliefs and practices of the Mormons. However, it was likely also fostered by the group and their obvious growth and prosperity, which aroused fear on the part of some that they might eventually be dominated or dispossessed by the sect.

In 1834 a mob destroyed the printing shop of the community newspaper and committed other acts of violence. Appeals to the governor, President Andrew Jackson, and Congress proved futile. The Mormons then formed their own militia in 1838—an action that aggravated the situation still further. Subsequently the governor issued what came to be known as the "Boggs Exterminating Order," and seventeen Mormons were killed by state forces.

The members of the sect moved the next year to Illinois, where they established a large colony called Nauvoo; but again they were soon at odds with the residents of nearby communities. Armed conflict broke out in 1844, and the state militia was ordered to defeat and disarm the Nauvoo Legion. Joseph Smith and his brother were arrested and, while awaiting trial for treason, were murdered by a mob.

After Smith's death, a division occurred within the church, and the newly elected president, Brigham Young, led one faction on a long trek westward to the Great Salt Lake area. There they established the "State of Deseret," which became the Territory of Utah in 1850. Young served not only as president of the church in Utah but also as governor of the territory from 1850 to 1854.

Efforts of the church met with great economic as well as spiritual success in Utah, but its members soon came once again under great popular and governmental pressure. This time the primary cause of the conflict was polygamy, or "plural marriage." There had been rumors in Illinois that Joseph Smith and some of the other leaders of the community engaged in polygamy: he claimed to have received a "revelation" concerning the practice the year before his death. Not until 1852, however, did Brigham Young, who ultimately married twenty-seven women in all, proclaim polygamy to be an official tenet of the church.

Polygamy was probably never practiced by many members of the Mormon church. But the idea of plural marriage in any case was repugnant to most Americans, who saw it as posing a serious threat to the traditional concept of the monogamous family unit as the bulwark of a stable society. The great public outcry led Congress in 1862 to pass the Morrill Act in order "to punish and prevent the practice of polygamy in the Territories."

Among others, George Reynolds, private secretary to Brigham Young, was prosecuted and convicted under the statute. A territorial court rejected his contention that the law could not be constitutionally applied to a Mormon who practiced polygamy in the belief that it was a religious duty. Reynolds appealed to the Supreme Court, and in REYNOLDS v. UNITED STATES (1878) (p. 49) that body handed down its first decision directly concerning an alleged violation of religious freedom as guaranteed by the First Amendment.

Confronted for the first time with specific litigation requiring location of the constitutional line of demarcation between religious rights of the individual and regulatory power of the federal government, the Court found it necessary to formulate the first of several "tests" or standards that it has since developed and applied to reach decisions—or at least to rationalize its decisions. No one test has been exclusively or consistently applied, and it has sometimes seemed that the justices groped for arguments to justify their preconceived conclusions.

In unanimously sustaining the statute as applied to Reynolds, the Court, speaking through Chief Justice Waite, announced a rather simplistic and antilibertarian "action-belief" doctrine as its guiding standard. That is, the First Amendment makes *belief* absolute, but not action based on that belief. As the Chief Justice said, "Congress was deprived of all legislative power over mere opinion, but was left free to reach actions which were in violation of social duties or subversive of good order." Or as he phrased it at another point: "Laws are made for the government of actions, and while they cannot interfere with mere religious belief and opinions, they may with practices." Interestingly, one may note the use in the opinion of the *argumentum ad horrendum* where Waite suggested that a contrary decision of the Court might later be used to justify human sacrifice as a religious practice or the efforts of a wife to burn herself on the funeral pyre of her husband because she believes it to be her religious duty.

[4] "Religious Marginality and the Free Exercise Clause," *The American Political Science Review* 77 (September 1983): 652-65. The study also found a much higher success rate for the claims. The authors attribute the great increase in cases to several causes among which are greater involvement of rapidly proliferating "marginal religions" in litigation; increase in population; availability of legal remedies under legislation such as Title VII of the Civil Rights Act of 1964, which was not available in earlier years; and the perception of a more favorable attitude on the part of the judges.

[5] Anthony A. Hoekema, *The Four Major Cults* (Grand Rapids: William B. Eerdmans Publishing Co., 1963) gives an excellent account of both the Mormon and Jehovah's Witnesses movements. Hoekema also discusses Christian Science and Seventh-day Adventism, which sometimes have been involved in religious rights litigations.

A dozen years later, in DAVIS v. BEASON (p. 52), another unanimous Court extended the "belief-action" dichotomy to allow punishment for even the advocacy of belief or for the association with others who believe in polygamy. Davis, a Mormon but not a practicing polygamist, had been convicted of violating a statute of the Idaho Territory by taking falsely an oath required of a voter. The oath was to the effect that not only was he not a bigamist but also was not a member of any organization that taught or encouraged its members to practice polygamy and he did not teach or encourage anyone to commit such a crime "either as a religious duty or otherwise." Observing that "[c]rime is not the less odious because sanctioned by what any particular sect may designate as religion," Justice Field again denied that the First Amendment was ever intended to be "invoked as a protection against legislation for the punishment of acts inimical to the peace, good order and morals of society."

In *Church of Jesus Christ of Latter-Day Saints* v. *United States*, another case decided in 1890, the Court upheld a federal statute revoking the charter of the Mormon Church and confiscating much of its property. These and other punitive actions taken against members of the church forced its president to issue an order in 1890 which renounced polygamous marriages and advised church members "to refrain from contracting any marriage forbidden by the law of the land." [6]

Utah was admitted as a state in 1896 under a constitution forbidding polygamous or plural marriages.

During a period in which the American people were not yet sensitized to minority rights, these legislative acts and decisions of the Court occasioned no outburst of public indignation. In general, they were regarded as a triumph for the forces of morality in their battle for order and decency. The "belief-action" test, which gave an extraordinarily narrow definition of the constitutional guarantee of "free exercise of religion," has not been specifically overruled by the Court. However, it has never again been advanced as the sole standard used to arrive at a decision, and since 1970 has seldom been cited as controlling. [7]

---

[6] Not all of the members of the church have followed this advice. Some Mormons have come in conflict with the law in more recent years and have fared no better in court than their forebears. In *Cleveland* v. *United States* (1946), the Supreme Court upheld the convictions of members of a fundamental Mormon sect for violation of the Mann "White Slave" Act when they transported their plural wives across state lines. The Court in 1955 let stand the decision of a Utah court which denied custody of their children to parents who taught them the now disavowed tenets concerning plural marriage (*In re Black*).

[7] Professor Laurence H. Tribe of Harvard University traces at considerable length the departure of the Court from the *Reynolds* belief-action doctrine, particularly subsequent to the pronouncement of new "tests" in *Sherbert* v. *Verner*, in *The Constitutional Protection of Individual Rights: Limits on Government Authority* (Mineola, N.Y.: The Foundation Press, Inc., 1978). Chapter 14 of this outstanding work is devoted to the topic "Rights of Religious Autonomy." Rodney K. Smith is highly critical of the Court's use of the belief-action dichotomy and the Jeffersonian concept of free exercise which permitted government to regulate beliefs when they resulted in acts against "peace and good order" in *Reynolds*, and is gratified by the abandonment of the test by today's Court. "Getting Off on the Wrong Foot and Back on Again: A Reexamination of the History of the Framing of the Religion Clauses of the First Amendment and a Critique of the *Reynolds* and *Everson* Decisions," *Wake Forest Law Review* 20 (Fall 1984): 569-642.

REYNOLDS v. UNITED STATES

98 U.S. 145
IN ERROR TO THE SUPREME COURT OF
THE TERRITORY OF UTAH
Motion Submitted February 13, 1878 — Decided
February 18, 1878
Argued November 14, 15, 1878 — Redecided January
4, 1879

⊥*Mr. CHIEF JUSTICE WAITE* delivered the ⌐153
opinion of the court:

This is an indictment for bigamy under Section 5352, Revised Statutes, which, omitting its exceptions, is as follows:

"Every person having a husband or wife living, who marries another, whether married or single, in a Territory, or other place over which the United States have exclusive jurisdiction, is guilty of bigamy, and shall be punished by a fine of not more than $500, and by imprisonment for a term of not more than five years."

The assignments of error, when grouped, present the following questions:

1. Was the indictment bad because found by a grand jury of less than sixteen persons?

2. Were the challenges of certain petit jurors by the accused improperly overruled?

3. Were the challenges of certain other jurors by the Government improperly sustained?

4. Was the testimony of Amelia Jane Schofield, given at a former trial for the same offense, but under another indictment, improperly admitted in evidence?

5. Should the accused have been acquitted if he married the second time, because he believed it to be his religious duty?

6. Did the court err in that part of the charge which directed the attention of the jury to the consequences of polygamy?

These questions will be considered in their order. [Discussion of first four questions omitted] ⊥   ⌐161

5. As to the defense of religious belief or duty.

On the trial, the plaintiff in error, the accused, proved that at the time of his alleged second marriage he was, and for many years before had been, a member of the Church of Jesus Christ of Latter-Day Saints, commonly called the Mormon Church, and a believer in its doctrines; that it was an accepted doctrine of that Church "That it was the duty of male members of said Church, circumstances permitting, to practice polygamy; . . . that this duty was enjoined by different books which the members of said Church believed to be of divine origin, and among others the Holy Bible, and also that the members of the Church believed that the practice of polygamy was directly enjoined upon the male members thereof by the Almighty God, in a revelation to Joseph Smith, the founder and prophet of said Church; that the failing or refusing to practice polygamy by such male members of said Church, when circumstances would admit, would be punished, and that the penalty for such failure and refusal would be damnation in the life to come." He also proved "That he had received permission from the recognized authorities in said Church to enter into polygamous marriage; . . . that Daniel H. Wells, one having authority in said Church to perform the marriage ceremony, married the said defendant on or about the time the crime is alleged to have been committed, to some woman by the name of Schofield, and that such marriage ceremony was performed under and pursuant to the doctrines of said Church."

Upon this proof he asked the court to instruct the jury that if they found from the evidence that he ⏌162 "was married as ⊥ charged (if he was married) in pursuance of and in conformity with what he believed at the time to be a religious duty, that the verdict must be 'not guilty.'" This request was refused, and the court did charge "That there must have been a criminal intent, but that if the defendant, under the influence of a religious belief that it was right— under an inspiration, if you please, that it was right—deliberately married a second time, having a first wife living, the want of consciousness of evil intent, the want of understanding on his part that he was committing a crime, did not excuse him; but the law inexorably in such case implies the criminal intent."

Upon this charge and refusal to charge the question is raised, whether religious belief can be accepted as a justification of an overt act made criminal by the law of the land. The inquiry is not as to the power of Congress to prescribe criminal laws for the Territories, but as to the guilt of one who knowingly violates a law which has been properly enacted, if he entertains a religious belief that the law is wrong.

Congress cannot pass a law for the government of the Territories which shall prohibit the free exercise of religion. The first amendment to the Constitution expressly forbids such legislation. Religious freedom is guaranteed everywhere throughout the United States, so far as congressional interference is concerned. The question to be determined is, whether the law now under consideration comes within this prohibition.

The word "religion" is not defined in the Constitution. We must go elsewhere, therefore, to ascertain its meaning, and nowhere more appropriately, we think, than to the history of the times in the midst of which the provision was adopted. The precise point of the inquiry is, what is the religious freedom which has been guaranteed?

Before the adoption of the Constitution, attempts were made in some of the Colonies and States to legislate not only in respect to the establishment of religion, but in respect to its doctrines and precepts as well. The people were taxed, against their will, for the support of religion, and sometimes for the support of particular sects to whose tenets they could

not and did not subscribe. Punishments were prescribed for a failure to attend upon public worship, and sometimes for entertaining ⊥ heretical opinions. The controversy upon this general subject was animated in many of the States, but seemed at last to culminate in Virginia. In 1784, the House of Delegates of that State having under consideration "A bill establishing provision for teachers of the Christian religion," postponed it until the next session, and directed that the bill should be published and distributed, and that the People be requested "to signify their opinion respecting the adoption of such a bill at the next session of the Assembly."

This brought out a determined opposition. Amongst others, Mr. Madison prepared a "Memorial and Remonstrance," which was widely circulated and signed, and in which he demonstrated that religion, or the duty we owe the Creator", was not within the cognizance of civil government. At the next session the proposed bill was not only defeated, but another, "for establishing religious freedom," drafted by Mr. Jefferson was passed. In the preamble of this Act, religious freedom is defined; and after a recital "That to suffer the civil magistrate to intrude his powers into the field of opinion, and to restrain the profession or propagation of principles on supposition of their ill tendency, is a dangerous fallacy which at once destroys all religious liberty," it is declared "that it is time enough for the rightful purposes of civil government for its officers to interfere when principles break out into overt acts against peace and good order." In these two sentences is found the true distinction between what properly belongs to the Church and what to the State.

In a little more than a year after the passage of this statute the convention met which prepared the Constitution of the United States. Of this convention Mr. Jefferson was not a member, he being then absent as minister to France. As soon as he saw the draft of the Constitution proposed for adoption, he, in a letter to a friend, expressed his disappointment at the absence of an express declaration insuring the freedom of religion, but was willing to accept it as it was, trusting that the good sense and honest intentions of the people would bring about the necessary alterations. ⊥ Five of the States, while adopting the ⏌164 Constitution, proposed amendments. Three, New Hampshire, New York and Virginia, included in one form or another a declaration of religious freedom in the changes they desired to have made, as did also North Carolina, where the convention at first declined to ratify the Constitution until the proposed amendments were acted upon. Accordingly, at the first session of the first Congress the amendment now under consideration was proposed with others by Mr. Madison. It met the views of the advocates of religious freedom, and was adopted. Mr. Jefferson afterwards, in reply to an address to him by a committee of the Danbury Baptist Association, took occasion to say: "Believing with you that religion is

⏌163

a matter which lies solely between man and his God; that he owes account to none other for his faith or his worship; that the legislative powers of the Government reach actions only, and not opinions, I contemplate with sovereign reverence that act of the whole American people which declared that their Legislature should 'make no law respecting an establishment of religion or prohibiting the free exercise thereof,' thus building a wall of separation between Church and State. Adhering to this expression of the Supreme will of the Nation in behalf of the rights of conscience, I shall see, with sincere satisfaction, the progress of those sentiments which tend to restore man to all his natural rights, convinced he has no natural right in opposition to his social duties." Coming as this does from an acknowledged leader of the advocates of the measure, it may be accepted almost as an authoritative declaration of the scope and effect of the amendment thus secured. Congress was deprived of all legislative power over mere opinion, but was left free to reach actions which were in violation of social duties or subversive of good order.

Polygamy has always been odious among the Northern and Western Nations of Europe and, until the establishment of the Mormon Church, was almost exclusively a feature of the life of Asiatic and African people. At common law, the second marriage was always void, and from the earliest history of England polygamy has been treated as an offense against society. After the establishment of the eccle⊥siastical courts, and until the time of James I., it was punished through the instrumentality of those tribunals, not merely because ecclesiastical rights had been violated, but because upon the separation of the ecclesiastical courts from the civil, the ecclesiastical were supposed to be the most appropriate for the trial of matrimonial causes and offenses against the rights of marriage; just as they were for testamentary causes and the settlement of the estates of deceased persons.

⌐165

By the Statute of 1 James I., ch. 11, the offense, if committed in England or Wales, was made punishable in the civil courts, and the penalty was death. As this statute was limited in its operation to England and Wales, it was at a very early period reenacted, generally with some modifications, in all the Colonies. In connection with the case we are now considering, it is a significant fact that on the 8th of December, 1788, after the passage of the Act establishing religious freedom, and after the convention of Virginia had recommended as an amendment to the Constitution of the United States the declaration in a Bill of Rights that "all men have an equal, natural and unalienable right to the free exercise of religion, according to the dictates of conscience," the Legislature of that State substantially enacted the Statute of James I., death penalty included, because as recited in the preamble, "It hath been doubted whether bigamy or polygamy be punishable by the laws of

this Commonwealth." From that day to this we think it may safely be said there never has been a time in any State of the Union when polygamy has not been an offense against society, cognizable by the civil courts and punishable with more or less severity. In the face of all this evidence, it is impossible to believe that the constitutional guaranty of religious freedom was intended to prohibit legislation in respect to this most important feature of social life. Marriage, while from its very nature a sacred obligation, is, nevertheless, in most civilized nations, a civil contract, and usually regulated by law. Upon it society may be said to be built, and out of its fruits spring social relations and social obligations and duties, with which government is necessarily required to deal. In fact, according as monogamous or polygamous marriages are allowed, do we find the principles on which the government of ⊥ the people, to a greater or less extent, rests. Professor Lieber says: polygamy leads to the patriarchal principle, and which, when applied to large communities, fetters the people in stationary despotism, while that principle cannot long exist in connection with monogamy. *Chancellor* Kent observes that this remark is equally striking and profound. An exceptional colony of polygamists under an exceptional leadership may sometimes exist for a time without appearing to disturb the social condition of the people who surround it; but there cannot be a doubt that, unless restricted by some form of constitution, it is within the legitimate scope of the power of every civil government to determine whether polygamy or monogamy shall be the law of social life under its dominion.

⌐166

In our opinion the statute immediately under consideration is within the legislative power of Congress. It is constitutional and valid as prescribing a rule of action for all those residing in the Territories, and in places over which the United States have exclusive control. This being so, the only question which remains is, whether those who make polygamy a part of their religion are excepted from the operation of the statute. If they are, then those who do not make polygamy a part of their religious belief may be found guilty and punished, while those who do must be acquitted and go free. This would be introducing a new element into criminal law. Laws are made for the government of actions, and while they cannot interfere with mere religious belief and opinions, they may with practices. Suppose one believed that human sacrifices were a necessary part of religious worship, would it be seriously contended that the civil government under which he lived could not interfere to prevent a sacrifice? Or if a wife religiously believed it was her duty to burn herself upon the funeral pile of her dead husband, would it be beyond the power of the civil government to prevent her carrying her belief into practice?

So here, as a law of the organization of society under the exclusive dominion of the United States, it is provided that plural marriages shall not be allowed. Can a man excuse his practices to the contrary because of his religious belief? ⊥ To permit this would be to make the professed doctrines of religious belief superior to the law of the land, and in effect to permit every citizen to become a law unto himself. Government could exist only in name under such circumstances.

A criminal intent is generally an element of crime, but every man is presumed to intend the necessary and legitimate consequences of what he knowingly does. Here the accused knew he had been once married, and that his first wife was living. He also knew that his second marriage was forbidden by law. When, therefore, he married the second time, he is presumed to have intended to break the law. And the breaking of the law is the crime. Every act necessary to constitute the crime was knowingly done, and the crime was, therefore, knowingly committed. Ignorance of a fact may sometimes be taken as evidence of a want of criminal intent, but not ignorance of the law. The only defense of the accused in this case is his belief that the law ought not to have been enacted. It matters not that his belief was a part of his professed religion; it was still belief, and belief only.

In *Regina* v. *Wagstaffe* the parents of a sick child, who omitted to call in medical attendance because of their religious belief that what they did for its cure would be effective, were held not to be guilty of manslaughter, while it was said the contrary would have been the result if the child had actually been starved to death by the parents, under the notion that it was their religious duty to abstain from giving it food. But when the offense consists of a positive act which is knowingly done, it would be dangerous to hold that the offender might escape punishment because he religiously believed the law which he had broken ought never to have been made. No case, we believe, can be found that has gone so far.

6. As to that part of the charge which directed the attention of the jury to the consequences of polygamy.

The passage complained of is as follows: "I think it not improper, in the discharge of your duties in this case, that you should consider what are to be the consequences to the innocent victims of this delusion. As this contest goes on, they multiply, ⊥ and there are pure-minded women and there are innocent children; innocent in a sense even beyond the degree of the innocence of childhood itself. These are to be the sufferers; and as jurors fail to do their duty, and as these cases come up in the Territory of Utah, just so do these victims multiply and spread themselves over the land."

While every appeal by the court to the passions or the prejudices of a jury should be promptly rebuked, and while it is the imperative duty of a reviewing court to take care that wrong is not done in this way,

we see no just cause for complaint in this case. Congress, in 1862, saw fit to make bigamy a crime in the Territories. This was done because of the evil consequences that were supposed to flow from plural marriages. All the court did was to call the attention of the jury to the peculiar character of the crime for which the accused was on trial, and to remind them of the duty they had to perform. There was no appeal to the passions, no instigation of prejudice. Upon the showing made by the accused himself, he was guilty of a violation of the law under which he had been indicted: and the effort of the court seems to have been not to withdraw the minds of the jury from the issue to be tried, but to bring them to it; not to make them partial, but to keep them impartial.

Upon a careful consideration of the whole case, we are satisfied that no error was committed by the court below, *and the judgment is consequently affirmed.*

DAVIS v. BEASON

133 U.S. 333

ON APPEAL FROM THE THIRD JUDICIAL
DISTRICT COURT OF
THE TERRITORY OF IDAHO

Argued December 9, 10, 1889 — Decided February 3, 1890

⊥ Statement by *Mr. Justice FIELD:*

In April, 1889, the appellant, Samuel D. Davis, was indicted in the District Court of the Third Judicial District of the Territory of Idaho, in the County of Oneida, in connection with divers persons named, and divers other persons whose names were unknown to the grand jury, for a conspiracy to unlawfully pervert and obstruct the due administration of the laws of the Territory in this, that they would unlawfully procure themselves to be admitted to registration as electors of said County of Oneida for the general election then next to occur in that county, when they were not entitled to be admitted to such registration, by appearing before the respective registrars of the election precincts in which they resided, and taking the oath prescribed by the Statute of the State, in substance as follows: "I do swear (or affirm) that I am a male citizen of the United States of the age of twenty-one years (or will be on the 6th day of November, 1888); and that I have (or will have) actually resided in this Territory four months and in this county for thirty days next preceding the day of the next ensuing election; that I have never been convicted of treason, felony or bribery; and that I am not registered or entitled to vote at any other place in this Territory; and I do further swear that I am not a bigamist or polygamist; that I am not a member of any order, organization or association which teaches, advises, counsels or encourages its members, devotees or any other person to commit the crime of bigamy or polygamy, or any other crime defined by law as a duty arising or resulting from membership in such order, organization or association, or which practices bigamy, polygamy or plural or celestial marriage as a doctrinal right of such organization; that I do not and will not, publicly or privately, or in any manner whatever, reach, advise, counsel or encourage any person to commit the crime of bigamy or polygamy, or any other crime defined by law, either as a religious duty or otherwise; that I do regard the Constitution of the United States and the laws thereof and the laws of this Territory, as interpreted by the courts, as the supreme laws of the land, the teachings of any order, organization or association to the contrary notwithstanding, so help me God," when, in truth, each of the defendants was ⊥ a member of an order, organization and association, namely, the Church of Jesus Christ of Latter-Day Saints, commonly known as the Mormon Church, which they knew taught, advised, counseled and encouraged its members and devotees to commit the crimes of bigamy and polygamy as duties arising and resulting from membership in said order, organization and association, and which order, organization and association, as they all knew, practiced bigamy and polygamy and plural and celestial marriage as doctrinal rights of said organization; and that in pursuance of said conspiracy the said defendants went before the registrars of different precincts of the county (which are designated) and took and had administered to them respectively the oath aforesaid.

The defendants demurred to the indictment, and the demurrer being overruled they pleaded separately not guilty. On the trial which followed on the 12th of September, 1889, the jury found the defendant Samuel D. Davis guilty as charged in the indictment. The defendant was thereupon sentenced to pay a fine of $500, and in default of its payment to be confined in the county jail of Oneida County for a term not exceeding 250 days, and was remanded to the custody of the sheriff until the judgment should be satisfied.

Soon afterwards, on the same day, the defendant applied to the court before which the trial was had, and obtained a writ of *habeas corpus*, alleging that he was imprisoned and restrained of his liberty by the sheriff of the county; that his imprisonment was by virtue of his conviction and the judgment mentioned and the warrant issued thereon; that such imprisonment was illegal; and that such illegality consisted in this: (1) that the facts in the indictment and record did not constitute a public offense, and the acts charged were not criminal or punishable under any statute or law of the territory; and (2) that so much of the statute of the territory as ⊥ provides that no person is entitled to register or vote at any election who is "a member of any order, organization or association which teaches, advises, counsels or encourages its members, devotees or any other person to commit the crime of bigamy or polygamy, or any

other crime defined by law, as a duty arising or resulting from membership in such order, organization or association, or which practices bigamy or polygamy or plural or celestial marriage as a doctrinal rite of such organization," is a "law respecting an establishment of re⊥ligion," in violation of the First Amendment of the Constitution, and void.

The court ordered the writ to issue, directed to the sheriff, returnable before it, at three o'clock in the afternoon of that day, commanding the sheriff to have the body of the defendant before the court at the hour designated, with the time and cause of his imprisonment, and to do and receive what should then be considered concerning him. On the return of the writ, the sheriff produced the body of the defendant and also the warrant of commitment under which he was held, and the record of the case showing his conviction for the conspiracy mentioned and the judgment thereon. To this return, the defendant, admitting the facts stated therein, excepted to their insufficiency to justify his detention. The court, holding that sufficient cause was not shown for the discharge of the defendant, ordered him to be remanded to the custody of the sheriff. From this judgment the defendant appealed to this court. . . .

⊥ *Mr. Justice FIELD* delivered the opinion of the court:

On this appeal our only inquiry is whether the District Court of the Territory had jurisdiction of the offense charged in the indictment of which the defendant was found guilty. If it had jurisdiction, we can go no farther. We cannot look into any alleged errors in its rulings on the trial of the defendant. The writ of *habeas corpus* cannot be turned into a writ of error to review the action of that court. Nor can we inquire whether the evidence established the fact alleged, that the defendant was a member of an order or organization known as the Mormon Church, called the Church of Jesus Christ of Latter-Day Saints, or the fact that the order or organization taught and counseled its members and devotees to commit the crimes of bigamy and polygamy as duties arising from membership therein. On this hearing we can only consider whether, these allegations being taken as true, an offense was committed of which the territorial court had jurisdiction to try the defendant. And on this point there can be no serious discussion or difference of opinion. Bigamy and polygamy are crimes by the laws of the civilized and Christian countries. They are crimes by the laws of the United States, and they are crimes by the laws of Idaho. They tend to destroy the purity of the marriage relation, to disturb the peace of families, to degrade woman and to debase man. Few crimes are more pernicious to the best interests of society and receive more general or more deserved punishment. To extend exemption from punishment for such crimes would be to shock the moral judgment of the community. To call their ⊥ advocacy a tenet of religion is to offend the common sense of mankind. If they are crimes, then to teach, advise and counsel their practice is to aid in their commission, and such teaching and counseling are themselves criminal and proper subjects of punishment, as aiding and abetting crime are in all other cases.

The term "religion" has reference to one's views of his relations to his Creator, and to the obligations they impose of reverence for his being and character, and of obedience to his will. It is often confounded with the *cultus* or form of worship of a particular sect, but is distinguishable from the latter. The First Amendment to the Constitution, in declaring that Congress shall make no law respecting the establishment of religion, or forbidding the free exercise thereof, was intended to allow everyone under the jurisdiction of the United States to entertain such notions respecting his relations to his Maker and the duties they impose as may be approved by his judgment and conscience, and to exhibit his sentiments in such form of worship as he may think proper, not injurious to the equal rights of others, and to prohibit legislation for the support of any religious tenets, or the modes of worship of any sect. The oppressive measures adopted, and the cruelties and punishments inflicted by the governments of Europe for many ages, to compel parties to conform in their religious beliefs and modes of worship to the views of the most numerous sect, and the folly of attempting in that way to control the mental operations of persons and enforce an outward conformity to a prescribed standard, led to the adoption of the Amendment in question. It was never intended or supposed that the Amendment could be invoked as a protection against legislation for the punishment of acts inimical to the peace, good order and morals of society. With man's relations to his Maker and the obligations he may think they impose, and the manner in which an expression shall be made by him of his belief on those subjects, no interference can be permitted, provided always the laws of society, designed to secure its peace and prosperity, and the morals of its people, are not interfered with. However free the exercise of religion may ⊥ be, it must be subordinate to the criminal laws of the country, passed with reference to actions regarded by general consent as properly the subjects of punitive legislation. There have been sects which denied as a part of their religious tenets that there should be any marriage tie, and advocated promiscuous intercourse of the sexes as prompted by the passions of their members. And history discloses the fact that the necessity of human sacrifices, on special occasions, has been a tenet of many sects. Should a sect of either of these kinds ever find its way into this country, swift punishment would follow the carrying into effect of its doctrines, and no heed would be given to the pretense that, as religious beliefs, their supporters could be protected in their exercise by the Constitution of the United States. Probably never before in the history of this country has it been seriously contended that the whole punitive power of the government, for acts recognized by the general consent of the Christian world in modern times as proper matters for prohibitory legislation, must be suspended in order that the tenets of a religious sect encouraging crime may be carried out without hindrance. . . .

⊥ It is assumed by counsel of the petitioner that, because no mode of worship can be established or religious tenets enforced in this country, therefore any form of worship may be followed and any tenets, however destructive of society, may be held and advocated, if asserted to be a part of the religious doctrines of those advocating and practicing them. But nothing is further from the truth. Whilst legislation for the establishment of a religion is forbidden, and its free exercise permitted, it does not follow that everything which may be so called can be tolerated. Crime is not the less odious because sanctioned by what any particular sect may designate as religion.

It only remains to refer to the laws which authorized the Legislature of the Territory of Idaho to prescribe the qualifications of voters and the oath they were required to take. The Revised Statutes provide that "the legislative power of every Territory shall extend to all rightful subjects of legislation not inconsistent with the Constitution and laws of the United States. But no law shall be passed interfering with the primary disposal of the soil; no tax shall be imposed upon the property of the United States; nor shall the lands or other property of nonresidents be taxed higher than the lands or other property of residents."

Under this general authority it would seem that the Territorial Legislature was authorized to prescribe any qualifications for voters calculated to secure obedience to its laws. But, in addition to the above law, section 1859 of the Revised Statutes ⊥ provides that "every male citizen above the age of twenty-one, including persons who have legally declared their intention to become citizens in any Territory hereafter organized, and who are actual residents of such Territory at the time of the organization thereof, shall be entitled to vote at the first election in such Territory, and to hold any office therein; subject, nevertheless, to the limitations specified in the next section," namely, that at all elections in any Territory subsequently organized by Congress, as well as at all elections in Territories already organized, the qualifications of voters and for holding office shall be such as may be prescribed by the Legislative Assembly of each Territory, subject, nevertheless, to the following restrictions:

First. That the right of suffrage and of holding office shall be exercised only by citizens of the United States above the age of twenty-one or persons above that age who have declared their intention to become such citizens;

Second. That the elective franchise or the right of holding office shall not be denied to any citizen on account of race, color or previous condition of servitude;

Third. That no soldier or sailor or other person in the army or navy, or attached to troops in the service of the United States, shall be allowed to vote unless he has made his permanent domicil in the Territory for six months; and,

Fourth. That no person belonging to the army or navy shall be elected to or hold a civil office or appointment in the Territory.

These limitations are the only ones placed upon the authority of Territorial Legislatures against granting the right of suffrage or of holding office. They have the power, therefore, to prescribe any reasonable qualifications of voters and for holding office not inconsistent with the above limitations. In our judgment, section 501 of the Revised Statutes of Idaho Territory, which provides that "no person under guardianship, *non compos mentis* or insane, nor any person convicted of treason, felony or bribery in this Territory, or in any other State or Territory in the Union, unless restored to civil rights; nor any person who is a bigamist or polygamist, or who teaches, advises, ⊥ counsels or encourages any person or persons to become bigamists or polygamists, or to commit any other crime defined by law, or to enter into what is known as plural or celestial marriage, or who is a member of any order, organization or association which teaches, advises, counsels or encourages its members or devotees or any other persons to commit the crime of bigamy or polygamy, or any other crime defined by law, either as a rite or ceremony of such order, organization or association, or otherwise, is permitted to vote at any election, or to hold any position or office of honor, trust or profit within this Territory," is not open to any constitutional or legal objection. With the exception of persons under guardianship or of unsound mind, it simply excludes from the privilege of voting, or of holding any office of honor, trust or profit, those who have been convicted of certain offenses, and those who advocate a practical resistance to the laws of the Territory and justify and approve the commission of crimes forbidden by it. The second subdivision of section 504 of the Revised Statutes of Idaho, requiring every person desiring to have his name registered as a voter to take an oath that he does not belong to an order that advises a disregard of the criminal law of the Territory, is not open to any valid legal objection to which our attention has been called.

The position that Congress has, by its Statute, covered the whole subject of punitive legislation against bigamy and polygamy, leaving nothing for territorial action on the subject, does not impress us as entitled to much weight. The Statute of Congress of March 22, 1882, amending a previous section of the Revised Statutes in reference to bigamy, declares

⌐347

"that no polygamist, bigamist or any person cohabiting with more than one woman, and no woman cohabiting with any of the persons described as aforesaid in this section, in any Territory or other place over which the United States have exclusive jurisdiction, shall be entitled to vote at any election held in any such Territory or other place, or be eligible for election or appointment to or be entitled to hold any office or place of public trust, honor or emolument in, under or for any such Territory or place, or under the United States."

⊥ This is a general law applicable to all Territories and other places under the exclusive jurisdiction of the United States. It does not purport to restrict the legislation of the Territories over kindred offenses or over the means for their ascertainment and prevention. The cases in which the legislation of Congress will supersede the legislation of a State or Territory, without specific provisions to that effect, are those in which the same matter is the subject of legislation by both. There the action of Congress may well be considered as covering the entire ground. But here there is nothing of this kind. The Act of Congress does not touch upon teaching, advising and counseling the practice of bigamy and polygamy, that is, upon aiding and abetting in the commission of those crimes, nor upon the mode adopted, by means of the oath required for registration, to prevent persons from being enabled by their votes to defeat the criminal laws of the country.

⌐348

The judgment of the court below is therefore affirmed.

The Jehovah's Witnesses Cases

Almost fifty years passed before the Supreme Court again dealt directly with the issue of religious liberty. The Jehovah's Witnesses, who like the Mormons were subjected to much mistreatment before they ultimately attained "respectability," provided the opportunity for the Court to develop a significant body of federal case law on the subject. In the years since 1938, approximately eighty cases involving the sect have been carried to the Supreme Court. All individuals, as well as religious bodies, owe this sometimes intolerant and belligerent—but always tenacious—group a debt of gratitude for forcing the Court to wrestle with issues which it sometimes would surely have preferred to avoid. In the process of thinking and rethinking the issues raised in the continuing litigation, the Court has been forced to develop and refine new formulae giving not only greater clarity but also greater breadth to the meaning of the free exercise clause.

The Jehovah's Witnesses movement, which denies that it is a religion as such, was organized in the 1870s by Charles Taze Russell; the followers were known for years as "Russellites." In 1884 the Watch Tower Bible and Tract Society was incorporated. On his death in 1916 Russell's position was filled by Joseph F. Rutherford, who was president of the group when it first began to attract wide public attention in the 1930s due to rapid growth and an unorthodox attitude toward both organized government and religious organizations.

Witnesses ordinarily refuse to vote, hold office, perform jury or military duty, or to cooperate or compromise with various other government regulations. Their most spectacular brushes with the law and the public probably arose through refusal to salute the flag, regarded as a "graven image" to which Exodus 20:4-5 forbids obeisance. Their distinctive interpretation of Old Testament texts prohibiting the eating of blood causes them to refuse blood transfusions for themselves and family members.

Organized religions enjoy no more respect from the Witnesses than does government. Their frequently repeated slogans proclaim that religion is a "snare" and a "racket," and their strongest invectives are reserved for the Roman Catholic Church.

Though they maintain modest kingdom halls, Jehovah's Witnesses rely for membership primarily on direct evangelism which takes them to the street corners and from door to door where they distribute tracts, books, and their regular publications, *Awake!* and *Watchtower.* "Contributions" for the printed materials are accepted, but they are given free if a contribution is not offered.

Every baptized Witness is considered a minister, which explains the sect's insistent claim for deferment from compulsory military service. There are two principal classes of ministers: (1) "publishers," who "publish the glad tidings" on a part-time basis and (2) "pioneers," who do not hold a secular job but spend their entire time working for the sect. At least in the early years the movement attracted primarily the disadvantaged and the alienated, who ranked low in both income and education.

In view of these unconventional doctrines and aggressive proselytizing tactics, it is not surprising that as the number of converts to the movement increased, both the public and public officials reacted negatively. Frequently the reaction took the form of mob violence against members of the group. Community and state officials moved more "legally" to curb the Witnesses by enacting new ordinances or redirecting existing laws at Witness techniques. Licensing laws, permit requirements, tax measures, anti-littering laws, sound truck regulations, anti-peddling ordinances— all these and more were utilized.

The Witnesses were not intimidated by this harassment. They pressed forward with perseverance in their active personal evangelism. Though they hold government in low esteem, they have not been the least reluctant to turn to one of its agencies to sustain them when they needed it. Vigorously and persistently they have called on the courts to protect their constitutional rights; and when state courts have failed to do so, they have sought to avail themselves of the opportunity presented by recent developments in the incorporation movement to appeal their cases to the United States Supreme Court. The first appeal—which challenged the ordinance of a small Georgia town requiring written permission of the city manager prior to distribution of circulars, handbills, and other advertising or literature—was dismissed by the Court in 1937 for lack of a substantial federal question. (*Coleman* v. *Griffen*).

Attorneys for the Witnesses then prepared another legal attack on the same ordinance. (*Lovell* v. *Griffen*) This appeal was accepted and considered by the Court, not on the basis of religious liberty, but on the closely related First Amendment guarantee of free press, which had been incorporated a few years earlier. A unanimous Court held the ordinance void on its face: it gave the city manager no reasonable guideline to govern his exercise of authority. His unfettered power of censorship through prior restraint was so great as to constitute a clear violation of freedom of press. The Court observed that freedom to publish without freedom to circulate would be of little value.

At the next session of the Court a similar ordinance of Irvington, New Jersey, was invalidated by a seven-to-one vote. (*Schneider* v. *Irvington*) Since both these cases were decided on free press grounds, the Court did not need to determine whether there might be a difference of degree in the right to distribute religious pamphlets as opposed to literature containing other ideas, and hence no pressure to reconsider the test governing free exercise of religion announced in the Mormon cases. [1]

In 1940 came the landmark case of CANTWELL v. CONNECTICUT (p. 60). Here, a Jehovah's Witness and his two sons were approaching persons on the streets of a predominantly Roman Catholic neighborhood of New Haven, Connecticut, asking permission to play for them a record entitled "Enemies," which contained a particularly vitriolic attack on the Roman Catholic Church. Although the listeners were incensed, no violence occurred. The father and sons were arrested, however, and eventually convicted of breach of the peace and of failure to obtain in advance a "certificate of approval" from the secretary of the Public Welfare Council. That official had the authority to withhold the permit if he was not satisfied that the cause represented by the applicant was a "religious one" or was a "bona fide object of charity and philanthropy and conforms to reasonable standards of efficiency and integrity."

Although the opinion written by Justice Roberts for a unanimous Court specified that nothing said in the opinion was "intended even remotely to imply that, under the cloak of religion, persons may, with impunity, commit frauds upon the public," it voided both the conviction of the Cantwells and the Connecticut statute.

The *Cantwell* decision has had great significance other than as a major victory for Jehovah's Witnesses. For the first time the Court specifically incorporated the Free Exercise Clause into the Fourteenth Amendment, thus applying it to the states. The Court also found it necessary in *Cantwell* to construct a doctrine for the determination of the limits of governmental control over religious freedom on a broader base than the "belief-action" test of the Mormon cases. Although the opinion pays its respects to this distinction, it clearly goes beyond: it warns that the power to regulate freedom to act must not be used in such a way as "unduly to infringe the protected freedom."

---

[1] Even after the free exercise clause was incorporated, the Court sometimes avoided the religious issue. For example, in *Martin* v. *Struthers* (1943), another Jehovah's Witness case, the majority opinion relied on speech and press grounds alone to invalidate a city ordinance making it unlawful to knock on doors or ring doorbells to summon the occupants to the door to receive handbills or other literature.

Justice Roberts also for the first time applied the liberal "clear and present danger" doctrine (first enunciated in Justice Holmes in the famous 1919 free speech case of *Schenck* v. *United States*) to the free exercise of religion. This requirement of a showing of clear and present danger to the public interest to justify state restraint of religion was to prove extremely significant, as the second flag salute case and others would show.

Some preliminary consideration was also given to a concept of "nondiscrimination" or "neutrality" when the opinion indicated that any classification using religion as a basis is invalid, whether the classification works to the advantage or disadvantage of a religious activity. The Court indicated that while a carefully drawn nondiscriminatory statute that incidentally infringes on religious groups or activities might be countenanced, a law drafted or applied specifically to disadvantage the activities of these groups is clearly unconstitutional. [2] Here, the standard was applied to the benefit of the Witnesses.

The same test sometimes worked to their detriment. In 1942 the Court, in JONES v. OPELIKA (p. 63), used it to uphold a practice which posed an extremely serious threat to the economically deprived group: the requirement of the payment of a tax for the distribution of literature. By a five-to-four vote the Court found that the ordinance did not discriminate against religious or other types of literature. The tax fell on all salesmen alike, and the First Amendment does not "require a subsidy in the form of fiscal exemption."

Justice Murphy, in dissent, sought to tie the Free Exercise Clause to the "preferred freedoms" concept. The Court had used this phrase in some speech and press cases after 1938 to insist on a "more exacting judicial scrutiny" of First Amendment guarantees than that given other constitutional rights. Murphy went further, however; he would elevate freedom of religion to a plane above even the other First Amendment rights. Those engaged in the dissemination of all ideas and opinions should enjoy a favored position over purely commercial endeavors, but a still higher level is reached when religious doctrines are involved. Even dearer than free speech and free press, he argued, is the right of individuals to worship freely, and "to carry their message or their gospel to every living creature."

Largely because of the appointment of Wiley B. Rutledge to fill the vacancy created by Justice Byrnes's resignation, the "preferred freedoms" doctrine became majority opinion the next year when the Court, by another five-to-four vote, overruled *Opelika* [3] in MURDOCK v. PENNSYLVANIA (p. 74). Writing for the new majority, Justice Douglas brushed aside the nondiscriminatory argument and clearly enunciated the preferred position of the First Amendment freedoms with a particular emphasis on religion as he sought to restore "to their high, constitutional position the liberties of itinerant evangelists who disseminate their religious beliefs and the tenets of their faith through distribution of literature."

Though some judges, such as Justice Frankfurter, who always referred to the concept as a "mischievous phrase," refused to accept the "preferred freedoms" test, it has often been adhered to implicitly, if not explicitly, and has been important in giving added dignity to religious rights. The next year the *Murdock* holding was extended in *Follett* v. *McCormick* to give tax immunity to a Jehovah's Witness whose sole source of income was the sale of religious books.

But the most dramatic public controversy involving Jehovah's Witnesses was incited by their refusal to permit their children to comply with the flag-salute requirement imposed by many public school boards. Such nonconformity is never popular; and as World War II approached with its mounting patriotic fervor, it became a highly emotional issue.

Children of members of the sect were frequently expelled as a result of refusal to participate in the flag salute. Their parents then came under legal pressures because of compulsory school attendance laws and were convicted in numerous state courts. At least three times between 1938 and 1940, the Witnesses appealed in vain to the Supreme Court for relief. In 1940, the year the Court heard the *Cantwell* case, it finally agreed to consider the flag-salute issue in MINERSVILLE SCHOOL DISTRICT v. GOBITIS (p. 82). Contrary to the decision in *Cantwell*, the Court, with only Justice Stone in eloquent dissent, found against the Witnesses' claim of violation of their constitutional rights. Justice Frankfurter used the nondiscrimination test to emphasize that the flag-salute requirement was a general law applicable to all and was not intended to restrict religious beliefs. He stressed the relationship between symbolism and national unity. Religion is a "precious right," he agreed, but it is not absolute; and when, as here, it collides with national security, "reasonable accommodations" must be made in an effort to "reconcile two rights in order to prevent either from destroying the other."

Seldom does a Court that votes eight-to-one then reverse itself in the brief span of three years. Such did happen here for a variety of reasons. Two changes in personnel occurred, when Justices Jackson and Rutledge replaced Justices Hughes and McReynolds. The Court was also likely affected both by the severe criticism to which its decision was subjected by legal scholars and many religious leaders and by the wave of public violence against the Witnesses by persons who apparently assumed that the Court, in rejecting the claims of the Witnesses, had rejected the movement. In an unprecedented move, three members of the Court in effect invited a rehearing of the flag-salute issue. Dissenting in *Jones* v. *Opelika I*, Justices Black, Douglas, and Murphy, who surprisingly had been in the *Gobitis* majority two years before, recanted. They had come to believe that *Gobitis* as well as *Opelika I* had been "wrongly decided."

The opportunity for reversal came quickly. In WEST VIRGINIA STATE BOARD OF EDUCATION v. BARNETTE (p. 87) the Court, by a six-to-three vote, struck down a West Virginia requirement different in no significant way

---

[2] This doctrine of "neutrality" has been proposed as the primary test for determining the limits of government with respect to both religion clauses by Professor Philip B. Kurland of the University of Chicago Law School. See *Religion and the Law: Of Church and State and the Supreme Court* (Chicago: Aldine Publishing Company, 1962).

[3] *Jones* v. *Opelika* was put back on the Court's docket in 1943. Because the issues were the same as those in *Murdock* v. *Pennsylvania*, they were argued together with that case. Hence, *Jones* v. *Opelika II* is merely a *per curiam* opinion explaining this fact.

from that involved in the *Gobitis* case. Relying primarily on freedom of speech and press rather than of religion, Justice Jackson for the majority measured the peaceful nonparticipation on the part of the students against the "clear and present danger" test, which he here read to mean "grave and immediate danger," and found insufficient grounds for state restraint. [4]

After a rather inauspicious beginning, the Jehovah's Witnesses have forged, through their unflagging persistence, a quite remarkable record of judicial victories before the Supreme Court; and they have ultimately won the vast majority of the cases appealed to the high tribunal. Yet, in some few instances the Court has denied their claims without later reversing itself. In 1941, in COX v. NEW HAMPSHIRE (p. 96), the Court upheld as a reasonable police regulation a city's requirement that Witnesses, like other groups, give notice and obtain a permit before staging a parade or procession on the public streets. The next year, in *Chaplinsky* v. *New Hampshire*, the Court sustained the conviction of a Witness for cursing in strong terms a city marshal who interfered with his street corner preaching. In the opinion for the Court, Justice Murphy who, though a Roman Catholic, ordinarily voted for the Witnesses, observed that he could not "conceive that cursing a public officer is the exercise of religion in any sense of the term." In 1944 the Court, recognizing the power of the state to protect children from physical harm or abuse even at the hands of religiously motivated parents or other relatives, upheld a state child labor law in PRINCE v. MASSACHUSETTS (p. 99) when applied to a nine-year-old girl who, in the company of her aunt, was distributing religious literature at night on a downtown street corner.

Prince v. *Massachusetts* has since been used by state courts as a precedent for state action ordering necessary blood transfusions for children of Jehovah's Witnesses when the parents refuse to agree to the transfusions. The Supreme Court has never considered the blood transfusion issue except as it has consistently denied certiorari from lower court decisions raising the point. The lower courts have regularly held that parents cannot on religious grounds deny their child a blood transfusion if such a transfusion is necessary to save the child's life. Court orders may be obtained authorizing the transfusion. Similar action may be taken with respect to a pregnant

woman who refuses a transfusion. Courts also ordinarily hold that parents with minor children will not be allowed to endanger the future welfare of the children by refusing on religious grounds to submit to transfusion.

Competent adults without minor children pose a greater problem when they refuse transfusions on religious grounds. Although most appellate courts uphold court-ordered transfusions even in these instances, there has been at least one case in which an Illinois court ruled that a competent adult without minor children could not, over her religiously based protestations, be compelled to receive a transfusion. [5]

In *Neimotko* v. *Maryland* (1951) the Supreme Court struck down denial of a permit by a city council to Jehovah's Witnesses who sought use of a city park for religious services after having received "unsatisfactory responses" to questions with respect to their attitude toward flag salutes and military service and to their interpretation of the Bible. The Court unanimously held the denial violative of both freedom of speech and of equal protection of the laws.

Although the Jehovah's Witnesses have ceased to be the main focus of controversies involving religious liberty, justices of succeeding courts have frequently resorted to the tests applied and refined in cases occasioned by Witnesses. The quest for new judicial standards has continued as cases involving individuals and groups as diverse as conscientious objectors to war, Sabbatarians,

---

[4] *Barnette* was the controlling precedent used in 1977 by a federal district court judge and the Court of Appeals for the Third Circuit in striking down a New Jersey statute requiring students to stand at "respectful attention" if they did not participate in the school's flag salute ceremony. (*Lipp* v. *Norris*) See also *Goetz* v. *Ansell* (1973) and *Banks* v. *Board of Public Instruction of Dade County, Florida* (1970). The Supreme Court also used *Barnette* as a precedent for holding that New Hampshire could not punish a Jehovah's Witness couple for covering up the state motto "Live Free or Die" on their automobile license plates, a motto which they considered to be repugnant to their moral, religious, and political beliefs. Chief Justice Burger, for the majority of six, agreed that the requirement that the motto be displayed was a less serious violation of personal liberty than coerced flag salute but he viewed the difference as one only of degree. In both instances the individual was being forced to express "an ideological point of view" he could not accept. "The First Amendment," he wrote, "protects the right of individuals to hold a point of view different from the majority and to refuse to foster, in the way New Hampshire commands, an idea they find morally objectionable." (*Wooley* v. *Maynard*, 1977)

[5] *In re Brooks* (1965). Some of the leading state cases involving the blood transfusion issue are: *Jehovah's Witnesses* v. *King County Hospital* (1968) in which the Supreme Court affirmed in a *per curiam* opinion a lower court ruling upholding a Washington law which allowed children in need of blood transfusions to be declared wards of the state if their parents, on religious grounds, withheld permission; *Raleigh Fitkin-Paul Morgan Memorial Hospital* v. *Anderson* (1964) which involved a pregnant woman; *John F. Kennedy Memorial Hospital* v. *Heston* (1971) in which an unmarried childless woman refused a transfusion. Cf. Ronald B. Flowers, "Freedom of Religion Versus Civil Authority in Matters of Health," in "The Uneasy Boundary: Church and State" *The Annals of the American Academy of Political and Social Science*, ed. Dean M. Kelley 446 (November 1979): 156-59.

Black Muslims [6] and the gentle Amish have made their way to the high court.

Two of these tests should be mentioned because together they seem to represent the present position of the Court: the "alternative means" test and the "compelling interest" rule. The "alternative means" test, although used earlier in free speech cases, was first advanced in connection with free exercise of religion in 1961 in BRAUNFELD v. BROWN (p. 316), a case in which the majority opinion upheld the Sunday closing laws against claims of violation of religious rights of Orthodox Jewish merchants. But the potential of the test for expanding religious liberty was exhibited two years later in SHERBERT v. VERNER (p. 145). There it was used to invalidate a state law denying unemployment compensation to a Seventh-day Adventist who could not obtain employment because of her refusal to work on Saturday. The rule forbids the state, as it seeks further to legitimate secular goals, to impose even an indirect burden on religious observances unless the state can show that there are no practicable less restrictive "alternative means" by which the legislative purpose can be achieved. The Court found no effective alternative means available to the state in *Braunfeld*; it did in *Sherbert*. Exemption could be granted from the statute for refusal to work for religious reasons.

The second rule imposes upon the state the necessity of justifying infringement of religious rights by a showing of nothing less than a "compelling" state interest that requires the encroachment. This rule was first advanced by the Court in *Sherbert*. It was given greater emphasis and clarity in 1972 in WISCONSIN v. YODER (p. 200), in which the Court upheld the right of Amish parents to take their children from public school after the eighth grade. Chief Justice Burger, in the majority opinion, placed an even heavier burden of proof on the state than verbalized in *Sherbert*, when he emphasized that the "compelling state interest" means that "[o]nly those interests of the highest order, and those not otherwise served can overbalance the legitimate claim to the free exercise of religion." (406 U.S. 205, 215)

In 1986, in her dissenting opinion in GOLDMAN v. WEINBERGER (p. 179), Justice O'Connor summed up her understanding of the tests applied by the present Court when she wrote:

> First, when the government attempts to deny a Free Exercise claim, it must show that an unusually important interest is at stake, whether that interest is denominated "compelling," "of the highest order," or "overriding." Second, the government must show that granting the requested exemption will do substantial harm to that interest, whether by showing that the means adopted is the "least restrictive" or "essential," or that the interest will not "otherwise be served." (106 S.Ct. 1310, 1325)

These tests involve, as have those previously used, judicial balancing of the competing interests of religious freedom and the goals which the state is seeking to achieve by restricting that freedom. Both tilt the scale heavily in favor of religion. Applied together, as in *Wisconsin* v. *Yoder*, they grant an extremely wide latitude to actions based on religious belief.

It is unrealistic to suggest that the Court of today, or even of tomorrow, will be willing to accept arguments for an absolute right of religious liberty any more than the Waite Court was willing a hundred years ago. In the succeeding years since the claims of the Mormons were summarily dismissed, however, the standards announced and the decisions rendered, though not without their inconsistencies and vacillations, have evidenced a philosophy of greatly expanded liberality on the part of the Court. It has accorded to the First Amendment commitment to free exercise of religion a position of honor second to none in its scale of constitutional values.

---

[6] The problems of conscientious objectors, Sabbatarians, and Amish are discussed in some detail at other points in the book. In recent years public and judicial controversies have sometimes arisen concerning the beliefs, activities, and ultimate goals of the Nation of Islam, or the Black Muslims, an aggressive black separatist religious group. Because of their strident demands for racial separation, members of this unconventional sect were sometimes considered racial extremists rather than a genuine religious group. In 1975, after the death of Elijah Muhammad, founder of the organization, his son Wallace took over the leadership of the group and made it less racist and much closer to classical Islam. His supporters began accepting white members, muted their militancy, and began working more nearly for the economic welfare of all poor people, not just blacks. The name of the group was changed to "American Muslim Mission" which was disbanded as a national organization in 1985 by Wallace who encouraged all its members to work with good Muslims everywhere. In 1978, Louis Farrakhan split with Muhammad over the revisions and reinstituted the nation of Isalam with much the same ideological stance that it had under Elijah Muhammad. For a good account of the various changes in the movement, see Lawrence H. Mamiga, "From Black Muslim to Bilalian: The Evolution of a Movement," *Journal for the Scientific Study of Religion* 21 (1982): 138-52.

Most litigation involving Black Muslims has developed from refusals of prison authorities to permit them to exercise their religious tenets to the same degree as prisoners of other religious persuasions. Some lower courts have sustained the denials on the basis of the recognized need for prison discipline and the possibility that the group's black supremacy arguments would tend to encourage challenges to the authority of white prison guards and officials. However, the lower court decisions have usually been reversed on appeal, particularly where rulings have been based on a summary determination that Black Muslims were not members of a bona fide religion.

In 1964 a Black Muslim case, *Cooper* v. *Pate*, was accepted by the U.S. Supreme Court. A federal district court in Illinois had rejected the claims of a Black Muslim prisoner that he had been discriminated against because of his religious beliefs by prison officials when they denied him the right to obtain his Qur'an and other Muslim literature, to have visits by Black Muslim ministers, and to attend religious services. A court of appeals affirmed the decision, but the Supreme Court in a brief *per curiam* opinion reversed the lower courts. The district court subsequently ruled that the challenged prison restrictions could be imposed only if a "clear and present danger to prison security" would result from the requested religious privileges. (Eight years later the Court in another *per curiam* opinion written in *Cruz* v. *Beto* extended the same free exercise rights to a Buddhist convict.) Other cases involving Black Muslim rights in prison are *Williford* v. *California* (1963), *Knuckles* v. *Prasse* (1971), and *Hutto* v. *Finney* (1978). Undoubtedly the most publicized Black Muslim case to reach the Supreme Court was that of world boxing champion Muhammad Ali who had been convicted for refusing to serve in the Vietnam War notwithstanding his claim of conscientious objector status. The conviction was set aside in a *per curiam* decision. *Cassius M. Clay, Jr. (Muhammad Ali)* v. *United States* (1971).

CANTWELL v. CONNECTICUT

310 U.S. 296
ON APPEAL AND WRIT OF CERTIORARI TO
THE SUPREME
COURT OF ERRORS OF THE STATE OF
CONNECTICUT

Argued March 29, 1940 — Decided May 20, 1940

⌐300   ⊥ *Mr. Justice ROBERTS* delivered the opinion of the Court:

Newton Cantwell and his two sons, Jesse and Russell, members of a group known as Jehovah's Witnesses, and claiming to be ordained ministers, were arrested in New Haven, Connecticut, and each was charged by information in five counts, with statutory and common law offenses. After trial in the Court of Common Pleas of New Haven County each of them was convicted on the third count, which charged a violation of § 6294 of the General Statutes of Connecticut, and on the fifth count, which charged commission of the common law offense of inciting a breach of the peace. On appeal to the Supreme Court the conviction of all three on the third count was affirmed. The conviction of Jesse Cantwell, on the fifth count, was also affirmed, but the conviction of Newton and Russell on that count was reversed and a new trial ordered as to them.

By demurrers to the information, by requests for rulings of law at the trial, and by their assignments of error in the State Supreme Court, the appellants pressed the contention that the statute under which the third count was drawn was offensive to the due process clause of the Fourteenth Amendment because, on its face and as construed and applied, it denied them freedom of speech and prohibited their ⌐301 free exercise of religion. In like manner ⊥ they made the point that they could not be found guilty on the fifth count, without violation of the Amendment.

We have jurisdiction on appeal from the judgments on the third count, as there was drawn in question the validity of a state statute under the federal Constitution, and the decision was in favor of validity. Since the conviction on the fifth count was not based upon a statute, but presents a substantial question under the federal Constitution, we granted the writ of certiorari in respect of it.

The facts adduced to sustain the convictions on the third count follow. On the day of their arrest the appellants were engaged in going singly from house to house on Cassius Street in New Haven. They were individually equipped with a bag containing books and pamphlets on religious subjects, a portable phonograph and a set of records, each of which, when played, introduced, and was a description of, one of the books. Each appellant asked the person who responded to his call for permission to play one of the records. If permission was granted he asked the person to buy the book described and, upon refusal, he solicited such contribution towards the publication of the pamphlets as the listener was willing

to make. If a contribution was received a pamphlet was delivered upon condition that it would be read.

Cassius Street is in a thickly populated neighborhood, where about ninety per cent of the residents are Roman Catholics. A phonograph record, describing a book entitled "Enemies," included an attack on the Catholic religion. None of the persons interviewed were members of Jehovah's witnesses.

The statute under which the appellants were charged provides:

"No person shall solicit money, services, subscriptions or any valuable thing for any alleged religious, charitable ⊥ or philanthropic cause, from other than ⌐302 a member of the organization for whose benefit such person is soliciting or within the county in which such person or organization is located unless such cause shall have been approved by the secretary of the public welfare council. Upon application of any person in behalf of such cause, the secretary shall determine whether such cause is a religious one or is a bona fide object of charity or philanthropy and conforms to reasonable standards of efficiency and integrity, and, if he shall so find, shall approve the same and issue to the authority in charge a certificate to that effect. Such certificate may be revoked at any time. Any person violating any provision to this section shall be fined not more than one hundred dollars or imprisoned not more than thirty days or both."

The appellants claimed that their activities were not within the statute but consisted only of distribution of books, pamphlets, and periodicals. The State Supreme Court construed the finding of the trial court to be that "in addition to the sale of the books and the distribution of the pamphlets the defendants were also soliciting contributions or donations of money for an alleged religious cause, and thereby came within the purview of the statute." It overruled the contention that the Act, as applied to the appellants, offends the due process clause of the Fourteenth Amendment, because it abridges or denies religious freedom and liberty of speech and press. The court stated that it was the solicitation that brought the appellants within the sweep of the Act and not their other activities in the dissemination of literature. It declared the legislation constitutional as an effort by the State to protect the public against fraud and imposition in the solicitation of funds for what purported to be religious, charitable, or philanthropic causes.

The facts which were held to support the conviction of Jesse Cantwell on the fifth count were that he stopped ⊥ two men in the street, asked, and received, permission to play a phonograph record, and ⌐303 played the record "Enemies," which attacked the religion and church of the two men, who were Catholics. Both were incensed by the contents of the record and were tempted to strike Cantwell unless he went away. On being told to be on his way he left their presence. There was no evidence that he was personally offensive or entered into any argument with those he interviewed.

The court held that the charge was not assault or breach of the peace or threats on Cantwell's part, but invoking or inciting others to breach of the peace, and that the facts supported the conviction of that offense.

First. We hold that the statute, as construed and applied to the appellants, deprives them of their liberty without due process of law in contravention of the Fourteenth Amendment. The fundamental concept of liberty embodied in that Amendment embraces the liberties guaranteed by the First Amendment. The First Amendment declares that Congress shall make no law respecting an establishment of religion or prohibiting the free exercise thereof. The Fourteenth Amendment has rendered the legislatures of the states as incompetent as Congress to enact such laws. The constitutional inhibition of legislation on the subject of religion has a double aspect. On the one hand, it forestalls compulsion by law of the acceptance of any creed or the practice of any form of worship. Freedom of conscience and freedom to adhere to such religious organization or form of worship as the individual may choose cannot be restricted by law. On the other hand, it safeguards the free exercise of the chosen form of religion. Thus the Amendment embraces two concepts,—freedom to believe and freedom to act. The first is absolute but, in the nature of things, ⌐304 the⊥ second cannot be. Conduct remains subject to regulation for the protection of society. The freedom to act must have appropriate definition to preserve the enforcement of that protection. In every case the power to regulate must be so exercised as not, in attaining a permissible end, unduly to infringe the protected freedom. No one would contest the proposition that a state may not, by statute, wholly deny the right to preach or to disseminate religious views. Plainly such a previous and absolute restraint would violate the terms of the guaranty. It is equally clear that a state may by general and non-discriminatory legislation regulate the times, the places, and the manner of soliciting upon its streets, and of holding meetings thereon; and may in other respects safeguard the peace, good order and comfort of the community, without unconstitutionally invading the liberties protected by the Fourteenth Amendment. The appellants are right in their insistence that the Act in question is not such a regulation. If a certificate is procured, solicitation is permitted without restraint but, in the absence of a certificate, solicitation is altogether prohibited.

The appellants urge that to require them to obtain a certificate as a condition of soliciting support for their views amounts to a prior restraint on the exercise of their religion within the meaning of the Constitution. The State insists that the Act, as construed by the Supreme Court of Connecticut, im-

poses no previous restraint upon the dissemination of religious views or teaching but merely safeguards against the perpetration of frauds under the cloak of religion. Conceding that this is so, the question remains whether the method adopted by Connecticut to ⊥ that end transgresses the liberty safeguarded by ⌐305 the Constitution.

The general regulation, in the public interest, of solicitation, which does not involve any religious test and does not unreasonably obstruct or delay the collection of funds, is not open to any constitutional objection, even though the collection be for a religious purpose. Such regulation would not constitute a prohibited previous restraint on the free exercise of religion or interpose an inadmissible obstacle to its exercise.

It will be noted, however, that the Act requires an application to the secretary of the public welfare council of the State; that he is empowered to determine whether the cause is a religious one, and that the issue of a certificate depends upon his affirmative action. If he finds that the cause is not that of religion, to solicit for it becomes a crime. He is not to issue a certificate as a matter of course. His decision to issue or refuse it involves appraisal of facts, the exercise of judgment, and the formation of an opinion. He is authorized to withhold his approval if he determines that the cause is not a religious one. Such a censorship of religion as the means of determining its right to survive is a denial of liberty protected by the First Amendment and included in the liberty which is within the protection of the Fourteenth.

The State asserts that if the licensing officer acts arbitrarily, capriciously, or corruptly, his action is subject to judicial correction. Counsel refer to the rule prevailing in Connecticut that the decision of a commission or an administrative official will be reviewed upon a claim that "it works material damage to individual or corporate rights, or invades or threatens such rights, or is so unreasonable as to justify judicial intervention, or is not consonant with justice, or that a legal duty has not ⊥ been per- ⌐306 formed." It is suggested that the statute is to be read as requiring the officer to issue a certificate unless the cause in question is clearly not a religious one; and that if he violates his duty his action will be corrected by a court.

To this suggestion there are several sufficient answers. The line between a discretionary and a ministerial act is not always easy to mark and the statute has not been construed by the State court to impose a mere ministerial duty on the secretary of the welfare council. Upon his decision as to the nature of the cause, the right to solicit depends. Moreover, the availability of a judicial remedy for abuses in the system of licensing still leaves that system one of previous restraint which, in the field of free speech and press, we have held inadmissible. A statute authorizing previous restraint upon the exercise of the guaranteed freedom by judicial decision after trial is as obnoxious to the Constitution as one providing for like restraint by administrative action.

Nothing we have said is intended even remotely to imply that, under the cloak of religion, persons may, with impunity, commit frauds upon the public. Certainly penal laws are available to punish such conduct. Even the exercise of religion may be at some slight inconvenience in order that the state may protect its citizens from injury. Without doubt a state may protect its citizens from fraudulent solicitation by requiring a stranger in the community, before permitting him publicly to solicit funds for any purpose, to establish his identity and his authority to act for the cause which he purports to represent. ⌐307 The state is likewise free to regulate the time⊥ and manner of solicitation generally, in the interest of public safety, peace, comfort or convenience. But to condition the solicitation of aid for the perpetuation of religious views or systems upon a license, the grant of which rests in the exercise of a determination by state authority as to what is a religious cause, is to lay a forbidden burden upon the exercise of liberty protected by the Constitution.

Second. We hold that, in the circumstances disclosed, the conviction of Jesse Cantwell on the fifth count must be set aside. Decision as to the lawfulness of the conviction demands the weighing of two conflicting interests. The fundamental law declares the interest of the United States that the free exercise of religion be not prohibited and that freedom to communicate information and opinion be not abridged. The state of Connecticut has an obvious interest in the preservation and protection of peace and good order within her borders. We must determine whether the alleged protection of the State's interest, means to which end would, in the absence of limitation by the federal Constitution, lie wholly within the State's discretion, has been pressed, in this instance, to a point where it has come into fatal collision with the overriding interest protected by the federal compact.

Conviction on the fifth count was not pursuant to a statute evincing a legislative judgment that street discussion of religious affairs, because of its tendency to provoke disorder, should be regulated, or a judgment that the playing of a phonograph on the streets should in the interest of comfort or privacy be limited or prevented. Violation of an Act exhibiting such a legislative judgment and narrowly drawn to prevent the supposed evil, would pose a question differing from that we must here answer. Such a declaration of the State's policy⊥ would weigh heavily in ⌐308 any challenge of the law as infringing constitutional limitations. Here, however, the judgment is based on a common law concept of the most general and undefined nature. The court below has held that the petitioner's conduct constituted the commission of an offense under the State law, and we accept this decision as binding upon us to that extent.

The offense known as breach of the peace embraces a great variety of conduct destroying or menacing public order and tranquillity. It includes not only violent acts but acts and words likely to produce violence in others. No one would have the hardihood to suggest that the principle of freedom of speech sanctions incitement to riot or that religious liberty connotes the privilege to exhort others to physical attack upon those belonging to another sect. When clear and present danger of riot, disorder, interference with traffic upon the public streets, or other immediate threat to public safety, peace, or order, appears, the power of the state to prevent or punish is obvious. Equally obvious is it that a state may not unduly suppress free communication of views, religious or other, under the guise of conserving desirable conditions. Here we have a situation analogous to a conviction under a statute sweeping in a great variety of conduct under a general and indefinite characterization, and leaving to the executive and judicial branches too wide a discretion in its application.

Having these considerations in mind, we note that Jesse Cantwell, on April 26, 1938, was upon a public street, where he had a right to be, and where he had a right peacefully to impart his views to others. There is no showing that his deportment was noisy, truculent, overbearing or offensive. He requested of two pedestrians permission to play to them a phonograph record. The permission was granted. It is not claimed that he⊥ intended to insult or affront the ⌐309 hearers by playing the record. It is plain that he wished only to interest them in his propaganda. The sound of the phonograph is not shown to have disturbed residents of the street, to have drawn a crowd, or to have impeded traffic. Thus far he had invaded no right or interest of the public or of the men accosted.

The record played by Cantwell embodies a general attack on all organized religious systems as instruments of Satan and injurious to man; it then singles out the Roman Catholic Church for strictures couched in terms which naturally would offend not only persons of that persuasion, but all others who respect the honestly held religious faith of their fellows. The hearers were in fact highly offended. One of them said he felt like hitting Cantwell and the other that he was tempted to throw Cantwell off the street. The one who testified he felt like hitting Cantwell said, in answer to the question "Did you do anything else or have any other reaction?" "No, sir, because he said he would take the victrola and he went." The other witness testified that he told Cantwell he had better get off the street before something happened to him and that was the end of the matter as Cantwell picked up his books and walked up the street.

Cantwell's conduct, in the view of the court below, considered apart from the effect of his communication upon his hearers, did not amount to a breach of the peace. One may, however, be guilty of the offense if he commit acts or make statements likely to provoke violence and disturbance of good order, even though no such eventuality be intended. Decisions to this effect are many, but examination discloses that, in practically all, the provocative language which was held to amount to a breach of the peace consisted of profane, indecent, or abusive remarks directed to the
⌐310 person of the hearer. Resort to epithets or ⊥ personal abuse is not in any proper sense communication of information or opinion safeguarded by the Constitution, and its punishment as a criminal act would raise no question under that instrument.

We find in the instant case no assault or threatening of bodily harm, no truculent bearing, no intentional discourtesy, no personal abuse. On the contrary, we find only an effort to persuade a willing listener to buy a book or to contribute money in the interest of what Cantwell, however misguided others may think him, conceived to be true religion.

In the realm of religious faith, and in that of political belief, sharp differences arise. In both fields the tenets of one man may seem the rankest error to his neighbor. To persuade others to his own point of view, the pleader, as we know, at times, resorts to exaggeration, to vilification of men who have been, or are, prominent in church or state, and even to false statement. But the people of this nation have ordained in the light of history, that, in spite of the probability of excesses and abuses, these liberties are, in the long view, essential to enlightened opinion and right conduct on the part of the citizens of a democracy.

The essential characteristic of these liberties is, that under their shield many types of life, character, opinion and belief can develop unmolested and unobstructed. Nowhere is this shield more necessary than in our own country for a people composed of many races and of many creeds. There are limits to the exercise of these liberties. The danger in these times from the coercive activities of those who in the delusion of racial or religious conceit would incite violence and breaches of the peace in order to deprive others of their equal right to the exercise of their liberties, is emphasized by events familiar to all. These and other transgressions of those limits the states
⌐311 appropriately may punish. ⊥

Although the contents of the record not unnaturally aroused animosity, we think that, in the absence of a statute narrowly drawn to define and punish specific conduct as constituting a clear and present danger to a substantial interest of the State, the petitioner's communication, considered in the light of the constitutional guaranties, raised no such clear and present menace to public peace and order

as to render him liable to conviction of the common law offense in question.

The judgment affirming the convictions on the third and fifth counts is reversed and the cause is remanded for further proceedings not inconsistent with this opinion.

Reversed.

JONES v. OPELIKA (No.280)

ON WRIT OF CERTIORARI TO
THE SUPREME COURT OF THE STATE OF
ALABAMA

BOWDEN v. FORT SMITH (No. 314)

ON WRIT OF CERTIORARI TO
THE SUPREME COURT OF THE STATE OF
ARKANSAS

JOBIN v. ARIZONA (No. 966)

ON APPEAL FROM
THE SUPREME COURT OF THE STATE OF
ARIZONA
316 U.S. 584
Argued February 5 and April 30, 1942 — Decided
June 8, 1942

⊥ *Mr. Justice REED* delivered the opinion of the   ⌐585
Court:

By writ of certiorari in Nos. 280 and 314 and by appeal in No. 966 we have before us the question of the constitu⊥tionality of various city ordinances im-   ⌐586
posing the license taxes upon the sale of printed matter for nonpayment of which the appellant, Jobin, and the petitioners, Jones, Bowden and Sanders, all members of the organization known as Jehovah's Witnesses, were convicted.

No. 280

The City of Opelika, Alabama, filed a complaint in the Circuit Court of Lee County charging petitioner Jones with violation of its licensing ordinance by selling books without a license, by operating as a Book Agent without a license, and by operating as a transient agent, dealer or distributor of books without a license. The license fee for Book Agents (Bibles excepted) was $10 per annum, that for transient agents, dealers or distributors of books $5. ⊥ Under   ⌐587
§ 1 of the ordinance all licenses were subject to revocation in the discretion of the City Commission, with or without notice. There is a clause providing for severance in case of invalidity of any section, condition or provision. Petitioner demurred, alleging that the ordinance because of unlimited discretion in revocation and requirement of a license was an unconstitutional encroachment upon freedom of the

press. During the trial without a jury these contentions, with the added claim of interference with freedom of religion, were renewed at the end of the city's case, and at the close of all the evidence. The court overruled these motions, and found petitioner guilty on evidence that without a license he had been displaying pamphlets in his upraised hand and walking on a city street selling them two for five cents. The court excluded as irrelevant testimony designed to show that the petitioner was an ordained minister, and that his activities ⊥ were in furtherance of his beliefs and the teachings of Jehovah's Witnesses. Once again by an unsuccessful motion for new trial the constitutional issues were raised. The Court of Appeals of Alabama reversed the conviction on appeal because it thought the unlimited discretion of the City Commission to revoke the licenses invalidated the ordinance. Without discussion of this point the Supreme Court of Alabama decided that non-discriminatory licensing of the sale of books or tracts was constitutional, reversed the Court of Appeals, and stayed execution pending certiorari. This Court, having granted certiorari, dismissed the writ for lack of a final judgment. The Court of Appeals thereupon entered a judgment sustaining the conviction, which was affirmed by the Alabama Supreme Court and is final. We therefore grant the petition for rehearing of the dismissal of the writ, and proceed with the consideration of the case.

⌐588

No. 315

⌐589 Petitioners Bowden and Sanders were arrested by police officers of Fort Smith, Arkansas, brought before the Municipal Court on charges of violation of City Ordinance No. 1172, and convicted. They appealed to the Sebastian Circuit Court, and there moved to dismiss on the ground that the ordinance was an unconstitutional restriction of freedom of religion and of the press, contrary to the Fourteenth Amendment. The circuit judge heard the case de novo without a jury on stipulated facts. The ordinance required a license "For each person peddling dry goods, notions, wearing apparel, household goods or other articles not herein or otherwise specifically mentioned $25 per month, $10 per week, $2.50 per day." ⊥ The petitioners, in the exercise of their beliefs concerning their duty to preach the gospel, admitted going from house to house without a license, playing phonographic transcriptions of Bible lectures, and distributing books setting forth their views to the residents in return for a contribution of twenty-five cents per book. When persons desiring books were unable to contribute, the books were in some instances given away free. The circuit judge concluded as a matter of law that the books were other articles and that petitioners were guilty of peddling without a license. A motion for new trial was denied. On appeal the Supreme Court of Arkansas held the ordinance constitutional on the authority of its previous decision in *Cook* v. *Harrison* and af-

firmed the convictions. This Court denied certiorari, but later, because of the similarity of the issues presented to those in the Jobin Case, No. 966, vacated the denial of certiorari and issued a writ.

No. 966

The City of Casa Grande, Arizona, by ordinance made it a misdemeanor for any person to carry on any occupation or business specified without first procuring a license. ⊥ Transient merchants, peddlers and street vendors were listed as subject to a quarterly license fee of $25.00, payable in advance. In the Superior Court of Pinal County Jobin was tried and convicted by a jury on a complaint charging that not having "a permanent place of business in the City", he there carried on the "business of peddling, vending, selling, offering for sale and soliciting the sale of ⊥ goods, wares and merchandise, to wit: pamphlets, books and publications without first having procured a license," contrary to the ordinance. The evidence for the state showed that without a license the appellant called at two homes and a laundry and offered for sale and sold books and pamphlets of a religious nature. At one home, accompanied by his wife, he was refused admission, but was allowed by the girl who came to the door to play a portable phonograph on the porch. The girl purchased one of his stock of books, "Religion," for a quarter, and received a pamphlet free. During the conversation he stated that he was an ordained minister preaching the gospel and quoted passages from the Bible. At the second home the lady of the house allowed him and his wife to enter and play the phonograph, but she refused to buy either books or pamphlets. When departing the appellant left some literature on the table although informed by the lady that it would not be read and had better be given to someone else. At the laundry the appellant introduced himself as one of the Jehovah's Witnesses and discussed with the proprietor their work and religion generally. The proprietor bought the book "Religion" for a quarter but declined to buy others at the same price. He was given a pamphlet free. When arrested the appellant stated that he was "selling religious books and preaching the gospel of the kingdom," and that because of his religious beliefs he would not take out a license. A motion at the close of the evidence for a directed verdict of acquittal on the ground that the ordinance violated the Fourteenth Amendment was denied. The jury was instructed to acquit unless it found the defendant was selling books or pamphlets. It returned a verdict of guilty. On appeal the Supreme Court of Arizona held that the ordinance, an "ordinary occupational license tax ordinance," did not deny freedom of religion and of the press and affirmed the conviction. An appeal to this Court ⊥ was allowed under § 237 of the Judicial Code, 28, USCA §344.

⌐590

⌐591

⌐592

The Opelika ordinance required book agents to pay $10.00 per annum, transient distributors of books (annual only) $5.00. The license fee in Casa Grande was $25 per quarter, that in Fort Smith ranged from $2.50 per day to $25 per month. All the fees were small, yet substantial. But the appellant and the petitioners, so far as the records disclose, advanced no claim and presented no proof in the courts below that these fees were invalid because so high as to make the cost of compliance a deterrent to the further distribution of their literature in those cities. Although petitioners in No. 314 contended that their enterprise was operated at a loss, there was no suggestion that they could not obtain from the same sources which now supply the funds to meet whatever deficit there may be sums sufficient to defray license fees also. The amount of the fees was not considered in the opinions below except for a bare statement by the Alabama court that the exaction was "reasonable," and neither the briefs nor the assignments of error in this Court have directed their attack specifically to that issue. Consequently there is not before us the question of the power to lay fees, objectionable in their effect because of their size, upon the constitutionally protected rights of free speech, press or the exercise of religion. If the size of the fees were to be considered, to reach a conclusion one would desire to know the estimated volume, the margin of profit, the solicitor's commission, the expense of policing and other pertinent facts of income and expense. In the circumstances we venture no opinion concerning the validity of license taxes if it were proved, or at least distinctly claimed, that the burden of the tax was a substantial clog upon activi|593 ties of the sort here involved. The ⊥ sole constitutional question considered is whether a non-discriminatory license fee, presumably appropriate in amount, may be imposed upon these activities.

We turn to the constitutional problem squarely presented by these ordinances. There are ethical principles of greater value to mankind than the guarantees of the Constitution, personal liberties which are beyond the power of government to impair. These principles and liberties belong to the mental and spiritual realm where the judgments and decrees of mundane courts are ineffective to direct the course of man. The rights of which our Constitution speaks have a more earthy quality. They are not absolutes to be exercised independently of other cherished privileges, protected by the same organic instrument. Conflicts in the exercise of rights arise and the conflicting forces seek adjustments in the courts, as do these parties, claiming on the one side the freedom of religion, speech and the press, guaranteed by the Fourteenth Amendment, and on the other the right to employ the sovereign power explicitly reserved to the State by the Tenth Amendment to ensure orderly living without which constitutional guarantees of civil liberties would be a mockery. Courts, no more than Constitutions, can intrude into the consciences of men or compel them to believe

contrary to their faith or think contrary ⊥ to their convictions, but courts are competent to adjudge the acts men do under color of a constitutional right, such as that of freedom of speech or of the press or the free exercise of religion and to determine whether the claimed right is limited by other recognized powers, equally precious to mankind. So the mind and spirit of man remain forever free, while his actions rest subject to necessary accommodation to the competing needs of his fellows. |594

If all expression of religion or opinion, however, were subject to the discretion of authority, our unfettered dynamic thoughts or moral impulses might be made only colorless and sterile ideas. To give them life and force, the Constitution protects their use. No difference of view as to the importance of the freedoms of press or religion exist. They are "fundamental personal rights and liberties." *Schneider* v. *Irvington*. To proscribe the dissemination of doctrines or arguments which do not transgress military or moral limits is to destroy the principal bases of democracy,—knowledge and discussion. One man, with views contrary to the rest of his compatriots, is entitled to the privilege of expressing his ideas by speech or broadside to anyone willing to listen or to read. Too many settled beliefs have in time been rejected to justify this generation in refusing a heating to its own dissentients. But that hearing may be limited by action of the proper legislative body to times, places and methods for the enlightenment of the community which, in view of existing social and economic conditions, are not at odds with the preservation of peace and good order.

This means that the proponents of ideas cannot determine entirely for themselves the time and place and manner for the diffusion of knowledge or for their evangelism, any more than the civil authorities may hamper or suppress the public dissemination of facts and prin⊥ciples by the people. The ordinary |595 requirements of civilized life compel this adjustment of interests. The task of reconcilement is made harder by the tendency to accept as dominant any contention supported by a claim of interference with the practice of religion or the spread of ideas. Believing as this nation has from the first that the freedoms of worship and expression are closely akin to the illimitable privileges of thought itself, any legislation affecting those freedoms is scrutinized to see that the interferences allowed are only those appropriate to the maintenance of a civilized society. The determination of what limitations may be permitted under such an abstract test rests with the legislative bodies, the courts, the executive and the people themselves guided by the experience of the past, the needs of revenue for law enforcement, the requirements and capacities of police protection, the dangers of disorder and other pertinent factors.

Upon the courts falls the duty of determining the validity of such enactments as may be challenged as unconstitutional by litigants. In dealing with these delicate adjustments this Court denies any place to administrative censorship of ideas or capricious approval of distributors. In *Lovell* v. *Griffin* the requirement of permission from the city manager invalidated the ordinance; in *Schneider* v. *Irvington*, that f a police officer. In the *Cantwell* Case, the secretary of the public welfare council was to determine whether the object of charitable solicitation was worthy. We held the requirement bad. Ordinances abso⊥lutely prohibiting the exercise of the right to disseminate information are a fortiori, invalid.

⌋596

The differences between censorship and complete prohibition, either of subject matter or the individuals participating, upon the one hand, and regulation of the conduct of individuals in the time, manner and place of their activities upon the other, are decisive. "One who is a martyr to a principle ... does not prove by his martyrdom that he has kept within the law," said Mr. Justice Cardozo concurring in *Hamilton* v. *University of California*, which held that conscientious objection to military training would not excuse a student, during his enrollment, from attending required courses in that science. There is to be noted, too, a distinction between non-discriminatory regulation of operations which are incidental to the exercise of religion or the freedom of speech or the press and those which are imposed upon the religious rite itself or the unmixed dissemination of information. Casual reflection verifies the suggestion that both teachers and preachers need to receive support for themselves as well as alms and benefactions for charity and the spread of knowledge. But when, as in these cases, the practitioners of these noble callings choose to utilize the vending of their religious books and tracts as a source of funds, the financial aspects of their transactions need not be wholly disregarded. To subject any religious or didactic group to a reasonable fee for their money-making activities does not require a finding that the licensed acts are purely commercial. It is enough that money is earned by the sale ⊥ of articles. A book agent cannot escape a license requirement by a plea that it is a tax on knowledge. It would hardly be contended that the publication of newspapers is not subject to the usual government fiscal exactions or the obligations placed by statutes on other business. The Constitution draws no line between a payment from gross receipts or a net income tax and a suitably calculated occupational license. Commercial advertising cannot escape control by the simple expedient of printing matter of public interest on the same sheet or handbill. Nor does the fact that to the participants a formation in the streets is an "information march," and "one of their ways of worship," suffice to exempt such a procession from a city ordinance which, narrowly construed, required a license for such parade.

⌋597

When proponents of religious or social theories use the ordinary commercial methods of sales of articles to raise propaganda funds, it is a natural and proper exercise of the power of the state to charge reasonable fees for the privilege of canvassing. Careful as we may and should be to protect the freedoms safeguarded by the Bill of Rights, it is difficult to see in such enactments a shadow of prohibition of the exercise of religion or of abridgement of the freedom of speech or the press. It is prohibition and unjustifiable abridgement which are interdicted, not taxation. Nor do we believe it can be fairly said that because such proper charges may be expanded into unjustifiable abridgements they are therefore invalid on their face. The freedoms claimed by those seeking relief here are guaranteed against abridgement by the Fourteenth Amendment. Its commands protect their rights. The legislative power of municipalities must yield when ⊥ abridgement is shown. If we were to assume, as is here argued, that the licensed activities involve religious rites, a different question would be presented. These are not taxes on free will offerings. But it is because we view these sales as partaking more of commercial than religious or educational transactions that we find the ordinances, as here presented, valid. A tax on religion or a tax on interstate commerce may alike be forbidden by the Constitution. It does not follow that licenses for selling Bibles or for manufacture of articles of general use, measured by extra-state sales, must fall. It may well be that the wisdom of American communities will persuade them to permit the poor and weak to draw support from the petty sales of religious books without contributing anything for the privilege of using the streets and conveniences of the municipality. Such an exemption, however, would be a voluntary, not a constitutionally enforced, contribution.

⌋598

In the ordinances of Casa Grande and Fort Smith, we have no discretionary power in the public authorities to refuse a license to anyone desirous of selling religious literature. No censorship of the material which enters into the books or papers is authorized. No religious symbolism is involved such as was urged against the flag salute in *Minersville School Dist.* v. *Gobitis*. For us there is no occasion to apply here the principles taught by that opinion. Nothing more is asked from one group than from another which uses similar methods of propagation. We see nothing in the collection of a non-discriminatory license fee, uncontested in amount, from those selling books or papers, which abridges the freedoms of worship, speech or press. As to the claim that even small license charges, if valid, will impose upon the itinerant colporteur a crushing ag⊥gregate, it is plain that if each single fee is, as we assume, commensurate with the activities licensed, then though the accumulation of fees from city to city may in time bulk large, he will have enjoyed a correlatively enlarged field of distribution. The First Amendment does not require a subsidy in the form of fiscal exemption. Ac-

⌋599

cordingly the challenge to the Fort Smith and Casa Grande ordinances fails.

There is an additional contention by petitioner as to the Opelika ordinance. It is urged that since the licenses were revocable, arbitrarily, by the local authorities, there can be no true freedom for petitioners in the dissemination of information because of the censorship upon their actions after the issuance of the license. But there has been neither application for nor revocation of a license. The complaint was bottomed on sales without a license. It was that charge against which petitioner claimed the protection of the Constitution. This issue he had standing to raise. From what has been said previously it follows that the objection to the unconstitutionality of requiring a license fails. There is no occasion, at this time, to pass on the validity of the revocation section, as it does not affect his present defense.

In *Lovell* v. *Griffin* we held invalid a statute which placed the grant of a license within the discretion of the licensing authority. By this discretion, the right to obtain a license was made an empty right. Therefore the formality of going through an application was naturally not deemed a prerequisite to insistence on a constitutional right. Here we have a very different situation. A license is required that may properly be required. The fact that such a license, if it were granted, may subse⊥quently be revoked does not necessarily destroy the licensing ordinance. The hazard of such revocation is much too contingent for us now to declare the licensing provisions to be invalid. *Lovell* v. *Griffin* has, in effect, held that discretionary control in the general area of free speech is unconstitutional. Therefore, the hazard that the license properly granted would be improperly revoked is far too slight to justify declaring the valid part of the ordinance, which is alone now at issue, also unconstitutional.

⊥600

The judgments in Nos. 280, 314 and 966 are *affirmed.*

Mr. CHIEF JUSTICE STONE:

The First Amendment, which the Fourteenth makes applicable to the states, declares: "Congress shall make no law respecting an establishment of religion, or prohibiting the free exercise thereof; or abridging the freedom of speech, or of the press." I think that the ordinance in each of these cases is on its face a prohibited invasion of the freedoms thus guaranteed, and that the judgment in each should be reversed.

The ordinance in the Opelika case should be held invalid on two independent grounds. One is that the annual tax in addition to the 50 cent "issuance fee" which the ordinance imposes is an unconstitutional restriction on those freedoms, for reasons which will presently appear. The other is that the requirement of a license for dissemination of ideas, when as here the license is revocable at will without cause and in the unrestrained discretion of administrative officers, is likewise an unconstitutional restraint on those freedoms.

The sole condition which the Opelika ordinance prescribes for grant of the license is payment of the designated annual tax and issuance fee. The privilege thus purchased, for the period of a year, is forthwith revocable in the unrestrained and unreviewable discretion of the ⊥ licensing commission without cause and without notice or opportunity for a hearing. The case presents in its baldest form the question whether the freedoms which the Constitution purports to safeguard can be completely subjected to uncontrolled administrative action. Only recently this Court was unanimous in holding void on its face the requirement of a license for the distribution of pamphlets which was to be issued in the sole discretion of a municipal officer. The precise ground of our decision was that the ordinance made enjoyment of the freedom which the Constitution guarantees contingent upon the uncontrolled will of administrative officers. We declared:

⊥601

"We think that the ordinance is invalid on its face. Whatever the motive which induced its adoption, its character is such that it strikes at the very foundation of the freedom of the press by subjecting it to license and censorship. The struggle for the freedom of the press was primarily directed against the power of the licensor. It was against that power that John Milton directed his assault by his 'Appeal for the Liberty of Unlicensed Printing.' And the liberty of the press became initially a right to publish '*without* a license what formerly could be published only *with* one.' While this freedom from previous restraint upon publication cannot be regarded as exhausting the guaranty of liberty, the prevention of that restraint was a leading purpose in the adoption of the constitutional provision."

That purpose cannot rightly be defeated by so transparent a subterfuge as the pronouncement that, while a license may not be required if its award is contingent upon the whim of an administrative officer, it may be if its retention and the enjoyment of the privilege which it purports to give are wholly contingent upon his whim. In either case enjoyment of the freedom is dependent upon the same contingency and the censorship is as effective ⊥ in one as in the other. Nor is any palliative afforded by the assertion that the defendant's failure to apply for a license deprives him of standing to challenge the ordinance because of its revocation provision, by the terms of which retention of the license and exercise of the privilege may be cut off at any time without cause.

⊥602

Indeed, the present ordinance is a more callous disregard of the constitutional right than that exhibited in *Lovell* v. *Griffin.* There at least the defendant might have been given a license if he had applied for it. In any event he would not have been compelled to pay a money exaction for a license to exercise the privilege of free speech—a license which if granted in this case would have been wholly illusory. Here the defendant Jones was prohibited from distributing his pamphlets at all unless he paid in advance a year's tax for the exercise of the privilege and subjected himself to termination of the license without cause, notice or hearing, at the will of city officials. To say that he who is free to withhold at will the privilege of publication exercises a power of censorship prohibited by the Constitution, but that he who has unrestricted power to withdraw the privilege does not, would be to ignore history and deny the teachings of experience, as well as to perpetuate the evils at which the First Amendment was aimed.

It is of no significance that the defendant did not apply for a license. As this Court has often pointed out, when a licensing statute is on its face a lawful exercise of regulatory power, it will not be assumed that it will be unlawfully administered in advance of an actual denial of application for the license. But here it is the prohibition of publication, save at the uncontrolled will of public officials, which transgresses constitutional limitations and makes the ordinance void on its face. The Constitution can hardly be thought to deny to one subjected to the restraints of such an ordinance the right to attack its constitutionality, because he has not yielded to its demands. . . . ⊥

⌊603

In all three cases the question presented by the record and fully argued here and below is whether the ordinances—which as applied penalize the defendants for not having paid the flat fee taxes levied—violate the freedom of speech, press, and religion guaranteed by the First and Fourteenth Amendments. Defendants' challenge to the ordinances, naming them, is a challenge to the substantial taxes which they impose, in specified amounts, and not to some tax of a different or lesser amount which some other ordinance might levy. In their briefs here they argue, as upon the records they are entitled to do, that the taxes are an unconstitutional burden on the

⌊604 right of ⊥ free speech and free religion comparable to license taxes which the Court has often held to be an inadmissible burden on interstate commerce. They argue also that the cumulative effect of such taxes, in town after town throughout the country, would be destructive of freedom of the press for all persons except those financially able to distribute their literature without soliciting funds for the support of their cause.

While these are questions which have been studiously left unanswered by the opinion of the Court, it seems inescapable that an answer must be given before the convictions can be sustained. Decision of them cannot rightly be avoided now by asserting that the amount of the tax has not been put in issue; that the tax is "uncontested in amount" by the de-

fendants, and can therefore be assumed by us to be "presumably appropriate," "reasonable," or "suitably calculated;" that it has not been proved that the burden of the tax is a substantial clog on the activities of the defendants, or that those who have defrayed the expense of their religious activities will not willingly defray the license taxes also. All these are considerations which would seem to be irrelevant to the question now before us—whether a flat tax, more than a nominal fee to defray the expenses of a regulatory license, can constitutionally be laid on a non-commercial, non-profit activity devoted exclusively to the dissemination of ideas, educational and religious in character, to those persons who consent to receive them.

Nor is the essential issue here disguised by the reiterated characterization of these exactions, not as taxes but as "fees"—a characterization to which the records lend no support. All these ordinances on their face purport to be an exercise of the municipality's taxing power. In none is there the slightest pretense by the taxing authority, or the slightest suggestion by the state court, that the "fee" is to defray expenses of the licensing system. The ⊥ ⌊605 amounts of the "fees," without more, demonstrate that such a contention is groundless. In No. 280, Opelika itself contends that the issue relates solely to its power to raise money for general revenue purposes, and the Supreme Court of Alabama referred to the levy as a "reasonable" "tax." The tax exacted by Opelika, on the face of the ordinance, is in addition to a 50 cent "issuance fee," which alone is presumably what the city deems adequate to defray the cost of administering the licensing system. Similarly in the Fort Smith and Casa Grande cases, the state courts sustained the ordinances as a tax, and nothing else. If this litigation has involved any controversy—and the state courts all seemed to think that it did—the controversy has been one solely relating to the power to tax, and not the power to collect a "fee" to support a licensing system which, as has already been indicated, has no regulatory purpose other than that involved in the raising of revenue.

This Court has often had occasion to point out that where the state may, as a regulatory measure, license activities which it is without constitutional authority to tax, it may charge a small or nominal fee sufficient to defray the expense of licensing, and similarly it may charge a reasonable fee for the use of its highways by interstate motor traffic which it cannot tax. But we are not concerned in these cases with a nominal fee for a regulatory license, which may be assumed for argument's sake to be valid. Here the licenses are not regulatory, save as the licenses conditioned upon payment of the tax may serve to restrain or suppress publication. None of the ordinances, if complied with, purports to or could control the time, place or manner of the distribution of the books and pamphlets concerned. None has any discernible relationship to the police ⊥ protec- ⌊606 tion or the good order of the community. The only condition and purpose of the licenses under all three ordinances is suppression of the specified distributions of literature in default of the payment of a substantial tax fixed in amount and measured neither by the extent of the defendants' activities under the license nor the amounts which they receive for and devote to religious purposes in the exercise of the licensed privilege. Opelika exacts a license fee for book agents of $10 per annum and of $5 per annum for transient distributors of books, in addition to a 50 cent "issuance fee" on each license. The Supreme Court of Alabama found it unnecessary to determine whether both or only one of these taxes was payable by defendant Jones. The Fort Smith tax of $25 a month or $10 a week or $2.50 a day is substantial in amount for transient distributors of literature of the character here involved; the Opelika exaction is even more onerous when applied against one who may be in the city for only a day or two; and the tax of $25 per quarter exacted by the Casa Grande ordinance, adopted in a community having an adult population of less than 1,000 and applied to distributions of literature like the present, is prohibitive in effect.

In considering the effect of such a tax on the defendants' activities it is important to note that the state courts have applied levies obviously devised for the taxation of business employments—in the first case the "business or vocation" of "book agent;" in the second the business of peddling specified types of merchandise or "other articles;" in the third, the practice of the callings of "peddlers, transient merchants and vendors"—to activities which concededly are not ordinary business or commercial transactions. As appears by stipulation or undisputed testimony, the defendants are Jehovah's Witnesses, engaged in spreading their religious doctrines in conformity to the teachings of St. Matthew, Matt. 10:11-14 and ⊥ 24:14, by going from city to city, from village to village, and house to house, to proclaim them. After asking and receiving permission from the householder, they play to him phonograph records and tender to him books or pamphlets advocating their religious views. For the latter they ask payment of a nominal amount, two to five cents for the pamphlets and twenty-five cents for books, as a contribution to the religious cause which they seek to advance. But they distribute the pamphlets, and sometimes the books, gratis when the householder is unwilling or unable to pay for them. The literature is published for such distribution by non-profit charitable corporations organized by Jehovah's Witnesses. The funds collected are used for the support of the religious movement and no one derives a profit from the publication and distribution of the literature. In the *Opelika* case the defendant's activities were confined to distribution of literature and solicitation of funds in the public streets.

⌐607

No one could doubt that taxation which may be freely laid upon activities not within the protection of the Bill of Rights could—when applied to the dissemination of ideas—be made the ready instrument for destruction of that right. Few would deny that a license tax laid specifically on the privilege of disseminating ideas would infringe the right of free speech. For one reason among others, if the state may tax the privilege it may fix the rate of tax and, through the tax, control or suppress the activity which it taxes. If the distribution of the literature had been carried on by the defendants without solicitation of funds, there plainly would have been no basis, either statutory or constitutional, for levying the tax. It is the collection of funds which has been seized upon to justify the extension, to the defendants' activities, of the tax laid upon business callings. But if we assume, despite our recent ⊥ decision in *Schneider* v. *Irvington*, that the essential character of these activities is in some measure altered by the collection of funds for the support of a religious undertaking, still it seems plain that the operation of the present flat tax is such as to abridge the privileges which the defendants here invoke.

⌐608

It lends no support to the present tax to insist that its restraint on free speech and religion is non-discriminatory because the same levy is made upon business callings carried on for profit, many of which involve no question of freedom of speech and religion and all of which involve commercial elements—lacking here—which for present purposes may be assumed to afford a basis for taxation apart from the exercise of freedom of speech and religion. The constitutional protection of the Bill of Rights is not to be evaded by classifying with business callings an activity whose sole purpose is the dissemination of ideas, and taxing it as business callings are taxed. The immunity which press and religion enjoy may sometimes be lost when they are united with other activities not immune. But here the only activities involved are the dissemination of ideas, educational and religious, and the collection of funds for the propagation of those ideas, which we have said is likewise the subject of constitutional protection.

The First Amendment is not confined to safeguarding freedom of speech and freedom of religion against discriminatory attempts to wipe them out. On the contrary the Constitution, by virtue of the First and the Fourteenth Amendments, has put those freedoms in a preferred position. Their commands are not restricted to cases where the protected privilege is sought out for attack. They extend at least to every form of taxation which, because it is a condition of the exercise of the privilege, is capable of being used to control or suppress it.

⊥ Even were we to assume—what I do not concede—that there could be a lawful non-discriminatory license tax of a percentage of the gross receipts collected by churches and other religious or-

⌐609

ders in support of their religious work, we have no such tax here. The tax imposed by the ordinances in these cases is more burdensome and destructive of the activity taxed than any gross receipts tax. The tax is for a fixed amount, unrelated to the extent of the defendants' activities or the receipts derived from them. It is thus the type of flat tax which, when applied to interstate commerce, has repeatedly been deemed by this Court to be prohibited by the commerce clause. When applied as it is here to activities involving the exercise of religious freedom, its vice is emphasized in that it is levied and paid in advance of the activities save only as others may volunteer to pay the tax. It requires a sizable out-of-pocket expense by someone who may never succeed in raising a penny in his exercise of the privilege which is taxed.

The defendants' activities, if taxable at all, are taxable only because of the funds which they solicit. But that solicitation is for funds for religious purposes, and the present taxes are in no way gauged to the receipts. The taxes are insupportable either as a tax on the dissemination of ideas or as a tax on the collection of funds for religious purposes. For on its face a flat license tax restrains in advance the freedom taxed and tends inevitably to suppress its exercise. The First Amendment prohibits all laws abridging freedom of press and religion, not merely some laws or all except tax laws. It is true that the constitutional guaranties of freedom of press and religion, like the commerce clause, make no distinction ⊥610 between fixed-sum ⊥ taxes and other kinds. But that fact affords no excuse for courts, whose duty is to enforce those guaranties, to close their eyes to the characteristics of a tax which render it destructive of freedom of press and religion.

We may lay to one side the Court's suggestion that a tax otherwise unconstitutional is to be deemed valid unless it is shown that there are none who, for religion's sake, will come forward to pay the unlawful exaction. The defendants to whom the ordinances have been applied have not paid it and there is nothing in the Constitution to compel them to seek the charity of others to pay it before protesting the tax. It seems fairly obvious that if the present taxes, laid in small communities upon peripatetic religious propagandists, are to be sustained, a way has been found for the effective suppression of speech and press and religion despite constitutional guaranties. The very taxes now before us are better adapted to that end than were the stamp taxes which so successfully curtailed the dissemination of ideas by eighteenth century newspapers and pamphleteers, and which were a moving cause of the American Revolution. Vivid recollections of the effect of those taxes on the freedom of press survived to inspire the adoption of the First Amendment.

Freedom of press and religion, explicitly guaranteed by the Constitution, must at least be entitled to the same freedom from burdensome taxation which

it has been thought that the more general phraseology of the commerce clause has extended to interstate commerce. Whatever doubts may be entertained as to this Court's function to relieve, unaided by Congressional legislation, from burdensome taxation under the commerce clause, ⊥ it cannot be ⊥611 thought that that function is wanting under the explicit guaranties of freedom of speech, press and religion. In any case the flat license tax can hardly become any the less burdensome or more permissible, when levied on activities within the protection extended by the First and Fourteenth Amendments both to the orderly communication of ideas, educational and religious, to persons willing to receive them, see *Cantwell* v. *Connecticut*, and to the practice of religion and the solicitation of funds in its support.

In its potency as a prior restraint on publication the flat license tax falls short only of outright censorship or suppression. The more humble and needy the cause, the more effective is the suppression.

Mr. Justice BLACK, Mr. Justice DOUGLAS and *Mr. Justice MURPHY* join in this opinion.

Mr. Justice MURPHY, with whom The *CHIEF JUSTICE, Mr. Justice BLACK*, and *Mr. Justice DOUGLAS* concur, dissenting:

When a statute is challenged as impinging on freedom of speech, freedom of the press, or freedom of worship, those historic privileges which are so essential to our political welfare and spiritual progress, it is the duty of this Court to subject such legislation to examination, in the light of the evidence adduced, to determine whether it is so drawn as not to impair the substance of those cherished freedoms in reaching its objective. Ordinances that may operate to restrict the circulation or dissemination of ideas on religious or other subjects should be framed with fastidious care and precise language to avoid undue encroachment on these fundamental liberties. And the protection of the Constitution must be extended to all, ⊥ not only to those whose views accord with ⊥612 prevailing thought but also to dissident minorities who energetically spread their beliefs. Being satisfied by the evidence that the ordinances in the cases now before us, as construed and applied in the state courts, impose a burden on the circulation and discussion of opinion and information in matters of religion, and therefore violate the petitioners' rights to freedom of speech, freedom of the press, and freedom of worship in contravention of the Fourteenth Amendment, I am obliged to dissent from the opinion of the Court.

It is not disputed that petitioners, Jehovah's Witnesses, were ordained ministers preaching the gospel, as they understood it, through the streets and from house to house, orally and by playing religious records with the consent of the householder, and by distributing books and pamphlets setting forth the tenets of their faith. It does not appear that their motives were commercial, but only that they were evangelizing their faith as they saw it. In No. 280 the trial court excluded as irrelevant petitioner's testimony that he was an ordained minister and that his activities on the streets of Opelika were in furtherance of his ministerial duties. The testimony of ten clergymen of Opelika that they distributed free religious literature in their churches, the cost of which was defrayed by voluntary contribution, and that they had never been forced to pay any license fee, was also excluded. It is admitted here that petitioner was a Jehovah's Witness and considered himself an ordained minister.

The Supreme Court of Arizona stated in No. 966 that appellant was "a regularly ordained minister of the denomination commonly known as Jehovah's Witnesses, . . . going from house to house in the city of Casa Grande preaching the gospel, as he understood it, by means of his ⊥ spoken word, by playing various records on a phonograph, with the approval of the householder, and by distributing printed books, pamphlets and tracts which set forth his views as to the meaning of the Bible. The method of distribution of these printed books, pamphlets and tracts was as follows: He first offered them for sale at various prices ranging from five to twenty-five cents each. If the householder did not desire to purchase any of them he then left a small leaflet summarizing some of the doctrines which he preached."

The facts were stipulated in No. 314. Each petitioner "claims to be an ordained minister of the gospel. . . . They do not engage in this work for any selfish reason but because they feel called upon to publish the news and preach the gospel of the Kingdom to all the world as a witness before the end comes. . . . They believe that the only effective way to preach is to go from house to house and make personal contact with the people and distribute to them books and pamphlets setting forth their views of Christianity." Petitioners "were going from house to house in the residential section within the city of Fort Smith . . . presenting to the residents of these houses various booklets, leaflets and periodicals setting forth their views of Christianity held by Jehovah's Witnesses." They solicited "a contribution of twenty-five cents for each book," but "these books in some instances are distributed free when the people wishing them are unable to contribute."

There is no suggestion in any of these three cases that petitioners were perpetrating a fraud, that they were demeaning themselves in any obnoxious manner, that their activities created any public disturbance or inconvenience, that private rights were contravened, or that the literature distributed was offensive to morals or created any "clear and present danger" to organized society.

The ordinance in each case is sought to be sustained as a system of non-discriminatory taxation of various busi⊥nesses, professions and vocations, including the distribution of books for which contributions are asked, for the sole purpose of raising revenue. Any inclination to take the position that petitioners, who were proselytizing by distributing informative literature setting forth their religious tenets, and whose activities were wholly unrelated to any commercial purposes, were not within the purview of these occupational tax ordinances, is foreclosed by the decisions of the state courts below to the contrary. As so construed the ordinances in effect impose direct taxes on the dissemination of ideas and the distribution of literature, relating to and dealing with religious matters, for which a contribution is asked in an attempt to gain converts, because those were petitioners' activities. Such taxes have been held to violate the Fourteenth Amendment, and that should be the holding here.

FREEDOM OF SPEECH AND FREEDOM OF THE PRESS

In view of the recent decisions of this Court striking down acts which impair freedom ⊥ of speech and freedom of the press no elaboration on that subject is now necessary. We have "unequivocally held that the streets are proper places for the exercise of the freedom of communicating information and disseminating opinion and that, though the states and municipalities may appropriately regulate the privilege in the public interest, they may not unduly burden or proscribe its employment in these public thoroughfares." *Valentine* v. *Chrestensen*, decided April 13, 1942. And as the distribution of pamphlets to spread information and opinion on the streets and from house to house for non-commercial purposes is protected from the prior restraint of censorship, so should it be protected from the burden of taxation.

The opinion of the Court holds that the amount of the tax is not before us and that a "non-discriminatory license fee, presumably appropriate in amount, may be imposed upon these activities." Both of these holdings must be rejected.

Where regulation or infringement of the liberty of discussion and the dissemination of information and opinion are involved, there are special reasons for testing the challenged statute on its face. That should be done here.

Consideration of the taxes leads to but one conclusion—that they prohibit or seriously hinder the distribution of petitioners' religious literature. The opinion of the Court admits that all the taxes are "substantial." The $25 quar⊥terly tax of Casa Grande approaches prohibition. The 1940 population of that town was 1,545. With so few potential purchasers it would take a gifted evangelist, indeed, in view of the antagonism generally encountered by Jehovah's Witnesses, to sell enough tracts at prices ranging from five to twenty-five cents to gross enough to pay the tax. While the amount is actually lower in Opelika and may be lower in Fort Smith in that it is possible to get a license for a short period, and while the circle of purchasers is wider in those towns, these exactions also place a heavy hand on petitioners' activities. The petitioners should not be subjected to such tribute.

But whatever the amount, the taxes are in reality taxes upon the dissemination of religious ideas, a dissemination carried on by the distribution of religious literature for religious reasons alone and not for personal profit. As such they place a burden on freedom of speech, freedom of the press, and the exercise of religion even if the question of amount is laid aside. Liberty of circulation is the very life blood of a free press, and taxes on the circulation of ideas have a long history of misuse against freedom of thought. And taxes on circulation solely for the purpose of revenue were success⊥fully resisted, prior to the adoption of the First Amendment, as interferences with freedom of the press. Surely all this was familiar knowledge to the framers of the Bill of Rights. We need not shut our eyes to the possibility that use may again be made of such taxes, either by discrimination in enforcement or otherwise, to suppress the unpalatable view of militant minorities such as Jehovah's Witnesses. As the evidence excluded in No. 280 tended to show, no attempt was made there to apply the ordinance to ministers functioning in a more orthodox manner than petitioner.

⌊617

Other objectionable features in addition to the factor of historical misuse exist. There is the unfairness present in any system of flat fee taxation, bearing no relation to the ability to pay. And there is the cumulative burden of many such taxes throughout the municipalities of the land, as the number of recent cases involving such ordinances abundantly demonstrates. The activities of Jehovah's ⊥ Witnesses are widespread, and the aggregate effect of numerous exactions, no matter how small, can conceivably force them to choose between refraining from attempting to recoup part of the cost of their literature, or else paying out large sums in taxes. Either choice hinders and may even possibly put an end to their activities. There is no basis, other than a refusal to consider the characteristics of taxes such as these, for any assumption that such taxes are "commensurate with the activities licensed." Nor is there any assurance that "a correlatively enlarged field of distribution" will insure sufficient proceeds even to meet such exactions, let alone leaving any residue for the continuation of petitioners' evangelization.

⌊618

Freedom of speech, freedom of the press, and freedom of religion all have a double aspect—freedom of thought and freedom of action. Freedom to think is absolute of its own nature; the most tyrannical government is powerless to control the inward workings of the mind. But even an aggressive mind is of no missionary value unless there is freedom of action, freedom to communicate its message to others by speech and writing. Since in any form of action there is a possibility of collision with the rights of others, there can be no doubt that this freedom to act is not absolute but qualified, being subject to regulation in the public interest which does not unduly infringe the right. However, there is no assertion here that the ordinances were regulatory, but if there were such a claim, they still should not be sustained. No abuses justifying regulation are advanced and the ordinances are not narrowly and precisely drawn to deal with actual, or even hypothetical evils, while at the same time preserving the substance of the right. ⊥ They impose a tax on the dissemination of information and opinion anywhere within the city limits, whether on the streets or from house to house. "As we have said, the streets are natural and proper places for the dissemination of information and opinion; and one is not to have the exercise of his liberty of expression in appropriate places abridged on the plea that it may be exercised elsewhere." *Schneider* v. *Irvington*. These taxes abridge that liberty.

⌊619

It matters not that petitioners asked contributions for their literature. Freedom of speech and freedom of the press cannot and must not mean freedom only for those who can distribute their broadsides without charge. There may be others with messages more vital but purses less full, who must seek some reimbursement for their outlay or else forego passing on their ideas. The pamphlet, an historic weapon against oppression, is today the convenient vehicle of those with limited resources because newspaper space and radio time are expensive and the cost of establishing such enterprises great. If freedom of speech and freedom of the press are to have any concrete meaning, people seeking to distribute information and opinion, to the end only that others shall have the benefit thereof, should not be taxed for circulating such matter. It is unnecessary to consider now the validity of such taxes on commercial enterprises engaged in the dissemination of ideas. Petitioners were not engaged in a traffic for profit. While the courts below held their activities were covered by the ⊥ ordinances, it is clear that they were seeking only to further their religious convictions by preaching the gospel to others.

⌊620

The exercise, without commercial motives, of freedom of speech, freedom of the press, or freedom of worship are not proper sources of taxation for general revenue purposes. In dealing with a permissible regulation of these freedoms and the fee charged in connection therewith, we emphasized the fact that the fee was not a revenue tax, but one to meet the expense incident to the administration of the Act and to the maintenance of public order, and stated only that, "There is nothing contrary to the Constitution in the charge of a fee limited to the purpose stated." *Cox* v. *New Hampshire*. The taxes here involved are ostensibly for revenue purposes; they are not regulatory fees. Respondents do not show that the instant activities of Jehovah's Witnesses create special problems causing a drain on the municipal coffers, or that these taxes are commensurate with any expenses entailed by the presence of the Witnesses. In the absence of such a showing I think no tax whatever can be levied on petitioners' activities in distributing their literature or disseminating their ideas. If the guaranties of freedom of speech and freedom of the press are to be preserved, municipalities should not be free to raise general revenue by taxes on the circulation of information and opinion in non-commercial causes; other sources can be found, the taxation of which will not choke off ideas. Taxes such as the instant ones violate petitioners' right to freedom of speech and freedom of the press, protected against state invasion by the Fourteenth Amendment.⊥

⌐621

FREEDOM OF RELIGION

Under the foregoing discussion of freedom of speech and freedom of the press any person would be exempt from taxation upon the act of distributing information or opinion of any kind, whether political, scientific, or religious in character, when done solely in an effort to spread knowledge and ideas, with no thought of commercial gain. But there is another, and perhaps more precious reason why these ordinances cannot constitutionally apply to petitioners. Important as free speech and a free press are to a free government and a free citizenry, there is a right even more dear to many individuals—the right to worship their Maker according to their needs and the dictates of their souls and to carry their message or their gospel to every living creature. These ordinances infringe that right, which is also protected by the Fourteenth Amendment.

Petitioners were itinerant ministers going through the streets and from house to house in different communities, preaching the gospel by distributing booklets and pamphlets setting forth their views of the Bible and the tenets of their faith. While perhaps not so orthodox as the oral sermon, the use of religious books is an old, recognized and effective mode of worship and means of proselytizing. For this petitioners were taxed. The mind rebels at the thought that a minister of any of the old established churches could be made to pay fees to the community before entering the pulpit. These taxes on petitioners' efforts to preach the "news of the Kingdom" should be struck down because they burden petitioners' right to worship the Diety in their own fashion and to spread the gospel as they understand it. There is here no contention that their manner of worship

gives rise to conduct which calls for regulation, and these ordinances are not aimed at any such practices.

One need only read the decisions of this and other courts in the past few years to see the unpopularity of Jehovah's Witnesses ⊥ and the difficulties put in their path because of their religious beliefs. An arresting parallel exists between the troubles of Jehovah's Witnesses and the struggles of various dissentient groups in the American colonies for religious liberty which culminated in the Virginia Statute for Religious Freedom, the Northwest Ordinance of 1787, and the First Amendment. In most of the colonies there was an established church, and the way of the dissenter was hard. All sects, including Quaker, Methodist, Baptist, Episcopalian, Separatist, Rogerine, and Catholic, suffered. Many of the non-conforming ministers were itinerants, and measures were adopted to curb their unwanted activities. The books of certain denominations were banned. Virginia and Connecticut had burdensome licensing requirements. Other states required oaths before one could preach which many ministers could not conscientiously take. ⊥ Research reveals no attempt to control or persecute by the more subtle means of taxing the function of preaching, or even any attempt to tap it as a source of revenue.

⌐622

⌐623

By applying these occupational taxes to petitioners' non-commercial activities, respondents now tax sincere efforts to spread religious beliefs, and a heavy burden falls upon a new set of itinerant zealots, the Witnesses. That burden should not be allowed to stand, especially if, as the excluded testimony in No. 280 indicates, the accepted clergymen of the town can take to their pulpits and distribute their literature without the impact of taxation. Liberty of conscience is too full of meaning for the individuals in this nation to permit taxation to prohibit or substantially impair the spread of religious ideas, even though they are controversial and run counter to the established notions of a community. If this Court is to err in evaluating claims that freedom of speech, freedom of the press, and freedom of religion have been invaded, far better that it err in being overprotective of these precious rights.

Mr. Justice BLACK, Mr. Justice DOUGLAS, Mr. Justice MURPHY:

The opinion of the Court sanctions a device which in our opinion suppresses or tends to suppress the free exercise of a religion practiced by a minority group. This is but another step in the direction which *Minersville School Dist.* v. *Gobitis* took against the same religious minority and is a logical extension of the principles upon which that decision rested. Since we joined in the opinion in the *Gobitis* Case, we think this is an ap⊥propriate occasion to state that we now believe that it was also wrongly decided. Certainly our democratic form of govern-

⌐624

ment functioning under the historic Bill of Rights has a high responsibility to accommodate itself to the religious views of minorities however unpopular and unorthodox those views may be. The First Amendment does not put the right freely to exercise religion in a subordinate position. We fear, however, that the opinions in these and in the *Gobitis* Case do exactly that.

MURDOCK v. PENNSYLVANIA

319 U.S. 105
ON WRIT OF CERTIORARI TO THE SUPERIOR COURT OF THE COMMONWEALTH OF PENNSYLVANIA
Argued March 10 and 11, 1943 — Decided May 3, 1943

⊥106   ⊥ *Mr. Justice DOUGLAS* delivered the opinion of the Court:

The City of Jeannette, Pennsylvania, has an ordinance, some forty years old, which provides in part:

"That all persons canvassing for or soliciting within said Borough, orders for goods, paintings, pictures, wares, or merchandise of any kind, or persons delivering such articles under orders so obtained or solicited, shall be required to procure from the Burgess a license to transact said business and shall pay to the Treasurer of said Borough therefore the following sums according to the time for which said license shall be granted.

"For one day $1.50, for one week seven dollars ($7.00), for two weeks twelve dollars ($12.00), for three weeks twenty dollars ($20.00), provided that the provisions of this ordinance shall not apply to persons selling by sample to manufacturers or licensed merchants or dealers doing business in said Borough of Jeannette."

Petitioners are "Jehovah's Witnesses." They went about from door to door in the City of Jeannette distributing literature and soliciting people to "purchase" certain religious books and pamphlets, all ⊥107 published by the ⊥ Watch Tower Bible & Tract Society. The "price" of the books was twenty-five cents each, the "price" of the pamphlets five cents each. In connection with these activities petitioners used a phonograph on which they played a record expounding certain of their views on religion. None of them obtained a license under the ordinance. Before they were arrested each had made "sales" of books. There was evidence that it was their practice in making these solicitations to request a "contribution," of twenty-five cents each for the books and five cents each for the pamphlets but to accept lesser sums or even to donate the volumes in case an interested person was without funds. In the present case some donations of pamphlets were made when books were purchased. Petitioners were convicted and fined for violation of the ordinance. Their judgments of conviction were sustained by the Superior Court of Pennsylvania against their contention that the ordi-

nance deprived them of the freedom of speech, press, and religion guaranteed by the First Amendment. Petitions for leave to appeal to the Supreme Court of Pennsylvania were denied. The cases are here on petitions for writs of certiorari which we granted along with the petitions for rehearing of *Jones* v. *Opelika* and its companion cases. ⊥   ⊥108

The First Amendment, which the Fourteenth makes applicable to the states, declares that "Congress shall make no law respecting an establishment of religion, or prohibiting the free exercise thereof; or abridging the freedom of speech, or of the press. . . ." It could hardly be denied that a tax laid specifically on the exercise of those freedoms would be unconstitutional. Yet the license tax imposed by this ordinance is in substance just that.

Petitioners spread their interpretations of the Bible and their religious beliefs largely through the hand distribution of literature by full or part time workers. They claim to follow the example of Paul, teaching "publickly, and from house to house." Acts 20:20. They take literally the mandate of the Scriptures, "Go ye into all the world, and preach the gospel to every creature." Mark 16:15. In doing so they believe that they are obeying a commandment of God.

The hand distribution of religious tracts is an age-old form of missionary evangelism—as old as the history of printing presses. It has been a potent force in various religious movements down through the years. This form of evangelism is utilized today on a large scale by various religious sects whose colporteurs carry the Gospel to thou⊥sands upon thou-   ⊥109 sands of homes and seek through personal visitations to win adherents to their faith. It is more than preaching; it is more than distribution of religious literature. It is a combination of both. Its purpose is as evangelical as the revival meeting. This form of religious activity occupies the same high estate under the First Amendment as do worship in the churches and preaching from the pulpits. It has the same claim to protection as the more orthodox and conventional exercises of religion. It also has the same claim as the others to the guarantees of freedom of speech and freedom of the press.

The integrity of this conduct or behavior as a religious practice has not been challenged. Nor do we have presented any question as to the sincerity of petitioners in their religious beliefs and practices, however misguided they may be thought to be. Moreover, we do not intimate or suggest in respecting their sincerity that any conduct can be made a religious rite and by the zeal of the practitioners swept into the First Amendment. *Reynolds* v. ⊥ *United States* and *Davis* v. *Beason* denied any   ⊥110 such claim to the practice of polygamy and bigamy. Other claims may well arise which deserve the same fate. We only hold that spreading one's religious beliefs or preaching the Gospel through distribution of religious literature and through personal visitations is an age-old type of evangelism with as high a claim to constitutional protection as the more orthodox types. The manner in which it is practiced at times gives rise to special problems with which the police power of the states is competent to deal. But that merely illustrates that the rights with which we are dealing are not absolutes. We are concerned, however, in these cases merely with one narrow issue. There is presented for decision no question whatsoever concerning punishment for any alleged unlawful acts during the solicitation. Nor is there involved here any question as to the validity of a registration system for colporteurs and other solicitors. The cases present a single issue—the constitutionality of an ordinance which as construed and applied requires religious colporteurs to pay a license tax as a condition to the pursuit of their activities.

The alleged justification for the exaction of this license tax is the fact that the religious literature is distributed with a solicitation of funds. Thus it was stated in *Jones* v. *Opelika* that when a religious sect uses "ordinary commercial methods of sales of articles to raise propaganda funds," it is proper for the state to charge "reasonable fees for the privilege of canvassing." Situations will arise where it will be difficult to determine whether a particular activity is religious or purely commercial. The distinction at times is vital. As we stated only the other day in *Jamison* v. *Texas*, "The state can prohibit the use of the streets for ⊥ the distribution of purely commercial leaflets, even though such leaflets may have 'a civic appeal, or a moral platitude' appended. *Valentine* v. *Chrestensen*. They may not prohibit the distribution of handbills in the pursuit of a clearly religious activity merely because the handbills invite the purchase of books for the improved understanding of the religion or because the handbills seek in a lawful fashion to promote the raising of funds for religious purposes." But the mere fact that the religious literature is "sold" by itinerant preachers rather than "donated" does not transform evangelism into a commercial enteprise. If it did, then the passing of the collection plate in church would make the church service a commercial project. The constitutional rights of those spreading their religious beliefs through the spoken and printed word are not to be gauged by standards governing retailers or wholesalers of books. The right to use the press for expressing one's views is not to be measured by the protection afforded commercial handbills. It should be remembered that the pamphlets of Thomas Paine were not distributed free of charge. It is plain that a religious organization needs funds to remain a going concern. But an itinerant evangelist however misguided or intolerant he may be, does not become a mere book agent by selling the Bible or religious tracts to help defray his expenses or to sustain him. Freedom of speech, freedom of the press, freedom of religion are available to all, not merely to those who can pay their own way. As we have said, the problem of drawing the line between a purely commercial activity and a religious one will at times be difficult. On this record it plainly cannot be said that petitioners were engaged in a commercial rather than a religious venture. It is a distortion of the facts of record to describe their activities as the occupation of selling books and pamphlets. And the Pennsylvania court did not rest the judgments of conviction on that basis, though it did find ⊥ that petitioners "sold" the literature. The Supreme Court of Iowa in *State* v. *Mead* described the selling activities of members of this same sect as "merely incidental and collateral" to their "main object which was to preach and publicize the doctrines of their order." That accurately summarizes the present record.

We do not mean to say that religious groups and the press are free from all financial burdens of government. We have here something quite different, for example, from a tax on the income of one who engages in religious activities or a tax on property used or employed in connection with those activities. It is one thing to impose a tax on the income or property of a preacher. It is quite another thing to exact a tax from him for the privilege of delivering a sermon. The tax imposed by the City of Jeannette is a flat license tax, the payment of which is a condition of the exercise of these constitutional privileges. The power to tax the exercise of a privilege is the power to control or suppress its enjoyment. Those who can tax the exercise of this religious practice can make its exercise so costly as to deprive it of the resources necessary for its maintenance. Those who can tax the privilege of engaging in this form of missionary evangelism can close its doors to all those who do not have a full purse. Spreading religious beliefs in this ancient and honorable manner would thus be denied the needy. Those who can deprive religious groups of their colporteurs can take from them a part of the vital power of the press which has survived from the Reformation.

It is contended, however, that the fact that the license tax can suppress or control this activity is unim⊥portant if it does not do so. But that is to disregard the nature of this tax. It is a license tax—a flat tax imposed on the exercise of a privilege granted by the Bill of Rights. A state may not impose a charge for the enjoyment of a right granted by the federal constitution. Thus, it may not exact a license tax for the privilege of carrying on interstate commerce, although it may tax the property used in, or the income derived from, that commerce, so long as those taxes are not discriminatory. A license tax applied to activities guaranteed by the First Amendment would have the same destructive effect. It is true that the First Amendment, like the commerce clause, draws no distinction between license taxes, fixed sum taxes, and other kinds of taxes. But that is no reason why we should shut our eyes to the nature

⊥112

⊥111

⊥113

of the tax and its destructive influence. The power to impose a license tax on the exercise of these freedoms is indeed as potent as the power of censorship which this Court has repeatedly struck down. For that reason the dissenting opinions in *Jones* v. *Opelika* stressed the nature of this type of tax. In that case as in the present ones, we have something very different from a registration system under which those going from house to house are required to give their names, addresses and other marks of identification to the authorities. In all of these cases the issuance of the permit or license is dependent on the payment of a license tax. And the license tax is fixed in amount and unrelated to the scope of the activities of petitioners or to their realized revenues. It is not a nominal fee ⊥ imposed as a regulatory measure to defray the expenses of policing the activities in question. It is in no way apportioned. It is a flat license tax levied and collected as a condition to the pursuit of activities whose enjoyment is guaranteed by the First Amendment. Accordingly, it restrains in advance those constitutional liberties of press and religion and inevitably tends to suppress their exercise. That is almost uniformly recognized as the inherent vice and evil of this flat license tax. As stated by the Supreme Court of Illinois in a case involving this same sect and an ordinance similar to the present one, a person cannot be compelled "to purchase, through a license fee or a license tax, the privilege freely granted by the Constitution." *Blue Island* v. *Kozul*. So, it may not be said that proof is lacking that these license taxes either separately or cumulatively have restricted or are likely to restrict petitioners' religious activities. On their face they are a restriction of the free exercise of those freedoms which are protected by the First Amendment.

The taxes imposed by this ordinance can hardly help but be as severe and telling in their impact on the freedom ⊥ of the press and religion as the "taxes on knowledge" at which the First Amendment was partly aimed. They may indeed operate even more subtly. Itinerant evangelists moving throughout a state or from state to state would feel immediately the cumulative effect of such ordinances as they become fashionable. The way of the religious dissenter has long been hard. But if the formula of this type of ordinance is approved, a new device for the suppression of religious minorities will have been found. This method of disseminating religious beliefs can be crushed and closed out by the sheer weight of the toll or tribute which is exacted town by town, village by village. The spread of religious ideas through personal visitations by the literature ministry of numerous religious groups would be stopped.

The fact that the ordinance is "non-discriminatory" is immaterial. The protection afforded by the First Amendment is not so restricted. A license tax certainly does not acquire constitutional validity because it classifies the privileges protected by the First Amendment along with the wares and merchandise of hucksters and peddlers and treats them all alike. Such equality in treatment does not save the ordinance. Freedom of press, freedom of speech, freedom of religion are in a preferred position.

It is claimed, however, that the ultimate question in determining the constitutionality of this license tax is whether the state has given something for which it can ask a return. That principle has wide applicability. But it is quite irrelevant here. This tax is not a charge for the enjoyment of a privilege or benefit bestowed by the state. The privilege in question exists apart from state authority. It is guaranteed the people by the Federal constitution.

Considerable emphasis is placed on the kind of literature which petitioners were distributing—its provocative, ⊥ abusive, and ill-mannered character and the assault which it makes on our established churches and the cherished faiths of many of us. But those considerations are not justification for the license tax which the ordinance imposes. Plainly a community may not suppress, or the state tax, the dissemination of views because they are unpopular, annoying or distasteful. If that device were ever sanctioned, there would have been forged a ready instrument for the suppression of the faith which any minority cherishes but which does not happen to be in favor. That would be a complete repudiation of the philosophy of the Bill of Rights.

Jehovah's Witnesses are not "above the law." But the present ordinance is not directed to the problems with which the police power of the state is free to deal. It does not cover, and petitioners are not charged with, breaches of the peace. They are pursuing their solicitations peacefully and quietly. Petitioners, moreover, are not charged with or prosecuted for the use of language which is obscene, abusive, or which incites retaliation. Nor do we have here, as we did in *Cox* v. *New Hampshire* and *Chaplinsky* v. *New Hampshire*, state regulation of the streets to protect and insure the safety, comfort, or convenience of the public. Furthermore, the present ordinance is not narrowly drawn to safeguard the people of the community in their homes against the evils of solicitations. As we have said, it is not merely a registration ordinance calling for an identification of the solicitors so as to give the authorities some basis for investigating strangers coming into the community. And the fee is not a nominal one, imposed as a regulatory measure and calculated to defray the expense of protecting those on the streets and at home against the abuses of solicitors. ⊥ Nor can the present ordinance survive if we assume that it has been construed to apply only to solicitation from house to house. The ordinance is not narrowly drawn to prevent or control abuses or evils arising from that activity. Rather, it sets aside the residential area as a prohibited zone, entry of which is denied petitioners unless the tax is paid. That restraint and one which is city wide in scope (*Jones* v. *Opelika*) are different only in degree. Each is an abridgment of freedom of press and a restraint on the free exercise of religion. They stand or fall together.

The judgment in *Jones* v. *Opelika* has this day been vacated. Freed from that controlling precedent, we can restore to their high, constitutional position the liberties of itinerant evangelists who disseminate their religious beliefs and the tenets of their faith through distribution of literature. The judgments are reversed and the causes are remanded to the Pennsylvania Superior Court for proceedings not inconsistent with this opinion.

Reversed.

The following dissenting opinions are applicable to *Jones* v. *Opelika* and *Murdock* v. *Pennsylvania.*

Mr. Justice REED, dissenting:

These cases present for solution the problem of the constitutionality of certain municipal ordinances levying a tax for the production of revenue on the sale ⊥118 of books ⊥ and pamphlets in the streets or from door to door. Decisions sustaining the particular ordinances were entered in the three cases first listed at the list term of this Court. In that opinion the ordinances were set out and the facts and issues stated. A rehearing has been granted. The present judgments vacate the old and invalidate the ordinances. The eight cases of this term involve canvassing from door to door only under similar ordinances, which are in the form stated in the Court's opinion. By a per curiam opinion of this day the Court affirms its acceptance of the arguments presented by the dissent of last term in *Jones* v. *Opelika*. The Court states its position anew in the *Jeannette* Cases.

This dissent does not deal with an objection which theoretically could be made in each case, to wit, that the licenses are so excessive in amount as to be prohibitory. This matter is not considered because that defense is not relied upon in the pleadings, the briefs or at the bar. No evidence is offered to show the amount is oppressive. An unequal tax, levied on the activities of distributors of informatory publications, would be a phase of discrimination against the freedom of speech, press or religion. Nor do we deal with discrimination against the petitioners, as individuals or as members of the group, calling themselves Jehovah's Witnesses. There is no contention in any of these cases that such discrimination is practiced in the application of the ordinances. Obviously an improper application by a city, which resulted in the arrest of witnesses and failure to enforce the ordinance against other groups, such as the Adventists, would raise entirely distinct issues.

A further and important disclaimer must be made in order to focus attention sharply upon the constitutional issue. This dissent does not express, directly or by inference, any conclusion as to the constitutional rights of state or federal governments to place a privilege tax upon the ⊥ soliciting of a ⊥119 free-will contribution for religious purposes. Petitioners suggest that their books and pamphlets are not sold but are given either without price or in appreciation of the recipient's gift for the furtherance of the work of the witnesses. The pittance sought, as well as the practice of leaving books with poor people without cost, gives strength to this argument. In our judgment, however, the plan of national distribution by the Watch Tower Bible & Tract Society, with its wholesale prices of five or twenty cents per copy for books, delivered to the public by the witnesses at twenty-five cents per copy, justifies the characterization of the transaction as a sale by all the state courts. The evidence is conclusive that the witnesses normally approach a prospect with an offer of a book for twenty-five cents. Sometimes, apparently rarely, a book is left with a prospect without payment. The quid pro quo is demanded. If the profit was greater, twenty cents or even one dollar, no difference in principle would emerge. The witness sells books to raise money for propagandising his faith, just as other religious groups might sponsor bazaars or peddle tickets to church suppers, or sell Bibles or prayer books for the same object. However high the purpose or noble the aims of the witness, the transaction has been found by the state courts to be a sale under their ordinances and, though our doubt was greater than it is, the state's conclusion would influence us to follow its determination. ⊥   ⊥120

In the opinion in *Jones* v. *Opelika* on the former hearing, attention was called to the differentiation between these cases of taxation and those of forbidden censorship, prohibition, or discrimination. There is no occasion to repeat what has been written so recently as to the constitutional right to tax the money raising activities of religious or didactic groups. There are, however, other reasons, not fully developed in that opinion, that add to our conviction that the Constitution does not prohibit these general occupational taxes.

The real contention of the Witnesses is that there can be no taxation of the occupation of selling books and pamphlets because to do so would be contrary to the due process clause of the Fourteenth Amendment, which now is held to have drawn the contents of the First Amendment into the category of individual rights protected ⊥ from state deprivation. Since ⊥121 the publications teach a religion which conforms to our standards of legality, it is urged that these ordinances prohibit the free exercise of religion and abridge the freedom of speech and of the press. . . . Is subjection to non-discriminatory, nonexcessive taxation in the distribution of religious literature, a prohibition of the exercise of religion or an abridgment of the freedom of the press? ⊥   ⊥122

Nothing has been brought to our attention which would lead to the conclusion that the contemporary advocates of the adoption of a Bill of Rights intended such an exemption. The words of the Amendment do not support such a construction. "Free" cannot be held to be without cost but rather its meaning must accord with the freedom guaranteed. "Free" means a privilege to print or pray without permission and without accounting to authority for one's actions. In the Constitutional Convention the proposal for a Bill of Rights of any kind received scant attention. In the course of the ratification of the Constitution, however, the absence of a Bill of Rights was used vigorously by the opponents of the new government. A number of the states suggested amendments. Where these suggestions have any bearing at all upon religion or free speech, they indicate nothing as to any feeling concerning taxation either of religious bodies or their evangelism. This was ⌐123 not because freedom of ⊥ religion or free speech was not understood. It was because the subjects were looked upon from standpoints entirely distinct from taxation.

The available evidence of Congressional action shows clearly that the draftsmen of the amendments had in mind the practice of religion and the right to be heard, rather than any abridgment or interference ⌐124 with either by taxa⊥tion in any form. The amend-
⌐125 ments were proposed by ⊥ Mr. Madison. He was careful to explain to the Congress the meaning of the amendment on religion. The draft was commented upon by Mr. Madison when it read: "no religion shall be established by law, nor shall the equal rights of conscience be infringed."

He said that he apprehended the meaning of the words on religion to be that Congress should not establish a religion and enforce the legal observation of it by law, nor compel men to worship God in any manner contrary to their conscience. No such specific interpretation of the amendment on freedom of expression has been found in the debates. The clearest is probably from Mr. Benson who said that "The committee who framed this report proceeded on the principle that these rights belonged to the people; they conceived them to be inherent; and all that they mean to provide against was their being infringed by the Government."

There have been suggestions that the English taxes on newspapers, springing from the tax act of 10 Anne, c. 19, § CI, influenced the adoption of the ⌐126 First Amendment. ⊥ These taxes were obnoxious but an examination of the sources of the suggestion is convincing that there is nothing to support it except the fact that the tax on newspapers was in existence in England and was disliked. The simple answer is that if there had been any purpose of Congress to prohibit any kind of taxes on the press, its knowledge of the abominated English taxes would have led it to ban them unequivocally.

It is only in recent years that the freedoms of the First Amendment have been recognized as among the fundamental personal rights protected by the Fourteenth Amendment from impairment by the states. Until then these liberties were not deemed to be guarded from state action by the Federal Constitution. The states placed ⊥ restraints upon them- ⌐127 selves in their own Constitutions in order to protect their people in the exercise of the freedoms of speech and of religion. Pennsylvania may be taken as a fair example. Its constitution reads:

"All men have a natural and indefeasible right to worship Almighty God according to the dictates of their own consciences; no man can of right be compelled to attend, erect or support any place of worship, or to maintain any ministry against his consent; no human authority can, in any case whatever, control or interfere with the rights of conscience and no preference shall ever be given by law to any religious establishments or modes of worship."

"No person who acknowledges the being of a God, and a future state of rewards and punishments shall, on account of his religious sentiments, be disqualified to hold any office or place of trust or profit under this Commonwealth."

"The printing press shall be free to every person who may undertake to examine the proceedings of the Legislature or any branch of government, and no law shall ever be made to restrain the right thereof. The free communication of thoughts and opinions is one of the invaluable rights of man, and every citizen may freely speak, write and print on any subject, being responsible for the abuse of that liberty. . . ."

It will be observed that there is no suggestion of freedom from taxation, and this statement is equally true of the other state constitutional provisions. It may be concluded that neither in the state or the federal constitutions was general taxation of church or press interdicted.

Is there anything in the decisions of this Court which indicates that church or press is free from the financial ⊥ burdens of government? We find noth- ⌐128 ing. Religious societies depend for their exemptions from taxation upon state constitutions or general statutes, not upon the Federal Constitution. This Court has held that the chief purpose of the free press guarantee was to prevent previous restraints upon publication. In *Grosjean* v. *American Press Co.*, it was said that the predominant purpose was to preserve "an untrammeled press as a vital source of public information." In that case, a gross receipts tax on advertisements in papers with a circulation of more than twenty thousand copies per week was held invalid because "a deliberate and calculated device in the guise of a tax to limit the circulation. . . ." There was this further comment:

"It is not intended by anything we have said to suggest that the owners of newspapers are immune from any of the ordinary forms of taxation for support of the government. But this is not an ordinary form of tax, but one single in kind, with a long history of hostile misuse against the freedom of the press."

It may be said, however, that ours is a too narrow, technical and legalistic approach to the problem of state taxation of the activities of church and press; that we should look not to the expressed or historical meaning of the First Amendment but to the broad principles of free speech and free exercise of religion which pervade our national way of life. It may be that the Fourteenth Amendment guarantees these principles rather than the more definite concept expressed in the First Amendment. This would mean that as a Court, we should determine what sort of ⊥129 liberty it is that the due process clause of ⊥ the Fourteenth Amendment guarantees against state restrictions on speech and church.

But whether we give content to the literal words of the First Amendment or to principles of the liberty of the press and the church, we conclude that cities or states may levy reasonable, non-discriminatory taxes on such activities as occurred in these ⊥130 cases. . . . ⊥

It is urged that such a tax as this may be used readily to restrict the dissemination of ideas. This must be conceded but the possibility of misuse does not make a tax unconstitutional. No abuse is claimed here. The ordinances in some of these cases are the general occupation license type covering many businesses. In the *Jeannette* prosecutions, the ordinance involved lays the usual tax on canvassing or soliciting sales of goods, wares and merchandise. It was passed in 1898. Every power of taxation or regulation is capable of abuse. Each one, to some extent, prohibits the free exercise of religion and abridges the freedom of the press, but that is hardly a reason for denying the power. If the tax is used oppressively, the law will protect the victims of such action.

This decision forces a tax subsidy notwithstanding our accepted belief in the separation of church and state. Instead of all bearing equally the burdens of government, this Court now fastens upon the communities the entire cost of policing the sales of religious literature. That the burden may be heavy is shown by the record in the *Jeannette* Cases. There are only eight prosecutions but one hundred and four ⊥131 witnesses solicited in Jeannette the day ⊥ of the arrests. They had been requested by the authorities to await the outcome of a test case before continuing their canvassing. The distributors of religious literature, possibly of all informatory publications, become today privileged to carry on their occupations without contributing their share to the support of the government which provides the opportunity for the exercise of their liberties.

Nor do we think it can be said, properly, that these sales of religious books are religious exercises.

The opinion of the Court in the *Jeannette* Cases emphasizes for the first time the argument that the sale of books and pamphlets is in itself a religious practice. The Court says the Witnesses "spread their interpretations of the Bible and their religious beliefs largely through the hand distribution of literature by full or parttime workers." "The hand distribution of religious tracts is an age-old form of missionary evangelism—as old as the history of printing presses." "It is more than preaching; it is more than distribution of religious literature. It is a combination of both. Its purpose is as evangelical as the revival meeting. This form of religious activity occupies the same high estate under the First Amendment as do worship in the churches and preaching from the pulpits." "Those who can tax the exercise of this religious practice can make its exercise so costly as to deprive it of the resources necessary for its maintenance." "The judgment in *Jones* v. *Opelika* has this day been vacated. Freed from that controlling precedent, we can restore to their high, constitutional position the liberties of itinerant evangelists who disseminate their religious beliefs and the tenets of their faith through distribution of literature." The record shows that books entitled "Creation" and "Salvation," as well as Bibles, were offered for sale. We shall assume the first two publications, also, are religious books. Certainly there can be no dissent from the statement that ⊥ selling reli- ⊥132 gious books is an age-old practice or that it is evangelism in the sense that the distributors hope the readers will be spiritually benefited. That does not carry us to the conviction, however, that when distribution of religious books is made at a price, the itinerant colporteur is performing a religious rite, is worshipping his Creator in his way. Many sects practice healing the sick as an evidence of their religious faith or maintain orphanages or homes for the aged or teach the young. These are, of course, in a sense, religious practices but hardly such examples of religious rites as are encompassed by the prohibition against the free exercise of religion.

And even if the distribution of religious books was a religious practice protected from regulation by the First Amendment, certainly the affixation of a price for the articles would destroy the sacred character of the transaction. The evangelist becomes also a book agent.

The rites which are protected by the First Amendment are in essence spiritual—prayer, mass, sermons, sacrament—not sales of religious goods. The card furnished each witness to identify him as an ordained minister does not go so far as to say the sale is a rite. It states only that the witnesses worship by exhibiting to people "the message of said gospel in printed form, such as the Bible, books, booklets and magazines and thus afford the people the opportunity of learning of God's gracious provision for them." On the back of the card appears: "You may contribute twenty-five cents to the Lord's work and receive a copy of this beautiful book." The sale of these religious books has, we think, relation to their religious exercises, similar to the "information march," said by the witnesses to be one of their "ways of worship" and by this Court to be subject to regulation by license in *Cox* v. *New Hampshire*.

⊥133 The attempted analogy in the dissenting opinion in *Jones* v. *Opelika*, which now be ⊥ comes the decision of this Court, between the forbidden burden of a state tax for the privilege of engaging in interstate commerce and a state tax on the privilege of engaging in the distribution of religious literature is wholly irrelevant. A state tax on the privilege of engaging in interstate commerce is held invalid because the regulation of commerce between the states has been delegated to the Federal Government. This grant includes the necessary means to carry the grant into effect and forbids state burdens without congressional consent. It is not the power to tax interstate commerce which is interdicted, but the exercise of that power by an unauthorized sovereign, the individual state. Although the fostering of commerce was one of the chief purposes for organizing the present Government, that commerce may be burdened with a tax by the United States. Commerce must pay its way. It is not exempt from any type of taxation if imposed by an authorized authority. The Court now holds that the First Amendment wholly exempts the church and press from a privilege tax, presumably by the national as well as the state governments.

The limitations of the Constitution are not maxims of social wisdom but definite controls on the legislative process. We are dealing with power, not its abuse. This late withdrawal of the power of taxation over the distribution activities of those covered by the First Amendment fixes what seems to us an unfortunate principle of tax exemption, capable of indefinite extension. We had thought that such an exemption required a clear and certain grant. This we do not find in the language of the First and Fourteenth Amendments. We are therefore of the opinion the judgments below should be affirmed.

⊥134   ⊥ *Mr. Justice ROBERTS, Mr. Justice FRANK-FURTER*, and *Mr. Justice JACKSON* join in this dissent.

Mr. Justice FRANKFURTER, dissenting:

While I wholly agree with the views expressed by *Mr. Justice REED*, the controversy is of such a nature as to lead me to add a few words.

A tax can be a means for raising revenue, or a device for regulating conduct, or both. Challenge to the constitutional validity of a tax measure requires that it be analyzed and judged in all its aspects. We must therefore distinguish between the questions that are before us in these cases and those that are not. It is altogether incorrect to say that the question here is whether a state can limit the free exercise of religion by imposing burdensome taxes. As the opinion of my *Brother REED* demonstrates, we have not here the question whether the taxes imposed in these cases are in practical operation an unjustifiable curtailment upon the petitioners' undoubted right to communicate their views to others. No claim is made that the effect of these taxes, either separately or cumulatively, has been, or is likely to be, to restrict the petitioners' religious propaganda activities in any degree. Counsel expressly disclaim any such contention. They insist on absolute immunity from any kind of monetary exaction for their occupation. Their claim is that no tax, no matter how trifling, can constitutionally be laid upon the activity of distributing religious literature, regardless of the actual effect of the tax upon such activity. That is the only ground upon which these ordinances have been attacked, that is the only question raised in or decided by the state courts; and that is the only question presented to us. No complaint is made against the size of the taxes. If an appropriate claim, indicating that the taxes were oppressive in their effect upon the petition⊥ers' activities, had been made, the issues here would be very different. No such claim has been made, and it would be gratuitous to consider its merits.   ⊥135

Nor have we occasion to consider whether these measures are invalid on the ground that they unjustly or unreasonably discriminate against the petitioners. Counsel do not claim, as indeed they could not, that these ordinances were intended to or have been applied to discriminate against religious groups generally or Jehovah's Witnesses particularly. No claim is made that the effect of the taxes is to hinder or restrict the activities of Jehovah's Witnesses while other religious groups, perhaps older or more prosperous, can carry on theirs. This question, too, is not before us.

It cannot be said that the petitioners are constitutionally exempt from taxation merely because they may be engaged in religious activities or because such activities may constitute an exercise of a constitutional right. It will hardly be contended, for example, that a tax upon the income of a clergyman would violate the Bill of Rights, even though the tax is ultimately borne by the members of his church. A clergyman, no less than a judge, is a citizen. And not only in time of war would neither willingly enjoy immunity from the obligations of citizenship. It is only fair that he also who preaches the word of God should share in the costs of the benefits provided by government to him as well as to the other members of the community. And so, no one would suggest that a clergyman who uses an automobile or the telephone in connection with his work thereby gains a constitutional exemption from taxes levied upon the use of automobiles or upon telephone calls. Equally alien is it to our constitutional system to suggest that the Constitution of the United States exempts church-held lands from state taxation. Plainly, a tax measure is not invalid under the federal Constitution merely because it falls upon persons engaged in activities of a religious nature. ⊥

⌐136

Nor can a tax be invalidated merely because it falls upon activities which constitute an exercise of a constitutional right. The First Amendment of course protects the right to publish a newspaper or a magazine or a book. But the crucial question is—how much protection does the Amendment give, and against what is the right protected? It is certainly true that the protection afforded the freedom of the press by the First Amendment does not include exemption from all taxation. A tax upon newspaper publishing is not invalid simply because it falls upon the exercise of a constitutional right. Such a tax might be invalid if it invidiously singled out newspaper publishing for bearing the burdens of taxation or imposed upon them in such ways as to encroach on the essential scope of a free press. If the Court could justifiably hold that the tax measures in these cases were vulnerable on that ground, I would unreservedly agree. But the Court has not done so, and indeed could not. . . . . ⊥

⌐137

As I read the Court's opinion, it does not hold that the taxes in the cases before us in fact do hinder or restrict the petitioners in exercising their constitutional rights. It holds that "The power to tax the exercise of a privilege is the power to control or suppress its enjoyment." This assumes that because the taxing power exerted in *Magnano Co.* v. *Hamilton*, the well-known oleomargarine tax case, may have had the effect of "controlling" or "suppressing" the enjoyment of a privilege and still was sustained by this Court, and because all exertions of the taxing power may have that effect, if perchance a particular exercise of the taxing power does have that effect, it would have to be sustained under our ruling in the *Magnano Co.* Case.

The power to tax, like all powers of government, legislative, executive and judicial alike, can be abused or perverted. The power to tax is the power to destroy only in the sense that those who have power can misuse it. Mr. Justice Holmes disposed of this smooth phrase as a constitutional basis for invalidating taxes when he wrote "The power to tax is not the power to destroy while this Court sits." *Panhandle Oil Co.* v. *Mississippi*. The fact that a power can be perverted does not mean that every exercise of the power is a perversion of the power. Thus, if a tax indirectly suppresses or controls the enjoyment of a constitutional privilege which a legislature cannot directly suppress or control, of course it is bad. But it is irrelevant that a tax can suppress or control if it does not. The Court holds that "Those who can tax the exercise of this religious practice can make its exercise so costly as to deprive it of resources nec-

essary for its maintenance." But this is not the same as saying that "Those who do tax the exercise of this religious practice have made its exercise so costly as to deprive it of the resources necessary for its maintenance." ⊥

⌐138

The Court could not plausibly make such an assertion because the petitioners themselves disavow any claim that the taxes imposed in these cases impair their ability to exercise their constitutional rights. We cannot invalidate the tax measures before us simply because there may be others, not now before us, which are oppressive in their effect. The Court's opinion does not deny that the ordinances involved in these cases have in no way disabled the petitioners to engage in their religious activities. It holds only that "Those who can tax the privilege of engaging in this form of missionary evangelism can close its doors to all those who do not have a full purse." I quite agree with this statement as an abstract proposition. Those who possess the power to tax might wield it in tyrannical fashion. It does not follow, however, that every exercise of the power is an act of tyranny, or that government should be impotent because it might be tyrannical. The question before us now is whether these ordinances have deprived the petitioners of their constitutional rights, not whether some other ordinances not now before us might be enacted which might deprive them of such rights. To deny constitutional power to secular authority merely because of the possibility of its abuse is as valid as to deny the basis of spiritual authority because those in whom it is temporarily vested may misuse it. . . . . ⊥

⌐139

It is strenuously urged that the Constitution denies a city the right to control the expression of men's minds and the right of men to win others to their views. But the Court is not divided on this proposition. No one disputes it. All members of the Court are equally familiar with the history that led to the adoption of the Bill of Rights and are equally zealous to enforce the constitutional protection of the free play of the human spirit. Escape from the real issue before us cannot be found in such generalities. The real issue here is not whether a city may charge for the dissemination of ideas but whether the states have power to require those who need additional facilities to help bear the cost of furnishing such facilities. Street hawkers make demands upon municipalities that involve the expenditure of dollars and cents, whether they hawk printed matter or other things. As the facts in these cases show, the cost of maintaining the peace, the additional demands upon governmental facilities for assuring security, involve outlays which have to be met. To say that the Constitution forbids the states to obtain the necessary revenue from the whole of a class that enjoys these benefits ⊥ and facilities, when in fact no discrimination is suggested as between purveyors of printed matter and purveyors of other things, and

⌐140

the exaction is not claimed to be actually burdensome, is to say that the Constitution requires not that the dissemination of ideas in the interest of religion shall be free but that it shall be subsidized by the state. Such a claim offends the most important of all aspects of religious freedom in this country, namely, that of the separation of church and state.

The ultimate question in determining the constitutionality of a tax measure is—has the state given something for which it can ask a return? There can be no doubt that these petitioners, like all who use the streets, have received the benefits of government. Peace is maintained, traffic is regulated, health is safeguarded—these are only some of the many incidents of municipal administration. To secure them costs money, and a state's source of money is its taxing power. There is nothing in the Constitution which exempts persons engaged in religious activities from sharing equally in the costs of benefits to all, including themselves, provided by government.

I cannot say, therefore, that in these cases the community has demanded a return for that which it did not give. Nor am I called upon to say that the state has demanded unjustifiably more than the value of what it gave, nor that its demand in fact cramps activities pursued to promote religious beliefs. No such claim was made at the bar, and there is no evidence in the records to substantiate any such claim if it had been made. Under these circumstances, therefore, I am of opinion that the ordinances in these cases must stand.

Mr. Justice JACKSON joins in this dissent.

MINERSVILLE SCHOOL DISTRICT v. GOBITIS

310 U.S. 586
ON WRIT OF CERTIORARI TO THE UNITED STATES CIRCUIT
COURT OF APPEALS FOR THE THIRD CIRCUIT
Argued April 25, 1940 — Decided June 3, 1940

⌞591   ⊥ *Mr. Justice FRANKFURTER* delivered the opinion of the Court:

A grave responsibility confronts this Court whenever in course of litigation it must reconcile the conflicting claims of liberty and authority. But when the liberty invoked is liberty of conscience, and the authority is authority to safeguard the nation's fellowship, judicial conscience is put to its severest test. Of such a nature is the present controversy.

Lillian Gobitis, aged twelve, and her brother William, aged ten, were expelled from the public schools of Minersville, Pennsylvania, for refusing to salute the national flag as part of a daily school exercise. The local Board of Education required both teachers and pupils to participate in this ceremony. The cere-

mony is a familiar one. The right hand is placed on the breast and the following pledge recited in unison: "I pledge allegiance to my flag, and to the Republic for which it stands; one nation indivisible, with liberty and justice for all." While the words are spoken, teachers and pupils extend their right hands in salute to the flag. The Gobitis family are affiliated with "Jehovah's Witnesses," for whom the Bible as the Word of God is the supreme authority. The children had been brought up conscientiously to believe that such a gesture of respect for the flag was forbidden by command of Scripture.   ⌞592

The Gobitis children were of an age for which Pennsylvania makes school attendance compulsory. Thus they were denied a free education, and their parents had to put them into private schools. To be relieved of the financial burden thereby entailed, their father on behalf of the children and in his own behalf, brought this suit. He sought to enjoin the authorities from continuing to exact participation in the flag-salute ceremony as a condition of his children's attendance at the Minersville school. After trial of the issues, Judge Maris gave relief in the District Court, on the basis of a thoughtful opinion, at a preliminary stage of the litigation; his decree was affirmed by the Circuit Court of Appeals. Since this decision ran counter to several per curiam dispositions of this Court, we granted certiorari to give the matter full reconsideration. By their able submissions, the Committee on the Bill of Rights of the American Bar Association and the American Civil Liberties Union, as friends of the Court, have helped us to our conclusion.

We must decide whether the requirement of participation in such a ceremony, exacted from a child who refuses ⊥ upon sincere religious grounds, infringes without due process of law the liberty guaranteed by the Fourteenth Amendment.   ⌞593

Centuries of strife over the erection of particular dogmas as exclusive or all-comprehending faiths led to the inclusion of a guarantee for religious freedom in the Bill of Rights. The First Amendment, and the Fourteenth through its absorption of the First, sought to guard against repetition of those bitter religious struggles by prohibiting the establishment of a state religion and by securing to every sect the free exercise of its faith. So pervasive is the acceptance of this precious right that its scope is brought into question, as here, only when the conscience of individuals collides with the felt necessities of society.

Certainly the affirmative pursuit of one's convictions about the ultimate mystery of the universe and man's relation to it is placed beyond the reach of law. Government may not interfere with organized or individual expression of belief or disbelief. Propagation of belief—or even of disbelief in the supernatural—is protected, whether in church or chapel, mosque or synagogue, tabernacle or meetinghouse. Likewise the Constitution assures generous immunity to the individual from imposition of penalties for offending, in the course of his own religious activities, the religious views of others, be they a minority or those who are dominant in government.

But the manifold character of man's relations may bring his conception of religious duty into conflict with the secular interests of his fellow-men. When does the constitutional guarantee compel exemption from doing what society thinks necessary for the promotion of some great common end, or from a penalty for conduct which appears dangerous to the general good? To state the ⊥ problem is to recall the truth that no single principle can answer all of life's complexities. The right to freedom of religious belief, however dissident and however obnoxious to the cherished beliefs of others—even of a majority—is itself the denial of an absolute. But to affirm that the freedom to follow conscience has itself no limits in the life of a society would deny that very plurality of principles which, as a matter of history, underlies protection of religious toleration. Our present task then, as so often the case with courts, is to reconcile two rights in order to prevent either from destroying the other. But, because in safeguarding conscience we are dealing with interests so subtle and so dear, every possible leeway should be given to the claims of religious faith.

⌊594

In the judicial enforcement of religious freedom we are concerned with a historic concept. The religious liberty which the Constitution protects has never excluded legislation of general scope not directed against doctrinal loyalties of particular sects. Judicial nullification of legislation cannot be justified by attributing to the framers of the Bill of Rights views for which there is no historic warrant. Conscientious scruples have not, in the course of the long struggle for religious toleration, relieved the individual from obedience to a general law not aimed at the promotion or restriction of religious beliefs. The mere possession of religious convictions ⊥ which contradict the relevant concerns of a political society does not relieve the citizen from the discharge of political responsibilities. The necessity for this adjustment has again and again been recognized. In a number of situations the exertion of political authority has been sustained, while basic considerations of religious freedom have been left inviolate. In all these cases the general laws in question, upheld in their application to those who refused obedience from religious conviction, were manifestations of specific powers of government deemed by the legislature essential to secure and maintain that orderly, tranquil, and free society without which religious toleration itself is unattainable. Nor does the freedom of speech assured by Due Process move in a more absolute circle of immunity than that enjoyed by religious freedom. Even if it were assumed that freedom of speech goes beyond the historic concept of full opportunity to utter and to disseminate views, however heretical or offensive to dominant opinion, and includes freedom from conveying what may be deemed an implied but

⌊595

rejected affirmation, the question remains whether school children, like the Gobitis children, must be excused from conduct required of all the other children in the promotion of national cohesion. We are dealing with an interest inferior to none in the hierarchy of legal values. National unity is the basis of national security. To deny the legislature the right to select appropriate means for its attainment presents a totally different order of problem from that of the propriety of subordinating the possible ugliness of littered streets to the free expression of opinion through distribution of handbills. ⊥

⌊596

Situations like the present are phases of the profoundest problem confronting a democracy—the problem which Lincoln cast in memorable dilemma: "Must a government of necessity be too *strong* for the liberties of its people, or too *weak* to maintain its own existence?" No mere textual reading or logical talisman can solve the dilemma. And when the issue demands judicial determination, it is not the personal notion of judges of what wise adjustment requires which must prevail.

Unlike the instances we have cited, the case before us is not concerned with an exertion of legislative power for the promotion of some specific need or interest of secular society—the protection of the family, the promotion of health, the common defense, the raising of public revenues to defray the cost of government. But all these specific activities of government presuppose the existence of an organized political society. The ultimate foundation of a free society is the binding tie of cohesive sentiment. Such a sentiment is fostered by all those agencies of the mind and spirit which may serve to gather up the traditions of a people, transmit them from generation to generation, and thereby create that continuity of a treasured common life which constitutes a civilization. "We live by symbols." The flag is the symbol of our national unity, transcending all internal differences, however large, within the framework of the Constitution. This Court has had occasion to say that ". . . the flag is the symbol of the Nation's power, the emblem of freedom in its truest, best sense . . . it signifies government resting on the consent of the governed; liberty regulated by law; the protection of the weak against the strong; security against the exercise of arbitrary power; and absolute safety for free institutions against foreign aggression." *Halter* v. *Nebraska.* ⊥

⌊597

The case before us must be viewed as though the legislature of Pennsylvania had itself formally directed the flag-salute for the children of Minersville; had made no exemption for children whose parents were possessed of conscientious scruples like those of the Gobitis family; and had indicated its belief in the desirable ends to be secured by having its public school children share a common experience at those periods of development when their minds are supposedly receptive to its assimilation, by an exercise appropriate in time and place and setting, and one designed to evoke in them appreciation of the nation's hopes and dreams, its sufferings and sacrifices. The precise issue, then, for us to decide is whether the legislatures of the various states and the authorities in a thousand counties and school districts of this country are barred from determining the appropriateness of various means to evoke that unifying sentiment without which there can ultimately be no liberties, civil or religious. To stigmatize legislative judgment in providing for this universal gesture of respect for the symbol of our national life in the setting of the common school as a lawless inroad on that freedom of conscience which the Constitution protects, would amount to no less than the pronouncement of pedagogical and psychological dogma in a field where courts possess no marked and certainly no ⊥ controlling competence. The influences which help toward a common feeling for the common country are manifold. Some may seem harsh and others no doubt are foolish. Surely, however, the end is legitimate. And the effective means for its attainment are still so uncertain and so unauthenticated by science as to preclude us from putting the widely prevalent belief in flag-saluting beyond the pale of legislative power. It mocks reason and denies our whole history to find in the allowance of a requirement to salute our flag on fitting occasions the seeds of sanction for obeisance to a leader.

⌞1598

The wisdom of training children in patriotic impulses by those compulsions which necessarily pervade so much of the educational process is not for our independent judgment. Even were we convinced of the folly of such a measure, such belief would be no proof of its unconstitutionality. For ourselves, we might be tempted to say that the deepest patriotism is best engendered by giving unfettered scope to the most crochety beliefs. Perhaps it is best, even from the standpoint of those interests which ordinances like the one under review seek to promote, to give to the least popular sect leave from conformities like those here in issue. But the courtroom is not the arena for debating issues of educational policy. It is not our province to choose among competing considerations in the subtle process of securing effective loyalty to the traditional ideals of democracy, while respecting at the same time individual idiosyncracies among a people so diversified in racial origins and religious allegiances. So to hold would in effect make us the school board for the country. That authority has not been given to this Court, nor should we assume it.

We are dealing here with the formative period in the development of citizenship. Great diversity of psychological and ethical opinion exists among us concerning the best way to train children for their place in society. Be ⊥ cause of these differences and because of reluctance to permit a single, iron-cast system of education to be imposed upon a nation compounded of so many strains, we have held that, even though public education is one of our most

⌞1599

cherished democratic institutions, the Bill of Rights bars a state from compelling all children to attend the public schools. But it is a very different thing for this Court to exercise censorship over the conviction of legislatures that a particular program or exercise will best promote in the minds of children who attend the common schools an attachment to the institutions of their country.

What the school authorities are really asserting is the right to awaken in the child's mind considerations as to the significance of the flag contrary to those implanted by the parent. In such an attempt the state is normally at a disadvantage in competing with the parent's authority, so long—and this is the vital aspect of religious toleration—as parents are unmolested in their right to counteract by their own persuasiveness the wisdom and rightness of those loyalties which the state's educational system is seeking to promote. Except where the transgression of constitutional liberty is too plain for argument, personal freedom is best maintained—so long as the remedial channels of the democratic process remain open and unobstructed—when it is ingrained in a people's habits and not enforced against popular policy by the coercion of adjudicated law. That the flag-salute is an allowable portion of a school program for those who do not invoke conscientious scruples is surely not debatable. But for us to insist that, though the ceremony may be ⊥ required, exceptional immunity must be given to dissidents, is to maintain that there is no basis for a legislative judgment that such an exemption might introduce elements of difficulty into the school discipline, might cast doubts in the minds of the other children which would themselves weaken the effect of the exercise.

⌞1600

The preciousness of the family relation, the authority and independence which give dignity to parenthood, indeed the enjoyment of all freedom, presuppose the kind of ordered society which is summarized by our flag. A society which is dedicated to the preservation of these ultimate values of civilization may in self-protection utilize the educational process of inculcating those almost unconscious feelings which bind men together in a comprehending loyalty, whatever may be their lesser differences and difficulties. That is to say, the process may be utilized so long as men's right to believe as they please, to win others to their way of belief, and their right to assemble in their chosen places of worship for the devotional ceremonies of their faith, are all fully respected.

Judicial review, itself a limitation on popular government, is a fundamental part of our constitutional scheme. But to the legislature no less than to courts is committed the guardianship of deeply-cherished liberties. Where all the effective means of inducing political changes are left free from interference, education in the abandonment of foolish legislation is itself a training in liberty. To fight out the wise use of legislative authority in the forum of public opinion and before legislative assemblies rather than to transfer such a contest to the judicial arena, serves to vindicate the self-confidence of a free people.

Reversed.

⊥ *Mr. Justice McREYNOLDS* concurs in the result. _|601

Mr. Justice STONE, dissenting:

I think the judgment below should be affirmed.

Two youths, now fifteen and sixteen years of age, are by the judgment of this Court held liable to expulsion from the public schools and to denial of all publicly supported educational privileges because of their refusal to yield to the compulsion of a law which commands their participation in a school ceremony contrary to their religious convictions. They and their father are citizens and have not exhibited by any action or statement of opinion, any disloyalty to the Government of the United States. They are ready and willing to obey all its laws which do not conflict with what they sincerely believe to be the higher commandments of God. It is not doubted that these convictions are religious, that they are genuine, or that the refusal to yield to the compulsion of the law is in good faith and with all sincerity. It would be a denial of their faith as well as the teachings of most religions to say that children of their age could not have religious convictions.

The law which is thus sustained is unique in the history of Anglo-American legislation. It does more than suppress freedom of speech and more than prohibit the free exercise of religion, which concededly are forbidden by the First Amendment and are violations of the liberty guaranteed by the Fourteenth. For by this law the state seeks to coerce these children to express a sentiment which, as they interpret it, they do not entertain, and which violates their deepest religious convictions. It is not denied that such compulsion is a prohibited infringement of personal liberty, freedom of speech and religion, guaranteed by the Bill of Rights, except in so far as it may be justified and supported as a proper exercise of the state's power over public education. Since the state,
⊥ in competition with parents, may through _|602
teaching in the public schools indoctrinate the minds of the young, it is said that in aid of its undertaking to inspire loyalty and devotion to constituted authority and the flag which symbolizes it, it may coerce the pupil to make affirmation contrary to his belief and in violation of his religious faith. And, finally, it is said that since the Minersville School Board and others are of the opinion that the country will be better served by conformity than by the observance of religious liberty which the Constitution prescribes, the courts are not free to pass judgment on the Board's choice.

Concededly the constitutional guaranties of personal liberty are not always absolutes. Government has a right to survive and powers conferred upon it are not necessarily set at naught by the express prohibitions of the Bill of Rights. It may make war and raise armies. To that end it may compel citizens to give military service and subject them to military training despite their religious objections. It may suppress religious practices dangerous to morals, and presumably those also which are inimical to public safety, health and good order. But it is a long step, and one which I am unable to take, to the position that government may, as a supposed educational measure and as a means of disciplining the young, compel public affirmations which violate their religious conscience.

The very fact that we have constitutional guaranties of civil liberties and the specificity of their command where freedom of speech and of religion are concerned require some accommodation of the powers which government normally exercises, when no question of civil liberty is involved, to the constitutional demand that those liberties be protected against the action of govern⊥ment itself. The state _|603
concededly has power to require and control the education of its citizens, but it cannot by a general law compelling attendance at public schools preclude attendance at a private school adequate in its instruction, where the parent seeks to secure for the child the benefits of religious instruction not provided by the public school. And only recently we have held that the state's authority to control its public streets by generally applicable regulations is not an absolute to which free speech must yield, and cannot be made the medium of its suppression any more than can its authority to penalize littering of the streets by a general law be used to suppress the distribution of handbills as a means of communicating ideas to their recipients.

In these cases it was pointed out that where there are competing demands of the interests of government and of liberty under the Constitution, and where the performance of governmental functions is brought into conflict with specific constitutional restrictions, there must, when that is possible, be reasonable accommodation between them so as to preserve the essentials of both and that it is the function of courts to determine whether such accommodation is reasonably possible. In the cases just mentioned the Court was of opinion that there were ways enough to secure the legitimate state end without infringing the asserted immunity, or that the inconvenience caused by the inability to secure that end satisfactorily through other means, did not outweigh freedom of speech or religion. So here, even if we believe that such compulsions will contribute to national unity, there are other ways to teach loyalty and patriotism which are the sources of national unity, than by compelling the pupil to affirm that which he does not believe and by ⊥ commanding a _|604 form of affirmance which violates his religious convictions. Without recourse to such compulsion the state is free to compel attendance at school and require teaching by instruction and study of all in our history and in the structure and organization of our government, including the guaranties of civil liberty which tend to inspire patriotism and love of country. I cannot say that government here is deprived of any interest or function which it is entitled to maintain at the expense of the protection of civil liberties by requiring it to resort to the alternatives which do not coerce an affirmation of belief.

The guaranties of civil liberty are but guaranties of freedom of the human mind and spirit and of reasonable freedom and opportunity to express them. They presuppose the right of the individual to hold such opinions as he will and to give them reasonably free expression, and his freedom, and that of the state as well, to teach and persuade others by the communication of ideas. The very essence of the liberty which they guarantee is the freedom of the individual from compulsion as to what he shall think and what he shall say, at least where the compulsion is to bear false witness to his religion. If these guaranties are to have any meaning they must, I think, be deemed to withhold from the state any authority to compel belief for the expression of it where that expression violates religious convictions, whatever may be the legislative view of the desirability of such compulsion.

History teaches us that there have been but few infringements of personal liberty by the state which have not been justified, as they are here, in the name of righteousness and the public good, and few which have not been directed, as they are now, at politically helpless minorities. The framers were not unaware that under the system which they created most ⌐605 governmental cur⊥tailments of personal liberty would have the support of a legislative judgment that the public interest would be better served by its curtailment than by its constitutional protection. I cannot conceive that in prescribing, as limitations upon the powers of government, the freedom of the mind and spirit secured by the explicit guaranties of freedom of speech and religion, they intended or rightly could have left any latitude for a legislative judgment that the compulsory expression of belief which violates religious convictions would better serve the public interest than their protection. The Constitution may well elicit expressions of loyalty to it and to the government which it created, but it does not command such expressions or otherwise give any indication that compulsory expressions of loyalty play any such part in our scheme of government as to override the constitutional protection of freedom of speech and religion. And while such expressions of loyalty, when voluntarily given, may promote national unity, it is quite another matter to say that their compulsory expression by children in violation of their own and their parents' religious convictions can be regarded as playing so important a part in our national unity as to leave school boards free to exact it despite the constitutional guaranty of freedom of religion. The very terms of the Bill of Rights preclude, it seems to me, any reconciliation of such compulsions with the constitutional guaranties by a legislative declaration that they are more important to the public welfare than the Bill of Rights.

But even if this view be rejected and it is considered that there is some scope for the determination by legislatures whether the citizen shall be compelled to give public expression of such sentiments contrary to his religion, I am not persuaded that we should refrain from passing upon the legislative judgment "as long as the remedial ⊥ channels of the democratic ⌐606 process remain open and unobstructed." This seems to me no more than the surrender of the constitutional protection of the liberty of small minorities to the popular will. We have previously pointed to the importance of a searching judicial inquiry into the legislative judgment in situations where prejudice against discrete and insular minorities may tend to curtail the operation of those political processes ordinarily to be relied on to protect minorities. And until now we have not hesitated similarly to scrutinize legislation restricting the civil liberty of racial and religious minorities although no political process was affected. Here we have such a small minority entertaining in good faith a religious belief, which is such a departure from the usual course of human conduct, that most persons are disposed to regard it with little toleration or concern. In such circumstances careful scrutiny of legislative efforts to secure conformity of belief and opinion by a compulsory affirmation of the desired belief, is especially needful if civil rights are to receive any protection. Tested by this standard, I am not prepared to say that the right of this small and helpless minority, including children having a strong religious conviction, whether they understand its nature or not, to refrain from an expression obnoxious to their religion, is to be overborne by the interest of the state in maintaining discipline in the schools.

The Constitution expresses more than the conviction of the people that democratic processes must be preserved at all costs. It is also an expression of faith and a command that freedom of mind and spirit must be preserved, which government must obey, if it is to adhere to that justice and moderation without which no free government can exist. For this reason it would seem that legislation which operates to repress the religious freedom of small minorities, which is admittedly within the scope of the protection of the Bill of Rights, must at least be subject to the same judicial scrutiny as legislation which we have recently held to infringe the constitutional liberty of religious and racial minorities.

With such scrutiny I cannot say that the inconveniences which may attend some sensible adjustment of school discipline in order that the religious convictions of these children may be spared, presents a problem so momentous or pressing as to outweigh the freedom from compulsory violation of religious faith which has been thought worthy of constitutional protection.

WEST VIRGINIA STATE BOARD OF EDUCATION V. BARNETTE

319 U.S. 624
ON APPEAL FROM THE DISTRICT COURT OF THE UNITED STATES
FOR THE SOUTHERN DISTRICT OF WEST VIRGINIA

Argued March 11, 1943 — Decided June 14, 1943

⊥625 ⊥ *Mr. Justice JACKSON* delivered the opinion of the Court:

Following the decision by this Court on June 3, 1940, in *Minersville School Dist.* v. *Gobitis*, the West Virginia legislature amended its statutes to require all schools therein to conduct courses of instruction in history, civics, and in the Constitutions of the United States and of the State for the purpose of teaching, fostering and perpetuating the ideals, principles and spirit of Americanism, and increasing the knowledge of the organization and machinery of the ⊥626 government." Appel⊥lant Board of Education was directed, with advice of the State Superintendent of Schools, to "prescribe the courses of study covering these subjects" for public schools. The Act made it the duty of private, parochial and denominational schools to prescribe courses of study "similar to those required for the public schools."

The Board of Education on January 9, 1942, adopted a resolution containing recitals taken largely from the Court's *Gobitis* opinion and ordering that the salute to the flag become "a regular part of the program of activities in the public schools,"that all teachers and pupils "shall be required to participate in the salute honoring the Nation represented by the Flag; provided, however, that refusal to salute the Flag be regarded as an Act of insubordination, and ⊥627 shall be dealt with accordingly." ⊥

The resolution originally required the "commonly accepted salute to the Flag" which it defined. Objections to the salute as "being too much like Hitler's" were raised by the Parent and Teachers Association, ⊥628 the Boy and Girl⊥ Scouts, the Red Cross, and the Federation of Women's Clubs. Some modification appears to have been made in deference to these objections, but no concession was made to Jehovah's Witnesses. What is now required is the "stiff-arm" salute, the saluter to keep the right hand raised with palm turned up while the following is repeated: "I ⊥629 pledge allegiance to the Flag of⊥ the United States of America and to the Republic for which it stands; one Nation, indivisible, with liberty and justice for all."

Failure to conform is "insubordination" dealt with by expulsion. Readmission is denied by statute until compliance. Meanwhile the expelled child is "unlawfully absent" and may be proceeded against as a delinquent. His parents or guardians are liable to prosecution, and if convicted are subject to fine not exceeding $50 and jail term not exceeding thirty days.

Appellees, citizens of the United States and of West Virginia, brought suit in the United States District Court for themselves and others similarly situated asking its injunction to restrain enforcement of these laws and regulations against Jehovah's Witnesses. The Witnesses are an unincorporated body teaching that the obligation imposed by law of God is superior to that of laws enacted by temporal government. Their religious beliefs include a literal version of Exodus, Chapter 20, verses 4 and 5, which says: "Thou shalt not make unto thee any graven image, or any likeness of anything that is in heaven above, or that is in the earth beneath, or that is in the water under the earth; thou shalt not bow down thyself to them, nor serve them." They consider that the flag is an "image" within this command. For this reason they refuse to salute it. ⊥   ⊥630

Children of this faith have been expelled from school and are threatened with exclusion for no other cause. Officials threaten to send them to reformatories maintained for criminally inclined juveniles. Parents of such children have been prosecuted and are threatened with prosecutions for causing delinquency.

The Board of Education moved to dismiss the complaint setting forth these facts and alleging that the law and regulations are an unconstitutional denial of religious freedom, and of freedom of speech, and are invalid under the "due process" and "equal protection" clauses of the Fourteenth Amendment to the Federal Constitution. The cause was submitted on the pleadings to a District Court of three judges. It restrained enforcement as to the plaintiffs and those of that class. The Board of Education brought the case here by direct appeal.

This case calls upon us to reconsider a precedent decision, as the Constitution throughout its history often has been required to do. Before turning to the *Gobitis* Case, however, it is desirable to notice certain characteristics by which this controversy is distinguished.

The freedom asserted by these appellees does not bring them into collision with rights asserted by any other individual. It is such conflicts which most frequently require intervention of the State to determine where the rights of one end and those of another begin. But the refusal of these persons to participate in the ceremony does not interfere with or deny rights of others to do so. Nor is there any question in this case that their behavior is peaceable and orderly. The sole conflict is between authority and rights of the individual. The State asserts power to condition access to public education on making a prescribed sign and profession and at the same time to coerce⊥ attendance by punishing both parent and child. The latter stand on a right of self-determination in matters that touch individual opinion and personal attitude.

|631

As the present *Chief Justice* said in dissent in the *Gobitis* Case, the State may "require teaching by instruction and study of all in our history and in the structure and organization of our government, including the guaranties of civil liberty, which tend to inspire patriotism and love of country." Here, however, we are dealing with a compulsion of students to declare a belief. They are not merely made acquainted with the flag salute so that they may be informed as to what it is or even what it means. The issue here is whether this slow and easily neglected route to aroused loyalties constitutionally may be short-cut by substituting a compulsory salute and slogan. This issue is not prejudiced by⊥ the Court's previous holding that where a State, without compelling attendance, extends college facilities to pupils who voluntarily enroll, it may prescribe military training as part of the course without offense to the Constitution. It was held that those who take advantage of its opportunities may not on ground of conscience refuse compliance with such conditions. In the present case attendance is not optional. That case is also to be distinguished from the present one because, independently of college privileges or requirements, the State has power to raise militia and impose the duties of service therein upon its citizens.

|632

There is no doubt that, in connection with the pledges, the flag salute is a form of utterance. Symbolism is a primitive but effective way of communicating ideas. The use of an emblem or flag to symbolize some system, idea, institution, or personality, is a short cut from mind to mind. Causes and nations, political parties, lodges and ecclesiastical groups seek to knit the loyalty of their followings to a flag or banner, a color or design. The State announces rank, function, and authority through crowns and maces, uniforms and black robes; the church speaks through the Cross, the Crucifix, the altar and shrine, and clerical raiment. Symbols of State often convey political ideas just as religious symbols come to convey theological ones. Associated with many of these symbols are appropriate gestures of acceptance or respect: a salute, a bowed or bated head, a bended knee. A person gets from a ⊥ symbol the meaning he puts into it, and what is one man's comfort and inspiration is another's jest and scorn.

|633

Over a decade ago Chief Justice Hughes led this Court in holding that the display of a red flag as a symbol of opposition by peaceful and legal means to organized government was protected by the free speech guaranties of the Constitution. Here it is the State that employs a flag as a symbol of adherence to government as presently organized. It requires the individual to communicate by word and sign his acceptance of the political ideas it thus bespeaks. Objection to the form of communication when coerced is an old one, well known to the framers of the Bill of Rights.

It is also to be noted that the compulsory flag salute and pledge requires affirmation of a belief and an attitude of mind. It is not clear whether the regulation contemplates that pupils forego any contrary convictions of their own and become unwilling converts to the prescribed ceremony or whether it will be acceptable if they simulate assent by words without belief and by a gesture barren of meaning. It is now a commonplace that censorship or suppression of expression of opinion is tolerated by our Constitution only when the expression presents a clear and present danger of action of a kind the State is empowered to prevent and punish. It would seem that involuntary affirmation could be commanded only on even more immediate and urgent grounds than silence. But here the power of com⊥pulsion is invoked without any allegation that remaining passive during a flag salute ritual creates a clear and present danger that would justify an effort even to muffle expression. To sustain the compulsory flag salute we are required to say that a Bill of Rights which guards the individual's right to speak his own mind, left it open to public authorities to compel him to utter what is not in his mind.

|634

Whether the First Amendment to the Constitution will permit officials to order observance of ritual of this nature does not depend upon whether as a voluntary exercise we would think it to be good, bad or merely innocuous. Any credo of nationalism is likely to include what some disapprove or to omit what others think essential, and to give off different overtones as it takes on different accents or interpretations. If official power exists to coerce acceptance of any patriotic creed, what it shall contain cannot be decided by courts, but must be largely discretionary with the ordaining authority, whose power to prescribe would no doubt include power to amend. Hence validity of the asserted power to force an American citizen publicly to profess any statement of belief or to engage in any ceremony of assent to one, presents questions of power that must be considered independently of any idea we may have as to the utility of the ceremony in question.

Nor does the issue as we see it turn on one's possession of particular religious views or the sincerity with which they are held. While religion supplies appellees' motive for enduring the discomforts of making the issue in this case, many citizens who do not share these religious views⊥ hold such a compulsory rite to infringe constitutional liberty of the individual. It is not necessary to inquire whether nonconformist beliefs will exempt from the duty to salute unless we first find power to make the salute a legal duty.

|635

The *Gobitis* decision, however, *assumed*, as did the argument in that case and in this, that power exists in the State to impose the flag salute discipline upon school children in general. The Court only examined and rejected a claim based on religious beliefs of immunity from an unquestioned general rule. The question which underlies the ⊥ flag salute controversy is whether such a ceremony so touching matters of opinion and political attitude may be imposed upon the individual by official authority under powers committed to any political organization under our Constitution. We examine rather than assume existence of this power and, against this broader definition of issues in this case, re-examine specific grounds assigned for the *Gobitis* decision.

1. It was said that the flag-salute controversy confronted the Court with "the problem which Lincoln cast in memorable dilemma: 'Must a government of necessity be too *strong* for the liberties of its people, or too *weak* to maintain its own existence?' " and that the answer must be in favor of strength.

We think these issues may be examined free of pressure or restraint growing out of such considerations.

It may be doubted whether Mr. Lincoln would have thought that the strength of government to maintain itself would be impressively vindicated by our confirming power of the state to expel a handful of children from school. Such oversimplification, so handy in political debate, often lacks the precision necessary to postulates of judicial reasoning. If validly applied to this problem, the utterance cited would resolve every issue of power in favor of those in authority and would require us to override every liberty thought to weaken or delay execution of their policies.

Government of limited power need not be anemic government. Assurance that rights are secure tends to diminish fear and jealousy of strong government, and by making us feel safe to live under it makes for its better support. Without promise of a limiting Bill of Rights it is ⊥ doubtful if our Constitution could have mustered enough strength to enable its ratification. To enforce those rights today is not to choose weak government over strong government. It is only to adhere as a means of strength to individual freedom of mind in preference to officially disciplined uniformity for which history indicates a disappointing and disastrous end.

The subject now before us exemplifies this principle. Free public education, if faithful to the ideal of secular instruction and political neutrality, will not be partisan or enemy of any class, creed, party, or faction. If it is to impose any ideological discipline, however, each party or denomination must seek to control, or failing that, to weaken the influence of the educational system. Observance of the limitations of the Constitution will not weaken government in the field appropriate for its exercise.

2. It was also considered in the *Gobitis* Case that functions of educational officers in states, counties

and school districts were such that to interfere with their authority "would in effect make us the school board for the country."

The Fourteenth Amendment, as now applied to the States, protects the citizen against the State itself and all of its creatures—Boards of Education not excepted. These have, of course, important, delicate, and highly discretionary functions, but none that they may not perform within the limits of the Bill of Rights. That they are educating the young for citizenship is reason for scrupulous protection of Constitutional freedoms of the individual, if we are not to strangle the free mind at its source and teach youth to discount important principles of our government as mere platitudes.

Such Boards are numerous and their territorial jurisdiction often small. But small and local authority may feel less sense of responsibility to the Constitution, and agencies of publicity may be less vigilant in calling it to ac ⊥ count. The action of Congress in making flag observance voluntary and respecting the conscience of the objector in a matter so vital as raising the Army contrasts sharply with these local regulations in matters relatively trivial to the welfare of the nation. There are village tyrants as well as village Hampdens, but none who acts under color of law is beyond reach of the Constitution.

3. The *Gobitis* opinion reasoned that this is a field "where courts possess no marked and certainly no controlling competence, that it is committed to the legislatures as well as the courts to guard cherished liberties and that it is constitutionally appropriate to "fight out the wise use of legislative authority in the forum of public opinion and before legislative assemblies rather than to transfer such a contest to the judicial arena," since all the "effective means of inducing political changes are left free."

The very purpose of a Bill of Rights was to withdraw certain subjects from the vicissitudes of political controversy, to place them beyond the reach of majorities and officials and to establish them as legal principles to be applied by the courts. One's right to life, liberty, and property, to free speech, a free press, freedom of worship and assembly, and other fundamental rights may not be submitted to vote; they depend on the outcome of no elections. ⊥

In weighing arguments of the parties it is important to distinguish between the due process clause of the Fourteenth Amendment as an instrument for transmitting the principles of the First Amendment and those cases in which it is applied for its own sake. The test of legislation which collides with the Fourteenth Amendment, because it also collides with the principles of the First, is much more definite than the test when only the Fourteenth is involved. Much of the vagueness of the due process clause disappears when the specific prohibitions of the First become its standard. The right of a State to regulate, for example, a public utility may well include, so far as the due prcoess test is concerned, power to impose all of the restrictions which a legislature may have a "rational basis" for adopting. But freedoms of speech and of press, of assembly, and of worship may not be infringed on such slender grounds. They are susceptible of restriction only to prevent grave and immediate danger to interests which the state may lawfully protect. It is important to note that while it is the Fourteenth Amendment which bears directly upon the State it is the more specific limiting principles of the First Amendment that finally govern this case.

Nor does our duty to apply the Bill of Rights to assertions of official authority depend upon our possession of marked competence in the field where the invasion of rights occurs. True, the task of translating the majestic generalities of the Bill of Rights, conceived as part of the pattern of liberal government in the eighteenth century, into concrete restraints on officials dealing with the problems of the twentieth century, is one to disturb self-confidence. These principles grew in soil which also produced a philosophy that the individual was the center of society, that his liberty was attainable through mere absence of governmental restraints, and that government should be entrusted with few controls and only ⌐640 the mildest supervi⊥sion over men's affairs. We must transplant these rights to a soil in which the laissez-faire concept or principle of non-interference has withered at least as to economic affairs, and social advancements are increasingly sought through closer integration of society and through expanded and strengthened governmental controls. These changed conditions often deprive precedents of reliability and cast us more than we would choose upon our own judgment. But we act in these matters not by authority of our competence but by force of our commissions. We cannot, because of modest estimates of our competence in such specialties as public education, withhold the judgment that history authenticates as the function of this Court when liberty is infringed.

4. Lastly, and this is the very heart of the *Gobitis* opinion, it reasons that "national unity is the basis of national security," that the authorities have "the right to select appropriate means for its attainment," and hence reaches the conclusion that such compulsory measures toward "national unity" are constitutional. Upon the verity of this assumption depends our answer in this case.

National unity as an end which officials may foster by persuasion and example is not in question. The problem is whether under our Constitution compulsion as here employed is a permissible means for its achievement.

Struggles to coerce uniformity of sentiment in support of some end thought essential to their time and country have been waged by many good as well as by evil men. Nationalism is a relatively recent phenomenon but at other times and places the ends have been racial or territorial security, support of a dynasty or regime, and particular plans for saving souls. As first and moderate methods to attain unity have failed, those bent on its accomplishment must resort to an ever increasing severity.⊥ As governmental ⌐641 pressure toward unity becomes greater, so strife becomes more bitter as to whose unity it shall be. Probably no deeper division of our people could proceed from any provocation than from finding it necessary to choose what doctrine and whose program public educational officials shall compel youth to unite in embracing. Ultimate futility of such attempts to compel coherence is the lesson of every such effort from the Roman drive to stamp out Christianity as a disturber of its pagan unity, the Inquisition, as a means to religious and dynastic unity, the Siberian exiles as a means to Russian unity, down to the fast failing efforts of our present totalitarian enemies. Those who begin coercive elimination of dissent soon find themselves exterminating dissenters. Compulsory unification of opinion achieves only the unanimity of the graveyard.

It seems trite but necessary to say that the First Amendment to our Constitution was designed to avoid these ends by avoiding these beginnings. There is no mysticism in the American concept of the State or of the nature or origin of its authority. We set up government by consent of the governed, and the Bill of Rights denies those in power any legal opportunity to coerce that consent. Authority here is to be controlled by public opinion, not public opinion by authority.

The case is made difficult not because the principles of its decision are obscure but because the flag involved is our own. Nevertheless, we apply the limitations of the Constitution with no fear that freedom to be intellectually and spiritually diverse or even contrary will disintegrate the social organization. To believe that patriotism will not flourish if patriotic ceremonies are voluntary and spontaneous instead of a compulsory routine is to make an unflattering estimate of the appeal of our institutions to free minds. We can have intellectual individualism⊥ and the ⌐642 rich cultural diversities that we owe to exceptional minds only at the price of occasional eccentricity and abnormal attitudes. When they are so harmless to others or to the State as those we deal with here, the price is not too great. But freedom to differ is not limited to things that do not matter much. That would be a mere shadow of freedom. The test of its substance is the right to differ as to things that touch the heart of the existing order.

If there is any fixed star in our constitutional constellation, it is that no official, high or petty, can prescribe what shall be orthodox in politics, nationalism, religion, or other matters of opinion or force citizens to confess by word or act their faith therein. If there are any circumstances which permit an exception, they do not now occur to us.

We think the action of the local authorities in compelling the flag salute and pledge transcends constitutional limitations on their power and invades the sphere of intellect and spirit which it is the purpose of the First Amendment to our Constitution to reserve from all official control.

The decision of this Court in *Minersville School Dist.* v. *Gobitis* and the holdings of those few per curiam decisions which preceded and foreshadowed it are overruled, and the judgment enjoining enforcement of the West Virginia Regulation is *affirmed*.

⌐643 *Mr. Justice ROBERTS* and *Mr. Justice REED* adhere to the views expressed by the Court in *Minersville School⊥ Dist* v. *Gobitis* and are of the opinion that the judgment below should be *reversed*.

Mr. Justice BLACK and *Mr. Justice DOUGLAS*, concurring:

We are substantially in agreement with the opinion just read, but since we originally joined with the Court in the *Gobitis* Case, it is appropriate that we make a brief statement of reasons for our change of view.

Reluctance to make the Federal Constitution a rigid bar against state regulation of conduct thought inimical to the public welfare was the controlling influence which moved us to consent to the *Gobitis* decision. Long reflection convinced us that although the principle is sound, its application in the particular case was wrong. We believe that the statute before us fails to accord full scope to the freedom of religion secured to the appellees by the First and Fourteenth Amendments.

The statute requires the appellees to participate in a ceremony aimed at inculcating respect for the flag and for this country. The Jehovah's Witnesses, without any desire to show disrespect for either the flag or the country, interpret the Bible as commanding, at the risk of God's displeasure, that they not go through the form of a pledge of allegiance to any flag. The devoutness of their belief is evidenced by their willingness to suffer persecution and punishment, rather than make the pledge.

No well ordered society can leave to the individuals an absolute right to make final decisions, unassailable by the State, as to everything they will or will not do. The First Amendment does not go so far. Religious faiths, honestly held, do not free individuals from responsibility to conduct themselves obediently to laws which are either imperatively necessary ⌐644 to protect society as a whole from grave ⊥ and pressingly imminent dangers or which, without any general prohibition, merely regulate time, place or manner of religious activity. Decision as to the constitutionality of particular laws which strike at the substance of religious tenets and practices must be

made by this Court. The duty is a solemn one, and in meeting it we cannot say that a failure, because of religious scruples, to assume a particular physical position and to repeat the words of a patriotic formula creates a grave danger to the nation. Such a statutory exaction is a form of test oath, and the test oath has always been abhorrent in the United States.

Words uttered under coercion are proof of loyalty to nothing but self-interest. Love of country must spring from willing hearts and free minds, inspired by a fair administration of wise laws enacted by the people's elected representatives within the bounds of express constitutional prohibitions. These laws must, to be consistent with the First Amendment, permit the widest toleration of conflicting viewpoints consistent with a society of free men.

Neither our domestic tranquillity in peace nor our martial effort in war depend on compelling little children to participate in a ceremony which ends in nothing for them but a fear of spiritual condemnation. If, as we think, their fears are groundless, time and reason are the proper antidotes for their errors. The ceremonial, when enforced against conscientious objectors, more likely to defeat than to serve its high purpose, is a handy implement for disguised religious persecution. As such, it is inconsistent with our Constitution's plan and purpose.

Mr. Justice MURPHY, concurring;

I agree with the opinion of the Court and join in it.

The complaint challenges an order of the State Board of Education which requires teachers and pupils to participate in the prescribed salute to the flag. For refusal to conform with the requirement the State law prescribes ex⊥pulsion. The offender is required by law to be treated as unlawfully absent from school and the parent or guardian is made liable to prosecution and punishment for such absence. Thus not only is the privilege of public education conditioned on compliance with the requirement, but noncompliance is virtually made unlawful. In effect compliance is compulsory and not optional. It is the claim of appellees that the regulation is invalid as a restriction on religious freedom and freedom of speech, secured to them against State infringement by the First and Fourteenth Amendments to the Constitution of the United States.

A reluctance to interfere with considered state action, the fact that the end sought is a desirable one, the emotion aroused by the flag as a symbol for which we have fought and are now fighting again,— all of these are understandable. But there is before us the right of freedom to believe, freedom to worship one's Maker according to the dictates of one's conscience, a right which the Constitution specifically shelters. Reflection has convinced me that as a judge I have no loftier duty or responsibility than to uphold that spiritual freedom to its farthest reaches.

The right of freedom of thought and of religion as guaranteed by the Constitution against State action includes both the right to speak freely and the right to refrain from speaking at all, except in so far as essential operations of government may require it for the preservation of an orderly society,—as in the case of compulsion to give evidence in court. Without wishing to disparage the purposes and intentions of those who hope to inculcate sentiments of loyalty and patriotism by requiring a declaration of allegiance as a feature of public education, or unduly belittle the benefits that may accrue therefrom, I am impelled to conclude that such a requirement is not essential to the maintenance of effective government and orderly society. To many it is deeply distasteful to join in a public chorus of affirmation of private belief. By some, in⊥cluding the members of this sect, it is apparently regarded as incompatible with a primary religious obligation and therefore a restriction on religious freedom. Official compulsion to affirm what is contrary to one's religious beliefs is the antithesis of freedom of worship which, it is well to recall, was achieved in this country only after what Jefferson characterized as the "severest contests in which I have ever been engaged."

⌐646

I am unable to agree that the benefits that may accrue to society from the compulsory flag salute are sufficiently definite and tangible to justify the invasion of freedom and privacy that is entailed or to compensate for a restraint on the freedom of the individual to be vocal or silent according to his conscience or personal inclination. The trenchant words in the preamble to the Virginia Statute for Religious Freedom remain unanswerable: ". . . all attempts to influence [the mind] by temporal punishments, or burdens, or by civil incapacitations, tend only to beget habits of hypocrisy and meanness, . . ." Any spark of love for country which may be generated in a child or his associates by forcing him to make what is to him an empty gesture and recite words wrung from him contrary to his religious beliefs is overshadowed by the desirability of preserving freedom of conscience to the full. It is in that freedom and the example of persuasion, not in force and compulsion, that the real unity of America lies.

Mr. Justice FRANKFURTER, dissenting:

One who belongs to the most vilified and persecuted minority in history is not likely to be insensible to the freedoms guaranteed by our Constitution. Were my purely personal attitude relevant I should wholeheartedly associate myself with the general libertarian views in the Court's opinion, representing as they do the thought and ⊥ action of a lifetime. But as judges we are neither Jew nor Gentile, neither Catholic nor agnostic. We owe equal at-

⌐647

tachment to the Constitution and are equally bound by our judicial obligations whether we derive our citizenship from the earliest or the latest immigrants to these shores. As a member of this Court I am not justified in writing my private notions of policy into the Constitution, no matter how deeply I may cherish them or how mischievous I may deem their disregard. The duty of a judge who must decide which of two claims before the Court shall prevail, that of a State to enact and enforce laws within its general competence or that of an individual to refuse obedience because of the demands of his conscience, is not that of the ordinary person. It can never be emphasized too much that one's own opinion about the wisdom or evil of a law should be excluded altogether when one is doing one's duty on the bench. The only opinion of our own even looking in that direction that is material is our opinion whether legislators could in reason have enacted such a law. In the light of all the circumstances, including the history of this question in this Court, it would require more daring than I possess to deny that reasonable legislators could have taken the action which is before us for review. Most unwillingly, therefore, I must differ from my brethren with regard to legislation like this. I cannot bring my mind to believe that the "liberty" secured by the Due Process Clause gives this Court authority to deny to the State of West Virginia the attainment of that which we all recognize as a legitimate legislative end, namely, the promotion of good citizenship, by employment of the means here chosen.

Not so long ago we were admonished that "the only check upon our own exercise of power is our own sense of self-restraint. For the removal of unwise laws from the statute books appeal lies not to the court but to the ballot and to the processes of democratic government."⊥ *United States* v. *Butler* (dissent). We have been told that generalities do not decide concrete cases. But the intensity with which a general principle is held may determine a particular issue, and whether we put first things first may decide a specific controversy.

⌐648

The admonition that judicial self-restraint alone limits arbitrary exercise of our authority is relevant every time we are asked to nullify legislation. The Constitution does not give us greater veto power when dealing with one phase of "liberty" than with another, or when dealing with grade school regulations than with college regulations that offend conscience as well was the case in *Hamilton* v. *University of California*. In neither situation is our function comparable to that of a legislature or are we free to act as though we were a super-legislature. Judicial self-restraint is equally necessary whenever an exercise of political or legislative power is challenged. There is no warrant in the constitutional basis of this Court's authority for attributing different rôles to it depending upon the nature of the challenge to the legislation. Our power does not vary according to the particular provision of the Bill of Rights which is invoked. The right not to have property taken without just compensation has, so far as the scope of judicial power is concerned, the same consitutional dignity as the right to be protected against unreasonable searches and seizures, and the latter has no less claim than freedom of the press or freedom of speech or religious freedom. In no instance is this Court the primary protector of the particular liberty that is invoked. This Court has recognized, what hardly could be denied, that all the provisions of the first ten Amendments are "specific" prohibitions, *United States* v. *Carolene Products Co.* But each specific Amendment, in so far as embraced within the Fourteenth Amendment, must be equally respected, and the function of this⊥ Court does not ⌐649 differ in passing on the constitutionality of legislation challenged under different Amendments. . . .

The framers of the federal Constitution might have chosen to assign an active share in the process of legislation to this Court. They had before them the well-known example of New York's Council of Revision, which had been functioning since 1777. After stating that "laws inconsistent with the spirit of this constitution, or with the public good, may be hastily and unadvisedly passed," the state constitution made the judges of New York part of the legislative process by providing that "all bills which have passed the senate and assembly shall, before they become laws," be presented to a Council of which the judges constituted a majority, "for their revisal and consideration." Art. 3, New York Constitution of 1777. Judges exercised this legislative function in ⌐650 New York⊥ for nearly fifty years. . . . But the framers of the Constitution denied such legislative powers to the federal judiciary. They chose instead to insulate the judiciary from the legislative function. They did not grant to this Court supervision over legislation.

The reason why from the beginning even the narrow judicial authority to nullify legislation has been viewed with a jealous eye is that it serves to prevent the full play of the democratic process. The fact that it may be an undemocratic aspect of our scheme of government does not call for its rejection or its disuse.

The precise scope of the question before us defines the limits of the constitutional power that is in issue. The State of West Virginia requires all pupils to share in the salute to the flag as part of school training in citizenship. The present action is one to enjoin the enforcement of this requirement by those in school attendance. We have not before us any attempt by the State to punish disobedient children or visit penal consequences on their parents. All that is in question is the right of the State to compel participation in this exercise by those who choose to attend the public schools.

We are not reviewing merely the action of a local school board. The flag salute requirement in this case comes before us with the full authority of the State of West Virginia. We are in fact passing judgment on "the power of the State as a whole." *Rippey* v. *Texas.* Practically we are passing upon the political power of each of the forty-eight states. Moreover, since the First Amendment has been read into the Fourteenth, our problem is precisely the same as it would be if we had before us an Act of Congress for the District of Columbia. To suggest that we are here con⊥cerned with the heedless action of some village   ⌐651 tyrants is to distort the augustness of the constitutional issue and the reach of the consequences of our decision.

Under our constitutional system the legislature is charged solely with civil concerns of society. If the avowed or intrinsic legislative purpose is either to promote or to discourage some religious community or creed, it is clearly within the constitutional restrictions imposed on legislatures and cannot stand. But it by no means follows that legislative power is wanting whenever a general non-discriminatory civil regulation in fact touches conscientious scruples or religious beliefs of an individual or a group. Regard for such scruples or beliefs undoubtedly presents one of the most reasonable claims for the exertion of legislative accommodation. It is, of course, beyond our power to rewrite the State's requirement, by providing exemptions for those who do not wish to participate in the flag salute or by making some other accommodations to meet their scruples. That wisdom might suggest the making of such accommodations and that school administration would not find it too difficult to make them and yet maintain the ceremony for those not refusing to conform, is outside our province to suggest. Tact, respect, and generosity toward variant views will always commend themselves to those charged with the duties of legislation so as to achieve a maximum of good will and to require a minimum of unwilling submission to a general law. But the real question is, who is to make such accommodations, the courts or the legislature?

This is no dry, technical matter. It cuts deep into one's conception of the democratic process—it concerns no less the practical differences between the means for making these accommodations that are open to courts and to legislatures. A court can only strike down. It can only say "This or that law is void." It cannot modify or qualify, it cannot make exceptions to a general require⊥ment. And it strikes   ⌐652 down not merely for a day. At least the finding of unconstitutionality ought not to have ephemeral significance unless the Constitution is to be reduced to the fugitive importance of mere legislation. When we are dealing with the Constitution of the United States, and more particularly with the great safeguards of the Bill of Rights, we are dealing with principles of liberty and justice "so rooted in the traditions and conscience of our people as to be ranked as fundamental"—something without which "a fair and enlightened system of justice would be impossible." *Palko* v. *Connecticut*. If the function of this Court is to be essentially no different from that of a legislature, if the considerations governing constitutional construction are to be substantially those that underlie legislation, then indeed judges should not have life tenure and they should be made directly responsible to the electorate. There have been many but unsuccessful proposals in the last sixty years to amend the Constitution to that end.

Conscientious scruples, all would admit, cannot stand against every legislative compulsion to do positive acts in conflict with such scruples. We have been told that such compulsions override religious scruples only as to major concerns of the state. But the determination of what is major and what is minor itself raises questions of policy. For the way in which men equally guided by reason appraise importance goes to the very heart of policy. Judges should be very diffident in setting their judgment against that of a state in determining what is and what is not a major concern, what means are appropriate to proper ends, and what is the total social cost in striking the balance of imponderables.

⌊653   What one can say with assurance is that the history out of which grew constitutional provisions for religious equal⊥ity and the writings of the great exponents of religious freedom— Jefferson, Madison, John Adams, Benjamin Franklin—are totally wanting in justification for a claim by dissidents of exceptional immunity from civic measures of general applicability, measures not in fact disguised assaults upon such dissident views. The great leaders of the American Revolution were determined to remove political support from every religious establishment. They put on an equality the different religious sects—Episcopalians, Presbyterians, Catholics, Baptists, Methodists, Quakers, Hugenots— which, as dissenters, had been under the heel of the various orthodoxies that prevailed in different colonies. So far as the state was concerned, there was to be neither orthodoxy nor heterodoxy. And so Jefferson and those who followed him wrote guaranties of religious freedom into our constitutions. Religious minorities as well as religious majorities were to be equal in the eyes of the political state. But Jefferson and the others also knew that minorities may disrupt society. It never would have occurred to them to write into the Constitution the subordination of the general civil authority of the state to sectarian scruples.

The constitutional protection of religious freedom terminated disabilities, it did not create new privileges. It gave religious equality, not civil immunity. Its essence is freedom from conformity to religious dogma, not freedom from conformity to law because of religious dogma. Religious loyalties may be exercised without hindrance from the state, not the state may not exercise that which except by leave of religious loyalties is within the domain of temporal power. Otherwise each individual could set up his own censor against obedience to laws conscientiously deemed for the public good by those whose business it is to make laws.

The prohibition against any religion establishment by the government placed denominations on an equal foot⊥ing—it assured freedom from support by   ⌊654 the government to any mode of worship and the freedom of individuals to support any mode of worship. Any person may therefore believe or disbelieve what he pleases. He may practice what he will in his own house of worship or publicly within the limits of public order. But the lawmaking authority is not circumscribed by the variety of religious beliefs, otherwise the constitutional guaranty would be not a protection of the free exercise of religion but a denial of the exercise of legislation.

The essence of the religious freedom guaranteed by our Constitution is therefore this: no religion shall either receive the state's support or incur its hostility. Religion is outside the sphere of political government. This does not mean that all matters on which religious organizations or beliefs may pronounce are outside the sphere of government. Were this so, instead of the separation of church and state, there would be the subordination of the state on any matter deemed within the sovereignty of the religious conscience. Much that is the concern of temporal authority affects the spiritual interests of men. But it is not enough to strike down a nondiscriminatory law that it may hurt or offend some dissident view. It would be too easy to cite numerous prohibitions and injunctions to which laws run counter if the variant interpretations of the Bible were made the tests of obedience to law. The validity of secular laws cannot be measured by their conformity to religious doctrines. It is only in a theocratic state that ecclesiastical doctrines measure legal right or wrong.

An act compelling profession of allegiance to a religion, no matter how subtly or tenuously promoted, is bad. But an act promoting good citizenship and national allegiance is within the domain of governmental authority and is therefore to be judged by the same considerations of power and of constitutionality as those involved in the many⊥ claims of im-   ⌊65⊥ munity from civil obedience because of religious scruples.

That claims are pressed on behalf of sincere religious convictions does not of itself establish their constitutional validity. Nor does waving the banner of religious freedom relieve us from examining into the power we are asked to deny the states. Otherwise the doctrine of separation of church and state, so cardinal in the history of this nation and for the liberty of our people, would mean not the disestablishment of a state church but the establishment of all churches and of all religious groups. . . .

Law is concerned with external behavior and not with the inner life of man. It rests in large measure upon compulsion. Socrates lives in history partly because he gave his life for the conviction that duty of obedience to secular law does not presuppose consent to its enactment or belief in its virtue. The consent upon which free government rests is the consent that comes from sharing in the process of making and unmaking laws. The state is not shut out from a domain because the individual conscience may deny the state's claim. The individual con⊥science may profess what faith it chooses. It may affirm and promote that faith—in the language of the Constitution, it may "exercise" it freely—but it cannot thereby restrict community action through political organs in matters of community concern, so long as the action is not asserted in a discriminatory way either openly or by stealth. One may have the right to practice one's religion and at the same time owe the duty of formal obedience to laws that run counter to one's beliefs. Compelling belief implies denial of opportunity to combat it and to assert dissident views. Quite another matter is submission to conformity of action while denying its wisdom or virtue and with ample opportunity for seeking its change or abrogation. . . .⊥

Parents have the privilege of choosing which schools they wish their children to attend. And the question here is whether the state may make certain requirements that seem to it desirable or important for the proper education of those future citizens who go to schools maintained by the states, or whether the pupils in those schools may be relieved from those requirements if they run counter to the consciences of their parents. Not only have parents the right to send children to schools of their own choosing but the state has no right to bring such schools "under a strict governmental control" or give affirmative direction⊥ concerning the intimate and essential details of such schools, intrust their control to public officers, and deny both owners and patrons reasonable choice and discretion in respect of teachers, curriculum, and textbooks." *Farrington* v. *Tokushige*. Why should not the state likewise have constitutional power to make reasonable provisions for the proper instruction of children in schools maintained by it?

When dealing with religious scruples we are dealing with an almost numberless variety of doctrines and beliefs entertained with equal sincerity by the particular groups for which they satisfy man's needs in his relation to the mysteries of the universe. There are in the United States more than 250 distinctive established religious denominations. In the state of Pennsylvania there are 120 of these, and in West Virginia as many as 65. But if religious scruples afford immunity from civic obedience to laws, they may be invoked by the religious beliefs of any individual even though he holds no membership in any sect or organized denomination. Certainly this Court cannot be called upon to determine what claims of conscience should be recognized and what should be rejected as satisfying the "religion" which the Constitution protects. That would indeed resurrect the very discriminatory treatment of religion which the Constitution sought forever to forbid. . . .

⊥We are told that a flag salute is a doubtful substitute for adequate understanding of our institutions. The states that require such a school exercise do not have to justify it as the only means for promoting good citizenship in children, but merely as one of diverse means for accomplishing a worthy end. We may deem it a foolish measure, but the point is that this Court is not the organ of government to resolve doubts as to whether it will fulfill its purpose. Only if there be no doubt that any rea-⊥sonable mind could entertain can we deny to the states the right to resolve doubts their way and not ours.

That which to the majority may seem essential for the welfare of the state may offend the consciences of a minority. But, so long as no inroads are made upon the actual exercise of religion by the minority, to deny the political power of the majority to enact laws concerned with civil matters, simply because they may offend the consciences of a minority, really means that the consciences of a minority are more sacred and more enshrined in the Constitution than the consciences of a majority.

We are told that symbolism is a dramatic but primitive way of communicating ideas. Symbolism is inescapable. Even the most sophisticated live by symbols. But it is not for this Court to make psychological judgments as to the effectiveness of a particular symbol in inculcating concededly indispensable feelings, particularly if the state happens to see fit to utilize the symbol that represents our heritage and our hopes. And surely only flippancy could be responsible for the suggestion that constitutional validity of a requirement to salute our flag implies equal validity of a requirement to salute a dictator. The significance of a symbol lies in what it represents. To reject the swastika does not imply rejection of the Cross. And so it beats repetition to say that it mocks reason and denies our whole history to find in the allowance of a requirement to salute our flag on fitting occasions the seeds of sanction for obeisance to a leader. To deny the power to employ educational symbols is to say that the state's educational system may not stimulate the imagination because this may lead to unwise stimulation.

The right of West Virginia to utilize the flag salute as part of its educational process is denied because, so it is argued, it cannot be justified as a means of meeting a "clear and present danger" to national unity. In passing it deserves to be noted that the four cases which unani⊥mously sustained the power of states to utilize such an educational measure arose and were all decided before the present World War. But to measure the state's power to make such regulations as are here resisted by the imminence of national danger is wholly to misconceive the origin and purpose of the concept of "clear and present danger." To apply such a test is for the Court to assume, however unwittingly a legislative responsibility that does not belong to it. To talk about "clear and present danger" as the touchstone of allowable educational policy by the states whenever school curricula may impinge upon the boundaries of individual conscience, is to take a felicitous phrase out of the context of the particular situation where it arose and for which it was adapted. Mr. Justice Holmes used the phrase "clear and present danger" in a case involving mere speech as a means by which alone to accomplish sedition in time of war. By that phrase he meant merely to indicate that, in view of the protection given to utterance by the First Amendment, in order that mere utterance may not be proscribed, "the words used are used in such circumstances and are of such a nature as to create a clear and present danger that will bring about the substantive evils that Congress has a right to prevent." *Schenck* v. *United States*. The "substantive evils about which he was speaking were inducement of insubordination in the military and naval forces of the United States and obstruction of enlistment while the country was at war. He was not enunciating a formal rule that there can be no restriction upon speech and, still less, no compulsion where conscience balks, unless imminent danger would thereby be wrought "to our institutions or our government."

The flag salute exercise has no kinship whatever to the oath tests so odious in history. For the oath test was one of the instruments for suppressing heretical ⌊664 beliefs. ⊥ Saluting the flag suppresses no belief nor curbs it. Children and their parents may believe what they please, avow their belief and practice it. It is not even remotely suggested that the requirement for saluting the flag involves the slightest restriction against the fullest opportunity on the part both of the children and of their parents to disavow as publicly as they choose to do so the meaning that others attach to the gesture of salute. All channels of affirmative free expression are open to both children and parents. Had we before us any act of the state putting the slightest curbs upon such free expression, I should not lag behind any member of this Court in striking down such an invasion of the right to freedom of thought and freedom of speech protected by the Constitution. . . .

⌊670   ⊥ Of course patriotism cannot be enforced by the flag salute. But neither can the liberal spirit be enforced by judicial invalidation of illiberal legislation. Our constant preoccupation with the constitutionality of legislation rather than with its wisdom tends to preoccupation of the American mind with a false value. The tendency of focusing attention on constitutionality is to make constitutionality synony-mous with wisdom, to regard a law as all right if it is constitutional. Such an attitude is a great enemy of liberalism. Particularly in legislation affecting freedom of thought and freedom of speech much which should offend a free-spirited society is constitutional. Reliance for the most precious interests of civilization, therefore, must be found outside of their vindication in courts of law. Only a persistent positive translation of the faith of a free society into the convictions and habits and actions of a community is the ultimate reliance against unabated temptations to fetter the human spirit.

COX v. NEW HAMPSHIRE

312 U.S. 569

ON APPEAL FROM THE SUPREME COURT OF THE STATE OF NEW HAMPSHIRE

Argued March 7, 1941 — Decided March 31, 1941

⊥ *Mr. Chief Justice HUGHES* delivered the opinion of the Court: ⌊570

Appellants are five "Jehovah's Witnesses" who, with sixty-three others of the same persuasion, were convicted in the municipal court of Manchester, New Hampshire, for violation of a state statute prohibiting a "parade or ⊥ procession" upon a public street without a special license.   ⌊571

Upon appeal, there was a trial de novo of these appellants before a jury in the Superior Court, the other defendants having agreed to abide by the final decision in that proceeding. Appellants were found guilty and the judgment of conviction was affirmed by the Supreme Court of the State.

By motions and exceptions, appellants raised the questions that the statute was invalid under the Fourteenth Amendment of the Constitution of the United States in that it deprived appellants of their rights of freedom of worship, freedom of speech and press, and freedom of assembly, vested unreasonable and unlimited arbitrary and discriminatory powers in the licensing authority, and was vague and indefinite. These contentions were overruled and the case comes here on appeal.

The statutory prohibition is as follows:

"No theatrical or dramatic representation shall be performed or exhibited, and no parade or procession upon any public street or way, and no open-air public meeting upon any ground abutting thereon, shall be permitted, unless a special license therefor shall first be obtained from the selectmen of the town, or from a licensing committee for cities hereinafter provided for."

⊥ The facts, which are conceded by the appellants to be established by the evidence, are these: The sixty-eight defendants and twenty other persons met at a hall in the City of Manchester on the evening of Saturday, July 8, 1939, "for the purpose of engaging in an information march." The company was divided into four or five groups, each with about fifteen to twenty persons. Each group then proceeded to a dif-   ⌊572 ferent part of the business district of the city and there "would line up in single-file formation and then proceed to march along the sidewalk, 'single-file,' that is, following one another." Each of the defendants carried a small staff with a sign reading "Religion is a Snare and a Racket" and on the reverse "Serve God and Christ the King." Some of the marchers carried placards bearing the statement "Fascism or Freedom. Hear Judge Rutherford and Face the Facts." The marchers also handed out printed leaflets announcing a meeting to be held at a later time in the hall from which they had started, where a talk on government would be given to the public free of charge. Defendants did not apply for a permit and none was issued.

⌐573   There was a dispute in the evidence as to the distance ⊥ between the marchers. Defendants said that they were from fifteen to twenty feet apart. The State insists that the evidence clearly showed that the "marchers were as close together as it was possible for them to walk." Appellants concede that this dispute is not material to the questions presented. The recital of facts which prefaced the opinion of the state court thus summarizes the effect of the march: "Manchester had a population of over 75,000 in 1930, and there was testimony that on Saturday nights in an hour's time 26,000 persons passed one of the intersections where the defendants marched. The marchers interfered with the normal sidewalk travel, but no technical breach of the peace occurred. The march was a prearranged affair, and no permit for it was sought, although the defendants understood that under the statute one was required."

Appellants urge that each of the defendants was a minister ordained to preach the gospel in accordance with his belief and that the participation of these ministers in the march was for the purpose of disseminating information in the public interest and was one of their ways of worship.

The sole charge against appellants was that they were "taking part in a parade or procession" on public streets without a permit as the statute required. They were not prosecuted for distributing leaflets, or for conveying information by placards or otherwise, or for issuing invitations to a public meeting, or for holding a public meeting, or for maintaining or expressing religious beliefs. Their right to do any one of these things apart from engaging in a "parade or procession" upon a public street is not here involved and the question of the validity of a statute addressed to any other sort of conduct than that complained of is not before us.

There appears to be no ground for challenging the ruling of the state court that appellants were in fact ⌐574   ⊥ engaged in a parade or procession upon the public streets. As the state court observed: "It was a march in formation, and its advertising and informatory purpose did not make it otherwise. . . . It is immaterial that its tactics were few and simple. It is enough that it proceeded in an ordered and close file as a collective body of persons on the city streets."

Civil liberties, as guaranteed by the Constitution, imply the existence of an organized society maintaining public order without which liberty itself would be lost in the excesses of unrestrained abuses. The authority of a municipality to impose regulations in order to assure the safety and convenience of the people in the use of public highways has never been regarded as inconsistent with civil liberties but rather as one of the means of safeguarding the good order upon which they ultimately depend. The control of travel on the streets of cities is the most familiar illustration of this recognition of social need. Where a restriction of the use of highways in that relation is designed to promote the public convenience in the interest of all, it cannot be disregarded by the attempted exercise of some civil right which in other circumstances would be entitled to protection. One would not be justified in ignoring the familiar red traffic light because he thought it his religious duty to disobey the municipal command or sought by that means to direct public attention to an announcement of his opinions. As regulation of the use of the streets for parades and processions is a traditional exercise of control by local government, the question in a particular case is whether that control is exerted so as not to deny or unwarrantedly abridge the right of assembly and the opportunities for the communication of thought and the discussion of public questions immemorially associated with resort to public places.

⊥ In the instant case, we are aided by the opinion   ⌐575 of the Supreme Court of the State which construed the statute and defined the limitations of the authority conferred for the granting of licenses for parades and processions. The court observed that if the clause of the Act requiring a license "for all open-air public meetings upon land contiguous to a highway" was invalid, that invalidity did not nullify the Act in its application to the other situations described. Recognizing the importance of the civil liberties invoked by appellants, the court thought it significant that the statute prescribed "no measures for controlling or suppressing the publication on the highways of facts and opinions, either by speech or by writing;" that communication "by the distribution of literature or by the display of placards and signs" was in no respect regulated by the statute; that the regulation with respect to parades and processions was applicable only "to organized formations of persons using the highways;" and that "the defendants, separately, or collectively in groups not constituting a parade or procession," were "under no contemplation of the Act." In this light, the court thought that interference with liberty of speech and writing seemed slight; that the distribution of pamphlets and folders by the groups "traveling in unorganized fashion" would have had as large a circulation, and that "signs carried by members of the groups not in marching formation would have been as conspicuous, as published by them while in parade or procession."

It was with this view of the limited objective of the statute that the state court considered and defined the duty of the licensing authority and the rights of the appellants to a license for their parade, with regard only to considerations of time, place and man-

⌐576 ner so as to ⊥ conserve the public convenience. The obvious advantage of requiring application for a permit was noted as giving the public authorities notice in advance so as to afford opportunity for proper policing. And the court further observed that, in fixing time and place, the license served "to prevent confusion by overlapping parades or processions, to secure convenient use of the streets by other travelers, and to minimize the risk of disorder." But the court held that the licensing board was not vested with arbitrary power or an unfettered discretion; that its discretion must be exercised with "uniformity of method of treatment upon the facts of each application, free from improper or inappropriate considerations and from unfair discrimination;" that a "systematic, consistent and just order of treatment, with reference to the convenience of public use of the highways, is the statutory mandate." The defendants, said the court, "had a right, under the Act, to a license to march when, where and as they did, if after a required investigation it was found that the convenience of the public in the use of the streets would not thereby be unduly disturbed, upon such conditions or changes in time, place and manner as would avoid disturbance."

If a municipality has authority to control the use of its public streets for parades or processions, as it undoubtedly has, it cannot be denied authority to give consideration, without unfair discrimination, to time, place and manner in relation to the other proper uses of the streets. We find it impossible to say that the limited authority conferred by the licensing provisions of the statute in question as thus construed by the state court contravened any constitutional right.

There remains the question of license fees which, as the court said, had a permissible range from $300 to a nominal amount. The court construed the Act as requiring "a reasonable fixing of the amount of

⌐577 the fee." "The ⊥ charge," said the court, "for a circus parade or a celebration procession of length, each drawing crowds of observers, would take into account the greater public expense of policing the spectacle, compared with the slight expense of a less expansive and attractive parade or procession, to which the charge would be adjusted." The fee was held to be not a revenue tax, but one to meet the expense incident to the administration of the Act and to the maintenance of public order in the matter licensed." There is nothing contrary to the Constitution in the charge of a fee limited to the purpose stated. The suggestion that a flat fee should have

been charged fails to take account of the difficulty of framing a fair schedule to meet all circumstances, and we perceive no constitutional ground for denying to local governments that flexibility of adjustment of fees which in the light of varying conditions would tend to conserve rather than impair the liberty sought.

There is no evidence that the statute has been administered otherwise than in the fair and non-discriminatory manner which the state court has construed it to require.

The decisions upon which appellants rely are not applicable. In *Lovell* v. *Griffin* the ordinance prohibited the distribution of literature of any kind at any time, at any place, and in any manner without a permit from the city manager, thus striking at the very foundation of the freedom of the press by subjecting it to license and censorship. In *Hague* v. *Committee for Industrial Organization*, the ordinance dealt with the exercise of the right of assembly for the purpose of communicating views; it did not make comfort or convenience in the use of streets the standard of official action but enabled the local official absolutely to refuse a permit on his mere opinion that such refusal would prevent "riots disturbances or disorderly as-

semblage." The ordi⊥nance thus created as the re-   ⌐578 cord disclosed, an instrument of arbitrary suppression of opinions on public questions. The court said that "uncontrolled official suppression of the privilege cannot be made a substitute for the duty to maintain order in connection with the exercise of the right." In *Schneider* v. *Irvington* the ordinance was directed at canvassing and banned unlicensed communication of any views, or the advocacy of any cause, from door to door, subject only to the power of a police officer to determine as a censor what literature might be distributed and who might distribute it. In *Cantwell* v. *Connecticut* the statute dealt with the solicitation of funds for religious causes and authorized an official to determine whether the cause was a religious one and to refuse a permit if he determined it was not, thus establishing a censorship of religion.

Nor is any question of peaceful picketing here involved, as in *Thornhill* v. *Alabama* and *Carlson* v. *California*. The statute, as the state court said, is not aimed at any restraint of freedom of speech, and there is no basis for an assumption that it would be applied so as to prevent peaceful picketing as described in the cases cited.

The argument as to freedom of worship is also beside the point. No interference with religious worship or the practice of religion in any proper sense is shown, but only the exercise of local control over the use of streets for parades and processions.

The judgment of the Supreme Court of New Hampshire is *affirmed*.

PRINCE v. MASSACHUSETTS

321 U.S. 158

APPEAL FROM THE SUPERIOR COURT OF
MASSACHUSETTS,
PLYMOUTH COUNTY

Argued December 14, 1943 — Decided January 31,
1944

⊥159   ⊥ *Mr. Justice RUTLEDGE* delivered the opinion
of the Court.

The case brings for review another episode in the
conflict between Jehovah's Witnesses and state authority. This time Sarah Prince appeals from convictions for violating Massachusetts' child labor laws,
by acts said to be a rightful exercise of her religious
convictions.

When the offenses were committed she was the
aunt and custodian of Betty M. Simmons, a girl nine
years of age. Originally there were three separate
⊥160 complaints. They ⊥ were, shortly, for (1) refusal to
disclose Betty's identity and age to a public officer
whose duty was to enforce the statutes; (2) furnishing her with magazines, knowing she was to sell
them unlawfully, that is, on the street; and (3) as
Betty's custodian, permitting her to work contrary to
law. The complaints were made, respectively, pursuant to §§ 79, 80 and 81 of Chapter 149, Gen. Laws
of Mass. The Supreme Judicial Court reversed the
conviction under the first complaint on state
grounds, but sustained the judgments founded in the
other two. They present the only questions for our
decision. These are whether §§ 80 and 81, as applied,
contravene the Fourteenth Amendment by denying
or abridging appellant's freedom of religion and by
denying to her the equal protection of the laws.

Sections 80 and 81 form parts of Massachusetts'
comprehensive child labor law. They provide methods for enforcing the prohibitions of § 69, which is as
follows:

"No boy under twelve and no girl under eighteen
shall sell, expose or offer for sale any newspapers,
magazines, periodicals or any other articles of mer-
⊥161 chandise of any ⊥ description, or exercise the trade
of bootblack or scavenger, or any other trade, in any
street or public place."

Sections 80 and 81, so far as pertinent, read:

"Whoever furnishes or sells to any minor any article of any description with the knowledge that the
minor intends to sell such article in violation of any
provision of sections sixty-nine to seventy-three, inclusive, or after having received written notice to
this effect from any officer charged with the enforcement thereof, or knowingly procures or encourages
any minor to violate any provisions of said sections,
shall be punished by a fine of not less than ten nor
more than two hundred dollars or by imprisonment
for not more than two months, or both." § 80.

"Any parent, guardian or custodian having a minor under his control who compels or permits such
minor to work in violation of any provision of sec-

tions sixty to seventy-four, inclusive, . . . shall for
the first offense be punished by a fine of not less
than two nor more than ten dollars or by imprisonment for not more than five days, or both;' . . ."
§ 81.

The story told by the evidence has become familiar. It hardly needs repeating, except to give setting
to the variations introduced through the part played
by a child of tender years. Mrs. Prince, living in
Brockton, is the mother of two young sons. She also
has legal custody of Betty Simmons, who lives with
them. The children too are Jehovah's Witnesses and
both Mrs. Prince and Betty testified they were ordained ministers. The former was accustomed to go
each week on the streets of Brockton to distribute
"Watchtower" and "Consolation," according to the
usual plan. She had permitted the children to ⊥ en-   ⊥162
gage in this activity previously, and had been warned
against doing so by the school attendance officer,
Mr. Perkins. But, until December 18, 1941, she generally did not take them with her at night.

That evening, as Mrs. Prince was preparing to
leave her home, the children asked to go. She at first
refused. Childlike, they resorted to tears; and, moth-
erlike, she yielded. Arriving downtown, Mrs. Prince
permitted the children "to engage in the preaching
work with her upon the sidewalks." That is, with
specific reference to Betty, she and Mrs. Prince took
positions about twenty feet apart near a street inter-
section. Betty held up in her hand, for passers-by to
see, copies of "Watchtower" and "Consolation."
From her shoulder hung the usual canvas magazine
bag, on which was printed: "Watchtower and Consolation 5 cents per copy." No one accepted a copy
from Betty that evening and she received no money.
Nor did her aunt. But on other occasions, Betty had
received funds and given out copies.

Mrs. Prince and Betty remained until 8:45 p.m. A
few minutes before this, Mr. Perkins approached
Mrs. Prince. A discussion ensued. He inquired and
she refused to give Betty's name. However, she
stated the child attended the Shaw School. Mr. Perkins referred to his previous warnings and said he
would allow five minutes for them to get off the
street. Mrs. Prince admitted she supplied Betty with
the magazines and said, "[N]either you nor anybody
else can stop me . . . This child is exercising her
God-given right and her constitutional right to
preach the gospel, and no creature has a right to interfere with God's commands." However, Mrs.
Prince and Betty departed. She remarked as she
went, "I'm not going through this any more. We've
been through it time and time again. I'm going home
and put the little girl to bed." It may be added that
testimony, by Betty, her aunt and others, was offered at the trials, and was ex⊥cluded, to show that   ⊥163
Betty believed it was her religious duty to perform
this work and failure would bring condemnation "to
everlasting destruction at Armageddon."

As the case reaches us, the questions are no longer open whether what the child did was a "sale" or an "offer to sell" within § 69 or was "work" within § 81. The state court's decision has foreclosed them adversely to appellant as a matter of state law. The only question remaining therefore is whether, as construed and applied, the statute is valid. Upon this the court said: "We think that freedom of the press and of religion is subject to incidental regulation to the slight degree involved in the prohibition of the selling of religious literature in streets and public places by boys under twelve and girls under eighteen, and in the further statutory provisions herein considered, which have been adopted as means of enforcing ⊥ that prohibition."

⊥164   Appellant does not stand on freedom of the press. Regarding it as secular, she concedes it may be restricted as Massachusetts has done. Hence, she rests squarely on freedom of religion under the First Amendment, applied by the Fourteenth to the states. She buttresses this foundation, however, with a claim of parental right as secured by the due process clause of the latter Amendment. These guaranties, she thinks, guard alike herself and the child in what they have done. Thus, two claimed liberties are at stake. One is the parent's, to bring up the child in the way he should go, which for appellant means to teach him the tenets and the practices of their faith. The other freedom is the child's, to observe these; and among them is "to preach the gospel . . . by public distribution" of "Watchtower" and "Consolation," in conformity with the scripture: "A little child shall lead them."

If by this position appellant seeks for freedom of conscience a broader protection than for freedom of the mind, it may be doubted that any of the great liberties insured by the First Article can be given higher place than the others. All have preferred position in our basic scheme. All are interwoven there together. Differences there are, in them and in the modes appropriate for their exercise. But they have unity in the charter's prime place because they have ⊥165   unity in their human sources and ⊥ functionings. Heart and mind are not identical. Intuitive faith and reasoned judgment are not the same. Spirit is not always thought. But in the everyday business of living, secular or otherwise, these variant aspects of personality find inseparable expression in a thousand ways. They cannot be altogether parted in law more than in life.

To make accommodation between these freedoms and an exercise of state authority always is delicate. It hardly could be more so than in such a clash as this case presents. On one side is the obviously earnest claim for freedom of conscience and religious practice. With it is allied the parent's claim to authority in her own household and in the rearing of her children. The parent's conflict with the state over control of the child and his training is serious enough when only secular matters are concerned. It

becomes the more so when an element of religious conviction enters. Against these sacred private interests, basic in a democracy, stand the interests of society to protect the welfare of children, and the state's assertion of authority to that end, made here in a manner conceded valid if only secular things were involved. The last is no mere corporate concern of official authority. It is the interest of youth itself, and of the whole community, that children be both safeguarded from abuses and given opportunities for growth into free and independent well-developed men and citizens. Between contrary pulls of such weight, the safest and most objective recourse is to the lines already marked out, not precisely but for guides, in narrowing the no man's land where this battle has gone on.

The rights of children to exercise their religion, and of parents to give them religious training and to encourage them in the practice of religious belief, as against preponderant sentiment and assertion of state power voicing it, have had recognition here, most recently in *West Virginia State Board of Education* v. *Barnette*. ⊥ Previously in *Pierce* v. *Society*   ⊥166 *of Sisters*, this Court had sustained the parent's authority to provide religious with secular schooling, and the child's right to receive it, as against the state's requirement of attendance at public schools. And in *Meyer* v. *Nebraska* children's rights to receive teaching in languages other than the nation's common tongue were guarded against the state's encroachment. It is cardinal with us that the custody, care and nurture of the child reside first in the parents, whose primary function and freedom include preparation for obligations the state can neither supply nor hinder. And it is in recognition of this that these decisions have respected the private realm of family life which the state cannot enter.

But the family itself is not beyond regulation in the public interest, as against a claim of religious liberty. And neither rights of religion nor rights of parenthood are beyond limitation. Acting to guard the general interest in youth's well being, the state as *parens patriae* may restrict the parent's control by requiring school attendance, regulating or prohibiting the child's labor and in many other ways. Its authority is not nullified merely because the parent grounds his claim to control the child's course of conduct on religion or conscience. Thus, he cannot claim freedom from compulsory vaccination for the child more than for himself on religious grounds. The right to practice religion freely does not include liberty to expose the community or the child ⊥ to   ⊥167 communicable disease or the latter to ill health or death. The catalogue need not be lengthened. It is sufficient to show what indeed appellant hardly disputes, that the state has a wide range of power for limiting parental freedom and authority in things affecting the child's welfare; and that this includes, to some extent, matters of conscience and religious conviction.

But it is said the state cannot do so here. This, first, because when state action impinges upon a claimed religious freedom, it must fall unless shown to be necessary for or conducive to the child's protection against some clear and present danger and, it is added, there was no such showing here. The child's presence on the street, with her guardian, distributing or offering to distribute the magazine, it is urged, was in no way harmful to her, nor in any event more so than the presence of many other children at the same time and place, engaged in shopping and other activities not prohibited. Accordingly, in view of the preferred position the freedoms of the First Article occupy, the statute in its present application must fall. It cannot be sustained by any presumption of validity. And, finally, it is said, the statute is, as to children, an absolute prohibition, not merely a reasonable regulation, of the denounced activity.

Concededly a statute or ordinance identical in terms with § 69, except that it is applicable to adults ⊥168 or all persons generally, would be invalid. ⊥ But the mere fact a state could not wholly prohibit this form of adult activity, whether characterized locally as a "sale" or otherwise, does not mean it cannot do so for children. Such a conclusion granted would mean that a state could impose no greater limitation upon child labor than upon adult labor. Or, if an adult were free to enter dance halls, saloons, and disreputable places generally, in order to discharge his conceived religious duty to admonish or dissuade persons from frequenting such places, so would be a child with similar convictions and objectives, if not alone then in the parent's company, against the state's command.

The state's authority over children's activities is broader than over like actions of adults. This is peculiarly true of public activities and in matters of employment. A democratic society rests, for its continuance, upon the healthy, well-rounded growth of young people into full maturity as citizens, with all that implies. It may secure this against impeding restraints and dangers within a broad range of selection. Among evils most appropriate for such action are the crippling effects of child employment, more especially in public places, and the possible harms arising from other activities subject to all the diverse ⊥169 influences of the street. It is too late now to doubt ⊥ that legislation appropriately designed to reach such evils is within the state's police power, whether against the parent's claim to control of the child or one that religious scruples dictate contrary action.

It is true children have rights, in common with older people, in the primary use of highways. But even in such use streets afford dangers for them not affecting adults. And in other uses, whether in work or in other things, this difference may be magnified. This is so not only when children are unaccompanied but certainly to some extent when they are with their parents. What may be wholly permissible

for adults therefore may not be so for children, either with or without their parents' presence.

Street preaching, whether oral or by handing out literature, is not the primary use of the highway, even for adults. While for them it cannot be wholly prohibited, it can be regulated within reasonable limits in accommodation to the primary and other incidental uses. But, for obvious reasons, notwithstanding appellant's contrary view, the validity of such a prohibition applied to children not accompanied by an older person hardly would seem open to question. The case reduces itself therefore to the question whether the presence of the child's guardian puts a limit to the state's power. That fact may lessen the likelihood that some evils the legislation seeks to avert will occur. But it cannot forestall all of them. The zealous though lawful exercise of the right to engage in propagandizing the community, whether in religious, political or other matters, may and at times does create situa⊥tions difficult enough for   ⊥170 adults to cope with and wholly inappropriate for children, especially of tender years, to face. Other harmful possibilities could be stated, of emotional excitement and psychological or physical injury. Parents may be free to become martyrs themselves. But it does not follow they are free, in identical circumstances, to make martyrs of their children before they have reached the age of full and legal discretion when they can make that choice for themselves. Massachusetts has determined that an absolute prohibition, though one limited to streets and public places and to the incidental uses proscribed, is necessity to accomplish its legitimate objectives. Its power to attain them is broad enough to reach these peripheral instances in which the parent's supervision may reduce but cannot eliminate entirely the ill effects of the prohibited conduct. We think that with reference to the public proclaiming of religion, upon the streets and in other similar public places, the power of the state to control the conduct of children reaches beyond the scope of its authority over adults, as is true in the case of other freedoms, and the rightful boundary of its power has not been crossed in this case.

In so ruling we dispose also of appellant's argument founded upon denial of equal protection. It falls with that based on denial of religious freedom, since in this instance the one is but another phrasing of the other. Shortly, the contention is that the street, for Jehovah's Witnesses and their children, is their church, since their conviction makes it so; and to deny them access to it for religious purposes as was done here has the same effect as excluding altar boys, youthful choristers, and other children from the edifices in which they practice their religious beliefs and worship. The argument hardly needs more than statement, after what has been said, to refute it. However Jehovah's Witnesses may conceive them, the public highways have not become their religious prop⊥erty merely by their assertion. And there is no   ⊥171 denial of equal protection in excluding their children from doing there what no other children may do.

Our ruling does not extend beyond the facts the case presents. We neither lay the foundation "for any [that is, every] state intervention in the indoctrination and participation of children in religion" which may be done "in the name of their health and welfare" nor give warrant for "every limitation on their religious training and activities." The religious training and indoctrination of children may be accomplished in many ways, some of which, as we have noted, have received constitutional protection through decisions of this Court. These and all others except the public proclaiming of religion on the streets, if this may be taken as either training or indoctrination of the proclaimer, remain unaffected by the decision.

The judgment is *Affirmed.*

Mr. Justice MURPHY, dissenting:

This attempt by the state of Massachusetts to prohibit a child from exercising her constitutional right to practice her religion on the public streets cannot, in my opinion, be sustained.

The record makes clear the basic fact that Betty Simmons, the nine-year old child in question, was engaged in a genuine religious, rather than commercial, activity. She was a member of Jehovah's Witnesses and had been taught the tenets of that sect by her guardian, the appellant. Such tenets included the duty of publicly distributing religious tracts on the street and from door to door. Pursuant to this religious duty and in the company of the appellant, Betty Simmons on the night of December 18, 1941, was standing on a public street corner and offering to distribute Jehovah's Witness literature to passers-by. There was no expectation of pecuniary profit to ⊥ herself or to appellant. It is undisputed, furthermore, that she did this of her own desire and with appellant's consent. She testified that she was motivated by her love of the Lord and that He commanded her to distribute this literature; this was, she declared, her way of worshiping God. She was occupied, in other words, in "an age-old form of missionary evangelism" with a purpose "as evangelical as the revival meeting." *Murdock* v. *Pennsylvania.*

Religious traning and activity, whether performed by adult or child, are protected by the Fourteenth Amendment against interference by state action, except insofar as they violate reasonable regulations adopted for the protection of public health, morals and welfare. Our problem here is whether a state, under the guise of enforcing its child labor laws, can lawfully prohibit girls under the age of eighteen and boys under the age of twelve from practicing their religious faith insofar as it involves the distribution or sale of religious tracts on the public streets. No question of freedom of speech or freedom of press is present and we are not called upon to determine the permissible restraints on those rights. Nor are any truancy or curfew restrictions in issue. The statutes in question prohibit all children within the specified age limits from selling or offering to sell "any newspapers, magazines, periodicals or any other articles of merchandise of any description . . . in any street or public place." Criminal sanctions are imposed on the parents and guardians who compel or permit minors in their control to engage in the prohibited transactions. The state court has construed these statutes to cover the activities here involved, thereby imposing an indirect restraint through the parents and guardians on the free exercise by minors of their religious beliefs. This indirect restraint is no less effective than a direct one. A square conflict between the con⊥stitutional guarantee of religious freedom and the state's legitimate interest in protecting the welfare of its children is thus presented.

As the opinion of the Court demonstrates, the power of the state lawfully to control the religious and other activities of children is greater than its power over similar activities of adults. But that fact is no more decisive of the issue posed by this case than is the obvious fact that the family itself is subject to reasonable regulation in the public interest. We are concerned solely with the reasonableness of this particular prohibition of religious activity by children.

In dealing with the validity of statutes which directly or indirectly infringe religious freedom and the right of parents to encourage their children in the practice of a religious belief, we are not aided by any strong presumption of the constitutionality of such legislation. On the contrary, the human freedoms enumerated in the First Amendment and carried over into the Fourteenth Amendment are to be presumed to be invulnerable and any attempt to sweep away those freedoms is prima facie invalid. It follows that any restriction or prohibition must be justified by those who deny that the freedoms have been unlawfully invaded. The burden was therefore on the state of Massachusetts to prove the reasonableness and necessity of prohibiting children from engaging in religious activity of the type involved in this case.

The burden in this instance, however, is not met by vague references to the reasonableness underlying child labor legislation in general. The great interest of the state in shielding minors from the evil vicissitudes of early life does not warrant every limitation on their religious training and activities. The reasonableness that justifies the prohibition of the ordinary distribution of literature in the public streets by children is not necessarily the rea⊥sonableness that justifies such a drastic restriction when the distribution is part of their religious faith. If the right of a child to practice its religion in that manner is to be forbidden by constitutional means, there must be convincing proof that such a practice constitutes a grave and immediate danger to the state or to the health, morals or welfare of the child. The vital freedom of religion, which is "of the very essence of a scheme of ordered liberty," *Palko* v. *Connecticut*, cannot be erased by slender references to the state's power to restrict the more secular activities of children.

The state, in my opinion, has completely failed to sustain its burden of proving the existence of any grave or immediate danger to any interest which it may lawfully protect. There is no proof that Betty Simmons' mode of worship constituted a serious menace to the public. It was carried on in an orderly, lawful manner at a public street corner. And "one who is rightfully on a street which the state has left open to the public carries with him there as elsewhere the constitutional right to express his views in an orderly fashion. This right extends to the communication of ideas by handbills and literature as well as by the spoken word." *Jamison* v. *Texas*. The sidewalk, no less than the cathedral or the evangelist's tent, is a proper place, under the Constitution, for the orderly worship of God. Such use of the streets is as necessary to the Jehovah's Witnesses, the Salvation Army and others who practice religion without benefit of conventional shelters as is the use of the streets for purposes of passage.

It is claimed, however, that such activity was likely to affect adversely the health, morals and welfare of the child. Reference is made in the majority opinion to "the crippling effects of child employment, more especially in pub⊥lic places, and the possible harms arising from other activities subject to all the diverse influences of the street." To the extent that they flow from participation in ordinary commercial activities, these harms are irrelevant to this case. And the bare possibility that such harms might emanate from distribution of religious literature is not, standing alone, sufficient justification for restricting freedom of conscience and religion. Nor can parents or guardians be subjected to criminal liability because of vague possibilities that their religious teachings might cause injury to the child. The evils must be grave, immediate, substantial. Yet there is not the slightest indication in this record, or in sources subject to judicial notice, that children engaged in distributing literature pursuant to their religious beliefs have been or are likely to be subject to any of the harmful "diverse influences of the street." Indeed, if probabilities are to be indulged in, the likelihood is that children engaged in serious religious endeavor are immune from such influences. Gambling, truancy, irregular eating and sleeping habits, and the more serious vices are not consistent with the high moral character ordinarily displayed by children fulfilling religious obligations. Moreover, Jehovah's Witness children invariably make their distributions in groups subject at all times to adult or parental control, as was done in this case. The dangers are thus exceedingly remote, to say the least. And the fact that the zealous exercise of the right to propagandize

⊥175

the community may result in violent or disorderly situations difficult for children to face is no excuse for prohibiting the exercise of that right.

No chapter in human history has been so largely written in terms of persecution and intolerance as the one dealing with religious freedom. From ancient times to the present day, the ingenuity of man has known no limits in its ability to forge weapons of oppression for use against ⊥ those who dare to express or practice unorthodox religious beliefs. And the Jehovah's Witnesses are living proof of the fact that even in this nation, conceived as it was in the ideals of freedom, the right to practice religion in unconventional ways is still far from secure. Theirs is a militant and unpopular faith, pursued with a fanatical zeal. They have suffered brutal beatings: their property has been destroyed; they have been harassed at every turn by the resurrection and enforcement of little used ordinances and statutes. To them, along with other present-day religious minorities, befalls the burden of testing our devotion to the ideals and constitutional guarantees of religious freedom. We should therefore hesitate before approving the application of a statute that might be used as another instrument of oppression. Religious freedom is too sacred a right to be restricted or prohibited in any degree without convincing proof that a legitimate interest of the state is in grave danger.

⊥176

Mr. Justice JACKSON:

The novel feature of this decision is this: the Court holds that a state may apply child labor laws to restrict or prohibit an activity of which, as recently as last term, it held: "This form of religious activity occupies the same high estate under the First Amendment as do worship in the churches and preaching from the pulpits. It has the same claim to protection as the more orthodox and conventional exercises of religion." ". . . the mere fact that the religious literature is sold by itinerant preachers rather than 'donated' does not transform evangelism into a commercial enterprise. If it did, then the passing of the collection plate in church would make the church service a commercial project. The constitutional rights of those spreading their religious beliefs through the spoken ⊥ and printed word are not to be gauged by standards governing retailers or wholesalers of books." *Murdock* v. *Pennsylvania*.

It is difficult for me to believe that going upon the streets to accost the public is the same thing for application of public law as withdrawing to a private structure for religious worship. But if worship in the churches and the activity of Jehovah's Witnesses on the streets "occupy the same high estate" and have the "same claim to protection" it would seem that child labor laws may be applied to both if to either. If the *Murdock* doctrine stands along with today's decision, a foundation is laid for any state intervention in the indoctrination and participation of chil-

⊥177

dren in religion, provided it is done in the name of their health or welfare.

This case brings to the surface the real basis of disagreement among members of this Court in previous Jehovah's Witness cases. Our basic difference seems to be as to the method of establishing limitations which of necessity bound religious freedom.

My own view may be shortly put: I think the limits begin to operate whenever activities begin to affect or collide with liberties of others or of the public. Religious activities which concern only members of the faith are and ought to be free—as nearly absolutely free as anything can be. But beyond these, many religious denominations or sects engage in collateral and secular activities intended to obtain means from unbelievers to sustain the worshippers and their leaders. They raise money, not merely by passing the plate to those who voluntarily attend services or by contributions by their own people, but by solicitations and drives addressed to the public by holding public dinners and entertainments, by various kinds ⊥ of sales and Bingo games and lotteries. All such money-raising activities on a public scale are, I think, Caesar's affairs and may be regulated by the state so long as it does not discriminate against one because he is doing them for a religious purpose, and the regulation is not arbitrary and capricious, in violation of other provisions of the Constitution.

The Court in the *Murdock* case rejected this principle of separating immune religious activities from secular ones in declaring the disabilities which the Constitution imposed on local authorities. Instead, the Court now draws a line based on age that cuts across both true exercise of religion and auxiliary secular activities. I think this is not a correct principle for defining the activities immune from regulation on grounds of religion, and *Murdock* overrules the grounds on which I think affirmance should rest. I have no alternative but to dissent from the grounds of affirmance of a judgment which I think was rightly decided, and upon right grounds, by the Supreme Judicial Court of Massachusetts.

Mr. Justice ROBERTS and *Mr. Justice FRANK-FURTER* join in this opinion.

CONSCIENTIOUS OBJECTION TO WAR

There is likely no more direct collision between the authority of government and the liberty of the individual than in the relationship of the state and the conscientious objector to war. Both legislative and judicial bodies have encountered great difficulty in seeking to reconcile the demands of national security and the preservation of individual liberty in this area. The problem is real in peacetime; it becomes acute in time of war or national emergency.[1]

Even in American colonial times, conscientious objection was a recognized problem. Quakers, Mennonites, and Brethren—have made pacifism a religious tenet—made up the great majority of such objectors. Although exceptions with regard to service in the militia were sometimes made on their behalf, colonial records are replete with instances of fines and imprisonments for refusal to bear arms.

During the American Revolution conscientious objectors suffered many inconveniences and some actual mistreatment at the hands of both individuals and government. Though there was no draft law at the time, public sentiment was such that pacifists were often considered traitors. In Pennsylvania, where the Quakers and Mennonites were most numerous, Benjamin Franklin, as a member of the Committee of Safety, interested himself the first year of the war in providing exemption from military service for the conscientious objector. The Pennsylvania Assembly responded by allowing exemption, provided an assessment of money approximating the expense and loss of time of those who served in the army was paid.

The Continental Congress in 1775 also took cognizance of the presence of conscientious objectors. That body acknowledged the position of the objectors by passing a resolution which read:

> As there are some people, who, from religious principles, cannot bear arms in any case, this Congress intend no violence to their consciences, but earnestly recommend it to them, to contribute liberally in this time of universal calamity, to the relief of their distressed brethren in the several colonies, and do all other services to their oppressed Country, which they can consistently with their religious principles.[2]

The United States Constitution as it was submitted to the states for ratification in 1787 contained no reference to the issue of conscientious objection. Three state ratifying conventions submitted proposals for amendments to exempt from military service those persons religiously opposed to bearing arms. Fear was expressed in Pennsylvania's convention that conscientious objectors might be coerced into military service. In the first Congress in 1789, James Madison proposed as part of a constitutional amendment a clause providing that "no person religiously scrupulous of bearing arms shall be compelled to render

---

[1] For an excellent discussion of the problem of conscientious objection through the World War II period, see Mulford Q. Sibley and Philip E. Jacob, *Conscription of Conscience: The American State and the Conscientious Objector, 1940-1947* (Ithaca, New York: Cornell University Press, 1952). More recent developments, with a particular emphasis on "selective" conscientious objection, are recounted in Kent Greenawalt, "All or Nothing at All: The Defeat of Selective Conscientious Objection," in Kurland, ed., *Church and State: The Supreme Court and the First Amendment*, ed. Philip B. Kurland (Chicago: University of Chicago Press, 1975), pp. 168-231

[2] *Journals of the Continental Congress, 1774-1789, May 10-September 20*, ed. Worthington C. Ford, 34 vols. (Washington: Government Printing Office, 1904-1937), vol. 2: 1775, p. 189.

military service in person."[3] The proposal was not adopted, but several state constitutions did include provisions of this type. When the first militia law was passed by Congress in 1792, there was some discussion as to the advisability of providing exemptions for conscientious objectors; a decision was finally made to leave the matter to the states.

Since there was no national conscription during the War of 1812 or the Mexican War, no special problem existed with respect to conscientious objectors in those wars, although a certain amount of pressure was brought to bear by local opinion and militia laws enacted by state legislatures. With the Civil War, however, came compulsory military service in both North and South, and conscientious objection became a live issue. The Federal Conscription Act of 1864 allowed conscientious objectors who were members of religious denominations with articles of faith that prohibited the bearing of arms to pay a substitute or to accept noncombatant duties. In the Confederacy, at least until 1864, similar provisions were made for members of certain designated pacifist denominations.

No conscription law existed during the Spanish-American War, but when the United States entered World War I, Congress again resorted to compulsory military service. The Selective Draft Act, passed on 18 May 1917, subjected all male citizens between the ages of twenty-one and thirty years of age to duty for the period of the emergency. The act exempted regularly ordained ministers and theological students from the draft. It further provided exemption from combatant duty for members of "any well-recognized religious sect or organization at present organized and existing and whose existing creed or principles forbid its members to participate in war in any form."[4]

While such conscientious objectors were thus exempted from combatant duties, no provision was made for objectors outside these recognized groups until the War Department ordered that persons with "personal scruples against war" be treated as conscientious objectors. Neither were there provisions for those who might have scruples against noncombatant service, and several hundred persons were imprisoned for refusal to undertake such service.

The constitutionality of the Draft Act was soon contested in a federal district court by a conscientious objector who was prosecuted on refusal to register. Among other contentions, he charged establishment of religion under the First Amendment where exemption was granted to members of recognized churches without similar treatment for others of like belief who were not members of a recognized pacifist church. A similar argument was made with regard to the exemptions of ministers and theological students. The district court, however, upheld the constitutionality of the Selective Draft Act, saying that the law was not one respecting an establishment of reli-

gion as contemplated in the First Amendment. (*United States* v. *Stephens* 1917)

The Supreme Court unanimously upheld the Draft Act in January 1918. Chief Justice White, speaking for the Court, brushed aside the argument that the exemption of certain religious groups constituted an establishment of religion:

> We pass without anything but statement the proposition that an establishment of a religion or an interference with the free exercise thereof repugnant to the First Amendment resulted from the exemption clauses of the act . . . because we think its unsoundness is too apparent to require us to do more (*Arver* v. *United States* [Selective Draft Law Cases], 245 U.S. 366, 389).

After the termination of World War I, conscientious objection ceased to be a pressing issue insofar as selective service was concerned. A decade later, however, the Court was confronted with the problem of the right of an individual to reserve conscientious scruples against military service in connection with the oath of allegiance prescribed for aliens applying for naturalization. The Naturalization Act of 1906 required an applicant for citizenship to declare under oath that he would "support and defend the Constitution and laws of the United States against all enemies, foreign and domestic, and bear true faith and allegiance to the same."[5]

In 1927 forty-nine-year old Madame Rosika Schwimmer, a native of Hungary and a well-known pacifist lecturer and writer, appeared before a federal district court to obtain her naturalization papers for American citizenship. One of a series of questions asked of all prospective citizens was the following: "If necessary, are you willing to take up arms in defense of this country?" This question had been inserted soon after World War I by the head of the Naturalization Service without any specific congressional authorization. Madame Schwimmer was willing to take the oath of allegiance without reservations, but in answer to the question, she stated that as an uncompromising pacifist she had no sense of nationalism and therefore would not personally take up arms, regardless of whether or not other women were compelled to do so.

Because of her refusal to answer the question affirmatively, the district court denied her application for naturalization. The circuit court reversed the district court, and the case went on certiorari to the Supreme Court, where by a six-to-three vote the Court held that her application should be denied. (UNITED STATES v. SCHWIMMER, p. 109)

Justice Butler spoke for the majority. He held that naturalized as well as native-born citizens owed the obligation of allegiance to the government. The burden was upon the applicant to prove that she had the qualifications specified in the statute. It is the duty of citizens to bear arms in defense of the country if the need should arise. Refusing to do so or holding and expressing opinions against this duty might serve to influence others to refuse to perform their obligations, and the safety of the country might be endangered. Religious scruples were not here involved because the applicant had no religion.

---

[3] *The Debates and Proceedings in the Congress of the United States: With An Appendix, Containing Important State Papers and Public Documents, and All the Laws of a Public Nature; With a Copious Index,* comp. Joseph Gales, 42 vols. (Washington: Gales & Seaton, 1834-1856), 1:451.

[4] Selective Draft Act, Ch. 15, 40 Stat. 76, 78 (1917).

[5] Act of 29 June 1906, Ch. 3592, 34 Stat. 596, 598 (1906).

Justice Holmes, joined by Justice Brandeis, filed a strong dissent. He emphasized the fact that the applicant was a woman of superior intelligence and character. Because of her sex and age she would not have been called upon to bear arms. Though he personally disagreed with Madame Schwimmer's pacifist optimism with respect to the abolition of war, Holmes made a strong plea for "freedom for the thought that we hate," and comparing her philosophy to that of the Quakers, said that he "would suggest that the Quakers have done their share to make the country what it is, that many citizens agree with the applicant's belief, and that I had not supposed hitherto that we regretted our inability to expel them because they believe more than some of us do in the teaching of the Sermon on the Mount." (279 U.S. 644, 655, [1929])

Two years later the Supreme Court again had occasion to interpret the Naturalization Act in a case which more directly involved a religious issue. Douglas C. Macintosh, Baptist professor at the Yale Divinity School and a chaplain with the Canadian Army during World War I, was denied naturalization because he refused to state in advance that he would fight in any war in which the country was involved. He qualified his answer by saying that he would take up arms only if he felt the war was morally justified; he was not willing to put allegiance to government before allegiance to the will of God.

By a five-to-four vote the Court upheld the denial of Macintosh's application. (UNITED STATES v. MACINTOSH, p. 112) Although the question again turned only on the interpretation of the naturalization statute, Justice Sutherland, in his opinion for the Court, went further than the majority opinion in *Schwimmer*. In what was in effect *obiter dictum*, he made it clear that concessions made to conscientious objectors were *privileges* conferred as a matter of grace by Congress and not constitutional rights. In dismissing the contention made by counsel for Macintosh that it was a constitutional principle that a citizen could not be forced to bear arms if he had conscientious scruples against doing so, Sutherland commented:

> This, if it means what it seems to say, is an astonishing statement. Of course, there is no such principle of the Constitution, fixed or otherwise. The conscientious objector is relieved from the obligation to bear arms in obedience to no constitutional provision, express or implied; but because, and only because, it has accorded with the policy of Congress thus to relieve him. (183 U.S. 605, 623)

Chief Justice Hughes wrote a vigorous dissent in which Justices Holmes, Brandeis, and Stone joined. He pointed out that the question here involved was not whether Congress had the right to exact a promise to bear arms as a requisite for naturalization. Rather, the issue was whether Congress had exacted such a commitment. The words used were general; he did not believe that such a demand could be implied for it was "directly opposed to the spirit of our institutions and to the historic practice of the Congress."

Although the *Schwimmer* and *Macintosh* decisions were widely criticized, they remained law for fifteen years. Their doctrine was utilized in 1934 to uphold suspension of several young men from the University of California at Los Angeles. As members of the Methodist Episcopal Church with conscientious scruples against military service, they refused to take the prescribed R.O.T.C. course in military science and tactics. (HAMILTON v. REGENTS OF THE UNIVERSITY OF CALIFORNIA, p. 118) Justice Butler denied that their suspension violated the Fourteenth Amendment as claimed: Government, federal and state, each in its own sphere owes a duty to the people within its jurisdiction to preserve itself in adequate strength to maintain peace and order and to insure the just enforcement of law. And every citizen owes the reciprocal duty, according to his capacity, to support and defend government against all enemies. (293 U.S. 245, 262) As has been observed at an earlier point (p. 4), Justice Cardozo's brief concurring opinion in *Hamilton* had great subsequent significance because there the assumption was first made that religious liberty as guaranteed in the First Amendment against the national government was protected by the Fourteenth Amendment against state action as well.

In 1945 the naturalization cases were again used as precedent by the Supreme Court in *In re Summers*, when it upheld denial of admission to the state bar to a conscientious objector. Although the applicant had expressed his willingness to take an oath to uphold the Constitution of Illinois, the Committee on Character and Fitness decided that his beliefs in nonviolence and his unwillingness to serve in the state militia would prevent his taking the requisite oath.

A year after the *Summers* decision, the Court reexamined the naturalization cases and came to the conclusion in GIROUARD v. UNITED STATES (p. 121) that they no longer stated the correct rule of law. Girouard, a Seventh-day Adventist, stated in his petition for naturalization that he was entirely willing to serve in any future war in a noncombatant capacity, but that he was forbidden by his conscience to bear arms. The United States District Court in Massachusetts admitted him to citizenship, but a court of appeals reversed the action on authority of the *Schwimmer* and *Macintosh* cases.

With Justice Douglas writing the opinion, the five-man Supreme Court majority held that in the absence of express language to the contrary, it was not to be assumed that Congress had intended to make a promise to bear arms a prerequisite to naturalization. The required oath did not specifically demand that aliens promise to bear arms, and Congress had not explicitly made the answering of the question with respect to willingness to bear arms a requirement for citizenship.

The bearing of arms, Justice Douglas said, is not the only way in which our institutions may be supported and defended. He pointed to such persons as civilian workers, Quakers, and nuclear physicists as examples of those who serve in as patriotic a way as those who enter military service. Although he agreed that the authority of government to provide for its defense is unchallenged, Justice Douglas concluded that

> The struggle for religious liberty has through the centuries been an effort to accommodate the demands of the State to the conscience of the individual. The victory for freedom of thought recorded in our Bill of Rights recognizes that in the domain of conscience there is a moral power higher than the State. (328 U.S. 61, 68)

Notwithstanding Justice Douglas's broad statement, the *Girouard* decision was not based on constitutional issues, but on the interpretation of the intent of Congress in the naturalization statutes. It held only that if aliens are to be kept from American citizenship because of conscientious objection, it must be done by clear statutory enactment. The statutory ambiguity was largely removed by the Naturalization Act of 1952, which provided that a conscientious objector can take the oath and become a citizen if he can prove "by clear and convincing evidence to the satisfaction of the naturalization court that he is opposed to the bearing of arms in the Armed Forces of the United States by reason of religious training and belief." [6]

In 1940, for the first time in its history, the United States departed from its traditional policy of maintaining a peacetime army of volunteers only. The conscientious objector provision of the Selective Training and Service Act was broader than its 1917 predecessor. Rather than requiring membership in a "well-recognized" religious group, it exempted from combatant service any person "who, by reason of religious training and belief, is conscientiously opposed to participation in war in any form." [7] It also provided for assignment to "work of national importance" for those conscientiously opposed to noncombatant service.

Construction of the phrase "religious training and belief" soon presented local draft boards and ultimately federal courts with grave difficulties. The phrase received conflicting interpretations from different courts of appeal when political, philosophical, and ethical objectors contended that although their objection did not result from any formalized religious training or beliefs, it was based upon a moral conscience that was religious in nature.

In 1948, Congress amended the statute to define the term "religious training and belief" to mean "an individual's belief in a relation to a Supreme Being involving duties superior to those arising from any human relation, but [not including] essentially political, sociological, or philosophical views or a merely personal moral code." [8]

This statutory language, found in section 6(j) of the act, was interpreted by the Supreme Court in 1965 in three cases decided under the style of UNITED STATES v. SEEGER (p. 124). All three of the men involved were conscientious objectors who had been convicted in federal district courts for refusal to submit to induction after Selective Service officials had rejected their claims for exemption. None of the three had a traditional concept of God. Seeger, for example, said that he preferred to leave open the question of his belief in a Supreme Being, but that his "skepticism or disbelief in the existence of God" did "not necessarily mean lack of faith in anything whatsoever." His, he stated, was a "belief in and devotion to goodness and virtue for their own sakes, and a religious faith in a purely ethical creed."

The Second Court of Appeals had not only reversed the district court's conviction of Seeger, the appeals court held that section 6(j), insofar as it required a theistic belief, was unconstitutional as a preferment of religion to irreligion in violation of the First Amendment. Justice Clark, for a unanimous Supreme Court, avoided the constitutional question but gave an extremely broad construction to section 6(j) in upholding the right of exemption for Seeger and his fellow appellants. Congress, Clark held, had not intended to restrict the exemption for conscientious objectors only to those who believe in a traditional God. The expression "Supreme Being," rather than "God," had been employed by Congress "so as to embrace all religions" while excluding "essentially political, sociological, or philosophical views." The test of belief required by the act is "whether a given belief that is sincere and meaningful occupies a place in the life of its possessor parallel to that filled by the orthodox belief in God of one who clearly qualifies for the exemption." (380 U.S. 163, 166) The Court emphasized that each claimant had based his conscientious objection on a religious belief.

An irritated Congress responded to the Court's reading of section 6(j) by amending the governing act in 1967. The new act removed the Supreme Being clause while retaining the restrictive phrase which ruled out inclusion of "essentially political, sociological, or philosophical views, or a merely personal moral code" as "religious training and belief." [9]

In 1969 the new provision was held unconstitutional by several district judges as a violation of the Establishment Clause of the First Amendment. The leading case was *United States* v. *Sisson* heard in the U.S. District Court in Boston. Sisson, a "selective" conscientious objector to the Vietnam War, based his objection on philosophical and political grounds. Judge Wyzanski held section 6(j) unconstitutional on two counts. On the basis of the Free Exercise Clause, he held that "no statute can require combat service of a conscientious objector whose principles are either religious or akin thereto." On Establishment Clause grounds he ruled that section 6(j) "invalidly discriminates in favor of certain types of religious objectors to the prejudice of Sisson." (297 F. Supp 902, 906, D., Mass. [1969]) Judge Wyzanski summed up his complaint against the provisions concerning exemption, saying: "In short, in the Draft Act Congress unconstitutionally discriminated against atheists, agnostics, and men like Sisson who, whether they be religious or not, are motivated in their objection to the draft by profound moral convictions of their beings." (297 F. Supp. 902, 911)

The Supreme Court, for procedural reasons, refused to take the Sisson case on appeal; but the next year, in WELSH v. UNITED STATES (p.132), it did give consideration to some of the questions raised in that case. Elliott A. Welsh II, a Los Angeles commodities broker, answered affirmatively the question as to whether his objection to participation in war was based on "religious training and belief." But he struck out the word "religious" and said that his beliefs had been formed by reading in the fields of history and sociology. Although he had first said that his beliefs were nonreligious, he later wrote his appeal board that his beliefs were "certainly religious in the ethical sense of the word."

---

[6] Immigration and Nationality Act, 66 Stat. 163, 258 (1952).
[7] 54 Stat. 885, 889 (1940).
[8] Selective Service Act of 1948, 62 Stat. 604, 613 (1948).

[9] Military Selective Service Act of 1967, 81 Stat. 100, 104 (1967); 50 U.S.C. App., Sec. 456(j) (1973).

Justice Black, for four members of an eight-man Court, refused to distinguish Welsh's views from those of Seeger; but to uphold the exemption claim without voiding section 6(j), he had to stretch the construction of the terminology even more than in the *Seeger* case. Black maintained that the restrictive clause did not have to be read to exclude persons with strong beliefs about the foreign and domestic affairs of the nation, nor did it deny exemption to those whose beliefs were grounded in good part "in considerations of public policy." He concluded that section 6(j) "exempts from military service all those whose consciences, spurred by deeply held moral, ethical, or religious beliefs, would give them no rest or peace if they allowed themselves to become a part of an instrument of war." (398 U.S. 333, 344)

Justice Harlan wrote a concurring opinion in which he acknowledged that he had erred in joining the majority in *Seeger* where the Court had upheld an exemption claim not based on a theistic belief. He felt that the Court had already gone too far in distorting the legislative intent of the act, and he refused to subscribe to the "lobotomy" now performed in the *Welsh* decision. Harlan would have preferred to hold the section unconstitutional as violating the establishment clause by giving a preference to the "religious" and disadvantaging those who belong to religions that do not worship a Supreme Being. However, he accepted Justice Black's "test" as merely a "patchwork of judicial making" to cure the "defects of underinclusion in section 6(j)" so that local draft boards could continue to administer the law.

As the unpopular war in Vietnam continued and opposition became more vocal, it was almost inevitable that the Court would eventually have to speak to the question of "selective" conscientious objection claims. [10] It did so in 1971 in the companion cases of GILLETTE v. UNITED STATES and NEGRE v. LARSEN (p. 137). Gillette, a rock musician from Yonkers, New York, expressed his willingness to take part in a war of national defense or a peacekeeping war sponsored by the United Nations, but he refused to enter the armed forces while the country was engaged in an "unjust war" in Vietnam. He based his opposition on a "a humanistic approach to religion." Negre, a gardener from California who was already in the Army, said that as a devout Roman Catholic he had a religious duty to distinguish "just" and "unjust" wars and to refuse to participate in such an "unjust" war as that in which Americans were involved in Vietnam. He therefore sought a discharge from the Army.

Justice Marshall, writing for himself and seven other members of the Court, upheld the power of Congress to rule out "selective" conscientious objection by granting exemptions only to those persons "conscientiously opposed to participation in war in any form." He denied that the statutory requirement of opposition to *all* wars to justify exemption results in discrimination among religions in violation of the First Amendment. He stated further that restricting exemptions to those opposed to participation in all wars serves to minimize the entanglement of government in religion. It also reduces the possibility of discrimination involved in the weighing of individual claims concerning "just" and "unjust" wars. He found the purposes of section 6(j) to be "neutral" and "secular," as required by the First Amendment. Finally, he noted the government's interest in procuring manpower and concluded that any "incidental burdens" imposed on particular persons were "strictly justified by substantial governmental interests that relate directly to the very impacts questioned." (401 U.S. 437, 462) Justice Douglas, in lone dissent, condemned the statute as a "a species of those which show an invidious discrimination in favor of religious persons and against others with like scruples." (401 U.S. 437, 468)

The Veteran's Readjustment Benefits Act of 1966 did not provide educational benefits for conscientious objectors who performed "alternative civilian service." [11] William Robison challenged that provision on behalf of himself and all others in a like situation as violative of both the Free Exercise Clause and the equal protection of the laws guarantee as applied to the federal government through the Due Process Clause of the Fifth Amendment. In *Johnson* v. *Robison* (1974) the Supreme Court, with only Justice Douglas dissenting, rejected both contentions.

Justice Brennan, for the majority, reasoned with respect to the Free Exercise Clause that if a conscientious objector could be imprisoned for refusal to serve in what he considered to be an unjust war, as the Court had held in *Gillette*, denial of educational benefits was only an "incidental" burden on Robison's free exercise of religion, if there was a burden at all. Speaking to the equal protection contention, he found the disruptions and disabilities caused military veterans and those who perform alternative services to be both quantitatively and qualitatively sufficiently different to constitute a rational basis for Congress' distinction as to privileges granted. Justice Douglas, in dissent, had no difficulty finding discrimination in the act and warned that "Where Government places a price on the free exercise of one's religious scruples it crosses the forbidden line." (415 U.S. 360, 390)

Later in the same year, in a *per curiam* opinion speaking principally to a very technical issue concerning the granting of injunctive relief, the Court in effect defeated an effort of the American Friends Service Committee and several of its conscientious objector employees to obtain a refund of that part of their withholding taxes used for military purposes. They contended that the withholding of taxes on salaries deprived them of their free exercise right to express their opposition on religious grounds to all wars through this form of protest. Justice Douglas was again the only dissenter. (*U.S.* v. *American Friends Service Committee*, 1974) Controversy

---

[10] Actually, in 1955, the Supreme Court had been faced with a most unusual "selective" conscientious objector case in *Sicurella* v. *United States*. There, a Jehovah's Witness had been denied exemption because of his expressed willingness to fight in a "theocratic war" on the orders of Jehovah and to justify the use of force in defending "his ministry, Kingdom interest . . . and his fellow brethren." The Court, in reversing his conviction, expressed doubt that Witness doctrine contemplated a theocratic war, and even stronger doubt that "the yardstick of Congress includes within its measure such spiritual wars between the powers of good and evil where the Jehovah's Witnesses, if they participate, will do so without carnal weapons." (345 U.S. 385, 391).

[11] Title 38 U.S.C., Sec. 1652(a) (1).

relating to the draft subsided at the conclusion of the Vietnam conflict. Interest was revived, however, when, following the Soviet invasion of Afghanistan, President Carter asked for and received approval of Congress for resumption of draft registration at age eighteen. He also sought an amendment to the Military Selective Service Act to allow registration of women. After much debate, Congress failed to amend the act or to appropriate funds to register women. On 2 July 1980, President Carter issued a proclamation ordering the registration. In *Rostker* v. *Goldberg* (1981) the Supreme Court by a vote of six-to-three upheld the registration provision against the charge that the equal protection of the law clause as applied to the federal government by the Fifth Amendment was violated by requiring registration of males only.

Although opposition to registration never reached the level of widespread indignation occasioned by the draft in earlier years, dissent existed and a considerable number of young men refused to register. Congress' response was to pass legislation in 1983 making male college students between the ages of eighteen and twenty-six who had failed to register ineligible for federal financial aid. By a vote of seven-to-two the Court upheld the constitutionality of the statute in *Selective Service System* v. *Minnesota Public Interest Research Group* (1984).

To punish those young men who failed to register, the government adopted a "passive enforcement policy" whereby only those who reported themselves in some way as having violated the law or who were reported by others were prosecuted. There was no provision for exemption on religious grounds in the draft registration requirements, and the government was undoubtedly aware that the system would result primarily in prosecutions of religious and moral objectors and of those who objected vocally to registration.

A number of cases in which the passive enforcement policy had been used were heard at the district court level; two made their way to the Supreme Court. One, *Wayte* v. *U.S.* (1985), received a full hearing, and the Court by a seven-to-two vote failed to accept Wayte's argument that he was being selectively punished for his expression of ideas in violation of the First and Fifth Amendments. The nation, reasoned Mr. Powell for the majority, has a compelling interest to ensure its safety, and the enforcement policy "placed no more limitation on speech than was necessary to ensure registration for the national defense." On the basis of the *Wayte* ruling, the case of Mark Schmucker, a Mennonite who had written a letter stating that registration would violate his religious conscience, was remanded to the Court of Appeals for the Sixth Circuit from which the case had come on certiorari for further consideration. (*U.S.* v. *Schmucker*, 1985)

In the absence of actual conscription, debate concerning exemption for conscientious objectors to war is today in abeyance. Should the nation again be forced to resort to a draft, however, both Congress and the Court can expect to be faced once more with difficult questions concerning not only the breadth of exemptions allowed but also the possibility of a constitutional *right* to conscientious objector exemptions. But because of the statutory revisions and the Court decisions of the last several decades, debate can begin at a much more advanced point than in 1917, when only members of "well-recognized" pacifist churches could claim the privilege of exemption from combatant duty.

UNITED STATES v. SCHWIMMER

279 U.S. 644
ON WRIT OF CERTIORARI TO THE UNITED STATES CIRCUIT
COURT OF APPEALS FOR THE SEVENTH CIRCUIT
Argued April 12, 1929 — Decided May 27, 1929
⊥*Mr. Justice* BUTLER delivered the opinion of   ⌐646
the court:

Respondent filed a petition for naturalization in the district court for the northern district of Illinois. The court found her unable, without mental reservation, to take the prescribed oath of allegiance and not attached to the principles of the Constitution of the United States and not well disposed to the good order and happiness of the same; and it denied her application. The circuit court of appeals reversed the decree and directed the district court to grant respondent's petition.

The Naturalization Act of June 16, 1906, requires:

"He [the applicant for naturalization] shall, before he is admitted to citizenship, declare on oath in open court . . . that he will support and defend the Constitution and laws of the United States against all enemies, foreign and domestic, and bear true faith and allegiance to the same." U.S.C. title 8, § 381.

"It shall be made to appear to the satisfaction of the court . . . that during that time [at least five years preceding the application] he has behaved as a man of good moral character, attached to the principles of the Constitution of the United States, and well disposed to the good order and happiness of the same. . . ." § 382.

Respondent was born in Hungary in 1877, and is a citizen of that country. She came to the United States in August, 1921, to visit and lecture, has resided in Illinois since the latter part of that month, declared her intention to become a citizen the following November, and filed petition for naturalization in September, 1926. On a preliminary form, she stated that she understood the prin⊥ciples of and   ⌐647
fully believed in our form of government and that she had read, and in becoming a citizen was willing to take, the oath of allegiance. Question 22 was this: "If necessary, are you willing to take up arms in defense of this country?" She answered: "I would not take up arms personally."

She testified that she did not want to remain subject to Hungary, found the United States nearest her ideals of a democratic republic, and that she could whole-heartedly take the oath of allegiance. She said: "I cannot see that a woman's refusal to take up arms is a contradiction to the oath of allegiance." For the fulfillment of the duty to support and defend the Constitution and laws, she had in mind other ways and means. She referred to her interest in civic life, to her wide reading and attendance at lectures and meetings, mentioned her knowledge of foreign languages and that she occasionally glanced through Hungarian, French, German, Dutch, Scandinavian, and Italian publications and said that she could imagine finding in meetings and publications attacks on the American form of government and she would conceive it her duty to uphold it against such attacks. She expressed steadfast opposition to any undemocratic form of government like proletariat, Fascist, white terror, or military dictatorships. "All my past work proves that I have always served democratic ideals and fought—though not with arms—against undemocratic institutions." She stated that before coming to this country she had defended American ideals and had defended America in 1924 during an international pacifist congress in Washington.

She also testified: "If . . . the United States can compel its women citizens to take up arms in the defense of the country,—something that no other civilized government has ever attempted,—I would not be able to comply with this requirement of American ⌐648 citizenship. In this ⊥ case I would recognize the right of the government to deal with me as it is dealing with its male citizens who for conscientious reasons refuse to take up arms."

The district director of naturalization by letter called her attention to a statement made by her in private correspondence: "I am an uncompromising pacifist . . . I have no sense of nationalism, only a cosmic consciousness of belonging to the human family." She answered that the statement in her petition demonstrated that she was an uncompromising pacifist. "Highly as I prize the privilege of American citizenship I could not compromise my way into it by giving an untrue answer to question 22, though for all practical purposes I might have done so, as even men of my age—I was forty-nine years old last September—are not called to take up arms. . . . That 'I have no nationalistic feeling' is evident from the fact that I wish to give up the nationality of my birth and to adopt a country which is based on principles and institutions more in harmony with my ideals. My 'cosmic consciousness of belonging to the human family' is shared by all those who believe that all human beings are the children of God."

And at the hearing she reiterated her ability and willingness to take the oath of allegiance without reservation and added: "I am willing to do everything that an American citizen has to do except fighting. If American women would be compelled to do that, I would not do that. I am an uncompromising pacifist. . . . I do not care how many other women fight, because I consider it a question of conscience. I am not willing to bear arms. In every other single way I am ready to follow the law and do everything that the law compels American citizens to do.

That is why I can take the oath of allegiance, because, as far as I can find out, there is nothing that I could be compelled to do that I cannot do. . . . With reference to spreading propaganda among the women throughout ⊥ the country about my being an uncompromising pacifist and not willing to fight, I am ⌐649 always ready to tell anyone who wants to hear it that I am an uncompromising pacifist and will not fight. In my writings and in my lectures I take up the question of war and pacifism if I am asked for that."

Except for eligibility to the Presidency, naturalized citizens stand on the same footing as do native-born citizens. All alike owe allegiance to the government, and the government owes to them the duty of protection. These are reciprocal obligations and each is a consideration for the other. But aliens can acquire such equality only by naturalization according to the uniform rules prescribed by the Congress. They have no natural right to become citizens, but only that which is by statute conferred upon them. Because of the great value of the privileges conferred by naturalization, the statutes prescribing qualifications and governing procedure for admission are to be construed with definite purpose to favor and support the government. And, in order to safeguard against admission of those who are unworthy or who for any reason fail to measure up to required standards, the law puts the burden upon every applicant to show by satisfactory evidence that he has the specified qualifications.

Every alien claiming citizenship is given the right to submit his petition and evidence in support of it. And, if the requisite facts are established, he is entitled as of right to admission. On applications for naturalization, the court's function is "to receive the testimony, to compare it with the law, and to judge on both law and fact." *Spratt* v. *Spratt*. We quite recently declared that: "Citizenship is a high privilege and when doubts exist concerning a grant of it, generally at least, ⊥ they should be resolved in favor of ⌐650 the United States and against the claimant." *United States* v. *Manzi*. And when, upon a fair consideration of the evidence adduced upon an application for citizenship, doubt remains in the mind of the court as to any essential matter of fact, the United States is entitled to the benefit of such doubt and the application should be denied.

That it is the duty of citizens by force of arms to defend our government against all enemies whenever necessity arises is a fundamental principle of the Constitution.

The common defense was one of the purposes for which the people ordained and established the Constitution. It empowers Congress to provide for such defense, to declare war, to raise and support armies, to maintain a navy, to make rules for the government and regulation of the land and naval forces, to provide for organizing, arming and disciplining the militia, and for calling it forth to execute the laws of the Union, suppress insurrections and repel invasions; it makes the President commander in chief of the army and navy and of the militia of the several states when called into the service of the United States; it declares that, a well-regulated militia being necessary to the security of a free state, the right of the people to keep and bear arms shall not be infringed. We need not refer to the numerous statutes that contemplate defense of the United States, its Constitution, and laws by armed citizens. This court, in the Selective Draft Law Cases speaking through *Chief Justice WHITE*, said that "the very conception of a just government and its duty to the citizen includes the reciprocal obligation of the citizen to render military service in case of need. . . ."

Whatever tends to lessen the willingness of citizens to discharge their duty to bear arms in the country's defense detracts from the strength and ⌐651 safety of the government. ⊥ And their opinions and beliefs as well as their behavior indicating a disposition to hinder in the performance of that duty are subjects of inquiry under the statutory provisions governing naturalization and are of vital importance, for if all or a large number of citizens oppose such defense the "good order and happiness" of the United States cannot long endure. And it is evident that the views of applicants for naturalization in respect of such matters may not be disregarded. The influence of conscientious objectors against the use of military force in defense of the principles of our government is apt to be more detrimental than their mere refusal to bear arms. The fact that, by reason of sex, age or other cause, they may be unfit to serve, does not lessen their purpose or power to influence others. It is clear from her own statements that the declared opinions of respondent as to armed defense by citizens against enemies of the country were directly pertinent to the investigation of her application. . . .

⌐652 The fact that she is an uncompromising pacifist with no sense of nation⊥alism but only a cosmic sense of belonging to the human family justifies belief that she may be opposed to the use of military force as contemplated by our Constitution and laws. And her testimony clearly suggests that she is disposed to exert her power to influence others to such opposition.

A pacifist in the general sense of the word is one who seeks to maintain peace and to abolish war. Such purposes are in harmony with the Constitution and policy of our government. But the word is also used and understood to mean one who refuses or is unwilling for any purpose to bear arms because of conscientious considerations and who is disposed to encourage others in such refusal. And one who is without any sense of nationalism is not well bound or held by the ties of affection to any nation or government. Such persons are liable to be incapable of the attachment for and devotion to the principles of

our Constitution that are required of aliens seeking naturalization.

It is shown by official records and everywhere well known that during the recent war there were found among those who described themselves as pacifists and conscientious objectors many citizens—though happily a minute part of all—who were unwilling to bear arms in that crisis and who refused to obey the laws of the United States and the lawful commands of its officers and encouraged such disobedience in others. Local boards found it necessary to issue a great number of noncombatant certificates, and several thousand who were called to camp made claim because of conscience for exemption from any form of military service. Several hundred were convicted and sentenced to imprisonment for offenses involving disobedience, desertion, propaganda and sedition. It is obvious that the acts of such offenders evidence a want of that attachment to the principles of the Constitution of which ⊥ the applicant is re- ⌐653 quired to give affirmative evidence by the Naturalization Act.

The language used by respondent to describe her attitude in respect of the principles of the Constitution was vague and ambiguous; the burden was upon her to show what she meant and that her pacifism and lack of nationalistic sense did not oppose the principle that it is a duty of citizenship by force of arms when necessary to defend the country against all enemies, and that her opinions and beliefs would not prevent or impair the true faith and allegiance required by the act. She failed to do so. The district court was bound by the law to deny her application.

The decree of the Circuit Court of Appeals is reversed.

The decree of the District Court is affirmed.

Mr. Justice HOLMES, dissenting:

The applicant seems to be a woman of superior character and intelligence, obviously more than ordinarily desirable as a citizen of the United States. It is agreed that she is qualified for citizenship except so far as the views set forth in a statement of facts "may show that the applicant is not attached to the principles of the Constitution of the United States and well disposed to the good order and happiness of the same, and except in so far as the same may show that she cannot take the oath of allegiance without a mental reservation." The views referred to are an extreme opinion in favor of pacifism and a statement that she would not bear arms to defend the Constitution. So far as the adequacy of her oath is concerned, I hardly can see how that is affected by the statement, inasmuch as she is a woman over fifty years of age, and would not be allowed to bear arms if she wanted ⊥ to. And as to the opinion the whole ex- ⌐654 amination of the applicant shows that she holds none of the now-dreaded creeds, but thoroughly believes in organized government and prefers that of the United States to any other in the world. Surely it cannot show lack of attachment to the principles of the Constitution that she thinks that it can be improved. I suppose that most intelligent people think that it might be. Her particular improvement looking to the abolition of war seems to me not materially different in its bearing on this case from a wish to establish cabinet government as in England, or a single house, or one term of seven years for the President. To touch a more burning question, only a judge mad with partisanship would exclude because the applicant thought that the 18th Amendment should be repealed.

Of course, the fear is that if a war came the applicant would exert activities such as were dealt with in *Schenck* v. *United States*. But that seems to me unfounded. Her position and motives are wholly different from those of *Schenck*. She is an optimist and states in strong and, I do not doubt, sincere words her belief that war will disappear and that the impending destiny of mankind is to unite in peaceful leagues. I do not share that optimism nor do I think that a philosophic view of the world would regard war as absurd. But most people who have known it regard it with horror, as a last resort, and, even if not yet ready for cosmopolitan efforts, would welcome any practicable combinations that would increase the power on the side of peace. The notion that the applicant's optimistic anticipations would make her a worse citizen is sufficiently answered by her examination, which seems to me a better argument for her admission than any that I can offer. Some of her answers might excite popular prejudice, but if there is any principle of the Constitution that more imperatively calls for attachment than any oth- ⊥ er it is the principle of free ⊥ thought—not free thought for those who agree with us but freedom for the thought that we hate. I think that we should adhere to that principle with regard to admission into, as well as to life within, this country. And, recurring to the opinion that bars this applicant's way, I would suggest that the Quakers have done their share to make the country what it is, that many citizens agree with the applicant's belief, and that I had not supposed hitherto that we regretted our inability to expel them because they believe more than some of us do in the teachings of the Sermon on the Mount.

⊥655

Mr. Justice BRANDEIS concurs in this opinion.

Mr. Justice SANFORD, dissenting:

I agree, in substance, with the views expressed by the Circuit Court of Appeals, and think its decree should be affirmed.

UNITED STATES v. MACINTOSH

283 U.S. 605
ON WRIT OF CERTIORARI TO THE UNITED STATES CIRCUIT
COURT OF APPEALS FOR THE SECOND CIRCUIT
Argued April 27, 1931 — Decided May 25, 1931
⊥ *Mr. Justice SUTHERLAND* delivered the opinion of the court: ⊥613

The respondent was born in the Dominion of Canada. He came to the United States in 1916, and in 1925 declared his intention to become a citizen. His petition for naturalization was presented to the federal district court for Connecticut, and that court, after hearing and consideration, denied the application upon the ground that, since petitioner would not promise in advance to bear arms in defense of the United States unless he believed the war to be morally justified, he was not attached to the principles of the Constitution. The circuit court of appeals reversed the decree and directed the district court to admit respondent to citizenship. . . .

⊥ Naturalization is a privilege, to be given, quali-   ⊥614
fied or withheld as Congress may determine, and which the alien may claim as of right only upon compliance with the terms which Congress imposes. That Congress regarded the admission to citizenship as a serious matter is apparent from the conditions and precautions with which it carefully surrounded the subject. . . .

⊥ Why does the statute require examination of the   ⊥616
applicant and witnesses in open court and under oath, and for what purpose is the government authorized to cross-examine concerning any matter *touching* or in any way *affecting* the right of naturalization? Clearly, it would seem, in order that the court and the government, whose power and duty in that respect these provisions take for granted, may discover whether the applicant is fitted for citizenship;—and to that end, by actual inquiry, ascertain, among other things, whether he has intelligence and good character; whether his oath to support and defend the Constitution and laws of the United States, and to bear true faith and allegiance to the same, will be taken without mental reservation or purpose inconsistent therewith; whether his views are compatible with the obligations and duties of American citizenship; whether he will upon his own part observe the laws of the land; whether he is willing to support the government in time of war, as well as in time of peace, and to assist in the defense of the country, not to the extent or in the manner that he may choose, but to such extent and in such manner as he lawfully may be required to do. These, at least, are matters which are of the essence of the statutory requirements, and in respect of which the mind and conscience of the applicant ⊥ may be probed by per-   ⊥617

tinent inquiries, as fully as the court, in the exercise of a sound discretion, may conclude is necessary. . . .

The applicant had complied with all the formal requirements of the law, and his personal character and conduct were shown to be good in all respects. His right to naturalization turns altogether upon the effect to be given to certain answers and qualifying statements made in response to interrogatories propounded to him.

Upon the preliminary form for petition for naturalization, the following questions, among others, appear: "20. Have you read the following oath of allegiance? [which is then quoted]. Are you willing to take this oath in becoming a citizen?" "22. If necessary, are you willing to take up arms in defense of this country?" In response to the questions designated 20, he answered "Yes." In response to the question designated 22, he answered, "Yes; but I ⌐618 should want to be free to judge of the neces⊥sity." By a written memorandum subsequently filed, he amplified these answers as follows:

"20 and 22. I am willing to do what I judge to be in the best interests of my country, but only in so far as I can believe that this is not going to be against the best interests of humanity in the long run. I do not undertake to support 'my country, right or wrong' in any dispute which may arise, and I am not willing to promise beforehand, and without knowing the cause for which my country may go to war, either that I will or that I will not 'take up arms in defense of this country,' however 'necessary' the war may seem to be to the government of the day.

It is only in a sense consistent with these statements that I am willing to promise to 'support and defend' the government of the United States 'against all enemies, foreign and domestic.' But, just because I am not certain that the language of questions 20 and 22 will bear the construction I should have to put upon it in order to be able to answer them in the affirmative, I have to say that I do not know that I can say 'Yes' in answer to these two questions."

Upon the hearing before the district court on the petition, he explained his position more in detail. He said that he was not a pacifist; that if allowed to interpret the oath for himself he would interpret it as not inconsistent with his position and would take it. He then proceeded to say that he would answer question 22 in the affirmative only on the understanding that he would have to believe that the war was morally justified before he would take up arms in it or give it his moral support. He was ready to give to the United States all the allegiance he ever had given or ever could give to any country, but he could not put allegiance to the government of any country before allegiance to the will of God. He did not anticipate engaging in any propaganda against the prosecution ⌐619 of a war which the ⊥ government had already declared and which it considered to be justified; but he

preferred not to make any absolute promise at the time of the hearing, because of his ignorance of all the circumstances which might affect his judgment with reference to such a war. He did not question that the government under certain conditions could regulate and restrain the conduct of the individual citizen, even to the extent of imprisonment. He recognized the principle of the submission of the individual citizen to the opinion of the majority in a democratic country; but he did not believe in having his own moral problems solved for him by the majority. The position thus taken was the only one he could take consistently with his moral principles and with what he understood to be the moral principles of Christianity. He recognized, in short, the right of the government to restrain the freedom of the individual for the good of the social whole; but was convinced, on the other hand, that the individual citizen should have the right respectfully to withhold from the government military services (involving, as they probably would, the taking of human life), when his best moral judgment would compel him to do so. He was willing to support his country, even to the extent of bearing arms, if asked to do so by the government, in any war which he could regard as morally justified.

There is more to the same effect, but the foregoing is sufficient to make plain his position.

These statements of the applicant fairly disclose that he is unwilling to take the oath of allegiance, except with these important qualifications: That he will do what he judges to be in the best interests of the country only in so far as he believes it will not be against the best interests of humanity in the long run; that he will not assist in the defense of the country by force of arms or give any war his moral support unless he believes it to be morally justified, however necessary the war might ⊥ seem to the gov- ⌐620 ernment of the day; that he will hold himself free to judge of the morality and necessity of the war, and, while he does not anticipate engaging in propaganda against the prosecution of a war declared and considered justified by the government, he prefers to make no promise even as to that; and that he is convinced that the individual citizen should have the right to withhold his military services when his best moral judgment impels him to do so. . . .

⊥ There are few finer or more exalted sentiments ⌐621 than that which finds expression in opposition to war. Peace is a sweet and holy thing, and war is a hateful and an abominable thing to be avoided by any sacrifice or concession that a free people can make. But thus far mankind has been unable to devise any method of indefinitely prolonging the one or of entirely abolishing the other; and, unfortunately, there is nothing which seems to afford ⊥ positive ⌐622 ground for thinking that the near future will witness the beginning of the reign of perpetual peace for which good men and women everywhere never cease to pray. The Constitution, therefore, wisely contemplating the ever present possibility of war, declares that one of its purposes is to "provide for the common defense." In express terms Congress is empowered "to declare war," which necessarily connotes the plenary power to wage war with all the force necessary to make it effective; and "to raise . . . armies," which necessarily connotes the like power to say who shall serve in them and in what way.

From its very nature the war power, when necessity calls for its exercise, tolerates no qualifications or limitations, unless found in the Constitution or in applicable principles of international law. In the words of John Quincy Adams,— "This power is tremendous; it is strictly constitutional; but it breaks down every barrier so anxiously erected for the protection of liberty, property and of life."

To the end that war may not result in defeat, freedom of speech may, by act of Congress, be curtailed or denied so that the morale of the people and the spirit of the army may not be broken by seditious utterances; freedom of the press curtailed to preserve our military plans and movements from the knowledge of the enemy; deserters and spies put to death without indictment or trial by jury; ships and supplies requisitioned; property of alien enemies, theretofore under the protection of the Constitution, seized without process and converted to the public use without compensation and without due process of law in the ordinary sense of that term; prices of food and other necessities of life fixed or regulated; railways taken over and operated by the government; and other drastic powers, wholly inadmissible in time of peace, exercised to meet the emergencies of war.

⌐623   ⊥ These are but illustrations of the breadth of the power; and it necessarily results from their consideration that whether any citizen shall be exempt from serving in the armed forces of the nation in time of war is dependent upon the will of Congress and not upon the scruples of the individual, except as Congress provides. That body, thus far, has seen fit, by express enactment, to relieve from the obligation of armed service those persons who belong to the class known as conscientious objectors; and this policy is of such long standing that it is thought by some to be beyond the possibility of alteration. Indeed, it seems to be assumed in this case that the privilege is one that Congress itself is powerless to take away. Thus it is said in the carefully prepared brief of respondent:

"To demand from an alien who desires to be naturalized an unqualified promise to bear arms in every war that may be declared, despite that fact that he may have conscientious religious scruples against doing so in some hypothetical future war, would mean that such an alien would come into our citizenry on an unequal footing with the native born, and

that he would be forced, as the price of citizenship, to forego a privilege enjoyed by others. That is the manifest result of the fixed principle of our Constitution, zealously guarded by our laws, that a citizen cannot be forced and need not bear arms in a war if he has conscientious religious scruples against doing so."

This, if it means what it seems to say, is an astonishing statement. Of course, there is no such principle of the Constitution, fixed or otherwise. The conscientious objector is relieved from the obligation to bear arms in obedience to no constitutional provision, express or implied; but because, and only because, it has accorded with the policy of Congress thus to relieve him. . . . ⊥ The privilege of the   ⌐624 native-born conscientious objector to avoid bearing arms comes not from the Constitution, but from the acts of Congress. That body may grant or withhold the exemption as in its wisdom it sees fit; and if it be withheld, the native-born conscientious objector cannot successfully assert the privilege. No other conclusion is compatible with the well-nigh limitless extent of the war powers as above illustrated, which include, by necessary implication, the power, in the last extremity, to compel the armed service of any citizen in the land, without regard to his objections or his views in respect of the justice or morality of the particular war or of war in general. In *Jacobson* v. *Massachusetts* this court, speaking of the liberties guaranteed to the individual by the 14th Amendment, said:

". . . and yet he may be compelled, by force if need be, against his will and without regard to his personal wishes or his pecuniary interests, or even his religious or political convictions, to take his place in the ranks of the army of his country and risk the chance of being shot down in its defense."

The applicant for naturalization here is unwilling to become a citizen with this understanding. He is unwilling to leave the question of his future military service to the wisdom of Congress where it belongs, and where every native-born or admitted citizen is obliged to leave it. In effect, he offers to take the oath of allegiance only with the qualification that the question whether the war is necessarily or morally justified must, so far as his support is concerned, be conclusively determined by reference to his opinion.

When he speaks of putting his allegiance to the will of God above his allegiance to the government, it is evident, in the light of his entire statement, that he means to make *his own interpretation* of the will of God the decisive test which shall conclude the government and stay its hand. We are a Christian people according to one another the equal right of religious freedom, and acknowledging with reverence the duty of obedience to the will of God. But, also, we are a nation with the duty to survive; a nation whose Constitution contemplates war as well as peace; whose government must go forward upon the assumption, and safely can proceed upon no other, that unqualified allegiance to the nation and submission and obedience to the laws of the land, as well those made for war as those made for peace, are not inconsistent with the will of God.

The applicant here rejects that view. He is unwilling to rely, as every native-born citizen is obliged to do, upon the probable continuance by Congress of the long established and approved practice of exempting the honest conscientious objector, while at the same time asserting his willingness to conform to whatever the future law constitutionally shall require of him; but discloses a present and fixed purpose to refuse to give his moral or armed support to any future war in which the country may be actually engaged, if, in his opinion, the war is not morally justified, the opinion of the nation as expressed by Congress to the contrary notwithstanding.

If the attitude of this claimant, as shown by his statements and the inferences properly to be deduced from them, be held immaterial to the question of his fitness for admission to citizenship, where shall the line be drawn? Upon what ground of distinction may we hereafter reject another applicant who shall express his willingness to re⊥spect any particular principle of the Constitution or obey any future statute only upon the condition that he shall entertain the opinion that it is morally justified? The applicant's attitude, in effect, is a refusal to take the oath of allegiance except in an altered form. The qualifications upon which he insists, it is true, are made by parol and not by the way of written amendment to the oath; but the subs favor of the United States and against the claimant."

The Naturalization Act is to be construed "with definite purpose to favor and support the government," and the United States is entitled to the benefit of any doubt which remains in the mind of the court as to any essential matter of fact. The burden was upon the applicant to show that his views were not opposed to "the principle that it is a duty of citizenship, by force of arms when necessary, to defend the country against all enemies, and that [his] opinions and beliefs would not prevent or impair the true faith and allegiance required by the act." *United States* v. *Schwimmer*. We are of opinion that he did not meet this requirement. The examiner and the court of first instance who heard and weighed the evidence and saw the applicant and witnesses so concluded. That conclusion, if we were in ⊥ doubt, would not be rejected except for good and persuasive reasons, which we are unable to find.

The decree of the Circuit Court of Appeals is reversed and that of the District Court is *affirmed.*

Mr. Chief Justice HUGHES dissenting:

I am unable to agree with the judgment in this case. It is important to note the precise question to be determined. It is solely one of law, as there is no controversy as to the facts. The question is not whether naturalization is a privilege to be granted or withheld. That it is such a privilege is undisputed. Nor, whether the Congress has the power to fix the conditions upon which the privilege is granted. That power is assumed. Nor, whether the Congress may in its discretion compel service in the army in time of war or punish the refusal to serve. That power is not here in dispute. Nor is the question one of the authority of Congress to exact a promise to bear arms as a condition of its grant of naturalization. That authority, for the present purpose, may also be assumed.

The question before the court is the narrower one whether the Congress has exacted such a promise. That the Congress has not made such an express requirement is apparent. The question is whether that exaction is to be implied from certain general words which do not, as it seems to me, either literally or historically, demand the implication. I think that the requirement should not be implied, because such a construction is directly opposed to the spirit of our institutions and to the historic practice of the Congress. It must be conceded that departmental zeal may not be permitted to outrun the authority conferred by statute. If such a promise is to be demanded, contrary to principles which have been respected as fundamental, the Congress should exact it in unequivocal ⊥ terms, and we should not, by judicial decision, attempt to perform what, as I see it, is a legislative function.

In examining the requirements for naturalization, we find that the Congress has expressly laid down certain rules which concern the opinions and conduct of the applicant. Thus it is provided that no person shall be naturalized "who disbelieves in or who is opposed to organized government, or who is a member of or affiliated with any organization entertaining and teaching such disbelief in or opposition to organized government, or who advocates or teaches the duty, necessity, or propriety of the unlawful assaulting or killing of any officer or officers, either of specific individuals or of officers generally, of the government of the United States, or of any other organized government, because of his or their official character, or who is a polygamist." Act of June 29, 1906. The respondent, Douglas Clyde Macintosh, entertained none of these disqualifying opinions and had none of the associations or relations disapproved. Among the specific requirements as to beliefs, we find none to the effect that one shall not be naturalized if by reason of his religious convictions he is opposed to war or is unwilling to promise to bear arms. In view of the questions which have repeatedly been brought to the attention of the Congress in relation to such beliefs, and having regard to the action of the Congress when its decision was of immediate importance in the raising of armies, the omission of such an express requirement from the naturalization statute is highly significant.

Putting aside these specific requirements as fully satisfied, we come to the general conditions imposed by the statute. We find one as to good behavior during the specified period of residence preceding application. No applicant could appear to be more exemplary than Macintosh. A Canadian by birth, he |629 first came to the United ⊥ States as a graduate student at the University of Chicago, and in 1907 he was ordained as a Baptist minister. In 1909 he began to teach in Yale University and is now a member of the faculty of the Divinity School, Chaplain of the Yale Graduate School, and Dwight Professor of Theology. After the outbreak of the Great War, he voluntarily sought appointment as a chaplain with the Canadian Army and as such saw service at the front. Returning to this country, he made public addresses in 1917 in support of the Allies. In 1918, he went again to France where he had charge of an American Y.M.C.A. hut at the front until the armistice, when he resumed his duties at Yale University. It seems to me that the applicant has shown himself in his behavior and character to be highly desirable as a citizen and, if such a man is to be excluded from naturalization, I think the disqualification should be found in unambiguous terms and not in an implication which shuts him out and gives admission to a host far less worthy.

The principal ground for exclusion appears to relate to the terms of the oath which the applicant must take. It should be observed that the respondent was willing to take the oath, and he so stated in his petition. But, in response to further inquiries, he explained that he was not willing "to promise beforehand" to take up arms, "without knowing the cause for which my country may go to war" and that "he would have to believe that the war was morally justified." He declared that "his first allegiance was to the will of God;" that he was ready to give to the United States "all the allegiance he ever had given or ever could give to any country, but that he could not put allegiance to the government of any country before allegiance to the will of God." The question then is whether the terms of the oath are to be taken as necessarily implying an assurance of willingness to bear arms, so that one whose conscientious convic- |630 tions or belief of the su ⊥ preme allegiance to the will of God will not permit him to make such an absolute promise, cannot take the oath and hence is disqualified for admission to citizenship.

The statutory provision as to the oath which is said to require this promise is this: "That he will support and defend the Constitution and laws of the United States against all enemies, foreign and domestic, and bear true faith and allegiance to the same." Act of June 29, 1906. That these general words have not been regarded as implying a promise to bear arms notwithstanding religious or conscientious scruples, or as requiring one to promise to put

allegiance to temporal power above what is sincerely believed to be one's duty of obedience to God, is apparent, I think, from a consideration of their history. This oath does not stand alone. It is the same oath in substance that is required by act of Congress of civil officers generally (except the President, whose oath is prescribed by the Constitution). The Congress, in prescribing such an oath for civil officers, acts under Article 6, § 3, of the Constitution, which provides: "The Senators and Representatives before mentioned, and the Members of the Several Legislatures, and all executive and judicial Officers, both of the United States and of the several States, shall be bound by Oath or Affirmation, to support this Constitution; but no religious test shall ever be required as a Qualification to any Office or public Trust under the United States." The general oath of office, in the form which has been prescribed by the Congress for over sixty years, contains the provision "that I will support and defend the Constitution of the United States against all enemies, foreign and domestic; that I will bear true faith and allegiance to the same; that I take this obligation freely, without any mental reservation or purpose of evasion." (Rev. Stat. § 1757, U.S.C. title 5, § 16.) It goes without ⊥ |631 saying that it was not the intention of the Congress in framing the oath to impose any religious test. When we consider the history of the struggle for religious liberty, the large number of citizens of our country from the very beginning, who have been unwilling to sacrifice their religious convictions, and in particular, those who have been conscientiously opposed to war and who would not yield what they sincerely believed to be their allegiance to the will of God, I find it impossible to conclude that such persons are to be deemed disqualified for public office in this country because of the requirement of the oath which must be taken before they enter upon their duties. The terms of the promise "to support and defend the Constitution of the United States against all enemies, foreign and domestic," are not, I think, to be read as demanding any such result. There are other and most important methods of defense, even in time of war, apart from the personal bearing of arms. We have but to consider the defense given to our country in the late war, both in industry and in the field, by workers of all sorts, by engineers, nurses, doctors and chaplains, to realize that there is opportunity even at such a time for essential service in the activities of defense which do not require the overriding of such religious scruples. I think that the requirement of the oath of office should be read in the light of our regard from the beginning for freedom of conscience. While it has always been recognized that the supreme power of government may be exerted and disobedience to its commands may be punished, we know that with many of our worthy citizens it would be a most heart-searching question if they were asked whether they would promise to obey a law believed to be in conflict with religious duty. Many of their most honored exemplars in the past have been willing to suffer imprisonment or even death rather than to make such a promise. And we also know, in particular, that a promise to engage |632 in ⊥ war by bearing arms, or thus to engage in a war believed to be unjust, would be contrary to the tenets of religious groups among our citizens who are of patriotic purpose and exemplary conduct. To conclude that the general oath of office is to be interpreted as disregarding the religious scruples of these citizens and as disqualifying them for office because they could not take the oath with such an interpretation would, I believe, be generally regarded as contrary not only to the specific intent of the Congress but as repugnant to the fundamental principle of representative government.

But the naturalization oath is in substantially the same terms as the oath of office to which I have referred. I find no ground for saying that these words are to be interpreted differently in the two cases. On the contrary, when the Congress reproduced the historic words of the oath of office in the naturalization oath, I should suppose that, according to familiar rules of interpretation, they should be deemed to carry the same significance.

The question of the proper interpretation of the oath is, as I have said, distinct from that of legislative policy in exacting military service. The latter is not dependent upon the former. But the long-established practice of excusing from military service those whose religious convictions oppose it confirms the view that the Congress in the terms of the oath did not intend to require a promise to give such service. The policy of granting exemptions in such cases has been followed from colonial times and is abundantly shown by the provisions of colonial and state statutes, of state constitutions, and of acts of Congress. . . .

|633 ⊥ Much has been said of the paramount duty to the state, a duty to be recognized, it is urged, even though it conflicts with convictions of duty to God. Undoubtedly that duty to the state exists within the domain of power, for government may enforce obedience to laws regardless of scruples. When one's belief collides with the power of the state, the latter is supreme within its sphere and submission or punishment follows. But, in the forum of conscience, duty to a moral power higher than the state has always been maintained. The reservation of that supreme obligation, as a matter of principle, would unquestionably be made by many of our conscientious and law-abiding citizens. The essence of religion is belief in a relation to God involving duties superior to |634 those ⊥ arising from any human relation. As was stated by Mr. Justice Field, in *Davis* v. *Beason*: "The term 'religion' has reference to one's views of his relations to his Creator, and to the obligations they impose of reverence for his being and character, and of obedience to his will." One cannot speak of

religious liberty, with proper appreciation of its essential and historic significance, without assuming the existence of a belief in supreme allegiance to the will of God. Professor Macintosh, when pressed by the inquiries put to him, stated what is axiomatic in religious doctrine. And, putting aside dogmas with their particular conceptions of deity, freedom of conscience itself implies respect for an innate conviction of paramount duty. The battle for religious liberty has been fought and won with respect to religious beliefs and practices, which are not in conflict with good order, upon the very ground of the supremacy of conscience within its proper field. What that field is, under our system of government, presents in part a question of constitutional law and also, in part, one of legislative policy in avoiding unnecessary clashes with the dictates of conscience. There is abundant room for enforcing the requisite authority of law as it is enacted and requires obedience, and for maintaining the conception of the supremacy of law as essential to orderly government without demanding that either citizens or applicants for citizenship shall assume by oath an obligation to regard allegiance to God as subordinate to allegiance to civil power. The attempt to exact such a promise, and thus to bind one's conscience by the taking of oaths or the submission to tests, has been the cause of many deplorable conflicts. The Congress has sought to avoid such conflicts in this country by respecting our happy tradition. In no sphere of legislation has the intention to prevent such clashes been more conspicuous than in relation to the bearing of arms. It would require strong evidence ⊥ that the Congress |635 intended a reversal of its policy in prescribing the general terms of the naturalization oath. I find no such evidence.

Nor is there ground, in my opinion, for the exclusion of Professor Macintosh because his conscientious scruples have particular reference to wars believed to be unjust. There is nothing new in such an attitude. Among the most eminent statesmen here and abroad have been those who condemned the action of their country in entering into wars they thought to be unjustified. Agreements for the renunciation of war presuppose a preponderant public sentiment against wars of aggression. If, while recognizing the power of Congress, the mere holding of religious or conscientious scruples against all wars should not disqualify a citizen from holding office in this country, or an applicant otherwise qualified from being admitted to citizenship, there would seem to be no reason why a reservation of religious or conscientious objection to participation in wars believed to be unjust should constitute such a disqualification.

Apart from the terms of the oath, it is said that the respondent has failed to meet the requirement of "attachment to the principles of the Constitution." Here, again, is a general phrase which should be construed, not in opposition to, but in accord with, the theory and practice of our government in relation to freedom of conscience. What I have said as to the provisions of the oath I think applies equally to this phase of the case.

The judgment in *United States* v. *Schwimmer* stands upon the special facts of that case, but I do not regard it as requiring a reversal of the judgment here. I think that the judgment below should be affirmed.

Mr. Justice HOLMES, Mr. Justice BRANDEIS and *Mr. Justice STONE* concur in this opinion.

HAMILTON v. REGENTS OF THE UNIVERSITY OF CALIFORNIA

293 U.S. 245
ON APPEAL FROM THE SUPREME COURT OF
THE STATE OF CALIFORNIA
Argued October 17 and 18, 1934 — Decided
December 3, 1934

⌐250 ⊥ *Mr. Justice BUTLER* delivered the opinion of the Court.

This is an appeal under § 237 (a), Judicial Code, U.S.C. title 28, § 344 (a), from a judgment of the highest court of California sustaining a state law that requires students at its university to take a course in military science and tactics the validity of which was by the appellants challenged as repugnant to the Constitution and laws of the United States.

The appellants are the above named minors and the fathers of each as his guardian *ad litem* and individually. They are taxpayers and citizens of the United States and of California. Appellees are the regents constituting a corporation created by the State to administer the university, its president and its provost. Appellants applied to the state supreme court for a writ of mandate compelling appellees to admit the minors into the university as students. So far as they are material to the questions presented here, the allegations of the petition are:

In October, 1933, each of these minors registered, became a student in the university and fully conformed to all its requirements other than that compelling him to take the course in military science and tactics in the Reserve Officers Training Corps which they assert to be an integral part of the military establishment of the United States and not connected in any way with the militia or military establishment of the State. The primary object of there establishing units of the training corps is to qualify students for ⌐251 appointment in the Officers Reserve ⊥ Corps. The courses in military training are those prescribed by the War Department. The regents require enrollment and participation of able-bodied male students who are citizens of the United States. These courses include instruction in rifle marksmanship, scouting and patrolling, drill and command, musketry, combat principles, and use of automatic rifles. Arms, equipment and uniforms for use of students in such courses are furnished by the War Department of the United States government.

These minors are members of the Methodist Episcopal Church and of the Epworth League and connected religious societies and organizations. For many years their fathers have been ordained ministers of that church. The Southern California Conference at its 1931 session adopted a resolution:

"With full appreciation of the heroic sacrifices of all those who have conscientiously and unselfishly served their country in times of war, but with the belief that the time has come in the unfolding light of the new day for the settlement of human conflicts by pacific means, and because we as Christians owe our first and supreme allegiance to Jesus Christ. Because the Methodist Episcopal Church in her General Conference of 1928 has declared: 'We renounce war as an instrument of national policy.' Because our nation led the nations of the world in signing the Paris Peace Pact, and the Constitution of the United States, Article 6, § 2, provides that: 'This Constitution and the laws of the United States which shall be made in pursuance thereof and all treaties made under authority of the United States shall be the Supreme Law of the Land.' Thus making the Paris Pact the supreme law of the land which declares: 'The high contracting parties agree that the settlement of all disputes or conflict—shall never be sought except by pacific means.'⊥ ⌐252

"Therefore we, the Southern California Conference, memorialize the General Conference which convenes in Atlantic City in May, 1932; to petition the United States Government to grant exemption from military service to such citizens who are members of the Methodist Episcopal Church, as conscientiously believe that participation in war is a denial of their supreme allegiance to Jesus Christ."

And in 1932 the General Conference of that Church adopted as a part of its tenets and discipline:

"We hold that our country is benefited by having as citizens those who unswervingly follow the dictates of their consciences. . . . Furthermore, we believe it to be the duty of the churches to give moral support to those individuals who hold conscientious scruples against participation in military training or military service. We petition the government of the United States to grant to members of the Methodist Episcopal Church who may be conscientious objectors to war the same exemption from military service as has long been granted to members of the Society of Friends and other similar religious organizations. Similarly we petition all educational institutions which require military training to excuse from such training any student belonging to the Methodist Episcopal Church who has conscientious scruples against it. We earnestly petition the government of the United States to cease to support financially all military training in civil educational institutions."

And the Southern California Conference at its 1933 session adopted the following:

"Reserve Officers' Training Corps— Recalling the action of the General Conference asking for exemption from military service for those members of our church to whom war and preparation for war is a violation of conscience, we request the authorities of our State Universities at Berkeley, Los Angeles and Tucson, to exempt Methodist students from the ⊥253 R.O.T.C. on the grounds of conscien⊥tious objection, and we hereby pledge the moral and official backing of this Conference, seeking such exemption, provided that it be understood that no conscientious objector shall participate in the financial profits of war. The Secretary of the Conference is asked to send copies of this paragraph to the governing boards of these institutions."

Appellants as members of that church accept and feel themselves morally, religiously and conscientiously bound by its tenets and discipline as expressed in the quoted conference resolutions; each is a follower of the teachings of Jesus Christ; each accepts as a guide His teachings and those of the Bible and holds as a part of his religious and conscientious belief that war, training for war and military training are immoral, wrong and contrary to the letter and spirit of His teaching and the precepts of the Christian religion.

Therefore these students at the beginning of the fall term in 1933 petitioned the university for exemption from military training and participation in the activities of the training corps, upon the ground of their religious and conscientious objection to war and to military training. Their petition was denied. Thereupon, through that church's bishop in California, they and their fathers petitioned the regents that military training be made optional in order that conscientious and religious objectors to war, training for war and military training might not be confronted with the necessity of violating and forswearing their beliefs or being denied the right of education in the state university to which these minors are entitled under the constitution and laws of the State of California and of the United States.

The regents refused to make military training optional or to exempt these students. Then, because of their religious and conscientious objections, they declined to take the prescribe course and solely upon that ground the regents by formal notification sus⊥254 pended them from ⊥ the university, but with leave to apply for readmission at any time conditioned upon their ability and willingness to comply with all applicable regulations of the university governing the matriculation and attendance of students. The university affords opportunity for education such as may not be had at any other institution in California except at a greater cost which these minors are not

able to pay. And they, as appellees at the time of their suspension well knew, are willing to take as a substitute for military training such other courses as may be prescribed by the university. . . .⊥   ⊥259

The petition is not to be understood as showing that students required by the regents' order to take the prescribed course thereby serve in the army or in any sense become a part of the military establishment of the United States. Nor is the allegation that the courses are prescribed by the War Department to be taken literally. We take judicial notice of the long-established voluntary co-operation between federal and state authorities in respect of the military instruction given in the land grant colleges. The War Department has not been empowered ⊥ to deter-   ⊥260 mine or in any manner to prescribe the military instruction in these institutions. The furnishing of officers, men and equipment conditioned upon the giving of courses and the imposing of discipline deemed appropriate, recommended or approved by the Department does not support the suggestion that the training is not exclusively prescribed and given under the authority of the State. The States are interested in the safety of the United States, the strength of its military forces and its readiness to defend them in war and against every attack of public enemies. Undoubtedly every State has authority to train its able-bodied male citizens of suitable age appropriately to develop fitness, should any such duty be laid upon them, to serve in the United States army or in state militia (always liable to be called forth by federal authority to execute the laws of the Union, suppress insurrection or repel invasion, Constitution, Art. I, § 8, cls. 12, 15 and 16) or as members of local constabulary forces, or as officers needed effectively to police the state. And, when made possible by the national government, the State in order more effectively to teach and train its citizens for these and like purposes may avail itself of the services of officers and equipment belonging to the military establishment of the United States. So long as its action is within retained powers and not inconsistent with any exertion of the authority of the national government and transgresses no right safeguarded to the citizen by the Federal Constitution, the State is the sole judge of the means to be employed and the amount of training to be exacted for the effective accomplishment of these ends.

⊥ The clauses of the Fourteenth Amendment in-   ⊥261 voked by appellants declare: "No State shall make or enforce any law which shall abridge the privileges or immunities of citizens of the United States; nor shall any State deprive any person of life, liberty or property, without due process of law." Appellants' contentions are that the enforcement of the order prescribing instruction in military science and tactics abridges some privilege or immunity covered by the first clause and deprives of liberty safeguarded by the second. The "privileges and immunities" protected are only those that belong to citizens of the United States as distinguished from citizens of the States—those that arise from the Constitution and laws of the United States as contrasted with those that spring from other sources. Appellants assert—unquestionably in good faith—that all war, preparation for war and the training required by the university are repugnant to the tenets and discipline of their church, to their religion and to their consciences. The "privilege" of attending the university as a student comes not from federal sources but is given by the State. It is not within the asserted protection. The only "immunity" claimed by these students is freedom from obligation to comply with the rule prescribing military training. But that "immunity" cannot be regarded as not within, or as distinguishable from, the "liberty" of which they claim to have been deprived by the enforcement of the regents' order. If the regents' order is not repugnant to the due process clause, then it does not violate the privileges and immunities ⊥ clause. Therefore we need only decide whether by state action the "liberty" of these students has been infringed.

⌐262

There need be no attempt to enumerate or comprehensively to define what is included in the "liberty" protected by the due process clause. Undoubtedly it does include the right to entertain the beliefs, to adhere to the principles and to teach the doctrines on which these students base their objections to the order prescribing military training. The fact that they are able to pay their way in this university but not in any other institution in California is without significance upon any constitutional or other question here involved. California has not drafted or called them to attend the university. They are seeking education offered by the State and at the same time insisting that they be excluded from the prescribed course solely upon grounds of their religious beliefs and conscientious objections to war, preparation for war and military education. Taken on the basis of the facts alleged in the petition, appellants' contentions amount to no more than an assertion that the due process clause of the Fourteenth Amendment as a safeguard of "liberty" confers the right to be students in the state university free from obligation to take military training as one of the conditions of attendance.

Viewed in the light of our decisions that proposition must at once be put aside as untenable.

Government, federal and state, each in its own sphere owes a duty to the people within its jurisdiction to preserve itself in adequate strength to maintain peace and order and to assure the just enforcement of law. And every citizen owes the reciprocal duty, according to his capacity, to support and defend government against all ⊥ enemies.

⌐263

United States v. *Schwimmer* involved a petition for naturalization by one opposed to bearing arms in defense of country. Holding the applicant not entitled to citizenship we said: "That it is the duty of citizens by force of arms to defend our government against all enemies whenever necessity arises is a fundamental principle of the Constitution. . . . Whatever tends to lessen the willingness of citizens to discharge their duty to bear arms in the country's defense detracts from the strength and safety of the Government."

In *United States* v. *Macintosh*, a later naturalization case, the applicant was unwilling, because of conscientious objections, to take unqualifiedly the statutory oath of allegiance which contains this statement: "That he will support and defend the Constitution and laws of the United States against all enemies, foreign and domestic, and bear true faith and allegiance to the same." His petition stated that he was willing if necessary to take up arms in defense of this country, "but I should want to be free to judge of the necessity." In amplification he said: "I do not undertake to support 'my country, right or wrong' in any dispute which may arise, and I am not willing to promise beforehand, and without knowing the cause for which my country may go to war, either that I will or that I will not 'take up arms in defense of this country,' however 'necessary' the war may seem to be to the government of the day." The opinion of this court quotes from petitioner's brief a statement to the effect that it is a "fixed principle of our Constitution, zealously guarded by our laws, that a citizen cannot be forced and need not bear arms in a war if he has conscientious religious scruples against doing so." And, referring to that part of the ⊥ argument in behalf of the applicant this court said: "This, if it means what it seems to say, is an astonishing statement, Of course, there is no such principle of the Constitution, fixed or otherwise. The conscientious objector is relieved from the obligation to bear arms in obedience to no constitutional provision, express or implied; but because, and only because, it has accorded with the policy of Congress thus to relieve him. . . . The privilege of the native-born conscientious objector to avoid bearing arms comes not from the Constitution but from the acts of Congress. That body may grant or withhold the exemption as in its wisdom it sees fit; and if it be withheld, the native-born conscientious objector cannot successfully assert the privilege. No other conclusion is compatible with the well-nigh limitless extent of the war powers as above illustrated, which include, by necessary implication, the power, in the last extremity, to compel the armed service of any citizen in the land, without regard to his objections or his views in respect of the justice or morality of the particular war or of war in general. In *Jacobson* v. *Massachusetts*, this Court [upholding a state compulsory vaccination law] speaking of the liberties guaranteed to the individual by the Fourteenth Amendment, said: '. . . and yet he may be compelled, by force if need be, against his will and without regard to his personal wishes or his pecuniary interests, or even his religious or political convic-

⌐264

tions, to take his place in the ranks of the army of his country and risk the chance of being shot down in its defense.' "

And see *University of Maryland* v. *Coale*, a case, similar to that now before us, decided against the contention of a student in the University of Maryland who on conscientious grounds objected to military training there required. His appeal to this Court was dismissed for the want of a substantial federal question. ⊥

Plainly there is no ground for the contention that the regents' order, requiring able-bodied male students under the age of twenty-four as a condition of their enrollment to take the prescribed instruction in military science and tactics, transgresses any constitutional right asserted by these appellants.

The contention that the regents' order is repugnant to the Briand-Kellogg Peace Pact requires little consideration. In that instrument the United States and the other high contracting parties declare that they condemn recourse to war for the solution of international controversies and renounce it as an instrument of national policy in their relations with one another and agree that the settlement or solution of all disputes or conflicts which may arise among them shall never be sought except by pacific means. Clearly there is no conflict between the regents' order and the provisions of this treaty.

Affirmed.

Mr. Justice CARDOZO [concurring].

Concurring in the opinion I wish to say an extra word.

I assume for present purposes that the religious liberty protected by the First Amendment against invasion by the nation is protected by the Fourteenth Amendment against invasion by the states.

Accepting that premise, I cannot find in the respondents' ordinance an obstruction by the state to "the free exercise" of religion as the phrase was understood by the founders of the nation, and by the generations that have followed. . . .

⊥ Instruction in military science is not instruction in the practice or tenets of a religion. Neither directly nor indirectly is government establishing a state religion when it insists upon such training. Instruction in military science, unaccompanied here by any pledge of military service, is not an interference by the state with the free exercise of religion when the liberties of the constitution are read in the light of a century and a half of history during days of peace and war. . . .

From the beginnings of our history Quakers and other conscientious objectors have been exempted as an act of grace from military service, but the exemption, when granted, has been coupled with a condition, at least in many instances, that they supply the army with a substitute or with the money necessary

to hire one. ⊥ For one opposed to force, the affront to conscience must be greater in furnishing men and money wherewith to wage a pending contest than in studying military science without the duty or the pledge of service. Never in our history has the notion been accepted, or even, it is believed, advanced, that acts thus indirectly related to service in the camp or field are so tied to the practice of religion as to be exempt, in law or in morals, from regulation by the state. On the contrary, the very lawmakers who were willing to give release from warlike acts had not thought that they were doing any ⊥ thing inconsistent with the moral claims of an objector, still less with his constitutional immunities, in coupling the exemption with these collateral conditions.

Manifestly a different doctrine would carry us to lengths that have never yet been dreamed of. The conscientious objector, if his liberties were to be thus extended, might refuse to contribute taxes in furtherance of a war, whether for attack or for defense, or in furtherance of any other end condemned by his conscience as irreligious or immoral. The right of private judgment has never yet been so exalted above the powers and the compulsion of the agencies of government. One who is a martyr to a principle—which may turn out in the end to be a delusion or an error—does not prove by his martyrdom that he has kept within the law.

I am authorized to state that *Mr. Justice BRANDEIS* and *Mr. Justice STONE* join in this opinion.

GIROUARD v. UNITED STATES

328 U.S. 61
ON WRIT OF CERTIORARI TO THE UNITED STATES CIRCUIT
COURT OF APPEALS FOR THE FIRST CIRCUIT

Argued March 4, 1946 — Decided April 22, 1946

⊥ Mr. Justice DOUGLAS delivered the opinion of the Court.

In 1943 petitioner, a native of Canada, filed his petition of naturalization in the District Court of Massachusetts. He stated in his application that he understood the prin⊥ciples of the government of the United States, believed in its form of government, and was willing to take the oath of allegiance which reads as follows:

"I hereby declare, on oath, that I absolutely and entirely renounce and abjure all allegiance and fidelity to any foreign prince, potentate, state, or sovereignty of whom or which I have heretofore been a subject or citizen; that I will support and defend the Constitution and laws of the United States of America against all enemies, foreign and domestic; that I will bear true faith and allegiance to the same; and that I take this obligation freely without any mental reservation or purpose of evasion: So Help Me God."

To the question in the application "If necessary, are you willing to take up arms in defense of this country?" he replied, "No (Non-combatant) Seventh Day Adventist." He explained that answer before the examiner by saying "it is a purely religious matter with me, I have no political or personal reasons other than that." He did not claim before his Selective Service board exemption from all military service, but only from combatant military duty. At the hearing in the District Court petitioner testified that he was a member of the Seventh Day Adventist denomination, of whom approximately 10,000 were then serving in the armed forces of the United States as non-combatants, especially in the medical corps; and that he was willing to serve in the army but would not bear arms. The District Court admitted him to citizenship. The Circuit Court of Appeals reversed, one judge dissenting. It took that action on the authority of *United States* v. *Schwimmer; United States* v. *Macintosh*, and *United States* v. *Bland*, saying that the facts of the present case brought it squarely within the principles of those ⌐63 cases. The case is here on ⊥ a petition for a writ of certiorari which we granted so that those authorities might be reexamined.

The *Schwimmer, Macintosh* and *Bland* Cases involved, as does the present one, a question of statutory construction. At the time of those cases, Congress required an alien, before admission to citizenship, to declare on oath in open court that "he will support and defend the Constitution and laws of the United States against all enemies, foreign and domestic, and bear true faith and allegiance to the same." It also required the court to be satisfied that the alien had during the five year period immediately preceding the date of his application "behaved as a man of good moral character, attached to the principles of the Constitution of the United States, and well disposed to the good order and happiness of the same." Those provisions were reenacted into the present law in substantially the same form.

While there are some factual distinctions between this case and the *Schwimmer* and *Macintosh* Cases, the *Bland* Case on its facts is indistinguishable. But the principle emerging from the three cases obliterates any factual distinction among them. As we recognized in *Re Summers*, they stand for the same general rule—that an alien who refuses to bear arms will not be admitted to citizenship. As an original proposition, we could not agree with that rule. The ⌐64 fallacies underlying ⊥ it were, we think, demonstrated in the dissents of Mr. Justice Holmes in the *Schwimmer* Case and of Mr. Chief Justice Hughes in the *Macintosh* Case.

The oath required of aliens does not in terms require that they promise to bear arms. Nor has Congress expressly made any such finding a prerequisite to citizenship. To hold that it is required is to read it into the Act by implication. But we could not assume that Congress intended to make such an abrupt and radical departure from our traditions unless it spoke in unequivocal terms.

The bearing of arms, important as it is, is not the only way in which our institutions may be supported and defended, even in times of great peril. Total war in its modern form dramatizes as never before the great cooperative effort necessary for victory. The nuclear physicists who developed the atomic bomb, the worker at his lathe, the seaman on cargo vessels, construction battalions, nurses, engineers, litter bearers, doctors, chaplains—these, too, made essential contributions. And many of them made the supreme sacrifice. Mr. Justice Holmes stated in the *Schwimmer* Case that "the Quakers have done their share to make the country what it is." And the annals of the recent war show that many whose religious scruples prevented them from bearing arms, nevertheless were unselfish participants in the war effort. Refusal to bear arms is not necessarily a sign of disloyalty or a lack of attachment to our institutions. One may serve his country faithfully and devotedly, though his religious scruples make it impossible for him to shoulder a rifle. Devotion to one's country can be as real and as enduring among non-combatants as among combatants. One may adhere to what he deems to be his obligation to God and yet assume all military risks to secure victory. The effort of war is indivisible; and those whose religious scruples prevent them from killing are no less patriots than those whose special traits or handicaps result in their ⊥ assignment to duties far behind the ⌐65 fighting front. Each is making the utmost contribution according to his capacity. The fact that his role may be limited by religious convictions rather than by physical characteristics has no necessary bearing on his attachment to his country or on his willingness to support and defend it to his utmost.

Petitioner's religious scruples would not disqualify him from becoming a member of Congress or holding other public offices. While Article 6, Clause 3 of the Constitution provides that such officials, both of the United States and the several States, "shall be bound by Oath or Affirmation, to support this Constitution," it significantly adds that no religious Test shall ever be required as a Qualification to any Office or public Trust under the United States." The oath required is in no material respect different from that prescribed for aliens under the Nationality Act. It has long contained the provision "that I will support and defend the Constitution of the United States against all enemies, foreign and domestic; that I will bear true faith and allegiance to the same; that I take this obligation freely, without any mental reservation or purpose of evasion." As Mr. Chief Justice Hughes stated in his dissent in the *Macintosh* Case, "the history of the struggle for religious liberty, the large number of citizens of our country from the very beginning, who have been unwilling to sacrifice their religious convictions, and in particular, those who have been conscientiously opposed to war and who would not yield what they sincerely believed to be their allegiance to the will of God"—these considerations make it impossible to conclude "that such persons are to be deemed disqualified for public office in this country because of the requirement of the oath which must be taken before they enter upon their duties."

There is not the slightest suggestion that Congress set a stricter standard for aliens seeking admission to citizen⊥ship than it did for officials who make and enforce the laws of the nation and administer its affairs. It is hard to believe that one need forsake his religious scruples to become a citizen but not to sit in the high councils of state.

As Mr. Chief Justice Hughes pointed out (*United States* v. *Macintosh*) religious scruples against bearing arms have been recognized by Congress in the various draft laws. This is true of the Selective Training and Service Act of [September 16] 1940 as it was of earlier acts. He who is inducted into the armed services takes an oath which includes the provision "that I will bear true faith and allegiance to the United States of America; that I will serve them honestly and faithfully against all their enemies whomsoever." Congress has thus recognized that one may adequately discharge his obligations as a citizen by rendering non-combatant as well as combatant services. This respect by Congress over the years for the conscience of those having ⊥ religious scruples against bearing arms is cogent evidence of the meaning of the oath. It is recognition by Congress that even in time of war one may truly support and defend our institutions though he stops short of using weapons of war.

That construction of the naturalization oath received new support in 1942. In the Second War Powers Act, Congress relaxed certain of the requirements for aliens who served honorably in the armed forces of the United States during World War II and provided machinery to expedite their naturalization. Residence requirements were relaxed, educational tests were eliminated, and no fees were required. But no change in the oath was made; nor was any change made in the requirement that the alien be attached to the principles of the Constitution. Yet it is clear that these new provisions cover non-combatants as well as combatants. If petitioner had served as a non-⊥combatant (as he was willing to do), he could have been admitted to citizenship by taking the identical oath which he is willing to take. Can it be that the oath means one thing to one who has served to the extent permitted by his religious scruples and another thing to one equally willing to serve but who has not had the opportunity? It is not enough to say that petitioner is not entitled to the benefits of the new Act since he did not serve in the armed forces. He is not seeking the benefits of the expedited procedure and the relaxed requirements. The oath which he must take is identical with the oath which both non-combatants and combatants must take. It would, indeed, be a strange construction to say that "support and defend the Constitution and laws of the United States of America against all enemies, foreign and domestic" demands something more from some than it does from others. That oath can hardly be adequate for one who is unwilling to bear arms because of religious scruples and yet exact from another a promise to bear arms despite religious scruples.

Mr. Justice Holmes stated in the *Schwimmer* Case: "if there is any principle of the Constitution that more imperatively calls for attachment than any other it is the principle of free thought—not free thought for those who agree with us but freedom for the thought that we hate. I think that we should adhere to that principle with regard to admission into, as well as to life within this country." The struggle for religious liberty has through the centuries been an effort to accommodate the demands of the State to the conscience of the individual. The victory for freedom of thought recorded in our Bill of Rights recognizes that in the domain of conscience there is a moral power higher than the State. Throughout the ages men have suffered death rather than subordinate their allegiance to God to the authority of the State. Freedom of religion guaranteed by the First Amendment is the product of that struggle. As we ⊥ recently stated in *United States* v. *Ballard*, "Freedom of thought, which includes freedom of religious belief, is basic in a society of free men. *West Virginia State Bd. of Edu.* v. *Barnette*." The test oath is abhorrent to our tradition. Over the years Congress has meticulously respected that tradition and even in time of war has sought to accommodate the military requirements to the religious scruples of the individual. We do not believe that Congress intended to reverse that policy when it came to draft the naturalization oath. Such an abrupt and radical departure from our traditions should not be implied. See *Schneiderman* v. *United States*. Cogent evidence would be necessary to convince us that Congress took that course.

We conclude that the *Schwimmer, Macintosh* and *Bland* Cases do not state the correct rule of law.

We are met, however, with the argument that even though those cases were wrongly decided, Congress has adopted the rule which they announced. The argument runs as follows: Many efforts were made to amend the law so as to change the rule announced by those cases; but in every instance the bill died in committee. Moreover, when the Nationality Act of 1940 was passed, Congress reenacted the oath in its pre-existing form, though at the same time it made extensive changes in the requirements and procedure for naturalization. From this it is argued that Congress adopted and reenacted the rule of the *Schwimmer, Macintosh,* and *Bland* Cases.

We stated in *Helvering* v. *Hallock* that "It would require very persuasive circumstances enveloping Congressional silence to debar this Court from reexamining its own doctrines." It is at best treacherous to find in Congressional silence alone the adoption of a controlling rule of law. We do not think under the circumstances of this legislative history that we can ⌐70 properly ⊥ place on the shoulders of Congress the burden of the Court's own error. The history of the 1940 Act is at most equivocal. It contains no affirmative recognition of the rule of the *Schwimmer*, *Macintosh* and *Bland* Cases. The silence of Congress and its inaction are as consistent with a desire to leave the problem fluid as they are with an adoption by silence of the rule of those cases. But for us, it is enough to say that since the date of those cases Congress never acted affirmatively on this question but once and that was in 1942. At that time, as we have noted, Congress specifically granted naturalization privileges to non-combatants who like petitioner were prevented from bearing arms by their religious scruples. That was affirmative recognition that one could be attached to the principles of our government and could support and defend it even though his religious convictions prevented him from bearing arms. And, as we have said, we cannot believe that the oath was designed to exact something more from one person than from another. Thus the affirmative action taken by Congress in 1942 negatives any inference that otherwise might be drawn from its silence when it reenacted the oath in 1940.

Reversed.

UNITED STATES v. SEEGER (No. 50)

ON WRIT OF CERTIORARI TO THE UNITED STATES CIRCUIT
COURT OF APPEALS FOR THE SECOND CIRCUIT

UNITED STATES v. JAKOBSON (No. 51)

ON WRIT OF CERTIORARI TO THE UNITED STATES CIRCUIT
COURT OF APPEALS FOR THE SECOND CIRCUIT

PETER v. UNITED STATES (No. 29)

ON WRIT OF CERTIORARI TO THE UNITED STATES CIRCUIT
COURT OF APPEALS FOR THE NINTH COURT
380 U.S. 163
Argued November 16 and 17, 1964 — Decided March 8, 1965

⊥ *Mr. Justice CLARK* delivered the opinion of the   ⌐164
Court.

These cases involve claims of conscientious objectors under § 6(j) of the Universal Military Training and Service Act, 50 USC App § 456(j) (1958 ed.), which exempts from combatant training and service in the armed forces of the United States those persons who by ⊥ reason of their religous training and   ⌐165
belief are conscientiously opposed to participation in war in any form. The cases were consolidated for argument and we consider them together although each involves different facts and circumstances. The parties raise the basic question of the constitutionality of the section which defines the term "religious training and belief," as used in the Act, as "an individual's belief in a relation to a Supreme Being involving duties superior to those arising from any human relation, but [not including] essentially political, sociological, or philosophical views or a merely personal moral code." The constitutional attack is launched under the First Amendment's Establishment and Free Exercise Clauses and is twofold: (1) The section does not exempt nonreligious conscientious objectors; and (2) it discriminates between different forms of religious expression in violation of the Due Process Clause of the Fifth Amendment. . . . We granted certiorari in each of the cases because of their importance in the administration of the Act.

We have concluded that Congress, in using the expression "Supreme Being" rather than the designation "God," was merely clarifying the meaning of religious training and belief so as to embrace all religions and to exclude essentially political, sociological or philosophical views. We believe that under this construction, the test of belief ⊥ "in a relation to a Supreme Being" is whether a given belief that is sincere and meaningful occupies a place in the life of its possessor parallel to that filled by the orthodox belief in God of one who clearly qualifies for the exemption. Where such beliefs have parallel positions in the lives of their respective holders we cannot say that one is "in a relation to a Supreme Being" and the other is not. We have concluded that the beliefs of the objectors in these cases meet these criteria, and, accordingly, we affirm the judgments in Nos. 50 and 51 and reverse the judgment in No. 29.

THE FACTS IN THE CASES

No. 50: Seeger was convicted in the District Court for the Southern District of New York of having refused to submit to induction in the armed forces. He was originally classified 1-A in 1953 by his local board, but this classification was changed in 1955 to 2-S (student) and he remained in this status until 1958 when he was reclassified 1-A. He first claimed exemption as a conscientious objector in 1957 after successive annual renewals of his student classification. Although he did not adopt verbatim the printed Selective Service System form, he declared that he was conscientiously opposed to participation in war in any form by reason of his "religious" belief; that he preferred to leave the question as to his belief in a Supreme Being open, "rather than answer 'yes' or 'no' "; that his "skepticism or disbelief in the existence of God" did "not necessarily mean lack of faith in anything whatsoever"; that his was a "belief in and devotion to goodness and virtue for their own sakes, and a religious faith in a purely ethical creed." He cited such personages as Plato, Aristotle and Spinoza for support of his ethical belief in intellectual and moral integrity "without belief in God, except in the remotest sense." His belief was found to be sincere, hon⊥est, and made in good faith; and his conscientious objection to be based upon individual training and belief, both of which included research in religious and cultural fields. Seeger's claim, however, was denied solely because it was not based upon a "belief in a relation to a Supreme Being" as required by § 6 (j) of the Act. At trial Seeger's counsel admitted that Seeger's belief was not in relation to a Supreme Being as commonly understood, but contended that he was entitled to the exemption because "under the present law Mr. Seeger's position would also include definitions of religion which have been stated more recently," and could be "accommodated" under the definition of religious training and belief in the Act. He was convicted and the Court of Appeals reversed, holding that the Supreme Being requirement of the section distinguished "between internally derived and externally compelled beliefs" and was, therefore, an "impermissible clas-

sification" under the Due Process Clause of the Fifth Amendment.

No. 51: Jakobson was also convicted in the Southern District of New York on a charge of refusing to submit to induction. On his appeal the Court of Appeals reversed on the ground that rejection of his claim may have rested on the factual finding, erroneously made, that he did not believe in a Supreme Being as required by § 6(j).

Jakobson was originally classified 1-A in 1953 and intermittently enjoyed a student classification until 1956. It was not until April 1958 that he made claim to noncombatant classification (1-A-O) as a conscientious objector. He stated on the Selective Service System form that he believed in a "Supreme Being" who was "Creator of Man" in the sense of being "ultimately responsible for the existence of" man and who was "the Supreme Reality" of which "the existence of man is the *result*." (Emphasis in the original.) He explained that his reli⊥gious and social thinking had developed after much meditation and thought. He had concluded that man must be "partly spiritual" and, therefore, "partly akin to the Supreme Reality"; and that his "most important religious law" was that "no man ought ever to wilfully sacrifice another man's life as a means to any other end. . . ." In December 1958 he requested a 1-O classification since he felt that participation in any form of military service would involve him in "too many situations and relationships that would be a strain on [his] conscience that [he felt he] must avoid." He submitted a long memorandum of "notes on religion" in which he defined religion as the "*sum and essence of one's basic attitudes to the fundamental problems of human existence,*" (emphasis in the original); he said that he believed in "Godness" which was "the Ultimate Cause for the fact of the Being of the Universe"; that to deny its existence would but deny the existence of the universe because "anything that Is, has an Ultimate Cause for its Being." There was a relationship to Godness, he stated, in two directions, i.e., "vertically, towards Godness directly," and "horizontally, toward Godness through Mankind and the World." He accepted the latter one. The Board classified him 1-A-O and Jakobson appealed. The hearing officer found that the claim was based upon a personal moral code and that he was not sincere in his claim. The Appeal Board classified him 1-A. It did not indicate upon what ground it based its decision, i.e., insincerity or a conclusion that his belief was only a personal moral code. The Court of Appeals reversed, finding that his claim came within the requirements of § 6(j). Because it could not determine whether the Appeal Board had found that Jakobson's beliefs failed to come within the statutory definition, or whether it had concluded that he lacked sincerity, it directed dismissal of the indictment.⊥

No. 29: Forest Britt Peter was convicted in the Northern District of California on a charge of refusing to submit to induction. In his Selective Service System form he stated that he was not a member of a religious sect or organization; he failed to execute section VII of the questionnaire but attached to it a quotation expressing opposition to war, in which he stated that he concurred. In a later form he hedged the question as to his belief in a Supreme Being by saying that it depended on the definition and he appended a statement that he felt it a violation of his moral code to take human life and that he considered this belief superior to his obligation to the state. As to whether his conviction was religious, he quoted with approval Reverend John Haynes Holmes' definition of religion as "the consciousness of some power manifest in nature which helps man in the ordering of his life in harmony with its demands . . . [;it] is the supreme expression of human nature; it is man thinking his highest, feeling his deepest, and living his best." The source of his conviction he attributed to reading and meditation "in our democratic American culture, with its values derived from the western religious and philosophical tradition." As to his belief in a Supreme Being, Peter stated that he supposed "you could call that a belief in the Supreme Being or God. These just do not happen to be the words I use." In 1959 he was classified 1-A, although there was no evidence in the record that he was not sincere in his beliefs. After his conviction for failure to report for induction the Court of Appeals, assuming arguendo that he was sincere, affirmed.

BACKGROUND OF § 6(J)

Chief Justice Hughes, in his opinion in *United States* v. *Macintosh*, enunciated the rationale behind ⌐170 the long recognition of conscientious objec⌐tion to participation in war accorded by Congress in our various conscription laws when he declared that "in the forum of conscience, duty to a moral power higher than the State has always been maintained." In a similar vein Harlan Fiske Stone, later Chief Justice, drew from the Nation's past when he declared that "both morals and sound policy require that the state should not violate the conscience of the individual. All our history gives confirmation to the view that liberty of conscience has a moral and social value which makes it worthy of preservation at the hands of the state. So deep in its significance and vital, indeed, is it to the integrity of man's moral and spiritual nature that nothing short of the self-preservation of the state should warrant its violation; and it may well be questioned whether the state which preserves its life by a settled policy of violation of the conscience of the individual will not in fact ultimately lose it by the process."

Governmental recognition of the moral dilemma posed for persons of certain religious faiths by the call to arms came early in the history of this country.

Various methods of ameliorating their difficulty were adopted by the Colonies, and were later perpetuated in state statutes and constitutions. Thus by the time of the Civil War there existed a state pattern of exempting conscientious objectors on religious grounds. In the Federal Militia Act of 1862 control of conscription was left primarily in the States. However, General Order No. 99, issued by the Adjutant General pursuant to that Act, provided for striking from the conscription list those who were exempted by the States; it also established a commutation or substitution system fashioned from earlier state enactments. With the Federal Conscription Act of 1863, ⌐ which ⌐171 enacted the commutation and substitution provisions of General Order No. 99, the Federal Government occupied the field entirely, and in the 1864 Draft Act, it extended exemptions to those conscientious objectors who were members of religious denominations opposed to the bearing of arms and who were prohibited from doing so by the articles of faith of their denominations. In that same year the Confederacy exempted certain pacifist sects from military duty.

The need for conscription did not again arise until World War I. The Draft Act of 1917 afforded exemptions to conscientious objectors who were affiliated with a "well-recognized religious sect or organization [then] organized and existing and whose existing creed or principles [forbade] its members to participate in war in any form. . . ." The Act required that all persons be inducted into the armed services, but allowed the conscientious objectors to perform noncombatant service in capacities designated by the President of the United States. Although the 1917 Act excused religious objectors only, in December 1917, the Secretary of War instructed that "personal scruples against war" be considered as constituting "conscientious objection." This Act, including its conscientious objector provisions was upheld against constitutional attack in the *Selective Draft Law Cases*.

In adopting the 1940 Selective Training and Service Act Congress broadened the exemption afforded in the 1917 Act by making it unnecessary to belong to a pacifist religious sect if the claimant's own opposition to war was based on "religious training and belief." Those found to be within the exemption were not ⌐ inducted into the armed services but ⌐172 were assigned to noncombatant service under the supervision of the Selective Service System. The Congress recognized that one might be religious without belonging to an organized church just as surely as minority members of a faith not opposed to war might through religious reading reach a conviction against participation in war. Indeed, the consensus of the witnesses appearing before the congressional committees was that individual belief—rather than membership in a church or sect—determined the duties that God imposed upon a person in his everyday conduct; and that "there is a higher loyalty than loyalty to this country, loyalty to God." Thus, while shifting the test from membership in such a church to one's individual belief the Congress nevertheless continued its historic practice of excusing from armed service those who believed that they owed an obligation, superior to that due the state, of not participating in war in any form.

Between 1940 and 1948 two courts of appeals held that the phrase "religious training and belief" did not include philosophical, social or political policy. Then in 1948 the Congress amended the language of the statute and declared that "religious training and belief" was to be defined as "an individual's belief in a relation to a Supreme Being involving duties superior to those arising from any human relation, but [not including] essentially political, sociological, or philosophical views or a merely personal moral code." The only significant mention of ⊥ this change in the provision appears in the report of the Senate Armed Services Committee recommending adoption. It said simply this: "This section reenacts substantially the same provisions as were found in subsection 5(g) of the 1940 act. Exemption extends to anyone who, because of religious training and belief in his relation to a Supreme Being, is conscientiously opposed to combatant military service or to both combatant and non-combatant military service."

INTERPRETATION OF § 6(J)

1. The crux of the problem lies in the phrase "religious training and belief" which Congress has defined as "belief in a relation to a Supreme Being involving duties superior to those arising from any human relation." In assigning meaning to this statutory language we may narrow the inquiry by noting briefly those scruples expressly excepted from the definition. The section excludes those persons who, disavowing religious belief, decide on the basis of essentially political, sociological or economic considerations that war is wrong and that they will have no part of it. These judgments have historically been reserved for the Government, and in matters which can be said to fall within these areas the conviction of the individual has never been permitted to override that of the state. The statute further excludes those whose opposition to war stems from a "merely personal moral code," a phrase to which we shall have occasion to turn later in discussing the application of § 6(j) to these cases. We also pause to take note of what is not involved in this litigation. No party claims to be an atheist or attacks the statute on this ground. The question is not, therefore, one between theistic and atheistic beliefs. We do not deal with ⊥ or intimate any decision on that situation in these cases. Nor do the parties claim the monotheistic belief that there is but one God; what they claim (with the possible exception of Seeger who bases his position here not on factual but on purely

constitutional grounds) is that they adhere to theism, which is the "Belief in the existence of a god or gods; . . . Belief in superhuman powers or spiritual agencies in one or many gods, as opposed to atheism." Our question, therefore, is the narrow one: Does the term "Supreme Being" as used in § 6(j) mean the orthodox God or the broader concept of a power or being, or a faith, "to which all else is subordinate or upon which all else is ultimately dependent"? Webster's New International Dictionary (Second Edition). In considering this question we resolve it solely in relation to the language of § 6(j) and not otherwise.

2. Few would quarrel, we think, with the proposition that in no field of human endeavor has the tool of language proved so inadequate in the communication of ideas as it has in dealing with the fundamental questions of man's predicament in life, in death or in final judgment and retribution. This fact makes the task of discerning the intent of Congress in using the phrase "Supreme Being" a complex one. Nor is it made the easier by the richness and variety of spiritual life in our country. Over 250 sects inhabit our land. Some believe in a purely personal God, some in a supernatural deity; others think of religion as a way of life envisioning as its ultimate goal the day when all men can live together in perfect understanding and peace. There are those who think of God as the depth of our being; others, such as the Buddhists, strive for a state of lasting rest through self-denial and inner purification; in Hindu philosophy, the Supreme Being ⊥ is the transcendental reality which is truth, knowledge and bliss. Even those religious groups which have traditionally opposed war in every form have splintered into various denominations: from 1940 to 1947 there were four denominations using the name "Friends;" the "Church of the Brethren" was the official name of the oldest and largest church body of four denominations composed of those commonly called Brethren; and the "Mennonite Church" was the largest of 17 denominations, including the Amish and Hutterites, grouped as "Mennonite bodies" in the 1936 report on the Census of Religious Bodies. This vast panoply of beliefs reveals the magnitude of the problem which faced the Congress when it set about providing an exemption from armed service. It also emphasizes the care that Congress realized was necessary in the fashioning of an exemption which would be in keeping with its long-established policy of not picking and choosing among religious beliefs.

In spite of the elusive nature of the inquiry, we are not without certain guidelines. In amending the 1940 Act, Congress adopted almost intact the language of Chief Justice Hughes in *United States* v. *Macintosh*:

"The essence of religion is belief in a relation to *God* involving duties superior to those arising from any human relation."

By comparing the statutory definition with those words, however, it becomes readily apparent that the Congress deliberately broadened them by substituting the phrase "Supreme Being" for the appellation "God." And in so doing it is also significant that Congress did not elaborate on the form or nature of this higher authority which it chose to designate as "Supreme Being." By so refraining it ⊥176 must have had in mind the admonitions of the ⊥ Chief Justice when he said in the same opinion that even the word "God" had myriad meanings for men of faith:

"[P]utting aside dogmas with their particular conceptions of deity, freedom of conscience itself implies respect for an innate conviction of paramount duty. The battle for religious liberty has been fought and won with respect to religious beliefs and practices, which are not in conflict with good order, upon the very ground of the supremacy of conscience within its proper field."

Moreover, the Senate Report on the bill specifically states that § 6(j) was intended to re-enact "substantially the same provisions as were found" in the 1940 Act. That statute, of course, refers to "religious training and belief" without more. Admittedly, all of the parties here purport to base their objection on religious belief. It appears, therefore, that we need only look to this clear statement of congressional intent as set out in the report. Under the 1940 Act it was necessary only to have a conviction based upon religious training and belief; we believe that is all that is required here. Within that phrase would come all sincere religious beliefs which are based upon a power or being, or upon a faith, to which all else is subordinate or upon which all else is ultimately dependent. The test might be stated in these words: A sincere and meaningful belief which occupies in the life of its possessor a place parallel to that filled by the God of those admittedly qualifying for the exemption comes within the statutory definition. This construction avoids imputing to Congress an intent to classify different religious beliefs, exempting some and excluding others, and is in accord with the well-established congressional policy of equal treatment for those whose opposition to service is grounded in ⊥177 their religious tenets. ⊥

3. The Government takes the position that since *Berman* v. *United States* was cited in the Senate Report on the 1948 Act, Congress must have desired to adopt the Berman interpretation of what constitutes "religious belief." Such a claim, however, will not bear scrutiny. First, we think it clear that an explicit statement of congressional intent deserves more weight than the parenthetical citation of a case which might stand for a number of things. Congress specifically stated that it intended to re-enact substantially the same provisions as were found in the 1940 Act. Moreover, the history of that Act reveals no evidence of a desire to restrict the concept of religious belief. On the contrary, the Chairman of the House Military Affairs Committee which reported out the 1940 exemption provisions stated:

"We heard the conscientious objectors and all of their representatives that we could possibly hear, and, summing it all up, their whole objection to the bill, aside from their objection to compulsory military training, was based upon the right of conscientious objection and in most instances to the right of the ministerial students to continue in their studies, and we have provided ample protection for those classes and those groups."

During the House debate on the bill, Mr. Faddis of Pennsylvania made the following statement:

"We have made provision to take care of conscientious objectors. I am sure the committee has had all the sympathy in the world with those who appeared claiming to have religious scruples against rendering military service in its various degrees. Some appeared who had conscientious scruples against handling lethal weapons, but who had no ⊥ scruples ⊥178 against performing other duties which did not actually bring them into combat. Others appeared who claimed to have conscientious scruples against participating in any of the activities that would go along with the Army. The committee took all of these into consideration and has written a bill which, I believe, will take care of all the reasonable objections of this class of people." 86 Cong. Rec. 11418 (1940).

Thus the history of the Act belies the notion that it was to be restrictive in application and available only to those believing in a traditional God. . . . ⊥   ⊥179

Section 6(j), then, is no more than a clarification of the 1940 provision involving only certain "technical amendments," to use the words of Senator Gurney. As such it continues the congressional policy of providing exemption from military service for those whose opposition ⊥ is based on grounds that can ⊥180 fairly be said to be "religious." To hold otherwise would not only fly in the face of Congress' entire action in the past; it would ignore the historic position of our country on this issue since its founding.

4. Moreover, we believe this construction embraces the ever-broadening understanding of the modern religious community. The eminent Protestant theologian, Dr. Paul Tillich, whose views the Government concedes would come within the statute, identifies God not as a projection "out there" or beyond the skies but as the ground of our very being. The Court of Appeals stated in No. 51 that Jakobson's views "parallel [those of] this eminent theologian rather strikingly." In his book, Systematic Theology, Dr. Tillich says:

"I have written of the God above the God of theism. . . . In such a state [of self-affirmation] the God of both religious and theological language disappears. But something remains, namely, the seriousness of that doubt in which meaning within meaninglessness is affirmed. The source of this affirmation of meaning within meaninglessness, of certitude within doubt, is not the God of traditional theism but the 'God above God,' the power of being, which works through those who have no name for it, ⊥181 not even the name God." ⊥

Another eminent cleric, the bishop of Woolwich, John A. T. Robinson, in his book, Honest To God (1963), states:

"The Bible speaks of a God 'up there.' No doubt its picture of a three-decker universe, of 'the heaven above, the earth beneath and the waters under the earth,' was once taken quite literally. . . ." "[Later] *in place of a God who is literally or physically 'up there' we have accepted, as part of our mental furniture, a God who is spiritually or metaphysically 'out there.'* . . . But now it seems there is no room for him, not merely in the inn, but in the entire universe: for there are no vacant places left. In reality, of course, our new view of the universe has made not the slightest difference. . . ."

"But the idea of a God spiritually or metaphysically 'out there' dies very much harder. Indeed, most people would be seriously disturbed by the thought that it should need to die at all. For it *is* their God, and they have nothing to put in its place. . . . Every one of us lives with some mental picture of a God 'out there,' a God who 'exists' above and beyond the world he made, a God 'to' whom we pray and to whom we 'go' when we die." "But the signs are that we are reaching the point at which the whole conception of a God 'out there,' which has served us so well since the collapse of the three-decker universe, is itself becoming more of a hindrance than a help." (Emphasis in original.)

The Schema of the recent Ecumenical Council in-
⊥182 cluded a most significant declaration on religion: ⊥

"The community of all peoples is one. One is their origin, for God made the entire human race live on all the face of the earth. One, too, is their ultimate end, God. Men expect from the various religions answers to the riddles of the human condition: What is man? What is the meaning and purpose of our lives? What is the moral good and what is sin? What are death, judgment, and retribution after death?

.   .   .   .   .

Ever since primordial days, numerous peoples have had a certain perception of that hidden power which hovers over the course of things and over the events that make up the lives of men; some have even come to know of a Supreme Being and Father. Religions in an advanced culture have been able to use more refined concepts and a more developed language in their struggle for an answer to man's religious questions.

.   .   .   .   .

"Nothing that is true and holy in these religions is scorned by the Catholic Church. Ceaselessly the Church proclaims Christ, 'the Way, the Truth, and the Life,' in whom God reconciled all things to Him-

self. The Church regards with sincere reverence those ways of action and of life, precepts and teachings which, although they differ from the ones she sets forth, reflect nonetheless a ray of that Truth which enlightens all men."

Dr. David Saville Muzzey, a leader in the Ethical Culture Movement, states in his book, Ethics As a Religion (1951), that "[e]verybody except the avowed atheists (and they are comparatively few) believes in some kind of God," and that "The proper question to ask, therefore, is ⊥ not the futile one, Do you be- ⊥183
lieve in God? but rather, What *kind* of God do you believe in?" Dr. Muzzey attempts to answer that question:

"Instead of positing a personal God, whose existence man can neither prove nor disprove, the ethical concept is founded on human experience. It is anthropocentric, not theocentric. Religion, for all the various definitions that have been given of it, must surely mean the devotion of man to the highest ideal that he can conceive. And that ideal is a community of spirits in which the latent moral potentialities of men shall have been elicited by their reciprocal endeavors to cultivate the best in their fellow men. What ultimate reality is we do not know; but we have the faith that it expresses itself in the human world as the power which inspires in men moral purpose."

"Thus the 'God' that we love is not the figure on the great white throne, but the perfect pattern, envisioned by faith, of humanity as it should be, purged of the evil elements which retard its progress toward 'the knowledge, love and practice of the right.' "

These are but a few of the views that comprise the broad spectrum of religious beliefs found among us. But they demonstrate very clearly the diverse manners in which beliefs, equally paramount in the lives of their possessors, may be articulated. They further reveal the difficulties inherent in placing too narrow a construction on the provisions of § 6 (j) and thereby lend conclusive support to the construction which we today find that Congress intended.

5. We recognize the difficulties that have always faced the trier of fact in these cases. We hope that the test that we lay down proves less onerous. The examiner is fur ⊥ nished a standard that permits con- ⊥184
sideration of criteria with which he has had considerable experience. While the applicant's words may differ, the test is simple of application. It is essentially an objective one, namely, does the claimed belief occupy the same place in the life of the objector as an orthodox belief in God holds in the life of one clearly qualified for exemption?

Moreover, it must be remembered that in resolving these exemption problems one deals with the beliefs of different individuals who will articulate them in a multitude of ways. In such an intensely personal area, of course, the claim of the registrant that his belief is an essential part of a religious faith must be given great weight. Recognition of this was implicit in this language, cited by the Berman court from *State* v. *Amana Society*:

"Surely a scheme of life designed to obviate [man's inhumanity to man], and by removing temptations, and all the allurements of ambition and avarice, to nurture the virtues of unselfishness, patience, love, and service, ought not to be denounced as not pertaining to religion *when its devotees regard it as an essential tenet of their religious faith.*"

The validity of what he believes cannot be questioned. Some theologians, and indeed some examiners, might be tempted to question the existence of the registrant's "Supreme Being" or the truth of his concepts. But these are inquiries foreclosed to Government. As Mr. Justice Douglas stated in *United States* v. *Ballard*: "Men may believe what they cannot prove. They may not be put to the proof of their religious doctrines or beliefs. Religious experiences which are as real as life to some may be ⌐185 incomprehensible to others." Local ⊥ boards and courts in this sense are not free to reject beliefs because they consider them "incomprehensible." Their task is to decide whether the beliefs professed by a registrant are sincerely held and whether they are, in his own scheme of things, religious.

But we hasten to emphasize that while the "truth" of a belief is not open to question, there remains the significant question whether it is "truly held." This is the threshold question of sincerity which must be resolved in every case. It is, of course, a question of fact—a prime consideration to the validity of every claim for exemption as a conscientious objector. The Act provides a comprehensive scheme for assisting the Appeal Boards in making this determination, placing at their service the facilities of the Department of Justice, including the Federal Bureau of Investigation and hearing officers. Finally, we would point out that in *Estep* v. *United States*, this Court held that:

"The provision making the decisions of the local boards 'final' means to us that Congress chose not to give administrative action under this Act the customary scope of judicial review which obtains under other statutes. It means that the courts are not to weigh the evidence to determine whether the classification made by the local boards was justified. The decisions of the local boards made in conformity with the regulations are final even though they may be erroneous. The question of jurisdiction of the local board is reached only if there is no basis in fact for the classification which it gave the registrant."

APPLICATION OF § 6(J) TO THE INSTANT CASES

As we noted earlier, the statutory definition excepts those registrants whose beliefs are based on a "merely personal moral code." The records in these ⌐186 cases, how⊥ever, show that at no time did any one of the applicants suggest that his objection was based on a "merely personal moral code." Indeed at the outset each of them claimed in his application that his objection was based on a religious belief. We have construed the statutory definition broadly and it follows that any exception to it must be interpreted narrowly. The use by Congress of the words "merely personal" seems to us to restrict the exception to a moral code which is not only personal but which is the sole basis for the registrant's belief and is in no way related to a Supreme Being. It follows, therefore, that if the claimed religious beliefs of the respective registrants in these cases meet the test that we lay down then their objections cannot be based on a "merely personal" moral code.

In Seeger, No. 50, the Court of Appeals failed to find sufficient "externally compelled beliefs." However, it did find that "it would seem impossible to say with assurance that [Seeger] is not bowing to 'external commands' in virtually the same sense as is the objector who defers to the will of a supernatural power." Of course, as we have said, the statute does not distinguish between externally and internally derived beliefs. Such a determination would, as the Court of Appeals observed, prove impossible as a practical matter, and we have found that Congress intended no such distinction.

The Court of Appeals also found that there was no question of the applicant's sincerity. He was a product of a devout Roman Catholic home; he was a close student of Quaker beliefs from which he said "much of [his] thought is derived"; he approved of their opposition to war in any form; he devoted his spare hours to the Amer⊥ican Friends Service Committee ⌐187 and was assigned to hospital duty.

In summary, Seeger professed "religious belief" and "religious faith." He did not disavow any belief "in a relation to a Supreme Being"; indeed he stated that "the cosmic order does, perhaps, suggest a creative intelligence." He decried the tremendous "spiritual" price man must pay for his willingness to destroy human life. In light of his beliefs and the unquestioned sincerity with which he held them, we think the Board, had it applied the test we propose today, would have granted him the exemption. We think it clear that the beliefs which prompted his objection occupy the same place in his life as the belief in a traditional diety holds in the lives of his friends, the Quakers. We are reminded once more of Dr. Tillich's thoughts:

"And if that word [God] has not much meaning for you, translate it, and speak of the depths of your life, of the source of your being, of your ultimate concern, *of what you take seriously without any reservation.* Perhaps, in order to do so, you must forget everything traditional that you have learned about God. . . ." Tillich, The Shaking of the Foundations 57 (1948). (Emphasis supplied.)

It may be that Seeger did not clearly demonstrate what his beliefs were with regard to the usual understanding of the term "Supreme Being." But as we have said Congress did not intend that to be the test. We therefore *affirm* the judgment in No. 50. . . . ⊥

⊥188

Mr. Justice DOUGLAS, concurring.

If I read the statute differently from the Court, I would have difficulties. For then those who embraced one religious faith rather than another would be subject to penalties; and that kind of discrimination, as we held in *Sherbert* v. *Verner*, would violate the Free Exercise Clause of the First Amendment. It would also result in a denial of equal protection by preferring some religions over others—an invidious discrimination that would run afoul of the Due Process Clause of the Fifth Amendment.

The legislative history of this Act leaves much in the dark. But it is, in my opinion, not a tour de force if we construe the words "Supreme Being" to include the cosmos, as well as an anthropomorphic entity. If it is a tour de force so to hold, it is no more so than other instances where we have gone to extremes to construe an Act of Congress to save it from demise on constitutional grounds. In a more extreme case than the present one we said that the words of a statute may be strained "in the candid service of avoiding a serious constitutional doubt." *United States* v. *Rumely.* ⊥

⊥189

The words "a Supreme Being" have no narrow technical meaning in the field of religion. Long before the birth of our Judeo-Christian civilization the idea of God had taken hold in many forms. Mention of only two—Hinduism and Buddhism—illustrates the fluidity and evanescent scope of the concept. In the Hindu *religion* the Supreme Being is conceived in the forms of several cult Deities. The chief of these, which stands for the Hindu Triad, are Brahma, Vishnu and Siva. Another Deity, and the one most widely worshipped, is Sakti, the Mother Goddess, conceived as power, both destructive and creative. Though Hindu religion encompasses the worship of many Deities, it believes in only one single God, the eternally existent One Being with his manifold attributes and manifestations. This idea is expressed in Rigveda, the earliest sacred text of the Hindus, in verse 46 of a hymn attributed to the mythical seer Dirghatamas (Rigveda, I, 164):

"They call it Indra, Mitra, Varuna and Agni
And also heavenly beautiful Garutman:
The Real is One, though sages name it variously—
They call it Agni, Yama, Matarisvan."

Indian *philosophy*, which comprises several schools of thought, has advanced different theories of the nature of the Supreme Being. According to the Upanisads, Hindu sacred texts, the Supreme Being is described as the power which creates and sustains everything, and to which the created things return upon dissolution. The word which is commonly used in the Upanisads to indicate the Supreme Being is

⊥190 Brahman. Philosophically, the ⊥ Supreme Being is

the transcendental Reality which is Truth, Knowledge, and Bliss. It is the source of the entire universe. In this aspect Brahman is Isvara, a personal Lord and Creator of the universe, an object of worship. But, in the view of one school of thought, that of Sankara, even this is an imperfect and limited conception of Brahman which must be transcended: to think of Brahman as the Creator of the material world is necessarily to form a concept infected with illusion, or maya—which is what the world really is, in highest truth. Ultimately, mystically, Brahman must be understood as without attributes, as neti neti (not this, not that).

Buddhism—whose advent marked the reform of Hinduism—continued somewhat the same concept. As stated by Nancy Wilson Ross, "God—if I may borrow that word for a moment—the universe, and man are one indissoluble existence, one total whole. Only THIS—capital THIS—is. Anything and everything that appears to us as an individual entity or phenomenon, whether it be a planet or an atom, a mouse or a man, is but a temporary manifestation of THIS in form; every activity that takes place, whether it be birth or death, loving or eating breakfast, is but a temporary manifestation of THIS in activity. When we look at things this way, naturally we cannot believe that each individual person has been endowed with a special and individual soul or self. Each one of us is but a cell, as it were, in the body of the Great Self, a cell that comes into being, performs its functions, and passes away, transformed into another manifestation. Though we have temporary individuality, that temporary, limited individuality is not either a true self or our true self. Our true self is the Great Self; our true body is the Body of Reality, or the Dharmakaya, to give it its technical Buddhist name." The World of Zen. ⊥   ⊥191

Does a Buddhist believe in "God" or a "Supreme Being"? That, of course, depends on how one defines "God," as one eminent student of Buddhism has explained:

"It has often been suggested that Buddhism is an atheistic system of thought, and this assumption has given rise to quite a number of discussions. Some have claimed that since Buddhism knew no God, it could not be a religion; others that since Buddhism obviously was a religion which knew no God, the belief in God was not essential to religion. These discussions assumed that *God* is an unambiguous term, which is by no means the case." Conze, Buddhism.

Dr. Conze then says that if "God" is taken to mean a personal Creator of the universe, then the Buddhist has no interest in the concept. But if "God" means something like the state of oneness with God as described by some Christian mystics, then the Buddhist surely believes in "God," since this state is almost indistinguishable from the Buddhist concept of Nirvana, "the supreme Reality; . . . the eternal, hidden and incomprehensible Peace."

And finally, if "God" means one of the many Deities in at least superficially polytheistic religion Hinduism, then Buddhism tolerates a belief in many Gods: "the Buddhists believe that a Faith can be kept alive only if it can be adapted to the mental habits of the average person. In consequence, we find that, in the earlier Scriptures, the deities of Brahmanism are taken for granted and that, later on, the Buddhists adopted the local Gods of any district to which they came."

When the present Act was adopted in 1948 we were a nation of Buddhists, Confucianists, and Taoists, as well as Christians. Hawaii, then a Territory, was indeed filled with Buddhists, Buddhism being ⊥192 "probably the major ⊥ faith, if Protestantism and Roman Catholicism are deemed different faiths." Stokes and Pfeffer, Church and State in the United States. Organized Buddhism first came to Hawaii in 1887 when Japanese laborers were brought to work on the plantations. There are now numerous Buddhist sects in Hawaii, and the temple of the Shin sect in Honolulu is said to have the largest congregation in the city. See Mulholland, Religion in Hawaii.

In the continental United States Buddhism is found "in real strength" in Utah, Arizona, Washington, Oregon, and California. "Most of the Buddhists in the United States are Japanese or Japanese-Americans; however, there are 'English' departments in San Francisco, Los Angeles, and Tacoma." Mead, Handbook of Denominations. The Buddhist Churches of North America, organized in 1914 as the Buddhist Mission of North America and incorporated under the present name in 1942, represent the Jodo Shinshu Sect of Buddhism in this country. This sect is the only Buddhist group reporting information to the annual Yearbook of American Churches. In 1961, the latest year for which figures are available, this group alone had 55 churches and an inclusive membership of 60,000; it maintained 89 church schools with a total enrollment of 11,150. Yearbook of American Churches. According to one source, the total number of Buddhists of all sects in North America is 171,000. See World Almanac.

When the Congress spoke in the vague general terms of a Supreme Being I cannot, therefore, assume that it was so parochial as to use the words in the narrow sense urged on us. I would attribute tolerance and sophistication to the Congress, commensurate with the religious complexion of our communities. In sum, I agree with the Court that any person opposed to war on the basis of a sincere belief, which in his life fills the same place as a be-
⊥193 ⊥lief in God fills in the life of an orthodox religionist, is entitled to exemption under the statute. None comes to us an avowedly irreligious person or as an atheist; one, as a sincere believer in "goodness and virtue for their own sakes." His questions and doubts on theological issues, and his wonder, are no more alien to the statutory standard than are the awe-inspired questions of a devout Buddhist.

WELSH v. UNITED STATES

398 U.S. 333
ON WRIT OF CERTIORARI TO THE UNITED STATES CIRCUIT
COURT OF APPEALS FOR THE NINTH CIRCUIT
Argued January 20, 1970 — Decided June 15, 1970

⊥ *Mr. Justice BLACK* announced the judgment of ⊥335 the Court and delivered an opinion in which *Mr. Justice DOUGLAS, Mr. Justice BRENNAN,* and *Mr. Justice MARSHALL* join.

The petitioner, Elliott Ashton Welsh II, was convicted by a United States District Judge of refusing to submit to induction into the Armed Forces in violation of 50 USC App § 462(a), and was on June 1, 1966, sentenced to imprisonment for three years. One of petitioner's defenses to the prosecution was that § 6(j) of the Universal Military Training and Service Act exempted him from combat and noncombat service because he was "by reason of religious training and belief . . . conscientiously opposed to participation in war in any form." After finding that there was no religious basis for petitioner's conscientious objector claim, the Court of Appeals, Judge Hamley dissenting, affirmed the conviction. We granted certiorari chiefly to review the contention that Welsh's conviction should be set aside on the basis on this Court's decision in *United States* v. *Seeger.* For the reasons to be stated, and without passing upon the constitutional arguments that have been raised, we vote to reverse this conviction because of its fundamental inconsistency with the *United States* v. *Seeger.*

The controlling facts in this case are strikingly similar to those in Seeger. Both Seeger and Welsh were brought up in religious homes and attended church in their childhood, but in neither case was this church one which taught its members not to engage in war at any time for ⊥ any reason. Neither ⊥336 Seeger nor Welsh continued his childhood religious ties into his young manhood, and neither belonged to any religious group or adhered to the teaching of any organized religion during the period of his involvement with the Selective Service System. At the time of registration for the draft, neither had yet come to accept pacifist principles. Their views on war developed only in subsequent years, but when their ideas did fully mature both made application to their local draft boards for conscientious objector exemptions from military service under § 6(j) of the Universal Military Training and Service Act. That section then provided in part:

"Nothing contained in this title shall be construed to require any person to be subject to combatant training and service in the armed forces of the United States who, by reason of religious training and belief, is conscientiously opposed to participation in war in any form. Religious training and belief in this connection means an individual's belief in a relation to a Supreme Being involving duties superior to those arising from any human relation, but does not include essentially political, sociological, or philosophical views or a merely personal moral code."

In filling out their exemption applications both Seeger and Welsh were unable to sign the statement that, as printed in the Selective Service form, stated "I am, by reason of my religious training and belief, conscien⊥tiously opposed to participation in war in any form." Seeger could sign only after striking the words "training and" and putting quotations marks around the word "religious." Welsh could sign only after striking the words "my religious training and." On those same applications, neither could definitely affirm or deny that he believed in a "Supreme Being," both stating that they preferred to leave the question open. But both Seeger and Welsh affirmed on those applications that they held deep conscientious scruples against taking part in wars where people were killed. Both strongly believed that killing in war was wrong, unethical, and immoral, and their consciences forbade them to take part in such an evil practice. Their objection to participating in war in any form could not be said to come from a "still, small voice of conscience"; rather, for them that voice was so loud and insistent that both men preferred to go to jail rather than serve in the Armed Forces. There was never any question about the sincerity and depth of Seeger's convictions as a conscientious objector, and the same is true of Welsh. In this regard the Court of Appeals noted, "[t]he government concedes that [Welsh's] beliefs are held with the strength of more traditional religious convictions." But in both cases the Selective Service System concluded that the beliefs of these men were in some sense insufficiently "religious" to qualify them for conscientious objector exemptions under the terms of § 6(j). Seeger's conscientious objector claim was denied "solely because it was not based upon a 'belief in a relation to a Supreme Being' as required by § 6(j) of the Act," *United States* v. *Seeger*, while Welsh was ⊥ denied the exemption because his Appeal Board and the Department of Justice hearing officer "could find no religious basis for the registrant's beliefs, opinions and convictions." Both Seeger and Welsh subsequently refused to submit to induction into the military and both were convicted of that offense. . . .⊥

In the case before us the Government seeks to distinguish our holding in *Seeger* on basically two grounds,⊥ both of which were relied upon by the Court of Appeals in affirming Welsh's conviction. First, it is stressed that Welsh was far more insistent and explicit than Seeger in denying that his views were religious. For example, in filling out their conscientious objector applications, Seeger put quotation marks around the word "religious," but Welsh struck the word "religious" entirely and later charac-

terized his beliefs as having been formed "by reading in the fields of history and sociology." The Court of Appeals found that Welsh had "denied that his objection to war was premised on religious belief" and concluded that "[t]he Appeal Board was entitled to take him at his word." We think this attempt to distinguish *Seeger* fails for the reason that it places undue emphasis on the registrant's interpretation of his own beliefs. The Court's statement in *Seeger* that a registrant's characterization of his own belief as "religious" should carry great weight, does not imply that his declaration that his views are nonreligious should be treated similarly. When a registrant states that his objections to war are "religious," that information is highly relevant to the question of the function his beliefs have in his life. But very few registrants are fully aware of the broad scope of the word "religious" as used in § 6(j), and accordingly a registrant's statement that his beliefs are nonreligious is a highly unreliable guide for those charged with administering the exemption. Welsh himself presents a case in point. Although he originally characterized his beliefs as nonreligious, he later upon reflection wrote a long and thoughtful letter to his Appeal Board in which he declared that his beliefs were "certainly religious in the ethical sense of the word:" He explained:

"I believe I mentioned taking of life as not being, for me, a religious wrong. Again, I assumed Mr. Brady (the Department of Justice hearing ⊥ officer) was using the word 'religious' in the conventional sense, and, in order to be perfectly honest did not characterize my belief as 'religious.' "

The Government also seeks to distinguish *Seeger* on the ground that Welsh's views, unlike Seeger's, were "essentially political, sociological, or philosophical views or a merely personal moral code." As previously noted, the Government made the same argument about Seeger, and not without reason, for Seeger's views had a substantial political dimension. In this case, Welsh's conscientious objection to war was undeniably based in part on his perception of world politics. In a letter to his local board, he wrote:

"I can only act according to what I am and what I see. And I see that the military complex wastes both human and material resources, that it fosters disregard for (what I consider a paramount concern) human needs and ends; I see that the means we employ to 'defend' our 'way of life' profoundly change that way of life. I see that in our failure to recognize the political, social, and economic realities of the world, we, *as a nation,* fail our responsibility *as a nation.*"

We certainly do not think that § 6(j)'s exclusion of those persons with "essentially political, sociological, or philosophical views or a merely personal moral code" should be read to exclude those who hold strong beliefs about our domestic and foreign affairs or even those whose conscientious objection to participation in all wars is founded to a substantial extent upon considerations of public policy. The two groups of registrants that obviously do fall within these exclusions from the exemption are those whose beliefs are not deeply held and those whose objection to war does not rest at all upon moral, ethical, or religious principle but instead rests solely upon ⊥ considerations of policy, pragmatism, or expediency. In applying § 6 (j)'s exclusion of those whose views are "essentially political, sociological, or philosophical" or of those who have a "merely personal moral code," it should be remembered that these exclusions are definitional and do not therefore restrict the category of persons who are conscientious objectors by "religious training and belief." Once the Selective Service System has taken the first step and determined under the standards set out here and in *Seeger* that the registrant is a "religious" conscientious objector, it follows that his views cannot be "essentially political, sociological, or philosophical." Nor can they be a "merely personal moral code."

Welsh stated that he "believe[d] the taking of life—anyone's life—to be morally wrong." In his original conscientious objector application he wrote the following:

"I believe that human life is valuable in and of itself; in its living; therefore I will not injure or kill another human being. This belief (and the corresponding 'duty' to abstain from violence toward another person) is not 'superior to those arising from any human relation.' On the contrary: *it is essential to every human relation.* I cannot, therefore, conscientiously comply with the Government's insistence that I assume duties which I feel are immoral and totally repugnant." Welsh elaborated his beliefs in later communications with Selective Service officials. On the basis of these beliefs and the conclusion of the Court of Appeals that he held them "with the strength of more traditional religious convictions," we think Welsh was clearly entitled to a conscientious objector exemption. Section ⊥ 6(j) requires no more. That section exempts from military service all those whose consciences, spurred by deeply held moral, ethical, or religious beliefs, would give them no rest or peace if they allowed themselves to become a part of an instrument of war.

The judgment is Reversed.

Mr. Justice BLACKMUN took no part in the consideration or decision of this case.

Mr. Justice HARLAN, concurring in the result.

Candor requires me to say that I joined the Court's opinion in *United States* v. *Seeger* only with the gravest misgivings as to whether it was a legitimate exercise in statutory construction, and today's decision convinces me that in doing so I made a mistake which I should now acknowledge.

In *Seeger* the Court construed § 6(j) of the Universal Military Training and Service Act so as to sustain a conscientious objector claim not founded on a theistic belief. ⊥

Today the prevailing opinion makes explicit its total elimination of the statutorily required religious content for a conscientious objector exemption. The prevailing opinion now says: "If an individual deeply and sincerely holds beliefs that are *purely ethical* or *moral* in source and content but that nevertheless impose upon him a duty of conscience to refrain from participating in any war at any time" (emphasis added), he qualifies for a § 6(j) exemption.

In my opinion, the liberties taken with the statute both in *Seeger* and today's decision cannot be justified in the name of the familiar doctrine of construing federal statutes in a manner that will avoid possible constitutional infirmities in them. There are limits to the permissible application of that doctrine, and, as I will undertake to show in this opinion, those limits were crossed in *Seeger*, and even more apparently have been exceeded in the present case. I therefore find myself unable to escape facing the constitutional issue that this case squarely presents: whether § 6(j) in limiting this draft exemption to those opposed to war in general because of theistic beliefs runs afoul of the religious clauses of the First Amendment. For reasons later appearing I believe it does, and on that basis I concur in the judgment reversing this conviction, and adopt the test announced by Mr. Justice Black, not as a matter of statutory construction, but as the touchstone for salvaging a congressional policy of long standing that would otherwise have to be nullified. . . .⊥

I

B

Against this legislative history it is a remarkable feat of judicial surgery to remove, as did *Seeger*, the theistic requirement of § 6(j). The prevailing opinion today, however, in the name of interpreting the will of Congress, has performed a lobotomy and completely transformed the statute by reading out of it any distinction between religiously acquired beliefs and those deriving from "essentially political, sociological, or philosophical views or a merely personal moral code. . . ."⊥

Unless we are to assume an Alice-in-Wonderland world where words have no meaning, I think it fair to say that Congress' choice of language cannot fail to convey to the discerning reader the very policy choice that the prevailing opinion today completely obliterates: that between conventional religions that usually have an organized and formal structure and dogma and a cohesive group identity, even when nontheistic, and cults that represent schools of thought and in the usual case are without formal structure or are, at most, loose and informal associations of individuals who share common ethical, moral, or intellectual views.

II

When the plain thrust of a legislative enactment can only be circumvented by distortion to avert an inevitable constitutional collision, it is only by exalting form over substance that one can justify this veering off the path that has been plainly marked by the statute. Such a course betrays extreme skepticism as to constitutionality, and, in this instance, reflects a groping to preserve the conscientious objector exemption at all cost.

I cannot subscribe to a wholly emasculated construction of a statute to avoid facing a latent constitutional question, in purported fidelity to the salutary doctrine of avoiding unnecessary resolution of constitutional issues, a principle to which I fully
⌐356 adhere. . . . ⊥

III

The constitutional question that must be faced in this case is whether a statute that defers to the individual's conscience only when his views emanate from adherence to theistic religious beliefs is within the power of Congress. Congress, of course, could, entirely consistently with the requirements of the Constitution, eliminate *all* exemptions for conscientious objectors. Such a course would be wholly "neutral" and, in my view, would not offend the Free Exercise Clause, for reasons set forth in my dis-
⌐357 senting opinion in *Sherbert* v. *Verner.* . . . ⊥

The "radius" of this legislation is the conscientiousness with which an individual opposes war in general, yet the statute, as I think it must be construed, excludes from its "scope" individuals motivated by teachings of non-theistic religions, and individuals guided by an inner ethical voice that bespeaks secular and not "religious" reflection. It not only accords a preference to the "religious" but also disadvantages adherents of religions that do not worship a Supreme Being. The constitutional infirmity cannot be cured, moreover, even by an impermissible construction that eliminates the theistic requirement and simply draws the line between religious and nonreligious. This in my view offends the Establishment
⌐358 Clause and is that kind of classification ⊥ that this Court has condemned. . . .

⌐365 ⊥ The policy of exempting religious conscientious objectors is one of longstanding tradition in this country and accords recognition to what is, in a diverse and "open" society, the important value of re-
⌐366 conciling in⊥dividuality of belief with practical exigencies whenever possible. It dates back to colonial times and has been perpetuated in state and federal conscription statutes. That it has been phrased in religious terms reflects, I assume, the fact that ethics and morals, while the concern of secular philosophy, have traditionally been matters taught by organized religion and that for most individuals spiritual and ethical nourishment is derived from that source. It further reflects, I would suppose, the

assumption that beliefs emanating from a religious source are probably held with great intensity.

When a policy has roots so deeply embedded in history, there is a compelling reason for a court to hazard the necessary statutory repairs if they can be made within the administrative framework of the statute and without impairing other legislative goals, even though they entail, not simply eliminating an offending section, but rather building upon it. Thus I am prepared to accept the prevailing opinion's conscientious objector test, not as a reflection of congressional statutory intent but as patch⊥work of   ⌐367 judicial making that cures the defect of underinclusion in § 6(j) and can be administered by local boards in the usual course of business. Like the prevailing opinion, I also conclude that petitioner's beliefs are held with the required intensity and consequently vote to *reverse* the judgment of conviction.

Mr. Justice WHITE, with whom The *Chief Justice* and *Mr. Justice STEWART* join, dissenting.

Whether or not *United States* v. *Seeger* accurately reflected the intent of Congress in providing draft exemptions for religious conscientious objectors to war, I cannot join today's construction of § 6(j) extending draft exemption to those who disclaim religious objections to war and whose views about war represent a purely personal code arising not from religious training and belief as the statute requires but from readings in philosophy, history, and sociology. Our obli⊥gation in statutory construction cases is to   ⌐368 enforce the will of Congress, not our own; and as *Mr. Justice HARLAN* has demonstrated, construing § 6(j) to include Welsh exempts from the draft a class of persons to whom Congress has expressly denied an exemption.

For me that conclusion should end this case. Even if Welsh is quite right in asserting that exempting religious believers is an establishment of religion forbidden by the First Amendment, he nevertheless remains one of those persons whom Congress took pains not to relieve from military duty. Whether or not § 6(j) is constitutional, Welsh had no First Amendment excuse for refusing to report for induction. If it is contrary to the express will of Congress to exempt Welsh, as I think it is, then there is no warrant for saving the religious exemption and the statute by redrafting it in this Court to include Welsh and all others like him. . . . ⊥   ⌐369

If I am wrong in thinking that Welsh cannot benefit from invalidation of § 6(j) on Establishment Clause grounds, I would nevertheless affirm his conviction; for I cannot hold that Congress violated the Clause in exempting from the draft all those who oppose war by reason of religious training and belief. In exempting religious conscientious objectors, Congress was making one of two judgments, perhaps both. First, § 6(j) may represent a purely practical judgment that religious objectors, however admirable, would be of no more use in combat than many others unqualified for military service. Exemption was not extended to them to further religious belief or practice but to limit military service to those who were prepared to undertake the fighting that the armed services have to do. On this basis, the exemption has neither the primary purpose nor the effect of furthering religion. As *Mr. Justice FRANKFURTER*, joined by *Mr. Justice HARLAN*, said, in a separate opinion in the Sunday Closing Law Cases, an establishment contention "can prevail only if the absence of any substantial legislative purpose other than a religious one is made to appear."

Second, Congress may have granted the exemption because otherwise religious objectors would be forced into conduct that their religions forbid and because ⊥ in the view of Congress to deny the exemption would violate the Free Exercise Clause or at least raise grave problems in this respect. True, this Court has more than once stated its unwillingness to construe the First Amendment, standing alone, as requiring draft exemptions for religious believers. But this Court is not alone in being obliged to construe the Constitution in the course of its work; nor does it even approach having a monopoly on the wisdom and insight appropriate to the task. Legislative exemptions for those with religious convictions against war date from colonial days. As Chief Justice Hughes explained in his dissent in *United States* v. *Macintosh*, the importance of giving immunity to those having conscientious scruples against bearing arms has consistently been emphasized in debates in Congress and such draft exemptions are " 'indicative of the actual operation of the principles of the Constitution.' " However this Court might construe the First Amendment, Congress has regularly steered clear of free exercise problems by granting exemptions to those who conscientiously oppose war on religious grounds. . . .⊥

Congress has the power "To raise and support Armies" and "To make all Laws which shall be necessary and proper for carrying into Execution" that power. Art I, § 8. The power to raise armies must be exercised consistently with the First Amendment which, among other things, forbids laws prohibiting the free exercise of religion. It is surely essential therefore—surely "necessary and proper"— in enacting laws for the raising of armies to take account of the First Amendment and to avoid possible violations of the Free Exercise Clause. If this was the course Congress took, then just as in *Katzenbach* v. *Morgan* where we accepted the judgment of Congress as to what legislation was appropriate to enforce the Equal Protection Clause of the Fourteenth Amendment, here we should respect congressional judgment accommodating the Free Exercise Clause and the power to raise armies. This involves no surrender of the Court's function as ultimate arbiter in disputes over interpretation of the Constitution. But it was

enough in *Katzenbach* "to perceive a basis upon which the Congress might resolve the conflict as it did," and plainly in the case before us there is an arguable basis for § 6(j) in the Free Exercise Clause since, without the exemption, the law would compel some members of the public to engage in combat ⊥ operations contrary to their religious convictions. Indeed, one federal court has recently held that to draft a man for combat service contrary to his conscientious beliefs would violate the First Amendment. There being substantial roots in the Free Exercise Clause for § 6(j) I would not frustrate congressional will by construing the Establishment Clause to condition the exemption for religionists upon extending the exemption also to those who object to war on nonreligious grounds.

We have said that neither support nor hostility, but neutrality, is the goal of the religion clauses of the First Amendment. "Neutrality," however, is not self-defining. If it is "favoritism" and not "neutrality" to exempt religious believers from the draft, is it "neutrality" and not "inhibition" of religion to compel religious believers to fight when they have special reasons for not doing so, reasons to which the Constitution gives particular recognition? It cannot be ignored that the First Amendment itself contains a religious classification. The Amendment protects belief and speech, but as a general proposition, the free speech provisions stop short of immunizing conduct from official regulation. The Free Exercise Clause, however, has a deeper cut: it protects conduct as well as religious belief and speech. "[I]t safeguards the free exercise of the chosen form of religion. Thus the Amendment embraces two concepts,—freedom to believe and freedom to act. The first is absolute but, in the nature of things, the second cannot be." *Cantwell* v. *Connecticut*. Although socially harmful acts may as a rule be banned despite the Free Exercise Clause even where religiously motivated, there is an area of conduct that cannot be forbidden to religious practitioners but which may be forbidden to others. ⊥ We should thus not labor to find a violation of the Establishment Clause when free exercise values prompt Congress to relieve religious believers from the burdens of the law at least in those instances where the law is not merely prohibitory but commands the performance of military duties that are forbidden by a man's religion. . . .

The Establishment Clause as construed by this Court unquestionably has independent significance; its function is not wholly auxiliary to the Free Exercise Clause. ⊥ It bans some involvements of the State with religion that otherwise might be consistent with the Free Exercise Clause. But when in the rationally based judgment or Congress free exercise of religion calls for shielding religious objectors from compulsory combat duty, I am reluctant to frustrate the legislative will by striking down the statutory exemption because it does not also reach those to whom the Free Exercise Clause offers no protection whatsoever.

I would affirm the judgment below.

GILLETTE v. UNITED STATES (No. 85)

ON WRIT OF CERTIORARI TO THE UNITED STATES CIRCUIT COURT OF APPEALS FOR THE SECOND CIRCUIT

NEGRE v. LARSEN (No. 325)

ON WRIT OF CERTIORARI TO THE UNITED STATES CIRCUIT COURT OF APPEALS FOR THE NINTH CIRCUIT
401 U.S. 437

Argued December 9, 1970 — Decided March 8, 1971

⌐439 ⊥ *Mr. Justice MARSHALL* delivered the opinion of the Court.

These cases present the question whether conscientious objection to a particular war, rather than objection to war as such, relieves the objector from responsibilities of military training and service. Specifically, we are called upon to decide whether conscientious scruples relating to a particular conflict are within the purview of established provisions relieving conscientious objectors to war from military service. Both petitioners also invoke constitutional principles barring government interference with the exercise of religion and requiring governmental neutrality in matters of religion.

In No. 85, petitioner Gillette was convicted of wilful failure to report for induction into the armed forces. Gillette defended on the ground that he should have been ruled exempt from induction as a conscientious objector to war. In support of his unsuccessful request for classification as a conscientious objector, this petitioner had stated his willingness to participate in a war of national defense or a war sponsored by the United Nations as a peace-keeping measure, but declared his opposition to American military operations in Vietnam, which he characterized as "unjust." Petitioner concluded that he could not in conscience enter and serve in the armed forces during the period of the Vietnam conflict. Gillette's view of his duty to abstain from any involvement in a war seen as unjust is, in his words, "based on a humanist approach to religion," and his personal decision concerning military service was guided by fundamental principles of conscience and deeply held views about the purpose and obligation of human existence. ⊥

⌐440

The District Court determined that there was a basis in fact to support administrative denial of exemption in Gillette's case. The denial of exemption was upheld, and Gillette's defense to the criminal charge rejected, not because of doubt about the sincerity or the religious character of petitioner's objection to military service, but because his objection ran to a particular war. In affirming the conviction, the Court of Appeals concluded that Gillette's conscientious beliefs "were specifically directed against the war in Vietnam," while the relevant exemption provision of the Military Selective Service Act of 1967, "requires opposition 'to participation in war in any form.'"

In No. 325, petitioner Negre, after induction into the Army, completion of basic training, and receipt of orders for Vietnam duty, commenced proceedings looking to his discharge as a conscientious objector to war. Application for discharge was denied, and Negre sought judicial relief by habeas corpus. The District Court found a basis in fact for the Army's rejection of petitioner's application for discharge. Habeas relief was denied, and the denial was affirmed on appeal, because, in the language of the Court of Appeals, Negre "objects to the war in Vietnam, not to all wars," and therefore does "not qualify for separation [from the Army], as a conscientious objector." Again, no question is raised as to the sincerity or the religious quality of this petitioner's views. In line with religious counseling, and numerous religious texts, Negre, ⊥ a devout Catholic, believes that it is his duty as a faithful Catholic to discriminate between "just" and "unjust" wars, and to forswear participation in the latter. His assessment of the Vietnam conflict as an unjust war became clear in his mind after completion of infantry training, and Negre is now firmly of the view that any personal involvement in that war would contravene his conscience and "all that I had been taught in my religious training."   ⌐441

We granted certiorari in these cases in order to resolve vital issues concerning the exercise of congressional power to raise and support armies, as affected by the religious guarantees of the First Amendment. We affirm the judgments below in both cases.

I

Each petitioner claims a nonconstitutional right to be relieved of the duty of military service in virtue of his conscientious scruples. Both claims turn on the proper construction of § 6(j) of the Military Selective Service Act of 1967 which provides:

"Nothing contained in this title . . . shall be construed to require any person to be subject to combatant training and service in the armed forces of the United States who, by reason of religious training and belief, is conscientiously opposed to participation in war in any form." ⊥   ⌐442

This language controls Gillette's claim to exemption, which was asserted administratively prior to the point of induction. Department of Defense Directive No. 1300.6 (May 10, 1968), prescribes that post-induction claims to conscientious objector sta-

tus shall be honored, if valid, by the various branches of the armed forces. Section 6(j) of the Act, as construed by the courts, is incorporated by the various service regulations issued pursuant to the Directive, and thus the standards for measuring claims of in-service objectors, such as Negre, are the same as the statutory tests applicable in a pre-induction
⌊443 situation. ⊥

For purposes of determining the statutory status of conscientious objection to a particular war, the focal language of § 6(j) is the phrase, "conscientiously opposed to participation in war in any form." This language, on a straightforward reading, can bear but one meaning; that conscientious scruples relating to war and military service must amount to conscientious opposition to participating personally in any war and all war. . . .

A different result cannot be supported by reliance on the materials of legislative history. Petitioners
⌊444 and ⊥ amici point to no episode or pronouncement in the legislative history of § 6(j), or of predecessor provisions, that tends to overthrow the obvious in-
⌊445 terpretation of the words themselves. ⊥

It is true that the legislative materials reveal a deep concern for the situation of conscientious objectors to war, who absent special status would be put to a hard choice between contravening imperatives of religion and conscience or suffering penalties. Moreover, there are clear indications that congressional reluctance to impose such a choice stems from a recognition of the value of conscientious action to the democratic community at large, and from respect for the general proposition that fundamental principles of conscience and religious duty may sometimes override the demands of the secular state. But there are countervailing considerations, which are also the concern of Congress, and the legislative materials simply do not support the view that Congress intended to recognize any conscientious claim whatever as a basis for relieving the claimant from the general responsibility or the various incidents of military service. The claim that is recognized by § 6(j) is
⌊446 a ⊥ claim of conscience running against war as such. This claim, not one involving opposition to a particular war only, was plainly the focus of congressional concern.

Finding little comfort in the wording or the legislative history of § 6(j), petitioners rely heavily on dicta in the decisional law dealing with objectors whose conscientious scruples ran against war as such, but who indicated certain reservations of an abstract nature. It is instructive that none of the cases relied upon embraces an interpretation of § 6(j) at variance with the construction we adopt today.

Sicurella v. *United States* presented the only previous occasion for this Court to focus on the "participation in war in any form" language of § 6(j). In Sicurella a Jehovah's Witness who opposed participation in secular wars was held to possess the requisite conscientious scruples concerning war,

although he was not opposed to participation in a "theocratic war" commanded by Jehovah. The Court noted that the "theocratic war" reservation was highly abstract—no such war had occurred since biblical times, and none was contemplated. Congress, on the other hand, had in mind "real shooting wars," and Sicurella's abstract reservations did not undercut his conscientious opposition to participating in such wars. Plainly, Sicurella cannot be read to support the claims of those, like petitioners, ⊥ who for a   ⌊447 variety of reasons consider one particular "real shooting war" to be unjust, and therefore oppose participation in that war. . . .

II

⊥ Both petitioners argue that § 6(j), construed to   ⌊448 cover only objectors to all war, violates the religious clauses of the First Amendment. The First Amendment provides that "Congress shall make no law respecting an establishment of religion, or prohibiting the free exercise thereof. . . ." Petitioners contend that Congress interferes with free exercise of religion by failing to relieve objectors to a particular war from military service, when the objection is religious or conscientious in nature. While the two religious clauses—pertaining to "free exercise" and ⊥ "estab-   ⌊449 lishment" of religion—overlap and interact in many ways, it is best to focus first on petitioners other contention, that § 6(j) is a law respecting the establishment of religion. For despite free exercise overtones, the gist of the constitutional complaint is that § 6(j) impermissibly discriminates among types of religious belief and affiliation.

On the assumption that these petitioners' beliefs concerning war have roots that are "religious" in nature, within the meaning of the Amendment as well as this Court's decisions construing § 6(j), petitioners ask how their claims to relief from military service can be permitted to fail, while other "religious" claims are upheld by the Act. It is a fact that § 6(j), properly construed, has this effect. Yet we cannot conclude in mechanical fashion, or at all, that the section works an establishment of religion . . .
⊥   ⌊450

A

The critical weakness of petitioners' establishment claim arises from the fact that § 6(j), on its face, simply does not discriminate on the basis of religious affiliation or religious belief, apart of course from beliefs concerning war. The section says that anyone who is conscientiously opposed to all war shall be relieved of military service. The specified objection must have a grounding in "religious training and belief," but no par ⊥ ticular sectarian affiliation or the-   ⌊451 ological position is required. The Draft Act of 1917 extended relief only to those conscientious objectors affiliated with some "well-recognized religious sect or organization" whose principles forbade members' participation in war, but the attempt to focus on particular sects apparently broke down in administrative practice, *Welsh* v. *United States*, and the 1940 Selective Training and Service Act discarded all sectarian restriction. Thereafter Congress has framed the conscientious objector exemption in broad terms compatible with "its long-established policy of not picking and choosing among religious beliefs." *United States* v. *Seeger.*

Thus, there is no occasion to consider the claim that when Congress grants a benefit expressly to adherents of one *religion*, courts must either nullify the grant or somehow extend the benefit to cover all religions. For § 6(j) does not single out any religious organization or religious creed for special treatment. Rather petitioners' contention is that since Congress has recognized one sort of conscientious objection concerning war, whatever its religious basis, the Establishment Clause commands that another, different objection be carved out and protected by the courts.

Properly phrased, petitioners' contention is that the special statutory status accorded conscientious objection to all war, but not objection to a particular war, works ⊥ a de facto discrimination among religions. This happens, say petitioners, because some religious faiths themselves distinguish between personal participation in "just" and in "unjust" wars, commending the former and forbidding the latter, and therefore adherents of some religious faiths— and individuals whose personal beliefs of a religious nature include the distinction—cannot object to all wars consistently with what is regarded as the true imperative of conscience. Of course, this contention of de facto religious discrimination, rendering § 6(j) fatally underinclusive, cannot simply be brushed aside. The question of governmental neutrality is not concluded by the observation that § 6(j) on its face makes no discrimination between religions, for the Establishment Clause forbids subtle departures from neutrality, "religious gerrymanders," as well as obvious abuses. . . .

For the reasons that follow, we believe that petitioners have failed to make the requisite showing with respect to § 6(j).

Section 6(j) serves a number of valid purposes having nothing to do with a design to foster or favor any sect, religion, or cluster of religions. There are considera⊥tions of a pragmatic nature, such as the hopelessness of converting a sincere conscientious objector into an effective fighting man, but no doubt the section reflects as well the view that "in the forum of conscience, duty to a moral power higher than the State has always been maintained." *United States* v. *Macintosh.* We have noted that the legislative materials show congressional concern for the hard choice that conscription would impose on conscientious objectors to war, as well as respect for the value of conscientious action and for the principle of supremacy of conscience.

⌊452

⌊453

Naturally the considerations just mentioned are affirmative in character, going to support the existence of an exemption rather than its restriction specifically to persons who object to all war. The point is that these affirmative purposes are neutral in the sense of the Establishment Clause. Quite apart from the question whether the Free Exercise Clause might require some sort of exemption, it is hardly impermissible for Congress to attempt to accommodate free exercise values, in line with "our happy tradition" of "avoiding unnecessary clashes with the dictates of conscience." *United States* v. *Macintosh.* . . .⊥

In the draft area for 30 years the exempting provision has focused on individual conscientious belief, not on sectarian affiliation. The relevant individual belief is simply objection to all war, not adherence to any extraneous theological viewpoint. And while the objection must have roots in conscience and personality that are "religious" in nature, this requirement has never been construed to elevate conventional piety or religiosity of any kind above the imperatives of a personal faith.

In this state of affairs it is impossible to say that § 6(j) intrudes upon "voluntarism," in religious life, or that the congressional purpose in enacting § 6(j) is to promote or foster those religious organizations that traditionally have taught the duty to abstain from participation in any war. A claimant, seeking judicial protection for his own conscientious beliefs, would be hard put to argue that § 6(j) encourages membership in putatively "favored" religious organizations, for the painful dilemma of the sincere conscientious objector arises precisely because he feels himself bound in conscience not to compromise his beliefs or affiliations.

B

We conclude not only that the affirmative purposes underlying § 6(j) are neutral and secular, but also that valid neutral reasons exist for limiting the exemption to objectors to all war, and that the section therefore cannot be said to reflect a religious preference.

⊥Apart from the Government's need for manpower, perhaps the central interest involved in the administration of conscription laws is the interest in maintaining a fair system for determining "who serves when not all serve." When the Government exacts so much, the importance of fair, evenhanded, and uniform decisionmaking is obviously intensified. The Government argues that the interest in fairness would be jeopardized by expansion of § 6(j) to include conscientious objection to a particular war. The contention is that the claim to relief on account of such objection is intrinsically a claim of uncertain dimensions, and that granting the claim in theory would involve a real danger of erratic or even dis-

⌊454

⌊455

criminatory decisionmaking in administrative practice.

A virtually limitless variety of beliefs are subsumable under the rubric, "objection to a particular war." All the factors that might go into nonconscientious dissent from policy, also might appear as the concrete basis of an objection that has roots as well in conscience and religion. Indeed, over the realm of possible situations, opposition to a particular war may more likely be political and nonconscientious, than otherwise. The difficulties of sort⊥ing the two, with a sure hand, are considerable. Moreover, the belief that a particular war at a particular time is unjust is by its nature changeable and subject to nullification by changing events. Since objection may fasten on any of an enormous number of variables, the claim is ultimately subjective, depending on the claimant's view of the facts in relation to his judgment that a given factor or congeries of factors colors the character of the war as a whole. In short, it is not at all obvious in theory what sorts of objections should be deemed sufficient to excuse an objector, and there is considerable force in the Government's contention that a program of excusing objectors to particular wars may be "impossible to conduct with any hope of reaching fair and consistent results. . . ."

For their part, petitioners make no attempt to provide a careful definition of the claim to exemption that they ask the courts to carve out and protect. They do not explain why objection to a particular conflict—much less an objection that focuses on a particular facet of a conflict—should excuse the objector from all military service whatever, even from military operations that are connected with the conflict at hand in remote or tenuous ways. They suggest no solution to the problems arising from the fact that altered circumstances may quickly render the objection to military service moot.

To view the problem of fairness and evenhanded decisionmaking, in the present context, as merely a commonplace chore of weeding out "spurious claims," is to minimize substantial difficulties of real concern to a responsible legislative body. For example, under the petitioners' unarticulated scheme for exemption, an objector's claim to exemption might be based on some feature of a current conflict that most would regard as incidental, ⊥ or might be predicated on a view of the facts that most would regard as mistaken. The particular complaint about the war may itself be "sincere," but it is difficult to know how to judge the "sincerity" of the objector's conclusion that the war in toto is unjust and that any personal involvement would contravene conscience and religion. . . .⊥

Of course, we do not suggest that Congress would have acted irrationally or unreasonably had it decided to exempt those who object to particular wars. Our analysis of the policies of § 6(j) is undertaken in order to determine the existence vel non of a neutral, secular justification for the lines Congress has drawn. We find that justifying reasons exist and therefore hold that the Establishment Clause is not violated.

III

⊥ Petitioners' remaining contention is that Congress interferes with the free exercise of religion by conscripting persons who oppose a particular war on grounds of conscience and religion. Strictly viewed, this complaint does not implicate problems of comparative treatment of different sorts of objectors, but rather may be examined in some isolation from the circumstance that Congress has chosen to exempt those who conscientiously object to all war. And our holding that § 6(j) comports with the Establishment Clause does not automatically settle the present issue. For despite a general harmony of purpose between the two religious clauses of the First Amendment, the Free Exercise Clause no doubt has a reach of its own.

Nonetheless, our analysis of § 6(j) for Establishment Clause purposes has revealed governmental interests of a kind and weight sufficient to justify under the Free Exercise Clause the impact of the conscription laws on those who object to particular wars. . . .⊥

The conscription laws, applied to such persons as to others, are not designed to interfere with any religious ritual or practice, and do not work a penalty against any theological position. The incidental burdens felt by persons in petitioners' position are strictly justified by substantial governmental interests that relate directly to the very impacts questioned. And more broadly, of course, there is the Government's interest in procuring the manpower necessary for military purposes, pursuant to the constitutional grant of power to Congress to raise and support armies.

IV

⊥ Since petitioners' statutory and constitutional claims to relief from military service are without merit, it follows that in Gillette's case (No. 85) there was a basis in fact to support administrative denial of exemption, and that in Negre's case (No. 325) there was a basis in fact to support the Army's denial of a discharge. Accordingly, the judgments below are

Affirmed.

Mr. Justice BLACK concurs in the Court's judgment and in Part I of the opinion of the Court.

Mr. Justice DOUGLAS, dissenting in *Gillette* v. *United States* (No. 85).

Gillette's objection is to combat service in the Vietnam war, not to wars in general, and the basis of his objection is his conscience. His objection does not put him into the statutory exemption which extends to one "who, by reason of religious training and belief, is conscientiously opposed to participation in war in any form."

He stated his views as follows:

"I object to any assignment in the United States Armed Forces while this unnecessary and unjust war is being waged, on the grounds of religious belief specifically 'Humanism.' This essentially means respect and love for man, faith in his inherent goodness and perfectability, and confidence in his capability to improve some of the pains of the human condition."

This position is substantially the same as that of Sisson in *United States* v. *Sisson* ⊥ where the District Court summarized the draftee's position as follows:

"Sisson's table of ultimate values is moral and ethical. It reflects quite as real, pervasive, durable, and commendable a marshalling of priorities as a formal religion. It is just as much a residue of culture, early training, and beliefs shared by companions and family. What another derives from the discipline of a church, Sisson derives from the discipline of conscience."

There is no doubt that the views of Gillette are sincere, genuine, and profound. The District Court in the present case faced squarely the issue presented in *Sisson* and being unable to distinguish the case on the facts, refused to follow *Sisson*.

The question, Can a conscientious objector, whether his objection be rooted in "religion" or in moral values, be required to kill? has never been answered by the Court. *Hamilton* v. *Regents*, did no more than hold that the Fourteenth Amendment did not require a State to make its university available to one who would not take military training. *United States* v. *Macintosh* denied naturalization to a person who "would not promise in advance to bear arms in defense of the United States unless he believed the war to be morally justified." The question of compelling a man to kill against his conscience was not squarely involved. Most of the talk in the majority opinion concerned "serving in the armed forces of the ⊥ Nation in time of war." Such service can, of course, take place in noncombatant roles. The ruling was that such service is "dependent upon the will of Congress and not upon the scruples of the individual, except as Congress provides." The dicta of the Court in the *Macintosh* case squint towards the denial of Gillette's claim, though as I have said, the issue was not squarely presented.

Yet if dicta are to be our guide, my choice is the dicta of Chief Justice Hughes who, dissenting in *Macintosh*, spoke as well for Justices Holmes, Brandeis, and Stone:

"Nor is there ground, in my opinion, for the exclusion of Professor Macintosh because his conscientious scruples have particular reference to

wars believed to be unjust. There is nothing new in such an attitude. Among the most eminent statesmen here and abroad have been those who condemned the action of their country in entering into wars they thought to be unjustified. Agreements for the renunciation of war presuppose a preponderant public sentiment against wars of aggression. If, while recognizing the power of Congress, the mere holding of religious or conscientious scruples against all wars should not disqualify a citizen from holding office in this country, or an applicant otherwise qualified from being admitted to citizenship, there would seem to be no reason why a reservation of religious or conscientious objection to participation in wars believed to be unjust should constitute such a disqualification."

I think the Hughes view is the constitutional view. It is true that the First Amendment speaks of the free exercise of religion, not of the free exercise of conscience or belief. Yet conscience and belief are the main ingredients of First Amendment rights. They are the ⊥ bedrock of free speech as well as religion. . . .

⊥ The law as written is a species of those which show an invidious discrimination in favor of religious persons and against others with like scruples. . . .⊥

I had assumed that the welfare of the single human soul was the ultimate test of the vitality of the First Amendment.

This is an appropriate occasion to give content to our dictum in *Board of Education* v. *Barnette*: "[F]reedom to differ is not limited to things that do not matter much. . . . The test of its sub⊥stance is the right to differ as to things that touch the heart of the existing order."

I would reverse this judgment.

Mr. Justice DOUGLAS, dissenting in *Negre* v. *Larsen* (No. 325).

I approach the facts of this case with some diffidence, as they involve doctrines of the Catholic Church in which I was not raised. But we have on one of petitioner's briefs an authoritative lay Catholic scholar, Dr. John T. Noonan, Jr., and from that brief I deduce the following:

Under the doctrines of the Catholic Church a person has a moral duty to take part in wars declared by his government so long as they comply with the tests of his church for just wars. Conversely, a Catholic has a moral duty not to participate in unjust wars.⊥

The Fifth Commandment, "Thou shalt not kill," provides a basis for the distinction between just and unjust wars. In the 16th century Francisco Victoria, Dominican master of the University of Salamanca and pioneer in international law, elaborated on the distinction. "If a subject is convinced of the injustice of a war, he ought not to serve in it, even on the command of his prince. This is clear, for no one can authorize the killing of an innocent person." He realized not all men had the information of the prince and his counsellors on the causes of a war, but where "the proofs and tokens of the injustice of the war may be such that ignorance would be no excuse even to the subjects" who are not normally informed, that ignorance will not be an excuse if they participate. Well over 400 years later, today, the Baltimore Catechism makes an exception to the Fifth Commandment for a "soldier fighting a just war."

No one can tell a Catholic that this or that war is either just or unjust. This is a personal decision that an individual must make on the basis of his own ⌐472 conscience after studying the facts.⊥

Like the distinction between just and unjust wars, the duty to obey conscience is not a new doctrine in the Catholic Church. When told to stop preaching by the Sanhedrin, to which they were subordinate by law, "Peter and the apostles answered and said, 'We must obey God rather than men.'" That duty has not changed. Pope Paul VI has expressed it as follows: "On his part, man perceives and acknowledges the imperatives of the divine law through the mediation of conscience. In all his activity a man is bound to follow his conscience, in order that he may come to God, the end and purpose of life."

While the fact that the ultimate determination of whether a war is unjust rests on individual con⌐473 science, the Church has provided guides. . . .⊥

⌐474 Louis Negre is a devout Catholic. In 1951 when he was four, his family immigrated to this country from ⊥ France. He attended Catholic schools in Bakersfield, California, until graduation from high school. Then he attended Bakersfield Junior College for two years. Following that, he was inducted into the Army.

At the time of his induction he had his own convictions about the Vietnam war and the Army's goals in the war. He wanted, however, to be sure of his convictions. "I agreed to myself that before making any decision or taking any type of stand on the issue, I would permit myself to see and understand the Army's explanation of its reasons for violence in Vietnam. For, without getting an insight on the subject, it would be unfair for me to say anything, without really knowing the answer."

On completion of his advanced infantry training, "I knew that if I would permit myself to go to Vietnam I would be violating my own concepts of natural law and would be going against all that I had been taught in my religious training." Negre applied for a discharge as a conscientious objector. His application was denied. He then refused to comply with an order to proceed for shipment to Vietnam. A general court-martial followed, but he was acquitted. After that he filed this application for discharge as a con⌐475 scientious objector.⊥

Negre is opposed under his religious training and beliefs to participation in any form in the war in Vietnam. His sincerity is not questioned. His application for a discharge, however, was denied because his religious training and beliefs led him to oppose only a particular war which according to his conscience was unjust.

For the reasons I have stated in my dissent in the *Gillette* case decided this day, I would reverse the judgment.

RELIGION AND THE RIGHT TO WORK

Although the right to work is not one of the enumerated rights guaranteed in the Constitution, the right to engage in a legitimate occupation for financial gain, free of unreasonable burden by government, is undoubtedly considered an inalienable right by the American people. Historically, the courts have ordinarily found that guarantee in the due process and equal protection of the laws provisions of the Fifth and Fourteenth Amendments. Occasionally, however, the right to work has become legally involved with the religion clauses of the First Amendment. A substantial number of these cases have in recent years made their way to the Supreme Court.

Because they went off primarily on the basis of Establishment Clause issues, the compulsory Sunday closing law cases decided by the Court in 1961 are discussed in Chapter 3. However, in two of the cases—BRAUNFELD v. BROWN (p. 316) and *Gallagher* v. *Crown Kosher Super Markets*—Orthodox Jewish merchants claimed that the laws of Pennsylvania and Massachusetts, by limiting their businesses to a five-day week, placed them at a great economic disadvantage in their competition with non-Sabbatarian storekeepers and placed an unreasonable burden on their free exercise of religion. The Court majority conceded that the laws did indeed impose an indirect burden on their religious rights, but maintained that the burden was not unreasonable and that there was no viable less restrictive alternative means by which the states could accomplish their secular objectives. Justice Stewart, in dissent, insisted that a state could not constitutionally compel "an Orthodox Jew to choose between his religious faith and his economic survival."

SHERBERT v. VERNER (p. 145), decided two years later, involved a similar yet different constitutional claim—that of an employee rather than a business owner and one in which the Free Exercise Clause is primary rather than secondary. Mrs. Adell Sherbert joined the Seventh-day Adventist Church in 1957. At the time, she was employed at a textile mill in the Spartanburg, South Carolina, area. She experienced no conflict between her job and her new religion because the mill worked a five-day week, but in 1959 the mill changed to a six-day week for all three shifts. The sixth work day was Saturday. She refused to work on Saturday and was dismissed by her employer.

After her discharge, Mrs. Sherbert applied to three other textile mills for five-day employment, but none was available. At that point she applied to the state Employment Security Commission for unemployment compensation. In her application she stated her willingness to work in other mills, or even in other industries, as long as Saturday work was not involved. The request for unemployment compensation was denied and she sued.

Two South Carolina courts upheld the findings of the Employment Security Commission that Mrs. Sherbert's refusal to accept Saturday employment disqualified her for unemployment benefits as a worker who failed to accept "suitable work when offered . . . by the employment office or the employer." At no time during the court proceedings was there any question about the sincerity of her beliefs or that prohibition of Saturday work is a basic belief of the Seventh-day Adventist Church.

In a seven-to-two decision, the Supreme Court reversed the lower courts and found in favor of the Sabbatarian. The Court held that to disqualify the appellant for unemployment benefits only because she refused to work on Saturday, a decision based firmly on her religious beliefs, was to impose an unconstitutional burden upon the free exercise of her religion. Withholding of benefits forced the appellant to choose between following the teachings of her religion and not working or receiving benefits, or abandoning one of the precepts of her religion in order to accept work. For the government to compel such a choice was clearly a violation of the Free Exercise Clause. "To condition the availability of benefits upon this appellant's willingness to violate a cardinal principle of her religious faith," wrote Justice Brennan for the majority, "effectively penalizes the free exercise of her constitutional liberties." (374 U.S. 398, 406)

The Court also denied that to decide in favor of the appellant was to "establish" the Seventh-day Adventist religion. To allow Sabbatarians to be the recipients of unemployment compensation along with Sunday worshippers merely reflects governmental neutrality in the area of religious differences. [1] Not to allow the benefits to Sabbatarians would show hostility to their religion.

Of interest is the fact that the two dissenters and even Justice Stewart, who concurred in the result of the decision, wrote that they believed this case was clearly inconsistent with the decision reached by the Court in *Braunfeld*. Indeed, they failed to see how *Braunfeld* could continue to stand in the light of this opinion. The injury suffered by Mr. Braunfeld when the Sunday closing law was upheld (i.e., having to close his business) was much greater than that which would have been suffered by Mrs. Sherbert if the Court had not found in her favor (i.e., losing twenty-two weeks of unemployment pay). In view of the expression of these doubts, it is rather surprising that the Sunday closing law dispute has not been taken to the Court again. This failure may be due to the fact that many Sunday laws have been repealed or modified and, except for sporadic holiday season efforts, existing laws have been largely ignored in more recent times by law enforcement officials; thus the weight of such laws is no longer so onerous to Sabbatarians. [2]

It has been said that, with the possible exception of WISCONSIN v. YODER (p. 200), the *Sherbert* case

broadens free exercise claims more than any previous decision of the Supreme Court. In the Sunday closing law cases the Court argued that if the state's laws had only an indirect effect on the Sabbatarians' exercise of religion, there was no basis for challenge of the laws. In the *Sherbert* case, however, the Court said that even indirect inhibitions of religious exercise could be challenged under the Free Exercise Clause. Furthermore, in the *Braunfeld* and *Crown Kosher Market* cases the Sabbatarians asked only to be left alone, to be able to practice their religion without economic damage to themselves. In the *Sherbert* case the Sabbatarian demanded that the state pay her money when she refused to work for religious reasons, and the Court held that she was entitled to that money. [3] In this case, the Court indeed gave the Free Exercise Clause a broad interpretation.

As has been mentioned earlier, the "least restrictive alternative means" test advanced by the Court in *Braunfeld* and subsequently used in *Sherbert* to the appellant's benefit, represented a significant development. *Sherbert*, in turn, established the requirement of a showing of "compelling state interest" to justify even incidental infringement of religious rights. Combined for use as a judicial standard, the two concepts had great potential for an extremely broad reading of free exercise rights.

This interpretation gained statutory status in 1972 when the Civil Rights Act of 1964 was amended to provide that "it shall be an unlawful employment practice for an employer . . . to . . . discharge any individual, or otherwise to discriminate against any individual with respect to his compensation, terms, conditions, or privileges of employment, because of such individual's . . . religion." The act also undertook to define religion as used in the revision, and incorporated a 1967 Equal Employment Opportunity Commission "guideline" for enforcement of the law when it provided:

> The term "religion" includes all aspects of religious observance and practice, as well as belief, unless an employer demonstrates that he is unable to reasonably accommodate to an employee's or prospective employee's religious observances or practice without undue hardship on the conduct of the employer's business. (Title VII, § 701(j) U.S.C., § 2000C(j)

The burden of proof with regard to undue hardship was placed on the employer.

This definition, together with the accompanying condition, was an effort to do by legislation what the Supreme Court had failed to do the year before because of a four-to-four deadlock in *Dewey* v. *Reynolds Metal Company*. In that case a federal Court of Appeals had upheld a company's refusal to accede to the demands of a Sabbatarian that the company make arrangements to accommodate his religious conviction. The evenly-divided vote had the effect of affirming the lower court's determination that existing law did not mandate the requested company action.

After the 1972 amendment, litigation quickly developed in an effort to determine the meaning of the requirement

---

[1] For an elaboration of this "neutrality" argument, cf. Wilber G. Katz, *Religion and American Constitutions* (Evanston, Ill.: Northwestern University Press, 1963), pp. 12-18, 97, 100, and the concurring opinion by Justice Brennan in ABINGTON SCHOOL DISTRICT v. SCHEMPP, (p. 402).

[2] Leo Pfeffer, *God, Caesar, and the Constitution: The Court as Referee of Church-State Confrontation* (Boston: Beacon Press, 1975), p. 333.

[3] *Ibid.*, p. 332. Pfeffer's entire section, pp. 330-37, is extremely helpful in understanding the issues this case raises.

for reasonable accommodation of employee religious needs without undue hardship on the part of the company. [4] In late 1976, the Court considered the amended law in *Parker Seal Company* v. *Cummins*. Paul Cummins was a supervisor in the Berea, Kentucky, plant of the Parker Seal Company. A member of the Worldwide Church of God, a Sabbatarian group, Cummins refused to work on Saturday. For more than a year the company accommodated Cummins' Sabbatarianism, although other supervisors were compelled to work on Saturday. When resentment developed among the other supervisors, Cummins was fired. The Sixth U.S. Circuit Court of Appeals found that the company had not made sufficient effort to accommodate Cummins. In a *per curiam* decision which did not include a written opinion, another divided Court (four-to-four with Justice Stevens disqualifing himself) affirmed the lower court's opinion to the benefit of Cummins.

However, in June 1977, the full Court, in TRANS WORLD AIRLINES, INC. v. HARDISON (p. 151), reversed the Eighth Circuit Court of Appeals which had found in favor of the Sabbatarian claims of another member of the same denomination. The Supreme Court refused to construe the 1972 statute as dictating that companies discriminate against some employees in order to satisfy the religious preferences of other employees. Justice Byron White, for the majority of seven, held that the law did not require the abandonment of neutral union seniority programs nor force employers to bear more than a minimal cost to accommodate workers who wished to have Saturday off for religious reasons. Justices Thurgood Marshall and William Brennan, in dissent, decried the undesirable impact on those Sabbatarians "who could be forced to live on welfare as the price they must pay for worshiping their God."

Four years later in THOMAS v. REVIEW BOARD OF INDIANA EMPLOYMENT SECURITY DIVISION (p. 158), the Court was again asked to rule on denial of unemployment compensation, this time with respect to a Jehovah's Witness who quit his job with a machinery company after he was transferred from the department where he had been employed in working with steel products for industrial use to one that produced turrets for military tanks. Thomas maintained that his religious beliefs forbade working in the production of armaments, but he was denied unemployment benefits on the strength of a state law which mandated such denial of compensation to any person voluntarily leaving a job "without good cause [arising] in connection with [his] work."

The Indiana Supreme Court found no undue burden on Eddie Thomas' right to free exercise of religion. It further held that for the state to provide benefits under such circumstances would in effect constitute an establishment of religion. But the United States Supreme Court by a vote of eight-to-one, denied both findings. Chief Justice Burger ruled that "Where the state conditions receipt of an important benefit upon conduct proscribed by a religious faith, or where it denies such a benefit because of conduct mandated by religious belief, thereby putting substantial pressure on an adherent to modify his

behavior and to violate his beliefs, a burden on religion exists." (450 U.S. 707, 717) The state, he explained, had not shown that this denial of benefits was the least restrictive means of achieving some compelling state interest. With respect to the establishment charge, he quoted from *Sherbert* in finding payment of benefits to reflect "nothing more than the governmental obligation of neutrality in the face of religious differences . . . " Justice Rehnquist, in dissent, complained that the decision added "mud to the already muddied waters of First Amendment jurisprudence."

It is certain that *Thomas* does not represent the Court's last encounter with questions concerning Sabbatarians and job termination, unemployment compensation, *reasonable accommodation* and *undue hardship*. Lower court decisions have kept the issues alive, [5] and in April 1986 the Supreme Court accepted for argument during its 1986-1987 term *Hobbie* v. *Unemployment Appeals Commission of Florida*, which involves another Seventh-day Adventist who was denied unemployment compensation benefits after being fired by a Florida jeweler for refusing to work on her Sabbath.

One week before adjournment of the 1985-86 session, the Court handed down a decision in a potentially highly significant case involving the balancing of religious rights on the part of a religiously affiliated school and a teacher's right to protection against sexual discrimination by that school. However, the decision of the Court in OHIO CIVIL RIGHTS COMMISSION v. DAYTON CHRISTIAN SCHOOLS (p. 164) went off on highly technical grounds and postponed the ultimate resolution of many of the questions raised.

Dayton Christian Schools operates three schools as part of its religious mission. To assure the desired fun-

---

[4] See, for example, *Johnson* v. *United States Postal Service* (1974) and *United States* v. *City of Albuquerque* (1975).

[5] See *Anderson* v. *General Dynamics Convair Aerospace Division* (1982) and *Turpen* v. *Missouri-Kansas-Texas Railroad Company* (1984). Two years before *Thomas* the Court refused to review a lower court's ruling that religious liberty similarly took precedence over the payment of union dues. (*International Association of Machinists and Aerospace Workers, AFL-CIO* v. *Anderson* [1979]). The Court in 1986 also granted certiorari in another case, *Ansonia Board of Education* v. *Philbrook* which raises the question of reasonable accommodation and undue hardship with respect to a teacher's right to use his/her personal leave for religious observances. Philbrook, a member of the Worldwide Church of God, found it necessary to be absent from school approximately six days each year. His contract with the school district entitled him to three days off with pay per year for religious observances, but forbade him to use any of his personal leave for that purpose. He offered two proposed accommodations which the board did not find acceptable.

Philbrook filed a complaint against the school and the teachers' union charging that the school's leave policies violated Title VII of the Civil Rights Act of 1964 and the Free Exercise Clause. The district court held that he had failed to prove religious discrimination. The Second Court of Appeals, however, found that he had established a prima facia case of discrimination under Title VII, and, reaching only the statutory question, reversed and remanded the decision of the district court.

Observing that "*Hardison* did not sound a death knell to the employer's duty to accommodate under Title VII," Judge Oakes said for the court, "Where the employer and the employee each propose a reasonable accommodation, Title VII requires the employer to accept the proposal the employee prefers unless that accommodation causes undue hardship on the employer's conduct of his business." (757 F.2d 476, 484) The appeals court did not accept the argument of the school board that accomodating Philbrook would constitute preferential treatment.

damentalist Christian commitment on the part of the board of directors and educational staff, all are required annually to sign a Statement of Faith of religious precepts. After working for five years as a teacher in the elementary school, Linda Hoskinson became pregnant and so informed the school officials. She also told them that she desired to keep teaching both during her pregnancy and in the following school year. She was, however, notified that her teaching contract would not be renewed because her teaching as a new parent would be in conflict with the school's philosophy that the mother should be in the home during the early years of child rearing.

On receipt of the notification, she consulted a lawyer who wrote a letter to the superintendent alleging the existence of discriminatory practices at the school. Shortly thereafter Mrs. Hoskinson was suspended effective immediately because she had violated the "biblical chain of command" for internal resolution of disputes which she had agreed in her contract to follow. The provision in her contract required that she "agree to follow the Biblical pattern of Matthew 18: 15-17 and Galations 6:1 and always give a good report (with) all differences . . . to be resolved by utilizing Biblical principles—always presenting a united front." In going to the attorney she had breached her contract.

The day after she was dismissed Mrs. Hoskinson filed a sex discrimination complaint with the Ohio Civil Rights Commission which, after preliminary investigation and failure to resolve the controversy by conciliation, notified the school that the commission would begin a hearing on the charge before an administrative hearing examiner. While the administrative proceedings were still pending, Dayton Christian Schools filed a suit in the United States District Court for the Southern District of Ohio, seeking an injunction to bar the administrative proceedings. Application of the Ohio Civil Rights Commission statutes to the employment practices of the schools based on sincerely held religious beliefs would, the suit contended, violate both the Free Exercise and Establishment Clauses.

That court refused to issue the injunction, holding that the state has a "compelling and overriding interest in eliminating sex discrimination in the employment setting" sufficient to justify "the slight infringement that may result in Plaintiff's free exercise rights." However, the Dayton Christian Schools appealed the district court's findings. The United States Court of Appeals for the Sixth Circuit reversed the decision, and ruled in favor of the school on free exercise and establishment grounds. The decision emphasized the potential for "highly intrusive" intervention and surveillance on the part of the commission in ruling on such matters as reinstatement and backpay, although these specific issues were not at the moment before the court.

By unanimous vote the Supreme Court reversed the decision of the court of appeals and remanded the case for further proceedings, but the Court split five-to-four as to the appropriateness of the action of the district court in taking jurisdiction over the suit in the first instance. Justice Rehnquist, for himself and four other justices, held that the district court should have abstained from adjudicating the case. He cited numerous precedents to the effect that, out of concern for comity and federalism, a

federal court should not enjoin a pending proceeding in state courts or state administrative bodies except in the "very unusual situation that an injunction is necessary to prevent great and immediate irreparable injury." The elimination of sex discrimination is an important state interest, and mere investigation by the commission to ascertain the real reason for Mrs. Hoskinson's discharge would violate no constitutional rights. "Even religious schools," said Justice Rehnquist, "cannot claim to be wholly free from state regulation," and constitutional claims resulting from a final commission order could properly be raised in state court.

Justice Stevens wrote for Justices Brennan, Marshall, and Blackmun. He concurred in the judgment and agreed with the majority that investigation of the charges by the commission and the holding of a hearing on the charges were not prohibited by the First Amendment. He disagreed, however, with the majority's contention that the district court should have abstained from adjudicating the case, thereby possibly delaying or denying the school a hearing in federal court as to the constitutionality of any provisional administrative remedy which the commission might determine. Although the merits of Mrs. Hoskinson's case were not spoken to, the decision does appear to have considerable significance in the larger area of liability of religious schools to investigation and hearing proceedings by civil rights commissions under state antidiscrimination laws. [6]

SHERBERT v. VERNER

374 U.S. 398
ON APPEAL FROM THE SUPREME COURT OF SOUTH CAROLINA
Argued April 24, 1963 — Decided June 17, 1963

⊥ *Mr. Justice BRENNAN* delivered the opinion of the Court.   ⌐399

Appellant, a member of the Seventh-day Adventist Church, was discharged by her South Carolina employer because she would not work on Saturday, the

---

[6] In 1985 a federal court of appeals affirmed a district court ruling that the Equal Employment Opportunity Commission had no jurisdiction under Title VII of the Civil Rights Act of 1964 with respect to alleged sexual discrimination in pastoral hiring. Carole Rayburn took her case to the EEOC and then to court when the Seventh-day Adventist Church in Takoma Park, Maryland, turned down her request for employment as an intern with assignment as an associate in pastoral care. The district court dismissed Rayburn's suit on the ground that government scrutiny of the hiring practices of the church would infringe on its freedom of religion.

Judge J. Harvie Williamson III of the Fourth Circuit Court of Appeals agreed that state scrutiny here would constitute both substantial infringement of free exercise of religion and impermissible entanglement. He argued that:

The right to choose ministers without government restriction . . . underlies the wellbeing of the religious community . . . for perpetuation of a church's existence may depend upon those whom it selects to preach its values, teach its message, and interpret its doctrines both to its membership and the world at large. (*Rayburn v. General Conference of Seventh-day Adventists*, 772 F. 2d 1164, 1168)

He cautioned, however, that decisions of churches may be subject to Title VII scrutiny where the decision "does not involve the church's spiritual functions."

Sabbath Day of her faith. When she was unable to obtain other employment because from conscientious scruples she would not take Saturday work, she filed ⊥400 a claim for ⊥ unemployment compensation benefits under the South Carolina Unemployment Compensation Act. That law provides that, to be eligible for benefits, a claimant must be "able to work and ⊥401 . . . available for work"; and, fur⊥ther, that a claimant is ineligible for benefits "[i]f . . . he has failed, without good cause . . . to accept available suitable work when offered him by the employment office or the employer. . . ." The appellee Employment Security Commission, in administrative proceedings under the statute, found that appellant's restriction upon her availability for Saturday work brought her within the provision disqualifying for benefits insured workers who fail, without good cause, to accept "suitable work when offered . . . by the employment office or the employer. . . ." The Commission's finding was sustained by the Court of Common Pleas for Spartanburg County. That court's judgment was in turn affirmed by the South Carolina Supreme Court, which rejected appellant's contention that, as applied to her, the disqualifying provisions of the South Carolina statute abridged her right to the free exercise of her religion secured under the Free Exercise Clause of the First Amendment through the Fourteenth Amendment. The State Supreme Court held specifically that appellant's ineligibility infringed no constitutional liberties because such a construction of the statute "places no restriction upon the appellant's freedom of religion nor does it in any way prevent her in the exercise of her right and freedom to observe her religious beliefs in accordance with the dictates of her conscience." We noted ⊥402 probable ⊥ jurisdiction of appellant's appeal. We reverse the judgment of the South Carolina Supreme Court and remand for further proceedings not inconsistent with this opinion.

I

The door of the Free Exercise Clause stands tightly closed against any governmental regulation of religious *beliefs* as such. Government may neither compel affirmation of a repugnant belief, nor penalize or discriminate against individuals or groups because they hold religious views abhorrent to the authorities; nor employ the taxing power to inhibit the dissemination of particular religious views. On ⊥403 the other hand, ⊥ the Court has rejected challenges under the Free Exercise Clause to governmental regulation of certain overt acts prompted by religious beliefs or principles, for "even when the action is in accord with one's religious convictions, [it] is not totally free from legislative restrictions." *Braunfeld* v. *Brown.* The conduct or actions so regulated have invariably posed some substantial threat to public safety, peace or order.

Plainly enough, appellant's conscientious objection to Saturday work constitutes no conduct prompted by religious principles of a kind within the reach of state legislation. If, therefore, the decision of the South Carolina Supreme Court is to withstand appellant's constitutional challenge, it must be either because her disqualification as a beneficiary represents no infringement by the State of her constitutional rights of free exercise, or because any incidental burden on the free exercise of appellant's religion may be justified by a "compelling state interest in the regulation of a subject within the State's constitutional power to regulate. . . ." *NAACP* v. *Button.*

II

We turn first to the question whether the disqualification for benefits imposes any burden on the free exercise of appellant's religion. We think it is clear that it does. In a sense the consequences of such a disqualification to religious principles and practices may be only an indirect result of welfare legislation within the State's general competence to enact; it is true that no criminal sanctions directly compel appellant to work a six-day week. But this is only the beginning, not the end, of our ⊥ inquiry. ⊥404 For "[i]f the purpose or effect of a law is to impede the observance of one or all religions or is to discriminate invidiously between religions, that law is constitutionally invalid even though the burden may be characterized as being only indirect." *Braunfeld* v. *Brown.* Here not only is it apparent that appellant's declared ineligibility for benefits derives solely from the practice of her religion, but the pressure upon her to forego that practice is unmistakable. The ruling forces her to choose between following the precepts of her religion and forfeiting benefits, on the one hand, and abandoning one of the precepts of her religion in order to accept work, on the other hand. Governmental imposition of such a choice puts the same kind of burden upon the free exercise of religion as would a fine imposed against appellant for her Saturday worship.

Nor may the South Carolina court's construction of the statute be saved from constitutional infirmity on the ground that unemployment compensation benefits are not appellant's "right" but merely a "privilege." It is too late in the day to doubt that the liberties of religion and expression may be infringed by the denial of or placing of conditions upon a benefit or privilege. . . .⊥   ⊥406

To condition the availability of benefits upon this appellant's willingness to violate a cardinal principle of her religious faith effectively penalizes the free exercise of her constitutional liberties.

Significantly South Carolina expressly saves the Sunday worshipper from having to make the kind of choice which we here hold infringes the Sabbatarian's religious liberty. When in times of "national emergency" the textile plants are authorized by the State Commissioner of Labor to operate on Sunday, "no employee shall be required to work on

Sunday . . . who is conscientiously opposed to Sunday work; and if any employee should refuse to work on Sunday on account of conscientious . . . objections he or she shall not jeopardize his or her seniority by such refusal or be discriminated against in any other manner." No question of the disqualification of a Sunday worshipper for benefits is likely to arise, since we cannot suppose that an employer will discharge him in violation of this statute. The unconstitutionality of the disqualification of the Sabbatarian is thus compounded by the religious discrimination which South Carolina's general statutory scheme necessarily effects.

III

We must next consider whether some compelling state interest enforced in the eligibility provisions of the South Carolina statute justifies the substantial infringement of appellant's First Amendment right. It is basic that no showing merely of a rational relationship to some colorable state interest would suffice; in this highly sensitive constitutional area, "[o]nly the gravest abuses, endangering paramount interests, give occasion for permissible limitation." ⌋407 *Thomas* v. *Collins*. ⊥ No such abuse or danger has been advanced in the present case. The appellees suggest no more than a possibility that the filing of fraudulent claims by unscrupulous claimants feigning religious objections to Saturday work might not only dilute the unemployment compensation fund but also hinder the scheduling by employers of necessary Saturday work. But that possibility is not apposite here because no such objection appears to have been made before the South Carolina Supreme Court, and we are unwilling to assess the importance of an asserted state interest without the views of the state court. Nor, if the contention had been made below, would the record appear to sustain it; there is no proof whatever to warrant such fears of malingering or deceit as those which the respondents now advance. Even if consideration of such evidence is not foreclosed by the prohibition against judicial inquiry into the truth or falsity of religious beliefs—a question as to which we intimate no view since it is not before us—it is highly doubtful whether such evidence would be sufficient to warrant a substantial infringement of religious liberties. For even if the possibility of spurious claims did threaten to dilute the fund and disrupt the scheduling of work, it would plainly be incumbent upon the appellees to demonstrate that no alternative forms of regulation would combat such abuses without infringing First Amend- ⌋408 ment rights.⊥

In these respects, then, the state interest asserted in the present case is wholly dissimilar to the interests which were found to justify the less direct burden upon religious practices in *Braunfeld* v. *Brown*. The Court recognized that the Sunday closing law which that decision sustained undoubtedly served "to make the practice of [the Orthodox Jewish merchants'] . . . religious beliefs more expensive." But the statute was nevertheless saved by a countervailing factor which finds no equivalent in the instant case—a strong state interest in providing one uniform day of rest for all workers. That secular objective could be achieved, the court found, only by declaring Sunday to be that day of rest. Requiring exemptions for Sabbatarians, while theoretically possible, appeared to present an administrative ⊥ prob- ⌋409 lem of such magnitude, or to afford the exempted class so great a competitive advantage, that such a requirement would have rendered the entire statutory scheme unworkable. In the present case no such justifications underlie the determination of the state court that appellant's religion makes her ineligible to receive benefits.

IV

In holding as we do, plainly we are not fostering the "establishment" of the Seventh-day Adventist religion in South Carolina, for the extension of unemployment benefits to Sabbatarians in common with Sunday worshippers reflects nothing more than the governmental obligation of neutrality in the face of religious differences, and does not represent that involvement of religious with secular institutions which it is the object of the Establishment Clause to forestall. Nor does the recognition of the appellant's right to unemployment benefits under the state statute serve to abridge any other person's religious liberties. Nor do we, by our decision today, declare the existence of a constitutional right to unemployment benefits on the part ⊥ of all persons whose religious ⌋410 convictions are the cause of their unemployment. This is not a case in which an employee's religious convictions serve to make him a nonproductive member of society. Finally, nothing we say today constrains the States to adopt any particular form or scheme of unemployment compensation. Our holding today is only that South Carolina may not constitutionally apply the eligibility provisions so as to constrain a worker to abandon his religious convictions respecting the day of rest. This holding but reaffirms a principle that we announced a decade and a half ago, namely that no State may "exclude individual Catholics, Lutherans, Mohammedans, Baptists, Jews, Methodists, Non-believers, Presbyterians, or the members of any other faith, *because of their faith, or lack of it*, from receiving the benefits of public welfare legislation." *Everson* v. *Board of Education*.

In view of the result we have reached under the First and Fourteenth Amendments' guarantee of free exercise of religion, we have no occasion to consider appellant's claim that the denial of benefits also deprived her of the equal protection of the laws in violation of the Fourteenth Amendment.

The judgment of the South Carolina Supreme Court is reversed and the case is remanded for further proceedings not inconsistent with this opinion.

It is so ordered.

Mr. Justice DOUGLAS, concurring.

The case we have for decision seems to me to be of small dimensions, though profoundly important. The question is whether the South Carolina law which denies unemployment compensation to a Seventh-day Adventist, who, because of her religion, has declined to work on her Sabbath, is a law "prohibiting the free exercise" of religion as those words are used in the First Amendment.⊥ It seems obvious to me that this law does run afoul of that clause.

⌊411

Religious scruples of Moslems require them to attend a mosque on Friday and to pray five times daily. Religious scruples of a Sikh require him to carry a regular or a symbolic sword. Religious scruples of a Jehovah's Witness teach him to be a colporteur, going from door to door, from town to town, distributing his religious pamphlets. Religious scruples of a Quaker compel him to refrain from swearing and to affirm instead. Religious scruples of a Buddhist may require him to refrain from partaking of any flesh, even of fish.

The examples could be multiplied, including those of the Seventh-day Adventist whose Sabbath is Saturday and who is advised not to eat some meats.

These suffice, however, to show that many people hold beliefs alien to the majority of our society— beliefs that are protected by the First Amendment but which could easily be trod upon under the guise of "police" or "health" regulations reflecting the majority's views.

Some have thought that a majority of a community can, through state action, compel a minority to observe their particular religious scruples so long as the majority's rule can be said to perform some valid secular function. ⊥ That was the essence of the Court's decision in the Sunday Blue Law Cases, a ruling from which I then dissented and still dissent.

⌊412

That ruling of the Court travels part of the distance that South Carolina asks us to go now. She asks us to hold that when it comes to a day of rest a Sabbatarian must conform with the scruples of the majority in order to obtain unemployment benefits.

The result turns not on the degree of injury, which may indeed be nonexistent by ordinary standards. The harm is the interference with the individual's scruples or conscience—an important area of privacy which the First Amendment fences off from government. The interference here is as plain as it is in Soviet Russia, where a churchgoer is given a second-class citizenship, resulting in harm though perhaps not in measurable damages.

This case is resolvable not in terms of what an individual can demand of government, but solely in terms of what government may not do to an individual in violation of his religious scruples. The fact that government cannot exact from me a surrender of one iota of my religious scruples does not, of course, mean that I can demand of government a sum of money, the better to exercise them. For the Free Exercise Clause is written in terms of what the government cannot do to the individual, not in terms of what the individual can exact from the government.

Those considerations, however, are not relevant here. If appellant is otherwise qualified for unemployment benefits, payments will be made to her not as a Seventh-day Adventist, but as an unemployed worker. Conceivably these payments will indirectly benefit her church, ⊥ but no more so than does the salary of any public employee. Thus, this case does not involve the problems of direct or indirect state assistance to a religious organization—matters relevant to the Establishment Clause, not in issue here.

⌊413

Mr. Justice STEWART, concurring in the result.

Although fully agreeing with the result which the Court reaches in this case, I cannot join the Court's opinion. This case presents a double-barreled dilemma, which in all candor I think the Court's opinion has not succeeded in papering over. The dilemma ought to be resolved.

I

Twenty-three years ago in *Cantwell* v. *Connecticut* the Court said that both the Establishment Clause and the Free Exercise Clause of the First Amendment were made wholly applicable to the States by the Fourteenth Amendment. In the intervening years several cases involving claims of state abridgment of individual religious freedom have been decided here—most recently *Braunfeld* v. *Brown,* and *Torcaso* v. *Watkins.* During the same period "cases dealing with the specific problems arising under the 'Establishment' Clause which have reached this Court are few in number." The most recent are last Term's *Engel* v. *Vitale,* and this Term's *Schempp* and *Murray* cases.

I am convinced that no liberty is more essential to the continued vitality of the free society which our Constitution guarantees than is the religious liberty protected by the Free Exercise Clause explicit in the First Amendment and imbedded in the Fourteenth. And I regret that on ⊥ occasion, and specifically in *Braunfeld* v. *Brown,* the Court has shown what has seemed to me a distressing insensitivity to the appropriate demands of this constitutional guarantee. By contrast I think that the Court's approach to the Establishment Clause has on occasion, and specifically in *Engel, Schempp* and *Murray,* been not only insensitive, but positively wooden, and that the Court has accorded to the Establishment Clause a meaning which neither the words, the history, nor

⌊414

the intention of the authors of that specific constitutional provision even remotely suggests.

But my views as to the correctness of the Court's decisions in these cases are beside the point here. The point is that the decisions are on the books. And the result is that there are many situations where legitimate claims under the Free Exercise Clause will run into head-on collision with the Court's insensitive and sterile construction of the Establishment Clause. The controversy now before us is clearly such a case. Because the appellant refuses to accept available jobs which would require her to work on Saturdays, South Carolina has declined to pay unemployment compensation benefits to her. Her refusal to work on Saturdays is based on the tenets of her religious faith. The Court says that South Carolina cannot under these circumstances declare her to be not "available for work" within the meaning of its statute because to do so would violate her constitutional right to the free exercise of her religion.

Yet what this Court has said about the Establishment Clause must inevitably lead to a diametrically opposite result. If the appellant's refusal to work on ⊥415 Saturdays ⊥ were based on indolence, or on a compulsive desire to watch the Saturday television programs, no one would say that South Carolina could not hold that she was not "available for work" within the meaning of its statute. That being so, the Establishment Clause as construed by this Court not only *permits* but affirmatively *requires* South Carolina equally to deny the appellant's claim for unemployment compensation when her refusal to work on Saturdays is based upon her religious creed. For, as said in *Everson* v. *Board of Education*, the Establishment Clause bespeaks "a government . . . stripped of all power . . . to support, or otherwise to assist any or all religions . . .," and no State "can pass laws which aid one religion. . . ." In Mr. Justice Rutledge's words, adopted by the Court today in *Schempp*, the Establishment Clause forbids "every form of public aid or support for religion." In the words of the Court in *Engel* v. *Vitale*, reaffirmed today in the *Schempp* case, the Establishment Clause forbids the "financial support of government" to be "placed behind a particular religious belief."

To require South Carolina to so administer its laws as to pay public money to the appellant under the circumstances of this case is thus clearly to require the State to violate the Establishment Clause as construed by this Court. This poses no problem for me, because I think the Court's mechanistic concept of the Establishment Clause is historically unsound and constitutionally wrong. I think the process of constitutional decision in the area of the relationships between government and religion demands considerably more than the invocation of broad-brushed rhetoric of the kind I have quoted. And I think that the guarantee of religious liberty

embodied in the Free Exercise Clause affirmatively requires government to create an atmosphere of hospitality and accommoda⊥tion to individual belief or ⊥416 disbelief. In short, I think our Constitution commands the positive protection by government of religious freedom—not only for a minority, however small—not only for the majority, however large—but for each of us.

South Carolina would deny unemployment benefits to a mother unavailable for work on Saturdays because she was unable to get a babysitter. Thus, we do not have before us a situation where a State provides unemployment compensation generally, and singles out for disqualification only those persons who are unavailable for work on religious grounds. This is not, in short, a scheme which operates so as to discriminate against religion as such. But the Court nevertheless holds that the State must prefer a religious over a secular ground for being unavailable for work—that state financial support of the appellant's religion is constitutionally required to carry out "the governmental obligation of neutrality in the face of religious differences. . . ."

Yet in cases decided under the Establishment Clause the Court has decreed otherwise. It has decreed that government must blind itself to the differing religious beliefs and traditions of the people. With all respect, I think it is the Court's duty to face up to the dilemma posed by the conflict between the Free Exercise Clause of the Constitution and the Establishment Clause as interpreted by the Court. It is a duty, I submit, which we owe to the people, the States, and the Nation, and a duty which we owe to ourselves. For so long as the resounding but fallacious fundamentalist rhetoric of some of our Establishment Clause opinions remains on our books, to be disregarded at will as in the present case, ⊥ or to ⊥417 be undiscriminatingly invoked as in the *Schempp* case, so long will the possibility of consistent and perceptive decision in this most difficult and delicate area of constitutional law be impeded and impaired. And so long, I fear, will the guarantee of true religious freedom in our pluralistic society be uncertain and insecure.

II

My second difference with the Court's opinion is that I cannot agree that today's decision can stand consistently with *Braunfeld* v. *Brown*. The Court says that there was a "less direct burden upon religious practices" in that case than in this. With all respect, I think the Court is mistaken, simply as a matter of fact. The *Braunfeld* case involved a state *criminal* statute. The undisputed effect of that statute, as pointed out by *Mr. Justice BRENNAN* in his dissenting opinion in that case, was that " 'Plaintiff, Abraham Braunfeld, will be unable to continue in his business if he may not stay open on Sunday and he will thereby lose his capital investment.' In other words, the issue in this case—and we do not understand either appellees or the Court to contend otherwise—is whether a State may put an individual to a choice between his business and his religion."

The impact upon the appellant's religious freedom in the present case is considerably less onerous. We deal here not with a criminal statute, but with the particularized administration of South Carolina's Unemployment Compensation Act. Even upon the unlikely assumption that the appellant could not find suitable non-Saturday employment, the appellant at the worst would be denied ⊥ a maximum of 22 weeks of compensation payments. I agree with the Court that the possibility of that denial is enough to infringe upon the appellant's constitutional right to the free exercise of her religion. But it is clear to me that in order to reach this conclusion the Court must explicitly reject the reasoning of *Braunfeld* v. *Brown*. I think the *Braunfeld* case was wrongly decided and should be overruled, and accordingly I concur in the result reached by the Court in the case before us.

Mr. Justice HARLAN, whom *Mr. Justice WHITE* joins, dissenting.

Today's decision is disturbing both in its rejection of existing precedent and in its implications for the future. The significance of the decision can best be understood after an examination of the state law applied in this case.

South Carolina's Unemployment Compensation Law was enacted in 1936 in response to the grave social and economic problems that arose during the depression of that period. As stated in the statute itself:

"Economic insecurity due to unemployment is a serious menace to health, morals and welfare of the people of this State; *involuntary unemployment* is therefore a subject of general interest and concern . . .; the achievement of social security requires protection against this greatest hazard of our economic life; this can be provided by encouraging the employers *to provide more stable employment and by the systematic accumulation of funds during periods of employment to provide benefits for periods of unemployment*, thus maintaining purchasing power and limiting the serious social consequences of poor relief assistance." (Emphasis added.) ⊥

Thus the purpose of the legislature was to tide people over, and to avoid social and economic chaos, during periods when *work was unavailable*. But at the same time there was clearly no intent to provide relief for those who for purely personal reasons were or became *unavailable for work*. In accordance with this design, the legislature provided that "[a]n unemployed insured worker shall be eligible to receive benefits with respect to any week *only* if the Commission finds that . . . [h]e is able to work and is available for work. . . ." (Emphasis added.)

The South Carolina Supreme Court has uniformly applied this law in conformity with its clearly expressed purpose. It has consistently held that one is not "available for work" if his unemployment has resulted not from the inability of industry to provide a job but rather from personal circumstances, no matter how compelling. The reference to "involuntary unemployment" in the legislative statement of policy, whatever a sociologist, philosopher, or theologian might say, has been interpreted not to embrace such personal circumstances.

In the present case all that the state court has done is to apply these accepted principles. Since virtually all of the mills in the Spartanburg area were operating on a six-day week, the appellant was "unavailable for work," and thus ineligible for benefits, when personal considera⊥tions prevented her from accepting employment on a full-time basis in the industry and locality in which she had worked. The fact that these personal considerations sprang from her religious convictions was wholly without relevance to the state court's application of the law. Thus in no proper sense can it be said that the State discriminated against the appellant on the basis of her religious beliefs or that she was denied benefits *because* she was a Seventh-day Adventist. She was denied benefits just as any other claimant would be denied benefits who was not "available for work" for personal reasons.

With this background, this Court's decision comes into clearer focus. What the Court is holding is that if the State chooses to condition unemployment compensation on the applicant's availability for work, it is constitutionally compelled to *carve out an exception*—and to provide benefits—for those whose unavailability is due to their religious convictions. Such a holding has particular significance in two respects. ⊥

First, despite the Court's protestations to the contrary, the decision necessarily overrules *Braunfeld* v. *Brown*, which held that it did not offend the "Free Exercise" Clause of the Constitution for a State to forbid a Sabbatarian to do business on Sunday. The secular purpose of the statute before us today is even clearer than that involved in *Braunfeld*. And just as in *Braunfeld*—where exceptions to the Sunday closing laws for Sabbatarians would have been inconsistent with the purpose to achieve a uniform day of rest and would have required case-by-case inquiry into religious beliefs—so here, an exception to the rules of eligibility based on religious convictions would necessitate judicial examination of those convictions and would be at odds with the limited purpose of the statute to smooth out the economy during periods of industrial instability. Finally, the indirect financial burden of the present law is far less than that involved in *Braunfeld*. Forcing a store owner to close his business on Sunday may well have the effect of depriving him of a satisfactory livelihood if his religious convictions require him to close on Saturday as well. Here we are dealing only with temporary benefits, amounting to a fraction of regular weekly wages and running for not more than 22 weeks. Clearly, any differences between this case and _422 *Braunfeld* cut against the present appellant. ⊥

Second, the implications of the present decision are far more troublesome than its apparently narrow dimensions would indicate at first glance. The meaning of today's holding, as already noted, is that the State must furnish unemployment benefits to one who is unavailable for work if the unavailability stems from the exercise of religious convictions. The State, in other words, must *single out* for financial assistance those whose behavior is religiously motivated, even though it denies such assistance to others whose identical behavior (in this case, inability to work on Saturdays) is not religiously motivated.

It has been suggested that such singling out of religious conduct for special treatment may violate the constitutional limitations on state action. My own view, however, is that at least under the circumstances of this case it would be a permissible accommodation of religion for the State, if it *chose* to do so, to create an exception to its eligibility requirements for persons like the appellant. The constitutional obligation of "neutrality" is not so narrow a channel that the slightest deviation from an absolutely straight course leads to condemnation. There are too many instances in which no such course can be charted, too many areas in which the pervasive activities of the State justify some special provision for religion to prevent it from being submerged by an all-embracing secularism. The State _423 violates its obligation of neutrality ⊥ when, for example, it mandates a daily religious exercise in its public schools, with all the attendant pressures on the school children that such an exercise entails. But there is, I believe, enough flexibility in the Constitution to permit a legislative judgment accommodating an unemployment compensation law to the exercise of religious beliefs such as appellant's.

For very much the same reasons, however, I cannot subscribe to the conclusion that the State is constitutionally *compelled* to carve out an exception to its general rule of eligibility in the present case. Those situations in which the Constitution may require special treatment on account of religion are, in my view, few and far between, and this view is amply supported by the course of constitutional litigation in this area. Such compulsion in the present case is particularly inappropriate in light of the indirect, remote, and insubstantial effect of the decision below on the exercise of appellant's religion and in light of the direct financial assistance to religion that today's decision requires.

For these reasons I respectfully dissent from the opinion and judgment of the Court.

TRANS WORLD AIRLINES, INC. v. HARDISON INTERNATIONAL ASSOCIATION OF MACHINISTS AND AEROSPACE WORKERS, AFL-CIO v. HARDISON

432 U.S. 63
ON WRITS OF CERTIORARI TO THE UNITED STATES COURT
OF APPEALS FOR THE EIGHTH CIRCUIT
Argued March 30, 1977 — Decided June 16, 1977
⊥ *Mr. Justice WHITE* delivered the opinion of _66 the Court.

Section 703 (a) (1) of the Civil Rights Act of 1964, Title VII, 42 U. S. C. § 2000e — 2 (a) (1), makes it an unlawful employment practice for an employer to discriminate against an employee or a prospective employee on the basis of his or her religion. At the time of the events involved here, a guideline of the Equal Employment Opportunity Commission (EEOC), 29 CFR § 1605.1 (b), required, as the Act itself now does, 42 U. S. C. § 2000e (j), that an employer, short of "undue hardship," make "reasonable accommodations" to the religious needs of its employees. The issue in this case is the extent of the employer's obligation under Title VII to accommodate an employee whose religious beliefs prohibit him from working on Saturdays.

I

We summarize briefly the facts found by the District Court.

Petitioner Trans World Airlines (TWA) operates a large maintenance and overhaul base in Kansas City, Mo. On June 5, 1967, respondent Larry G. Hardison was hired by TWA to work as a clerk in the Stores Department at its Kansas City base. Because of its essential role in the Kansas City operation, the Stores Department must operate 24 hours per day, 365 days per year, and whenever an employee's job in that department is not filled, an employee must be ⊥ shifted from another department, or a supervisor _67 must cover the job, even if the work in other areas may suffer.

Hardison, like other employees at the Kansas City base, was subject to a seniority system contained in a collective-bargaining agreement that TWA maintains with petitioner International Association of Machinists and Aerospace Workers (IAM). The seniority system is implemented by the union steward through a system of bidding by employees for particular shift assignments as they become available. The most senior employees have first choice for job and shift assignments, and the most junior employees are required to work when the union steward is unable to find enough people willing to work at a particular time or in a particular job to fill TWA's needs.

In the spring of 1968 Hardison began to study the religion known as the Worldwide Church of God. One of the tenets of that religion is that one must observe the Sabbath by refraining from performing any work from sunset on Friday until sunset on Saturday. The religion also proscribes work on certain specified religious holidays.

When Hardison informed Everett Kussman, the manager of the Stores Department, of his religious conviction regarding ⊥ observance of the Sabbath, Kussman agreed that the union steward should seek a job swap for Hardison or a change of days off; that Hardison would have his religious holidays off whenever possible if Hardison agreed to work the traditional holidays when asked; and that Kussman would try to find Hardison another job that would be more compatible with his religious beliefs. The problem was temporarily solved when Hardison transferred to the 11 p.m.-7 a.m. shift. Working this shift permitted Hardison to observe his Sabbath.

The problem soon reappeared when Hardison bid for and received a transfer from Building 1, where he had been employed, to Building 2, where he would work the day shift. The two buildings had entirely separate seniority lists; and while in Building 1 Hardison had sufficient seniority to observe the Sabbath regularly, he was second from the bottom on the Building 2 seniority list.

In Building 2 Hardison was asked to work Saturdays when a fellow employee went on vacation. TWA agreed to permit the union to seek a change of work assignments for Hardison, but the union was not willing to violate the seniority provisions set out in the collective-bargaining contract, and Hardison had insufficient seniority to bid for a shift having Saturdays off.

A proposal that Hardison work only four days a week was rejected by the company. Hardison's job was essential, and on weekends he was the only available person on his shift to perform it. To leave the position empty would have impaired Supply Shop functions, which were critical to airline operations; to fill Hardison's position with a supervisor or an ⊥ employee from another area would simply have undermanned another operation; and to employ someone not regularly assigned to work Saturdays would have required TWA to pay premium wages.

When an accommodation was not reached, Hardison refused to report for work on Saturdays. A transfer to the twilight shift proved unavailing since that schedule still required Hardison to work past sundown on Fridays. After a hearing, Hardison was discharged on grounds of insubordination for refusing to work during his designated shift.

Hardison, having first invoked the administrative remedy provided by Title VII, brought this action for injunctive relief in the United States District Court against TWA and IAM, claiming that his discharge by TWA constituted religious discrimination in violation of Title VII, 42 U. S. C. § 2000e — 2 (a) (1). He also charged that the union had discriminated against him by failing to represent him adequately in his dispute with TWA and by depriving him of his right to exercise his religious beliefs. Hardison's claim of religious discrimination rested on 1967 EEOC guidelines requiring employers "to make reasonable accommodations to the religious needs of employees" whenever such accommodation would not work an "undue hardship," 29 CFR § 1605.1, 32 Fed. Reg. 10298 (1967), and on similar language adopted by Congress in the 1972 amendments to Title VII, 42 U. S. C. § 2000e (j).

After a bench trial, the District Court ruled in favor of the defendants. Turning first to the claim against the union, the District Court ruled that although the 1967 EEOC guidelines were applicable to unions, the union's duty to accommodate Hardison's belief did not require it to ignore its seniority system as Hardison appeared to claim. As for Hardison's ⊥ claim against TWA, the District Court rejected at the outset TWA's contention that requiring it in any way to accommodate the religious needs of its employees would constitute an unconstitutional establishment of religion. As the District Court construed the Act, however, TWA had satisfied its "reasonable accommodation" obligations, and any further accommodation would have worked an undue hardship on the company.

The Eighth Circuit Court of Appeals reversed the judgment for TWA. It agreed with the District Court's constitutional ruling, but held that TWA had not satisfied its duty to accommodate. Because it did not appear that Hardison had attacked directly the judgment in favor of the union, the Court of Appeals affirmed that judgment without ruling on its substantive merits.

In separate petitions for certiorari TWA and IAM contended that adequate steps had been taken to accommodate Hardison's religious observances and that to construe the statute to require further efforts at accommodation would create an establishment of religion contrary to the First Amendment of the Constitution. TWA also contended that the Court of Appeals improperly ignored the District Court's findings of fact.

We granted both petitions for certiorari. Because we agree with petitioners that their conduct was not a violation of Title VII, we need not reach the other questions presented.

II

⊥ The Court of Appeals found that TWA had committed an unlawful employment practice under § 703 (a) (1) of the Act, 42 U. S. C. § 2000e-2 (a) (1), which provides:

"(a) It shall be an unlawful employment practice for an employer—

"(1) to fail or refuse to hire or to discharge any individual, or otherwise to discriminate against any individual with respect to his compensation, terms, conditions, or privileges of employment, because of such individual's race, color, religion, sex, or national origin."

The emphasis of both the language and the legislative history of the statute is on eliminating discrimination in employment; similarly situated employees are not to be treated differently solely because they differ with respect to race, color, religion, sex, or national origin. This is true regardless of whether ⊥ the discrimination is directed against majorities or minorities.

The prohibition against religious discrimination soon raised the question of whether it was impermissible under § 703 (a) (1) to discharge or refuse to hire a person who for religious reasons refused to work during the employer's normal work-week. In 1966 an EEOC guideline dealing with this problem declared that an employer had an obligation under the statute "to accommodate to the reasonable religious needs of employees . . . where such accommodation can be made without serious inconvenience to the conduct of the business."

In 1967 the EEOC amended its guidelines to require employers "to make reasonable accommodations to the religious needs of employees and prospective employees where such accommodation can be made without undue hardship on the conduct of the employer's business." The Commission did not suggest what sort of accommodations are "reasonable" or when hardship to an employer becomes "undue."

⊥ This question—the extent of the required accommodation—remained unsettled when this Court affirmed by an equally divided Court the Sixth Circuit's decision in *Dewey* v. *Reynolds Metals Co.*. The discharge of an employee who for religious reasons had refused to work on Sundays was there held by the Court of Appeals not to be an unlawful employment practice because the manner in which the employer allocated Sunday work assignments was discriminatory in neither its purpose nor effect; and consistent with the 1967 EEOC guidelines, the employer had made a reasonable accommodation of the employee's beliefs by giving him the opportunity to secure a replacement for his Sunday work.

In part "to resolve by legislation" some of the issues raised in *Dewey* (remarks of Sen. Randolph), Congress included the following definition of religion in its 1972 amendments to Title VII:

"The term 'religion' includes all aspects of religious observance and practice, as well as belief, unless an employer demonstrates that he is unable to reasonably accom⊥modate to an employee's or prospective employee's religious observance or practice without undue hardship on the conduct of the employer's business." Title VII § 701 (j), 42 U. S. C. §

2000e (j). The intent and effect of this definition was to make it an unlawful employment practice under § 703 (a) (1) for an employer not to make reasonable accommodations, short of undue hardship, for the religious practices of his employees and prospective employees. But like the EEOC guidelines, the statute provides no guidance for determining the degree of accommodation that is required of an employer. The brief legislative history of § 701 (j) is likewise of little assistance in this regard. The proponent of the measure, Senator Jennings ⊥ Randolph, expressed his general desire "to assure that freedom from religious discrimination in the employment of workers is for all time guaranteed by law," but he made no attempt to define the precise circumstances under which the "reasonable accommodation" requirement would be applied.

In brief, the employer's statutory obligation to make reasonable accommodation for the religious observances of its employees, short of incurring an undue hardship, is clear, but the reach of that obligation has never been spelled out by Congress or by Commission guidelines. With this in mind, we turn to a consideration of whether TWA has met its obliga⊥tion under Title VII to accommodate the religious observances of its employees.

III

The Court of Appeals held that TWA had not made reasonable efforts to accommodate Hardison's religious needs under the 1967 EEOC guidelines in effect at the time the relevant events occurred. In its view, TWA had rejected three reasonable alternatives, any one of which would have satisfied its obligation without undue hardship. First, within the framework of the seniority system, TWA could have permitted Hardison to work a four-day week, utilizing in his place a supervisor or another worker on duty elsewhere. That this would have caused other shop functions to suffer was insufficient to amount to undue hardship in the opinion of the Court of Appeals. Second—according to the Court of Appeals, also within the bounds of the collective-bargaining contract—the company could have filled Hardison's Saturday shift from other available personnel competent to do the job, of which the court said there were at least 200. That this would have involved premium overtime pay was not deemed an undue hardship. Third, TWA could have arranged a "swap between Hardison and another employee either for another shift or for the Sabbath days." In response to the assertion that this would have involved a breach of the senior⊥ity provisions of the contract, the court noted that it had not been settled in the courts whether the required statutory accommodation to religious needs stopped short of transgressing seniority rules, but found it unnecessary to decide the issue because, as the Court of Appeals saw the record, TWA had not sought, and the union had therefore not declined to entertain, a possible variance from the seniority provisions of the collective-bargaining agreement. The company had simply left the entire matter to the union steward who the Court of Appeals said "likewise did nothing."

We disagree with the Court of Appeals in all relevant respects. It is our view that TWA made reasonable efforts to accommodate and that each of the Court of Appeals' suggested alternatives would have been an undue hardship within the meaning of the statute as construed by the EEOC guidelines.

A

It might be inferred from the Court of Appeals' opinion and from the brief of the EEOC in this Court that TWA's efforts to accommodate were no more than negligible. The findings of the District Court, supported by the record, are to the contrary. In summarizing its more detailed findings, the District Court observed: "TWA established as a matter of fact that it did take appropriate action to accommodate as required by Title VII. It held several meetings with plaintiff at which it attempted to find a solution to plaintiff's problems. It did accommodate plaintiff's observance of his special religious holidays. It authorized the union steward to search for someone who would swap shifts, which apparently was normal procedure."

It is also true that TWA itself attempted without success to find Hardison another job. The District Court's view was that TWA had done all that could reasonably be expected within the bounds of the seniority system.

⊥78   ⊥The Court of Appeals observed, however, that the possibility of a variance from the seniority system was never really posed to the union. This is contrary to the District Court's findings and to the record. The District Court found that when TWA first learned of Hardison's religious observances in April, 1968, it agreed to permit the union's steward to seek a swap of shifts or days off but that "the steward reported that he was unable to work out scheduling changes and that he understood no one was willing to swap days with plaintiff." Later, in March 1969, at a meeting held just two days before Hardison first failed to report for his Saturday shift, TWA again "offered to accommodate plaintiff's religious observance by agreeing to any trade of shifts that plaintiff and the union could work out. Any shift or change was impossible within the seniority framework and the union was not willing to violate the seniority provisions set out in the contract to make a shift or change." As the record shows, Hardison himself testified that Kussman was willing, but the union was not, to work out a shift or job trade with another employee.

We shall say more about the seniority system, but at this juncture it appears to us that the system itself represented a significant accommodation to the needs, both religious and secular, of all of TWA's employees. As will become apparent, the seniority system represents a neutral way of minimizing the number of occasions when an employee must work on a day that he would prefer to have off. Additionally, recognizing that weekend work schedules are the least popular, the company made further accommodation by reducing its work force to a bare minimum on those days.

B

We are also convinced, contrary to the Court of Appeals, that TWA cannot be faulted for having failed itself to work ⊥ out a shift or job swap for   ⊥79 Hardison. Both the union and TWA had agreed to the seniority system; the union was unwilling to entertain a variance over the objections of men senior to Hardison; and for TWA to have arranged unilaterally for a swap would have amounted to a breach of the collective-bargaining agreement.

(1)

Hardison and the EEOC insist that the statutory obligation to accommodate religious needs takes precedence over both the collective-bargaining contract and the seniority rights of TWA's other employees. We agree that neither a collective-bargaining contract nor a seniority system may be employed to violate the statute, but we do not believe that the duty to accommodate requires TWA to take steps inconsistent with the otherwise valid agreement. Collective bargaining, aimed at effecting workable and enforceable agreements between management and labor, lies at the core of our national labor policy, and seniority provisions are universally included in these contracts. Without a clear and express indication from Congress, we cannot agree with Hardison and the EEOC that an agreed-upon seniority system must give way when necessary to accommodate religious observances. The issue is important and warrants some discussion.

⊥Any employer who, like TWA, conducts an   ⊥80 around-the-clock operation is presented with the choice of allocating work schedules either in accordance with the preferences of its employees or by involuntary assignment. Insofar as the varying shift preferences of its employees complement each other, TWA could meet its manpower needs through voluntary work scheduling. In the present case, for example, Hardison's supervisor foresaw little difficulty in giving Hardison his religious holidays off since they fell on days that most other employees preferred to work, while Hardison was willing to work on the traditional holidays that most other employees preferred to have off.

Whenever there are not enough employees who choose to work a particular shift, however, some employees must be assigned to that shift even though it is not their first choice. Such was evidently the case with regard to Saturday work; even though TWA cut back its weekend work force to a skeleton crew, not enough employees chose those days off to staff the Stores Department through voluntary scheduling. In these circumstances, TWA and IAM agreed to give first preference to employees who had worked in a particular department the longest.

Had TWA nevertheless circumvented the seniority system by relieving Hardison of Saturday work and ordering a senior employee to replace him, it would have denied the latter his shift preference so that Hardison could be given his. The senior employee would also have been deprived of his contractual rights under the collective-bargaining agreement.

It was essential to TWA's business to require Saturday and Sunday work from at least a few employees even though most employees preferred those days off. Allocating the burdens of weekend work was a matter for collective bargaining. In considering criteria to govern this allocation, TWA and the union had two alternatives: adopt a neutral system, such as seniority, a lottery, or rotating shifts; or ⊥81 allocate days off in ⊥ accordance with the religious needs of its employees. TWA would have had to adopt the latter in order to assure Hardison and others like him of getting the days off necessary for strict observance of their religion, but it could have done so only at the expense of others who had strong, but perhaps nonreligious reasons for not working on weekends. There were no volunteers to relieve Hardison on Saturdays, and to give Hardison Saturdays off, TWA would have had to deprive another employee of his shift preference at least in part because he did not adhere to a religion that observed the Saturday Sabbath.

Title VII does not contemplate such unequal treatment. The repeated, unequivocal emphasis of both the language and the legislative history of Title VII is on eliminating discrimination in employment, and such discrimination is proscribed when it is directed against majorities as well as minorities. Indeed, the foundation of Hardison's claim is that TWA and IAM engaged in religious *discrimination* in violation of § 703 (a) (1) when they failed to arrange for him to have Saturdays off. It would be anomalous to conclude that by "reasonable accommodation" Congress meant that an employer must deny the shift and job preference of some employees, as well as deprive them of their contractual rights, in order to accommodate or prefer the religious needs of others, and we conclude that Title VII does not require an employer to go that far.

(2)

Our conclusion is supported by the fact that seniority systems are afforded special treatment under Title VII itself. Section 703 (h) provides in pertinent part: "Notwithstanding any other provision of this sub-chapter, it shall not be an unlawful employment practice for an employer to apply different standards of compensation, or different terms, condi-

tions, or privileges of em⊥ployment pursuant to a ⊥82 bona fide seniority or merit system . . . provided that such differences are not the result of an intention to discriminate because of race, color, religion, sex, or national origin. . . ." "[T]he unmistakable purpose of § 703 (h) was to make clear that the routine application of a bona fide seniority system would not be unlawful under Title VII." *International Brotherhood of Teamsters* v. *United States*. Section 703 (h) is "a definitional provision; as with other provisions of § 703, subsection (h) delineates which employment practices are illegal and thereby prohibited and which are not." *Franks* v. *Bowman Transportation Co., Inc.*. Thus, absent a discriminatory purpose, the operation of a seniority system cannot be an unlawful employment practice even if the system has some discriminatory consequences.

There has been no suggestion of discriminatory intent in this case. "The seniority system was not designed with the intention to discriminate against religion nor did it act to lock members of any religion into a pattern wherein their freedom to exercise their religion was limited. It was coincidental that in plaintiff's case the seniority system acted to compound his problems in exercising his religion." The Court of Appeals' conclusion that TWA was not limited by the terms of its seniority system was in substance nothing more than a ruling that operation of the seniority system was itself an unlawful employment practice even though no discriminatory purpose had been shown. That ruling is plainly inconsistent with the dictates of § 703 (h), both on its face and as interpreted in the recent decisions of this Court.

⊥ As we have said, TWA was not required by Title ⊥83 VII to carve out a special exception to its seniority system in order to help Hardison to meet his religious obligations.

⊥ C   ⊥84

The Court of Appeals also suggested that TWA could have permitted Hardison to work a four-day week if necessary in order to avoid working on his Sabbath. Recognizing that this might have left TWA short-handed on the one shift each week that Hardison did not work, the court still concluded that TWA would suffer no undue hardship if it were required to replace Hardison either with supervisory personnel or with qualified personnel from other departments. Alternatively, the Court of Appeals suggested that TWA could have replaced Hardison on his Saturday shift with other available employees through the payment of premium wages. Both of these alternatives would involve costs to TWA, either in the form of lost efficiency in other jobs or as higher wages.

To require TWA to bear more than a *de minimus* cost in order to give Hardison Saturdays off is an undue hardship. Like abandonment of the seniority system, to require TWA to bear additional costs when no such costs are incurred to give other employees the days off that they want would involve unequal treatment of employees on the basis of their religion. By suggesting that TWA should incur certain costs in order to give Hardison Saturdays off the Court of Appeals would in effect require TWA to finance an additional Saturday off and then to choose the employee who will enjoy it on the basis of his religious beliefs. While incurring extra costs to secure a replacement for Hardison might remove the necessity of compelling another employee to work in⊥voluntarily in Hardison's place, it would not change the fact that the privilege of having Saturdays off would be allocated according to religious beliefs. |85

As we have seen, the paramount concern of Congress in enacting Title VII was the elimination of discrimination in employment. In the absence of clear statutory language or legislative history to the contrary, we will not readily construe the statute to require an employer to discriminate against some employees in order to enable others to observe their Sabbath.

Reversed.

Mr. Justice MARSHALL, with whom *Mr. Justice BRENNAN* joins, dissenting.

One of the most intractable problems arising under Title VII of the Civil Rights Act of 1964, has been whether an employer is guilty of religious discrimination when he discharges an employee (or refuses to hire a job applicant) because of the employee's religious practices. Particularly troublesome has been the plight of adherents to minority faiths who do not observe the holy days on which most businesses are closed—Sundays, Christmas, and Easter—but who need time off for their own days of religious observance. The Equal Employment Opportunity Commission has grappled with this problem in two sets of regulations, and in a long line of decisions. Initially the Commission concluded that an employer was "free under Title VII to establish a normal workweek . . . generally applicable to all employees," and that an employee could not "demand any alteration in [his work schedule] to accommodate his religious needs." Eventually, however, the Commission changed its view and decided that employers must reasonably accommodate such requested schedule changes except where "undue hardship" would result—for example, "where the employee's needed work cannot be per⊥formed by another employee of substantially similar qualifications during the period of absence." In amending Title VII in 1972 Congress confronted the same problem, and adopted the second position of the EEOC. Both before and after the 1972 amendment the lower courts have considered at length the circumstances in which employers must accommodate the religious practices of employees, |86

reaching what the Court correctly describes as conflicting results. And on two occasions this Court has attempted to provide guidance to the lower courts, only to find ourselves evenly divided. *Parker Seal Co.* v. *Cummins; Dewey* v. *Reynolds Metals Co.*.

Today's decision deals a fatal blow to all efforts under Title VII to accommodate work requirements to religious practices. The Court holds, in essence, that although the EEOC regulations and the Act state that an employer must make reasonable adjustments in his work demands to take account of religious observances, the regulation and Act do not ⊥ really mean what they say. An employer, the Court concludes, need not grant even the most minor special privilege to religious observers to enable them to follow their faith. As a question of social policy, this result is deeply troubling, for a society that truly values religious pluralism cannot compel adherents of minority religions to make the cruel choice of surrendering their religion or their job. And as a matter of law today's result is intolerable, for the Court adopts the very position that Congress expressly rejected in 1972, as if we were free to disregard congressional choices that a majority of this Court thinks unwise. I therefore dissent. |87

I

With respect to each of the proposed accommodations to respondent's religious observances that the Court discusses, it ultimately notes that the accommodation would have required "unequal treatment," in favor of the religious observer. That is quite true. But if an accommodation can be rejected simply because it involves preferential treatment, then the regulation and the statute, while brimming with "sound and fury," ultimately "signif[y] nothing."

The accommodation issue by definition arises only when a neutral rule of general applicability conflicts with the religious practices of a particular employee. In some of the reported cases, the rule in question has governed work attire; in other cases it has required attendance at some religious function; in still other instances, it has compelled membership in a union; and in the largest class of cases, it has concerned work schedules. What all these cases have in common is an employee who could comply with the rule only by violating what the employee views as a religious commandment. In each ⊥ instance, the question is whether the employee is to be exempt from the rule's demands. To do so will always result in a privilege being "allocated according to religious beliefs," unless the employer gratuitously decides to repeal the rule in toto. What the statute says, in plain words, is that such allocations are required unless "undue hardship" would result. |88

The point is perhaps best made by considering a not-altogether-hypothetical example. See EEOC Decision No. 71-779, 1973 CCH EEOC Decisions ¶ 6180 (Dec. 21, 1970). Assume that an employer requires all employees to wear a particular type of hat at work in order to make the employees readily identifiable to customers. Such a rule obviously does not, on its face, violate Title VII, and an employee who altered the uniform for reasons of taste could be discharged. But a very different question would be posed by the discharge of an employee who, for religious reasons, insisted on wearing, over her hair a tightly fitted scarf which was visible through the hat. In such a case the employer could accommodate this religious practice without undue hardship—or any hardship at all. Yet as I understand the Court's analysis—and nothing in the Court's response, is to the contrary—the accommodation would not be required because it would afford the privilege of wearing scarfs to a select few based on their religious beliefs. The employee thus would have to give up either the religious practice or the job. This, I submit, makes a mockery of the statute.

In reaching this result, the Court seems almost oblivious to the legislative history of the 1972 amendment to Title VII which is briefly recounted in the Court's opinion. That history is far more instructive than the Court allows. After the EEOC promulgated its second set of guidelines requiring reasonable accommodations unless undue hardship would result, at least two courts issued decisions questioning, whether the guidelines were consistent with Title VII. ⊥These courts reasoned, in language strikingly similar to today's decision, that to excuse religious observers from neutral work rules would "discriminate against . . . other employees" and "constitute unequal administration of the collective-bargaining agreement." *Dewey* v. *Reynolds Metals Co.* They therefore refused to equate "religious discrimination with failure to accommodate." When Congress was reviewing Title VII in 1972, Senator Jennings Randolph informed the Congress of these decisions which, he said, had "clouded" the meaning of religious discrimination. 118 Cong. Rec. 706 (1972). He introduced an amendment, tracking the language of the EEOC regulation, to make clear that Title VII requires religious accommodation, even though unequal treatment would result. The primary purpose of the amendment, he explained, was to protect Saturday Sabbatarians like himself from employers who refuse "to hire or to continue in employment employees whose religious practices rigidly require them to abstain from work in the nature of hire on particular days." His amendment was unanimously approved by the Senate on a roll call vote, and was accepted by the Conference Committee, whose report was approved by both Houses. Yet the Court today, in rejecting any accommodation that involves preferential treatment, follows the *Dewey* decision in direct contravention of congressional intent.

The Court's interpretation of the statute, by effectively nullifying it, has the singular advantage of making consideration of petitioners' constitutional

⊥89

challenge unnecessary. The Court does not even rationalize its construction on this ground, however, nor could it, since "resort to an alternative construction to avoid deciding a constitutional question is appro⊥priate only when such a course is 'fairly possible' or when the statute provides a 'fair alternative' construction." *Swain* v. *Pressley*. Moreover, while important constitutional questions would be posed by interpreting the law to compel employers (or fellow employees) to incur substantial costs to aid the religious observer, not all accommodations are costly, and the constitutionality of the statute is not placed in serious doubt simply because it sometimes requires an exemption from a work rule. Indeed, this Court has repeatedly found no Establishment Clause problems in exempting religious observers from state-imposed duties, *e.g.*, *Wisconsin* v. *Yoder*; *Sherbert* v. *Verner*; *Zorach* v. *Clauson*, even when the exemption was in no way compelled by the Free Exercise Clause, *e.g.*, *Gillette* v. *United States*; *Welsh* v. *United States* (*White, J.*, dissenting); *Sherbert* v. *Verner* (*Harlan, J.*, dissenting); *Braunfeld* v. *Brown*, (dictum); *McGowan* v. *Maryland*, (*Frankfurter, J.*, concurring). If the State does not establish ⊥ religion over nonreligion by excusing religious practitioners from obligations owed the State, I do not see how the State can be said to establish religion by requiring employers to do the same with respect to obligations owed the employer. Thus, I think it beyond dispute that the Act does—and, consistently with the First Amendment, can—require employers to grant privileges to religious observers as part of the accommodation process.

⊥90

⊥91

II

Once it is determined that the duty to accommodate sometimes requires that an employee be exempted from an otherwise valid work requirement, the only remaining question is whether this is such a case: did TWA prove that it exhausted all reasonable accommodations, and that the only remaining alternatives would have caused undue hardship on TWA's business. To pose the question is to answer it, for all that the District Court found TWA had done to accommodate respondent's Sabbath observance was that it "held several meetings with [respondent] . . . [and] authorized the union steward to search for someone who would swap shifts." *Hardison* v. *TWA*. To conclude that TWA, one of the largest air carriers in the Nation, would have suffered undue hardship had it done anything more defies both reason and common sense.

The Court implicitly assumes that the only means of accommodation open to TWA were to compel an unwilling employee to replace respondent; to pay premium wages to a voluntary substitute; or to employ one less person during ⊥ respondent's Sabbath shift. Based on this assumption, the Court seemingly finds that each alternative would have involved un-

⊥92

due hardship not only because respondent would have given a special privilege, but also because either another employee would have been deprived of rights under the collective-bargaining agreement, or because "more than a *de minimus* cost" would have been imposed on TWA. But the Court's myopic view of the available options is not supported by either the District Court's findings or the evidence adduced at trial. Thus, the Court's conclusion cannot withstand analysis, even assuming that its rejection of the alternatives it does discuss is justifiable.

_|93   ⊥To begin with, the record simply does not support the Court's assertion, made without accompanying citations, that "[t]here were no volunteers to relieve Hardison on Saturdays." Everett Kussman, the manager of the department in which respondent worked, testified that he had made no effort to find volunteers, and the Union stipulated that its steward had not done so either. Thus, contrary to the Court's assumption, there may have been one or more employees who, for reasons of either sympathy or personal convenience, willingly would have

_|94   substi⊥tuted for respondent on Saturdays until respondent could either regain the non-Saturday shift he had held for the three preceding months or transfer back to his old department where he had sufficient seniority to avoid Saturday work. Alternatively, there may have been an employee who preferred respondent's Thursday-Monday daytime shift to his own; in fact, respondent testified that he had informed Kussman and the Union steward that the clerk on the Sunday-Thursday night shift (the "graveyard" shift) was dissatisfied with his hours. Thus, respondent's religious observance might have been accommodated by a simple trade of days or shifts without necessarily depriving any employee of

_|95   his or her contractual rights and without ⊥ imposing significant costs on TWA. Of course it is also possible that no trade—or none consistent with the seniority system—could have been arranged. But the burden under the EEOC regulation is on TWA to establish that a reasonable accommodation was not possible. Because it failed either to explore the possibility of a voluntary trade or to assure that its delegate, the Union steward, did so, TWA was unable to meet its burden.

Nor was a voluntary trade the only option open to TWA that the Court ignores; to the contrary, at least two other options are apparent from the record. First, TWA could have paid overtime to a voluntary replacement for respondent—assuming that someone would have been willing to work Saturdays for premium pay—and passed on the cost to respondent. In fact, one accommodation Hardison suggested would have done just that by requiring Hardison to work overtime when needed at regular pay. Under this plan, the total overtime cost to the employer—and the total number of overtime hours available for other employees—would not have reflected Hardison's Sabbath absences. Alternatively, TWA could have

transferred respondent back to his previous department where he had accumulated substantial seniority, as respondent also suggested. Admittedly, both options would have violated the collective-bargaining agreement; the former because the agreement required that employees working over forty hours per week receive premium pay, and the latter because the agreement prohibited employees from trans⊥ferring departments more than once every six _|96 months. But neither accommodation would have deprived any other employee of rights under the contract or violated the seniority system in any way. Plainly an employer cannot avoid his duty to accommodate by signing a contract that precludes all reasonable accommodations; even the Court appears to concede as much. Thus I do not believe it can be even seriously argued that TWA would have suffered "undue hardship" to its business had it required respondent to pay the extra costs of his replacement, or had it transferred respondent to his former department.

What makes this case most tragic, however, is not that respondent Hardison has been needlessly deprived of his livelihood simply because he chose to follow the dictates of his conscience. Nor is the tragedy of the case exhausted by the impact it will have on thousands of Americans like Hardison who could be forced to live on welfare as the price they must pay for ⊥ worshipping their God. The ultimate tragedy _|97 edy is that despite Congress' best efforts, one of this Nation's pillars of strength—our hospitality to religious diversity—has been seriously eroded. All Americans will be a little poorer until today's decision is erased. I respectfully dissent.

THOMAS v. REVIEW BOARD OF INDIANA EMPLOYMENT SECURITY DIVISION

450 U.S. 707
ON WRIT OF CERTIORARI TO THE SUPREME COURT
OF THE STATE OF INDIANA
Argued October 7, 1980 — Decided April 6, 1981
⊥ *Chief Justice BURGER* delivered the opinion of _|709 the Court.

We granted certiorari to consider whether the State's denial of unemployment compensation benefits to the petitioner, a Jehovah's Witness who terminated his job because his religious beliefs forbade participation in the production of armaments, constituted a violation of his First Amendment right to free exercise of religion.

I

Thomas terminated his employment in the Blaw-Knox Foundry and Machinery Company when he was transferred from the roll foundry to a department that produced turrets for military tanks. He claimed his religious beliefs prevented him from participating in the production of war materials. The respondent Review Board denied him unemployment compensation benefits by applying disqualifying provisions of the Indiana Employment Security Act.⊥

Thomas, a Jehovah's Witness, was hired initially to work in the roll foundry at Blaw-Knox. The function of that department was to fabricate sheet steel for a variety of industrial uses. On his application form, he listed his membership in the Jehovah's Witnesses, and noted that his hobbies were Bible study and Bible reading. However, he placed no conditions on his employment; and, he did not describe his religious tenets in any detail on the form.

Approximately a year later, the roll foundry closed, and Blaw-Knox transferred Thomas to a department that fabricated turrets for military tanks. On his first day at this new job, Thomas realized that the work he was doing was weapons related. He checked the bulletin board where inplant openings were listed, and discovered that all of the remaining departments at Blaw-Knox were engaged directly in the production of weapons. Since no transfer to another department would resolve his problem, he asked for a layoff. When that request was denied, he quit, asserting that he could not work on weapons without violating the principles of his religion. The record does not show that he was offered any nonweapons work by his employer, or that any such work was available.

Upon leaving Blaw-Knox, Thomas applied for unemployment compensation benefits under the Indiana Employment Security Act. At an administrative hearing where he was ⊥ not represented by counsel, he testified that he believed that contributing to the production of arms violated his religion. He said that when he realized that his work on the tank turret line involved producing weapons for war, he consulted another Blaw-Knox employee—a friend and fellow Jehovah's Witness. The friend advised him that working on weapons parts at Blaw-Knox was not "unscriptural." Thomas was not able to "rest with" this view, however. He concluded that his friend's view was based upon a less strict reading of Witness' principles than his own.

When asked at the hearing to explain what kind of work his religious convictions would permit, Thomas said that he would have no difficulty doing the type of work that he had done at the roll foundry. He testified that he could, in good conscience, engage indirectly in the production of materials that might be used ultimately to fabricate arms— for example, as an employee of a raw material supplier or of a roll foundry.

The hearing referee found that Thomas' religious beliefs specifically precluded him from producing or directly aiding in the manufacture of items used in warfare. He also found that Thomas had terminated

his employment because of these religious convictions. The referee reported:

"Claimant continually searched for a transfer to another department which would not be so armament related; ⊥ however, this did not materialize, and prior to the date of his leaving, claimant requested a layoff, which was denied; and on November 6, 1975, *claimant did quit due to his religious convictions.*"

The referee concluded nonetheless that Thomas' termination was not based upon a "good cause [arising] in connection with [his] work," as required by the Indiana unemployment compensation statute. Accordingly, he was held not entitled to benefits. The Review Board adopted the referee's findings and conclusions, and affirmed the denial of benefits.

The Indiana Court of Appeals, accepting the finding that Thomas terminated his employment "due to his religious convictions," reversed the decision of the Review Board, and held that § 22-4-15-1, as applied, improperly burdened Thomas' right to the free exercise of his religion. Accordingly, it ordered the Board to extend benefits to Thomas. *Thomas* v. *Review Board.*

The Supreme Court of Indiana, dividing 3-2, vacated the decision of the Court of Appeals, and denied Thomas benefits. *Thomas* v. *Review Board.* With reference to the Indiana unemployment compensation statute, the court said:

"It is not intended to facilitate changing employment or to provide relief for those who quit work voluntarily for personal reasons. Voluntary unemployment is not compensable under the purpose of the Act, which is to provide benefits for persons unemployed through no fault of their own.

"Good cause which justifies voluntary unemployment must ⊥ be job-related and objective in character."

The court held that Thomas had quit voluntarily for personal reasons, and therefore did not qualify for benefits.

In discussing the petitioner's Free Exercise claim, the court stated: "[A] personal philosophical choice rather than a religious choice, does not rise to the level of a first amendment claim." The Court found the basis and the precise nature of Thomas' belief unclear—but it concluded that the belief was more "personal philosophical choice" than religious belief. Nonetheless, it held that, even assuming that Thomas quit for religious reasons, he would not be entitled to benefits: under Indiana law, a termination motivated by religion is not for "good cause" objectively related to the work.

The Indiana court concluded that denying Thomas benefits would create only an indirect burden on his free exercise right and that the burden was justified by the legitimate state interest in preserving the integrity of the insurance fund and maintaining a stable work force by encouraging workers not to leave their jobs for personal reasons.

Finally, the court held that awarding unemployment compensation benefits to a person who terminates employment voluntarily for religious reasons, while denying such benefits to persons who terminate for other personal but nonreligious reasons, would violate the Establishment Clause of the First Amendment.

The judgment under review must be examined in light of our prior decisions, particularly *Sherbert* v. *Verner.*

II

Only beliefs rooted in religion are protected by the Free Exercise Clause, which, by its terms, gives special protection to the exercise of religion. *Sherbert* v. _|714 *Verner; Wis⊥consin* v. *Yoder.* The determination of what is a "religious" belief or practice is more often than not a difficult and delicate task, as the division in the Indiana Supreme Court attests. However, the resolution of that question is not to turn upon a judicial perception of the particular belief or practice in question; religious beliefs need not be acceptable, logical, consistent, or comprehensible to others in order to merit First Amendment protection.

In support of his claim for benefits, Thomas testified:

"Q. And then when it comes to actually producing the tank itself, hammering it out; that you will not do. . . .

"A. That's right, that's right when . . . I'm daily faced with the knowledge that these are tanks. . . .

. . . . .

"A. I really could not, you know, conscientiously continue to work with armaments. It would be against all of the . . . religious principles that . . . I have come to learn. . . ."

Based upon this and other testimony, the referee held that Thomas "quit due to his religious convictions." The Review Board adopted that finding, and the finding is not challenged in this Court.

The Indiana Supreme Court apparently took a different view of the record. It concluded that "although the claimant's reasons for quitting were described as religious, it was unclear what his belief was, and what the religious basis of his belief was." In that court's view, Thomas had made a merely "personal philosophical choice rather than a reli-_|715 gious choice."⊥

In reaching its conclusion, the Indiana court seems to have placed considerable reliance on the facts that Thomas was "struggling" with his beliefs and that he was not able to "articulate" his belief precisely. It noted, for example, that Thomas admitted before the referee that he would not object to "working for United States Steel or Inland Steel . . . produc[ing]

the raw product necessary for the production of any kind of tank . . . [because I] would not be a direct party to whoever they shipped it to [and] would not be . . . chargeable in . . . conscience. . . ." *Thomas* v. *Review Board.*

The court found this position inconsistent with Thomas' stated opposition to participation in the production of armaments. But, Thomas' statements reveal no more than that he found work in the roll foundry sufficiently insulated from producing weapons of war. We see, therefore, that Thomas drew a line, and it is not for us to say that the line he drew was an unreasonable one. Courts should not undertake to dissect religious beliefs because the believer admits that he is "struggling" with his position or because his beliefs are not articulated with the clarity and precision that a more sophisticated person might employ.

The Indiana court also appears to have given significant weight to the fact that another Jehovah's Witness had no scruples about working on tank turrets; for that other Witness, at least, such work was "scripturally" acceptable. Intrafaith differences of that kind are not uncommon among followers of a particular creed, and the judicial process is singularly ill equipped to resolve such differences in relation to the Religion Clauses. One can, of course, imagine an asserted claim so bizarre, so clearly nonreligious in motivation, as not to be entitled to protection under the Free Exercise Clause; but that is not the case here, and the guarantee of free exercise is not limited to beliefs which are shared by all of the members ⊥   _|716 of a religious sect. Particularly in this sensitive area, it is not within the judicial function and judicial competence to inquire whether the petitioner or his fellow worker more correctly perceived the commands of their common faith. Courts are not arbiters of scriptural interpretation.

The narrow function of a reviewing court in this context is to determine whether there was an appropriate finding that petitioner terminated his work because of an honest conviction that such work was forbidden by his religion. Not surprisingly, the record before the referee and the Review Board was not made with an eye to the microscopic examination often exercised in appellate judicial review. However, judicial review is confined to the facts as found and conclusions drawn. On this record, it is clear that Thomas terminated his employment for religious reasons.

III
A

More than 30 years ago, the Court held that a person may not be compelled to choose between the exercise of a First Amendment right and participation in an otherwise available public program. A state may not "exclude individual Catholics, Lutherans, Mohammedans, Baptists, Jews, Methodists, Non-believers, Presbyterians, or the members of any other faith, because of their faith, or lack of it, from receiving the benefits of public welfare legislation." *Everson* v. *Board of Education.*

Later, in *Sherbert*, the Court examined South Carolina's attempt to deny unemployment compensation benefits to a Sabbatarian who declined to work on Saturday. In sustaining her right to receive benefits, the Court held:

"The ruling [disqualifying Mrs. Sherbert from benefits because of her refusal to work on Saturday in violation of her faith] forces her to choose between following the ⊥ precepts of her religion and forfeiting benefits, on the one hand, and abandoning one of the precepts of her religion in order to accept work, on the other hand. Governmental imposition of such a burden puts the same kind of burden upon the free exercise of religion as would a fine imposed against [her] for her Saturday worship."

⌐717

The respondent Review Board argues, and the Indiana Supreme Court held, that the burden upon religion here is only the indirect consequence of public welfare legislation that the state clearly has authority to enact. "Neutral objective standards must be met to qualify for compensation." *Thomas* v. *Review Board*, Indiana requires applicants for unemployment compensation to show that they left work for "good cause in connection with the work."

A similar argument was made and rejected in *Sherbert*, however. It is true that, as in *Sherbert*, the Indiana law does not *compel* a violation of conscience. But, "this is only the beginning, not the end, of our inquiry." In a variety of ways we have said that "a regulation neutral on its face may, in its application, nonetheless offend the constitutional requirement for governmental neutrality if it unduly burdens the free exercise of religion." *Wisconsin* v. *Yoder.* Cf. *Walz* v. *Tax Commissioner.*

Here, as in *Sherbert*, the employee was put to a choice between fidelity to religious belief or cessation of work; the coercive impact on Thomas is indistinguishable from *Sherbert*, where the Court held:

"[N]ot only is it apparent that appellant's declared ineligibility for benefits derives solely from the practices of her religion, but the pressure upon her to forego that practice is unmistakable."

Where the state conditions receipt of an important benefit upon conduct proscribed by a religious faith, or where it denies ⊥ such a benefit because of conduct mandated by religious belief, thereby putting substantial pressure on an adherent to modify his behavior and to violate his beliefs, a burden upon religion exists. While the compulsion may be indirect, the infringement upon free exercise is nonetheless substantial.

⌐718

The State also contends that *Sherbert* is inapposite because, in that case, the employee was dismissed by the employer's action. But we see that Mrs. Sherbert was dismissed because she refused to work on Saturdays after the plant went to a six-day workweek. Had Thomas simply presented himself at the Blaw-Knox plant turret line but refused to perform any assigned work, it must be assumed that he, like Sherbert, would have been terminated by the employer's action, if no other work was available. In both cases, the termination flowed from the fact that the employment, once acceptable, became religiously objectionable because of changed conditions.

B

The mere fact that the petitioner's religious practice is burdened by a governmental program does not mean that an exemption accommodating his practice must be granted. The state may justify an inroad on religious liberty by showing that it is the least restrictive means of achieving some compelling state interest. However, it is still true that "[t]he essence of all that has been said and written on the subject is that only those interests of the highest order can overbalance legitimate claims to the free exercise of religion." *Wisconsin* v. *Yoder.*

The purposes urged to sustain the disqualifying provision of the Indiana unemployment compensation scheme are twofold: (1) to avoid the widespread unemployment and the consequent burden on the fund resulting if people were permitted to leave jobs for "personal" reasons; and (2) to ⊥ avoid a detailed probing by employers into job applicants' religious beliefs. These are by no means unimportant considerations. When the focus of the inquiry is properly narrowed, however, we must conclude that the interests advanced by the state do not justify the burden placed on free exercise of religion.

⌐719

There is no evidence in the record to indicate that the number of people who find themselves in the predicament of choosing between benefits and religious beliefs is large enough to create "widespread unemployment," or even to seriously affect unemployment—and no such claim was advanced by the Review Board. Similarly, although detailed inquiry by employers into applicants' religious beliefs is undesirable, there is no evidence in the record to indicate that such inquiries will occur in Indiana, or that they have occurred in any of the states that extend benefits to people in the petitioner's position. Nor is there any reason to believe that the number of people terminating employment for religious reasons will be so great as to motivate employers to make such inquiries.

Neither of the interests advanced is sufficiently compelling to justify the burden upon Thomas' religious liberty. Accordingly, Thomas is entitled to receive benefits unless, as the state contends and the Indiana court held, such payment would violate the Establishment Clause.

IV

The respondent contends that to compel benefit payments to Thomas involves the state in fostering a religious faith. There is, in a sense, a "benefit" to Thomas deriving from his religious beliefs, but this manifests no more than the tension between the two Religious Clauses which the Court resolved in *Sherbert*:

"In holding as we do, plainly we are not fostering the 'establishment' of the Seventh Day Adventist re- ⌋720 ligion ⊥ in South Carolina, for the extension of unemployment benefits to Sabbatarians in common with Sunday worshippers reflects nothing more than the governmental obligation of neutrality in the face of religious differences, and does not represent that involvement of religious with secular institutions which it is the object of the Establishment Clause to forestall." *Sherbert* v. *Verner*.

See also *Wisconsin* v. *Yoder; Walz* v. *Tax Commission of the City of New York; O'Hair* v. *Andrus*.

Unless we are prepared to overrule *Sherbert*, Thomas cannot be denied the benefits due him on the basis of the findings of the referee, the Review Board and the Indiana Court of Appeals that he terminated his employment because of his religious convictions.

Reversed.

Justice BLACKMUN joins parts I, II, and III of the Court's opinion. As to Part IV thereof, he concurs in the result.

Justice REHNQUIST, dissenting:

The Court today holds that the State of Indiana is constitutionally required to provide direct financial assistance to a person solely on the basis of his religious beliefs. Because I believe that the decision today adds mud to the already muddied waters of First Amendment jurisprudence, I dissent.

I

The Court correctly acknowledges that there is a "tension" between the Free Exercise and Establishment Clauses of the First Amendment of the United States Constitution. Although the relationship of the two clauses has been the subject of much commen- ⌋721 tary, the "tension" is a fairly recent ⊥ vintage, unknown at the time of the framing and adoption of the First Amendment. The causes of the tension, it seems to me, are three-fold. First, the growth of social welfare legislation during the latter part of the 20th century has greatly magnified the potential for conflict between the two clauses, since such legislation touches the individual at so many points in his life. Second, the decision by this Court that the First Amendment was "incorporated" into the Fourteenth Amendment and thereby made applicable against the States, *Stromberg* v. *California; Cantwell* v. *Connecticut*, similarly multiplied the number of instances in which the "tension" might arise. The third, and perhaps most important, cause of the ten-

sion is our overly expansive interpretation of *both* clauses. By broadly construing both clauses, the Court has constantly narrowed the channel between the Scylla and Charybdis through which any state or federal action must pass in order to survive constitutional scrutiny.

None of these developments could have been foreseen by those who framed and adopted the First Amendment. The First Amemdement was adopted well before the growth of much social welfare legislation and at a time when the Federal Government was in a real sense considered a government of limited delegated powers. Indeed, the principal argument against adopting the Constitution *without* a "Bill of Rights" was not that such an enactment would be *undesirable* but that it was *unnecessary* because of the limited nature of the Federal Government. So long as the government enacts little social welfare legislation, as was the case in 1791, there are few occasions in which the two clauses may conflict. Moreover, as originally enacted, the First Amendment applied only to the Federal Government, not the government of the States. *Barron* v. *Baltimore*. The Framers could hardly anticipate *Barron* being superseded by the "selective incorporation" doctrine adopted by the Court, a decision which greatly expanded the number of stat⊥utes which would be ⌋722 subject to challenge under the First Amendment. Because those who drafted and adopted the First Amendment could not have foreseen either the growth of social welfare legislation or the incorporation of the First Amendment into the Fourteenth Amendment, we simply do not know how they would view the scope of the two clauses.

II

The decision today illustrates how far astray the Court has gone in interpreting the Free Exercise and Establishment Clauses of the First Amendment. Although the Court holds that a State is constitutionally required to provide direct financial assistance to persons solely on the basis of their religious beliefs and recognizes the "tension" between the two clauses, it does little to help resolve that tension or to offer meaningful guidance to other courts which must decide cases like this on a day-by-day basis. Instead, it simply asserts that there is no Establishment Clause violation here and leaves tension between the two Religion Clauses to be resolved on a case-by-case basis. As suggested above, however, I believe that the "tension" is largely of this Court's own making, and would diminish almost to the vanishing point if the clauses were properly interpreted.

Just as it did in *Sherbert* v. *Verner*, the Court today reads the Free Exercise Clause more broadly than is warranted. As to the proper interpretation of the Free Exercise Clause, I would accept the decision of *Braunfeld* v. *Brown* and the dissent in *Sherbert*. In *Braunfeld*, we held that Sunday Closing laws do not violate the First Amendment rights of Sabbatarians. Chief Justice Warren explained that the statute did not make unlawful any religious practices of appellants; it simply made the practice of their religious beliefs more expensive. We concluded that "to strike down, without the most critical scrutiny, legislation which imposes only an indirect burden on the exercise of religion, *i.e.* legislation which does ⊥723 not ⊥ make unlawful the religious practice itself, would radically restrict the operating latitude of the legislature." Likewise in this case, it cannot be said that the State discriminated against Thomas on the basis of his religious beliefs or that he was denied benefits *because* he was a Jehovah's Witness. Where, as here, a State has enacted a general statute, the purpose and effect of which is to advance the State's secular goals, the Free Exercise Clause does not in my view require the State to conform that statute to the dictates of religious conscience of any group. As Justice Harlan recognized in his dissent in *Sherbert* v. *Verner*, "Those situations in which the Constitution may require special treatment on account of religion are . . . few and far between." Like him I believe that although a State could choose to grant exemptions to religious persons from state unemployment regulations, a State is not constitutionally ⊥724 compelled to do so. ⊥

The Court's treatment of the Establishment Clause issue is equally unsatisfying. Although today's decision requires a State to provide direct financial assistance to persons solely on the basis of their religious beliefs, the Court nonetheless blandly assures us, just as it did in *Sherbert*, that its decision "plainly" does not foster the "establishment" of religion. I would agree that the Establishment Clause, properly interpreted, would not be violated if Indiana ⊥725 volun⊥tarily chose to grant unemployment benefits to those persons who left their jobs for religious reasons. But I also believe that the decision below is inconsistent with many of our prior Establishment Clause cases. Those cases, if faithfully applied, would require us to hold that such voluntary action by a State *did* violate the Establishment Clause.

Justice Stewart noted this point in his concurring opinion in *Sherbert*. He observed that decisions like *Sherbert*, and the one rendered today, squarely conflict with the more extreme language of many of our prior Establishment Clause cases. In *Everson* v. *Board of Education* the Court stated that the Establishment Clause bespeaks a "government . . . stripped of all power . . . to support, or otherwise to assist any or all religions . . .," and no State "can pass laws which aid one religion [or] all religions." In *Torcaso* v. *Watkins* the Court asserted that the government cannot "constitutionally pass laws or impose requirements which aid all religions as against non-believers." And in *School District of Abington Township* v. *Schempp* the Court adopted Justice Rutledge's words in *Everson* that the Establishment

Clause forbids "every form of public aid or support for religion." See also *Engel* v. *Vitale*.

In recent years the Court has moved away from the mechanistic "no-aid-to-religion" approach to the Establishment Clause and has stated a three-part test to determine the constitutionality of governmental aid to religion. See *Lemon* v. *Kurtzman; Committee for Public Education & Religious Liberty* v. *Nyquist*. First, the statute must serve a secular legislative purpose. Second, it must have a "primary effect" that neither advances nor inhibits religion. And third, the State and its administration must avoid excessive entanglement with religion. *Walz* v. *Tax Commission.* ⊥   ⊥726

It is not surprising that the Court today makes no attempt to apply those principles to the facts of this case. If Indiana were to legislate what the Court today requires—an unemployment compensation law which permitted benefits to be granted to those persons who quit their jobs for religious reasons—the statute would "plainly" violate the Establishment Clause as interpreted in such cases as *Lemon* and *Nyquist*. First, although the unemployment statute as a whole would be enacted to serve a secular legislative purpose, the proviso would clearly serve only a religious purpose. It would grant financial benefits for the sole purpose of accommodating religious beliefs. Second, there can be little doubt that the primary effect on the proviso would be to "advance" religion by facilitating the exercise of religious belief. Third, any statute including such a proviso would surely "entangle" the State in religion far more than the mere grant of tax exemptions, as in *Walz*, or the award of tuition grants and tax credits, as in *Nyquist*. By granting financial benefits to persons solely on the basis of their religious beliefs, the State must necessarily inquire whether the claimant's belief is "religious" and whether it is sincerely held. Otherwise any dissatisfied employee may leave his job without cause and claim that he did so because his own particular beliefs required it.

It is unclear from the Court's opinion whether it has temporarily retreated from its expansive view of the Establishment Clause, or wholly abandoned it. I would welcome the latter. Just as I think that Justice Harlan in *Sherbert* correctly stated the proper approach to free exercise questions, I believe that Justice Stewart, dissenting in *School District* v. *Schempp*, accurately stated the reach of the Establishment Clause. He explained that the Establishment Clause is limited to "government support of proselytizing activities of religious sects by throwing the weight of secular authorities behind the dissemination of religious tenets." See *McCollum* v. *Board of Education*. (Reed, J., dissenting) ⊥ (impermissible aid is only "purposeful assistance directly to the church itself or to some religious group . . . performing ecclesiastical functions.") Conversely, governmental assistance which does not have the ef-   ⊥727 fect of "inducing" religious belief, but instead merely "accommodates" or implements an independent religious choice does not impermissibly involve the government in religious choices and therefore does not violate the Establishment Clause of the First Amendment. I would think that in this case, as in *Sherbert*, had the state voluntarily chosen to pay unemployment compensation benefits to persons who left their jobs for religious reasons, such aid would be constitutionally permissible because it redounds directly to the benefit of the individual. Accord, *Wolman* v. *Walter* (upholding various disbursements made to pupils in parochial schools).

In sum, my difficulty with today's decision is that it reads the Free Exercise Clause too broadly and it fails to squarely acknowledge that such a reading conflicts with many of our Establishment Clause cases. As such, the decision simply exacerbates the "tension" between the two clauses. If the Court were to construe the Free Exercise Clause as it did in *Braunfeld* and the Establishment Clause as Justice Stewart did in *Schempp*, the circumstances in which there would be a conflict between the two clauses would be few and far between. Although I heartily agree with the Court's tacit abandonment of much of our rhetoric about the Establishment Clause, I regret that the Court cannot see its way clear to restore what was surely intended to have been a greater degree of flexibility to the federal and state governments in legislating consistently with the Free Exercise Clause. Accordingly, I would affirm the judgment of the Indiana Supreme Court.

OHIO CIVIL RIGHTS COMMISSION v. DAYTON CHRISTIAN SCHOOLS

ON APPEAL FROM THE UNITED STATES COURT OF APPEALS FOR THE SIXTH CIRCUIT

Argued March 26, 1986 — Decided June 27, 1986
JUSTICE REHNQUIST delivered the opinion of the Court.

Appellee Dayton Christian Schools, Inc. (Dayton) and various individuals brought an action in the United States District Court for the Southern District of Ohio under 42 U.S.C. § 1983, seeking to enjoin a pending state administrative proceeding brought against Dayton by appellant Ohio Civil Rights Commission (Commission). Dayton asserted that the Free Exercise and Establishment Clauses of the First Amendment prohibited the Commission from exercising jurisdiction over it or from punishing it for engaging in employment discrimination. The District Court refused to issue the injunction on grounds that any conflict between the First Amendment and the administrative proceedings was not yet ripe, and that in any case the proposed action of the Commission violated neither the Free Exercise nor

the Establshment Clause of the First and Fourteenth Amendments. The Court of Appeals for the Sixth Circuit reversed, holding that the exercise of jurisdiction and the enforcement of the statute would impermissibly burden appellees' rights under the Free Exercise Clause and would result in excessive entanglement under the Establishment Clause. We postponed the question of jurisdiction pending consideration of the merits. We now conclude that we have jurisdiction, and we reverse, holding that the District Court should have abstained under our cases beginning with *Younger* v. *Harris*.

Dayton is a private nonprofit corporation that provides education at both the elementary and secondary school levels. It was formed by two local churches, the Patterson Park Brethren Church and the Christian Tabernacle, and it is regarded as a "nondenominational" extension of the Christian education ministries of these two chruches. Dayton's corporate charter establishes a Board of Directors (Board) to lead the corporation in both spiritual and temporal matters. The charter also includes a section entitled, "Statement of Faith," which serves to restrict membership on the Board and the educational staff to persons who subscribe to a particular set of religious beliefs. The Statement of Faith requires each Board or staff member to be a born-again Christian and to reaffirm his or her belief annually in the Bible, the Trinity, the nature and mission of Jesus Christ, the doctrine of original sin, the role of the Holy Ghost, the resurrection and judgment of the dead, the need for Christian unity, and the divine creation of human beings.

The Board has elaborated these requirements to include a belief in the internal resolution of disputes through the "biblical chain of command." The core of this doctrine, rooted in passages from the New Testament, is that one Christian should not take another Christian into courts of the State. Teachers are expected to present any grievance they may have to their immediate supervisor, and to acquiesce in the final authority of the Board, rather than to pursue a remedy in civil court. The Board has sought to ensure compliance with this internal dispute resolution doctrine by making it a contractual condition of employment.

Linda Hoskinson was employed as a teacher at Dayton during the 1978-1979 school year. She subscribed to the Statement of Faith and expressly agreed to resolve disputes internally through the biblical chain of command. In January 1979, she informed her principal, James Rakestraw, that she was pregnant. After consulting with his superiors, Rakestraw informed Hoskinson that her employment contract would not be renewed at the end of the school year because of Dayton's religious doctrine that mothers should stay home with their preschool age children. Instead of appealing this decision internally, Hoskinson contacted an attorney who sent a letter to Dayton's Superintendent, Claude Schindler, threatening litigation based on state and federal sex discrimination laws if Dayton did not agree to rehire Hoskinson for the coming school year.

Upon receipt of this letter, Schindler informed Hoskinson that she was suspended immediately for challenging the nonrenewal decision in a manner inconsistent with the internal dispute resolution doctrine. The Board reviewed this decision and decided to terminate Hoskinson. It stated that the sole reason for her termination was her violation of the internal dispute resolution doctrine, and it rescinded the earlier nonrenewal decision because it said that she had not received adequate prior notice of the doctrine concerning a mother's duty to stay home with her young children.

Hoskinson filed a complaint with appellant Ohio Civil Rights Commission (Commission), alleging that Dayton's nonrenewal decision constituted sex discrimination, in violation of Ohio Rev. Code Ann. § 4112.02(A) (Supp. 1985), and that its termination decision penalized her for asserting her rights, in violation of Ohio Rev. Code Ann. § 4112.02(I) (Supp. 1985). The Commission notified Dayton that it was conducting a preliminary investigation into the matter, and repeatedly urged Dayton to consider private settlement, warning that failure to do so could result in a formal adjudication of the matter.

The Commission eventually determined that there was probable cause to believe that Dayton had discriminated against Hoskinson based on her sex and had retaliated against her for attempting to assert her rights in violation of § 4112(A) and (I). Pursuant to Ohio Rev. Code Ann. § 4112.05(B) (Supp. 1985), it sent Dayton a proposed Conciliation Agreement and Consent Order that would have required Dayton to reinstate Hoskinson with back pay, and would have prohibited Dayton from taking retaliatory action against any employee for participating in the preliminary investigation. The Commission warned Dayton that failure to accede to this proposal or an acceptable counteroffer would result in formal administrative proceedings being initiated against it. When Dayton failed to respond, the Commission initiated administrative proceedings against it by filing a complaint. Dayton answered the complaint by asserting that the First Amendment prevented the Commission from exercising jurisdiction over it since its actions had been taken pursuant to sincerely held religious beliefs.

While these administrative proceedings were pending, Dayton filed this action against the Commission in the United States District Court for the Southern District of Ohio under 42 U.S.C. § 1983, seeking a permanent injunction of the state proceedings on the ground that any investigation of Dayton's hiring process or any imposition of sanctions for Dayton's nonrenewal or termination decisions would violate the Religion Clauses of the First Amendment. The Commission filed a motion to dismiss, arguing, *inter alia*, that the District Court should refrain from enjoining the administrative proceedings based on federal abstention doctrines. It also filed various documents defending its action on the merits.

Without addressing the abstention argument, the District Court refused to issue the injunction. The Court of Appeals for the Sixth Circuit reversed, as previously noted, holding that the exercise of such jurisdiction would violate both the Free Exercise and the Establishment Clauses of the First Amendment.

We hold that we have appellate jurisdiction under 28 U.S.C. § 1254(2) to review the decision of the Court of Appeals. That statute authorizes an appeal to this Court "by a party relying on a State statute held by a court of appeals to be invalid as repugnant to the Constitution." This authority embraces cases holding a state statute unconstitutional as applied to the facts of the case. Here there is no doubt that the decision by the Court of Appeals satisfies this test. The court expressly held that Ohio Rev. Code Ann. § 4112 (Supp. 1985) is repugnant to the Free Exercise and Establishment Clauses as applied to authorize the administrative body to investigate the charges against Dayton and decide whether to impose sanctions.

Having taken jurisdiction over the decision below, we now turn to whether the Distict Court should have exercised jurisdiction over the case itself. We conclude that the District Court should have abstained from adjudicating this case under *Younger* v. *Harris* and later cases. The Commission urged such abstention in the District Court, and on oral argument here. Dayton has filed a post argument brief urging that the Commission has waived any claim to abstention because it had stipulated in the District Court that that court had jurisdiction of the action. We think, however, that this argument misconceives the nature of *Younger* abstention. It does not arise from lack of jurisdiction in the District Court, but from strong policies counseling against the exercise of such jurisdiction where particular kinds of state proceedings have already been commenced. A State may of course voluntarily submit to federal jurisdiction even though it might have had a tenable claim for abstention. See *Brown* v. *Hotel Employees*; *Ohio Bureau of Employment Services* v. *Hodory*; *Sosna* v. *Iowa*. But in each of these cases the State expressly urged this Court or the District Court to proceed to an adjudication of the constitutional merits. We think there was no similar consent or waiver here, and we therefore address the issue of whether the District Court should have abstained from deciding the case.

In *Younger* v. *Harris*, we held that a federal court should not enjoin a pending state criminal proceeding except in the very unusual situation that an injunction is necessary to prevent great and immediate irreparable injury. We justified our decision both on equitable principles and on the "more vital consideration" of the proper respect for the fundamental role of States in our federal system. Because of our concerns for comity and federalism, we thought that it was "perfectly natural for our cases to repeat time and time again that the *normal* thing to do when federal courts are asked to enjoin pending proceedings in state courts is not to issue such injunctions". *Younger*

We have since recognized that our concern for comity and federalism is equally applicable to certain other pending state proceedings. We have applied the *Younger* principle to civil proceedings in which important state interests are involved. *Huffman* v. *Pursue, Ltd.*; *Juidice* v. *Vail*; *Trainor* v. *Hernandez*; *Moore* v. *Sims*. We have also applied it to state administrative proceedings in which important state interests are vindicated, so long as in the course of those proceedings the federal plaintiff would have a full and fair opportunity to litigate his constitutional claim. We stated in *Gibson* v. *Berryhill*, that "administrative proceedings looking toward the revocation of a license to practice medicine may in proper circumstances command the respect due court proceedings." Similarly, we have held that federal courts should refrain from enjoining lawyer disciplinary proceedings initiated by state ethics committees if the proceedings are within the appellate jursidiction of the appropriate State Supreme Court. *Middlesex County Ethics Committee* v. *Garden State Bar Assn.* Because we found that the administrative proceedings in *Middlesex* were "judicial in nature" from the outset, it was not essential to the decision that they had progressed to state court review by the time we heard the federal injunction case.

We think the principles enunciated in these cases govern the present one. We have no doubt that the elimination of prohibited sex discrimination is a sufficiently important state interest to bring the present case within the ambit of the cited authorities. We also have no reason to doubt that Dayton will receive an adequate opportunity to raise its constitutional claims. Dayton contends that the mere exercise of jurisdiction over it by the state administrative body violates its First Amendment rights. But we have repeatedly rejected the argument that a constitutional attack on state procedures themselves "automatically vitiates the adequacy of those procedures for purposes of the *Younger-Huffman* line of cases." *Moore.* Even religious schools cannot claim to be wholly free from some state regulation. *Wisconsin* v. *Yoder* We therefore think that however Dayton's constitutional claim should be decided on the merits, the Commission violates no constitutional rights by merely investigating the circumstances of Hoskinson's discharge in this case, if only to ascertain whether the ascribed religious-based reason was in fact the reason for the discharge.

Dayton also contends that the administrative proceedings do not afford the opportunity to level constitutional challenges against the potential sanctions for the alleged sex discrimination. In its reply brief in this Court, the Commission cites several rulings to demonstrate that religious justifications for otherwise illegal conduct are considered by it. See, *e.g.*, *In re St. Mary of the Falls*, No. 948 (1975). Dayton in turn relies on a decision of the Supreme Court of Ohio, *Mobil Oil Corp.* v. *Rocky River*, in which that court held that a local zoning commission could not consider constitutional claims. But even if Ohio law is such that the Commission may not consider the constitutionality of the statute under which it operates, it would seem an unusual doctrine, and one not supported by the cited case, to say that the Commission could not construe its own statutory mandate in the light of federal constitutional principles. In any event, it is sufficient under *Middlesex* that constitutional claims may be raised in state court judicial review of the administrative proceeding. Section 4112.06 of Ohio Rev. Code Ann. (1980) provides that any "respondent claiming to be aggrieved by a final order of the commission . . . may obtain judicial review thereof." Dayton cites us to no Ohio authority indicating that this provision does not authorize judicial review of claims that agency action violates the United States Constitution.

The judgment of the Court of Appeals is therefore reversed and the case remanded for further proceedings consistent with this opinion.

It is so ordered.

Justice STEVENS, with whom Justice BRENNAN, Justice MARSHALL, and Justice BLACKMUN join, concurring in the judgment.

Appellee Dayton Christian Schools, Inc., employed Mrs. Linda Hoskinson as a teacher. Shortly after learning that she was pregnant, the School refused to renew Mrs. Hoskinson's teaching contract for the next academic year. The two reasons for this decision, according to the School, were (1) the School's belief that Mrs. Hoskinson should remain at home to supervise the care for her forthcoming child; and (2) the School's belief that Mrs. Hoskinson had violated the "Biblical chain of command" by consulting an attorney regarding her disagreement with the School's conviction that she remain at home.

After her termination, Mrs. Hoskinson filed a sex discrimination charge against the School with appellant Ohio Civil Rights Commission. The Commission investigated her charge and, upon finding probable cause to believe that the School had violated § 4112 of the Ohio Revised Code, scheduled a hearing. The School thereupon filed this action in Federal District Court seeking declaratory and injunctive relief.

In the District court, the School argued that the Ohio antidiscrimination statute violates the First Amendment Religion Clauses as applied to sectarian schools. The District Court determined that "[t]he only conduct on the part of the Commission that is presently being threatened with sufficient immediacy and reality to present a justiciable controversy is the investigation, which has already taken place, and the pending hearing on the complaint filed by the [Commission] concerning the discharge of Mrs. Hoskinson." 578 F. Supp. 1004, 1029 On the merits, the District Court concluded that the Commission's investigation and adjudication of sex discrimination charges was constitutional. The court recognized that "the statute *could* be applied in any number of ways that could impermissibly interfere with" appellees' religious freedom, but it concluded that these concerns—which relate to the possible remedies that might or might not be ordered if a violation is found—were "hypothetical or speculative" and therefore not ripe on the current state of the record.

The Court of Appeals reversed. It recognized that the School "challenge[d] only the [Commission's] exercise of jurisdiction and its issuance of the complaint in this case." 766 F. 2d 932, 950, n. 31 It further acknowledged that "an order of reinstatement or backpay is not at issue in this case." It nevertheless determined that the "chilling knowledge" that the School's selection criteria for teachers "will be reevaluated, and, perhaps, adjusted by the state applying secular criteria" placed an impermissible burden on appellees' religious freedoms. Looking into the future, the Court of Appeals also concluded that the "highly intrusive nature" of backpay and reinstatement, as well as the "continuing surveillance implicated by the conciliation agreement proposed by the Commission" and rejected by the School, "revealed the 'significant risk that the First Amendment will be infringed.'"

Like the majority, I agree with the District Court that neither the investigation of certain charges nor the conduct of a hearing on those charges is prohibited by the First Amendment: "the Commission violates no constitutional rights by merely investigating the circumstances of Hoskinson's discharge in this case, if only to ascertain whether the ascribed religious-based reason was in fact the reason for the discharge."

I further agree with the District Court that any challenge to a possibly intrusive remedy is premature at this juncture. As the majority points out, the Commission recognizes religious justifications for conduct that might otherwise be illegal. Thus, although § 4112.02 forbids discrimination on the basis of religion, the Commission has dismissed complaints alleging religious discrimination by religious educational institutions, see *Menz* v. *St. Pius School*, No. 3823 (1983), and in particular has dismissed complaints by teachers against sectarian schools for limiting employment to instructors who subscribe to the appropriate faith, see *In re St. Michael's School*, No. 2726 (1976); *In re St. Mary of the Falls*, No. 948 (1975). It bears emphasis that the

Commission dismissed these complaints only *after* investigating charges of discrimination, finding probable cause that the statute had been violated, and holding a hearing on the complaint. It therefore follows that the Commission's finding of probable cause and decision to schedule a hearing in this case does not also mean that the Commission intends to impose *any* sanction, let alone a sanction in derogation of the First Amendment's Religion Clauses. In view of this fact, the District Court was entirely correct in concluding that appellees' constitutional challenge to the remedial provisions of the Ohio statute is not ripe for review. Accordingly, I concur in the judgment.

RELIGIOUS TESTS FOR PUBLIC SERVICE OR BENEFITS

Although Article VI of the United States Constitution forbids religious tests for federal office, many states retained, and sometimes enforced, such tests. Several of the original state constitutions excluded from office or even disfranchised nonbelievers, Catholics, and Jews. Only Christians were eligible for the office of governor in Massachusetts and Maryland. The governor was required to be a Protestant in four other states. Similar requirements were often imposed on witnesses and jurors, and a number of states specifically banned ministers of the gospel from holding public office.

Delaware in 1792 became the first state to adopt a constitutional provision forbidding religious tests as a requirement for public office. Many other states followed suit; and even in those states where archaic constitutional requirements of oaths remained, they were largely ignored. Because there had been few attempts to enforce them, there was little governing case law. By 1946 the Supreme Court was able to say with confidence in *Girouard* v. *United States*: "The test oath is abhorrent to our tradition."

Fifteen years after this statement, the Court found it necessary to consider for the first time a religious test oath in TORCASO v. WATKINS (p. 171). The case came to the Court from Maryland. In 1776 the state had adopted its first constitution, which guaranteed the right to hold public office to all who would subscribe to a "declaration of a belief in the Christian religion." In 1864 the constitution was revised to require either "a declaration of belief in the Christian religion," or the belief "in the existence of God, and in a future state of rewards and punishments."

The 1867 constitution kept only the requirement of "a declaration of belief in the existence of God." In 1922 the Maryland attorney general ruled that it was still mandatory that every state official be "required in some definite way" to declare his belief in the existence of God.

Almost forty years later Roy Torcaso was appointed to the minor state office of notary public. As an atheist, he refused to take the mandatory oath and was consequently denied his commission. Torcaso appealed to the state circuit court, claiming that the required oath violated the First and Fourteenth Amendments as well as Article VI of the original Constitution. The circuit court rejected his arguments, and the Maryland Court of Appeals affirmed the decision of the lower state court. Torcaso then took his case to the Supreme Court.

The unanimous Court used the First Amendment—by then applicable to the states—to invalidate Maryland's oath requirement as an invasion of the appellant's "freedom of belief and religion." Therefore, it did not have to consider the question raised by Torcaso of whether Article VI of the Constitution applied to state officers.

In his opinion, Justice Black denied that, as the Maryland Court of Appeals had assumed, the Court had in any way repudiated its strong position taken in EVERSON v. BOARD OF EDUCATION OF EWING TOWNSHIP (p. 461) concerning limitations imposed by the Establishment Clause. He reaffirmed the *Everson* statement that neither a state nor the federal government could "force a person to profess a belief or disbelief in any religion."

The *Torcaso* decision is significant for several reasons. It denies categorically that religious tests for office can be imposed at any level of government. It holds that the First Amendment forbids different treatment by government of believers and nonbelievers, thus guaranteeing freedom of irreligion as well as religion. In *Torcaso*, the Court also accepted an expanded concept of religion. It emphasized that no distinction could be shown between "those religions based on a belief in the existence of God" and such nontheistic religions as Buddhism, Taoism, Ethical Culture, and Secular Humanism. [1]

Gradually the states repealed their constitutional bans on the holding of public officers by ministers. By 1975 only Tennessee retained the restrictive provision and that only as applied to service in the legislature. In 1976 the restriction was extended to candidates for the state constitutional convention to be held the next year. Paul A. McDaniel, the ordained minister of a Baptist church in Chattanooga, filed for election to the convention. Selma Cash Paty, an opposing candidate, brought suit seeking McDaniel's disqualification, but McDaniel was overwhelmingly elected. The state court in which the suit was filed found the provision to be violative of the First and Fourteenth Amendments, but the Supreme Court of Tennessee reversed the holding. According to that body, the disqualification did not place a burden on "religious action . . . [only] in the lawmaking process of government—where religious action is absolutely prohibited by the establishment clause."

The United States Supreme Court, in MCDANIEL v. PATY (1978) (p.172), with Justice Blackmun not participating, unanimously invalidated the restriction. However, four separate opinions were written expressing at least three different rationales for voiding the statute in question. Chief Justice Burger, joined by Justices Powell,

Rehnquist, and Stevens, held the disqualification unconstitutional but sought to distinguish the ruling from that of *Torcaso*, where the Court had found a violation of freedom of religious *belief* to result from the religious oath required of officeholders. Instead, this opinion emphasized denial of religious *action* by the Tennessee statute.

Justice Brennan, joined by Justice Marshall, concurred in the judgment, but Brennan contended that *Torcaso* governed and that both belief and exercise of that belief had been infringed. Justice Stewart also concurred that *Torcaso* governed, arguing that more than action was involved. But Stewart was apparently unwilling to join Brennan and Marshall in all their reasoning.

In his separate concurring opinion, Justice White relied not on the Free Exercise Clause of the First Amendment but rather on the Equal Protection Clause of the Fourteenth. While expressing understanding for the state's desire to maintain separation between church and state, White found this action both unnecessary to accomplish that purpose and unconstitutional. On equal protection grounds, he contended that the law discriminated against legislators because its restriction did not apply to officials of the other two branches.

Situations have sometimes arisen in which, although no formal religious test was imposed, individuals have been forced to decide between sacrificing a desire for a position or benefit from government and religious conviction. There, too, a substantial, though indirect, burden is imposed on free exercise of religion.

Chief Justice Burger recognized this burden when, in writing the majority opinion in 1981 in THOMAS v. REVIEW BOARD OF INDIANA EMPLOYMENT SECURITY DIVISION (p. 158), he said that:

> Where the state conditions receipt of an important benefit upon conduct proscribed by a religious faith, or where it denies such a benefit because of conduct mandated by religious belief, thereby putting substantial pressure on an adherent to modify his behavior and violate his beliefs, a burden upon religion exists. While the compulsion may be indirect, the infringement upon free exercise is nonetheless substantial. (450 U.S. 707, 717-18)

In 1986, a case involving a clear conflict between continued service in the military and adherence to a strongly held religious obligation was heard and decided by the Supreme Court. Civilian courts have traditionally exhibited great deference toward military regulations governing the conduct of service personnel. Different standards prevail in weighing constitutional rights of members of the military services, or even of civilians while on military enclaves, from those used by the courts for persons engaged in ordinary civilian pursuits. The Supreme Court has, for example, upheld the authority of a base commander to prohibit political speeches or demonstrations on a military base and the requirement that prior approval be obtained from the appropriate commander before distribution of leaflets or even petitions to members of Congress and the Secretary of Defense. [2] As the majority opinion of the Court observed in a highly publicized case arising from the Vietnam conflict, that body has con-

---

[1] In 1965 the Maryland Court of Appeals acted on the basis of the *Torcaso* holding to void a requirement that all jurors swear to a belief in God. The state court there accepted the contention of a Buddhist that exclusion of nonbelievers in God from the grand jury and the jury that had indicted and convicted him had violated his constitutional rights. *Schowgurow* v. *State* (1965) One of the claims of the "New Christian Right," in its criticism of public schools and promotion of "Christian schools" is that the public schools are, as a matter of fact, teaching a religion: secular humanism. Frequently spokespersons for this view have cited *Torcaso*, pointing to the reference to secular humanism in footnote #11 of that decision as a confirmation of the claim that secular humanism is a religion.

---

[2] *Greer* v. *Spock*, (1976); *Brown* v. *Glines*, (1980); *Secretary of the Navy* v. *Huff*, (1980).

sistently held that "the military is, by necessity, a specialized society separate from civilian society." [3]

Obviously, then, an individual entering military service can expect limitations on certain constitutional rights that he or she would take for granted as a civilian. Simcha Goldman, an Orthodox Jew and ordained rabbi serving as a clinical psychologist at the mental clinic at March Air Force Base, discovered in 1981 how limited his rights really were when he ran afoul of an Air Force regulation that forbade the wearing of headgear while indoors, except by on-duty security police. As a male Orthodox Jew, he felt a strong religious obligation to cover his head with a yarmulke indoors as well as out. He had worn the yarmulke indoors on duty at the hospital, covering it with his regulation service cap while outdoors, for four years without formal complaint.

Only after he apparently incurred the wrath of a military prosecutor by testifying as a defense witness in a court-martial was a complaint filed against Goldman for violation of the headgear regulation. He subsequently received a letter of reprimand from the hospital commander, together with a warning that failure to comply with the regulation could result in a court-martial. The commander also withdrew an earlier recommendation that Goldman's request to extend his active duty be approved, and replaced it with a negative recommendation.

Goldman contended that the headgear regulation infringed his First Amendment right to free exercise of his religious belief, and appealed to a federal district court. The district court permanently enjoined the Air Force from enforcing the regulation against him, but the Court of Appeals for the District of Columbia reversed the decision. The appellate court ruling went on writ of certiorari to the Supreme Court, was argued in January 1986, and the Court's holding in GOLDMAN v. WEINBERGER (p. 179) was announced the following March.

By a five-to-four vote, with Justice Rehnquist writing for the majority, the Court upheld the regulation as applied to Goldman. Chief Justice Burger and Justices White, Powell, and Stevens joined in the opinion. A concurring opinion was written by Justice Stevens joined by White and Powell. Separate dissenting opinions were filed by Justices Brennan, Blackmun, and O'Connor. Justice Marshall joined Brennan and O'Connor in their dissents.

Justice Rehnquist's relatively brief opinion for the majority emphasized the ordinary high degree of judicial deference to military regulations, saying, "Our review of military regulations challenged on First Amendment grounds is far more deferential than constitutional reviews of similar laws or regulations designed for civilian society." (106 S.Ct. 1310, 1313) The Court, therefore, would not challenge the professional judgment of the Air Force that habits of discipline and unity essential to military discipline and morale were furthered by the outfitting of personnel in standardized uniforms for the "subordination of personal preferences and identities in favor of the overall group mission." (106 S.Ct. 1310, 1315) Although regulations against wearing of religious apparel might well be objectionable to Goldman and others, "the First Amendment does not require the military to accommodate such

practices in the face of its view that they would detract from the uniformity sought by the dress regulations." (106 S.Ct. 1310, 1315)

Justice Brennan, in dissent, lamented that the Court had abdicated "its role as principal expositor of the Constitution and protector of individual liberties in favor of credulous deference to unsupported assertions of military necessity." (106 S.Ct. 1310, 1316) "The Court and the military services," he said, "have presented patriotic Orthodox Jews with a painful dilemma—the choice between fulfilling a religious obligation and serving their country. Should the draft be reinstated, compulsion will replace choice." (106 S.Ct. 1310, 1322) He called on Congress to act to correct this denial of constitutional rights. Congress was quick to respond. In less than two weeks, legislation was introduced in both the Senate and the House to permit military personnel to wear "unobtrusive" religious apparel while on duty. The House version spoke directly to Goldman when it prohibited denial of the wearing of "any inconspicuous religious symbol, such as a yarmulke." However, at the time of this writing, none of those proposals had become law.

The Supreme Court in 1985 passed up an opportunity to speak to the question of a state's denial of another important benefit—the privilege of driving a car in that state—because an applicant for a driver's license refused to comply with a requirement which she contended unconstitutionally burdened the free exercise of her religious beliefs.

Although she was not a member of an organized church, Frances J. Quaring refused on religious grounds to have her photograph taken and attached to her driver's license as required by Nebraska law. She maintained that the requirement imposed an excessive burden on her sincerely held religious belief that the Second Commandment expressly forbids the making of any graven images or likeness of anything in creation. A federal district court upheld her contention and enjoined state officials from refusing to issue her a license without the photograph.

The United States Court of Appeals for the Eighth Circuit upheld the issuance of the injunction against the state's claim that providing the exemption on religious grounds would create an impermissible establishment of religion. The court failed to find sufficient compelling state interest or undue administrative burden to justify the infringement of Quaring's religious liberty. The exemption mandated by the district court, the appellate court held, was a reasonable accommodation of religion and did not constitute an establishment of religion. The Supreme Court granted certiorari, but in a *per curiam* opinion announced that it affirmed the judgment of the Court of Appeals by an equally divided (four-to-four) vote. [4]

In the last weeks of the 1985-1986 session the Court heard and decided another case involving a choice between receiving a governmental benefit and adhering to a religious commitment. Stephen Roy, a Native American descended from the Abenaki Indian Tribe, refused to comply with the government's requirement that he furnish the Social Security numbers of the members of his family

---

[3] *Parker* v. *Levy*, (1974).

[4] *Jensen* v.*Quaring*, (1985); case below: *Quaring* v. *Peterson*, (1984).

to state welfare agencies in order to receive benefits under the Aid to Families with Dependent Children and Food Stamp programs. Roy, his wife, and another five-year-old daughter had Social Security numbers, but he had recently decided that to obtain a Social Security number for his two-year-old daughter, Little Bird of the Snow, and allow the government to make routine use of that number would violate his religious beliefs as a Native American that control of one's life is essential to the attainment of spiritual purity and to "becoming a holy person." Uses of a number over which she had no control would "rob the spirit" of his daughter.[5]

The Pennsylvania Department of Public Welfare responded to Roy's refusal by stopping AFDC and medical benefits for the child and taking steps to reduce food stamps which the family was receiving. He filed suit in a federal district court, claiming the right of exemption from the requirement on free exercise grounds. After an extended hearing, the trial court agreed with his argument and enjoined the Secretary of Health and Human Services from using or disseminating the Social Security number which, as became evident during the trial, had already been issued to the child. Both federal and state officials were also enjoined from denying benefits until Little Bird of the Snow's sixteenth birthday due to refusal to provide a Social Security number.

In an extremely complex decision, the Court vacated the judgment of the trial court, but the justices spoke with a unique mix of opinions and votes. Chief Justice Burger, writing his final church-state majority opinion for the Court, divided the opinion into three parts. Seven of his colleagues joined in Parts I and II. Only Justice Powell and Rehnquist joined him in Part III. Justice Blackmun filed a separate opinion concurring in part, as did Justice Stevens. Justice O'Connor, joined by Justices Brennan and Marshall, filed an opinion concurring in part and dissenting in part; Justice White dissented alone. To make the decision even more confusing, Justices Blackmun and Stevens raised questions on mootness and ripeness grounds as to whether the issues involved should even be considered by the Court.

In Parts I and II of his opinion for the Court with which seven other justices agreed, Chief Justice Burger upheld the requirement of the Social Security number for eligibility for the benefits in question and the right of the government to make use of the account in the administration of the AFDC plan. He agreed that the Free Exercise Clause protects an individual against some forms of government compulsion, but it does not, he said, "afford an individual a right to dictate the conduct of the government's internal procedures."

With respect to Roy's claim of harm done to his daughter's spirit, Burger said:

---

[5] Two years earlier the United States Court of Appeals for the Ninth Circuit had heard an appeal from the District Court for the Northern District of California ruling in which that court upheld denial of benefits under the Aid to Families and Dependent Children to a parent who refused to obtain a Social Security number for a child. He claimed that the requirement infringed his religious belief that the Book of Revelation condemns the use of a universal number such as a Social Security number as the "mark of the beast," by means of which the Antichrist endeavors to control mankind. The court of appeals reversed and remanded the decision of the district court. (*Callahan* v. *Woods*, 1984)

Never to our knowledge has the Court interpreted the First Amendment to require the Government *itself* to behave in ways that the individual believes will further his or her spiritual development or that of his or her family. The Free Exercise Clause simply cannot be understood to require the Government to conduct its own internal affairs in ways that comport with the religious beliefs of particular citizens. Just as the Government may not insist that appellees engage in any set form of religious observance, so appellees may not demand that the Government join in their chosen religious practices by refraining from using a number to identify their daughter. (l06 S.Ct. 2147, 2152)

It was Part III of the opinion which stirred debate among the justices, and for good reason. There the Chief Justice sought to advance a significantly less strenuous standard for determining the constitutionality of government interference with free exercise claims. He expressed his recognition of the importance of various government benefits today, but he sought to distinguish denial of those benefits by a "uniformly applicable statute neutral on its face" as being of a different and less intrusive nature than government action making religiously inspired activity illegal or compelling conduct found objectionable for religious reasons. This distinction, he argued, entitled the government to "wide latitude," and justified a less strict test than the "least restrictive means of accomplishing a compelling state interest" standard developed and applied in *Sherbert, Yoder,* and *Thomas.* Instead, he would say that in cases involving denial of government benefits the government could meet its burden of proof when it "demonstrates that a challenged requirement for government benefits, neutral and uniform in its application, is a reasonable means of promoting a legitimate public interest." A quite different standard, indeed.

The Free Exercise Clause, he said, did not mandate that Congress grant a special exemption from its religiously neutral statutory requirement to Roy. "Appellees," he said

may not use the Free Exercise Clause to demand government benefits, but only on their own terms, particularly where that insistence works a demonstrable disadvantage to the Government in the administration of the programs. As the Court has recognized before, given the diversity of beliefs in our pluralistic society and the necessity of providing governments with sufficient operating latitude, some incidental neutral restraints on the free exercise of religion are inescapable. (106 S.Ct. 2147, 2158)

Had the Chief Justice's more relaxed standard, expounded in Part III, prevailed with a majority of the Court, BOWEN v. ROY (p. 187), which attracted almost no public attention when released, might well have become a landmark decision because of the significant weakening of the standard applied by the Court to governmental restraint of free exercise of religion. Only Justices Rehnquist and Powell joined the Chief Justice in that part of the opinion.

Justice O'Connor agreed that the government's stated goal for requiring the Social Security number as preventing fraud and abuse in the welfare system was "both laudable and compelling," and she joined Parts I and II of the opinion. However, she took the Chief Justice sharply to task in her "dissent in part" for his proposed departure from the least restrictive means—compelling state interest test. The test he proposed to substitute, she said, had "no basis in precedent and relegates a serious First Amendment value to the barest level of minimal scrutiny that the Equal Protection Clause already provides." She reviewed the precedents for the test which had prevailed in recent years and concluded that "Only an especially important governmental interest pursued by narrowly tailored means can justify exacting a sacrifice of First Amendment freedoms as the price for an equal share of the rights, benefits, and privileges enjoyed by other citizens." (106 S.Ct. 2147, 2167) Justice White dissented, stating simply that *Thomas* and *Sherbert* controlled the case at hand.

It should perhaps be noted that Justice William Rehnquist voted with Chief Justice Burger in all parts of his opinion. His recent elevation to be Chief Justice obviously could mean that the more relaxed test may be advanced again at a later date, given his demonstrated stance in free exercise cases.

TORCASO v. WATKINS

367 U.S. 488
ON APPEAL FROM THE COURT OF APPEALS OF MARYLAND
Argued April 24, 1961 — Decided June 19, 1961

⊥489 ⊥ *Mr. Justice BLACK* delivered the opinion of the Court.

Article 37 of the Declaration of Rights of the Maryland Constitution provides: "[N]o religious test ought ever to be required as a qualification for any office of profit or trust in this State, other than a declaration of belief in the existence of God. . . ."

The appellant Torcaso was appointed to the office of Notary Public by the Governor of Maryland but was refused a commission to serve because he would not declare his belief in God. He then brought this action in a Maryland Circuit Court to compel issuance of his commission, charging that the State's requirement that he declare this belief violated "the First and Fourteenth Amendments to the Constitution of the United States. . . ." *

There is, and can be, no dispute about the purpose or effect of the Maryland Declaration of Rights requirement before us—it sets up a religious test which
⊥490 was designed to ⊥ and, if valid, does bar every person who refuses to declare a belief in God from holding a public "office of profit or trust" in Maryland. The power and authority of the State of Mary-

---

* Appellant also claimed that the State's test oath requirement violates the provision of Art. VI of the Federal Constitution that "no religious Test shall ever be required as a Qualification to any Office or public Trust under the United States." Because we are reversing the judgment on other grounds, we find it unnecessary to consider appellant's contention that this provision applies to state as well as federal offices.

land thus is put on the side of one particular sort of believers—those who are willing to say they believe in "the existence of God." It is true that there is much historical precedent for such laws. Indeed, it was largely to escape religious test oaths and declarations that a great many of the early colonists left Europe and came here hoping to worship in their own way. It soon developed, however, that many of those who had fled to escape religious test oaths turned out to be perfectly willing, when they had the power to do so, to force dissenters from their faith to take test oaths in conformity with that faith. This brought on a host of laws in the new Colonies imposing burdens and disabilities of various kinds upon varied beliefs depending largely upon what group happened to be politically strong enough to legislate in favor of its own beliefs. The effect of all this was the formal or practical "establishment" of particular religious faiths in most of the Colonies, with consequent burdens imposed on the free exercise of the faiths of non-favored believers.

There were, however, wise and farseeing men in the Colonies—too many to mention—who spoke out against test oaths and all the philosophy of intolerance behind them. . . .

⊥ When our Constitution was adopted, the desire   ⊥491 to put the people "securely beyond the reach" of religious test oaths brought about the inclusion in Article VI of that document of a provision that, "no religious Test shall ever be required as a Qualification to any Office or public Trust under the United States." Article VI supports the accuracy of our observation in *Girouard* v. *United States* that "[t]he test oath is abhorrent to our tradition." Not satisfied, however, with Article VI and other guarantees in the original Constitution, the First Congress proposed and the States very shortly thereafter ⊥   ⊥492 adopted our Bill of Rights, including the First Amendment. That Amendment broke new constitutional ground in the protection it sought to afford to freedom of religion, speech, press, petition and assembly. Since prior cases in this Court have thoroughly explored and documented the history behind the First Amendment, the reasons for it, and the scope of the religious freedom it protects, we need not cover that ground again. What was said in our prior cases we think controls our decision here.

In *Cantwell* v. *Connecticut* we said: "The First Amendment declares that Congress shall make no law respecting an establishment of religion or prohibiting the free exercise thereof. The Fourteenth Amendment has rendered the legislatures of the states as incompetent as Congress to enact such laws. . . . Thus the Amendment embraces two concepts,—freedom to believe and freedom to act. The first is absolute but, in the nature of things, the second cannot be."

Later we decided *Everson* v. *Board of Education* and said this: "The 'establishment of religion' clause of the First Amendment means at least this: Neither

⌐493 a state nor ⊥ the Federal Government can set up a church. Neither can pass laws which aid one religion, aid all religions, or prefer one religion over another. Neither can force nor influence a person to go to or to remain away from church against his will or force him to profess a belief or disbelief in any religion. No person can be punished for entertaining or professing religious beliefs or disbeliefs, for church attendance or non-attendance. No tax in any amount, large or small, can be levied to support any religious activities or institutions, whatever they may be called, or whatever form they may adopt to teach or practice religion. Neither a state nor the Federal Government can, openly or secretly, participate in the affairs of any religious organizations or groups and *vice versa*. In the words of Jefferson, the clause against establishment of religion by law was intended to erect 'a wall of separation between church and State.' "

While there were strong dissents in the Everson case, they did not challenge the Court's interpretation of the First Amendment's coverage as being too broad, but thought the Court was applying that interpretation too narrowly to the facts of that case. Not long afterward in *Illinois ex rel. McCollum* v. *Board of Education*, we were urged to repudiate as dicta the above-quoted Everson interpretation of the scope of the First Amendment's coverage. We declined to do this, but instead strongly reaffirmed what had been said in Everson, calling attention to the fact that both the majority and the minority in Everson had agreed on the principles declared in this part of the Everson opinion. And a concurring opinion in McCollum, written by Mr. Justice Frankfurter and joined by the other Everson dissenters, said this: "We are all agreed that the First and Fourteenth Amendments have a secular reach far more pene-

⌐494 trat ⊥ ing in the conduct of Government than merely to forbid an 'established church.' . . . We renew our conviction that 'we have staked the very existence of our country on the faith that complete separation between the state and religion is best for the state and best for religion.' "

The Maryland Court of Appeals thought, and it is argued here, that this Court's later holding and opinion in *Zorach* v. *Clauson* had in part repudiated the statement in the *Everson* opinion quoted above and previously reaffirmed in *McCollum*. But the Court's opinion in *Zorach* specifically stated: "We follow the *McCollum* case." Nothing decided or written in *Zorach* lends support to the idea that the Court there intended to open up the way for government, state or federal, to restore the historically and constitutionally discredited policy of probing religious beliefs by test oaths or limiting public offices to persons who have, or perhaps more properly profess to have, a belief in some particular kind of religious concept.

⌐495 ⊥ We repeat and again reaffirm that neither a State nor the Federal Government can constitution-

ally force a person "to profess a belief or disbelief in any religion." Neither can constitutionally pass laws or impose requirements which aid all religions as against nonbelievers, and neither can aid those religions based on a belief in the existence of God as against those religions founded on different beliefs. *

In upholding the State's religious test for public office the highest court of Maryland said: "The petitioner is not compelled to believe or disbelieve, under threat of punishment or other compulsion. True, unless he makes the declaration of belief he cannot hold public office in Maryland, but he is not compelled to hold office."

The fact, however, that a person is not compelled to hold public office cannot possibly be an excuse for barring him ⊥ from office by state-imposed criteria ⌐496 forbidden by the Constitution. This was settled by our holding in *Wieman* v. *Updegraff*. We there pointed out that whether or not "an abstract right to public employment exists," Congress could not pass a law providing " '. . . that no federal employee shall attend Mass or take any active part in missionary work.' "

This Maryland religious test for public office unconstitutionally invades the appellant's freedom of belief and religion and therefore cannot be enforced against him.

The judgment of the Court of Appeals of Maryland is accordingly reversed and the cause is remanded for further proceedings not inconsistent with this opinion.

Reversed and remanded.

Mr. Justice FRANKFURTER and Mr. Justice HARLAN concur in the result.

McDANIEL v. PATY

435 U.S. 618
ON APPEAL FROM THE SUPREME COURT OF THE
STATE OF TENNESSEE
Argued December 5, 1977 — Decided April 19, 1978

⊥ *Mr. Chief Justice BURGER* announced the ⌐620 judgment of the Court and delivered an opinion in which *Mr. Justice POWELL, Mr. Justice REHNQUIST*, and *Mr. Justice STEVENS* joined.

The question presented by this appeal is whether a Tennessee statute barring "Ministers of the Gospel, or priest[s] of any denomination whatever" from serving as delegates to the State's limited constitutional convention deprived appellant McDaniel, an ordained minister, of the right to the free exercise of religion guaranteed by the First Amendment and

---

* Among religions in this country which do not teach what would generally be considered a belief in the existence of God are Buddhism, Taoism, Ethical Culture, Secular Humanism and others.

made applicable to the States by the Fourteenth Amendment. The First Amendment forbids all laws "prohibiting the free exercise" of religion. ⊥

I

In its first constitution, in 1796, Tennessee disqualified ministers from serving as legislators. *

That disqualifying provision has continued unchanged since its adoption; it is now Art. IX, § 1 of the state constitution. The state legislature applied this provision to candidates for delegate to the State's 1977 limited constitutional convention when it enacted Chapter 848, Section 4 of the 1976 Tennessee Public Acts: "Any citizen of the state who can qualify for membership in the House of Representatives of the General Assembly may become a candidate for delegate to the convention. . . ."

McDaniel, an ordained minister of a Baptist Church in Chattanooga, Tenn., filed as a candidate for delegate to the constitutional convention. An opposing candidate, appellee Selma Cash Paty, sued in the Chancery Court for a declaratory judgment that McDaniel was disqualified to serve as a delegate and for a judgment striking his name from the ballot. Chancellor Franks of the Chancery Court held that § 4 of ch. 848 violated the First and Fourteenth Amendments to the Federal Constitution and declared McDaniel eligible for the office of delegate. Accordingly, McDaniel's name remained on the ballot and in the ensuing election he was elected by a vote almost equal to that of three opposing candidates.

After the election, the Tennessee Supreme Court reversed the Chancery Court, holding that the disqualification of clergy imposed no burden upon "religious belief" and restricted "religious action . . . [only] in the law making process of government—where religious action is absolutely prohibited by the establishment clause. . . ." ⊥ The state interest in preventing the establishment of religion and in avoiding the divisiveness and tendency to channel political activity along religious lines, resulting from clergy participation in political affairs, were deemed by that court sufficiently weighty to justify the disqualification, notwithstanding the guarantee of the Free Exercise Clause.

We noted probable jurisdiction.

II
A

The disqualification of ministers from legislative office was a practice carried from England by seven of the original States; later six new States similarly excluded clergymen from some political offices. In England the practice of excluding clergy from the House of Commons was justified on a variety of grounds: to prevent dual office holding, that is, membership by a minister in both Parliament and Convocation; to insure that the priest or deacon devoted himself to his "sacred calling" rather than to "such mundane activities as were appropriate to a member of the House of Commons"; and to prevent ministers, who after 1533 were subject to the Crown's powers over the benefices of the clergy, from using membership in Commons to diminish its independence by increasing the influence of the King and the nobility.

The purpose of the several States in providing for disqualification was primarily to assure the success of a new political experiment, the separation of church and state. ⊥ Prior to 1776, most of the 13 colonies had some form of an established, or government-sponsored, church. Even after ratification of the First Amendment, which prohibited the Federal Government from following such a course, some States continued pro-establishment provisions. Massachusetts, the last State to accept disestablishment, did so in 1833.

In light of this history and a widespread awareness during that period of undue and often dominant clerical influence in public and political affairs here, in England, and on the Continent, it is not surprising that strong views were held by some that one way to assure dis-establishment was to keep clergymen out of public office. Indeed, some of the foremost political philosophers and statesmen of that period held such views regarding the clergy. Earlier, John Locke argued for confining the authority of the English clergy "within the bounds of the church, nor can it in any manner be extended to civil affairs; because the church itself is a thing absolutely separate and distinct from the commonwealth." Thomas Jefferson initially advocated such a position in his 1783 draft of a constitution for Virginia. James Madison, however, disagreed and vigorously urged ⊥ the position which in our view accurately reflects the spirit and purpose of the Religion Clauses of the First Amendment. Madison's response to Jefferson's position was:

"Does not The exclusion of Ministers of the Gospel as such violate a fundamental principle of liberty by punishing a religious profession with the privation of a civil right? does it [not] violate another article of the plan itself which exempts religion from the cognizance of Civil power? does it not violate justice by at once taking away a right and prohibiting a compensation for it? does it not in fine violate impartiality by shutting the door against the Ministers of one Religion and leaving it open for those of every other."

Madison was not the only articulate opponent of clergy disqualification. When proposals were made

---

* "Whereas ministers of the gospel are, by their profession, dedicated to God and the care of Souls, and ought not to be diverted from the great duties of their functions; therefore, no ministers of the gospel, or priest of any denomination whatever, shall be eligible to a seat in either House of the legislature." Tenn. Const. of 1796, Art. VIII, § 1.

earlier to prevent clergymen from holding public office, John Witherspoon, a Presbyterian minister, president of Princeton University, and the only clergyman to sign the Declaration of Independence, made a cogent protest and, with tongue in cheek, offered an amendment to a provision much like that challenged here: "No clergyman, of any denomination, shall be capable of being elected a member of the Senate or House of Representatives, because (here insert the grounds of offensive disqualification, which I have been able to discover) Provided always, and it is the true intent and meaning of this part of the constitution, that if at any time he shall be completely deprived of the clerical character by those by whom he was invested with it, as by deposition for cursing and swearing, drunkenness or uncleanness, he shall then be fully restored to all the privileges of ⫫625 a free ⊥ citizen; his offense [of being a clergyman] shall no more be remembered against him; but he may be chosen either to the Senate or House of Representatives, and shall be treated with all the respect due to his *brethren*, the other members of Assembly."

As the value of the dis-establishment experiment was perceived, 11 of the 13 States disqualifying the clergy from some types of public office gradually abandoned that limitation. New York, for example, took that step in 1846 after delegates to the State's constitutional convention argued that the exclusion of clergymen from the legislature was an "odious distinction." Only Maryland and Tennessee continued their clergy disqualification provisions into this century and, in 1974, a three judge District Court held Maryland's provision violative of the First and Fourteenth Amendments' guarantees of the free exercise of religion. Today Tennessee remains the only State excluding ministers from certain public offices.

The essence of this aspect of our national history is that in all but a few States the selection or rejection of clergymen for public office soon came to be viewed as something safely left to the good sense and desires of the people.

B

This brief review of the history of clergy disqualification provisions also amply demonstrates, however, that, at least during the early segment of our national life, those provisions enjoyed the support of responsible American statesmen and were accepted as having a rational basis. Against this background we do not lightly invalidate a statute enacted pursuant to a provision of a state constitution which has been sustained by its highest court. The challenged provision came to the Tennessee Supreme Court clothed with the presumption of validity to which that court was bound to give deference.

⫫626 ⊥ However, the right to the free exercise of religion unquestionably encompasses the right to preach, proselyte, and perform other similar religious functions, or, in other words, to be a minister of the

type McDaniel was found to be. *Murdock* v. *Pennsylvania; Cantwell* v. *Connecticut.* Tennessee also acknowledges the right of its adult citizens generally to seek and hold office as legislators or delegates to the state constitutional convention. Yet under the clergy disqualification provision, McDaniel can not exercise both rights simultaneously because the State has conditioned the exercise of one on the surrender of the other. Or, in James Madison's words, the State is "punishing a religious profession with the privation of a civil right." In so doing, Tennessee has encroached upon McDaniel's right to the free exercise of religion, "[T]o condition the availability of benefits [including access to the ballot] upon this appellant's willingness to violate a cardinal principle of [his] religious faith [by surrendering his religiously impelled ministry] effectively penalizes the free exercise of [his] constitutional liberties." *Sherbert* v. *Verner.*

If the Tennessee disqualification provision were viewed as depriving the clergy of a civil right solely because of their religious beliefs, our inquiry would be at an end. The Free Exercise Clause categorically forbids government from regulating, prohibiting or rewarding religious beliefs as such. *Sherbert* v. *Verner; Cantwell* v. *Connecticut.* In *Torcaso* v. *Watkins* the Court reviewed the Maryland constitutional requirement that all holders of "any office of profit or trust in this State" declare their belief in the existence of God. In striking down the Maryland requirement, the Court did not evaluate the interests assertedly justifying it but rather held that it violated freedom of religious belief.

In our view, however, *Torcaso* does not govern. By its ⊥ terms, the Tennessee disqualification operates ⫫627 against McDaniel because of his *status* as a "minister" or "priest." The meaning of those words is, of course, a question of state law. And although the question has not been examined extensively in state law sources, such authority as is available indicates that ministerial status is defined in terms of conduct and activity rather than in terms of belief. Because the Tennessee disqualification is directed primarily at status, acts and conduct it is unlike the requirement in *Torcaso*, which focused on *belief.* Hence, the Free Exercise Clause's absolute prohibition of infringements on the "freedom to believe" is inapposite here.

This does not mean, of course, that the disqualification escapes judicial scrutiny or that McDaniel's activity does not enjoy significant First Amendment protection. The Court ⊥ recently declared in *Wis-* ⫫62 *consin* v. *Yoder:* "The essence of all that has been said and written on the subject is that only those interests of the highest order and those not otherwise served can overbalance legitimate claims to the free exercise of religion."

Tennessee asserts that its interest in preventing the establishment of a state religion is consistent with the Establishment Clause and thus of the highest order. The constitutional history of the several States reveals that generally the interest in preventing establishment prompted the adoption of clergy disqualification provisions; Tennessee does not appear to be an exception to this pattern. There is no occasion to inquire whether promoting such an interest is a permissible legislative goal, however, for Tennessee has failed to demonstrate that its views of the dangers of clergy participation in the political process have not lost whatever validity they may once have enjoyed. The essence of the rationale underlying the Tennessee restriction on ministers is that if elected to public office they will necessarily |629 exercise ⊥ their powers and influence to promote the interests of one sect or thwart the interests of another thus pitting one against the others, contrary to the anti-establishment principle with its command of neutrality. See *Walz* v. *Tax Commission*. However widely that view may have been held in the 18th century by many, including enlightened statesmen of that day, the American experience provides no persuasive support for the fear that clergymen in public office will be less careful of antiestablishment interests or less faithful to their oaths of civil office than their unordained counterparts.

We hold that § 4 of ch. 848, violates McDaniel's First Amendment right to the free exercise of his religion made applicable to the States by the Fourteenth Amendment. Accordingly, the judgment of the Tennessee Supreme Court is reversed and the case is remanded to that court for further proceedings not inconsistent with this opinion.

Reversed and remanded.

Mr. Justice BLACKMUN took no part in the consideration or decision of this case.

Mr. Justice BRENNAN, with whom *Mr. Justice MARSHALL* joins, concurring in the judgment.

I would hold that § 4 of the legislative call to the Tennessee constitutional convention, to the extent |630 that it incorporates ⊥ Art. IX, § 1, of the Tennessee Constitution, violates both the Free Exercise and Establishment Clauses of the First Amendment as applied to the States through the Fourteenth Amendment. I therefore concur in the reversal of the judgment of the Tennessee Supreme Court.

I

The Tennessee Supreme Court sustained Tennessee's exclusion on the ground that it "does not infringe upon religious belief or religious action within the protection of the free exercise clause[, and] that such indirect burden as may be imposed upon ministers and priests by excluding them from the lawmaking process of government is justified by the compelling state interest in maintaining the wall of

separation between church and state." In reaching this conclusion, the state court relied on two interrelated propositions which are inconsistent with decisions of this Court. The first is that a distinction may be made between "religious belief or religious action" on the one hand, and the "career or calling" of the ministry on the other. The court states that "[i]t is not religious belief, but the career or calling, by which one is identified as dedicated to the full time promotion of the religious objectives of a particular religious sect, that disqualifies." The second is that the disqualification provision does not interefere with the free exercise of religion because the practice of the ministry is left unimpaired; only candidacy for legislative office is proscribed.

⊥ The characterization of the exclusion as one |631 burdening appellant's "career or calling" and not religious belief cannot withstand analysis. Clearly freedom of belief protected by the Free Exercise Clause embraces freedom to profess or practice that belief, even including doing so to earn a livelihood. One's religious belief surely does not cease to enjoy the protection of the First Amendment when held with such depth of sincerity as to impel one to join the ministry.

Whether or not the provision discriminates among religions (and I accept for purposes of discussion the State Supreme ⊥ Court's construction that it does |632 not), it establishes a religious classification involvement in protected religious activity—governing the eligibility for office which I believe is absolutely prohibited. The provision imposes a unique disability upon those who exhibit a defined level of intensity of involvement in protected religious activity. Such a classification as much imposes a test for office based on religious conviction as one based on denominational preference. A law which limits political participation to those who eschew prayer, public worship, or the ministry as much establishes a religious test as one which disqualifes Catholics, or Jews, or Protestants. *Wieman* v. *Updegraff*. Because the challenged provision establishes as a condition of office the willingness to eschew certain protected religious practices, *Torcaso* v. *Watkins* compels the conclusion that it violates the Free Exercise Clause. *Torcaso* struck down Maryland's requirement that an appointee to the office of Notary Public declare his belief in the existence of God expressly disavowing "the historically and constitutionally discredited policy of probing religious beliefs by test oaths or limiting public offices to persons who have, or perhaps more properly profess to have, a belief in some particular kind ⊥ of religious concept." That principle |633 equally condemns the religious qualification for elective office imposed by Tennessee.

The second proposition—that the law does not interfere with free exercise because it does not directly prohibit religious activity, but merely conditions eligibility for office on its abandonment—is also squarely rejected by precedent. In *Sherbert* v. *Verner*

a state statute disqualifying from unemployment
compensation benefits persons unwilling to work on
Saturdays was held to violate the Free Exercise
Clause as applied to a Sabbatarian whose religious
faith forbade Saturday work. That decision turned
upon the fact that "The ruling forces her to choose
between following the precepts of her religion and
forfeiting benefits, on the one hand, and abandoning
one of the precepts of her religion in order to accept
work, on the other hand. Governmental imposition
of such a choice puts the same kind of burden upon
the free exercise of religion as would a fine imposed
against appellant for her Saturday worship." Similarly, in "prohibiting legislative service because of a
person's leadership role in a religious faith," Tennessee's disqualification provision imposed an unconstitutional penalty upon appellant's exercise of
his religious faith.

⊥634 ⊥ Nor can Tennessee's political exclusion be distinguished from *Sherbert's* welfare disqualification
as the Tennessee court thought, by suggesting that
the unemployment compensation involved in *Sherbert* was necessary to sustain life while participation
in the Constitutional Convention is a voluntary activity not itself compelled by religious belief. *Torcaso*
answers that contention. There we held that "[t]he
fact . . . that a person is not compelled to hold public office cannot possibly be an excuse for barring
him from office by state-imposed criteria forbidden
by the Constitution."

The opinion of the Tennessee Supreme Court
makes clear that the statute requires appellant's disqualification solely because he is a minister of a religious faith. If appellant were to renounce his
ministry, presumably he could regain eligibility for
elective office, but if he does not, he must forego an
opportunity for political participation he otherwise
would enjoy. *Sherbert* and *Torcaso* compel the conclusion that because the challenged provision requires appellant to purchase his right to engage in
the ministry by sacrificing his candidacy it impairs
the free exercise of his religion.

The plurality recognizes that *Torcaso* held "categorically forbid[den]," a provision disqualifying from
political office on the basis of religious belief, but
draws what I respectfully suggest is a sophistic distinction between that holding and Tennessee's disqualification provision. The purpose of the
Tennessee provision is not to regulate activities associated with a ministry, such as dangerous snake-
handling or human sacrifice, which the State validly
could prohibit, but to bar from political office persons regarded as deeply committed to religious
participation because of that participation—
participation itself not regarded as harmful by the
State and which therefore must be conceded to be
protected. As the plurality recognizes, petitioner was
disqualified because he "fill[ed] a 'leadership role in
⊥635 religion,' and . . . 'dedicated ⊥ [himself] to the full
time *promotion* of the religious objectives of a partic-

ular religious sect.' (emphasis added)." According to
the plurality, McDaniel could not be and was not in
fact barred for *his* belief in religion, but was barred
because of his commitment to persuade or lead others to accept that belief. I simply cannot fathom why
the Free Exercise Clause "categorically forbids"
hinging qualification for office on the *act* of declaring a belief in religion, but not on the act of discussing that belief with others. ⊥   ⊥636

II

The State Supreme Court's justification of the
prohibition, echoed here by the State, as intended to
prevent those most intensely involved in religion
from injecting sectarian goals and policies into the
lawmaking process, and thus to avoid fomenting religious strife or the fusing of church with state affairs,
itself raises the question whether the exclusion violates the Establishment Clause. As construed, the exclusion manifests patent hostility toward, not
nonneutrality in respect of, religion, forces or influences a minister or priest to abandon his ministry as
the price of public office, and in sum, has a primary
effect which inhibits religion. See *Everson* v. *Board
of Education; McCollum* v. *Board of Education; Torcaso* v. *Watkins; Lemon* v. *Kurtzman; Meek* v. *Pittenger.*

⊥ The fact that responsible statesmen of the day,   ⊥637
including some of the United States Constitution's
Framers, were attracted by the concept of clergy disqualification does not provide historical support for
concluding that those provisions are harmonious
with the Establishment Clause. Notwithstanding the
presence of such provisions in seven state constitutions when the Constitution was being written, the
Framers refused to follow suit. That the disqualification provisions contained in state constitutions contemporaneous with the United States Constitution
and the Bill of Rights cannot furnish a guide concerning the understanding of the harmony of such
provisions with the Establishment Clause is evident
from the presence in state constitutions, side-by-side
with disqualification clauses, of provisions which
would have clearly contravened the First Amendment had it applied to the States, such as those creating an official church, and limiting political office
to Protestants or theistic believers generally. In
short, the regime of religious liberty embodied in
state constitutions was very different from that established by the Constitution of the United States.
When, with the adoption of the Fourteenth Amendment, the strictures of the First Amendment became
wholly applicable to the States, see *Cantwell* v. *Connecticut; Everson* v. *Board of Education*, earlier conceptions of permissible state action with respect to
religion—including those regarding clergy disqualification—were superseded.

Our decisions interpreting the Establishment
Clause have aimed at maintaining erect the wall between church and State. ⊥ State governments, like   ⊥638

the Federal Government, have been required to refrain from favoring the tenets or adherents of any religion or of religion over nonreligion, from insinuating themselves in ecclesiastical affairs or disputes, and from establishing programs which unnecessarily or excessively entangle government with religion. On the other hand, the Court's decisions have indicated that the limits of permissible governmental action with respect to religion under the Establishment Clause must reflect an appropriate accommodation of our heritage as a religious people whose freedom to develop and preach religious ideas and practices is protected by the Free Exercise Clause. Thus, we have rejected as unfaithful to our constitutionally protected tradition of religious liberty, any conception of the Religion Clauses as stating a "strict no-aid" theory or as stating a unitary principle, that "religion may not be used as a basis for classification for purposes of governmental action, whether that action be the conferring of rights or privileges or the imposition of duties or obliga⊥tions." Such rigid conceptions of neutrality have been tempered by constructions upholding religious classifications where necessary to avoid "[a] manifestation of . . . hostility [toward religion] at war with our national tradition as embodied in the First Amendment's guaranty of the free exercise of religion." *McCollum* v. *Board of Education.* This understanding of the interrelationship of the Religion Clauses has permitted government to take religion into account when necessary to further secular purposes unrelated to the advancement of religion, and to exempt, when possible, from generally applicable governmental regulation individuals whose religious beliefs and practices would otherwise thereby be infringed, or to create without state involvement an atmosphere in which voluntary religious exercise may flourish.

Beyond these limited situations in which government may take cognizance of religion for purposes of accommodating our traditions of religious liberty, government may not use religion as a basis of classification for the imposition of duties, penalties, privileges or benefits. "State power is no more to be used so as to handicap religions, than it is to favor them." *Everson* v. *Board of Education.*

Tennessee nevertheless invokes the Establishment Clause to excuse the imposition of a civil disability upon those deemed ⊥ to be deeply involved in religion. In my view, that Clause will not permit much less excuse or condone the deprivation of religious liberty here involved.

Fundamental to the conception of religious liberty protected by the Religion Clauses is the idea that religious beliefs are a matter of voluntary choice by individuals and their associations, and that each sect is entitled to "flourish according to the zeal of its adherents and the appeal of its dogma." *Zorach* v. *Clauson.* Accordingly, religious ideas, no less than any other, may be the subject of debate which is

"uninhibited, robust, and wide-open . . ." *New York Times Co.* v. *Sullivan.* Government may not interfere with efforts to proselyte or worship in public places. *Kunz* v. *New York.* It may not tax the dissemination of religious ideas. *Murdock* v. *Pennsylvania.* It may not seek to shield its citizens from those who would solicit them with their religious beliefs. *Martin* v. *City of Struthers.*

That public debate of religious ideas, like any other, may arouse emotion, may incite, may foment religious divisiveness and strife does not rob it of constitutional protection. *Cantwell* v. *Connecticut;* cf. *Terminiello* v. *Chicago.* The mere fact that a purpose of the Establishment Clause is to reduce or eliminate religious divisiveness or strife, does not place religious discussion, association, or political participation in a status less preferred than rights of discussion, association and political participation generally. "Adherents of particular faiths and individual churches frequently take strong positions on public ⊥ issues including . . . vigorous advocacy of legal or constitutional positions. Of course, churches as much as secular bodies and private citizens have that right." *Walz* v. *Tax Commission.*

The State's goal of preventing sectarian bickering and strife may not be accomplished by regulating religious speech and political association. The Establishment Clause does not license government to treat religion and those who teach or practice it, simply by virtue of their status as such, as subversive of American ideals and therefore subject to unique disabilities. Cf. *Wieman* v. *Updegraff.* Government may not inquire into the religious beliefs and motivations of officeholders—it may not remove them from office merely for making public statements regarding religion, nor question whether their legislative actions stem from religious conviction. Cf. *Bond* v. *Floyd.*

In short, government may not as a goal promote "safe-thinking" with respect to religion and fence out from political participation those, such as ministers, whom it regards as overinvolved in religion. Religionists no less than members of any other group enjoy the full measure of protection afforded speech, association and political activity generally. The Establishment Clause, properly understood, is a shield against any attempt by government to inhibit religion as it has done here; *Abington School District* v. *Schempp.* It may not be used as a sword to justify repression of religion or its adherents from any aspect of public life.

⊥ Our decisions under the Establishment Clause prevent government from supporting or involving itself in religion or from becoming drawn into ecclesiastical disputes. These prohibitions naturally tend, as they were designed to, to avoid channelling political activity along religious lines and to reduce any tendency toward religious divisiveness in society. Beyond enforcing these prohibitions, however, government may not go. The antidote which the Constitution provides against zealots who would inject sectarianism into the political process is to subject their ideas to refutation in the marketplace of ideas and their platforms to rejection at the polls. With these safeguards, it is unlikely that they will succeed in inducing government to act along religiously divisive lines, and, with judicial enforcement of the Establishment Clause, any measure of success they achieve must be short-lived, at best.

Mr. Justice STEWART, concurring in the judgment.

Like *Mr. Justice BRENNAN*, I believe that *Torcaso* v. *Watkins* controls this case. There, the Court held that Maryland's refusal to commission Torcaso as a Notary Public because he would not declare his belief in God violated the First Amendment, as incorporated by the Fourteenth. The offense against the First and Fourteenth Amendments lay not simply in requiring an oath, but in "limiting public offices to persons who have, or perhaps more properly profess to have, a belief in some particular kind of religious concept." As the Court noted, "The Fact . . . that a person is not compelled to hold public of- |643 fice cannot possibly be ⊥ an excuse for barring him from office by state-imposed criteria forbidden by the Constitution." Except for the fact that Tennessee bases its disqualification not on a person's statement of belief but on his decision to pursue a religious vocation as directed by his belief, that case is indistinguishable from this one—and that sole distinction is without constitutional consequence.

Mr. Justice WHITE, concurring in the judgment.

While I share the view of my Brothers that Tennessee's disqualification of ministers from serving as delegates to the State's constitutional convention is constitutionally impermissible, I disagree as to the basis for this invalidity. Rather than relying on the Free Exercise Clause, as do the other Members of the Court, I would hold Chapter 848, Section 4 of the 1976 Tennessee Public Acts unconstitutional under the Equal Protection Clause of the Fourteenth Amendment.

The plurality states that § 4 "has encroached upon McDaniel's right to the free exercise of religion," but fails to explain in what way McDaniel has been deterred in the observance of his religious beliefs. Certainly he has not felt compelled to abandon the ministry as a result of the challenged statute, nor has |644 he been required to disavow any of his ⊥ religious beliefs. Because I am not persuaded that the Tennessee statute in any way interferes with McDaniel's ability to exercise his religion as he desires, I would not rest the decision on the Free Exercise Clause but instead would turn to McDaniel's argument that the statute denies him equal protection of the laws.

Our cases have recognized the importance of the right of an individual to seek elective office and ac-

cordingly have afforded careful scrutiny to state regulations burdening that right. In *Lubin* v. *Panish*, for example, we noted: "This legitimate state interest, however, must be achieved by a means that does not unfairly or unnecessarily burden either a minority party's or an individual candidate's equally important interest in the continued availability of political opportunity. The interests involved are not merely those of parties or individual candidates; the voters can assert their preferences only through candidates or parties or both and it is this broad interest that must be weighed in the balance. The right of a party or an individual to a place on a ballot is entitled to protection and is intertwined with the rights of voters."

Recognizing that "the rights of voters and the rights of candidates do not lend themselves to neat separation . . .," *Bullock* v. *Carter*. The Court has required States to provide substantial justification for any requirement that prevents a class of citizens from gaining ballot access and has held unconstitutional state laws requiring the payment of prohibitively large filing fees, requiring the payment of even moderate fees by indigent candidates, and ⊥ having |64 the effect of excluding independent and minority party candidates from the ballot.

The restriction in this case, unlike the ones challenged in the previous cases, is absolute on its face: there is no way in which a Tennessee minister can qualify as a candidate for the State's constitutional convention. The State's asserted interest in this absolute disqualification is its desire to maintain the required separation between church and State. While the State recognizes that not all ministers would necessarily allow their religious commitments to interfere with their duties to the State and to their constituents, it asserts that the potential for such conflict is sufficiently great to justify § 4's candidacy disqualification.

Although the State's interest is a legitimate one, close scrutiny reveals that the challenged law is not "reasonably necessary to the accomplishment of . . ." that objective. *Bullock*. All 50 States are required by the First and Fourteenth Amendments to maintain a separation between church and State, and yet all of the States other than Tennessee are able to achieve this objective without burdening ministers' rights to candidacy. This suggests that the underlying assumption on which the Tennessee statute is based—that a minister's duty to the superiors of his church will interefere with his governmental service—is unfounded. Moreover, the rationale of the Tennessee statute is undermined by the fact that it is both underinclusive and overinclusive. While the State asserts an interest in keeping religious and governmental interests separate, the disqualification of ministers applies only to legislative positions, and not to executive and judicial offices. On the other hand, that statute's sweep is so overly broad, for it applies with equal force to those ministers whose religious beliefs would not prevent them from properly discharging their duties as constitutional convention delegates.

⊥646   ⊥ The facts of this case show that the voters of McDaniel's district desired to have him represent them at the limited constitutional convention. Because I conclude that the State's justification for frustrating the desires of these voters and for depriving McDaniel and all other ministers of the right to seek this position is insufficient, I would hold § 4 unconstitutional as a violation of the Equal Protection Clause.

GOLDMAN v. WEINBERGER

106 S.Ct. 1310
ON WRIT OF CERTIORARI TO THE UNITED STATES COURT OF
APPEALS FOR THE DISTRICT OF COLUMBIA CIRCUIT
Argued January 14, 1986 — Decided March 25, 1986
Justice REHNQUIST delivered the opinion of the Court.

Petitioner S. Simcha Goldman contends that the Free Exercise Clause of the First Amendment to the United States Constitution permits him to wear a yarmulke while in uniform, notwithstanding an Air Force regulation mandating uniform dress for Air Fore personnel. The District Court for the District of Columbia permanently enjoined the Air Force from enforcing its regulation against petitioner and from penalizing him for wearing his yarmulke. The court of Appeals for the District of Columbia Circuit reversed on the ground that the Air Force's strong interest in discipline justified the strict enforcement of its uniform dress requirements. We granted certiorari because of the importance of the question, and now affirm.

Petitioner Goldman is an Orthodox Jew and ordained rabbi. In 1973, he was accepted into the Armed Forces Health Professions Scholarship Program and placed on inactive reserve status in the Air Force while he studied clinical psychology at Loyola University of Chicago. During his three years in the scholarship program, he received a monthly stipend and an allowance for tuition, books, and fees. After completing his Ph.D. in psychology, petitioner entered active service in the United States Air Force as a commissioned officer, in accordance with a requirement that participants in the scholarship program serve one year of active duty for each year of subsidized education. Petitioner was stationed at March Air Force Base in Riverside, California, and served as a clinical psychologist at the mental health clinic on the base.

Until 1981, petitioner was not prevented from wearing his yarmulke on the base. He avoided controversy by remaining close to his duty station in the health clinic and by wearing his service cap over the yarmulke when out of doors. But in April 1981, after he testified as a defense witness at a court-martial wearing his yarmulke but not his service cap, opposing counsel lodged a complaint with Colonel Joseph Gregory, the Hospital Commander, arguing that petitioner's practice of wearing his yarmulke was a violation of Air Force Regulation (AFR) 35-10. This regulation states in pertinent part that "[h]eadgear will not be worn . . . [w]hile indoors except by armed security police in the performance of their duties."

Colonel Gregory informed petitioner that wearing a yarmulke while on duty does indeed violate AFR 35-10, and ordered him not to violate this regulation outside the hospital. Although virtually all of petitioner's time on the base was spent in the hospital, he refused. Later, after petitioner's attorney protested to the Air Force General Counsel, Colonel Gregory revised his order to prohibit petitioner from wearing the yarmulke even in the hospital. Petitioner's request to report for duty in civilian clothing pending legal resolution of the issue was denied. The next day he received a formal letter of reprimand, and was warned that failure to obey AFR 35-10 could subject him to a court-martial. Colonel Gregory also withdrew a recommendation that petitioner's application to extend the term of his active service be approved, and substituted a negative recommendation.

Petitioner then sued respondent Secretary of Defense and others, claiming that the application of AFR 35-10 to prevent him from wearing his yarmulke infringed upon his First Amendment freedom to exercise his religious beliefs. The United States District Court for the District of Columbia preliminarily enjoined the enforcement of the regulation, 530 F. Supp. 12 (1981), and then after a full hearing permanently enjoined the Air Force from prohibiting petitioner from wearing a yarmulke while in uniform. Respondents appealed to the Court of Appeals for the District of Columbia Circuit, which reversed. As an initial matter, the Court of Appeals determined that the appropriated level of scrutiny of a military regulation that clashes with a constitutional right is neither strict scrutiny nor rational basis. Instead, it held that a military regulation must be examined to determine whether "legitimate military ends are sought to be achieved," and whether it is "designed to accommodate the individual right to an appropriate degree." Applying this test, the court concluded that "the Air Force's interest in uniformity renders the strict enforcement of its regulation permissible." The full Court of Appeals denied a petition for rehearing en banc, with three judges dissenting.

Petitioner argues that AFR 35-10, as applied to him, prohibits religiously motivated conduct and should therefore be analyzed under the standard enunciated in *Sherbert* v. *Verner*. But we have repeatedly held that "the military is, by necessity, a specialized society separate from civilian society."

Parker v. *Levy.* "[T]he military must insist upon a respect for duty and a discipline without counterpart in civilian life," *Schlesinger* v. *Councilman*, in order to prepare for and perform its vital role.

Our review of military regulations challenged on First Amendment grounds is far more deferential than constitutional review of similar laws or regulations designed for civilian society. The military need not encourage debate or tolerate protest to the extent that such tolerance is required of the civilian state by the First Amendment; to accomplish its mission the military must foster instinctive obedience, unity, commitment, and esprit de corps. The essence of military service "is the subordination of the desires and interests of the individual to the needs of the service." *Orloff* v. *Willoughby.*

These aspects of military life do not, of course, render entirely nugatory in the military context the guarantees of the First Amendment. But "within the military community there is simply not the same [individual] autonomy as there is in the larger civilian community." *Parker* v. *Levy.* In the context of the present case, when evaluating whether military needs justify a particular restriction on religiously motivated conduct, courts must give great deference to the professional judgment of military authorities concerning the relative importance of a particular military interest. Not only are courts "'ill-equipped to determine the impact upon discipline that any particular intrusion upon military authority might have,'" *Chappell* v. *Wallace*, but the military authorities have been charged by the Executive and Legislative Branches with carrying out our Nation's military policy. "Judicial deference . . . is at its apogee when legislative action under the congressional authority to raise and support armies and make rules and regulations for their governance is challenged." *Rostker* v. *Goldberg.*

The considered professional judgment of the Air Force is that the traditional outfitting of personnel in standardized uniforms encourages the subordination of personal preferences and identifies in favor of the overall group mission. Uniforms encourage a sense of hierarchical unity by tending to eliminate outward individual distinctions except for those of rank. The Air Force considers them as vital during peacetime as during war because its personnel must be ready to provide an effective defense on a moment's notice; the necessary habits of discipline and unity must be developed in advance of trouble. We have acknowledged that "[t]he inescapable demands of military procedures and orders must be virtually reflex with no time for debate or reflection." *Chappell* v. *Wallace.*

To this end, the Air Force promulgated AFR 35-10, a 190-page document, which states that "Air Force members will wear the Air Force uniform while performing their military duties, except when authorized to wear civilian clothes on duty." The rest of the document describes in minute detail all of the various items of apparel that must be worn as part of the Air Force uniform. It authorizes a few individualized options with respect to certain pieces of jewelry and hair style, but even these are subject to severe limitations. In general, authorized headgear may be worn only out of doors. Indoors, "[h]eadgear [may] not be worn . . . except by armed security police in the performance of their duties." A narrow exception to this rule exists for headgear worn during indoor religious ceremonies. In addition, military commanders may in their discretion permit visible religious headgear and other such apparel in designated living quarters and nonvisible items generally.

Petitioner Goldman contends that the Free Exercise Clause of the First Amendment requires the Air Force to make an exception to its uniform dress requirements for religious apparel unless the accoutrements create a "clear danger" of undermining discipline and esprit de corps. He asserts that in general, visible but "unobtrusive" apparel will not create such a danger and must therefore be accommodated. He argues that the Air Force failed to prove that specific exception for his practice of wearing an unobtrusive yarmulke would threaten discipline. He contends that the Air Force's assertion to the contrary is mere *ipse dixit*, with no support from actual experience or a scientific study in the record, and is contradicted by expert testimony that religious exceptions to AFR 35-10 are in fact desirable and will increase morale by making the Air Force a more humane place.

But whether or not expert witnesses may feel that religious exceptions to AFR 35-10 are desirable is quite beside the point. The desirability of dress regulations in the military is decided by the appropriate military officials, and they are under no constitutional mandate to abandon their considered professional judgment. Quite obviously, to the extent the regulations do not permit the wearing of religious apparel such as a yarmulke, a practice described by petitioner as silent devotion akin to prayer, military life may be more objectionable for petitioner and probably others. But the First Amendment does not require the military to accommodate such practices in the face of its view that they would detract from the uniformity sought by the dress regulations. The Air Force has drawn the line essentially between religious apparel which is visible and that which is not, and we hold that those portions of the regulations challenged here reasonably and evenhandedly regulate dress in the interest of the military's perceived need for uniformity. The First Amendment therefore does not prohibit them from being applied to petitioner even though their effect is to restrict the wearing of the headgear required by his religious beliefs.

The judgment of the Court of Appeals is *Affirmed.*

Justice STEVENS, with whom *Justice WHITE* and *Justice POWELL* join, concurring.

Captain Goldman presents an especially attractive case for an exception from the uniform regulations that are applicable to all other Air Force personnel. His devotion to this faith is readily apparent. The yarmulke is a familiar and accepted sight. In addition to its religious significance for the wearer, the yarmulke may evoke the deepest respect and admiration—the symbol of a distinguished tradition and an eloquent rebuke to the ugliness of anti-Semitism. Captain Goldman's military duties are performed in a setting in which a modest departure from the uniform regulation creates almost no danger of impairment of the Air Force's military mission. Moreover, on the record before us, there is reason to believe that the policy of strict enforcement against Captain Goldman had a retaliatory motive—he had worn his yarmulke while testifying on behalf of a defendant in a court-martial proceeding. Nevertheless, as the case has been argued, I believe we must test the validity of the Air Force's rule not merely as it applies to Captain Goldman but also as it applies to all service personnel who have sincere religious beliefs that may conflict with one or more military commands.

Justice BRENNAN is unmoved by the Government's concern "that while a yarmulke might not seem obtrusive to a Jew, neither does a turban to a Sikh, a saffron robe to a Satchidananda Ashram-Integral Yogi, nor do dreadlocks to a Rastafarian." He correctly points out that "turbans, saffron robes, and dreadlocks are not before us in this case," and then suggests that other cases may be fairly decided by reference to a reasonable standard based on "functional utility, health and safety considerations, and the goal of a polished, professional appearance." As the Court has explained, this approach attaches no weight to the separate interest in uniformity itself. Because professionals in the military service attach great importance to that plausible interest in uniformity itself. Because professionals in the military service attach great importance to that plausible interest, it is one that we must recognize as legitimate and rational even though personal experience or admiration for the performance of the "rag-tag band of soldiers" that won us our freedom in the revolutionary war might persuade us that the Government has exaggerated the importance of that interest.

The interest in uniformity, however, has a dimension that is of still greater importance for me. It is the interest in uniform treatment for the members of all religious faiths. The very strength of Captain Goldman's claim creates the danger that a similar claim on behalf of a Sikh or a Rastafarian might readily be dismissed as "so extreme, so unusual, or so faddish an image that public confidence in his ability to perform his duties will be destroyed." If exceptions from dress code regulations are to be granted on the basis of a multifactored test such as that proposed by *Justice BRENNAN,* inevitably the decisionmaker's evaluation of the character and the sincerity of the requestor's faith—as well as the probable reaction of the majority to the favored treatment of a member of that faith—will play a critical part in the decision. For the difference between a turban or a dreadlock on the one hand, and a yarmulke on the other, is not merely a difference in "appearance"—it is also the difference between a Sikh or a Rastafarian, on the one hand, and an Orthodox Jew on the other. The Air Force has no business drawing distinctions between such persons when it is enforcing commands of universal application.

As the Court demonstrates, the rule that is challenged in this case is based on a neutral, completely objective standard—visibility. It was not motivated by hostility against, or any special respect for, any religious faith. An exception for yarmulkes would represent a fundamental departure from the true principle of uniformity that supports that rule. For that reason, I join the Court's opinion and its judgment.

Justice BRENNAN, with whom *Justice MARSHALL* joins, dissenting.

Simcha Goldman invokes this Court's protection of his First Amendment right to fulfill one of the traditional religious obligations of a male Orthodox Jew—to cover his head before an omnipresent God. The Court's response to Goldman's request is to abdicate its role as principal expositor of the Constitution and protector of individual liberties in favor of credulous deference to unsupported assertions of military necessity. I dissent.

I

In ruling that the paramount interests of the Air Force override Dr. Goldman's free exercise claim the Court overlooks the sincere and serious nature of his constitutional claim. It suggests that the desirability of certain dress regulations, rather than a First Amendment right, is at issue. The Court declares that in selecting dress regulations, "military officials are under no constitutional mandate to abandon their considered professional judgment." If Dr. Goldman wanted to wear a hat to keep his head warm or to cover a bald spot I would join the majority. Mere personal preferences in dress are not constitutionally protected. The First Amendment, however, restrains the Government's ability to prevent an Orthodox Jewish serviceman from, or punish him for, wearing a yarmulke.

The Court also attempts, unsuccessfully, to minimize the burden that was placed on Dr. Goldman's rights. The fact that "the regulations don't permit the wearing of . . . a yarmulke," does not simply render military life for observant Orthodox Jews "objectionable." It sets up an almost absolute bar to the fulfillment of a religious duty. Dr. Goldman spent most of his time in uniform indoors, where the dress code forbade him even from covering his head with his service cap. Consequently, he was asked to violate the tenets of his faith virtually every minute of every work day.

II
A

Dr. Goldman has asserted a substantial First Amendment claim, which is entitled to meaningful review by this Court. The Court, however, evades its responsibility by eliminating, in all but name only, judicial review of military regulations that interfere with the fundamental constitutional rights of service personnel.

Our cases have acknowledged that in order to protect our treasured liberties, the military must be able to command service members to sacrifice a great many of the individual freedoms they enjoyed in the civilian community and to endure certain limitations on the freedoms they retain. Notwithstanding this acknowledgment, we have steadfastly maintained that "'our citizens in uniform may not be stripped of basic rights simply because they have doffed their civilian clothes.'" *Chappell* v. *Wallace*. And, while we have hesitated, due to our lack of expertise concerning military affairs and our respect for the delegated authority of a coordinate branch, to strike down restrictions on individual liberties which could reasonably be justified as necessary to the military's vital function, we have never abdicated our obligation of judicial review.

Today the Court eschews its constitutionally mandated role. It adopts for review of military decisions affecting First Amendment rights a subrational-basis standard—absolute, uncritical "deference to the professional judgment of military authorities." If a branch of the military declares one of its rules sufficiently important to outweigh a service person's constitutional rights, it seems that the Court will accept that conclusion, no matter how absurd or unsupported it may be.

A deferential standard of review, however, need not, and should not, mean that the Court must credit arguments that defy common sense. When a military service burdens the free exercise rights of its members in the name of necessity, it must provide, as an initial matter and at a minimum, *credible* explanation of how the contested practice is likely to interfere with the proffered military interest. Unabashed *ipse dixit* cannot outweigh a constitutional right.

In the present case, the Air Force asserts that its interests in discipline and uniformity would be undermined by an exception to the dress code permitting observant male Orthodox Jews to wear yarmulkes. The Court simply restates these asser-

tions without offering any explanation how the exception Dr. Goldman requests reasonably could interfere with the Air Force's interests. Had the Court given actual consideration to Goldman's claim, it would have been compelled to decide in his favor.

B
1

The Government maintains in its brief that discipline is jeopardized whenever exceptions to military regulations are granted. Service personnel must be trained to obey even the most arbitrary command reflexively. Non-Jewish personnel will perceive the wearing of a yarmulke by an Orthodox Jew as an unauthorized departure from the rules and will begin to question the principle of unswerving obedience. Thus shall our fighting forces slip down the treacherous slope toward unkempt appearance, anarchy, and, ultimately, defeat at the hands of our enemies.

The contention that the discipline of the armed forces will be subverted if Orthodox Jews are allowed to wear yarmulkes with their uniforms surpasses belief. It lacks support in the record of this case and the Air Force offers no basis for it as a general proposition. While the perilous slope permits the services arbitrarily to refuse exceptions requested to satisfy mere personal preferences, before the Air Force may burden free exercise rights it must advance, at the *very least*, a rational reason for doing so.

Furthermore, the Air Force cannot logically defend the content of its rule by insisting that discipline depends upon absolute adherence to whatever rule is established. If, as General Usher admitted at trial, the dress code codified religious exemptions from the "no-headgear-indoors" regulation, then the wearing of a yarmulke would be sanctioned by the code and could not be considered an unauthorized deviation from the rules.

2

The Government also argues that the services have an important interest in uniform dress, because such dress establishes the preeminence of group identity, thus fostering esprit de corps and loyalty to the service that transcends individual bonds. In its belief, the Government characterizes the yarmulke as an assertion in individuality and as a badge of religious and ethnic identity, strongly suggesting that, as such, it could drive a wedge of divisiveness between members of the services.

First, the purported interests of the Air Force in complete uniformity of dress and in elimination of individuality or visible identification with any group other than itself are belied by the service's own regulations. The dress code expressly abjures the need for total uniformity:

"(1) The American public and its elected representatives draw certain conclusions on military effectiveness based on what they see; that is, the image the Air Force presents. The image must instill public confidence and leave no doubt that the service member lives by a common standard and responds to military order and discipline.

"(2) Appearance in uniform is an important part of this image. . . . Neither the Air Force nor the public expects absolute uniformity of appearance. Each member has the right, within limits, to express individuality through his or her appearance. However, the image of a disciplined service member who can be relied on to do his or her job excludes the extreme, the unusual, and the fad."

It cannot be seriously contended that a serviceman in a yarmulke presents so extreme, so unusual, or so faddish an image that public confidence in his ability to perform his duties will be destroyed. Under the Air Force's own standards, then, Dr. Goldman should have and could have been granted an exception to wear his yarmulke.

The dress code also allows men to wear up to three rings and one identification bracelet of "neat and conservative," but non-uniform, design. This jewelry is apparently permitted even if, as is often the case with rings, it associates the wearer with a denominational school or a religious or secular fraternal organization. If these emblems of religious, social, and ethnic identity are not deemed to be unacceptably divisive, the Air Force cannot rationally justify its bar against yarmulkes on that basis.

Moreover, the services allow, and rightly so, other manifestations of religious diversity. It is clear to all service personnel that some members attend Jewish services, some Christian, some Islamic, and some yet other religious services. Barracks mates see Mormons wearing temple garments, Orthodox Jews wearing tzitzit, and Catholics wearing crosses and scapulars. That they come from different faiths and ethnic backgrounds is not a secret that can or should be kept from them.

I find totally implausible the suggestion that the overarching group identity of the Air Force would be threatened if Orthodox Jews were allowed to wear yarmulkes with their uniforms. To the contrary, a yarmulke worn with a United States military uniform is an eloquent reminder that the shared and proud identity of United States serviceman embraces and unites religious and ethnic pluralism.

Finally, the Air Force argues that while Dr. Goldman describes his yarmulke as an "unobtrusive" addition to his uniform, obtrusiveness is a purely relative, standardless judgment. The Government notes that while a yarmulke might not seem obtrusive to a Jew, neither does a turban to a Sikh, a saffron robe to a Satchidananda Ashram-Integral Yogi, nor do dreadlocks to a Rastafarian. If the Court were to require the Air Force to permit yarmulkes, the service must also allow all of these other forms of dress and grooming.

The Government dangles before the Court a classic parade of horribles, the specter of a brightly-colored,

"rag-tag band of soldiers." Although turbans, saffron robes, and dreadlocks are not before us in this case and must each be evaluated against the reasons a service branch offers for prohibiting personnel from wearing them while in uniform, a reviewing court could legitimately give deference to dress and grooming rules that have a *reasoned* basis in, for example, functional utility, health and safety considerations, and the goal of a polished, professional appearance. AFR 35-10, ¶ 1-12a and 1-12a(1) (1978) (identifying neatness, cleanliness, safety, and military image as the four elements of the dress code's "high standard of dress and personal appearance"). It is the lack of any reasoned basis for prohibiting yarmulkes that is so striking here.

Furthermore, contrary to its intimations, the Air Force has available to it a familiar standard for determining whether a particular style of yarmulke is consistent with a polished, professional military appearance—the "neat and conservative" standard by which the service judges jewelry. No rational reason exists why yarmulkes cannot be judged by the same criterion. Indeed, at argument Dr. Goldman declared himself willing to wear whatever style and color yarmulke the Air Force believes best comports with its uniform.

3

Department of Defense directive 1300.17 (June 18, 1985) grants commanding officers the discretion to permit service personnel to wear religious items and apparel that are not visible with the uniform, such as crosses, temple garments, and scapulars. *Justice STEVENS* favors this "visibility test" because he believes that it does not involve the Air Force in drawing distinctions among faiths. He rejects functional utility, health, and safety considerations, and similar grounds as criteria for religious exceptions to the dress code, because he fears that these standards will allow some service persons to satisfy their religious dress and grooming obligations, while preventing others from fulfilling theirs. But, the visible/not visible standard has that same effect. Furthermore, it restricts the free exercise rights of a larger number of service persons. The visibility test permits "only" individuals whose outer garments and grooming are indistinguishable from those of mainstream Christians to fulfill their religious duties. In my view, the Constitution requires the selection of criteria that permit the greatest possible number of persons to practice their faiths freely.

Implicit in *Justice STEVENS'* concurrence, and in the Government's arguments, is what might be characterized as a fairness concern. It would be unfair to allow Orthodox Jews to wear yarmulkes, while prohibiting members of other minority faiths with visible dress and grooming requirements from wearing their saffron robes, dreadlocks, turbans, and so forth. While I appreciate and share this concern for the feelings and the free exercise rights of members of these other faiths, I am baffled by this formulation of the problem. What puzzles me is the implication that a neutral standard that could result in the disparate treatment of Orthodox Jews and, for example, Sikhs is *more* troublesome or unfair than the existing neutral standard that does result in the different treatment of Christians, on the one hand, and Orthodox Jews and Sikhs on the other. *Both* standards are constitutionally suspect; before either can be sustained, it must be shown to be a narrowly tailored means of promoting important military interests.

I am also perplexed by the related notion that for purposes of constitutional analysis religious faiths may be divided into two categories—those with visible dress and grooming requirements and those without. This dual category approach seems to incorporate an assumption that fairness, the First Amendment, and, perhaps, Equal Protection, require all faiths belonging to the same category to be treated alike, but permit a faith in one category to be treated differently from a faith belonging to the other category. The practical effect of this categorization is that, under the guise of neutrality and evenhandedness, majority religions are favored over distinctive minority faiths. This dual category analysis is fundamentally flawed and leads to a result that the First Amendment was intended to prevent. Under the Constitution there is only *one* relevant category—*all* faiths. Burdens placed on the free exercise rights of members of one faith must be justified independently of burdens placed on the rights of members of another religion. It is not enough to say that Jews cannot wear yarmulkes simply because Rastafarians might not be able to wear dreadlocks.

Unless the visible/not visible standard for evaluating requests for religious exceptions to the dress code promotes a significant military interest, it is constitutionally impermissible. *Justice STEVENS* believes that this standard advances an interest in the "uniform treatment" of all religions. As I have shown, that uniformity is illusory, unless uniformity means uniformly accommodating majority religious practices and uniformly rejecting distinctive minority practices. But, more directly, Government agencies are not free to define their own interests in uniform treatment of different faiths. That function has been assigned to the First Amendment. The First Amendment requires that burdens on free exercise rights be justified by independent and important interests that promote the function of the agency. The only independent military interest furthered by the visibility standard is uniformity of dress. And, that interest, as I demonstrated in Part II B §2, *supra*, does not support a prohibition against yarmulkes.

The Air Force has failed utterly to furnish a credible explanation why an exception to the dress code permitting Orthodox Jews to wear neat and con-

servative yarmulkes while in uniform is likely to interfere with its interest in discipline and uniformity. We cannot "distort the Constitution to approve all that the military may deem expedient." *Korematsu* v. *United States* (Jackson, J., dissenting). Under any meaningful level of judicial review, Simcha Goldman should prevail.

III

Through our Bill of Rights, we pledged ourselves to attain a level of human freedom and dignity that had no parallel in history. Our constitutional commitment to religious freedom and acceptance of religious pluralism is one of our greatest achievements in that noble endeavor. Almost 200 years after the First Amendment was drafted, tolerance and respect for all religions still set us apart from most other countries and draws to our shores refugees from religious persecution from around the world.

Guardianship of this precious liberty is not the exclusive domain of federal courts. It is the responsibility as well of the States and of the other branches of the Federal Government. Our military services have a distinguished record of providing for many of the religious needs of their personnel. But that they have satisfied much of their constitutional obligation does not remove their actions from judicial scrutiny. Our Nation has preserved freedom of religion, not through trusting to the good faith of individual agencies of government alone, but through the constitutionally mandated vigilant oversight and checking authority of the judiciary.

It is not the province of the federal courts to second-guess the professional judgments of the military services, but we are bound by the Constitution to assure ourselves that there exists a rational foundation for assertions of military necessity when they interfere with the free exercise of religion. "The concept of military necessity is seductively broad," and military decisionmakers themselves are as likely to succumb to its allure as are the courts and the general public. Definitions of necessity are influenced by decisionmakers' experiences and values. As a consequence, in pluralistic societies such as ours, institutions dominated by a majority are inevitably, if inadvertently, insensitive to the needs and values of minorities when these needs and values differ from those of the majority. The military, with its strong ethic of conformity and unquestioning obedience, may be particularly impervious to minority needs and values. A critical function of the Religion Clauses of the First Amendment is to protect the rights of members of minority religions against quiet erosion by majoritarian social institutions that dismiss minority beliefs and practices as unimportant, because unfamiliar. It is the constitutional role of this Court to ensure that this purpose of the First Amendment be realized.

The Court and the military services have presented patriotic Orthodox Jews with a painful dilemma—the choice between fulfilling a religious obligation and serving their country. Should the draft be reinstated, compulsion will replace choice. Although the pain the services inflict on Orthodox Jewish servicemen is clearly the result of insensitivity rather than design, it is unworthy of our military because it is unnecessary. The Court and the military have refused these servicemen their constitutional rights; we must hope that Congress will correct this wrong.

Justice BLACKMUN, dissenting.

I would reverse the judgment of the Court of Appeals, but for reasons somewhat different from those respectively enunciated by *Justice BRENNAN* and *Justice O'CONNOR*. I feel that the Air Force is justified in considering not only the costs of allowing Captain Goldman to cover his head indoors, but also the cumulative costs of accommodating constitutionally indistinguishable requests for religious exemptions. Because, however, the Government has failed to make any meaningful showing that either set of costs is significant, I dissent from the Court's rejection of Goldman's claim.

The Government concedes that Goldman wears his yarmulke out of sincere religious conviction. For Goldman, as for many other Jews, "a yarmulke is an expression of respect for God . . . intended to keep the wearer aware of God's presence." If the Free Exercise Clause of the First Amendment means anything, it must mean that an individual's desire to follow his or her faith is not simply another personal preference, to be accommodated by government when convenience allows. Indeed, this Court has read the Clause, I believe correctly, to require that "only those interests of the highest order and those not otherwise served can overbalance legitimate claims to the free exercise of religion." *Wisconsin v. Yoder.* In general, government "may justify an inroad on religious liberty only by showing that it is the least restrictive means of achieving some compelling state interest." *Thomas v. Review Board of Indiana Employment Security Div.* The clear import of *Sherbert, Yoder,* and *Thomas* is that this showing must be made even when the inroad results from the "evenhanded" application of a facially neutral requirement. "Rules are rules" is not by itself a sufficient justification for infringing religious liberty.

Nor may free exercise rights be compromised simply because the military says they must be. To be sure, application of the First Amendment to members of the armed services must take into account "the different character of the military community and of the military mission." *Parker v. Levy.* As *Justice BRENNAN and Justice O'CONNOR* point out, however, military personnel do not forfeit their constitutional rights as a price of enlistment. Except as otherwise required by "interests of the highest or-

der," soldiers as well as civilians are entitled to follow the dictates of their faiths.

In my view, this case does not require us to determine the extent to which the ordinary test for inroads on religious freedom must be modified in the military context, because the Air Force has failed to produce even a minimally credible explanation for its refusal to allow Goldman to keep his head covered indoors. I agree with the Court that deference is due the considered judgment of military professionals that, as a general matter, standardized dress serves to promote discipline and esprit de corps. But Goldman's modest supplement to the Air Force uniform clearly poses by itself no threat to the Nation's military readiness. Indeed, the District Court specifically found that Goldman has worn a yarmulke on base for years without any adverse effect on his performance, any disruption of operations at the base, or any complaints from other personnel.

The Air Force argues that it has no way of distinguishing fairly between Goldman's request for an exemption and the potential requests of others whose religious practices may conflict with the appearance code, perhaps in more conspicuous ways. In theory, this argument makes some sense. Like any rules prescribing a uniform, the Air Force dress code is by nature arbitrary; few of its requirements could be defended on purely functional grounds. Particularly for personnel such as Goldman who serve in noncombat roles, variations from the prescribed attire frequently will interfere with no military goals other than those served by uniformity itself. There thus may be no basis on which to distinguish some variations from others, aside from the degree to which they detract from the overall image of the service, a criterion that raises special constitutional problems when applied to religious practices. To allow noncombat personnel to wear yarmulkes but not turbans or dreadlocks because the latter seem more obtrusive—or, as *Justice BRENNAN* suggests, less "polished" and "professional,"—would be to discriminate in favor of this country's more established, mainstream religions, the practices of which are more familiar to the average observer. Not only would conventional faiths receive special treatment under such an approach; they would receive special treatment precisely "because" they are conventional. In general, I see no constitutional difficulty in distinguishing between religious practices based on how difficult it would be to accommodate them, but favoritism based on how unobtrusive a practice appears to the majority could create serious problems of equal protection and religious establishment, problems the Air Force clearly has a strong interest in avoiding by drawing an objective line at visibility.

The problem with this argument, it seems to me, is not doctrinal but empirical. The Air Force simply has not shown any reason to fear that a significant number of enlisted personnel and officers would request religious exemptions that could not be denied on neutral grounds such as safety, let alone that granting these requests would noticeably impair the overall image of the service. The Air Force contends that the potential for such disruption was demonstrated at trial through the introduction of an Army publication discussing the beliefs and practices of a variety of religious denominations, some of which have traditions or requirements involving attire. See Department of the Army Pamphlet No. 165-13-1, Religious Requirements and Practices of Certain Selected Groups: A Handbook Supplement for Chaplains (1980). But that publication provides no indication whatsoever as to how many soldiers belong to the denominations it describes, or as to how many are likely to seek religious exemptions from the dress code.

In these circumstances, deference seems unwarranted. Reasoned military judgments, of course, are entitled to respect, but the military has failed to show that this particular judgment with respect to Captain Goldman is a reasoned one. If, in the future, the Air Force is besieged with requests for religious exemptions from the dress code, and those requests cannot be distinguished on functional grounds from Goldman's, the service may be able to argue credibly that circumstances warrant a flat rule against any visible religious apparel. That, however, would be a case different from the one at hand.

Justice O'CONNOR, with whom *Justice MARSHALL* joins, dissenting.

The issue posed in this case is whether, consistent with the Free Exercise Clause of the First Amendment, the Air Force may prohibit Captain Goldman, an Orthodox Jewish psychologist, from wearing a yarmulke while he is in uniform on duty inside a military hospital.

The Court rejects Captain Goldman's claim without even the slightest attempt to weigh his asserted right to the free exercise of his religion against the interest of the Air Force in uniformity of dress within the military hospital. No test for Free Exercise claims in the military context is even articulated, much less applied. It is entirely sufficient for the Court if the military perceives a need for uniformity.

Justice STEVENS acknowledges that "Captain Goldman's military duties are performed in a setting in which a modest departure from the uniform regulation creates almost no danger of impairment of the Air Force's military mission." Nevertheless, *Justice STEVENS* is persuaded that a governmental regulation based on *any* "neutral, completely objective standard," will survive a free exercise challenge.

In contrast, *Justice BRENNAN* recognizes that the Court "overlooks the sincere and serious nature of [the] constitutional claim." He properly notes that, even with respect to military rules and regulations, the courts have a duty to weigh sincere First

Amendment claims of its members against the necessity of the particular application of the rule. But *Justice BRENNAN* applies no particular test or standard to determine such claims.

Justice BLACKMUN focuses on the particular ways in which the military may pursue its interest in uniformity, but nonetheless declines "to determine the extent to which the ordinary test for inroads on religious freedom must be modified in the military context."

I believe that the Court should attempt to articulate and apply an appropriate standard for a free exercise claim in the military context, and should examine Captain Goldman's claim in light of that standard.

Like the Court today in this case involving the military, the Court in the past has had some difficulty, even in the civilian context, in articulating a clear standard for evaluating free exercise claims that result from the application of general state laws burdening religious conduct. In *Sherbert* v. *Verner*, and *Thomas* v. *Review Board*, the Court required the States to demonstrate that their challenged policies were "the least restrictive means of achieving some compelling state interest" in order to deprive claimants of unemployment benefits when the refusal to work was based on sincere religious beliefs. In *Wisconsin* v. *Yoder*, the Court noted that "only those interests of the highest order and those not otherwise served can overbalance legitimate claims to the free exercise of religion" in deciding that the Amish were exempt from a State's requirement that children attend school through the age of 16. In *United States* v. *Lee*, the Court stated that "[t]he State may justify a limitation on religious liberty by showing that it is essential to accomplish an overriding governmental interest," and held that the Amish could not exempt themselves from the Social Security system on religious grounds.

These tests, though similar, are not identical. One can, however, glean at least two consistent themes from this Court's precedents. First, when the government attempts to deny a Free Exercise claim, it must show that an unusually important interest is at stake, whether that interest is denominated "compelling," "of the highest order," or "overriding." Second, the government must show that granting the requested exemption will do substantial harm to that interest, whether by showing that the means adopted is the "least restrictive" or "essential," or that the interest will not "otherwise be served." These two requirements are entirely sensible in the context of the assertion of a free exercise claim. First, because the government is attempting to override an interest specifically protected by the Bill of Rights, the government must show that the opposing interest it asserts is of especial importance before there is any chance that its claim can prevail. Second, since the Bill of Rights is expressly designed to protect the individual against the aggregated and sometimes intolerant powers of the state, the government must show that the interest asserted will in fact be substantially harmed by granting the type of exemption requested by the individual.

There is no reason why these general principles should not apply in the military, as well as the civilian, context. As this Court has stated unanimously, " 'our citizens in uniform may not be stripped of basic rights simply because they have doffed their civilian clothes.' " *Chappell* v.*Wallace*. Furthermore, the test that one can glean from this Court's decisions in the civilian context is sufficiently flexible to take into account the special importance of defending our Nation without abandoning completely the freedoms that make it worth defending.

The first question that the Court should face here, therefore, is whether the interest that the Government asserts against the religiously based claim of the individual is of unusual importance. It is perfectly appropriate at this step of the analysis to take account of the special role of the military. The mission of our armed services is to protect our Nation from those who would destroy all our freedoms. I agree that, in order to fulfill that mission, the military is entitled to take some freedoms from its members. As the Court notes, the military " 'must insist upon a respect for duty and a discipline without counterpart in civilian life.' " The need for military discipline and esprit de corps is unquestionably an especially important governmental interest.

But the mere presence of such an interest cannot, as the majority implicitly believes, end the analysis of whether a refusal by the Government to honor the free exercise of an individual's religion is constitutionally acceptable. A citizen pursuing even the most noble cause must remain within the bounds of the law. So, too, the Government may, even in pursuing its most compelling interests, be subject to specific restraints in doing so. The second question in the analysis of a Free Exercise claim under this Court's precedents must also be reached here: will granting an exemption of the type requested by the individual do substantial harm to the especially important governmental interest?

I have no doubt that there are many instances in which the unique fragility of military discipline and esprit de corps necessitates rigidity by the Government when similar rigidity to preserve an assertedly analogous interest would not pass constitutional muster in the civilian sphere. Nonetheless, as *Justice BRENNAN* persuasively argues, the Government can present no sufficiently convincing proof in *this* case to support an assertion that granting an exemption of the type requested here would do substantial harm to military discipline and esprit de corps.

First, the Government's asserted need for absolute uniformity is contradicted by the Government's own exceptions to its rule. As *Justice BRENNAN* notes, an Air Force dress code in force at the time of Captian Goldman's service states: "Neither the Air Force nor the public expects absolute uniformity of appearance. Each member has the right, within limits, to express individuality through his or her appearance. However, the image of a disciplined service member who can be relied on to do his or her job excludes the extreme, the unusual, and the fad." Furthermore, the Government does not assert, and could not plausibly argue, that petitioner's decision to wear his yarmulke while indoors at the hospital presents a threat to health or safety. And finally, the District Court found as fact that in this particular case, far from creating discontent or indiscipline in the hospital where Captain Goldman worked, "[f]rom September 1977 to May 7, 1981, *no objection* was raised to Goldman's wearing of his yarmulke while in uniform.

In the rare instances where the military has not consistently or plausibly justified its asserted need for rigidity of enforcement, and where the individual seeking the exemption establishes that the assertion by the military of a threat to discipline or esprit de corps is in his or her case completely unfounded, I would hold that the Government's policy of uniformity must yield to the individual's assertion of the right of free exercise of religion. On the facts of this case, therefore, I would require the Government to accommodate the sincere religious belief of Captain Goldman. Napoleon may have been correct to assert that, in the military sphere, morale is to all other factors as three is to one, but contradicted assertions of necessity by the military do not on the scales of justice bear a similarly disproportionate weight to sincere religious beliefs of the individual.

I respectfully dissent.

BOWEN v. ROY

106 S.Ct. 2147

ON APPEAL FROM THE UNITED STATES DISTRICT COURT FOR THE MIDDLE DISTRICT OF PENNSYLVANIA

Argued January 14, 1986 — Decided June 11, 1986

Chief Justice BURGER announced the judgment of the Court and delivered the opinion of the Court with respect to Parts I and II, and an opinion with respect to Part III, in which *Justice POWELL* and *Justice REHNQUIST* join.

The question presented is whether the Free Exercise Clause of the First Amendment compels the government to accommodate a religiously-based objection to the statutory requirements that a Social Security number be provided by an applicant seeking to receive certain welfare benefits and that the States use these numbers in administering the benefit programs.

I

Appellees Stephen J. Roy and Karen Miller applied for and received benefits under the Aid to Families with Dependent Children program and the Food Stamp program. They refused to comply, however, with the requirement, contained in 42 U.S.C. § 602 (a)(25) and 7 U.S.C. § 2025 (e), that participants in these programs furnish their state welfare agencies with the Social Security numbers of the members of their household as a condition of receiving benefits. Appellees contended that obtaining a Social Security number for their two-year-old daughter, Little Bird of the Snow, would violate their Native American religious beliefs. The Pennsylvania Department of Public Welfare thereafter terminated AFDC and medical benefits payable to appellees on the child's behalf and instituted proceedings to reduce the level of food stamps that appellees' household was receiving. Appellees then filed this action against the Secretary of the Pennsylvania Department of Public Welfare, the Secretary of Health and Human Services, and the Secretary of Agriculture, arguing that the Free Exercise Clause entitled them to an exemption from the Social Security number requirement. In their complaint, appellees stated that "[t]he sole basis" for the denial of welfare benefits was "Mr. Roy's refusal to obtain a Social Security Number for Little Bird of the Snow," and thus requested injunctive relief, damages, and benefits. In the statement of "undisputed facts," the parties agreed that Little Bird of the Snow did not have a Social Security number.

At trial, Roy testified that he had recently developed a religious objection to obtaining a Social Security number for Little Bird of the Snow. Roy is a Native American descended from the Abenaki Tribe, and he asserts a religious belief that control over one's life is essential to spiritual purity and indispensable to "becoming a holy person." Based on recent conversations with an Abenaki chief, Roy believes that technology is "robbing the spirit of man." In order to prepare his daughter for greater spiritual power, therefore, Roy testified to his belief that he must keep her person and spirit unique and that the uniqueness of the Social Security number as an identifier, coupled with the other uses of the number over which she has no control, will serve to "rob the spirit" of his daughter and prevent her from attaining greater spiritual power.

For purposes of determining the breadth of Roy's religious concerns, the trial judge raised the possibility of using the phonetics of his daughter's name to derive a Social Security number. Although Roy saw "a lot of good" in this suggestion, he stated it would violate his religious beliefs because the special number still would apply uniquely and identify her. Roy also testified that his religious objection would not be satisfied even if the Social Security Adminis-

tration appended the daughter's full tribal name to her Social Security number.

In Roy's own testimony, he emphasized the evil that would flow simply from *obtaining* a number. On the last day of trial, however, a federal officer inquired whether Little Bird of the Snow already had a Social Security number; he learned that a number had been assigned—under first name "Little", middle name "Bird of the Snow", and last name "Roy."

The Government at this point suggested that the case had become moot because, under Roy's beliefs, Little Bird of the Snow's spirit had already been "robbed." Roy, however, was recalled to the stand and testified that her spirit would be robbed only by "use" of the number. Since no known use of the number had yet been made, Roy expressed his belief that her spirit had not been damaged. The District Court concluded that the case was not moot because of Roy's beliefs regarding "use" of the number. ("Roy believes that the establishment of a Social Security number for Little Bird of the Snow, without more, has not 'robbed her spirit,' but widespread use of the Social Security number by the federal or state governments in their computer systems would have that effect").

After hearing all of the testimony, the District Court denied appellees' request for damages and benefits, but granted injunctive relief. Based on the testimony of the Government's experts and the obvious fact that many people share certain names, the District Court found that "[u]tilization in the computer system of the name of a benefit recipient alone frequently is not sufficient to ensure the proper payment of benefits." The court nevertheless concluded that the public "interest in maintaining an efficient and fraud resistant system can be met without requiring use of a Social Security number for Little Bird of the Snow," elaborating that: "It appears to the Court that the harm that the Government might suffer if [appellees] prevailed in this case would be, at worst, that one or perhaps a few individuals could fraudulently obtain welfare benefits. Such a result would obtain only if (1) Little Bird of the Snow attempted fraudulently to obtain welfare benefits or someone else attempted fraudulently to obtain such benefits using Little Bird of the Snow's name *and* (2) identification procedures available to the Defendants that do not require utilization of a Social Security number failed to expose the fraud. This possibility appears to the Court to be remote." Citing our decision in *United States* v. *Lee*, the court entered an injunction containing two basic components. *First*, the Secretary of Health and Human Services was "permanently restrained from making any use of the social security number which was issued in the name of Little Bird of the Snow Roy and from disseminating the number to any agency, individual, business entity, or any other third party." *Second*, the federal and state defendants were enjoined until Little Bird of the Snow's 16th birthday from denying Roy cash assistance, medical assistance, and food stamps "because of the [appellees'] refusal to provide a Social Security number for her."

We noted probable jurisdiction and we reverse.

II

Appellees raise a constitutional challenge to two features of the statutory scheme here. They object to Congress's requirement that a state AFDC plan "*must . . .* provide (A) that, *as a condition of eligibility* under the plan, *each* applicant for or recipient of aid *shall* furnish to the State agency his Social Security account number." 42 U.S.C. § 602 (a)(25) (emphasis added). They also object to Congress's requirement that "such State agency *shall utilize* such account numbers . . . in the administration of such plan." *Ibid.* (emphasis added). We analyze each of these contentions, turning to the latter contention first.

Our cases have long recognized a distinction between the freedom of individual belief, which is absolute, and the freedom of individual conduct, which is not absolute. This case implicates only the latter concern. Roy objects to the statutory requirement that state agencies "shall utilize" Social Security numbers not because it places any restriction on what he may believe or what he may do, but because he believes the use of the number may harm his daughter's spirit.

Never to our knowledge has the Court interpreted the First Amendment to require the Government *itself* to behave in ways that the individual believes will further his or her spiritual development or that of his or her family. The Free Exercise Clause simply cannot be understood to require the Government to conduct its own internal affairs in ways that comport with the religious beliefs of particular citizens. Just as the Government may not insist that appellees engage in any set form of religious observance, so appellees may not demand that the Government join in their chosen religious practices by refraining from using a number to identify their daughter. "[T]he Free Exercise Clause is written in terms of what the government cannot do to the individual, not in terms of what the individual can extract from the government." *Sherbert* v. *Verner*, (Douglas, J., concurring).

As a result, Roy may no more prevail on his religious objection to the Government's use of a Social Security number for his daughter than he could on a sincere religious objection to the size or color of the Government's filing cabinets. The Free Exercise Clause affords an individual protection from certain forms of governmental compulsion; it does not afford an individual a right to dictate the conduct of the Government's internal procedures.

As Roy points out, eight years ago Congress passed a Joint Resolution concerning American Indian reli-

gious freedom that provides guidance with respect to this case. As currently codified, the Resolution provides: "On and after August 11, 1978, it shall be the policy of the United States to protect and preserve for American Indians their inherent right of freedom to believe, express, and exercise the traditional religions of the American Indian, Eskimo, Aleut, and Native Hawaiians, including but not limited to access to sites, use and possession of sacred objects, and the freedom to worship through ceremonials and traditional rites." 42 U.S.C. § 1996. That Resolution—with its emphasis on protecting the freedom to believe, express, and exercise a religion— accurately identifies the mission of the Free Exercise Clause itself. The Federal Government's use of a Social Security number for Little Bird of the Snow does not itself in any degree impair Roy's "freedom to believe, express, and exercise" his religion. Consequently, appellees' objection to the statutory requirement that each State agency "shall utilize" a Social Security number in the administration of its plan is without merit. It follows that their request for an injunction against use of the Social Security number in processing benefit applications should have been rejected. We therefore hold that the portion of the District Court's injunction that permanently restrained the Secretary from making any use of the Social Security number that had been issued in the name of Little Bird of the Snow Roy must be vacated.

III

Roy also challenges Congress' requirement that a state AFDC plan "*must . . .* provide (A) that, *as a condition of eligibility* under the plan, *each* applicant for or recipient of aid *shall furnish* to the State agency his Social Security account number." The First Amendment's guarantee that "Congress shall make no law . . . prohibiting the free exercise" of religion holds an important place in our scheme of ordered liberty, but the Court has steadfastly maintained that claims of religious conviction do not automatically entitle a person to fix unilaterally the conditions and terms of dealings with the government. Not all burdens on religion are unconstitutional. This was treated recently in *United States* v. *Lee*: "To maintain an organized society that guarantees religious freedom to a great variety of faiths requires that some religious practices yield to the common good. Religious beliefs can be accommodated, but there is a point at which accommodation would 'radically restrict the operating latitude of the legislature.' "

The statutory requirement that applicants provide a Social Security number is wholly neutral in religious terms and uniformly applicable. There is no claim that there is any attempt by Congress to discriminate invidiously or any covert suppression of particular religious beliefs. The administrative requirement does not create any danger of censorship or place a direct condition or burden on the dissemination of religious views. It does not intrude on the organization of a religious institution or school. It may indeed confront some applicants for benefits with choices, but in no sense does it affirmatively compel appellees, by threat of sanctions, to refrain from religiously motivated conduct or to engage in conduct that they find objectionable for religious reasons. Rather, it is appellees who seek benefits from the Government and who assert that, because of certain religious beliefs, they should be excused from compliance with a condition that is binding on all other persons who seek the same benefits from the Government.

This is far removed from the historical instances of religious persecution and intolerance that gave concern to those who drafted the Free Exercise Clause of the First Amendment. We are not unmindful of the importance of many government benefits today or of the value of sincerely-held religious beliefs. However, while we do not believe that no government compulsion is involved, we cannot ignore the reality that denial of such benefits by a uniformly applicable statute neutral on its face is of a wholly different, less intrusive nature than affirmative compulsion or prohibition, by threat of penal sanctions, for conduct that has religious implications.

This distinction is clearly revealed in the Court's opinions. Decisions rejecting religious-based challenges have often recited the fact that a mere denial of a governmental benefit by a uniformly applicable statute does not constitute infringement of religious liberty. In *Hamilton* v. *Regents of the University of California*, for example, the Court rejected a religious challenge by students to military courses required as part of their curriculum, explaining: "The fact that they are able to pay their way in this university but not in any other institution in California is without significance upon any constitutional or other question here involved. California has not drafted or called them to attend the university. They are seeking education offered by the State and at the same time insisting that they be excluded from the prescribed course solely upon grounds of their religious beliefs and conscientious objections to war. . . ." In cases upholding First Amendment challenges, on the other hand, the Court has often relied on the showing that compulsion of certain activity with religious significance was involved. In *West Virginia Board of Education* v. *Barnette*, for example, the Court distinguished the earlier *Hamilton* holding and upheld a challenge to a flag salute requirement: "Here . . . we are dealing with a compulsion of students to declare a belief. . . . This issue is not prejudiced by the Court's previous holding that where a State, without compelling attendance, extends college facilities to pupils who voluntarily enroll, it may prescribe military training as part of

the course without offense to the Constitution. It was held that those who take advantage of its opportunities may not on ground of conscience refuse compliance with such conditions. *Hamilton* v. *Regents*. In the present case attendance is not optional." The distinction between governmental compulsion and conditions relating to governmental benefits contained in these two cases was emphasized by *Justice BRENNAN* in his concurring opinion in *Abington School District* v. *Schempp*: "The different results of [*Hamilton* and *Barnette*] are attributable only in part to a difference in the strength of the particular state interests which the respective statutes were designed to serve. Far more significant is the fact that *Hamilton* dealt with the voluntary attendance at college of young adults, while *Barnette* involved the compelled attendance of young children at elementary and secondary schools. This distinction warrants a difference in constitutional results." We have repeatedly emphasized this distinction: In rejecting a Free Exercise challenge in *Bob Jones University* v. *United States*, for example, we observed that the "[d]enial of tax benefits will inevitably have a substantial impact on the operation of private religious schools, but will not prevent those schools from observing their religious tenets."

We conclude then that government regulation that indirectly and incidentally calls for a choice between securing a governmental benefit and adherence to religious beliefs is wholly different from governmental action or legislation that criminalizes religiously inspired activity or inescapably compels conduct that some find objectionable for religious reasons. Although the denial of government benefits over religious objection can raise serious Free Exercise problems, these two very different forms of government action are not governed by the same constitutional standard. A governmental burden on religious liberty is not insulated from review simply because it is indirect, *Thomas* v. *Review Board*, but the nature of the burden is relevant to the standard the Government must meet to justify the burden.

The general governmental interests involved here buttress this conclusion. Governments today grant a broad range of benefits; inescapably at the same time the administration of complex programs requires certain conditions and restrictions. Although in some situations a mechanism for individual consideration will be created, a policy decision by a government that it wishes to treat all applicants alike and that it does not wish to become involved in case-by-case inquires into the genuineness of each religious objection to such condition or restrictions is entitled to substantial deference. Moreover, legitimate interests are implicated in the need to avoid any appearance of favoring religious over nonreligious applicants.

The test applied in cases like *Wisconsin* v. *Yoder* is not appropriate in this setting. In the enforcement of a facially neutral and uniformly applicable requirement for the administration of welfare programs reaching many million of people, the Government is entitled to wide latitude. The Government should not be put to the strict test applied by the District Court; that standard required the Government to justify enforcement of the use of Social Security number requirement as the least restrictive means of accomplishing a compelling state interest. Absent proof of an intent to discriminate against particular religious beliefs or against religion in general, the Government meets its burden when it demonstrates that a challenged requirement for governmental benefits, neutral and uniform in its application, is a reasonable means of promoting a legitimate public interest.

We reject appellees' contention that *Sherbert* and *Thomas* compel affirmance. The statutory conditions at issue in those cases provided that a person was not eligible for unemployment compensation benefits if, "without good cause," he had quit work or refused available work. The "good cause" standard created a mechanism for individualized exemptions. If a state creates a mechanism, its refusal to extend an exemption to an instance of religious hardship suggests a discriminatory intent. Thus, as was urged in *Thomas*, to consider a religiously motivated resignation to be "without good cause" tends to exhibit hostility, not neutrality, towards religion. (*Thomas* and *Sherbert* may be viewed "as a protection against unequal treatment rather than a grant of favored treatment for the members of the religious sect"). In those cases, therefore, it was appropriate to require the State to demonstrate a compelling reason for denying the requested exemption.

Here there is nothing whatever suggesting antagonism by Congress towards religion generally or towards any particular religious beliefs. The requirement that applicants provide a Social Security number is facially neutral and applies to all applicants for the benefits involved. Congress has made no provision for individual exemptions to the requirement in the two statutes in question. Indeed, to the contrary, Congress has specified that a state AFDC plan "*must . . . provide (A) that, as a condition of eligibility* under the plan, *each* applicant for or recipient of aid *shall* furnish to the State agency his Social Security account number," 42 U.S.C. § 602 (a)(25) (emphasis added), and that "[s]tate agencies *shall* (1) *require, as a condition of eligibility* for participation in the food stamp program, that *each* household member furnish to the State agency their Social Security account number," 7 U. S. C. § 2025(e) (emphasis added). Nor are these requirements relics from the past; Congress made the requirement mandatory for the food stamp program in 1981. Congress also recently extended to several other aid programs the mandatory requirement that the States use Social Security numbers in verifying eligibility for benefits.

The Social Security number requirement clearly promotes a legitimate and important public interest.

No one can doubt that preventing fraud in these benefits programs is an important goal. As Representative Richmond explained in support of the bill that made the Social Security number requirement mandatory for the Food Stamp program, "We know that however generously motivated Americans may be to furnish resources to the poor to enable them to survive, . . . they understandably object if they believe that those resources are being abused or wasted. . . .

"We want to be certain that the food stamp program is run as efficiently and as error-free as possible.

"We want applicants and recipients constantly to be aware that the Congress does not and will not tolerate any refusal to disclose earnings accurately, and underreporting of welfare or other assistance program benefits, any efforts to evade the work requirement or any other attempts to take advantage of the program and dollars intended only for those who completely satisfy the stringent eligibility requirements set forth in sections 5 and 7 of the Food Stamp Act of 1977 and further tightened this year and in this bill." 127 Cong. Rec. 24783 (1981). We also think it plain that the Social Security number requirement is a reasonable means of promoting that goal. The programs at issue are of truly staggering magnitude. Each year roughly 3.8 million families receive $7.8 billion through federal funded AFDC programs and 20 million persons receive $11 billion in food stamps. The Social Security program itself is the largest domestic governmental program in the United States today, distributing approximately $51 billion monthly to 36 million recipients. Because of the tremendous administrative problems associated with managing programs of this size, the District Court found that "Social Security numbers are used in making the determination that benefits in the programs are properly paid and that there is no duplication of benefits or failure of payment. . . . Utilization in the computer system of the name of a benefit recipient alone frequently is not sufficient to ensure the proper payment of benefits." Social Security numbers are unique numerical identifiers and are used pervasively in these programs. The numbers are used, for example, to keep track of persons no longer entitled to receive food stamps because of past fraud or abuses of the program. Moreover, the existence of this unique numerical identifier creates opportunities for ferreting out fraudulent applications through computer "matching" techniques. One investigation, "Project Match," compared Federal employee files against AFDC and Medicaid files to determine instances of Government employees receiving welfare benefits improperly. Data from 26 states were examined, and 9,000 individuals were identified as receiving duplicate welfare payments. While undoubtedly some fraud escapes detection in spite of such investigations, the President's Private Sector Survey on Cost Control, known more popularly as the "Grace Commission," recently reported that matching "is the Federal Government's most cost-effective tool for verification or investigation in the prevention and detection of fraud, waste and abuse." 7 The President's Private Sector Survey on Cost Control, Management Office Selected Issues—Information Gap in the Federal Government 90 (1984).

The importance of the Social Security number to these matching techniques is illustrated by the facts of this case. The District Court found that "efficient operation of these [matching] programs requires the use of computer systems that utilize unique numerical identifiers such as the Social Security number." It further found that exempting even appellees alone from this requirement could result in "one or perhaps a few individuals . . . fraudulently obtain[ing] welfare benefits," a prospect the court termed "remote." The District Court's assessment of this probability seems quite dubious. But in any event, we know of no case obligating the government to tolerate a slight risk of "one or perhaps a few individuals" fraudulently obtaining benefits in order to satisfy a religious objection to a requirement designed to combat that very risk. Appellees may not use the Free Exercise Clause to demand government benefits, but only on their own terms, particularly where that insistence works a demonstrable disadvantage to the Government in the administration of the program.

As the Court has recognized before, given the diversity of beliefs in our pluralistic society and the necessity of providing governments with sufficient operating latitude, some incidental neutral restraints on the free exercise of religion are inescapable. As a matter of legislative policy, a legislature might decide to make religious accommodations to a general and neutral system of awarding benefits, "[b]ut our concern is not with the wisdom of legislation but with its constitutional limitation." *Braunfeld* v. *Brown.* We conclude that the Congress's refusal to grant appellees a special exemption does not violate the Free Exercise Clause.

The judgment of the District Court is reversed, and the case is remanded for further proceedings consistent with this opinion.

Reversed

Justice BLACKMUN, concurring in part.

I join only Parts I and II of the opinion written by *The CHIEF JUSTICE.*

In August 1983, appellees Stephen J. Roy and Karen Miller sued to prevent the Government from requiring them to provide a Social Security number for their two-year-old daughter, Little Bird of the Snow, as a condition for obtaining food stamps and welfare benefits for the child. They object to the Social Security number requirement because of their sincere religious conviction that the Government's widespread use of a unique numerical identifier for

their daughter will deprive her of spiritual power. After it developed at trial that the Government already had a Social Security number for Little Bird of the Snow, the District Court enjoined the Government not only from denying benefits to her based on her parents' failure to provide a Social Security number, but also from using or disseminating the number already in the Government's possession until the child's 16th birthday.

I agree with the Court that the District Court erred in enjoining the Government's internal use of Little Bird of the Snow's Social Security number. It is easy to understand the rationale for that part of the District Court's injunction: appellees argue plausibly that the Government's threat to put the Social Security number into active use if they apply for benefits for their daughter requires them to choose between the child's physical sustenance and the dictates of their faith, the same dilemma created by the Government's initial requirement that appellees themselves supply a Social Security number for Little Bird of the Snow. They claim that, absent some compelling state interest, the Government should refrain from acting in ways that appellees believe on religious grounds will harm their daughter's spiritual development.

Although this argument has some facial appeal, I conclude, for the reasons stated in Part II of the Court's opinion, that it stretches the Free Exercise Clause too far. Consequently, I agree that the portion of the District Court's judgment that enjoins the Government from using or disseminating the Social Security number already assigned to Little Bird of the Snow must be vacated. I would also vacate the remainder of the judgment and remand the case for further proceedings, because once the injunction against use or dissemination is set aside, it is unclear on the record presently before us whether a justiciable controversy remains with respect to the rest of the relief ordered by the District Court. Roy and Miller evidently objected to the Social Security number requirement primarily because they did not want the *Government* to be able to use a unique numerical identifier for Little Bird of the Snow, and that injury cannot be redressed if, as the Court today holds, the Government cannot be enjoined from using the pre-existing number. It is possible, however, that appellees still would have an independent religious objection to their being forced to cooperate actively with the Government by themselves providing their daughter's Social Security number on benefit applications.

In my view, the record is ambiguous on this score. In rejecting the Government's argument that the existence of the number rendered the case moot, the District Court found that Roy "feels compelled by his religious belief to avoid any use of that number and, to that end, has refused to provide the number to the Defendants in order to receive welfare benefits for Little Bird of the Snow." It is unclear whether the "use" to which the District Court referred included use by Roy and Miller, or just the more extensive use of the number by the Government. And even if the court meant to refer only to use by the Government, it is not clear that appellees do not also have an independent religious objection to the requirement that *they* provide a Social Security number for their daughter.

On the other hand, even if appellees do have such an objection, vacating the District Court's injunction against governmental use or dissemination of the number may moot this case in other ways. Regardless of whether Roy and Miller are required to provide their daughter's Social Security number on applications for benefits, they may simply be unwilling to apply for benefits without an assurance that the application will not trigger the use of the number. Conversely, it is possible that the Government, in a welcome display of reasonableness, will decide that since it already has a Social Security number for Little Bird of the Snow, it will not insist that appellees resupply it.

Since the proceedings on remand might well render unnecessary any discussion of whether appellees constitutionally may be required to provide a Social Security number for Little Bird of the Snow in order to obtain government assistance on her behalf, that question could be said not to be properly before us. I nonetheless address it, partly because the rest of the court has seen fit to do so, and partly because I think it is not the kind of difficult constitutional question that we should refrain from deciding except when absolutely necessary. Indeed, for the reasons expressed by *Justice O'CONNOR*, I think the question requires nothing more than a straightforward application of *Sherbert*, *Thomas*, and *Wisconsin* v. *Yoder*. If it proves necessary to reach the issue on remand, I agree with *Justice O'CONNOR* that, on the facts as determined by the District Court, the Government may not deny assistance to Little Bird of the Snow solely because her parents' religious convictions prevent them from supplying the Government with a Social Security number for their daughter.

Justice STEVENS, concurring in part and concurring in the result.

Members of the Abenaki Indian Tribe are unquestionably entitled to the same constitutional protection against governmental action "prohibiting the free exercise" of their religion as are the adherents of other faiths. Our respect for the sincerity of their religious beliefs does not, however, relieve us from the duty to identify the precise character of the two quite different claims that the parents of Little Bird of the Snow have advanced. They claim, first, that they are entitled to an injunction preventing the Government from making any use of a Social Security number assigned to Little

Bird of the Snow; and second, they are entitled to receive a full allowance of food stamps and cash assistance for Little Bird of the Snow without providing a Social Security number for her.

As the Court holds in Part II of its opinion, which I join, the first claim must fail because the Free Exercise Clause does not give an individual the right to dictate the Government's method of recordkeeping. The second claim, I submit, is either moot or not ripe for decision.

I

In order to understand the precise nature and current posture of appellees' claims, it is necessary to emphasize an extremely unusual feature of this case. At the outset of the litigation, the parties assumed—indeed, they stipulated to—a critical fact that was discovered to be inaccurate on the last day of the trial. Although the parties believed that Little Bird of the Snow did not have a Social Security number, the District Court found, and the parties now agree, that she has had a Social Security number since birth. The contrary belief had been central to the parties' perception of the litigation, and to the requested relief. It is thus also central to the state of the record as we find it.

At the state agency administrative hearing on the threatened withdrawal of certain benefits, the issue had been framed as whether to affirm a decision "determining the appellant's daughter, Little Bird of the Snow, ineligible for public assistance and Medical Assistance because the appellant would not apply for a Social Security Number for her." In their complaint, Little Bird's parents alleged that "[t]he sole basis" for the denial of welfare benefits was "Mr. Roy's refusal to obtain a Social Security Number for Little Bird of the Snow" and thus requested injunctive relief, damages, and benefits. In the statement of "undisputed facts," the parties stipulated that Little Bird of the Snow did not have a Social Security number. In the District Court's opinion denying summary judgment, the Court began its opinion by observing that Roy and Miller "have refused to obtain a Social Security number for their 2-year-old daughter, Little Bird of the Snow, on the ground that doing so would be contrary to their Native Abenaki Indian religious beliefs." At trial, Roy's counsel introduced his case by emphasizing that Little Bird of the Snow, unlike the other members of the family, did not have a Social Security number and thus had not been exposed to the evil that the number represents. In Roy's own testimony, he emphasized the evil that would follow from *obtaining* a number. On the last day of trial, however, in response to questions, a federal official inquired, during a court recess, whether Little Bird of the Snow already had a Social Security number and discovered that she had been assigned a Social Security number at birth.

This discovery had a dramatic impact on the litigation, and on the judgment under review. Because there was no longer any apparent basis for the dispute, the Government suggested that the case had become moot. Roy, however, responded to the discovery by changing his request for relief and asking for a cancellation of the existing number.

Concluding that the discovery did not moot the case, the District Court denied the request for damages and benefits, but granted injunctive relief. The injunction—the judgment that we are considering—contains two basic components. First, the Secretary of Health and Human Services is "permanently restrained from making any use of the social security number which was issued in the name Little Bird of the Snow Roy and from disseminating the number to any agency, individual, business entity, or any other third party." Second, the federal and state defendants are enjoined until Little Bird of the Snow's 16th birthday from denying Roy cash assistance, medical assistance, and food stamps "because of the Plaintiffs' refusal to provide a social security number for her." Of course, if the injunction preventing the Secretary from making use of the already existing number had not been granted, there would have been no apparent impediment to providing the benefits that had previously been denied.

As the case comes to us, the first question to be decided is whether the District Court erred in effectively canceling the number that had already been issued for Little Bird of the Snow and that established the appellees' eligibility for the benefits in dispute. The Court correctly holds that the District Court did err and that "the portion of the District Court's injunction that permanently restrained the Secretary from making any use of the Social Security number that had been issued in the name of Little Bird of the Snow Roy must be vacated." Having so held, however, the Court should pause to consider whether any other constitutional issue need be addressed. For, as the Court demonstrates, an objection to the Government's use of a Social Security number, and a possible objection to "providing" the number when the Government already has it, pose very different constitutional problems.

II

Once we vacate the injunction preventing the Government from making routine use of the number that has already been assigned to Little Bird of the Snow, there is nothing disclosed by the record to prevent the appellees from receiving the payments that are in dispute. Indeed, since the Government itself suggested to the District Court that the case had become moot as soon as it was learned that a Social Security number already existed, it is obvious that the Government perceives no difficulty in making the requested payments in the future. The only issue that prevented the case from becoming moot was the claim asserted by Roy that he was entitled to an in-

junction that effectively canceled the existing number. Since that issue has now been resolved, nothing remains of the case.

Neither Roy nor the Government has pointed to anything in the record suggesting that Roy will be under any further obligation to "provide" a Social Security number for Little Bird of the Snow. Even if one makes the unsupported assumption that Roy may object to filing certain forms in the future, there is a conspicuous lack of evidence and findings concerning the extent to which such requirements might impose a burden either on Roy, or on any other person who finds difficulty in providing information on pertinent forms.

The absence of this information in the record is significant. Current regulations suggest that assistance for such difficulties may well be available in the programs at issue, particularly for those with mental, physical, and linguistic handicaps that prevent completion of the required forms, or other required steps in the application process. To the extent that other food stamp and welfare applicants are, in fact, offered exceptions and special assistance in response to their inability to "provide" required information, it would seem that a religious inability should be given no less deference. For our recent free exercise cases suggest that religious claims should not be disadvantaged in relation to other claims.

These considerations highlight the fact that, if this case is not moot, it surely is not ripe. The case, as litigated, simply bears no resemblance to the currently abstract question about what the Government may require if it seeks a Social Security number that it already has.

Consistent with our longstanding principles of constitutional adjudication, we should decide nothing more than is actually necessary to dispose of the precise dispute before the Court, and nothing more than is fairly presented by the record and the factual findings. Because the District Court has not made findings about the extent to which other exceptions and assistance are available for those who cannot, or do not, "provide" required information, and because there is nothing in the record to suggest that the Government will not pay the benefits in dispute as soon as the District Court's injunction against the use of the number has been vacated, I concur in the judgment vacating the remainder of the injunction. No matter how interesting, or how clear their answers may appear to be, however, I would not address the hypothetical questions debated by *The CHIEF JUSTICE* and *Justice O'CONNOR* because they are not properly presented by the record in this case.

Justice O'CONNOR, with whom *Justice BRENNAN* and *Justice MARSHALL* join, concurring in part and dissenting in part.

I join Parts I and II of *The CHIEF JUSTICE's* opinion and I would vacate only a portion of the injunction issued by the District Court.

I

I believe that appellees cannot pursue their free exercise claim based solely on the actions of the Government with respect to the use of a Social Security number already in its possession, or with respect to any other identification number the Government may wish to assign and use in connection with its administration of its welfare assistance program. Accordingly, I join parts I and II of *The CHIEF JUSTICE's* opinion, and I would vacate that portion of the District Court's judgment that enjoins the Government from using or disseminating the Social Security number already assigned to Little Bird of the Snow.

In all, eight members of the Court believe that the District Court's injunction was overbroad in preventing the Government from using information already in its possession.

A logical next step on the facts of this case is to consider whether the case is moot. Only two members of the Court believe that the case is, or may be, moot. I agree with *The CHIEF JUSTICE*, that the case is not moot.

The District Court enjoined the Government not only from disseminating or using the Social Security number already in its possession, but "from denying Plaintiff Roy cash assistance and medical assistance benefits for Little Bird of the Snow for the Plaintiffs' failure to provide a Social Security number for her." Because of this portion of the District Court's injunction, we continue to have before us a live case or controversy. Mr. Roy sought in part an injunction that "restrai[ns the Government] from denying cash assistance and medical assistance to Little Bird of the Snow for failure to provide a Social Security Number." The District Court granted that relief. The Government still refuses to concede that it should now provide welfare benefits to Little Bird of the Snow, even though it now claims to possess Little Bird of the Snow's Social Security number, and even though the Solicitor General has been "advised by the Social Security Administration that the agency itself assigns [Social Security numbers] to persons who are required by federal law to have one but decline to complete an application." Because the Government contests the District Court's decision that the Government may not deny welfare benefits to Little Bird of the Snow despite its acknowledgement of appellees' sincere religious objections, Mr. Roy may properly press his suit. Although the Government properly challenges part of the District Court's injunction as overbroad, it seeks to overturn the rest of the injunction only on the grounds that the District Court improperly applied the substantive standards of the First Amendment.

II

Given that a majority of the Court believes that the Government may use and disseminate information already in its possession, and given that the case is not moot, there is probably less remaining in this case than meets the eye. The interest asserted by the Government before the District Court could be wholly served after accommodating appellee's sincere religious beliefs, and the interests remaining after vacating the overbroad portion of the injunction are certainly no more difficult to pursue.

The Government has identified its goal as preventing fraud and abuse in the welfare system, a goal that is both laudable and compelling. The District Court, however, soundly rejected the Government's assertion that provision of the Social Security number was necessary to prevent such fraud and abuse. Among the means for which the Social Security number is used to reduce such fraud is "cross-matching," in which various computerized lists are compared with the welfare rolls to detect unreported income, individuals claimed as part of more than one household, and other fraudulent practices. As now appears the Government not only has the Social Security number it wants for Little Bird of the Snow, but it can also use it. But even under the erroneous assumption of the District Court that no such number was available for use, that court found as a fact that, while cross-matching is "more difficult" without Social Security numbers, "[t]he file on a particular benefit recipient can be identified and cross-matching performed, if the recipient's full name, date of birth, and parents' names are entered into the computerized systems." The District Court's generalized evaluation of the asserted indispensability of the Social Security number similarly undermines the Government's claim here: "*The government's interest* in preventing Little Bird of the Snow from fraudulently receiving welfare benefits *can be satisfied without requiring a Social Security number* for Little Bird of the Snow." (emphasis added).

Faced with these facts, however, *The CHIEF JUSTICE* not only believes appellees themselves must provide a Social Security number to the Government before receiving benefits, but he also finds it necessary to invoke a new standard to be applied to test the validity of government regulations under the Free Exercise Clause. He would uphold any facially neutral and uniformly applicable governmental requirement if the Government shows its rule to be "a reasonable means of promoting a legitimate public interest." Such a test has no basis in precedent and relegates a serious First Amendment value to the barest level of minimal scrutiny that the Equal Protection Clause already provides. I would apply our long line of precedents to hold that the Government must accommodate a legitimate free exercise claim unless pursuing an especially important interest by narrowly tailored means.

This Court has stated: "Where the state conditions receipt of an important benefit upon conduct proscribed by a religious faith, or where it denies such a benefit because of conduct mandated by religious belief, thereby putting substantial pressure on an adherent to modify his behavior and to violate his beliefs, a burden upon religion exists." *Thomas* v. *Review Board of Indiana Employment Security Division*. Indeed, *The CHIEF JUSTICE* appears to acknowledge at least that the law at issue here involves governmental compulsion. ("We do not believe that no government compulsion is involved"). The Free Exercise Clause is therefore clearly implicated in this case.

Once it has been shown that a governmental regulation burdens the free exercise of religion, "only those interests of the highest order and those not otherwise served can overbalance legitimate claims to the free exercise of religion." *Wisconsin* v. *Yoder*. This Court has consistently asked the Government to demonstrate that unbending application of its regulation to the religious objector "is essential to accomplish an overriding governmental interest," *United States* v. *Lee*, or represents "the least restrictive means of achieving some compelling state interest," *Thomas* v. *Review Board*. Only an especially important governmental interest pursued by narrowly tailored means can justify exacting a sacrifice of First Amendment freedoms as the price for an equal share of the rights, benefits, and privileges enjoyed by other citizens.

Granting an exemption to Little Bird of the Snow, and to the handful of others who can be expected to make a similar religious objection to providing the Social Security number in conjunction with the receipt of welfare benefits, will not demonstrably diminish the Government's ability to combat welfare fraud. The District Court found that the governmental appellants had hardly shown that a significant number of other individuals were likely to make a claim similar to that at issue here: "There have been four reported cases involving challenges to the Social Security number requirement for welfare benefits based upon the contention that the number violates sincerely held religious beliefs of the welfare recipient." The danger that a religious exemption would invite or encourage fraudulent applications seeking to avoid cross-matching performed with the use of Social Security numbers is remote on the facts as found by the District Court: few would-be lawbreakers would risk arousing suspicion by requesting an exemption granted only to a very few. And the sincerity of the appellees' religious beliefs is here undisputed. There is therefore no reason to believe that our previous standard for determining whether the Government must accommodate a free exercise claim does not apply.

Bob Jones University v. *United States* does not support *The CHIEF JUSTICE's* analysis. The Court states in that case: "The governmental interest at stake here is compelling. . . . [T]he Government has a fundamental, overriding interest in eradicating racial discrimination in education—discrimination that prevailed, with official approval, for the first 165 years of this Nation's constitutional history. That governmental interest substantially outweighs whatever burden denial of tax benefits places on petitioners' exercise of their religious beliefs. The interests asserted by petitioners cannot be accommodated with that compelling governmental interest, see *United States* v. *Lee*, and no 'less restrictive means,' see *Thomas* v. *Review Board of Indiana Employment Security Div.*, are available to achieve the governmental interest." See also *id.*, (" 'The State may justify a limitation on religious liberty by showing that it is *essential* to accomplish an *overriding* governmental interest' ") (emphasis added) (quoting *United States* v. *Lee*). It is clear that the Court in *Bob Jones University* did not adopt anything like the legitimate interest/rational means test propounded by *The CHIEF JUSTICE*, but rather continued to require the Government to show pursuit of an especially important interest by narrowly tailored means. In addition, the interest that the Court in *Bob Jones University* balanced against asserted religious interests was not merely a compelling governmental interest but a *constitutional* interest. Here, although prevention of welfare fraud is concededly a compelling interest, the Government asserts only administrative efficiency as its reason for refusing to exempt appellees from furnishing the Social Security number. The District Court found that assertion sorely wanting, and our conclusion that part of the resulting injunction was overbroad only makes the Government's assertion less plausible. Surely the fact that the Court was willing in *Bob Jones University* to give overriding weight to the government's interest in eradicating the scourge of racial discrimination does not mean that the Court must also give overriding weight to the unanchored anxieties of the welfare bureaucracy.

Hamilton v. *Regents of the University of California* also fails to support *The CHIEF JUSTICE's* construction of a new test. When the Court decided *Hamilton*, it had not yet applied, and did not in *Hamilton* apply, the Free Exercise Clause to actions of the States. The Court's discussion in *Hamilton* of the state university's decision to require military training is therefore limited to a generalized analysis under the Fourteenth Amendment of whether the state's policy deprived the would-be students of "life, liberty, or property." The Court concluded that no such deprivation was involved when the state "ha[d] not drafted or called [the individuals] to . . . war."

This Court's opinions have never turned on so slender a reed as whether the challenged requirement is merely a "reasonable means of promoting a legitimate public interest." *The CHIEF JUSTICE* appears to believe that the added inconvenience to the State of administering a selective exemption overbalances any burden on individual religious exercise. But this Court has held that administrative inconvenience is not alone sufficient to justify a burden of free exercise unless it creates problems of substantial magnitude. See *Sherbert* v. *Verner*. And as Part II of *The CHIEF JUSTICE's* opinion makes clear, there is essentially no administrative burden imposed on the Government in this case.

Appellants have rested their case on vague allegations of administrative inconvenience and harm to the public fisc that are wholly unsubstantiated by the record and the findings of the District Court. The Court simply cannot, consistent with its precedents, distinguish this case from the wide variety of factual situations in which the Free Exercise Clause indisputably imposes significant constraints upon government. Indeed, five members of the Court agree that *Sherbert* and *Thomas*, in which the Government was required to accommodate sincere religious beliefs, control the outcome of this case to the extent it is not moot.

The CHIEF JUSTICE's distinction between this case and the Court's previous decisions on free exercise claims—that here "it is appellees who seek benefits from the Government and who assert that . . . they should be excused from compliance with a condition that is binding on all other persons who seek the same benefits from the Government," has been directly rejected. The fact that the underlying dispute involves an award of benefits rather than an exaction of penalties does not grant the Government license to apply a different version of the Constitution: "[Welfare] benefits are a matter of statutory entitlement for persons qualified to receive them. Their termination involves state action that adjudicates important rights. The constitutional challenge cannot be answered by an argument that public assistance benefits are 'a "privilege" and not a "right." ' *Shapiro* v. *Thompson*. Relevant constitutional restraints apply as much to the withdrawal of public assistance benefits as to disqualification for unemployment compensation, *Sherbert* v. *Verner*". *Goldberg* v. *Kelly*. See also *Sherbert* v. *Verner*, ("It is too late in the day to doubt that the liberties of religion and expression may be infringed by the denial of or placing of conditions upon a benefit or privilege"). The fact that appellees seek exemption from a precondition that the Government attaches to an award of benefits does not, therefore, generate a meaningful distinction between this case and one where appellees seek an exemption from the Government's imposition of penalties upon them. Even if the Founding Fathers did not live in a society with the "broad range of benefits [and] complex programs" that the Federal Government administers today, they constructed a society in which the Constitution placed express limits upon governmental

actions limiting the freedoms of that society's members. The rise of the welfare state was not the fall of the Free Exercise Clause.

Our precedents have long required the Government to show that a compelling state interest is served by its refusal to grant a religious exemption. The Government here has clearly and easily met its burden of showing that the prevention of welfare fraud is a compelling governmental goal. If the Government could meet its compelling needs only by refusing to grant a religious exemption, and chose a narrowly tailored means to do so, then the Government would prevail. But the Government has failed to show that granting a religious exemption to those who legitimately object to providing a Social Security number will do any harm to its compelling interest in preventing welfare fraud.

I would merely vacate that portion of the injunction issued by the District Court that enjoins the Government from using or disseminating the Social Security number already in its possession.

Justice WHITE, dissenting.

Being of the view that *Thomas* v. *Review Board*, and *Sherbert* v. *Verner*, control this case, I cannot join the Court's opinion and judgment.

FREE EXERCISE AND PUBLIC EDUCATION

In the landmark *Brown* v. *Board of Education* school desegregation decision, Chief Justice Warren wrote for a unanimous Court, "Today education is perhaps the most important function of state and local governments." There is no doubt that in pursuance of this function states may enact and enforce compulsory attendance statutes mandating attendance at public or private schools within designated ages.

The compulsory school attendance laws of Wisconsin required children in that state to attend school until they reached age sixteen. Notwithstanding the requirement, the fourteen- and fifteen-year-old children of Jonas Yoder, Wallace Miller, and Adin Yutzy were not enrolled in school, and their parents were convicted of violating the law and fined a nominal amount. Their defense was that their sincerely held religious beliefs as members of the Old Order Amish and Conservative Amish Mennonite Church forbade their sending the children to school past the eighth grade.

The religious group to which Jonas Yoder and his fellow religionists belonged was not one of the new and exotic "cults" of the 1960s. Its history goes back to the sixteenth century, at which time there were many attempts to reform the Roman Catholic church—attempts which resulted in separate "Protestant" groups. The principal leaders of these groups were Martin Luther, Huldreich Zwingli, Henry VIII, and somewhat later, John Calvin. With the exception of the one initiated by Henry VIII, these attempts at reform were theological in nature, i.e., they tried to reform the church by calling it back to what the different reformers considered to be the New Testament form of Christianity.

However, another Protestant group also originated in the sixteenth century: the anabaptists emerged in 1525 after and because of their disagreements with Zwingli's reforms in Zurich, Switzerland. The Anabaptists were of the opinion that none of the earlier reformers had gone far enough in their break with Rome. Although the reformers had started in the right direction, they had not followed their own ideas to logical conclusions and consequently had not conformed their Christian lives and thought to the New Testament pattern. The Anabaptists attempted to be meticulously faithful to New Testament ideas and styles of faith and thus to take reformatory ideas to completion. Because of their attitudes, the Anabaptists have been labeled by historians as "the Radical Reformation" or "the Left Wing of the Reformation."

Basic to Anabaptist theology was the idea that the "world" was totally evil and corrupt and that their church was a community of saints. Consequently, the faithful should remain as distinct and separate from the world as possible. The Anabaptists demanded that should Christians from any other church want to join their group, they would have to be baptized into the community of saints in order to become separate from the world: believer's baptism by immersion. The saints considered this to be the only true baptism, but their opponents, all of whom believed in infant baptism, believed it was unnecessary rebaptism. Thus the origin of their name: "Anabaptist" means "rebaptizer," a name of derision given them by their detractors.

One of the problems with other churches, including the Protestant movements, was that they were willing to be state churches, thus bringing the church and the world into close contact. The Anabaptists insisted that there should be a separation of church and state, a principle which made them unique in the sixteenth century.

Although not the founder of the movement, Menno Simons, a converted Roman Catholic priest, became the leader of the nonviolent Dutch Anabaptists. Because he exerted such influential leadership the Dutch Anabaptists came to be called "Mennonites."

In order to maintain congregational discipline and personal sainthood, the Mennonites practiced both excommunication, or the "ban," and "shunning." If a member should fail to maintain the strictly righteous life or should violate the congregation's moral standards, that one would, after admonition, be excommunicated and subjected to social ostracism.

Near the end of the seventeenth century the Mennonite group began to lose momentum, partly because of persecution, partly because of acculturation. The rigorous moral discipline of the group began to decline, and the practice of shunning was infrequently exercised. In the 1690s a Swiss Mennonite lamented the decline in internal moral discipline and sought to revive it. Jakob Ammann led a portion of the Mennonites, chiefly in Alsace, in a revival of the old ways, i.e., a reassertion of the ideal of the church as a highly disciplined community of saints, maintained by the practices of excommunication and shunning. This group, called the Amish after Jakob Ammann, has survived as the strictest of all the Mennonite groups, particularly that branch called the Old Order Amish.

Coming to this country as early as 1727, primarily to escape persecution in Europe, the Amish settled in America throughout the eighteenth and the first quarter of the nineteenth centuries. Only in North America have the name and the distinctive theology and practices of the Amish survived. A principal feature of the group has been adherence to custom and extreme reluctance to change; consequently, the Old Order Amish continue to be a virtual carbon copy of their seventeenth-century conservative forebears. Like their ancestors, contemporary Amish have two favorite passages of Scripture: Romans 12:2, "Do not be conformed to this world, but be transformed by the renewal of your mind, that you may prove what is the will of God, what is good and acceptable and perfect" (RSV), and 2 Corinthians 6:14: "Do not be unequally yoked together with unbelievers; for what fellowship does righteousness have with unrighteousness? and what communion does light have with darkness?" (RSV) These passages mean to the Amish that they should not be like other people in the world, and they have striven mightily to maintain their distinctiveness and individuality.

In order to maintain their character as a community of saints in the midst of a pagan world, the Amish have adopted a distinctive life style which self-consciously sets them apart from the rest of the world. The life style is comprehensive, ranging from unique dress and language to avoidance of modern conveniences.

The Amish recognize the need for a basic elementary education even in their simple agricultural pursuits, and do not object to their children attending school through the eighth grade. But to send their children beyond this level of formal education would expose them to ideas and attitudes that are incompatible with the Amish faith and way of life. Thus, they have chosen to limit their children's formal education in order to avoid the corruption which would inevitably come from massive exposure to the thinking of the outside world. The Amish claim they have the right to do so as one of their constitutionally guaranteed religious rights, overruling any state's compulsory school attendance law. [1]

It is interesting that the Amish did not themselves initiate the litigation discussed here. Given their attitudes toward education, they obviously had no college graduates or lawyers of their own. In addition, Amish efforts to avoid contact with the corrupting world have meant that they have traditionally participated in the civil processes, including the judicial, as little as possible. The *Yoder* litigation was initiated by people who were concerned for the right of the Amish to maintain their religious attitudes and life style. The proceedings were supported by an organization called the National Committee for Amish Religious Freedom which solicited funds from the public to finance the proper forwarding of the case. The case for the Amish was argued before the Supreme Court by William B. Ball, a Roman Catholic.

---

[1] The excellent studies of the history and culture of the Amish are Willaim R. Estep, *The Anabaptist Story*, rev. ed.,(Grand Rapids, Mich: Wm. B. Eerdmans Publishing Co., 1975); Franklin H. Littell, *The Origins of Sectarian Protestantism: A Study of the Anabaptist View of the Church* (New York: The Macmillan Co., 1964) and John A. Hostetler, *Amish Society*, 3d. ed. (Baltimore: The Johns Hopkins Press, 1980).

Writing for a unanimous Court (Justice Douglas dissented in part), Chief Justice Burger used the "compelling state interest—no alternative means" applied first for the protection of religious rights in SHERBERT v. VERNER (p. 145) and BRAUNFELD v. BROWN (p. 316) to uphold the claims of Yoder and the other parents that enforcement of Wisconsin's school attendance law against the Amish abridged their free exercise of religion. He said:

> The essence of all that has been said and written on the subject is that only those interests of the highest order and those not otherwise served can overbalance legitimate claims to the free exercise of religion. We can accept it as settled, therefore, that, however strong the State's interest in universal compulsory education, it is by no means absolute to the exclusion or subordination of all other interests. (406 U.S. 205, 215)

The Chief Justice emphasized the long and honorable history of the Amish and spoke approvingly of their "qualities of reliability, self reliance, and dedication to work." He made it clear both that the Court did not wish to become a school board or legislative body and that the Court's holding was limited to the self-sufficient Amish who would look after their own.

Justice Douglas dissented "in part" because he felt that the Court had considered only the religious rights of the parents. Only one child had been queried by the Wisconsin courts as to her views toward high school education. Because "children themselves have constitutionally protectible interests," all of the children should be heard to ascertain their preferences with respect to additional education, without which their lives might be "stunted and deformed." Justice Douglas also complained that the Chief Justice's emphasis on the "law and order" record of the Amish was quite irrelevant. "A religion is a religion," he said, "irrespective of what the misdemeanor or felony records of its members might be."

With few exceptions, cases involving religion and education which have been decided by the Supreme Court have related, as *Yoder*, to problems in elementary and secondary schools. In 1981 the Court was confronted with a difficult question at the university level.

As has been noted frequently, the religion clauses of the First Amendment often conflict with rather than complement one another. In COMMITTEE FOR PUBLIC EDUCATION AND RELIGIOUS LIBERTY v. NYQUIST (p. 504), the Supreme Court itself recognized that "it may often not be possible to promote free exercise without intruding on establishment." The inevitable tension between the clauses often necessitates a balancing of constitutional rights and limitations.

To add further to the Court's dilemma, sometimes as in WIDMAR v. VINCENT (p. 210) a third freedom—in this instance free speech—becomes involved. In 1972, the Board of Curators of the University of Missouri at Kansas City adopted a resolution forbidding the use of campus facilities "for purposes of religious worship or religious teaching by either student or nonstudent groups." The Board maintained that such regulation was mandated by the establishment clauses of both the United States and Missouri Constitutions. On the basis of this regulation, Cornerstone, an organization of active Christian students,

was denied permission to hold group Bible studies in university facilities. This denial came four years after the group had begun holding such meetings with permission from university authorities.

To members of Cornerstone, this denial represented not a defense of the Establishment Clause but rather a violation of their right to free exercise of religion. Eleven student members brought suit challenging the regulation in federal district court. That court found the regulation not only justifiable but required by the Establishment Clause of the First Amendment. This decision was subsequently reversed by a court of appeals which ruled that the state's interest in achieving the extreme degree of separation sought was not sufficiently compelling to justify "content-based" discrimination against the religious speech of the Cornerstone members.

On appeal to the Supreme Court, Justice Powell wrote the opinion for seven members of the Court. Justice Stevens concurred in the judgment; Justice White dissented alone. The majority opinion stated flatly: "Here the UMKC has discriminated against student groups and speakers based on their desire to use a generally open forum to engage in religious worship and discussion." (454 U.S. 263, 268) As the Court viewed the case, the question was whether the university could exclude a group because of the content of their speech when there was no reason to believe that the "primary effect of the public forum would be to advance religion" or to "confer any imprimatur of state approval on religious sects or practices." The Court found that the university could not so discriminate against religious activity and discussion by enforcing a "content-based exclusion of religious speech." In this instance the need for protection of free exercise of religion and freedom of speech outweighed the university's concept of the demands of the Establishment Clause.

Only one week later the Court made clear, in *Brandon v. Board of Education of Guilderland School District*, that it was not prepared to extend the *Widmar* ruling to public high school campuses. The school board at Guilderland High School near Albany, New York, denied permission to a group called Students for Voluntary Prayer to meet each day before classes in an unused classroom. The school board's action was upheld by the Second U.S. Circuit Court of Appeals; and the Supreme Court, without comment, left that ruling intact. The effect of the two decisions was to emphasize that the Court still adhered to the distinction that it first drew in 1971 in TILTON v. RICHARDSON (p. 498) between public colleges and universities on the one hand and elementary and secondary schools on the other when it upheld a federal construction grant to a church-related college that would undoubtedly have been struck down if made to a lower level school. As will be seen in Chapter 4, the Court in 1986 in BENDER v. WILLIAMSPORT (p. 270), by the narrowest possible vote, again avoided ruling on the merits of the "equal access" question, this time by use of the standing rule.

WISCONSIN v. YODER

406 U.S. 205
ON CERTIORARI TO THE SUPREME COURT
OF WISCONSIN
Argued December 8, 1971 — Decided May 15, 1972

⊥207   ⊥ *Mr. Chief Justice BURGER* delivered the opinion of the Court.

On petition of the State of Wisconsin, we granted the writ of certiorari in this case to review a decision of the Wisconsin Supreme Court holding that respondents' convictions of violating the State's compulsory school-attendance law were invalid under the Free Exercise Clause of the First Amendment to the United States Constitution made applicable to the States by the Fourteenth Amendment. For the reasons hereafter stated we affirm the judgment of the Supreme Court of Wisconsin.

Respondents Jonas Yoder and Wallace Miller are members of the Old Order Amish religion, and respondent Adin Yutzy is a member of the Conservative Amish Mennonite Church. They and their families are residents of Green County, Wisconsin. Wisconsin's compulsory school-attendance law required them to cause their children to attend public or private school until reaching age 16 but the respondents declined to send their children, ages 14 and 15, to public school after they completed the eighth grade. The children were not enrolled in any private school, or within any recognized exception to the compulsory-attendance law, and they are conceded to be subject to the Wisconsin statute.

⊥208   ⊥On complaint of the school district administrator for the public schools, respondents were charged, tried, and convicted of violating the compulsory-attendance law in Green County Court and were fined the sum of $5 each. Respondents de-
⊥209   fended on the ground that the applica⊥tion of the compulsory-attendance law violated their rights under the First and Fourteenth Amendments. The trial testimony showed that respondents believed, in accordance with the tenets of Old Order Amish communities generally, that their children's attendance at high school, public or private, was contrary to the Amish religion and way of life. They believed that by sending their children to high school, they would not only expose themselves to the danger of the censure of the church community, but, as found by the county court, also endanger their own salvation and that of their children. The State stipulated that respondent's religious beliefs were sincere.

In support of their position, respondents presented as expert witnesses scholars on religion and education whose testimony is uncontradicted. They expressed their opinions on the relationship of the Amish belief concerning school attendance to the more general tenets of their religion, and described the impact that compulsory high school attendance could have on the continued survival of Amish com-

munities as they exist in the United States today. The history of the Amish ⊥ sect was given in some ⊥210 detail, beginning with the Swiss Anabaptists of the 16th century who rejected institutionalized churches and sought to return to the early, simple, Christian life de-emphasizing material success, rejecting the competitive spirit, and seeking to insulate themselves from the modern world. As a result of their common heritage, Old Order Amish communities today are characterized by a fundamental belief that salvation requires life in a church community separate and apart from the world and worldly influence. This concept of life aloof from the world and its values is central to their faith.

A related feature of Old Order Amish communities is their devotion to a life in harmony with nature and the soil, as exemplified by the simple life of the early Christian era that continued in America during much of our early national life. Amish beliefs require members of the community to make their living by farming or closely related activities. Broadly speaking, the Old Order Amish religion pervades and determines the entire mode of life of its adherents. Their conduct is regulated in great detail by the *Ordnung*, or rules, of the church community. Adult baptism, which occurs in late adolescence, is the time at which Amish young people voluntarily undertake heavy obligations, not unlike the Bar Mitzvah of the Jews, to abide by the rules of the church community.

Amish objection to formal education beyond the eighth grade is firmly grounded in these central religious concepts. They object to the high school, and higher education generally, because the values they teach ⊥ are in marked variance with Amish values ⊥211 and the Amish way of life; they view secondary school education as an impermissible exposure of their children to a "worldly" influence in conflict with their beliefs. The high school tends to emphasize intellectual and scientific accomplishments, self-distinction, competitiveness, wordly success, and social life with other students. Amish society emphasizes informal learning-through-doing; a life of "goodness," rather than a life of intellect; wisdom, rather than technical knowledge; community welfare, rather than competition; and separation from, rather than integration with, contemporary worldly society.

Formal high school education beyond the eighth grade is contrary to Amish beliefs, not only because it places Amish children in an environment hostile to Amish beliefs with increasing emphasis on competition in class work and sports and with pressure to conform to the styles, manners, and ways of the peer group, but also because it takes them away from their community, physically and emotionally, during the crucial and formative adolescent period of life. During this period, the children must acquire Amish attitudes favoring manual work and self-reliance and the specific skills needed to perform the adult role of an Amish farmer or housewife. They must learn to enjoy physical labor. Once a child has learned basic reading, writing, and elementary mathematics, these traits, skills, and attitudes admittedly fall within the category of those best learned through example and "doing" rather than in a classroom. And, at this time in life, the Amish child must also grow in his faith and his relationship to the Amish community if he is to be prepared to accept the heavy obligations imposed by adult baptism. In short, high school attendance with teachers who are not of the Amish faith—and may even be hostile to it—interposes a serious barrier to the integration of the Amish child ⊥ into the Amish religious community. Dr. John Hostetler, one of the experts on Amish society, testified that the modern high school is not equipped, in curriculum or social environment, to impart the values promoted by Amish society.

⊥212

The Amish do not object to elementary education through the first eight grades as a general proposition because they agree that their children must have basic skills in the "three R's" in order to read the Bible, to be good farmers and citizens, and to be able to deal with non-Amish people when necessary in the course of daily affairs. They view such a basic education as acceptable because it does not significantly expose their children to wordly values or interfere with their development in the Amish community during the crucial adolescent period. While Amish accept compulsory elementary education generally, wherever possible they have established their own elementary schools in many respects like the small local schools of the past. In the Amish belief higher learning tends to develop values they reject as influences that alienate man from God.

On the basis of such considerations Dr. Hostetler testified that compulsory high school attendance could not only result in great psychological harm to Amish children, because of the conflicts it would produce, but would also, in his opinion, ultimately result in the destruction of the Old Order Amish church community as it exists in the United States today. The testimony of Dr. Donald A. Erickson, an expert witness on education, also showed that the Amish succeed in preparing their high school age children to be productive members of the Amish community. He described their system of learning through doing the skills directly relevant to their adult roles in the Amish community as "ideal" and perhaps superior to ordinary high school education. The evidence also showed that the Amish have an excellent ⊥ record as lawabiding and generally self-sufficient members of society.

⊥213

Although the trial court in its careful findings determined that the Wisconsin compulsory school-attendance law "does interfere with the freedom of the Defendants to act in accordance with their sincere religious belief" it also concluded that the requirement of high school attendance until age 16 was a "reasonable and constitutional" exercise of governmental power, and therefore denied the motion to dismiss the charges. The Wisconsin Circuit Court af-

firmed the convictions. The Wisconsin Supreme Court, however, sustained respondents' claim under the Free Exercise Clause of the First Amendment and reversed the convictions. A majority of the court was of the opinion that the State had failed to make an adequate showing that its interest in "establishing and maintaining an educational system overrides the defendants' right to the free exercise of their religion."

I

There is no doubt as to the power of a State, having a high responsibility for education of its citizens, to impose reasonable regulations for the control and duration of basic education. Providing public schools ranks at the very apex of the function of a State. Yet even this paramount responsibility was, in *Pierce*, made to yield to the right of parents to provide an equivalent education in a privately operated system. There the Court held that Oregon's statute compelling attendance in a public school from age eight to age 16 unreasonably interfered with the interest of parents in directing the rearing of their offspring, including their education in church-operated schools. As that case suggests, the values of parental direction of the religious upbringing ⊥ and education of their children in their early and formative years have a high place in our society. Thus, a State's interest in universal education, however highly we rank it, is not totally free from a balancing process when it impinges on fundamental rights and interests, such as those specifically protected by the Free Exercise Clause of the First Amendment, and the traditional interest of parents with respect to the religious upbringing of their children so long as they, in the words of *Pierce*, "prepare [them] for additional obligations."

⊥214

It follows that in order for Wisconsin to compel school attendance beyond the eighth grade against a claim that such attendance interferes with the practice of a legitimate religious belief, it must appear either that the State does not deny the free exercise of religious belief by its requirement, or that there is a state interest of sufficient magnitude to override the interest claiming protection under the Free Exercise Clause. Long before there was general acknowledgment of the need for universal formal education, the Religion Clauses had specifically and firmly fixed the right to free exercise of religious beliefs, and buttressing this fundamental right was an equally firm, even if less explicit, prohibition against the establishment of any religion by government. The values underlying these two provisions relating to religion have been zealously protected, sometimes even at the expense of other interests of admittedly high social importance. The invalidation of financial aid to parochial schools by government grants for a salary subsidy for teachers is but one example of the extent to which courts have gone in this regard, notwithstanding that such aid programs were legislatively determined to be in the public interest and the service of sound educational policy by States and by Congress.

⌐215   ⊥ The essence of all that has been said and written on the subject is that only those interests of the highest order and those not otherwise served can overbalance legitimate claims to the free exercise of religion. We can accept it as settled, therefore, that, however strong the State's interest in universal compulsory education, it is by no means absolute to the exclusion or subordination of all other interests.

II

We come then to the quality of the claims of the respondents concerning the alleged encroachment of Wisconsin's compulsory school-attendance statute on their rights and the rights of their children to the free exercise of the religious beliefs they and their forebears have adhered to for almost three centuries. In evaluating those claims we must be careful to determine whether the Amish religious faith and their mode of life are, as they claim, inseparable and interdependent. A way of life, however virtuous and admirable, may not be interposed as a barrier to reasonable state regulation of education if it is based on purely secular considerations; to have the protection of the Religion Clauses, the claims must be rooted in religious belief. Although a determination of what is "religious" belief or practice entitled to constitutional protection may present a most delicate question, the very concept of ordered liberty

⌐216   precludes ⊥ allowing every person to make his own standards on matters of conduct in which society as a whole has important interests. Thus, if the Amish asserted their claims because of their subjective evaluation and rejection of the contemporary secular values accepted by the majority, much as Thoreau rejected the social values of his time and isolated himself at Walden Pond, their claims would not rest on a religious basis. Thoreau's choice was philosophical and personal rather than religious, and such belief does not rise to the demands of the Religion Clauses.

Giving no weight to such secular considerations, however, we see that the record in this case abundantly supports the claim that the traditional way of life of the Amish is not merely a matter of personal preference, but one of deep religious conviction, shared by an organized group, and intimately related to daily living. That the Old Order Amish daily life and religious practice stem from their faith is shown by the fact that it is in response to their literal interpretation of the Biblical injunction from the Epistle of Paul to the Romans, "be not conformed to this world. . . ." This command is fundamental to the Amish faith. Moreover, for the Old Order Amish, religion is not simply a matter of theocratic belief. As the expert witnesses explained, the Old Order Amish religion pervades and determines virtually their entire way of life, regulating it with the detail of the

Talmudic diet through the strictly enforced rules of the church community.

The record shows that the respondents' religious beliefs and attitude toward life, family, and home have remained constant—perhaps some would say static—in a period of unparalleled progress in human knowledge generally and great changes in education. The re⊥spondents freely concede, and indeed assert   ⌐217 as an article of faith, that their religious beliefs and what we would today call "life style" have not altered in fundamentals for centuries. Their way of life in a church-oriented community, separated from the outside world and "worldly" influences, their attachment to nature and the soil, is a way inherently simple and uncomplicated, albeit difficult to preserve against the pressure to conform. Their rejection of telephones, automobiles, radios, and television, their mode of dress, of speech, their habits of manual work do indeed set them apart from much of contemporary society; these customs are both symbolic and practical.

As the society around the Amish has become more populous, urban, industrialized, and complex, particularly in this century, government regulation of human affairs has correspondingly become more detailed and pervasive. The Amish mode of life has thus come into conflict increasingly with requirements of contemporary society exerting a hydraulic insistence on conformity to majoritarian standards. So long as compulsory education laws were confined to eight grades of elementary basic education imparted in a nearby rural schoolhouse, with a large proportion of students of the Amish faith, the Old Order Amish had little basis to fear that school attendance would expose their children to the worldly influence they reject. But modern compulsory secondary education in rural areas is now largely carried on in a consolidated school, often remote from the student's home and alien to his daily home life. As the record so strongly shows, the values and programs of the modern secondary school are in sharp conflict with the fundamental mode of life mandated by the Amish religion; modern laws requiring compulsory secondary education have accordingly engendered great concern and conflict. ⊥ The conclusion   ⌐218 is inescapable that secondary schooling, by exposing Amish children to worldly influences in terms of attitudes, goals, and values contrary to beliefs, and by substantially intefering with the religious development of the Amish child and his integration into the way of life of the Amish faith community at the crucial adolescent stage of development, contravenes the basic religious tenets and practice of the Amish faith, both as to the parent and the child.

The impact of the compulsory-attendance law on respondents' practice of the Amish religion is not only severe, but inescapable, for the Wisconsin law affirmatively compels them, under threat of criminal sanction, to perform acts undeniably at odds with fundamental tenets of their religious beliefs. Nor is the impact of the compulsory-attendance law confined to grave interference with important Amish religious tenets from a subjective point of view. It carries with it precisely the kind of objective danger to the free exercise of religion that the First Amendment was designed to prevent. As the record shows, compulsory school attendance to age 16 for Amish children carries with it a very real threat of undermining the Amish community and religious practice as they exist today; they must either abandon belief and be assimilated into society at large, or be forced to migrate to some other and more tolerant region.

⊥219 ⊥ In sum, the unchallenged testimony of acknowledged experts in education and religious history, almost 300 years of consistent practice, and strong evidence of a sustained faith pervading and regulating respondents' entire mode of life support the claim that enforcement of the State's requirement of compulsory formal education after the eighth grade would gravely endanger if not destroy the free exercise of respondents' religious beliefs.

III

Neither the findings of the trial court nor the Amish claims as to the nature of their faith are challenged in this Court by the State of Wisconsin. Its position is that the State's interest in universal compulsory formal secondary education to age 16 is so great that it is paramount to the undisputed claims of respondents that their mode of preparing their youth for Amish life, after the traditional elementary education, is an essential part of their religious belief and practice. Nor does the State undertake to meet the claim that the Amish mode of life and education is inseparable from and a part of the basic tenets of their religion—indeed, as much a part of their religious belief and practices as baptism, the confessional, or a sabbath may be for others.

Wisconsin concedes that under the Religion Clauses religious beliefs are absolutely free from the State's control, but it argues that "actions," even though religiously grounded, are outside the protection of the First Amendment. But our decisions have ⊥220 rejected the idea that ⊥ religiously grounded conduct is always outside the protection of the Free Exercise Clause. It is true that activities of individuals, even when religiously based, are often subject to regulation by the States in the exercise of their undoubted power to promote the health, safety, and general welfare, or the Federal Government in the exercise of its delegated powers. But to agree that religiously grounded conduct must often be subject to the broad police power of the State is not to deny that there are areas of conduct protected by the Free Exercise Clause of the First Amendment and thus beyond the power of the State to control, even under regulations of general applicability. This case, therefore, does not become easier because respondents were convicted for their "actions" in refusing to send their children to the public high school; in this con-

text belief and action cannot be neatly confined in logic-tight compartments.

Nor can this case be disposed of on the grounds that Wisconsin's requirement for school attendance to age 16 applies uniformly to all citizens of the State and does not, on its face, discriminate against religions or a particular religion, or that it is motivated by legitimate secular concerns. A regulation neutral on its face may, in its application, nonetheless offend the constitutional requirement for governmental neutrality if it unduly burdens the free exercise of religion. The Court must not ignore the danger that an exception ⊥ from a general obliga- ⊥221 tion of citizenship on religious grounds may run afoul of the Establishment Clause, but that danger cannot be allowed to prevent any exception no matter how vital it may be to the protection of values promoted by the right of free exercise. . . .

We turn, then, to the State's broader contention that its interest in its system of compulsory education is so compelling that even the established religious practices of the Amish must give way. Where fundamental claims of religious freedom are at stake, however, we cannot accept such a sweeping claim; despite its admitted validity in the generality of cases, we must searchingly examine the interests that the State seeks to promote by its requirement for compulsory education to age 16, and the impediment to those objectives that would flow from recognizing the claimed Amish exemption.

The State advances two primary arguments in support of its system of compulsory education. It notes, as Thomas Jefferson pointed out early in our history, that some degree of education is necessary to prepare citizens to participate effectively and intelligently in our open political system if we are to preserve freedom and independence. Further, education prepares individuals to be self-reliant and self-sufficient participants in society. We accept these propositions.

⊥ However, the evidence adduced by the Amish in ⊥222 this case is persuasively to the effect that an additional one or two years of formal high school for Amish children in place of their long-established program of informal vocational education would do little to serve those interests. Respondents' experts testified at trial, without challenge, that the value of all education must be assessed in terms of its capacity to prepare the child for life. It is one thing to say that compulsory education for a year or two beyond the eighth grade may be necessary when its goal is the preparation of the child for life in modern society as the majority live, but it is quite another if the goal of education be viewed as the preparation of the child for life in the separated agrarian community that is the keystone of the Amish faith.

The State attacks respondents' position as one fostering "ignorance" from which the child must be protected by the State. No one can question the State's duty to protect children from ignorance but this argument does not square with the facts disclosed in the record. Whatever their idiosyncrasies as seen by the majority, this record strongly shows that the Amish community has been a highly successful social unit within our society, even if apart from the conventional "mainstream." Its members are productive and very law-abiding members of society; they reject public welfare in any of its usual modern forms. The Congress itself recognized their self-sufficiency by authorizing exemption of such groups as the Amish from the obligation to pay social security taxes.

⊥223   ⊥ It is neither fair nor correct to suggest that the Amish are opposed to education beyond the eighth grade level. What this record shows is that they are opposed to conventional formal education of the type provided by a certified high school because it comes at the child's crucial adolescent period of religious development. Dr. Donald Erickson, for example, testified that their system of learning-by-doing was an "ideal system" of education in terms of preparing Amish children for life as adults in the Amish community, and that "I would be inclined to say they do a better job in this than most of the rest of us do." As he put it, "These people aren't purporting to be learned people, and it seems to me the self-sufficiency of the community is the best evidence I can point to—whatever is being done seems to function well."

We must not forget that in the Middle Ages important values of the civilization of the Western World were preserved by members of religious orders who isolated themselves from all worldly influences against great obstacles. There can be no assumption
⊥224   that today's majority is ⊥ "right" and the Amish and others like them are "wrong." A way of life that is odd or even erratic but interferes with no rights or interests of others is not to be condemned because it is different.

The State, however, supports its interest in providing an additional one or two years of compulsory high school education to Amish children because of the possibility that some such children will choose to leave the Amish community, and that if this occurs they will be ill-equipped for life. The State argues that if Amish children leave their church they should not be in the position of making their way in the world without the education available in the one or two additional years the State requires. However, on this record, that argument is highly speculative. There is no specific evidence of the loss of Amish adherents by attrition, nor is there any showing that upon leaving the Amish community Amish children, with their practical agricultural training and habits of industry and self-reliance, would become burdens on society because of educational shortcomings. Indeed, this argument of the State appears to rest primarily on the State's mistaken assumption, already noted, that the Amish do not provide any education for their children beyond the eighth grade, but allow

them to grow in "ignorance." To the contrary, not only do the Amish accept the necessity for formal schooling through the eighth grade level, but continue to provide what has been characterized by the undisputed testimony of expert educators as an "ideal" vocational education for their children in the adolescent years.

There is nothing in this record to suggest that the Amish qualities of reliability, self-reliance, and dedication to work would fail to find ready markets in today's society. Absent some contrary evidence supporting the ⊥ State's position, we are unwilling to   ⊥225 assume that persons possessing such valuable vocational skills and habits are doomed to become burdens on society should they determine to leave the Amish faith, nor is there any basis in the record to warrant a finding that an additional one or two years of formal school education beyond the eighth grade would serve to eliminate any such problem that might exist.

Insofar as the State's claim rests on the view that a brief additional period of formal education is imperative to enable the Amish to participate effectively and intelligently in our democratic process, it must fall. The Amish alternative to formal secondary school education has enabled them to function effectively in their day-to-day life under self-imposed limitations on relations with the world, and to survive and prosper in contemporary society as a separate, sharply identifiable and highly self-sufficient community for more than 200 years in this country. In itself this is strong evidence that they are capable of fulfilling the social and political responsibilities of citizenship without compelled attendance beyond the eighth grade at the price of jeopardizing their free exercise of religious belief. When Thomas Jefferson emphasized the need for education as a bulwark of a free people against tyranny, there is nothing to indicate he had in mind compulsory education through any fixed age beyond a basic education. Indeed, the Amish communities singularly parallel and reflect many of the virtues of Jefferson's ideal of the "sturdy yeoman" who would form the basis of what he considered as the ⊥ ideal of a democratic society.   ⊥226 Even their idosyncratic separateness exemplifies the diversity we profess to admire and encourage.

The requirement for compulsory education beyond the eighth grade is a relatively recent development in our history. Less than 60 years ago, the educational requirements of almost all of the States were satisfied by completion of the elementary grades, at least where the child was regularly and lawfully employed. The inde⊥pendence and successful social func-   ⊥227 tioning of the Amish community for a period approaching almost three centuries and more than 200 years in this country are strong evidence that there is at best a speculative gain, in terms of meeting the duties of citizenship, from an additional one or two years of compulsory formal education. Against this background it would require a more particularized showing from the State on this point to justify the severe interference with religious freedom such additional compulsory attendance would entail.

We should also note that compulsory education and child labor laws find their historical origin in common humanitarian instincts, and that the age limits of both laws have been coordinated to achieve their related objectives. In the context of this case, such considera⊥tions, if anything, support rather than detract from respondents' position. The origins of the requirement for school attendance to age 16, an age falling after the completion of elementary school but before completion of high school, are not entirely clear. But to some extent such laws reflected the movement to prohibit most child labor under age 16 that culminated in the provisions of the Federal Fair Labor Standards Act of 1938. It is true, then, that the 16-year child labor age limit may to some degree derive from a contemporary impression that children should be in school until that age. But at the same time, it cannot be denied that, conversely, the 16-year education limit reflects, in substantial measure, the concern that children under that age not be employed under conditions hazardous to their health, or in work that should be performed by adults.

The requirement of compulsory schooling to age 16 must therefore be viewed as aimed not merely at providing educational opportunities for children, but as an alternative to the equally undesirable consequence of unhealthful child labor displacing adult workers, or, on the other hand, forced idleness. The two kinds of statutes—compulsory school attendance and child labor laws—tend to keep children of certain ages off the labor market and in school; this regimen in turn provides opportunity to prepare for a livelihood of a higher order than that which children could pursue without education and protects their health in adolescence.

In these terms, Wisconsin's interest in compelling the school attendance of Amish children to age 16 emerges as somewhat less substantial than requiring such attend⊥ance for children generally. For, while agricultural employment is not totally outside the legitimate concerns of the child labor laws, employment of children under parental guidance and on the family farm from age 14 to age 16 is an ancient tradition that lies at the periphery of the objectives of such laws. There is no intimation that the Amish employment of their children on family farms is in any way deleterious to their health or that Amish parents exploit children at tender years. Any such inference would be contrary to the record before us. Moreover, employment of Amish children on the family farm does not present the undesirable economic aspects of eliminating jobs that might otherwise be held by adults.

IV

Finally, the State, on authority of *Prince* v. *Massachusetts*, argues that a decision exempting Amish children from the State's requirement fails to recognize the substantive right of the Amish child to a secondary education, and fails to give due regard to the power of the State as *parens patriae* to extend the benefit of secondary education to children regardless of the wishes of their parents. Taken at its broadest sweep, the Court's language in *Prince*, might be read to give support to the State's position. However, the Court was not confronted in *Prince* with a situation comparable to that of the Amish as revealed in this record; this is shown by the ⊥ Court's severe characterization of the evils that it thought the legislature could legitimately associate with child labor, even when performed in the company of an adult. The Court later took great care to confine *Prince* to a narrow scope in *Sherbert* v. *Verner*, when it stated: "On the other hand, the Court has rejected challenges under the Free Exercise Clause to governmental regulation of certain overt acts prompted by religious beliefs or principles, for 'even when the action is in accord with one's religious convictions, [it] is not totally free from legislative restrictions.' *Braunfeld* v. *Brown*. The conduct or actions so regulated have invariably posed some substantial threat to public safety, peace or order."

This case, of course, is not one in which any harm to the physical or mental health of the child or to the public safety, peace, order, or welfare has been demonstrated or may be properly inferred. The record is to the contrary, and any reliance on that theory would find no support in the evidence.

Contrary to the suggestion of the dissenting opinion of *Mr. Justice DOUGLAS*, our holding today in no degree depends on the assertion of the religious interest of the child as contrasted with that of the parents. It is the parents who are subject to prosecution here for failing to cause their children to attend school, and it ⊥ is their right of free exercise, not that of their children, that must determine Wisconsin's power to impose criminal penalties on the parent. The dissent argues that a child who expresses a desire to attend public high school in conflict with the wishes of his parents should not be prevented from doing so. There is no reason for the Court to consider that point since it is not an issue in the case. The children are not parties to this litigation. The State has at no point tried this case on the theory that respondents were preventing their children from attending school against their expressed desires, and indeed the record is to the contrary. The State's position from the outset has been that it is empowered to apply its compulsory-attendance law to Amish parents in the same manner as to other parents—that is, without regard to the wishes of the child. That is the claim we reject today.

⊥228

⊥229

⊥230

⊥231

Our holding in no way determines the proper resolution of possible competing interests of parents, children, and the State in an appropriate state court proceeding in which the power of the State is asserted on the theory that Amish parents are preventing their minor children from attending high school despite their expressed desires to the contrary. Recognition of the claim of the State in such a proceeding would, of course, call into question traditional concepts of parental control over the religious upbringing and education of their minor children recognized in this Court's past decisions. It is clear that such an intrusion by a State into family decisions in the area of religious training would give rise to grave questions of religious freedom comparable to those raised here ⊥ and those presented in *Pierce* v. | 232 *Society of Sisters*. On this record we neither reach nor decide those issues.

The State's argument proceeds without reliance on any actual conflict between the wishes of parents and children. It appears to rest on the potential that exemption of Amish parents from the requirements of the compulsory-education law might allow some parents to act contrary to the best interests of their children by foreclosing their opportunity to make an intelligent choice between the Amish way of life and that of the outside world. The same argument could, of course, be made with respect to all church schools short of college. There is nothing in the record or in the ordinary course of human experience to suggest that non-Amish parents generally consult with children of ages 14-16 if they are placed in a church school of the parents' faith.

Indeed it seems clear that if the State is empowered, as *parens patriae*, to "save" a child from himself or his Amish parents by requiring an additional two years of compulsory formal high school education, the State will in large measure influence, if not determine, the religious future of the child. Even more markedly than in *Prince*, therefore, this case involves the fundamental interest of parents, as contrasted with that of the State, to guide the religious future and education of their children. The history and culture of Western civilization reflect a strong tradition of parental concern for the nurture and upbringing of their children. This primary role of the parents in the upbringing of their children is now established beyond debate as an enduring American tradition. If not the first, perhaps the most significant statements of the Court in this area are found in *Pierce* v. *Society of Sisters*, in which the Court observed: "Under the doctrine of *Meyer* v. *Ne-*| 233 *braska*, we think it entirely plain that the Act ⊥ of 1922 unreasonably interferes with the liberty of parents and guardians to direct the upbringing and education of children under their control. As often heretofore pointed out, rights guaranteed by the Constitution may not be abridged by legislation which has no reasonable relation to some purpose within the competency of the State. The fundamen-

tal theory of liberty upon which all governments in this Union repose excludes any general power of the State to standardize its children by forcing them to accept instruction from public teachers only. The child is not the mere creature of the State; those who nurture him and direct his destiny have the right, coupled with the high duty, to recognize and prepare him for additional obligations."

The duty to prepare the child for "additional obligations," referred to by the Court, must be read to include the inculcation of moral standards, religious beliefs, and elements of good citizenship. *Pierce*, of course, recognized that where nothing more than the general interest of the parent in the nurture and education of his children is involved, it is beyond dispute that the State acts "reasonably" and constitutionally in requiring education to age 16 in some public or private school meeting the standards prescribed by the State.

However read, the Court's holding in *Pierce* stands as a charter of the rights of parents to direct the religious upbringing of their children. And, when the interests of parenthood are combined with a free exercise claim of the nature revealed by this record, more than merely a "reasonable relation to some purpose within the competency of the State" is required to sustain the validity of the State's requirement under the First Amendment. To be sure, the power of the parent, even when linked to a free exercise claim, may be subject to limitation under *Prince* ⊥ if it appears that parental decisions will | 234 jeopardize the health or safety of the child, or have a potential for significant social burdens. But in this case, the Amish have introduced persuasive evidence undermining the arguments the State has advanced to support its claims in terms of the welfare of the child and society as a whole. The record strongly indicates that accommodating the religious objections of the Amish by foregoing one, or at most two, additional years of compulsory education will not impair the physical or mental health of the child, or result in an inability to be self-supporting or to discharge the duties and responsibilities of citizenship, or in any other way materially detract from the welfare of society.

In the face of our consistent emphasis on the central values underlying the Religion Clauses in our constitutional scheme of government, we cannot accept a *parens patriae* claim of such all-encompassing scope and with such sweeping potential for broad and unforeseeable application as that urged by the State.

V

For the reasons stated we hold, with the Supreme Court of Wisconsin, that the First and Fourteenth Amendments prevent the State from compelling respondents to cause their children to attend formal high school to age 16. Our disposition of this case, however, in no way ⊥ alters our recognition of the | 235 obvious fact that courts are not school boards or legislatures, and are ill-equipped to determine the "necessity" of discrete aspects of a State's program of compulsory education. This should suggest that courts must move with great circumspection in performing the sensitive and delicate task of weighing a State's legitimate social concern when faced with religious claims for exemption from generally applicable educational requirements. It cannot be overemphasized that we are not dealing with a way of life and mode of education by a group claiming to have recently discovered some "progressive" or more enlightened process for rearing children for modern life.

Aided by a history of three centuries as an identifiable religious sect and a long history as a successful and self-sufficient segment of American society, the Amish in this case have convincingly demonstrated the sincerity of their religious beliefs, the interrelationship of belief with their mode of life, the vital role that belief and daily conduct play in the continued survival of Old Order Amish communities and their religious organization, and the hazards presented by the State's enforcement of a statute generally valid as to others. Beyond this, they have carried the even more difficult burden of demonstrating the adequacy of their alternative mode of continuing informal vocational education in terms of precisely those overall interests that the State advances in support of its program of compulsory high ⌐236 school education. In light of this con⊥vincing showing, one that probably few other religious groups or sects could make, and weighing the minimal difference between what the State would require and what the Amish already accept, it was incumbent on the State to show with more particularity how its admittedly strong interest in compulsory education would be adversely affected by granting an exemption to the Amish.

Nothing we hold is intended to undermine the general applicability of the State's compulsory school-attendance statutes or to limit the power of the State to promulgate reasonable standards that, while not impairing the free exercise of religion, provide for continuing agricultural vocational education under parental and church guidance by the Old Order Amish or others similarly situated. The States have had a long history of amicable and effective relationships with church-sponsored schools, and there is no basis for assuming that, in this related context, reasonable standards cannot be established concerning the content of the continuing vocational education of Amish children under parental guidance, provided always that state regulations are not inconsistent with what we have said in this opinion.

Affirmed.

Mr. Justice POWELL and *Mr. Justice REHN-QUIST* took no part in the consideration or decision of this case.

⊥*Mr. Justice STEWART*, with whom *Mr. Justice* ⌐237 *BRENNAN* joins, concurring.

This case involves the constitutionality of imposing criminal punishment upon Amish parents for their religiously based refusal to compel their children to attend public high schools. Wisconsin has sought to brand these parents as criminals for following *their* religious beliefs, and the Court today rightly holds that Wisconsin cannot constitutionally do so.

This case in no way involves any questions regarding the right of the children of Amish parents to attend public high schools, or any other institutions of learning, if they wish to do so. As the Court points out, there is no suggestion whatever in the record that the religious beliefs of the children here concerned differ in any way from those of their parents. Only one of the children testified. The last two questions and answers on her cross-examination accurately sum up her testimony:

"Q. So I take it then, Frieda, the only reason you are not going to school, and did not go to school since last September, is because of *your* religion?

"A. Yes.

"Q. That is the only reason?

"A. Yes." (Emphasis supplied.)

It is clear to me, therefore, that this record simply does not present the interesting and important issue discussed in Part II of the dissenting opinion of *Mr. Justice DOUGLAS*. With this observation, I join the opinion and the judgment of the Court.

Mr. Justice WHITE, with whom *Mr. Justice BRENNAN* and *Mr. Justice STEWART* join, concurring.

Cases such as this one inevitably call for a delicate balancing of important but conflicting interests. I join the opinion and judgment of the Court because I cannot ⊥ say that the State's interest in requiring ⌐238 two more years of compulsory education in the ninth and tenth grades outweighs the importance of the concededly sincere Amish religious practice to the survival of that sect.

This would be a very different case for me if respondents' claim were that their religion forbade their children from attending any school at any time and from complying in any way with the educational standards set by the State. Since the Amish children are permitted to acquire the basic tools of literacy to survive in modern society by attending grades one through eight and since the deviation from the State's compulsory-education law is relatively slight, I conclude that respondents' claim must prevail, largely because "religious freedom—the freedom to believe and to practice strange and, it may be, foreign creeds—has classically been one of the highest values of our society." *Braunfeld* v. *Brown*.

The importance of the state interest asserted here cannot be denigrated, however: "Today, education is perhaps the most important function of state and local governments. Compulsory school attendance laws and the great expenditures for education both demonstrate our recognition of the importance of education to our democratic society. It is required in the performance of our most basic public responsibilities, even service in the armed forces. It is the very foundation of good citizenship. Today it is a principal instrument in awakening the child to cultural values, in preparing him for later professional training; and in helping him to adjust normally to his environment." *Brown* v. *Board of Education*.

⊥239   ⊥ As recently as last Term, the Court reemphasized the legitimacy of the State's concern for enforcing minimal educational standards, *Lemon* v. *Kurtzman*. *Pierce* v. *Society of Sisters* lends no support to the contention that parents may replace state educational requirements with their own idiosyncratic views of what knowledge a child needs to be a productive and happy member of society; in *Pierce*, both the parochial and military schools were in compliance with all the educational standards that the State had set, and the Court held simply that while a State may posit such standards, it may not pre-empt the educational process by requiring children to attend public schools. In the present case, the State is not concerned with the maintenance of an educational system as an end in itself, it is rather attempting to nurture and develop the human potential of its children, whether Amish or non-Amish: to expand their knowledge, broaden their sensibilities, kindle their imagination, foster a spirit of free inquiry, and increase their human understanding and tolerance. It is possible that most Am-

⊥240 ish ⊥ children will wish to continue living the rural life of their parents, in which case their training at home will adequately equip them for their future role. Others, however, may wish to become nuclear physicists, ballet dancers, computer programmers, or historians, and for these occupations, formal training will be necessary. There is evidence in the record that many children desert the Amish faith when they come of age. A State has a legitimate interest not only in seeking to develop the latent talents of its children but also in seeking to prepare them for the life style that they may later choose, or at least to provide them with an option other than the life they have led in the past. In the circumstances of this case, although the question is close, I am unable to say that the State has demonstrated that Amish children who leave school in the eighth grade will be intellectually stultified or unable to acquire new academic skills later. The statutory minimum school attendance age set by the State is, after all, only 16.

Decision in cases such as this and the administration of an exemption for Old Order Amish from the State's compulsory school-attendance laws will inevitably involve the kind of close and perhaps repeated scrutiny of religious practices, as is exemplified in today's opinion, which the Court has heretofore been anxious to avoid. But such entanglement does not create a forbidden establishment of religion where it is essential to implement free ⊥ exercise values ⊥241 threatened by an otherwise neutral program instituted to foster some permissible, nonreligious state objective. I join the Court because the sincerity of the Amish religious policy here is uncontested, because the potentially adverse impact of the state requirement is great, and because the State's valid interest in education has already been largely satisfied by the eight years the children have already spent in school.

Mr. Justice DOUGLAS, dissenting in part.

I

I agree with the Court that the religious scruples of the Amish are opposed to the education of their children beyond the grade schools, yet I disagree with the Court's conclusion that the matter is within the dispensation of parents alone. The Court's analysis assumes that the only interests at stake in the case are those of the Amish parents on the one hand, and those of the State on the other. The difficulty with this approach is that, despite the Court's claim, the parents are seeking to vindicate not only their own free exercise claims, but also those of their highschool-age children.

It is argued that the right of the Amish children to religious freedom is not presented by the facts of the case, as the issue before the Court involves only the Amish parents' religious freedom to defy a state criminal statute imposing upon them an affirmative duty to cause their children to attend high school.

First, respondents' motion to dismiss in the trial court expressly asserts, not only the religious liberty of the adults, but also that of the children, as a defense to the prosecutions. It is, of course, beyond question that the parents have standing as defendants in a criminal prosecution to assert the religious interests of their ⊥ children as a defense. ⊥242 Although the lower courts and a majority of this Court assume an identity of interest between parent and child, it is clear that they have treated the religious interest of the child as a factor in the analysis.

Second, it is essential to reach the question to decide the case, not only because the question was squarely raised in the motion to dismiss, but also because no analysis of religious-liberty claims can take place in a vacuum. If the parents in this case are allowed a religious exemption, the inevitable effect is to impose the parents' notions of religious duty upon their children. Where the child is mature enough to express potentially conflicting desires, it would be an invasion of the child's rights to permit such an imposition without canvassing his views. As in *Prince v. Massachusetts*, it is an imposition resulting from this very litigation. As the child has no other effective forum, it is in this litigation that his rights should be considered. And, if an Amish child desires to attend high school, and is mature enough to have that desire respected, the State may well be able to override the parents' religiously motivated objections.

⊥243   ⊥ Religion is an individual experience. It is not necessary, nor even appropriate, for every Amish child to express his views on the subject in a prosecution of a single adult. Crucial, however, are the views of the child whose parent is the subject of the suit. Frieda Yoder has in fact testified that her own religious views are opposed to high-school education. I therefore join the judgment of the Court as to respondent Jonas Yoder. But Frieda Yoder's views may not be those of Vernon Yutzy or Barbara Miller. I must dissent, therefore, as to respondents Adin Yutzy and Wallace Miller as their motion to dismiss also raised the question of their children's religious liberty.

II

This issue has never been squarely presented before today. Our opinions are full of talk about the power of the parents over the child's education. And we have in the past analyzed similar conflicts between parent and State with little regard for the views of the child. Recent cases, however, have clearly held that the children themselves have constitutionally protectible interests.

These children are "persons" within the meaning of the Bill of Rights. We have so held over and over again. In *Haley v. Ohio*, we extended the protection of the Fourteenth Amendment in a state trial of a 15-year-old boy. In *In re Gault*, we held that "neither the Fourteenth Amendment nor the Bill of Rights is for adults alone." In *In re Winship*, we held that a 12-year-old boy, when charged with an act which would be a crime if committed by an adult, was entitled to procedural safeguards contained in the Sixth Amendment.

⊥244   ⊥ In *Tinker v. Des Moines School District*, we dealt with 13-year-old, 15-year-old, and 16-year-old students who wore armbands to public schools and were disciplined for doing so. We gave them relief, saying that their First Amendment rights had been abridged.

"Students in school as well as out of school are 'persons' under our Constitution. They are possessed of fundamental rights which the State must respect, just as they themselves must respect their obligations to the State."

In *Board of Education v. Barnette*, we held that schoolchildren, whose religious beliefs collided with a school rule requiring them to salute the flag, could

not be required to do so. While the sanction included expulsion of the students and prosecution of the parents, the vice of the regime was its interference with the child's free exercise of religion. We said: "Here . . . we are dealing with a compulsion of students to declare a belief."

· · · · ·

On this important and vital matter of education, I think the children should be entitled to be heard. While the parents, absent dissent, normally speak for the entire family, the education of the child is a matter on which the child will often have decided views. He may want to be a pianist or an astronaut or an oceanog⊥rapher. To do so he will have to break   ⊥245 from the Amish tradition.

It is the future of the student, not the future of the parents, that is imperiled by today's decision. If a parent keeps his child out of school beyond the grade school, then the child will be forever barred from entry into the new and amazing world of diversity that we have today. The child may decide that that is the preferred course, or he may rebel. It is the student's judgment, not his parents', that is essential if we are to give full meaning to what we have said about the Bill of Rights and of the right of students to be masters of their own destiny. If he is harnessed to the Amish way of life ⊥ by those in authority over him   ⊥246 and if his education is truncated, his entire life may be stunted and deformed. The child, therefore, should be given an opportunity to be heard before the State gives the exemption which we honor today.

The views of the two children in question were not canvassed by the Wisconsin courts. The matter should be explicitly reserved so that new hearings can be held on remand of the case.

III

I think the emphasis of the Court on the "law and order" record of this Amish group of people is quite irrelevant. A religion is a religion irrespective of what the misdemeanor or felony records of its members might be. I am not at all sure how the Catholics, Episcopalians, the Baptists, Jehovah's Witnesses, the Unitarians, and my own Presbyterians would make out if subjected to such a test. It is, of course, true that if a group or society was organized to perpetuate crime and if that is its motive, we would have rather startling problems akin to those that were raised when some years back a particular sect was challenged here as operating on a fraudulent basis. But no such factors are present here, and the Amish, whether with a high or low crim⊥inal re-   ⊥247 cord, certainly qualify by all historic standards as a religion within the meaning of the First Amendment.

The Court rightly rejects the notion that actions, even though religiously grounded, are always outside the protection of the Free Exercise Clause of the First Amendment. In so ruling, the Court departs from the teaching of *Reynolds* v. *United States*, where it was said concerning the reach of the Free Exercise Clause of the First Amendment, "Congress was deprived of all legislative power over mere opinion, but was left free to reach actions which were in violation of social duties or subversive of good order." In that case it was conceded that polygamy was a part of the religion of the Mormons. Yet the Court said, "It matters not that his belief [in polygamy] was a part of his professed religion: it was still belief, and belief only."

Action, which the Court deemed to be antisocial, could be punished even though it was grounded on deeply held and sincere religious convictions. What we do today, at least in this respect, opens the way to give organized religion a broader base than it has ever enjoyed; and it even promises that in time *Reynolds* will be overruled.

In another way, however, the Court retreats when in reference to Henry Thoreau it says his "choice ⌐248 was philo⊥sophical and personal rather than religious, and such belief does not rise to the demands of the Religion Clauses." That is contrary to what we held in *United States* v. *Seeger*, where we were concerned with the meaning of the words "religious training and belief" in the Selective Service Act, which were the basis of many conscientious objector claims. We said: "Within that phrase would come all sincere religious beliefs which are based upon a power or being, or upon a faith, to which all else is subordinate or upon which all else is ultimately dependent. The test might be stated in these words: A sincere and meaningful belief which occupies in the life of its possessor a place parallel to that filled by the God of those admittedly qualifying for the exemption comes within the statutory definition. This construction avoids imputing to Congress an intent to classify different religious beliefs, exempting some and excluding others, and is in accord with the well-established congressional policy of equal treatment for those whose opposition to service is grounded in their religious tenets. . . ."

⌐249   ⊥I adhere to these exalted views of "religion" and see no acceptable alternative to them now that we have become a Nation of many religions and sects, representing all of the diversities of the human race.

WIDMAR v. VINCENT

454 U.S. 263
ON WRIT OF CERTIORARI TO THE UNITED
STATES COURT OF
APPEALS FOR THE EIGHTH CIRCUIT
Argued October 6, 1981 — Decided December 8,
1981

⌐264   ⊥*Justice POWELL* delivered the opinion of the Court.

This case presents the question whether a state university, which makes its facilities generally ⌐265 available for the activities ⊥of registered student groups, may close its facilities to a registered student group desiring to use the facilities for religious worship and religious discussion.

I

It is the stated policy of the University of Missouri at Kansas City to encourage the activities of student organizations. The University officially recognizes over 100 student groups. It routinely provides University facilities for the meetings of registered organizations. Students pay an activity fee of $41 per semester (1978-1979) to help defray the costs to the University.

From 1973 until 1977 a registered religious group named Cornerstone regularly sought and received permission to conduct its meetings in University facilities. In 1977, however, the University informed the group that it could no longer meet in University buildings. The exclusion was based on a regulation, adopted by the Board of Curators in 1972, that prohibits the use of University buildings or grounds "for purposes of religious worship or religious teaching."

⊥Eleven University students, all members of Cornerstone, brought suit to challenge the regulation in Federal District Court for the Western District of Missouri. They alleged that the University's discrimination against religious activity and discussion violated their rights to free exercise of religion, equal protection, and freedom of speech under the First and Fourteenth Amendments to the Constitution of the United States.   ⌐266

Upon cross motions for summary judgment, the District Court upheld the challenged regulation. *Chess* v. *Widmar*. It found the regulation not only justified, but required, by the Establishment Clause of the Federal Constitution. Under *Tilton* v. *Richardson*, the court reasoned, the State ⊥could not ⌐267 provide facilities for religious use without giving prohibited support to an institution of religion. The District Court rejected the argument that the University could not discriminate against religious speech on the basis of its content. It found religious speech entitled to less protection than other types of expression.

The Court of Appeals for the Eighth Circuit reversed. *Chess* v. *Widmar*. Rejecting the analysis of the District Court, it viewed the University regulation as a content-based discrimination against religious speech, for which it could find no compelling justification. The Court held that the Establishment Clause does not bar a policy of equal access, in which facilities are open to groups and speakers of all kinds. According to the Court of Appeals, the "primary effect" of such a policy would not be to advance religion, but rather to further the neutral purpose of developing students' " 'social and cultural awareness as well as [their] intellectual curiosity,' " (quoting from the University bulletin's description of the student activities program).

We now affirm.

II

Through its policy of accommodating their meetings, the University has created a forum generally open for use by student groups. Having done so, the University has assumed an obligation to justify its discriminations and exclusions under applicable constitutional norms. The Constitution forbids a State to enforce certain exclusions from a forum generally open to the public, even if it was not required to create the forum in the first place. See, *e.g., City of Madison Joint School District* v. *Wisconsin Public Employment Relations Comm'n* (although a State may conduct business in private session, "where the State has opened a forum for direct citizen involvement," exclusions bear a heavy burden of justification); *Southeastern Promotions, Ltd.* v. *Conrad* (because municipal theater was a public forum, city could not exclude a production without satisfying constitutional safeguards applicable to prior restraints).

The University's institutional mission, which it describes as providing a *"secular* education" to its students, does not exempt its actions from constitutional scrutiny. With respect to persons entitled to be there, our cases leave no doubt that the First ⌐269 Amendment ⊥rights of speech and association extend to the campuses of state universities. See, *e.g., Healy* v. *James; Tinker* v. *Des Moines Independent School District; Shelton* v. *Tucker.*

Here the University of Missouri has discriminated against student groups and speakers based on their desire to use a generally open forum to engage in religious worship and discussion. These are forms of speech and association protected by the First Amendment. See, *e.g., Heffron* v. *International Soc'y for Krishna Consciousness, Inc.; Niemotko* v. *Maryland; Saia* v. *New York.* In order to justify discrimi- ⌐270 na⊥tory exclusion from a public forum based on the religious content of a group's intended speech, the University must therefore satisfy the standard of review appropriate to content-based exclusions. It must show that its regulation is necessary to serve a compelling state interest and that it is narrowly drawn to achieve that end. See *Carey* v. *Brown.*

III

In this case the University claims a compelling interest in maintaining strict separation of church and State. It derives this interest from the "Establishment Clauses" of both the Federal and Missouri Constitutions.

A

⌐271 The University first argues that it cannot offer its facilities to religious groups and speakers on the terms available to ⊥other groups without violating the Establishment Clause of the Constitution of the United States. We agree that the interest of the University in complying with its constitutional obliga-

tions may be characterized as compelling. It does not follow, however, that an "equal access" policy would be incompatible with this Court's Establishment Clause cases. Those cases hold that a policy will not offend the Establishment Clause if it can pass a three-pronged test: "First, the [governmental policy] must have a secular legislative purpose; second, its principal or primary effect must be one that neither advances nor inhibits religion . . . ; finally, the [policy] must not foster 'an excessive government entanglement with religion.' " *Lemon* v. *Kurtzman.* See *Committee for Public Education* v. *Regan; Roemer* v. *Maryland Public Works Bd.*

In this case two prongs of the test are clearly met. Both the District Court and the Court of Appeals held that an open-forum policy, including nondiscrimination against religious speech, would have a secular purpose and would ⊥avoid entanglement ⌐272 with religion. But the District Court concluded, and the University argues here, that allowing religious groups to share the limited public forum would have the "primary effect" of advancing religion.

⊥The University's argument misconceives the na- ⌐273 ture of this case. The question is not whether the creation of a religious forum would violate the Establishment Clause. The University has opened its facilities for use by student groups, and the question is whether it can now exclude groups because of the content of their speech. See *Healy* v. *James.* In this context we are unpersuaded that the primary effect of the public forum, open to all forms of discourse, would be to advance religion.

We are not oblivious to the range of an open forum's likely effects. It is possible—perhaps even foreseeable—that religious groups will benefit from access to University facilities. But this Court has explained that a religious organization's enjoyment of merely "incidental" benefits does not violate the prohibition against the "primary advancement" of religion. *Committee for Public Education* v. *Nyquist;* ⊥see, *e.g., Roemer* v. *Board of Public Works; Hunt* ⌐274 v. *McNair; McGowan* v. *Maryland.*

We are satisfied that any religious benefits of an open forum at UMKC would be "incidental" within the meaning of our cases. Two factors are especially relevant.

First, an open forum in a public university does not confer any imprimatur of State approval on religious sects or practices. As the Court of Appeals quite aptly stated, such a policy "would no more commit the University . . . to religious goals," than it is "now committed to the goals of the Students for a Democratic Society, the Young Socialist Alliance," or any other group eligible to use its facilities. *Chess* v. *Widmar.*

Second, the forum is available to a broad class of non-religious as well as religious speakers; there are over 100 recognized student groups at UMKC. The provision of benefits to so broad a spectrum of groups is an important index of secular effect. See, *e.g., Wolman* v. *Walter; Committee for Public Education* v. *Nyquist.* If the Establishment Clause barred the extension of general benefits to religious groups, "a church could not be protected by the police and fire depart⊥ments, or have its public sidewalk kept in repair." *Roemer* v. *Maryland* (plurality opinion); quoted in *Committee for Public Education* v. *Regan.* At least in the absence of empirical evidence that religious groups will dominate UMKC's open forum, we agree with the Court of Appeals that the advancement of religion would not be the forum's "primary effect."

⊥275

B

Arguing that the State of Missouri has gone further than the Federal Constitution in proscribing indirect State support for religion, the University claims a compelling interest in complying with the applicable provisions of the Missouri Constitution.

The Missouri courts have not ruled whether a general policy of accommodating student groups, applied equally to those wishing to gather to engage in religious and non-religious speech, would offend the State Constitution. We need not, however, determine how the Missouri courts would decide this issue. It is also unnecessary for us to decide whether, under the Supremacy Clause, a state interest, derived from its own constitution, could ever outweigh free ⊥speech interests protected by the First Amendment. We limit our holding to the case before us.

⊥276

On one hand, respondents' First Amendment rights are entitled to special constitutional solicitude. Our cases have required the most exacting scrutiny in cases in which a State undertakes to regulate speech on the basis of its content. See, *e.g., Carey* v. *Brown; Police Dept.* v. *Mosley.* On the other hand, the State interest asserted here—in achieving greater separation of church and State than is already ensured under the Establishment Clause of the Federal Constitution—is limited by the Free Exercise Clause and in this case by the Free Speech Clause as well. In this constitutional context, we are unable to recognize the State's interest as sufficiently "compelling" to justify content-based discrimination against respondents' religious speech.

IV

Our holding in this case in no way undermines the capacity of the University to establish reasonable time, place, and manner regulations. Nor do we question the right of the University to make academic judgments as to how best to allocate scarce resources or "to determine for itself on academic grounds who may teach, what may be taught, how it shall be taught, and who may be admitted to study." *Sweezy* v. *New Hampshire* (Frankfurter, J., concurring in the judgment); see *Regents of the Univ. of Cal.* v. *Bakke* (opinion of Powell. J.. announcing the judgment of the Court). Fi⊥nally, we affirm the continuing validity of cases, *e.g., Healy* v. *James,* that

⊥277

recognize a University's right to exclude even First Amendment activities that violate reasonable campus rules or substantially interfere with the opportunity of other students to obtain an education.

The basis for our decision is narrow. Having created a forum generally open to student groups, the University seeks to enforce a content-based exclusion of religious speech. Its exclusionary policy violates the fundamental principle that a state regulation of speech should be content-neutral, and the University is unable to justify this violation under applicable constitutional standards.

For this reason, the decision of the Court of Appeals is,

Affirmed.

Justice STEVENS, concurring in the judgment.

As the Court recognizes, every university must "make academic judgments as to how best to allocate scarce resources." The Court appears to hold, however, that those judgments must "serve a compelling state interest" whenever they are based, even in part, on the content of speech. This conclusion apparently flows from the Court's suggestion that a student activities program—from which the public may be excluded—must be managed as though it were a "public forum." In my opinion, the use of the terms "compelling ⊥state interest" and "public forum" to analyze the question presented in this case may needlessly undermine the academic freedom of public universities.

⊥278

Today most major colleges and universities are operated by public authority. Nevertheless, their facilities are not open to the public in the same way that streets and parks are. University facilities—private or public—are maintained primarily for the benefit of the student body and the faculty. In performing their learning and teaching missions, the managers of a university routinely make countless decisions based on the content of communicative materials. They select books for inclusion in the library, they hire professors on the basis of their academic philosophies, they select courses for inclusion in the curriculum, and they reward scholars for what they have written. In addition, in encouraging students to participate in extracurricular activities, they necessarily make decisions concerning the content of those activities.

Because every university's resources are limited, an educational institution must routinely make decisions concerning the use of the time and space that is available for extracurricular activities. In my judgment, it is both necessary and appropriate for those decisions to evaluate the content of a proposed student activity. I should think it obvious, for example, that if two groups of 25 students requested the use of a room at a particular time—one to view Mickey Mouse cartoons and the other to rehearse an amateur performance of Hamlet—the First Amendment would not require that the room be reserved for the group that submitted its application first. Nor do I see why a university should have to establish a "compelling state interest" to defend its decision to permit one group to use the facility and not the other. In my opinion, a university should be allowed to decide for itself whether a program that illuminates the genius of Walt Disney be given precedence over one that may duplicate material adequately covered in the classroom. Judgments of ⊥ this kind should be made by academicians, not by federal judges, and their standards for decision should not be encumbered with ambiguous phrases like "compelling state interest."

⊥ Thus, I do not subscribe to the view that a public university has no greater interest in the content of student activities than the police chief has in the content of a soap box oration on Capitol Hill. A university legitimately may regard some subjects as more relevant to its educational mission than others. But the university, like the police officer, may not allow its agreement or disagreement with the viewpoint of a particular speaker to determine whether access to a forum will be granted. If a state university is to deny recognition to a student organization—or is to give it a lesser right to use school facilities than other student groups—it must have a valid reason for doing so. *Healy* v. *James.*

In this case I agree with the Court that the University has not established a sufficient justification for its refusal to allow the Cornerstone group to engage in religious worship on the campus. The primary reason advanced for the discriminatory treatment is the University's fear of violating the Establishment Clause. But since the record discloses no danger ⊥ that the University will appear to sponsor any particular religion, and since student participation in the Cornerstone meetings is entirely voluntary, the Court properly concludes that the University's fear is groundless. With that justification put to one side, the University has not met the burden that is imposed on it by *Healy.*

Nor does the University's reliance on the Establishment Clause of the Missouri State Constitution provide a sufficient justification for the discriminatory treatment in this case. As I have said, I believe that the University may exercise a measure of control over the agenda for student use of school facilities, preferring some subjects over others, without needing to identify so-called "compelling state interests." Quite obviously, however, the University could not allow a group of Republicans or Presbyterians to meet while denying Democrats or Mormons the same privilege. It seems apparent that the policy under attack would allow groups of young philosophers to meet to discuss their skepticism that a Supreme Being exists, or a group of political scientists to meet to debate the accuracy of the view that religion is the "opium of the people." If school facilities may be used to discuss anti-clerical doctrine, it

seems to me that comparable use by a group desiring to express a belief in God must also be permitted. The fact that their expression of faith includes ceremonial conduct is not, in my opinion, a sufficient reason for suppressing their discussion entirely.

Accordingly, although I do not endorse the Court's reasoning, I concur in its judgment.

⊥ *Justice WHITE*, dissenting.

In affirming the decision of the Court of Appeals, the majority rejects petitioners' argument that the Establishment Clause of the Constitution prohibits the use of university buildings for religious purposes. A state university may permit its property to be used for purely religious services without violating the First and Fourteenth Amendments. With this I agree. See *Committee for Public Education* v. *Nyquist* (White, J., dissenting); *Lemon* v. *Kurtzman* (Opinion of White, J.). The Establishment Clause, however, sets limits only on what the State may do with respect to religious organizations; it does not establish what the State is *required* to do. I have long argued that Establishment Clause limits on state action which incidentally aids religion are not as strict as the Court has held. The step from the permissible to the necessary, however, is a long one. In my view, just as there is room under the Religion Clauses for state policies that may have some beneficial effect on religion, there is also room for state policies that may incidentally burden religion. In other words, I believe the states to be a good deal freer to formulate policies that affect religion in divergent ways than does the majority. See *Sherbert* v. *Verner* (Harlan, J., dissenting). The majority's position will inevitably lead to those contradictions and tensions between the Establishment and Free Exercise Clauses warned against by Justice Stewart in *Sherbert* v. *Verner.*

The university regulation at issue here provides in pertinent part: "No University buildings or grounds (except chapels as herein provided) may be used for purposes of religious worship or religious teaching by either student or nonstudent groups. Student congregations of local ⊥ churches or of recognized denominations or sects, although not technically recognized campus groups, may use the facilities . . . under the same regulations that apply to recognized campus organizations, provided that no University facilities may be used for purposes of religious worship or religious teaching."

Although there may be instances in which it would be difficult to determine whether a religious group used university facilities for "worship" or "religious teaching," rather than for secular ends, this is not such a case. The regulation was applied to respondents' religious group, Cornerstone, only after the group explicitly informed the University that it sought access to the facilities for the purpose of offering prayer, singing hymns, reading scripture, and teaching biblical principles. Cornerstone described their meetings as follows: "Although these meetings would not appear to a casual observer to correspond precisely to a traditional worship service, there is no doubt that worship is an important part of the general atmosphere." The issue here is only whether the University ⊥ regulation as applied and interpreted in this case is impermissible under the federal Constitution. If it is impermissible, it is because it runs afoul of either the Free Speech or the Free Exercise Clause of the First Amendment.

A large part of respondents' argument, accepted by the court below and accepted by the majority, is founded on the proposition that because religious worship uses speech, it is protected by the Free Speech Clause of the First Amendment. Not only is it protected, they argue, but religious worship *qua* speech is not different from any other variety of protected speech as a matter of constitutional principle. I believe that this proposition is plainly wrong. Were it right, the Religion Clauses would be emptied of any independent meaning in circumstances in which religious practice took the form of speech. Although the majority describes this argument as "novel," I believe it to be clearly supported by our previous cases. Just last term, the Court found it suffi⊥ciently obvious that the Establishment Clause prohibited a state from posting a copy of the Ten Commandments on the classroom wall that a statute requiring such a posting was summarily struck down. *Stone* v. *Graham.* That case necessarily presumed that the state could not ignore the religious content of the written message, nor was it permitted to treat that content as it would, or must treat, other—secular—messages under the First Amendment's protection of speech. Similarly, the Court's decisions prohibiting prayer in the public schools rest on a content-based distinction between varieties of speech: as a speech act, apart from its content, a prayer is indistinguishable from a biology lesson. See *School District of Abington Township* v. *Schempp; Engel* v. *Vitale.* Operation of the Free Exercise Clause is equally dependent, in certain circumstances, on recognition of a content-based distinction between religious and secular speech. Thus, in *Torcaso* v. *Watkins* the Court struck down, as violative of the Free Exercise Clause, a state requirement that made a declaration of belief in God a condition of state employment. A declaration is again a speech act, but it was the content of the speech that brought the case within the scope of the Free Exercise Clause.

If the majority were right that no distinction may be drawn between verbal acts of worship and other verbal acts, all of these cases would have to be reconsidered. Although I agree that the line may be difficult to draw in many cases, surely the majority cannot seriously suggest that no line may ever be drawn. If that were the case, the majority would ⊥ have to uphold the University's right to offer a

class entitled "Sunday Mass." Under the majority's view, such a class would be—as a matter of constitutional principle—indistinguishable from a class entitled "The History of the Catholic Church."

There may be instances in which a state's attempt to disentangle itself from religious worship would intrude upon secular speech about religion. In such a case, the state's action would be subject to challenge under the Free Speech Clause of the First Amendment. This is not such a case. This case involves religious worship only; the fact that that worship is accomplished through speech does not add anything to respondents' argument. That argument must rely upon the claim that the state's action impermissibly interferes with the free exercise of respondents' religious practices. Although this is a close question, I conclude that it does not.

Plausible analogies on either side suggest themselves. Respondents argue, and the majority agrees, that by permitting any student group to use its facilities for communicative purposes other than religious worship, the University has created a "public forum." With ample ⊥ support, they argue that the state may not make content-based distinctions as to what groups may use, or what messages may be conveyed in, such a forum. See *Police Department of Chicago* v. *Mosley, Cox* v. *Louisiana.* The right of the religious to nondiscriminatory access to the public forum is well established. See *Niemotko* v. *Maryland; Murdock* v. *Pennsylvania.* Moreover, it is clear that there are bounds beyond which the University could not go in enforcing its regulation: I don't suppose it could prevent students from saying grace before meals in the school cafeteria, or prevent distribution of religious literature on campus.

Petitioners, on the other hand, argue that allowing use of their facilities for religious worship is constitutionally indistinguishable from directly subsidizing such religious services: It would "[fund] a specifically religious activity in an otherwise substantially secular setting." *Hunt* v. *McNair.* They argue that the fact that secular student groups are entitled to the in-kind subsidy at issue here does not establish that a religious group is entitled to the same subsidy. They could convincingly argue, for example, that a state University that pays for basketballs for the basketball team is not thereby required to pay for bibles for a group like Cornerstone.

⊥ A third analogy suggests itself, one that falls between these two extremes. There are a variety of state policies which incidentally benefit religion that this Court has upheld without implying that they were constitutionally required of the state. See *Board of Education* v. *Allen* (state loan of textbooks to parochial school students); *Zorach* v. *Clauson* (release of students from public schools, during school hours, to perform religious activities away from the school grounds); *Everson* v. *Board of Education* (state provision of transportation to parochial school students). **Provision of university facilities on** a uniform basis to all student groups is not very different from provision of text books or transportation. From this perspective the issue is not whether the state must, or must not, open its facilities to religious worship; rather, it is whether the state may choose not to do so.

Each of these analogies is persuasive. Because they lead to different results, however, they are of limited help in reaching a decision here. They also demonstrate the difficulty in reconciling the various interests expressed in the Religion Clauses. In my view, therefore, resolution of this case is best achieved by returning to first principles. This requires an assessment of the burden on respondents' ability freely to exercise their religious beliefs and practices and of the state's interest in enforcing its regulation.

Respondents complain that compliance with the regulation would require them to meet "about a block and a half" from campus under conditions less comfortable than those previously available on campus. I view this burden on free exer⊥cise as minimal. Because the burden is minimal, the state need do no more than demonstrate that the regulation furthers some permissible state end. The state's interest in avoiding claims that it is financing or otherwise supporting religious worship—in maintaining a definitive separation between church and state—is such an end. That the state truly does mean to act toward this end is amply supported by the treatment of religion in the state constitution. Thus, I believe the interest of the state is sufficiently strong to justify the imposition of the minimal burden on respondents' ability freely to exercise their religious beliefs.

On these facts, therefore, I cannot find that the application of the regulation to prevent Cornerstone from holding religious worship services in university facilities violates the First and Fourteenth Amendments. I would not hold as the majority does that if a university permits students and others to use its property for secular purposes, it must also furnish facilities to religious groups for the purposes of worship and the practice of their religion. Accordingly, I would reverse the judgment of the Court of Appeals.

FREE EXERCISE AND TAXATION

At any level of government the power to tax is essential to effective operation of that government: without funds government cannot survive. The primary purpose of taxation is therefore correctly perceived to be the raising of revenue. A secondary, and highly significant, objective of taxation may sometimes be regulation of or even prohibition of certain practices thought to be detrimental to society. The taxing power may also be used to encourage or induce individuals or organizations to take positive action to further contemporary governmental objectives.

Even general neutral tax laws and their exemption provisions often raise legal problems as to their applicability to religious organizations. It has for long been argued by some, for example, that the virtually universal policy of exempting church property from taxation is unconstitutional. As will be discussed at a later point, it was not until 1970

that in WALZ v. TAX COMMISSION (p. 278), the Supreme Court spoke definitely and positively to that practice with respect to church property used solely for religious worship. Since that time both Congress and the courts have wrestled with related questions concerning property and income of church activities beyond the immediate scope of the decision. Such a question was involved in *St. Martin Evangelical Lutheran Church v. South Dakota* (1980). In this case the issue was whether a church must pay unemployment compensation taxes imposed by the Federal Unemployment Tax Act (FUTA) on employees who work in the church's parochial school. The Lutheran church and academy involved in the litigation argued that to subject them to the tax would violate both the Free Exercise and Establishment Clauses.

The statute at bar provided exemption from the taxes with respect to "service performed—(1) in the employ of (A) a church or convention or association of churches, or (B) an organization . . . which is operated, supervised, controlled, or principally supported by a church or a convention or association of churches." The taxing authorities tried to interpret the word "church" to mean only the actual place of worship—the church building—thus making the employees of a church-related school subject to the collection of the FUTA taxes. After reviewing the legislative history of the act, the Court concluded that such a construction contradicted the phrasing of the statute itself: the employees of a church-related school are "in the employ of a church or convention or association of churches" and are thus eligible for exemption under the act from the collection of the contested taxes. The fact that the Court refused to allow such a narrow definition of the words under question is likely to have wide implications since this or very similar language is used in other statutes, particularly in various places in the Internal Revenue Code.

Later that year the Court heard oral arguments in another case requiring the balancing of free exercise claims against congressional power to tax. Edwin D. Lee, self-employed Pennsylvania farmer and carpenter, refused on religious grounds to withhold or to pay Social Security taxes on wages he paid several Old Order Amish employees. Lee, also a member of that religious group, believed that each individual has the responsibility for caring for those in need in his community, and he maintained it was contrary to his religious tenets either to pay Social Security taxes or to accept Social Security benefits.

When the government brought suit for payment of the taxes, a federal district judge upheld Lee's refusal to pay. The judge cited a 1965 federal law exempting self-employed Amish and members of other religious groups whose religious beliefs forbid payment of the tax or receipt of benefits. The government appealed the decision, contending that the law in question applies only to taxes that a self-employed individual would pay on his own income, not to the tax paid on the compensation of his employees.

In February 1982 Chief Justice Burger, writing for a unanimous Court in UNITED STATES v. LEE (p. 219), upheld the government's contention that the statutory exemption applied only to self-employed individuals, and did not apply to Lee—an employer—and his employees. Burger then turned to the broader question of whether there was a constitutionally required exemption. He agreed that compulsory participation of the Amish in the Social Security system interfered with their free exercise rights, but he noted that "Not all burdens on religion are unconstitutional." Government, he said, may justify a restraint on religious liberty by showing that the limitation is necessary for accomplishment of an overriding government interest.

The Social Security program is a vital nationwide government service and only by mandatory participation can it be kept fiscally sound. Religious beliefs can be accommodated, but a system forced to accommodate the great variety of religious beliefs in the area of taxation would be difficult if not impossible to administer. Religious practices must sometimes yield to the public good. Said the Chief Justice:

> Congress and the courts have been sensitive to the needs flowing from the Free Exercise Clause, but every person cannot be shielded from all the burdens incident to exercising every aspect of the right to practice religious beliefs. When followers of a particular sect enter into commercial activity as a matter of choice, the limits they accept on their own conduct as a matter of conscience and faith are not to be superimposed on the statutory schemes which are binding on others in that activity. (455 U.S. 252, 262)

Justice Stevens concurred in the judgment, but expressed his belief that the heavy burden now imposed upon government to justify the applicability of general neutral laws to individual conscientious objectors should be shifted to the objector to demonstrate that "there is a unique reason for allowing him a special exemption from a valid law of general applicability." [1]

Several cases have in recent years dealt with the issue of the use of tax exemptions to coerce compliance with government policy. In *First Unitarian Church* v. *County of Los Angeles* (1958), the Court considered a California constitutional provision that made as a condition for tax exemption the signing of an oath stating that the applicant for exemption would not advocate overthrow of the government by force, violence, or unlawful means. The First Unitarian Church of Los Angeles refused to sign the oath, claiming that the state had no right to compel a church to sign an oath affirming any doctrine, advocacy, or belief. In reaching its decision, the Court did not deal with the substantive question of whether the state could condition tax exemption upon acceptance of state-defined beliefs or activities. Rather it said simply that, in order to deny the tax exemption, the state would have to demonstrate that a particular church did in fact advocate overthrow of the government. It was not permissible to withhold the exemption merely because a church would not sign the oath.

Christian Echoes National Ministry v. *United States* (1973) also concerned the exemption issue. The ministry of fundamentalist evangelist Billy James Hargis was denied tax exemption by the IRS because the Hargis organization was substantially involved in political activities in violation of IRS regulations. A tax-exempt religious or educational organization may not use a substantial part of its activities or assets to influence legislation or to participate in a political campaign on behalf of a candidate. Because the Hargis organization did both, the IRS withdrew its tax exemption. After the federal court of appeals up-

---

[1] In 1984 the United States Court of Appeals for the Tenth Circuit agreed with an Oklahoma City minister that his situation differed from that of Lee, an employer. As a minister opposed to public insurance on religious grounds, he would have been entitled to exemption from self-employed taxes had he filed for exemption within the time frame provided in the governing statute. He had not done so, however, so the court upheld the denial of the exemption by the IRS and Tax Court. Such interference with his free exercise of religion as resulted from the tax was overridden by the government's interest in "maintaining the financial stability of the social security system." Congress could, the court observed, constitutionally remove all exemptions from payment of the tax if it so chose. *Ballinger* v. *Commissioner of Internal Revenue* (1984). Two years later, the Bethel Baptist Church, a fundamentalist congregation in Sellersville, Pennsylvania, received the same ruling from a federal district judge when it challenged the constitutionality of the Social Security Act as amended in 1983 and 1984. Prior to the amendments, churches could choose to participate in the Social Security system on a voluntary basis. By the 1984 amendment, churches were required to affirmatively choose not to be a part of the system if they did not wish to contribute to social security. If they did elect for religious reasons not to participate in the program, their employees would have to pay the tax applicable to self-employed persons—a greater amount than an employee would contribute at the employee rate. The church did not make the election and in 1984 paid $17,795.04 on wages subject to social security taxes. Subsequently the church filed a claim for refund of the amount paid and challenged the constitutionality of the amendments on free exercise, establishment, and equal protection grounds. District Judge Caldwell held, consistent with *Lee* and *Ballinger* that the government's overriding compelling interest in maintaining the integrity of the revenue system outweighed the religious claims; he similarly found no violation of the Equal Protection of the Laws Clause. (*Bethel Baptist Church* v. *United States* (1986)

held the IRS revocation, the Supreme Court denied certiorari.

In this controversy, the Christian Echoes Ministry was supported by a large number of religious groups across the theological spectrum. They were, and are, concerned about two dimensions of their relationship with the IRS. The first is that "substantial political participation" means whatever the IRS says it means. That is, there are no objective guidelines as to how much a group may engage in political activity or advocacy before it is in danger of losing its tax exemption. The second dimension is the more crucial one: Does the government have the right to set limits on the activities and speech of religious institutions as they address public issues? [2]

The most publicized controversy concerning the use of tax exemption to bring about compliance with government policy involved Bob Jones University. A fundamentalist Christian school in the strictest sense of the word, it affirms a literalistic view of the Bible, assuming the world to be essentially evil and dominated by atheistic, pagan attitudes. Interracial dating and marriages are said to be forbidden by the Bible. Consequently, prior to 1971, the university accepted no black students. After that time, married black people were accepted as students; later, unmarried blacks were admitted. However, rules were introduced which prohibit interracial dating and marriage, upon penalty of being expelled.

In the 1970s, as the result of extended judicial and administrative interpretation of civil rights laws, certain federal officials determined that racially segregated or discriminatory schools, including church-related colleges, should lose federal benefits and/or tax exemption. These policies were applied to Bob Jones University through litigation initiated by various federal agencies, principally the IRS. That agency declared that the school should lose its tax exempt status because it at first refused to admit black students and, later, did not treat them equally.

Bob Jones University sued to recover tax exempt status, arguing that its treatment of blacks was a matter of deeply and sincerely held religious faith and thus was protected by the Free Exercise Clause of the First Amendment. Articulated somewhat more broadly, the issue may be described as follows: Government control over admission policies of church schools deprives these institutions of the right to make decisions that may very well rest on theological or ecclesiastical bases. Further, such government policy negates the judgment of a

church college regarding the best means to accomplish goals that the college has set for itself.

In litigation against the IRS, the university won at the trial court level but lost in the appeals court (*Bob Jones University* v. *United States* [1980]). When the university asked the Supreme Court to consider its grievance, the case was consolidated with *Goldsboro Christian Schools* v. *United States* (involving a North Carolina school with virtually identical racial theology and tax problems as Bob Jones) and granted a hearing. However, in January 1982 the Reagan administration (by means of a memorandum from the Justice Department to the Supreme Court, requesting that the case be declared moot) announced that the tax exemption for these schools and any others similarly situated was being restored. After a tremendous cry of protest from blacks and other civil rights advocates, the administration promptly retreated from the original announcement. President Ronald Reagan affirmed that he was firmly opposed to racial discrimination and was asking Congress to pass legislation to withdraw tax exemption from racially discriminatory institutions, including church-related schools. Seeking to explain its actions, the Reagan administration announced that public policy should be made by the legislative branch, not by the regulations of executive agencies.

Congress soon indicated, however, that it had no intention of obliging the President. The issue was further complicated when in February the Court of Appeals in the District of Columbia issued an interim order barring the administration from granting exemptions to "any school that unlawfully discriminates on the basis of race." The Justice Department then filed papers with the Supreme Court stating that its earlier request that the *Bob Jones-Goldsboro* case be vacated as moot was no longer appropriate because of the order of the Court of Appeals.

The administration sought permission from the Court to file a brief arguing that there was no basis in congressional legislation for the Internal Revenue Service's eleven-year policy of denying exemptions to schools that discriminate on racial grounds. Meanwhile, Bob Jones University and Goldsboro Christian Schools asked the Court to reverse the federal appeals court ruling. In March the Supreme Court accepted the government brief.

In May 1983 the Court, with only Justice Rehnquist in dissent, affirmed the judgments of the Court of Appeals in the two cases. Chief Justice Burger delivered the opinion for the Court in BOB JONES UNIVERSITY v. UNITED STATES and GOLDSBORO CHRISTIAN SCHOOLS v. UNITED STATES (p. 222). The Chief Justice interpreted congressional intent with respect to entitlement to tax exemptions provided for in the Internal Revenue Code to mean that entitlement was to depend not only on an institution's falling within one of the designated eight categories set forth, but on "meeting certain common law standards of charity—namely, that an institution seeking tax-exempt status must serve a public purpose and not be contrary to established public policy." (461 U.S. 574, 586)

Racial discrimination is clearly contrary to public policy, and the IRS therefore acted properly in July 1970 when it concluded that tax-exempt status would no longer be granted to private schools practicing racial discrimination, nor would gifts to such schools be treated as charitable

---

[2] A case of tremendous significance is at the time of this writing pending before a federal district court in New York: if successful, the suit would revoke the tax exemption of the Roman Catholic Church. The litigation brought by Abortion Rights Mobilization and twenty other pro-choice groups and individuals against the United States Catholic Conference and National Conference of Catholic Bishops—contends that the Church has violated section 501(c)(3) of the tax code which provides that tax exempt organizations cannot "participate in, or intervene in . . . any political campaign on behalf of any candidate for public office." It is charged that the Church has violated the prohibition through its consistent efforts to support or oppose candidates based on their stance on the abortion issue. Obviously, the suit has grave implications not only for the Roman Catholic Church, but for all churches because of the financial benefit which accrues to them through tax deductibility of contributions.

deductions for income tax purposes. The immediate responsibility for interpreting the Internal Revenue Code falls upon the administrative agency. Congress obviously has the power to modify improper IRS rulings, but Congress had been "acutely aware" of the controversial determinations for twelve years and by failing to modify them had in effect acquiesced in and ratified the IRS action.

The majority opinion then spoke to the contention that the construction given the code by the IRS violated First Amendment free exercise rights of religious schools engaging in racial discrimination on the basis of "sincerely held religious beliefs." The Chief Justice agreed that the Court recognized that government regulation of religious beliefs was prohibited; however, it had also consistently recognized that not all burdens on actions based on religious beliefs are forbidden. Some government interests are so compelling as to justify regulation of religiously based conduct. Eradication of racial discrimination in education is such a compelling state interest which "substantially outweighs whatever burden denial of tax benefits places on petitioners' exercise of their religious beliefs." (461 U.S. 574, 604)

Justice Powell concurred in the judgment of the Court, but in a separate opinion he expressed his concern with the "broader implications" of the majority opinion. He was particularly troubled by the conformity which the opinion seemed to mandate, as if suggesting that the "primary function of a tax-exempt organization is to act on behalf of the Government in carrying out governmentally approved policies." Powell assumed that one of the important purposes of tax exemption to private nonprofit schools and other groups is to provide alternative choices and "encourage diverse, indeed often sharply conflicting activities and viewpoints." If tax exemption was to be denied, Congress should so provide. "The contours of public policy," he concluded, "should be determined by Congress, not by judges or the IRS."

Justice Rehnquist, in dissent, agreed that there is a strong national policy against racial discrimination and that Congress could legislate to further that policy through denial of tax exemption. The Court had erred, he argued, in assuming that Congress had adopted the 1970 IRS ruling by failure to pass legislation negating it. He, like Justice Powell, maintained that "this Court should not legislate for Congress."[3]

Beginning at least as early as the encounters of the Jehovah's Witnesses with license fees and taxes on income from sale of religious publications in the 1930s, unpopular, unorthodox religious movements have been made painfully aware that the taxing power can be one of the most successful devices used by unfriendly authorities to limit or to harass their efforts. These incidents have most often occurred at the local level, and the courts—at least the appellate courts—have most often come to the rescue of the beleaguered groups.

In the seventies and eighties the Unification Church, having met with widespread negative governmental action, has succeeded the Jehovah's Witnesses as today's most litigated religious movement. Numerous cases have been brought in both state and federal courts against, or on behalf of, the "Moonies," as members of the movement are derogatorily designated. The most highly publicized suits have concerned either the alleged "mind control" and "brainwashing" techniques of the Unification Church or the "deprogramming" activities of Ted Patrick and others who gained considerable public attention for their forcible abduction of young, or sometimes not so young, Unification converts followed by strenuous psychological efforts to cause them to recant and return to their former religious commitment and lifestyle.[4]

However, the litigation most costly in terms of time, finance, and leadership has emanated from tax conflicts. For five years the church was involved in a tax battle with New York City. In 1977 that city's tax commission denied the Church's request for real estate tax exemption for three New York properties—which together served as headquarters for the worldwide movement—on the ground that the primary purpose of the Unification Church was political and economic rather than religious. The church appealed to the Appellate Division of the New York Supreme Court which, finding the record insufficient for review, appointed a special referee to acquire the necessary information to ascertain whether the commission had acted arbitrarily and capriciously in denying the claim for exemption.

The referee determined that while the primary purpose of the Church was religious, the commission had not acted arbitrarily and capriciously because the political motives and activities of the Church were such as to deny exemption. The Appellate Division approved the report of the referee, but rejected his finding that the church's primary purpose was religious.

---

[3] For further discussion of the case see "Bob Jones University v. United States: Paying the Price of Prejudice—Loss of Tax Exempt Status," Mercer Law Review 35 (Spring 1984): 937-63, and Charles O. Gavin and Neal Devins, "A Tax Policy Analysis of Bob Jones University v. United States," Vanderbilt Law Review 36 (November 1983): 1353-82.

[4] See such state and lower federal court cases as Katz v. Superior Court (1977), Colombrito v. Kelly (1985), and Molko and Leal v. HSA (1986). Responding to great public concern about the proliferation of "cults," particularly after the Jonestown tragedy in 1978, investigations of the cult movement were conducted in numerous state legislatures and Congress as well. In response to alleged brainwashing by adherents of the Unification Church, conservatorship bills to allow state appointment of conservators for a person who had fallen under the control of a group to the point that his or her judgment had been impaired were introduced in at least seven legislatures. The New York legislature actually passed such a bill in 1980, which would allow the state to appoint conservators for persons who had "become closely and regularly associated with a group which practices the use of deception in the recruitment of members and which engages in systematic food or sleep deprivation or isolation from family or unusually long work schedules and such persons for whom the temporary conservator is to be appointed has undergone a sudden and radical change in behavior, lifestyle, habits and attitudes, and has become unable to care for his welfare and that his judgment has become impaired to the extent that he is unable to understand the need for such care." (11122-A Section 1, New York 25 March 1980) The bill was vetoed by Governor Hugh L. Carey as both unconstitutional and unworkable. Perceptive accounts of the events of the period are found in David G. Bromley and Anson D. Shupe, Jr., Strange Gods: The Great American Cult Scare (Boston: Beacon Press, 1981) and James E. Wood, Jr., "Editorial: New Religions and the First Amendment," Journal of Church and State 24 (Autumn 1982): 457-62.

On further appeal, the Court of Appeals of New York in 1982 reversed the denial of tax exemption and, citing *Watson*, *Barnette*, and *Ballard*, said: "As stated, it is not the province of civil authorities to indulge in such distillation as to what is to be denominated religious and what political or economic. It is for religious bodies themselves, rather than the courts or administrative agencies to define by their teachings and activities what their religion is." *The Holy Spirit Association for the Unification of World Christianity* v. *The Tax Commission of the City of New York* (435 N.E. 2d 662, 668 [1982])

In December 1981 a criminal suit was filed in the United Sates District Court for the Southern District of New York which soon overshadowed all previous Unification Church litigation, and which caused grave concern on the part of many individuals and church groups not ordinarily sympathetic with the goals and methods of the Unification Church. After a five-year investigation by the IRS, the suit was brought against Reverend Sun Myung Moon, founder and leader of the Church, and his financial aide. They were indicted on thirteen counts relating to federal tax evasion—filing false tax returns, submitting false documents, perjury, obstruction of justice, etc. Because he feared prejudice on the part of most potential jurors, Reverend Moon asked for but was denied a non-jury trial. He was represented by eminent Harvard Law Professor Lawrence H. Tribe.

The case revolved primarily around the question of whether bank accounts in a New York bank and stock in a corporation, both held in Moon's name, were for his personal use and financial benefit as the government contended, or whether he held them as a trustee, and living embodiment of the faith, in behalf of the Unification Church (in which case the interest and dividends would be tax exempt).

After a six-week trial, Moon was found guilty on all counts and Judge Gerard L. Goettel, who had carefully sought to keep the trial free from religious overtones, sentenced him to concurrent prison terms of eighteen months and levied a fine of $25,000 plus court costs. The case was appealed to the Court of Appeals for the Second Circuit which upheld the verdict by a two-to-one vote. In 1984 the Supreme Court refused to review the case and Reverend Moon served thirteen of the eighteen-month sentence.

That the entire proceeding caused great concern to many individuals and religious and civil rights groups is evidenced by the extraordinary number of *amici curiae* briefs filed in Moon's behalf. Sixteen briefs were filed by forty individuals and religious and civil rights groups as varied as United States Senators Orrin G. Hatch and Eugene J. McCarthy, the National Council of Christ in the U.S.A., the Presbyterian Church (USA), the National Association of Evangelicals, the African Methodist Episcopal Church, the Church of Jesus Christ of Latter Day Saints, the Southern Christian Leadership Conference, and the Catholic League for Religion and Civil Rights.

The briefs objected not only to what their authors regarded as excessive governmental interference in the internal financial procedures of churches but also to the selective prosecution of a controversial religious leader. They pointed out that the practice of a church holding its funds and property in the name of the pastor is not peculiar to the Unification Church. Thus Moon's conviction had ominous forebodings, particularly for those poorer, less highly organized churches where the pastor may be the only paid employee available to handle funds and financial accounting.

Many persons have commented on the selective prosecution aspect of the case. Trial judge Goettel himself recognized the unusual nature of the case against Reverend Moon when he said, "I am not so naive as to believe that if Reverend Moon was a noncontroversial person whose religion was Pollyannish, who nobody took exception to, that the government would not have as much interest in looking at his taxes as they did." [5]

Senator Orrin Hatch, who chaired a Senate subcommittee which looked into the Moon prosecution, expressed his misgivings about the entire proceeding in a letter to attorney Edward Bennett Williams:

In my opinion, Rev. Moon's is an extremely important religious freedom case. In a very real way, it has sent a message of how present day America deals with unpopular religions seeking sanctuary on our shores. Sadly, the message is not a good one . . . . The Moon case sends a strong signal that if one's views are unpopular enough, this country will find a way not to tolerate, but to convict. [6]

Whatever Reverend Sun Myung Moon's real motives may have been, what happened to him serves once again to emphasize the potential for control of unpopular religious movements that lies in the power to tax.

UNITED STATES v. LEE

455 U.S. 252

ON APPEAL FROM THE UNITED STATES DISTRICT COURT FOR THE WESTERN DISTRICT OF PENNSYLVANIA

Argued November 2, 1981 — Decided February 23, 1982

⊥*Chief Justice BURGER* delivered the opinion of the Court.   ⊥254

We noted probable jurisdiction to determine whether imposition of social security taxes is unconstitutional as applied to persons who object on religious grounds to receipt of public insurance benefits and to payment of taxes to support public insurance funds. The District Court concluded that the Free Exercise Clause prohibits forced payment of social security taxes when payment of taxes and receipt of benefits violates the taxpayer's religion. We reverse.

I

Appellee, a member of the Old Order Amish, is a self-employed farmer and carpenter. From 1970 to 1977, appellee employed several other Amish to work on his farm and in his carpentry shop. He failed to

---

[5] Quoted in Leo Pfeffer, *Religion, State and the Burger Court* (Buffalo, N.Y.: Prometheus Books, 1984), p. 13.
[6] *Unification News*, September 1985, p. 5.

file the quarterly social security tax returns required of employers, withhold social security tax from his employees or pay the employer's share of social security taxes.

_|255 In 1978, the Internal Revenue Service assessed appellee in excess of $27,000 for unpaid employment taxes; he paid $91—⊥ the amount owed for the first quarter of 1973—and then sued in the United States District Court for the Western District of Pennsylvania for a refund, claiming that imposition of the social security taxes violated his First Amendment Free Exercise rights and those of his Amish employees.

The District Court held the statutes requiring appellee to pay social security and unemployment insurance taxes unconstitutional as applied. The court noted that the Amish believe it sinful not to provide for their own elderly and needy and therefore are religiously opposed to the national social security system. The court also accepted appellee's contention that the Amish religion not only prohibits the acceptance of social security benefits, but also bars all contributions by Amish to the social security system. The District Court observed that in light of their beliefs, Congress has accommodated self-employed Amish and self-employed members of other religious groups with similar beliefs by providing exemptions from social security taxes. 26 U. S. C. § 1402(g). The court's holding was based on both

_|256 ⊥the exemption statute for the self-employed and the First Amendment; appellee and others "who fall within the carefully circumscribed definition provided in 1402(g) are relieved from paying the employer's share of [social security taxes] as it is an unconstitutional infringement upon the free exercise of their religion."

Direct appeal from the judgment of the District Court was taken pursuant to 28 U. S. C. § 1252.

II

The exemption provided by § 1402(g) is available only to self-employed individuals and does not apply to employers or employees. Consequently, appellee and his employees are not within the express provisions of § 1402(g). Thus any exemption from payment of the employer's share of social security taxes must come from a constitutionally-required exemption.

A

The preliminary inquiry in determining the existence of a constitutionally-required exemption is

_|257 whether the payment ⊥of social security taxes and the receipt of benefits interferes with the Free Exercise rights of the Amish. The Amish believe that there is a religiously based obligation to provide for their fellow members the kind of assistance contemplated by the social security system. Although the government does not challenge the sincerity of this belief, the government does contend that payment of

social security taxes will not threaten the integrity of the Amish religious belief or observance. It is not within "the judicial function and judicial competence," however, to determine whether appellee or the government has the proper interpretation of the Amish faith; "[c]ourts are not arbiters of scriptural interpretation." *Thomas* v. *Review Bd. of Indiana Employment Sec.* We therefore accept appellee's contention that both payment and receipt of social security benefits is forbidden by the Amish faith. Because the payment of the taxes or receipt of benefits violates Amish religious beliefs, compulsory participation in the social security system interferes with their Free Exercise rights.

The conclusion that there is a conflict between the Amish faith and the obligations imposed by the social security system is only the beginning, however, and not the end of the inquiry. Not all burdens on religion are unconstitutional. The state may justify a limitation on religious liberty by showing that it is essential to accomplish an overriding governmental inter⊥est.   _|258

B

Because the social security system is nationwide, the governmental interest is apparent. The social security system in the United States serves the public interest by providing a comprehensive insurance system with a variety of benefits available to all participants, with costs shared by employers and employees. The social security system is by far the largest domestic governmental program in the United States today, distributing approximately $11 billion monthly to 36 million Americans. The design of the system requires support by mandatory contributions from covered employers and employees. This mandatory participation is indispensable to the fiscal vitality of the social security system. "[W]idespread individual voluntary coverage under social security . . . would undermine the soundness of the social security program." S. Resp. No. 404, 89th Cong., 1st Sess., Pt. III, U. S. Code Cong. & Admin. News (1965), pp. 1943, 2056. Moreover, a comprehensive national social security system providing for voluntary participation would be almost a contradiction in terms and difficult, if not impossible, to administer. Thus, the government's interest in as-⊥suring mandatory and continuous participation in and contribution to the social security system is very high.   _|259

C

The remaining inquiry is whether accommodating the Amish belief will unduly interfere with fulfillment of the governmental interest. In *Braunfeld* v. *Brown* this Court noted that "to make accommodation between the religious action and an exercise of state authority is a particularly delicate task . . . because resolution in favor of the State results in the choice to the individual of either abandoning his religious principle or facing . . . prosecution." The difficulty in attempting to accommodate religious beliefs in the area of taxation is that "we are a cosmopolitan nation made up of people of almost every conceivable religious preference." *Braunfeld.* The Court has long recognized that balance must be struck between the values of the comprehensive social system, which rests on a complex of actuarial factors, and the consequences of allowing religiously based exemptions. To maintain an organized society that guarantees religious freedom to a great variety of faiths requires that some religious practices yield to the common good. Religious beliefs can be accommodated, but there is a point at which accommodation would "radically restrict the operating latitude of the legislature." *Braunfeld.*

Unlike the situation presented in *Wisconsin* v. *Yoder,* it would be difficult to accommodate the ⌐260 comprehen⊥sive social security system with myriad exceptions flowing from a wide variety of religious beliefs. The obligation to pay the social security tax initially is not fundamentally different from the obligation to pay income taxes; the difference—in theory at least—is that the social security tax revenues are segregated for use only in furtherance of the statutory program. There is no principled way, however, for purposes of this case, to distinguish between general taxes and those imposed under the Social Security Act. If, for example, a religious adherent believes war is a sin, and if a certain percentage of the federal budget can be identified as devoted to war-related activities, such individuals would have a similarly valid claim to be exempt from paying that percentage of the income tax. The tax system could not function if denominations were allowed to challenge the tax system because tax payments were spent in a manner that violates their religious belief. Because the broad public interest in maintaining a sound tax system is of such a high order, religious belief in conflict with the payment of taxes affords no basis for resisting the tax.

III

Congress has accommodated, to the extent compatible with a comprehensive national program, the practices of those who believe it a violation of their faith to participate in the social security system. In § 1402(g) Congress granted an exemption, on religious grounds, to self-employed Amish and others. Confining the § 1402(g) exemption to the self-⌐261 ⊥employed provided for a narrow category which was readily identifiable. Self-employed persons in a religious community having its own "welfare" system are distinguishable from the generality of wage earners employed by others.

Congress and the courts have been sensitive to the needs flowing from the Free Exercise Clause, but every person cannot be shielded from all the burdens incident to exercising every aspect of the right to practice religious beliefs. When followers of a particular sect enter into commercial activity as a matter of choice, the limits they accept on their own conduct as a matter of conscience and faith are not to be superimposed on the statutory schemes which are binding on others in that activity. Granting an exemption from social security taxes to an employer operates to impose the employer's religious faith on the employees. Congress drew a line in § 1402(g), exempting the self-employed Amish but not all persons working for an Amish employer. The tax imposed on employers to support the social security system must be uniformly applicable to all, except as Congress provides explicitly otherwise.

Accordingly, the judgment of the District Court is reversed and the case remanded for proceedings consistent with this opinion.

Reversed and remanded.

Justice STEVENS, concurring in the judgment.

The clash between appellee's religious obligation and his civic obligation is irreconcilable. He must violate either an Amish belief or a federal statute. According to the Court, the religious duty must prevail unless the Government shows ⊥that enforcement of ⌐262 the civic duty "is essential to accomplish an overriding governmental interest." That formulation of the constitutional standard suggests that the Government always bears a heavy burden of justifying the application of neutral general laws to individual conscientious objectors. In my opinion, it is the objector who must shoulder the burden of demonstrating that there is a unique reason for allowing him a special exemption from a valid law of general applicability.

Congress already has granted the Amish a limited exemption from social security taxes. As a matter of administration, it would be a relatively simple matter to extend the exemption to the taxes involved in this case. As a matter of fiscal policy, an enlarged exemption probably would benefit the social security system because the nonpayment of these taxes by the Amish would be more than offset by the elimination of their right to collect benefits. In view of the fact that the Amish have demonstrated their capacity to care for their own, the social cost of eliminating this relatively small group of dedicated believers would be minimal. Thus, if we confine the analysis to the Government's interest in rejecting the particular claim to an exemption at stake in this case, the constitutional standard as formulated by the Court has not been met.

The Court rejects the particular claim of this appellee, not because it presents any special problems, but rather because of the risk that a myriad of other claims would be too difficult to process. The Court overstates the magnitude of this risk because the Amish claim applies only to a small religious community with an established welfare system of its

⌐263 own. ⊥ Nevertheless, I agree with the Court's conclusion that the difficulties associated with processing other claims to tax exemption on religious grounds justify a rejection of this claim. I believe, however, that this reasoning supports the adoption of a different constitutional standard than the Court purports to apply.

The Court's analysis supports a holding that there is virtually no room for a "constitutionally-required exemption" on religious grounds from a valid tax law that is entirely neutral in its general application. Because I agree with that holding, I concur in the judgment.

BOB JONES UNIVERSITY
v.
UNITED STATES

GOLDSBORO CHRISTIAN SCHOOLS, INC.
v.
UNITED STATES

461 U.S. 574

ON WRIT OF CERTIORARI TO THE UNITED STATES
COURT OF APPEALS FOR THE FOURTH CIRCUIT

Argued October 12, 1982 — Decided May 24, 1983

⌐577 ⊥ *CHIEF JUSTICE BURGER* delivered the opinion of the Court.

We granted certiorari to decide whether petitioners, nonprofit private schools that prescribe and enforce racially discriminatory admissions standards on the basis of religious doctrine, qualify as tax exempt organizations under § 501(c)(3) of the Internal Revenue Code of 1954.

I
A

Until 1970, the Internal Revenue Service granted tax-exempt status to private schools, without regard to their racial admissions policies, under § 501(c)(3), ⌐578 and granted chari⊥table deductions for contributions to such schools under § 170 of the Code, 26 U.S.C. § 170.

On January 12, 1970 a three-judge District Court for the District of Columbia issued a preliminary injunction prohibiting the IRS from according tax-exempt status to private schools in Mississippi that discriminated as to admissions on the basis of race. *Green* v. *Kennedy.* Thereafter, in July 1970, the IRS concluded that it could "no longer legally justify allowing tax-exempt status [under § 501(c)(3)] to private schools which practice racial discrimination." At the same time, the IRS announced that it could not "treat gifts to such schools as charitable deduc-

tions for income tax purposes [under §170]." By letter dated November 30, 1970 the IRS formally notified private schools, including those involved in this case, of this change in policy, "applicable to all private schools in the United States at all levels of education."

On June 30, 1971 the three-judge District Court issued its opinion on the merits of the Mississippi challenge. *Green* v. *Connally.* That court approved the IRS' amended construction of the Tax Code. The court also held that racially discriminatory private schools were not entitled to exemption under § 501(c)(3) and that donors were not entitled to deductions for contributions to such schools under § 170. The court permanently enjoined the Commissioner of ⊥ Internal Revenue from approving tax-exempt ⌐579 status for any school in Mississippi that did not publicly maintain a policy of nondiscrimination.

The revised policy on discrimination was formalized in Revenue Ruling 71-447, 1971-2 Cum. Bull. 230: "Both the courts and the Internal Revenue Service have long recognized that the statutory requirement of being 'organized and operated exclusively for religious, charitable, . . . or educational purposes' was intended to express the basic common law concept [of 'charity']. . . . All charitable trusts, educational or otherwise, are subject to the requirement that the purpose of the trust may not be illegal or contrary to public policy." Based on the "national policy to discourage racial discrimination in education," the IRS ruled that "a private school not having a racially nondiscriminatory policy as to students is not 'charitable' within the common law concepts reflected in sections 170 and 501(c)(3) of the Code."

The application of the IRS construction of these provisions to petitioners, two private schools with racially discriminatory admissions policies, is now before us.

B
No. 81-3, Bob Jones University v. United States

Bob Jones University is a nonprofit corporation located in Greenville, South Carolina. Its purpose is "to conduct an institution ⊥ of learning . . . , ⌐580 giving special emphasis to the Christian religion and the ethics revealed in the Holy Scriptures." The corporation operates a school with an enrollment of approximately 5,000 students, from kindergarten through college and graduate school. Bob Jones University is not affiliated with any religious denomination, but is dedicated to the teaching and propagation of its fundamentalist Christian religious beliefs. It is both a religious and educational institution. Its teachers are required to be devout Christians, and all courses at the University are taught according to the Bible. Entering students are screened as to their religious beliefs, and their public and private conduct is strictly regulated by standards promulgated by University authorities.

The sponsors of the University genuinely believe that the Bible forbids interracial dating and marriage. To effectuate these views, Negroes were completely excluded until 1971. From 1971 to May 1975, the University accepted no applications from unmarried Negroes, but did accept applications from Negroes married within their race.

Following the decision of the United States Court of Appeals for the Fourth Circuit in *McCrary* v. *Runyon*, prohibiting racial exclusion from private schools, the University revised its policy. Since May 29, 1975, the University has permitted unmarried Negroes to enroll; but a disciplinary rule prohibits interracial dating and marriage. That rule reads: *There is to be no interracial dating.*

1. Students who are partners in an interracial marriage will be expelled.

⊥ 2. Students who are members of or affiliated with any group or organization which holds as one of its goals or advocates interracial marriage will be expelled.

3. Students who date outside their own race will be expelled.

4. Students who espouse, promote, or encourage others to violate the University's dating rules and regulations will be expelled.

The University continues to deny admission to applicants engaged in an interracial marriage or known to advocate interracial marriage or dating.

Until 1970, the IRS extended tax-exempt status to Bob Jones University under § 501(c)(3). By the letter of November 30, 1970, that followed the injunction issued in *Green* v. *Kennedy*, the IRS formally notified the University of the change in IRS policy, and announced its intention to challenge the tax-exempt status of private schools practicing racial discrimination in their admissions policies.

After failing to obtain an assurance of tax exemption through administrative means, the University instituted an action in 1971 seeking to enjoin the IRS from revoking the school's tax-exempt status. That suit culminated in *Bob Jones University* v. *Simon,* in which this Court held that the Anti-Injunction Act of the Internal Revenue Code, 26 U.S.C. § 7421(a), prohibited the University from obtaining judicial review by way of injunctive action before the assessment or collection of any tax.

Thereafter, on April 16, 1975, the IRS notified the University of the proposed revocation of its tax-exempt status. On January 19, 1976, the IRS officially revoked the University's tax-exempt status, effective as of December 1, 1970, the day after the University was formally notified of the change in IRS policy. The University subsequently filed returns under the Federal Unemployment Tax Act for the period from December 1, 1970, to December 31, 1975, and paid a tax ⊥ totalling $21.00 on one em-

ployee for the calendar year of 1975. After its request for a refund was denied, the University instituted the present action, seeking to recover the $21.00 it had paid to the IRS. The Government counterclaimed for unpaid federal unemployment taxes for the taxable years 1971 through 1975, in the amount of $489,675.59, plus interest.

The United States District Court for the District of South Carolina held that revocation of the University's tax-exempt status exceeded the delegated powers of the IRS, was improper under the IRS rulings and procedures, and violated the University's rights under the Religion Clauses of the First Amendment. The court accordingly ordered the IRS to pay the University the $21.00 refund it claimed and rejected the IRS counterclaim.

The Court of Appeals for the Fourth Circuit, in a divided, opinion, reversed. Citing *Green* v. *Connally*, with approval, the Court of Appeals concluded that § 501(c)(3) must be read against the background of charitable trust law. To be eligible for an exemption under that section, an institution must be "charitable" in the common law sense, and therefore must not be contrary to public policy. In the court's view, Bob Jones University did not meet this requirement, since its "racial policies violated the clearly defined public policy, rooted in our Constitution, condemning racial discrimination and, more specifically, the government policy against subsidizing racial discrimination in education, public or private." The court held that the IRS acted within its statutory authority in revoking the University's tax-exempt status. Finally, the Court of Appeals rejected petitioner's arguments that the revocation of the tax exemption violated the Free Exercise and Establishment Clauses of the First Amendment. The case was remanded to the District Court with instructions to dismiss the University's claim for a refund and to reinstate the Government's counterclaim.

⊥ C

No. 81-1, Goldsboro Christian Schools, Inc. v. *United States*

Goldsboro Christian Schools is a nonprofit corporation located in Goldsboro, North Carolina. Like Bob Jones University, it was established "to conduct an institution of learning . . . , giving special emphasis to the Christian religion and the ethics revealed in the Holy scriptures." The school offers classes from kindergarten through high school, and since at least 1969 has satisfied the State of North Carolina's requirements for secular education in private schools. The school requires its high school students to take Bible-related courses, and begins each class with prayer.

Since its incorporation in 1963, Goldsboro Christian Schools has maintained a racially discriminatory admissions policy based upon its interpretation of the Bible. Goldsboro has for the most part accepted only Caucasians. On occasion, however, the school has accepted children from racially mixed marriages in which one of the parents is Caucasian.

Goldsboro never received a determination by the IRS that it was an organization entitled to tax exemption under § 501(c)(3). Upon audit of Goldsboro's records for the years 1969 through 1972, the IRS determined that Goldsboro was not an organization described in § 501(c)(3), and therefore was required to pay taxes under the Federal Insurance Contribution Act and the Federal Unemployment Tax Act.

⊥584   ⊥ Goldsboro paid the IRS $3,459.93 in withholding, social security, and unemployment taxes with respect to one employee for the years 1969 through 1972. Thereafter, Goldsboro filed a suit seeking refund of that payment, claiming that the school had been improperly denied § 501(c)(3) exempt status. The IRS counterclaimed for $160,073.96 in unpaid social security and unemployment taxes for the years 1969 through 1972, including interest and penalties.

The District Court for the Eastern District of North Carolina decided the action on cross-motions for summary judgment. In addressing the motions for summary judgment, the court assumed that Goldsboro's racially discriminatory admissions policy was based upon a sincerely held religious belief. The court nevertheless rejected Goldsboro's claim to tax-exempt status under § 501(c)(3), finding that "private schools maintaining racially discriminatory admissions policies violate clearly declared federal policy and, therefore, must be denied the federal tax benefits flowing from qualification under Section 501(c)(3)." The court also rejected Goldsboro's arguments that denial of tax-exempt status violated the Free Exercise and Establishment Clauses of the First Amendment. Accordingly, the court entered summary judgment for the Government on its counterclaim.

The Court of Appeals for the Fourth Circuit affirmed. That court found an "identity for present purposes" between the *Goldsboro* case and the *Bob Jones University* case, which had been decided ⊥585 shortly ⊥ before by another panel of that court, and affirmed for the reasons set forth in *Bob Jones University.*

We granted certiorari in both cases, and we affirm in each.

II

A

In Revenue Ruling 71-447, the IRS formalized the policy first announced in 1970, that § 170 and § 501(c)(3) embrace the common law "charity" concept. Under that view, to qualify for a tax exemption pursuant to § 501(c)(3), an institution must show, first, that it falls within one of the eight categories expressly set forth in that section, and second, that its activity is not contrary to settled public policy.

Section 501(c)(3) provides that "[c]orporations . . . organized and operated exclusively for religious, charitable . . . or educational purposes" are entitled to tax exemption. Petitioners argue that the plain language of the statute guarantees them tax-exempt status. They emphasize the absence of any language in the statute expressly requiring all exempt organizations to be "charitable" in the common law sense, and they contend that the disjunctive "or" separating the categories in § 501(c)(3) precludes such a reading. Instead, they argue that if an institution falls within one or more of ⊥ the specified cate- ⊥586 gories it is automatically entitled to exemption, without regard to whether it also qualifies as "charitable." The Court of Appeals rejected that contention and concluded that petitioners' interpretation of the statute "tears section 501(c)(3) from its roots." *United States* v. *Bob Jones University.*

It is a well-established canon of statutory construction that a court should go beyond the literal language of a statute if reliance on that language would defeat the plain purpose of the statute: "The general words used in the clause . . . , taken by themselves, and literally construed, without regard to the object in view, would seem to sanction the claim of the plaintiff. But this mode of expounding a statute has never been adopted by any enlightened tribunal—because it is evident that in many cases it would defeat the object which the Legislature intended to accomplish. And it is well settled that, in interpreting a statute, the court will not look merely to a particular clause in which general words may be used, *but will take in connection with it the whole statute . . . and the objects and policy of the law . . . .*" *Brown* v. *Duchesne.*

Section 501(c)(3) therefore must be analyzed and construed within the framework of the Internal Revenue Code and against the background of the Congressional purposes. Such an examination reveals unmistakable evidence that, underlying all relevant parts of the Code, is the intent that entitlement to tax exemption depends on meeting certain common law standards of charity—namely, that an institution seeking tax-exempt status must serve a public purpose and not be contrary to established public policy.

This "charitable" concept appears explicitly in § 170 of the Code. That section contains a list of organizations virtually identical to that contained in § 501(c)(3). It is apparent that Congress intended that list to have the same meaning in both ⊥ sections. In ⊥587 § 170, Congress used the list of organizations in defining the term "charitable contributions." On its face, therefore, § 170 reveals that Congress' intention was to provide tax benefits to organizations serving charitable purposes. The form of § 170 simply makes plain what common sense and history tell us: in enacting both § 170 and ⊥ § 501(c)(3), Congress ⊥588 sought to provide tax benefits to charitable organizations, to encourage the development of private institutions that serve a useful public purpose or supplement or take the place of public institutions of the same kind.

Tax exemptions for certain institutions thought beneficial to the social order of the country as a whole, or to a particular community, are deeply rooted in our history, as in that of England. The origins of such exemptions lie in the special privileges that have long been extended to charitable trusts.

More than a century ago, this Court announced the caveat that is critical in this case: "[I]t has now become an established principle of American law, that courts of chancery will sustain and protect . . . a gift . . . to public charitable uses, *provided the same is consistent with local laws and public policy* . . . ." *Perin* v. *Carey* (emphasis added). Soon after that, in 1878, the Court commented: "A charitable use, *where neither law nor public policy forbids,* may be applied to almost any thing *that tends to promote the well-doing and well-being of social man.*" *Ould* v. *Washington Hospital for Foundlings* (emphasis added). ⊥ In 1891, in a restatement of the English law of charity which has long been recognized as a leading authority in this country, Lord MacNaghten stated: "'Charity' in its legal sense comprises four principal divisions: trusts for the relief of poverty; *trusts for the advancement of education;* trusts for the advancement of religion; and trusts for *other purposes beneficial to the community,* not falling under any of the preceding heads." *Commissioners* v. *Pemsel* (emphasis added). These statements clearly reveal the legal background against which Congress enacted the first charitable exemption statute in 1894: charities were to be given preferential treatment because they provide a benefit to society.

What little floor debate occurred on the charitable exemption provision of the 1894 Act and similar sections of later statutes leaves no doubt that Congress deemed the specified organizations entitled to tax benefits because they served desirable public purposes. ⊥ In floor debate on a similar provision in 1917, for example, Senator Hollis articulated the rationale: "For every dollar that a man contributes to these public charities, educational, scientific, or otherwise, the public gets 100 percent." In 1924, this Court restated the common understanding of the charitable exemption provision: "Evidently the exemption is made in recognition of the benefit which the public derives from corporate activities of the class named, and is intended to aid them when not conducted for private gain." *Trinidad* v. *Sagrada Orden.*

In enacting the Revenue Act of 1938, Congress expressly reconfirmed this view with respect to the charitable deduction provision: "The exemption from taxation of money and property devoted to charitable and other purposes is based on the theory that the Government is compensated for the loss of revenue by its relief from financial burdens which would otherwise have to be met by appropriations from other public funds, and by the benefits resulting from the promotion of the general welfare."

⊥ A corollary to the public benefit principle is the requirement, long recognized in the law of trusts, that the purpose of a charitable trust may not be illegal or violate established public policy. In 1861, this Court stated that a public charitable use must be "consistent with local laws and public policy," *Perin* v. *Carey.* Modern commentators and courts have echoed that view.

When the Government grants exemptions or allows deductions all taxpayers are affected; the very fact of the exemption or deduction for the donor means that other taxpayers can be said to be indirect and vicarious "donors." Charitable exemptions are justified on the basis that the exempt entity confers a public benefit—a benefit which the society or the community may not itself choose or be able to provide, or which supplements and advances the work of public institutions already supported by tax revenues. History but ⊥ tresses logic to make clear that, to warrant exemption under § 501(c)(3), an institution must fall within a category specified in that section and must demonstrably serve and be in harmony with the public interest. The institution's purpose must not be so at odds with the common community conscience as to undermine any public benefit that might otherwise be conferred.

B

We are bound to approach these questions with full awareness that determinations of public benefit and public policy are sensitive matters with serious implications for the institutions affected; a declaration that a given institution is not "charitable" should be made only where there can be no doubt that the activity involved is contrary to a fundamental public policy. But there can no longer be any doubt that racial discrimination in education violates deeply and widely accepted views of elementary justice. Prior to 1954, public education in many places still was conducted under the pall of ⊥ *Plessy* v. *Ferguson;* racial segregation in primary and secondary education prevailed in many parts of the country. This Court's decision in *Brown* v. *Board of Education,* signalled an end to that era. Over the past quarter of a century, every pronouncement of this Court and myriad Acts of Congress and Executive Orders attest a firm national policy to prohibit racial segregation and discrimination in public education.

An unbroken line of cases following *Brown* v. *Board of Education* establishes beyond doubt this Court's view that racial discrimination in education violates a most fundamental national public policy, as well as rights of individuals. "The right of a student not to be segregated on racial grounds in schools . . . is indeed so fundamental and pervasive that it is embraced in the concept of due process of law." *Cooper* v. *Aaron*. In *Norwood* v. *Harrison*, we dealt with a non-public institution: "[A] private school—even one that discriminates—fulfills an important educational function; *however, . . . [that] legitimate educational function cannot be isolated from ⊥ discriminatory practices . . . [D]iscriminatory treatment exerts a pervasive influence on the entire educational process.*" (Emphasis added).

⌊594

Congress, in Titles IV and VI of the Civil Rights Act of 1964, clearly expressed its agreement that racial discrimination in education violates a fundamental public policy. Other sections of that Act, and numerous enactments since then, testify to the public policy against racial discrimination.

The Executive Branch has consistently placed its support behind eradication of racial discrimination. Several years before this Court's decision in *Brown* v. *Board of Education*, President Truman issued Executive Orders prohibiting racial discrimination in federal employment decisions and in classifications for the Selective Service. In 1957, President Eisenhower employed military forces to ensure compliance with federal standards in school desegregation programs. And in 1962, President Kennedy announced: "[T]he granting of federal assistance for . . . housing and related facilities from which Americans are excluded because of their race, color, creed, or national origin is unfair, unjust, and inconsistent with the public policy of ⊥ the United States as manifested in its Constitution and laws." These are but a few of numerous Executive Orders over the past three decades demonstrating the commitment of the Executive Branch to the fundamental policy of eliminating racial discrimination.

⌊595

Few social or political issues in our history have been more vigorously debated and more extensively ventilated than the issue of racial discrimination, particularly in education. Given the stress and anguish of the history of efforts to escape from the shackles of the "separate but equal" doctrine of *Plessy* v. *Ferguson,* it cannot be said that educational institutions that, for whatever reasons, practice racial dicrimination, are institutions exercising "beneficial and stabilizing influences in community life," *Walz* v. *Tax Commission*, or should be encouraged by having all taxpayers share in their support by way of special tax status.

There can thus be no question that the interpretation of § 170 and § 501(c)(3) announced by the IRS in 1970 was correct. That it may be seen as belated does not undermine its soundness. It would be wholly incompatible with the concepts underlying tax exemption to grant the benfit of tax-exempt status to racially discriminatory educational entities, which "exer[t] a pervasive influence on the entire educational process." *Norwood* v. *Harrison*. Whatever may be the rationale for such private schools' policies, and however sincere the rationale may be, racial discrimination in education is contrary to public pol-

icy. Racially discriminatory educational institutions cannot be viewed as conferring a public benefit within the "charitable" concept discussed ear⊥lier, or within the Congressional intent underlying § 170 and § 501(c)(3).

⌊596

C

Petitioners contend that, regardless of whether the IRS properly concluded that racially discriminatory private schools violate public policy, only Congress can alter the scope of § 170 and § 501(c)(3). Petitioners accordingly argue that the IRS overstepped its lawful bounds in issuing its 1970 and 1971 rulings.

Yet ever since the inception of the tax code, Congress has seen fit to vest in those administering the tax laws very broad authority to interpret those laws. In an area as complex as the tax system, the agency Congress vests with administrative responsibility must be able to exercise its authority to meet changing conditions and new problems. Indeed as early as 1918, Congress expressly authorized the Commissioner "to make all needful rules and regulations for the enforcement" of the tax laws. Revenue Act of 1918, Ch. 18 § 1309, 40 Stat. 1057, 1143 (1919). The same provision, so essential to efficient and fair administration of the tax laws, has appeared in tax codes ever since; and this Court has long recognized the primary authority of the IRS and its predecessors in construing the Internal Revenue Code.

Congress, the source of IRS authority, can modify IRS rulings it considers improper; and courts exercise review over IRS actions. In the first instance, however, the responsibil⊥ity for construing the Code falls to the IRS. Since Congress cannot be expected to anticipate every conceivable problem that can arise or to carry out day-to-day oversight, it relies on the administrators and on the courts to implement the legislative will. Administrators, like judges, are under oath to do so.

⌊597

In § 170 and § 501(c)(3), Congress has identified categories of traditionally exempt institutions and has specified certain additional requirements for tax exemption. Yet the need for continuing interpretation of those statutes is unavoidable. For more than 60 years, the IRS and its predecessors have constantly been called upon to interpret these and comparable provisions, and in doing so have referred consistently to principles of charitable trust law. In Treas. Reg. 45, art. 517(1) (1921), for example, the IRS denied charitable exemptions on the basis of proscribed political activity before the Congress itself added such conduct as a disqualifying element. In other instances, the IRS has denied charitable exemptions to otherwise qualified entities because they served too limited a class of people and thus did not provide a truly "public" benefit under the common law test. Some years before the issuance of the rulings challenged in these cases, the IRS also ruled that contributions to community recreational facilities would not be deductible and that the facilities themselves would not be entitled to tax-exempt status, unless those facilities were open to all on a racially nondiscriminatory basis. These rulings reflect the Commissioner's continuing duty to interpret and apply the Internal Revenue Code.

Guided, of course, by the Code, the IRS has the responsibility, in the first instance, to determine ⌊598 whether a particu⊥lar entity is "charitable" for purposes of § 170 and § 501(c)(3). This in turn may necessitate later determinations of whether given activities so violate public policy that the entities involved cannot be deemed to provide a public benefit worthy of "charitable" status. We emphasize, however, that these sensitive determinations should be made only where there is no doubt that the organization's activities violate fundamental public policy.

On the record before us, there can be no doubt as to the national policy. In 1970, when the IRS first issued the ruling challenged here, the position of all three branches of the Federal Government was unmistakably clear. The correctness of the Commissioner's conclusion that a racially discriminatory private school "is not 'charitable' within the common law concepts reflected in . . . the Code" is wholly consistent with what Congress, the Executive and the courts had repeatedly declared before 1970. Indeed, it would be anomalous for the Executive, Legislative and Judicial Branches to reach conclusions that add up to a firm public policy on racial discrimination, and at the same time have the IRS blissfully ignore what all three branches of the Federal Government had declared. Clearly an educa-⌊599 tional institution engaging in ⊥ practices affirmatively at odds with this declared position of the whole government cannot be seen as exercising a "beneficial and stabilizing influenc[e] in community life," *Walz* v. *Tax Commission*, and is not "charitable," within the meaning of § 170 and § 501(c)(3). We therefore hold that the IRS did not exceed its authority when it announced its interpretation of § 170 and § 501(c)(3) in 1970 and 1971.

D

The actions of Congress since 1970 leave no doubt that the IRS reached the correct conclusion in exercising its authority. It is, of course, not unknown for independent agencies or the Executive Branch to misconstrue the intent of a statute; Congress can and often does correct such misconceptions, if the courts have not done so. Yet for a dozen years Congress has been made aware—acutely aware—of the IRS rulings of 1970 and 1971. As we noted earlier, few issues have been the subject of more vigorous and widespread debate and discussion in and out of Congress than those related to racial segregation in education. Sincere adherents advocating contrary views have ventilated the subject for well over three

decades. Failure on Congress to modify the IRS rulings of 1970 and 1971, of which Congress was, by its own studies and by public discourse, constantly reminded; and Congress' awareness of the denial of tax-exempt status for racially discriminatory schools when enacting other and related legislation make out an unusually strong case of legislative acquiescence in and ratification by implication of the 1970 and 1971 rulings.

⊥ Ordinarily, and quite appropriately, courts are ⌊600 slow to attribute significance to the failure of Congress to act on particular legislation. We have observed that "unsuccessful attempts at legislation are not the best of guides to legislative intent," *Red Lion Broadcasting Co.* v. *FCC*. Here, however, we do not have an ordinary claim of legislative acquiecence. Only one month after the IRS announced its position in 1970, Congress held its first hearings on this precise issue. Exhaustive hearings have been held on the issue at various times since then. These include hearings in February 1982, after we granted review in this case.

Nonaction by Congress is not often a useful guide, but the non-action here is significant. During the past 12 years there have been no fewer than 13 bills introduced to overturn the IRS interpretation of § 501(c)(3). Not one of these bills has emerged from any committee, although Congress has enacted numerous other amendments to § 501 during this same period, including an amendment to § 501(c)(3) itself. It is hardly conceivable that Congress—and in this setting, any Member of Congress—was not abundantly ⊥ aware of what was going on. In view of its ⌊601 prolonged and acute awareness of so important an issue, Congress' failure to act on the bills proposed on this subject provides added support for concluding that Congress acquiesced in the IRS rulings of 1970 and 1971.

The evidence of Congressional approval of the policy embodied in Revenue Ruling 71-447 goes well beyond the failure of Congress to act on legislative proposals. Congress affirmatively manifested its acquiescence in the IRS policy when it enacted the present § 501(i) of the Code. That provision denies tax-exempt status to social clubs whose charters or policy statements provide for "discrimination against any person on the basis of race, color, or religion." Both the House and Senate committee reports on that bill articulated the national policy against granting tax exemptions to racially discriminatory private clubs.

Even more significant is the fact that both reports focus on this Court's affirmance of *Green* v. *Connally,* as having established that "discrimination on account of race is inconsistent with an *educational institution's* tax exempt status." These references in Congressional committee reports on an enactment denying tax exemptions to racially discriminatory private social clubs cannot be read ⊥ other than as ⌊602 indicating approval of the standards applied to racially discriminatory private schools by the IRS subsequent to 1970, and specifically of Revenue Ruling 71-447.

III

Petitioners contend that, even if the Commissioner's policy is valid as to nonreligious private schools, that policy cannot constitutionally be applied to schools that engage in racial discrimination on the basis of sincerely held religious beliefs. ⊥ As to such schools, it is argued that the IRS construction of § 170 and § 501(c)(3) violates their free exercise rights under the Religion Clauses of the First Amendment. This contention presents claims not heretofore considered by this Court in precisely this context.

⌊603

This Court has long held the Free Exercise Clause of the First Amendment an absolute prohibition against governmental regulation of religious beliefs. As interpreted by this Court, moreover, the Free Exercise Clause provides substantial protection for lawful conduct grounded in religious belief. However, "[n]ot all burdens on religion are unconstitutional. . . . The state may justify a limitation on religious liberty by showing that it is essential to accomplish an overriding governmental interest." *United States* v. *Lee.*

On occasion this Court has found certain governmental interests so compelling as to allow even regulations prohibiting religiously based conduct. In *Prince* v. *Massachusetts*, for example, the Court held that neutrally cast child labor laws prohibiting sale of printed materials on public streets could be applied to prohibit children from dispensing religious literature. The Court found no constitutional infirmity in "excluding [Jehovah's Witness children] from doing there what no other children may do." Denial of tax benefits will inevitably have a substan-

⌊604

⊥tial impact on the operation of private religious schools, but will not prevent those schools from observing their religious tenets.

The governmental interest at stake here is compelling. As discussed in Part II(B), *supra,* the government has a fundamental, overriding interest in eradicating racial discrimination in education—discrimination that prevailed, with official approval, for the first 165 years of this Nation's history. That governmental interest substantially outweighs whatever burden denial of tax benefits places on petitioners' exercise of their religious beliefs. The interests asserted by petitioners cannot be accommodated with that compelling governmental interest; and no "less restrictive means" are available to achieve the governmental interest.

⌊605

⊥IV

The remaining issue is whether the IRS properly applied its policy to these petitioners. Petitioner Goldsboro Christian Schools admits that it "main-

tain[s] racially discriminatory policies," but seeks to justify those policies on grounds we have fully discussed. The IRS properly denied tax-exempt status to Goldsboro Christian Schools.

Petitioner Bob Jones University, however, contends that it is not racially discriminatory. It emphasizes that it now allows all races to enroll, subject only to its restrictions on the conduct of all students, including its prohibitions of association between men and women of different races, and of interracial marriage. Although a ban on intermarriage or interracial dating applies to all races, decisions of this Court firmly establish that discrimination on the basis of racial affiliation and association is a form of racial discrimination. We therefore find that the IRS properly applied Revenue Ruling 71-447 to Bob Jones University.

The judgments of the Court of Appeals are, accordingly,

Affirmed.

⊥ *Justice POWELL,* concurring in part and concurring in the judgment.   ⌊606

I join the Court's judgment, along with part III of its opinion holding that the denial of tax exemptions to petitioners does not violate the First Amendment. I write separately because I am troubled by the broader implications of the Court's opinion with respect to the authority of the Internal Revenue Service (IRS) and its construction of §§ 170(c) and 501(c)(3) of the Internal Revenue Code.

I

Federal taxes are not imposed on organizations "operated exclusively for religious, charitable, scientific, testing for public safety, literary, or educational purposes . . . ." 26 U.S.C. § 510(c)(3). The Code also permits a tax deduction for contributions made to these organizations. § 170(c). It is clear that petitioners, organizations incorporated for educational purposes, fall within the language of the statute. It also is clear that the language itself does not mandate refusal of tax-exempt status to any private school that maintains a racially discriminatory admissions policy. Accordingly, there is force in Justice REHNQUIST's argument that §§ 170(c) and 501(c)(3) should be construed as setting forth the only criteria Congress has established for qualification as a tax-exempt organization. Indeed, were we writing prior to the history detailed in the Court's opinion, this could well be the construction I would adopt. But there has been a decade of acceptance that is persuasive in the circumstances of this case, and I conclude that there are now sufficient reasons for accepting the IRS's construction of the Code as proscribing ⊥ tax exemptions for schools that   ⌊607
discriminate on the basis of race as a matter of policy.

I cannot say that this construction of the Code, adopted by the IRS in 1970 and upheld by the Court of Appeals below, is without logical support. The statutory terms are not self-defining, and it is plausible that in some instances an organization seeking a tax exemption might act in a manner so clearly contrary to the purposes of our laws that it could not be deemed to serve the enumerated statutory purposes. And, as the Court notes, if any national policy is sufficiently fundamental to constitute such an overriding limitation on the availability of tax-exempt status under § 501(c)(3), it is the policy against racial discrimination in education. Finally, and of critical importance for me, the subsequent actions of Congress present "an unusually strong case of legislative acquiescence in and ratification by implication of the [IRS] 1970 and 1971 rulings" with respect to racially discriminatory schools. In particular, Congress' enactment of § 501(i) in 1976 is strong evidence of agreement with these particular IRS rulings.

⌐608

⊥ II

I therefore concur in the Court's judgment that tax-exempt status under §§ 170(c) and 501(c)(3) is not available to private schools that concededly are racially discriminatory. I do not agree, however, with the Court's more general explanation of the justifications for the tax exemptions provided to charitable organizations. The Court states: "Charitable exemptions are justified on the basis that the exempt entity confers a public benefit—a benefit which the society or the community may not itself choose or be able to provide, or which supplements and advances the work of public institutions already supported by tax revenues. History buttresses logic to make clear that, to warrant exemption under § 501(c)(3), an institution must fall within a category specified in that section and must demonstrably serve and be in harmony with the public interest. The institution's purpose must not be so at odds with the common community conscience as to undermine any public benefit that might otherwise be conferred." Applying this test to petitioners, the Court concludes that "[c]learly an educational instititution engaging in practices affirmatively at odds with [the] declared position of the whole government cannot be seen as exercising a 'beneficial and stabilizing influenc[e] in community life,' . . . and is not 'charitable' within the meaning of § 170 and § 501(c)(3)."

With all respect, I am unconvinced that the critical question in determining tax-exempt status is whether an individual organization provides a clear "public benefit" as defined by the Court. Over 106,000 organizations filed § 501(c)(3) returns in

⌐609

1981. ⊥ I find it impossible to believe that all or even most of those organizations could prove that they "demonstrably serve and [are] in harmony with the public interest" or that they are "beneficial and

stabilizing influences in community life." Nor I am prepared to say that petitioners, because of their racially discriminatory policies, necessarily contribute nothing of benefit to the community. It is clear from the substantially secular character of the curricula and degrees offered that petitioners provide educational benefits.

Even more troubling to me is the element of conformity that appears to inform the Court's analysis. The Court asserts that an exempt organization must "demonstrably serve and be in harmony with the public interest," must have a purpose that comports with "the common community conscience," and must not act in a manner "affirmatively at odds with [the] declared position of the whole government." Taken together, these passages suggest that the primary function of a tax-exempt organization is to act on behalf of the Government in carrying out governmentally approved policies. In my opinion, such a view of § 501(c)(3) ignores the important role played by tax exemptions in encouraging diverse, indeed often sharply conflicting, activities and viewpoints. As Justice BRENNAN has observed, private, nonprofit groups receive tax exemptions because "each group contributes to the diversity of association, viewpoint, and enterprise essential to a vigorous, pluralistic society." *Walz* (BRENNAN J., concurring). Far from representing an effort to reinforce any perceived "common community conscience," the provision of tax exemptions to nonprofit groups is one indispensable means of limiting the influence of governmental orthodoxy on important areas of community life.

⊥ Given the importance of our tradition of plu-   ⌐610
ralism, "[t]he interest in preserving an area of untrammeled choice for private philanthropy is very great." *Jackson* v. *Statler Foundation*.

I do not suggest that these considerations always are or should be dispositive. Congress, of course, may find that some organizations do not warrant tax-exempt status. In this case I agree with the Court that Congress has determined that the policy against racial discrimination in education should override the countervailing interest in permitting unorthodox private behavior.

⊥ I would emphasize, however, that the balancing   ⌐611
of these substantial interests is for *Congress* to perform. I am unwilling to join any suggestion that the Internal Revenue Service is invested with authority to decide which public policies are sufficiently "fundamental" to require denial of tax exemptions. Its business is to administer laws designed to produce revenue for the Government, not to promote "public policy." As former IRS commissioner Kurtz has noted, questions concerning religion and civil rights "are far afield from the more typical tasks of tax administrators—determining taxable income." Kurtz, Difficult Definitional Problems in Tax Administration: Religion and Race, 23 Catholic Lawyer 301, 301

(1978). This Court often has expressed concern that the scope of an agency's authorization be limited to those areas in which the agency fairly may be said to have expertise, and this concern applies with special force when the asserted administrative power is one to determine the scope of public policy. As Justice BLACKMUN has noted, "where the philanthropic organization is concerned, there appears to be little to circumscribe the almost unfettered power of the Commissioner. This may be very well so long as one subscribes to the particular brand of social policy the Commissioner happens to be advocating ⊥ at the time . . . , but application of our tax laws should not operate in so fickle a fashion. Surely, social policy in the first instance is a matter for legislative concern." *Commissioner* v. *"Americans United"* (BLACKMUN, J., dissenting).

|612

III

The Court's decision upholds IRS Revenue Ruling 71-447, and thus resolves the question whether tax-exempt status is available to private schools that openly maintain racially discriminatory admissions policies. There no longer is any justification for *Congress* to hesitate—as it apparently has—in articulating and codifying its desired policy as to tax exemptions for discriminatory organizations. Many questions remain, such as whether organizations that violate other policies should receive tax-exempt status under § 501(c)(3). These should be legislative policy choices. It is not appropriate to leave the IRS "on the cutting edge of developing national policy." The contours of public policy should be determined by Congress, not by judges or the IRS.

Justice REHNQUIST, dissenting.

The Court points out that there is a strong national policy in this country against racial discrimination. To the extent that the Court states that Congress in furtherance of this policy could deny tax-exempt status to educational institutions that promote racial discrimination, I readily agree. But, unlike the Court, I am convinced that Congress simply has failed to take this action and, as this Court has said over and over again, regardless of our view on the propriety of Congress' failure to legislate we are not constitutionally empowered to act for them.

In approaching this statutory construction question the Court quite adeptly avoids the statute it is construing. This I am sure is no accident, for there is nothing in the language ⊥ of § 501(c)(3) that supports the result obtained by the Court. Section 501(c)(3) provides tax-exempt status for: "Corporations, and any community chest, fund, or foundation, organized and operated exclusively for religious, charitable, scientific, testing for public safety, literary, or educational purposes, or to foster national or international amateur sports competition (but only if

|613

no part of its activities involve the provision of athletic facilities or equipment), or for the prevention of cruelty to children or animals, no part of the net earnings of which inures to the benefit of any private shareholder or individual, no substantial part of the activities of which is carrying on propaganda, or otherwise attempting, to influence legislation (except as otherwise provided in subsection (h)), and which does not participate in, or intervene in (including the publishing or distributing of statements), any political campaign on behalf of any candidate for public office." With undeniable clarity, Congress has explicitly defined the requirements for § 501(c)(3) status. An entity must be (1) a corporation, or community chest, fund, or foundation, (2) organized for one of the eight enumerated purposes, (3) operated on a nonprofit basis, and (4) free from involvement in lobbying activities and political campaigns. Nowhere is there to be found some additional, undefined public policy requirement.

The Court first seeks refuge from the obvious reading of § 501(c)(3) by turning to § 170 of the Internal Revenue Code which provides a tax deduction for contributions made to § 501(c)(3) organizations. In setting forth the general rule, § 170 states: "There shall be allowed as a deduction any charitable contribution (as defined in subsection (c)) payment of which is made within the taxable year. A charitable contribution shall be allowable as a deduction only if ver⊥ified under regulations prescribed by the Secretary." The Court seizes the words "charitable contribution" and with little discussion concludes that "[o]n its face, therefore, § 170 reveals that Congress' intention was to provide tax benefits to organizations serving charitable purposes," intimating that this implies some unspecified common law charitable trust requirement.

|614

The Court would have been well advised to look to subsection (c) where, as § 170(a)(1) indicates, Congress has defined a "charitable contribution": "For purposes of this section, the term 'charitable contribution' means a contribution or gift to or for the use of . . . [a] corporation, trust, or community chest, fund, or foundation . . . organized and operated exclusively for religious, charitable, scientific, literary, or educational purposes, or to foster national or international amateur sports competition (but only if no part of its activities involve the provision of athletic facilities or equipment), or for the prevention of cruelty to children or animals; . . . no part of the net earnings of which inures to the benefit of any private shareholder or individual; and . . . which is not disqualified for tax exemption under section 501(c)(3) by reason of attempting to influence legislation, and which does not participate in, or intervene in (including the publishing or distributing of statements), any political campaign on behalf of any candidate for public office." Plainly, § 170(c) simply tracks the requirements set forth in § 501(c)(3). Since § 170 is no more than a mirror of §

501(c)(3) and, as the Court points out, § 170 followed § 501(c)(3) by more than two decades, it is at best of little usefulness in finding the meaning of § 501(c)(3).

Making a more fruitful inquiry, the Court next turns to the legislative history of § 501(c)(3) and finds that Congress in⊥tended in that statute to offer a tax benefit to organizations that Congress believed were providing public benefit. I certainly agree. But then the Court leaps to the conclusion that this history is proof Congress intended that an organization seeking § 501(c)(3) status "must fall within a category specified in that section and *must demonstrably serve and be in harmony with the public interest.*" (emphasis added). To the contrary, I think that the legislative history of § 501(c)(3) unmistakably makes clear that *Congress has decided* what organizations are serving a public purpose and providing a public benfit within the meaning of § 501(c)(3) and has clearly set forth in § 501(c)(3) the characteristics of such organizations. In fact, there are few examples which better illustrate Congress' effort to define and re-define the requirements of a legislative act.

The first general income tax law was passed by Congress in the form of the Tariff Act of 1894. A provision of that Act provided an exemption for "corporations, companies, or associations organized and conducted solely for charitable, religious, or educational purposes." Ch. 349, § 32, 28 Stat. 509, 556 (1894). The income tax portion of the 1894 Act was held unconstitutional by this Court, but a similar exemption appeared in the Tariff Act of 1909 which imposed a tax on corporate income. The 1909 Act provided an exemption for "any corporation or association organized and operated exclusively for religious, charitable, or educational purposes, no part of the net income of which inures to the benefit of any private stockholder or individual."

With the ratification of the Sixteenth Amendment, Congress again turned its attention to an individual income tax with the Tariff Act of 1913. And again, in the direct predecessor of § 501(c)(3), a tax exemption was provided for "any corporation or association organized and operated exclusively for religious, charitable, scientific, or educational purposes, ⊥ no part of the net income of which inures to the benefit of any private stockholder or individual." In subsequent acts Congress continued to broaden the list of exempt purposes. The Revenue Act of 1918 added an exemption for corporations or associations organized "for the prevention of cruelty to children or animals." 1076 (1918). The Revenue Act of 1921 expanded the groups to which the exemption applied to include "any community chest, fund, or foundation" and added "literary" endeavors to the list of exempt purposes. The exemption remained unchanged in the Revenue Acts of 1924, 1926, 1928, and 1932. In the Revenue Act of 1934

Congress added the requirement that no substantial part of the activities of any exempt organization can involve the carrying on of "propaganda" or "attempting to influence legislation." Again, the exemption was left unchanged by the Revenue Acts of 1936 and 1938.

The tax laws were overhauled by the Internal Revenue Code of 1939, but this exemption was left unchanged. When the 1939 Code was replaced with the Internal Revenue Code of 1954, the exemption was adopted in full in the present § 501(c)(3) with the addition of "testing for public safety" as an exempt purpose and an additional restriction that tax-exempt organizations could not "participate in, or intervene in (including the publishing or distributing of statements), any political campaign on behalf of any candidate for public office." Then in 1976 the statute was again amended adding to the purposes for which an exemption would be authorized, "to foster national or international ama⊥teur sports competition," provided the activities did not involve the provision of athletic facilities or equipment.

One way to read the opinion handed down by the Court today leads to the conclusion that this long and arduous refining process of § 501(c)(3) was certainly a waste of time, for when enacting the original 1894 statute Congress intended to adopt a common law term of art, and intended that this term of art carry with it all of the common law baggage which defines it. Such a view, however, leads also to the unsupportable idea that Congress has spent almost a century adding illustrations simply to clarify an already defined common law term.

Another way to read the Court's opinion leads to the conclusion that even though Congress has set forth *some* of the requirements of a § 501(c)(3) organization, it intended that the IRS additionally require that organizations meet a higher standard of public interest, not stated by Congress, but to be determined and defined by the IRS and the courts. This view I find equally unsupportable. Almost a century of statutory history proves that Congress itself intended to decide what § 501(c)(3) requires. Congress has expressed its decision in the plainest of terms in § 501(c)(3) by providing that tax-exempt status is to be given to any corporation, or community chest, fund, or foundation that is organized for one of the eight enumerated purposes, operated on a nonprofit basis, and uninvolved in lobbying activities or political campaigns. The IRS certainly is empowered to adopt regulations for the enforcement of these specified requirements, and the courts have authority to resolve challenges to the IRS's exercise of this power, but Congress has left it to neither the IRS nor the courts to select or add to the requirements of § 501(c)(3).

The Court suggests that unless its new requirement be added to § 501(c)(3), nonprofit organizations formed to teach pick-pockets and terrorists

⌐618 would necessarily acquire tax-ex⊥empt status. Since the Court does not challenge the characterization of *petitioners* as "educational" institutions within the meaning of § 501(c)(3), and in fact states several times in the course of its opinion that petitioners *are* educational institutions, it is difficult to see how this argument advances the Court's reasoning for disposing of petitioners' cases.

But simply because I reject the Court's heavy-handed creation of the requirement that an organization seeking § 501(c)(3) status must "serve and be in harmony with the public interest," does not mean that I would deny to the IRS the usual authority to adopt regulations further explaining what Congress meant by the term "educational." The IRS has fully exercised that authority in 26 CFR § 1.501(c)(3)-1(d)(3), which provides:

"(3) *Educational defined*—(i)*In general.* The term "educational", as used in section 501(c)(3), relates to—

"(a) The instruction or training of the individual for the purpose of improving or developing his capabilities; or

"(b) The instruction of the public on subjects useful to the individual and beneficial to the community.

"An organization may be educational even though it advocates a particular position or viewpoint so long as it presents a sufficiently full and fair exposition of the pertinent facts as to permit an individual or the public to form an independent opinion or conclusion. On the other hand, an organization is not educational if its principal function is the mere presentation of unsupported opinion.

"(ii) *Examples of educational organizations.* The following are examples of organizations which, if they otherwise meet the requirements of this section, are educational:

⌐619 ⊥ *"Example (1).* An organization, such as a primary or secondary school, a college, or a professional or trade school, which has a regularly scheduled curriculum, a regular faculty, and a regularly enrolled body of students in attendance at a place where the educational activities are regularly carried on.

"Example (2). An organization whose activities consist of presenting public discussion groups, forums, panels, lectures, or other similar programs. Such programs may be on radio or television.

"Example (3). An organization which presents a course of instruction by means of correspondence or through the utilization of television or radio.

"Example (4). Museums, zoos, planetariums, symphony orchestras, and other similar organizations."

I have little doubt that neither the "Fagin School for Pickpockets" nor a school training students for guerrilla warfare and terrorism in other countries would meet the definitions contained in the regulations.

Prior to 1970, when the charted course was abruptly changed, the IRS had continuously interpreted § 501(c)(3) and its predecessors in accordance

with the view I have expressed above. This, of course, is of considerable significance in determining the intended meaning of the statute.

In 1970 the IRS was sued by parents of black public school children seeking to enjoin the IRS from according tax-exempt status under § 501(c)(3) to private schools in Mississippi that discriminated against blacks. The IRS answered, consistent with its long standing position, by maintaining a lack of authority to deny the tax-exemption if the schools met the specified requirements of § 501(c)(3). Then "[i]n the midst of this litigation", *Green* v. *Connaly,* aff'd per curiam sub nom. *Coit* v. *Green* and in the face of a preliminary injunc⊥tion, the IRS changed ⌐620 its position and adopted the view of the plaintiffs.

Following the close of the litigation, the IRS published its new position in Revenue Ruling 71-447, stating that "a school asserting a right to the benefits provided for in section 501(c)(3) of the Code as being organized and operated exclusively for educational purposes must be a common law charity in order to be exempt under that section." The IRS then concluded that a school that promotes racial discrimination violates public policy and therefore cannot qualify as a common law charity. The circumstances under which this change in interpretation was made suggest that it is entitled to very little deference. But even if the circumstances were different, the latter-day wisdom of the IRS has no basis in § 501(c)(3).

Perhaps recognizing the lack of support in the statute itself, or in its history, for the 1970 IRS change in interpretation, the Court finds that "[t]he actions of Congress since 1970 leave no doubt that the IRS reached the correct conclusion in exercising its authority," concluding that there is "an unusually strong case of legislative acquiescence in and ratification by implication of the 1970 and 1971 rulings." The Court relies first on several bills introduced to overturn the IRS interpretation of § 501(c)(3). But we have said before, and it is equally applicable here, that this type of congressional inaction is of virtually no weight in determining legislative intent. These bills and related hearings indicate litle more than that a vigorous debate has existed in Congress concerning the new IRS position.

The Court next asserts that "Congress affirmatively manifested its acquiescence in the IRS policy when it enacted the present § 501(i) or the Code," a provision that "denies tax exempt status to social clubs whose charters or policy state⊥ments provide ⌐621 for" racial discrimination. Quite to the contrary, it seems to me that in § 501(i) Congress showed that when it wants to add a requirement prohibiting racial discrimination to one of the tax-benefit provisions, it is fully aware of how to do it.

The Court intimates that the Ashbrook and Dornan Amendments also reflect an intent by Congress to acquiesce in the new IRS positon. The amendments were passed to limit certain enforcement procedures proposed by the IRS in 1978 and 1979 for determining whether a school operated in a racially nondiscriminatory fashion. The Court points out that in proposing his amendment, Congressman Ashbrook stated: "'My amendment very clearly indicates on its face that all the regulations in existence as of August 22, 1978, would not be touched.'" The Court fails to note that Congressman Ashbrook also said: "The IRS has no authority to create public policy. . . . So long as the Congress has not acted to set forth a national policy respecting denial of tax exemptions to private schools, it is improper for the IRS or any other branch of the Federal Government to seek denial of tax-exempt status. . . . There exists but a single responsibility which is proper for the Internal Revenue Service: To serve as tax collector." In the same debate, Congressman Grassley asserted: "Nobody argues that racial discrimination should receive preferred tax status in the United States. However, the IRS should not be making these decisions on the agency's own discretion. Congress should make these decisions." The same debates are filled with other similar statements. While on the whole these debates do not show conclusively that Congress believed the IRS had exceeded its authority with the 1970 change in position, they likewise are ⊥ far less than a showing of acquiescence in and ratification of the new position.

⌐622

This Court continuously has been hesitant to find ratification through inaction. This is especially true where such a finding "would result in a construction of the statute which not only is at odds with the language of the section in question and the pattern of the statute taken as a whole, but also is extremely far reaching in terms of the virtually untrammeled and unreviewable power it would vest in a regulatory agency." *SEC* v. *Sloan.* Few cases would call for more caution in finding ratification by acquiescence than the present one. The new IRS interpretation is not only far less than a long standing administrative policy, it is at odds with a position maintained by the IRS, and unquestioned by Congress, for several decades prior to 1970. The interpretation is unsupported by the statutory language, it is unsupported by legislative history, the interpretation has led to considerable controversy in and out of Congress, and the interpretation gives to the IRS a broad power which until now Congress had kept for itself. Where in addition to these circumstances Congress has shown time and time again that it is ready to enact positive legislation to change the tax code when it desires, this Court has no business finding that Congress has adopted the new IRS position by failing to enact legislation to reverse it.

I have no disagreement with the Court's finding that there is a strong national policy in this country opposed to racial discrimination. I agree with the Court that Congress has the power to further this policy by denying § 501(c)(3) status to organizations that practice racial discrimination. But as of yet Congress has failed to do so. Whatever the reasons for the failure, this Court should not legislate for Congress.

⊥ Petitioners are each organized for the "instruction or training of the individual for the purpose of improving or developing his capabilities," and thus are organized for "educational purposes" within the meaning of § 501(c)(3). Petitioners' nonprofit status is uncontested. There is no indication that either petitioner has been involved in lobbying activities or political campaigns. Therefore, it is my view that unless and until Congress affirmatively amends § 501(c)(3) to require more, the IRS is without authority to deny petitioners § 501(c)(3) status. For this reason, I would reverse the Court of Appeals.

⌐623

SOLICITATION BY RELIGIOUS GROUPS

Solicitation of financial contributions door-to-door and in public places by religious groups is clearly subject to reasonable nondiscriminatory regulation by the state or local community as a protection against fraud, injury, or undue violation of privacy. The community may within reason regulate the time, place, and manner of the solicitation. However, regulation must be accomplished through narrowly drawn, nondiscriminatory statutes designed to protect the legitimate interests of the public without unduly interfering with the free exercise of religion.

In too many instances this has not been the primary goal of these regulations. They are sometimes seen as a convenient means to disadvantage or harass currently unpopular religious movements. The statute to be used may already be in place or it may be especially tailored to the characteristics of the targeted group. Even statutes which appear on the surface to be neutral and nondiscriminatory may be administered with a selectively uneven hand when applied to unpopular religious groups.

Many of the early Jehovah's Witnesses' cases discussed earlier in this chapter involved efforts to restrain or prohibit fund solicitation by that widely despised group. Few of the measures survived the scrutiny of the Court.

As was true of the doughty Jehovah's Witnesses of the 1940s, members of today's unorthodox, aggressive sects are most likely to be involved in litigation testing the scope of the free exercise guarantee. Members of the International Society for Krishna Consciousness (ISKCON), known also as Hare Krishna, have in recent years attracted much public attention by their unusual dress and persistent efforts to sell religious literature and to solicit donations in public places such as airports.

Hare Krishnas maintain that these actions constitute a ritual (*Sankirtan*) essential to their religion. Because their activities have intimidated and frightened some and irritated many, practitioners have been subjected to various restrictive efforts on the part of state and local authorities. With mixed results, the constitutionality of these regulations has been challenged by ISKCON in state and federal courts.

In 1981, in HEFFRON v. INTERNATIONAL SOCIETY FOR KRISHNA CONSCIOUSNESS (p. 235) the United States Supreme Court dealt with the problem when it reviewed a decision of the Minnesota Supreme Court. The Minnesota Agriculture Society, which operates a state fair, required all persons, groups, or firms desiring to sell, exhibit, or distribute materials at the fair to do so at a booth rented from the Society. Representatives of organizations were free to move about the fairgrounds and communicate their views orally. The regulation, as applied to Hare Krishna members, was voided by the Minnesota Supreme Court as unconstitutionally restricting their practice of Sankirtan. The rule, as the court agreed, was applied without discrimination and did not prevent representatives of organizations involved from moving freely about the fairgrounds to communicate orally their views to patrons of the fair.

The majority opinion of the Supreme Court, written by Justice White, reversed the Minnesota high court. He found the state's interest in orderly movement of crowds and avoidance of congestion sufficient justification for the challenged rule. The case was decided primarily on free speech grounds. Observing that it is settled law that the First Amendment does not guarantee the right to communicate one's views at all times and places in any manner desired, Justice White expressed the view of the Court that the even-handed rental of booths to all applicants and the freedom allowed the Hare Krishna to propagate their views orally constituted sufficient alternative outlets for expression of ideas.

The sect, said the Court's opinion, gained no special claim to protection as compared to other religious groups merely by ritualizing the process:

> That organization and its ritual of Sankirtan have no special claim to First Amendment protection as compared to that of other religions who also distribute literature and solicit funds. None of our cases suggest that the inclusion of peripatetic solicitation as part of a church ritual entitles church members to solicitation rights in a public forum superior to those of members of other religious groups that raise money but do not purport to ritualize the process. (452 U.S. 640, 652)

The opinion stated further that religious groups in general enjoy under present circumstances no greater right to communicate, distribute literature, and solicit than "other organizations having social, political, or other ideological messages to proselytize."

Justice Brennan, joined by Justices Marshall and Stevens, dissented, contending that the state could have drafted a more narrowly drawn restriction to achieve its legitimate interest in crowd control. Justice Blackmun concurred in part and dissented in part.

Another governmental effort to restrict solicitation in public places had enjoyed less success when it went before the Supreme Court the year before the *Heffron* decision in *Village of Schaumburg* v. *Citizens for a Better Environment* (1980). In this case, no specific religious group was involved and the decision was based on the freedom of speech clause. However, Justice White—who later also wrote for the majority in *Heffron*—cited and discussed numerous Jehovah's Witnesses cases of the 1930s and 1940s. The decision invalidated an ordinance which prohibited door-to-door or on-street solicitation of contributions by charitable organizations, including churches, that did not use at least 75 percent of their

receipts for charitable purposes. The Court found the 75 percent requirement to be insufficiently related to legitimate government interests in protecting the public against "fraud, crime, and undue annoyance" and held it to be constitutionally overbroad in violation of the First and Fourteenth Amendments. Only Justice Rehnquist would have upheld Schaumburg's ordinance.

Although the decision was based on Establishment Clause and Equal Protection Clause grounds and is therefore discussed in more detail under that heading (p. 336), LARSON v. VALENTE (p. 337), decided the next year, also involved Minnesota restrictions on solicitation as applied to another controversial religious movement—the Unification Church—against whom the law had been primarily aimed from its inception. The statute before the Court required registration and disclosure from only those religious organizations that solicited more than one-half of their contributions from nonmembers.

The Court, by a five-to-four vote, with Justice Brennan speaking for the majority, struck down the application of the registration and reporting act to the Unification Church as preferring one religion over another and effecting the "selective legislative imposition of burdens and advantages upon particular denominations."

In 1983 the city commission of Clearwater, Florida, Western Hemisphere headquarters of the Church of Scientology, enacted an extremely burdensome solicitation ordinance. The broadly drawn ordinance required charitable organizations to register with the city, keep detailed records, disclose the sources and uses of their contributions, and refrain from engaging in fraudulent solicitation practices. On the complaint of ten or more individuals, the soliciting organization would be required to submit to an investigation by the city attorney. Although the ordinance was rather obviously aimed at the unpopular Church of Scientology, it also applied, of course, to mainstream religious and charitable organizations.

Americans United for Separation of Church and State, joined by the National Council of Churches, the American Jewish Committees, and the Suncoast Baptist Church of Clearwater, attacked the ordinance in a federal district court alleging violation of the Free Exercise and Establishment Clauses as well as free speech, free press, due process, equal protection, the commerce clause, and the right to privacy. The Church of Scientology filed a separate suit. The city commission, responding to the protests, repealed the first ordinance and passed a second less oppressive measure.

The district court held the original ordinance unconstitutional and permanently enjoined its enforcement. It held the second ordinance to be facially constitutional. The two cases were then joined and went to the United States Court of Appeals for the Eleventh Circuit. That court held that the issue of the constitutionality of the repealed ordinance was at the time moot and should not have been heard by the district court. The appellate court also raised serious questions with respect to proof of standing on the part of the challenging organizations and remanded the cases to the district court with instructions that they be dismissed. Though the cases were technically lost by those who brought them, they obviously had a positive effect. The controversy and accompanying publicity caused the city commission to reconsider its action in enacting the harsh solicitation measure, which would not only have had a chilling effect on the activities of all charitable and religious groups in Clearwater but might, if accepted by the courts, have been adopted as a model for other communities desiring to harass unpopular movements.

HEFFRON v. INTERNATIONAL SOCIETY FOR KRISHNA CONSCIOUSNESS

452 U.S. 640

ON WRIT OF CERTIORARI TO THE SUPREME COURT
OF THE STATE OF MINNESOTA

Argued April 20, 1981 — Decided June 22, 1981

⌐642   ⊥Justice WHITE delivered the opinion of the Court.

The question presented for review is whether a State, consistent with the First and Fourteenth Amendments, may require a religious organization desiring to distribute and sell religious literature and to solicit donations at a state fair to conduct those activities only at an assigned location within the fairgrounds even though application of the rule limits the religious practices of the organization.

I

⌐643   ⊥Each year, the Minnesota Agricultural Society (Society), a public corporation organized under the laws of Minnesota, operates a state fair on a 125-acre state-owned tract located in St. Paul, Minn. The Fair is conducted for the purpose of "exhibiting . . . the agricultural, stock-breeding, horticultural, mining, mechanical, industrial, and other products and resources of the state, including proper exhibits and expositions of the arts, human skills, and sciences." The Fair is a major public event and attracts visitors from all over Minnesota as well as from other parts of the country. During the past 5 years, the average total attendance for the 12-day fair has been 1,320,000 persons. The average daily attendance on weekdays has been 115,000 persons and on Saturdays and Sundays 160,000.

The Society is authorized to make all "bylaws, ordinances, and rules, not inconsistent with law, which it may deem necessary or proper for the government of the fair grounds . . . ." Under this authority, the Society promulgated Minnesota State Fair Rule 6.05 which provides in relevant part that: "Sale or distribution of any merchandise, including printed or written material except under license issued [by] the Society and/or from a duly-licensed location shall be a misdemeanor."

As Rule 6.05 is construed and applied by the Society, "all persons, groups or firms which desire to sell, exhibit or distribute materials during the annual State Fair must do so only from fixed locations on the fairgrounds." Although the Rule does not prevent organizational representatives from walking about the fairgrounds and communicating the organ⊥ization's views with fair patrons in face-to-face discussions, it does require that any exhibitor conduct its sales, distribution, and fund solicitation operations from a booth rented from the Society. Space in the fairgrounds is rented to all comers in a nondiscriminatory fashion on a first-come, first-served basis with the rental charge based on the size and location of the booth. The rule applies alike to nonprofit, charitable, and commercial enterprises.

⌐644

One day prior to the opening of the 1977 Minnesota State Fair, respondents International Society for Krishna Consciousness, Inc. (ISKCON), an international religious society espousing the views of the Krishna religion, and Joseph Beca, head of the Minneapolis ISKCON temple, filed suit against numerous state officials seeking a declaration that Rule 6.05, both on its face and as applied, violated respondents' rights under the First Amendment, and seeking injunctive relief ⊥prohibiting enforcement of the Rule against ISKCON and its members. Specially, ISKCON asserted that the Rule would suppress the practice of Sankirtan, one of its religious rituals, which enjoins its members to go into public places to distribute or sell religious literature and to solicit donations for the support of the Krishna religion. The trial court entered temporary orders to govern the conduct of the parties during the 1977 Fair. When that event concluded and after a hearing, the trial court granted the state officials' motion for summary judgment, upholding the constitutionality of Rule 6.05. Relying on the reasoning in *ISKCON* v. *Evans*, the court found that the State's interest "in providing all fair goers and concessionaries with adequate and equal access to each other and in providing a minimum of ⊥congestion of the fairgrounds" was sufficient to sustain Rule 6.05's limitations as applied to respondents. The court, however, provided that respondents were free to "[r]oam throughout those areas of the fairgrounds generally open to the public for the purpose of discussing with others their religious beliefs."

⌐646

On appeal, the Minnesota Supreme Court reversed, holding that Rule 6.05, as applied to respondents, unconstitutionally restricted the Krishnas' religious practice of Sankirtan. The court rejected the Society's proffered justifications for the Rule as inadequate to warrant the restriction. Furthermore, the application of Rule 6.05 to ISKCON was not essential to the furtherance of the State's interests in that those interests could be served by means less restrictive of respondents' First Amendment rights. We granted the state officials' petition for writ of certiorari in light of the important constitutional issues presented and the conflicting results reached in similar cases in various lower courts.

II

|647   ⊥The State does not dispute that the oral and written dissemination of the Krishnas' religious views and doctrines is protected by the First Amendment. See *Schneider* v. *State; Lovell* v. *City of Griffin.* Nor does it claim that this protection is lost because the written materials sought to be distributed are sold rather than given away or because contributions or gifts are solicited in the course of propagating the faith. Our cases indicate as much. *Murdock* v. *Pennsylvania; Village of Schaumburg* v. *Citizens for a Better Environment.* See *Cantwell* v. *Connecticut.*

It is also common ground, however, that the First Amendment does not guarantee the right to communicate one's views at all times and places or in any manner that may be desired. *Adderley* v. *Florida; Poulos* v. *New Hampshire*; see *Cox* v. *Louisiana.* As the Minnesota Supreme Court recognized, the activities of ISKCON, like those of others protected by the First Amendment, are subject to reasonable time, place, and manner restrictions. *Grayned* v. *City of Rockford; Adderley* v. *Florida; Kovacs* v. *Cooper; Cox*
|648   v. *New Hampshire.* "We have often ap⊥proved restrictions of that kind provided that they are justified without reference to the content of the regulated speech, that they serve a significant governmental interest, and that in doing so they leave open ample alternative channels for communication of the information." *Virginia State Board of Pharmacy* v. *Virginia Citizens Consumer Council*; see also *Consolidated Edison Co.* v. *Public Service Commission.* The issue here, as it was below, is whether Rule 6.05 is a permissible restriction on the place and manner of communicating the views of the Krishna religion, more specifically, whether the Society may require the members of ISKCON who desire to practice Sankirtan at the State Fair to confine their distribution, sales, and solicitation activities to a fixed location.

A major criterion for a valid time, place and manner restriction is that the restriction "may not be based upon either the content or subject matter of the speech." *Consolidated Edison Co.* v. *Public Ser-*
|649   *vice Commission.* Rule 6.05 ⊥qualifies in this respect, since as the Supreme Court of Minnesota observed, the Rule applies evenhandedly to all who wish to distribute and sell written materials or to solicit funds. No person or organization, whether commercial or charitable, is permitted to engage in such activities except from a booth rented for those purposes.

Nor does Rule 6.05 suffer from the more covert forms of discrimination that may result when arbitrary discretion is vested in some governmental authority. The method of allocating space is a straightforward first-come, first-served system. The Rule is not open to the kind of arbitrary application that this Court has condemned as inherently incon-

sistent with a valid time, place, and manner regulation because such discretion has the potential for becoming a means of suppressing a particular point of view. See *Shuttlesworth* v. *Birmingham; Cox* v. *Louisiana; Staub* v. *City of Baxley; Largent* v. *Texas; Cantwell* v. *Connecticut; Schneider* v. *State; Hague* v. *C.I.O.*

A valid time, place, and manner regulation must also "serve a significant governmental interest." *Virginia Board* v. *Citizens Council.* See *Grayned* v. *City of Rockford.* Here, the principal justification asserted by the State in support of Rule 6.05 is the need to maintain the orderly movement of ⊥the crowd given |650 the large number of exhibitors and persons attending the Fair.

The fairgrounds comprise a relatively small area of 125 acres, the bulk of which is covered by permanent buildings, temporary structures, parking lots, and connecting thoroughfares. There were some 1400 exhibitors and concessionaires renting space for the 1977 and 1978 Fairs, chiefly in permanent and temporary buildings. The Fair is designed to exhibit to the public an enormous variety of goods, services, entertainment and other matters of interest. This is accomplished by confining individual exhibitors to fixed locations, with the public moving to and among the booths or other attractions, using streets and open spaces provided for that purpose. Because the Fair attracts large crowds—an average of 115,000 patrons on weekdays and 160,000 on Saturdays and Sundays—it is apparent that the State's interest in the orderly movement and control of such an assembly of persons is a substantial consideration.

As a general matter, it is clear that a State's interest in protecting the "safety and convenience" of persons using a public forum is a valid governmental objective. See *Grayned* v. *City of Rockford; Cox* v. *New Hampshire.* Furthermore, consideration of a forum's special attributes is relevant to the constitutionality of a regulation since the significance of the governmental ⊥interest must be assessed in light of |65▮ the characteristic nature and function of the particular forum involved. See, *e.g., Grayned* v. *City of Rockford; Lehman* v. *City of Shaker Heights.* This observation bears particular import in the present case since respondents make a number of analogies between the fairgrounds and city streets which have "immemorially been held in trust for the use of the public and, . . . have been used for purposes of assembly, communicating thoughts between citizens, and discussing public questions." *Hague* v. *C.I.O.* See *Kunz* v. *New York.* But it is clear that there are significant differences between a street and the fairgrounds. A street is continually open, often uncongested, and constitutes not only a necessary conduit in the daily affairs of a locality's citizens, but also a place where people may enjoy the open air or the company of friends and neighbors in a relaxed environment. The Minnesota Fair, as described above, is a temporary event attracting great numbers of visitors who come to the event for a short period to see and experience the host of exhibits and attractions at the Fair. The flow of the crowd and demands of safety are more pressing in the context of the Fair. As such, any comparisons to public streets are necessarily inexact.

The Minnesota Supreme Court recognized that the State's interest in the orderly movement of a large crowd and in avoiding congestion was substantial and that Rule 6.05 furthered that interest significantly. Nevertheless, the Minnesota Supreme Court declared that the case did not turn on the "importance of the state's undeniable interest in pre-⊥venting the widespread disorder that would surely exist if no regulation such as Rule 6.05 were in effect" but upon the significance of the State's interest in avoiding whatever disorder would likely result from granting members of ISKCON an exemption from the Rule. Approaching the case in this way, the court concluded that although some disruption would occur from such an exemption, it was not of sufficient concern to warrant confining the Krishnas to a booth. The court also concluded that, in any event, the rule was not essential to the furtherance of the State's interest in crowd control, which could adequately be served by less intrusive means.

⌐652

As we see it, the Minnesota Supreme Court took too narrow a view of the State's interest in avoiding congestion and maintaining the orderly movement of fair patrons on the fairgrounds. The justification for the Rule should not be measured by the disorder that would result from granting an exemption solely to ISKCON. That organization and its ritual of Sankirtan have no special claim to First Amendment protection as compared to that of other religions who also distribute literature and solicit funds. None of our cases suggest that the inclusion of peripatetic solicitation as part of a church ritual entitles church members to solicitation rights in a public forum superior to those of members of other religious groups that raise money but do not purport to ritualize the process. Nor for present purposes do religious organizations enjoy rights to communicate, distribute, and solicit on the fairgrounds superior to those of other organizations having social, political, or other ideological messages to ⊥proselytize. These nonreligious organizations seeking support for their activities are entitled to rights equal to those of religious groups to enter a public forum and spread their views, whether by soliciting funds or by distributing literature.

⌐653

If Rule 6.05 is an invalid restriction on the activities of ISKCON, it is no more valid with respect to the other social, political, or charitable organizations that have rented booths at the Fair and confined their distribution, sale, and fund solicitation to those locations. Nor would it be valid with respect to other organizations that did not rent booths, either because they were unavailable due to a lack of space or because they chose to avoid the expense involved, but that would in all probability appear in the fairgrounds to distribute, sell, and solicit if they could freely do so. The question would also inevitably arise as to what extent the First Amendment also gives commercial organizations a right to move among the crowd to distribute information about or to sell their wares as respondents claim they may do.

ISKCON desires to proselytize at the fair because it believes it can successfully communicate and raise funds. In its view, this can be done only by intercepting fair patrons as they move about, and if success is achieved, stopping them momentarily or for longer periods as money is given or exchanged for literature. This consequence would be multiplied many times over if Rule 6.05 could not be applied to confine such transactions by ISKCON and others to fixed locations. Indeed, the court below agreed that without Rule 6.05 there would be widespread disorder at the fairgrounds. The court also recognized that some disorder would inevitably result from exempting the Krishnas from the Rule. Obviously, there would be a much larger threat to the State's interest in crowd control if all other religious, nonreligious, and noncommercial organizations could likewise move freely about the fairgrounds distributing and selling literature and soliciting funds at will.

⊥ Given these considerations, we hold that the State's interest in confining distribution, selling, and fund solicitation activities to fixed locations is sufficient to satisfy the requirement that a place or manner restriction must serve a substantial state interest. By focusing on the incidental effect of providing an exemption from Rule 6.05 to ISKCON, the Minnesota Supreme Court did not take into effect the fact that any such exemption cannot be meaningfully limited to ISKCON, and as applied to similarly situated groups would prevent the State from furthering its important concern with managing the flow of the crowd. In our view, the Society may apply its Rule and confine the type of transactions at issue to designated locations without violating the First Amendment.

⌐654

For similar reasons, we cannot agree with the Minnesota Supreme Court that Rule 6.05 is an unnecessary regulation because the State could avoid the threat to its interest posed by ISKCON by less restrictive means, such as penalizing disorder or disruption, limiting the number of solicitors, or putting more narrowly drawn restrictions on the location and movement of ISKCON's representatives. As we have indicated, the inquiry must involve not only ISKCON, but also all other organizations that would be entitled to distribute, sell or solicit if the booth rule may not be enforced with respect to ISKCON. Looked at in this way, it is quite improbable that the alternative means suggested by the Minnesota Supreme Court would deal adequately with the problems posed by the much larger number of distributors and solicitors that would be present on the fairgrounds if the judgment below were affirmed.

For Rule 6.05 to be valid as a place and manner restriction, it must also be sufficiently clear that alternative forums for the expression of respondents' protected speech exist despite the effects of the Rule. Rule 6.05 is not vulnerable on this ground. First, the Rule does not prevent ISKCON from practicing Sankirtan anywhere outside the fairgrounds. More importantly, the Rule has not been shown to deny access within the forum in question. Here, the Rule ⌊655 does not exclude ISKCON from ⊥ the fairgrounds, nor does it deny that organization the right to conduct any desired activity at some point within the forum. Its members may mingle with the crowd and orally propagate their views. The organization may also arrange for a booth and distribute and sell literature and solicit funds from that location on the fairgrounds itself. The Minnesota State Fair is a limited public forum in that it exists to provide a means for a great number of exhibitors temporarily to present their products or views, be they commercial, religious, or political, to a large number of people·in an efficient fashion. Considering the limited functions of the Fair and the combined area within which it operates, we are unwilling to say that Rule 6.05 does not provide ISKCON and other organizations with an adequate means to sell and solicit on the fairgrounds. The First Amendment protects the right of every citizen to "reach the minds of willing listeners and to do so there must be opportunity to win their attention." *Kovacs* v. *Cooper*. Rule 6.05 does not unnecessarily limit that right within the fairgrounds.

⌊656   ⊥ The judgment of the Supreme Court of Minnesota is reversed and the case is remanded for further proceedings not inconsistent with this opinion.

So ordered.

Justice BRENNAN, with whom *Justice MARSHALL* and *Justice STEVENS* join, concurring in part and dissenting in part.

As the Court recognizes, the issue in this case is whether Minnesota State Fair Rule 6.05 constitutes a reasonable time, place, and manner restriction on respondents' exercise of protected First Amendment rights. See *Schad* v. *Borough of Mt. Ephraim*; *Grayned* v. *City of Rockford*. In deciding this issue, the Court considers, *inter alia*, whether the regulation serves a significant governmental interest and whether that interest can be served by a less intrusive restriction. The Court errs, however, in failing to apply its analysis separately to each of the protected First Amendment activities restricted by Rule 6.05. Thus, the Court fails to recognize that some of the State's restrictions may be reasonable while others may not.

Rule 6.05 restricts three types of protected First Amendment activity: distribution of literature, sale of literature, and solicitation of funds. See *Village of Schaumburg* v. *Citizens for a Better Environment; Murdock* v. *Pennsylvania; Jamison* v. *Texas; Schneider* v. *State; Lovell* v. *City of Griffin*. No individual or group is permitted to engage in these activities at the Minnesota State Fair except from preassigned, rented booth locations. Violation of this rule constitutes a misdemeanor, and violators are subject to arrest and expulsion from the fairgrounds.

The State advances three justifications for its booth rule. The justification relied upon by the Court today is the State's ⊥ interest in maintaining ⌊657 the orderly movement of the crowds at the fair. The second justification, relied upon by the dissenting Justices below, is the State's interest in protecting its fairgoers from fraudulent, deceptive, and misleading solicitation practices. The third justification, based on the "captive audience" doctrine, is the State's interest in protecting its fairgoers from annoyance and harassment.

I quite agree with the Court that the State has a significant interest in maintaining crowd control on its fairgrounds. See *Grayned* v. *City of Rockford; Cox* v. *New Hampshire*. I also have no doubt that the State has a significant interest in protecting its fairgoers from fraudulent or deceptive solicitation practices. See *Village of Schaumburg* v. *Citizens for a Better Environment; Virginia State Bd. of Pharmacy* v. *Virginia Citizens Consumer Council*. Indeed, because I believe on this record that this latter interest is substantially furthered by a Rule that restricts sales and solicitation activities to fixed booth locations, where the State will have the greatest opportunity to police and prevent possible deceptive practices, I would hold that Rule 6.05's restriction on those particular forms of First Amendment expression is justified as an anti-fraud measure. Accordingly, I join the judgment of the Court insofar as it upholds Rule 6.05's restriction on sales and solicitations. However, because I believe that the booth rule is an overly intrusive means of achieving the State's interest in crowd control, and because I cannot accept the validity of the State's third asserted justification, I dissent from the Court's approval of Rule 6.05's restriction on the distribution of literature.

⊥ As our cases have long noted, once a governmen- ⌊658 tal regulation is shown to impinge upon basic First Amendment rights, the burden falls on the government to show the validity of its asserted interest and the absence of less intrusive alternatives. See, *e.g., Schneider* v. *State*. The challenged "regulation must be narrowly tailored to further the State's legitimate interest." *Grayned* v. *City of Rockford*. Minnesota's Rule 6.05 does not meet this test.

The Minnesota State Fair is an annual 12-day festival of people and ideas. Located on permanent fairgrounds comprising approximately 125 acres, the fair attracts an average of 115,000 visitors on weekdays and 160,000 on Saturdays and Sundays. Once the fairgoers pay their admission fees, they are permitted to roam the fairgrounds at will, visiting booths, meeting friends, or just milling about. Significantly, each and every fairgoer, whether political candidate, concerned citizen, or member of a religious group, is free to give speeches, engage in face-to-face advocacy, campaign, or proselytize. No restrictions are placed on any fairgoer's right to speak at any time, at any place, or to any person. Thus, if on a given day 5,000 members of ISKCON came to the fair and paid their admission fees, all 5,000 would be permitted to wander throughout the fairgrounds, delivering speeches to ⊥whomever they wanted, about whatever they wanted. Moreover, because this right does not rest on Sankirtan or any other religious principle, it can be exercised by every political candidate, partisan advocate, and common citizen who has paid the price of admission. All share the identical ⊥right to move peripatetically and speak freely throughout the fairgrounds.

Because of Rule 6.05, however, as soon as a proselytizing member of ISKCON hands out a free copy of the Bhagavad-Gita to an interested listener, or a political candidate distributes his campaign brochure to a potential voter, he becomes subject to arrest and removal from the fairgrounds. This constitutes a significant restriction on First Amendment rights. By prohibiting distribution of literature outside the booths, the fair officials sharply limit the number of fairgoers to whom the proselytizers and candidates can communicate their messages. Only if a fairgoer affirmatively seeks out such information by approaching a booth does Rule 6.05 fully permit potential communicators to exercise their First Amendment rights.

In support of its crowd control justification, the State contends that if fairgoers are permitted to distribute literature, large crowds will gather, blocking traffic lanes and causing safety problems. As counsel for the State asserted at oral argument: "it seems to me that if you had [distribution] activity going on with not just the Krishnas but 10 or 20 or 30 representatives from perhaps 30 to 60 or 70 groups, that inevitably is going to draw more attention and going to cause or create more or less moving pockets or moving congested crowds. . . . If all of a sudden the crowd becomes aware of the fact that dozens of people are walking around passing out materials and they're going to ⊥inevitably be attracted by that. Whereas, they wouldn't be if people were just talking."

But the State has failed to provide any support for these assertions. It has made no showing that relaxation of its booth rule would create additional disorder in a fair that is already characterized by the robust and unrestrained participation of hundreds of thousands of wandering fairgoers. See *ISKCON* v. *Barber*. If fairgoers can make speeches, engage in face-to-face proselytizing, and buttonhole prospective supporters, they can surely distribute literature to members of their audience without significantly adding to the State's asserted crowd control problem. Cf. *Martin* v. *City of Struthers*. (Murphy, J. concurring) (invalidating ordinance that banned house-to-house distribution of handbills but did not ban house-to-house proselytizing). The record is devoid of any evidence that the 125-acre fairgrounds could not accommodate peripatetic distributors of literature just as easily as it now accommodates peripatetic speechmakers and proselytizers.

⊥Relying on a general, speculative fear of disorder, the State of Minnesota has placed a significant restriction on respondents' ability to exercise core First Amendment rights. This restriction is not narrowly drawn to advance the State's interests, and for that reason is unconstitutional. "[U]ndifferentiated fear or apprehension of disturbance is not enough to overcome the right to freedom of expression." *Tinker* v. *Des Moines Ind. Comm. School Dist.* If the State had a reasonable concern that distribution in certain parts of the fairgrounds—for example, entrances and exits—would cause disorder, it could have drafted its rule to prohibit distribution of literature at those points. If the State felt it necessary to limit the number of persons distributing an organization's literature, it could, within reason, have done that as well. It had no right, however, to ban all distribution of literature outside the booths. A State "may serve its legitimate interests, but it must do so by narrowly drawn regulations designed to serve those ⊥interests without unnecessarily interfering with First Amendment freedoms. . . . 'Broad prophylactic rules in the area of free expression are suspect. Precision of regulation must be the touchstone. . . .'" *Village of Schaumburg* v. *Citizens for a Better Environment*, quoting *NAACP* v. *Button.* Accord, *Grayned* v. *City of Rockford.*

Because I believe that the State could have drafted a more narrowly-drawn restriction on the right to distribute literature without undermining its interest in maintaining crowd control on the fairgrounds, I would affirm that part of the judgment below that strikes down Rule 6.05 as it applies to distribution of literature.

Justice BLACKMUN, concurring in part and dissenting in part.

For the reasons stated by Justice Brennan, I believe that Minnesota State Fair Rule 6.05 is unconstitutional as applied to the distribution of literature. I also agree, however, that the Rule is *constitutional* as applied to the sale of literature and the solicitation of funds. I reach this latter conclusion by a different route than does Justice Brennan for I am not persuaded that, under the Court's precedents, the State's interest in protecting fairgoers from fraudulent solicitation ⊥or sales practices justifies Rule 6.05's restrictions of those activities.

In *Village of Schaumburg* v. *Citizens for a Better Environment* the Court stressed that a community's

interest in preventing fraudulent solicitations must
be met by narrowly drawn regulations that do not
unnecessarily interfere with First Amendment freedoms. It there held that possibility of fraud in "door-
to-door" or "on-street" solicitations could be countered "by measures less intrusive than a direct prohibition on solicitation," such as disclosure provisions
and penal laws prohibiting fraudulent misrepresentations. I see no reason why the same considerations
are not applicable here. There is nothing in this record to suggest that it is more difficult to police
fairgrounds for fraudulent solicitations than it is to
police an entire community's streets; just as fraudulent solicitors may "melt into a crowd" at the fair, so
also may door-to-door solicitors quickly move on after consummating several transactions in a particular neighborhood. Indeed, since respondents have
offered to wear identifying tags and since the fairgrounds are an enclosed area, it is at least arguable
that it is easier to police the fairgrounds than a community's streets.

Nonetheless, I believe that the State's substantial
interest in maintaining crowd control and safety on
the fairgrounds does justify Rule 6.05's restriction on
solicitation and sales activities not conducted from a
booth. As the Court points out, "[t]he flow of the
⌊665 crowd and demands of ⊥safety are more pressing in
the context of the Fair" than in the context of a
typical street. While I agree with Justice Brennan
that the State's interest in order does not justify restrictions upon distribution of literature, I think that
common-sense differences between literature distribution, on the one hand, and solicitation and
sales, on the other, suggest that the latter activities
present greater crowd control problems than the former. The distribution of literature does not require
that the recipient stop in order to receive the message the speaker wishes to convey; instead, the recipient is free to read the message at a later time. For
this reason, literature distribution may present even
fewer crowd control problems than the oral proselytizing that the State already allows upon the fairgrounds. In contrast, as the dissent in the Minnesota
Supreme Court observed, sales and the collection of
solicited funds not only require the fairgoer to stop,
but also "engender additional confusion . . . because
they involve acts of exchanging articles for money,
fumbling for and dropping money, making change,
etc." Rules restricting the exchange of money to
booths have been upheld in analogous contexts, see
e.g., *International Society for Krishna Consciousness* v. *Eaves* (Atlanta airports), and for similar reasons I would uphold Rule 6.05 insofar as it applies to
solicitation and sales.

4 THE ESTABLISHMENT OF RELIGION

The development of the Establishment Clause and some aspects of its application have been described in the opening essay of this book (pp. Iff). Now the clause must be examined more extensively in preparation for the cases which have been argued and decided specifically on establishment grounds. Interpretation of the Establishment Clause has not been an easy matter; its meaning is not self-evident. Part of the problem of interpretation stems from lack of clarity concerning what the framers of the Constitution intended when they wrote the clause. Although the justices of the Supreme Court have on occasion appealed to the intentions of the authors of the Constitution in arriving at their decisions, there is no unanimity about what the authors had in mind when they composed the clause. Clearly, they intended to eliminate the possibility of an established church in the new nation; but when one gets beyond that, agreement as to their intent ceases. According to one authority, "Historical data can throw some light on the purposes behind such language, but all too often 'intention of the framers' has been a rhetorical device employed by partisans to read their own policy preferences into the Constitution." [1]

The uncertainty of determining the founders' intent has resulted in at least two basic approaches to the interpretation of the Establishment Clause. One of these may be labeled the "accommodationist" or "no preference" approach. This viewpoint argues that so long as the state does not single out one religious group for support to the exclusion of all others, there is nothing wrong with a cooperative relationship between government and religious institutions. In this interpretation, government could provide aid for religious institutions as long as the aid was imparted fairly and without favoritism.

The accommodationist view gained great visibility, at both the scholarly and popular levels, in the 1980s. Some scholars examined the debates leading up to the writing and ratification of the Constitution and the Bill of Rights and concluded that the founders intended only to remove religious requirements for public office, prevent the creation of a national church or religion, protect freedom of conscience in matters of religion against invasion by the national government, and leave the states to deal with questions of religion as they saw fit. [2] Consequently,

> there appears to be no historical evidence that the First Amendment was intended to preclude Federal government aid to religion when it was provided on a nondiscriminatory basis. Nor does there appear to be any historical evidence that the First Amendment was intended to provide an *absolute separation or independence* of religion and the national state. [3]

This view was also adopted by the administration of Ronald Reagan. Attorney General Edwin Meese III explicitly said: "It has been and will continue to be the policy of this administration to press for a Jurisprudence of Original Intention." He applied this concept to religion just as Professor Cord had done. [4]

---

[1] Charles H. Pritchett, *The American Constitution*, 3d ed. (New York: McGraw-Hill, 1977), p. 32; Cf. also Arthur Sutherland, "Historians, Lawyers, and 'Establishment of Religion,'" in *Religion and the Public Order*, Donald A. Giannella, ed., no. 5 (Ithaca, N.Y.: Cornell University Press, 1969), pp. 45-46.

[2] Robert L. Cord, *Separation of Church and State: Historical Fact and Current Fiction* (New York: Lambeth Press, 1982), p. 15. This book is one of the principal exponents of the "intentionalist" position, which is also accommodationist, and argues it forcefully.

[3] Ibid. (emphasis in original)

[4] Address before the American Bar Association, Washington, D. C., July 9, 1985, transcript Superintendent of Documents classification number J1.34:M47, p. 17.

Accommodationism gained popular recognition and support as a result of the rise of the "New Christian Right," which gained high visibility because of the outspokenness of its leaders, many of whom were television evangelists, because of its alleged impact on politics (beginning with the election of 1980), and because of the attention given to it by the media. Here the accommodationism went beyond that of most scholars, for many in the "New Christian Right" believed that the nation was founded on Christian or, somewhat more broadly, Judaeo-Christian principles, although they acknowledged that the founders never intended to give government support to any particular denomination of Christianity. [5]

The other major approach to interpreting the Establishment Clause is the "separationist" or "no aid" approach. According to this view, not only should the state not aid or support one religious group, it should not aid any, even if this could be done on a basis of equality. Government and religion should neither depend upon nor aid each other. There is to be strict separation between government and religion. [6] This view is said to grow out of the views of many of the framers of the Constitution, notably Jefferson and Madison. For example, in Jefferson's "A Bill for Establishing Religious Freedom" and Madison's "Memorial and Remonstrance" (see Appendices A and B), the idea is clearly expressed, in a variety of ways, that religion should be independent of government interference. This has been interpreted to mean that not even nondiscriminatory, even-handed aid is permissible. In the words of one leading exponent of this view, "in the minds of the fathers of our Constitution, independence of religion and government was the alpha and omega of democracy and freedom." [7]

Many would say that to place all views of church-state relationships in these two categories only is an oversimplification. Professor Carl H. Esbeck has provided five very useful categories to delineate various perceptions of the proper relationship between religion and civil authority which go beyond Establishment Clause analysis, but which nonetheless are useful in this context. Although his article spells out the categories in great detail, he summarizes them as follows:

> Strict separationists are alone in regarding religion as principally a private and an individualistic phenomenon that should little influence public affairs and matters of state. Additionally, strict separationism is the only model unwilling to recognize ontological status in the law for churches and other religious organizations. To the extent that religious societies have legal defenses against interference by the state, they are only the sum of the individual rights derived from the organization's members. Institutional separationists maintain that an ultimate

world view transcends and unifies the state and thereby limits it by holding the state in account to this "higher law." Moreover, this overarching public philosophy is properly theistic and heavily informed by Judeo-Christian thought, as is the history and tradition of all Western nations. Pluralistic separationists regard this talk of a universalistic public consensus as smacking of civil religion, a tendency toward self-righteous nationalism fueled by nativist religion. They view the modern nation-state as strictly a human invention, not an entity divinely instituted. Nonpreferentialists would permit government to favor religion on a basis that does not give preference to one religion over another. Thus, unlike the three separationist models, nonpreferentialists would allow the state to aid religion-in-general while not aiding those professing no religious belief. Finally, restorationists are the only type that would bind the state to a particular confession of faith and would assign to civil officials limited duties in defense of the dominant religion. [8]

The judicial interpretation of the Establishment Clause has a relatively short history that dates from EVERSON v. BOARD OF EDUCATION (p. 461), decided in 1947. Prior to Everson there were a few cases which seemed to raise Establishment Clause questions, but they were decided on other grounds. In 1899 the Court considered Bradfield v. Roberts, in which a challenge was made to the expenditure of federal money for the improvement of a hospital owned and operated by an order of Catholic nuns. The case was handled as a matter of corporation law. So long as the hospital fulfilled its contract (i.e., to treat illness), the Court held that its operation by a religious order was of no consequence. The Establishment Clause was not used as a basis for the decision.

In 1908 the Court decided Quick Bear v. Leupp, which involved the federal government's holding in trust some money which belonged to Indians. The Court decided that the money could be used to pay for the education of Indian children in Catholic schools because it was the Indians' money, not the government's.

The 1925 case of PIERCE v. SOCIETY OF SISTERS (p. 458) challenged an Oregon law requiring that all able-bodied children of school age attend public school. The Court held that the law was unconstitutional; but the decision was made on the basis of the Fourteenth Amendment, not the First.

A final case which seemed to raise Establishment Clause issues was COCHRAN v. BOARD OF EDUCATION (p. 460), decided in 1930. The question was whether Louisiana could use state funds to provide textbooks for students attending parochial schools. Holding that the program was constitutional, the Court again based its argument upon the Fourteenth Amendment, rather than the First.

One can surmise that there were at least three reasons why no Establishment Clause litigation was decided by the Court prior to 1947. First, persons who wanted to challenge the use of tax monies in support of religious in-

---

[5] Cf. Tim LaHaye, Battle for the Mind (Old Tappan, N.J.: Fleming H. Revell Co., 1980), pp. 37-38; Jerry Falwell, Listen, America! (Garden City, N.Y.: Doubleday and Co., 1980), pp. 16, 27. Rus Walton, One Nation Under God (Old Tappan, N.J.: Fleming H. Revell Co., 1975), at p. 23 says, "The Constitution was designed to perpetuate a Christian order." (emphasis in original)

[6] Richard E. Morgan, The Politics of Religious Conflict (New York: Pegasus, 1968), pp. 20-26.

[7] Leo Pfeffer, Church, State, and Freedom, rev. ed. (Boston: Beacon Press, 1967) p. 127.

[8] Carl H. Esbeck, "Five Views of Church-State Relations in Contemporary American Thought," Brigham Young University Law Review (Fall 1986):np (emphasis added)

stitutions or practices encountered extreme difficulty in obtaining standing to sue. (Cf. below pp. 246-249.) Second, many states have statutory or constitutional provisions that are more specific than those of the federal Constitution in prohibiting use of governmental funds for particular religious activities. These prohibitions tend to minimize state involvement in religious matters. Third, the application of the Establishment Clause to the states is a relatively recent development. [9] Indeed, it is commonly understood that the *Everson* case was the first in which the Establishment Clause was incorporated into the Fourteenth Amendment. The case setting the precedent for incorporation, *Gitlow* v. *New York*, had been decided in 1925. In 1940, in CANTWELL v. CONNECTICUT, the Court made the following observation:

> The First Amendment declares that Congress shall make no law respecting an establishment of religion or prohibiting the free exercise thereof. The Fourteenth Amendment has rendered the legislatures of the states as incompetent as Congress to enact such laws. 310 U.S. 296, 303. (Cf. p. 61.)

In spite of this broad language, *Cantwell* was decided solely on a free exercise question. As a result, the Establishment Clause was not specifically applied to the states until *Everson*.

The issue in *Everson* was whether state tax money could be used to reimburse parents for the cost of transporting children by bus to parochial schools. A New Jersey taxpayer sued in a state court (taxpayer suits being permissible under New Jersey law), claiming that such use of state money was a violation of the Establishment Clause made applicable to the states by the Fourteenth Amendment. The plaintiff based his argument on the broad language in *Cantwell*. The Supreme court accepted the case because it raised a compelling federal question.

In writing the opinion of the Court, Justice Black included a paragraph defining the limits of the Establishment Clause, a paragraph which is frequently quoted:

> The "establishment of religion" clause of the First Amendment means at least this: Neither a state nor the Federal Government can set up a church. Neither can pass laws which aid one religion, aid all religions, or prefer one religion over another. Neither can force nor influence a person to go to or to remain away from church against his will or force him to profess a belief or disbelief in religion. No person can be punished for entertaining or professing religious beliefs or disbeliefs, for church attendance or non-attendance. No tax in any amount, large or small, can be levied to support any religious activities or institutions, whatever they may be called, or whatever form they may adopt to teach or practice religion. Neither a state nor the Federal Government can, openly or secretly, participate in the affairs of any religious organizations or groups and *vice versa*. In the words of Jefferson, the clause against establishment of religion by law was in-

tended to erect "a wall of separation between church and State." 330 U.S. 1, 15-16 (1947) (p. 464)

In the light of this separationist language, many were surprised when Justice Black and four colleagues found that reimbursements for transportation were not a violation of the Establishment Clause.

In the paragraph quoted above, as elsewhere in the majority opinion, Justice Black simply assumed that the precedent of incorporation of the Establishment Clause into the Fourteenth Amendment was well established. He did not argue in support of the concept. For him the Establishment Clause should be applied to the states; the Court has followed that procedure in all subsequent Establishment Clause cases since *Everson*.

It should be noted that since *Everson* many have raised both theoretical and practical objections to the concept of incorporation. How can the Due Process and Equal Protection Clauses of the Fourteenth Amendment apply the Establishment Clause to the states if the aid challenged under that clause does not oppress anyone either in beliefs or religious exercise? How can a state's right be imposed as a prohibition on a state (thus showing that the Fourteenth Amendment is logically inconsistent with reference to the Establishment Clause)? Incorporation interposes federal judges between the people and their local and state legislatures and state courts. [10] Objections to incorporation, particularly as it applies to religion, were expressed forcefully as a part of the Reagan administration's "jurisprudence of original intent."

> And nowhere else has the principle of federalism been dealt so politically violent and constitutionally suspect a blow as by the theory of incorporation. . . . The point, of course, is that the Establishment Clause of the First Amendment was designed to prohibit Congress from establishing a national church. The belief was that the Constitution should not allow Congress to designate a particular faith or sect as politically above the rest. But to have argued, as is popular today, that the amendment demands a strict neutrality between religion and irreligion would have struck the founding generation as bizarre. The purpose was to prohibit religious tyranny, not to undermine religion generally. [11]

However, several commentators have pointed out that no Supreme Court justice since 1925 (*Gitlow* v. *New York*) has questioned the validity of incorporation. That is true. Not even the most accommodationist of the justices writing in the cases included in this book questioned the correctness of the concept of incorporation.

Although *Everson* articulated a strict separationist view of the Establishment Clause, subsequent cases have fol-

---

[9] Paul G. Kauper, *Religion and the Constitution* (Baton Rouge: Louisiana State University Press, 1964), p. 53. Cf. p. 4 for a discussion of the incorporation of the First Amendment into the Fourteenth.

[10] As representative of this literature see Mark DeWolfe Howe, *The Garden and the Wilderness: Religion and Government in American Constitutional History* (Chicago: University of Chicago Press, 1965), pp. 136-139 and Joseph M. Snee, S.J., "Religious Disestablishment and the Fourteenth Amendment," *Washington University Law Quarterly* (December 1954): 371-407. For a review of objections to incorporating the Establishment Clause and attempts to answer them, see Justice Brennan's concurring opinion in ABINGTON TOWNSHIP SCHOOL DISTRICT v. SCHEMPP 373 U.S. 203 at 253-258 (pp. 409)

[11] Edwin Meese III, Address before the American Bar Association, p. 14.

lowed it with varying degrees of rigidity. In McCOLLUM v. BOARD OF EDUCATION (1948) (p. 382), Justice Black again wrote the opinion for the Court and adhered to the separationism of the *Everson* rhetoric. The *McCollum* opinion declared that a plan to offer released time religious education on public school premises during the school day was unconstitutional. Four years later, however in ZORACH v. CLAUSON (p. 393), Justice Douglas' majority opinion rather dramatically departed from a strict separationist approach to the Establishment Clause. This opinion found a New York program of released time instruction constitutional because it was done away from school premises and there was no coercion to get the children to go, although three dissenters, including Justice Black, disagreed with the contention that there was no coercion. Justice Douglas began with the assumption that we are a religious people and concluded that the state encouragement and cooperation with religion is not state aid but rather "follows the best of our traditions."

In 1962 the Court decided the first of the prayer cases, ENGEL v. VITALE (p. 397). Here the Court returned to the more absolutist view of the Establishment Clause articulated, but not implemented, by *Everson*, which is not surprising since Justice Black authored the *Engel* opinion. In finding government-written prayer unconstitutional, Justice Black wrote:

> The Establishment Clause, unlike the Free Exercise Clause, does not depend upon any showing of direct governmental compulsion and is violated by the enactment of laws which establish official religion whether those laws operate directly to coerce nonobserving individuals or not. 370 U.S. 421, 430 (p. 399)

From *Everson* to *Engel* there is not a clear line of interpretation of the Establishment Clause. *Everson*, *McCollum*, and *Engel* represent a hard-line separationist, "no aid" approach; but *Zorach* represents a much more flexible, almost accommodationist, "no preference" approach. In this period there were no clear guidelines as to how the clause should be interpreted.

Clarification of the situation began with ABINGTON TOWNSHIP SCHOOL DISTRICT v. SCHEMPP, decided in 1963 (p. 402). In that case, involving compulsory prayer and Bible reading in the public schools, Justice Clark set forth two tests which must be applied in order to determine a program's constitutionality under the Establishment Clause. Concerning such legislation, Justice Clark wrote:

> The test may be stated as follows: what are the purpose and the primary effect of the enactment? If either is the advancement or inhibition of religion then the enactment exceeds the scope of legislative power as circumscribed by the Constitution. That is to say that to withstand the strictures of the Establishment Clause there must be a secular legislative purpose and a primary effect that neither advances nor inhibits religion. 374 U.S. 203, 222 (p. 407)

Some have suggested that the "secular purpose" part of this test had been used two years before in the Sunday closing law cases, particularly McGOWAN v. MARYLAND (p. 292), in which the laws, which originally had the purpose of compelling observance of the Chris-

tian day of worship, were found constitutional because they now had a secular purpose of providing a day of rest. But in those cases the secular purpose of only Sunday closing laws was at issue, whereas in the *Schempp* opinion the test was generalized to apply not solely to the cases at bar but to all legislation involving the Establishment Clause.

In 1970 a third test was set forth, this time by Chief Justice Burger in WALZ v. TAX COMMISSION (p. 278). This case challenged the legality of tax exemptions for properties used for religious worship. In finding tax exemptions constitutional, the Chief Justice declared that the elimination of exemptions would cause government officials to evaluate church property for tax purposes and, in the case of default, to initiate legal proceedings against the churches, thus causing "excessive entanglement" between government and religion. He reasoned:

> Granting tax exemptions to churches necessarily operates to afford an indirect economic benefit and also gives rise to some, but yet a lesser, involvement than taxing them. In analyzing either alternative the questions are whether it is a continuing one calling for official and continuing surveillance leading to an impermissible degree of entanglement. 397 U.S. 664, 674 (p.280)

(The "secular purpose," "primary effect," and "excessive entanglement" tests are frequently called the "Lemon test" because they were first used together in LEMON v. KURTZMAN (p. 480).)

In *Walz*, Justice Harlan mentioned that practices such as tax exemption may also cause political controversy, a different kind of government involvement in religious life that also ought to be avoided. In some of the cases subsequent to *Walz*, the possibility of political divisiveness was mentioned, e.g., proponents of government aid to parochial schools trying to influence legislatures and/or candidates while opponents try to blunt their efforts. In these cases the warning was given that political division along religious lines was the very kind of thing the Establishment Clause was intended to avoid. From time to time different justices, usually when writing in dissent, have argued that the political divisiveness dimension of the entanglement test should be raised to the level of a fourth test for interpreting the Establishment Clause. But the suggestion has never been implemented.

Through 1982, the Court steered a middle course between the rigid separationism of *Everson* and *Engel* and the flexible accommodationism of *Zorach*. The three tests were applied in such a way that there can be indirect aid to a religious institution if the purpose of the legislation is secular, if its primary effect is neither to aid nor to inhibit religion, and if the involvement between a religious institution and government is not excessive. Words such as "primary" and "excessive" are not totally clear in meaning, but they allowed courts a measure of flexibility in interpreting the Establishment Clause, thus permitting them to avoid hostility to religion (cf. *Zorach*, p. 393) without lowering the bars to direct aid to religion.

The three components of the test are independent of each other. Thus, a law may pass two of the tests, fail one, and be declared unconstitutional.

The purpose of the "secular purpose" test is to ascertain the government's intent in a piece of legislation, to see whether or not it was designed to advance or inhibit religion. If either purpose is present, the law is unconstitutional. Since its introduction, however, the "secular purpose" test has not been the deciding factor in most of the cases that have come before the Court, primarily because legislatures have become more sophisticated in writing a secular purpose into their legislative enactments, although as recently as STONE v. GRAHAM (1980) (p. 432) and WALLACE v. JAFFREE (1985) (p. 434) state statutes were struck down because they lacked a secular purpose.

The "primary effect" test goes beyond the intent of the law to determine its effect as it is implemented and enforced. The primary effect of the law must be neither to advance nor to inhibit religion, although this language leaves open the possibility of some slight or indirect aid. The effect of a law may be determined first by an analysis of the religious permeation of the recipient institution. That is, how religious is the institution receiving aid? There are some institutions which are pervasively religious, e.g. churches. Others are less thoroughly permeated by religion, e.g. parochial schools. Still others are only slightly permeated by religion; they are collaterally religious, e.g., many church-affiliated colleges and universities. The more pervasively religious the institution receiving aid, the more likely it is that the law will be found unconstitutional as a violation of the establishment clause.

A second factor in the application of the "primary effect" test is that of severability. That is, how independent of its religious function is the secular function of the institution receiving aid? Are the functions sufficiently distinct from each other so that state aid flows only to the secular function and not to the religious function? If so, the program under scrutiny will probably pass the "primary effect" test; if not, it will fail.

The "excessive entanglement" test is related, at least in part, to the "primary effect" test. That is, if a program is of such a nature that it requires regular government inspection or surveillance to make sure the effect of the program is not aiding or hindering religion, that surveillance itself is a violation of the Establishment Clause because it brings government and religion into too much interaction. Supervisory observation to remedy the impermissible effect of the aid program, if done on a continual and extensive basis, constitutes excessive and forbidden entanglement. [12]

Between *Walz* and LARSON v. VALENTE (1982) (p. 337), the three tests were used in all Establishment Clause cases. The Court's attitude during that period is summarized in COMMITTEE FOR PUBLIC EDUCATION v. NYQUIST (p. 504), referring to the three-part test: "these previous Establishment Clause decisions dictate that to pass muster under the Establishment Clause the law in question *must* conform to the test." [13] And in 1982, in LARKIN v. GRENDEL'S DEN (p. 332): "This Court has

consistently held that a statute *must* satisfy three criteria to pass muster under the Establishment Clause." [14] But earlier in that same year, the Court's consistent use of the tests had begun to waver. In *Larson*, the Court declared that the tests were applicable to laws "affording a benefit to *all* religions," not to laws "that discriminate *among* religions." [15] The case was decided on equal protection grounds: the statute was given strict scrutiny and judged to be discriminating between religions.

In subsequent cases, the results and the rhetoric showed much less commitment to the use of the "*Lemon* test." In MARSH v. CHAMBERS (p. 350) the Court did not even mention the three-part test, much less apply it. Rather, an argument from history was used to find the employment of chaplains in state legislatures to be constitutional. In MUELLER v. ALLEN (p. 552) and LYNCH v. DONNELLY (p. 359) the tests were utilized to reach the decision, but in the process language was used which made it appear that they were used more out of convenience than commitment. In referring to the three-part test, *Mueller* says: "While this principle is well settled, our cases have also emphasized that it provides 'no more than [a] helpful signpost' in dealing with Establishment Clause challenges." [16] In *Lynch*: "But, we have repeatedly emphasized our unwillingness to be confined to any single test or criterion in this sensitive area." [17] In that same case, Justice O'Connor, concurring, suggested a redefinition of the three-part test, in which the purpose and effect prongs would prohibit government endorsement or disapproval of religion, i.e., when a law makes adherence to religion relevant to a person's standing in the political community. The entanglement prong would prohibit only institutional entanglement of religion with government, not any and all kinds of entanglement. She repeated this view in WALLACE v. JAFFREE (1986) (p. 434), adding, over against Justice Rehnquist, who proposed that the three-part test be abandoned, that she was not yet ready to discard the test, although, by the time of her dissent in AGUILAR v. FELTON (p. 559), her thinking had changed to the point that she was virtually willing to abandon the entanglement part of it. Justice Stevens, writing for the majority in *Jaffree*, employed the three-part test and used Justice O'Connor's concept that the secular purpose prong is violated if the law endorses religion. He called that the dispositive point in the case. In a concurring opinion, Justice Powell described the three-part test as "the only coherent test a majority of the Court has ever adopted." Far from wanting to abandon it or even to reinterpret it, he counseled against criticizing the test.

Taken together, the cases between 1982 and 1986 show that there developed among the justices a lack of unanimity about the meaning and applicability of the

---

[12] These principles of interpreting the Establishment Clause are derived in part from the very helpful article by Denise Cote, "Establishment Clause Analysis of Legislative and Administrative Aid to Religion", *Columbia Law Review* 74 (1974): 1175-1202. Cf. also Ronald B. Flowers, "The Supreme Court's Three Tests of the Establishment Clause", *Religion in Life* 45 (Spring 1976): 41-52

[13] 413 U.S. 756 at 772-773. (emphasis added)

[14] 459 U.S. 116 at 123. (emphasis added)

[15] 456 U.S. 228 at 252. However, the Court did go on to say that the statute at issue in *Larson* was violative of the entanglement test.

[16] 463 U.S. 388 at 394, quoting *Hunt* v. *McNair* 413 U.S. 734 at 741 (1973).

[17] 465 U.S. 668 at 679. The cases cited which illustrated that the Court had "repeatedly" been unwilling to be bound to a particular Establishment Clause analysis were TILTON v. RICHARDSON (p. 498) and *Nyquist*, in both of which the three-part test was employed.

"*Lemon* test." Consistency was the loser in this development.

Coincidentally with the emergence of evidence that the justices were not of one mind on how to apply (or even whether to keep) the three-part test, the Court began to waver between a separationist interpretation of the Establishment Clause, which had been its tendency prior to 1982, and an accommodationist one. In *Marsh* the Court found state-paid chaplains to legislatures to be consistent with the Constitution. *Mueller* allowed state income tax deductions to help finance children's tuitions to both public and private, including church-related, schools. *Lynch* declared that cities may constitutionally finance the erection and display of a nativity scene and went so far as to say: "Nor does the Constitution require complete separation of church and state; *it affirmatively mandates accommodation*, not merely tolerance, of all religions, and forbids hostility toward any." [18] However, the Court did not completely adopt an accommodationist stance. In *Jaffree* a law mandating a minute of silence for meditation or voluntary prayer was declared unconstitutional, as were plans to provide government-paid teachers in parochial schools in AGUILAR v. FELTON (p. 559) and GRAND RAPIDS SCHOOL DISTRICT v. BALL (p. 567). Strict separationists were despondent at the end of the 1984 term of the Court, since they were convinced that the accommodationism of that term forecast a grim future. But their confidence in the separationism of the Court returned by the end of the 1985 term, in spite of the fact that the Court showed some uncertainty about its Establishment Clause doctrine.

STANDING TO SUE

With good reason the American people have looked upon the Supreme Court of the United States as the ultimate defender of the dual constitutional principles of religious liberty and separation of church and state. However, the Court has not always proved receptive to challenges to governmental actions alleged to violate those principles, especially when brought by individuals or groups in the absence of criminal prosecution by the state.

All courts exercise a measure of control over their dockets, but the Supreme Court possesses a unique discretion as to what will be considered. Constitutional and statutory provisions fix some jurisdictional and procedural limits; but to a remarkable degree the Court, through self-imposed restraints, determines the cases and issues it will hear on appeal from state and lower federal courts. Through this supervisory power and the governing judicial precedents, the Court also exerts great control over the dockets of the lower federal courts. Judicial answers to significant constitutional questions have frequently been avoided or delayed because the courts declined to take jurisdiction over the cases in which they were raised. Since the restraints are largely self-imposed, the Court is free to overlook or reconsider them should it become convinced either that the query has become so critical as to demand response or that the times are more propitious for that response.

In the exercise of control over its work load, the Supreme Court has developed over the years a considerable number of rules, understandings, and procedural techniques which can be invoked. [19] The Court, for example, will not render "advisory opinions," that is, will not give answers to hypothetical questions. It insists that there be an actual "case or controversy" with a concrete set of facts in which adverse parties have a substantial legal interest. An appeal may also be rejected as involving a "political," as opposed to a "justiciable," question.

"Standing to sue" is the procedural requirement that has most often created a problem for those seeking to question the constitutionality of a practice of government as infringing one or both of the religion clauses. This important but complicated and nebulous concept has been held to mean that the party bringing the suit must convince the Court that the interest presented is a substantial and legally protected interest; that it has been injured or is in direct danger of such injury; and that it is a personal right peculiar to him or her—not just one shared with all other persons generally. Obviously, proof of these requisites is a formidable assignment, particularly if the Court is not sympathetic to the substance of the appellant's cause.

One avenue of attack, which was until 1968 unavailable in federal courts due to the Supreme Court's interpretation of standing, is the taxpayer's suit. This is a rather commonly used method of contesting the constitutionality of municipal and state actions. The theory of such litigation is that the taxpayer has standing because if tax money taken by government is used for an unconstitutional purpose, the taxpayer, in effect, has been deprived of property without due process of law.

In 1923 the Supreme Court was confronted with such a suit when Mrs. Frothingham, a citizen of the District of Columbia, challenged the constitutionality of the Federal Maternity Act of 1921. A unanimous Court denied Mrs. Frothingham's standing to sue, saying with respect to the status of a United States taxpayer: "His interest in the moneys of the Treasury—partly realized from taxation and partly from other sources—is shared with millions of others; is comparatively minute and indeterminable; and the effect upon future taxation of any payment out of the funds, so remote, fluctuating and uncertain that no basis is afforded for an appeal to the preventive powers of a court of equity." (262 U.S. 447, 487)

Because *Frothingham* v. *Mellon* related only to federal taxpayers' suits, it did not inhibit continued use of such litigation at the state level. Appeals of these decisions to the Supreme Court have sometimes been accepted, sometimes rejected. The Court has never enunciated a clear doctrine as to what extent the standing issue is resolved through acceptance of a case by the state court. In 1952, for example, two residents of New Jersey challenged the practice of Bible reading in a public high

---

[18] 465 U.S. 668 at 673 (emphasis added)

[19] A helpful discussion of these "maxims of judicial self-restraint" can be found in Henry J. Abraham, *The Judicial Process: An Introductory Analysis of the Courts of the United States, England, and France*, 5th ed. (New York: Oxford University Press, 1985), pp. 369-92; see also C. Herman Pritchett, *The American Constitution*, 3d ed. (New York: McGraw-Hill Book Co., 1977), pp. 129-36.

school. One sued as a taxpayer, the other both as a taxpayer and as a parent of a pupil in the school. When the New Jersey court ruled in favor of the challenged practice, appeal was made to the Supreme Court. The appeal was denied on the basis of lack of standing in *Doremus* v. *Board of Education*, the Court noting that one plaintiff was only a taxpayer and that the other plaintiff's child was no longer a student in the school. Justice Jackson distinguished the situation in *Doremus* where there was no increase in cost of education, from that in EVERSON v. BOARD OF EDUCATION (p. 461) in which the Court had accepted an appeal of the same state's school busing practices. *Everson*, he said, "showed a measurable appropriation or disbursement of school-district funds occasioned solely by the activities complained of." He made no mention of COCHRAN v. LOUISANA STATE BOARD OF EDUCATION (p. 460), where the Court had seemingly accepted jurisdiction because the state court had assumed the presence of standing.

Although the theoretical position of the Court was thus left rather unclear, it soon became evident that the Court was substantially relaxing its standing requirement with respect to the review of state taxpayers' suits in which there was an allegation of denial of constitutional rights. The same year the Court rejected the *Doremus* case, it accepted jurisdiction in ZORACH v. CLAUSON (p. 393). There the petitioners sought appeal based on their status as parents of children in a school in which released time was used. It would have been difficult to show any added tax burden resulting from the practice involved. Ten years later the Court took and decided ENGEL v. VITALE (p. 397) without even discussing the question of standing.

The body of the text of the Court's opinion in ABINGTON TOWNSHIP SCHOOL DISTRICT v. SCHEMPP (1963) (p. 402) was likewise silent as to the question of standing. The only reference to the issue is found in a footnote to Justice Clark's opinion. There, in this rather inconspicuous spot, he indicated that the Court had made a major concession with respect to standing for those presenting challenges based on the Establishment Clause. He wrote: "But the requirements for standing to challenge state action under the Establishment Clause, unlike those relating to the Free Exercise Clause, do not include proof that particular religious freedoms are infringed." (374 U.S. 844, 859) He then commented that the interests of the school children and the parents who were affected by the laws and practices in question would "surely suffice" to give them standing.

In 1968 the appeal of a young school teacher, who had sought an injunction from a state court seeking to prevent enforcement of the Arkansas "monkey law" against her, was accepted and upheld in EPPERSON v. ARKANSAS (p. 428), although the state had neither undertaken to enforce the statute nor given any evidence that it ever intended to. It is most unlikely that an earlier Court would have seriously considered the appeal. [20]

In the early 1960s, *Frothingham* v. *Mellon* took on added significance for both supporters and opponents of state aid to parochial schools as bills providing for federal aid to education were hotly debated in each session of Congress. Separationists feared that the holding in the 1923 case would prevent any judicial review as to the constitutionality of the provisions for parochial aid, which the act would almost certainly contain. Amendments were repeatedly attached to the proposals to provide for judicial review by means of taxpayers' suits, but the comprehensive Federal Elementary and Secondary Aid to Education Act was passed in 1965 without any such condition. Under the leadership of Senator Sam Ervin of North Carolina, new measures which would have granted standing to challenge alleged violations of the First Amendment were introduced in the Senate, only to die in the House. [21]

In the face of these legislative defeats, seven taxpayers in 1967 brought suit against the 1965 act in a federal district court in New York. They sought to enjoin the Secretary of Health, Education, and Welfare, on constitutional grounds, from spending funds under the act for services and textbooks for religious schools. The district court dismissed the case (*Flast* v. *Gardner*) for lack of standing under the Frothingham rule, but the Supreme Court granted certiorari and heard the case in 1968 as FLAST v. COHEN (p. 249). [22]

Without passing on the constitutionality of the Elementary and Secondary Education Act itself, and without expressly overruling *Frothingham* the Supreme Court, by an eight-to-one vote, lowered the barrier against taxpayer suits challenging federal expenditures as violations of the Establishment Clause. Such suits could be entertained, said Chief Justice Warren, provided a taxpayer could demonstrate a two-point "nexus": "First, the taxpayer must establish a logical link between that status and the type of legislative enactment attacked . . . Secondly, the taxpayer must establish a nexus between that status and the precise nature of the constitutional infringement alleged." (392 U.S. 83, 102) To establish the second nexus, the taxpayer must prove that the challenged statute exceeds limits imposed by the Constitution on the exercise of the taxing and spending power. Appellants here had met all the tests and were now free to pursue their suits on its merits in the appropriate court.

---

[20]Leo Pfeffer says of *Epperson* that it illustrates the point "that there is no way to make the Supreme Court take a case when it does not want to, and not much way of stopping it from taking a case when it wants to take it." *God, Caesar, and the Constitution, The Court as Referee of Church-State Confrontation* (Boston: Beacon Press, 1975), p. 222.

[21]However, Representative Emanuel Celler, at the insistence of the National Council of Churches, read into the record an assurance that judicial review would be available to resolve any constitutional issues arising under the act.

[22]The significance attached to the case is indicated by the individuals and interest groups that were involved in the Supreme Court hearing. Senator Ervin filed an *amicus curiae* brief for the Americans for Public Schools et al. and joined Leo Pfeffer and other attorneys in arguing the cause for the appellants. *Amici curiae* briefs were also filed on behalf of appellants by the National Council of Churches, Protestants and Other Americans United for Separation of Church and State, the American Jewish Committee, and the Council of Chief State School Officers. Solicitor General E. N. Griswold argued on behalf of Cohen, and *amici curiae* briefs were filed for the A.F.L.-C.I.O., the National Jewish Commission on Law and Public Affairs, and various private parties. Because of the practical requirement of legal expertise and substantial sums of money to bring such suits, participation of such groups is essential.

Justice Douglas concurred in the opinion but would have preferred to go further and overturn *Frothingham* completely. That the majority of the Court was not willing to do so but, instead, rather narrowly limited the breach in the *Frothingham* rule to First Amendment establishment claims is significant in itself. It indicates the high priority the justices attached to those claims.

The Supreme Court has never passed on the constitutionality of the Elementary and Secondary Education Act since the 1968 decision. Nevertheless, FLAST v. COHEN (p. 249), is a landmark decision. It not only removed an almost insurmountable barrier to challenges of federal aid to church-related schools but also opened more widely the doors of federal courts to taxpayer suits against *state* aid. The significance of the latter development is attested to by the number of such cases subsequently accepted and decided.

In 1982 the Burger Court backed away from the door opened in *Flast* by a narrow vote of five-to-four in VALLEY FORGE CHRISTIAN COLLEGE v. AMERICANS UNITED FOR SEPARATION OF CHURCH AND STATE (p. 258). The *Valley Forge* case arose in 1976 when Americans United and four of its employees filed suit in a United States district court in Pennsylvania. They challenged the action of the then Department of Health, Education, and Welfare when that government agency conveyed, without charge, seventy acres of land and the buildings of a "surplus" government hospital to a denominational school then called Northeast Bible College. The suit charged violation of the Establishment Clause and alleged that each member of the organization dedicated to separation of church and state "would be deprived of the fair and constitutional use of his (her) tax dollars." The district court failed to find standing and dismissed the complaint. Appeal was sought, and the Third Court of Appeals held that the claimants had standing as citizens who had shown a "particular and concrete injury" to a "personal, constitutional right," if not as taxpayers.

Justice Rehnquist wrote the majority opinion of the Supreme Court and was joined by Justices Burger, White, Powell, and O'Connor. Rehnquist agreed with the district court that those seeking to bring the suit had "failed to allege that they have suffered any actual or concrete injury beyond a generalized grievance common to all taxpayers." On rather narrow technical grounds, he distinguished the fact situations here from that in *Flast*: in that case it was *congressional* action and exercise of the Taxing and Spending Clause of Article I which was challenged. In the instant case it was action by an *executive* department and an exercise of congressional power under the Property Clause of Article IV.

The opinion saw no basis for creation of a "hierarchy of constitutional values" that would justify a standard of easier court access to those invoking religious rights. Justice Rehnquist also struck out at separationist groups such as Americans United:

> Their claim that the government has violated the Establishment Clause does not provide a special license to roam the country in search of governmental wrongdoing and to reveal their discoveries in federal court. The federal courts were simply not constituted as ombudsmen of the general welfare. (454 U.S. 464, 487)

At another point he commented that "standing is not measured by the intensity of the litigant's interest or the fervor of his advocacy."

Joined by Justices Marshall and Blackmun, Justice Brennan wrote an acid dissent, citing the majority opinion as "a stark example of the unfortunate trend of resolving cases at the 'threshold' while obscuring the nature of the underlying rights and interests at stake." Brennan charged that the Court was "blind to history" when it sought to distinguish the case from *Flast*, and he contended, "Surely . . . a taxpayer must have standing at the time that he learns of the Government's alleged Establishment Clause violation to seek equitable relief in order to halt the continuing and intolerable burden on his pocketbook, his conscience, and his constitutional rights." (454 U.S. 464, 490-91, 509)

In a separate dissent, Justice Stevens argued that *Flast* has given a special position to establishment claims and would not allow for the "drawing of a tenuous distinction between the Spending Clause and the Property Clause." The *Valley Forge* decision, by limiting access to those able to prove direct, personal, actual injury, undoubtedly made suits against federal action on establishment grounds much more difficult and therefore much less likely to be brought.

The degree to which the Court will ultimately retreat toward its pre-*Flast* stance is not yet clear. However, there is no doubt that the Burger Court has continued to move away from the more liberalized standing policy of the Warren Court. For example, in 1984, in a case not involving church-state issues, the Court in *Allen* v. *Wright* denied standing to parents with black children in public schools undergoing desegregation who sought to challenge regulations of the IRS concerning tax-exemption entitlement of private schools which discriminate against blacks. Justice Brennan, as in the *Valley Forge* case, complained bitterly that, "Once again the Court 'uses' standing to slam the courthouse door against plaintiffs who are entitled to full consideration of their claims on the merits." (104 S.Ct. 3315, 3333) Justice Stevens also filed a dissenting opinion in which Justice Blackmun joined.

Two years later the Court again invoked lack of standing to avoid ruling, at least temporarily, on the highly controversial issue of "equal access," a practice which will be discussed at a later point. (p. 381) The voting alignment of the judges was noticeably different in BENDER v. WILLIAMSPORT AREA SCHOOL DISTRICT (p. 270) from that in *Valley Forge* and *Allen* v. *Wright*. In *Bender* it was Justices Stevens, Brennan, Blackmun, and Marshall, joined this time by Justice O'Connor, who "used" standing to refrain from a decision on the merits of an appellant's claim.

In 1981, a group of high school students in Williamsport, Pennsylvania, organized "Petros," a club which they said would promote "spiritual growth and positive attitudes in the lives of its members." After consulting with the school district's legal counsel, the principal and superintendent denied the request of members of the organization to meet on campus during the school's activity period to read scripture, discuss religious matters, and pray. When the negative decision was upheld by the school board, the students and their parents filed suit in the United States District Court for the Middle District of

Pennsylvania, alleging that the exclusion of Petros because of its religious activities violated the First Amendment.

The district court ruled that the school board would not have violated the Establishment Clause by authorizing Petros to meet on the same basis as other student groups. Rather, refusal to allow meetings had impermissibly infringed upon the students' right of free speech. The school board voted eight-to-one not to appeal the ruling, and Petros resumed its meetings.

Later, however, John C. Youngman, Jr., the only school board dissenter, appealed to the United States Court of Appeals for the Third Circuit. In 1984 that court held that the board authorization ultimately given to the club to meet had the primary effect of advancing religion and that teacher monitoring of the meetings involved an excessive entanglement of government and religion.

The Supreme Court granted the students' petition for certiorari and the case was argued 15 October 1985, at which time it became evident that the question of Mr. Youngman's standing to bring suit was a crucial issue. On 25 March 1986 the Court, by a vote of five-to-four, decided that he did not have standing to appeal as an individual, as a member of the board, or as a parent, and that the Court of Appeals had no jurisdiction to hear the appeal. The judgment of the appellate court was therefore vacated. Mr. Youngman, said Justice Stevens for the majority, had been sued not as an individual or a parent but in his official capacity as a member of the school board. As the lone dissenter, he had no standing to appeal a decision of the board, and he had not asserted a parental interest during the district court proceedings.

It may well be that Justices Brennan, Stevens, Blackmun, and Marshall were willing to invoke the standing rule, after having criticized its use in earlier situations, because they feared that if the case was decided on its merits, equal access would gain the approval of a majority of the Court and thus apply the favorable decision of the local district court to the national scene. The action taken by the Supreme Court limited the immediate effect of the lower court's decision to only the Williamsport Area School District.

Chief Justice Burger, writing for Justices White and Rehnquist, would have accepted Youngman's standing as a parent of a student at Williamsport High and would have proceeded to the constitutional issue of granting the religious group equal access to the student activity forum. He, as did Justice Powell in a separate dissent, saw WIDMAR v. VINCENT (p. 210) as controlling.

Justice Powell made his position quite clear when he wrote, "I do not believe—particularly in this age of massive media information—that the few years difference in age between high school and college students justifies departing from *Widmar*" (106 S.Ct. 1326, 1339). Although Justice O'Connor voted with the majority in failing to find standing, her earlier interpretations of the Establishment Clause indicate that she would likely vote to uphold an equal access statute if decided by the Court on substantive grounds. Other equal access cases already in the lower federal courts will likely give the members of the Court an early opportunity to express themselves more fully on the constitutional merits of the practice.

FLAST v. COHEN

392 U.S. 83
ON APPEAL FROM THE UNITED STATES
DISTRICT COURT FOR
THE SOUTHERN DISTRICT OF NEW YORK
Argued March 12, 1968 — Decided June 10, 1968

⊥*Mr. Chief Justice WARREN* delivered the opinion of the Court.   ⌐85

In *Frothingham* v. *Mellon* this Court ruled that a federal taxpayer is without standing to challenge the constitutionality of a federal statute. That ruling has stood for 45 years as an impenetrable barrier to suits against Acts of Congress brought by individuals who can assert only the interest of federal taxpayers. In this case, we must decide whether the *Frothingham* barrier should be lowered when a taxpayer attacks a federal statute on the ground that it violates the Establishment and Free Exercise Clauses of the First Amendment.

Appellants filed suit in the United States District Court for the Southern District of New York to enjoin the allegedly unconstitutional expenditure of federal funds under Titles I and II of the Elementary and Secondary Education Act of 1965. The complaint alleged that the seven appellants had as a common attribute that "each pay[s] income taxes of the United States," and it is clear from the complaint that the appellants were resting their standing to maintain the action solely on their status as federal taxpayers. The appellees, who are charged by Congress with administering the Elementary and Secondary Education Act of 1965, were sued in their official capacities.

The gravamen of the appellants' complaint was that federal funds appropriated under the Act were being used to finance instruction in reading, arithmetic, and other subjects in religious schools, and to purchase textbooks ⊥and other instructional materials for use in such schools. Such expenditures were alleged to be in contravention of the Establishment and Free Exercise Clauses of the first Amendment. Appellants' constitutional attack focused on the statutory criteria which state and local authorities must meet to be eligible for federal grants under the Act. Title I of the Act establishes a program for financial assistance to local educational agencies for the education of low-income families. Federal payments are made to state educational agencies, which pass the payments on in the form of grants to local educational agencies. Under § 205 of the Act, a local educational agency wishing to have a plan or program funded by a grant must submit the plan or program to the appropriate state educational agency for approval. The plan or program must be "consistent with such basic criteria as the [appellee United States Commissioner of Education] may establish." The specific criterion of that section attacked by the appellants is the requirement "that, to the extent consistent with the number of educationally deprived children in the school district of the local educational agency who are enrolled in private elementary and secondary schools, such agency has made provision for including special educational services and arrangements (such as dual enrollment, educational radio and television, and mobile educational services and equipment) in which such children can participate. . . ."

Under § 206 of the Act, the Commissioner of Education is given broad powers to supervise a State's participation in Title I programs and grants. Title II of the Act establishes a program of federal grants for the acquisition of school library resources, textbooks, ⊥87 ⊥and other printed and published instructional materials "for the use of children and teachers in public and private elementary and secondary schools." A State wishing to participate in the program must submit a plan to the Commissioner for approval, and the plan must "provide assurance that to the extent consistent with law such library resources, textbooks, and other instructional materials will be provided on an equitable basis for the use of children and teachers in private elementary and secondary schools in the State. . . ."

While disclaiming any intent to challenge as unconstitutional all programs under Title I of the Act, the complaint alleges that federal funds have been disbursed under the Act, "with the consent and approval of the [appellees]," and that such funds have been used and will continue to be used to finance "instruction in reading, arithmetic and other subjects and for guidance in religious and sectarian schools" and "the purchase of textbooks and instructional and library materials for use in religious and sectarian schools." Such expenditures of federal tax funds, appellants alleged, violate the First Amendment because "they constitute a law respecting an establishment of religion" and because "they prohibit the free exercise of religion on the part of the [appellants] . . . by reason of the fact that they constitute compulsory taxation for religious purposes." The complaint asked for a declaration that appellees' actions in approving the expenditure of federal funds for the alleged purposes were not authorized by the Act or, in the alternative, that if appellees' actions are deemed within the authority and intent of the Act, "the Act is to that extent unconstitutional and void." The complaint also prayed ⊥88 for an injunction to enjoin appel⊥lees from approving any expenditure of federal funds for the allegedly unconstitutional purposes. The complaint further requested that a three-judge court be convened.

The Government moved to dismiss the complaint on the ground that appellants lacked standing to maintain the action. District Judge Frankel, who considered the motion, recognized that *Frothingham* v. *Mellon* provided "powerful" support for the Government's position, but he ruled that the standing question was of sufficient substance to warrant the convening of a three-judge court to decide the question. The three-judge court received briefs and heard arguments limited to the standing question, and the court ruled on the authority of *Frothingham* that appellants lacked standing. Judge Frankel dissented. From the dismissal of their complaint on that ground, appellants appealed directly to this Court and we noted probable jurisdiction. For reasons explained at length below, we hold that appellants do have standing as federal taxpayers to maintain this action, and the judgment below must be reversed. . . .

⊥This Court first faced squarely the question ⊥91 whether a litigant asserting only his status as a taxpayer has standing to maintain a suit in a federal court in *Frothingham* v. *Mellon*, and that decision must be the starting point for analysis in this case. The taxpayer in *Frothingham* attacked as unconstitutional the Maternity Act of 1921, which established a federal program of grants to those States which would undertake programs to reduce maternal and infant mortality. The taxpayer alleged that Congress, in enacting the challenged statute, had exceeded the powers delegated to it under Article I of the Constitution and had invaded the legislative province reserved to the several States by the Tenth Amendment. The taxpayer complained that the result of the allegedly unconstitutional enactment would be to increase her future federal tax ⊥liability ⊥92 and "thereby take her property without due process of law." The Court noted that a federal taxpayer's "interest in the moneys of the Treasury. . . is comparatively minute and indeterminable" and that the effect upon future taxation, of any payment out of the [Treasury's] funds, . . . [is] remote, fluctuating and uncertain." As a result, the Court ruled that the taxpayer had failed to allege the type of "direct injury" necessary to confer standing.

Although the barrier *Frothingham* erected against federal taxpayer suits has never been breached, the decision has been the source of some confusion and the object of considerable criticism. The confusion has developed as commentators have tried to determine whether *Frothingham* establishes a constitutional bar to taxpayer suits or whether the Court was simply imposing a rule of self-restraint which was not constitutionally compelled. The conflicting viewpoints are reflected in the arguments made to this Court by the parties in this case. The Government has pressed upon us the view that *Frothingham* announced a constitutional rule, compelled by the Article III limitations on federal court jurisdiction and grounded in considerations of the doctrine of separation of powers. Appellants, however, insist that ⊥*Frothingham* expressed no more than a policy of ⊥93 judicial self-restraint which can be disregarded when compelling reasons for assuming jurisdiction over a taxpayer's suit exist. The opinion delivered in *Frothingham* can be read to support either position. The concluding sentence of the opinion states that, to take jurisdiction of the taxpayer's suit, "would be not to decide a judicial controversy, but to assume a position of authority over the governmental acts of another and co-equal department, an authority which plainly we do not possess." Yet the concrete reasons given for denying standing to a federal taxpayer suggest that the Court's holding rests on something less than a constitutional foundation. For example, the Court conceded that standing had previously been conferred on municipal taxpayers to sue in that capacity. However, the Court viewed the interest of a federal taxpayer in total federal tax revenues as "comparatively minute and indeterminable" when measured against a municipal taxpayer's interest in a smaller city treasury. This suggests that the petitioner in *Frothingham* was denied standing not because she was a taxpayer but because her tax bill was not large enough. In addition, the Court spoke of the "attendant inconveniences" of entertaining that taxpayer's suit because it might open the door of federal courts to countless such suits "in respect of every other appropriation act and statute whose administration requires the outlay of public money, and whose validity may be questioned." Such a statement suggests pure policy considerations.

⊥94 ⊥To the extent that *Frothingham* has been viewed as resting on policy considerations, it has been criticized as depending on assumptions not consistent with modern conditions. For example, some commentators have pointed out that a number of corporate taxpayers today have a federal tax liability running into hundreds of millions of dollars, and such taxpayers have a far greater monetary stake in the Federal Treasury than they do in any municipal treasury. To some degree, the fear expressed in *Frothingham* that allowing one taxpayer to sue would inundate the federal courts with countless similar suits has been mitigated by the ready availability of the devices of class actions and joinder under the Federal Rules of Civil Procedure, adopted subsequent to the decision in *Frothingham*. Whatever the merits of the current debate over *Frothingham*, its very existence suggests that we should undertake a fresh examination of the limitations upon standing to sue in a federal court and the application of those limitations to taxpayer suits. . . .

⊥101 ⊥Thus, in terms of Article III limitations on federal court jurisdiction, the question of standing is related only to whether the dispute sought to be adjudicated will be presented in an adversary context and in a form historically viewed as capable of judicial resolution. It is for that reason that the emphasis in standing problems is on whether the party invoking federal court jurisdiction has "a personal stake in the outcome of the controversy" and whether the dispute touches upon "the legal relations of parties having adverse legal interests." A taxpayer may or may not have the requisite personal stake in the outcome, depending upon the circum-

stances of the particular case. Therefore, we find no absolute bar in Article III to suits by federal taxpayers challenging allegedly unconstitutional federal taxing and spending programs. There remains, however, the problem of determining the circumstances under which a federal taxpayer will be deemed to have the personal stake and interest that impart the necessary concrete adverseness to such litigation so that standing can be conferred on the taxpayer *qua* taxpayer consistent with the constitutional limitations of Article III.

The various rules of standing applied by federal courts have not been developed in the abstract. Rather, they have been fashioned with specific reference to the status asserted by the party whose standing is challenged and to the type of question he wishes to have adjudicated. We have noted that, in deciding the question of standing, it is not relevant that the substantive issues in the litigation might be nonjusticiable. However, our decisions ⊥establish   ⊥102 that, in ruling on standing, it is both appropriate and necessary to look to the substantive issues for another purpose, namely, to determine whether there is a logical nexus between the status asserted and the claim sought to be adjudicated. For example, standing requirements will vary in First Amendment religion cases depending upon whether the party raises an Establishment Clause claim or a claim under the Free Exercise Clause. Such inquiries into the nexus between the status asserted by the litigant and the claim he presents are essential to assure that he is a proper and appropriate party to invoke federal judicial power. Thus, our point of reference in this case is the standing of individuals who assert only the status of federal taxpayers and who challenge the constitutionality of a federal spending program. Whether such individuals have standing to maintain that form of action turns on whether they can demonstrate the necessary stake as taxpayers in the outcome of the litigation to satisfy Article III requirements.

The nexus demanded of federal taxpayers has two aspects to it. First, the taxpayer must establish a logical link between that status and the type of legislative enactment attacked. Thus, a taxpayer will be a proper party to allege the unconstitutionality only of exercises of congressional power under the taxing and spending clause of Art. I, § 8, of the Constitution. It will not be sufficient to allege an incidental expenditure of tax funds in the administration of an essentially regulatory statute. This requirement is consistent with the limitation imposed upon state-taxpayer standing in federal courts in *Doremus* v. *Board of Education*. Secondly, the taxpayer must establish a nexus between that status and the precise nature of the constitutional infringement alleged. Under this requirement, the taxpayer must show that the challenged enactment exceeds ⊥specific   ⊥103 constitutional limitations imposed upon the exercise of the congressional taxing and spending power and not simply that the enactment is generally beyond the powers delegated to Congress by Art. I, § 8. When both nexuses are established, the litigant will have shown a taxpayer's stake in the outcome of the controversy and will be a proper and appropriate party to invoke a federal court's jurisdiction.

The taxpayer-appellants in this case have satisfied both nexuses to support their claim of standing under the test we announce today. Their constitutional challenge is made to an exercise by Congress of its power under Art. I, § 8, to spend for the general welfare, and the challenged program involves a substantial expenditure of federal tax funds. In addition, appellants have alleged that the challenged expenditures violate the Establishment and Free Exercise Clauses of the First Amendment. Our history vividly illustrates that one of the specific evils feared by those who drafted the Establishment Clause and fought for its adoption was that the taxing and spending power would be used to favor one religion over another or to support religion in general. James Madison, who is generally recognized as the leading architect of the religion clauses of the First Amendment, observed in his famous Memorial and Remonstrance Against Religious Assessments that "the same authority which can force a citizen to contribute three pence only of his property for the support of any one establishment, may force him to conform to any other establishment in all cases whatsoever." The concern of Madison and his supporters was quite clearly that religious liberty ultimately would ⊥104 be the victim if ⊥government could employ its taxing and spending powers to aid one religion over another or to aid religion in general. The Establishment Clause was designed as a specific bulwark against such potential abuses of governmental power, and that clause of the First Amendment operates as a specific constitutional limitation upon the exercise by Congress of the taxing and spending power conferred by Art. I, § 8.

The allegations of the taxpayer in *Frothingham* v. *Mellon* were quite different from those made in this case, and the result in *Frothingham* is consistent with the test of taxpayer standing announced today. The taxpayer in *Frothingham* attacked a federal spending program and she, therefore, established the ⊥105 first nexus ⊥ required. However, she lacked standing because her constitutional attack was not based on an allegation that Congress, in enacting the Maternity Act of 1921, had breached a specific limitation upon its taxing and spending power. The taxpayer in *Frothingham* alleged essentially that Congress, by enacting the challenged statute, had exceeded the general powers delegated to it by Art. I, § 8, and that Congress had thereby invaded the legislative province reserved to the States by the Tenth Amendment. To be sure, Mrs. Frothingham made the additional allegation that her tax liability would be increased as a result of the allegedly unconstitutional enactment, and she framed that allegation in

terms of a deprivation of property without due process of law. However, the Due Process Clause of the Fifth Amendment does not protect taxpayers against increases in tax liability, and the taxpayer in *Frothingham* failed to make any additional claim that the harm she alleged resulted from a breach by Congress of the specific constitutional limitations imposed upon an exercise of the taxing and spending power. In essence, Mrs. Frothingham was attempting to assert the States' interest in their legislative prerogatives and not a federal taxpayer's interest in being free of taxing and spending in contravention of specific constitutional limitations imposed upon Congress' taxing and spending power.

We have noted that the Establishment Clause of the First Amendment does specifically limit the taxing and spending power conferred by Art. I, § 8. Whether the Constitution contains other specific limitations can be determined only in the context of future cases. However, whenever such specific limitations are found, we believe a taxpayer will have a clear stake as a taxpayer in assuring that they are not breached by Congress. Consequently, we hold that a taxpayer will have stand⊥ing consistent with ⊥106 Article III to invoke federal judicial power when he alleges that congressional action under the taxing and spending clause is in derogation of those constitutional provisions which operate to restrict the exercise of the taxing and spending power. The taxpayer's allegation in such cases would be that his tax money is being extracted and spent in violation of specific constitutional protections against such abuses of legislative power. Such an injury is appropriate for judicial redress, and the taxpayer has established the necessary nexus between his status and the nature of the allegedly unconstitutional action to support his claim of standing to secure judicial review. Under such circumstances, we feel confident that the questions will be framed with the necessary specificity, that the issues will be contested with the necessary adverseness and that the litigation will be pursued with the necessary vigor to assure that the constitutional challenge will be made in a form traditionally thought to be capable of judicial resolution. We lack that confidence in cases such as *Frothingham* where a taxpayer seeks to employ a federal court as a forum in which to air his generalized grievances about the conduct of government or the allocation of power in the Federal System.

While we express no view at all on the merits of appellants' claims in this case, their complaint contains sufficient allegations under the criteria we have outlined to give them standing to invoke a federal court's jurisdiction for an adjudication on the merits.

Reversed.

⊥ *Mr. Justice DOUGLAS*, concurring.   ⊥107

While I have joined the opinion of the Court, I do not think that the test it lays down is a durable one for the reasons stated by my *Brother HARLAN*. I think, therefore, that it will suffer erosion and in time result in the demise of *Frothingham* v. *Mellon*. It would therefore be the part of wisdom, as I see the problem, to be rid of *Frothingham* here and now.

I do not view with alarm, as does my *Brother HARLAN*, the consequences of that course. *Frothingham*, decided in 1923, was in the heyday of substantive due process, when courts were sitting in judgment on the wisdom or reasonableness of legislation. The claim in *Frothingham* was that a federal regulatory Act dealing with maternity deprived the plaintiff of property without due process of law. When the Court used substantive due process to determine the wisdom or reasonableness of legislation, it was indeed transforming itself into the Council of Revision which was rejected by the Constitutional Convention. It was that judicial attitude, not the theory of standing to sue rejected in *Frothingham*, that involved "important hazards for the continued effectiveness of the federal judiciary," to borrow a phrase from my *Brother HARLAN*. A contrary result in *Frothingham* in that setting might well have accentuated an ominous trend to judicial supremacy.

But we no longer undertake to exercise that kind of power. Today's problem is in a different setting.

Most laws passed by Congress do not contain even a ghost of a constitutional question. The "political" decisions, as distinguished from the "justiciable" ones, occupy most of the spectrum of congressional action. The case or controversy requirement comes into play only when the Federal Government does something that affects a person's life, his liberty, or his property. The wrong may be slight or it may be ⊥108 grievous. Madison in denouncing ⊥ state support of churches said the principle was violated when even "three pence" was appropriated to that cause by the Government. It therefore does not do to talk about taxpayers' interest as "infinitesimal." The restraint on "liberty" may be fleeting and passing and still violate a fundamental constitutional guarantee. The "three pence" mentioned by Madison may signal a monstrous invasion by the Government into church affairs, and so on. . . .

⊥111   ⊥ The judiciary is an indispensable part of the operation of our federal system. With the growing complexities of government it is often the one and only place where effective relief can be obtained. If the judiciary were to become a super-legislative group sitting in judgment on the affairs of people, the situation would be intolerable. But where wrongs to individuals are done by violation of specific guarantees, it is abdication for courts to close their doors.

Marshall wrote in *Marbury* v. *Madison* that if the judiciary stayed its hand in deference to the legislature, it would give the legislature "a practical and real omnipotence." My *Brother HARLAN'S* view would do just that, for unless Congress created a procedure through which its legislative creation could be challenged quickly and with ease, the momentum of what it had done would grind the dissenter under.

We have a Constitution designed to keep government out of private domains. But the fences have often been broken down; and *Frothingham* denied effective machinery to restore them. The Constitution even with the judicial gloss it has acquired plainly is not adequate to protect the individual against the growing bureaucracy in the Legislative and Executive Branches. He faces a formidable opponent in government, even when he is endowed with funds and with courage. The individual is almost certain to be plowed under, unless he has a well-organized active political group to speak for him. The church is one. The press is another. The union is a third. But if a powerful sponsor is lacking, individual liberty withers—in spite of glowing opinions and resounding constitutional phrases.

I would not be niggardly therefore in giving private attorneys general standing to sue. I would certainly not ⊥ wait for Congress to give its blessing to our de-   ⊥112 ciding cases clearly within our Article III jurisdiction. To wait for a sign from Congress is to allow important constitutional questions to go undecided and personal liberty unprotected.

There need be no inundation of the federal courts if taxpayers' suits are allowed. There is a wise judicial discretion that usually can distinguish between the frivolous question and the substantial question, between cases ripe for decision and cases that need prior administrative processing, and the like. When the judiciary is no longer "a great rock" in the storm, as Lord Sankey once put it, when the courts are niggardly in the use of their power and reach great issues only timidly and reluctantly, the force of the Constitution in the life of the Nation is greatly weakened. . . .

We have recently reviewed the host of devices ⊥ used by the States to avoid opening to Negroes   ⊥113 public facilities enjoyed by whites. There is a like process at work at the federal level in respect to aid to religion. The efforts made to insert in the law an express provision which would allow federal aid to sectarian schools to be reviewable in the courts was defeated. The mounting federal aid to sectarian schools is notorious and the subterfuges numerous.

⊥ I would be as liberal in allowing taxpayers   ⊥114 standing to object to these violations of the First Amendment as I would in granting standing to people to complain of any invasion of their rights under the Fourth Amendment or the Fourteenth or under any other guarantee in the Constitution itself or in the Bill of Rights.

Mr. Justice STEWART, concurring.

I join the judgment and opinion of the Court, which I understand to hold only that a federal taxpayer has standing to assert that a specific expenditure of federal funds violates the Establishment

Clause of the First Amendment. Because that clause plainly prohibits taxing and spending in aid of religion, every taxpayer can claim a personal constitutional right not to be taxed for the support of a religious institution. The present case is thus readily distinguishable from *Frothingham* v. *Mellon* where the taxpayer did not rely on an explicit constitutional prohibition but instead questioned the scope of the powers delegated to the national legislature by Article I of the Constitution.

As the Court notes, "one of the specific evils feared by those who drafted the Establishment Clause and fought for its adoption was that the taxing and spending power would be used to favor one religion over another or to support religion in general." Today's decision no more than recognizes that the appellants have a clear stake as taxpayers in assuring that they not be compelled to contribute even "three pence . . . of [their] property for the support of any one establishment." In concluding that the appellants therefore have standing to sue, we do not undermine the salutary principle, established by *Frothingham* and reaffirmed today, that a taxpayer may not "employ a federal court as a forum in which to air his generalized grievances about the conduct of government or the allocation of power in the Federal System."

⌐115   ⊥*Mr. Justice FORTAS*, concurring.

I would confine the ruling in this case to the proposition that a taxpayer may maintain a suit to challenge the validity of a federal expenditure on the ground that the expenditure violates the Establishment Clause. As the Court's opinion recites, there is enough in the constitutional history of the Establishment Clause to support the thesis that this Clause includes a *specific* prohibition upon the use of the power to tax to support an establishment of religion. There is no reason to suggest, and no basis in the logic of this decision for implying, that there may be other types of congressional expenditures which may be attacked by a litigant solely on the basis of his status as a taxpayer.

I agree that *Frothingham* does not foreclose today's result. I agree that the congressional powers to tax and spend are limited by the prohibition upon Congress to enact laws "respecting an establishment of religion." This thesis, slender as its basis is, provides a direct nexus, as the Court puts it, between the use and collection of taxes and the congressional action here. Because of this unique "nexus," in my judgment, it is not far-fetched to recognize that a taxpayer has a special claim to status as a litigant in a case raising the "establishment" issue. This special claim is enough, I think, to permit us to allow the suit, coupled, as it is, with the interest which the taxpayer and all other citizens have in the church-state issue. In terms of the structure and basic philosophy of our constitutional government, it would

be difficult to point to any issue that has a more intimate, pervasive, and fundamental impact upon the life of the taxpayer—and upon the life of all citizens.

Perhaps the vital interest of a citizen in the establishment issue, without reference to his taxpayer's status, ⊥would be acceptable as a basis for this challenge. We need not decide this. But certainly, I believe, we must recognize that our principle of judicial scrutiny of legislative acts which raise important constitutional questions requires that the issue here presented—the separation of state and church—which the Founding Fathers regarded as fundamental to our constitutional system—should be subjected to judicial testing. This is not a question which we, if we are to be faithful to our trust, should consign to limbo, unacknowledged, unresolved, and undecided.   ⌐116

On the other hand, the urgent necessities of this case and the precarious opening through which we find our way to confront it, do not demand that we open the door to a general assault upon exercises of the spending power. The status of taxpayer should not be accepted as a launching pad for an attack upon any target other than legislation affecting the Establishment Clause.

Mr. Justice HARLAN, dissenting.

The problems presented by this case are narrow and relatively abstract, but the principles by which they must be resolved involve nothing less than the proper functioning of the federal courts, and so run to the roots of our constitutional system. The nub of my view is that the end result of *Frothingham* v. *Mellon* was correct, even though, like others, I do not subscribe to all of its reasoning and premises. Although I therefore agree with certain of the conclusions reached today by the Court, I cannot accept the standing doctrine ⊥that it substitutes for *Frothingham*, for it seems to me that this new doctrine rests on premises that do not withstand analysis. Accordingly, I respectfully dissent.   ⌐117

I

It is desirable first to restate the basic issues in this case. The question here is not, as it was not in *Frothingham*, whether "a federal taxpayer is without standing to challenge the constitutionality of a federal statute." It could hardly be disputed that federal taxpayers may, as taxpayers, contest the constitutionality of tax obligations imposed severally upon them by federal statute. Such a challenge may be made by way of defense to an action by the United States to recover the amount of a challenged tax debt, or to a prosecution for willful failure to pay or to report the tax. Moreover, such a challenge may provide the basis of an action by a taxpayer to obtain the refund of a previous tax payment.

The lawsuits here and in *Frothingham* are fundamentally different. They present the question whether federal taxpayers *qua* taxpayers may, in suits in which they do not contest the validity of their previous or existing tax obligations, challenge the constitutionality of the uses for which Congress has authorized the expenditure of public funds. These differences in the purposes of the cases are reflected in differences in the litigants' interests. An action brought to contest the validity of tax liabilities assessed to the plaintiff is designed to vindicate interests that are personal and proprietary. The wrongs alleged and the relief sought by such a plaintiff are unmistakably private; only secondarily are his interests representative of those of the general ⌐118 population. I take ⊥ it that the Court, although it does not pause to examine the question, believes that the interests of those who as taxpayers challenge the constitutionality of public expenditures may, at least in certain circumstances, be similar. Yet this assumption is surely mistaken.

The complaint in this case, unlike that in *Frothingham*, contains no allegation that the contested expenditures will in any fashion affect the amount of these taxpayers' own existing or foreseeable tax obligations. Even in cases in which such an allegation is made, the suit cannot result in an adjudication either of the plaintiff's tax liabilities or of the propriety of any particular level of taxation. The relief available to such a plaintiff consists entirely of the vindication of rights held in common by all citizens. It is thus scarcely surprising that few of the state courts that permit such suits require proof either that the challenged expenditure is consequential in amount or that it is likely to affect significantly the plaintiff's own tax bill; these courts have at least impliedly recognized that such allegations are surplusage, useful only to preserve the form of an obvious fiction.

Nor are taxpayers' interests in the expenditure of public funds differentiated from those of the general public by any special rights retained by them in their tax payments. The simple fact is that no such rights can sensibly be said to exist. Taxes are ordinarily levied by the United States without limitations of purpose; absent such a limitation, payments received by the Treasury in satisfaction of tax obligations lawfully created become part of the Government's general funds. The national legislature is required by ⌐119 the Constitution to ⊥ exercise its spending powers to "provide for the common Defence and general Welfare." Whatever other implications there may be to that sweeping phrase, it surely means that the United States holds its general funds, not as stakeholder or trustee for those who have paid its imposts, but as surrogate for the population at large. Any rights of a taxpayer with respect to the purposes for which those funds are expended are thus subsumed in, and extinguished by, the common rights of all citizens. To characterize taxpayers' interests in such expenditures as proprietary or even personal either deprives those terms of all meaning or postulates for taxpayers a *scintilla juris* in funds that no longer are theirs. . . .

II

⊥ As I understand it, the Court's position is that it ⌐121 is unnecessary to decide in what circumstances public actions should be permitted, for it is possible to identify situations in which taxpayers who contest the constitutionality of federal expenditures assert "personal" rights and interests. This position, if supportable, would of course avoid many of the difficulties of this case; indeed, if the Court is correct, its extended exploration of the subtleties of Article III is entirely unnecessary. But, for reasons that follow, I believe that the Court's position is untenable.

The Court's analysis consists principally of the observation that the requirements of standing are met if a taxpayer has the "requisite personal stake in the outcome" of his suit. This does not, of course, resolve the standing problem; it merely restates it. The Court implements this standard with the declaration that taxpayers will be "deemed" to have the necessary personal interest if their suits satisfy two criteria; *first*, the challenged expenditure must form part of a federal spending program, and not merely be "incidental" to a regulatory program; and *second*, the constitutional provision under which the plaintiff claims must be a "specific limitation" upon Congress' spending powers. The difficulties with these criteria are many and severe, but it is enough for the moment to emphasize that they are not in any sense a measurement of any plaintiff's interest in the outcome of any suit. As even a cursory examination of ⊥ the criteria will show, the Court's standard for the ⌐122 determination of standing and its criteria for the satisfaction of that standard are entirely unrelated.

It is surely clear that a plaintiff's interest in the outcome of a suit in which he challenges the constitutionality of a federal expenditure is not made greater or smaller by the unconnected fact that the expenditure is, or is not, "incidental" to an "essentially regulatory" program. An example will illustrate the point. Assume that two independent federal programs are authorized by Congress, that the first is designed to encourage a specified religious group by the provision to it of direct grants-in-aid, and that the second is designed to discourage all other religious groups by the imposition of various forms of discriminatory regulation. Equal amounts are appropriated by Congress for the two programs. If a taxpayer challenges their constitutionality in separate suits, are we to suppose, as evidently does the Court, that his ⊥ "personal stake" in the suit involving the ⌐123 second is necessarily smaller than it is in the suit involving the first, and that he should therefore have standing in one but not the other?

Presumably the Court does not believe that regulatory programs are necessarily less destructive of First Amendment rights, or that regulatory programs are necessarily less prodigal of public funds than are grants-in-aid, for both these general propositions are demonstrably false. The Court's disregard of regulatory expenditures is not even a logical consequence of its apparent assumption that taxpayer-plaintiffs assert essentially monetary interests, for it surely cannot matter to a taxpayer *qua* taxpayer whether an unconstitutional expenditure is used to hire the services of regulatory personnel or is distributed among private and local governmental agencies as grants-in-aid. His interest as taxpayer arises, if at all, from the fact of an unlawful expenditure, and not as a consequence of the expenditure's form. Apparently the Court has repudiated the emphasis in *Frothingham* upon the amount of the plaintiff's tax bill, only to substitute an equally irrelevant emphasis upon the form of the challenged expenditure.

The Court's second criterion is similarly unrelated to its standard for the determination of standing. The intensity of a plaintiff's interest in a suit is not measured, even obliquely, by the fact that the constitutional provision under which he claims is, or is not, a "specific limitation" upon Congress' spending powers. Thus, among the claims in *Frothingham* was the assertion that the Maternity Act deprived the petitioner of property without due process of law. The Court has evidently concluded that this claim did not confer standing because the Due Process Clause of the Fifth Amendment is not a specific lim-

⏊124 itation upon the spending ⏊powers. Disregarding for the moment the formidable obscurity of the Court's categories, how can it be said that Mrs. Frothingham's interests in her suit were, as a consequence of her choice of a constitutional claim, necessarily less intense than those, for example, of the present appellants? I am quite unable to understand how, if a taxpayer believes that a given public expenditure is unconstitutional, and if he seeks to vindicate that belief in a federal court, his interest in the suit can be said necessarily to vary according to the constitutional provision under which he states his claim. . . .

⏊125   ⏊Although the Court does not altogether explain its position, the essence of its reasoning is evidently that a taxpayer's claim under the Establishment Clause is "not merely one of ultra vires," but one which instead asserts "an abridgment of individual religious liberty" and a "governmental infringement of individual rights protected by the Constitution." It must first be emphasized that this is apparently not founded upon any "preferred" position for the First Amendment, or upon any asserted unavailability of other plaintiffs. The Court's position is instead that, because of the Establishment Clause's historical purposes, taxpayers retain rights under it quite different from those held by them under other constitutional provisions.

The difficulties with this position are several. First, we have recently been reminded that the historical purposes of the religious clauses of the First

Amendment are significantly more obscure and complex than this Court has heretofore acknowledged. Careful students ⏊of the history of the Establishment Clause have found that "it is impossible to give a dogmatic interpretation of the First Amendment, and to state with any accuracy the intention of the men who framed it. . . ." Above all, the evidence seems clear that the First Amendment was not intended simply to enact the terms of Madison's Memorial and Remonstrance against Religious Assessments. I do not suggest that history is without relevance to these questions, or that the use of federal funds for religious purposes was not a form of establishment that many in the 18th century would have found objectionable. I say simply that, given the ultimate obscurity of the Establishment Clause's historical purposes, it is inappropriate for this Court to draw fundamental distinctions among the several constitutional commands upon the supposed authority of isolated dicta extracted from the clause's complex history. In particular, I have not found, and the opinion of the Court has not adduced, historical evidence that properly permits the Court to distinguish, as it has here, among the Establishment Clause, the Tenth Amendment, and the Due Process Clause of the Fifth Amendment as limitations upon Congress' taxing and spending powers.   ⏊126

⏊The Court's position is equally precarious if it is   ⏊127
assumed that its premise is that the Establishment Clause is in some uncertain fashion a more "specific" limitation upon Congress' powers than are the various other constitutional commands. It is obvious, first, that only in some Pickwickian sense are any of the provisions with which the Court is concerned "specific[ally]" limitations upon spending, for they contain nothing that is expressly directed at the expenditure of public funds. The specificity to which the Court repeatedly refers must therefore arise, not from the provisions' language, but from something implicit in their purposes. But this Court has often emphasized that Congress' powers to spend are coterminous with the purposes for which, and methods by which, it may act, and that the various constitutional commands applicable to the central government, including those implicit both in the Tenth Amendment and in the General Welfare Clause, thus operate as limitations upon spending. I can attach no constitutional significance to the various degrees of specificity with which these limitations appear in the terms or history of the Constitution. If the Court accepts the proposition, as I do, ⏊that the number and scope of public actions   ⏊128
should be restricted, there are, as I shall show, methods more appropriate, and more nearly permanent, than the creation of an amorphous category of constitutional provisions that the Court has deemed, without adequate foundation, "specific limitations" upon Congress' spending powers.

Even if it is assumed that such distinctions may properly be drawn, it does not follow that federal taxpayers hold any "personal constitutional right" such that they may each contest the validity under the Establishment Clause of all federal expenditures. The difficulty, with which the Court never comes to grips, is that taxpayers' suits under the Establishment Clause are not in these circumstances meaningfully different from other public actions. If this case involved a tax specifically designed for the support of religion, as was the Virginia tax opposed by Madison in his Memorial and Remonstrance, I would agree that taxpayers have rights under the religious clauses of the First Amendment that would permit them standing to challenge the tax's validity in the federal courts. But this is not such a case, and appellants challenge an expenditure, not a tax. Where no such tax is involved, a taxpayer's complaint can consist only of an allegation that public funds have been, or shortly will be, expended for purposes inconsistent with the Constitution. The taxpayer cannot ask the return of any portion of his previous tax payments, cannot prevent the collection of any existing tax debt, and cannot demand an adjudication of the propriety of any particular level of taxation. His tax payments are received for the general purposes of the United States, and are, upon proper receipt, lost in the general revenues. The interests he ⊥represents, and the rights he espouses, are, as they are in all public actions, those held in common by all citizens. To describe those rights and interests as personal, and to intimate that they are in some unspecified fashion to be differentiated from those of the general public, reduces constitutional standing to a word game played by secret rules.

⊥Apparently the Court, having successfully circumnavigated the issue, has merely returned to the proposition from which it began. A litigant, it seems, will have standing if he is "deemed" to have the requisite interest, and "if you . . . have standing, then you can be confident you are" suitably interested.

III

It seems to me clear that public actions, whatever the constitutional provisions on which they are premised, may involve important hazards for the continued effectiveness of the federal judiciary. Although I believe such actions to be within the jurisdiction conferred upon the federal courts by Article III of the Constitution, there surely can be little doubt that they strain the judicial function and press to the limit judicial authority. There is every reason to fear that unrestricted public actions might well alter the allocation of authority among the three branches of the Federal Government. It is not, I submit, enough to say that the present members of the Court would not seize these opportunities for abuse, for such actions would, even without conscious abuse, go far toward the final transformation of this Court into the Council of Revision which, despite Madison's support, was rejected by the Constitutional Convention. I do not doubt that there must be "some effectual power in the government to restrain or correct the infractions" of ⊥the Constitution's several commands, but neither can I suppose that such power resides only in the federal courts. We must as judges recall that, as Mr. Justice Holmes wisely observed, the other branches of the Government "are ultimate guardians of the liberties and welfare of the people in quite as great a degree as the courts." *Missouri, Kansas & Texas R. Co.* v. *May*. The powers of the federal judiciary will be adequate for the great burdens placed upon them only if they are employed prudently, with recognition of the strengths as well as the hazards that go with our kind of representative government.

Presumably the Court recognizes at least certain of these hazards, else it would not have troubled to impose limitations upon the situations in which, and purposes for which, such suits may be brought. Nonetheless, the limitations adopted by the Court are, as I have endeavored to indicate, wholly untenable. This is the more unfortunate because there is available a resolution of this problem that entirely satisfies the demands of the principle of separation of powers. This Court has previously held that individual litigants have standing to represent the public interest, despite their lack of economic or other personal interests, if Congress has appropriately authorized such suits. I would adhere to that principle. Any hazards to the ⊥proper allocation of authority among the three branches of the Government would be substantially diminished if public actions had been pertinently authorized by Congress and the President. I appreciate that this Court does not ordinarily await the mandate of other branches of the Government, but it seems to me that the extraordinary character of public actions, and of the mischievous, if not dangerous, consequences they involve for the proper functioning of our constitutional system, and in particular of the federal courts, makes such judicial forbearance the part of wisdom. It must be emphasized ⊥that the implications of these questions of judicial policy are of fundamental significance for the other branches of the Federal Government.

Such a rule could readily be applied to this case. Although various efforts have been made in Congress to authorize public actions to contest the validity of federal expenditures in aid of religiously affiliated schools and other institutions, no such authorization has yet been given.

This does not mean that we would, under such a rule, be enabled to avoid our constitutional responsibilities, or that we would confine to limbo the First Amendment or any other constitutional command. The question here is not, despite the Court's unarticulated premise, whether the religious clauses of the First Amendment are hereafter to be enforced by the federal courts; the issue is simply whether an *additional* category of plaintiffs, heretofore excluded

⊥129

⊥130

⊥131

⊥132

⊥133

from those courts, are to be permitted to maintain suits. The recent history of this Court is replete with illustrations that questions involving the religious clauses will not, if federal taxpayers are prevented from contesting federal expenditures, be left "unacknowledged, unresolved, and undecided."

Accordingly, for the reasons contained in this opinion, I would affirm the judgment of the District Court.

VALLEY FORGE CHRISTIAN COLLEGE v. AMERICANS UNITED FOR SEPARATION OF CHURCH AND STATE

454 U.S. 464
ON WRIT OF CERTIORARI TO THE UNITED STATES COURT OF
APPEALS FOR THE THIRD CIRCUIT
Argued November 4, 1981 — Decided January 12, 1982

⊥466   ⊥*Justice REHNQUIST* delivered the opinion of the Court.

I

Article IV, Section 3, Clause 2 of the Constitution vests Congress with the "Power to dispose of and make all needful Rules and Regulations respecting the . . . Property belonging to the United States." Shortly after the termination of hostilities in the Second World War, Congress enacted the Federal Property and Administrative Services Act of 1949, 63 Stat. 377, 40 U. S. C. § 471 *et seq.* (1976 ed. and Supp. III). The Act was designed, in part, to provide "an economical and efficient system for . . . the disposal of surplus property." 63 Stat. 378, 40 U. S. C. § 471. In furtherance of this policy, federal agencies are directed to maintain adequate inventories of the property under their control and to identify excess property for transfer to other agencies able to use it. See 63 Stat. 384, 40 U. S. C. § 483(b), (c). Property that has outlived its usefulness to the federal government is declared "surplus" and may be transferred to ⊥467   pri⊥vate or other public entities. See generally 63 Stat. 385, as amended, 40 U. S. C. § 484.

The Act authorizes the Secretary of Health, Education, and Welfare (now the Secretary of Education) to assume responsibility for disposing of surplus real property "for school, classroom, or other educational use." 63 Stat. 387, as amended, 40 U. S. C. § 484(k)(1). Subject to the disapproval of the Administrator of General Services, the Secretary may sell or lease the property to nonprofit, tax exempt educational institutions for consideration that takes into account "any benefit which has accrued or may accrue to the United States" from the transferee's use of the property. 63 Stat. 387, 40 U. S. C. §

484(k)(1)(A), (C). By regulation, the Secretary has provided for the computation of a "public benefit allowance," which discounts the transfer price of the property "on the basis of benefits to the United States from the use of such property for educational purposes." 34 CFR § 12.9(a)(1980).

The property which spawned this litigation was acquired by the Department of the Army in 1942, as part of a larger tract of approximately 181 acres of land northwest of Philadelphia. The Army built on that land the Valley Forge General Hospital, and for 30 years thereafter, that hospital provided medical care for members of the Armed Forces. In April 1973, as part of a plan to reduce the number of military ⊥installations in the United States, the Secre- ⊥468 tary of Defense proposed to close the hospital, and the General Services Administration declared it to be "surplus property."

The Department of Health, Education, and Welfare (HEW) eventually assumed responsibility for disposing of portions of the property, and in August 1976, it conveyed a 77-acre tract to petitioner, the Valley Forge Christian College. The appraised value of the property at the time of conveyance was $577,500. This appraised value was discounted, however, by the Secretary's computation of a 100% public benefit allowance, which permitted petitioner to acquire the property without making any financial payment for it. The deed from HEW conveyed the land in fee simple with certain conditions subsequent, which required petitioner to use the property for 30 years solely for the educational purposes described in petitioner's application. In that description, petitioner stated its intention to conduct "a program of education . . . meeting the accrediting standards of the State of Pennsylvania, The American Association of Bible Colleges, the Division of Education of the General Council of the Assemblies of God and the Veterans Administration."

Petitioner is a nonprofit educational institution operating under the supervision of a religious order known as the Assemblies of God. By its own description, petitioner's purpose is "to offer systematic training on the collegiate level to men and women for Christian service as either ministers or laymen." Its degree programs reflect this orientation by providing courses of study "to train leaders for church related ministries." Faculty members ⊥must "have ⊥469 been baptized in the Holy Spirit and be living consistent Christian lives," and all members of the college administration must be affiliated with the Assemblies of God. In its application for the 77-acre tract, petitioner represented that, if it obtained the property, it would make "additions to its offerings in the arts and humanities," and would strengthen its "psychology" and "counselling" courses to provide services in inner city areas.

In September 1976, respondents Americans United for Separation of Church and State, Inc. (Americans United), and four of its employees, learned of the conveyance through a news release. Two months later, they brought suit in the United States District Court for the Eastern District of Pennsylvania to challenge the conveyance on the ground that it violated the Establishment Clause of the First Amendment. In its amended complaint, Americans United described itself as a nonprofit organization composed of 90,000 "taxpayer members." The complaint asserted that each member "would be deprived of the fair and constitutional use of his (her) tax dollar for constitutional purposes in violation of his (her) rights under the First Amendment of the United States Constitution." Respondents sought a declaration that the conveyance was null and void, and an order compelling petitioner to transfer the property back to the United States.

On petitioner's motion, the District Court granted summary judgment and dismissed the complaint. The court found that respondents lacked standing to sue as taxpayers under *Flast* v. *Cohen*, and had "failed to allege that they have suffered any actual or concrete injury beyond a generalized grievance common to all taxpayers."

⊥Respondents appealed to the Court of Appeals for the Third Circuit, which reversed the judgment of the District Court by a divided vote. All members of the court agreed that respondents lacked standing as taxpayers to challenge the conveyance under *Flast* v. *Cohen* since that case extended standing to taxpayers *qua* taxpayers only to challenge congressional exercises of the power to tax and spend conferred by Art. I, § 8, of the Constitution, and this conveyance was authorized by legislation enacted under the authority of the Property Clause, Art. IV, § 3, cl. 2. Notwithstanding this significant factual difference from *Flast*, the majority of the Court of Appeals found that respondents also had standing merely as "citizens," claiming " 'injury in fact' to their shared individuated right to a government that 'shall make no law respecting the establishment of religion.' " In the majority's view, this "citizen standing" was sufficient to satisfy the "case or controversy" requirement of Art. III. One judge, perhaps sensing the doctrinal difficulties with the majority's extension of standing, wrote separately, expressing his view that standing was necessary to satisfy "the need for an available plaintiff," without whom "the Establishment Clause would be rendered virtually unenforceable" by the Judiciary. The dissenting judge expressed the view that respondents' allegations constituted a "generalized grievance . . . too abstract to satisfy the injury in fact component of standing." He therefore concluded that their standing to contest the transfer was barred by this Court's decisions in *Schlesinger* v. *Reservists Committee to Stop the War* and *United States* v. *Richardson*.

Because of the unusually broad and novel view of standing to litigate a substantive question in the federal courts adopted by the Court of Appeals, we granted certiorari, and we now reverse.

II

⊥Article III of the Constitution limits the "judicial power" of the United States to the resolution of "cases" and "controversies." The constitutional power of federal courts cannot be defined, and indeed has no substance, without reference to the necessity "to adjudge the legal rights of litigants in actual controversies." *Liverpool Steamship Co.* v. *Commissioners of Emigration*. The requirements of Art. III are not satisfied merely because a party requests a court of the United States to declare its legal rights, and has couched that request for forms of relief historically associated with courts of law in terms that have a familiar ring to those trained in the legal process. The judicial power of the United States defined by Art. III is not an unconditioned authority to determine the constitutionality of legislative or executive acts. The power to declare the rights of individuals and to measure the authority of governments, this Court said 90 years ago, "is legitimate only in the last resort, and as a necessity in the determination of real, earnest and vital controversy." *Chicago & Grand Trunk R. Co.* v. *Wellman*. Otherwise, the power "is not judicial . . . in the sense in which judicial power is granted by the Constitution to the courts of the United States." *United States* v. *Ferreira*.

As an incident to the elaboration of this bedrock requirement, this Court has always required that a litigant have "standing" to challenge the action sought to be adjudicated in the lawsuit. The term "standing" subsumes a blend of constitutional requirements and prudential considerations, see *Warth* v. *Seldin*, and it has not always been clear in the opinions of this Court whether particular features of the "standing" requirement have been required by Art. III *ex proprio vigore*, or whether they are requirements that the Court itself has erected and which were not compelled by the language of the Constitution. See *Flast* v. *Cohen*.

⊥A recent line of decisions, however, has resolved that ambiguity, at least to the following extent: at an irreducible minimum, Art. III requires the party who invokes the court's authority to "show that he personally has suffered some actual or threatened injury as a result of the putatively illegal conduct of the defendant," *Gladstone, Realtors* v. *Village of Bellwood*, and that the injury "fairly can be traced to the challenged action" and "is likely to be redressed by a favorable decision," *Simon* v. *Eastern Kentucky Welfare Rights Org.* In this manner does Art. III limit the federal judicial power "to those disputes which confine federal courts to a role consistent with a system of separated powers and which are traditionally thought to be capable of resolution through the judicial process." *Flast* v. *Cohen*.

The requirement of "actual injury redressable by the court," *Simon*, serves several of the "implicit policies embodied in Article III," *Flast*. It tends to assure that the legal questions presented to the court will be resolved, not in the rarified atmosphere of a debating society, but in a concrete factual context conducive to a realistic appreciation of the consequences of judicial action. The "standing" requirement serves other purposes. Because it assures an actual factual setting in which the litigant asserts a claim of injury in fact, a court may decide the case with some confidence that its decision will not pave the way for lawsuits which have some, but not all, of the facts of the case actually decided by the court.

⌐473   ⊥ The Art. III aspect of standing also reflects a due regard for the autonomy of those persons likely to be most directly affected by a judicial order. The federal courts have abjured appeals to their authority which would convert the judicial process into "no more than a vehicle for the vindication of the value interests of concerned bystanders." *United States* v. *SCRAP*. Were the federal courts merely publicly funded forums for the ventilation of public grievances or the refinement of jurisprudential understanding, the concept of "standing" would be quite unnecessary. But the "cases and controversies" language of Art. III forecloses the conversion of courts of the United States into judicial versions of college debating forums. As we said in *Sierra Club* v. *Morton*: "The requirement that a party seeking review must allege facts showing that he is himself adversely affected . . . does serve as at least a rough attempt to put the decision as to whether review will be sought in the hands of those who have a direct stake in the outcome."

The exercise of judicial power, which can so profoundly affect the lives, liberty, and property of those to whom it extends, is therefore restricted to litigants who can show "injury in fact" resulting from the action which they seek to have the Court adjudicate.

The exercise of the judicial power also affects relationships between the coequal arms of the national government. The effect is, of course, most vivid when a federal court declares unconstitutional an act of the Legislative or Executive branch. While the exercise of that "ultimate and supreme function," *Chicago & Grand Trunk R. Co.* v. *Wellman*, is a formidable means of vindicating individual rights, when employed unwisely or unnecessarily it is also the ultimate threat to the continued effectiveness of the federal courts performing that role. While the propriety of such action by a federal court has been

⌐474   recognized since ⊥ *Marbury* v. *Madison*, it has been recognized as a tool of last resort on the part of the federal judiciary throughout its nearly 200 years of existence: "[R]epeated and essentially head-on confrontations between the life-tenured branch and the representative branches of government will not, in the long run, be beneficial to either. The public confidence essential to the former and the vitality critical to the latter may well erode if we do not exercise self-restraint in the utilization of our power to

negative the actions of the other branches." *United States* v. *Richardson*. Proper regard for the complex nature of our constitutional structure requires neither that the judicial branch shrink from a confrontation with the other two coequal branches of the federal government, nor that it hospitably accept for adjudication claims of constitutional violation by other branches of government where the claimant has not suffered cognizable injury. Thus this Court has "refrain[ed] from passing upon the constitutionality of an act [of the representative branches] unless obliged to do so in the proper performance of our judicial function, when the question is raised by a party whose interests entitle him to raise it." *Blair* v. *United States*. The importance of this precondition should not be underestimated as a means of "defin[ing] the role assigned to the judiciary in a tripartite allocation of power." *Flast* v. *Cohen*.

Beyond the constitutional requirements, the federal judiciary has also adhered to a set of prudential principles that bear on the question of standing. Thus, this Court has held that "the plaintiff generally must assert his own legal rights and interests, and cannot rest his claim to relief on the legal rights or interests of third parties." *Warth* v. *Seldin*. In addition, even when the plaintiff has al⊥leged re-   ⌐475 dressable injury sufficient to meet the requirements of Art. III, the Court has refrained from adjudicating "abstract questions of wide public significance" which amount to "generalized grievances," pervasively shared and most appropriately addressed in the representative branches. Finally, the Court has required that the plaintiff's complaint fall within "the zone of interests to be protected or regulated by the statute or constitutional guarantee in question." *Data Processing Service* v. *Camp*.

Merely to articulate these principles is to demonstrate their close relationship to the policies reflected in the Art. III requirement of actual or threatened injury amenable to judicial remedy. But neither the counsels of prudence nor the policies implicit in the "case or controversy" requirement should be mistaken for the rigorous Art. III requirements themselves. Satisfaction of the former cannot substitute for a demonstration of " 'distinct and palpable injury' . . . that is likely to be redressed if the requested relief is granted." *Gladstone, Realtors* v. *Village of Bellwood*. That requirement states a limitation on judicial power, not merely a factor to be balanced in the weighing of so-called "prudential" considerations.

We need not mince words when we say that the concept of "Art. III standing" has not been defined with complete consistency in all of the various cases decided by this Court which have discussed it, nor when we say that this very fact is probably proof that the concept cannot be reduced to a one-sentence or one-paragraph definition. But of one thing we may be sure: Those who do not possess Art. III standing may ⊥ not litigate as suitors in the courts   ⌐476 of the United States. Art. III, which is every bit as important in its circumscription of the judicial power of the United States as in its granting of that power, is not merely a troublesome hurdle to be overcome if possible so as to reach the "merits" of a lawsuit which a party desires to have adjudicated; it is a part of the basic charter promulgated by the framers of the Constitution at Philadelphia in 1787, a charter which created a general government, provided for the interaction between that government and the governments of the several States, and was later amended so as to either enhance or limit its authority with respect to both States and individuals.

III

The injury alleged by respondents in their amended complaint is the "depriv[ation] of the fair and constitutional use of [their] tax dollar." As a result, our discussion ⊥must begin with *Frothingham* v. *Mellon*. In that action a taxpayer brought suit challenging the constitutionality of the Maternity Act of 1921, which provided federal funding to the States for the purpose of improving maternal and infant health. The injury she alleged consisted of the burden of taxation in support of an unconstitutional regime, which she characterized as a deprivation of property without due process. "Looking through forms of words to the substance of [the] complaint," the Court concluded that the only "injury" was the fact "that officials of the executive branch of the government are executing and will execute an act of Congress asserted to be unconstitutional." Any tangible effect of the challenged statute on the plaintiff's tax burden was "remote, fluctuating, and uncertain." In rejecting this as a cognizable injury sufficient to establish standing, the Court admonished: "The party who invokes the power [of judicial review] must be able to show not only that the statute is invalid but that he has sustained or is immediately in danger of sustaining some direct injury as the result of its enforcement, and not merely that he suffers in some indefinite way in common with people generally. . . . Here the parties plaintiff have no such case."

Following the decision in *Frothingham*, the Court confirmed that the expenditure of public funds in an allegedly unconstitutional manner is not an injury sufficient to confer standing, even though the plaintiff contributes to the public coffers as a taxpayer. In *Doremus* v. *Board of Education* plaintiffs brought suit as citizens and taxpayers, claiming that a New Jersey law which authorized public school teachers in the classroom to read passages from ⊥the Bible violated the Establishment Clause of the First Amendment. The Court dismissed the appeal for lack of standing: "This Court has held that the interests of a taxpayer in the moneys of the federal treasury are too indeterminable, remote, uncertain and indirect to furnish a basis for an appeal to the

preventive powers of the Court over their manner of expenditure. . . . Without disparaging the availability of the remedy by taxpayer's action to restrain unconstitutional acts which result in direct pecuniary injury, we reiterate what the Court said of a federal statute as equally true when a state Act is assailed: The party who invokes the power must be able to show not only that the statute is invalid but that he has sustained or is immediately in danger of sustaining some direct injury as the result of its enforcement, and not merely that he suffers in some indefinite way in common with people generally." In short, the Court found that plaintiffs' grievance was "not a direct dollars-and-cents injury but is a religious difference." A case or controversy did not exist, even though the "clash of interests [was] real and . . . strong."

The Court again visited the problem of taxpayer standing in *Flast* v. *Cohen*. The taxpayer plaintiffs in *Flast* sought to enjoin the expenditure of federal funds under the Elementary and Secondary Education Act of 1965, which they alleged were being used to support religious schools in violation of the Establishment Clause. The Court developed a two-part test to determine whether the plaintiffs had standing to sue. First, because a taxpayer alleges injury only by virtue of his liability for taxes, the Court held that "a taxpayer will be a proper party to allege the unconstitutionality only of exercises of congressional power under the taxing and spending clause of Art. I, § 8, of the Constitu⊥tion." Second, the Court required the taxpayer to "show that the challenged enactment exceeds specific constitutional limitations upon the exercise of the taxing and spending power and not simply that the enactment is generally beyond the powers delegated to Congress by Art. I, § 8."

The plaintiffs in *Flast* satisfied this test because "[t]heir constitutional challenge [was] made to an exercise by Congress of its power under Art. I, § 8, to spend for the general welfare," and because the Establishment Clause, on which plaintiffs' complaint rested, "operates as a specific constitutional limitation upon the exercise by Congress of the taxing and spending power conferred by Art. I, § 8." The Court distinguished *Frothingham* v. *Mellon* on the ground that Mrs. Frothingham had relied, not on a specific limitation on the power to tax and spend, but on a more general claim based on the Due Process Clause. Thus, the Court reaffirmed that the "case or controversy" aspect of standing is unsatisfied "where a taxpayer seeks to employ a federal court as a forum in which to air his generalized grievances about the conduct of government or the allocation of power in the Federal System."

Unlike the plaintiffs in *Flast*, respondents fail the first prong of the test for taxpayer standing. Their claim is deficient in two respects. First, the source of their complaint is not a congressional action, but a decision by HEW to transfer a parcel of federal property. *Flast* limited taxpayer standing to challenges directed "only [at] exercises of congressional power." See *Schlesinger* v. *Reservists Committee to Stop the War* (denying standing because the taxpayer plaintiffs "did not challenge an enactment under Art. I, § 8, but rather the action of the Executive Branch").

⌐480 ⊥ Second, and perhaps redundantly, the property transfer about which respondents complain was not an exercise of authority conferred by the taxing and spending clause of Art. I, § 8. The authorizing legislation, the Federal Property and Administrative Services Act of 1949, was an evident exercise of Congress' power under the Property Clause, Art. IV, § 3, cl. 2. Respondents do not dispute this conclusion, and it is decisive of any claim of taxpayer standing under the *Flast* precedent.

⌐481 ⊥ Any doubt that once might have existed concerning the rigor with which the *Flast* exception to the *Frothingham* principle ought to be applied should have been erased by this Court's recent decisions in *United States* v. *Richardson* and *Schlesinger* v. *Reservists Committee to Stop the War*. In *Richardson*, the question was whether the plaintiff had standing as a federal taxpayer to argue that legislation which permitted the Central Intelligence Agency to withhold from the public detailed information about its expenditures violated the Accounts Clause of the Constitution. We rejected plaintiff's claim of standing because "his challenge [was] not addressed to the taxing or spending power, but to the statutes regulating the CIA." The "mere recital" of those claims "demonstrate[d] how far he [fell] short of the standing criteria of *Flast* and how neatly he [fell] within the *Frothingham* holding left undisturbed."

The claim in *Schlesinger* was marred by the same deficiency. Plaintiffs in that case argued that the Incompatibility Clause of Art. I prevented certain Members of Congress from holding commissions in the Armed Forces Reserve. We summarily rejected their assertion of standing as taxpayers because they "did not challenge an enactment under Art. I, § 8, but rather the action of the Executive Branch in permitting Members of Congress to maintain their Reserve status."

⌐482 ⊥ Respondents, therefore, are plainly without standing to sue as taxpayers. The Court of Appeals apparently reached the same conclusion. It remains to be seen whether respondents have alleged any other basis for standing to bring this suit.

IV

Although the Court of Appeals properly doubted respondents' ability to establish standing solely on the basis of their taxpayer status, it considered their allegations of taxpayer injury to be "essentially an assumed role." "Plaintiffs have no reason to expect, nor perhaps do they care about, any personal tax saving that might result should they prevail. The crux of the interest at stake, the plaintiffs argue, is found in the Establishment Clause, not in the supposed loss of money as such. As a matter of primary identity, therefore, the plaintiffs are not so much taxpayers as separationists. . . ." In the court's view, respondents had established standing by virtue of an " 'injury in fact' to their shared individuated right to a government that 'shall make no law respecting the establishment of religion.' " The court distinguished this "injury" from "the question of 'citizen standing' as such." Although citizens generally could not establish standing simply by claiming an interest in governmental observance of the Constitution, respondents had "set forth instead a particular and concrete injury" to a "personal constitutional right."

The Court of Appeals was surely correct in recognizing that the Art. III requirements of standing are not satisfied by "the abstract injury in nonobservance of the Constitution asserted by . . . citizens." *Schlesinger* v. *Reservists Committee to Stop the War*. This Court repeatedly has rejected claims of standing predicated on " 'the right, possessed by every citizen, to require that the ⊥ Government be administered according to law. . . .' *Fairchild* v. *Hughes*." *Baker* v. *Carr*. See *Schlesinger* v. *Reservists Committee to Stop the War*; *Laird* v. *Tatum*; *Ex parte Levitt*. Such claims amount to little more than attempts "to employ a federal court as a forum in which to air. . . generalized grievances about the conduct of government." *Flast* v. *Cohen*.

In finding that respondents had alleged something more than "the generalized interest of all citizens in constitutional governance," *Schlesinger*, the Court of Appeals relied on factual differences which we do not think amount to legal distinctions. The court decided that respondents' claim differed from those in *Schlesinger* and *Richardson*, which were predicated, respectively, on the Incompatibility and Accounts Clauses, because "it is at the very least arguable that the Establishment Clause creates in each citizen a 'personal constitutional right' to a government that does not establish religion." The court found it unnecessary to determine whether this "arguable" proposition was correct, since it judged the mere allegation of a legal right sufficient to confer standing.

This reasoning process merely disguises, we think with a rather thin veil, the inconsistency of the court's result with our decisions in *Schlesinger* and *Richardson*. The plaintiffs in those cases plainly asserted a "personal right" to have the government act in accordance with their views of the Constitution; indeed, we see no barrier to the *assertion* of such claims with respect to any constitutional provision. But assertion of a right to a particular kind of government conduct, which the government has violated by acting differently, cannot alone satisfy the requirements of Art. III without draining those requirements of meaning.

⊥Nor can *Schlesinger* and *Richardson* be distinguished on the ground that the Incompatibility and Accounts Clauses are in some way less "fundamental" than the Establishment Clause. Each establishes a norm of conduct which the federal government is bound to honor—to no greater or lesser extent than any other inscribed in the Constitution. To the extent the Court of Appeals relied on a view of standing under which the Art. III burdens diminish as the "importance" of the claim on the merits increases, we reject that notion. The requirement of standing "focuses on the party seeking to get his complaint before a federal court and not on the issues he wishes to have adjudicated." *Flast* v. *Cohen.* Moreover, we know of no principled basis on which to create a hierarchy of constitutional values or a complementary "sliding scale" of standing which might permit respondents to invoke the judicial power of the United States. ⊥"The proposition that all constitutional provisions are enforceable by any citizen simply because citizens are the ultimate beneficiaries of those provisions has no boundaries." *Schlesinger* v. *Reservists Committee to Stop the War.*

The complaint in this case shares a common deficiency with those in *Schlesinger* and *Richardson.* Although they claim that the Constitution has been violated, they claim nothing else. They fail to identify any personal injury suffered by the plaintiffs *as a consequence* of the alleged constitutional error, other than the psychological consequence presumably produced by observation of conduct with which one disagrees. That is not an injury sufficient to confer standing under Art. III, even though the disagreement is phrased in ⊥constitutional terms. It is evident that respondents are firmly committed to the constitutional principle of separation of church and State, but standing is not measured by the intensity of the litigant's interest or the fervor of his advocacy. "[T]hat concrete adverseness which sharpens the presentation of issues," *Baker* v. *Carr,* is the anticipated consequence of proceedings commenced by one who has been injured in fact; it is not a permissible substitute for the showing of injury itself.

In reaching this conclusion, we do not retreat from our earlier holdings that standing may be predicated on noneconomic injury. See, *e.g., United States* v. *SCRAP; Data Processing Service* v. *Camp.* We simply cannot see that respondents have alleged an *injury* of *any* kind, economic or otherwise, sufficient to confer standing. Respondents com⊥plain of a transfer of property located in Chester County, Pennsylvania. The named plaintiffs reside in Maryland and Virginia; their organizational headquarters are located in Washington, D.C. They learned of the transfer through a news release. Their claim that the government has violated the Establishment Clause does not provide a special license to roam the country in search of governmental wrongdoing and to reveal their discoveries in federal court. The federal courts were simply not constituted as ombudsmen of the general welfare.

V

⊥The Court of Appeals in this case ignored unambiguous limitations on taxpayer and citizen standing. It appears to have done so out of the conviction that enforcement of the Establishment Clause demands special exceptions from the requirement that a plaintiff allege " 'distinct and palpable injury to himself,' . . . that is likely to be redressed if the requested relief is granted." *Gladstone, Realtors* v. *Village of Bellwood* (quoting *Warth* v. *Seldin).* The court derived precedential comfort from *Flast* v. *Cohen*: "The underlying justification for according standing in *Flast* it seems, was the implicit recognition that the Establishment Clause does create in every citizen a personal constitutional right, such that any citizen, including taxpayers, may contest under that clause the constitutionality of federal expenditures." The concurring opinion was even more direct. In its view, "statutes alleged to violate the Establishment Clause may not have an ⊥individual impact sufficient to confer standing in the traditional sense." To satisfy "the need for an available plaintiff," and thereby to assure a basis for judicial review, respondents should be granted standing because, "as a practical matter, no one is better suited to bring this lawsuit and thus vindicate the freedoms embodied in the Establishment Clause."

Implicit in the foregoing is the philosophy that the business of the federal courts is correcting constitutional errors, and that "cases and controversies" are at best merely convenient vehicles for doing so and at worst nuisances that may be dispensed with when they become obstacles to that transcendent endeavor. This philosophy has no place in our constitutional scheme. It does not become more palatable when the underlying merits concern the Establishment Clause. Respondents' claim of standing implicitly rests on the presumption that violations of the Establishment Clause typically will not cause injury sufficient to confer standing under the "traditional" view of Art. III. But "[t]he assumption that if respondents have no standing to sue, no one would have standing, is not a reason to find standing." *Schlesinger* v. *Reservists Committee to Stop the War* This view would convert standing into a requirement that must be observed only when satisfied. Moreover, we are unwilling to assume that injured parties are nonexistent simply because they have not joined respondents in their suit. The law of averages is not a substitute for standing.

Were we to accept respondents' claim of standing in this case, there would be no principled basis for confining our exception to litigants relying on the Establishment Clause. Ultimately, that exception derives from the idea that the judicial power requires nothing more for its invocation than important is-

sues and able litigants. The existence of injured
⊥parties who might not wish to bring suit becomes
irrelevant. Because we are unwilling to countenance
such a departure from the limits on judicial power
contained in Art. III, the judgment of the Court of
Appeals is reversed.

It is so ordered.

Justice BRENNAN, with whom _Justice MAR-
SHALL_ and _Justice BLACKMUN_ join, dissenting.

A plaintiff's standing is a jurisdictional matter for
Article III courts, and thus a "threshold question" to
be resolved before turning attention to more "substantive" issues. See _Linda R. S._ v. _Richard D._ But
in consequence there is an impulse to decide difficult
questions of substantive law obliquely in the course
of opinions purporting to do nothing more than determine what the Court labels "standing"; this accounts for the phenomenon of opinions, such as the
one today, that tend merely to obfuscate, rather than
inform, our understanding of the meaning of rights
under the law. The serious by-product of that practice is that the Court disregards its constitutional
responsibility when, by failing to acknowledge the
protections afforded by the Constitution, it uses
"standing to slam the courthouse door against plaintiffs who are entitled to full consideration of their
claims on the merits."

The opinion of the Court is a stark example of this
unfortunate trend of resolving cases at the "threshold" while obscur⊥ing the nature of the underlying
rights and interests at stake. The Court waxes eloquent on the blend of prudential and constitutional
considerations that combine to create our misguided
"standing" jurisprudence. *But not one word is said
about the Establishment Clause right that the plaintiff seeks to enforce.* And despite its past recitation
of our standing decisions, the opinion utterly fails,
except by the sheerest form of *ipse dixit*, to explain
why this case is unlike *Flast* v. *Cohen*, and is controlled instead by *Frothingham* v. *Mellon*.

I

There is now much in the way of settled doctrine
in our understanding of the injury-in-fact requirement of Article III. At the core is the irreducible
minimum that persons seeking judicial relief from an
Article III court have "such a personal stake in the
outcome of the controversy as to assure that concrete adverseness which sharpens the presentation of
issues upon which the court so largely depends. . . ." *Baker* v. *Carr*. See *Duke Power Co.* v.
Carolina Environmental Study Group. Cases of this
Court have identified the two essential components
of this "personal stake" requirement. Plaintiff must
have suffered, or be threatened with, some "distinct
and palpable injury," *Warth* v. *Seldin*. In addition,
there must be some causal connection between plaintiff's asserted injury and defendant's challenged ac-

tion. *Simon* v. *Eastern Ky. Welfare Rights Org.;
Arlington Heights* v. *Metropolitan Housing Development Corp.* The Constitution requires an Article III
court to ascertain that both requirements are met
before proceeding to exercise its authority on behalf
of any plaintiff, whether the form of relief requested
is equitable or monetary.

But the existence of Article III injury "often turns
on the nature and source of the claim asserted."
Warth v. *Seldin.* ⊥Neither "palpable injury" nor
"causation" is a term of unvarying meaning. There
is much in the way of "mutual understandings" and
"common law traditions" that necessarily guides the
definitional inquiry. *In addition*, the Constitution,
and by legislation the Congress, may impart a new,
and on occasion unique, meaning to the terms "injury" and "causation" in particular statutory or constitutional contexts. The Court makes a fundamental
mistake when it determines that a plaintiff has failed
to satisfy the two-pronged "injury-in-fact" test, or
indeed any other test of "standing," without first determining whether the Constitution or a statute defines injury, and creates a cause of action for redress
of that injury, in precisely the circumstance
presented to the Court.

It may of course happen that a person believing
himself injured in some obscure manner by government action will be held to have no legal right under
the constitutional or statutory provision upon which
he relies, and will not be permitted to complain of
the invasion of another person's "rights." It ⊥is
quite another matter to employ the the rhetoric of
"standing" to deprive a person, whose interest is
clearly protected by the law, of the opportunity to
prove that his own rights have been violated. It is in
precisely that dissembling enterprise that the Court
indulges today.

The "case and controversy" limitation of Article
III overrides no other provision of the Constitution.
To construe that Article to deny standing "to the
class for whose sake [a] constitutional protection is
given," *Jones* v. *United States*, quoting *Hatch* v.
Reardon, simply turns the Constitution on its head.
Article III was designed to provide a ⊥hospitable
forum in which persons enjoying rights under the
Constitution could assert those rights. How are we to
discern whether a particular person is to be afforded
a right of action in the courts? The Framers did not,
of course, employ the modern vocabulary of
standing. But this much is clear: The drafters of the
Bill of Rights surely intended that the particular
beneficiaries of their legacy should enjoy rights legally enforceable in courts of law. See *West Virginia
State Bd. of Educ.* v. *Barnette*.

With these observations in mind, I turn to the
problem of taxpayer standing in general, and this
case in particular.

II
A

Frothingham v. *Mellon* involved a challenge to the Maternity Act of 1921, which provided financial grants to states that agreed to cooperate in programs designed to reduce infant and maternal mortality. Apellant contended that Congress, in enacting the program, had exceeded its authority under Article I, and had intruded on authority reserved to the States. The Court described Mrs. Frothingham's claim as follows: "[T]his plaintiff alleges . . . that she is a taxpayer of the United States; and her contention, though not clear, seems to be that the effect of the appropriations complained of will be to increase the burden of future taxation and thereby take her property without due process of law. The right of a taxpayer to enjoin the execution ⊥of a federal appropriation act, on the ground that it is invalid and will result in taxation for illegal purposes, has never been passed upon by this Court."

⌐495

The Court conceded that it had historically treated the interest of a *municipal* taxpayer in the application of the municipality's funds as sufficiently direct and immediate to warrant injunctive relief to prevent misuse. *Bradfield* v. *Roberts*, in which the Court permitted a federal taxpayer to present an Establishment Clause challenge to the use of federal money for the construction of hospital buildings in the District of Columbia, was held to fall within this rule because it was appropriate to treat the District of Columbia as a municipality. But the Court distinguished Mrs. Frothingham's action against the United States: "[T]he relation of a taxpayer of the United States to the Federal Government is very different. His interest in the moneys of the Treasury—partly realized from taxation and partly from other sources—is shared with millions of others; is comparatively minute and indeterminable; and the effect upon future taxation, of any payment out of the funds, so remote, fluctuating and uncertain, that no basis is afforded for an appeal to the preventive powers of a court of equity.

⌐496

⊥ "The administration of any statute, likely to produce additional taxation to be imposed upon a vast number of taxpayers, the extent of whose several liability is indefinite and constantly changing, is essentially a matter of public and not of individual concern."

After noting the importance of judicial restraint, the Court concluded: "The party who invokes the [judicial] power must be able to show not only that the statute is invalid but that he has sustained or is immediately in danger of sustaining some direct injury as the result of its enforcement, and not merely that he suffers in some indefinite way in common with people generally."

Frothingham's reasoning remains obscure. The principal interpretive difficulty lies in the manner in which *Frothingham* chose to blend the language of

policy with seemingly absolute statements about jurisdiction. For example, the Court commented with significance on the sheer number of taxpayers who might have raised a claim similar to that of Mrs. Frothingham. Yet it can hardly be argued that the Constitution bars from federal court a plaintiff who has suffered injury merely because others are similarly aggrieved. "[S]tanding is not to be denied simply ⊥because many people suffer the same injury." *United States* v. *SCRAP*. And it is equally clear that the Constitution draws no distinction between injuries that are large, and those that are comparatively small. The line between more dollars and less is no valid constitutional measure. Cf. *Everson* v. *Board of Education* (Rutledge, J., dissenting). The only distinction that a Constitution guaranteeing justice to all can recognize is one between some injury and none at all.

⌐497

Frothingham also stressed the indirectness of the taxpayer's injury. But, *as a matter of Article III standing*, if the causal relationship is sufficiently certain, the length of the causal chain is irrelevant. See *Warth* v. *Seldin*. The financial stake of a federal taxpayer in the outcome of a lawsuit challenging an allegedly unlawful federal expenditure is not qualitatively different from that of a state or a municipal taxpayer attacking a local expenditure. More importantly, the injury suffered by a taxpayer is not dependent on the extent of his tax payment. The concept of taxpayer injury necessarily recognizes the continuing stake of the taxpayer in the disposition of the Treasury to which he ⊥has contributed his taxes, and his right to have those funds put to lawful uses. Until *Frothingham* there was nothing in our precedents to indicate that this concept, so comfortably applied to municipal taxpayers, was inconsistent with the framework of rights and remedies established by the Federal Constitution.

⌐498

The explanation for the limit on federal taxpayer "standing" imposed by *Frothingham* must be sought in more substantive realms. Justice Harlan, dissenting in *Flast*, came close to identifying what I consider the unstated premise of the *Frothingham* rule: "[The] taxpayer's complaint can consist only of an allegation that public funds have been, or shortly will be, expended for purposes inconsistent with the Constitution. The taxpayer cannot ask the return of any portion of his previous tax payments, cannot prevent the collection of any existing tax debt, and cannot demand an adjudication of the propriety of any particular level of taxation. His tax payments are received for the general purposes of the United States, and are, upon proper receipt, lost in the general revenues."

⊥ In a similar vein, the Government argued in *Flast* that taxpayer suits involve only a disagreement by the taxpayer with the uses to which tax revenues were committed, and that the resolution of such disagreements is entrusted to branches of the Federal Government other than the judiciary. The argu-

⌐499

ments of both the Government and Justice Harlan are phrased, as they must be, not in the language of "standing," but of "legal rights" and "justiciable issues."

The *Frothingham* rule may be seen as founded solely on the prudential judgment by the Court that precipitate and unnecessary interference in the activities of a coequal branch of government should be avoided. Alternatively, *Frothingham* may be construed as resting upon an unarticulated, constitutionally established barrier between Congress' power to tax and its power to spend, which barrier makes it analytically impossible to mount an assault on the former through a challenge to the latter. But it is sufficient for present purposes to say that *Frothingham* held that the federal taxpayer has no continuing legal interest in the affairs of the Treasury analogous to a shareholder's continuing interest in the conduct of a corporation.

Whatever its provenance, the general rule of *Frothingham* displays sound judgment: Courts must be circumspect in dealing with the taxing power in order to avoid unnecessary intrusion into the functions of the legislative and executive branches. Congress' *purpose* in taxing will not ordinarily effect the validity of the tax. Unless the tax *operates* unconstitutionally, see *e.g., Murdock* v. *Pennsylvania*, the taxpayer may not object to the use of his funds. Mrs. Frothingham's argument, that the use of tax funds for purposes unauthorized by the Constitution amounted to a violation of due process, did not provide her with the required legal interest because the Due Process Clause of the Fifth Amendment does not protect taxpayers against increases in tax liability. See *Flast* v. *Cohen.* Mrs. Frothingham's claim
|500 was thus reduced ⊥to an assertion of "the States' interest in their legislative prerogatives," a third-party claim that could properly be barred. But in *Flast* the Court faced a different sort of constitutional claim, and found itself compelled to retreat from the general assertion in *Frothingham* that taxpayers have *no* interest in the disposition of their tax payments. To understand why *Frothingham's* bar necessarily gave way in the face of an Establishment Clause claim, we must examine the right asserted by a taxpayer making such a claim.

B

In 1947, nine Justices of this Court recognized that the Establishment Clause does impose a very definite restriction on the power to tax. The Court held in *Everson* v. *Board of Education* that the " 'establishment of religion' clause of the First Amend-
|501 ment means at least this:" ⊥ "No tax in any amount, large or small, can be levied to support any religious activities or institutions, whatever they may be called, or whatever form they may adopt, to teach or practice religion."

The members of the Court could not have been more explicit. "One of our basic rights is to be free of

taxation to support a transgression of the constitutional command that the authorities 'shall make no law respecting an establishment of religion, or prohibiting the free exercise thereof.' " "[A]part from efforts to inject religious training or exercises and sectarian issues into the public schools, the only serious threat to maintaining that complete and permanent separation of religion and civil power which the First Amendment commands is through the use of the taxing power to support religion, religious establishments, or establishments having a religious foundation whatever their form or special religious function. . . . [M]oney taken by taxation from one is not to be used or given to support another's religious training or belief, or indeed one's own."

In determining whether the law challenged in *Everson* was one "respecting an establishment of religion," the Court did not fail to examine the historic meaning of the constitutional language, "particularly with respect to the imposition of taxes." For as Justice Rutledge pointed out in his dissent, "No provision of the Constitution is more closely tied to or given content by its generating history than the religious clause of the First Amendment. It is at once the refined product and the terse summation of that history." That history bears a brief repetition in the present context.

Many of the early settlers of this Nation came here to escape the tyranny of laws that compelled the support of government-sponsored churches and that inflicted punishments for the failure to pay establishment taxes and tithes. But the inhabitants of the various colonies soon dis⊥played a capacity to |502 recreate the oppressive practices of the countries that they had fled. Once again persons of minority faiths were persecuted, and again such persons were subjected—this time by the colonial governments— to tithes and taxes for support of religion. *Reynolds* v. *United States.*

"These practices became so commonplace as to shock the freedom-loving colonials into a feeling of abhorrence. The imposition of taxes to pay ministers' salaries and to build and maintain churches and church property aroused their indignation. It was these feelings which found expression in the First Amendment." *Everson.*

In 1784-1785, before the adoption of the Constitution, the continuing conflict between those who saw state aid to religion as but the natural expression of "commonly shared" religious sentiments, and those who saw such support as a threat to the very notion of civil government, culminated in the battle fought in the Virginia House of Delegates over "a bill establishing provision for teachers of the Christian religion." *Reynolds.* The introduction of that bill in the state assembly prompted James Madison to prepare and circulate his famous "Memorial and Remonstrance Against Religious Assessments," imploring the legislature to establish and maintain the complete separation of religion and civil authority, and thus to reject the bill. In the end, the bill was rejected by the Virginia legislature, and in its place Madison succeeded in securing the enactment of a "A Bill for Establishing Religious Freedom," first introduced in the Virginia General Assembly seven ⌐503 years earlier by Thomas Jefferson. ⊥Because Madison and Jefferson played such leading roles in the events leading to the adoption of the First Amendment, the *Everson* opinions did not hesitate to reproduce the partial text of their Virginia bill as a primary source for understanding the objectives, and protections, afforded by the more concise phrasing of the Establishment Clause. Extracts from that bill also bear repeating in the present context. The preamble provided, in part: "[T]o compel a man to furnish contributions of money for the propagation of opinions which he disbelieves, is sinful and tyrannical; that even the forcing him to support this or that teacher of his own religious persuasion, is depriving him of the comfortable liberty of giving his contributions to the particular pastor, whose morals he would make his pattern." 12 Hennings Stat. 85.

Its operative language emphatically stated: "That no man shall be compelled to frequent or support any religious worship, place or ministry whatsoever, nor shall be enforced, restrained, molested, or burthened in his body or goods, nor shall otherwise suffer on account of his religious opinions or belief. . . ." *Id.*, at 86.

Justice Rutledge summed up Madison's views in the following terms: "In no phase was he more unrelentingly absolute than in opposing state support or aid by taxation. Not even 'three pence' contribu- ⌐504 tion was thus to be exacted from ⊥ any citizen for such a purpose. Tithes had been the lifeblood of establishment before and after other compulsions disappeared. Madison and his coworkers made no exceptions or abridgments to the complete separation [between church and state] they created. Their objection was not to small tithes. It was to any tithes whatsoever. 'If it were lawful to impose a small tax for religion, the admission would pave the way for oppressive levies.' Not the amount, but 'the principle of the assessment' was wrong." *Everson.*

It is clear in the light of this history, that one of the primary purposes of the Establishment Clause was to prevent the use of tax monies for religious purposes. *The taxpayer was the direct and intended beneficiary of the prohibition on financial aid to religion.* This basic understanding of the meaning of the Establishment Clause explains why the Court in *Ev- erson*, while rejecting appellant's claim on the mer- ⌐505 its, ⊥perceived the issue presented there as it did. The appellant sued "in his capacity as a district taxpayer" challenging the actions of the Board of Education in passing a resolution providing reimbursement to parents for the cost of transporting their children to parochial schools, and seeking to have that resolution "set aside." Appellant's Establishment Clause claim was precisely that the "statute

. . . forced inhabitants to pay taxes to help support and maintain" church schools. It seems obvious that all the Justices who participated in *Everson* would have agreed with Justice Jackson's succinct statement of the question presented: "Is it constitutional to tax this complainant to pay the cost of carrying pupils to Church schools of one specified denomination?" Given this view of the issues, could it fairly be doubted that this taxpayer alleged injury in precisely the form that the Establishment Clause sought to make actionable?

C

In *Flast* v. *Cohen* federal taxpayers sought to challenge the Department of Health, Education, and Welfare's administration of the Elementary and Second⊥ary Education Act of 1965: specifically the ⌐506 Department's practice of allowing funds distributed under that Act to be used to finance instruction in religious schools. Appellants urged that the use of federal funds for such a purpose violated the Establishment and Free Exercise Clauses of the First Amendment, and sought a declaration that this use of federal funds was not authorized by the Act, or that to the extent the use was authorized, the Act was "unconstitutional and void." Appellants further sought an injunction to bar appellees from approving any expenditure of funds for the allegedly unconstitutional purposes. The *Frothingham* rule stood as a seemingly absolute barrier to the maintenance of the claim. The Court held, however, that the *Frothingham* barrier could be overcome by any claim that met both requirements of a two part "nexus" test.

The Justices who participated in *Flast* were not unaware of the Court's continued recognition of a federally cognizable "case or controversy" when a *local* taxpayer seeks to challenge as unconstitutional the use of a *municipality's* funds—⊥the propriety of ⌐507 which had, of course, gone unquestioned in *Everson*. The Court was aware as well of the rule stated in *Doremus* v. *Board of Education* that the interest of a taxpayer, even one raising an Establishment Clause claim, was limited to the actions of a government involving the expenditure of funds. But in reaching its holding, it is also quite clear that the Court was responding, not only to *Everson's* continued acceptance of municipal taxpayer actions but also to *Everson's* exposition of the history and meaning of the Establishment Clause. See *Flast*.

It is at once apparent that the test of standing formulated by the Court in *Flast* sought to reconcile the developing doctrine of taxpayer "standing" with the Court's historical understanding that the Establishment Clause was intended to prohibit the Federal Government from using tax funds for the advancement of religion, and thus the constitutional imperative of taxpayer standing in certain cases brought pursuant to the Establishment Clause. The two-

⌐508 pronged "nexus" test offered by the Court, despite its general language, is ⊥best understood as "a determinant of standing of plaintiffs alleging only injury as taxpayers who challenge alleged violations of the Establishment and Free Exercise Clauses of the First Amendment," and not as a general statement of standing principles. *Schlesinger* v. *Reservists Committee to Stop the War; Flast.* The test explains what forms of governmental action may be attacked by someone alleging *only* taxpayer status, and, without ruling out the possibility that history might reveal another similarly founded provision, explains why an Establishment Clause claim is treated differently from any other assertion that the federal government has exceeded the bounds of the law in allocating its largesse. Thus, consistent with *Doremus, Flast* required, as the first prong of its test, that the taxpayer demonstrate a logical connection between his taxpayer status and the type of legislation attacked. Appellants' challenge to a program of grants to educational institutions clearly satisfied this first requirement. As the second prong, consistent with the prohibition of taxpayer claims of the kind advanced in *Frothingham*, appellants were required to show a connection between their status and the precise nature of the infringement alleged. They had no difficulty meeting this requirement: the Court agreed that the Establishment Clause jealously protects taxpayers from diversion of their funds to the support of religion through the offices of the Federal Government.

⌐509 ⊥ The nexus test that the Court "announced" sought to maintain necessary continuity with prior cases, and set forth principles to guide future cases involving taxpayer standing. But *Flast* did not depart from the principle that no judgment about standing should be made without a fundamental understanding of the rights at issue. The two-part *Flast* test did not supply the rationale for the Court's decision, but rather its exposition: That rationale was supplied by an understanding of the nature of the restrictions on government power imposed by the Constitution and the intended beneficiaries of those restrictions.

It may be that Congress can tax for *almost* any reason, or for no reason at all. There is, so far as I have been able to discern, but one constitutionally imposed limit on that authority. Congress cannot use tax money to support a church, or to encourage religion. That is "*the* forbidden exaction." *Everson* v. *Board of Education* (emphasis added). See *Flast.* In absolute terms the history of the Establishment Clause of the First Amendment makes this clear. History also makes it clear that the federal taxpayer is a singularly "proper and appropriate party to invoke a federal court's jurisdiction" to challenge a federal bestowal of largesse as a violation of the Establishment Clause. Each, and indeed every, federal taxpayer suffers precisely the injury that the Establishment Clause guards against when the Federal Government directs that funds be taken from the pocketbooks of the citizenry and placed into the coffers of the ministry.

A taxpayer cannot be asked to raise his objection to such use of his funds at the time he pays his tax. Apart from the unlikely circumstance in which the Government announced in advance that a particular levy would be used for religious subsidies, taxpayers could hardly assert that they were being injured until the Government actually lent its support to a religious venture. Nor would it be reasonable to require him to address his claim to those officials charged with the collec⊥tion of federal taxes. Those officials ⌐510 would be without the means to provide appropriate redress—there is no practical way to segregate the complaining taxpayer's money from that being devoted to the religious purpose. Surely, then, a taxpayer must have standing at the time that he learns of the Government's alleged Establishment Clause violation to seek equitable relief in order to halt the continuing and intolerable burden on his pocketbook, his conscience, and his constitutional rights.

III

Blind to history, the Court attempts to distinguish this case from *Flast* by wrenching snippets of language from our opinions, and by perfunctorily applying that language under color of the first prong of *Flast's* two-part nexus test. The tortuous distinctions thus produced are specious, at best: at worst, they are pernicious to our constitutional heritage.

First, the Court finds this case different from *Flast* because here the "source of [plaintiff's] complaint is not a *congressional* action, but a decision by HEW to transfer a parcel of federal property" (emphasis added). This attempt at distinction cannot withstand scrutiny. *Flast* involved a challenge to the actions of the Commissioner of Education, and other officials of HEW, in disbursing funds under the Elementary and Secondary Education Act of 1965 to "religious and sectarian" schools. Plaintiffs disclaimed "any intention to challenge all programs under . . . the Act." *Flast.* Rather, they claimed that defendant-administrators' approval of such expenditures was not authorized by the Act, or alternatively, to the extent the expenditure was authorized, the Act was "unconstitutional and void." In the present case, respondents challenge HEW's grant of property pursuant to the Federal Property and Administrative Services Act of 1949, seeking to enjoin HEW "from making a grant of this and other property to the [defendant] so long as such grant will violate the Establishment Clause." It may be that the Court is concerned with the adequacy of respondents' pleading; re⊥spondents have not, in so many words, ⌐511 asked for a declaration that the "Federal Property and Administrative Services Act is unconstitutional and void to the extent that it authorizes HEW's actions." I would not construe their complaint so narrowly.

More fundamentally, no clear division can be drawn in this context between actions of the legislative branch and those of the executive branch. To be sure, the First Amendment is phrased as a restriction on Congress' legislative authority; this is only natural since the Constitution assigns the authority to legislate and appropriate only to the Congress. But it is difficult to conceive of an expenditure for which the last governmental actor, either implementing directly the legislative will, or acting within the scope of legislatively delegated authority, is not an Executive Branch official. The First Amendment binds the Government as a whole, regardless of which branch is at work in a particular instance.

The Court's second purported distinction between this case and *Flast* is equally unavailing. The majority finds it "decisive" that the Federal Property and Administrative Services Act of 1949 "was an evident exercise of Congress' power under the Property Clause, Art. IV, § 3, cl. 2," while the government action in *Flast* was taken under the Art. I, § 8. The Court relies on *United States* v. *Richardson* and *Schlesinger* v. *Reservists Committee to Stop the War* to support the distinction between the two clauses, noting that those cases involved alleged deviations from the requirements of Art. I, § 9, cl. 7, and Art. I, § 6, cl. 2, respectively. The standing defect in each case was *not*, however, the failure to allege a violation of the Spending Clause; rather, the taxpayers in those cases had not complained of the distribution of government largesse, and thus failed to meet the essential requirement of taxpayer standing recognized in *Doremus*.

⌐512   It can make no constitutional difference in the case before us whether the donation to the defendant here was in the form of a cash grant to build a facility, see *Tilton* v. *Richard⊥son*, or in the nature of a gift of property including a facility already built. That this is a meaningless distinction is illustrated by *Tilton*. In that case, taxpayers were afforded standing to object to the fact that the Government had not received adequate assurance that if the property that it financed for use as an educational facility was later converted to religious uses, it would receive full value for the property, as the Constitution requires. The complaint here is precisely that, although the property at issue is actually being used for a sectarian purpose, the government has not received, nor demanded, full value payment. Whether undertaken pursuant to the Property Clause or the Spending Clause, the breach of the Establishment Clause, and the relationship of the taxpayer to that breach, is precisely the same.

IV

⌐513   ⊥ Plainly hostile to the Framers' understanding of the Establishment Clause, and *Flast's* enforcement of that understanding, the Court vents that hostility under the guise of standing, "to slam the courthouse door against plaintiffs who [as the Framers intended] are entitled to full consideration of their [Establishment Clause] claims on the merits." *Barlow* v. *Collins*. Therefore, I dissent.

Justice STEVENS, dissenting.

In Parts I, II, and III of his dissenting opinion, *Justice BRENNAN* demonstrates that respondent taxpayers have standing to mount an Establishment Clause challenge against the Federal Government's transfer of property worth $1,300,000 to the Assembly of God. For the Court to hold that plaintiffs' ⊥standing depends on whether the Government's   ⌐514 transfer was an exercise of its power to spend money, on the one hand, or its power to dispose of tangible property, on the other, is to trivialize the standing doctrine.

One cannot read the Court's opinion and the concurring opinions of Justice Stewart and Justice Fortas in *Flast* v. *Cohen* without forming the firm conclusion that the plaintiffs' invocation of the Establishment Clause was of decisive importance in resolving the standing issue in that case. Justice Fortas made this point directly: "I agree that the congressional powers to tax and spend are limited by the prohibition upon Congress to enact laws 'respecting an establishment of religion.' This thesis, slender as its basis is, provides a direct 'nexus,' as the Court puts it, between the use and collection of taxes and the congressional action here. Because of this unique 'nexus,' in my judgment, it is not far-fetched to recognize that a taxpayer has a special claim to status as a litigant in a case raising the 'establishment' issue. This special claim is enough, I think, to permit us to allow the suit, coupled, as it is, with the interest which the taxpayer and all other citizens have in the church-state issue. In terms of the structure and basic philosophy of our constitutional government, it would be difficult to point to any issue that has a more intimate, pervasive, and fundamental impact upon the life of the taxpayer— and upon the life of all citizens.

"Perhaps the vital interest of a citizen in the establishment issue, without reference to his taxpayer's status, would be acceptable as a basis for this challenge. We need not decide this. But certainly, I believe, we must recognize that our principle of judicial scrutiny of legislative acts which raise important constitutional questions requires that the issue here presented—the separation of state and church—which the Founding Fathers re⊥garded as   ⌐515 fundamental to our constitutional system—should be subjected to judicial testing. This is not a question which we, if we are to be faithful to our trust, should consign to limbo, unacknowledged, unresolved, and undecided.

"On the other hand, the urgent necessities of this case and the precarious opening through which we find our way to confront it, do not demand that we open the door to a general assault upon exercises of the spending power. The status of taxpayer should not be accepted as a launching pad for an attack upon any target other than legislation affecting the Establishment Clause."

Today the Court holds, in effect, that the Judiciary has no greater role in enforcing the Establishment Clause than in enforcing other "norm[s] of conduct which the federal government is bound to honor," such as the Accounts Clause, *United States* v. *Richardson*, and the Incompatibility Clause, *Schlesinger* v. *Reservists Committee to Stop the War*. Ironically, however, its decision rests on the premise that the difference between a disposition of funds pursuant to the Spending Clause and a disposition of realty pursuant to the Property Clause is of fundamental jurisprudential significance. With all due respect, I am persuaded that the essential holding of *Flast* v. *Cohen* attaches special importance to the Establishment Clause and does not permit the drawing of a tenuous distinction between the Spending Clause and the Property Clause.

For this reason, and for the reasons stated in Parts I, II, and III of Justice Brennan's opinion, I would affirm the judgment of the Court of Appeals.

BENDER v. WILLIAMSPORT AREA SCHOOL DISTRICT

106 S. Ct. 1326
ON WRIT OF CERTIORARI TO THE UNITED STATES COURT OF APPEALS FOR THE THIRD CIRCUIT
Argued October 15, 1985 — Decided March 25, 1986
Justice STEVENS delivered the opinion of the Court.

This case raises an important question of federal appellate jurisdiction that was not considered by the Court of Appeals: Whether one member of a School Board has standing to appeal from a declaratory judgment against the Board. We conclude that although the School Board itself had a sufficient stake in the outcome of the litigation to appeal, an individual Boardmember cannot invoke the Board's interest in the case to confer standing upon himself.

I

In September 1981 a group of high school students in Williamsport, Pennsylvania, formed a club called "Petros" for the purpose of promoting "spiritual growth and positive attitudes in the lives of its members." The group asked the Principal of the high school for permission to meet on school premises during student activity periods scheduled during the regular schoolday on Tuesdays and Thursdays. The Principal allowed Petros to hold an organizational meeting that was attended by approximately 45 students. At that meeting passages of scripture were read and some students prayed. There is no evidence

that any students, or parents, expressed any opposition or concern about future meetings of Petros. The Principal nevertheless advised the group that they could not hold any further meetings until he had discussed the matter with the School Superintendent. The Superintendent, in turn, advised the students that he would respond to their written request for recognition after he received "competent legal advice [from the School District's Solicitor] as to the propriety of approving establishment of the proposed prayer club" on school premises.

On November 16, 1981, the Principal and the Superintendent met with representatives of Petros and advised them that "based on the Solicitor's legal opinion, their request must be denied." The legal opinion is not a part of the record; nor does the record contain any evidence that the Principal, the Superintendent, or any other person except the Solicitor had voiced any opposition to the proposed meetings by Petros. Indeed, Petros was informed that it could meet off school premises and "would be given released time during the activity period" if it could secure "a location and an adult supervisor, preferably a clergyman" for their meetings.

The students thereafter wrote a letter to the Chairman of the Williamsport Area School Board appealing the Superintendent's decision. At a meeting held January 19, 1982, the Board upheld the Superintendent's decision and "denied the appeal on the basis of the Solicitor's opinion."

II

On June 2, 1982, 10 of the students filed suit in the United States District Court against Williamsport Area School District, the 9 members of the School Board, the Superintendent of the District, and the Principal of the high school. Although there is a general allegation in the first paragraph of the complaint that the action was brought against the defendants "in their individual and official capacities," the specific allegation concerning each of the named members of the Board was in this form: "John C. Youngman, Jr., is a member of the Williamsport Areas School Board and is sued in that capacity." The complaint alleged that the defendants' refusal to recognize "Petros" and to allow it to meet on the same basis as other student groups because of its religious activities violated the First Amendment. The complaint prayed for declaratory and injunctive relief.

One answer was filed on behalf of all the defendants. Although they admitted most of the material allegations of the complaint, they alleged that they had "requested and received in writing an opinion from the school district solicitor and legal counsel that it would be unlawful, improper and unconstitutional to recognize said group as a student organization."

After plaintiffs completed their discovery (defendants took no depositions), the parties filed cross-motions for summary judgment supported by affidavits, the deposition testimony, and statements of material fact not in dispute. On November 9, 1982, the District Court entered an order finding that the record was incomplete. It thereupon directed the parties to submit affidavits or other documentation concerning "the exact nature of the activity period, the type of activities or clubs that have been, and would be, approved, and what proposed groups, if any, have been denied approval." After that additional information was supplied, and after the case had been fully briefed, the District Court on May 12, 1983, filed a detailed and carefully written opinion in which it stated: "Presently before the court are the parties' cross-motions for summary judgment. . . . Although the case presents only a question of law, this is not to say that the facts are unimportant. On the contrary, the undisputed facts are of paramount importance to the resolution of the legal question presented in this case. A slight change in the facts could very well have dictated a contrary decision.

"After carefully reviewing those facts, and after giving full consideration to all pertinent legal authority, the court concludes that because the defendant school district is not constitutionally required to deny the plaintiffs the opportunity to meet, by doing so solely on constitutional grounds it has impermissibly burdened their free-speech rights. Accordingly, summary judgment will be granted in favor of the plaintiffs." 563 F. Supp., at 699-700. The final order entered by the District Court was a ruling "in favor of the plaintiffs and against the defendants on plaintiffs' freedom of speech claim." No injunction was entered, and no relief was granted against any defendant in his individual capacity. The District Court, in effect, merely held that the Board's attorney was incorrect in his legal advice.

The School District did not challenge the judgment of the District Court in any way. It made no motion for a stay and took no appeal. Instead, it decided to comply with the judgment and to allow Petros to conduct the meetings it had requested.

However, John C. Youngman, Jr., who was then still a member of the Board, did file a timely notice of appeal.

III

In the Court of Appeals no one raised any question about Mr. Youngman's standing to appeal. The court did note that all of the original plaintiffs had graduated from high school, but it granted a motion to add additional plaintiffs who were currently enrolled students in order to prevent the case from becoming moot. Neither the majority nor the dissenting opinion even mentioned Mr. Youngman.

After repeatedly stressing "the crucial role which the particular facts play in every first amendment analysis," the majority of the Court of Appeals held "that the particular circumstances disclosed by this record and present at the Williamsport Area High School lead to the inexorable conclusion that the constitutional balance of interests tilts against permitting the Petros activity to be conducted within the school as a general activity program."

In dissent, Judge Adams suggested that the majority had implicitly adopted a *per se* rule because of its concern about "the possibility of unconstitutional extensions of the Williamsport arrangement elsewhere," instead of performing the "more difficult adjudicative task [of carefully sifting the facts] on a case-by-case basis."

The importance of the question presented by the students' petition for certiorari persuaded us that the case merited plenary review. After granting certiorari, however, we noticed that neither the Board nor any of the defendants except Mr. Youngman opposed the students' position and that only Mr. Youngman had challenged the District Court's judgment by invoking the jurisdiction of the Court of Appeals. We therefore find it necessary to answer the question whether Mr. Youngman had a sufficient stake in the outcome of the litigation to support appellate jurisdiction. The parties and the *amici* have identified three different capacities in which Mr. Youngman may have had standing to appeal—as an individual, as a member of the Board, and as a parent.

IV

Before considering each of the standing theories, it is appropriate to restate certain basic principles that limit the power of every federal court. Federal courts are not courts of general jurisdiction; they have only the power that is authorized by Article III of the Constitution and the statutes enacted by Congress pursuant thereto. See, *e.g., Marbury* v.*Madison.* For that reason, every federal appellate court has a special obligation to "satisfy itself not only of its own jurisdiction, but also that of the lower courts in a cause under review," even though the parties are prepared to concede it. *Mitchell* v. *Maurer.* "And if the record discloses that the lower court was without jurisdiction this court will notice the defect, although the parties make no contention concerning it. [When the lower federal court] lack[s] jurisdiction, we have jurisdiction on appeal, not of the merits but merely for the purpose of correcting the error of the lower court in entertaining the suit." *United States* v. *Corrick*

This obligation to notice defects in a court of appeals' subject-matter jurisdiction assumes a special importance when a constitutional question is presented. In such cases we have strictly adhered to the standing requirements to ensure that our deliberations will have benefit of adversary presentation and a full development of the relevant facts. Thus, as we emphasized in *Valley Forge Christian College* v. *Americans United for Separation of Church and*

State, Inc.: "[A]t an irreducible minimum, Art. III requires the party who invokes the court's authority to 'show that he personally has suffered some actual or threatened injury as a result of the putatively illegal conduct of the defendant,' *Gladstone, Realtors* v. *Village of Bellwood,* and that the injury 'fairly can be traced to the challenged action' and 'is likely to be redressed by a favorable decision,' *Simon* v. *Eastern Kentucky Welfare Rights Org. . . .*

.   .   .   .   .   .

"The requirement of 'actual injury redressable by the court,' *Simon,* serves several of the 'implicit policies embodied in Article III,' *Flast.* It tends to assure that the legal questions presented to the court will be resolved, not in the rarified atmosphere of a debating society, but in a concrete factual context conducive to a realistic appreciation of the consequences of judicial action. The 'standing' requirement serves other purposes. Because it assures an actual factual setting in which the litigant asserts a claim of injury in fact, a court may decide the case with some confidence that its decision will not pave the way for lawsuits which have some, but not all, of the facts of the case actually decided by the court."

V

The first paragraph of the complaint alleged that the action was brought against the defendants "in their individual and official capacities." There is, however, nothing else in the complaint, or in the record on which the District Court's judgment was based, to support the suggestion that relief was sought against any School Board member in his or her *individual* capacity. Certainly the District Court's judgment granted no such relief. Accordingly, to paraphrase our holding in *Brandon* v. *Holt,* "[t]he course of proceedings . . . make it abundantly clear that the action against [Mr. Youngman] was in his official capacity and only in that capacity." Since the judgment against Mr. Youngman was not in his individual capacity, he had no standing to appeal in that capacity.

VI

As a member of the School Board sued in his official capacity Mr. Youngman has no personal stake in the outcome of the litigation and therefore did not have standing to file the notice of appeal. As we held in *Brandon* v. *Holt,* "a judgment against a public servant 'in his official capacity' imposes liability on the entity that he represents provided, of course, the public entity received notice and an opportunity to respond." We repeated this point in *Kentucky* v. *Graham*: "Official-capacity suits . . . 'generally represent only another way of pleading an action against an entity of which an officer is an agent.' *Monell* v. *New York City Dept. of Social Services* As long as the government entity receives notice and an opportunity to respond, an official-capacity suit is,

in all respects other than name, to be treated as a suit against the entity. *Brandon* It is *not* a suit against the official personally, for the real party in interest is the entity. Thus, while an award of damages against an official in his personal capacity can be executed only against the official's personal assets, a plaintiff seeking to recover on a damages judgment in an official-capacity suit must look to the government entity itself."

Mr. Youngman's status as a School Board member does not permit him to "step into the shoes of the Board" and invoke its right to appeal. In this case, Mr. Youngman was apparently the lone dissenter in a decision by the other eight members of the School Board to forgo an appeal. Generally speaking, members of collegial bodies do not have standing to perfect an appeal the body itself has declined to take. The Court of Appeals for the District of Columbia so held in *Smuck* v. *Hobson*: "We also find that Mr. Smuck has no appealable interest as a member of the Board of Education. While he was in that capacity a named defendant, the Board of Education was undeniably the principal figure and could have been sued alone as a collective entity. Appellant Smuck had a fair opportunity to participate in its defense, and in the decision not to appeal. Having done so, he has no separate interest as an individual in the litigation. The order directs the Board to take certain actions. But since its decisions are made by vote as a collective whole, there is no apparent way in which Smuck as an individual could violate the decree and thereby become subject to enforcement proceedings."

VII

At oral argument Mr. Youngman advised the Court that he is the parent of at least one student attending the Williamsport Area High School and that as a matter of conscience he is opposed to prayer activities on school premises during regular school hours. The Solicitor General submits that Mr. Youngman's status as a parent provides an adequate predicate for federal appellate jurisdiction.

Mr. Youngman's status as an aggrieved parent, however, like any other kindred fact showing the existence of a justiciable "case" or "controversy" under Art. III, must affirmatively appear in the record. As the first *Justice HARLAN* observed, "the presumption . . . is that the court below was without jurisdiction" unless "the contrary appears affirmatively from the record." *King Bridge Co.* v. *Otoe County* That lack of standing was not noticed by either party matters not, for as we said in *Mansfield C. & L. M. R. Co.* v. *Swan*: "[T]he rule, springing from the nature and limits of the judicial power of the United States, is inflexible and without exception, which requires this court, of its own motion, to deny its own jurisdiction, and, in the exercise of its appellate power, that of all other courts of the United States, in all cases where such jurisdiction does not affirmatively appear in the record on which, in the exercise of that power, it is called to act. On every writ of error or appeal, the first and fundamental question is that of jurisdiction, first, of this court, and then of the court from which the record comes. This question the court is bound to ask and answer for itself, even when not otherwise suggested, and without respect to the relation of the parties to it." Moreover, because it is not "sufficient that jurisdiction may be inferred argumentatively from averments in the pleadings," *Grace* v. *American Central Ins. Co.,* it follows that the necessary factual predicate may not be gleaned from the briefs and arguments themselves. This "first principle of federal jurisdiction" applies "whether the case is at the trial stage or the appellate stage." P. Bator, P. Mishkin, D. Shapiro, & H. Wechsler, Hart and Wechsler's The Federal Courts and the Federal System 835-836 (2d ed. 1973).

There is nothing in the record indicating anything about Mr. Youngman's status as a parent. Nor is anything in the record to indicate that he or his children have suffered any injury as a result of the District Court's judgment, or as a result of the activities of Petros subsequent to the entry of that judgment. For all that appears in the record, Mr. Youngman and his children might even be active supporters of Petros.

The reasons why Mr. Youngman may not take an appeal in his individual capacity also foreclose an appeal in his capacity as a parent. His interest as a parent in the outcome of the litigation differs from his interest as a member of the School Board which, as we have already noted, is legally that of a "different legal personage." Since Mr. Youngman was not sued as a parent in the District Court, he had no right to participate in the proceedings in that court in that capacity without first filing an appropriate motion or pleading setting forth the claim or defense that he desired to assert. Thus, even if one were amenable to the dissent's unprecedented (and unexplained) suggestion that the principle governing determination of subject matter jurisdiction should be relaxed on appeal, the proposed exception for litigants who were "proper part[ies]" in the District Court would not help Mr. Youngman because he could not perfect an appeal in either capacity in which he was a "party" in the District Court, *i.e.,* as a School Board member sued in his individual capacity or as a Board member sued in his official capacity. Tacitly conceding Mr. Youngman's lack of standing on these two bases, the dissent instead would confer standing on Mr. Youngman as a parent—a capacity in which he plainly was not a party in the District Court and to which, therefore, the dissent's reasoning does not apply. Having failed to assert his parental interest in the District Court— or to adduce any factual support for that interest in this Court—Mr. Youngman has no right to prosecute an appeal in his capacity as a parent.

We therefore hold that because the Court of Appeals was without jurisdiction to hear the appeal, it was without authority to decide the merits. Accordingly, the judgment of the Court of Appeals is vacated, and the case is remanded with instructions to dismiss the appeal for want of jurisdiction.

It is so ordered.

Justice MARSHALL, concurring.

I join *Justice STEVENS'* opinion for the Court. I write separately to emphasize that the parties cannot, as the Solicitor General and *The CHIEF JUSTICE* contend, invoke the Article III jurisdiction of this Court through a belated nontestimonial statement by Mr. Youngman that he is a parent of a child in the Williamsport Area High School.

This lawsuit on appeal was *not* "the same dispute between the same parties" as the one conducted in the District Court. The dispute litigated in the District Court was one between certain students wishing to conduct prayer group activities as part of an official school activity period, on the one hand, and a school board that refused them permission to do so, on the other. Mr. Youngman participated in that lawsuit only as a member of the school board, sued in his official capacity. The real party in interest in that lawsuit was the board. That controversy ended with the entry of the District Court judgment; the school board, voting 8-1 with Mr. Youngman in the minority, abandoned its earlier position and agreed to allow plaintiffs to conduct the prayer group activities they sought. There was therefore nothing left to litigate between those parties.

The lawsuit sought to be litigated on appeal is a different one. This dispute, under *The CHIEF JUSTICE's* theory, is one between Mr. Youngman, asserting that he is a parent of a child in the Williamsport Area High School whose First Amendment rights would be infringed by his attendance at a school whose activities impermissibly advance religion, on the one hand, and students seeking to conduct prayer group activities, on the other. The school board itself is nowhere to be found. I do not contest that Mr. Youngman could pursue this dispute on appeal had he intervened in the lawsuit in his capacity as a parent. Absent such intervention, it is conceivable that Mr. Youngman might bottom his standing to raise such an argument on facts in the record setting out his status as a parent. There are, however, no such facts anywhere in the extensive record in this case. There is not one word in the *record* indicating that Mr. Youngman is a father at all. Nor did Mr. Youngman claim such status in his Notice of Appeal.

In fact, the Brief for Respondent filed in this Court suggests that Mr. Youngman did *not* have a child in the Williamsport Area High School when he filed his notice of appeal from the District Court's decision on June 10, 1983. Benjamin Youngman, rather, apparently is claimed to have begun study at that school several months later, in the fall of 1983. Assertions in the parties' briefs are not part of the record for purposes of determining our jurisdiction. This discrepancy, however, illustrates the wisdom of our long-established rule requiring that the facts supporting our Article III jurisdiction "appea[r] affirmatively from the record." *King Bridge Co.* v. *Otoe County*

Because no facts appear in the record supporting Mr. Youngman's status as the parent of a child enrolled in the Williamsport Area High School opposed to petitioners' activities, I join the opinion and judgment of the Court vacating the judgment below and remanding with instructions to dismiss the appeal for want of jurisdiction.

Chief Justice BURGER, with whom *Justice WHITE* and *Justice REHNQUIST* join, dissenting.

I agree with the Court that the judgment of the District Court allowing Petros to meet during the student extra-curricular activity period must be reinstated. Because Respondent Youngman had standing to appeal, however, I would reach the merits of this dispute and reverse the judgment of the Court of Appeals.

I

Mr. Youngman is a parent of a student at Williamsport High School; as a matter of conscience he is opposed to prayer activities on school premises during school hours. As this Court has repeatedly held, parents have standing to challenge conditions in public schools that their children attend. See *Engel* v. *Vitale*; *Zorach* v. *Clauson*. The Court's principal objection to Youngman's standing as a parent stems from his failure " 'to allege facts demonstrating that he is a proper party to invoke judicial resolution of the dispute and the exercise of the court's remedial powers.' " *Warth* v. *Seldin* It is, of course, perfectly sensible to impose such pleading burdens upon the plaintiff who initiates the litigation. These burdens, however, need not be placed upon a properly named defendant, like Mr. Youngman, who seeks to invoke the jurisdiction of the Court of Appeals. Once the jurisdiction of the District Court over a particular dispute is established, it seems clear that the same dispute between the same parties will remain within the Article III powers of the courts on appeal. To be sure, we require that the case-or-controversy requirement be met throughout the course of the litigation. But the method for determining whether the case-or-controversy exists and the burdens placed on the parties should not, indeed cannot, be the same on appeal as in the District Court. At the District Court stage, the facts required by *Warth* should normally appear on the face of the complaint. At the appellate

stage, however, the "complaining party" does not allege any facts but merely identifies himself as a party to the case in the District Court and challenges the validity of that decision. Only if the appellant's standing is challenged must he allege facts sufficient to convince the Court of Appeals that he is a proper party to pursue the appeal. Here, petitioners not only failed to challenge Youngman's standing before the Court of Appeals, they also conceded that, had they challenged Youngman's standing, he would have satisfied the *Warth* standing test.

II

I would reach the issue the Court granted certiorari to address: whether the Establishment Clause requires a public high school to prevent a student-initiated, student-led group from meeting during an extracurricular activity period.

The Establishment Clause prohibits Congress and, through the Fourteenth Amendment, the States from passing any law "respecting an establishment of religion." As we have observed on other occasions, the precise contours of this prohibition remain unclear. But it is common ground that nothing in the Establishment Clause requires the State to suppress a person's speech merely because the *content* of the speech is religious in character. In *McDaniel* v. *Paty*, *Justice BRENNAN* emphasized in his opinion concurring in the judgment that "[t]he Establishment Clause does not license government to treat religion and those who teach or practice it, simply by virtue of their status as such, as subversive of American ideals and therefore subject to unique disabilities." And more recently, in *Widmar* v. *Vincent*, we held that the Establishment Clause did not justify a university's content-based exclusion of religious speech from a forum generally open to student groups.

Widmar clearly controls the resolution of this case. Petros is a student-initiated and student-led group seeking the same forum available to other student extracurricular activity groups. The students would have been allowed to meet to discuss moral philosophy or Marxism, to practice French, or to play chess; but, since they chose to worship, the school decided that it could not allow the group to meet without violating the Establishment Clause.

The Court of Appeals agreed that the Establishment Clause prohibited Petros from meeting on school premises because to allow them to meet could have been misinterpreted by other students as active state support of religion. Under that analysis, because an individual's discussion of religious beliefs may be confused by others as being that of the State, both must be viewed as the same. Yet the several commands of the First Amendment require vision capable of distinguishing between *state* establishment of religion, which is prohibited by the Establishment Clause, and *individual* participation and advocacy of religion which, far from being prohibited by the Establishment Clause, is affirmatively protected by the Free Exercise and Free Speech Clauses of the First Amendment. If the latter two commands are to retain any vitality, utterly un-proven, subjective impressions of some hypothetical students should not be allowed to transform *individual* expression of religious belief into *state* advancement of religion.

No one would contend that the State would be authorized to dismantle a church erected by private persons on private property because overwhelming evidence showed that other members of the community *thought* the church was owned and operated by the State. That the "primary effect" of state inaction might turn out to advance the cause of organized religion has no bearing upon the threshold question of whether the challenged activity is conducted by the State or by individuals.

The Establishment Clause mandates state neutrality, not hostility, toward religion. As *Justice BLACK* stated for the Court in *Everson* v. *Board of Education*, the First Amendment "requires the state to be neutral in its relations with groups of religious believers and non-believers; it does not require the state to be their adversary. State power is no more to be used so as to handicap religions than it is to favor them." In *Zorach* v. *Clauson*, the Court upheld a state law allowing schools to release students, during school hours, so that they could receive religious instruction elsewhere. Although the state did not compel students to go to religious classes, the program undoubtedly advanced the cause of religion. *Justice DOUGLAS*, writing for the Court, eloquently rejected the suggestion that the program thereby violated the Establishment Clause: "We are a religious people whose institutions presuppose a Supreme Being. We guarantee the freedom to worship as one chooses. We make room for as wide a variety of beliefs and creeds as the spiritual needs of man deem necessary. We sponsor an attitude on the part of government that shows no partiality to any one group and that lets each flourish according to the zeal of its adherents and the appeal of its dogma. When the state encourages religious instruction or cooperates with religious authorities by adjusting the schedule of public events to sectarian needs, it follows the best of our traditions. For it then respects the religious nature of our people and accommodates the public service to their spiritual needs. To hold that it may not would be to find in the Constitution a requirement that the government show a callous indifference to religious groups."

By granting the student prayer group equal access to the student activity forum, the order of the District Court "follows the best of our traditions" and is wholly consistent with the Constitution. Although I would have reached this issue on the merits, it is appropriate that the Court, by vacating the judgment of the Court of Appeals, restores the sound analysis and judgment of the District Court.

Justice POWELL, dissenting.

I agree with *The CHIEF JUSTICE* that respondent has standing to appeal, and also agree with much of his dissenting opinion. I write briefly to say that on its merits, this case is controlled by *Widmar* v. *Vincent*.

As in that case, respondent School District simply had "created a forum generally open for use by student groups." The School District provided thirty-minute periods on Tuesdays and Thursdays for high school students to meet in groups in separate school rooms for extracurricular activities, including discussion or debate on any subject of their choosing. A religious group was formed for reading passages of scripture and for prayer. Although there were no complaints by students, faculty, or parents, on the basis of a legal opinion the principal advised the group that it could not meet during these periods. As *The CHIEF JUSTICE* observes in his dissent, this is "a student-initiated and student-led group seeking the same forum available to other student extracurricular activity groups." At the time of this suit, there was a total of twenty-five identified groups, each organized by students. All of these groups were free to discuss any subject other than a religious one.

In *Widmar*, under essentially the same circumstances, we held that the University of Missouri at Kansas City had "discriminated against student groups and speakers based on their desire to use a generally open forum to engage in religious worship and discussion. These are forms of speech and association protected by the First Amendment." The only arguable distinction between *Widmar* and this case is that *Widmar* involved university students while the groups here are composed of high school students. We did note in *Widmar* that university students are "less impressionable than younger students and should be able to appreciate that the University's policy is one of neutrality to a religion." Other decisions, however, have recognized that the First Amendment rights of speech and association extend also to high school students. I do not believe—particularly in this age of massive media information—that the few years difference in age between high school and college students justifies departing from *Widmar*. I accordingly dissent.

TAX EXEMPTION TO RELIGIOUS INSTITUTIONS

Although the United States Supreme Court has given attention to a wide range of Establishment and Free Exercise Clause questions, the relationship between churches and taxation remains largely unexplored. The reason for this is primarily historical.

Tax exemption for religious institutions and leaders is an ancient and virtually universal concept, nearly always to be found wherever an establishment of religion has existed. Consequently, tax exemption for the established church was found in all but a few of the early American colonies. Even after the First Amendment was ratified most states continued to grant tax exemptions to religious institutions. So it is today: many states have constitutional or statutory provisions for exemption. A major rationale for this practice is that the state's power to tax is the power to control and thus the concept of separation of church and state demands that churches should be tax-exempt. Another justification for exemption is that it has been widely assumed that churches perform a valuable service for the community in that they promote a moral ideology necessary to a stable society. Furthermore, it is often noted that churches perform certain social functions which otherwise would require state performance at public expense (e.g., care of the aged and orphans). Tax exemptions, it has been argued, are in exchange for these services. Opponents of exemptions have contended that to exempt churches is to give them an indirect state subsidy: a violation of the Establishment Clause. But, because of the long-standing historical precedent for tax exemption and the rationale behind it, until recently the Supreme Court refused to accept any cases challenging the practice.

In 1970, the Court agreed to hear a case involving the issue of property tax exemptions for churches. Frederick Walz, a New York lawyer, bought a piece of property in New York City specifically for the purpose of initiating a case that would eliminate such exemptions. He claimed that because the churches in New York were tax-exempt, he, as a taxpayer, was required to make an indirect contribution to those religious bodies. Thus, he claimed that tax exemptions on property used for religious worship were a violation of the Establishment Clause.

The Court, in WALZ v. TAX COMMISSION (p. 278), sustained the tax exemption on the basis of three arguments. First, Chief Justice Burger, the author of the opinion, pointed out that legislation creating the tax exemption did not grant it to churches only, but rather that churches were part of a large class of eleemosynary institutions which provide helpful services to the community. Consequently, the legislation had the effect of neither advancing nor inhibiting religion. Second, if the civil authority were to levy taxes on churches, it would be necessary to assess the taxable property, collect the taxes, and proceed with tax foreclosures in case of nonpayment. This kind of activity would bring churches and civil authorities into close proximity and foster an excessive entanglement between them. By not taxing the churches, the involvement between church and state was kept to a lesser, and more acceptable, level. (This excessive entanglement argument became the third part of the test for interpreting the Establishment Clause.) Finally, the argument from history was used. American churches had been exempt from property taxes for two centuries and it could be demonstrated that exemption had not led to an established church.

Dealing only with property used solely for religious worship, the *Walz* case left untouched an area fraught with controversy, that of "unrelated business income." Since the inception of income taxes, churches have been exempt from paying taxes on money earned from businesses that are totally unrelated to the religious mission of the church. Until 1950, in the federal tax system, unrelated business income of educational institutions and other charitable organizations was also exempt from income taxes. But in that year Congress took the exemption away from all organizations except churches. Churches operated radio stations, gasoline stations, apartment houses, steel mills, and even, in one instance, a girdle and brassiere factory. No other charitable institutions except churches were exempted from paying federal taxes on such income. Naturally, there was opposition to such preferential treatment of churches, even among most church leaders. However, the Supreme Court has never ruled on the constitutionality of such exemption.

The closest the Court has come to dealing with this issue was the case of *Diffenderfer* v. *Central Baptist Church of Miami, Florida* (1972). The church owned a parking lot on which its members parked when they came to Sunday worship. The rest of the week the church sold spaces on its lot, which made it a commercial enterprise exempt from city and state property taxes. A suit was filed claiming that such an arrangement violated the Establishment Clause. In 1971 the Court agreed to hear the case. Between acceptance of the case and oral arguments Florida changed its law so that the parking lot in question and other religious properties would be subject to taxation in proportion to the time they were operated commercially. Because of the change in the law, the Court declared the case moot and passed up its chance to grapple with the question of whether government may constitutionally exempt from taxation church-owned property used for commercial purposes.

Meanwhile, Congress passed the Tax Reform Act of 1969. Under this statute, churches were placed in the same category as other charitable institutions, namely, their unrelated businesses and the income derived therefrom were made subject to federal taxes. However, the effective date of the act for churches was 1 January 1976, thus giving them time to adjust their activities to the provisions of the act and, of course, more years to enjoy paying no taxes on unrelated business income. In creating the legislation, Congress determined that all § 501(c)(3) organizations,[1] including religious organizations,

---

[1] Section 501(c)(3) of the Internal Revenue Code (26 U.S.C. § 501(c)(3)) is the section which defines organizations which are exempt from income taxes because of their public service nature. It says, in pertinent part, that the following are exempt from paying income tax: "Corporations, and any community chest, fund, or foundation, organized and operated exclusively for religious, charitable, scientific, testing for public safety, literary, or educational purposes, . . . no part of the net earnings of which inures to the benefit of any private shareholder or individual, no substantial part of the activities of which is carrying on propaganda, or otherwise attempting, to influence legislation . . . and which does not participate in, or intervene in . . . any political campaign on behalf of any candidate for public office."

must file Internal Revenue Service (IRS) Form 990. [2] Given the amount and type of information required, churches were greatly concerned about the necessity to file the form. Furthermore, they believed that it would involve the government in internal church affairs, impermissible under the Establishment Clause.

In response to the concern of religious leaders, Congress initially agreed to exempt churches and conventions and associations of churches from having to file the form. In response to a Utah senator's concern that some units in the Mormon church known as "auxiliaries" be included in the exemption, the Senate added that word to the exempting legislation. Later, when a conference committee met to resolve differences between the House and Senate versions of the bill, the qualifying word "integrated" was added. Thus the amended § 6033 limited the mandatory exemption from filing informational returns to "churches, their integrated auxiliaries, and conventions or associations of churches." [3]

Because the term "integrated auxiliaries" was not the subject of extensive hearings or debate, the interpretation and application of its meaning was left to the IRS. To determine which church organizations were to be recognized as integrated auxiliaries, in 1977 the IRS devised a three-part test:

(5)(i) For the purposes of this title, the term "integrated auxiliary of a church" means an organization:

(a) Which is exempt from taxation as an organization described in section 501(c)(3);

(b) Which is affiliated . . . with a church; and

(c) Whose principal activity is exclusively religious. [4]

The definition went on to ascribe the following meaning to "exclusively religious":

(ii) An organization's principal activity will not be considered to be exclusively religious if that activity is educational, literary, charitable, or of another nature (other than religious) that would serve as a basis for exemption under section 501(c)(3). [5]

An "affiliated" organization is one "either controlled by or associated with a church or a convention or association of churches." [6]

Since the IRS did not consider the "principal activity" of an organization to be "exclusively religious" if that activity itself would have qualified the organization for tax exemption under § 501(c)(3), an organization such as a denominational children's home or retirement home, or a church-related college was not considered an integrated auxiliary of a church body. That meant that such organizations had to file Form 990. Much worse, in the minds of most leaders of religious groups, the government was now in the position of defining the ministry of organizations related to churches.

The case of the Tennessee Baptist Children's Homes (TBCH) is illustrative of the problem. [7] The child care facility was established in 1891 and was, from the first, committed to providing a Christian environment for homeless or neglected children. It has had the goal of providing a highly regimented environment within which it could develop the physical, intellectual, and spiritual growth of children, including indoctrinating them in or converting them to the Baptist faith. At the time of the litigation, TBCH operated four child care facilities in Tennessee.

In 1977, shortly after the IRS promulgated its definition of "integrated auxiliary," it informed TBCH that the homes conformed to the first two criteria, mentioned above, to be considered an integrated auxiliary of its parent church, but it did not meet the third, i.e., TBCH's principal activity was not exclusively religious because its services were dedicated to the entire community and, in addition, because its operation of child care facilities would qualify it for § 501(c)(3) status on a basis other than religious. Consequently, TBCH would have to file Form 990.

The administrators of TBCH refused to accept the IRS's definition and to file the required form. The IRS assessed penalties and interest, which TBCH paid. The Homes also requested refund of the penalty payments, which the IRS denied. In 1983 TBCH filed suit in federal district court, requesting recovery of the penalty payments and a redefinition of their activity, insisting that their principal activity was exclusively religious. TBCH also requested that the IRS pay all its attorney's fees and court costs and that the court declare that Treasury Regulation § 1.6033-2(g)(1)(i) & (g)(5), which required TBCH to file Form 990, is unconstitutional. The trial court found in TBCH's favor on the main issue, i.e., that TBCH's principal activity is exclusively religious, that it did not have to file Form 990, and that the IRS should return the penalty payments. However, the court denied the request for attorney's fees and refused to rule on the constitutionality of the regulation. On appeal by the IRS, a court of appeals affirmed all parts of the district court's decision.

The testimony by the government in this case illustrated exactly what church leaders feared as the worst result of the "exclusively religious" requirement of the regulations. Government lawyers argued that because TBCH provided for children such nonreligious services as food, shelter, medical expenses, and education, it is not exclusively religious, since similar services would be provided by a secular child-care facility. In the appeal, a government lawyer declared that "religious activity is limited only to the conduct of worship." That, of course, puts the government in the position of defining the ministry of a church-related institution and prevents all but places

---

[2] 26 U.S.C. § 6033 requires that Form 990, a financial information form, should be filed annually and requires disclosure, among other things, of gross income; costs incurred in obtaining income; expenditures for exempt purposes; assets; liabilities; net worth; total contributions; names and addresses of substantial contributors; names, addresses, and compensation of officers, directors, trustees, and highly paid employees; a detailed description of any activities engaged in that have not previously been reported to the IRS; copies of all governing instruments; and amounts spent directly or indirectly on behalf of a candidate for public office.

It should be noted that this requirement imposed no taxes on the affected exempt organizations, but merely compelled churches, in this case, to disclose information that the IRS thought necessary to implement the Internal Revenue laws.

[3] 26 U.S.C. § 6033(a)(2)(A).

[4] Treasury Regulation § 1.6033-2(g)(5).

[5] Treasury Regulation § 1.6033-2(g)(5)(ii).

[6] Treasury Regulation § 1.6033-2(g)(5)(iii).

[7] *Tennessee Baptist Children's Homes* v. *United States*. For another example, cf. *Lutheran Social Services of Minnesota* v. *United States*.

where worship is conducted from being exempt from filing Form 990. Fortunately, from the viewpoint of churches, the courts found against the government's position. [8]

The court of appeals decision in the Tennessee Homes case was handed down 14 May 1986. Just prior to that, on 6 May 1986, the IRS announced a change in policy which may have made the bulk of that litigation moot. When the detrimental aspects of the "integrated auxiliary" and "exclusively religious" dimensions of the IRS code became clear to church leaders, they formed a committee of representatives from a number of denominations and requested a dialogue with IRS officials. The result of those conversations was a modification of the IRS rules about exemption from having to file Form 990 (although some believe that the change would not have come about solely because of the conversations, but that litigation such as the Tennessee Homes case and some decisions against the government helped considerably). The change was the issuance of Revenue Procedure 86-23, which asserted that internally supported affiliates of churches or conventions or associations of churches would be exempt from filing. Under this interpretation, an organization is considered internally supported unless it both:

> (1) Offers admissions, goods, services, or facilities for sale, other than on an incidental basis, to the general public (except goods, services, or facilities sold at a nominal charge or substantially less than cost), and
>
> (2) normally receives more than 50 percent of its support from a combination of governmental sources; public solicitation of contributions (such as through a community fund drive); and receipts from the sale of admissions, goods, performance of services, or furnishing of facilities in activities that are not unrelated trades or businesses. [9]

This change was widely hailed by religious leaders as again making institutions such as denominational orphanages and church-related colleges exempt from having to file Form 990 and, perhaps more importantly, effectively prevents the government from declaring the ministry of such organizations to be nonreligious. Although the Supreme Court had never heard a tax case involving governmental definitions of religion and ministry, it may be that the new attitude on the part of the IRS will effectively remove that issue from the possibility of litigation.

The Court has dealt with other tax-related cases in which the Establishment Clause was not involved. Those are discussed in this book beginning on page 215.

---

[8] A very similar result was found in the federal court of appeals in *Lutheran Social Services of Minnesota* v. *United States.*
[9] Revenue Procedure 86-23, 6 May 1986.

WALZ v. TAX COMMISSION OF THE CITY OF NEW YORK

397 U.S. 664
ON APPEAL FROM THE COURT OF APPEALS
OF THE STATE OF NEW YORK
Argued November 19, 1969 — Decided May 4, 1970

⊥*Mr. Chief Justice BURGER* delivered the opinion of the Court.   ⌐666

Appellant, owner of real estate in Richmond County, New York, sought an injunction in the New York courts to prevent the New York City Tax Commission from granting property tax exemptions to religious organizations for religious properties used solely for religious worship. The exemption from state taxes is authorized by Art. 16, § 1, of the New York Constitution, which provides: "Exemptions from taxation may be granted only by general laws. Exemptions may be altered or repealed except those exempting real or personal property used exclusively for religious, educational or ⊥charitable purposes as   ⌐667 defined by law and owned by any corporation or association organized or conducted exclusively for one or more of such purposes and not operating for profit."

The essence of appellant's contention was that the New York State Tax Commission's grant of an exemption to church property indirectly requires the appellant to make a contribution to religious bodies and thereby violates provisions prohibiting establishment of religion under the First Amendment which under the Fourteenth Amendment is binding on the States.

Appellee's motion for summary judgment was granted and the Appellate Division, New York Supreme Court, and the New York Court of Appeals affirmed. We noted jurisdiction and affirm.

I

Prior opinions of this Court have discussed the development and historical background of the First Amendment in detail. It would therefore serve no useful purpose to review in detail the background of the Establishment and Free ⊥Exercise Clauses of   ⌐668 the First Amendment or to restate what the Court's opinions have reflected over the years.

It is sufficient to note that for the men who wrote the Religious Clauses of the First Amendment the "establishment" of a religion connoted sponsorship, financial support, and active involvement of the sovereign in religious activity. In England, and in some Colonies at the time of the separation in 1776, the Church of England was sponsored and supported by the Crown as a state, or established, church; in other countries "establishment" meant sponsorship by the sovereign of the Lutheran or Catholic Church. The exclusivity of established churches in the 17th and 18th centuries, of course, was often carried to prohibition of other forms of worship.

The Establishment and Free Exercise Clauses of the First Amendment are not the most precisely drawn portions of the Constitution. The sweep of the absolute prohibitions in the Religion Clauses may have been calculated; but the purpose was to state an objective, not to write a statute. In attempting to articulate the scope of the two Religious Clauses, the Court's opinions reflect the limitations inherent in formulating general principles on a case-by-case basis. The considerable internal inconsistency in the opinions of the Court derives from what, in retrospect, may have been too sweeping utterances on aspects of these clauses that seemed clear in relation to the particular cases but have limited meaning as general principles.

The Court has struggled to find a neutral course between the two Religion Clauses, both of which are cast in absolute terms, and either of which, if expanded to a ⊥logical extreme, would tend to clash with the other. For example, in *Zorach* v. *Clauson*, *Mr. Justice DOUGLAS*, writing for the Court, noted: "The First Amendment however, does not say that in every and all respects there shall be a separation of Church and State."

"We sponsor an attitude on the part of government that shows no partiality to any one group and that lets each flourish according to the zeal of its adherents and the appeal of its dogma."

Mr. Justice HARLAN expressed something of this in his dissent in *Sherbert* v. *Verner*, saying that the constitutional neutrality imposed on us "is not so narrow a channel that the slightest deviation from an absolutely straight course leads to condemnation."

The course of constitutional neutrality in this area cannot be an absolutely straight line; rigidity could well defeat the basic purpose of these provisions, which is to insure that no religion be sponsored or favored, none commanded, and none inhibited. The general principle deducible from the First Amendment and all that has been said by the Court is this: that we will not tolerate either governmentally established religion or governmental interference with religion. Short of those expressly proscribed governmental acts there is room for play in the joints productive of a benevolent neutrality which will permit religious exercise to exist without sponsorship and without interference.

Each value judgment under the Religion Clauses must therefore turn on whether particular acts in question are intended to establish or interfere with religious beliefs and practices or have the effect of doing so. Adherence to the policy of neutrality that derives from an accommodation of the Establishment and Free Exercise Clauses ⊥has prevented the kind of involvement that would tip the balance toward government control of churches or governmental restraint on religious practice.

Adherents of particular faiths and individual churches frequently take strong positions on public issues including, as this case reveals in the several briefs *amici*, vigorous advocacy of legal or constitutional positions. Of course, churches as much as secular bodies and private citizens have that right. No perfect or absolute separation is really possible; the very existence of the Religion Clauses is an involvement of sorts—one which seeks to mark boundaries to avoid excessive entanglement.

The hazards of placing too much weight on a few words or phrases of the Court is abundantly illustrated within the pages of the Court's opinion in *Everson*. *Mr. Justice BLACK*, writing for the Court's majority, having said the First Amendment "means at least this: Neither a state nor the Federal Government can . . . pass laws which aid one religion, aid all religions, or prefer one religion over another," yet had no difficulty in holding that "Measured by these standards, we cannot say that the First Amendment prohibits New Jersey from spending tax-raised funds to pay the bus fares of parochial school pupils as a part of a general program under which it pays the fares of pupils attending public and other schools. *It is undoubtedly true that children are helped to get to church schools. There is even a possibility that some of the children might not be sent to the church schools if the parents were compelled to pay their children's bus fares out of their own pockets. . . .*" (Emphasis added.)

⊥ The Court did not regard such "aid" to schools teaching a particular religious faith as any more a violation of the Establishment Clause than providing "state-paid policemen, detailed to protect children . . . [at the schools] from the very real hazards of traffic. . . ."

Mr. Justice Jackson, in perplexed dissent in *Everson*, noted that "the undertones of the opinion, advocating complete and uncompromising separation . . . seem utterly discordant with its conclusion. . . ."

Perhaps so. One can sympathize with Mr. Justice Jackson's logical analysis but agree with the Court's eminently sensible and realistic application of the language of the Establishment Clause. In *Everson* the Court declined to construe the Religion Clauses with a literalness that would undermine the ultimate constitutional objective as illuminated by history. Surely, bus transportation and police protection to pupils who receive religious instruction "aid" that particular religion to maintain schools that plainly tend to assure future adherents to a particular faith by having control of their total education at an early age. No religious body that maintains schools would deny this as an affirmative if not dominant policy of church schools. But if as in *Everson* buses can be provided to carry and policemen to protect church school pupils, we fail to see how a broader range of police and fire protection given equally to all churches, along with nonprofit hospitals, art galleries, and libraries receiving the same tax exemption, is different for purposes of the Religion Clauses.

Similarly, making textbooks available to pupils in parochial schools in common with public schools was surely an "aid" to the sponsoring churches because it relieved those churches of an enormous aggregate cost |672 ⊥ for those books. Supplying of costly teaching materials was not seen either as manifesting a legislative purpose to aid or as having a primary effect of aid contravening the First Amendment. *Board of Education* v. *Allen.* In so doing the Court was heeding both its own prior holdings and our religious tradition. *Mr. Justice DOUGLAS,* in *Zorach* v. *Clauson* after recalling that we "are a religious people whose institutions presuppose a Supreme Being," went on to say: "We make room for as wide a variety of beliefs and creeds as the spiritual needs of man deem necessary. . . . *When the state encourages religions instruction . . . it follows the best of our traditions.* For it then respects the religious nature of our people and accommodates the public service to their spiritual needs." (Emphasis added.)

With all the risks inherent in programs that bring about administrative relationships between public education bodies and church-sponsored schools, we have been able to chart a course that preserved the autonomy and freedom of religious bodies while avoiding any semblance of established religion. This is a "tight rope" and one we have successfully traversed.

II

The legislative purpose of the property tax exemption is neither the advancement nor the inhibition of religion; it is neither sponsorship nor hostility. New York, in common with the other States, has determined that certain entities that exist in a harmonious relationship to the community at large, and that foster its "moral or mental improvement," should not be inhibited in their activities by property taxation or the hazard of loss of those properties for non-|673 payment of taxes. It ⊥ has not singled out one particular church or religious group or even churches as such; rather, it has granted exemption to all houses of religious worship within a broad class of property owned by nonprofit, quasi-public corporations which include hospitals, libraries, playgrounds, scientific, professional, historical and patriotic groups. The State has an affirmative policy that considers these groups as beneficial and stabilizing influences in community life and finds this classification useful, desirable, and in the public interest. Qualification for tax exemption is not perpetual or immutable; some tax-exempt groups lose that status when their activities take them outside the classification and new entities can come into being and qualify for exemption.

Governments have not always been tolerant of religious activity, and hostility toward religion has taken many shapes and forms—economic, political, and sometimes harshly oppressive. Grants of exemption historically reflect the concern of authors of constitutions and statutes as to the latent dangers inherent in the imposition of property taxes; exemption constitutes a reasonable and balanced attempt to guard against those dangers. The limits of permissible state accommodation to religion are by no means co-extensive with the noninterference mandated by the Free Exercise Clause. To equate the two would be to deny a national heritage with roots in the Revolution itself. We cannot read New York's statute as attempting to establish religion; it is simply sparing the exercise of religion from the burden of property taxation levied on private profit institutions.

⊥ We find it unnecessary to justify the tax exemp- |674 tion on the social welfare services of "good works" that some churches perform for parishioners and others—family counselling, aid to the elderly and the infirm, and to children. Churches vary substantially in the scope of such services; programs expand or contract according to resources and need. As public-sponsored programs enlarge, private aid from the church sector may diminish. The extent of social services may vary, depending on whether the church serves an urban or rural, a rich or poor consituency. To give emphasis to so variable an aspect of the work of religious bodies would introduce an element of governmental evaluation and standards as to the worth of particular social welfare programs, thus producing a kind of continuing day-to-day relationship which the policy of neutrality seeks to minimize. Hence, the use of a social welfare yardstick as a significant element to qualify for tax exemption could conceivably give rise to confrontations that could escalate to constitutional dimensions.

Determining that the legislative purpose of tax exemption is not aimed at establishing, sponsoring, or supporting religion does not end the inquiry, however. We must also be sure that the end result—the effect—is not an excessive government entanglement with religion. The test is inescapably one of degree. Either course, taxation of churches or exemption, occasions some degree of involvement with religion. Elimination of exemption would tend to expand the involvement of government by giving rise to tax valuation of church property, tax liens, tax foreclosures, and the direct confrontations and conflicts that follow in the train of those legal processes.

Granting tax exemptions to churches necessarily operates to afford an indirect economic benefit and also gives rise to some, but yet a lesser, involvement than taxing ⊥ them. In analyzing either alternative |675 the questions are whether the involvement is excessive, and whether it is a continuing one calling for official and continuing surveillance leading to an impermissible degree of entanglement. Obviously a direct money subsidy would be a relationship pregnant with involvement and, as with most governmental grant programs, could encompass sustained and detailed administrative relationships for enforcement of statutory or administrative standards, but that is not this case. The hazards of churches supporting government are hardly less in their potential than the hazards of governments supporting churches; each relationship carries some involvement rather than the desired insulation and separation. We cannot ignore the instances in history when church support of government led to the kind of involvement we seek to avoid.

The grant of a tax exemption is not sponsorship since the government does not transfer part of its revenue to churches but simply abstains from demanding that the church support the state. No one has ever suggested that tax exemption has converted libraries, art galleries, or hospitals into arms of the state or employees "on the public payroll." There is no genuine nexus between tax exemption and establishment of religion. As Mr. Justice Holmes commented in a related context "a page of ⊥ history is worth a volume of logic." *New York Trust Co.* v. *Eisner.* The exemption creates only a minimal and remote involvement between church and state and far less than taxation of churches. It restricts the fiscal relationship between church and state, and tends to complement and reinforce the desired separation insulating each from the other.

Separation in this context cannot mean absence of all contact; the complexities of modern life inevitably produce some contact and the fire and police protection received by houses of religious worship are no more than incidental benefits accorded all persons or institutions within a State's boundaries, along with many other exempt organizations. The appellant has not established even an arguable quantitative correlation between the payment of an ad valorem property tax and the receipt of these municipal benefits.

All of the 50 States provide for tax exemption of places of worship, most of them doing so by constitutional guarantees. For so long as federal income taxes have had any potential impact on churches— over 75 years— religious organizations have been expressly exempt from the tax. Such treatment is an "aid" to churches no more and no less in principle than the real estate tax exemption granted by States. Few concepts are more deeply embedded in the fabric of our national life, beginning with pre-Revolutionary colonial times, than for the government to exercise at the very least this kind of benevolent neutrality toward churches and religious exer ⊥ cise generally so long as none was favored over others and none suffered interference.

It is significant that Congress, from its earliest days, has viewed the Religion Clauses of the Constitution as authorizing statutory real estate tax exemption to religious bodies. In 1802 the 7th Congress enacted a taxing statute for the County of Alexandria, adopting the 1800 Virginia statutory pattern which provided tax exemptions for churches. As early as 1813 the 12th Congress refunded import duties paid by religious societies on the importation of religious articles. During this period the City Council of Washington, D.C., acting under congressional authority, enacted a series of real and personal property assessments which uniformly exempted church property. In 1870 the Congress specifically exempted all churches in the District of Colum ⊥ bia and appurtenant grounds and property "from any and all taxes or assessments, national, municipal, or county."

It is obviously correct that no one acquires a vested or protected right in violation of the Constitution by long use, even when that span of time covers our entire national existence and indeed predates it. Yet an unbroken practice of according the exemption to churches, openly and by affirmative state action, not covertly or by state inaction, is not something to be lightly cast aside. Nearly 50 years ago Mr. Justice Holmes stated: "[I]f a thing has been practised for two hundred years by common consent, it will need a strong case for the Fourteenth Amendment to affect it." *Jackman* v. *Rosenbaum.*

Nothing in this national attitude toward religious tolerance and two centuries of uninterrupted freedom from taxation has given the remotest sign of leading to an established church or religion and on the contrary it has operated affirmatively to help guarantee the free exercise of all forms of religious beliefs. Thus, it is hardly useful to suggest that tax exemption is but the "foot in the door" or the "nose of the camel in the tent" leading to an established church. If tax exemption can be seen as the first step toward "establishment" of religion, as *Mr. Justice DOUGLAS* fears, the second step has been long in coming. Any move which realistically "establishes" a church or tends to do so can be dealt with "while this Court sits."

Mr. Justice Cardozo commented in The Nature of the Judicial Process (1921) on the "tendency of a prin ⊥ ciple to expand itself to the limit of its logic"; such expansion must always be contained by the historical frame of reference of the principle's purpose and there is no lack of vigilance on this score by those who fear religious entanglement in government.

The argument that making "fine distinctions" between what is and what is not absolute under the Constitution is to render us a government of men, not laws, gives too little weight to the fact that it is an essential part of adjudication to draw distinctions, including fine ones, in the process of interpreting the Constitution. We must frequently decide, for example, what are "reasonable" searches and seizures under the Fourth Amendment. Determining what acts of government tend to establish or interfere with religion falls well within what courts have long been called upon to do in sensitive areas.

It is interesting to note that while the precise question we now decide has not been directly before the Court previously, the broad question was dis-

|676

|677

|678

|679

cussed by the Court in relation to real estate taxes
assessed nearly a century ago on land owned by and
adjacent to a church in Washington, D.C. At the
time Congress granted real estate tax exemptions to
buildings devoted to art, to institutions of public
charity, libraries, cemeteries, and "church buildings,
and grounds actually occupied by such buildings." In
denying tax exemption as to land owned by but not
used for the church, but rather to produce income,
the Court concluded: "In the exercise of this [taxing]
power, Congress, like any State legislature unrestricted by constitutional provisions, may at its discretion wholly exempt certain classes of property
⌐680   from taxation, or ⊥ may tax them at a lower rate
than other property." *Gibbons* v. *District of Columbia.*

It appears that at least up to 1885 this Court, reflecting more than a century of our history and
uninterrupted practice, accepted without discussion
the proposition that federal or state grants of tax exemption to churches were not a violation of the Religious Clauses of the First Amendment. As to the
New York statute, we now confirm that view.

Affirmed.

Mr. Justice BRENNAN, concurring.

I concur for reasons expressed in my opinion in
Abington Township v. *Schempp.* I adhere to the
view there stated that to give concrete meaning to
the Establishment Clause, "the line we must draw
between the permissible and the impermissible is one
which accords with history and faithfully reflects the
understanding of the Founding Fathers. It is a line
which the Court has consistently sought to mark in
its decisions expounding the religious guarantees of
the First Amendment. What the Framers meant to
foreclose, and what our decisions under the Establishment Clause have forbidden, are those involvements of religious with secular institutions which (a)
serve the essentially religious activities of religious
institutions; (b) employ the organs of government for
essentially religious purposes; or (c) use essentially
religious means to serve governmental ends, where
secular means would suffice. When the secular and
religious institutions become involved in such manner, there inhere in the relationship precisely those
⌐681   ⊥ dangers—as much to church as to state—which
the Framers feared would subvert religious liberty
and the strength of a system of secular government.
On the other hand, there may be myriad forms of involvements of government with religion which do
not import such dangers and therefore should not, in
my judgment, be deemed to violate the Establishment Clause." Thus, in my view, the history, purpose, and operation of real property tax exemptions
for religious organizations must be examined to determine whether the Establishment Clause is
breached by such exemptions.

I

The existence from the beginning of the Nation's
life of a practice, such as tax exemptions for religious
organizations, is not conclusive of its constitutionality. But such practice is a fact of considerable import in the interpretation of abstract constitutional
language. On its face, the Establishment Clause is
reasonably susceptible of different interpretations regarding the exemptions. This Court's interpretation
of the clause, accordingly, is appropriately influenced
by the reading it has received in the practices of the
Nation. As Mr. Justice Holmes observed in an analogous context, in resolving such questions of interpretation "a page of history is worth a volume of
logic." *New York Trust Co.* v. *Eisner.* The more
longstanding and widely accepted a practice, the
greater its impact upon constitutional interpretation.
History is particularly compelling in the present case
because of the undeviating acceptance given religious
tax exemptions from our earliest days as a Nation.
Rarely if ever has this Court considered the constitutionality of a practice for which the historical support is so overwhelming.

⊥ The Establishment Clause, along with the other   ⌐682
provisions of the Bill of Rights, was ratified by the
States in 1791. Religious tax exemptions were not an
issue in the petitions calling for the Bill of Rights, in
the pertinent congressional debates, or in the debates preceding ratification by the States. The absence of concern about the exemptions could not
have resulted from failure to foresee the possibility
of their existence, for they were widespread during
colonial days. Rather, it seems clear that the exemptions were not among the evils which the Framers
and Ratifiers of the Establishment Clause sought to
avoid. Significantly, within a decade after ratification, at least four States passed statutes exempting
the property of religious organizations from taxation.

Although the First Amendment may not have applied to the States during this period, practice in
Virginia at the time is nonetheless instructive. The
Commonwealth's efforts to separate church and state
provided the direct antecedents of the First Amendment, ⊥ and Virginia remained unusually sensitive   ⌐683
to the proper relation between church and state
during the years immediately following ratification
of the Establishment Clause. Virginia's protracted
movement to disestablish the Episcopal Church culminated in the passage on January 24, 1799, of "An
ACT to repeal certain acts, and to declare the construction of the [Virginia] bill of rights and constitution, concerning religion." The 1799 Act stated that
the Virginia Bill of Rights had "excepted from the
powers given to the [civil] government the power of
reviving any species of ecclesiastical or church government . . . by referring the subject of religion to
conscience" and that the repealed measures had "bestowed property upon [the Anglican] church," had
"asserted a legislative right to establish any religious

sect" and had "incorporated religious sects, all of which is inconsistent with the principles of the constitution, and of religious freedom, and manifestly tends to the reestablishment of a national church." Yet just one year after the passage of this Act, Virginia reenacted a measure exempting from taxation property belonging to "any . . . college, houses for divine worship, or seminary of learning." This exemption dated at least from 1777 and had been reaffirmed immediately before and after ratification of the First Amendment. It may reasonably be inferred that the Virginians did not view the exemption for "houses of divine worship" as an establishment of religion.

Similarly, in 1784 the New York Legislature repealed colonial acts establishing the Episcopal |684 Church in several counties of the State. ⊥Yet in 1799, the legislature provided that "no house or land belonging to . . . any church or place of public worship . . . nor any college or incorporated academy, nor any school house . . . alms house or property belonging to any incorporated library, shall be taxed by virtue of this act." And early practice in the District of Columbia—governed from the outset by the First Amendment—mirrored that in the States. In 1802 the Corporation of the City of Washington, under authority delegated by Congress, exempted "houses for public worship" from real property taxes.

Thomas Jefferson was President when tax exemption was first given Washington churches, and James Madison sat in sessions of the Virginia General Assembly which voted exemptions for churches in that Commonwealth. I have found no record of their personal views on the respective acts. The absence of |685 such a record is itself ⊥significant. It is unlikely that two men so concerned with the separation of church and state would have remained silent had they thought the exemptions established religion. And if they had not either approved the exemptions, or been mild in their opposition, it is probable that their views would be known to us today. Both Jefferson and Madison wrote prolifically about issues they felt important, and their opinions were well known to contemporary chroniclers. See, for example, the record preserved of Madison's battle in 1784-1785 against the proposal in the Virginia Assembly to levy a general tax to support "teachers of the Christian religion," in the dissenting opinion of *Mr. Justice DOUGLAS.* Much the same can be said of the other Framers and Ratifiers of the Bill of Rights who remained active in public affairs during the late 18th and early 19th centuries. The adoption of the early exemptions without controversy, in other words, strongly suggests that they were not thought incompatible with constitutional prohibitions against involvements of church and state.

The exemptions have continued uninterrupted to the present day. They are in force in all 50 States. No judicial decision, state or federal, has ever held that they violate the Establishment Clause. In 1886,

for example, this Court in *Gibbons* v. *District of Columbia*, rejected on statutory grounds a church's claim for the exemption of certain of its land under congressional statutes exempting Washington churches and appurtenant ground from real property taxes. But the Court ⊥gave not the slightest hint |686 that it ruled against the church because, under the First Amendment, *any* exemption would have been unconstitutional. To the contrary, the Court's opinion implied that nothing in the Amendment precludes exemption of church property: "We are not disposed to deny that grounds left open around a church, not merely to admit light and air, but also used to add to its beauty and attractiveness, may, if not used or intended to be used for any other purpose, be exempt from taxation under these statutes."

Mr. Justice Holmes said that "[i]f a thing has been practised for two hundred years by common consent, it will need a strong case for the Fourteenth Amendment to affect it. . . ." *Jackman* v. *Rosenbaum Co.* For almost 200 years the view expressed in the actions of legislatures and courts has been that tax exemptions for churches do not threaten "those consequences which the Framers deeply feared" or "tend to promote the type of interdependence between religion and state which the First Amendment was designed to prevent." An examination both of the governmental purposes for granting the exemptions and of the type of ⊥church-state relationship |687 that has resulted from their existence makes clear that no "strong case" exists for holding unconstitutional this historic practice.

II

Government has two basic secular purposes for granting real property tax exemptions to religious organizations. First, these organizations are exempted because they, among a range of other private, nonprofit organizations contribute to the well-being of the community in a variety of nonreligious ways, and thereby bear burdens that would otherwise either have to be met by general taxation, or be left undone, to the detriment of the community. Thus, New York exempts "[r]eal property owned by a corporation or association ⊥organized exclusively for the |688 moral or mental improvement of men and women, or for religious, bible, tract, charitable, benevolent, missionary, hospital, infirmary, educational, public playground, scientific, literary, bar association, library, patriotic, historical or cemetery purposes, for the enforcement of laws relating to children or animals, or for two or more such purposes. . . ."

Appellant seeks to avoid the force of this secular purpose of the exemptions by limiting his challenge to "exemptions from real property taxation to religious organizations on real property used exclusively for religious purposes." Appellant assumes, apparently, that church-owned property is used for ex- ·clusively religious purposes if it does not house a hospital, orphanage, weekday school or the like. Any assumption that a church building itself is used for exclusively religious activities, however, rests on a simplistic view of ordinary church operations. As the appellee's brief cogently observes, "the public welfare activities and the sectarian activities of religious institutions are . . . intertwined. . . . Often a particular church will use the same personnel, facilities and source of funds to carry out both its secular and religious activities." Thus, the same people who gather in church facilities for religious worship and study may return to these facilities to participate in Boy Scout activities, to promote antipoverty causes, to discuss public issues, or to listen to chamber music. Accordingly, the funds used to maintain the facilities as a place for religious worship and study also maintain them as a place for secular activities beneficial to the community as a whole. Even during formal worship services, churches frequently collect the ⌊689 funds used to finance ⊥their secular operations and make decisions regarding their nature.

Second, government grants exemptions to religious organizations because they uniquely contribute to the pluralism of American society by their religious activities. Government may properly include religious institutions among the variety of private, non-profit groups which receive tax exemptions, for each group contributes to the diversity of association, viewpoint and enterprise essential to a vigorous, pluralistic society. To this end, New York extends its exemptions not only to religious and social service organizations but also to scientific, literary, bar, library, patriotic and historical groups, and generally to institutions "organized exclusively for the moral or mental improvement of men and women." The very breadth of this scheme of exemptions negates any suggestion that the State intends to single out religious organizations for special preference. The scheme is not designed to inject any religious activity into a nonreligious context, as was the case with school prayers. No particular activity of a religious organization—for example, the propagation of its beliefs—is specially promoted by the exemptions. They merely facilitate the existence of a broad range of private, non-profit organizations, among them religious groups, by leaving each free to come into existence, then to flourish or wither, without being burdened by real property taxes.

III

Although governmental purposes for granting religious exemptions may be wholly secular, exemptions can nonetheless violate the Establishment Clause if ⌊690 they result in ⊥extensive state involvement with religion. Accordingly, those who urge the exemptions unconstitutionality argue that exemptions are the equivalent of governmental subsidy of churches. General subsidies of religious activities would, of course, constitute impermissible state involvement with religion.

Tax exemptions and general subsidies, however, are qualitatively different. Though both provide economic assistance, they do so in fundamentally different ways. A subsidy involves the direct transfer of public monies to the subsidized enterprise and uses resources exacted from taxpayers as a whole. An exemption, on the other hand, involves no such transfer. It assists the exempted enterprise only passively, by relieving a privately funded venture of the burden of paying taxes. In other words, ⊥"[i]n the case of ⌊691 direct subsidy, the state forcibly diverts the income of both believers and nonbelievers to churches," while "[i]n the case of an exemption, the state merely refrains from diverting to its own uses income independently generated by churches through voluntary contributions." Giannella, Religious Liberty, Nonestablishment, and Doctrinal Development, 81 Harv. L. Rev. 513, 553 (1968). Thus, "the symbolism of tax exemption is significant as a manifestation that organized religion is not expected to support the state; by the same token the state is not expected to support the church." Freund, Public Aid to Parochial Schools, 82 Harv. L. Rev. 1680, 1687, n. 16 (1969). Tax exemptions, accordingly, constitute mere passive state involvement with religion and not the affirmative involvement characteristic of outright governmental subsidy.

Even though exemptions produce only passive state involvement with religion, nonetheless some argue that their termination would be desirable as a means of reducing the level of church-state contact. But it cannot realistically be said that termination of religious tax exemptions would quantitatively lessen the extent of state involvement with religion. Appellee contends that "[a]s a practical matter, the public welfare activities and the sectarian activities of religious institutions are so intertwined that they cannot be separated for the purpose of determining eligibility for tax exemptions." If not impossible, the separation would certainly involve extensive state investigation into church operations and finances. Moreover, the termination of exemptions would give rise, as the Court says, to the necessity for "tax valuation of church property, tax liens, tax foreclosures and the direct confrontations and conflicts which follow in the train of those legal processes." ⊥Tax- ⌊692 ation, further, would bear unequally on different churches, having its most disruptive effect on those with the least ability to meet the annual levies assessed against them. And taxation would surely influence the allocation of church resources. By diverting funds otherwise available for religious or public service purposes to the support of the Government, taxation would necessarily affect the extent of church support for the enterprises which they now promote. In many instances, the public service activities would bear the brunt of the reallocation, as churches looked first to maintain their places and programs of worship. In short, the cessation of exemptions would have a significant impact on religious organizations. Whether Government grants or withholds the exemptions, it is going to be involved with religion.

IV

Against the background of this survey of the history, purpose and operation of religious tax exemptions, I must conclude that the exemptions do not "serve the essentially religious activities of religious institutions." Their principal effect is to carry out secular purposes—the encouragement of public service activities and of a pluralistic society. During their ordinary operations, most churches engage in |693 activities of a secular nature ⊥which benefit the community; and all churches by their existence contribute to the diversity of association, viewpoint, and enterprise so highly valued by all of us.

Nor do I find that the exemptions "employ the organs of government for essentially religious purposes." To the extent that the exemptions further secular ends, they do not advance "essentially religious purposes." To the extent that purely religious activities are benefited by the exemptions, the benefit is passive. Government does not affirmatively foster these activities by exempting religious organizations from taxes, as it would were it to subsidize them. The exemption simply leaves untouched that which adherents of the organization bring into being and maintain.

Finally, I do not think that the exemptions "use essentially religious means to serve governmental ends, where secular means would suffice." The means churches use to carry on their public service activities are not "essentially religious" in nature. They are the same means used by any purely secular organization—money, human time and skills, physical facilities. It is true that each church contributes to the pluralism of our society through its purely religious activities, but the state encourages these activities not because it champions religion *per se* but because it values religion among a variety of private, nonprofit enterprises which contribute to the diversity of the Nation. Viewed in this light, there is no nonreligious substitute for religion as an element in our societal mosaic, just as there is no nonliterary substitute for literary groups.

As I said in *Schempp*, the First Amendment does not invalidate "the propriety of certain tax . . . exemptions which incidentally benefit churches and religious institutions, along with many secular charities and nonprofit organizations. . . . [R]eligious institutions simply share benefits which |694 government makes generally available ⊥to educational, charitable, and eleemosynary groups. There is no indication that taxing authorities have used such benefits in any way to subsidize worship or foster belief in God."

Opinion of *Mr. Justice HARLAN*.

While I entirely subscribe to the result reached today and find myself in basic agreement with what *The CHIEF JUSTICE* has written, I deem it appropriate, in view of the radiations of the issues involved, to state those considerations that are, for me, controlling in this case and lead me to conclude that New York's constitutional provision, as implemented by its real property law, does not offend the Establishment Clause. Preliminarily, I think it relevant to face up to the fact that it is far easier to agree on the purpose that underlies the First Amendment's Establishment and Free Exercise Clauses than to obtain agreement on the standards that should govern their application. What is at stake as a matter of policy is preventing that kind and degree of government involvement in religious life that, as history teaches us, is apt to lead to strife and frequently strain a political system to the breaking point. . . .

⊥*Mr. Justice DOUGLAS*, dissenting. |700

Petitioner is the owner of real property in New York and is a Christian. But he is not a member of any of the religious organizations, "rejecting them as hostile." The New York statute exempts from taxation real property "owned by a corporation or association organized exclusively for . . . religious . . . purposes" and used "exclusively for carrying out" such purpose. Yet nonbelievers who own realty are taxed at the usual rate. The question in the case therefore is whether believers—organized in church groups—can be made exempt from real estate taxes, merely because they are believers, while nonbelievers, whether organized or not, must pay the real estate taxes.

My *Brother HARLAN* says he "would suppose" that the tax exemption extends to "groups whose avowed tenets may be antitheological, atheistic and agnostic." If it does, then the line between believers and nonbelievers has not been drawn. But, with all respect, there is not even a suggestion in the present record that the statute covers property used exclusively by organizations for "antitheological purposes," "atheistic purposes" or "agnostic purposes."

In *Torcaso* v. *Watkins* we held that ⊥a State |701 could not bar an atheist from public office in light of the freedom of belief and religion guaranteed by the First and Fourteenth Amendments. Neither the State nor the Federal Government, we said, "can constitutionally pass laws or impose requirements which aid all religions as against nonbelievers, and neither can aid those religions based on a belief in the existence of God as against those religions founded on different beliefs."

That principle should govern this case.

There is a line between what a State may do in encouraging "religious" activities, *Zorach* v. *Clauson*, and what a State may not do by using its resources to promote "religious" activities, *McCollum* v. *Board of Education*, or bestowing benefits because of them. Yet that line may not always be clear. Closing public schools on Sunday is in the former category; subsidizing churches, in my view, is in the latter. Indeed I would suppose that in common understanding one of the best ways to "establish" one or more religions is to subsidize them, which a tax exemption does. The State may not do that any more than it may prefer "those who believe in no religion over those who do believe." *Zorach* v. *Clauson.*

In affirming this judgment the Court largely overlooks the revolution initiated by the adoption of the Fourteenth Amendment. That revolution involved the imposition of new and far-reaching constitutional restraints on the States. Nationalization of many civil liberties has been the consequence of the Fourteenth Amendment, reversing the historic position that the foundations of those liberties rested largely in state law.

The process of the "selective incorporation" of various provisions of the Bill of Rights into the Fourteenth Amendment, although often provoking ⌊702 lively disagree⊥ment at large as well as among the members of this Court, has been a steady one. It started in 1896 with *Chicago, B. & Q. R. Co.* v. *Chicago* in which the Court held that the Fourteenth Amendment precluded a State from taking private property for public use without payment of just compensation, as provided in the Fifth Amendment. The first direct holding as to the incorporation of the First Amendment into the Fourteenth occurred in 1931 in *Stromberg* v. *California*, a case involving the right of free speech, although that holding in *Stromberg* had been foreshadowed in 1925 by the Court's opinion in *Gitlow* v. *New York*. As regards the religious guarantees of the First Amendment, the Free Exercise Clause was expressly deemed incorporated into the Fourteenth Amendment in 1940 in *Cantwell* v. *Connecticut*, although that holding had been foreshadowed in 1923 and 1934 by the Court's dicta in *Meyer* v. *Nebraska* and *Hamilton* v. *Regents*. The Establishment Clause was not incorporated in the Fourteenth Amendment until *Everson* v. *Board of Education* was decided in 1947.

Those developments in the last 30 years have had unsettling effects. It was, for example, not until 1962 that state-sponsored, sectarian prayers were held to violate the Establishment Clause. *Engel* v. *Vitale.* That decision brought many protests, for the habit of putting one sect's prayer in public schools had long been practiced. Yet if the Catholics, controlling one school board, could put their prayer into one group of public schools, the Mormons, Baptists, Moslems, Presbyterians, and others could do the same, once they got control. And so the seeds of Establishment would grow and a secular institution would be used to serve a sectarian end.

⌊703   ⊥*Engel* was as disruptive of traditional state practices as was *Stromberg.* Prior to *Stromberg*, a State could arrest an unpopular person who made a

rousing speech on the charge of disorderly conduct. Since *Stromberg*, that has been unconstitutional. And so the revolution occasioned by the Fourteenth Amendment has progressed as Article after Article in the Bill of Rights has been incorporated in it and made applicable to the States. Hence the question in the present case makes irrelevant the "two centuries of uninterrupted freedom from taxation," referred to by the Court. If history be our guide, then tax exemption of church property in this country is indeed highly suspect, as it arose in the early days when the church was an agency of the state. The question here, though, concerns the meaning of the Establishment Clause and the Free Exercise Clause made applicable to the States for only a few decades at best.

With all due respect the governing principle is not controlled by *Everson* v. *Board of Education. Everson* involved the use of public funds to bus children to parochial as well as to public schools. Parochial schools teach religion; yet they are also educational institutions offering courses competitive with public schools. They prepare students for the professions and for activities in all walks of life. Education in the secular sense was combined with religious indoctrination at the parochial schools involved in *Everson.* Even so, the *Everson* decision was five to four and, though one of the five, I have since had grave doubts about it, because I have become convinced that grants to institutions teaching a sectarian creed violate the Establishment Clause.

⊥This case, however, is quite different. Education   ⌊704 is not involved. The financial support rendered here is to the church, the place of worship. A tax exemption is a subsidy. Is my *Brother* BRENNAN correct in saying that we would hold that state or federal grants to churches, say, to construct the edifice itself would be unconstitutional? What is the difference between that kind of subsidy and the present subsidy?

The problem takes us back where Madison was in 1784 and 1785 when he battled the *Assessment Bill* in Virginia. That bill levied a tax for the support of Christian churches, leaving to each taxpayer the choice as to "what society of Christians" he wanted the tax paid; and absent such designation, the tax was to go for education. Even so, Madison was unrelenting in his opposition. As stated by Mr. Justice Rutledge: "The modified Assessment Bill passed second reading in December, 1784, and was all but enacted. ⊥Madison and his followers, however,   ⌊705 maneuvered deferment of final consideration until November, 1785. And before the Assembly reconvened in the fall he issued his historic Memorial and Remonstrance." *Everson* v. *Board of Education.*

The *Remonstrance* stirred up such a storm of popular protest that the Assessment Bill was defeated.

The *Remonstrance* covers some aspects of the present subsidy, including Madison's protest in paragraph 3 to a requirement that any person be compelled to contribute even "three pence" to support a church. All men, he maintained in ¶4, enter society "on equal conditions" including the right to free exercise of religion: "Whilst we assert for ourselves a freedom to embrace, to profess and to observe the Religion which we believe to be of divine origin, we cannot deny an equal freedom to those whose minds have not yet yielded to the evidence which has convinced us. If this freedom be abused, it is an offence against God, not against man: To God, therefore, not to men, must an account of it be rendered. As the Bill violates equality by subjecting some to peculiar burdens; so it violates the same principle, by granting to others peculiar exemptions."

Madison's assault on the *Assessment Bill* was in fact an assault based on both the concepts of "free exercise" and "establishment" of religion later entered into the First Amendment. ⊥Madison, whom we recently called "the leading architect of the religious clauses of the First Amendment," *Flast* v. *Cohen*, was indeed their author and chief promoter. As Mr. Justice Rutledge said: "All the great instruments of the Virginia struggle for religious liberty thus became warp and woof of our constitutional tradition, not simply by the course of history, but by the common unifying force of Madison's life, thought and sponsorship. He epitomized the whole of that tradition in the Amendment's compact, but nonetheless comprehensive, phrasing." *Everson* v. *Board of Education.*

The Court seeks to avoid this historic argument as to the meaning of "establishment" and "free exercise" by relying on the long practice of the States in granting the subsidies challenged here.

Certainly government may not lay a tax on either worshiping or preaching. In *Murdock* v. *Pennsylvania* we ruled on a state license tax levied on religious colporteurs as a condition to pursuit of their activities. In holding the tax unconstitutional we said: "The power to tax the exercise of a privilege is the power to control or suppress its enjoyment. *Magnano Co.* v. *Hamilton.* Those who can tax the exercise of this religious practice can make its exercise so costly as to deprive it of the resources necessary for its maintenance. Those who can tax the privilege of engaging in this form of missionary evangelism can close its doors to all those who do not have a full purse. Spreading religious beliefs in this ancient and honorable manner would thus be denied the needy. Those who can deprive religious groups of their colporteurs can take from them a part of ⊥the vital power of the press which has survived from the Reformation."

Churches, like newspapers also enjoying First Amendment rights, have no constitutional immunity from all taxes. As we said in *Murdock*: "We do not mean to say that religious groups and the press are free from all financial burdens of government. We have here something quite different, for example, from a tax on the income of one who engages in religious activities or a tax on property used or employed in connection with those activities. It is one thing to impose a tax on the income or property of a preacher. It is quite another thing to exact a tax from him for the privilege of delivering a sermon."

State aid to places of worship, whether in the form of direct grants, or tax exemption, takes us back to the *Assessment Bill* and the *Remonstrance.* The church *qua* church would not be entitled to that support from believers and from nonbelievers alike. Yet the church *qua* nonprofit, charitable institution is one of many that receives a form of subsidy through tax exemption. To be sure, the New York statute does not single out the church for grant or favor. It includes churches in a long list of nonprofit organizations: for the moral or mental improvement of men and women; for charitable, hospital, or educational purposes; for playgrounds; for scientific or literary objects; for bar associations; for medical societies; for libraries; for patriotic and historical purposes; for cemeteries; for the enforcement of laws relating to children or animals; for opera ⊥houses, fraternal organizations; for academies of music; for veterans' organizations; pharmaceutical societies; and for dental societies. While the beneficiaries cover a wide range, "atheistic," "agnostic," or "antitheological" groups do not seem to be included.

Churches perform some functions that the State would constitutionally be empowered to perform. I refer to nonsectarian social welfare operations such as the care for orphaned children and the destitute and people who are sick. A tax exemption to agencies performing those functions would therefore be as constitutionally proper as the grant of direct subsidies to them. Under the First Amendment the State may not, however, provide worship if private groups fail to do so. As Mr. Justice Jackson said: "[A State] may socialize utilities and economic enterprises and make taxpayers' business out of what conventionally had been private business. It may make public business of individual welfare, health, education, entertainment or security. But it cannot make public business of religious worship or instruction, or of attendance at religious institutions of any character. . . . That is a difference which the Constitution sets up between religion and almost every other subject matter of legislation, a difference which goes to the very root of religious freedom and which the Court is overlooking today." *Everson* v. *Board of Education.*

That is a major difference between churches on the one hand and the rest of the nonprofit organizations on the other. Government could provide or finance operas, hospitals, historical societies, and all the rest because they represent social welfare programs within ⊥the reach of the police power. In contrast, government may not provide or finance worship because of the Establishment Clause any more than it may single out "atheistic" or "agnostic" centers or groups and create or finance them.

The Brookings Institution, writing in 1933, before the application of the Establishment Clause of the First Amendment to the States, said about tax exemptions of religious groups: "Tax exemption, no matter what its form, is essentially a government grant or subsidy. Such grants would seem to be justified only if the purpose for which they are made is one for which the legislative body *would be equally willing to make* a direct appropriation from public funds equal to the amount of the exemption. This test would not be met except in the case where the exemption is granted to encourage certain activities of private interests, which, if not thus performed, would have to be assumed by the government at an expenditure at least as great as the value of the exemption."

Since 1947 when the Establishment Clause was made applicable to the States, that Report would have to state that the exemption would be justified only where "the legislative body *could make*" an appropriation for the cause.

On the record of this case, the church *qua* nonprofit, charitable organization is intertwined with the church *qua* church. A church may use the same facilities, resources, and personnel in carrying out both its secular and its sectarian activities. The two are unitary and on the present record have not been ⌐710 separated one from ⊥the other. The state has a public policy of encouraging private public welfare organizations, which it desires to encourage through tax exemption. Why may it not do so and include churches *qua* welfare organizations on a nondiscriminatory basis? That avoids, it is argued, a discrimination against churches and in a real sense maintains neutrality toward religion which the First Amendment was designed to foster. Welfare services, whether performed by churches or by nonreligious groups, may well serve the public welfare.

Whether a particular church seeking an exemption for its welfare work could constitutionally pass muster would depend on the special facts. The assumption is that the church is a purely private institution, promoting a sectarian cause. The creed, teaching, and beliefs of one may be undesirable or even repulsive to others. Its sectarian faith sets it apart from all others and makes it difficult to equate its constituency with the general public. The extent that its facilities are open to all may only indicate the nature of its proselytism. Yet though a church covers up its religious symbols in welfare work, its welfare activities may merely be a phase of sectarian activity. I have said enough to indicate the nature of this tax exemption problem.

Direct financial aid to churches or tax exemptions to the church *qua* church is not, in my view, even arguably permitted. Sectarian causes are certainly not antipublic and many would rate their own church or perhaps all churches as the highest form of welfare. The difficulty is that sectarian causes must remain in the private domain not subject to public control

or subsidy. That seems to me to be the requirement of the Establishment Clause. As Edmond Cahn said: "In America, Madison submitted most astutely, the rights of conscience must be kept not only free but *equal* as well. And in view of the endless varia⊥tions—not only among the numerous sects, ⌐711 but also among the organized activities they pursued and the relative emotional values they attached to their activities—how could any species of government assistance be considered genuinely equal from sect to sect? If, for example, a state should attempt to subsidize all sectarian schools without discrimination, it would necessarily violate the principle of equality because certain sects felt impelled to conduct a large number of such schools, others few, others none. How could the officers of government begin to measure the intangible factors that a true equality of treatment would involve, i.e., the relative intensity of religious attachment to parochial education that the respective groups required of their lay and clerical members? It would be presumptuous even to inquire. Thus, just as in matters of race our belated recognition of intangible factors has finally led us to the maxim 'separate therefore unequal,' so in matters of religion Madison's immediate recognition of intangible factors led us promptly to the maxim 'equal therefore separate.' Equality was out of the question without total separation." E. Cahn, Confronting Injustice 186-187 (1966).

The exemptions provided here insofar as welfare projects are concerned may have the ring of neutrality. But subsidies either through direct grant or tax exemption for sectarian causes, whether carried on by church *qua* church or by church *qua* welfare agency, must be treated differently, lest we in time allow the church *qua* church to be on the public payroll, which, I fear, is imminent.

⊥As stated by my *Brother BRENNAN* in *Abing-* ⌐712 *ton School Dist.* v. *Schempp*, (concurring opinion), "It is not only the nonbeliever who fears the injection of sectarian doctrines and controversies into the civil polity, but in as high degree it is the devout believer who fears the secularization of a creed which becomes too deeply involved with and dependent upon the government."

Madison as President vetoed a bill incorporating the Protestant Episcopal Church in Alexandria, Virginia, as being a violation of the Establishment Clause. He said, *inter alia*: ". . . the bill vests in the said incorporated church an authority to provide for the support of the poor and the education of poor children of the same, an authority which, being altogether superfluous if the provision is to be the result of pious charity, would be a precedent for giving to religious societies as such a legal agency in carrying into effect a public and civil duty."

He also vetoed a bill which reserved a parcel of federal land "for the use" of the Baptist Church, as violating the Establishment Clause.

What Madison would have thought of the present state subsidy to churches—a tax exemption as distinguished from an outright grant—no one can say with certainty. The fact that Virginia early granted church tax exemptions cannot be credited to Madison. Certainly he seems to have been opposed. In his paper "Monopolies, Perpetuities, Corporations, Ecclesiastical Endowments" he wrote: "Strongly guarded as is the separation between Religion & ⊥713 Govt in the Constitution of the United ⊥States the danger of encroachment by Ecclesiastical Bodies, may be illustrated by precedents already furnished in their short history." And he referred, *inter alia*, to the "attempt in Kentucky for example, where it was proposed to exempt Houses of Worship from taxes." From these three statements, Madison, it seems, opposed all state subsidies to churches.

We should adhere to what we said in *Torcaso* v. *Watkins* that neither a State nor the Federal Government "can constitutionally pass laws or impose requirements *which aid all religions as against nonbelievers*, and neither can aid those religions based on a belief in the existence of God as against those religions founded on different beliefs." (Emphasis added.)

Unless we adhere to that principle, we do not give full support either to the Free Exercise Clause or to the Establishment Clause.

If a church can be exempted from paying real estate taxes, why may not it be made exempt from paying special assessments? The benefits in the two cases differ only in degree; and the burden on nonbelievers is likewise no different in kind.

⊥714 ⊥The religiously used real estate of the churches today constitutes a vast domain. Their assets total over $141 billion and their annual income at least $22 billion. And the extent to which they are feeding from the public trough in a variety of forms is alarming.

We are advised that since 1968 at least five States have undertaken to give subsidies to parochial and other private schools—Pennsylvania, Ohio, New York, Connecticut, and Rhode Island. And it is reported that under two federal Acts, the Act of April 11, 1965, 79 Stat. 27, and the Act of November 8, 1965, 79 Stat. 1219, *billions of dollars* have been granted to parochial and other private schools.

The federal grants to elementary and secondary schools under 79 Stat. 27 were made to the States which in turn made advances to elementary and secondary schools. Those amounts are not available.

But the federal grants to private institutions of higher education are revealed in Department of Health, Education, and Welfare, Digest of Educational Statistics. These show in billions of dollars the following:

1965-66	$1.4 billion
1966-67	$1.6 billion
1967-68	$1.7 billion
1968-69	$1.9 billion
1969-70	$2.1 billion

⊥It is an old, old problem. Madison adverted to it: ⊥715 "Are there not already examples in the U.S. of ecclesiastical wealth equally beyond its object and the foresight of those who laid the foundation of it? In the U.S. there is a double motive for fixing limits in this case, because wealth may increase not only from additional gifts, but from exorbitant advances in the value of the primitive one. In grants of vacant lands, and of lands in the vicinity of growing towns & Cities the increase of value is often such as if forseen, would essentially controul the liberality confirming them. The people of the U. S. owe their Independence & their liberty, to the wisdom of descrying in the minute tax of 3 pence on tea, the magnitude of the evil comprized in the precedent. Let them exert the same wisdom, in watching agst every evil lurking under plausible disguises, and growing up from small beginnings."

⊥If believers are entitled to public financial sup- ⊥716 port, so are nonbelievers. A believer and nonbeliever under the present law are treated differently because of the articles of their faith. Believers are doubtless comforted that the cause of religion is being fostered by this legislation. Yet one of the mandates of the First Amendment is to promote a viable, pluralistic society and to keep government neutral, not only between sects but between believers and nonbelievers. The present involvement of government in religion may seem *de minimis*. But it is, I fear, a long step down the Establishment path. Perhaps I have been misinformed. But as I have read the Constitution and its philosophy, I gathered that independence was the price of liberty.

I conclude that this tax exemption is unconstitutional.

SUNDAY WORK

A type of legislation that seems to be narrow in focus but which raises interesting church-state questions is that compelling observance of Sunday as a day of rest. Stated simply, this legislation prohibits most commercial activities on Sunday because of the state's strong interest in providing a day of rest for its population. These laws have been called a type of public welfare legislation.

There are, however, some exemptions from the general restrictions on Sunday labor. Exempted commercial enterprises are those involving "necessaries," i.e., those things which must be available to people all the time to enhance their safety, comfort, and enjoyment. Consequently, in addition to the sale of such items as food and drugs on Sunday, enterprises such as professional sports, amusement parks, and ice cream parlors are allowed to operate on the day of rest. The laws are intended to have the effect of prohibiting most people from working on Sunday so that they may rest, but allowing businesses which provide for basic human needs or which facilitate rest and recreation for the majority to remain open. The scope of this type of legislation and the extent and complexity of exemptions are clearly detailed in the cases that follow.

In the western world, the concept of a special day of rest goes back many centuries before the beginning of the Christian era. In the Ten Commandments one reads:

Remember the sabbath day, to keep it holy. Six days you shall labor, and do all your work; but the seventh day is a sabbath to the Lord your God; in it you shall not do any work, you, or your son, or your daughter, your manservant, or your maidservant, or your cattle, or the sojourner who is within your gates; for in six days the Lord made heaven and earth, the sea, and all that is in them, and rested the seventh day; therefore the Lord blessed the sabbath day and hallowed it. (Exodus 20:8-11, RSV)

As this passage indicates, the day of rest was to be the seventh day. It was of such strong religious significance that this rest day became obligatory for observant Jews.

Early in the second century of the Christian era a new day of rest gained widespread acceptance in the western world. The Christian religion, in commemoration of the resurrection of Jesus, adopted Sunday as its day of rest. Again, the day had very strong religious significance. In A.D. 321, as a part of the process which made Christianity the official religion of the Roman Empire, the Emperor Constantine decreed that Sunday be a day of rest. This law set the trend for most governments down to the present; the Sunday observance law has had a very wide acceptance.

In colonial America, the first Sunday observance law was promulgated in Virginia in 1610. It commanded that

no man or woman shall dare to violate or breake the Sabboth by any gaming, publique or private abroad, or at home, but duly sanctifie and observe the same, both himselfe and his familie, by preparing themselves at home with private prayer, that they may be the better fitted for the publique, according to the commandments of God, and the orders of our Church, as also every man and woman shall repaire in the morning to the divine service, and Sermons preached upon the Sabboth day, and in the afternoon to divine service, and Catechising, upon paine of the first fault to lose their provision, and allowance for the whole weeke following, for the second to lose the said allowance, and also to be whipt, and for the third to suffer death. [1]

Later, laws were added which specifically prohibited the sale of merchandise and goods on Sunday. Statutes of this type were found in all the colonies. After the adoption of the First Amendment, provisions requiring church attendance were dropped, but prohibitions against commercial activities on Sunday were retained. A very comprehensive presentation of the history of this type of legislation is given in the Supreme Court decisions themselves, especially the concurring opinion of Justice Frankfurter in McGOWAN v. MARYLAND (p. 292). [2]

The religious groups most directly affected by such laws are Jews and Seventh-day Adventists. Jews have always regarded the Biblical passage quoted above as divine law so that observant Jews believe that they have the obligation to observe the Sabbath (from sundown Friday to sundown Saturday, according to Biblical law) as a day of worship, meditation on religious themes, and cessation from work. Sabbath rest is a very important part of one's total religious life. Seventh-day Adventists, although definitely a Christian group, believe that the coming of Christ did not remove from the truly religious person the obligation to observe the seventh day as the day of worship. Because God, by resting from the labor of creation on the seventh day, established that pattern of life from the beginning of history, Adventists believe that it is a pattern which ought to be faithfully and carefully observed.

Observant Jews and Seventh-day Adventists have an obvious objection to Sunday laws: these statutes place an economic burden on Sabbatarians. The Sabbatarian refrains from doing business on Saturday because of religious belief while nonsabbatarian competitors proceed with business as usual; then one must not work on Sunday because of the Sunday law. While religion and the law have combined to allow him/her to work only five days in the week, nonsabbatarians have been able to work six. Consequently, the Sabbatarian argues that the Sunday law compels him/her to suffer an economic disadvantage because of religious belief.

In dealing with this issue, the Supreme Court, in 1961, handed down four decisions on the same day. Two of the cases dealt primarily with the Establishment Clause; two dealt primarily with the Free Exercise Clause. (Because the arguments were essentially the same in each type of case, only two cases, the most important of each type, are included in this book.)

In McGOWAN v. MARYLAND (p. 292) the establishment argument was raised by neither Jew nor Seventh-day Adventist, but by a discount store's employees who had been arrested for selling forbidden items on Sunday. Their argument was that the Sunday law was a violation of the Establishment Clause because it gave state sanction and coercion to the observance of the Christian day of worship. Because the state compelled the observance of the Christian day of worship, they had not been able to do business, thus suffering economic injury. [3]

The other case that raised primarily Establishment Clause consideration was *Two Guys from Harrison-Allentown, Inc.* v. *McGinley*. Essentially the same as the *McGowan* case, this case challenged a Pennsylvania statute. There were enough different facts, including questions about the term of a district attorney, to cause the

---

[1] H. Shelton Smith, Robert T. Handy, and Lefferts A. Loetscher, *American Christianity: An Historical Interpretation with Representative Documents*, 2 vols. (New York: Charles Scribner's Sons, 1960), 1:43.

[2] Additional historical material about Sunday laws may be found in Anson Phelps Stokes, *Church and State in the United States*, 3:153-76, and Leo Pfeffer, *Church, State, and Freedom* (Boston: Beacon Press, 1967), pp. 270-87.

[3] The appellants objected to the law on free exercise grounds also. But because they were challenging the law strictly on grounds of economic injury, and because they did not demonstrate that their own religious exercise had been affected, the Court set that question aside and dealt only with the establishment question. They also challenged the law on other than church-state grounds: specifically, that the Sunday law was a violation of the Equal Protection Clause of the Fourteenth Amendment. The opinions show that the Court was not persuaded by that argument.

Court to write a separate opinion, but its decision on the church-state issues was the same as in *McGowan*.

The primary case in which the free exercise issue was raised was BRAUNFELD v. BROWN (p. 316). Here the appellants were Orthodox Jews challenging a Pennsylvania statute. Although they also raised equal protection and establishment objections to the law, the case was decided on their free exercise contention. Appellants argued that they suffered economic injury not only because the state gave its sanction to the Christian day of worship but because, as practicing Jews, they were put at a competitive disadvantage by requirements of their religion (the argument spelled out above).

The other free exercise case was *Gallagher* v. *Crown Kosher Super Market*. The appellees were Orthodox Jews engaged in the kosher food business in Massachusetts. Because most of their customers were Orthodox Jews who were required by their religion to eat kosher food, and because they had traditionally done about one-third of their weekly business on Sunday, they argued that the state's Sunday law prohibited the free exercise of both themselves and their customers.

In all four cases, the Court found the Sunday laws to be constitutional. In this series of cases the Court used the "argument from history." That is, from time to time the Court, in finding a law constitutional or unconstitutional, will base its findings on the history of the practice under scrutiny. Has this practice been engaged in for a long time or did it originate rather recently? In either case, has it always been done the same way, or has the purpose and/or effect of the law changed during its history? The Court found the laws constitutional in these cases because the original Sunday laws had changed with the passage of time. Although they originally had a religious purpose, i.e., to protect the Christian day of worship for its proper observance, they had been secularized in that they had come to be regarded only as laws to provide a day of rest for laboring people. They no longer had a religious purpose, so they could not be said to be a violation of the Establishment Clause. The argument from history is frequently used in conjunction with other arguments to determine the constitutionality of the act. (Cf. WALZ v. TAX COMMISSION (p. 278), WISCONSIN v. YODER (p. 200), and Justice Brennan's concurring opinion in ABINGTON SCHOOL DISTRICT v. SCHEMPP (p.402)). In these Sunday law cases, however, the argument from history is essentially the determining factor in declaring the statutes constitutional, as it is in the more recent MARSH v. CHAMBERS (p. 350).

One should note that the dissent of Justice Douglas, which is included in the *McGowan* decision, applies to all four cases. It was the only dissent on the two Establishment Clause cases. In the free exercise cases, however, Justices Brennan and Stewart joined Douglas in dissent, making the vote six-to-three. The separate opinion of Justice Frankfurter, included in the *McGowan* case, was in essence a concurring opinion and was meant to apply to all four cases.

In these cases the Court mentioned that states could provide alternate ways of meeting their secular goals without imposing on the religious activities of Sabbatarians, e.g., they could designate Sunday as the day of rest but provide exemptions for those whose religion

required rest on another day, but they were not constitutionally required to do so. In 1962, in *Arlan's Department Store* v. *Kentucky*, the Court considered a law which contained such an exemption. The plaintiffs argued that in allowing Sabbatarians to keep their stores open on Sunday, while compelling nonsabbatarians to close theirs, the state was preferring religion over nonreligion, a violation of the Establishment Clause. The Court dismissed the appeal, stating that it did not present a substantial federal question, allowing the state courts' affirmation of the exemption to stand.

In *Kentucky Commission on Human Rights* v. *Kerns Bakery* a bakery employee, who had experienced religious conversion, refused to work on Sunday. When he was fired he sought relief through the state's civil rights commission, which found that the company could have accommodated plaintiff's work without "undue hardship," which it was required to do by a state law which forbade discrimination against an employee whose religious belief prevented work on his/her Sabbath. When the bakery contested the commission's decision in state court, the court ruled that the law was a violation of the Establishment Clause. On appeal, the state's highest court reversed, ruling that the law had the purpose of advancing equal employment opportunities for members of all faiths, that the law did not promote any religion in terms of either state sanction or finances, and that it did not unduly entangle religion and state. The United States Supreme Court refused to grant certiorari in 1983, allowing this state statute, which was virtually identical with the federal Civil Rights Act of 1964, to stand as not being violative of the Establishment Clause.

Finally, in 1985 the Court decided THORNTON v. CALDOR (p. 321), a case that dealt with the issue of whether a statute designed to accommodate the religious sensibilities of employees was contrary to Establishment Clause principles. (Between *McGowan* and *Braunfeld* in 1961 and *Thornton* the Court decided several other workplace cases, but they were decided on grounds other than establishment and are discussed elsewhere in this book (p. 142)). In 1977 Connecticut revised its Sunday closing law and Caldor, Inc. began opening some of its stores on Sunday. One of those was where Donald E. Thornton worked. A Presbyterian, Thornton worked on Sundays for a while, but then asked to be relieved of Sunday work in line with a Connecticut law which exempted from work on their Sabbath all those who requested such relief. The company responded with suggestions for alternative work schedules which were to Thornton's disadvantage and, indeed, transferred him to a different store in the chain at a reduced salary. Thornton resigned and appealed to the State Board of Mediation and Arbitration, claiming that the company had acted contrary to the statute. The Board and a state court found in Thornton's favor. The Supreme Court of Connecticut reversed, holding that the statute itself violated all three parts of the "*Lemon* test" of the Establishment Clause.

The United States Supreme Court, voting eight-to-one, agreed with the Connecticut Supreme Court, although it focused only on the "primary effect" test, rather than all three. Chief Justice Burger argued for the majority that the law mandated that one who observed a Sabbath day as a matter of religious conviction *must* be free from work that day by request, no matter what sort of burden it placed on employers and fellow employees. "The statute arms Sabbath observers with an absolute and unqualified right not to work on whatever day they designate as their Sabbath." Consequently, the law effectively made the Sabbath concerns of workers dominant over all secular concerns at the workplace. Such a law has the impermissible primary effect of advancing religion.

It is interesting to note that Thornton had died before the case reached the State Supreme Court. The case was carried on by the administrator of his estate. Neither the state court nor the United States Supreme Court declared the case moot, probably because Connecticut had intervened on behalf of Thornton and thus remained as a party who could be affected by the result. The result was not what the state had hoped for, however.

McGOWAN v. MARYLAND

366 U.S. 420
ON APPEAL FROM THE COURT OF APPEALS
OF MARYLAND
Argued December 8, 1960 — Decided May 29, 1961

⌐422   ⊥ *Mr. Chief Justice WARREN* delivered the opinion of the Court.

The issues in this case concern the constitutional validity of Maryland criminal statutes, commonly known as Sunday Closing Laws or Sunday Blue Laws. These statutes, with exceptions to be noted hereafter, generally proscribe all labor, business and other commercial activities on Sunday. The questions presented are whether the classifications within the statutes bring about a denial of equal protection of the law, whether the laws are so vague as to fail to give reasonable notice of the forbidden conduct and therefore violate due process, and whether the statutes are laws respecting an establishment of religion or prohibiting the free exercise thereof.

Appellants are seven employees of a large discount department store located on a highway in Anne Arundel County, Maryland. They were indicted for the Sunday sale of a three-ring loose-leaf binder, a can of floor wax, a stapler and staples, and a toy submarine in violation of Md. Ann. Code, Art. 27, § 521. Generally, this section prohibited, throughout the State, the Sunday sale of all merchandise except the retail sale of tobacco products, confectioneries, milk, ⌐423 bread, fruits, gasoline, oils, greases, ⊥drugs and medicines, and newspapers and periodicals. Recently amended, this section also now excepts from the general prohibition the retail sale in Anne Arundel County of all foodstuffs, automobile and boating accessories, flowers, toilet goods, hospital supplies and souvenirs. It now further provides that any retail establishment in Anne Arundel County which does not employ more than one person other than the owner may operate on Sunday.

Although appellants were indicted only under § 521, in order properly to consider several of the broad constitutional contentions, we must examine the whole body of Maryland Sunday laws. Several sections of the Maryland statutes are particularly relevant to evaluation of the issues presented. Section 492 of Md. Ann. Code, Art. 27, forbids all persons from doing any work or bodily labor on Sunday and forbids permitting children or servants to work on that day or to engage in fishing, hunting and unlawful pastimes or recreations. The section excepts all works of necessity and charity. Section 522 of Md. Ann. Code, Art. 27, disallows the opening or use of any dancing saloon, opera house, bowling alley or barber shop on Sunday. However, in addition to the exceptions noted above, Md. Ann. Code, Art. 27, § 509, exempts, for Anne Arundel County, the Sunday operation of any bathing beach, bathhouse, dancing saloon and amusement park, and activities incident thereto and retail sales of merchandise customarily sold at, or incidental to, the operation of the aforesaid occupations and businesses. Section 90 of Md. Ann. Code, Art. 2B, makes generally unlawful the sale of alcoholic beverages on Sunday. However, this section, and immediately succeeding ones, provide various immunities for the Sunday sale of different kinds of alcoholic beverages, at different hours during the day, by vendors holding different types of licenses, in different political divisions of the State— particularly ⊥ in Anne Arundel County.   ⌐424

The remaining statutory sections concern a myriad of exceptions for various counties, districts of counties, cities and towns throughout the State. Among the activities allowed in certain areas on Sunday are such sports as football, baseball, golf, tennis, bowling, croquet, basketball, lacrosse, soccer, hockey, swimming, softball, boating, fishing, skating, horseback riding, stock car racing and pool or billiards. Other immunized activities permitted in some regions of the State include group singing or playing of musical instruments; the exhibition of motion pictures; dancing; the operation of recreation centers, picnic grounds, swimming pools, skating rinks and miniature golf courses. The taking of oysters and the hunting or killing of game is generally forbidden, but shooting conducted by organized rod and gun clubs is permitted in one county. In some of the subdivisions within the State, the exempted Sunday activities are sanctioned throughout the day; in others, they may not commence until early afternoon or evening; in many, the activities may only be conducted during the afternoon and late in the evening. Certain localities do not permit the allowed Sunday activity to be carried on within one hundred yards of any church where religious services are being held. Local ordinances and regulations concerning certain limited activities supplement the State's statutory scheme. In Anne Arundel County, for example, slot machines, pinball machines and bingo may be played on Sunday.

Among other things, appellants contended at the trial that the Maryland statutes under which they were charged were contrary to the Fourteenth Amendment for the reasons stated at the outset of this opinion. Appellants were convicted and each was fined five dollars and costs. The Maryland Court ⌐425 of Appeals affirmed; ⊥on appeal, we noted probable jurisdiction.

I

Appellants argue that the Maryland statutes violate the "Equal Protection" Clause of the Fourteenth Amendment on several counts. First, they contend that the classifications contained in the statutes concerning which commodities may or may not be sold on Sunday are without rational and substantial relation to the object of the legislation. Specifically, appellants allege that the statutory exemptions for the Sunday sale of the merchandise mentioned above render arbitrary the statute under which they were convicted. Appellants further allege that § 521 is capricious because of the exemptions for the operation of the various amusements that have been listed and because slot machines, pin-ball machines, and bingo are legalized and are freely played on Sunday.

The standards under which this proposition is to be evaluated have been set forth many times by this Court. Although no precise formula has been developed, the Court has held that the Fourteenth Amendment permits the States a wide scope of discretion in enacting laws which affect some groups of citizens differently than others. The constitutional safeguard is offended only if the classification rests on grounds wholly irrelevant to the achievement of the State's objective. State legislatures are presumed to have acted within their constitutional power de- ⌐426 spite the fact that, in practice, their laws ⊥result in some inequality. A statutory discrimination will not be set aside if any state of facts reasonably may be conceived to justify it.

It would seem that a legislature could reasonably find that the Sunday sale of the exempted commodities was necessary either for the health of the populace or for the enhancement of the recreational atmosphere of the day— that a family which takes a Sunday ride into the country will need gasoline for the automobile and may find pleasant a soft drink or fresh fruit; that those who go to the beach may wish ice cream or some other item normally sold there; that some people will prefer alcoholic beverages or games of chance to add to their relaxation; that newspapers and drug products should always be available to the public.

The record is barren of any indication that this apparently reasonable basis does not exist, that the statutory distinctions are invidious, that local tradition and custom might not rationally call for this ⌐427 legislative treatment. ⊥Likewise, the fact that these exemptions exist and deny some vendors and operators the day of rest and recreation contemplated by the legislature does not render the statutes violative

of equal protection since there would appear to be many valid reasons for these exemptions, as stated above, and no evidence to dispel them.

Secondly, appellants contend that the statutory arrangement which permits only certain Anne Arundel County retailers to sell merchandise essential to, or customarily sold at, or incidental to, the operation of bathing beaches, amusement parks et cetera is contrary to the "Equal Protection" Clause because it discriminates unreasonably against retailers in other Maryland counties. But we have held that the Equal Protection Clause relates to equality between persons as such, rather than between areas and that territorial uniformity is not a constitutional prerequisite. With particular reference to the State of Maryland, we have noted that the prescription of different substantive offenses in different counties is generally a matter for legislative discretion. We find no invidious discrimination here.

Thirdly, appellants contend that this same statutory provision, Art. 27, § 509, violates the "Equal Protection" Clause because it permits only certain merchants within Anne Arundel County (operators of bathing beaches and amusement parks et cetera) to sell merchandise customarily sold at these places while forbidding its sale by other vendors of this merchandise, such as appellants' employer. Here again, it would seem that a legislature ⊥could rea- ⌐428 sonably find that these commodities, necessary for the health and recreation of its citizens, should only be sold on Sunday by those vendors at the locations where the commodities are most likely to be immediately put to use. Such a determination would seem to serve the consuming public and at the same time secure Sunday rest for those employees, like appellants, of all other retail establishments. In addition, the enforcement problems which would accrue if large retail establishments, like appellants' employer, were permitted to remain open on Sunday but were restricted to the sale of the merchandise in question would be far greater than the problems accruing if only beach and amusement park vendors were exempted. Here again, there has been no indication of the unreasonableness of this differentiation. On the record before us, we cannot say that these statutes do not provide equal protection of the laws.

II

Another question presented by appellants is whether Art. 27, § 509, which exempts the Sunday retail sale of "merchandise essential to, or customarily ⊥sold at, or incidental to, the operation of" bath- ⌐429 ing beaches, amusement parks et cetera in Anne Arundel County, is unconstitutionally vague. We believe that business people of ordinary intelligence in the position of appellants' employer would be able to know what exceptions are encompassed by the statute either as a matter of ordinary commercial knowledge or by simply making a reasonable investigation at a nearby bathing beach or amusement park within the county. Under these circumstances, there is no necessity to guess at the statute's meaning in order to determine what conduct it makes criminal. Questions concerning proof that the items appellants sold were customarily sold at, or incidental to the operation of, a bathing beach or amusement park were not raised in the Maryland Court of Appeals, nor are they raised here. Thus, we cannot consider the matter.

III

The final questions for decision are whether the Maryland Sunday Closing Laws conflict with the Federal Constitution's provisions for religious liberty. First, appellants contend here that the statutes applicable to Anne Arundel County violate the constitutional guarantee of freedom of religion in that the statutes' effect is to prohibit the free exercise of religion in contravention of the First Amendment, made applicable to the States by the Fourteenth Amendment. But appellants allege only economic injury to themselves; they do not allege any infringement of their own religious freedoms due to Sunday closing. In fact, the record is silent as to what appellants' religious beliefs are. Since the general rule is that "a litigant may only assert his own constitutional rights or immunities," *United States* v. *Raines*, we hold that appellants have no standing to raise this contention. Furthermore, since appellants do not specifically allege that the statutes infringe upon the religious beliefs of the department store's ⌐430 present or prospective patrons, we ⊥ have no occasion here to consider the standing question of *Pierce* v. *Society of Sisters*. Those persons whose religious rights are allegedly impaired by the statutes are not without effective ways to assert these rights. Appellants present no weighty countervailing policies here to cause an exception to our general principles.

Secondly, appellants contend that the statutes violate the guarantee of separation of church and state in that the statutes are laws respecting an establishment of religion contrary to the First Amendment, made applicable to the States by the Fourteenth Amendment. If the purpose of the "establishment" clause was only to insure protection for the "free exercise" of religion, then what we have said above concerning appellants' standing to raise the "free exercise" contention would appear to be true here. However, the writings of Madison, who was the First Amendment's architect, demonstrate that the establishment of a religion was equally feared because of its tendencies to political tyranny and subversion of civil authority. Thus, in *Everson* v. *Board of Education*, the Court permitted a district taxpayer to challenge, on "establishment" grounds, a state statute which authorized district boards of education to reimburse parents for fares paid for the transportation of their children to both public and Catholic

schools. Appellants here concededly have suffered direct economic injury, allegedly due to the imposition on them of the tenets of the Christian religion. We find that, in these circum⊥stances, these appellants ⌐431 have standing to complain that the statutes are laws respecting an establishment of religion.

The essence of appellants' "establishment" argument is that Sunday is the Sabbath day of the predominant Christian sects; that the purpose of the enforced stoppage of labor on that day is to facilitate and encourage church attendance; that the purpose of setting Sunday as a day of universal rest is to induce people with no religion or people with marginal religious beliefs to join the predominant Christian sects; that the purpose of the atmosphere of tranquility created by Sunday closing is to aid the conduct of church services and religious observance of the sacred day. In substantiating their "establishment" argument, appellants rely on the wording of the present Maryland statutes, on earlier versions of the current Sunday laws and on prior judicial characterizations of these laws by the Maryland Court of Appeals. Although only the constitutionality of § 521, the section under which appellants have been convicted, is immediately before us in this litigation, inquiry into the history of Sunday Closing Laws in our country, in addition to an examination of the Maryland Sunday closing statutes in their entirety and of their history, is relevant to the decision of whether the Maryland Sunday law in question is one respecting an establishment of religion. There is no dispute that the original laws which dealt with Sunday labor were motivated by religious forces. But what we must decide is whether present Sunday legislation, having undergone extensive changes from the earliest forms, still retains its religious character.

Sunday Closing Laws go far back into American history, having been brought to the colonies with a background of English legislation dating to the thirteenth century. In 1237, Henry III forbade the frequenting of markets on ⊥Sunday; the Sunday ⌐432 showing of wools at the staple was banned by Edward III in 1354; in 1409, Henry IV prohibited the playing of unlawful games on Sunday; Henry VI proscribed Sunday fairs in churchyards in 1444 and, four years later, made unlawful all fairs and markets and all showings of any goods or merchandise; Edward VI disallowed Sunday bodily labor by several injunctions in the mid-sixteenth century; various Sunday sports and amusements were restricted in 1625 by Charles I. The law of the colonies to the time of the Revolution and the basis of the Sunday laws in the States was 29 Charles II, c. 7 (1677). It provided, in part: "For the better observation and keeping holy the Lord's day, commonly called Sunday: be it enacted . . . that all the laws enacted and in force concerning the observation of the day, *and repairing to the church thereon*, be carefully put in execution; and that all and every person and persons whatsoever shall upon every Lord's day apply themselves to the observation of the same, by exercising themselves thereon in the duties of piety and true religion, publicly and privately; and that no tradesman, artificer, workman, laborer, or other person whatsoever, *shall do or exercise any worldly labor or business or work* of their ordinary callings upon the Lord's day, or any part thereof (works of necessity and charity only excepted); . . . and that no person or persons whatsoever shall publicly cry, show forth, or expose for sale any wares, merchandise, fruit, herbs, goods, or chattels, whatsoever, upon the Lord's day, or any part thereof. . . ." (Emphasis added).

⊥433 ⊥Observation of the above language, and of that of the prior mandates, reveals clearly that the English Sunday legislation was in aid of the established church.

The American colonial Sunday restrictions arose soon after settlement. Starting in 1650, the Plymouth Colony proscribed servile work, unnecessary traveling, sports, and the sale of alcoholic beverages on the Lord's day and enacted laws concerning church attendance. The Massachusetts Bay Colony and the Connecticut and New Haven Colonies enacted similar prohibitions, some even earlier in the seventeenth century. The religious orientation of the colonial statutes was equally apparent. For example, a 1629 Massachusetts Bay instruction began, "And to the end the Sabbath may be celebrated in a religious manner. . . ." A 1653 enactment spoke of Sunday activities "which things tend much to the dishonor of God, the reproach of religion, and the profanation of his holy Sabbath, the sanctification whereof is sometimes put for all duties immediately respecting the service of God. . . ." These laws persevered after the Revolution and, at about the time of the First Amendment's adoption, each of the colonies had laws of some sort restricting Sunday labor.

⊥434 But, despite the strongly religious origin of these laws, beginning before the eighteenth century, nonreligious ⊥arguments for Sunday closing began to be heard more distinctly and the statutes began to lose some of their totally religious flavor. In the middle 1700's, Blackstone wrote, "[T]he keeping one day in the seven holy, as a time of relaxation and refreshment as well as for public worship, is of admirable service to a state considered merely as a civil institution. It humanizes, by the help of conversation and society, the manners of the lower classes; which would otherwise degenerate into a sordid ferocity and savage selfishness of spirit; it enables the industrious workman to pursue his occupation in the ensuing week with health and cheerfulness."

A 1788 English statute dealing with chimney sweeps, in addition to providing for their Sunday religious affairs, also regulated their hours of work. The preamble to a 1679 Rhode Island enactment stated that the reason for the ban on Sunday employment was that "persons being evil minded, have

presumed to employ in servile labor, more than necessity requireth, their servants. . . ." The New York law of 1788 omitted the term "Lord's day" and substituted "the first day of the week commonly called Sunday." Similar changes marked the Maryland statutes, discussed below. With the advent of the First Amendment, the colonial provisions requiring church attendance were soon repealed.

More recently, further secular justifications have been advanced for making Sunday a day of rest, a day when people may recover from the labors of the week just passed and may physically and mentally prepare for the week's work to come. In England, during the First World War, a committee investigating the health conditions of munitions workers reported that "if the maximum output is to be secured and maintained for any length of ⊥time, a weekly period of rest must be allowed. . . . On economic and social grounds alike this weekly period of rest is best provided on Sunday." ⊥435

The proponents of Sunday closing legislation are no longer exclusively representatives of religious interests. Recent New Jersey Sunday legislation was supported by labor groups and trade associations; modern English Sunday legislation was promoted by the National Federation of Grocers and supported by the National Chamber of Trade, the Drapers' Chamber of Trade, and the National Union of Shop Assistants.

Throughout the years, state legislatures have modified, deleted from and added to their Sunday statutes. As evidenced by the New Jersey laws mentioned above, current changes are commonplace. Almost every State in our country presently has some type of Sunday regulation and over forty possess a relatively comprehensive system. Some of our States now enforce their Sunday legislation through Departments of Labor. Thus have Sunday laws evolved from the wholly religious sanctions that originally were enacted.

Moreover, litigation over Sunday closing laws is not novel. Scores of cases may be found in the state appellate courts relating to sundry phases of Sunday enactments. Religious objections have been raised there on numerous occasions but sustained only once, in *Ex parte Newman*; and that decision was overruled three years later, in *Ex parte Andrews*. A substantial number of cases in varying postures bearing ⊥on state Sunday legislation have reached this Court. Although none raising the issues now presented have gained plenary hearing, language used in some of these cases further evidences the evolution of Sunday laws as temporal statutes. Mr. Justice Field wrote in *Soon Hing* v. *Crowley*: "Laws setting aside Sunday as a day of rest are upheld, not from any right of the government to legislate for the promotion of religious observances, but from its right to protect all persons from the physical and moral debasement which comes from uninterrupted labor. Such laws have always been deemed benefi- ⊥436 cent and merciful laws, especially to the poor and dependent, to the laborers in our factories and workshops and in the heated rooms of our cities; and their validity has been sustained by the highest courts of the States. . . ."

⊥437 ⊥ Before turning to the Maryland legislation now here under attack, an investigation of what historical position Sunday Closing Laws have occupied with reference to the First Amendment should be undertaken.

This Court has considered the happenings surrounding the Virginia General Assembly's enactment of "An act for establishing religious freedom," written by Thomas Jefferson and sponsored by James Madison, as best reflecting the long and intensive struggle for religious freedom in America, as particularly relevant in the search for the First Amendment's meaning. In 1776, nine years before the bill's

⊥438 ⊥ passage, Madison co-authored Virginia's Declaration of Rights which provided, *inter alia*, that "all men are equally entitled to the free exercise of religion, according to the dictates of conscience. . . ." Virginia had had Sunday legislation since early in the seventeenth century; in 1776, the laws penalizing "maintaining any opinions in matters of religion, *forbearing to repair to church*, or the exercising any mode of worship whatsoever" (emphasis added), were repealed, and all dissenters were freed from the taxes levied for the support of the established church. The Sunday labor prohibitions remained; apparently, they were not believed to be inconsistent with the newly enacted Declaration of Rights. Madison had sought also to have the Declaration expressly condemn the existing Virginia establishment. This hope was finally realized when "A Bill for Establishing Religious Freedom" was passed in 1785. In this same year, Madison presented to Virginia legislators "A Bill for Punishing . . . Sabbath Breakers" which provided, in part: "If any person on Sunday shall himself be found labouring at his own or any other trade or calling, or shall employ his apprentices, servants or slaves in labour, or other business, except it be in the ordinary houshold offices of daily necessity, or other work of necessity or charity, he shall forfeit the sum of ten shillings for every such offence, deeming every apprentice, servant, or slave so employed, and every day he shall be so employed as constituting a distinct offence."

This became law the following year and remained during the time that Madison fought for the First Amendment in the Congress. It was the law of Vir-

⊥439 ginia, and similar ⊥ laws were in force in other States, when Madison stated at the Virginia ratification convention: "Happily for the states, they enjoy the utmost freedom of religion. . . . Fortunately for this commonwealth, a majority of the people are decidedly against any exclusive establishment. I believe it to be so in the other states. . . . I can appeal to my uniform conduct on this subject, that I have warmly supported religious freedom."

In 1799, Virginia pronounced "An act for establishing religious freedom" as "a true exposition of the principles of the bill of rights and constitution," and repealed all subsequently enacted legislation deemed inconsistent with it. Virginia's statute banning Sunday labor stood. . . .

⊥ But in order to dispose of the case before us, we   ⊥440 must consider the standards by which the Maryland statutes are to be measured. Here, a brief review of the First Amendment's background proves helpful. The First Amendment states that "Congress shall make no law respecting an establishment of religion. . . ." The Amendment was proposed by James Madison on June 8, 1789, in the House of Representatives. It then read, in part: "The civil rights of none shall be abridged on account of religious belief or worship, *nor shall any national religion be established* nor shall the full and equal rights of conscience be in any manner, or on any pretext, infringed." (Emphasis added.)

We are told that Madison added the word "national" to meet the scruples of States which then had an established church. ⊥ After being referred to   ⊥441 committee, it was considered by the House, on August 15, 1789, acting as a Committee of the Whole. Some assistance in determining the scope of the Amendment's proscription of establishment may be found in that debate.

In its report to the House, the committee, to which the subject of amendments to the Constitution had been submitted, recommended the insertion of the language, "no religion shall be established by law." Mr. Gerry "said it would read better if it was, that no religious doctrine shall be established by law." Mr. Madison "said, he apprehended the meaning of the words to be, that Congress should not establish a religion, and enforce the legal observation of it by law, nor compel men to worship God in any manner contrary to their conscience. . . . He believed that the people feared one sect might obtain a pre-eminence, or two combine together, and establish a religion to which they would compel others to conform."

The Amendment, as it passed the House of Representatives nine days later, read, in part: "Congress shall make no law establishing religion. . . ."

It passed the Senate on September 9, 1789, reading, in part: "Congress shall make no law establishing articles of faith, or a mode of worship. . . ."

An early commentator opined that the "real object of the amendment was . . . to prevent any national ecclesiastical establishment, which should give to an hierarchy the exclusive patronage of the national government." 3 Story, Commentaries on the Constitution of the United States, 728. But, the First Amendment, in its final form, ⊥ did not simply bar a   ⊥442 congressional enactment *establishing a church*; it forbade all laws *respecting an establishment of religion*. Thus, this Court has given the Amendment a "broad interpretation . . . in the light of its history and the evils it was designed forever to suppress. . . ." *Everson* v. *Board of Education*. It has found that the First and Fourteenth Amendments afford protection against religious establishment far more extensive than merely to forbid a national or state church. Thus, in *McCollum* v. *Board of Education*, the Court held that the action of a board of education, permitting religious instruction during school hours in public school buildings and requiring those children who chose not to attend to remain in their classrooms, to be contrary to the "Establishment" Clause.

However, it is equally true that the "Establishment" Clause does not ban federal or state regulation of conduct whose reason or effect merely happens to coincide or harmonize with the tenets of some or all religions. In many instances, the Congress or state legislatures conclude that the general welfare of society, wholly apart from any religious considerations, demands such regulation. Thus, for temporal purposes, murder is illegal. And the fact that this agrees with the dictates of the Judaeo-Christian religions while it may disagree with others does not invalidate the regulation. So too with the questions of adultery and polygamy. The same could be said of theft, fraud, etc., because those offenses were also proscribed in the Decalogue. . . .

⊥444   ⊥In light of the evolution of our Sunday Closing Laws through the centuries, and of their more or less recent emphasis upon secular considerations, it is not difficult to discern that as presently written and administered, most of them, at least, are of a secular rather than of a religious character, and that presently they bear no relationship to establishment of religion as those words are used in the Constitution of the United States.

Throughout this century and longer, both the federal and state governments have oriented their activities very largely toward improvement of the health, safety, recreation and general well-being of
⊥445   our citizens. Nu⊥merous laws affecting public health, safety factors in industry, laws affecting hours and conditions of labor of women and children, week-end diversion at parks and beaches, and cultural activities of various kinds, now point the way toward the good life for all. Sunday Closing Laws, like those before us, have become part and parcel of this great governmental concern wholly apart from their original purposes or connotations. The present purpose and effect of most of them is to provide a uniform day of rest for all citizens; the fact that this day is Sunday, a day of particular significance for the dominant Christian sects, does not bar the State from achieving its secular goals. To say that the States cannot prescribe Sunday as a day of rest for these purposes solely because centuries ago such laws had their genesis in religion would give a constitutional interpretation of hostility to the public welfare rather than one of mere separation of church and State.

We now reach the Maryland statutes under review. The title of the major series of sections of the Maryland Code dealing with Sunday closing—Art. 27, §§ 492-534C—is "Sabbath Breaking"; § 492 proscribes work or bodily labor on the "Lord's day," and forbids persons to "profane the Lord's day," by gaming, fishing et cetera; § 522 refers to Sunday as the "Sabbath day." As has been mentioned above, many of the exempted Sunday activities in the various localities of the State may only be conducted during the afternoon and late evening; most Christian church services, of course, are held on Sunday morning and early Sunday evening. Finally, as previously noted, certain localities do not permit the allowed Sunday activities to be carried on within one hundred yards of any church where religious services are being held. This is the totality of the evidence of religious purpose which may be gleaned from the face of the present statute and from its operative effect.

⊥The predecessors of the existing Maryland   ⊥446
Sunday laws are undeniably religious in origin. The first Maryland statute dealing with Sunday activities, enacted in 1649, was entitled "An Act concerning Religion." It made it criminal to "profane the Sabbath or Lords day called Sunday by frequent swearing, drunkennes or by any uncivill or disorderly recreation, or by working on that day when absolute necessity doth not require it." A 1692 statute entitled "An Act for the Service of Almighty God and the Establishment of the Protestant Religion within this Province," after first stating the importance of keeping the Lord's Day holy and sanctified and expressing concern with the breach of its observance throughout the State, then enacted a Sunday labor prohibition which was the obvious precursor of the present § 492. There was a re-enactment in 1696 entitled "An Act for Sanctifying & keeping holy the Lord's Day Commonly called Sunday." By 1723, the Sabbath-breaking section of the statute assumed the present form of § 492, omitting the specific prohibition against Sunday swearing and the patently religiously motivated title.

There are judicial statements in early Maryland decisions which tend to support appellants' position. In an 1834 case involving a contract calling for delivery on Sun⊥day, the Maryland Court of Appeals re-   ⊥447
marked that "Ours is a christian community, and a day set apart as the day of rest, is the day consecrated by the resurrection of our Saviour, and embraces the twenty-four hours next ensuing the midnight of Saturday." *Kilgour* v. *Miles*. This language was cited with approval in *Judefind* v. *State*. It was also stated there: "It is undoubtedly true that rest from secular employment on Sunday does have a tendency to foster and encourage the Christian religion—of all sects and denominations that observe that day—as rest from work and ordinary occupation enables many to engage in public worship who probably would not otherwise do so. But it would scarcely be asked of a Court, in what professes to be

a Christian land, to declare a law unconstitutional because it requires rest from bodily labor on Sunday, (except works of necessity and charity,) and *thereby* promotes the cause of Christianity. If the Christian religion is, incidentally or otherwise, benefited or fostered by having this day of rest, as it undoubtedly is, there is all the more reason for the enforcement of laws that help to preserve it. Whilst Courts have generally sustained Sunday laws as 'civil regulations,' their decisions will have no less weight if they are shown to be in accordance with divine law as well as human."

But it should be noted that, throughout the *Judefind* decision, the Maryland court specifically rejected the contention that the laws interfered with religious liberty and stated that the laws' purpose was to provide the "advantages of having a weekly day of rest, 'from a mere physical and political standpoint.' "

Considering the language and operative effect of the current statutes, we no longer find the blanket

⌐448 prohibition ⊥against Sunday work or bodily labor. To the contrary we find that § 521 of Art. 27, the section which appellants violated, permits the Sunday sale of tobaccos and sweets and a long list of sundry articles which we have enumerated above; we find that § 509 of Art. 27 permits the Sunday operation of bathing beaches, amusement parks and similar facilities; we find that Art. 2B, § 28, permits the Sunday sale of alcoholic beverages, products strictly forbidden by predecessor statutes; we are told that Anne Arundel County allows Sunday bingo and the Sunday playing of pinball machines and slot machines, activities generally condemned by prior Maryland Sunday legislation. Certainly, these are not works of charity or necessity. Section 521's current stipulation that shops with only one employee may remain open on Sunday does not coincide with a religious purpose. These provisions, along with those which permit various sports and entertainments on Sunday, seem clearly to be fashioned for the purpose of providing a´ Sunday atmosphere of recreation, cheerfulness, repose and enjoyment. Coupled with the general proscription against other types of work, we believe that the air of the day is one of relaxation rather than one of religion.

The existing Maryland Sunday laws are not simply verbatim re-enactments of their religiously oriented antecedents. Only § 492 retains the appellation of "Lord's day" and even that section no longer makes recitation of religious purpose. It does talk in terms of "profan[ing] the Lord's day," but other sections

⌐449 permit the activities ⊥previously thought to be profane. Prior denunciation of Sunday drunkenness is now gone. Contemporary concern with these statutes is evidenced by the dozen changes made in 1959 and by the recent enactment of a majority of the exceptions.

Finally, the relevant pronouncements of the Maryland Court of Appeals dispel any argument that the statutes' announced purpose is religious. In *Hiller* v. *Maryland*, the court had before it a Baltimore ordinance prohibiting Sunday baseball. The court said: "What the eminent chief judge said with respect to police enactments which deal with the protection of the public health, morals and safety apply with equal force to those which are concerned with the peace, order and quiet of the community on Sunday, for these social conditions are well recognized heads of the police power. Can the Court say that this ordinance has no real and substantial relation to the peace and order and quiet of Sunday, as a day of rest, in the City of Baltimore?"

And the Maryland court declared in its decision in the instant case: "The legislative plan is plain. It is to compel a day of rest from work, permitting only activities which are necessary or recreational." *McGowan* v. *State*. After engaging in the close scrutiny demanded of us when First Amendment liberties are at issue, we accept the State Supreme Court's determination that the statutes' present purpose and effect is not to aid religion but to set aside a day of rest and recreation.

But this does not answer all of appellants' contentions. We are told that the State has other means at its disposal ⊥to accomplish its secular purpose, oth-   ⌐45 er courses that would not even remotely or incidentally give state aid to religion. On this basis, we are asked to hold these statutes invalid on the ground that the State's power to regulate conduct in the public interest may only be executed in a way that does not unduly or unnecessarily infringe upon the religious provisions of the First Amendment. However relevant this argument may be, we believe that the factual basis on which it rests is not supportable. It is true that if the State's interest were simply to provide for its citizens a periodic respite from work, a regulation demanding that everyone rest one day in seven, leaving the choice of the day to the individual, would suffice.

However, the State's purpose is not merely to provide a one-day-in-seven work stoppage. In addition to this, the State seeks to set one day apart from all others as a day of rest, repose, recreation and tranquility—a day which all members of the family and community have the opportunity to spend and enjoy together, a day on which there exists relative quiet and disassociation from the everyday intensity of commercial activities, a day on which people may visit friends and relatives who are not available during working days.

⊥Obviously, a State is empowered to determine   ⌐45 that a rest-one-day-in-seven statute would not accomplish this purpose; that it would not provide for a general cessation of activity, a special atmosphere of tranquility, a day which all members of the family or friends and relatives might spend together. Furthermore, it seems plain that the problems involved in enforcing such a provision would be exceedingly more difficult than those in enforcing a common-day-of-rest provision.

Moreover, it is common knowledge that the first day of the week has come to have special significance as a rest day in this country. People of all religions and ⊥people with no religion regard Sunday as a time for family activity, for visiting friends and relatives, for late sleeping, for passive and active entertainments, for dining out, and the like. Sunday is a day apart from all others. The cause is irrelevant; the fact exists. It would seem unrealistic for enforcement purposes and perhaps detrimental to the general welfare to require a State to choose a common day of rest other than that which most persons would select of their own accord. For these reasons, we hold that the Maryland statutes are not laws respecting an establishment of religion.

The distinctions between the statutes in the case before us and the state action in *McCollum* v. *Board of Education*, the only case in this Court finding a violation of the "Establishment" Clause, lend further substantiation to our conclusion. In *McCollum*, state action permitted religious instruction in public school buildings during school hours and required students not attending the religious instruction to remain in their classrooms during that time. The Court found that this system had the effect of coercing the children to attend religious classes; no such coercion to attend church services is present in the situation at bar. In *McCollum*, the only alternative available to the nonattending students was to remain in their classrooms; the alternatives open to nonlaboring persons in the instant case are far more diverse. In *McCollum*, there was direct cooperation between state officials and religious ministers; no such direct participation exists under the Maryland laws. In *McCollum*, tax-supported buildings were used to aid religion; in the ⊥instant case, no tax monies are being used in aid of religion.

Finally, we should make clear that this case deals only with the constitutionality of § 521 of the Maryland statute before us. We do not hold that Sunday legislation may not be a violation of the "Establishment" Clause if it can be demonstrated that its purpose—evidenced either on the face of the legislation, in conjunction with its legislative history, or in its operative effect—is to use the State's coercive power to aid religion.

Accordingly, the decision is *Affirmed*.

.　.　.　.　.

⊥Separate opinion of *Mr. Justice FRANK-FURTER*, whom *Mr. Justice HARLAN* joins. *

So deeply do the issues raised by these cases cut that it is not surprising that no one opinion can

---

* NOTE: This opinion applies also to *Two Guys from Harrison-Allentown, Inc.*, v. *McGinley, Braunfeld et al.* v. *Brown*, and *Gallagher* v. *Crown Kosher Super Market*.

wholly express the views even of all the members of the Court who join in its result. Individual opinions in constitutional controversies have been the practice throughout the Court's history. Such expression of differences in view or even in emphasis converging toward the same result makes for the clarity of candor and thereby enhances the authority of the judicial process.

For me considerations are determinative here which call for separate statement. The long history of Sunday legislation, so decisive if we are to view the statutes now ⊥attacked in a perspective wider than that which is furnished by our own necessarily limited outlook, cannot be conveyed by a partial recital of isolated instances or events. The importance of that history derives from its continuity and fullness—from the massive testimony which it bears to the evolution of statutes controlling Sunday labor and to the forces which have, during three hundred years of Anglo-American history at the least, changed those laws, transmuted them, made them the vehicle of mixed and complicated aspirations. Since I find in the history of these statutes insights controllingly relevant to the constitutional issues before us, I am constrained to set that history forth in detail. And I also deem it incumbent to state how I arrive at concurrence with *The CHIEF JUSTICE'S* principal conclusions without drawing on *Everson* v. *Board of Education*.

I

Because the long colonial struggle for disestablishment—the struggle to free all men, whatever their theological views, from state-compelled obligation to acknowledge and support state-favored faiths—made indisputably fundamental to our American culture the principle that the enforcement of religious belief as such is no legitimate concern of civil government, this Court has held that the Fourteenth Amendment embodies and applies against the States freedoms that are loosely indicated by the not rigidly precise but revealing phrase "separation of church and state." The general principles of church-state separation were found to be included in the Amendment's Due Process Clause in view of the meaning which the presuppositions of our society infuse into the concept of "liberty" protected by the clause. This is the source of the limitations imposed upon the States. To the extent that those limitations ⊥are akin to the restrictions which the First Amendment places upon the action of the central government, it is because—as with the freedom of thought and speech of which Mr. Justice Cardozo spoke in *Palko* v. *Connecticut*—it is accurate to say concerning the principle that a government must neither establish nor suppress religious belief, that "With rare aberrations a pervasive recognition of that truth can be traced in our history, political and legal."

But the several opinions in *Everson* and *McCollum*, and in *Zorach* v. *Clauson* make sufficiently clear that"separation" is not a self-defining concept.

"[A]greement, in the abstract, that the First Amendment was designed to erect a 'wall of separation between church and State,' does not preclude a clash of views as to what the wall separates." By its nature, religion—in the comprehensive sense in which the Constitution uses that word—is an aspect of human thought and action which profoundly relates the life of man to the world in which he lives. Religious beliefs pervade, and religious institutions have traditionally regulated, virtually all human activity. It is a postulate of American life, reflected specifically in the First Amendment to the Constitution but not there alone, that those beliefs and institutions shall continue, as the needs and longings of the people shall inspire them, to exist, to function, to grow, to wither, and to exert with whatever innate strength they may contain their many influences upon men's conduct, free of the dictates and directions of the state. However, this freedom does not and cannot furnish the adherents of religious creeds entire insulation from every civic obligation. As the state's interest in the individual becomes more comprehensive, its concerns and the concerns of religion perforce overlap. State codes and the dictates of ⌐462 faith touch the same activities. ⊥Both aim at human good, and in their respective views of what is good for man they may concur or they may conflict. No constitutional command which leaves religion free can avoid this quality of interplay.

Innumerable civil regulations enforce conduct which harmonizes with religious canons. State prohibitions of murder, theft and adultery reinforce commands of the decalogue. Nor do such regulations, in their coincidence with tenets of faith, always support equally the beliefs of all religious sects: witness the civil laws forbidding usury and enforcing monogamy. Because these laws serve ends which are within the appropriate scope of secular state interest, they may be enforced against those whose religious beliefs do not proscribe, and even sanction, the activity which the law condemns.

This is not to say that government regulations which find support in their appropriateness to the achievement of secular, civil ends are invariably valid under the First or Fourteenth Amendment, whatever their effects in the sphere of religion. If the value to society of achieving the object of a particular regulation is demonstrably outweighed by the impediment to which the regulation subjects those whose religious practices are curtailed by it, or if the object sought by the regulation could with equal effect be achieved by alternative means which do not substantially impede those religious practices, the regulation cannot be sustained. This was the ground upon which the Court struck down municipal license taxes as applied to religious colporteurs in *Follett* v. *Town of McCormick, Murdock* v. *Pennsylvania*, and *Jones* v. *Opelika*. In each of those cases it was be- ⌐463 lieved that the State's need for revenue, which could be ⊥satisfied by taxing any of a variety of sources,

did not justify a levy imposed upon an activity which in the light of history could reasonably be viewed as sacramental. But see *Cox* v. *New Hampshire*, in which the Court, balancing the public benefits secured by a regulatory measure against the degree of impairment of individual conduct expressive of religious faith which it entailed, sustained the prohibition of an activity similarly regarded by its practicants as sacramental. And see *Prince* v. *Massachusetts*.

Within the discriminating phraseology of the First Amendment, distinction has been drawn between cases raising "establishment" and "free exercise" questions. Any attempt to formulate a bright-line distinction is bound to founder. In view of the competion among religious creeds, whatever "establishes" one sect disadvantages another, and vice versa. But it is possible historically, and therefore helpful analytically—no less for problems arising under the Fourteenth Amendment, illuminated as that Amendment is by our national experience, than for problems arising under the First—to isolate in general terms the two largely overlapping areas of concern reflected in the two constitutional phrases, "establishment" and "free exercise," and which emerge more ⊥or less clearly from the background of ⌐464 events and impulses which gave those phrases birth.

In assuring the free exercise of religion, the Framers of the First Amendment were sensitive to the then recent history of those persecutions and impositions of civil disability with which sectarian majorities in virtually all of the Colonies had visited deviation in the matter of conscience. This protection of unpopular creeds, however, was not to be the full extent of the Amendment's guarantee of freedom from governmental intrusion in matters of faith. The battle in Virginia, hardly four years won, where James Madison had led the forces of disestablishment in successful opposition to Patrick Henry's proposed Assessment Bill levying a general tax for the support of Christian teachers, was a vital and compelling ⊥memory in 1789. The lesson of that ⌐465 battle, in the words of Jefferson's Act for Establishing Religious Freedom, whose passage was its verbal embodiment, was "that to compel a man to furnish contributions of money for the propagation of opinions which he disbelieves, is sinful and tyrannical; that even the forcing him to support this or that teacher of his own religious persuasion, is depriving him of the comfortable liberty of giving his contributions to the particular pastor, whose morals he would make his pattern, and whose powers he feels most persuasive to righteousness, and is withdrawing from the ministry those temporal rewards, which proceeding from an approbation of their personal conduct, are an additional incitement to earnest and unremitting labours for the instruction of mankind. . . ." What Virginia had long practiced, and what Madison, Jefferson and others fought to end, was the extension of civil government's support to religion in a manner which made the two in some degree interdependent, and thus threatened the freedom of each. The purpose of the Establishment Clause was to assure that the national legislature would not exert its power in the service of any purely religious end; that it would not, as Virginia and virtually all of the Colonies had done, make of religion, as religion, an object of legislation.

Of course, the immediate object of the First Amendment's prohibition was the established church as it had been known in England and in most of the Colonies. But with foresight those who drafted and adopted the words, "Congress shall make no law respecting an establishment of religion," did not limit the constitutional proscription to any particular, dated form of state-supported theological venture. ⌊466 The Establishment Clause withdrew from ⊥ the sphere of legitimate legislative concern and competence a specific, but comprehensive, area of human conduct: man's belief or disbelief in the verity of some transcendental idea and man's expression in action of that belief or disbelief. Congress may not make these matters, as such, the subject of legislation, nor, now, may any legislature in this country. Neither the National Government nor, under the Due Process Clause of the Fourteenth Amendment, a State may, by any device, support belief or the expression of belief for its own sake, whether from conviction of the truth of that belief, or from conviction that by the propagation of that belief the civil welfare of the State is served, or because a majority of its citizens, holding that belief, are offended when all do not hold it.

With regulations which have other objectives the Establishment Clause, and the fundamental separationist concept which it expresses, are not concerned. These regulations may fall afoul of the constitutional guarantee against infringement of the free exercise or observance of religion. Where they do, they must be set aside at the instance of those whose faith they prejudice. But once it is determined that a challenged statute is supportable as implementing other substantial interests than the promotion of belief, the guarantee prohibiting religious "establishment" is satisfied.

To ask what interest, what object, legislation serves, of course, is not to psychoanalyze its legislators, but to examine the necessary effects of what they have enacted. If the primary end achieved by a form of regulation is the affirmation or promotion of religious doctrine—primary, in the sense that all secular ends which it purportedly serves are derivative from, not wholly independent of, the advancement of religion—the regulation is beyond the power of the state. This was the case in *McCollum.* Or if a statute ⌊467 furthers both secular and religious ends ⊥ by means unnecessary to the effectuation of the secular ends alone—where the same secular ends could equally be attained by means which do not have consequences for promotion of religion—the statute cannot stand.

A State may not endow a church although that church might inculcate in its parishioners moral concepts deemed to make them better citizens, because the very *raison d'être* of a church, as opposed to any other school of civilly serviceable morals, is the predication of religious doctrine. However, inasmuch as individusls are free, if they will, to build their own churches and worship in them, the State may guard its people's safety by extending fire and police protection to the churches so built. It was on the reasoning that parents are also at liberty to send their children to parochial schools which meet the reasonable educational standards of the State, *Pierce v. Society of Sisters*, that this Court held in the *Everson* case that expenditure of public funds to assure that children attending every kind of school enjoy the relative security of buses, rather than being left to walk or hitchhike, is not an unconstitutional "establishment," even though such an expenditure may cause some children to go to parochial schools who would not otherwise have gone. The close division of the Court in *Everson* serves to show what nice questions are involved in applying to particular governmental action the proposition, undeniable in the abstract, that not every regulation some of whose practical effects may facilitate the observance of a religion by its adherents affronts the requirement of church-state separation.

In an important sense, the constitutional prohibition of religious establishment is a provision of more comprehensive availability than the guarantee of free exercise, insofar as both give content to the prohibited fusion of church and state. The former may be invoked by the corporate operator of a seven-day department store whose ⊥ state-compelled Sunday ⌊468 closing injures it financially—or by the department store's employees, whatever their faith, who are convicted for violation of a Sunday statute—as well as by the Orthodox Jewish retailer or consumer who claims that the statute prejudices him in his ability to keep his faith. But it must not be forgotten that the question which the department store operator and employees may raise in their own behalf is narrower than that posed by the case of the Orthodox Jew. Their "establishment" contention can prevail only if the absence of any substantial legislative purpose other than a religious one is made to appear.

In the present cases the Sunday retail sellers and their employees and customers, in attacking statutes banning various activites on a day which most Christian creeds consecrate, do assert that these statutes have no other purpose. They urge, first, that the legislators' motives ⊥ were religious. But the pri- ⌊469 vate and unformulated influences which may work upon legislation are not open to judicial probing. "The decisions of this court from the beginning lend no support whatever to the assumption that the judiciary may restrain the exercise of lawful power on the assumption that a wrongful purpose or motive has caused the power to be exerted." *McCray* v.

United States. "Inquiry into the hidden motives which may move [a legislature] to exercise a power constitutionally conferred upon it is beyond the competency of courts." *Sonzinsky* v. *United States.* These litigants also argue, however, that when the state statutory provisions are regarded in their legislative context religion is apparent on their face: they point to the use of the terms "Lord's day" and "Sabbath" and "desecration," to exceptions whose hours permit activities only at times on Sunday when religious services are customarily not held, to explicit prohibition of otherwise permitted activity in the vicinity of churches, to regulations which condition the allowance of conduct on its consistency with the "due observance" of the day. Of course, since these various provisions regarding exemption from the Sunday ban of certain recreational activities have no possible application to the litigants in the present cases, they are not themselves before the Court, and their constitutionality is not now in issue. But they are put forward as evidence of the purpose of the statutes which are attacked here, and as such we may properly look to them, and also to the history of the body of state Sunday regulations, which, it is urged, further demonstrates sectarian creedal purpose. As a basis for appraising these arguments that ⌐470 the statutes are religious legislation, and pre⊥liminary to determining the claims of infringement of conscience raised in the *Gallagher* and *Braunfeld* cases, it is necessary to survey the long historical development and present-day position of civil Sunday regulation.

II

For these purposes the span of centuries which saw the enunciation of the Fourth Commandment, Constantine's edict proscribing labor on the venerable day of the Sun, and the Sunday prohibitions of Carlovingian, Merovingian and Saxon rulers, and later of the English kings of the thirteenth and fourteenth centuries, may be passed over. What is of concern here is the Sunday institution as it evolved in modern England, the American Colonies, and the States of the Union under the Constitution. The first significant English Sunday regulation, for this purpose, was the statute of Henry VI in 1448 which, after reciting "the abominable injuries and offences done to Almighty God, and to his Saints, . . . because of fairs and markets upon their high and principal feasts, . . . in which principal and festival days, for great earthly covetise, the people is more willingly vexed, and in bodily labour soiled, than in other . . . days, . . . as though they did nothing remember the horrible defiling of their souls in buying and selling, with many deceitful lies and false per-⌐471 jury, with drunkenness and strifes, and so spe⊥cially withdrawing themselves and their servants from divine service . . . ," ordained that all fairs and markets should cease to show forth goods or merchandise on Sundays, Good Friday, and the principal

feast days. A short-lived ordinance of Edward VI a century later, limiting the ban on bodily labor to Sundays and enumerated holy days, demonstrated in its preamble a similar sectarian purpose, and in 1625 Charles I, announcing that "there is nothing more acceptable to·God than the true and sincere service and worship of him . . . and that the holy keeping of the Lord's day is a principal part of the true service of God," prohibited all meetings of the people out of their parishes for sports and pastimes on Sunday, and all bear-baiting, bull-baiting, interludes, common plays, and other unlawful exercises and pastimes on that day. Several years later the same king declared it reproachful of God and religion, and hence made it un⊥lawful, for butchers to slaughter or carriers, ⌐472 drovers, waggoners, etc., to travel on the Lord's day; then, in 1677, "For the better Observation and keeping Holy the Lord's Day," the statute which is still the basic Sunday law of Britain, was enacted: "that all and every Person and Persons whatsoever, shall on every Lord's Day apply themselves to the Observation of the same, by exercising themselves thereon in the Duties of Piety and true Religion, publickly and privately; . . . and that no Tradesman, Artificer, Workman, Labourer or other Person whatsoever, shall do or exercise any worldly Labour, Business or Work of their ordinary Callings, upon the Lord's Day, or any part thereof (Works of Necessity and Charity only excepted;). . . and that no Person or Persons whatsoever, shall publickly cry, shew forth, or expose to Sale, any Wares, Merchandizes, Fruit, Herbs, Goods or Chattels whatsoever, upon the Lord's Day. . . ." In 1781, a ⊥statute reciting ⌐473 that various public entertainments and explications of scriptural texts by incompetent persons tended "to the great encouragement of irreligion and profaneness," closed all rooms and houses in which public entertainment, amusement or debates, for an admission charge, were held.

These Sunday laws were indisputably works of the English Establishment. Their prefatory language spoke their religious inspiration, exceptions made from time to time were expressly limited to preserve inviolable the hours of the divine service, and in their administration ⊥a spirit of inquisitorial piety ⌐474 was evident. But even in this period of religious predominance, notes of a secondary civil purpose could be heard. Apart from the counsel of those who had from the time of the Reformation insisted that the Fourth Commandment itself embodied a precept of social rather than sacramental significance, claims ⊥were asserted in the eighteenth century on behalf ⌐475 of Sunday rest, in part, in the service of health and welfare. Blackstone wrote that ". . . besides the notorious indecency and scandal of permitting any secular business to be publicly transacted on that day in a country professing Christianity, and the corruption of morals which usually follows its profanation, the keeping one day in the seven holy, as a time of relaxation and refreshment as well as for public worship, is of admirable service to a state, considered merely as a civil institution. It humanizes, by the help of conversation and society, the manners of the lower classes, which would otherwise degenerate into a sordid ferocity and savage selfishness of spirit; it enables the industrious workman to pursue his occupation in the ensuing week with health and cheerfulness; it imprints on the minds of the people that sense of their duty to God so necessary to make ⊥476 them good citizens, but which yet ⊥would be worn out and defaced by an unremitted continuance of labor, without any stated times of recalling them to the worship of their Maker." In 1788 the schedule to the act obligated master chimney sweeps to have their apprentices washed at least once a week, providing that on Sunday the master should send the apprentice to worship, should allow him to have religious instruction, and should not allow him to wear his sweeping dress; the act also regulated the sweeps' hours of work. In 1832 a Commons Select Committee on the Observance of the Sabbath heard the testimony of a medical doctor as to the physically injurious effects of seven-day unremitted labor, and although the report of the Committee reveals a primarily religious cast of mind, it discloses also a sensitivity to the plight of the journeyman bakers, seven thousand of whom had petitioned the House for one day's repose weekly, and to the wishes of shopkeepers and tradesmen forced by competition to work on Sunday, although "most desirous of a day of rest." The Committee recommended the enactment of severer sanctions for Lord's day violations: "The objects to be attained by Legislation may be considered to be, first, a solemn and decent outward Observance of the Lord's-day, as that portion of the week which is set apart by Divine Command for Public Worship; and next, the securing to every member of the Community without any exception, and however low his station, the uninterrupted enjoyment of that Day of Rest which has been in Mercy provided for him, and the privilege of employing it, as well in ⊥477 ⊥the sacred Exercises for which it was ordained, as in the bodily relaxation which is necessary for his well-being, and which, though a secondary end, is nevertheless, also of high importance."

But, whatever the nature of the propulsions underlying state-enforced Sunday labor stoppage during these centuries before the twentieth, it is clear that its effect was the creation of an institution of Sunday as a day apart. The origins of the institution were religious, certainly, but through long-established usage it had become a part of the life of the English people. It was a day of rest not merely in a physical, hygienic sense, but in the sense of a recurrent time in the cycle of human activity when the rhythms of existence changed, a day of particular associations which came to have their own autonomous value for life. When that value was threatened by the pressures of the Industrial Revolution, agita-

tion began for new ⊥legislative action to preserve ⊥478 the traditional English Sunday.

At the turn of the century, the Factory and Workshop Act, 1901, prohibited the Sunday employment of women and children in industrial establishments. The Shops Act, 1912, in its institution of a five-and-a-half-day week for shop assistants, built upon the base of existing Sunday closing law. When during the war the pressures of ⊥national defense ⊥479 compelled continuous factory operation, a Committee of the Ministry of Munitions appointed to investigate industrial fatigue as this affected the health and efficiency of munitions workers, recommended to Parliament reinauguration of Sunday work stoppage. . . . ". . . [I]f the maximum output is to be secured and maintained for any length of time, a weekly period of rest must be allowed. . . . On economic and social grounds alike this weekly period of rest is best provided on Sunday. . . ."

⊥ In 1936 the conflict between the economic pres- ⊥480 sures for seven-day commercial activity and the resistance to those pressures culminated in the Shops (Sunday Trading Restriction) Act of that year, which, with a complex pattern of exceptions, prohibited Sunday trading upon pain of penalties more severe, and hence better calculated to assure obedience, than the nominal fines which had obtained under the seventeenth century Lord's day ban. The Parliamentary Debates on the 1936 Act are instructive. With extremely rare exceptions, no intimation of religious purpose is to be discovered in them. The opening speech by Mr. Loftus who introduced the bill is representative: ". . . [I]t is a Bill which is necessary to secure the family life and liberty of hundreds of thousands of our people. . . .

                    .   .   .   .   .

⊥ ". . . I will explain to the House that there are ⊥481 thousands of shopkeepers who hate opening on Sunday—they dislike the whole idea—but are forced to open because their neighbours open. They are forced to open not for the sake of the Sunday trading, but because if they let their customers get into the habit on Sunday of going to other shops they may lose their week-day custom. . . . They have the right to a holiday on Sunday, to be able to rest from work on that day and to go out into the parks or into the country on a summer day. That is the liberty for which they are asking, and that is the liberty which this Bill would give to them. As regards the support behind the Bill, it is promoted by the Early Closing Association, with 300 affiliated associations, and the National Federation of Grocers, representing 400,000 individual shops, and is supported by the National Chamber of Trade, the Drapers' Chamber of Trade, the National Federation of the Boot Trade, and as regards the employes—and this is important—it is supported by the National

Union of Shop Assistants and by the National Union of Distributive Workers."

Speakers asserted the necessity for maintaining "the traditional quality of the Sunday in this country. . . ."

⊥482   ⊥Thus the English experience demonstrates the intimate relationship between civil Sunday regulation and the interest of a state in preserving to its people a recurrent time of mental and physical recuperation from the strains and pressures of their ordinary labors. It demonstrates also, of course, the intimate historical connection between the choice of

⊥483   Sunday as this time of rest and the doctrines ⊥of the Christian church. Long before the emergence of modern notions of government, religion had set Sunday apart. Through generations, the people were accustomed to it as a day when ordinary uses ceased. If it might once—or elsewhere—have been equally practicable to fulfill the same need of the workers and traders for periodic relaxation by the selection of some other cycle, it was no longer practicable in England. Some hypothetical man might do better with one-day-in-eight, or one-day-in-four, but the Englishman was used to one-day-in-seven. And that day was Sunday. Through associations fostered by tradition, that day had a character of its own which became in itself a cultural asset of importance: a release from the daily grind, a preserve of mental peace, an opportunity for self-disposition. Certainly, legislative fiat could have attempted to switch the day to Tuesday. But Parliament, naturally enough, concluded that such an attempt might prove as futile as the ephemeral decade of the French Republic of 1792.

III

⊥484   ⊥In England's American settlements, too, civil Sunday regulation early became an institution of importance in shaping the colonial pattern of life. Every Colony had a law prohibiting Sunday labor.

⊥485   These had been enacted ⊥in many instances prior to the last quarter of the seventeenth century, and they were continued in force throughout the period

⊥486   that preceded the adoption of the Federal ⊥Constitution and the Bill of Rights. This is not in itself, of course, indicative of the purpose of those laws, or of their consistency with the guarantee of religious freedom which the First Amendment, restraining the power of the central Government, secured. Most of the States were only partly disestablished in 1789. Only in Virginia and in Rhode Island, which had never had an establishment, had the ideal of complete church-state separation been realized. Other States were fast approaching that ideal, however, and everywhere the spirit of liberty in religion was in the ascendant. Ratifying Conventions in New York, New Hampshire and North Carolina, as well as in Virginia and Rhode Island, proposed an anti-establishment amendment to the Constitution or signified that in

their understanding the Constitution embodied such a safeguard. All of these five States had Sunday laws at the time that their Conventions spoke. Indeed, in four of the five, their legislatures had reaffirmed the Sunday labor ban within five years or less immediately prior to that date.

⊥The earlier among the colonial Sunday statutes   ⊥487 were unquestionably religious in purpose. Their preambles recite that profanation of the Lord's day "to the great Reproach of the Christian Religion," or "to the great offence of the Godly welafected among us," must be suppressed; that "the keeping holy the Lord's day, is a principal part of the true service of God"; that neglecting the Sabbath "pulls downe the judgments of God upon that place or people that suffer the same. . . ." The first Pennsylvania Sunday law announces a purpose "That Looseness, irreligion, and Atheism may not Creep in under pretense of Conscience. . . ." Sometimes ⊥reproach of God   ⊥488 is made an operative element of the offense. Prohibitions of Sunday labor are frequently coupled with admonitions that all persons shall "carefully apply themselves to Duties of Religion and Piety, publickly and privately . . . ," and are found in comprehensive ecclesiastical codes which also prohibit blasphemy, lay taxes for the support of the church, or compel attendance at divine services.

⊥But even the seventeenth century legislation   ⊥489 does not show an exclusively religious preoccupation. The same Pennsylvania law which speaks of the suppression of atheism also ordains Sunday rest "for the ease of the Creation," and shows solicitude that servants, as well as their masters, may be free on that day to attend such spiritual pursuits as they may wish. The Rhode Island Assembly in 1679 enacted: "Voted, Whereas there hath complaint been made that sundry persons being evill minded, have pre⊥   ⊥490 sumed to employ in servile labor, more than necessity requireth, their servants, and alsoe hire other mens' servants and sell them to labor on the first day of the week: . . . bee it enacted. . . . That if any person or persons shall employ his servants or hire and employ any other man's servant or servants, and set them to labor as aforesaid [he shall be penalized]."

⊥In the latter half of the eighteenth century, the   ⊥491 Sunday laws, while still giving evidence of concern for the "immorality" of the practices they prohibit, tend no longer to be prefixed by preambles in the form of theological treatises. Now it appears to be the community, rather than the Deity, which is offended by Sunday labor. New York's statute of 1788 no longer refers to the Lord's day, but to "the first day of the week commonly called Sunday." Where preambles do appear, they display a duplicity of purpose. . . .

⊥More significant is the history of Sunday legislation in Virginia. Even before the English statute of   ⊥492 29 Charles II, that Colony had had laws compelling Sunday attendance at worship and forbidding

Sunday labor. In 1776, the General Convention at Williamsburg adopted a Declaration of Rights, providing *inter alia*, that ". . . all men are equally entitled to the free exercise of religion, according to the dictates of conscience . . . ," and in the same year the acts of Parliament compelling church attendance and punishing deviation in belief were declared void, dissenters were exempted from the tax for support of the established church, and the levy of that tax was suspended. Eight years later came the battle over the Assessment Bill. Under Madison's leadership the forces supporting entire freedom of religion wrote the definitive quietus to the Virginia establishment, and Jefferson's Bill for Establishing Religious Freedom was enacted in 1786. . . . ⊥In this bill breathed the full amplitude of the spirit which inspired the First Amendment, and this Court has looked ⊥to the bill, and to the Virginia history which surrounded its enactment, as a gloss on the signification of the Amendment. The bill was drafted for the Virginia Legislature as No. 82 of the Revised Statutes returned to the Assembly by Jefferson and Wythe on June 18, 1779. Bill No. 84 of the Revision provided: "If any person on Sunday shall himself be found labouring at his own or any other trade or calling, or shall employ his apprentices, servants or slaves in labour, or other business, except it be in the ordinary household offices of daily necessity, or other work of necessity or charity, he shall forfeit the sum of ten shillings. . . ."

This bill was presented to the Assembly by Madison in 1785, and was enacted in 1786. Apparently neither Thomas Jefferson nor James Madison regarded it as ⊥repugnant to religious freedom. Nor did the Virginia legislators who thirteen years later reaffirmed the Bill for Establishing Religious Freedom as "a true exposition of the principles of the bill of rights and constitution," by repealing all laws which they deemed inconsistent with it. The Sunday law of 1786 was not among those repealed.

IV

Legislation currently in force in forty-nine of the fifty States illegalizes on Sunday some form of conduct lawful if performed on weekdays. In several States only one or a few activities are banned—the sale of alcoholic beverages, hunting, barbering, pawnbroking, trad⊥ing in automobiles—but thirty-four jurisdictions broadly ban Sunday labor, or the employment of labor, or selling or keeping open for sale, or some two or more of these comprehensive categories of affairs. In many of these States, and in others having no state-wide prohibition of industrial or commercial activity, municipal Sunday ordinances are ubiquitous. Most of these regulations are the product of many reenactments and amendments. Although some are still built upon the armatures ⊥of earlier statutes, they are all, like the laws of Maryland, Massachusetts and Pennsylvania which are before us in these cases, recently reconsidered legis-

lation. As expressions of state policy, they must be deemed as contemporary as their latest-enacted exceptions in favor of moving pictures or severer bans of Sunday motor vehicle trading. In all, they reflect a widely felt present-day need, for whose satisfaction old laws are shaped and new laws enacted.

To be sure, the Massachusetts statute now before the Court, and statutes in Pennsylvania and Maryland, still call Sunday the "Lord's day" or the "Sabbath." So do the Sunday laws in many other States. But the con⊥tinuation of seventeenth century language does not of itself prove the continuation of the purposes for which the colonial governments enacted these laws, or that these are the purposes for which their successors of the twentieth have retained them and modified them. We know, ⊥for example, that Committees of the New York Legislature, considering that State's Sabbath Laws on two occasions more than a century apart, twice recommended no repeal of those laws, both times on the ground that the laws did not involve "any partisan religious issue, but ⊥rather economic and health regulation of the activities of the people on a universal day of rest," and that a Massachusetts legislative committee rested on the same views. Sunday legislation has been supported not only ⊥by such clerical organizations as the Lord's Day Alliance, but also by labor and trade groups. The interlocking sections of the Massachusetts Labor Code construct their six-day-week provisions upon the basic premise of Sunday ⊥rest. Other States have similar laws. When in Pennsylvania motion pictures were excepted from the Lord's day statute, a day-of-rest-in-seven clause for motion picture personnel was written into the exempting statute to ⊥fill the gap. Puerto Rico's closing law, which limits the weekday hours of commercial establishments as well as proscribing their Sunday operation, does not express a religious purpose. Rhode Island and South Carolina now enforce portions of their Sunday employment bans through their respective Departments of Labor. It cannot be fairly denied that the institution of Sunday as a time whose occupations and atmosphere differ from those of other days of the week has now been a portion of the American cultural scene since well before the Constitution; that for many millions of people life has a hebdomadal rhythm in which this day, with all its particular associations, is the recurrent note of repose. Cultural history establishes not a few practices and prohibitions religious in origin which are retained as secular ⊥institutions and ways long after their religious sanctions and justifications are gone. In light of these considerations, can it reasonably be said that no substantial non-⊥ecclesiastical purpose relevant to a well-ordered social life exists for Sunday restrictions?

It is urged, however, that if a day of rest were the legislative purpose, statutes to secure it would take some other form than the prohibition of activity on Sunday. Such statutes, it is argued, would provide

⌐1493

⌐1494

⌐1495

⌐1496

⌐1497

⌐1498

⌐1499

⌐1500

⌐1501

⌐1502

⌐1503

⌐1504

⌐1505

⌐506 for one day's labor ⊥stoppage in seven, leaving the choice of the day to the individual; or, alternatively, would fix a common day of rest on some other day— Monday or Tuesday. But, in all fairness, certainly, it would be impossible to call unreasonable a legislative finding that these suggested alternatives were unsatisfactory. A provision for one day's closing per week, at the option of every particular enterpriser, might be disruptive of families whose members are employed by different enterprises. Enforcement might be more difficult, both because violation would be less easily discovered and because such a law would not be seconded, as is Sunday legislation, by the community's moral temper. More important, one-day-a-week laws do not accomplish all that is accomplished by Sunday laws. They provide only a periodic physical rest, not that atmosphere of entire community repose which Sunday has traditionally brought and which, a legislature might reasonably believe, is necessary to the welfare of those who for ⌐507 ⊥many generations have been accustomed to its recuperative effects.

The same considerations might also be deemed to justify the choice of Sunday as the single common day when labor ceases. For to many who do not regard it sacramentally, Sunday is nevertheless a day of special, long-established associations, whose particular temper makes it a haven that no other day could provide. The will of a majority of the community, reflected in the legislative process during scores of years, presumably prefers to take its leisure on Sunday. The spirit of any people expresses in goodly measure the heritage which links it to its past. Disruption of this heritage by a regulation which, like the unnatural labors of Claudius' shipwrights, does not divide the Sunday from the week, might prove a measure ill-designed to secure the desirable community repose for which Sunday legislation is designed. At all events, Maryland, Massachusetts and Pennsylvania, like thirty-one other States with similar regulations, could reasonably so find. Certainly, from failure to make a substitution for Sunday in securing a socially desirable day of surcease from subjection to labor and routine a purpose cannot be derived to establish or promote religion.

The question before the Court in these cases is not a new one. During a hundred and fifty years Sunday laws have been attacked in state and federal courts as disregarding constitutionally demanded Church-State separation, or infringing protected religious freedoms, or on the ground that they subserved no end within the legitimate compass of legislative power. One California court in 1858 held California's ⌐508 Sunday statute unconstitutional. ⊥That decision was overruled three years later. Every other appellate court that has considered the question has found the ⌐509 statutes supportable as civil regulations and ⊥not repugnant to religious freedom. These decisions are assailed as latter-day justifications upon specious civil grounds of legislation whose religious purposes

were either overlooked or concealed by the judges ⌐510 who passed upon it. ⊥Of course, it is for this Court ultimately to determine whether federal constitutional guarantees are observed or undercut. But this does not mean that we are to be indifferent to the unanimous opinion of genera⊥tions of judges who, ⌐511 in the conscientious discharge of obligations as solemn as our own, have sustained the Sunday laws as not inspired by religious purpose. The Court did not ignore that opinion in *Friedman* v. *New York; McGee* v. *North Carolina; Kidd* v. *Ohio*; and *Ullner* v. *Ohio*, dismissing for want of a substantial federal question appeals from state decisions sustaining Sunday laws which were obnoxious to the same objections urged in the present cases. I cannot ignore that consensus of view now. The statutes of Maryland, Massachusetts and Pennsylvania which we here examine are not constitutionally forbidden fusions of church and state.

V

⊥Appellees in the *Gallagher* case and appellants in ⌐512 the *Braunfeld* case contend that, as applied to them, Orthodox Jewish retailers and their Orthodox Jewish customers, the Massachusetts Lord's day statute and the Pennsylvania Sunday retail sales act violate the Due Process Clause of the Fourteenth Amendment because, in effect, the statutes deter the exercise and observance of their religion. The argument runs that by compelling the Sunday closing of retail stores and thus making unavailable for business and shopping uses one-seventh part of the week, these statutes force them either to give up the Sabbath observance—an essential part of their faith—or to forego advantages enjoyed by the non-Sabbatarian majority of the communnity. They point out, moreover, that because of the prevailing five-day working week of a large proportion of the population, Sunday is a day peculiarly profitable to retail sellers and peculiarly convenient to retail shoppers. The records in these cases support them in this.

The claim which these litigants urge assumes a number of aspects. First, they argue that any one-common-day-⊥of-closing regulation which selected a ⌐513 day other than their Sabbath would be *ipso facto* unconstitutional in its application to them because of its effect in preferring persons who observe no Sabbath, therefore creating economic pressures which urge Sabbatarians to give up their usage. The creation of this pressure by the Sunday statutes, it is said, is not so necessary a means to the achievement of the ends of day-of-rest legislation as to justify its employment when weighed against the injury to Sabbatarian religion which it entails. Six-day-week regulation, with the closing day left to individual choice, is urged as a more reasonable alternative.

Second, they argue that even if legitimate state interests justify the enforcement against persons generally of a single common day of rest, the choice of Sunday as that day violates the rights of religious freedom of the Sabbatarian minority. By choosing a day upon which Sunday-observing Christians worship and abstain from labor, the statutes are said to discriminate between religions. The Sunday observer may practice his faith and yet work six days a week, while the observer of the Jewish Sabbath, his competitor, may work only during five days, to the latter's obvious disadvantage. Orthodox Jewish shoppers whose jobs occupy a five-day week have no week-end shopping day, while Sunday-observing Christians do. Leisure to attend Sunday services, and relative quiet throughout their duration, is assured by law, but no equivalent treatment is accorded to Friday evening and Saturday services. Sabbatarians feel that the power of the State is employed to coerce their observance of Sunday as a holy day; that the State accords a recognition to Sunday Christian doctrine which is withheld from Sabbatarian creeds. All of these prejudices could be avoided, it is argued, without impairing the effectiveness of common-day-of-rest regulation, either by fixing as the rest time some day which is held sacred _|514_ by no sect, or by pro⊥viding for a Sunday work ban from which Sabbatarians are excepted, on condition of their abstaining from labor on Saturday. Failure to adopt these alternatives in lieu of Sunday statutes applicable to Sabbatarians is said to constitute an unconstitutional choice of means.

Finally, it is urged that if, as means, these statutes *are* necessary to the goals which they seek to attain, nevertheless the goals themselves are not of sufficient value to society to justify the disadvantage which their attainment imposes upon the religious exercise of Sabbatarians.

The first of these contentions has already been discussed. The history of Sunday legislation convincingly demonstrates that Sunday statutes may serve other purposes than the provision merely of one day of physical stoppage in seven. These purposes fully justify common-day-of-rest statutes which choose Sunday as the day.

In urging that an exception in favor of those who observe some other day as sacred would not defeat the ends of Sunday legislation, and therefore that failure to provide such an exception is an unnecessary—hence an unconstitutional—burden on Sabbatarians, the *Gallagher* appellees and *Braunfeld* appellants point to such exceptions in twenty-one of the thirty-four jurisdictions which have statutes banning labor or employment or the selling of goods on Sunday. Actually, in less than half of these twenty-_|515_ one States does the exemption extend to ⊥sales activity as well as to labor. There are tenable reasons why a legislature might choose not to make such an exception. To whatever extent persons who come within the exception are present in a community, their activity would disturb the atmosphere of general repose and reintroduce into Sunday the business tempo of the week. Administration would be more difficult, with violations less evident and, in effect,

two or more days to police ⊥instead of one. If it is _|516_ assumed that the retail demand for consumer items is approximately equivalent on Saturday and on Sunday, the Sabbatarian, in proportion as he is less numerous, and hence the competition less severe, might incur through the exception a competitive advantage over the non-Sabbatarian, who would then be in a position, presumably, to complain of discrimination against *his* religion. Employers who wished to avail themselves of the exception would have to employ only their co-religionists, and there might be introduced into private employment practices an element of religious differentiation which a legislature could regard as undesirable.

Finally, a relevant consideration which might cause a State's lawmakers to reject exception for observers of another day than Sunday is that administration of such a provision may require judicial inquiry into religious belief. A legislature could conclude that if all that is made requisite to qualify for the exemption is an abstinence from labor on some other day, there would be nothing to prevent an enterpriser from closing on his slowest business day, to take advantage of the whole of ⊥the profitable _|517_ week-end trade, thereby converting the Sunday labor ban, in effect, into a day-of-rest-in-seven statute, with choice of the day left to the individual. All of the state exempting statutes seem to reflect this consideration. Ten of them require that a person claiming exception "conscientiously" believe in the sanctity of another day or "conscientiously" observe another day as the Sabbath. Five demand that he keep another day as "holy time." Three allow the exemption only to members of a "religious" society observing another day, and a fourth provides for proof of membership in such a society by the certificate of a preacher or of any three adherents. In Illinois the claimant must observe some day as a "Sabbath," and in New Jersey he must prove that he devotes that day to religious exercises. Connecticut, one of the jurisdictions demanding conscientious belief, requires in addition that he who seeks the benefit of the exception file a notice of such belief with the prosecuting attorney.

⊥ Indicative of the practical administrative dif- _|518_ ficulties which may arise in attempts to effect, consistently with the purposes of Sunday closing legislation, an exception for persons conscientiously observing another day as Sabbath, are the provisions of § 53 of the British Shops Act, 1950, continuing in substance § 7 of the Shops (Sunday Trading Restriction) Act, 1936. These were the product of experience with earlier forms of exemptions which had proved unsatisfactory, and the new 1936 provisions were enacted only after the consideration and rejection of a number of proposed alternatives. They allow shops ⊥which are registered under the section _|519_ and which remain closed on Saturday to open for trade until 2 p.m. on Sunday. Applications for registration must contain a declaration that the shop occupier "conscientiously objects on religious grounds to carrying on trade or business on the Jewish Sabbath," and any person who, to procure registration, "knowingly or recklessly makes an untrue statement or untrue representation," is subject to fine and imprisonment. Whenever upon representations made to them the local authorities find reason to believe that a registered occupier is not a person of the Jewish religion or "that a conscientious objection on religious grounds . . . is not genuinely held," the authorities may furnish particulars of the case to a tribunal established after consultation with the London Committee of Deputies of the British Jews, which tribunal, if in their opinion the occupier is not a person of the Jewish religion or does not genuinely hold a conscientious objection to trade on the Jewish Sabbath, shall so report to the local authorities; and upon this report the occupier's registration is to be ⌐520 revoked. Surely, in light of the delicate ⊥enforcement problems to which these provisions bear witness, the legislative choice of a blanket Sunday ban applicable to observers of all faiths cannot be held unreasonable. A legislature might in reason find that the alternative of exempting Sabbatarians would impede the effective operation of the Sunday statutes, produce harmful collateral effects, and entail, itself, a not inconsiderable intrusion into matters of religious faith. However preferable, personally, one might deem such an exception, I cannot find that the Constitution compels it.

It cannot, therefore, be said that Massachusetts and Pennsylvania have imposed gratuitous restrictions upon the Sunday activities of persons observing the Orthodox Jewish Sabbath in achieving the legitimate secular ends at which their Sunday statutes may aim. The remaining question is whether the importance to the public of those ends is sufficient to outweigh the restraint upon the religious exercise of Orthodox Jewish practicants which the restriction entails. The nature of the legislative purpose is the preservation of a traditional institution which assures to the community a time during which the mind and body are released from the demands and distractions of an increasingly mechanized and competition-driven society. The right to this ⌐521 ⊥release has been claimed by workers and by small enterprises, especially by retail merchandisers, over centuries, and finds contemporary expression in legislation in three-quarters of the States. The nature of the injury which must be balanced against it is the economic disadvantage to the enterpriser, and the inconvenience to the consumer, which Sunday regulations impose upon those who choose to adhere to the Sabbatarian tenets of their faith.

These statutes do not make criminal, do not place under the onus of civil or criminal disability, any act which is itself prescribed by the duties of the Jewish or other religions. They do create an undeniable financial burden upon the observers of one of the fundamental tenets of certain religious creeds, a burden which does not fall equally upon other forms of observance. This was true of the tax which this Court held an unconstitutional infringement of the free exercise of religion in *Follett* v. *Town of McCormick*. But unlike the tax in *Follett*, the burden which the Sunday statutes impose is an incident of the only feasible means to achievement of their particular goal. And again unike *Follett*, the measure of the burden is not determined by fixed legislative decree, beyond the power of the individual to alter. Upon persons who earn their livelihood by activities not prohibited on Sunday, and upon those whose jobs require only a five-day week, the burden is not considerable. Like the customers of Crown Kosher Super Market in the *Gallagher* case, they are inconvenienced in their shopping. This is hardly to be assessed as an injury of preponderant constitutional weight. The burden on retail sellers competing with Sunday-observing and non-observing retailers is considerably greater. But, without minimizing the fact of this disadvantage, the legislature may have concluded that its severity might be offset by the industry and commercial initiative of the individual merchant. More is demanded of him, admittedly, whether in the ⊥form of additional labor or of material sacrifices, than is demanded of those who do not choose to keep his Sabbath. More would be demanded of him, of course, in a State in which there were no Sunday laws and in which his competitors chose—like "Two Guys From Harrison-Allentown"—to do business seven days a week. In view of the importance of the community interests which must be weighed in the balance, is the disadvantage wrought by the non-exempting Sunday statutes an impermissible imposition upon the Sabbatarian's religious freedom? Every court which has considered the question during a century and a half has concluded that it is not. This Court so concluded in *Friedman* v. *New York*. On the basis of the criteria for determining constitutionality, as opposed to what one might desire as a matter of legislative policy, a contrary conclusion cannot be reached.

VI

Two further grounds of unconstitutionality are urged in all these cases, based upon the selection in the challenged statutes of the activities included in, or excluded ⊥from, the Sunday ban. First it is ⌐523 argued that, if the aim of the statutes is to secure a day of peace and repose, the laws of Massachusetts and Maryland, by their exceptions, and the retail sales act of Pennsylvania, by its enumeration of the articles whose sale is forbidden, operate so imperfectly in the service of this aim—show so little rational relation to it—that they must be accounted as arbitrary and therefore violative of due process. The extensive range of recreational and commercial Sunday activity permitted in these States is said to deprive the statutes of any reasonable basis. The distinctions drawn by the laws between what may be sold or done and what may not, it is claimed, are un-supported by reason. Second, these claimants argue that the same discriminations between items which may and may not be sold, and in some cases between the persons who may and those who may not sell identical items, deprive them of the equal protection of the laws.

Although these contentions require the Court to examine separately and with particularity the provi-sions of each of the three States' statutes which are attacked, the general considerations which govern these cases are the same. It is clear that in fash-ioning legislative remedies by fine distinctions to fit specific needs, "The range of the State's discretion is large." *Bain Peanut Co.* v. *Pinson.* This is especially so where, by the nature of its subject, regulation must take account of traditional and prevailing local customs. "The Constitution does not require things which are different in fact or opinion to be treated in law as though they were the same." *Tigner* v. *Texas.* "Evils in the same field may be of different dimen-sions and proportions, requiring different remedies. Or so the legislature may think. . . . Or the reform may take one step at a time, addressing itself to the |524   phase of the ⊥problem which seems most acute to the legislative mind. . . . The legislature may select one phase of one field and apply a remedy there, ne-glecting the others." *Williamson* v. *Lee Optical, Inc.*

Neither the Due Process nor the Equal Protection Clause demands logical tidiness. No finicky or exact conformity to abstract correlation is required of leg-islation. The Constitution is satisfied if a legislature responds to the practical living facts with which it deals. Through what precise points in a field of many competing pressures a legislature might most suitably have drawn its lines is not a question for ju-dicial re-examination. It is enough to satisfy the Constitution that in drawing them the principle of reason has not been disregarded. And what degree of uniformity reason demands of a statute is, of course, a function of the complexity of the needs which the statute seeks to accommdate.

In the case of Sunday legislation, an extreme com-plexity of needs is evident. This is so, first, because one of the prime objectives of the legislation is the preservation of an atmosphere—a subtle desidera-tum, itself the product of a peculiar and changing set of local circumstances and local traditions. But in addition, in the achievement of that end, however formulated, numerous compromises must be made. Not all activity can halt on Sunday. Some of the very operations whose doings most contribute to the rush and clamor of the week must go on throughout that day as well, whether because life depends upon them, or because the cost of stopping and restarting them is simply too great, or because to be without their services would be more disruptive of peace than to have them to continue. Many activities have a double aspect: providing entertainment or recreation |525   for some persons, they ⊥entail labor and workday

tedium for others. . . . ⊥Moreover, the variation |526 from activity to activity in the degree of disturbance which Sunday operation entails, and the similar var-iation in degrees of temptation to flout the law, and in degrees of ability to absorb and ignore various le-gal penalties, make exceedingly difficult the devising of effective, yet comprehensively fair, schemes of sanctions.

Early in the history of the Sunday laws there de-veloped mechanisms which served to adapt their wide general prohibitions both to practical exigencies and to the evolving concerns and desires of the pub-lic. Where it was found that persons in certain ac-tivities tended with particular frequency to engage in violations, those activities were singled out for harsher punishment. On the other hand, practices found necessary or convenient to popular habits were specifically excepted from the ban. Under the basic English Sunday statute, 29 Charles II, c. 7, a wide general exception obtained for "Works of Necessity ⊥ and Charity"; this provision found its way into the |527 American colonial laws, and has descended into all of their successors currently in force. The effect of the phrase has been to give the courts a wide range of discretion in determining exceptions. But reasonable men can and do differ as to what is "necessity." In every juris⊥diction legislatures, presumably deeming |528 themselves fitter tribunals for decisions of this sort than were courts, acted to resolve the question against, or in favor of, various particular activities. Some pursuits were expressly declared not works of necessity, or were specially banned. ⊥Others were |529 expressly permitted: series of exceptions, giving the laws resiliency in the course of cultural change, pro-liferated. Today, the general pattern in over half of the States and in England is similar. Broad general pro⊥hibitions are qualified by numerous precise ex- |530 emptions, often with provision for local variation within a State, and are frequently bolstered by spe-cial provisions more heavily penalizing named activi-ties. The regulations of Maryland, Massachusetts and Pennsylvania are not atypical in this regard, al-though they are undoubtedly among the more complex of the statutory patterns.

The degree of explicitness of these provisions in so many jurisdictions demonstrates the intricacy of the adjustments which they are designed to make. . . . ⊥Certainly, when relevant considerations of policy |531 demand decisions and distinctions so fine, courts must accord to the legislature a wide range of power to classify and to delineate. It is true that, unlike their virtually unanimous attitude on the issue of re-ligious freedom, state courts have not always sus-tained Sunday legislation against the charge of unconstitutional discrimination. Statutes and ordi-nances have been struck down as arbitrary or as violative of state constitutional prohibitions ⊥of |532 special legislation. A far greater number of courts, in similar classes of cases, have sustained the legisla-tion. But the very diversity of judicial opinion as to

⌐533 what is rea⊥sonable classification—like the conflicting views on what is such "necessity" as will justify Sunday operations—testifies that the question
of inclusion with regard to Sunday bans is one where
⌐534 judgments rationally differ, and hence ⊥where a
State's determinations must be given every fair presumption of a reasonable support in fact. The restricted scope of this Court's review of state regulatory legislation under the Equal Protection Clause
⌐535 is of long ⊥standing. The applicable principles are
that a state statute may not be struck down as offensive of equal protection in its schemes of classification unless it is obviously arbitrary, and that,
except in the case of a statute whose discriminations
are so patently without reason that no conceivable
situation of fact could be found to justify them, the
claimant who challenges the statute bears the burden
of affirmative demonstration that in the actual state
of facts which surround its operation, its classifications lack rationality.

When these standards are applied, first, to the
Maryland statute challenged in the *McGowan* case,
appellants' claim under the Due Process and Equal
Protection Clauses show themselves clearly untenable. Counsel contend that the Sunday sales
prohibition, Md. Code Ann., 1957, Art. 27, § 521, is
rendered arbitrary by its exception of retail sales of
⌐536 tobacco items and soft drinks, ⊥ice and ice cream,
confectionery, milk, bread, fruit, gasoline products,
newspapers and periodicals, and of drugs and
medical supplies by apothecaries—by the further exemption in Anne Arundel County, under § 509, of
certain recreational activities and sales incidental to
them—and by the permissibility under other state
and local regulations of various amusements and
public entertainments on Sunday, Sunday beer and
liquor sales, and Sunday pinball machines and bingo.
The short answer is that these kinds of commodity
exceptions, and most of these exceptions for amusements and entertainments, can be found in the comprehensive Sunday statutes of England, Puerto Rico,
a dozen American States, and many other countries
having uniform-day-of-rest legislation. Surely un-
reason cannot be so widespread. The notion that,
with these matters excepted, the Maryland statute
lacks all rational foundation is baseless. The exceptions relate to products and services which a legislature could reasonably find necessary to the physical
and mental health of the people or to their recreation and relaxation on a day of repose. Other sales
activity and, under Art. 27, § 492, all other labor, are
forbidden. That more or fewer activities than fall
within the exceptions could with equal rationality
have been excluded from the general ban does not
make irrational the selection which has actually been
made. There is presented in this record not a trace of
evidence as to the habits and customs of the population of Maryland or of Anne Arundel County, nothing that suggests that the pattern of legislation
which their representatives have devised is not rea-

sonably related to local circumstances determining
their ways of ⊥life. Appellants have wholly failed to   ⌐537
meet their burden of proof.

Counsel for McGowan urge that the allowance,
limited to Anne Arundel County, of retail sales of
merchandise customarily sold at bathing beaches,
bathhouses, amusement parks and dancing saloons,
violates the equal protection of the laws both by discriminating between Anne Arundel retailers and
those in other counties, and by discriminating
among classes of persons within Anne Arundel
County who compete in sales of the same articles.
Clearly appellants, who were convicted for selling
within the county, would not ordinarily have
standing to raise the issue of possible discrimination
against out-of-county merchants; in any event, on
this record, it is dubious that the contention was adequately raised below. Suffice to say, for purposes of
the due process issue which appellants did raise, that
the provision of different Sunday regulations for different regions of a State is not *ipso facto* arbitrary.

As for the asserted discrimination in favor of those
who sell at the beach or the park articles not permitted to ⊥be sold elsewhere, the answer must be   ⌐538
that between such beach-side enterprisers and the
general suburban merchandising store at which appellants are employed there is a reasonable line of
demarcation. The reason of the exemption dictates
the human logic of its scope. The legislature has
found it desirable that persons seeking certain forms
of recreation on Sunday have the convenience of
purchasing on that day items which add enjoyment
to the recreation and which, perhaps, could not or
would not be provided for by a vacationer prior to
the day of his Sunday outing. On the other hand, the
policy of securing to the maximum possible number
of distributive employees their Sunday off might reasonably preclude allowing every retail establishment
in the county to open to serve this convenience. A
tenable resolution, surely, is to permit these particular sales only on the premises where the items will be
needed and used. The enforcement problem which
could arise from permitting general merchandising
outlets to open for the sale of these items alone, but
not for the sale of thousands of other items at adjacent counters and shelves, might in itself justify
the limitation of the exception to the group of on-
the-premises merchants who are less likely to stock
articles extraneous to the use of the enumerated
amusement facilities.

The Massachusetts statute attacked in the *Gallagher* case contains a wider range of exceptions but,
again, none that this record shows to be patently
baseless and therefore constitutionally impermissible. The court below believed that reason was offended by such provisions as those which allow,
apparently, digging for clams but not dredging for
oysters, or which permit certain professional sports
during the hours from 1:30 to 6:30 p.m. while restricting their amateur counterparts to 2 to 6, or

which make lawful (as the court below read the statute) Sunday pushcart vending by conscientious Sabbatarians, but not ⊥Sunday vending within a building. But the record below, on the basis of which a federal court has been asked to enjoin the enforcement of a state statute, contains no evidence concerning clam-digging or oyster-dredging, nothing to indicate that these two activities have anything more in common—requiring similar treatment— than that in each there is involved the pursuit of mollusca. There is nothing in the record concerning professional or amateur athletic events, and certainly nothing to support the conclusion that the problem of Sunday regulation of pushcarts is so similar to the problem of Sunday regulation of indoor markets as to require uniform treatment for both. These various differently treated situations may be different in fact, or they may not. A statute is not to be struck down on supposition.

It is true, as appellees there claim, that Crown Kosher Super Market may not sell on Sunday products which other retail establishments may sell on that day: bread (which may be sold during certain hours by innkeepers, common victuallers, confectioners and fruiterers, and, along with other bakery products, by bakers), confectionery, frozen desserts and dessert mix, and soda water (which may be sold by innkeepers, common victuallers, confectioners and fruiterers, and druggists), tobacco (which may be sold by innkeepers, common victuallers, druggists, and regular newsdealers), etc. (The sale of drugs and newspapers on Sunday is permitted generally.) But although Crown Kosher undoubtedly suffers an element of competition disadvantage from these provisions, the provisions themselves are not irrational. Their purpose, apparently, is to permit dealers specializing in certain products whose distribution on Sunday is regarded as necessary, to sell those products and also such other among the same group ⊥of necessaries as are generally found sold together with the products in which they specialize, thus fostering the maximum dissemination of the permitted products with the minimum number of retail employees required to work to disseminate them. Shops such as newsdealers, druggists, and confectioners may in Massachusetts tend, for all we know, to be smaller, less noisy, more widely distributed so that access to them from residential areas entails less traveling, than is the case with other stores. They may tend to hire fewer employees. They may present, because they specialize in products whose sale is permitted, less of a policing problem than would general markets selling these and many other products. Again there is nothing in the record to support the conclusion that Massachusetts has failed to afford to the Crown Kosher Super Market treatment which is equivalent to that enjoyed by all other retailers of a class not rationally distinguishable from Crown. "The prohibition of the Equal Protection Clause goes no further than the invidious discrimination.

We cannot say that that point has been reached here." *Williamson* v. *Lee Optical, Inc.*

Nor, on the record of the *McGinley* case, can any other conclusion be reached as to the 1959 Pennsylvania Sunday retail sales act. Appellants in this case argue that to punish by a fine of up to one hundred dollars per sale—or two hundred dollars per sale within one year after the first offense—the retail selling of some twenty enumerated broad categories of commodities, while punishing all other sales and laboring activity by the four-dollars-per-Sunday ⊥fine fixed by the earlier Lord's day statute, is arbitrary and violative of equal protection. But the court below found, and in this it is supported by the legislative history of the 1959 act, that the enactment providing severer penalties for these classes of sales was responsive to the appearance in the Commonwealth, only shortly before the act's passage, of a new kind of large-scale mercantile enterprise which, absorbing without difficulty a four-dollar-a-week fine, made a profitable business of persistent violation of the earlier statute. These new enterprises may have attracted a disturbing volume of Sunday traffic; they may have employed more retail salesmen, and under different conditions, than other kinds of businesses in the State; some of the legislators, apparently, so believed. The danger may have been apprehended that not only would these violations of long-standing State legislation continue, but that competition would force upon other enterprises which had for years closed on Sunday. Under this threat the 1959 statute was designed. It applies not only to the new merchandisers—if that were so, quite obviously, different constitutional problems would arise. Rather it singles out the area where a danger has been most evident, and within that area treats all business enterprises equally. That in so doing it may have drawn the line between the sale of a sofa cover, punished by a hundred-dollar fine, and the sale of an automobile seat cover, punished by a four dollar fine, is not sufficient to void the legislation. "[A] State may classify with reference to the evil to be prevented, and . . . if the class discriminated against is or reasonably might be considered to define those from whom the evil mainly is to be feared, it properly may be ⊥picked out. A lack of abstract symmetry does not matter. The question is a practical one dependent upon experience. The demand for symmetry ignores the specific difference that experience is supposed to have shown to mark the class. It is not enough to invalidate the law that others may do the same thing and go unpunished, if, as a matter of fact, it is found that the danger is characteristic of the class named." Mr. Justice Holmes, in *Patsone* v. *Pennsylvania*.

Even less should a legislature be required to hew the line of logical exactness where the statutory distinction challenged is merely one which sets apart offenses subject to penalties of differing degrees of severity, not one which divides the lawful from the unlawful. "Judgment on the deterrent effect of the various weapons in the armory of the law can lay little claim to scientific basis. Such judgment as yet is largely a prophecy based on meager and uninterpreted experience. . . .

". . . Moreover, the whole problem of deterrence is related to still wider considerations affecting the temper of the community in which law operates. The traditions of a society, the habits of obedience to law, the effectiveness of the law-enforcing agencies, are all peculiarly matters of time and place. They are thus matters within legislative competence." *Tigner* v. *Texas.* Appellants in *McGinley*, like appellants in the *McGowan* and appellees in the *Gallagher* cases, have had full opportunity to demonstrate the arbitrariness of the statute which they challenge. On this record they have entirely failed to satisfy the burden which they carry.

The *Braunfeld* case, however, comes here in a different posture. Appellants, plaintiffs below, allege in ⊥543 their ⊥amended complaint that the 1959 Pennsylvania Sunday retail sales act is irrational and arbitrary. The three-judge court dismissed the amended complaint for failure to state a claim. Speaking for myself alone and not for *Mr. Justice HARLAN* on this point, I think that this was too summary a disposition. However difficult it may be for appellants to prove what they allege, they must be given an opportunity to do so if they choose to avail themselves of it, in view of the Court's decisions in this series of cases. I would remand No. 67 to the District Court.

.   .   .   .   .

⊥561   ⊥ *Mr. Justice DOUGLAS*, dissenting. *

The question is not whether one day out of seven can be imposed by a State as a day of rest. The question is not whether Sunday can by force of custom and habit be retained as a day of rest. The question is whether a State can impose criminal sanctions on those who, unlike the Christian majority that makes up our society, worship on a different day or do not share the religious scruples of the majority.

If the "free exercise" of religion were subject to reasonable regulations, as it is under some constitutions, or if all laws "respecting the establishment of religion" were not proscribed, I could understand how rational men, representing a predominantly Christian civilization, might think these Sunday laws did not unreasonably interfere with anyone's free exercise of religion and took no step toward a burdensome establishment of any religion.

But that is not the premise from which we start, as there is agreement that the fact that a State, and not the Federal Government, has promulgated these Sunday laws does not change the scope of the power asserted. For the classic view is that the First Amendment should be applied to the States with the same firmness as it is enforced against the Federal Government. ⊥The most explicit statement perhaps ⊥562 was in *Board of Education* v. *Barnette*: "In weighing arguments of the parties it is important to distinguish between the due process clause of the Fourteenth Amendment as an instrument for transmitting the principles of the First Amendment and those cases in which it is applied for its own sake. The test of legislation which collides with the Fourteenth Amendment, because it also collides with the principles of the First, is much more definite than the test when only the Fourteenth is involved. Much of the vagueness of the due process clause disappears when the specific prohibitions of the First become its standard. The right of a State to regulate, for example, a public utility may well include, so far as the due process test is concerned, power to impose all of the restrictions which a legislature may have a 'rational basis' for adopting. But freedoms of speech and of press, of assembly, and of worship may not be infringed on such slender grounds. They are susceptible of restriction only to prevent grave and immediate danger to interests which the State may lawfully protect. It is important to note that while it is the Fourteenth Amendment which bears directly upon the State it is the more specific limiting principles of the First Amendment that finally govern this case."

With that as my starting point I do not see how a State can make protesting citizens refrain from doing innocent acts on Sunday because the doing of those acts offends sentiments of their Christian neighbors.

The institutions of our society are founded on the belief that there is an authority higher than the authority of the State; that there is a moral law which the State is powerless to alter; that the individual possesses rights, conferred by the Creator, which government must respect. ⊥The Declaration of In- ⊥563 dependence stated the now familiar theme: "We hold these Truths to be self-evident, that all Men are created equal, that they are endowed by their Creator with certain unalienable Rights, that among these are Life, Liberty, and the Pursuit of Happiness."

And the body of the Constitution as well as the Bill of Rights enshrined those principles.

The Puritan influence helped shape our constitutional law and our common law as Dean Pound has said: The Puritan "put individual conscience and individual judgment in the first place." For these reasons we stated in *Zorach* v. *Clauson*, "We are a religious people whose institutions presuppose a Supreme Being."

But those who fashioned the First Amendment decided that if and when God is to be served, His service will not be motivated by coercive measures of government. "Congress shall make no law respecting an establishment of religion, or prohibiting the free exercise thereof"—such is the command of the First Amendment made applicable to the State by reason of the Due Process Clause of the Fourteenth. This means, as I understand it, that if a religious leaven is to be worked into the affairs of our people, it is to be done by individuals and groups, not by the Government. This necessarily means, *first*, that the dogma,

_____

* NOTE: This opinion applies also to *Two Guys From Harrison-Allentown, Inc.*, v. *McGinley; Braunfeld et al.* v. *Brown*; and *Gallagher* v. *Crown Kosher Super Market, Inc.*

creed, scruples, or practices of no religious group or sect are to be preferred over those of any others; *second*, that no one shall be interfered with by government for practicing the religion of his choice; *third*, that the State cannot compel one so to conduct himself as not to offend the religious scruples of another. The idea, as I understand it, was to limit the power of government to act in religious matters, ⊥not to limit the freedom of religious men to act religiously nor to restrict the freedom of atheists or agnostics.

⊥564

The First Amendment commands government to have no interest in theology or ritual; it admonishes government to be interested in allowing religious freedom to flourish—whether the result is to produce Catholics, Jews, or Protestants, or to turn the people toward the path of Buddha, or to end in a predominantly Moslem nation, or to produce in the long run atheists or agnostics. On matters of this kind government must be neutral. This freedom plainly includes freedom *from* religion with the right to believe, speak, write, publish and advocate antireligious programs. Certainly the "free exercise" clause does not require that everyone embrace the theology of some church or of some faith, or observe the religious practices of any majority or minority sect. The First Amendment by its "establishment" clause prevents, of course, the selection by government of an "official" church. Yet the ban plainly extends farther than that. We said in *Everson* v. *Board of Education* that it would be an "establishment" of a religion if the Government financed one church or several churches. For what better way to "establish" an institution than to find the fund that will support it? The "establishment" clause protects citizens also against any law which selects any religious custom, practice, or ritual, puts the force of government behind it, and fines, imprisons, or otherwise penalizes a person for not observing it. The Government plainly could not join forces with one religious group and decree a universal and symbolic circumcision. Nor could it require all children to be baptized or give tax exemptions only to those whose children were baptized.

Could it require a fast from sunrise to sunset throughout the Moslem month of Ramadan? I should think not. ⊥Yet, why then can it make criminal the doing of other acts, as innocent as eating, during the day that Christians revere?

⊥565

Sunday is a word heavily overlaid with connotations and traditions deriving from the Christian roots of our civilization that color all judgments concerning it. . . .

The issue of these cases would therefore be in better focus if we imagined that a state legislature, controlled by orthodox Jews and Seventh-Day Adventists, passed a law making it a crime to keep a shop open on Saturdays. Would a Baptist, Catholic, Methodist, or Presbyterian be compelled to obey that law or go to jail or pay a fine? Or suppose Moslems grew in political strength here and got a law through a state legislature making it a crime to keep a shop open on Fridays. Would the rest of us have to submit under the fear of criminal sanctions?

Dr. John Cogley recently summed up the dominance of the three-religion influence in our affairs: "For the foreseeable future, it seems, the United States is going to be a three-religion nation. At the present time all three are characteristically 'Amer-⊥ican,' some think flavorlessly so. For religion in America is almost uniformly 'respectable,' bourgeois, and prosperous. In the Protestant world the 'church' mentality has triumphed over the more venturesome spirit of the 'sect.' In the Catholic world, the mystical is muted in favor of booming organization and efficiently administered good works. And in the Jewish world the prophet is too frequently without honor, while the synagogue emphasis is focused on suburban togetherness. There are exceptions to these rules, of course; each of the religious communities continues to cast up its prophets, its rebels and radicals. But a Jeremiah, one fears, would be positively embarrassing to the present position of the Jews; a Francis of Assisi upsetting the complacency of American Catholics would be rudely dismissed as a fanatic; and a Kierkegaard, speaking with an American accent, would be considerably less welcome than Norman Vincent Peale in most Protestant pulpits."

⊥566

This religious influence has extended far, far back of the First and Fourteenth Amendments. Every Sunday School student knows the Fourth Commandment:

"Remember the sabbath day to keep it holy.

"Six days shalt thou labour, and do all thy work:

"But the seventh day is the sabbath of the LORD thy God: in it thou shalt not do any work, thou, nor thy son, nor thy daughter, thy manservant, nor thy ⊥maidservant, nor thy cattle, nor thy stranger that is within thy gates:

⊥567

"For in six days the LORD made heaven and earth, the sea, and all that in them is, and rested the seventh day: wherefore the LORD blessed the sabbath day, and hallowed it." Exodus 20:8-11

This religious mandate for observance of the Seventh Day became, under Emperor Constantine, a mandate for observance of the First Day "in conformity with the practice of the Christian Church." This religious mandate has had a checkered history, but in general its command, enforced now by the ecclesiastical authorities, now by the civil authorities, and now by both, has held good down through the centuries. The general pattern of these laws in the United States was set in the eighteenth century and derives, most directly, from a seventeenth century English statute. Judicial comment on the ⊥Sunday laws has always been a mixed bag. Some judges have asserted that the statutes have a "purely" civil aim, *i.e.*, limitation of work time and provision for a common and universal leisure. But other judges have recognized the religious significance of Sunday and that the laws existed to enforce the maintenance of that significance. In general, both threads of argument have continued to interweave in the case law on the subject. Prior to the time when the First Amendment was held applicable to the States by reason of the Due Process Clause of the Fourteenth, the Court at least by *obiter dictum* approved State Sunday laws on three occasions: *Soon Hing* v. *Crowley; Hen-*

⊥568

nington v. *Georgia; Petit* v. *Minnesota.* And in *Friedman* v. *New York*, the Court, by a divided vote, dismissed "for want of a substantial federal question" an appeal from a New York decision upholding the validity of a Sunday law against an attack based on the First Amendment.

The *Soon Hing, Hennington*, and *Petit* cases all rested on the police power of the State—the right to safeguard the health of the people by requiring the cessation of normal activities one day out of seven. The Court in the *Soon Hing* case rejected the idea that Sunday laws rested on the power of government "to legislate for the promotion of religious observances." The New York Court of Appeals in the *Friedman* case followed the reasoning of the earlier cases.

|569   ⊥ The Massachusetts Sunday law involved in one of these appeals was once characterized by the Massachusetts court as merely a civil regulation providing for a "fixed period of rest." *Commonwealth* v. *Has.* That decision was, according to the District Court in the *Gallagher* case, "an *ad hoc* improvisation" made "because of the realization that the Sunday law would be more vulnerable to constitutional attack under the state Constitution if the religious motivation of the statute were more explicitly avowed." Certainly prior to the *Has* case, the Massachusetts courts had indicated that the aim of the Sunday law was religious. After the *Has* case the Massachusetts court construed the Sunday law as a religious measure. In *Davis* v. *Somerville*, it was said: "Our Puritan ancestors intended that the day should be not merely a day of rest from labor, but also a day devoted to public and private worship and to religious meditation and repose, undisturbed by secular cares or amusements. They saw fit to enforce the observance of the day by penal legislation, and the statute regulations which they devised for that purpose have continued in force, without any substantial modification, to the present time."

In *Commonwealth* v. *White*, the court refused to liberalize its construction of an exception in its Sunday law for works of "necessity." That word, it said, "was originally inserted to secure the obser-

|570   vance of the Lord's day in accordance with ⊥ the view of our ancestors, and it ever since has stood and still stands for the same purpose." In *Commonwealth* v. *McCarthy*, the court reiterated that the aim of the law was "to secure respect and reverence for the Lord's day."

The Pennsylvania Sunday laws before us in Nos. 36 and 67 have received the same construction. "Rest and quiet, on the Sabbath day, with the right and privilege of public and private worship, undisturbed by any mere worldly employment, are exactly what the statute was passed to protect." *Sparhawk* v. *Union Passenger R. Co.* A recent pronouncement by the Pennsylvania Supreme Court is found in *Commonwealth* v. *American Baseball Club.* "Christianity is part of the common law of Pennsylvania . . . and its people are christian people. Sunday is the holy day among christians."

The Maryland court, in sustaining the challenged law in No. 8, relied on *Judefind* v. *State* and *Le-*

vering v. *Park Commissioner.* In the former the court said: "It is undoubtedly true that rest from secular employment on Sunday does have a tendency to foster and encourage the Christian religion—of all sects and denominations that observe that day—as rest from work and ordinary occupation enables many to engage in public worship who probably would not otherwise do so. But it would scarcely be asked of a Court, in what professes to be a Christian land, to declare a law unconstitutional because it requires rest from bodily labor on Sunday, (except works of necessity and charity,) and *thereby* promotes the ⊥ cause of Christianity. If the Christian |57▮ religion is, incidentally or otherwise, benefited or fostered by having this day of rest, as it undoubtedly is, there is all the more reason for the enforcement of laws that help to preserve it."

In the *Levering* case the court relied on the excerpt from the *Judefind* decision just quoted.

We have then in each of the four cases Sunday laws that find their source in Exodus, that were brought here by the Virginians and by the Puritans, and that are today maintained, construed, and justified because they respect the views of our dominant religious groups and provide a needed day of rest.

The history was accurately summarized a century ago by Chief Justice Terry of the Supreme Court of California in *Ex parte Newman:* "The truth is, however much it may be disguised, that this one day of rest is a purely religious idea. Derived from the Sabbatical institutions of the ancient Hebrew, it has been adopted into all the creeds of succeeding religious sects throughout the civilized world; and whether it be the Friday of the Mohammedan, the Saturday of the Israelite, or the Sunday of the Christian, it is alike fixed in the affections of its followers, beyond the power of eradication, and in most of the States of our Confederacy, the aid of the law to enforce its observance has been given under the pretence of a civil, municipal, or police regulation."

That case involved the validity of a Sunday law under a provision of the California Constitution guaranteeing the "free exercise" of religion. Justice Burnett stated why he concluded that the ⊥ Sunday |57▮ law, there sought to be enforced against a man selling clothing on Sunday, infringed California's constitution: "Had the act made Monday, instead of Sunday, a day of compulsory rest, the constitutional question would have been the same. The fact that the Christian *voluntarily* keeps holy the first day of the week, does not authorize the Legislature to make that observance *compulsory.* The Legislature can not compel the citizen to do that which the Constitution leaves him free to do or omit, at his election. The act violates as much the religious freedom of the Christian as of the Jew. Because the conscientious views of the Christian compel him to keep Sunday as a Sabbath, he has the right to object, when the Legislature invades his freedom of religious worship, and assumes the power to compel him to do that which he has right to omit if he pleases. The principle is the same, whether the act of the Legislature *compels* us to do that which we wish to do, or not to do. . . .

"Under the Constitution of this State, the Legislature can not pass any act, the legitimate effect of which is *forcibly* to establish any merely religious truth, or enforce any merely religious observances. The Legislature has no power over such a subject. When, therefore, the citizen is sought to be compelled by the Legislature to do any affirmative religious act, or to refrain from doing anything, because it violates simply a religious principle or observance, the act is unconstitutional."

The Court picks and chooses language from various decisions to bolster its conclusion that these Sunday laws in the modern setting are "civil regulations." No matter how much is written, no matter what is said, the parentage of these laws is the Fourth Commandment; and they ⊥ serve and satisfy the religious predispositions of our Christian communities. After all, the labels a State places on its laws are not binding on us when we are confronted with a constitutional decision. We reach our own conclusion as to the character, effect, and practical operation of the regulation in determining its constitutionality.

It seems to me plain that by these laws the States compel one, under sanction of law, to refrain from work or recreation on Sunday because of the majority's religious views about that day. The State by law makes Sunday a symbol of respect or adherence. Refraining from work or recreation in deference to the majority's religious feelings about Sunday is within every person's choice. By what authority can government compel it?

Cases are put where acts that are immoral by our standards but not by the standards of other religious ⊥ groups are made criminal. That category of cases, until today, has been a very restricted one confined to polygamy *(Reynolds* v. *United States)* and other extreme situations. The latest example is *Prince* v. *Massachusetts,* which upheld a statute making it criminal for a child under twelve to sell papers, periodicals, or merchandise on a street or in any public place. It was sustained in spite of the finding that the child thought it was her religious duty to perform the act. But that was a narrow holding which turned on the effect which street solicitation might have on the child-solicitor: "The state's authority over children's activities is broader than over like actions of adults. This is peculiarly true of public activities and in matters of employment. A democratic society rests, for its continuance, upon the healthy, well-rounded growth of young people into full maturity as citizens, with all that implies. It may secure this against impeding restraints and dangers within a broad range of selection. Among evils most appropriate for such action are the crippling effects of child employment, more especially in public places, and the possible harms arising from other activities subject to all the diverse influences of the street. It is too late now to doubt that legislation appropriately designed to reach such evils is within the state's police power, whether against the parent's claim to control of the child or one that religious scruples dictate contrary action."

None of the acts involved here implicates minors. None of the actions made constitutionally criminal today involves the doing of any act that any society has deemed to be immoral.

The conduct held constitutionally criminal today embraces the selling of pure, not impure, food; wholesome, ⊥ not noxious articles. Adults, not minors, are involved. The innocent acts, now constitutionally classified as criminal, emphasize the drastic break we make with tradition.

These laws are sustained because, it is said, the First Amendment is concerned with religious convictions or opinion, not with conduct. But it is a strange Bill of Rights that makes it possible for the dominant religious group to bring the minority to heel because the minority, in the doing of acts which intrinsically are wholesome and not antisocial, does not defer to the majority's religious beliefs. Some have religious scruples against eating pork. Those scruples, no matter how bizarre they might seem to some, are within the ambit of the First Amendment. Is it possible that a majority of a state legislature having those religious scruples could make it criminal for the nonbeliever to sell pork? Some have religious scruples against slaughtering cattle. Could a state legislature, dominated by that group, make it criminal to run an abattoir?

The Court balances the need of the people for rest, recreation, late sleeping, family visiting and the like against the command of the First Amendment that no one need bow to the religious beliefs of another. There is in this realm no room for balancing. I see no place for it in the constitutional scheme. A legislature of Christians can no more make minorities conform to their weekly regime than a legislature of Moslems, or a legislature of Hindus. The religious regime of every group must be respected—unless it crosses the line of criminal conduct. But no one can be forced to come to a halt before it, or refrain from doing things that would offend it. That is my reading of the Establishment Clause and the Free Exercise Clause. Any other reading imports, I fear, an element common in other societies but foreign to us. . . .

⊥ The State can, of course, require one day of rest a week: one day when every shop or factory is closed. Quite a few States make that requirement. Then the "day of rest" becomes purely and simply a health measure. But the Sunday laws operate differently. They force minorities to obey the majority's religious feelings of what is due and proper for a Christian community; they provide a coercive spur to the "weaker brethren," to those who are indifferent to the claims of a Sabbath through apathy or scruple. Can there be any doubt that Christians, now aligned vigorously in favor of these laws, would be as strongly opposed if they were prosecuted under a Moslem law that forbade them from engaging in secular activities on days that violated Moslem scruples?

There is an "establishment" of religion in the constitutional sense if any practice of any religious group has the sanction of law behind it. There is an interference with the "free exercise" of religion if

⌐577 what in conscience one ⊥can do or omit doing is required because of the religious scruples of the community. Hence I would declare each of those laws unconstitutional as applied to the complaining parties, whether or not they are members of a sect which observes as its Sabbath a day other than Sunday.

When these laws are applied to Orthodox Jews, as they are in No. 11 and in No. 67, or to Sabbatarians their vice is accentuated. If the Sunday laws are constitutional, kosher markets are on a five-day week. Thus those laws put an economic penalty on those who observe Saturday rather than Sunday as the Sabbath. For the economic pressures on these minorities, created by the fact that our communities are predominantly Sunday-minded, there is no recourse. When, however, the State uses its coercive powers—here the criminal law—to compel minorities to observe a second Sabbath, not their own, the State undertakes to aid and "prefer one religion over another"—contrary to the command of the Constitution.

In large measure the history of the religious clause of the First Amendment was a struggle to be free of economic sanctions for adherence to one's religion. A small tax was imposed in Virginia for religious education. Jefferson and Madison led the fight against the tax, Madison writing his famous Memorial and Remonstrance against that law. As a result, the tax measure was defeated and instead Virginia's famous "Bill for Religious Liberty," written by Jefferson, was enacted. That Act provided: "That no man shall be compelled to frequent or support any religious worship, place, or ministry whatsoever, nor shall be enforced, restrained, molested, or burthened in his ⌐578 body or goods, nor shall other⊥wise suffer on account of his religious opinions or belief. . . ."

The reverse side of an "establishment" is a burden on the "free exercise" of religion. Receipt of funds from the State benefits the established church directly; laying an extra tax on nonmembers benefits the established church indirectly. Certainly the present Sunday laws place Orthodox Jews and Sabbatarians under extra burdens because of their religious opinions or beliefs. Requiring them to abstain from their trade or business on Sunday reduces their work-week to five days, unless they violate their religious scruples. This places them at a competitive disadvantage and penalizes them for adhering to their religious beliefs.

"The sanction imposed by the state for observing a day other than Sunday as holy time is certainly more serious economically than the imposition of a license tax for preaching," which we struck down in *Murdock* v. *Pennsylvania* and in *Follett* v. *McCormick*. The special protection which Sunday laws give the dominant religious groups and the penalty they place on minorities whose holy day is Saturday constitute, in my view, state interference with the "free exercise" of religion.

⌐579 ⊥I dissent from applying criminal sanctions against any of these complainants since to do so implicates the States in religious matters contrary to the constitutional mandate. Reverend Allan C. Parker, Jr., Pastor of the ⊥South Park Presbyterian ⌐580 Church, Seattle, Washington, has stated my views: "We forget that, though Sunday-worshiping Christians are in the majority in this country among religious people, we do not have the right to force our practice upon the minority. Only a Church which deems itself without error and intolerant of error can justify its intolerance of the minority.

"A Jewish friend of mine runs a small business establishment. Because my friend is a Jew his business is closed each Saturday. He respects my right to worship on Sunday and I respect his right to worship on Saturday. But there is a difference. As a Jew he closes his store voluntarily so that he will be able to worship his God in his fashion. Fine! But, as a Jew living under Christian inspired Sunday closing laws, he is required to close his store on Sunday so that I will be able to worship my God in my fashion.

"Around the corner from my church there is a small Seventh Day Baptist Church. I disagree with the Seventh Day Baptists on many points of doctrine. Among the tenets of their faith which which I disagree is the 'seventh day worship.' But they are good neighbors and fellow Christians, and while we disagree we respect one another. The good people of my congregation set aside their jobs on the first day of the week and gather in God's house for worship. Of course, it is easy for them to set aside their jobs since Sunday closing laws—inspired by the Church—keep them from their work. At the Seventh Day Baptist church the people set aside ⊥their jobs ⌐581 on Saturday to worship God. This takes real sacrifice because Saturday is a good day for business. But that is not all— they are required by law to set aside their jobs on Sunday while more orthodox Christians worship.

". . . I do not believe that because I have set aside Sunday as a holy day I have the right to force all men to set aside that day also. Why should my faith be favored by the State over any other man's faith?"

With all deference, none of the opinions filed today in support of the Sunday laws has answered that question.

BRAUNFELD v. BROWN

366 U.S. 599
ON APPEAL FROM THE UNITED STATES
DISTRICT COURT FOR
THE EASTERN DISTRICT OF
PENNSYLVANIA
Argued December 8, 1960 — Decided May 29, 1961

⊥*Mr. Chief Justice* WARREN announced the ⌐600 judgment of the Court and an opinion in which *MR. Justice* BLACK, *Mr. Justice* CLARK, and *Mr. Justice* WHITTAKER concur.

This case concerns the constitutional validity of the application to appellants of the Pennsylvania criminal statute, enacted in 1959, which proscribes the Sunday retail sale of certain enumerated commodities. Among the questions presented are whether the statute is a law ⊥respecting an establishment ⌐601 of religion and whether the statute violates equal protection. Since both of these questions, in reference to this very statute, have already been answered in the negative, *Two Guys from Harrison-Allentown, Inc.*, v. *McGinley*, and since appellants present nothing new regarding them, they need not be considered here. Thus, the only question for consideration is whether the statute interferes with the free exercise of appellants' religion.

Appellants are merchants in Philadelphia who engage in the retail sale of clothing and home furnishings within the proscription of the statute in issue. Each of the appellants is a member of the Orthodox Jewish faith, which requires the closing of their places of business and a total abstention from all manner of work from nightfall each Friday until nightfall each Saturday. They instituted a suit in the court below seeking a permanent injunction against the enforcement of the 1959 statute. Their complaint, as amended, alleged that appellants had previously kept their places of business open on Sunday; that each of appellants had done a substantial amount of business on Sunday, compensating somewhat for their closing on Saturday; that Sunday closing will result in impairing the ability of all appellants to earn a livelihood and will render appellant Braunfeld unable to continue in his business, thereby losing his capital investment; that the statute is unconstitutional for the reasons stated above. . . .

Appellants contend that the enforcement against them of the Pennsylvania statute will prohibit the free exercise ⊥of their religion because, due to the statute's compulsion to close on Sunday, appellants will suffer substantial economic loss, to the benefit of their non-Sabbatarian competitors, if appellants also continue their Sabbath observance by closing their businesses on Saturday; that this result will either compel appellants to give up their Sabbath observance, a basic tenet of the Orthodox Jewish faith, or will put appellants at a serious economic disadvantage if they continue to adhere to their Sabbath. Appellants also assert that the statute will operate so as to hinder the Orthodox Jewish faith in gaining new adherents. And the corollary to these arguments is that if the free exercise of appellants' religion is impeded, that religion is being subjected to discriminatory treatment by the State. . . .

⊥Concededly, appellants and all other persons who wish to work on Sunday will be burdened economically by the State's day of rest mandate; and appellants point out that their religion requires them to refrain from work on Saturday as well. Our inquiry then is whether, in these circumstances, the First and Fourteenth Amendments forbid application of the Sunday Closing Law to appellants.

Certain aspects of religious exercise cannot, in any way, be restricted or burdened by either federal or state legislation. Compulsion by law of the acceptance of any creed or the practice of any form of worship is strictly forbidden. The freedom to hold religious beliefs and opinions is absolute. Thus, in *West Virginia State Board of Education* v. *Barnette* this Court held that state action compelling school children to salute the flag, on pain of expulsion from public school, was contrary to the First and Fourteenth Amendments when applied to those students whose religious beliefs forbade saluting a flag. But this is not the case at bar; the statute before us does not make criminal the holding of any religious belief or opinion, nor does it force anyone to embrace any religious belief or to say or believe anything in conflict with his religious tenets.

However, the freedom to act, even when the action is in accord with one's religious convictions, is not totally free from legislative restrictions. As pointed out in *Reynolds* v. *United States*, legislative power over mere opinion is forbidden but it may reach people's actions when they are found to be in violation of important social duties or subversive of good order, even when ⊥ the actions are demanded by one's religion. . . .

And, in the *Barnette* case, the Court was careful to point out that "The freedom asserted by these appellees does not bring them into collision with rights asserted by any other individual. It is such conflicts which most frequently require intervention of the State to determine where the rights of one end and those of another begin. . . . It is . . . to be noted that the compulsory flag salute and ⊥pledge requires *affirmation of a belief* and an *attitude of mind.*" (Emphasis added.)

Thus, in *Reynolds* v. *United States*, this Court upheld the polygamy conviction of a member of the Mormon faith despite the fact that an accepted doctrine of his church then imposed upon its male members the *duty* to practice polygamy. And, in *Prince* v. *Massachusetts* this Court upheld a statute making it a crime for a girl under eighteen years of age to sell any newspapers, periodicals or merchandise in public places despite the fact that a child of the Jehovah's Witnesses faith believed that it was her religious *duty* to perform this work.

It is to be noted that, in the two cases just mentioned, the religious practices themselves conflicted with the public interest. In such cases, to make accommodation between the religious action and an exercise of state authority is a particularly delicate task because resolution in favor of the State results in the choice to the individual of either abandoning his religious principle or facing criminal prosecution.

But, again, this is not the case before us because the statute at bar does not make unlawful any religious practices of appellants; the Sunday law simply regulates a secular activity and, as applied to appellants, operates so as to make the practice of their religious beliefs more expensive. Furthermore, the law's effect does not inconvenience all members of the Orthodox Jewish faith but only those who believe it necessary to work on Sunday. And even these are not faced with as serious a choice as forsaking their religious practices or subjecting themselves to criminal prosecution. Fully recognizing that the alter⊥natives open to appellants and others similarly situated—retaining their present occupations and incurring economic disadvantage or engaging in some other commercial activity which does not call for either Saturday or Sunday labor—may well result in some financial sacrifice in order to observe their religious beliefs, still the option is wholly different than when the legislation attempts to make a religious practice itself unlawful.

To strike down, without the most critical scrutiny, legislation which imposes only an indirect burden on the exercise of religion, *i. e.*, legislation which does not make unlawful the religious practice itself, would radically restrict the operating latitude of the legislature. Statutes which tax income and limit the amount which may be deducted for religious contributions impose an indirect economic burden on the observance of the religion of the citizen whose religion requires him to donate a greater amount to his church; statutes which require the courts to be closed on Saturday and Sunday impose a similar indirect burden on the observance of the religion of the trial lawyer whose religion requires him to rest on a weekday. The list of legislation of this nature is nearly limitless.

Needless to say, when entering the area of religious freedom, we must be fully cognizant of the particular protection that the Constitution has accorded it. Abhorrence of religious persecution and intolerance is a basic part of our heritage. But we are a cosmopolitan nation made up of people of almost every conceivable religious preference. These denominations number almost three hundred. Consequently, it cannot be expected, much less required, that legislators enact no law regulating conduct that may in some way result in an economic disadvantage to some religious sects and not to others because of the special practices of the various religions. We do not believe that such an effect is an absolute test ⊥for determining whether the legislation violates the freedom of religion protected by the First Amendment.

Of course, to hold unassailable all legislation regulating conduct which imposes solely an indirect burden on the observance of religion would be a gross oversimplification. If the purpose or effect of a law is to impede the observance of one or all religions or is to discriminate invidiously between religions, that law is constitutionally invalid even though the burden may be characterized as being only indirect. But if the State regulates conduct by enacting a general law within its power, the purpose and effect of which is to advance the State's secular goals, the statute is valid despite its indirect burden on religious observance unless the State may accomplish its purpose by means which do not impose such a burden.

As we pointed out in *McGowan* v. *Maryland*, we cannot find a State without power to provide a weekly respite from all labor and, at the same time, to set one day of the week apart from the others as a day of rest, repose, recreation and tranquillity—a day when the hectic tempo of everyday existence ceases and a more pleasant atmosphere is created, a day which all members of the family and community have the opportunity to spend and enjoy together, a day on which people may visit friends and relatives who are not available during working days, a day when the weekly laborer may best regenerate himself. This is particularly true in this day and age of increasing state concern with public welfare legislation.

⊥Also, in *McGowan*, we examined several suggested alternative means by which it was argued that the State might accomplish its secular goals without even remotely or incidentally affecting religious freedom. We found there that a State might well find that those alternatives would not accomplish bringing about a general day of rest. We need not examine them again here.

However, appellants advance yet another means at the State's disposal which they would find unobjectionable. They contend that the State should cut an exception from the Sunday labor proscription for those people who, because of religious conviction, observe a day of rest other than Sunday. By such regulation, appellants contend, the economic disadvantages imposed by the present system would be removed and the State's interest in having all people rest one day would be satisfied.

A number of States provide such an exemption, and this may well be the wiser solution to the problem. But our concern is not with the wisdom of legislation but with its constitutional limitation. Thus, reason and experience teach that to permit the exemption might well undermine the State's goal of providing a day that, as best possible, eliminates the atmosphere of commercial noise and activity. Although not dispositive of the issue, enforcement problems would be more difficult since there would be two or more days to police rather than one and it would be more difficult to observe whether violations were occurring.

Additional problems might also be presented by a regulation of this sort. To allow only people who rest on a day other than Sunday to keep their businesses open on that day might well provide these people with an economic advantage over their competitors who must ⊥remain closed on that day; this might cause the Sunday-observers to complain that their religions are being discriminated against. With this competitive advantage existing, there could well be the temptation for some, in order to keep their businesses open on Sunday, to assert that they have religious convictions which compel them to close their businesses on what had formerly been their least profitable day. This might make necessary a state-conducted inquiry into the sincerity of the individual's religious beliefs, a practice which a State might believe would itself run afoul of the spirit of constitutionally protected religious guarantees. Finally, in order to keep the disruption of the day at a minimum, exempted employers would probably have to hire employees who themselves qualified for the exemption because of their own religious beliefs, a practice which a State might feel to be opposed to its general policy prohibiting religious discrimination in hiring. For all of these reasons, we cannot say that the Pennsylvania statute before us is invalid, either on its face or as applied.

Mr. Justice HARLAN concurs in the judgment. *Mr. Justice BRENNAN* and *Mr. Justice STEW-* |610 *ART* concur in ⊥our disposition of appellants' claims under the Establishment Clause and the Equal Protection Clause. *Mr. Justice FRANK-FURTER* and *Mr. Justice HARLAN* have rejected appellants' claim under the Free Exercise Clause in a separate opinion.

Accordingly, the decision is *Affirmed.*

Mr. Justice BRENNAN, concurring and dissenting.

I agree with *The CHIEF JUSTICE* that there is no merit in appellants' establishment and equal-protection claims. I dissent, however, as to the claim that Pennsylvania has prohibited the free exercise of appellants' religion.

The Court has demonstrated the public need for a weekly surcease from worldly labor, and set forth the considerations of convenience which have led the Commonwealth of Pennsylvania to fix Sunday as the time for that respite. I would approach this case differently, from the point of view of the individuals whose liberty is—concededly—curtailed by these enactments. For the values of the First Amendment, as embodied in the Fourteenth, look primarily towards the preservation of personal liberty, rather than towards the fulfillment of collective goals.

The appellants are small retail merchants, faithful practitioners of the Orthodox Jewish faith. They allege—and the allegation must be taken as true, since the case comes to us on a motion to dismiss the complaint—that ". . . one who does not observe the Sabbath [by refraining from labor] . . . cannot be an |611 Orthodox Jew." ⊥In appellants' business area Friday night and Saturday are busy times; yet appellants, true to their faith, close during the Jewish Sabbath, and make up some, but not all, of the business thus lost by opening on Sunday. "Each of the plaintiffs," the complaint continues, "does a substantial amount of business on Sundays, and the ability of the plaintiffs to earn a livelihood will be greatly impaired by closing their business establishment on Sundays." Consequences even more drastic are alleged: "Plaintiff, Abraham Braunfeld, will be unable to continue in his business if he may not stay open on Sunday and he will thereby lose his capital investment." In other words, the issue in this case—and we do not understand either appellees or the Court to contend otherwise—is whether a State may put an individual to a choice between his business and his religion. The Court today holds that it may. But I dissent, believing that such a law prohibits the free exercise of religion.

The first question to be resolved, however, is somewhat broader than the facts of this case. That question concerns the appropriate standard of constitutional adjudication in cases in which a statute is assertedly in conflict with the First Amendment, whether that limitation applies of its own force, or as absorbed through the less definite words of the Fourteenth Amendment. The Court in such cases is not confined to the narrow inquiry whether the challenged law is rationally related to some legitimate legislative end. Nor is the case decided by a finding that the State's interest is substantial and important, as well as rationally justifiable. This canon of adjudication was clearly stated by Mr. Justice Jackson, speaking for the Court in *West Virginia State Board of Education* v. *Barnette:* "In weighing arguments of the parties it is important to distinguish between the due process clause of the Fourteenth Amendment as an instrument for |612 ⊥transmitting the principles of the First Amendment and those cases in which it is applied for its own sake. The test of legislation which collides with the Fourteenth Amendment, because it also collides with the principles of the First, is much more definite than the test when only the Fourteenth is involved. Much of the vagueness of the due process clause disappears when the specific prohibitions of the First become its standard. The right of a State to regulate, for example, a public utility may well include, so far as the due process test is concerned, power to impose all of the restrictions which a legislature may have a 'rational basis' for adopting. But freedoms of speech and of press, of assembly, and of worship may not be infringed on such slender grounds. They are susceptible of restriction only to prevent grave and immediate danger to interests which the State may lawfully protect. It is important to note that while it is the Fourteenth Amendment which bears directly upon the State it is the more specific limiting principles of the First Amendment that finally govern this case."

This exacting standard has been consistently applied by this Court as the test of legislation under all clauses of the First Amendment, not only those specifically dealing with freedom of speech and of the press. For religious freedom—the freedom to believe and to practice strange and, it may be, foreign creeds—has classically been one of the highest values of our society. Even the most concentrated and fully articulated attack on this high standard has seemingly admitted its validity in principle, while ⊥de- |613 ploring some incidental phraseology. The honored place of religious freedom in our constitutional hierarchy, suggested long ago by the argument of counsel in *Permoli* v. *Municipality No. 1 of the City of New Orleans* and foreshadowed by a prescient footnote in *United States* v. *Carolene Products Co.* must now be taken to be settled. Or at least so it appeared until today. For in this case the Court seems to say, without so much as a deferential nod towards that high place which we have accorded religious freedom in the past, that any substantial state interest will justify encroachments on religious practice, at least if those encroachments are cloaked in the guise of some nonreligious public purpose.

Admittedly, these laws do not compel overt affirmation of a repugnant belief, as in *Barnette*, nor do they prohibit outright any of appellants' religious practices, as did the federal law upheld in *Reynolds* v. *United States* cited by the Court. That is, the laws do not say that appellants must work on Saturday. But their effect is that appellants may not simultaneously practice their religion and their trade, without being hampered by a substantial competitive disadvantage. Their effect is that no one may at one and the same time be an Orthodox Jew and compete effectively with his Sunday-observing fellow tradesmen. This clog upon the exercise of religion, this state-imposed burden on Orthodox Judaism, has exactly the same economic effect as a tax levied upon the sale of religious literature. And yet, such a tax, when applied in the form of an excise or license fee, was held invalid in *Follett* v. *Town of McCormick.* All this the Court, as I read its opinion, concedes.

What, then, is the compelling state interest which impels the Commonwealth of Pennsylvania to ⌐614 impede ⊥ appellants' freedom of worship? What overbalancing need is so weighty in the constitutional scale that it justifies this substantial, though indirect, limitation of appellants' freedom? It is not the desire to stamp out a practice deeply abhorred by society, such as polygamy, as in *Reynolds*, for the custom of resting one day a week is universally honored, as the Court has amply shown. Nor is it the State's traditional protection of children, as in *Prince* v. *Massachusetts* for appellants are reasoning and fully autonomous adults. It is not even the interest in seeing that everyone rests one day a week, for appellants' religion requires that they take such a rest. It is the mere convenience of having everyone rest on the same day. It is to defend this interest that the Court holds that a State need not follow the alternative route of granting an exemption for those who in good faith observe a day of rest other than Sunday.

It is true, I suppose, that the granting of such an exemption would make Sundays a little noisier, and the task of police and prosecutor a little more difficult. It is also true that a majority—21—of the 34 States which have general Sunday regulations have exemptions of this kind. We are not told that those States are significantly noisier, or that their police

are significantly more burdened, than ⊥ Penn- ⌐615 sylvania's. Even England, not under the compulsion of a written constitution, but simply influenced by considerations of fairness, has such an exemption for some activities. The Court conjures up several difficulties with such a system which seem to me more fanciful than real. Non-Sunday observers might get an unfair advantage, it is said. A similar contention against the draft exemption for conscientious objectors (another example of the exemption technique) was rejected with the observation that "its unsoundness is too apparent to require" discussion. *Selective Draft Law Cases.* However widespread the complaint, it is legally baseless, and the State's reliance upon it cannot withstand a First Amendment claim. We are told that an official inquiry into the good faith with which religious beliefs are held might be itself unconstitutional. But this Court indicated otherwise in *United States* v. *Ballard.* Such an inquiry is no more an infringement of religious freedom than the requirement imposed by the Court itself in *McGowan* v. *Maryland*, decided this day, that a plaintiff show that his good-faith religious beliefs are hampered before he acquires standing to attack a statute under the Free Exercise Clause of the First Amendment. Finally, I find the Court's mention of a problem under state anti-discrimination statutes almost chimerical. Most such statutes provide that hiring may be made on a religious basis if religion is a *bona fide* occupational qualification. It happens, moreover, that Pennsylvania's statute has such a provision.

In fine, the Court, in my view, has exalted administrative convenience to a constitutional level high enough to ⊥justify making one religion economically disadvantageous. The Court would justify this result on the ground that the effect on religion, though substantial, is indirect. The Court forgets, I think, a warning uttered during the congressional discussion of the First Amendment itself: ". . . the rights of conscience are, in their nature, of peculiar delicacy, and will little bear the gentlest touch of governmental hand. . . ."

I would reverse this judgment and remand for a trial of appellants' allegations, limited to the free-exercise-of-religion issue.

Mr. Justice STEWART, dissenting.

I agree with substantially all that *Mr. Justice BRENNAN* has written. Pennsylvania has passed a law which compels an Orthodox Jew to choose between his religious faith and his economic survival. That is a cruel choice. It is a choice which I think no State can constitutionally demand. For me this is not something that can be swept under the rug and forgotten in the interest of enforced Sunday togetherness. I think the impact of this law upon these appellants grossly violates their constitutional right to the free exercise of their religion.

ESTATE OF THORNTON v. CALDOR, INC.

105 S.Ct. 2914
ON WRIT OF CERTIORARI TO THE
SUPREME COURT OF CONNECTICUT
Argued November 7, 1984 — Decided June 26, 1985
CHIEF JUSTICE BURGER delivered the opinion of the Court.

We granted certiorari to decide whether a state statute that provides employees with the absolute right not to work on their chosen Sabbath violates the Establishment Clause of the First Amendment.

I

In early 1975, petitioner's decedent Donald E. Thornton began working for respondent Caldor, Inc., a chain of New England retail stores; he managed the men's and boys' clothing department in respondent's Waterbury, Connecticut, store. At that time, respondent's Connecticut stores were closed on Sundays pursuant to state law. Conn. Gen. Stat. §§ 53—300 to 53—303 (1958).

In 1977, following the state legislature's revision of the Sunday-closing laws, respondent opened its Connecticut stores for Sunday business. In order to handle the expanded store hours, respondent required its managerial employees to work every third or fourth Sunday. Thornton, a Presbyterian who observed Sunday as his Sabbath, initially complied with respondent's demand and worked a total of 31 Sundays in 1977 and 1978. In October 1978, Thornton was transferred to a management position in respondent's Torrington store; he continued to work on Sundays during the first part of 1979. In November 1979, however, Thornton informed respondent that he would no longer work on Sundays because he observed that day as his Sabbath; he invoked the protection of Conn. Gen. Stat. § 53—303e(b) (Supp. 1962-1984), which provides: "No person who states that a particular day of the week is observed as his Sabbath may be required by his employer to work on such day. An employee's refusal to work on his Sabbath shall not constitute grounds for his dismissal."

Thornton rejected respondent's offer either to transfer him to a management job in a Massachusetts store that was closed on Sundays, or to transfer him to a nonsupervisory position in the Torrington store at a lower salary. In March 1980, respondent transferred Thornton to a clerical position in the Torrington store; Thornton resigned two days later and filed a grievance with the State Board of Mediation and Arbitration alleging that he was discharged from his manager's position in violation of Conn. Gen. Stat. § 53—303e(b).

Respondent defended its action on the ground that Thornton had not been "discharged" within the meaning of the statute; respondent also urged the Board to find that the statute violated Article 7 of the Connecticut Constitution as well as the Establishment Clause of the First Amendment. After holding an evidentiary hearing the Board evaluated the sincerity of Thornton's claim and concluded it was based on a sincere religious conviction; it issued a formal decision sustaining Thornton's grievance. The Board framed the statutory issue as follows, "[i]f a discharge for refusal to work Sunday hours occurred and Sunday was the Grievant's Sabbath . . . ," § 53—303e(b) would be violated; the Board held that respondent had violated the statute by "discharg[ing] Mr. Thornton as a management employee for refusing to work . . . [on] Thornton's . . . Sabbath." The Board ordered respondent to reinstate Thornton with back pay and compensation for lost fringe benefits. The Superior Court, in affirming that ruling, concluded that the statute did not offend the Establishment Clause.

The Supreme Court of Connecticut reversed, holding the statute did not have a "clear secular purpose." By authorizing each employee to designate his own Sabbath as a day off, the statute evinced the "unmistakable purpose . . . [of] allow[ing] those persons who wish to worship on a particular day the freedom to do so." The court then held that the "primary effect" of the statute was to advance religion because the statute "confers its 'benefit' on an explicitly religious basis. Only those employees who designate a Sabbath are entitled not to work on that particular day, and may not be penalized for so doing." The court noted that the statute required the State Mediation Board to decide which religious activities may be characterized as an "observance of Sabbath" in order to assess employees' sincerity, and concluded that this type of inquiry is "exactly the type of 'comprehensive, discriminating and continuing state surveillance' . . . which creates excessive governmental entanglements between church and state." We granted certiorari. We affirm.

II

Under the Religion Clauses, Government must guard against activity that impinges on religious freedom, and must take pains not to compel people to act in the name of any religion. In setting the appropriate boundaries in Establishment Clause cases, the Court has frequently relied on our holding in *Lemon* for guidance, and we do so here. To pass constitutional muster under *Lemon* a statute must not only have a secular purpose and not foster excessive entanglement of government with religion, its primary effect must not advance or inhibit religion.

The Connecticut statute challenged here guarantees every employee, who "states that a particular day of the week is observed as his Sabbath," the right not to work on his chosen day. The State has thus decreed that those who observe a Sabbath any day of the week as a matter of religious conviction must be relieved of the duty to work on that day, no matter what burden or inconvenience this imposes on the employer or fellow workers. The statute arms Sabbath observers with an absolute and unqualified right not to work on whatever day they designate as their Sabbath.

In essence, the Connecticut statute imposes on employers and employees an absolute duty to conform their business practices to the particular religious practices of the employee by enforcing observance of the Sabbath the employee unilaterally designates. The State thus commands that Sabbath religious concerns automatically control over all secular interests at the workplace; the statute takes no account of the convenience or interests of the employer or those of other employees who do not observe a Sabbath. The employer and others must adjust their affairs to the command of the State whenever the statute is invoked by an employee.

There is no exception under the statute for special circumstances, such as the Friday Sabbath observer employed in an occupation with a Monday through Friday schedule—a school teacher, for example; the statute provides for no special consideration if a high percentage of an employer's workforce asserts rights to the same Sabbath. Moreover, there is no exception when honoring the dictates of Sabbath observers would cause the employer substantial economic burdens or when the employer's compliance would require the imposition of significant burdens on other employees required to work in place of the Sabbath observers. Finally, the statute allows for no consideration as to whether the employer has made reasonable accommodation proposals.

This unyielding weighting in favor of Sabbath observers over all other interests contravenes a fundamental principle of the Religion Clauses, so well articulated by Judge Learned Hand: " The First Amendment . . . gives no one the right to insist that in pursuit of their own interests others must conform their conduct to his own religious necessities." *Otten* v. *Baltimore & Ohio R. Co.* As such, the statute goes beyond having an incidental or remote effect of advancing religion. The statute has a primary effect that impermissibly advances a particular religious practice.

III

We hold that the Connecticut statute, which provides Sabbath observers with an absolute and unqualified right not to work on their Sabbath, violates the Establishment Clause of the First Amendment. Accordingly, the judgment of the Supreme Court of Connecticut is affirmed.

Affirmed.

Justice REHNQUIST dissents.

Justice O'CONNOR, with whom *Justice MARSHALL* joins, concurring.

The court applies the test enunciated in *Lemon* v. *Kurtzman,* and concludes that Conn. Gen. Stat. § 53—303e(b) has a primary effect that impermissibly advances religion. I agree, and I join the Court's opinion and judgment. In my view, the Connecticut Sabbath law has an impermissible effect because it conveys a message of endorsement of the Sabbath observance.

All employees, regardless of their religious orientation, would value the benefit which the statute bestows on Sabbath observers—the right to select the day of the week in which to refrain from labor. Yet Connecticut requires private employers to confer this valued and desirable benefit only on those employees who adhere to a particular religious belief. The statute singles out Sabbath observers for special and, as the Court concludes, absolute protection without according similar accommodation to ethical and religious beliefs and practices of other private employees. There can be little doubt that an objective observer or the public at large would perceive this statutory scheme precisely as the Court does today. The message conveyed is one of endorsement of a particular religious belief, to the detriment of those who do not share it. As such, the Connecticut statute has the effect of advancing religion, and cannot withstand Establishment Clause scrutiny.

I do not read the Court's opinion as suggesting that the religious accommodation provisions of Title VII of the Civil Rights Act are similarly invalid. These provisions preclude employment discrimination based on a person's religion and require private employers to reasonably accommodate the religious practices of employees unless to do so would cause undue hardship to the employer's business. 42 U.S.C. § 2000e(j) and 2000e—2(a)(l). Like the Connecticut Sabbath law, Title VII attempts to lift a burden on religious practice that is imposed by *private* employers, and hence it is not the sort of accommodation statute specifically contemplated by the Free Exercise Clause. The provisions of Title VII must therefore manifest a valid secular purpose and effect to be valid under the Establishment Clause. In my view, a statute outlawing employment discrimination based on race, color, religion, sex, or national origin has the valid secular purpose of assuring employment opportunity to all groups in our pluralistic society. Since Title VII calls for reasonable rather than absolute accommodation and extends that requirement to all religious beliefs and practices rather than protecting only the Sabbath observance, I believe an objective observer would perceive it as an antidiscrimination law rather than an endorsement of religion or a particular religious practice.

RELIGION IN LABOR RELATIONS

In recent years religious spokesmen have frequently expressed grave concern with respect to what they consider to be excessive intrusion by government into the affairs of religious organizations and their agencies. As the comment and cases in this book indicate, this intervention has taken many forms: use of the taxing power to aid or disadvantage religious groups, requirement of submission of voluminous forms and reports, regulation of religious fund-raising activities, even infiltration of church groups by government agents in an effort to destroy the sanctuary movement.

Some few cases have reached the Supreme Court with respect to government intervention in what, broadly viewed, might be designated religion and labor relations. They raised in various ways the question of the part that government may play in the regulation of religious organizations and those who work for them.

NATIONAL LABOR RELATIONS BOARD v. THE CATHOLIC BISHOP OF CHICAGO (1979) (p. 325) concerned unionization of lay teachers in schools controlled by the Catholic church. When unions sought to represent lay teachers in schools involved in this litigation, the NLRB ordered representation elections. Catholic school authorities insisted that the NLRB lacked jurisdiction to intervene in the dispute. For the NLRB to claim otherwise, they argued, would impermissibly entangle a government agency in religious matters. When elections were held and the parochial schools refused to bargain with unions chosen by lay teachers, the NLRB found the schools guilty of unfair labor practices. Subsequently, these schools challenged the NLRB order to bargain. In resulting litigation, a federal court of appeals found in favor of the Catholic schools. The Seventh Circuit Court of Appeals, on constitutional grounds, held that the National Labor Relations Act violated the First Amendment's religion clauses when applied to parochial school teachers.

The Supreme Court, on appeal, also recognized that NLRB jurisdiction over parochial schools would raise difficult constitutional questions, but there was a legitimate prior question as to whether that jurisdiction existed. Traditionally, the Court has insisted that an act of Congress ought not be construed to violate the Constitution if statutory construction will suffice; thus, the Court examined the legislative history of the National Labor Relations Act. Careful analysis convinced five justices that Congress had not intended church-operated schools to be covered by the statute. Consequently, they ruled that the NLRB did not have authority to order Catholic schools to bargain with unions representing lay teachers. By dealing with this case at the statutory level the Court was able to avoid the more difficult question of whether the NLRB's action amounted to excessive governmental entanglement forbidden by the Establishment Clause.

From 1978 to 1980, the Supreme Court heard three more NLRB cases with titles that suggest church-state controversies, but which were not decided on that basis. In National Labor Relations Board v. Baptist Hospital and Beth Israel Hospital v. National Labor Relations Board, the Court ruled that the NLRB is empowered to issue rules governing places where hospital employees may solicit coworkers on behalf of labor organizations. Such places include gift shops, employee cafeterias, and the first-floor waiting rooms. However, the Court ruled that the NLRB could not compel hospitals to permit solicitation in areas where patients would be affected, such as corridors and waiting rooms on floors where patients are cared for.

Although Baptist Hospital and Beth Israel Hospital involved work rules in institutions related to religious organizations, this litigation had nothing to do with First Amendment issues. A similar case is that of National Labor Relations Board v. Yeshiva University. Here, faculty members were seeking to unionize and to bargain with the Jewish university, which refused to bargain. The Court agreed with university administrators that all full-time Yeshiva faculty members could be classified as "managerial employees" and were not covered by the NLRA; thus, the university could not be compelled to bargain under NLRB rules.

In 1980 a variation of the situation in Catholic Bishop was involved in National Labor Relations Board v. Bishop Ford Central Catholic High School. There a Catholic high school was governed by lay trustees of an independent corporation although the Christian mission of the school was obvious. When the NLRB claimed authority over labor disputes at the school, a federal court of appeals held that, notwithstanding the governing structure, the school carried out its services as a "church operated" agency, and therefore, as the Court had held in Catholic Bishop, was not subject to the authority of the NLRB. The Supreme Court let the lower court decision stand without opinion.

Three years later the United States District Court for the Southern District of New York heard a case which arose when the Lay Faculty Association, representing 343 lay teachers employed by the Catholic High School Association, filed charges with the New York State Labor Relations Board alleging unfair labor practices by the association. The Catholic High School Association sought a declaratory judgment from the Court that the State Labor Relations Board's assertion of jurisdiction over it constituted both a burden on its free exercise of religion and an excessive entanglement of church and state under the Establishment Clause.

District Judge Lasker found no basic differences in the fact situation here and that of the Catholic Bishop case except that the labor board here was a state rather than federal agency and that the New York statute was unquestionably intended to cover parochial school-lay teacher labor relations. Both parties agreed to the religious character of the schools and that they were "church-operated" as the term was used in Catholic Bishop. The constitutional issue was therefore clear.

The district judge found it unnecessary to determine whether the act violated the Free Exercise Clause. In light of the clear violation of the Establishment Clause the type and extent of state scrutiny required to monitor lay faculty employment conditions would inevitably result in excessive entanglement between church and state. The Constitution, said Judge Lasker, "does limit the kind and degree of state scrutiny of religious practices." The teachers union appealed to the Court of Appeals for the Second Circuit which examined both the free exercise and establishment issues, and by a two-to-one vote reversed the lower court's decision. It held that the indirect and incidental burden imposed on religion by the government's intervention was justified by a compelling state interest in collective bargaining. With respect to the constraints of the Establishment Clause, the court failed to find a degree of government surveillance sufficient to justify a charge of administrative entanglement. The primary goal of government in collective bargaining is to bring the parties to the bargaining table and then leave them to work out their problems. The fact that the board would necessarily be precluded by the First Amendment from looking into asserted religious motives does not preclude its exercise of jurisdiction. By limiting the board to the protection of teachers from unlawful discharge for non-religiously motivated causes, the court had satisfactorily accommodated the interests of church and state. Using the analogy of keeping the camel's nose out of the tent, the majority opinion held that the accommodation "firmly tethers the State Board's jurisdiction outside the constitutional tent that protects the Association's First Amendment rights." [1] The Supreme Court may at a later time have an opportunity to examine this assessment.

In the mid-1970s, officials of church-related colleges and universities complained bitterly about oppressive, time-consuming federal regulations and reports. Several federal agencies undertook to require church-related agencies and institutions, even including theological seminaries, to report employment and admissions statistics by race, sex and religion, even though they received no government funds. Two examples gained notoriety in the early 1980s. In *Mississippi College* v. *Equal Employment Opportunity Commission*, the college, owned and operated by the Mississippi Baptist Convention, resisted the government agency's command to supply personnel data. A female part-time instructor, not a Baptist, was passed over for a position when the college hired a male Baptist instead. She filed a grievance with EEOC, claiming discrimination. EEOC requested detailed information on Mississippi College's hiring practices to determine if the college had violated the female's rights. College authorities refused to supply the information, claiming that the government's demand for information promoted entanglement of government with religion and violated the college's religious freedom to prefer Baptist instructors. The Fifth Court of Appeals, reversing the lower court, found against Mississippi College. The Supreme Court allowed that decision to stand.

The other example involves Southwestern Baptist Theological Seminary in Fort Worth, Texas. Under EEOC regulations, all institutions of higher learning with fifteen or more employees are required to file form EEO-6, which requests data on the compensation, tenure, race, sex, and national origin of employees. Beginning in 1975, the Seminary refused to file the form on the grounds that the presumed jurisdiction of EEOC over the Seminary violated the religion clauses of the First Amendment. EEOC sued the Seminary to compel compliance. The federal district court ruled in favor of the Seminary, saying that EEOC did not have jurisdiction over the school, a wholly religious entity. The Court of Appeals for the Fifth Circuit agreed in 1981 that the Seminary has the status of a church and consequently those who teach or have supervision of teaching are ministers. It ruled that EEOC data does not have to be reported on them, but nonteaching

personnel (support people and administrators) are not ministers, according to the Court of Appeals, and are subject to EEOC jurisdiction. (*Southwestern Baptist Theological Seminary* v. *Equal Employment Opportunity Commission.*) The Seminary, which represented all six Southern Baptist seminaries in the litigation, disagreed with this opinion and early in 1982 asked the Supreme Court to consider the case, but the Court denied review.

In 1977 the Secretary of Labor brought an action in the United States District Court for the Western District of Arkansas against the Tony and Susan Alamo Foundation, a nonprofit religious corporation which operated a number of commercial businesses ranging from hog farms and candy production to retail clothing and motels. These businesses were staffed primarily by "associates," most of whom were former drug addicts, derelicts, or criminals receiving as pay in-kind benefits such as food, clothing, shelter, and medical benefits rather than cash. In the suit the associates asserted that they considered themselves to be volunteers working "only for religious and evangelical reasons."

The suit alleged violations by the foundation of the minimum wage, overtime, and recordkeeping provisions of the Fair Labor Standards Act. The district court held the foundation to be an enterprise, though non-profit in nature, "engaged in ordinary commercial activities in competition with other commercial businesses." The associates were "employees" within the meaning of the FLSA although receiving wages in another form than cash, and the foundation was therefore subject to the act.

The court denied the claim that application of the act to the foundation violated the Free Exercise and Establishment Clauses. The Eighth Court of Appeals subsequently also rejected the claim; the Supreme Court granted certiorari, and, after hearing, affirmed the decisions of the lower courts, *Alamo Foundation* v. *Secretary of Labor* (1985).

Justice White delivered the opinion for a unanimous Court. He agreed with the court of appeals that it was difficult to conclude that the extensive commercial enterprise of the foundation was "nothing but a religious liturgy engaged in bringing good news to a pagan world," and said that "by entering the economic arena and trafficking in the marketplace, the foundation has subjected itself to the standards Congress has prescribed for the benefit of employees." (471 U.S. 290, 294) The mixture of religious motivations with commercial objectives does not justify the payment of substandard wages nor alter the effect of a business on interstate commerce. The Fair Labor Standards Act does not expressly or by implication grant exemption to commercial activities carried on by religious organizations, and has been consistently so interpreted by the Secretary of Labor.

Justice White did not find that inclusion in the program actually burdened the free exercise of the religious rights of the claimants or result in excessive government entanglement in the affairs of the religious foundation. The recordkeeping requirements particularly objected to by the foundation as fostering excessive entanglement, applied only to the foundation's commercial activities, and would have no effect on evangelical activities. The Establishment Clause, he noted, does not exempt religious or-

---

[1] *Catholic High School Association of the Archdiocese of New York* v. *Culvert* 753 F. 2d 1161, 1169 (1985).

ganizations from such governmental actions as fire inspections and zoning and building laws, and the FLSA's recordkeeping requirements, "while perhaps more burdensome in terms of paperwork, are not significantly more intrusive into religious affairs."

As can be seen, the Court has, with respect to questions concerning labor and religion, avoided constitutional issues where possible, and has been generally resistant to government intervention except where the religious organization involved is rather clearly engaged in commercial activities in competition with other commercial businesses and the challenged government regulations impose a minimum burden. This is a relatively new area of law; tension and controversy will likely continue to increase as government regulation becomes ever more pervasive.

NATIONAL LABOR RELATIONS BOARD v.
THE CATHOLIC BISHOP OF CHICAGO

440 U.S. 490
ON WRIT OF CERTIORARI TO THE UNITED STATES COURT OF
APPEALS FOR THE SEVENTH CIRCUIT
Argued October 30, 1978 — Decided March 21, 1979

⌐491   ⊥ *Mr. Chief Justice BURGER* delivered the opinion of the Court.

This case arises out of the National Labor Relations Board's exercise of jurisdiction over lay faculty members at two groups of Catholic high schools. We granted certiorari to consider two questions: (a) Whether teachers in schools operated by a church to teach both religious and secular subjects are within the jurisdiction granted by the National Labor Relations Act; and (b) if the Act authorizes such jurisdiction, does its exercise violate the guarantees of the Religion Clauses of the First Amendment?

I

⌐492   ⊥ One group of schools is operated by the Catholic Bishop of Chicago, a corporation sole; the other group is operated by the Diocese of Fort Wayne-South Bend, Inc. The group operated by the Catholic Bishop of Chicago consists of two schools, Quigley North and Quigley South. Those schools are termed "minor seminaries" because of their role in educating high school students who may become priests. At one time, only students who manifested a positive and confirmed desire to be priests were admitted to the Quigley schools. In 1970, the requirement was changed so that students admitted to these schools need not show a definite inclination toward the priesthood. Now the students need only be recommended by their parish priest as having a potential for the priesthood or for Christian leadership. The schools continue to provide special religious instruction not offered in other Catholic secondary

schools. The Quigley schools also offer essentially the same college-preparatory curriculum as public secondary schools. Their students participate in a variety of extracurricular activities which include secular as well as religious events. The schools are recognized by the State and accredited by a regional educational organization.

The Diocese of Fort Wayne-South Bend, Inc., has five high schools. Unlike the Quigley schools, the special recom⊥mendation of a priest is not a prereq-   ⌐493 uisite for admission. Like the Quigley schools, however, these high schools seek to provide a traditional secular education but oriented to the tenets of the Roman Catholic faith; religious training is also mandatory. These schools are similarly certified by the State.

In 1974 and 1975, separate representation petitions were filed with the Board by interested union organizations for both the Quigley and the Fort Wayne-South Bend schools; representation was sought only for lay teachers. The schools challenged the assertion of jurisdiction on two grounds: (a) that they do not fall within the Board's discretionary jurisdictional criteria; and (b) that the Religion Clauses of the First Amendment preclude the Board's jurisdiction. The Board rejected the jurisdictional arguments on the basis of its decision in *Roman Catholic Archdiocese of Baltimore.* There the Board explained that its policy was to decline jurisdiction over religiously sponsored organizations "only when they are completely religious, not just religiously associated." Because neither group of schools was found to fall within the Board's "completely religious" category, the Board ordered elections. *Catholic Bishop of Chicago.*

⊥ In the Board-supervised election at the Quigley   ⌐494 schools, the Quigley Education Alliance, a union affiliated with the Illinois Education Association, prevailed and was certified as the exclusive bargaining representative for 46 lay teachers. In the Diocese of Fort Wayne-South Bend, the Community Alliance for Teachers of Catholic High Schools, a similar union organization, prevailed and was certified as the representative for the approximately 180 lay teachers. Notwithstanding the Board's order, the schools declined to recognize the unions or to bargain. The unions filed unfair labor practice complaints with the Board under §§ 8(a)(1) and (5) of the National Labor Relations Act, 29 U.S.C. §§ 158(a)(1) and (5). The schools opposed the General Counsel's motion for summary judgment, again challenging the Board's exercise of jurisdiction over religious schools on both statutory and constitutional grounds.

The Board reviewed the record of previous proceedings and concluded that all of the arguments had been raised or could have been raised in those earlier proceedings. Since the arguments had been rejected previously, the Board granted summary judgment, holding that it had properly exercised its statutory discretion in asserting jurisdiction over these schools. The Board concluded that the schools had violated the Act and ordered that they cease their unfair labor practices and that they bargain collec- ⌐495 tively with the unions. *Catholic ⊥ Bishop of Chicago; Diocese of Fort Wayne-South Bend, Inc.*

II

The schools challenged the Board's orders in peti- tions to the Court of Appeals for the Seventh Circuit. That court denied enforcement of the Board's orders. The court considered the Board's ac- tions in relation to its discretion in choosing to ex- tend its jurisdiction only to religiously affiliated schools that were not "completely religious." It con- cluded that the Board had not properly exercised its discretion, because the Board's distinction between "completely religious" and "merely religiously as- sociated" failed to provide a workable guide for the exercise of discretion: "We find the standard itself to be a simplistic black or white, purported rule con- taining no borderline demarcation of where 'com- pletely religious' takes over or, on the other hand, ceases. In our opinion the dichotomous 'completely religious—merely religiously associated' standard provides no workable guide to the exercise of discre- tion. The determination that an institution is so completely a religious entity as to exclude any viable secular components obviously implicates very sensi- tive questions of faith and tradition. *See, e.g.,* [*Wis- consin* v.] *Yoder.*"

The Court of Appeals recognized that the rejection of the Board's policy as to church-operated schools meant that the Board would extend its jurisdiction ⌐496 to all church-operated ⊥ schools. The court therefore turned to the question of whether the Board could exercise that jurisdiction, consistent with constitu- tional limitations. It concluded that both the Free Exercise Clause and the Establishment Clause of the First Amendment foreclosed the Board's jurisdiction. It reasoned that from the initial act of certifying a union as the bargaining agent for lay teachers the Board's action would impinge upon the freedom of church authorities to shape and direct teaching in accord with the requirements of their religion. It an- alyzed the Board's action in this way: "At some point, factual inquiry by courts or agencies into such matters [separating secular from religious training] would almost necessarily raise First Amendment problems. If history demonstrates, as it does, that Roman Catholics founded an alternative school sys- tem for essentially religious reasons and continued to maintain them as an 'integral part of the religious mission of the Catholic Church,' *Lemon* v. *Kurtzman,* courts and agencies would be hard pressed to take official or judicial notice that these purposes were undermined or eviscerated by the determination to offer such secular subjects as math- ematics, physics, chemistry, and English literature."

The court distinguished local regulations which re- quired fire inspections or state laws mandating attendance, reasoning that they did not "have the clear inhibiting potential upon the relationship be- tween teachers and employers with which the present Board order is directly concerned." The court held that interference with management pre- rogatives, found acceptable in an ordinary commer- cial setting, was not acceptable in an area protected by the First Amendment. "The real difficulty is found in the chilling aspect that the requirement of bargaining will impose on the exercise of the bish- ops' control of the religious mission of the schools."

III

⊥ The Board's assertion of jurisdiction over pri- ⌐497 vate schools is, as we noted earlier, a relatively recent development. Indeed, in 1951 the Board indi- cated that it would not exercise jurisdiction over nonprofit, educational institutions because to do so would not effectuate the purposes of the Act. *Trust- ees of Columbia University in the City of New York.* In 1970, however, the Board pointed to what it saw as an increased involvement in commerce by educa- tional institutions and concluded that this required a different position on jurisdiction. In *Cornell Univer- sity,* the Board overruled its *Columbia University* de- cision. *Cornell University* was followed by the assertion of jurisdiction over nonprofit, private sec- ondary schools. *Shattuck School.* The Board now asserts jurisdiction over all private, nonprofit, educa- tional institutions with gross annual revenues that meet its jurisdictional requirements whether they are secular or religious. See, *e.g., Academia San Jorge* (advisory opinion stating that Board would not as- sert jurisdiction over Catholic educational institution which did not meet jurisdictional standards); *Wind- sor School, Inc.* (declining jurisdiction where private, proprietary school did not meet jurisdictional amounts).

The broad assertion of jurisdiction has not gone unchallenged. But the Board has rejected the conten- tion that the Religion Clauses of the First Amend- ment bar the extension of its jurisdiction to church- operated schools. Where the Board has declined to exercise jurisdiction, it has done so only on the grounds of the employer's minimal impact on com- merce. Thus, in *Association of Hebrew Teachers of Metropolitan Detroit,* the Board did not assert juris- diction over the Association which offered ⊥ courses ⌐498 in Jewish culture in after-school classes, a nursery school, and a college. The Board termed the Associa- tion an "isolated instance of [an] atypical employer." It explained: "Whether an employer falls within a given 'class' of enterprise depends upon those of its activities which are predominant and give the em- ploying enterprise its character. . . . [T]he fact that an employer's activity . . . is dedicated to a sectari- an religious purpose is not a sufficient reason for the Board to refrain from asserting jurisdiction." In the same year the Board asserted jurisdiction over an Association chartered by the State of New York to operate diocesan high schools. *Henry M. Hald High School Assn.* It rejected the argument that its assertion of jurisdiction would produce excessive governmental entanglement with religion. In the Board's view, the Association had chosen to entangle itself with the secular world when it decided to hire lay teachers.

When it ordered an election for the lay professional employees at five parochial high schools in Baltimore in 1975, the Board reiterated its belief that exercise of its jurisdiction is not contrary to the First Amendment: "[T]he Board's policy in the past has been to decline jurisdiction over similar institutions only when they are completely religious, not just religiously associated, and the Archdiocese concedes that instruction is not limited to religious subjects. That the Archdiocese seeks to provide an education based on Christian principles does not lead to a contrary conclusion. Most religiously associated institutions seek to operate in conformity with ⊥ their religious tenets." *Roman Catholic Archdiocese of Baltimore.*

The Board also rejected the First Amendment claims in *Cardinal Timothy Manning, Roman Catholic Archbishop of the Archdiocese of Los Angeles*: "Regulation of labor relations does not violate the First Amendment when it involves a *minimal intrusion* on religious conduct and is necessary to obtain [the Act's] objective." (Emphasis added.)

The Board thus recognizes that its assertion of jurisdiction over teachers in religious schools constitutes some degree of intrusion into the administration of the affairs of church-operated schools. Implicit in the Board's distinction between schools that are "completely religious" and those "religiously associated" is also an acknowledgment of some degree of entanglement. Because that distinction was measured by a school's involvement with commerce, however, and not by its religious association, it is clear that the Board never envisioned any sort of religious litmus test for determining when to assert jurisdiction. Nevertheless, by expressing its traditional jurisdictional standards in First Amendment terms, the Board has plainly recognized that intrusion into this area could run afoul of the Religion Clauses and hence preclude jurisdiction on constitutional grounds.

IV

That there are constitutional limitations on the Board's actions has been repeatedly recognized by this Court even while acknowledging the broad scope of the grant of jurisdiction. The First Amendment, of course, is a limitation on the power of Congress. Thus, if we were to conclude that the Act granted the challenged jurisdiction over these teachers we would be required to decide whether that was con-

stitutionally permissible under the Religion Clauses of the First Amendment.

⊥ Although the respondents press their claims under the Religion Clauses, the question we consider first is whether Congress intended the Board to have jurisdiction over teachers in church-operated schools. In a number of cases the Court has heeded the essence of Mr. Chief Justice Marshall's admonition in *Murray* v. *The Charming Betsy*, by holding that an Act of Congress ought not be construed to violate the Constitution if any other possible construction remains available. Moreover, the Court has followed this policy in the interpretation of the Act now before us and related statutes.

In *Machinists* v. *Street*, for example, the Court considered claims that serious First Amendment questions would arise if the Railway Labor Act were construed to allow compulsory union dues to be used to support political candidates or causes not approved by some members. The Court looked to the language of the Act and the legislative history and concluded that they did not permit union dues to be used for such political purposes, thus avoiding "serious doubt of [the Act's] constitutionality."

Similarly in *McCulloch* v. *Sociedad Nacional de Marineros de Honduras*, a case involving the Board's assertion of jurisdiction over foreign seamen, the Court declined to read the National Labor Relations Act so as to give rise to a serious question of separation of powers which in turn would have implicated sensitive issues of the authority of the Executive over relations with foreign nations. The international implications of the case led the Court to describe it as involving "public questions particularly high in the scale of our national interest." Because of those questions the Court held that before sanctioning the Board's exercise of jurisdiction " 'there must be present the affirmative intention of the Congress clearly expressed.' " (quoting *Benz* v. *Compania Naviera Hidalgo*).

⊥ The values enshrined in the First Amendment plainly rank high "in the scale of our national values." In keeping with the Court's prudential policy it is incumbent on us to determine whether the Board's exercise of its jurisdiction here would give rise to serious constitutional questions. If so, we must first identify "the affirmative intention of the Congress clearly expressed" before concluding that the Act grants jurisdiction.

V

In recent decisions involving aid to parochial schools we have recognized the critical and unique role of the teacher in fulfilling the mission of a church-operated school. What was said of the schools in *Lemon* v. *Kurtzman* is true of the schools in this case: "Religious authority necessarily pervades the school system." The key role played by teachers in such a school system has been the predi-

⊥499

⊥500

⊥501

cate for our conclusions that governmental aid channeled through teachers creates an impermissible risk of excessive governmental entanglement in the affairs of the church-operated schools. For example, in *Lemon* we wrote: "In terms of potential for involving some aspect of faith or morals *in secular subjects*, a textbook's content is ascertainable, but a teacher's handling of a subject is not. We cannot ignore the danger that a teacher under religious control and discipline poses to the separation of the religious from the purely secular aspects of pre-college education. The conflict of functions inheres in the situation." (Emphasis added.)

Only recently we again noted the importance of the teacher's function in a church school: "Whether the subject is 'remedial reading,' 'advanced reading,' or simply 'reading,' a teacher remains a teacher, and the danger that religious doctrine will become intertwined with secular instruction persists." *Meek* v. ⌐502 *Pittenger.* Cf. ⊥ *Wolman* v. *Walter.* Good intentions by government—or third parties—can surely no more avoid entanglement with the religious mission of the school in the setting of mandatory collective bargaining than in the well-motivated legislative efforts consented to by the church-operated schools which we found unacceptable in *Lemon, Meek,* and *Wolman.*

The Board argues that it can avoid excessive entanglement since it will resolve only factual issues such as whether an anti-union animus motivated an employer's action. But at this stage of our consideration we are not compelled to determine whether the entanglement is excessive as we would were we considering the constitutional issue. Rather, we make a narrow inquiry whether the exercise of the Board's jurisdiction presents a significant risk that the First Amendment will be infringed.

Moreover, it is already clear that the Board's actions will go beyond resolving factual issues. The Court of Appeals' opinion refers to charges of unfair labor practices filed against religious schools. The court observed that in those cases the schools had responded that their challenged actions were mandated by their religious creeds. The resolution of such charges by the Board, in many instances, will necessarily involve inquiry into the good faith of the position asserted by the clergy-administrators and its relationship to the school's religious mission. It is not only the conclusions that may be reached by the Board which may impinge on rights guaranteed by the Religion Clauses, but also the very process of inquiry leading to findings and conclusions.

The Board's exercise of jurisdiction will have at least one other impact on church-operated schools. The Board will be called upon to decide what are ⌐503 "terms and conditions of ⊥employment" and therefore mandatory subjects of bargaining. Although the Board has not interpreted that phrase as it relates to educational institutions, similar state provisions provide insight into the effect of mandatory bargaining.

The Oregon Court of Appeals noted that "nearly everything that goes on in the schools affects teachers and is therefore arguably a 'condition of employment.'" *Springfield Education Assn.* v. *Springfield School Dist. No. 19.*

The Pennsylvania Supreme Court aptly summarized the effect of mandatory bargaining when it observed that the "introduction of a concept of mandatory collective bargaining, regardless of how narrowly the scope of negotiation is defined, necessarily represents an encroachment upon the former autonomous position of management." *Pennsylvania Labor Relations Board* v. *State College Area School Dist.* Inevitably the Board's inquiry will implicate sensitive issues that open the door to conflicts between clergy-administrators and the Board, or conflicts with negotiators for unions. What we said in *Lemon* applies as well here: "[p]arochial schools involve substantial religious activity and purpose.

"The substantial religious character of these church-related schools gives rise to entangling church-state relationships of the kind the Religion Clauses sought to avoid."

Mr. Justice Douglas emphasized this in his concurring opinion in *Lemon,* noting "the admitted and obvious fact that the *raison d'être* of parochial schools is the propagation of a religious faith."

⊥The church-teacher relationship in a church- ⌐50 operated school differs from the employment relationship in a public or other nonreligious school. We see no escape from conflicts flowing from the Board's exercise of jurisdiction over teachers in church-operated schools and the consequent serious First Amendment questions that would follow. We therefore turn to an examination of the National Labor Relations Act to decide whether it must be read to confer jurisdiction that would in turn require a decision on the constitutional claims raised by respondents.

VI

There is no clear expression of an affirmative intention of Congress that teachers in church-operated schools should be covered by the Act. Admittedly, Congress defined the Board's jurisdiction in very broad terms; we must therefore examine the legislative history of the Act to determine whether Congress contemplated that the grant of jurisdiction would include teachers in such schools.

In enacting the National Labor Relations Act in 1935, Congress sought to protect the right of American workers to bargain collectively. The concern that was repeated throughout the debates was the need to assure workers the right to organize to counterbalance the collective activities of employers which had been authorized by the National Industrial Recovery Act. But congressional attention focused on employment in private industry and on industrial recovery.

Our examination of the statute and its legislative history indicates that Congress simply gave no consideration to church-operated schools. It is not without significance, however, that the Senate Committee on Education and Labor chose a college professor's dispute with the college as an example of ⊥employer-employee relations *not* covered by the Act. |505

Congress' next major consideration of the jurisdiction of the Board came during the passage of the Labor Management Relations Act of 1947—the Taft-Hartley Act. In that Act Congress amended the definition of "employer" in § 2 of the original Act to exclude nonprofit hospitals. There was some discussion of the scope of the Board's jurisdiction but the consensus was that nonprofit institutions in general did not fall within the Board's jurisdiction because they did not affect commerce.

The most recent significant amendment to the Act was passed in 1974, removing the exemption of nonprofit hospitals. The Board relies upon that amendment as showing that Congress approved the Board's exercise of jurisdiction over church-operated ⊥schools. A close examination of that legislative |506 history, however, reveals nothing to indicate an affirmative intention that such schools be within the Board's jurisdiction. Since the Board did not assert jurisdiction over teachers in a church-operated school until after the 1974 amendment, nothing in the history of the amendment can be read as reflecting Congress' tacit approval of the Board's action.

During the debate there were expressions of concern about the effect of the bill on employees of religious hospitals whose religious beliefs would not permit them to join a union. The result of those concerns was an amendment which reflects congressional sensitivity to First Amendment guarantees: "Any employee of a health care institution who is a member of and adheres to established and traditional tenets or teachings of a bona fide religion, body, or sect which has historically held conscientious objections to joining or financially supporting labor organizations shall not be required to join or financially support any labor organization as a condition of employment; except that such employee may be required, in lieu of periodic dues and initiation fees, to pay sums equal to such dues and initiation fees to a nonreligious charitable fund exempt from taxation under section 501(c)(3) of title 26, chosen by such employee from a list of at least three such funds, designated in a contract between such institution and a labor organization, or if the contract fails to designate such funds, then to any such fund chosen by the employee."

The absence of an "affirmative intention of the Congress clearly expressed" fortifies our conclusion that Congress did not contemplate that the Board would require church-operated schools to grant recognition to unions as bargaining agents for their teachers.

The Board relies heavily upon *Associated Press* v. *NLRB*. ⊥There the Court held that the First |507 Amendment was no bar to the application of the Act to the Associated Press, an organization engaged in collecting information and news throughout the world and distributing it to its members. Perceiving nothing to suggest that application of the Act would infringe First Amendment guarantees of press freedoms, the Court sustained Board jurisdiction. Here, on the contrary, the record affords abundant evidence that the Board's exercise of jurisdiction over teachers in church-operated schools would implicate the guarantees of the Religion Clauses.

Accordingly, in the absence of a clear expression of Congress' intent to bring teachers in church-operated schools within the jurisdiction of the Board, we decline to construe the Act in a manner that could in turn call upon the Court to resolve difficult and sensitive questions arising out of the guarantees of the First Amendment Religion Clauses.

Affirmed.

⊥*Mr. Justice BRENNAN*, with whom *Mr. Justice WHITE, Mr. Justice MARSHALL*, and *Mr. Justice BLACKMUN* join, dissenting. |508

The Court today holds that coverage of the National Labor Relations Act does not extend to lay teachers employed by church-operated schools. That construction is plainly wrong in light of the Act's language, its legislative history, and this Court's precedents. It is justified solely on the basis of a canon of statutory construction seemingly invented by the Court for the purpose of deciding this case. I dissent.

I

The general principle of construing statutes to avoid unnecessary constitutional decisions is a well-settled and salutary ⊥one. The governing canon, |509 however, is *not* that expressed by the Court today. The Court requires that there be a "clear expression of an affirmative intention of Congress" before it will bring within the coverage of a broadly worded regulatory statute certain persons whose coverage might raise constitutional questions. But those familiar with the legislative process know that explicit expressions of congressional intent in such broadly inclusive statutes are not commonplace. Thus, by strictly or loosely applying its requirement, the Court can virtually remake congressional enactments. This flouts Mr. Chief Justice Taft's admonition "that amendment may not be substituted for construction, and that a court may not exercise legislative functions to save [a] law from conflict with constitutional limitation." *Yu Cong Eng* v. *Trinidad.*

⊥The settled canon for construing statutes wherein constitutional questions may lurk was stated in |510 *Machinists* v. *Street*, cited by the Court: " 'When the validity of an act of the Congress is drawn in question, and even if a serious doubt of constitutionality is raised, it is a cardinal principle that this Court will first ascertain whether a construction of the statute is *fairly possible* by which the question may be avoided.' *Crowell* v. *Benson"* (emphasis added).

This limitation to constructions that are "fairly possible," and "reasonable," see *Yu Cong Eng* v. ⌐511 *Trinidad*, acts as a ⊥ brake against wholesale judicial dismemberment of congressional enactments. It confines the judiciary to its proper role in construing statutes, which is to interpret them so as to give effect to congressional intention. The Court's new "affirmative expression" rule releases that brake.

II

The interpretation of the National Labor Relations Act announced by the Court today is not "fairly possible." The Act's wording, its legislative history, and the Court's own precedents leave "the intention of the Congress . . . revealed too distinctly to permit us to ignore it because of mere misgivings as to power." *Moore Ice Cream Co.* v. *Rose.* Section 2(2) of the Act, 29 U.S.C. § 152(2), defines "employer" as ". . . any person acting as an agent of an employer, directly or indirectly, *but shall not include* the United States or any wholly owned Government corporation, or any Federal Reserve Bank, or any State or political subdivision thereof, or any person subject to the Railway Labor Act, as amended from time to time, or any labor organization (other than when acting as an employer), or anyone acting in the capacity of officer or agent of such labor organization." (Emphasis added.)

Thus, the Act covers all employers not within the eight express exceptions. The Court today substitutes amendment for construction to insert one more exception—for church-operated schools. This is a particularly transparent violation of the judicial role: The legislative history reveals that Congress itself considered and rejected a very similar amendment.

The pertinent legislative history of the NLRA begins with the Wagner Act of 1935, 49 Stat. 449. Section 2(2) of that Act, identical in all relevant respects to the current section, excluded from its cov-⌐512 erage neither church-operated schools ⊥nor any other private nonprofit organization. Accordingly, in applying that Act, the National Labor Relations Board did not recognize an exception for nonprofit employers, even when religiously associated. An argument for an implied nonprofit exemption was rejected because the design of the Act was as clear then as it is now: "[N]either charitable institutions nor their employees are exempted from operation of the Act by its terms, although certain other employers and employees are exempted." *Central Dispensary & Emergency Hospital.* Both the lower courts and this Court concurred in the Board's construction.

The Hartley bill, which passed the House of Representa⊥tives in 1947, would have provided the ⌐5⌐ exception the Court today writes into the statute: "The term 'employer' . . . shall not include . . . any corporation, community chest, fund, or foundation organized and operated exclusively for *religious*, charitable, scientific, literary, or *educational* purposes, . . . no part of the net earnings of which inures to the benefit of any private shareholder or individual. . . ." (Emphasis added.)

But the proposed exception was not enacted. The bill reported by the Senate Committee on Labor and Public Welfare did not contain the Hartley exception. Instead, the Senate proposed an exception limited to nonprofit hospitals, and passed the bill in that form. The Senate version was accepted by the House in conference, thus limiting the exception ⊥for nonprofit employers to nonprofit hospitals.   ⌐5⌐

Even that limited exemption was ultimately repealed in 1974. In doing so, Congress confirmed the view of the Act expressed here: that it was intended to cover all employers—including nonprofit employers—unless expressly excluded, and that the 1947 amendment excluded only nonprofit hospitals. ⊥Moreover, it is significant that in considering the   ⌐5⌐ 1974 amendments, the Senate expressly rejected an amendment proposed by Senator Ervin that was analogous to the one the Court today creates—an amendment to exempt nonprofit hospitals operated by religious groups. Senator Cranston, floor manager of the Senate Committee bill and primary opponent of the proposed religious exception, explained: "[S]uch an exception for religiously affiliated hospitals would seriously erode *the existing national policy which holds religiously affiliated institutions generally such as* proprietary nursing homes, residential communities, and *educational facilities to the same standards as their nonsectarian counterparts."* (Emphasis added.)

⊥In construing the Board's jurisdiction to exclude   ⌐5⌐ church-operated schools, therefore, the Court today is faithful to neither the statute's language nor its history. Moreover, it is also untrue to its own precedents. "This Court has consistently declared that in passing the National Labor Relations Act, Congress intended to and did vest in the Board the fullest *jurisdictional* breadth constitutionally permissible under the commerce Clause. *NLRB* v. *Reliance Fuel Oil Corp.* (emphasis in original). As long as an employer is within the reach of Congress' power under the Commerce Clause—and no one doubts that respondents are—the Court has held him to be covered by the Act regardless of the nature of his activity. Indeed, *Associated Press* v. *NLRB* construed the Act to ⊥cover editorial employees of a nonprofit   ⌐5⌐ news-gathering organization despite a claim—precisely parallel to that made here—that their inclusion rendered the Act in violation of the First Amendment. Today's opinion is simply unable to explain the grounds that distinguish that case from this one.

Thus, the available authority indicates that Congress intended to include—not exclude—lay teachers of church-operated schools. The Court does not counter this with evidence that Congress *did* intend an exception it never stated. Instead, despite the legislative history to the contrary, it construes the Act as excluding lay teachers only because Congress did not state explicitly that they were covered. In Mr. Justice Cardozo's words, this presses "avoidance of a ⊥ difficulty . . . to the point of disingenuous evasion." *Moore Ice Cream Co.* v. *Rose*.

_|518

III

Under my view that the NLRA includes within its coverage lay teachers employed by church-operated schools, the constitutional questions presented would have to be reached. I do not now do so only because the Court does not. I repeat for emphasis, however, that while the resolution of the constitutional question is not without difficulty, it is irresponsible to avoid it by a cavalier exercise in statutory interpretation which succeeds only in defying congressional intent. A statute is not "a nose of wax to be changed from that which the plain language imports. . . ." *Yu Cong Eng* v. *Trinidad*.

RELIGIOUS INSTITUTION FUNCTIONING AS A GOVERNMENTAL AGENCY

A city is a complex organism made up of a variety of components which may be summarized under the headings "residential," "commercial," and "charitable," the latter category containing such institutions as schools, churches and synagogues, hospitals, and museums. It is understandable that those in the residential and charitable categories desire to be protected from the bustle and commotion of the commercial (although not to have businesses so far away as to be inconvenient), so cities have zoning laws designed to protect the public health, safety, tranquility, morals, and general welfare of the community. Because religious institutions are in the charitable category, it sometimes happens that the creation or enforcement of zoning laws take on First Amendment dimensions.

An example is the case of *Incorporated Village of Roslyn Harbor* v. *Jewish Reconstruction Synagogue*. A small congregation of Jews purchased a residence to use as a synagogue. The zoning law required that religious institutions be 100 feet from the property line. The residence purchased was only twenty-nine feet from the line. Although there was enough room on the lot for a structure to be in compliance with the zoning requirements, the congregation did not have the funds either to build a new structure or to move the house currently on the lot. The congregation petitioned the city for an exception, but some of the nearby residents objected. In litigation, New York's highest court ruled in favor of the synagogue, holding that to enforce strictly the ordinance against a congregation financially unable to achieve compliance

was a denial of its free exercise of religion. The United States Supreme Court refused to hear the case. [1]

In *Lakewood, Ohio, Congregation of Jehovah's Witnesses* v. *City of Lakewood*, the religious group did not fare so well. A city zoning ordinance excluded church buildings in nearly ninety percent of a residential area. A congregation of Jehovah's Witnesses wanted to build a Kingdom Hall but was unable to do so because the allowable ten percent of land in the area already had church buildings. The Witnesses claimed that the law did not have a direct relation to public health, safety, or welfare. The city replied that the Kingdom Hall would be disruptive in the neighborhood because of the members' coming and going during the several meetings they had each week. The zoning board had the power to make exceptions, but refused to do so. In litigation, federal courts at both levels upheld the board's right to refuse. They rejected the congregation's argument that the ordinance prevented its free exercise of religion. The building of a church building is not a religious act. The ordinance did not prevent the Witnesses from worshiping, it just prevented their worshiping in a particular building. The city's interest in orderly residential areas was a justifiable burden on the group's religious exercise because it was so indirect. The Supreme Court allowed the decision to stand. [2]

In these cases the Supreme Court denied certiorari. The Court has historically given legislatures and zoning boards wide latitude to create zoning boundaries and to grant or withhold exceptions, so long as all interested parties are given adequate notice and the opportunity to request exceptions or express grievances. This reluctance to hear zoning cases included even those with First Amendment dimensions. An exception to that generalization, however, was LARKIN v. GRENDEL'S DEN (1982) (p. 332), perhaps because of the unusual facts of the case.

Massachusetts had a statute which prohibited the sale of alcoholic beverages within 500 feet of a school or a church if the governing body of the school or church filed a written objection to the application for a liquor license. In Cambridge a restaurant known as Grendel's Den applied for an alcoholic beverage license. It was located within ten feet of the Holy Cross Armenian Catholic Parish. The church, as it was allowed to do under the law, objected to the application (apparently because Grendel's Den was so close to the church and probably also because there were 25 other liquor licensees within 500 feet of the church). After seeking administrative relief, with no success, the restaurant sued in federal court, claiming, among other things, that the law violated the Establishment Clause. Both levels of federal courts agreed that the statute was unconstitutional on establishment grounds. The Supreme Court affirmed that ruling.

Chief Justice Burger, writing for himself and seven others, agreed that the statute had a secular purpose: to protect spiritual, cultural, and educational institutions from the noise and possible disturbances associated with

---

[1] See *City of Evanston* v. *Lubavitch Chabad House of Illinois*, a similar case with an identical result.

[2] The material covered in this and the preceding paragraph is derived from Leo Pfeffer, *Religion, State, and the Burger Court*, (Buffalo, NY: Prometheus Books, 1984), pp. 282-86.

liquor outlets. In short, there was nothing wrong with zoning statutes which insulated churches from businesses selling alcoholic beverages. They could do so either by having an absolute ban on liquor outlets within a prescribed distance from churches, schools, etc., or by having a procedure by which those objecting to being close to liquor outlets could be heard. The problem with this particular statute was that it was the church itself which was permitted to veto a liquor application. Because the church assumed a role normally residing in a governmental agency, the statute failed the other two parts of the "*Lemon* test." The statute had no provisions requiring that a church give the reasons that it took the action that it did; it was standardless. In this circumstance, churches could employ the law for religious goals, e.g., "favoring liquor licenses for members of that congregation or adherents of that faith." There was no evidence that that had been done in this case, but the potential was there. Also, the appearance of cooperation between a church and the zoning commission provided a symbolic benefit to religion in the minds of many. The cumulative effect was that the statute had a primary effect which advanced religion.

Furthermore, the arrangement which gave the churches the potential for advancing their religion under protection of law, i.e., that churches were granted veto power, also created excessive entanglement between church and state. It "enmeshe[d] churches in the exercise of substantial governmental powers" and created the danger of political fragmentation and divisiveness along religious lines. "Ordinary human experience and a long line of cases teach that few entanglements could be more offensive to the spirit of the Constitution."

Justice Rehnquist, in dissent, called this a silly case. Apparently the other Justices did not think so. But even if it is not silly, what is its significance? After all, footnote seven said that it applied to no zoning statute other than that in Massachusetts. Also, it had a very narrow factual basis. But it at least signals states that they may not exercise their power under the Twenty-first Amendment in a way which infringes on the Establishment Clause.[3] It also notifies legislatures that religious institutions may never serve in a governmental capacity. Finally, from time to time in Establishment Clause cases, the Justices have debated the weight to be given to the "political divisiveness" dimension of the entanglement portion of the three-part test. Never has it been used alone to decide a case. Chief Justice Burger did not use it in such a way here, but he did give it such visibility that it will probably continue to be taken seriously so long as the three-part test remains viable.

---

[3] The opinion makes this point in footnote five. The Twenty-first Amendment, ratified in 1933, repeals the Eighteenth and asserts that each state shall have administration over the transportation or importation of liquor into the state. Massachusetts had argued in this litigation that that amendment justified the statute under consideration.

LARKIN v. GRENDEL'S DEN

459 U.S. 116
ON APPEAL FROM THE UNITED STATES
COURT OF APPEALS FOR THE FIRST
CIRCUIT
Argued October 4, 1981 — Decided December 13,
1982

⊥*Chief Justice BURGER* delivered the opinion of ⊥117 the Court.

The question presented by this appeal is whether a Massachusetts statute, which vests in the governing bodies of churches and schools the power effectively to veto applications for liquor licenses within a five hundred foot radius of the church or school, violates the Establishment Clause of the First Amendment or the Due Process Clause of the Fourteenth Amendment.

I
A

Appellee operates a restaurant located in the Harvard Square area of Cambridge, Massachusetts. The Holy Cross Armenian Catholic Parish is located adjacent to the restaurant; the back walls of the two buildings are ten feet apart. In 1977, appellee applied to the Cambridge License Commission for approval of an alcoholic beverages license for the restaurant.

Section 16C of Chapter 138 of the Massachusetts General Laws provides: "Premises . . . located within a radius of five hundred feet of a church or school shall not be licensed for the sale of alcoholic beverages if the governing body of such church or school files written objection thereto."

⊥ Holy Cross Church objected to appellee's appli- ⊥118 cation, expressing concern over "having so many licenses *so* near" (emphasis in original). The License Commission voted to deny the application, citing only the objection of Holy Cross Church and noting that the church "is within 10 feet of the proposed location."

On appeal, the Massachusetts Alcoholic Beverages Control Commission upheld the License Commission's action. The Beverages Control Commission found that "the church's objection under Section 16C was the only basis on which the [license] was denied."

Appellee then sued the License Commission and the Beverages Control Commission in United States District Court. Relief was sought on the grounds that § 16C, on its face and as applied, violated the Equal Protection and Due Process Clauses of the Fourteenth Amendment, the Establishment Clause of the First Amendment, and the Sherman Act.

The suit was voluntarily continued pending the decision of the Massachusetts Supreme Judicial Court in a similar challenge to § 16C, *Arno* v. *Alcoholic Beverages Control Commission*. In *Arno*, the Massachusetts court characterized § 16C as delegating a ⊥ "veto power" to the specified institutions, but up- ⊥119 held the statute against Due Process and Establishment Clause challenges. Thereafter, the District Court denied appellants' motion to dismiss.

On the parties' cross-motion for summary judgment, the District Court declined to follow the Massachusetts Supreme Judicial Court's decision in *Arno*. The District Court held that § 16C violated the Due Process Clause and the Establishment Clause and held § 16C void on its face. The District Court rejected appellee's equal protection arguments, but held that the state's actions were not immune from antitrust review under the doctrine of *Parker* v. *Brown*. It certified the judgment to the first Circuit Court of Appeals pursuant to 28 U.S.C. § 1292, and the Court of Appeals accepted certification.

A panel of the First Circuit, in a divided opinion, reversed the District Court on the Due Process and Establishment Clause arguments, but affirmed its antitrust analysis.

Appellee's motion for rehearing *en banc* was granted and the *en banc* court, in a divided opinion, affirmed the District Court's judgment on Establishment Clause grounds without reaching the due process or antitrust claims.

B

The Court of Appeals noted that appellee does not contend that § 16C lacks a secular purpose, and turned to the question of "whether the law 'has the *direct* and *immediate* effect of advancing religion' as contrasted with 'only a *remote* and *incidental* effect advantageous to religious institutions,'" (emphasis in original), quoting *Committee for Public Education* v. *Nyquist*. The court concluded that § 16C confers a ⌐120 direct and substantial ⊥ benefit upon religions by "the grant of a veto power over liquor sales in roughly one million square feet . . . of what may be a city's most commercially valuable sites."

The court acknowledged that § 16C "extends its benefit beyond churches to schools," but concluded that the inclusion of schools "does not dilute [the statute's] forbidden religious classification," since § 16C does not "encompass all who are otherwise similarly situated to churches in all respects except dedication to 'divine worship.'" In the view of the Court of Appeals, this "explicit religious discrimination," provided an additional basis for its holding that § 16C violates the Establishment Clause.

The court found nothing in the Twenty-First Amendment to alter its conclusion, and affirmed the District Court's holding that § 16C is facially unconstitutional under the Establishment Clause of the First Amendment.

We noted probable jurisdiction and we affirm.

II

A

Appellants contend that the State may, without impinging on the Establishment Clause of the First Amendment, enforce what it describes as a "zoning" law in order to shield schools and places of divine worship from the presence nearby of liquor dispensing establishments. It is also contended that a zone of protection around churches and schools is essential to protect diverse centers of spiritual, educational and cultural enrichment. It is to that end that the State has vested in the governing bodies of all schools, public or private, and all churches, the power to prevent the issu⊥ance of liquor licenses for any ⌐121 premises within 500 feet of their institutions.

Plainly schools and churches have a valid interest in being insulated from certain kinds of commercial establishments, including those dispensing liquor. Zoning laws have long been employed to this end, and there can be little doubt about the power of a state to regulate the environment in the vicinity of schools, churches, hospitals and the like by exercise of reasonable zoning laws.

We have upheld reasonable zoning ordinances regulating the location of so-called "adult" theaters, see *Young* v. *American Mini Theaters, Inc.;* and in *Grayned* v. *City of Rockford* we recognized the legitimate governmental interest in protecting the environment around certain institutions when we sustained an ordinance prohibiting willfully making, on grounds adjacent to a school, noises which are disturbing to the good order of the school sessions.

The zoning function is traditionally a governmental task requiring the "balancing [of] numerous competing considerations," and courts should properly "refrain from reviewing the merits of [such] decisions, absent a showing of arbitrariness or irrationality." *Village of Arlington Heights* v. *Metropolitan Housing Development Corp.* Given the broad powers of states under the Twenty-First Amendment, judicial deference to the legislative exercise of zoning powers by a city council or other legislative zoning body is especially appropriate in the area of liquor ⊥ regulation. ⌐122

However, § 16C is not simply a legislative exercise of zoning power. As the Massachusetts Supreme Judicial Court concluded, § 16C delegates to private, nongovernmental entities power to veto certain liquor license applications, *Arno* v. *Alcoholic Beverages Control Commission*. This is a power ordinarily vested in agencies of government. See, *e.g., California* v. *LaRue*, commenting that a "state agency . . . is itself the repository of the State's power under the Twenty-First Amendment." We need not decide whether, or upon what conditions, such power may ever be delegated to nongovernmental entities; here, of two classes of institutions to which the legislature has delegated this important decision-making power, one is secular, but one is religious. Under these circumstances, the deference normally due a legislative zoning judgment is not merited.

B

The purposes of the First Amendment guarantees relating to religion were twofold: to foreclose state interferences with the practice of religious faiths, and to foreclose the establishment of a state religion familiar in other Eighteenth Century systems. Religion and government, each insulated from the other, could then coexist. Jefferson's idea of a "wall," ⊥ was a useful figurative illustration to emphasize the concept of separateness. Some limited and incidental entanglement between church and state authority is inevitable in a complex modern society, but the concept of a "wall" of separation is a useful signpost. Here that "wall" is substantially breached by vesting discretionary governmental powers in religious bodies.

This Court has consistently held that a statute must satisfy three criteria to pass muster under the Establishment Clause: "First, the statute must have a secular legislative purpose; second, its principal or primary effect must be one that neither advances nor inhibits religion . . . ; finally, the statute must not foster 'an excessive government entanglement with religion.'" *Lemon* v. *Kurtzman.* Independent of the first of those criteria, the statute, by delegating a governmental power to religious institutions, inescapably implicates the Establishment Clause.

The purpose of § 16C, as described by the District Court, is to "protec[t] spiritual, cultural, and educational centers from the 'hurly-burly' associated with liquor outlets." There can be little doubt that this embraces valid secular legislative purposes. However, these valid ⊥ secular objectives can be readily accomplished by other means—either through an absolute legislative ban on liquor outlets within reasonable prescribed distances from churches, schools, hospital and like institutions, or by ensuring a hearing for the views of affected institutions at licensing proceedings where, without question, such views would be entitled to substantial weight.

⊥Appellants argue that § 16C has only a remote and incidental effect on the advancement of religion. The highest court in Massachusetts, however, has construed the statute as conferring upon churches a veto power over governmental licensing authority. Section 16C gives churches the right to determine whether a particular applicant will be granted a liquor license, or even which one of several competing applicants will receive a license.

The churches' power under the statute is standardless, calling for no reasons, findings, or reasoned conclusions. That power may therefore be used by churches to promote goals beyond insulating the church from undesirable neighbors; it could be employed for explicitly religious goals, for example, favoring liquor licenses for members of that congregation or adherents of that faith. We can assume that churches would act in good faith in their exercise of the statutory power, yet § 16C does not by its terms require that churches' power be used in a religiously neutral way. "[T]he potential for conflict inheres in the situation," *Levitt* v. *Committee for Public Education;* and appellants have not suggested any "effective means of guaranteeing" that the delegated power "will be used exclusively for secular, neutral, and nonideological purposes." *Committee for Public Education* v. *Nyquist.* In addition, the mere appearance of a joint exercise of legislative authority by Church and State provides a significant symbolic benefit to ⊥ religion in the minds of some by reason of the power conferred. It does not strain our prior holdings to say that the statute can be seen as having a "primary" and "principal" effect of advancing religion.

Turning to the third phase of the inquiry called for by *Lemon* v. *Kurtzman,* we see that we have not previously had occasion to consider the entanglement implications of a statute vesting significant governmental authority in churches. This statute enmeshes churches in the exercise of substantial governmental powers contrary to our consistent interpretation of the Establishment Clause; "[t]he objective is to prevent, as far as possible, the intrusion of either [Church or State] into the precincts of the other." *Lemon* v. *Kurtzman.* We went on in that case to state: "Under our system the choice has been made that government is to be entirely excluded from the area of religious instruction *and churches excluded from the affairs of government.* The Constitution decrees that religion must be a private matter for the individual, the family, and the institutions of private choice, and that while some involvement and entanglement are inevitable, lines must be drawn." (emphasis added)

Our contemporary views do no more than reflect views approved by the Court more than a century ago: "The structure of our government has, for the preservation of civil liberty, rescued the temporal institutions from religious interference. On the other hand, it has secured religious liberty from the invasion of the civil authority." *Watson* v. *Jones.*

As these and other cases make clear, the core rationale underlying the Establishment Clause is preventing "a fusion of governmental and religious functions." *Abington School Dis⊥trict* v. *Schempp.* The Framers did not set up a system of government in which important, discretionary governmental powers would be delegated to or shared with religious institutions.

Section 16C substitutes the unilateral and absolute power of a church for the reasoned decisionmaking of a public legislative body acting on evidence and guided by standards, on issues with significant economic and political implications. The challenged statute thus enmeshes churches in the processes of government and creates the danger of "[p]olitical fragmentation and divisiveness along religious lines." *Lemon* v. *Kurtzman.* Ordinary human experience and a long line of cases teach that few entanglements could be more offensive to the spirit of the Constitution.

The judgment of the Court of Appeals is affirmed.

So ordered.

Justice REHNQUIST, dissenting.

Dissenting opinions in previous cases have commented that "great" cases, like "hard" cases, make ⊥128 bad law. ⊥ Today's opinion suggests that a third class of cases—silly cases—also make bad law. The Court wrenches from the decision of the Massachusetts Supreme Judicial Court the word "veto," and rests its conclusion on this single term. The aim of this effort is to prove that a quite sensible Massachusetts liquor zoning law is apparently some sort of sinister religious attack on secular government reminiscent of St. Bartholomew's Night. Being unpersuaded, I dissent.

In its original form, § 16C imposed a flat ban on the grant of alcoholic beverages licenses to any establishment located within 500 feet of a church or a school. This statute represented a legislative determination that worship and liquor sales are generally not compatible uses of land. The majority concedes, as I believe it must, that "an absolute legislative ban on liquor outlets within reasonable prescribed distances from churches, schools, hospitals, and like institutions," would be valid.

Over time, the legislature found that it could meet its goal of protecting people engaged in religious activities from liquor-related disruption with a less absolute prohibition. Rather than set out elaborate formulae or require an administrative agency to make findings of fact, the legislature settled on the simple expedient of asking churches to object if a proposed liquor outlet would disturb them. Thus, under the present version of § 16C, a liquor outlet within 500 feet of a church or school can be licensed unless the affected institution objects. The flat ban, which the majority concedes is valid, is more protective of churches and more restrictive of liquor sales than the present § 16C.

The evolving treatment of the grant of liquor licenses to outlets located within 500 feet of a church or a school seems to me to be the sort of legislative refinement that we should encourage, not forbid in the name of the First Amendment. If a particular ⊥129 church or a particular school located within the ⊥ 500-foot radius chooses not to object, the state has quite sensibly concluded that there is no reason to prohibit the issuance of the license. Nothing in the Court's opinion persuades me why the more rigid prohibition would be constitutional, but the more flexible not.

The Court rings in the metaphor of the "wall between church and state," and the "three part test" developed in *Walz* v. *Tax Commission*, to justify its result. However, by its frequent reference to the statutory provision as a "veto," the Court indicates a belief that § 16C effectively constitutes churches as third houses of the Massachusetts legislature. Surely we do not need a three part test to decide whether the grant of actual legislative power to churches is within the proscription of the Establishment Clause of the First and Fourteenth Amendments. The question in this case is not whether such a statute would be unconstitutional, but whether § 16C is such a statute. The Court in effect answers this question in the first sentence of its opinion without any discussion or statement of reasons. I do not think the question is so trivial that it may be answered by simply affixing a label to the statutory provision.

Section 16C does not sponsor or subsidize any religious group or activity. It does not encourage, much less compel, anyone to participate in religious activities or to support religious institutions. To say that it "advances" religion is to strain at the meaning of that word.

The Court states that § 16C "advances" religion because there is no guarantee than objections will be made "in a religiously neutral way." It is difficult to understand what the Court means by this. The concededly legitimate purpose of the statute is to protect citizens engaging in religious and educational activities from the incompatible activities of liquor outlets and their patrons. The only way to decide whether these activities are incompatible with one another in the case of a church is to ask whether the activities of liquor outlets and their patrons may interfere with religious ⊥ activity; this question cannot, in any ⊥130 meaningful sense, be "religiously neutral." In this sense, the flat ban of the original § 16C is no different from the present version. Whether the ban is unconditional or may be invoked only at the behest of a particular church, it is not "religiously neutral" so long as it enables a church to defeat the issuance of a liquor license when a similarly situated bank could not do the same. The state does not, in my opinion, "advance" religion by making provision for those who wish to engage in religious activities, as well as those who wish to engage in educational activities, to be unmolested by activities at a neighboring bar or tavern that have historically been thought incompatible.

The Court is apparently concerned for fear that churches might object to the issuance of a license for "explicitly religious reasons, such as "favoring liquor licenses for members of that congregation or adherents of that faith." If a church were to seek to advance the interests of its members in this way, there would be an occasion to determine whether it had violated any right of an unsuccessful applicant for a liquor license. But our ability to discern a risk of such abuse does not render § 16C violative of the Establishment Clause. The state can constitutionally protect churches from liquor for the same reasons it can protect them from fire and other harm.

The heavy First Amendment artillery that the Court fires at this sensible and unobjectionable Massachusetts statute is both unnecessary and unavailing. I would reverse the judgment of the Court of Appeals.

UNEQUAL GOVERNMENT TREATMENT OF RELIGIOUS GROUPS

Those in the media who report on religion and even scholars of religion frequently refer to "mainstream" or "mainline" religious groups. By these terms they refer to such denominations as Methodists, Baptists, Catholics, Episcopalians, Lutherans, etc. But the very terminology implies that there are other groups which are not "mainline," but rather are smaller, perhaps marginal in vitality, perhaps questionable in their theology (at least, from a "mainstream" point of view), and sometimes are led by people who are perceived (again, by the "mainstream") to be cunning and dishonest. In short, these nonmainline religious groups are regarded, in the best light, as curiosities and, in the worst, as unsavory and even dangerous. [1] These groups are frequently called "sects" or "cults" and, while these terms are acceptable and useful in the vocabulary of the Sociologist of Religion, in popular parlance they usually mean "strange," "weird," and, to say the very least, "unpopular." [2]

In times when fear of such groups has been intense, it has not been unusual for governments, often through their taxing power, to try to curb, if not destroy, these unpopular religions. The groups have sometimes responded with litigation, claiming that the government has violated their free exercise of religion. The Jehovah's Witnesses were the principal unpopular group in the 1930s and 1940s and governments singled them out for restrictive legislation: unequal treatment. This produced a great body of case law, much of which is reproduced earlier in this book. With the new wave of hysteria over cults in the 1970s and 1980s, unequal treatment of religions has come up in the courts again. Although there are many lower court cases, the Supreme Court had dealt with only one at the time of this writing, and it was decided on establishment grounds, rather than free exercise. [3] That case is LARSON v. VALENTE, (1982) (p. 337).

---

[1] See J. Gordon Melton, *The Encyclopedia of American Religions* (Wilmington, NC: McGrath Publishing Co., 1978), 2 vols., for a listing and description of the over 1,200 religious bodies in this country, including between 500 and 600 "alternative religions," another name for the kind of groups described here.

[2] See Ronald B. Flowers, *Religion in Strange Times: The 1960s and 1970s* (Macon, GA: Mercer University Press, 1984), especially pp. 85-111 for a popular exposition of what sects and cults are, set in the context of the latest anxiety about such groups in this country. For information on the theology and structure of such groups see J. Gordon Melton, *Encyclopedic Handbook of Cults in America* and *Biographical Dictionary of American Cult and Sect Leaders*, both published by Garland Publishing Company of New York, 1986.

[3] The recent literature on cults and even on their legal problems is voluminous; some of it is included in the bibliography in this book. A good overview, aimed particularly at the legal issues, is Leo Pfeffer, *Religion, State, and the Burger Court* (Buffalo, NY: Prometheus Books, 1984), pp. 201-34. See also Thomas Robbins, William C. Shepherd, and James McBride, eds., *Cults, Culture, and the Law: Perspectives on New Religious Movements* (Chico, CA: Scholars Press, 1985).

The thing which most bothered people about cults was not their theology; in fact even those who were very concerned about cults usually came to know the theology of the group only after they had already formed their opposition to it. The two things about the most unpopular cults which elicited opposition were the way they won converts and the way they raised revenue. In terms of the former, cults were frequently accused of "brainwashing," "mind control," and/or "instant hypnotism." [4] In terms of the latter, both Hare Krishna and the Unification Church (the "Moonies") were singled out for criticism. Although members of Hare Krishna from time to time did solicit funds in other public places, they came to be identified in the popular mind with attempting to sell books and solicit donations in airports. Members of the Unification Church (the official name of which is The Holy Spirit Association for the Unification of World Christianity) frequented airports, shopping centers, street corners, and other public places to sell things (frequently flowers and/or candy) and to ask for contributions. They were often persistent in their efforts and some people found them annoying. That was compounded by the popular perception that the church members/sales people, mostly young people of late high school or college age, were essentially enslaved in this activity (they had been brainwashed, according to popular lore), working long hours under adverse conditions, and that the revenue went primarily to the personal fortune of the founder and leader of the group, Rev. Sun Myung Moon. It was these perceptions, whether or not they were true (they probably were greatly overstated), which forms the background of *Larson*.

In 1961 Minnesota adopted its Charitable Solicitation Act, designed to protect the public from fraudulent collections of funds. It required charitable organizations to register with the state's Department of Commerce before they could solicit contributions. Thereafter the registered organizations had to submit annual reports of receipts, expenditures for management, fundraising, and public education, and descriptions of transfers of property or funds out of state. If a report showed that a group had spent more than thirty percent of its income for administrative costs, its registry would be canceled and it could no longer solicit contributions within the state. Religious groups were exempt from the requirement. In 1978, however, apparently because of a growing concern about the type of fund raising done by cults, described above, Minnesota changed its law by adding a fifty percent rule. Simply stated, the amended law said that if a religious group received more than half of its revenue from its own membership, it would continue to be exempt from the Solicitation Act. But if a group received less than half of its revenue from its own membership, i.e., if more than half its contributions came from the general public, such as people in airports or shopping centers, it would have to register and file the financial disclosure forms. Almost immediately after the amendment, the Minnesota Department of Commerce wrote to the Unification Church saying that it was now required to register.

The Church initiated litigation, claiming that the fifty percent rule, among other things, denied its members re-

---

[4] This issue is discussed in chapters three and five of this book.

ligious freedom and that it discriminated between religious organizations, contrary to the Establishment Clause. When the case reached the Supreme Court, the courts below had ruled, with some slight exceptions, that the law was in violation of the Establishment Clause. The Court affirmed.

On the question of standing, which the appeals court had questioned, Minnesota now claimed that the Unification Church was not a religious organization and thus would not be exempt from statutory requirements even if the fifty percent rule were declared unconstitutional. Justice Brennan, writing for the Court, disagreed, saying that the fifty percent rule applied only to religious organizations. When Minnesota requested the Church's registration, it must have assumed that the Church was a religious organization. Furthermore, application of the Act to the Church would cause it injury by means of its filing requirements. For both of these reasons, the Church had standing to sue.

On the merits of the case, the Court began with the assumption that the Establishment Clause commands that one denomination cannot be officially preferred over another. Since the Act seemed to apply to religious groups unequally, it was subject to strict scrutiny by the Court. Clearly Minnesota had a significant interest in protecting its citizens from fraudulent charitable organizations. But unless the statute at bar was "closely fitted" to accomplishing that purpose, it would be declared unconstitutional.

Minnesota made three arguments for the legitimacy of its law: (1) members of a religious body can and will exercise supervision over its solicitation activities when more than fifty percent of its contributions come from members; (2) following from the first, membership control is an adequate safeguard against improper solicitations of the public by the organization; and (3) the need for public disclosure of solicitation revenues and procedures rises in proportion with the percentage of nonmember contributions. The Court found all three arguments lacking. In regard to the first, there simply was nothing in the record to support the idea that members of the group are more attentive to the supervision of its solicitation when they contributed more than half. The existence of the Act itself contradicted the second: the state passed the legislation because of the belief that charitable organizations soliciting from the public cannot be relied upon to regulate themselves. Simple mathematics showed the third argument to be wrong. In short, the fifty percent rule treated religious groups differently, which was contrary to the Establishment Clause. Consequently, the Unification Church could not be compelled to register and report under that provision of the statute. [5]

This case was decided without using the three-part "*Lemon* test." However, the opinion was written by Justice Brennan, who believed in the enduring applicability of the test. [6] But in this case the test was not applicable, he said, because the "*Lemon* test" is designed "to apply to laws affording a uniform benefit to *all* religion and not to laws "that discriminate *among* religions" like the case at bar. But if the test *were* to be applied, it was clear to him that the fifty percent rule would fail the entanglement prong because it discriminated between denominations and thus ran the risk of politicizing religion.

The four dissenters did not address the constitutional issue of the case, but simply argued that the lower court's decision in favor of the Unification Church should be set aside on essentially technical grounds, e.g., the Church's lack of standing to sue.

LARSON v. VALENTE

456 U.S. 228
ON APPEAL FROM THE UNITED STATES
COURT OF APPEALS FOR THE EIGHTH
CIRCUIT
Argued December 9, 1981 — Decided April 21, 1982
⊥ *Justice BRENNAN* delivered the opinion of the   ⌐230
Court.

The principal question presented by this appeal is whether a Minnesota statute, imposing certain registration and reporting requirements upon only those religious organizations that solicit more than fifty per cent of their funds from nonmembers, discriminates against such organizations in violation of the Establishment Clause of the First Amendment.

I

Appellants are John R. Larson, Commissioner of Securities, and Warren Spannaus, Attorney General, of the State of Minnesota. They are, by virtue of their offices, responsible for the implementation and enforcement of the Minnesota Charitable Solicitation Act, Minn. Stat. §§ 309.50-309.61 (1969 and Supp. 1982). This Act, in effect since 1961, provides for a system of registration and disclosure respecting ⊥ charitable organizations, and is designed to   ⌐231 protect the contributing public and charitable beneficiaries against fraudulent practices in the solicitation of contributions for purportedly charitable purposes. A charitable organization subject to the Act must register with the Minnesota Department of Commerce before it may solicit contributions within the State. With certain specified exceptions, all charitable organizations registering under § 309.52 must file an extensive annual report with the Department, detailing, *inter alia*, their total receipts and income from all sources, their cost of management, fundraising, and public education, and their transfers of property or funds out of the State, along with a description of the recipients and purposes of those

---

[5] In a footnote the Court said that there might be other ways in which Minnesota could protect its citizens from fraudulent solicitation by religious groups. It just could not do it by statutorily treating them differently.

[6] In MARSH v. CHAMBERS, decided the year after *Larson*, the test was not even mentioned in the opinion. Justice Brennan, writing in dissent, referred to the test as "our settled doctrine" and chided the Court for not using it.

transfers. The Department is authorized by the Act to deny or withdraw the registration of any charitable organization if the Department finds that it would be in "the public interest" to do so and if the organization is found to have engaged in fraudulent, deceptive, or dishonest practices. Further, a charitable organization is deemed ineligible to maintain its registration under the Act if it expends or agrees to expend an "unreasonable amount" for management, general, and fundraising costs, with those costs being presumed unreasonable if they exceed thirty per cent of the organization's total income and revenue.

From 1961 until 1978, all "religious organizations" were exempted from the requirements of the Act. But effective March 29, 1978, the Minnesota Legislature amended the Act so as to include a "fifty per cent rule" in the exemption provision covering religious organizations. This fifty per cent rule provided that only those religious organizations that received ⌐232 more than half of their total con⊥tributions from members or affiliated organizations would remain exempt from the registration and reporting requirement of the Act.

Shortly after the enactment of § 309.515, subd. 1(b), the Department notified appellee Holy Spirit Association for the Unification of World Christianity (Unification Church) that it was required to register under the Act because of the newly enacted provision. Appellees Valente, Barber, Haft, and Korman, claiming to be followers of the tenets of the ⌐233 Unifica⊥tion Church, responded by bringing the present action in the United States District Court for the District of Minnesota. Appellees sought a declaration that the Act, on its face and as applied to them through § 309.151, subd. 1(b)'s fifty per cent rule, constituted an abridgment of their First Amendment rights of expression and free exercise of religion, as well as a denial of their right to equal protection of the laws, guaranteed by the Fourteenth ⌐234 Amendment; appellees also sought ⊥ temporary and permanent injunctive relief. Appellee Unification Church was later joined as a plaintiff by stipulation of the parties, and the action was transferred to a United States Magistrate.

After obtaining a preliminary injunction, appellees moved for summary judgment. Appellees' evidentiary support for this motion included a "declaration" of appellee Haft, which described in some detail the origin, "religious principles," and practices of the Unification Church. The declaration stated that among the activities emphasized by the Church were "door-to-door and public-place proselytizing and solicitation of funds to support the Church," and that the application of the Act to the Church through § 309.515, subd. 1(b)'s fifty percent rule would deny its members their "religious freedom". Appellees also argued that by discriminating among religious organizations, § 309.515, subd. 1(b)'s fifty per cent rule violated the Establishment Clause.

Appellants replied that the Act did not infringe appellees' freedom to exercise their religious beliefs. Appellants sought to distinguish the present case from *Murdock* v. *Pennsylvania*, where this Court invalidated a municipal ordinance that had required the licensing of Jehovah's Witnesses who solicited donations in exchange for ⊥ religious literature, by arguing that unlike the activities of the petitioners in *Murdock*, appellees' solicitations bore no substantial relationship to any religious expression, and that they were therefore outside the protection of the First Amendment. Appellants also contended that the Act did not violate the Establishment Clause. Finally, appellants argued that appellees were not entitled to challenge the Act until they had demonstrated that the Unification Church was a religion and that its fundraising activities were a religious practice.

The Magistrate determined, however, that it was not necessary for him to resolve the questions of whether the Unification Church was a religion, and whether appellees' activities were religiously motivated, in order to reach the merits of appellees' claims. Rather he found that the "overbreadth" doctrine gave appellees standing to challenge the Act's constitutionality. On the merits, the Magistrate held that the Act was facially unconstitutional with respect to religious organizations, and was therefore entirely void as to such organizations, because § 309.515, subd. 1(b)'s fifty per cent rule failed the second of the three Establishment Clause "tests" set forth by this Court in *Lemon* v. *Kurtzman*. The Magistrate also held on due ⊥ process grounds that certain provisions of the Act were unconstitutional as applied to any groups or persons claiming the religious-organization exemption from the Act. The Magistrate therefore recommended, *inter alia*, that appellees be granted the declarative and permanent injunctive relief that they had sought—namely, a declaration that the Act was unconstitutional as applied to religious organizations and their members, and an injunction against enforcement of the Act as to any religious organization. Accepting these recommendations, the District Court entered summary judgment in favor of appellees on these issues.

On appeal, the United States Court of Appeals for the Eighth Circuit affirmed in part and reversed in part. On the issue of standing, the Court of Appeals affirmed the District Court's application of the overbreadth doctrine, citing *Village of Schaumburg* v. *Citizens for Better Environment* for ⊥ the proposition that "a litigant whose own activities are unprotected may nevertheless challenge a statute by showing that it substantially abridges the First Amendment rights of other parties not before the court." On the merits, the Court of Appeals affirmed the District Court's holding that the "inexplicable religious classification" embodied in the fifty per cent rule of § 309.515, subd. 1(b), violated the Establishment Clause. Applying the Minnesota rule of severability, the Court of Appeals also held that §

309.515, subd. 1(b), as a whole should not be stricken from the Act, but that the fifty per cent rule should be stricken from § 309.515, subd. 1(b). But the court disagreed with the District Court's conclusion that appellees and others should enjoy the religious-organization exemption from the Act merely by claiming to be such organizations: The court held that proof of religious-organization status was required in order to gain the exemption, and left the question of appellees' status "open . . . for further development." The Court of Appeals accordingly vacated the judgment of the District Court and remanded the action for entry of a modified injunction and for further appropriate proceedings. We noted probable jurisdiction.

⊥238

⊥ II

Appellants argue that appellees are not entitled to be heard on their Establishment Clause claims. Their rationale for this argument has shifted, however, as this litigation has progressed. Appellant's position in the courts below was that the Unification Church was not a religion, and more importantly that appellees' solicitations were not connected with any religious purpose. From these premises appellants concluded that appellees were not entitled to raise their Establishment Clause claims until they had demonstrated that their activities were within the protection of that Clause. The courts below rejected this conclusion, instead applying the overbreadth doctrine in order to allow appellees to raise their Establishment Clause claims. In this Court, appellants have taken an entirely new tack. They now argue that the Unification Church is not a "religious organization" within the meaning of Minnesota Charitable Solicitation Act, and that the Church therefore would not be entitled to an exemption under § 309.515, subd. 1(b), even if the fifty per cent rule were declared unconstitutional. From this new premise appellants conclude that the courts below erred in invalidating § 309.515 subd. 1(b)'s fifty per cent rule without first requiring appellees to demonstrate that they would have been able to maintain their exempt status but for that rule, and thus that its adoption had caused them injury in fact. We have considered both of appellants' rationales, and hold that neither of them has merit.

"The essence of the standing inquiry is whether the parties seeking to invoke the court's jurisdiction have 'alleged such a personal stake in the outcome of the controversy as to assure ⊥ that concrete adverseness which sharpens the presentation of issues upon which the court so largely depends for illumination of difficult constitutional questions.' " *Duke Power Co.* v. *Carolina Environmental Study Group*, quoting *Baker* v. *Carr*. This requirement of a "personal stake" must consist of "a 'distinct and palpable injury . . . ' to the plaintiff," *Duke Power Co.*," quoting *Warth* v. *Seldin*, and "a 'fairly

⊥239

traceable' causal connection between the claimed injury and the challenged conduct," *Duke Power Co.*, quoting *Arlington Heights* v. *Metropolitan Housing Dev. Corp.* Application of these constitutional standards to the record before us and the factual findings of the District Court convince us that the Art. III requirements for standing are plainly met by appellees.

Appellants argue in this Court that the Unification Church is not a "religious organization" within the meaning of the Act, and therefore that appellees cannot demonstrate injury in fact. We note at the outset, however, that in the years before 1978 the Act contained a general exemption provision for all religious organizations, and that during those years the Unification Church was not required by the State to register and report under the Act. It was only in 1978, shortly after the addition of the fifty per cent rule to the religious-organization exemption, that the State first attempted to impose the requirements of the Act upon the Unification Church. And when the State made this attempt, it deliberately chose to do so in express and exclusive reliance upon the newly enacted fifty per cent rule of § 309.515, subd. 1(b). The present suit was initiated by appellees in direct response to that attempt by the State to force the Church's registration. It is thus plain that appellants' ⊥ stated rationale for the application of the Act to appellees was that § 309.515, subd. 1(b), *did* apply to the Unification Church. But § 309.515 subd. 1(b), by its terms applies only to religious organizations. It follows, therefore, that an essential premise of the State's attempt to require the Unification Church to register under the Act by virtue of the fifty per cent rule in § 309.515, subd. 1(b), is that the Church *is* a religious organization. It is logically untenable for the State to take the position that the Church is not such an organization, because that position destroys an essential premise of the exercise of statutory authority at issue in this suit.

⊥240

In the courts below, the State joined issue precisely on the premise that the fifty per cent rule of § 309.515, subd. 1(b), was sufficient authority in itself to compel appellees' registration. The adoption of that premise precluded the position ⊥ that the Church is not a religious organization. And it remains entirely clear that if we were to uphold the constitutionality of the fifty per cent rule, the State would without more, insist upon the Church's registration. In this Court, the State has changed its position, and purports to find independent bases for denying the Church an exemption from the Act. Considering the development of this case in the courts below, and recognizing the premise inherent in the State's attempt to apply the fifty per cent rule to appellees, we do not think that the State's change of position renders the controversy between these parties any less concrete. The fact that appellants chose to apply § 309.515, subd. 1(b), and its fifty per cent rule as the sole statutory authority requiring the Church to register under

⊥241

the Act compels the conclusion that, at least for purposes of this suit challenging that State application, the Church is indeed a religious organization within the meaning of the Act.

With respect to the question of injury in fact, we again take as the starting point of our analysis the fact that the State attempted to use § 309.515, subd. 1(b)'s fifty per cent rule in order to compel the Unification Church to register and report under the Act. That attempted use of the fifty per cent rule as the State's instrument of compulsion necessarily gives appellees standing to challenge the constitutional validity of the rule. The threatened application of § 309.515, subd. 1(b), and its fifty per cent rule to the Church surely amounts to a distinct and palpable injury to appellees: It disables them from soliciting contributions in the State of Minnesota unless the Church complies with registration and reporting requirements that are hardly *de minimis*. Just as surely, there is a fairly traceable causal connection between the claimed injury and the challenged conduct—here, between the claimed disabling and the threatened application of § 309.515, subd. 1(b), and its fifty per cent rule.

⊥242   ⊥ Of course, the Church cannot be assured of a continued religious-organization exemption even in the absence of the fifty per cent rule. Appellees have not yet shown an entitlement to the entirety of the broad injunctive relief that they sought in the District Court—namely, a permanent injunction barring the State from subjecting the Church to the registration and reporting requirements of the Act. But that fact by no means detracts from the palpability of the particular and discrete injury caused to appellees by the State's threatened application of § 309.515, subd. 1(b)'s fifty per cent rule. The Church may indeed be compelled, ultimately, to register under the Act on some ground other than the fifty per cent rule, and while this fact does affect the nature of the relief that can properly be granted to appellees on the present record, it does not deprive this Court of jurisdiction to hear the present case. In sum, contrary to appellants' suggestion, appellees have clearly demonstrated injury in fact.

Justice REHNQUIST's dissent attacks appellees' Art. III standing by arguing that appellees "have failed to show that a favorable decision of this Court will redress the injuries of which they complain." This argument follows naturally from the dissent's premise that the only meaningful relief that can be given to appellees is a total exemption from the requirements of the Act. But the argument, like the premise, is incorrect. This litigation began after the State attempted to compel the Church to register and report under the Act solely on the authority of § 309.515, subd. 1(b)'s fifty per cent rule. If that rule is declared unconstitutional, as appellees have requested, then the Church cannot be required to register and report under the Act by virtue of that rule. Since that rule was the sole basis for the State's at-

tempt to compel registration that gave ⊥ rise to the   ⊥243
present suit, a discrete injury of which appellees now complain will indeed be completely redressed by a favorable decision of this Court.

Furthermore, if the fifty per cent rule of § 309.515, subd. 1(b), is declared unconstitutional, then the Church cannot be compelled to register and report under the Act unless the Church is determined not to be a religious organization. And as the Court of Appeals below observed: "[A] considerable burden is on the state, in questioning a claim of a religious nature. Strict or narrow construction of a statutory exemption for religious organizations is not favored. *Washington Ethical Society* v. *District of Columbia*." At the very least, then, a declaration that § 309.515, subd. 1(b)'s fifty per cent rule is unconstitutional would put the State to the task of demonstrating that the Unification Church is not a religious organization within the meaning of the Act—and such a task is surely more burdensome than that of demonstrating that the Church's proportion of nonmember contributions exceeds fifty per cent. Thus appellees will be given substantial and meaningful relief by a favorable decision of this Court.

⊥ Since we conclude that appellees have estab-   ⊥244
lished Art. III standing, we turn to the merits of the case.

III
A

The clearest command of the Establishment Clause is that one religious denomination cannot be officially preferred over another. Before the Revolution, religious establishments of differing denominations were common throughout the Colonies. But the Revolutionary generation emphatically disclaimed that European legacy, and "applied the logic of secular liberty to the condition of religion and the churches." If Parliament had lacked the authority to tax unrepresented colonists, then by the same token the newly independent States should be powerless to tax their citizens for the support of a denomination to which they did not belong. The ⊥ force of this   ⊥245
reasoning led to the abolition of most denominational establishments at the state level by the 1780's, and led ultimately to the inclusion of the Establishment Clause in the First Amendment in 1791.

This constitutional prohibition of denominational preferences is inextricably connected with the continuing vitality of the Free Exercise Clause. Madison once noted: "Security for civil rights must be the same as that for religious rights. It consists in the one case in the multiplicity of interests and in the other in the multiplicity of sects." Madison's vision—freedom for all religion being guaranteed by free competition between religions—naturally assumed that every denomination would be equally at liberty to exercise and propagate its beliefs. But such equality would be impossible in an atmosphere of official denominational preference. Free exercise thus can be guaranteed only when legislators—and voters—are required to accord to their own religions the very same treatment given to small, new, or unpopular denominations. As *Justice JACKSON* noted in another context, "there is no more effective practical guaranty against arbitrary and unreasonable government than to require that the principles of law which officials would impose upon a minority ⊥ must be imposed generally." *Railway Express Agency, Inc.* v. *New York* (concurring opinion).

⌐246

Since *Everson* v. *Board of Education* this Court has adhered to the principle, clearly manifested in the history and logic of the Establishment Clause, that no State can "pass laws which aid one religion" or that "prefer one religion over another." This principle of denominational neutrality has been restated on many occasions. In *Zorach* v. *Clauson*, we said that "[t]he government must be neutral when it comes to competition between sects." In *Epperson* v. *Arkansas*, we stated unambiguously: "The First Amendment mandates governmental neutrality between religion and religion, . . . The State may not adopt programs or practices . . . which 'aid or oppose' any religion. . . . This prohibition is absolute." And *Justice GOLDBERG* cogently articulated the relationship between the Establishment Clause and Free Exercise Clause when he said that "[t]he fullest realization of true religious liberty requires that government . . . effect no favoritism among sects . . . and that it work deterrence of no religious belief." *Abington School District* In short, when we are presented with a state law granting a denominational preference, our precedents demand that we treat the law as suspect and that we apply strict scrutiny in adjudging its constitutionality.

B

The fifty per cent rule of § 309.515, subd. 1(b), clearly grants denominational preference of the sort consistently and firmly deprecated in our precedents. Consequently, ⊥ that rule must be invalidated unless it is justified by a compelling governmental interest, cf. *Widmar* v. *Vincent*, and unless it is closely fitted to further that interest, *Murdock* v. *Pennsylvania*. With that standard of review in mind, we turn to an examination of the governmental interest asserted by appellants.

⌐247

⊥ Appellants assert, and we acknowledge, that the State of Minnesota has a significant interest in protecting its citizens from abusive practices in the solicitation of funds for charity, and that this interest retains importance when the solicitation is conducted by a religious organization. We thus agree with the Court of Appeals that the Act, "viewed as a whole, has a valid secular purpose," and we will therefore assume, *arguendo*, that the Act generally is addressed to a sufficiently "compelling" governmental interest. But our inquiry must focus more narrowly, upon the distinctions drawn by § 309.515, subd. 1(b), itself: Appellants must demonstrate that the challenged fifty per cent rule is closely fitted to further the interest that it assertedly serves.

⌐248

Appellants argue that § 309.515, subd. 1(b)'s distinction between contributions solicited from members and from nonmembers is eminently sensible. They urge that members are reasonably assumed to have significant control over the solicitation of contributions from themselves to their organization, and over the expenditure of the funds that they contribute, as well. Further, appellants note that as a matter of Minnesota law, members of organizations have greater access than nonmembers to the financial records of the organization. Appellants conclude: "Where the safeguards of membership funding do not exist, the need for public disclosure is obvious. . . .

". . .As public contributions increase as a percentage of total contributions, the need for public disclosure increases. . . . The particular point at which public disclosure should be required . . . is a determination for the legislature. In this case, the Act's 'majority' distinction is a compelling point, since it is at this point that the organization becomes predominantly public-funded."

We reject the argument, for it wholly fails to justify the only aspect of § 309.515, subd. 1(b), under attack—the selective fifty per cent rule. Appellants' argument is based on three distinct premises: that members of a religious organiza⊥tion can and will exercise supervision and control over the organization's solicitation activities when membership contributions exceed fifty per cent; that membership control, assuming its existence, is an adequate safeguard against abusive solicitations of the public by the organization; and that the need for public disclosure rises in proportion with the *percentage* of nonmember contributions. Acceptance of all three of these premises is necessary to appellants' conclusion, but we find no substantial support for any of them in the record.

⌐249

Regarding the first premise, there is simply nothing suggested that would justify the assumption that a religious organization will be supervised and controlled by its members simply because they contribute more than half of the organization's solicited income. Even were we able to accept appellants' doubtful assumption that members will *supervise* their religious organization under such circumstances, the record before us is wholly barren of support for appellants' further assumption that members will effectively *control* the organization if they contribute more than half of its solicited income. Appellants have offered no evidence whatever that members of religious organizations exempted ⊥ by § 309.515, subd. 1(b)'s fifty per cent rule in fact control their organizations. Indeed, the legislative history of § 309.515, subd. 1(b), indicated precisely

⌐250

to the contrary. In short, the first premise of appellants' argument has no merit.

Nor do appellants offer any stronger justification for their second premise—that membership control is an adequate safeguard against abusive solicitations of the public by the organization. This premise runs directly contrary to the central thesis of the entire Minnesota charitable solicitations Act—namely, that charitable organizations soliciting contributions from the public cannot be relied upon to regulate themselves, and that state regulation is accordingly necessary. Appellants offer nothing to suggest why religious organizations should be treated any differently in this respect. And even if we were to assume that the members of religious organizations have some incentive, absent in nonreligious organizations, to protect the interests of nonmembers solicited by the organization, appellants' premise would still ⊥ fail to justify the fifty per cent rule: Appellants offer no reason why the members of religious organizations exempted under § 309.515, subd. 1(b)'s fifty per cent rule should have any *greater* incentive to protect nonmembers than the members of non-exempted religious organizations have. Thus we also reject appellants' second premise as without merit.

Finally, we find appellants' third premise—that the need for public disclosure rises in proportion with the *percentage* of nonmember contributions—also without merit. The flaw in appellants' reasoning here may be illustrated by the following example. Church A raises $10 million, 20 per cent from nonmembers. Church B raises $50,000, 60 per cent from non-members. Appellants would argue that although the public contributed $2 million to Church A and only $30,000 to Church B, there is less need for public disclosure with respect to Church A than with respect to Church B. We disagree; the need for public disclosure more plausibly rises in proportion with the *absolute amount*, rather than with the *percentage*, of nonmember contributions. The State of Minnesota has itself adopted this view elsewhere in § 309.515: With qualifications not relevant here, charitable organizations that receive annual nonmember contributions of less than $10,000 are exempted from the registration and reporting requirements of the Act.

We accordingly conclude that appellants have failed to demonstrate that the fifty per cent rule in § 309.515, subd. 1(b), is "closely fitted" to further a "compelling governmental interest."

C

In *Lemon* v. *Kurtzman*, we announced three "tests" that a statute must pass in order to avoid the prohibition of the Establishment Clause. ⊥ "First, the statute must have a secular legislative purpose; second, its principal or primary effect must be one that neither advances nor inhibits religion, *Board of Education* v. *Allen*; finally, the statute must not foster 'an excessive governmental entanglement with religion.' *Walz* v. *Tax Comm'n*"

As our citations of *Board of Education* v. *Allen* and *Walz* v. *Tax Comm'n* indicated, the *Lemon* v. *Kurtzman* "test" are intended to apply to laws affording a uniform benefit to *all* religions, and not to provisions, like § 309.515, subd. 1(b)'s fifty per cent rule, that discriminate *among* religions. Although application of the *Lemon* tests is not necessary to the disposition of the case before us, those tests do reflect the same concerns that warranted the application of strict scrutiny to § 309.515, subd. 1(b)'s fifty per cent rule. The Court of Appeals found that rule to be invalid under the first two *Lemon* tests. We view the third of those tests as most directly implicated in the present case. *Justice HARLAN* well described the problems of entanglement in his separate opinion in *Walz*, where he observed that governmental involvement in programs concerning religion "may be so direct or in such degree as to engender a risk of politicizing religion. . . . [R]eligious groups inevitably represent certain points of view and not infrequently assert them in the political arena, as evidenced by the continuing debate respecting birth control and abortion laws. Yet history cautions that political fragmentation on sectarian lines must be guarded ⊥ against. . . . [G]overnment participation in certain programs, whose very nature is apt to entangle the state in details of administration and planning, may escalate to the point of inviting undue fragmentation."

The Minnesota statute challenged here is illustrative of this danger. By their "very nature," the distinctions drawn by § 309.515, subd. 1(b), and its fifty per cent rule "engender a risk of politicizing religion"—a risk, indeed, that has already been substantially realized.

It is plain that the principal effect of the fifty per cent rule in § 309.515, subd. 1(b), is to impose the registration and reporting requirements of the Act on some religious organizations but not on others. It is also plain that, as the Court of Appeals noted, "[t]he benefit conferred [by exemption] constitutes a substantial advantage; the burden of compliance with the Act is certainly not *de minimis*." We do not suggest that the burdens of compliance with the Act would be intrinsically impermissible if they were imposed evenhandedly. But this statute does not operate evenhandedly, nor was it designed to do so: The fifty per ⊥ cent rule of § 309.515, subd. 1(b), effects the *selective* legislative imposition of burdens and advantages upon particular denominations. The "risk of politicizing religion" that inheres in such legislation is obvious, and indeed is confirmed by the provision's legislative history. For the history of § 309.515, subd. 1(b)'s fifty per cent rule demonstrates that the provision was drafted with the explicit intention of including particular religious denominations and excluding others. For example, the second sentence of an early draft of § 309.515, subd. 1(b), read: "A religious society or organization which solicits from its religious affiliates who are qualified under this subdivision and who are represented in a body or convention *that elects and controls the governing board of the religious society or organization* is exempt from the requirements of . . . Sections 309.52 and 309.53." The legislative history discloses that the legislators perceived that the italicized language would bring a Roman Catholic Archdiocese within the Act, that the legislators did not want the amendment to have that effect and that an amendment deleting the italicized clause was passed in committee for the sole purpose of exempting the Archdiocese from the provisions of the Act. On the other hand, there were certain religious organizations that the legislators did not want to exempt from the Act. One State Senator explained that the fifty per cent rule was "an attempt to deal with the religious organizations which are soliciting on the street and soliciting by direct mail, but who are not substantial religious institutions in . . . our state." Another Senator said, "what you're trying to get at here is the people that are running around airports and running around streets and soliciting people and you're trying to remove them from the exemption that normally applies to religious organizations." Still another Senator, who ap⊥parently had mixed feelings about the proposed provision, stated, "I'm not sure why we're so hot to regulate the Moonies anyway."

⌊255

In short, the fifty per cent rule's capacity—indeed, its express design—to burden or favor selected religious denominations led the Minnesota Legislature to discuss the characteristics of various sects with a view towards "religious gerrymandering," *Gillette* v. *United States.* As *The CHIEF JUSTICE* stated in *Lemon:* "This kind of state inspection and evaluation of the religious content of a religious organization is fraught with the sort of entanglement that the Constitution forbids. It is a relationship pregnant with dangers of excessive government direction . . . of churches."

IV

In sum, we conclude that the fifty per cent rule of § 309.515, subd. 1(b), is not closely fitted to the furtherance of any compelling governmental interest asserted by appellants, and that the provision therefore violates the Establishment Clause. Indeed, we think that § 309.515, subd. 1(b)'s fifty per cent rule sets up precisely the sort of official denominational preference that the Framers of the First Amendment forbade. Accordingly, we hold that appellees cannot be compelled to register and report under the Act on the strength of that provision.

The judgment of the Court of Appeals is *Affirmed.*

⌊256   ⊥ *Justice STEVENS, concurring.*

As the Court points out, invalidation of the 50-percent rule would require the State to shoulder

the considerable burden of demonstrating that the Unification Church is not a religious organization if the State persists in its attempt to require the Church to register and file financial statements. The burden is considerable because the record already establishes a prima facie case that the Church is a religious organization, and because a strict construction of a statutory exemption for religious organizations is disfavored and may give rise to constitutional questions. *Justice REHNQUIST* therefore is plainly wrong when he asserts in dissent that "invalidation of the fifty percent rule will have absolutely no effect on the Association's obligation to register and report as a *charitable organization* under the Act." (emphasis in original) The 50-percent rule has caused appellees a significant injury in fact because it has ⊥   ⌊257 substituted a simple method of imposing registration and reporting requirements for a more burdensome and less certain method of accomplishing that result. I therefore agree with the Court's conclusion that the appellees have standing to challenge the 50-percent rule in this case.

The more difficult question for me is whether the Court's policy of avoiding the premature adjudication of constitutional issues counsels postponement of any decision on the validity of the 50-percent rule until after the Unification Church's status as a religious organization within the meaning of the Minnesota statute is finally resolved. My difficulty stems from the fact that the trial and resolution of the statutory issue will certainly generate additional constitutional questions. Therefore, it is clear that at least one decision of constitutional moment is inevitable. Under these circumstances, it seems to me that reaching the merits is consistent with our "policy of strict necessity in disposing of constitutional issues," *Rescue Army* v. *Municipal Court.* ⊥ More-   ⌊258 over, a resolution of the question that has been fully considered by the District Court and by the Court of Appeals and that has been fully briefed and argued in this Court is surely consistent with the orderly administration of justice.

I agree with the Court's resolution of the Establishment Clause issue. Accordingly, I join the Court's opinion.

Justice WHITE, with whom Justice REHNQUIST joins, dissenting.

I concur in the dissent of *Justice REHNQUIST* with respect to standing. I also dissent on the merits.

I

It will be helpful first to indicate what occurred in the lower courts and what the Court now proposes to do. Based on two reports of a Magistrate, the District Court held unconstitutional the Minnesota limitation denying an exemption to religious organizations receiving less than 50 percent of their funding from their own members. The Magistrate recommended this action on the ground that the limitation could not pass muster under the second criterion set down in *Lemon* v. *Kurtzman* for identifying an unconstitutional establishment of religion—that the principal or primary effect of the statute is one that neither enhances nor inhibits religion. The 50-percent limitation failed this test because it subjected some churches to far more rigorous requirements than others, the effect being to "severely inhibit plaintiff's religious activities." This created a preference offensive to the Establishment Clause. The Magistrate relied on the inhibiting effect of the 50-percent rule without ref⊥erence to whether or not it was the principal or primary effect of the limitation. In any event, the Magistrate recommended, and the District Court agreed, that the exemption from registration be extended to all religious organizations.

⌐259

The Court of Appeals agreed with the District Court that the 50-percent rule violated the Establishment Clause. Its ruling, however, was on the ground that the limitation failed to satisfy the first *Lemon* criterion—that the statute have a secular rather than a religious purpose. The court conceded that the Act as a whole had the valid secular purpose of preventing fraudulent or deceptive practices in the solicitation of funds in the name of charity. The court also thought freeing certain organizations from regulation served a valid purpose because for those organizations public disclosure of funding would not significantly enhance the availability of information to contributors. Patriotic and fraternal societies that limit solicitation to voting members and certain charitable organizations that do not solicit in excess of $10,000 annually from the public fell into this category. But the court found no sound secular legislative purpose for the 50-percent limitation with respect to religious organizations because it "appears to be designed to shield favored sects, while continuing to burden other sects." The challenged provision, the Court of Appeals said, "expressly separates two classes of religious organizations and makes the separation for no valid secular purpose that has been suggested by defendants. Inexplicable disparate treatment will not generally be attributed to accident; it seems much more likely that at some stage of the legislative process special solicitude for particular religious organizations affected the choice of statutory language. The resulting discrimination is constitutionally invidious." The Court of Appeals went on to say that if it were necessary to apply the second part of the *Lemon* test, the provision would also fail to survive that examination because it advantaged some organizations and disadvantaged others.

⌐260

⊥ In this Court, the case is given still another treatment. The *Lemon* v. *Kurtzman* tests are put aside because they are applicable only to laws affording uniform benefit to all religions, not to provisions that discriminate among religions. Rather, in cases of denominational preference, the Court says that "our precedents demand that we treat the law as suspect and that we apply strict scrutiny in adjudging its constitutionality." The Court then invalidates the challenged limitation.

It does so by first declaring that the 50-percent rule makes explicit and deliberate distinctions between different religious organizations. The State's submission that the 50-percent limitation is a law based on secular criteria which happens not to have an identical effect on all religious organizations is rejected. The Court then holds that the challenged rule is not closely fitted to serve any compelling state interest and rejects each of the reasons submitted by the State to demonstrate that the distinction between contributions solicited from members and from nonmembers is a sensible one. Among others, the Court rejects the proposition that membership control is an adequate safeguard against deceptive solicitations of the public. The ultimate conclusion is that the exemption provision violates the Establishment Clause.

II

I have several difficulties with this disposition of the case. First, the Court employs a legal standard wholly different from that applied in the courts below. The premise for the Court's standard is that the challenged provision is a deliberate and explicit legislative preference for some religious denominations over others. But there was no such finding in the District Court. That court proceeded under the second *Lemon* test and then relied only on the disparate impact of the provision. There was no finding of a discriminatory or preferential legislative purpose. If this case is to be judged by a standard not employed by the courts below and if the ⊥ new standard involves factual issues or even mixed questions of law and fact that have not been addressed by the District Court, the Court should not itself purport to make these factual determinations. It should remand to the District Court.

⌐261

In this respect, it is no answer to say that the Court of Appeals appeared to find, although rather tentatively, that the state legislature had acted out of intentional denominational preferences. That court was no more entitled to supply the missing factual predicate for a different legal standard than is this Court. It is worth noting that none of the Court of Appeals' judges on the panel in this case is a resident of Minnesota.

Second, apparently realizing its lack of competence to judge the purposes of the Minnesota Legislature other than by the words it used, the Court disposes in a footnote of the State's claim that the 50-percent rule is a neutral, secular criterion that has disparate impact among religious organizations. The limitation, it is said, "is not simply a facially neutral statute" but one that makes "explicit and deliberate distinctions between different religious organizations." The rule itself, however, names no churches or denominations that are entitled to or denied the exemption. It neither qualifies nor disqualifies a church based on the kind or variety of its religious belief. Some religions will qualify and some will not, but this depends on the source of their contributions, not on their brand of religion.

To say that the rule on its face represents an explicit and deliberate preference for some religious beliefs over others is not credible. The Court offers no support for this assertion other than to agree with the Court of Appeals that the limitation might burden the less well organized denominations. This conclusion, itself, is a product of assumption and speculation. It is contrary to what the State insists is readily evident from a list of those charitable organizations that have registered under the Act and of those that are exempt. It is claimed that both categories include not only well-established, but also not so well-estab⊥lished, organizations. The Court appears to concede that the Minnesota law at issue does not constitute an establishment of religion merely because it has a disparate impact. An intentional preference must be expressed. To find that intention on the face of the provision at issue here seems to me to be patently wrong.

Third, I cannot join the Court's easy rejection of the State's submission that a valid secular purpose justifies basing the exemption on the percentage of external funding. Like the Court of Appeals, the majority accepts the prevention of fraudulent solicitation as a valid, even compelling, secular interest. Hence, charities, including religious organizations, may be required to register if the State chooses to insist. But here the State has excused those classes of charities it thought had adequate substitute safeguards or for some other reason had reduced the risk which is being guarded against. Among those exempted are various patriotic and fraternal organizations that depend only on their members for contributions. The Court of Appeals did not question the validity of this exemption because of the built-in safeguards of membership funding. The Court of Appeals, however, would not extend the same reasoning to permit the State to exempt religious organizations receiving more than half of their contributions from their members while denying exemption to those who rely on the public to a greater extent. This Court, preferring its own judgment of the realities of fundraising by religious organizations to that of the state legislature, also rejects the State's submission that organizations depending on their members for more than half of their funds do not pose the same degree of danger as other religious organizations. In the course of doing so, the Court expressly disagrees with the notion that members in general can be relied upon to control their organizations.

⊥ I do not share the Court's view of our omniscience. The State has the same interest in requiring registration by organizations soliciting most of their funds from the public as it would have in requiring any charitable organization to register, including a religious organization, if it wants to solicit funds. And if the State determines that its interest in preventing fraud does not extend to those who do not raise a majority of their funds from the public, its interest in imposing the requirement on others is not thereby reduced in the least. Furthermore, as the State suggests, the legislature thought it made good sense, and the courts, including this one, should not so readily disagree.

Fourth, and finally, the Court agrees with the Court of Appeals and the District Court that the exemption must be extended to all religious organizations. The Court of Appeals noted that the exemption provision, so construed, could be said to prefer religious organizations over nonreligious organizations and hence amount to an establishment of religion. Nevertheless, the Court of Appeals did not further address the question, and the Court says nothing of it now. Arguably, however, there is a more evident secular reason for exempting religious organizations who rely on their members to a great extent than there is to exempt all religious organizations, including those who raise all or nearly all of their funds from the public.

Without an adequate factual basis, the majority concludes that the provision in question deliberately prefers some religious denominations to others. Without an adequate factual basis, it rejects the justification offered by the State. It reaches its conclusions by applying a legal standard different from that considered by either of the courts below.

I would reverse the judgment of the Court of Appeals.

⊥ *Justice REHNQUIST*, with whom *The CHIEF JUSTICE*, *Justice WHITE*, and *Justice O'CONNOR* join, dissenting.

From the earliest days of the Republic it has been recognized that "[t]his Court is without power to give advisory opinions. *Hayburn's Case*". The logical corollary of this limitation has been the Court's "long . . . considered practice not to decide abstract, hypothetical or contingent questions, or to decide any constitutional question in advance of the necessity for its decision." Such fundamental principles notwithstanding, the Court today delivers what is at best an advisory constitutional pronouncement. The advisory character of the pronouncement is all but conceded by the Court itself, when it acknowledges in the closing footnote of its opinion that appellees must still "prove that the Unification Church is a religious organization within the meaning of the Act" before they can avail themselves of the Court's extension of the exemption contained in the Minnesota statute. Because I find the Court's standing analysis wholly unconvincing, I respectfully dissent.

I

Part II of the Court's opinion concluded that appellees have standing to challenge § 309.515, subd. 1(b), of the Minnesota Charitable Solicitation Act (Act), because they have "plainly met" the case-or-controversy requirements of Art. III. This conclusion is wrong. Its error can best be demonstrated by first reviewing three factual aspects of the case which are either misstated or disregarded in the Court's opinion.

First, the Act applies to appellees not by virtue of the "fifty percent rule," but by virtue of § 309.52. That provision requires "charitable organizations" to register with the Securities and Real Estate Division of the Minnesota Department of Commerce. ⌐265 The Holy Spirit Association for the ⊥ Unification of World Christianity (Association) constitutes such a "charitable organization" because it "engages in or purports to engage in solicitation" for a "religious . . . purpose." Only after an organization is brought within the coverage of the Act by § 309.52 does the question of exemption arise. The exemption provided by the fifty percent rule of § 309.515, subd. 1(b), one of several exemptions within the Act, applies only to "religious organizations." Thus, unless the Association is a "religious organization" within the meaning of the Act, the fifty percent rule has absolutely nothing to do with the Association's duty to register and report as a "charitable organization" soliciting funds in Minnesota. This more-than-semantic distinction apparently is misunderstood by the Court, for it repeatedly asserts that the Association is required to register "under the Act *by virtue of* the fifty percent rule of § 309.515, subd. 1(b)."

Second, the State's effort to enforce the Act against the Association was based on the Association's status as a "charitable organization" within the meaning of § 309.52. The State initially sought registration from the Association by letter: "From the nature of your solicitation it appears that [the Association] must complete a Charitable Organization Registration Statement and submit it to the ⌐266 Minnesota Department of Commerce." ⊥ When the Association failed to register within the allotted time, the State commenced "routine enforcement procedures" by filing a complaint in Minnesota state court. The complaint alleges that "charitable organizations" are required by § 309.52 to register with the State, that the Association comes within the § 309.50, subd. 4, definition of "charitable organizations," and that "[t]he [Association] has failed to file a registration statement and financial information with the Minnesota Department of Commerce, resulting in a violation of Minn. Stat. § 309.52." This complaint, which never once mentions the fifty percent rule of § 309.515, subd. 1(b), nor characterizes the Association as a "religious organization," is still

pending in Minnesota District Court, having been stayed by stipulation of the parties to this lawsuit. Because today's decision does nothing to impair the statutory basis of the complaint, or the State's reason for filing it, the State may proceed with its enforcement action before the ink on this Court's judgment is dry.

⊥ Third, appellees have never proved, and the lower courts have never found, that the Association is a "religious organization" for purposes of the fifty percent rule. The District Court expressly declined to make such a finding—"This court is not presently in a position to rule whether the [Association] is, in fact, a religious organization within the Act," and the Court of Appeals was content to decide the case despite the presence of this " 'unresolved factual dispute concerning the true character of [appellees'] organization,' " (quoting *Village of Schaumburg* v. *Citizens for Better Environment*). The absence of such a finding is significant, for it is by no means clear that the Association would constitute a "religious organization" for purposes of the § 309.515, subd. 1(b), exemption. The appellees' assertion in the District Court that their actions were religious was "directly contradict[ed]" by a "heavy testimonial barrage against the [Association's] claim that it is a religion."

⊥ II

The Court's opinion recognizes that the proper standing of appellees in this case is a constitutional prerequisite to the exercise of our Art. III power. To invoke that power, appellees must satisfy Art. III's case-or-controversy requirement by showing that they have a personal stake in the outcome of the controversy, consisting of a distinct and palpable injury. See also *Glad⊥stone, Realtors* v. *Village of Bellwood; Duke Power Co.* v. *Carolina Environmental Study Group.* I do not disagree with the Court's conclusion that the threatened application of the Act to appellees constitutes injury in fact.

But injury in fact is not the only requirement of Art. III. The appellees must also show that their injury "fairly can be traced to the challenged action of the defendant." *Simon* v. *Eastern Kentucky Welfare Rights Org.* The Court purports to find such causation by use of the following sophism: "there is a fairly traceable causal connection between the claimed injury and the challenged conduct—here, between the claimed disabling and the threatened application of § 309.515, subd. 1(b), and its fifty per cent rule."

As was demonstrated above, that statute and the State require the Association to register because it is a "charitable organization" under § 309.52, not because of the fifty percent requirement contained in the exemption for religious organizations. Indeed, at this point in the litigation the fifty percent rule is entirely inapplicable to appellees because they have not shown that the Association is a "religious organization." Therefore, any injury to appellees resulting from the registration and reporting requirements is *caused* by § 309.52, not, as the Court concludes, by "the . . . threatened application of § 309.515, subd. 1(b)'s fifty per cent rule." Having failed to establish that the fifty percent rule is causally connected to their injury, appellees at this point lack standing to challenge it.

The error of the Court's analysis is even more clearly demonstrated by a closely related and equally essential requirement of Art. III. In addition to demonstrating an injury which is caused by the challenged provision, appellees must show "that the exercise of the Court's remedial powers would redress the claimed injuries." *Duke Power Co.* v. *Carolina Environmental Study Group*. The importance ⊥ of redressability, an aspect of standing which has been recognized repeatedly by this Court, is of constitutional dimension: "[W]hen a plaintiff's standing is brought into issue the relevant inquiry is whether, assuming justiciability of the claim, the plaintiff has shown an injury to himself that is likely to be redressed by a favorable decision. Absent such a showing, exercise of its power by a federal court would be gratuitous and thus inconsistent with the Art. III limitation." *Simon* v. *Eastern Kentucky Welfare Rights Org.*

⊥270

Appellees have failed to show that a favorable decision of this Court will redress the injuries of which they complain. By affirming the decision of the Court of Appeals, the Court today extends the exemption of § 309.515, subd. 1(b), to all "religious organizations" soliciting funds in Minnesota. But because appellees have not shown that the Association is a "religious organization" under that provision, they have not shown that they will be entitled to this newly expanded exemption. This uncertainty is expressly recognized by the Court: ⊥ "We agree with the Court of Appeals that appellees and others claiming the benefits of the religious-organization exemption should not automatically enjoy those benefits. Rather, in order to receive them, appellees may be required by the State to prove that the Unification Church is a religious organization within the meaning of the Act." If the appellees fail in this proof—a distinct possibility given the State's "heavy testimonial barrage against [the Association's] claim that it is a religion,"—this court will have rendered a purely advisory opinion. In so doing, it will have struck down a state statute at the behest of a party without standing, contrary to the undeviating teaching of the cases previously cited. Those cases, I believe, require remand for a determination of whether the Association is a "religious organization" as that term is used in the Minnesota statute.

⊥271

III

There can be no doubt about the impropriety of the Court's action this day. "If there is one doctrine more deeply rooted than any other in the process of constitutional adjudication, it is that we ought not to pass on questions of constitutionality . . . unless such adjudication is unavoidable." *Spector Motor ⊥ Service, Inc.* v. *McLaughlin* Nowhere does this doctrine have more force than in cases such as this one, where the defect is a possible lack of Art. III jurisdiction due to want of standing on the part of the party which seeks the adjudication. "Considerations of propriety, as well as long-established practice, demand that we refrain from passing upon the constitutionality of [legislative Acts] unless obliged to do so in the proper performance of our judicial function, when the question is raised by a party whose interests entitle him to raise it." *Blair* v. *United States*, quoted in *Ashwander* v. *TVA*. (Brandeis, J., concurring). The existence of injury in fact does not alone suffice to establish such an interest. "The necessity that the plaintiff who seeks to invoke judicial power stand to profit in some personal interest remains an Art. III requirement. A federal court cannot ignore this requirement without overstepping its assigned role in our system of adjudicating only actual cases and controversies." *Simon* v. *Eastern Kentucky Welfare Rights Org*

⊥272

IV

In sum, the Court errs when it finds that appellees have standing to challenge the constitutionality of § 309.515, subd. 1(b). Although injured to be sure, appellees have not demonstrated that their injury was caused by the fifty percent rule or will be redressed by its invalidation. This is not to say that appellees can never prove causation or redressability, only that they have not done so at this point. The case should be remanded to permit such proof. Until such time as the requirements of Art. III clearly have been satisfied, this Court should refrain from rendering significant constitutional decisions.

LEGISLATIVE CHAPLAINS

Although the case included in this anthology of Supreme Court opinions has to do with the constitutionality of chaplains for legislatures, the topic has broader dimensions. This is because chaplains also serve in other government institutions, notably the military, prisons, and hospitals. Because chaplains are clergy whose salary is paid by the government, the church-state question, of course, is whether the maintenance of chaplains is a violation of the Establishment Clause; is it an instance of government supporting and advancing religion?

In terms of the military, prisons, and government hospitals, it is commonly understood that these kinds of chaplaincies are constitutional because of their peculiar location. Persons in the military, for example, are compelled by the government (even if they have voluntarily enlisted) to be in an environment other than their normal one. Those who are religious are not able to practice their religion as they normally would. Consequently, government, which requires them to be in their new location, has an obligation to provide them an opportunity to practice their religion. So, even though the providing of chaplains with government funds might appear to violate the Establishment Clause, the Free Exercise Clause requires government to supply the opportunity for religious behavior, thus justifying the "violation." (Of course, those in government hospitals, unlike those in the military or prison, are not in their abnormal environment because of government action. But because they are in a context in which the free exercise of religion is limited, government provides chaplaincy services.)

The Supreme Court has not heard a case on the constitutionality of the institutional chaplaincy, but the concept is illustrated by the recent case of *Katkoff* v. *Marsh*. The plaintiffs were two law school students who, as taxpayers, sued to declare the Army chaplaincy program unconstitutional as a violation of the Establishment Clause. The federal district court found that they had standing, because they were attacking an action of Congress under the Taxing and Spending Clause of Article I of the Constitution (to tax and spend "to provide for the common Defense") and because they were asserting a specific constitutional limitation on Congress' power to tax and spend (the Establishment Clause), as they are required to do under FLAST v. COHEN (p. 249) and VALLEY FORGE CHRISTIAN COLLEGE v. AMERICANS UNITED FOR SEPARATION OF CHURCH AND STATE (p. 258). On the merits of the case, the plaintiffs argued that it was unconstitutional for the government to finance the chaplaincy and that the way for the military to retain the benefits that it claimed were inherent in the chaplaincy program would be for the chaplains to be civilians, selected and financed by various denominations. The military claimed the chaplaincy proffered the benefits of the maintenance of good morale among military personnel and securing their right to exercise freely their religious preferences. The court found in favor of the military, citing the need for judicial deference to military judgment and that the chaplaincy program is not "a real threat to the Establishment Clause."

On appeal, the court of appeals affirmed the lower court in its deference to the judgment of Congress and the military in military matters and agreed with the concept that affording personnel the opportunity to worship prevented the chaplain program from being unconstitutional. The court stated the concept well:

> Since the program meets the requirement of voluntariness by leaving the practice of religion solely to the individual soldier, who is free to worship or not as he chooses without fear of any discipline or stigma, it might be viewed as not proscribed by the Establishment Clause. Indeed, if the Army prevented soldiers from worshipping in their own communities by removing them to areas where religious leaders of their persuasion and facilities were not available it could be accused of violating the Establishment Clause *unless* it provided them with a chaplaincy since its conduct would amount to inhibiting religion. . . . Unless the Army provided a chaplaincy it would deprive the soldier of his right under the Establishment Clause not to have religion inhibited and of his right under the Free Exercise Clause to practice his freely chosen religion. (755 F.2d. 223, 231-32, 234, emphasis in original)

At the time this is being written, *Katcoff* had not been sent forward to the Supreme Court. It may never be, especially since the trial court commented that the case had the flavor of being "more the grist of a moot court competition than a case or controversy to occupy the energies of a federal court." The appeals court, referring to plaintiffs' suggestion of a civilian chaplaincy financed by various denominations, said "plaintiffs' proposal is so inherently impractical as to border on the frivolous" and, at another place, called it a "will-o'-the-wisp" proposal. (The likelihood of appeal is also diminished by the Supreme Court's 1986 reaffirmation of the necessity of judicial deference to military judgment on how to run the military in GOLDMAN v. WEINBERGER (p.179)). The case does have the value, however, of eliciting clear expositions of the traditional argument for the constitutionality of chaplaincy programs in the military (and state prisons and hospitals). [1]

The reference to the voluntary nature of religious worship under the ministrations of a military chaplain are reminiscent of an earlier case, *Anderson* v. *Laird*. The controversy here was over compulsory chapel or church attendance at the United States Army, Navy, and Air Force Academies. The plaintiffs, cadets and midshipmen, claimed that required attendance at religious exercises violated both the Establishment and Free Exercise Clauses. The military argued that the requirement was not for the purpose of promoting religion or encouraging participation in worship, although a cadet was free to worship. Rather, the purpose of chapel attendance was to teach the officers-in-training the role and function of religion in the lives of others. Since these cadets someday would be in command over others, often in stressful situations, it was important that they be aware of the significance of religion in people's lives. What better place to learn that than in the worship context, where religion was in action? So the sole reason for the requirement was to provide the opportunities for cadets to observe others in worship, a legitimate and important part of their military training.

The federal district court noted the tradition of judicial deference to military judgment in things military and agreed with the rationale just described, which meant that the requirement had a secular purpose and not a primary effect which advanced religion. Consequently, the compulsory chapel attendance was constitutional.

The Court of Appeals for the District of Columbia Circuit reversed in a *per curiam* decision. However, two judges felt the need to comment. The essence of the comments was that while military judgment demands judicial respect, those under military discipline are not deprived of all constitutional rights. This becomes apparent in the case of compulsory religious activity. Forced worship was one of the evils the Framers of the Constitution opposed and so it has been throughout American history. The military cannot make it otherwise, especially on such specious grounds as a distinction between "worship" and "attendance" (the military had argued that "the requirement to attend is not a requirement to worship"). The service academies' requirements were clearly unconstitutional, since they had a religious purpose, had the

---

[1] Discussion of some cases about religion in prisons, involving the Free Exercise Clause, may be found at p. 59.

primary effect of advancing religion (providing a captive audience for worship), and violated the Free Exercise Clause as well. The Supreme Court refused to hear the case, allowing this judgment to stand.

The question of chaplains in legislatures is somewhat more difficult, since it cannot be claimed by defenders of the practice that legislators are entitled to chaplains because they are denied religious freedom by their service in the legislature. The traditional method of attack has been taxpayers challenging the constitutionality of the expenditure of government funds for the maintenance of legislative chaplains. A significant case of this type was *Elliott* v. *White* (1928). The plaintiff claimed that the expenditure of federal funds to maintain chaplains in the United States House of Representatives, Senate, Army, and Navy was a violation of the Establishment Clause and sought an injunction to prohibit the Treasurer of the United States from spending such funds. Although plaintiff claimed to sue as a citizen, not as a taxpayer, the Court of Appeals for the District of Columbia denied standing under the doctrine of *Frothingham* v. *Mellon* (see the discussion of standing above (p.246) and dismissed the challenge against the legislative chaplains.

When, in 1981, a similar challenge was launched in *Murray* v. *Morton,* a federal district court again denied plaintiff standing, asserting that *Elliott* v. *White* had not been superseded by *Flast* v. *Cohen.* (*Valley Forge* had not yet been decided.) The court did comment, in passing, that if a Senator or Representative filed suit, a court *might* hold that such a plaintiff's standing would not be denied by the *Elliott* precedent. On appeal, the case was argued before the entire Court of Appeals for the District of Columbia. Between the argument and the decision, the Supreme Court handed down MARSH v. CHAMBERS (p. 350), so when the appeals court did decide the case, it did not mention standing at all, but simply said that *Marsh* made it obvious that a challenge to the public funding of congressional chaplains had no validity.

What was this *Marsh* case? It was a challenge against the public funding of a chaplain in the legislature of Nebraska, brought by a member of the legislature. The challenge was three-fold: (1) the state funding of a chaplain promoted religion and thus violated the Establishment Clause, (2) the fact that Nebraska had employed a chaplain of one denomination (Presbyterian) for sixteen years impermissibly preferred one religion over others, and (3) the fact that the chaplain's prayers usually had a Judaeo-Christian content resulted in preference of one religion over others.

A federal district court found that the existence of a chaplain and the saying of prayers in the legislature were constitutional, but the state's paying for such services was not. The court of appeals took a broader approach and found that the chaplain program failed all three parts of the Establishment Clause test.

The Supreme Court reversed that judgment. Chief Justice Burger, writing for himself and five other justices, pointed to the fact that at the federal level and in most of the states, there was a long tradition of legislative chaplains. Most specifically, the First Congress, following the precedent established by the Continental Congress, "adopted the policy of selecting a chaplain to open each session with prayer." The Congress passed a law authorizing the payment of such chaplains from government funds. Just three days later, these same legislators finalized the wording of the First Amendment. The inescapable conclusion from this is that the Framers of the Constitution must not have seen any inconsistency between the government-paid chaplain program and the concept of separation of church and state. Neither did the Court.

> In light of the unambiguous and unbroken history of more than 200 years, there can be no doubt that the practice of opening legislative sessions with prayer has become part of the fabric of our society. To invoke Divine guidance on a public body entrusted with making laws is not, in these circumstances, an "establishment" of religion or a step toward establishment; it is simply a tolerable acknowledgment of beliefs widely held among the people of this country. (463 U.S. 783, 792)

In terms of the specific challenges to the Nebraska chaplain, none of them invalidated the program. The fact that only one chaplain had been appointed for sixteen years merely shows that the legislature was satisfied with his work, not because he was of a particular denomination. Paying the chaplain with state funds is not unconstitutional. Again, look to the precedent of the Framers of the Constitution. The practice has a long history; in Nebraska, over 100 years. The content of the prayers, in this case predominantly Judeo-Christian, is not relevant to constitutionality so long as they are not used to inculcate any particular religion or to proselytize anyone. There was no evidence of that in this case.

In *Marsh* the Court did not use the three-part "*Lemon* test" to reach its decision. Rather, it relied exclusively on an argument from history. This was a great concern to strict separationists, because they knew that more often than not the use of the test had led the Court to maintain what Jefferson had called the "wall of separation" between church and state. They were afraid that if the Court abandoned its use of the test, it might also take a more "accommodationist" view of the relation between church and state, as, indeed, it had done in this case.[2]

That the "*Lemon* test" had not been used was unacceptable to Justice Brennan, who wrote a dissent in which Justice Marshall joined. It was clear to him that "our settled doctrine" should have been employed. If it had been, the legislative chaplaincy would have failed all three parts for the following reasons:

---

[2] The fears of separationists seemed to be realized in *Katkoff* v. *Marsh,* a challenge to the military chaplaincy described above. The district court decision mentioned the "*Lemon* test," but, citing the precedent of *Marsh,* specifically declined to use it, using rather the test of "whether the Program is 'a real threat to the Establishment Clause,'" quoting *Marsh.* It found the chaplaincy constitutional. At the appeal level, the court commented that the chaplaincy program in the military would clearly fail all three parts of the Establishment Clause test. However, establishment cases should not be considered in a vacuum. Here the chaplaincy program related not only to the Establishment Clause, but also to the War Power Clause of Article 1, § 8 of the Constitution and to the Free Exercise Clause. These dimensions were enough to save the chaplaincy. The court did not cite *Marsh* exactly at that point, but earlier had pointed out that *Marsh* had shown that it was possible to decide an establishment case without using the test.

Legislative prayer clearly violates the principles of neutrality and separation that are embedded within the Establishment Clause. It is contrary to the fundamental message of *Engel* and *Schempp*. It intrudes on the right to conscience by forcing some legislators either to participate in a "prayer opportunity," with which they are in basic disagreement, or to make their disagreement a matter of public comment by declining to participate. It forces all residents of the State to support a religious exercise that may be contrary to their own beliefs. It requires the State to commit itself on fundamental theological issues. It has the potential of degrading religion by allowing a religious call to worship to be intermeshed with a secular call to order. And it injects religion into the political sphere by creating the potential that each and every selection of a chaplain, or consideration of a particular prayer, or even reconsideration of the practice itself, will provoke a political battle along religious lines and ultimately alienate some religiously identified group of citizens. (463 U.S. 783, 808)

Because *Marsh* found the practice of having legislative chaplains to be constitutional, any subsequent attacks on the concept would have to take a narrower and more novel approach. In late 1985 *Kurtz* v. *Kennickell* represented such a tactic. A taxpayer sued the Public Printer, the Secretary of the Treasury, and the Treasurer of the United States, seeking to prevent the publication of the annual compilation of the prayers offered by the chaplains of the Senate and House of Representatives (although the House ceased such publication in 1978). The federal district court, after finding that the plaintiff successfully negotiated the barriers of *Flast* and *Valley Forge* and thus had standing, set the case aside pending a discussion in the Senate Committee on Rules and Administration, which was poised on the brink of a reconsideration of the policy of publishing the prayers of the Senate Chaplain. [3] The court noted that the documents for both sides were in place so that if the Senate did not take up the matter in a timely manner, or if it decided to continue publishing the prayers, the case could be resumed and heard on the merits.

MARSH v. CHAMBERS

463 U.S. 783
ON WRIT OF CERTIORARI TO THE UNITED STATES COURT OF APPEALS FOR THE EIGHTH CIRCUIT
Argued April 20, 1983 — Decided July 5, 1983

⊥784 ⊥ *Chief Justice* BURGER delivered the opinion of the Court.

The question presented is whether the Nebraska Legislature's practice of opening each legislative day with a prayer by a chaplain paid by the State violates the Establishment Clause of the First Amendment.

I

The Nebraska Legislature begins each of its sessions with a prayer offered by a chaplain who is chosen biennially by the Executive Board of the Legislative Council and paid out of ⊥ public funds. ⊥785 Robert E. Palmer, a Presbyterian minister, has served as chaplain since 1965 at a salary of $319.75 per month for each month the legislature is in session.

Ernest Chambers is a member of the Nebraska Legislature and a taxpayer of Nebraska. Claiming that the Nebraska Legislature's chaplaincy practice violates the Establishment Clause of the First Amendment, he brought this action under 42 U.S.C. § 1983, seeking to enjoin enforcement of the practice. After denying a motion to dismiss on the ground of legislative immunity, the District Court held that the Establishment Clause was not breached by the prayers, but was violated by paying the chaplain from public funds. It therefore enjoined the Legislature from using public funds to pay the chaplain; it declined to enjoin the policy of beginning sessions with prayers. Cross-appeals were taken.

The Court of Appeals for the Eighth Circuit rejected arguments that the case should be dismissed on Tenth Amendment, legislative immunity, standing or federalism grounds. On the merits of the chaplaincy issue, the court refused to treat respondent's challenges as separable issues as the District Court had done. Instead, the Court of Appeals assessed the practice as a whole because "[p]arsing out [the] ⊥ elements" would lead to "an incongruous ⊥786 result."

Applying the three-part test of *Lemon* v. *Kurtzman*, the court held that the chaplaincy practice violated all three elements of the test: the purpose and primary effect of selecting the same minister for 16 years and publishing his prayers was to promote a particular religious expression; use of state money for compensation and publication led to entanglement. Accordingly, the Court of Appeals modified the District Court's injunction and prohibited the State from engaging in any aspect of its established chaplaincy practice.

We granted certiorari limited to the challenge to the practice of opening sessions with prayers by a State-employed clergyman and we reverse.

II

The opening of sessions of legislative and other deliberative public bodies with prayer is deeply embedded in the history and tradition of this country. From colonial times through the founding of the Republic and ever since, the practice of legislative prayer has coexisted with the principles of disestablishment and religious freedom. In the very courtrooms in which the United States District Judge and later three Circuit Judges heard and decided this case, the proceedings opened with an announcement

---

[3] "Periodic Printing of the Chaplain's Prayers," *Congressional Record—Senate* 131 (October 29, 1985): S14277.

that concluded, "God save the United States and this Honorable Court." The same invocation occurs at all sessions of this Court.

⊥ The tradition in many of the colonies was, of course, linked to an established church, but the Continental Congress, beginning in 1774, adopted the traditional procedure of opening its sessions with a prayer offered by a paid chaplain. Although prayers were not offered during the Constitutional Convention, the First Congress, as one of ⊥ its early items of business, adopted the policy of selecting a chaplain to open each session with prayer. Thus, on April 7, 1789, the Senate appointed a committee "to take under consideration the manner of electing Chaplains." On April 9, 1789, a similar committee was appointed by the House of Representatives. On April 25, 1789, the Senate elected its first chaplain; the House followed suit on May 1, 1789. A statute providing for the payment of these chaplains was enacted into law on Sept. 22, 1789.

On Sept. 25, 1789, three days after Congress authorized the appointment of paid chaplains, final agreement was reached on the language of the Bill of Rights. Clearly the men who wrote the First Amendment Religion Clause did not view paid legislative chaplains and opening prayers as a violation of that Amendment, for the practice of opening sessions with prayer has continued without interruption ever since that early session of Congress. It has also been followed con⊥sistently in most of the states, including Nebraska, where the institution of opening legislative sessions with prayer was adopted even before the State attained statehood.

⊥ Standing alone, historical patterns cannot justify contemporary violations of constitutional guarantees, but there is far more here than simply historical patterns. In this context, historical evidence sheds light not only on what the draftsmen intended the Establishment Clause to mean, but also on how they thought that Clause applied to the practice authorized by the First Congress—their actions reveal their intent. An act "passed by the first Congress assembled under the Constitution, many of whose members had taken part in framing that instrument, . . . is contemporaneous and weighty evidence of its true meaning". *Wisconsin* v. *Pelican Ins. Co.*

In *Walz* v. *Tax Comm'n* we considered the weight to be accorded to history: "It is obviously correct that no one acquires a vested or protected right in violation of the Constitution by long use, even when that span of time covers our entire national existence and indeed predates it. Yet an unbroken practice . . . is not something to be lightly cast aside." No more is Nebraska's practice of over a century, consistent with two centuries of national practice, to be cast aside. It can hardly be thought that in the same week Members of the First Congress voted to appoint and to pay a Chaplain for each House and

also voted to approve the draft of the First Amendment for submission to the States, they intended the Establishment Clause of the Amendment to forbid what they had just declared acceptable. In applying the First Amendment to the states through the Fourteenth Amendment, *Cantwell* v. *Connecticut*, it would be incongruous to interpret that clause as imposing more strin⊥gent First Amendment limits on the States than the draftsmen imposed on the Federal Government.

This unique history leads us to accept the interpretation of the First Amendment draftsmen who saw no real threat to the Establishment Clause arising from a practice of prayer similar to that now challenged. We conclude that legislative prayer presents no more potential for establishment that the provision of school transportation, *Everson* v. *Board of Education*, beneficial grants for higher education, *Tilton* v. *Richardson*, or tax exemptions for religious organizations, *Walz.*

Respondent cites *Justice BRENNAN's* concurring opinion in *Abington School Dist.* v. *Schempp* and argues that we should not rely too heavily on "the advice of the Founding Fathers" because the messages of history often tend to be ambiguous and not relevant to a society far more heterogeneous than that of the Framers. Respondent also points out that John Jay and John Rutledge opposed the motion to begin the first session of the Continental Congress with prayer.

We do not agree that evidence of opposition to a measure weakens the force of the historical argument; indeed it infuses it with power by demonstrating that the subject was considered carefully and the action not taken thoughtlessly, by force of long tradition and without regard to the problems posed by a pluralistic society. Jay and Rutledge specifically grounded their objection on the fact that the delegates to the Congress "were so divided in religious sentiments . . . that [they] could not join in the same act of worship." Their ob⊥jection was met by Samuel Adams, who stated that "he was no bigot, and could hear a prayer from a gentleman of piety and virtue, who was at the same time a friend to his country."

This interchange emphasizes that the delegates did not consider opening prayers as a proselytizing activity or as symbolically placing the government's "official seal of approval on one religious view." Rather, the Founding Fathers looked at invocations as "conduct whose . . . effect . . . harmonize[d] with the tenets of some or all religions." *McGowan* v. *Maryland.* The Establishment Clause does not always bar a state from regulating conduct simply because it "harmonizes with religious canons." *Id.* Here, the individual claiming injury by the practice is an adult, presumably not readily susceptible to "religious indoctrination", or peer pressure.

In light of the unambiguous and unbroken history of more than 200 years, there can be no doubt that the practice of opening legislative sessions with prayer has become part of the fabric of our society. To invoke Divine guidance on a public body entrusted with making the laws is not, in these circumstances, an "establishment" of religion or a step toward establishment; it is simply a tolerable acknowledgement of beliefs widely held among the people of this country. As *Justice DOUGLAS* observed, "[w]e are a religious people whose institutions presuppose a Supreme Being." *Zorach* v. *Clauson*

III

We turn then to the question of whether any features of the Nebraska practice violate the Establishment Clause. ⊥ Beyond the bare fact that a prayer is offered, three points have been made: first, that a clergyman of only one denomination—Presbyterian—has been selected for 16 years; second, that the chaplain is paid at public expense; and third, that the prayers are in the Judeo-Christian tradition. Weighed against the historical background, these factors do not serve to invalidate Nebraska's practice.

The Court of Appeals was concerned that Palmer's long tenure has the effect of giving preference to his religious views. We, no more than Members of the Congresses of this century, can perceive any suggestion that choosing a clergyman of one denomination advances the beliefs of a particular church. To the contrary, the evidence indicates that Palmer was reappointed because his performance and personal qualities were acceptable to the body appointing him. Palmer was not the only clergyman heard by the Legislature; guest chaplains have officiated at the request of various legislators and as substitutes during Palmer's absences. Absent proof that the chaplain's reappointment stemmed from an impermissible motive, we con⊥clude that his long tenure does not in itself conflict with the Establishment Clause.

Nor is the compensation of the chaplain from public funds a reason to invalidate the Nebraska Legislature's chaplaincy; remuneration is grounded in historic practice initiated, as we noted earlier, by the same Congress that adopted the Establishment Clause of the First Amendment. The Continental Congress paid its chaplain, as did some of the states. Currently, many state legislatures and the United States Congress provide compensation for their chaplains. Nebraska has paid its chaplain for well over a century. The content of the prayer is not of concern to judges where, as here, there is no indication that the prayer opportunity has been exploited to proselytize or advance any one, ⊥ or to disparage any other, faith or belief. That being so, it is not for us to embark on a sensitive evaluation or to parse the content of a particular prayer.

We do not doubt the sincerity of those, who like respondent, believe that to have prayer in this context risks the beginning of the establishment the Founding Fathers feared. But this concern is not well founded, for as *Justice GOLDBERG* aptly observed in his concurring opinion in *Abington*: "It is of course true that great consequences can grow from small beginnings, but the measure of constitutional adjudication is the ability and willingness to distinguish between real threat and mere shadow." The unbroken practice for two centuries in the National Congress, for more than a century in Nebraska and in many other states, gives abundant assurance that there is no real threat "while this Court sits," *Panhandle Oil Co.* v. *Mississippi ex rel. Knox* (Holmes, J., dissenting).

The judgment of the Court of Appeals is *Reversed.*

Justice BRENNAN, with whom *Justice MARSHALL* joins, dissenting.

The Court today has written a narrow and, on the whole, careful opinion. In effect, the Court holds that officially sponsored legislative prayer, primarily on account of its "unique history," is generally exempted from the First Amendment's prohibition against "the establishment of religion." The Court's opinion is consistent with dictum in at least one of our prior decisions, and its limited rationale should pose little threat to the overall fate of the Establishment Clause. Moreover, disagreement with the Court ⊥ requires that I confront the fact that some twenty years ago, in a concurring opinion in one of the cases striking down official prayer and ceremonial Bible reading in the public schools, I came very close to endorsing essentially the result reached by the Court today. Nevertheless, after much reflection, I have come to the conclusion that I was wrong then and that the Court is wrong today. I now believe that the practice of official invocational prayer, as it exists in Nebraska and most other State Legislatures, is unconstitutional. It is contrary to the doctrine as well the underlying purposes of the Establishment Clause, and it is not saved either by its history or by any of the other considerations suggested in the Court's opinion.

I respectfully dissent.

I

The Court makes no pretense of subjecting Nebraska's practice of legislative prayer to any of the formal "tests" that have traditionally structured our inquiry under the Establishment Clause. That it fails to do so is, in a sense, a good thing, for it simply confirms that the Court is carving out an exception to the Establishment Clause rather than reshaping Establishment Clause doctrine to accommodate legislative prayer. For my purposes, however, I must begin by demonstrating what should be obvious: that, if the Court were to judge legislative prayer through the unsentimental eye of our settled doctrine, it would have to strike it down as a clear violation of the Establishment Clause.

The most commonly cited formulation of prevailing Establishment Clause doctrine is found in *Lemon* v. *Kurtzman*: ⊥ "Every analysis in this area must begin with consideration of the cumulative criteria developed by the Court over many years. Three such tests may be gleaned from our cases. First, the statute [at issue] must have a secular legislative purpose; second, its principal or primary effect must be one that neither advances nor inhibits religion; finally, the statute must not foster 'an excessive government entanglement with religion.' "

That the "purpose" of legislative prayer is preeminently religious rather than secular seems to me to be self-evident. "To invoke Divine guidance on a public body entrusted with making the laws," is nothing but a religious act. Moreover, whatever secular functions legislative prayer might play—formally opening the legislative session, getting the members of the body to quiet down, and imbuing them with a sense of seriousness and high purpose—could so plainly be performed in a purely nonreligious fashion that to claim a secular purpose for the prayer is an insult to the per⊥fectly honorable individuals who instituted and continue the practice.

The "primary effect" of legislative prayer is also clearly religious. As we said in the context of officially sponsored prayers in the public schools, "prescribing a particular form of religious worship," even if the individuals involved have the choice not to participate, places "indirect coercive pressure upon religious minorities to conform to the prevailing officially approved religion. . . ." *Engel* v. *Vitale* More importantly, invocations in Nebraska's legislative halls explicitly link religious beliefs and observance to the power and prestige of the State. "[T]he mere appearance of a joint exercise of legislative authority by Church and State provides a significant symbolic benefit to religion in the minds of some by reason of the power conferred." *Larkin* v. *Grendel's Den*

Finally, there can be no doubt that the practice of legislative prayer leads to excessive "entanglement" between the State and religion. *Lemon* pointed out that "entanglement" can take two forms: First, a state statute or program might involve the state impermissibly in monitoring and overseeing ⊥ religious affairs. In the case of legislative prayer, the process of choosing a "suitable" chaplain, whether on a permanent or rotating basis, and insuring that the chaplain limits himself or herself to "suitable" prayers, involves precisely the sort of supervision that agencies of government should if at all possible avoid.

Second, excessive "entanglement" might arise out of "the divisive political potential" of a state statute or program. "Ordinarily political debate and division, however vigorous or even partisan, are normal and healthy manifestations of our democratic system of government, but political division along religious lines was one of the principal evils against which the First Amendment was intended to protect. The political divisiveness of such conflict is a threat to the normal political process." *Lemon* In this case, this second aspect of entanglement is also clear. The controversy between Senator Chambers and his colleagues, which had reached the stage of difficulty and rancor long before this lawsuit was brought, has split the Nebraska ⊥ Legislature precisely on issues of religion and religious conformity. The record in this case also reports a series of instances, involving legislators other than Senator Chambers, in which invocations by Reverend Palmer and others led to controversy along religious lines. And in general, the history of legislative prayer has been far more eventful—and divisive—than a hasty reading of the Court's opinion might indicate.

In sum, I have no doubt that, if any group of law students were asked to apply the principles of *Lemon* to the question ⊥ of legislative prayer, they would nearly unanimously find the practice to be unconstitutional.

II

The path of formal doctrine, however, can only imperfectly capture the nature and importance of the issues at stake in this case. A more adequate analysis must therefore take ⊥ into account the underlying function of the Establishment Clause, and the forces that have shaped its doctrine.

A

Most of the provisions of the Bill of Rights, even if they are not generally enforceable in the absence of state action, nevertheless arise out of moral intuitions applicable to individuals as well as governments. The Establishment Clause, however, is quite different. It is, to its core, nothing less and nothing more than a statement about the proper role of *government* in the society that we have shaped for ourselves in this land.

The Establishment Clause embodies a judgment, born of a long and turbulent history, that, in our society, religion "must be a private matter for the individual, and family, and the institutions of private choice. . . ." *Lemon* v. *Kurtzman* "Government in our democracy, state and national, must be neutral in matters of religious theory, doctrine, and practice. It may not be hostile to any religion or to the advocacy of no-religion; and it may not aid, foster, or promote one religion or religious theory against another or even against the militant opposite. The First Amendment mandates governmental neutrality between religion and nonreligion." *Epperson* v. *Arkansas* "In the words of Jefferson, the clause against establishment of religion by law was intended to

¹⁷⁹⁷

¹⁷⁹⁸

¹⁷⁹⁹

¹⁸⁰⁰

¹⁸⁰¹

¹⁸⁰²

erect 'a wall of separation between church and state.'" *Everson* v. *Board of Education*

⊥803   ⊥ The principles of "separation" and "neutrality" implicit in the Establishment Clause serve many purposes. Four of these are particularly relevant here.

The first, which is most closely related to the more general conceptions of liberty found in the remainder of the First Amendment, is to guarantee the individual right to conscience. The right to conscience, in the religious sphere, is not only implicated when the government engages in direct or indirect coercion. It is also implicated when the government requires individuals to support the practices of a faith with which they do not agree. "[T]o compel a man to furnish contributions of money for the propagation of [religious] opinions which he disbelieves, is sinful and tyrannical; . . . even . . . forcing him to support this or that teacher of his own religious persuasion, is depriving him of the comfortable liberty of giving his contributions to the particular pastor, whose morals he should make his pattern. . . ." *Everson* v. *Board of Education*

The second purpose of separation and neutrality is to keep the state from interfering in the essential autonomy of religious life, either by taking upon itself

⊥804   the decision of reli⊥gious issues, or by unduly involving itself in the supervision of religious institutions or officials.

The third purpose of separation and neutrality is to prevent the trivialization and degradation of religion by too close an attachment to the organs of government. The Establishment Clause "stands as an expression of principle on the part of the Founders of our Constitution that religion is too personal, too sacred, too holy to permit its 'unhallowed perversion' by a civil magistrate." *Engel* v. *Vitale*, quoting the Memorial and Remonstrance.

⊥805   ⊥ Finally, the principles of separation and neutrality help assure that essentially religious issues, precisely because of their importance and sensitivity, not become the occasion for battle in the political arena. With regard to most issues, the Government may be influenced by partisan argument and may act as a partisan itself. In each case, there will be winners and losers in the political battle, and the losers' most common recourse is the right to dissent and the right to fight the battle again another day. With regard to matters that are essentially religious, however, the Establishment Clause seeks that there should be no political battles, and that no American

⊥806   should at any point feel alien⊥ated from his government because that government has declared or acted upon some "official" or "authorized" point of view on a matter of religion.

B

The imperatives of separation and neutrality are not limited to the relationship of government to religious institutions or denominations, but extend as

well to the relationship of government to religious beliefs and practices. In *Torcaso* v. *Watkins*, for example, we struck down a state provision requiring a religious oath as a qualification to hold office, not only because it violated principles of free exercise of religion, but also because it violated the principles of non-establishment of religion. And, of course, in the pair of cases that hang over this one like a reproachful set of parents, we held that official prayer and prescribed Bible reading in the public schools represent a serious encroachment on the Establishment Clause. As we said in *Engel*, "[i]t is neither sacreligious nor anti-religious to say that each separate government in this country should stay out of the business of writing or sanctioning official prayers and leave that purely religious function to the people themselves and to those the people choose to look to for religious guidance."

Nor should it be thought that this view of the Establishment Clause is a recent concoction of an overreaching judi⊥ciary. Even before the First   ⊥807 Amendment was written, the Framers of the Constitution broke with the practices of the Articles of Confederation and many state constitutions, and did not invoke the name of God in the document. This "omission of a reference to the Deity was not inadvertent; nor did it remain unnoticed." Moreover, Thomas Jefferson and Andrew Jackson, during their respective terms as President, both refused on Establishment Clause grounds to declare national days of thanksgiving or fasting. And James Madison, writing subsequent to his own Presidency on essentially the very issue we face today, stated: "Is the appointment of Chaplains to the two Houses of Congress consistent with the Constitution, and with the pure principle of religious freedom?

"In strictness, the answer on both points must be in the negative. The Constitution of the U.S. forbids everything like an establishment of a national religion. The law appointing Chaplains establishes a religious worship for the national representatives, to be performed by Ministers of religion, elected by a majority of ⊥ them; and these are to be paid out of the   ⊥808 national taxes. Does not this involve the principle of a national establishment, applicable to a provision for a religious worship for the Constituent as well as of the representative Body, approved by the majority, and conducted by Ministers of religion paid by the entire nation." Fleet, Madison's "Detached Memoranda," 3 Wm. & Mary Quarterly 534, 588 (1946).

C

Legislative prayer clearly violates the principles of neutrality and separation that are embedded within the Establishment Clause. It is contrary to the fundamental message of *Engel* and *Schempp*. It intrudes on the right to conscience by forcing some legislators either to participate in a "prayer opportunity," with which they are in basic disagreement, or to make

their disagreement a matter of public comment by
declining to participate. It forces all residents of the
State to support a religious exercise that may be contrary to their own beliefs. It requires the State to
commit itself on fundamental theological issues. It
has the potential for degrading religion by allowing a
religious call to worship to be intermeshed with a
secular call to order. And it injects religion into the
political sphere by creating the potential that each
and every selection of a chaplain, or consideration of
a particular prayer, or even reconsideration of the
practice itself, will provoke a political battle along
religious lines and ultimately alienate some religiously identified group of citizens.

⊥809

⊥D

One response to the foregoing account, of course,
is that "neutrality" and "separation" do not exhaust
the full meaning of the Establishment Clause as it
has developed in our cases. It is indeed true that
there are certain tensions inherent in the First
Amendment itself, or inherent in the role of religion
and religious belief in any free society, that have
shaped the doctrine of the Establishment Clause,
and required us to deviate from an absolute adherence to separation and neutrality. Nevertheless,
these considerations, although very important, are
also quite specific, and where none of them is
present, the Establishment Clause gives us no warrant simply to look the other way and treat an unconstitutional practice as if it were constitutional.
Because the Court occasionally suggests that some of
these considerations might apply here, it becomes
important that I briefly identify the most prominent
of them and explain why they do not in fact have
any relevance to legislative prayer.

(1)

A number of our cases have recognized that religious institutions and religious practices may, in
certain contexts, receive the benefit of government
programs and policies generally available, on the basis of some secular criterion, to a wide class of similarly situated nonreligious beneficiaries, and the
precise cataloguing of those contexts is not necessarily an easy task. I need not tarry long here,
however, because the provision for a daily official in-
⊥810 vocation by a nonmember officer of ⊥ a legislative
body could by no stretch of the imagination appear
anywhere in that catalogue.

(2)

Conversely, our cases have recognized that religion
can encompass a broad, if not total, spectrum of concerns, overlapping considerably with the range of
secular concerns, and that not every governmental
act which coincides with or conflicts with a particular religious belief is for that reason an establishment
of religion. The Court seems to suggest at one point

that the practices of legislative prayer may be excused on this ground, but I cannot really believe that
it takes this position seriously. The practice of legislative prayer is nothing like the statutes we considered in *McGowan* and *Harris* v. *McRae;* prayer is not
merely "conduct whose . . . effect . . . harmonizes
with the tenets of some or all religions," prayer is
fundamentally and necessarily religious. "It is prayer
which distinguishes religious phenomena from all
those which resemble them or lie near to them, from
the moral sense, for example, or aesthetic feeling."
Engel

(3)

We have also recognized that Government cannot,
without adopting a decidedly *anti*-religious point of
view, be forbid⊥den to recognize the religious beliefs   ⊥811
and practices of the American people as an aspect of
our history and culture. Certainly, bona fide classes
in comparative religion can be offered in the public
schools. And certainly, the text of Abraham Lincoln's Second Inaugural Address which is inscribed
on a wall of the Lincoln Memorial need not be
purged of its profound theological content. The practice of offering invocations at legislative sessions
cannot, however, simply be dismissed as "a tolerable
acknowledgment of beliefs widely held among the
people of this country." "Prayer is religion *in act*."
"Praying means to take hold of a word, the end, so
to speak, of a line that leads to God." Reverend Palmer and other members of the clergy who offer invocations at legislative sessions are not museum
pieces, put on display once a day for the edification
of the legislature. Rather, they are engaged by the
legislature to lead it—as a body—in an act of religious worship. If upholding the practice requires
denial of this fact, I suspect that many supporters of
legislative prayer would feel that they had been
handed a pyrrhic victory.

(4)

Our cases have recognized that the purposes of the
Establishment Clause can sometimes conflict. For
example, in *Walz* v. *Tax Commissioner*, we upheld
tax exemptions for religious institutions in part because subjecting those institutions to taxation might
foster serious administrative entanglement. Here,
however, no ⊥ such tension exists; the State can   ⊥812
vindicate *all* the purposes of the Establishment
Clause by abolishing legislative prayer.

(5)

Finally, our cases recognize that, in one important
respect, the Constitution is *not* neutral on the subject of religion: Under the Free Exercise Clause, religiously motivated claims of conscience may give rise
to constitutional rights that other strongly-held beliefs do not. Moreover, even when the government is
not compelled to do so by the Free Exercise Clause,

it may to some extent act to facilitate the opportunities of individuals to practice their religion. This is
not, however, a case in which a State is accommodating individual religious interests. We are not
faced here with the right of the legislature to allow
⊥813   its members to offer prayers during the course of ⊥
general legislative debate. We are certainly not faced
with the right of legislators to form voluntary groups
for prayer or worship. We are not even faced with
the right of the state to employ members of the clergy to minister to the private religious needs of individual legislators. Rather, we are faced here with the
regularized practice of conducting official prayers, on
behalf of the entire legislature, as part of the order of
business constituting the formal opening of every
single session of the legislative term. If this is Free
Exercise, the Establishment Clause has no meaning
whatsoever.

III

With the exception of the few lapses I have already
noted, each of which is commendably qualified so as
to be limited to the facts of this case, the Court says
almost nothing contrary to the above analysis. Instead, it holds that "the practice of opening legislative sessions with prayer has become part of the
fabric of our society," and chooses not to interfere. I
sympathize with the Court's reluctance to strike
down a practice so prevalent and so ingrained as legislative prayer. I am, however, unconvinced by the
Court's arguments, and cannot shake my conviction
that legislative prayer violates both the letter and
the spirit of the Establishment Clause.

A

The Court's main argument for carving out an exception sustaining legislative prayer is historical.
The Court cannot—and does not—purport to find a
pattern of "undeviating acceptance," *Walz*, of legislative prayer. It also disclaims exclusive reliance on
the mere longevity of legislative prayer. The Court
does, however, point out that, only three days before
the First Congress reached agreement on the final
wording of the Bill of Rights, it authorized the ap-
⊥814   pointment of paid chaplains for ⊥ its own proceedings, and the Court argues that in light of this
"unique history," the actions of Congress reveal its
intent as to the meaning of the Establishment
Clause. I agree that historical practice is "of considerable import in the interpretation of abstract constitutional language," *Walz*. This is a case, however,
in which—absent the Court's invocation of history—
there would be no question that the practice at issue
was unconstitutional. And despite the surface appeal
of the Court's argument, there are at least three reasons why specific historical practice should not in
this case override that clear constitutional imperative.

First, it is significant that the Court's historical
argument does not rely on the legislative history of

the Establishment Clause itself. Indeed, that formal
history is profoundly unilluminating on this and
most other subjects. Rather, the Court assumes that
the Framers of the Establishment Clause would not
have themselves authorized a practice that they
thought violated the guarantees contained in the
clause. This assumption, however, is questionable.
Legislators, influenced by the passions and exigencies of the moment, the pressure of constituents and
colleagues, and the press of business, do not always
pass sober constitutional judgment on every piece of
legislation they enact, and this ⊥ must be assumed   ⊥815
to be as true of the members of the First Congress as
any other. Indeed, the fact that James Madison, who
voted for the bill authorizing the payment of the
first congressional chaplains, later expressed the
view that the practice was unconstitutional, is instructive on precisely this point. Madison's later
views may not have represented so much a change of
mind as a change of *role*, from a member of Congress
engaged in the hurley-burley of legislative activity to
a detached observer engaged in unpressured reflection. Since the latter role is precisely the one with
which this Court is charged, I am not at all sure that
Madison's later writings should be any less influential in our deliberations than his earlier vote.

Second, the Court's analysis treats the First
Amendment simply as an Act of Congress, as to
whose meaning the intent of Congress is the single
touchstone. Both the Constitution and its amendments, however, became supreme law only by virtue
of their ratification by the States, and the understanding of the States should be as relevant to our
analysis as the understanding of Congress. This observation is especially compelling in consid⊥ering   ⊥816
the meaning of the Bill of Rights. The first 10
Amendments were not enacted because the members
of the First Congress came up with a bright idea one
morning; rather, their enactment was forced upon
Congress by a number of the States as a condition
for their ratification of the original Constitution. To
treat any practice authorized by the First Congress
as presumptively consistent with the Bill of Rights is
therefore somewhat akin to treating any action of a
party to a contract as presumptively consistent with
the terms of the contract. The latter proposition, if
it were accepted, would of course resolve many of the
heretofore perplexing issues in contract law.

Finally, and most importantly, the argument tend-
ered by the Court is misguided because the
Constitution is not a static document whose
meaning of every detail is fixed for all time by the
life experience of the Framers. We have recognized
in a wide variety of constitutional contexts that the
practices that were in place at the time any particular guarantee was enacted into the Constitution do
not necessarily fix forever the meaning of that guarantee. To be truly faithful to the Framers, "our use
of the history of their time must limit itself to broad
purposes, not specific practices." *Abington School*

Dist. v. *Schempp.* Our primary task must be to translate "the majestic generalities of the Bill of Rights, conceived as part of the pattern of liberal government in the eighteenth century, into concrete restraints on officials dealing with the ⊥ problems of the twentieth century. . . ." *West Virginia State Bd. of Education* v. *Barnette*

⌐817

The inherent adaptability of the Constitution and its amendments is particularly important with respect to the Establishment Clause. "[O]ur religious composition makes us a vastly more diverse people than were our forefathers. . . . In the face of such profound changes, practices which may have been objectionable to no one in the time of Jefferson and Madison may today be highly offensive to many persons, the deeply devout and the nonbelievers alike." *Schempp.* President John Adams issued during his Presidency a number of official proclamations calling on all Americans to engage in Christian prayer. *Justice STORY*, in his treatise on the Constitution, contended that the "real object" of the First Amendment "was, not to countenance, much less to advance Mahometanism, Judaism, or infidelity, by prostrating Christianity; but to exclude all rivalry among Christian sects. . . ." Whatever deference Adams' actions and Story's views might once have deserved in this Court, the Establishment Clause must now be read in a very different light. Similarly, the members of the First Congress should be treated, not as sacred figures whose every action must be emulated, but as the authors of a document meant to last for the ages. Indeed, a proper respect for the Framers themselves forbids us to give so static and lifeless a meaning to their work. To my mind, the Court's focus here on a narrow piece of history is, in a fundamental sense, a betrayal of the lessons of history.

⌐818

⊥ B

Of course, the Court does not rely entirely on the practice of the First Congress in order to validate legislative prayer. There is another theme which, although implicit, also pervades the Court's opinion. It is exemplified by the Court's comparison of legislative prayer with formulaic recitation of "God save the United States and this Honorable Court." It is also exemplified by the Court's apparent conclusion that legislative prayer is, at worst, a "mere shadow" on the Establishment Clause rather than a "real threat" to it. Simply put, the Court seems to regard legislative prayer as at most a *de minimis* violation, somehow unworthy of our attention. I frankly do not know what should be the proper disposition of features of our public life such as "God save the United States and this Honorable Court," "In God We Trust," "One Nation Under God," and the like. I might well adhere to the view expressed in *Schempp* that such mottos are consistent with the Establishment Clause, not because their import is *de minimis,*

but because they have lost any true religious significance. Legislative invocations, however, are very different.

First of all, as *Justice STEVENS'* dissent so effectively highlights, legislative prayer, unlike mottos with fixed wordings, can easily turn narrowly and obviously sectarian. I agree with the Court that the federal judiciary should not sit as a board of censors on individual prayers, but to my mind the better way of avoiding that task is by striking down all official legislative invocations.

⊥ More fundamentally, however, *any* practice of legislative prayer, even if it might look "non-sectarian" to nine Justices of the Supreme Court, will inevitably and continuously involve the state in one or another religious debate. Prayer is serious business—serious theological business—and it is not a mere "acknowledgment of beliefs widely held among the people of this country" for the State to immerse itself in that business. Some religious individuals or groups find it theologically problematic to engage in joint religious exercises predominantly influenced by faiths not their own. Some might object even to the attempt to fashion a "non-sectarian" prayer. Some would find it impossible to participate in any "prayer opportunity," marked by ⊥ Trinitarian references. Some would find a prayer *not* invoking the name of Christ to represent a flawed view of the relationship between human beings and God. Some might find any petitionary prayer to be improper. Some might find any prayer that lacked a petitionary element to be deficient. Some might be troubled by what they consider shallow public prayer, or non-spontaneous prayer, or prayer without adequate spiritual preparation or concentration. Some might, of course, have *theological* objections to any prayer sponsored by an organ of government. Some ⊥ might object on theological grounds to the level of political neutrality generally expected of government-sponsored invocational prayer. And some might object on theological grounds to the Court's requirement, that prayer, even though religious, not be proselytizing. If these problems arose in the context of a religious objection to some otherwise decidedly secular activity, then whatever remedy there is would have to be found in the Free Exercise Clause. But, in this case, we are faced with potential religious objections to an activity at the very center of religious life, and it is simply beyond the competence of government, and inconsistent with our conceptions of liberty, for the state to take upon itself the role of ecclesiastical arbiter.

⌐819

⌐820

⌐821

IV

The argument is made occasionally that a strict separation of religion and state robs the nation of its spiritual identity. I believe quite the contrary. It may be true that individuals cannot be "neutral" on the question of religion. But the judgment of the Establishment Clause is that neutrality by the organs of *government* on questions of religion is both possible and imperative. Alexis de Tocqueville wrote the following concerning his travels through this land in the early 1830s: "The religious atmosphere of the country was the first thing that struck me on arrival in the United States. . . .

"In France I had seen the spirits of religion and of freedom almost always marching in opposite directions. In America I found them intimately linked together in joint reign over the same land.

⌐1822   ⊥ "My longing to understand the reason for this phenomenon increased daily.

"To find this out, I questioned the faithful of all communions; I particularly sought the society of clergymen, who are the depositaries of the various creeds and have a personal interest in their survival. . . . I expressed my astonishment and revealed my doubts to each of them; I found that they all agreed with each other except about details; all thought that the main reason for the quiet sway of religion over the country was the complete separation of church and state. I have no hesitation in stating that throughout my stay in America I met nobody, lay or cleric, who did not agree about that." *Democracy in America,* 295. More recent history has only confirmed de Tocqueville's observations. If the Court had struck down legislative prayer today, it would likely have stimulated a furious reaction. But it would also, I am convinced, have invigorated both the "spirit of religion" and the "spirit of freedom."

I respectfully dissent.

Justice STEVENS, dissenting.

In a democratically elected legislature, the religious beliefs of the chaplain tend to reflect the faith of the
⌐1823   majority of the ⊥ lawmakers' constituents. Prayers may be said by a Catholic priest in the Massachusetts Legislature and by a Presbyterian minister in the Nebraska Legislature, but I would not expect to find a Jehovah's Witness or a disciple of Mary Baker Eddy or the Reverend Moon serving as the official chaplain in any state legislature. Regardless of the motivation of the majority that exercises the power to appoint the chaplain, it seems plain to me that the designation of a member of one religious faith to serve as the sole official chaplain of a state legislature for a period of 16 years constitutes the preference of one faith over another in violation of the Establishment Clause of the First Amendment.

The Court declines to "embark on a sensitive evaluation or to parse the content of a particular prayer." Perhaps it does so because it would be unable to explain away the clearly sectarian content of some of the prayers given by Nebraska's chaplain.
⌐1824   Or perhaps the Court is unwilling to ⊥ acknowledge that the tenure of the chaplain must inevitably be conditioned on the acceptability of that content to the silent majority.

I would affirm the judgment of the Court of Appeals.

GOVERNMENT-SPONSORED NATIVITY SCENES

A recurring question in church-state relations has been whether government may finance or sponsor religious symbols. The Christmas season has spawned the bulk of these controversies because communities across the country routinely supported nativity scenes.[1] Over the years a multitude of cases has been tried over whether such sponsorship is a violation of the Establishment Clause, i.e., is it a way of government's promoting a particular religion at the expense of others? Courts have answered both "yes" and "no." Until 1983 the Supreme Court had consistently avoided the dispute by simply denying appeals from decisions of the state and lower federal courts. But in that year the Court finally granted certiorari to such a case coming from Pawtucket, Rhode Island and handed down its decision in LYNCH v. DONNELLY (p. 359) 5 March 1984.

The case involved an elaborate 40,000 square feet exhibit erected each Christmas for forty years by the city in cooperation with the downtown retail merchants' association in a park that was owned by a nonprofit organization. In addition to a live Santa Claus, a Santa Claus house, a wishing well, a banner reading "Seasons Greetings," and assorted reindeer, elves, and other figures, the display included a crèche complete with Mary, Joseph, the child Jesus, and other figures which ordinarily constitute the nativity scene. Various Pawtucket residents and members of the Rhode Island affiliate of the American Civil Liberties Union challenged inclusion of the crèche in the display and a United States district court held that the city's action violated the Establishment Clause in that the city had "tried to endorse and promulgate religious beliefs" thus bestowing "more than a remote and incidental benefit on Christianity." The decision was affirmed by a divided Court of Appeals for the First Circuit, but by a five-to-four decision the Supreme Court reversed the lower courts.

In the majority opinion Chief Justice Burger acknowledged the desirability of preventing undue intrusion by either church or state into the "precincts of the other," called attention to Thomas Jefferson's wall of separation, and tested the action of the city of Pawtucket against the three-part test prescribed in LEMON v. KURTZMAN (p. 480). However, he restated his often-expressed belief that total separation is not possible and maintained that the Court had consistently "declined to take a rigid, absolutist view of the Establishment Clause." He granted that the wall of separation was a "useful figure of speech" but insisted that the "metaphor itself is not a wholly accurate description of the practical aspects of the relationship that in fact exists between church and state."

---

[1] There have been controversies over government sponsorship and/or erection of other religious symbols, e.g., crosses, the lowering of the American flag to half-staff on Good Friday, and city seals which display religious symbols. These issues are discussed in Leo Pfeffer, *Religion, State, and the Burger Court* (Buffalo, NY: Prometheus Books, 1984), pp. 127-36 and Joseph Conn, "With This, We Conquer," *Church and State* 38 (March 1985): 9-10.

Emphasizing that the Constitution mandates government accommodation of religions with hostility toward none, he cited the many instances in the country's history which evidenced official governmental recognition of the role of religion in American life. He agreed that the Court had in recent years often used the three part "*Lemon* test*"* in ascertaining the line of separation, but the members of the Court had, he said, "repeatedly emphasized our unwillingness to be confined to any single test or criterion in this sensitive area." He then proceeded to find a secular purpose in Pawtucket's inclusion of the "passive" crèche as part of its traditional holiday display, no primary effect of advancing religion in violation of the Establishment Clause, since the nativity scene simply contributed to the festive character of the holiday season, and no entanglement of religion and the state or undue divisiveness resulting from the ownership and use of the crèche by the city.

Justice O'Connor wrote a concurring opinion to suggest, as she put it, "a clarification of our Establishment Clause doctrine." The "*Lemon* test*"*, she said, quoting from MUELLER v. ALLEN (p. 552), "provides 'no more than [a] helpful guidepost' in dealing with Establishment Clause challenges." She then read that test as "focusing on the evils of government endorsement or disapproval of religion" and held that inclusion of the crèche in the larger display had the secular purpose of celebration of a public holiday by use of its "traditional symbols." Pawtucket did not intend, by inclusion of the nativity scene, to "endorse the Christian beliefs represented by the crèche."

Justice Brennan, joined in dissent by Justices Marshall, Blackmun, and Stevens, sought to narrow the scope of the decision. Although he saw the Pawtucket action as an "impermissible endorsement of a particular faith," he emphasized that the majority opinion had not spoken to the question of public displays on public property of distinctively religious symbols standing alone, removed from the context of the particular holiday setting with the inclusion of secular figures. Brennan saw some cause for encouragement in the fact that the Court had at least returned to acknowledgement of the "*Lemon* test" after ignoring it in MARSH v. CHAMBERS (p. 350), but he observed that the Court's "less than vigorous application of the '*Lemon* test' suggests that its commitment to those standards may only be superficial." He agreed that no single formula could resolve all Establishment Clause problems, but he obviously resented the majority's insistence that the test set forth in *Lemon* was simply "one path that may be followed or not at the Court's option."

Justice Blackmun also wrote a dissent, joined by Justice Stevens. He, too, would have used the "*Lemon* test" to invalidate the Pawtucket display. In addition, he complained bitterly about the trivialization of religion inherent in the arrangement: "The crèche has been relegated to the role of a neutral harbinger of the holiday season, useful for commercial purposes, but devoid of any inherent meaning and incapable of enhancing the religious tenor of a display of which it is an integral part. The city has its victory—but it is a Pyrrhic one indeed. . . . Surely, this is a misuse of a sacred symbol."

The Supreme Court had another opportunity to speak to the question of nativity scenes during its 1984-85 term

in *Board of Trustees of the Village of Scarsdale* v. *McCreary*. In Scarsdale, New York a crèche committee had for twenty-four years placed a nativity scene in a public park. In 1981 the city refused permission because some had argued that the Christmas display favored Christianity over other religions. The crèche committee initiated legal proceedings. A federal district court ruled that the display did violate the Establishment Clause and upheld the city's denial. A court of appeals reversed. Citing the recently-decided *Lynch*, the court ruled that the city could not deny the committee the opportunity to display the nativity scene on public land. Many were pleased that the Supreme Court agreed to hear the case because they thought that it would clarify the *Lynch* opinion. In *McCreary* the nativity scene was not part of a larger Christmas display with secular holiday symbols such as Santa Claus as in *Lynch*; it stood alone. Many believed that *McCreary* might be decided differently from *Lynch*. That both views were argued on the Court is shown by the fact that the decision was handed down as a four-to-four deadlock, Justice Powell not having participated in the case. A tie vote allows the ruling of the lower court to stand, so the village was required to allow the nativity scene to be erected. But such an opinion also is not broadly applicable and does not establish any legal precedent, so the issue of the standing-alone nativity scene was left unanswered.

LYNCH v. DONNELLY

465 U.S. 668
ON WRIT OF CERTIORARI TO THE UNITED
STATES COURT
OF APPEALS FOR THE FIRST CIRCUIT
Argued October 4, 1983 — Decided March 5, 1984

The *CHIEF JUSTICE* delivered the opinion of the Court.   ⌐670

We granted certiorari to decide whether the Establishment Clause of the First Amendment prohibits a municipality ⊥ from including a crèche, or Nativity scene, in its annual Christmas display.   ⌐671

I

Each year, in cooperation with the downtown retail merchants' association, the City of Pawtucket, Rhode Island, erects a Christmas display as part of its observance of the Christmas holiday season. The display is situated in a park owned by a nonprofit organization and located in the heart of the shopping district. The display is essentially like those to be found in hundreds of towns or cities across the Nation—often on public grounds—during the Christmas season. The Pawtucket display comprises many of the figures and decorations traditionally associated with Christmas, including, among other things, a Santa Claus house, reindeer pulling Santa's sleigh, candy-striped poles, a Christmas tree, carolers, cutout figures representing such characters as a clown, an elephant, and a teddy bear, hundreds of colored lights, a large banner that reads "SEASONS GREETINGS," and the crèche at issue here.

All components of this display are owned by the City.

The crèche, which has been included in the display for 40 or more years, consists of the traditional figures, including the Infant Jesus, Mary and Joseph, angels, shepherds, kings, and animals, all ranging in heights from 5" to 5'. In 1973, when the present crèche was acquired, it cost the City $1365; it now is valued at $200. The erection and dismantling of the crèche cost the City about $20 per year; nominal expenses are incurred in lighting the crèche. No money has been expended on its maintenance for the past 10 years.

Respondents, Pawtucket residents and individual members of the Rhode Island affiliate of the American Civil Liberties Union, and the affiliate itself, brought this action in the United States District Court for Rhode Island, challenging the City's inclusion of the crèche in the annual display. The District Court held that the City's inclusion of the crèche in the annual display violates the Establishment Clause, which is binding on the states through the ⊥Fourteenth Amendment. The District Court found | 672 that, by including the crèche in the Christmas display, the City has "tried to endorse and promulgate religious beliefs," and that "erection of the crèche has the real and substantial effect of affiliating the City with the Christian beliefs that the crèche represents." This "appearance of official sponsorship," it believed, "confers more than a remote and incidental benefit on Christianity." Last, although the court acknowledged the absence of administrative entanglement, it found that excessive entanglement has been fostered as a result of the political divisiveness of including the crèche in the celebration. The City was permanently enjoined from including the crèche in the display.

A divided panel of the Court of Appeals for the First Circuit affirmed. We granted certiorari, and we reverse.

II
A

This Court has explained that the purpose of the Establishment and Free Exercise Clauses of the First Amendment is "to prevent, as far as possible, the intrusion of either [the church or the state] into the precincts of the other." *Lemon* v. *Kurtzman.* At the same time, however, the Court has recognized that "total separation is not possible in an absolute sense. Some relationship between government and religious organizations is inevitable." *Ibid.* In every Establishment Clause case, we must reconcile the inescapable tension between the objective or preventing unnecessary intrusion of either the church or the state upon the other, and the reality that, as the Court has so often noted, total separation of the two is not possible.

| 673   ⊥ The Court has sometimes described the Religion Clauses as erecting a "wall" between church and state. The concept of a "wall" of separation is a useful figure of speech probably deriving from views of Thomas Jefferson. The metaphor has served as a reminder that the Establishment Clause forbids an established church or anything approaching it. But the metaphor itself is not a wholly accurate description of the practical aspects of the relationship that in fact exists between church and state.

No significant segment of our society and no institution within it can exist in a vacuum or in total or absolute isolation from all the other parts, much less from government. "it has never been thought either possible or desirable to enforce a regime of total separation. . ." *Committee for Public Education & Religious Liberty v. Nyquist.* Nor does the Constitution require complete separation of church and state; it affirmatively mandates accommodation, not merely tolerance, of all religions, and forbids hostility toward any. Anything less would require the "callous indifference" we have said was never intended by the Establishment Clause. Indeed, we have observed, such hostility would bring us into "war with our national tradition as embodied in the First Amendment's guaranty of the free exercise of religion." *McCollum.*

B

The Court's interpretation of the Establishment Clause has comported with what history reveals was the contemporaneous understanding of its guarantees. A significant example ⊥of the contem- | 674 poraneous understanding of that Clause is found in the events of the first week of the First Session of the First Congress in 1789. In the very week that Congress approved the Establishment Clause as part of the Bill of Rights for submission to the states, it enacted legislation providing for paid chaplains for the House and Senate. In *Marsh* v. *Chambers,* we noted that seventeen Members of that First Congress had been Delegates to the Constitutional Convention where freedom of speech, press and religion and antagonism toward an established church were subjects of frequent discussion. We saw no conflict with the Establishment Clause when Nebraska employed members of the clergy as official Legislative Chaplains to give opening prayers at sessions of the state legislature.

The interpretation of the Establishment Clause by Congress in 1789 takes on special significance in light of the Court's emphasis that the First Congress "was a Congress whose constitutional decisions have always been regarded, as they should be regarded, as of the greatest weight in the interpretation of that fundamental instrument," *Myers* v. *United States.*

It is clear that neither the seventeen draftsmen of the Constitution who were Members of the First Congress, not the Congress of 1789, saw any establishment problem in the employment of congressional Chaplains to offer daily prayers in the Congress, a practice that has continued for nearly two centuries. It would be difficult to identify a more striking example of the accommodation of religious belief intended by the Framers.

C

There is an unbroken history of official acknowledgment by all three branches of government of the role of religion in American life from at least 1789. Seldom in our opinions was this more affirmatively expressed than in *Justice DOUGLAS'* opinion for the Court validating a program allowing release of ⊥public school students from classes to attend off-campus religious exercises. Rejecting a claim that the program violated the Establishment Clause, the Court asserted pointedly: "We are a religious people whose institutions presuppose a Supreme Being." *Zorach* v. *Clauson.*

Our history is replete with official references to the value and invocation of Divine guidance in deliberations and pronouncements of the Founding Fathers and contemporary leaders. Beginning in the early colonial period long before Independence, a day of Thanksgiving was celebrated as a religious holiday to give thanks for the bounties of Nature as gifts from God. President Washington and his successors proclaimed Thanksgiving, with all its religious overtones, a day of national celebration and Congress made it a National Holiday more than a century ago. That holiday has not lost its theme of expressing thanks for Divine aid any more than has Christmas lost its religious significance.

⊥Executive Orders and other official announcements of Presidents and of the Congress have proclaimed both Christmas and Thanksgiving National Holidays in religious terms. And, by Acts of Congress, it has long been the practice that federal employees are released from duties on these National Holidays, while being paid from the same public revenues that provide the compensation of the Chaplains of the Senate and the House and the military services. Thus, it is clear that Government has long recognized—indeed it has subsidized—holidays with religious significance.

Other examples of reference to our religious heritage are found in the statutorily prescribed national motto "In God We Trust," which Congress and the President mandated for our currency, and in the language "One nation under God," as part of the Pledge of Allegiance to the American flag. That pledge is recited by thousands of public school children—and adults—every year.

Art galleries supported by public revenues display religious paintings of the 15th and 16th centuries, predominantly inspired by one religious faith. The National Gallery in ⊥Washington, maintained with Government support, for example, has long exhibited masterpieces with religious messages, notably the Last Supper, and paintings depicting the Birth of Christ, the Crucifixion, and the Resurrection, among many others with explicit Christian themes and messages. The very chamber in which oral arguments on this case were heard is decorated with a notable and permanent—not seasonal—symbol of religion: Moses with Ten Commandments. Congress has long provided chapels in the Capitol for religious worship and meditation.

There are countless other illustrations of the Government's acknowledgment of our religious heritage and governmental sponsorship of graphic manifestations of that heritage. Congress has directed the President to proclaim a National Day of Prayer each year "on which [day] the people of the United States may turn to God in prayer and meditation at churches, in groups, and as individuals." Our Presidents have repeatedly issued such Proclamations. Presidential Proclamations and messages have also been issued to commemorate Jewish Heritage Week, and the Jewish High Holy Days. One cannot look at even this brief resume without finding that our history is pervaded by expressions of religious beliefs such as are found in *Zorach.* Equally pervasive is the evidence of accommodation of all faiths and all forms of religious expression, and hostility toward none. Through this accommoda⊥tion, as *Justice DOUGLAS* observed, governmental action has "follow[ed] the best of our traditions" and "respect[ed] the religious nature of our people."

III

This history may help explain why the Court consistently has declined to take a rigid, absolutist view of the Establishment Clause. We have refused "to construe the Religion Clauses with a literalness that would undermine the ultimate constitutional objective *as illuminated by history.*" *Walz* v. *Tax Commission.* In our modern, complex society, whose traditions and constitutional underpinnings rest on and encourage diversity and pluralism in all areas, an absolutist approach in applying the Establishment Clause is simplistic and has been uniformly rejected by the Court.

Rather than mechanically invalidating all governmental conduct or statutes that confer benefits or give special recognition to religion in general or to one faith—as an absolutist approach would dictate—the Court has scrutinized challenged legislation or official conduct to determine whether, in reality, it establishes a religion or religious faith, or tends to do so. Joseph Story wrote a century and a half ago:

"The real object of the [First] Amendment was . . .to prevent any national ecclesiastical establishment, which should give to an hierarchy the exclusive patronage of the national government." 3 Story, Commentaries on the Constitution of the United States 728 (1833).

In each case, the inquiry calls for line drawing; no fixed, *per se* rule can be framed. The Establishment Clause like the Due Process Clauses is not a precise, detailed provision in a legal code capable of ready application. The purpose of the Establishment Clause "was to state an objective, not to write a statute." *Walz* The line between permissible relationships and those barred by the Clause can no ⊥ more be straight and unwavering than due process can be defined in a single stroke or phrase or test. The Clause erects a "blurred, indistinct, and variable barrier depending on all the circumstances of a particular relationship." *Lemon*

|679

In the line-drawing process we have often found it useful to inquire whether the challenged law or conduct has a secular purpose, whether its principal or primary effect is to advance or inhibit religion, and whether it creates an excessive entanglement of government with religion. But, we have repeatedly emphasized our unwillingness to be confined to any single test or criterion in this sensitive area. In two cases, the Court did not even apply the *Lemon* "test." We did not, for example, consider that analysis relevant in *Marsh*. Nor did we find *Lemon* useful in *Larson* v. *Valente*, where there was substantial evidence of overt discrimination against a particular church.

In this case, the focus of our inquiry must be on the crèche in the context of the Christmas season. In *Stone*, for example, we invalidated a state statute requiring the posting of a copy of the Ten Commandments on public classroom walls. But the Court carefully pointed out that the Commandments were posted purely as a religious admonition, not "integrated into the school curriculum, where the Bible may constitutionally be used in an appropriate study of history, civilization, ethics, comparative religion or the like." Similarly, in *Abington*, although the Court struck down the practices in two States requiring daily Bible readings in public schools, it specifically noted that nothing in the Court's holding was intended to "indicat[e] that such study of the Bible or of religion, when presented objectively as part of a secular program of education, may not be effected consist⊥ently with the First Amendment." Focus exclusively on the religious component of any activity would inevitably lead to its invalidation under the Establishment Clause.

|680

The Court has invalidated legislation or governmental action on the ground that a secular purpose was lacking, but only when it has concluded there was no question that the statute or activity was motivated wholly by religious considerations. Even where the benefits to religion were substantial, as in *Everson, Board of Education* v. *Allen, Walz,* and *Tilton*. We saw a secular purpose and no conflict with the Establishment Clause.

The District Court inferred from the religious nature of the crèche that the City has no secular purpose for the display. In so doing, it rejected the City's claim that its reasons for including the crèche are essentially the same as its reasons for sponsoring the display as a whole. The District Court plainly

erred by focusing almost exclusively on the crèche. When viewed in the proper context of the Christmas Holiday season, it is apparent that, on this record, there is insufficient evidence to establish that the inclusion of the crèche is a purposeful or surreptitious effort to express some kind of subtle governmental advocacy of a particular religious message. In a pluralistic society a variety of motives and purposes are implicated. The City, like the Congresses and Presidents, however, has principally taken note of a significant historical religious event long celebrated in the Western World. The crèche in the display depicts the historical origins of this traditional event long recognized as a National Holiday.

⊥The narrow question is whether there is a secular purpose for Pawtucket's display of the crèche. The display is sponsored by the City to celebrate the Holiday and to depict the origins of that Holiday. These are legitimate secular purposes. The District Court's inference, drawn from the religious nature of the crèche, that the City has no secular purpose was, on this record, clearly erroneous.

|68*

The District Court found that the primary effect of including the crèche is to confer a substantial and impermissible benefit on religion in general and on the Christian faith in particular. Comparisons of the relative benefits to religion of different forms of governmental support are elusive and difficult to make. But to conclude that the primary effect of including the crèche is to advance religion in violation of the Establishment Clause would require that we view it as more beneficial to and more an endorsement of religion, for example, than expenditure of large sums of public money for textbooks supplied throughout the country to students attending church-sponsored schools, expenditure of public funds for transportation of ⊥students to church-sponsored schools, federal grants for college building of church-sponsored institutions of higher education combining secular and religious education, noncategorical grants to church-sponsored colleges and universities, and the tax exemptions for church properties sanctioned in *Walz*. It would also require that we view it as more of an endorsement of religion that the Sunday Closing Laws upheld in *McGowan* v. *Maryland*, the release time program for religious training in *Zorach*, and the legislative prayers upheld in *Marsh*.

|68

We are unable to discern a greater aid to religion deriving from inclusion of the crèche than from these benefits and endorsements previously held not violative of the Establishment Clause. What was said about the legislative prayers in *Marsh*, and implied about the Sunday Closing Laws in *McGowan* is true of the City's inclusion of the crèche: its "reason or effect merely happen to coincide or harmonize with the tenets of some . . . religions."

This case differs significantly from *Larkin* v. *Grendel's Den*, and *McCollum*, where religion was sub⊥stantially aided. In *Grendel's Den*, important

|68*

governmental power—a licensing veto authority—had been vested in churches. In *McCollum,* government had made religious instruction available in public school classrooms; the State had not only used the public school buildings for the teaching of religion, it had "afford[ed] sectarian groups an invaluable aid . . .[by] provid[ing] pupils for their religious classes through use of the State's compulsory public school machinery." No comparable benefit to religion is discernible here.

The dissent asserts some observers may perceive that the City has aligned itself with the Christian faith by including a Christian symbol in its display and that this serves to advance religion. We can assume, *arguendo,* that the display advances religion in a sense; but our precedents plainly contemplate that on occasion some advancement of religion will result from governmental action. The Court has made it abundantly clear, however, that "not every law that confers an 'indirect,' 'remote,' or 'incidental' benefit upon [religion] is, for that reason alone, constitutionally invalid." *Nyquist.* Here, whatever benefit to one faith or religion or to all religions, is indirect, remote and incidental; display of the crèche is no more an advancement or endorsement of religion than the Congressional and Executive recognition of the origins of the Holiday itself as "Christ's Mass," or the exhibition of literally hundreds of religious paintings in governmentally supported museums.

The District Court found that there had been no administrative entanglement between religion and state resulting from the City's ownership and use of the crèche. But it went on to hold that some political divisiveness was engendered by this litigation. Coupled with its finding of an impermissible sectarian purpose and effect, this persuaded the court that there was "excessive entanglement." The Court of ⌐684 Appeals expressly declined to ⊥accept the District Court's finding that inclusion of the crèche has caused political divisiveness along religious lines, and noted that this Court has never held that political divisiveness alone was sufficient to invalidate government conduct.

Entanglement is a question of kind and degree. In this case, however, there is no reason to disturb the District Court's finding on the absence of administrative entanglement. There is no evidence of contact with church authorities concerning the content or design of the exhibit prior to or since Pawtucket's purchase of the crèche. No expenditures for maintenance of the crèche have been necessary; and since the City owns the crèche, now valued at $200, the tangible material it contributes is *de minimis.* In many respects the display requires far less ongoing, day-to-day interaction between church and state than religious paintings in public galleries. There is nothing here, of course, like the "comprehensive, dis-

criminating, and continuing state surveillance" or the "enduring entanglement" present in *Lemon.*

The Court of Appeals correctly observed that this Court has not held that political divisiveness alone can serve to invalidate otherwise permissible conduct. And we decline to so hold today. This case does not involve a direct subsidy to church-sponsored schools or colleges, or other religious institutions, and hence no inquiry into potential political divisiveness is even called for. In any event, apart from this litigation there is no evidence of political friction or divisiveness over the crèche in the 40-year history of Pawtucket's Christmas celebration. The District Court stated that the inclusion of the crèche for the 40 years has been "marked by no apparent dissension" and that the display has had a "calm history." Curiously, it went on to hold that the political divisiveness engendered by this lawsuit was evidence of excessive entanglement. A litigant cannot, by the very act of commencing a lawsuit, however, create the ap⊥pearance of divisiveness and then ex-   ⌐685 ploit it as evidence of entanglement.

We are satisfied that the City has a secular purpose for including the crèche, that the City has not impermissibly advanced religion, and that including the crèche does not create excessive entanglement between religion and government.

IV

Justice BRENNAN describes the crèche as a "re-creation of an event that lies at the heart of Christian faith." The crèche, like a painting, is passive; admittedly it is a reminder of the origins of Christmas. Even the traditional, purely secular displays extant at Christmas, with or without a crèche, would inevitably recall the religious nature of the Holiday. The display engenders a friendly community spirit of good will in keeping with the season. The crèche may well have special meaning to those whose faith includes the celebration of religious masses, but none who sense the origins of the Christmas celebration would fail to be aware of its religious implications. That the display brings people into the central city, and serves commercial interests and benefits merchants and their employees, does not, as the dissent points out, determine the character of the display. That a prayer invoking Divine guidance in Congress is preceded and followed by debate and partisan conflict over taxes, budgets, national defense, and myriad mundane subjects, for example, has never been thought to demean or taint the sacredness of the invocation.

Of course the crèche is identified with one religious faith but no more so than the examples we have set out from prior cases in which we found no conflict with the Establishment ⊥Clause. It would   ⌐686 be ironic, however, if the inclusion of a single symbol of a particular historic religious event, as part of a celebration acknowledged in the Western World for

20 centuries, and in this country by the people, by the Executive Branch, by the Congress, and the courts for two centuries, would so "taint" the City's exhibit as to render it violative of the Establishment Clause. To forbid the use of this one passive symbol—the crèche—at the very time people are taking note of the season with Christmas hymns and carols in public schools and other public places, and while the Congress and Legislatures open sessions with prayers by paid chaplains would be a stilted over-reaction contrary to our history and to our holdings. If the presence of the crèche in this display violates the Establishment Clause, a host of other forms of taking official note of Christmas, and of our religious heritage, are equally offensive to the The Court has acknowledged that the "fears and political problems" that gave rise to the Religion Clauses in the 18th century are of far less concern today. We are unable to perceive the Archbishop of Canterbury, the Vicar of Rome, or other powerful religious leaders behind every public acknowledgement of the religious heritage long officially recognized by the three constitutional branches of government. Any notion that these symbols pose a real danger of establishment of a state church is far-fetched indeed.

V

That this Court has been alert to the constitutionally expressed opposition to the establishment of religion is shown in numerous holdings striking down statutes or programs as violative of the Estab-

⊥687 lishment Clause. ⊥The most recent example of this careful scrutiny is found in the case invalidating a municipal ordinance granting to a church a virtual veto power over the licensing of liquor establishments near the church. *Grendel's Den.* Taken together these cases abundantly demonstrate the Court's concern to protect the genuine objectives of the Establishment Clause. It is far too late in the day to impose a crabbed reading of the Clause on the country.

VI

We hold that, notwithstanding the religious significance of the crèche, the City of Pawtucket has not violated the Establishment Clause of the First Amendment. Accordingly, the judgment of the Court of Appeals is reversed.

It is so ordered.

Justice O'CONNOR, concurring.

I concur in the opinion of the Court. I write separately to suggest a clarification of our Establishment Clause doctrine. The suggested approach leads to the same result in this case as that taken by the Court, and the Court's opinion, as I read it, is consistent with my analysis.

I

The Establishment Clause prohibits government from making adherence to a religion relevant in any way to a person's standing in the political community. Government can run afoul of that prohibition in two principal ways. One is ex⊥cessive entanglement ⊥688 with religious institutions, which may interfere with the independence of the institutions, give the institutions access to government or governmental powers not fully shared by nonadherents of the religion, and foster the creation of political constituencies defined along religious lines. The second and more direct infringement is government endorsement or disapproval of religion. Endorsement sends a message to nonadherents that they are outsiders, not full members of the political community, and an accompanying message to adherents that they are insiders, favored members of the political community. Disapproval sends the opposite message.

Our prior cases have used the three-part test articulated in *Lemon* v. *Kurtzman,* as a guide to detecting these two forms of unconstitutional government action. It has never been entirely clear, however, ⊥ how the three parts of the test relate to the princi- ⊥689 ples enshrined in the Establishment Clause. Focusing on institutional entanglement and on endorsement or disapproval of religion clarifies the *Lemon* test as an analytical device.

II

In this case, as even the District Court found, there is no institutional entanglement. Nevertheless, the appellees contend that the political divisiveness caused by Pawtucket's display of its crèche violates the excessive-entanglement prong of the *Lemon* test. The Court's opinion follows the suggestion in *Mueller* v. *Allen,* and concludes that "no inquiry into potential political divisiveness is even called for" in this case. In my view, political divisiveness along religious lines should not be an independent test of constitutionality.

Although several of our cases have discussed political divisiveness under the entanglement prong of *Lemon,* we have never relied on divisiveness as an independent ground for holding a government practice unconstitutional. Guessing the potential for political divisiveness inherent in a government practice is simply too speculative an enterprise, in part because the existence of the litigation, as this case illustrates, itself may affect the political response to the government practice. Political divisiveness is admittedly an evil addressed by the Establishment Clause. Its existence may be evidence that institutional entanglement is excessive or that a government practice is perceived as an endorsement of religion. But the constitutional inquiry should focus ultimately on the character of the government activity that might cause such divisiveness, not on the divisiveness itself. The entanglement prong of the

Lemon test properly limited to institutional entanglement.

⊥ III

The central issue in this case is whether Pawtucket has endorsed Christianity by its display of the crèche. To answer that question, we must examine both what Pawtucket intended to communicate in displaying the crèche and what message the City's display actually conveyed. The purpose and effect prongs of the *Lemon* test represent these two aspects of the meaning of the City's action.

The meaning of a statement to its audience depends both on the intention of the speaker and on the "objective" meaning of the statement in the community. Some listeners need not rely solely on the words themselves in discerning the speaker's intent: they can judge the intent by, for example, examining the context of the statement or asking questions of the speaker. Other listeners do not have or will not seek access to such evidence of intent. They will rely instead on the words themselves; for them the message actually conveyed may be something not actually intended. If the audience is large, as it always is when government "speaks" by word or deed, some portion of the audience will inevitably receive a message determined by the "objective" content of the statement, and some portion will inevitably receive the intended message. Examination of both the subjective and the objective components of the message communicated by a government action is therefore necessary to determine whether the action carries a forbidden meaning.

The purpose prong of the *Lemon* test asks whether government's actual purpose is to endorse or disapprove of religion. The effect prong asks whether, irrespective of government's actual purpose, the practice under review in fact conveys a message of endorsement or disapproval. An affirmative answer to either question should render the challenged practice invalid.

A

The purpose prong of the *Lemon* test requires that a government activity have a secular purpose. That requirement ⊥ is not satisfied, however, by the mere existence of some secular purpose, however dominated by religious purposes. In *Stone* v. *Graham,* for example, the Court held that posting copies of the Ten Commandments in schools violated the purpose prong of the *Lemon* test, yet the State plainly had some secular objectives, such as instilling most of the values of the Ten Commandments and illustrating their connection to our legal system. The proper inquiry under the purpose prong of *Lemon,* I submit, is whether the government intends to convey a message of endorsement or disapproval of religion.

Applying that formulation to this case, I would find that Pawtucket did not intend to convey any message of endorsement of Christianity or disapproval of nonChristian religions. The evident purpose of including the crèche in the larger display was not promotion of the religious content of the crèche but celebration of the public holiday through its traditional symbols. Celebration of public holidays, which have cultural significance even if they also have religious aspects, is a legitimate secular purpose.

The District Court's finding that the display of the crèche had no secular purpose was based on erroneous reasoning. The District Court believed that it should ascertain the City's purpose in displaying the crèche separate and apart from the general purpose in setting up the display. It also found that, because the tradition-celebrating purpose was suspect in the court's eyes, the City's use of an unarguably religious symbol "raises an inference" of intent to endorse. When viewed in light of correct legal principles, the District Court's finding of unlawful purpose was clearly erroneous.

B

Focusing on the evil of government endorsement or disapproval of religion makes clear that the effect prong of the *Lemon* test is properly interpreted not to require invalidation of a government practice merely because it in fact causes, ⊥ even as a primary effect, advancement or inhibition of religion. The laws upheld in *Walz* v. *Tax commission,* (tax exemption for religious, educational, and charitable organizations), in *McGowan* v. *Maryland,* (mandatory Sunday closing law), and in *Zorach* v. *Clauson,* (released time from school for off-campus religious instruction), had such effects, but they did not violate the Establishment Clause. What is crucial is that a government practice not have the effect of communicating a message of government endorsement or disapproval of religion. It is only practices having the effect, whether intentionally or unintentionally, that make religion relevant, in reality or public perception, to status in the political community.

Pawtucket's display of its crèche, I believe, does not communicate a message that the government intends to endorse the Christian beliefs represented by the crèche. Although the religious and indeed sectarian significance of the crèche as the district court found, is not neutralized by the setting, the overall holiday setting changes what viewers may fairly understand to be the purpose of the display—as a typical museum setting, though not neutralizing the religious content of a religious painting, negates any message of endorsement of the content. The display celebrates a public holiday, and no one contends that declaration of that holiday is understood to be an endorsement of religion. The holiday itself has very strong secular components and traditions. Government celebration of the holiday, which is extremely common, generally is not understood to endorse the religious content of the holiday, just as government celebration of Thanksgiving is not so understood. The crèche is a traditional symbol of the holiday that is very commonly displayed along with purely secular symbols, as it was in Pawtucket.

These features combine to make the government's display of the crèche in this particular physical setting no more an endorsement of the religion than |693 such governmental "acknowl⊥edgments" of religion as legislative prayers of the type approved in *Marsh* v. *Chambers*, government declaration of Thanksgiving as a public holiday, printing of "In God We Trust" on coins, and opening court sessions with "God save the United States and this honorable court." Those government acknowledgments of religion serve, in the only ways reasonably possible in our culture, the legitimate secular purposes of solemnizing public occasions, expressing confidence in the future, and encouraging the recognition of what is worth of appreciation in society. For that reason, and because of their history and ubiquity, those practices are not understood as conveying government approval of particular religious beliefs. The display of the crèche likewise serves a secular purpose— celebration of a public holiday with traditional symbols. It cannot fairly be understood to convey a message of government endorsement of religion. It is significant in this regard that the crèche display apparently caused no political divisiveness prior to the filing of this lawsuit, although Pawtucket had incorporated the crèche in its annual Christmas display for some years. For these reasons, I conclude that Pawtucket's display of the crèche does not have the effect of communicating endorsement of Christianity.

The District Court's subsidiary findings on the effect test are consistent with this conclusion. The court found as facts that the crèche has a religious content, that it would not be seen as an insignificant part of the display, that its religious content is not neutralized by the setting, that the display is celebratory and not instructional, and that the city did not seek to counteract any possible religious message. These findings do not imply that the crèche communicates government approval of Christianity. The District Court also found, however, that the government was understood to place its imprimatur on the religious content of the crèche. But whether a government activity communicates endorsement of religion is not a question of simple historical fact. |694 ⊥Although evidentiary submissions may help answer it, the question is, like the question whether racial or sex-based classifications communicate an invidious message, in large part a legal question to be answered on the basis of judicial interpretation of social facts. The District Court's conclusion concerning the effect of Pawtucket's display of its crèche was in error as a matter of law.

IV

Every government practice must be judged in its unique circumstances to determine whether it constitutes an endorsement or disapproval of religion. In making that determination, courts must keep in mind both the fundamental place held by the Establishment Clause in our constitutional scheme and the myriad, subtle ways in which Establishment Clause values can be eroded. Government practices that purport to celebrate or acknowledge events with religious significance must be subjected to careful judicial scrutiny.

The City of Pawtucket is alleged to have violated the Establishment Clause by endorsing the Christian beliefs represented by the crèche included in its Christmas display. Giving the challenged practice the careful scrutiny it deserves, I cannot say that the particular crèche display at issue in this case was intended to endorse or had the effect of endorsing Christianity. I agree with the Court that the judgment below must be reversed.

Justice BRENNAN, with whom *Justice MARSHALL*, *Justice BLACKMUN* and *Justice STEVENS* join, dissenting.

The principles announced in the compact phrases of the Religion Clauses have, as the Court today reminds us, proven difficult to apply. Faced with that uncertainty, the Court properly looks for guidance to the settled test announced in *Lemon* v. *Kurtzman*, for assessing whether a challenged governmental practice involves an impermissible step toward the establishment of religion. Applying that test to this case, the ⊥Court reaches an essentially narrow result which turns largely upon the particular holiday context in which the City of Pawtucket's nativity scene appeared. The Court's decision implicitly leaves open questions concerning the constitutionality of the public display on public property of a crèche standing alone, or the public display of other distinctively religious symbols such as a cross. Despite the narrow contours of the Court's opinion, our precedents in my view compel the holding that Pawtucket's inclusion of a life-sized display depicting the biblical description of the birth of Christ as part of its annual Christmas celebration is unconstitutional. Nothing in the history of such practices or the setting in which the City's crèche is presented obscures or diminishes the plain fact that Pawtucket's action amounts to an impermissible governmental endorsement of a particular faith.

I

Last Term, I expressed the hope that the Court's decision in *Marsh* v. *Chambers* would prove to be only a single, aberrant departure from our settled method ⊥of analyzing Establishment Clauses cases. That the Court today returns to the settled analysis of our prior cases gratifies that hope. At the same time the Court's less than vigorous application of the *Lemon* test suggests that its commitment to those standards may only be superficial. After reviewing the Court's opinion, I am convinced that this case appears hard not because the principles of decision are obscure, but because the Christmas holiday seems so familiar and agreeable. Although the ⊥Court's reluctance to disturb a community's chosen method of celebrating such an agreeable holiday is understandable, that cannot justify the Court's departure from controlling precedent. In my view, Pawtucket's maintenance and display at public expense of a symbol as distinctively sectarian as a crèche simply cannot be squared with our prior cases. And it is plainly contrary to the purposes and values of the Establishment Clause to pretend, as the Court does, that the otherwise secular setting of Pawtucket's nativity scene dilutes in some fashion the crèche singular religiosity, or that the City's annual display reflects nothing more than an "acknowledgment" of our shared national heritage. Neither the character of the Christmas holiday itself, nor our heritage of religious expression supports this result. Indeed, our remarkable and precious religious diversity as a nation which the Establishment Clause seeks to protect, runs directly counter to today's decision.

A

As we have sought to meet new problems arising under the Establishment Clause, our decisions, with few exceptions, have demanded that a challenged governmental practice satisfy the following criteria: "First, the [practice] must have a secular legislative purpose; second, its principal or primary effect must be one that neither advances nor inhibits religion; finally, [it] must not foster 'an excessive government entanglement with religion.'" *Lemon* v. *Kurtzman.*

⊥This well-defined three-part test expresses the essential concerns animating the Establishment Clause. Thus, the test is designed to ensure that the organs of government remain strictly separate and apart from religious affairs, for "a union of government and religion tends to destroy government and degrade religion." *Engel* v. *Vitale.* And it seeks to guarantee that government maintains a position of neutrality with respect to religion and neither advances nor inhibits the promulgation and practice of religious beliefs. *Everson* v. *Board of Education.* ("Neither [a State nor the Federal Government] can pass laws which aid one religion, aid all religions, or prefer one religion over another"). In this regard, we must be alert in our examination of any challenged practice not only for an official establishment of religion, but also for those other evils at which the Clause was aimed—"sponsorship, financial support, and active involvement of the sovereign in religious

activity." *Committee for Public Education* v. *Nyquist.*

Applying the three-part test to Pawtucket's crèche, I am persuaded that the City's inclusion of the crèche in its Christmas display simply does not reflect a "clearly secular purpose." *Nyquist* Unlike the typical case in which the record reveals some contemporaneous expression of a clear purpose to advance religion, or, conversely, a clear secular purpose, ⊥ here we have no explicit statement of purpose by Pawtucket's municipal government accompanying its decision to purchase, display and maintain the crèche. Governmental purpose may nevertheless be inferred. For instance, in *Stone* v. *Graham,* this Court found, despite the state's avowed purpose of reminding school children of the secular application of the commands of the Decalogue, that the "preeminent purpose for posting the Ten Commandments on schoolroom walls is plainly religious in nature." In the present case, the City claims that its purposes were exclusively secular. Pawtucket sought, according to this view, only to participate in the celebration of a national holiday and to attract people to the downtown area in order to promote pre-Christmas retail sales and to help engender the spirit of goodwill and neighborliness commonly associated with the Christmas season.

Despite these assertions, two compelling aspects of this case indicate that our generally prudent "reluctance to attribute unconstitutional motives" to a governmental body, *Mueller* v. *Allen,* should be overcome. First, as was true in *Larkin* v. *Grendel's Den,* all of Pawtucket's "valid secular objectives can be readily accomplished by other means." Plainly, the City's interest in celebrating the holiday and in promoting both retail sales and goodwill are fully served by the elaborate display of Santa Claus, reindeer, and wishing wells that are already a part of Pawtucket's annual Christ⊥mas display. More importantly, the nativity scene, unlike every other element of the Hodgson Park display, reflects a sectarian exclusivity that the avowed purposes of celebrating the holiday season and promoting retail commerce simply do not encompass. To be found constitutional, Pawtucket's seasonal celebration must at least be non-denominational and not serve to promote religion. The inclusion of a distinctively religious element like the crèche, however, demonstrates that a narrower sectarian purpose lay behind the decision to include a nativity scene. That the crèche retained this religious character for the people and municipal government of Pawtucket is suggested by the Mayor's testimony at trial in which he stated that for him, as well as others in the City, the effort to eliminate the nativity scene from Pawtucket's Christmas celebration "is a step towards establishing another religion, non-religion that it may be." Plainly, the City and its leaders understood that the inclusion of the crèche in its display would serve the

⊥701 wholly religious purpose ⊥ of "keep[ing] 'Christ in Christmas.'" From this record, therefore, it is impossible to say with the kind of confidence that was possible in *McGowan* v. *Maryland,* that a wholly secular goal predominates.

The "primary effect" of including a nativity scene in the City's display is, as the District Court found, to place the government's imprimatur of approval on the particular religious beliefs exemplified by the crèche. Those who believe in the message of the nativity receive the unique and exclusive benefit of public recognition and approval of their views. For many, the City's decision to include the crèche as part of its extensive and costly efforts to celebrate Christmas can only mean that the prestige of the government has been conferred on the beliefs associated with the crèche, thereby providing "a significant symbolic benefit to religion. . ." *Larkin* v. *Grendel's Den.* The effect on minority religious groups, as well as on those who may reject all religion, is to convey the message that their views are not similarly worthy of public recognition nor entitled to public support. It was precisely this sort of religious chauvinism that the Establishment Clause was intended forever to prohibit. In this case, as in *Engel* v. *Vitale,* "[w]hen the power, prestige and fi-
⊥702 nancial support of government is placed behind ⊥ a particular religious belief, the indirect coercive pressure upon religious minorities to conform to the prevailing officially approved religion is plain." Our decision in *Widmar* v. *Vincent* rests upon the same principle. There the Court noted that a state university policy of "equal access" for both secular and religious groups would "not confer any imprimatur of State approval" on the religious groups permitted to use the facilities because "a broad spectrum of groups" would be served and there was no evidence that religious groups would dominate the forum. Here, by contrast, Pawtucket itself owns the crèche and instead of extending similar attention to a "broad spectrum" of religious and secular groups, it has singled out Christianity for special treatment.

Finally, it is evident that Pawtucket's inclusion of a crèche as part of its annual Christmas display does pose a significant threat of fostering "excessive entanglement." As the Court notes, the District Court found no administrative entanglement in this case, primarily because the City had been able to administer the annual display without extensive consultation with religious officials. Of course, there is no reason to disturb that finding, but it is worth noting that after today's decision, administrative entanglements may well develop. Jews and other non-Christian groups, prompted perhaps by the Mayor's remark that he will include a Menorah in future displays, can be expected to press government for inclusion of their symbols, and faced with such requests, government will have to become involved in accommodating the various demands. Cf. *Committee for Public Education* v. *Nyquist,* ("competing efforts [by

religious groups] to gain and maintain the support of government" may "occasio[n] considerable civil strife"). More importantly, although no political divisiveness was apparent in Pawtucket ⊥ prior to the   ⊥703 filing of respondents' lawsuit, that act, as the District Court found, unleashed powerful emotional reactions which divided the City along religious lines. The fact that calm had prevailed prior to this suit does not immediately suggest the absence of any division on the point for, as the District Court observed, the quiescence of those opposed to the crèche may have reflected nothing more than their sense of futility in opposing the majority. Of course, the Court is correct to note that we have nevertheless, repeatedly emphasized that "too close a proximity" between religious and civil authorities, may represent a "warning signal" that the values embodied in the Establishment Clause are at risk. *Committee for Public Education* v. *Nyquist.* Furthermore, the Court should not blind itself to the fact that because com⊥munities differ in religious composition, the   ⊥704 controversy over whether local governments may adopt religious symbols will continue to fester. In many communities, non-Christian groups can be expected to combat practices similar to Pawtucket's; this will be so especially in areas where there are substantial non-Christian minorities.

In sum, considering the District Court's careful findings of fact under the three-part analysis called for by our prior cases, I have no difficulty concluding that Pawtucket's display of the crèche is unconstitutional.

⊥ B   ⊥705

The Court advances two principal arguments to support its conclusion that the Pawtucket crèche satisfies the *Lemon* test. Neither is persuasive.

First. The Court, by focusing on the holiday "context" in which the nativity scene appeared, seeks to explain away the clear religious import of the crèche as both a symbol of Christian beliefs and a symbol of the City's support for those beliefs. Thus, although the Court concedes that the City's inclusion of the nativity scene plainly serves "to depict the origins" of Christmas as a "significant historical religious event," and that the crèche "is identified with one religious faith," we are nevertheless expected to believe that Pawtucket's use of the crèche does not signal the City's support for the sectarian symbolism that the nativity scene evokes. The effect of the crèche, of course, must be gauged not only by its inherent re⊥ligious significance but also by the   ⊥706 overall setting in which it appears. But it blinks reality to claim, as the Court does, that by including such a distinctively religious object as the crèche in its Christmas display, Pawtucket has done no more than make use of a "traditional" symbol of the holiday, and has thereby purged the crèche of its religious content and conferred only an "incidental and indirect" benefit on religion.

The court's struggle to ignore the clear religious effect of the crèche seems to me misguided for several reasons. In the first place, the City has positioned the crèche in a central and highly visible location within the Hodgson Park display. The District Court's findings in this regard are unambiguous:

"Despite the small amount of ground covered by the crèche, viewers would not regard the crèche as an insignificant part of the display. It is an almost life sized tableau marked off by a white picket fence. Furthermore, its location lends the crèche significance. The crèche faces the Roosevelt Avenue bus stops and access stairs where the bulk of the display is placed. Moreover, the crèche is near two of the most enticing parts of the display for children—Santa's house and the talking wishing well. Although the Court recognizes that one cannot see the crèche from all possible vantage points, it is clear from the City's own photos that people standing at the two bus shelters and looking down at the display will see the crèche centrally and prominently positioned." 525 F.Supp., at 1176-1177.

Moreover, the City has done nothing to disclaim government approval of the religious significance of the crèche, to suggest that the crèche represents only one religious symbol among many others that might be included in a seasonal display truly aimed at providing a wide catalogue of ethnic and religious celebrations, or to disassociate itself from the religious content of the crèche. In *Abington School Dist.* v. ⊥707 *Schempp* we noted that reading aloud ⊥ from the Bible would be a permissible schoolroom exercise only if it was "presented objectively as part of a secular program of education" that would remove any message of governmental endorsement of religion. Similarly, when the Court of Appeals for the District of Columbia approved the inclusion of a crèche as part of a national "Pageant of Peace" on federal parkland adjacent to the White House, it did so on the express condition that the government would erect "explanatory plaques" disclaiming any sponsorship of religious beliefs associated with the crèche. *Allen* v. *Morton.* In this case, by contrast, Pawtucket has made no effort whatever to provide a similar cautionary message.

Third, we have consistently acknowledged that an otherwise secular setting along does not suffice to justify a governmental practice that has the effect of aiding religion. In *Hunt* v. *McNair*, for instance, we observed that "aid may normally be thought to have a primary effect of advancing religion . . . when it [supports] a specifically religious activity in an otherwise secular setting." The demonstrably secular context of public education, therefore, did not save the challenged practice of school prayer in *Engel* or in *Schempp.* Similarly, in *Tilton* v. *Richardson*, despite the generally secular thrust of the financing legislation under review, the Court unanimously struck down that aspect of the program which permitted church-related institutions eventually to assume total control over the use of buildings constructed with federal aid.

⊥ Finally, and most importantly, even in the context of Pawtucket's seasonal celebration, the crèche ⊥708 retains a specifically Christian religious meaning. I refuse to accept the notion implicit in today's decision that non-Christians would find that the religious content of the crèche is eliminated by the fact that it appears as part of the City's otherwise secular celebration of the Christmas holiday. The nativity scene is clearly distinct in its purpose and effect from the rest of the Hodgson Park display for the simple reason that it is the only one rooted in a biblical account of Christ's birth. It is the chief symbol of the characteristically Christian belief that a divine Savior was brought into the world and that the purpose of this miraculous birth was to illuminate a path toward salvation and redemption. For Christians, that path is exclusive, precious and holy. But for those who do not share these beliefs, the symbolic re-enactment of the birth of a divine being who has been miraculously incarnated as a man stands as a dramatic reminder of their differences with Christian faith. When government appears to sponsor such reli⊥giously inspired views, we cannot say that ⊥709 the practice is "so separate and so indisputably marked off from the religious function, that [it] may fairly be viewed as reflect[ing] a neutral posture toward religious institutions." *Nyquist.* To be excluded on religious grounds by one's elected government is an insult and an injury that, until today, could not be countenanced by the Establishment Clause.

Second. The Court also attempts to justify the crèche by entertaining a beguilingly simple, yet faulty syllogism. The Court begins by noting that government may recognize Christmas day as a public holiday; the Court then asserts that the crèche is nothing more than a traditional element of Christmas celebrations; and it concludes that the inclusion of a crèche as part of a government's annual Christmas celebration constitutionally permissible. The Court apparently believes that once it finds that the designation of Christmas as a public holiday is constitutionally acceptable, it is then free to conclude that virtually every form of governmental association with the celebration of the holiday is also constitutional. The vice of this dangerously superficial argument is that it overlooks the fact that the Christmas holiday in our national culture contains both secular and sectarian elements. To say that government may recognize the holiday's traditional, secular elements of ⊥ gift-giving, public festivities and community ⊥710 spirit, does not mean that government may indiscriminately embrace the distinctively sectarian aspects of the holiday. Indeed, in its eagerness to approve the crèche, the Court has advanced a rationale so simplistic that it would appear to allow the Mayor of Pawtucket to participate in the celebration of a Christmas mass, since this would be just another unobjectionable way for the City to "celebrate the holiday." As is demonstrated below, the Court's logic is fundamentally flawed both because it obscures the reason why public designation of Christmas day as a holiday is constitutionally acceptable, and blurs the distinction between the secular aspects of Christmas and its distinctively religious character, as exemplified by the crèche.

When government decides to recognize Christmas day as a public holiday, it does no more than accommodate the calendar of public activities to the plain fact that many Americans will expect on that day to spend time visiting with their families, attending religious services, and perhaps enjoying some respite from pre-holiday activities. The Free Exercise Clause, of course, does not necessarily compel the government to provide this accommodation, but neither is the Establishment Clause offended by such a step. Because it is clear that the celebration of Christmas has both secular and sectarian elements, it may well be that by taking note of the holiday, the government is simply seeking to serve the same kinds of wholly secular goals—for instance, promoting goodwill and a common day of rest—that were found to justify Sunday Closing laws in *McGowan*. If public officials go further and participate in the *secular* celebration ⊥ of Christmas—by, for example, [711] decorating public places with such secular images as wreaths, garlands or Santa Claus figures—they move closer to the limits of their constitutional power but nevertheless remain within the boundaries set by the Establishment Clause. But when those officials participate in or appear to endorse the distinctively religious elements of this otherwise secular event, they encroach upon First Amendment freedoms. For it is at that point that the government brings to the forefront the theological content of the holiday, and places the prestige, power and financial support of a civil authority in the service of a particular faith.

The inclusion of a crèche in Pawtucket's otherwise secular celebration of Christmas clearly violates these principles. Unlike such secular figures as Santa Claus, reindeer and carolers, a nativity scene represents far more than a mere "traditional" symbol of Christmas. The essence of the crèche's symbolic purpose and effect is to prompt the observer to experience a sense of simple awe and wonder appropriate to the contemplation of one of the central elements of Christian dogma—that God sent His son into the world to be a Messiah. Contrary to the Court's suggestion, the crèche is far from a mere representation of a "particular historic religious event." It is, instead, but understood as a mystical re-creation of an event that lies at the heart of Christian faith. To [712] suggest, as the Court does, ⊥ that such a symbol is merely "traditional" and therefore no different from Santa's house or reindeer is not only offensive to those for whom the crèche has profound significance, but insulting to those who insist for religious or personal reasons that the story of Christ is in no sense a part of "history" nor an unavoidable element of our national "heritage."

For these reasons, the crèche in this context simply cannot be viewed as playing the same role that an ordinary museum display does. The Court seems to assume that forbidding Pawtucket from displaying a crèche would be tantamount to forbidding a state college from including the Bible or Milton's Paradise Lost in a course on English literature. But in those cases the religiously-inspired materials are being considered solely as literature. The purpose is plainly not to single out the particular religious beliefs that may have inspired the authors, but to see in these writings the outlines of a larger imaginative universe shared with other forms of literary expression. The same may be said of a course devoted to the study of art; when the course turns to Gothic architecture, the emphasis is not on the religious beliefs which the cathedrals exalt, but rather upon the "aesthetic consequences of [such religious] thought."

⊥ In this case, by contrast, the crèche plays no [71?] comparable secular role. Unlike the poetry of Paradise Lost which students in a literature course will seek to appreciate primarily for aesthetic or historical reasons, the angels, shepherds, Magi and infant of Pawtucket's nativity scene can only be viewed as symbols of a particular set of religious beliefs. It would be another matter if the crèche were displayed in a museum setting, in the company of other religiously-inspired artifacts, as an example, among many, of the symbolic representation of religious myths. In that setting, we would have objective guarantees that the crèche could suggest that a particular faith had been singled out for public favor and recognition. The effect of Pawtucket's crèche, however, is not confined by any of these limiting attributes. In the absence of any other religious symbols or of any neutral disclaimer, the inescapable effect of the crèche will be to remind the average observer of the religious roots of the celebration he is witnessing and to call to mind the scriptural message that the nativity symbolizes. The fact that Pawtucket has gone to the trouble of making such an elaborate public celebration and of including a crèche in that otherwise secular setting inevitably serves to reinforce the sense that the City means to express solidarity with the Christian message of the crèche and to dismiss other faiths as unworthy of similar attention and support.

II

Although the Court's relaxed application of the *Lemon* test to Pawtucket's crèche is regrettable, it is at least understandable and properly limited to the particular facts of this case. The Court's opinion, however, also sounds a broader ⊥ and more trou- [71] bling theme. Involving the celebration of Thanksgiving as a public holiday, the legend "In God We Trust" on our coins, and the proclamation "God save the United States and this Honorable Court" at the opening of judicial sessions, the Court asserts, without explanation, that Pawtucket's inclusion of a crèche in its annual Christmas display poses no more of threat to Establishment Clause values than these other official "acknowledgments" of religion.

Intuition tells us that some official "acknowledgment" is inevitable in a religious society if government is not to adopt a stilted indifference to the religious life of the people. It is equally true, however, that if government is to remain scrupulously neutral in matters of religious conscience, as our Constitution requires, then it must avoid those overly broad acknowledgments of religious practices that may imply governmental favoritism toward one set of religious beliefs. This does not mean, of course, that public officials may not take account, when necessary, of the separate existence and significance of the religious institutions and practices in the society they govern. Should government choose to incorporate some arguably religious element into its public ceremonies, that acknowledgment must be impartial; it must not tend to promote one faith or handicap another; and it should not sponsor religion generally over non-religion. Thus, in a series of decisions concerned with such acknowledgments, we have repeatedly held that any active form of public acknowledgment of religion indicating sponsorship or endorsement is forbidden. E.g., *Stone* v. *Graham* (posting of Ten Commandments in schoolroom); *Epperson* v. *Arkansas* (prohibition on teaching principles of Darwinian evolution); *Abington School Dist.* v. *Schempp* (mandatory Bible-reading at beginning ⊥715 of ⊥ school day); *Engel* v. *Vitale* (mandatory reading of state-composed prayer); *Illinois ex rel. McCollum* v. *Board of Education* (use of public-school facilities for religious instruction).

Despite this body of case law, the Court has never comprehensively addressed the extent to which government may acknowledge religion by, for example, incorporating religious references into public ceremonies and proclamations, and I do not presume to offer a comprehensive approach. Nevertheless, it appears from our prior decisions that at least three principles—tracing the narrow channels which government acknowledgments must follow to satisfy the Establishment Clause—may be identified. First, although the government may not be compelled to do so by the Free Exercise Clause, it may, consistently with the Establishment Clause, act to accommodate to some extent the opportunities of individuals to practice their religion. That is the essential meaning, I submit, of this Court's decision in *Zorach* v. *Clauson,* finding that government does not violate the Establishment Clause when it simply chooses to "close its doors or suspend its operations as to those who want to repair to their religious sanctuary for worship or instruction." And for me that principle would justify government's decision to declare December 25th a public holiday.

Second, our cases recognize that while a particular governmental practice may have derived from religious motivations and retain certain religious connotations, it is nonetheless permissible for the government to pursue the practice when it is continued today solely for secular reasons. As this Court noted with reference to Sunday Closing Laws in *McGowan* v. *Maryland,* the mere fact that a governmental practice coincides to some extent with certain religious beliefs does not render it unconstitutional. Thanksgiving Day, in my view, fits easily within this princi⊥ple, for despite its religious ⊥716 antecedents, the current practice of celebrating Thanksgiving is unquestionably secular and patriotic. We all may gather with our families on that day to give thanks both for personal and national good fortune, but we are free, given the secular character of the holiday, to address that gratitude either to a divine beneficence or to such mundane sources as good luck or the country's abundant natural wealth.

Finally, we have noted that government cannot be completely prohibited from recognizing in its public actions the religious beliefs and practices of the American people as an aspect of our national history and culture. While I remain uncertain about these questions, I would suggest that such practices as the designation of "In God We Trust" as our national motto, or the references to God contained in the Pledge of Allegiance can best be understood, in Dean Rostow's apt phrase, as a form a "ceremonial deism," protected from Establishment Clause scrutiny chiefly because they have lost through rote repetition any significant religious content. ⊥ Moreover, ⊥717 these references are uniquely suited to serve such wholly secular purposes as solemnizing public occasions, or inspiring commitment to meet some national challenge in a manner that simply could not be fully served in our culture if government were limited to purely non-religious phrases. The practices by which the government has long acknowledged religion are therefore probably necessary to serve certain secular functions, and that necessity, coupled with their long history, gives those practices an essentially secular meaning.

The crèche fits none of these categories. Inclusion of the crèche is not necessary to accommodate individual religious expression. This is plainly not a case in which individual residents of Pawtucket have claimed the right to place a crèche as part of a wholly private display on public land. Nor is the inclusion of the crèche necessary to serve wholly secular goals; it is clear that the City's secular purposes of celebrating the Christmas holiday and promoting retail commerce can be fully served without the crèche. And the crèche, because of its unique association with Christianity, is clearly more sectarian than those references to God that we accept in ceremonial phrases or in other contexts that assure neutrality. The religious works on display at the National Gallery, Presidential references to God during an Inaugural Address, or the national motto present no risk of establishing religion. To be sure, our understanding of these expressions may begin in contemplation of some religious element, but it does not end there. Their message is dominantly secular. In contrast, the message of the crèche begins and ends with reverence for a particular image of the divine.

By insisting that such a distinctively sectarian message is merely an unobjectionable part of our "religious heritage," the Court takes a long step back⌐718 wards ⊥ to the days when *Justice BREWER* could arrogantly declare for the Court that "this is a Christian nation." *Church of Holy Trinity* v. *United States.* Those days, I had thought, were forever put behind us by the Court's decision in *Engel* v. *Vitale* in which we rejected a similar argument advanced by the State of New York that its Regent's Prayer was simply an acceptable part of our "spiritual heritage."

III

The American historical experience concerning the public celebration of Christmas, if carefully examined, provides no support for the Court's decision. The opening sections of the Court's opinion, while seeking to rely on historical evidence, do no more than recognize the obvious: because of the strong religious currents that run through our history, an inflexible or absolutistic enforcement of the Establishment Clause would be both imprudent and impossible. This observation is at once uncontroversial and unilluminating. Simply enumerating the various ways in which the Federal Government has recognized the vital role religion plays in our society does nothing to help decide the question presented in this case.

Indeed, the Court's approach suggests a fundamental misapprehension of the proper uses of history in constitutional interpretation. Certainly, our decisions reflect the fact that an awareness of historical practice often can provide a useful guide in interpreting the abstract language of the Establishment Clause. But historical acceptance of a particular practice alone is never sufficient to justify a challenged governmental action, since, as the Court has rightly observed, "no one acquires a vested or protected right in violation of the Constitution by long use, even when that span of time covers our entire national existence and indeed predates it." *Walz.*
⌐719 ⊥ Attention to the details of history should not blind us to the cardinal purposes of the Establishment Clause, nor limit our central inquiry in these cases—whether the challenged practices "threaten those consequences which the Framers deeply feared." *Abington School Dist.* v. *Schempp.* In recognition of this fact, the Court has, until today, con-

sistently limited its historical inquiry to the particular practice under review.

In *McGowan,* for instance, the Court carefully canvassed the entire history of Sunday Closing laws from the Colonial period up to modern times. On the basis of this analysis, we concluded that while such laws were rooted in religious motivations, the current purpose was to serve the wholly secular goal of providing a uniform day of rest for all citizens. Our inquiry in *Walz* was similarly confined to the special history of the practice under review. There the Court found a pattern of "undeviating acceptance" over the entire course of the Nation's history of according property-tax exemptions to religious organizations, a pattern which supported our finding that the practice did not violate the Religion Clauses. Finally, where direct inquiry into the Framer's intent reveals that the First Amendment was not understood to prohibit a particular practice, we have found such an understanding compelling. Thus, in *Marsh* v. *Chambers,* after marshalling the historical evidence which indicated that the First Congress had authorized the appointment of paid chaplains for its own proceedings only three days before it reached agreement on the final wording of the Bill of Rights, the Court concluded on the basis of this "unique history" that the modern-day practice of opening legislative sessions with prayer was constitutional.

Although invoking these decisions in support of its result, the Court wholly fails to discuss the history of the public celebration of Christmas or the use of publicly-displayed nativity scene. The Court, instead, simply asserts, without any historical analysis or support whatsoever, that the now familiar ⊥ cele- ⌐720 bration of Christmas springs from an unbroken history of acknowledgement "by the people, by the Executive Branch, by the Congress, and the courts for two centuries. . . ." The Court's complete failure to offer any explanation of its assertion is perhaps understandable, however, because the historical record points in precisely the opposite direction. Two features of this history are worth noting. First, at the time of the adoption of the Constitution and the Bill of Rights, there was no settled pattern of celebrating Christmas, either as a purely religious holiday or as a public event. Second, the historical evidence, such as it is, offers no uniform pattern of widespread acceptance of the holiday and indeed suggests that the development of Christmas as a public holiday is a comparatively recent phenomenon.

The intent of the Framers with respect to the public display of nativity scenes is virtually impossible to discern primarily because the widespread celebration of Christmas did not emerge in its present form until well into the nineteenth century. Carrying a well-defined Puritan hostility to the celebration of Christ's birth with them to the New World, the founders of the Massachusetts Bay Colony pursued a vigilant policy of opposition to any public celebration of the holiday. ⊥ To the Puritans, the celebra- ⌐721 tion of Christmas represented a "Popish" practice lacking any foundation in Scripture. This opposition took legal form in 1659 when the Massachusetts Colony made the observance of Christmas day, "by abstinence from labor, feasting or any other way," an offense punishable by fine. Although the Colony eventually repealed this ban in 1681, the Puritan objection remained firm.

During the eighteenth century, sectarian division over the celebration of the holiday continued. As increasing numbers of members of the Anglican and the Dutch and German Reformed churches arrived, the practice of celebrating Christmas as a purely religious holiday grew. But denominational differences continued to dictate differences in attitude toward the holiday. American Anglicans, who carried with them the Church of England's acceptance of the holiday, Roman Catholics, and various German groups all made the celebration of Christmas a vital part of their religious life. By contrast, many nonconforming Protestant groups, including the Presbyterians, Congregationalists, Baptists and Methodists, continued to regard the holiday with suspicion and antagonism well into the nineteenth century. This pattern of sec⊥tarian division concerning the holiday suggests that for the Framers of the Establishment Clause, who were acutely sensitive to such sectarian controversies, no single view of how government should approach the celebration of Christmas would be possible.

Many of the same religious sects that were devotedly opposed to the celebration of Christmas on purely religious grounds, were also some of the most vocal and dedicated foes of established religions in the period just prior to the Revolutionary War. The Puritans, and later the Presbyterians, Baptists and Methodists, generally associated the celebration of Christmas with the elaborate and, in their view, sacrilegious celebration of the holiday by the Church of England, and also with, for them, the more sinister theology of "Popery." In the eyes of these dissenting religious sects, therefore, the groups most closely associated with estab⊥lished religion—the Churches of England and of Rome—were also most closely linked to the profane practice of publicly celebrating Christmas. For those who authored the Bill of Rights, it seems reasonable to suppose that the public celebration of Christmas would have been regarded as at least a sensitive matter, if not deeply controversial. As we have repeatedly observed, the Religion Clauses were intended to ensure a benign regime of competitive disorder among all denominations, so that each sect was free to vie against the others for the allegiance of its followers without state interference. The historical record, contrary to the Court's uninformed assumption, suggests that at the very least conflicting views toward the celebration of Christmas were an important element of that com-

petition at the time of the adoption of the Constitution.

Furthermore, unlike the religious tax exemptions upheld in *Walz*, the public display of nativity scenes as part of governmental celebrations of Christmas does not come to us supported by an unbroken history of widespread acceptance. It was not until 1836 that a State first granted legal recognition to Christmas as a public holiday. This was followed in the period between 1845 and 1865, by twenty-eight jurisdictions which included Christmas day as a legal holiday. Congress did not follow the States' lead until 1870 when it established December 25th, along with the Fourth of July, New Year's Day, and Thanksgiving, as a legal holiday in the District of Columbia. This pattern of legal recognition tells us only that ⊥ public acceptance of the holiday was gradual and that the practice—in stark contrast to the record presented in either *Walz* or *Marsh*—did not take on the character of a widely recognized holiday until the middle of the nineteenth century.

The historical evidence with respect to public financing and support for governmental displays of nativity scenes is even more difficult to gauge. What is known suggests that German immigrants who settled in Pennsylvania early in the eighteenth century, presumably drawing upon European traditions, were probably the first to introduce nativity scenes to the American celebration of Christmas. It also appears likely that this practice expanded as more Roman Catholic immigrants settled during the nineteenth century. From these modest beginnings, the familiar crèche scene developed and gained widespread acceptance, much less official endorsement, until the twentieth century.

In sum, there is no evidence whatsoever that the Framers would have expressly approved a Federal celebration of the Christmas holiday including public displays of a nativity ⊥ scene; accordingly, the Court's repeated invocation of the decision in *Marsh*, is not only baffling, it is utterly irrelevant. Nor is there any suggestion that publicly financed and supported displays of Christmas crèches are supported by a record of widespread, undeviating acceptance that extends throughout our history. Therefore, our prior decisions which relied upon concrete, specific historical evidence to support a particular practice simply have no bearing on the question presented in this case. Contrary to today's careless decision, those prior cases have all recognized that the "illumination" provided by history must always be focused on the particular practice at issue in a given case. Without that guiding principle and the intellectual discipline it imposes, the Court is at sea, free to select random elements of America's varied history solely to suit the views of five Members of this Court.

IV

Under our constitutional scheme, the role of safeguarding our "religious heritage" and of promoting religious beliefs is reserved as the exclusive prerogative of our nation's churches, religious institutions and spiritual leaders. Because the Framers of the Establishment Clause understood that "religion is too personal, too sacred, too holy to permit its 'unhallowed perversion' by civil [authorities]," *Engel* v. *Vitale,* the clause demands that government play no role in this effort. The Court today brushes aside these concerns by insisting that Pawtucket has done nothing more than include a "traditional" symbol of Christmas in its celebration of this national holiday, thereby muting the religious content of the crèche. But the City's action should be recognized for what it is: a coercive, though perhaps small, step toward establishing the sectarian preferences of the majority at the expense of the minority, accomplished by placing public facilities and funds in support of the religious symbolism and theological tidings that the crèche conveys. As *Justice FRANKFURTER,* writing in *McGowan* v. *Maryland,* observed, the Establishment Clause "withdr[aws] from the sphere of legitimate legislative concern and competence a specific, but comprehensive area of human conduct: man's belief or disbelief in the verity of some transcendental idea and man's expression in action of that belief or disbelief." That the Constitution sets this realm of thought and feeling apart from the pressures and antagonisms of government is one of its supreme achievements. Regrettably, the Court today tarnishes that achievement.

⌐726

I dissent.

Justice BLACKMUN, with whom *Justice STEVENS* joins, dissenting.

As *Justice BRENNAN* points out, the logic of the Court's decision in *Lemon* v. *Kurtzman* compels an affirmance here. If that case and its guidelines mean anything, the presence of Pawtucket's crèche in a municipally sponsored display must be held to be a violation of the First Amendment.

Not only does the Court's resolution of this controversy make light of our precedents, but also, ironically, the majority does an injustice to the crèche and the message it manifests. While certain persons, including the Mayor of Pawtucket, undertook a crusade to "keep Christ in Christmas," the Court today has declared that presence virtually irrelevant. The majority urges that the display, "with or without a crèche," "recall[s] the religious nature of the Holiday," and "engenders a friendly community spirit of good will in keeping with the season." Before the District Court, an expert witness for the city made ⊥ a similar, though perhaps more candid, point, stating that Pawtucket's display invites people "to participate in the Christmas spirit, brotherhood,

⌐727

peace, and let loose with their money." The crèche has been relegated to the role of a neutral harbinger of the holiday season, useful for commercial purposes, but devoid of any inherent meaning and incapable of enhancing the religious tenor of a display of which it is an integral part. The city has its victory—but it is a Pyrrhic one indeed.

The import of the Court's decision is to encourage use of the crèche in a municipally sponsored display, a setting where Christians feel constrained in acknowledging its symbolic meaning and non-Christians feel alienated by its presence. Surely, this is a misuse of a sacred symbol. Because I cannot join the court in denying either the force of our precedents or the sacred message that is at the core of the crèche, I dissent and join *Justice BRENNAN'S* opinion.

GOVERNMENT AID TO RELIGIOUS INSTITUTIONS OR VOCATIONS

In 1986 the Court was called upon to decide whether a state may provide financial aid to an individual who is preparing for a religious vocation in WITTERS v. WASHINGTON DEPARTMENT OF SERVICES FOR THE BLIND (p. 375). Larry Witters, who suffered from a degenerative eye condition, applied for aid from the Washington State Commission for the Blind. The Commission had the mandate, under state law, to provide special education and/or assistance in training for professional life for persons with visual handicaps. Witters thus was eligible to receive state financial assistance. The problem was that he was enrolled in a private Christian college in order to prepare for a career in the ministry. Because of that, the Commission denied Witters aid, pursuant to the provisions in the State Constitution which forbade the use of any public funds for supporting or assisting in religious instruction.

After Witters exhausted all administrative remedies, with no success, he filed suit in state court to obtain the funds to which he felt he was entitled under state law. The court also denied him aid, holding that the State Constitution would not allow it. When he appealed to the State Supreme Court, he got the same answer, with one difference. The Washington Supreme Court decided the case, not on the basis of the Washington Constitution, but on the Establishment Clause of the United States Constitution. Relying on the "primary effect" test, the court said that for Witters to receive state rehabilitation funds and apply them to education for the ministry would have the impermissible primary effect of advancing religion.

The United States Supreme Court, in a unanimous verdict, reversed that judgment. It found that the state program of aid to the handicapped clearly had a secular purpose: it was designed solely to aid a particular category of persons, not defined by religion, to be able to take their place in society as productive citizens. When it came to the second prong of the Establishment Clause test, the Court disagreed with the court below. Using language which has a "child benefit" sound, Justice Marshall for the Court noted that under the Washington program the money is paid directly to the student who then transfers it to the educational institution of his or her choice. Consequently, if any of the state money goes to a religious school, it is because the student chose to spend it there, not because of any state action. This being true, it is clear that there is no financial incentive for the student to undertake religious education: the amount of money made available is the same regardless of the type of school chosen. Furthermore, there was no reason to think that even if Witters were to be allowed to use the state money for ministerial training that a significant amount of the aggregate money Washington spent on educational aid for the handicapped would be used for religious education. Consequently:

> On the facts we have set out, it does not seem appropriate to view any aid ultimately flowing to the Inland Empire School of the Bible as resulting from a *state* action sponsoring or subsidizing religion. Nor does the mere circumstance that petitioner has chosen to use neutrally available state aid to help pay for his religious education confer any message of state endorsement of religion.

The Court chose not to consider the case on entanglement grounds because that test had not been argued in the courts below. It should also be noted, however, that the Court did not judge the case against Washington constitutional provisions, but rather sent the case back to the Washington Supreme Court for consideration on those grounds. But at least the program was not unconstitutional as measured against the United States Constitution.

The Court said that the free choice of the recipient of state money about how to use that money insulated the state from the charge of aid to religion. If that sounds similar to the language used in MUELLER v. ALLEN (p. 552) (the tax credit for assistance in paying parochial school tuition is triggered by the decision of the parent to send a child to private or parochial school, not by any state action), it did to some members of the Court, as well. Justices Powell and O'Connor chided the Court for failing to cite *Mueller* as a precedent for the concept as it was used in *Witters* and alerted jurists that it should be thought of as support for the idea that

> state programs that are wholly neutral in offering educational assistance to a class defined without reference to religion do not violate the second part of the *Lemon* v. *Kurtzman* test, because any aid to religion results from the private choices of individual beneficiaries. (Justice Powell, concurring)

WITTERS v. WASHINGTON DEPARTMENT OF SERVICES FOR THE BLIND

106 S.Ct. 748
ON WRIT OF CERTIORIARI TO THE
SUPREME COURT OF WASHINGTON
Argued November 6, 1985 — Decided January 27, 1986

Justice MARSHALL delivered the opinion of the Court.

The Washington Supreme Court ruled that the First Amendment precludes the State of Washington from extending assistance under a state vocational rehabilitation assistance program to a blind person studying at a Christian college and seeking to become a pastor, missionary, or youth director. Finding no such federal constitutional barrier on the record presented to us, we reverse and remand.

I

Petitioner Larry Witters applied in 1979 to the Washington Commission for the Blind for vocational rehabilitation services pursuant to Wash. Rev. Code § 74.16.181 (1981). That statute authorized the Commission, *inter alia*, to "[p]rovide for special education and/or training in the professions, business or trades" so as to "assist visually handicapped persons to overcome vocational handicaps and to obtain the maximum degree of self-support and self-care." Petitioner, suffering from a progressive eye condition, was eligible for vocational rehabilitation assistance under the terms of the statute. He was at the time attending Inland Empire School of the Bible, a private Christian college in Spokane, Washington, and studying bible, ethics, speech, and church administration in order to equip himself for a career as a pastor, missionary, or youth director.

The Commission denied petitioner aid. It relied on an earlier determination embodied in a Commission policy statement that "[t]he Washington State constitution forbids the use of public funds to assist an individual in the pursuit of a career or degree in theology or related areas," and on its conclusion that petitioner's training was "religious instruction" subject to that ban. That was affirmed by a state hearings examiner, who held that the Commission was precluded from funding petitioner's training "in light of the State Constitution's prohibition against the state directly or indirectly supporting a religion." The hearings examiner cited Wash. Const. Art. I, § 11, providing in part that "no public money or property shall be appropriated for or applied to any religious worship, exercise or instruction, or the support of any religious establishment," and Wash. Const., Art. IX, § 4, providing that "[a]ll schools maintained or supported wholly or in part by the public funds shall be forever free from sectarian control or influence." That ruling in turn, was upheld on internal administrative appeal.

Petitioner then instituted an action in state superior court for review of the administrative decision; the court affirmed on the same state-law grounds cited by the agency. The State Supreme Court affirmed as well. The Supreme Court, however, declined to ground its ruling on the Washington Constitution. Instead, it explicitly reserved judgment on the state constitutional issue and chose to base its ruling on the Establishment Clause of the Federal Constitution. The court stated: "The Supreme Court has developed a 3-part test for determining the constitutionality of state aid under the establishment clause of the First Amendment. 'First, the statute must have a secular legislative purpose; second, its principal or primary effect must be one that neither advances nor inhibits religion . . .; finally, the statute must not foster "an excessive government entanglement with religion." ' *Lemon* v. *Kurtzman.* To withstand attack under the establishment clause, the challenged state action must satisfy each of the three criteria." *Witters* v. *Commission for the Blind.*

The Washington court had no difficulty finding the "secular purpose prong of that test satisfied. Applying the second prong, however, that of "principal or primary effect," the court held that "provision of financial assistance by the State to enable someone to become a pastor, missionary, or church youth director clearly has the primary effect of advancing religion." The court, therefore held that provision of aid to petitioner would contravene the Federal Constitution. In light of that ruling, the court saw no need to reach the "entanglement" prong; it stated that the record was in any case inadequate for such an inquiry.

We granted certiorari, and we now reverse.

II

The Establishment Clause of the First Amendment has consistently presented this Court with difficult questions of interpretation and application. We acknowledge in *Lemon* v. *Kurtzman,* that "we can only dimly perceive the lines of demarcation in this extraordinarily sensitive area of constitutional law." Nonetheless, the Court's opinions in this area have at least clarified "the broad contours of our inquiry," *Committee for Public Education* v. *Nyquist,* and are sufficient to dispose of this case.

We are guided, as was the court below, by the three-part test set out by this Court in *Lemon.* Our analysis relating to the first prong of that test is simple: all parties concede the unmistakably secular purpose of the Washington program. That program was designed to promote the well-being of the visually handicapped through the provision of vocational rehabilitation services, and no more than a minuscule amount of the aid awarded under the program is likely to flow to religious education. No party suggests that the State's "actual purpose" in creating the program was to endorse religion, *Wallace* v. *Jaffree,* or that the secular purpose articulated by the legislature is merely "sham." *Wallace.*

The answer to the question posed by the second prong of the *Lemon* test is more difficult. We conclude, however, that extension of aid to petitioner is not barred on that ground either. It is well-settled that the Establishment Clause is not violated every time money previously in the possession of a State is conveyed to a religious institution. For example, a State may issue a paycheck to one of its employees, who may then donate all or part of that paycheck to a religious institution, all without constitutional barrier; and the State may do so even knowing that the employee so intends to dispose of his salary. It is equally well-settled, on the other hand, that the State may not grant aid to a religious school, whether cash or in-kind, where the effect of the aid is "that of a direct subsidy to the religious school" from the State. *Grand Rapids School District* v. *Ball.* Aid may have that effect even though it takes the form of aid to students or parents. The question presented is whether, on the facts as they appear in the record before us, extension of aid to petitioner and the use of that aid by petitioner to support his religious education is a permissible transfer similar to the hypothetical salary donation described above, or is an impermissible "direct subsidy."

Certain aspects of Washington's program are central to our inquiry. As far as the record shows, vocational assistance provided under the Washington program is paid directly to the student, who transmits it to the educational institution of his or her choice. Any aid provided under Washington's program that ultimately flows to religious institutions does so only as a result of the genuinely independent and private choices of aid recipients. Washington's program is "made available generally without regard to the sectarian-nonsectarian, or public-nonpublic nature of the institution benefited," *Committee for Public Education* v. *Nyquist,* and is in no way skewed towards religion. It is not one of "the ingenious plans for channeling state aid to sectarian schools that periodically reach this Court. It creates no financial incentive for students to undertake sectarian education. It does not tend to provide greater or broader benefits for recipients who apply their aid to religious education, nor are the full benefits of the program limited, in large part or in whole, to students at sectarian institutions. On the contrary, aid recipients have full opportunity to expend vocational rehabilitation aid on wholly secular education, and as a practical matter have rather greater prospects to do so. Aid recipients' choices are made among a huge variety of possible careers, of which only a small handful are sectarian. In this case, the fact that aid goes to individuals means that the decision is to support religious education is made by the individual, not by the State.

Further, and importantly, nothing in the record indicated that, if petitioner succeeds, any significant portion of the aid expended under the Washington program as a whole will end up flowing to religious education. The function of the Washington program is hardly "to provide desired financial support for nonpublic, sectarian institutions." *Nyquist.* The program, providing vocational assistance to the visually handicapped, does not seem well-suited to serve as the vehicle for such a subsidy. No evidence has been presented indicating that any other person has ever sought to finance religious education or activity pursuant to the State's program. The combination of these factors, we think, makes the link between the state and the school petitioner wishes to attend a highly attenuated one.

On the facts we have set out, it does not seem appropriate to view any aid ultimately flowing to the Inland Empire School of the Bible as resulting from a *state* action sponsoring or subsidizing religion. Nor does the mere circumstance that petitioner has chosen to use neutrally available state aid to help pay for his religious education confer any message of state endorsement of religion. Thus, while *amici* supporting respondent are correct in pointing out that aid to a religious institution unrestricted in its potential uses, if properly attributable to the State, is "clearly prohibited under the Establishment Clause," *Grand Rapids*, because it may subsidize the religious functions of that institution, that observation is not apposite to this case. On the facts present here, we think the Washington program works no state support of religion prohibited by the Establishment Clause.

III

We therefore reject the claim that, on the record presented, extension of aid under Washington's vocational rehabilitation program to finance petitioner's training at a Christian college to become a pastor, missionary, or youth director would advance religion in a manner inconsistent with the Establishment Clause of the First Amendment. On remand, the state court is of course free to consider the applicability of the "far stricter" dictates of the Washington state constitution, see *Witters* v. *Commission for the Blind*. It may also choose to reopen the factual record in order to consider the arguments made by respondent. We decline petitioner's invitation to leapfrog consideration of those issues by holding that the Free Exercise Clause *requires* Washington to extend vocational rehabilitation aid to petitioner regardless of what the state constitution commands or further factual development reveals, and we express no opinion on the matter.

The judgment of the Washington Supreme Court is reversed, and the case is remanded for further proceeding not inconsistent with this opinion.

It is so ordered.

Justice WHITE, concurring.

I remain convinced that the Court's decision finding constitutional violations where a state provides aid to private schools or their students misconstrue the Establishment Clause and disserve the public interest. Even under the cases in which I was in dissent, however, I agree with the Court that the Washington Supreme Court erred in this case. Hence, I join the Court's opinion and judgment. At the same time, I agree with most of *Justice POWELL's* concurring opinion with respect to the relevance of *Mueller* v. *Allen*, to this case.

Justice POWELL, with whom *The CHIEF JUSTICE* and *Justice REHNQUIST* join, concurring.

The Court's omission of *Mueller* v. *Allen* from its analysis may mislead courts and litigants by suggesting that *Mueller* is somehow inapplicable to cases such as this one. I write separately to emphasize that *Mueller* strongly supports the result we reach today.

As the Court states, the central question in this case is whether Washington's provision of aid to handicapped students has the "principal or primary effect" of advancing religion. *Lemon* v. *Kurtzman*. *Mueller* makes the answer clear: state programs that are wholly neutral in offering educational assistance to a class defined without reference to religion do not violate the second part of the *Lemon* v. *Kurtzman* test, because any aid to religion results from the private choices of individual beneficiaries. Thus, in *Mueller*, we sustained a tax deduction for certain educational expenses, even though the great majority of beneficiaries were parents of children attending sectarian schools. We noted the state's traditionally broad taxing authority, but the decision rested principally on two other factors. First, the deduction was equally available to parents of public school children and parents of children attending private schools. Second, any benefit to religion resulted from the "numerous, private choices of individual parents of school-age children." *Mueller*.

The state program at issue here provides aid to handicapped students when their studies are likely to lead to employment. Aid does not depend on whether the student wishes to attend a public university or a private college, nor does it turn on whether the student seeks training for a religious or a secular career. It follows that under *Mueller* the state's program does not have the "principal or primary effect" of advancing religion.

The Washington Supreme Court reached a different conclusion because if found that the program had the practical effect of aiding religion *in this particular case*. In effect, the court analyzed the cases as if the Washington legislature had passed a private bill that awarded respondent free tuition to pursue religious studies.

Such an analysis conflicts with both common sense and established precedent. Nowhere in *Mueller* did we analyze the effect of Minnesota's tax deduction on the parents who were parties to the case; rather, we looked to the nature and consequences of the program *viewed as a whole*. The same is true of our evaluation of the tuition reimbursement programs at issue in *Nyquist*, and *Sloan* v. *Lemon*. This is the appropriate perspective for this case as well. Viewed in the proper light, the Washington program easily satisfies the second prong of the *Lemon* test.

I agree, for the reasons stated by the Court, that the State's program has a secular purpose, and that no entanglement challenge is properly raised on this record. I therefore join the Court's judgment. On the understanding that nothing we do today lessens the authority of our decision in *Mueller*, I join the Court's opinion as well.

Justice O'CONNOR, concurring in the judgment and concurring in part.

I join Parts I and III of the Court's opinion, and concur in the judgment. I also agree with the Court that both the purpose and effect of Washington's program of aid to handicapped students are secular. As *Justice POWELL's* separate opinion persuasively argues, the Court's opinion in *Mueller* v. *Allen* makes clear that "state programs that are wholly neutral in offering educational assistance to a class defined without reference to religion do not violate the second part of the *Lemon* v. *Kurtzman* test, because any aid to religion results from the private decisions of beneficiaries." The aid to religion at issue here is the result of petitioner's private choice. No reasonable observer is likely to draw from the facts before us an inference that the state itself is endorsing a religious practice or belief.

RELIGION AND PUBLIC EDUCATION

Public education, as it is understood today, developed out of a philosophy of education that existed during the colonial period of American history. The school was thought of as an arm of the church and its curriculum was permeated with religion. Nevertheless, not all the colonies had exactly the same attitudes about education; hence they implemented their educational philosophies in different ways. In the southern colonies, for example, there was virtually no general program of education in the seventeenth century. One reason for this was that in these colonies the established church, the Church of England, was liturgically (ritualistically) oriented and thus the least Bible-centered of all Protestant groups. Consequently, there was no religious compulsion for widespread literacy. Primarily as the result of the eighteenth century revival known as the Great Awakening, an interest in literacy for Bible reading did develop throughout the colonies, and education in the south became what education had been in the New England and middle colonies since the early seventeenth century.

In the middle colonies, schools were started early in the colonial period. The general pattern was for them to be founded, financed, and operated by the local church and clergy. There appears to have been little relationship between these schools and civil government, but the vast majority of the schools were inseparably linked with churches and had religion as a major part of their curricula.

In New England, schools were supported by a general tax collected by the civil government. However, due to a strong Congregationalist establishment in each of the colonies (except Rhode Island), the schools had definite religious dimensions. The religious character of these schools is illustrated by Massachusetts Bay's legislation passed in 1647 to create its township school system. "It being one chief project of that old deluder, Satan, to keep men from the knowledge of the Scriptures," the law stipulated "that learning may not be buried in the graves of our fathers in the church and commonwealth, the Lord assisting our endeavors . . ." schools were to be established in every township in the colony. It was necessary to educate people so that they could read their Bibles and discern God's will in it. [1]

But the schools were not destined to maintain their religious character. As a result of several factors, schools in the national period ceased to be controlled by sponsoring churches and became less obviously sectarian in their teaching. One of these factors was that many of the states had written into their constitutions provisions for religious liberty and nonestablishment comparable to that in the national Constitution, thus eliminating the possibility of state-supported, church-related schools. Furthermore, since there were so many different religious groups with such diverse theologies, it became clear to some that if education were allowed to remain under church sponsorship, it would be eternally fragmented and would participate in the competition, and sometimes hostility, that existed among the denominations. There was also the rationalistic distaste for sectarian religion which was widespread at the end of the eighteenth and the beginning of the nineteenth centuries. Rationalists believed that historically religion had worked to keep people in ignorance. They did not anticipate that religion would reverse itself and provide the enlightened education which was needed in the new nation.

But perhaps the strongest reason for removal of education from control of the churches was that a democracy required an educated citizenry. Particularly for those with rationalist leanings, although others understood this as well, the basis for government by the consent of the governed was rational and humane debate about the affairs of government. In a nation as diverse as this one, it would be necessary for the various opinions of individuals and groups to be expressed in civic dialogue in order that democratic government might function. Such dialogue would require a literate citizenry. This requirement that people participate intelligently in political debate and decisions suggested the need for universal schooling. Thus, if there were really to be separation of church and state, if the educational process were to be insulated from sectarian strife, and if this entire process were so necessary for the civil state to function, then education ought to be undertaken by the civil state. Consequently, the new nation moved toward the creation of a new institution, the common school sponsored by the different states in the union. Furthermore, this school was to be secular, totally avoiding teaching the tenets of sectarian religion.

Public schools, however, did not become totally secular. In the minds of those in the public school movement, the schools were not only to educate people so that they could participate in political debate, but also they were to train Americans to be moral, law-abiding citizens. In the process of instilling morality, religion was reintroduced into the schools. Advocates of the public schools, most of whom were rationalists, believed that the essence of Christianity lay in its moral principles. They argued that if

---

[1] Leo Pfeffer, *Church, State and Freedom*, rev. ed. (Boston: Beacon Press, 1967), pp. 321-24.

the public schools were to make people more fit for citizenship by instilling civic morality, then one could do no better than to teach the moral precepts of Christianity. To allow sectarian religion to intrude into the public schools would be divisive and would take up the students' time with irrelevant and meaningless issues. Thus the public schools were to be secular. But to make education secular was to exclude *only* sectarian particularities, *not* the *essence of religion.* Many were insistent on the necessity of including within the public school curriculum those items in which all Christians believed and upon which they all agreed, i.e., belief in the existence of God and the moral order. In short, in the nineteenth century the developing public schools included a definite religious dimension, what might be called a "lowest common denominator Christianity," or, as it turned out, a "lowest common denominator Protestantism".

In the light of these trends, one is not surprised at Professor Sidney Mead's conclusion that Americans, in the absence of an established church, adopted the public school as their established church. The schools took over the function which had always been assigned to the establishment in other countries, namely, making citizens moral. [2]

Although most Protestant religious leaders agreed that public schools should teach values or morality to promote good citizenship, in the early part of the twentieth century many of them became concerned that not enough was being done to teach the theological content of the Christian faith. There was a growing concern that American children were religiously illiterate, that the public schools were unable to do any more to correct that problem, and that the Sunday schools were not doing enough. Part of the problem was that the public schools commanded so much of the students' time and the Sunday schools so little. Was there a way the public school could be made to cooperate with the church in the religious education of children without reintroducing sectarian strife? An arrangement termed "released time" was devised to fill this need and was inaugurated in Gary, Indiana, in 1914. With the consent of parents, students could be released from the public schools for specified periods of time each week in order to go to churches or synagogues (since by this time Protestants had to take the existence of Catholics and Jews seriously) for instruction in their own faith, returning to the school at the end of the instruction to resume their normal study.

In 1940 the "Gary plan" was inaugurated in Champaign, Illinois. A rather significant alteration in the plan was that the religious classes were held in public school buildings. For a specified time each week, religious teachers would come into the classrooms to teach their particular religion. Students who desired religious instruction were assigned classes which were religiously homo-geneous; nonparticipants were relocated to do some other school task or to bide their time until the religious instruction was ended.

Mrs. Vashti McCollum, whose son was a nonparticipant, challenged the plan in court. She claimed that it was a violation of the Establishment Clause, which by this time had been applied to the states. [3] In the 1948 case of McCOLLUM v. BOARD OF EDUCATION (p. 382), the Supreme Court agreed with that contention. Writing for the majority, Justice Black stated that released time aided religious groups in spreading their faiths through improper use of the tax-established and tax-supported public school system. Moreover, the state's compulsory school attendance laws were used to enable the teachers of religion to gain a captive audience. "This," he wrote, "is not separation of Church and State."

The released time issue was not dead, however. In 1952, in ZORACH v. CLAUSON (p. 393), the Court considered a New York law that provided for the release of children who had parental permission to attend religious classes off the public school campus. The location of instruction was the only essential difference between the plans in New York and Champaign. In a majority opinion written by Justice Douglas, the Court upheld the constitutionality of New York's released time statute. Calling attention to the fact that religion has always played a large role in the life of the American people, Justice Douglas argued that by allowing children to be released for religious instruction the public schools were doing nothing more than adjusting their schedules to the religious interests of their constituents. Far from being a violation of the Establishment Clause, such a plan was following the best of our national traditions. To do any less would show governmental hostility to religion, which would be unconstitutional.

Three separate, vigorous dissenting opinions were written by Justices Black, Frankfurter, and Jackson. The thrust of the dissents was that the location of religion classes was irrelevant. As long as school was in session for nonparticipants in religious instruction, the roll was checked, and truancy was forbidden, state machinery was still operating to provide a captive audience for the teaching of religion. The dissents in the *Zorach* case are among the most barbed that have been written in church-state cases.

The expectation of many Americans that public schools should have some religious quality came to the surface forcefully in the prayer and Bible reading cases. The first of these was ENGEL v. VITALE (p. 397), decided in 1962. The Board of Regents of New York's public schools composed a prayer and urged local school districts to cause it to be said by their pupils at the beginning of each school day. About 10 per cent of the school districts in New York complied with the recommendation, including the one in New Hyde Park, the defendant in this case. The regents had written the prayer as a part of their broad program of moral and spiritual training in the schools, an attempt to combat communism and juvenile delinquency. Knowing that the prayer could not be sec-

[2] Sidney E. Mead, *The Lively Experiment: The Shaping of Christianity in America* (New York: Harper and Row, 1963), pp. 66-68. An extremely helpful history of the relationship between religion and the public schools is Robert Michaelsen, *Piety in the Public School: Trends and Issues in the Relationship Between Religion and the Public School in the United States* (New York: The Macmillan Company, 1970). Cf. also Michaelsen's article "The Public Schools and 'America's Two Religions,'" *Journal of Church and State* 8 (Autumn 1966): 380-400.

[3] Cf. Vashti C. McCollum, *One Woman's Fight* (Boston: Beacon Press, 1951).

tarian, they wrote one which would be denominationally neutral (although some critics called it a perfect example of the "public school religion" referred to earlier in this essay, what was also called by some a "to whom it may concern prayer").

Writing for a majority of eight, Justice Black pointed out that the New York program was clearly unconstitutional, in spite of the fact that the prayer showed no denominational preference and that students who did not want to participate could be excused. Enactment of the law was a violation of the Establishment Clause, whether or not compulsion could be shown:

> . . . we think that the constitutional prohibition against laws respecting an establishment of religion must at least mean that in this country it is not part of the business of government to compose official prayers for any group of the American people to recite as a part of a religious program carried on by government. . . . The New York laws officially prescribing the Regents' prayer are inconsistent both with the purposes of the Establishment Clause and with the Establishment Clause itself. (370 U.S. 421, 425, 433) (pp. 398, 399).

A storm of protest erupted after the *Engel* decision. The Court had taken God out of the classroom; it had secularized the public schools! Some even suggested the schools had been made open prey to communism! In spite of the uproar, in 1963 the Court agreed to hear two other cases in this sensitive area. The first, ABINGTON TOWNSHIP SCHOOL DISTRICT v. SCHEMPP (p. 402), involved a Pennsylvania law providing that at least ten verses of the Bible should be read at the beginning of each school day in each public school in the state. Reading was to be without comment and students could request to be excused. The other case, *Murray* v. *Curlett*, was a challenge to a Maryland law that provided for reading, without comment, of a chapter of the Bible and/or recitation of the Lord's Prayer as a part of the opening exercises in the state's public schools. These two cases were decided together under the *Schempp* title. As noted above (p. 244), in this case the Court set forth the "secular purpose" and "primary effect" tests for interpreting the Establishment Clause. Applied to the cases at bar, the tests invalidated the devotional exercises in public schools. Clearly, the law required religious exercises that did not have a secular purpose but did have the primary effect of advancing religion. Consequently, the exercises were unconstitutional. *Engel* had held that state-written prayers for public school use were unconstitutional. *Schempp* went beyond that to say that required recitation of the Lord's Prayer or any other prayer was a violation of the Establishment Clause, as was the devotional reading of the Bible.

Although virtually unnoticed by the press and the general public at the time, the Court did suggest that academic teaching of religion in a nondevotional or a nonevangelistic way and as a part of the public schools' regular secular program of instruction was not only constitutional but was actually a good idea. In more recent years educators have developed strategies and curricular materials to accomplish that goal.

The issue of what could be taught in a public school classroom was presented in the strange case of EP-PERSON v. ARKANSAS (p. 428). In 1928 Arkansas had passed a law that prohibited teaching evolution in public schools. In 1965 the school administration of Little Rock adopted a biology textbook that contained the theory of evolution. A tenth-grade biology teacher, Mrs. Susan Epperson, was faced with dilemma. The school board had adopted the book, but if she should teach it and the law were enforced, she would be guilty of a criminal offense and subject to dismissal. Consequently, she initiated litigation to invalidate the law. Mrs. Epperson was joined by a parent who had two sons attending the school in which she taught.

When the case reached the Supreme Court, the "monkey law" was found to be unconstitutional because of failure to pass the "secular purpose" test. It was clear to the Court that the law was enacted in order to impose upon the school curriculum a particular theological viewpoint of the nature of human beings.

Strangely, this case did not present the kind of controversy which is normally assumed to be necessary for plaintiffs to have standing to sue. The Arkansas law had never been enforced, and there was no indication that it would be. By the time the case reached the Supreme Court, it was not known whether Mrs. Epperson was still teaching in Little Rock (she was not), or whether the two students were still subject to the biology course in question, or even whether they were still in school. The case was virtually an abstract question. But the Court accepted it, apparently to say finally and definitively what had been held in *McCollum*, *Engel*, and *Schempp*, but deviated from slightly in *Zorach*: the Establishment Clause insists that public schools must be secular both in their curricula and related programs. (The question of the teaching of evolution in public schools was resurrected in the early 1980s, the issue being whether "creation science" should be given "balanced treatment" with evolution. [Cf. pp. 576.] Late in the 1985 term the Court agreed to hear sometime in 1986 or 1987 *Edwards* v. *Aguillard*, a Louisiana creation science case.)

The year *Epperson* was decided, 1968, fairly accurately marks the end of the radical 1960s and the beginning of a public trend toward conservatism. As this tendency toward religious, political, and cultural conservatism gained momentum, public schools came under increasing scrutiny and criticism. The charge was frequently made that public schools had lost both their quality in teaching academic subjects and their ability to impart morality and values. Critics of the schools saw much evidence of these failures in rising crime rates; increasing unemployment, especially among the youth; the general lack of morality in society; and lack of discipline and respect for authority in the schools themselves, not to mention the fact that many students graduating from high school were hardly literate. Some critics, and they were many as the "Christian Right" gained momentum and visibility, went so far as to say that all the troubles of society were attributable to the fact that the Supreme Court's prayer decisions of 1962 and 1963 had taken religion and morality out of the schools; further, they contended that those decisions had initiated a trend toward secularism in America. Consequently, efforts were made to reverse the results and effects of those decisions.

One effort to that end was the law passed by Kentucky in 1978 which mandated that a copy of the Ten Commandments, 16 x 20 inches and of durable material, be posted in every public school classroom in the state. At the bottom of each of these posters was to be printed a disclaimer of any religious intent or meaning. Nevertheless, each poster was to point out that the Ten Commandments were integral to the secular legal code of the western world, including the United States. To further protect the plan from being rejected by the judiciary, the statute provided that the posters should be purchased by funds coming from private, voluntary contributions. The project was directed and pushed through the legislature by the Lexington Heritage Foundation, which apparently intended to be the solicitor and conduit of private contributions that would support the act.

The law was challenged in court by William Stone, an attorney for the Kentucky Civil Liberties Union, and others. They contended that it violated both the Establishment and Free Exercise Clauses. (Graham, the defendant, was the state Superintendent of Public Instruction.) The state trial court found the act to be constitutional in that its purpose was secular and that it neither advanced nor inhibited religion, as did the state Supreme Court.

Without having heard oral arguments, the U.S. Supreme Court decided this case by means of an unsigned opinion. It disagreed with the Kentucky courts. Going no farther than the first part of its Establishment Clause test, the Court held that the statute did not have a secular purpose. The purpose of the statute was plainly religious: to promote the moral concepts espoused by the Judaeo-Christian tradition. The fact that the state said that the statute had a secular purpose, articulated by the disclaimer on the posters, did not necessarily mean this was true. That the Ten Commandments contain admonitions on worshipping and showing proper respect for the deity prevents them from being only secular law. Support of the program by voluntary contributions was irrelevant because the very posting of the commandments under the auspices of a state statute constituted, in itself, a violation of the Establishment Clause. As one might suspect, there was considerable disagreement with this decision in Kentucky and across the nation among religious conservatives.

One of the most visible efforts to put religion back into the public schools was to restore prayer, to circumvent the *Engel* and *Schempp* decisions. From 1963 on there had been attempts to amend the Constitution to permit voluntary, nondenominational prayer in the schools—efforts that had never been successful. Given that lack of success (although Ronald Reagan, throughout his presidency, continued to support the idea), another strategy was proposed, primarily under the leadership of Senator Jesse Helms of North Carolina. Senator Helms repeatedly introduced legislation to remove questions of prayer in the public schools from the jurisdiction of the federal courts. The idea gained some popularity with the advent of the Reagan administration, but lost momentum after

Mr. Reagan's first attorney general argued against it. [4] In the meantime, there were many instances of schools going ahead with prayer and devotional exercises as if *Engel* and *Schempp* had never been handed down. Consequently, there were many cases in the lower courts having to do with prayer in the public schools.

Finally, the Supreme Court accepted WALLACE v. JAFFREE (1986) (p. 434). When it became clear that the Court was not inclined to change its rulings banning compulsory or state-prepared prayers in the public schools, many state legislatures or local school boards introduced a "minute of silence" at the beginning of each school day. Alabama was one of those states. In 1978 a statute provided for a minute of silence "for meditation." In 1981 the words "or voluntary prayer" were added to the law. At that point litigation was initiated, challenging the revised law as a violation of the Establishment Clause. The Court declared the revised law to be unconstitutional. It was clear that when the legislature added the new words it intended to characterize prayer as a favored practice, a violation of the secular purpose prong of the three-part test. Although there was some negative reaction from the religious and political right wing that this was just one more example of the Court's anti-religious bias, the decision did not prohibit prayer. Two concurring opinions and the majority opinion itself asserted that a mere moment of silence during the school day would be appropriate and that it *could* be used for voluntary prayer.

Another way to insert religion into public schools was the subject of BENDER v. WILLIAMSPORT (1986) (p. 270). High school students, who had formed a religious club, "Petros," had been prohibited from meeting during the regularly scheduled activity hour before the beginning of curricular offerings, even though a wide variety of other student clubs routinely met during that time. The students sued, claiming a denial of free speech and the free exercise of religion. The school board defended on the belief that to allow the students to meet on school property would be government sponsorship of religion, a violation of the Establishment Clause.

In 1981 the Supreme Court had dealt with a similar issue at the university level, WIDMAR v. VINCENT (p. 210). There the Court developed a concept which has come to be called a "limited public forum," i.e., the university makes facilities available to a wide variety of student groups to meet and discuss whatever is on their minds. This open forum is limited because it is confined to the students of the institution and their invited guests, not the general public. Relying on this concept from *Widmar*, the District Court held that "Petros" had the right to meet as a part of the limited open forum the high school provided for other student groups. The fact that the school did not create any special conditions for the religious club or even encourage it to meet (it was entirely student-initiated), showed that the school had a secular purpose in creating the forum and that to allow "Petros" to meet as one among many student groups and equal with them all showed that the practice did not have the primary effect of promoting religion or creating excessive entangle-

[4] "Attorney General Speaks Out on Court Stripping," *Congressional Record—Senate* (May 6, 1982): S4726-S4730.

ment between the school and religion. In addition, to deny only "Petros" the right to meet discriminated against speech with religious content, a violation of students' free speech rights.

When *Bender* reached the Supreme Court, it was not decided on the merits, but rather on a standing issue. (Cf. pp. 270). The Court vacated the ruling of the Court of Appeals (which had denied the students the right to meet) and affirmed the decision of the District Court, in effect upholding the right of students to meet at non-curricular hours of the school day for even prayer and worship, so long as the meeting was a part of a regular program of meetings by student organizations on a variety of academic and nonacademic subjects. (In 1984 the Equal Access Act became law (20 U.S.C. §§ 4071-4074). Although the Act is much longer, the following excerpt contains its essence:

> It shall be unlawful for any public secondary school which receives Federal financial assistance and which has a limited open forum to deny equal access or a fair opportunity to, or discriminate against, any students who wish to conduct a meeting within that limited open forum on the basis of the religious, political, philosophical, or other content of the speech at such meetings.

It thus formalized essentially the District Court's decision in *Bender*. Since the Supreme Court did not decide the case on the merits, it did not even allude to the constitutionality of the Equal Access Act.)

McCOLLUM v. BOARD OF EDUCATION

333 U.S. 203
ON APPEAL FROM THE SUPREME COURT OF ILLINOIS
Argued December 8, 1947 — Decided March 8, 1948

⌐204   ⌐ *Mr. Justice BLACK* delivered the opinion of the Court.

This case relates to the power of a state to utilize its tax-supported public school system in aid of reli-
⌐205 gious ⌐instruction insofar as that power may be restricted by the First and Fourteenth Amendments to the Federal Constitution.

The appellant, Vashti McCollum, began this action for mandamus against the Champaign Board of Education in the Circuit Court of Champaign County, Illinois. Her asserted interest was that of a resident and taxpayer of Champaign and of a parent whose child was then enrolled in the Champaign public schools. Illinois has a compulsory education law which, with exceptions, requires parents to send their children, aged seven to sixteen, to its tax-supported public schools where the children are to remain in attendance during the hours when the schools are regularly in session. Parents who violate this law commit a misdemeanor punishable by fine unless the children attend private or parochial schools which meet educational standards fixed by the State. District boards of education are given gen-

eral supervisory powers over the use of the public school buildings within the school districts.

Appellant's petition for mandamus alleged that religious teachers, employed by private religious groups, were permitted to come weekly into the school buildings during the regular hours set apart for secular teaching, and then and there for a period of thirty minutes substitute their religious teaching for the secular education provided under the compulsory education law. The petitioner charged that this joint public-school religious-group program violated the First and Fourteenth Amendments to the United States Constitution. The prayer of her petition was that the Board of Education be ordered to "adopt and enforce rules and regulations prohibiting all instruction in and teaching of religious education in all public schools in Champaign School District Number 71, . . . and in all public school houses and buildings in said district when occupied by public schools."

⌐ The board first moved to dismiss the petition on   ⌐206 the ground that under Illinois law appellant had no standing to maintain the action. This motion was denied. An answer was then filed, which admitted that regular weekly religious instruction was given during school hours to those pupils whose parents consented and that those pupils were released temporarily from their regular secular classes for the limited purpose of attending the religious classes. The answer denied that this coordinated program of religious instruction violated the State or Federal Constitution. Much evidence was heard, findings of fact were made, after which the petition for mandamus was denied on the ground that the school's religious instruction program violated neither the federal nor state constitutional provisions invoked by the appellant. On appeal the State Supreme Court affirmed. Appellant appealed to this Court and we noted probable jurisdiction on June 2, 1947.

The appellees press a motion to dismiss the appeal on several grounds, the first of which is that the judgment of the State Supreme Court does not draw in question the "validity of a statute of any State as required by 28 U.S.C. § 344 (a). This contention rests on the admitted fact that the challenged program of religious instruction was not expressly authorized by statute. But the State Supreme Court has sustained the validity of the program on the ground that the Illinois statutes granted the board authority to establish such a program. This holding is sufficient to show that the validity of an Illinois statute was drawn in question within the meaning of 28 U.S.C. § 344 (a). A second ground for the motion to dismiss is that the appellant lacks standing to maintain the action, a ground which is also without merit. ⌐ A third ground for the motion is that the   ⌐20 appellant failed properly to present in the State Supreme Court her challenge that the state program violated the Federal Constitution. But in view of the express rulings of both state courts on this question the argument cannot be successfully maintained. The motion to dismiss the appeal is denied.

Although there are disputes between the parties as to various inferences that may or may not properly be drawn from the evidence concerning the religious program, the following facts are shown by the record without dispute. In 1940 interested members of the Jewish, Roman Catholic, and a few of the Protestant faiths formed a voluntary association called the Champaign Council on Religious Education. They obtained permission from the Board of Education to offer classes in religious instruction to public school pupils in grades four to nine inclusive. Classes were made up of pupils whose parents signed printed cards requesting that their children be permitted to attend; they were held weekly, thirty minutes for ⊥208 ⊥ the lower grades, forty-five minutes for the higher. The council employed the religious teachers at no expense to the school authorities, but the instructors were subject to the approval and supervision of the superintendent of schools. The classes were taught in ⊥209 three ⊥ separate religious groups by Protestant teachers, Catholic priests, and a Jewish rabbi, although for the past several years there have apparently been no classes instructed in the Jewish religion. Classes were conducted in the regular classrooms of the school building. Students who did not choose to take the religious instruction were not released from public school duties; they were required to leave their classrooms and go to some other place in the school building for pursuit of their secular studies. On the other hand, students who were released from secular study for the religious instructions were required to be present at the religious classes. Reports of their presence or absence were to be made to their secular teachers.

The foregoing facts, without reference to others that appear in the record, show the use of tax-supported property for religious instruction and the close cooperation between the school authorities and the religious council in promoting religious education. The operation of the State's compulsory education system thus assists and is integrated with the program of religious instruction carried on by separate religious sects. Pupils compelled by law to go to ⊥210 school for secular education are released ⊥ in part from their legal duty upon the condition that they attend the religious classes. This is beyond all question a utilization of the tax-established and tax-supported public school system to aid religious groups to spread their faith. And it falls squarely under the ban of the First Amendment (made applicable to the States by the Fourteenth) as we interpreted it in *Everson* v. *Board of Educa-* ⊥211 *tion.* . . . ⊥ The majority in the *Everson* case, and the minority agreed that the First Amendment's language, properly interpreted, had erected a wall of separation between Church and State. They disagreed as to the facts shown by the record and as to

the proper application of the First Amendment's language to those facts.

Recognizing that the Illinois program is barred by the First and Fourteenth Amendments if we adhere to the views expressed both by the majority and the minority in the *Everson* case, counsel for the respondents challenge those views as dicta and urge that we reconsider and repudiate them. They argue that historically the First Amendment was intended to forbid only government preference of one religion over another, not an impartial governmental assistance of all religions. In addition they ask that we distinguish or overrule our holding in the *Everson* case that the Fourteenth Amendment made the "establishment of religion" clause of the First Amendment applicable as a prohibition against the States. After giving full consideration to the arguments presented we are unable to accept either of these contentions.

To hold that a state cannot consistently with the First and Fourteenth Amendments utilize its public school system to aid any or all religious faiths or sects in the dissemination of their doctrines and ideals does not, as counsel urge, manifest a governmental hostility to religion or religious teachings. A manifestation of such hostility would be at war with our national tradition as embodied in the First Amendment's guaranty of the free ⊥ exercise of religion. For the First Amendment rests upon the premise that both religion and government can best work to achieve their lofty aims if each is left free from the other within its respective sphere. Or, as we said in the *Everson* case, the First Amendment has erected a wall between Church and State which must be kept high and impregnable.   ⊥212

Here not only are the State's tax-supported public school buildings used for the dissemination of religious doctrines. The State also affords sectarian groups an invaluable aid in that it helps to provide pupils for their religious classes through use of the State's compulsory public school machinery. This is not separation of Church and State.

The cause is reversed and remanded to the State Supreme Court for proceedings not inconsistent with this opinion.

Reversed and remanded.

Mr. Justice FRANKFURTER delivered the following opinion, in which *Mr. Justice JACKSON, Mr. Justice RUTLEDGE* and *Mr. Justice BURTON* join. *

We dissented in *Everson* v. *Board of Education,* because in our view the Constitutional principle requiring separation of Church and State compelled invalidation of the ordinance sustained by the majority. Illinois has here authorized the commingling

---

* Mr. Justice RUTLEDGE and Mr. Justice BURTON concurred also in the Court's opinion.

of sectarian with secular instruction in the public schools. The Constitution of the United States forbids this.

This case, in the light of the *Everson* decision, demonstrates anew that the mere formulation of a relevant Constitutional principle is the beginning of the solution of a problem, not its answer. This is so |213 because the mean⊥ing of a spacious conception like that of the separation of Church from State is unfolded as appeal is made to the principle from case to case. We are all agreed that the First and the Fourteenth Amendments have a secular reach far more penetrating in the conduct of Government than merely to forbid an "established church." But agreement, in the abstract, that the First Amendment was designed to erect a "wall of separation between church and State," does not preclude a clash of views as to what the wall separates. Involved is not only the Constitutional principle but the implications of judicial review in its enforcement. Accommodation of legislative freedom and Constitutional limitations upon that freedom cannot be achieved by a mere phrase. We cannot illuminatingly apply the "wall-of-separation" metaphor until we have considered the relevant history of religious education in America, the place of the "released time" movement in that history, and its precise manifestation in the case before us.

To understand the particular program now before us as a conscientious attempt to accommodate the allowable functions of Government and the special concerns of the Church within the framework of our Constitution and with due regard to the kind of society for which it was designed, we must put this Champaign program of 1940 in its historic setting. Traditionally, organized education in the Western world was Church education. It could hardly be otherwise when the education of children was primarily study of the Word and the ways of God. Even in the Protestant countries, where there was a less close identification of Church and State, the basis of education was largely the Bible, and its chief purpose inculcation of piety. To the extent that the State intervened, it used its authority to further aims of the Church.

The emigrants who came to these shores brought this view of education with them. Colonial schools |214 certainly ⊥started with a religious orientation. When the common problems of the early settlers of the Massachusetts Bay Colony revealed the need for common schools, the object was the defeat of "one chief project of that old deluder, Satan, to keep men from the knowledge of the Scriptures." The Laws and Liberties of Massachusetts, 1648 edition.

The evolution of colonial education, largely in the service of religion, into the public school system of today is the story of changing conceptions regarding the American democratic society, of the functions of State-maintained education in such a society, and of the role therein of the free exercise of religion by the people. The modern public school derived from a philosophy of freedom reflected in the First Amendment. It is appropriate to recall that the Remonstrance of James Madison, an event basic in the history of religious liberty, was called forth by a proposal which involved support to religious education. As the momentum for popular education increased and in turn evoked strong claims for State support of religious education, contests not unlike that which in Virginia had produced Madison's Remonstrance appeared in various forms in other States. New York and Massachusetts provide famous chapters in the history that established dissociation of religious teaching from State-maintained schools. In New York, the rise of the common schools led, despite fierce sectarian opposition, to the barring of tax funds to church schools, and later to any school in which sectarian doctrine was ⊥taught. In Mas- |215 sachusetts, largely through the efforts of Horace Mann, all sectarian teachings were barred from the common school to save it from being rent by denominational conflict. The upshot of these controversies, often long and fierce, is fairly summarized by saying that long before the Fourteenth Amendment subjected the States to new limitations, the prohibition of furtherance by the State of religious instruction became the guiding principle, in law and feeling, of the American people. In sustaining Stephen Girard's will, this Court referred to the inevitable conflicts engendered by matters "connected with religious polity" and particularly "in a country composed of such a variety of religious sects as our country." *Vidal* v. *Girard's Executors*. That was more than one hundred years ago.

Separation in the field of education, then, was not imposed upon unwilling States by force of superior law. In this respect the Fourteenth Amendment merely reflected a principle then dominant in our national life. To the extent that the Constitution thus made it binding upon the States, the basis of the restriction is the whole experience of our people. Zealous watchfulness against fusion of secular and religious activities by Government itself, through any of its instruments but especially through its educational agencies, was the democratic response of the American community to the particular needs of a young and growing nation, unique in the composition of its ⊥people. A totally different situation else- |216 where, as illustrated for instance by the English provisions for religious education in State-maintained schools, only serves to illustrate that free societies are not cast in one mould. Different institutions evolve from different historic circumstances.

It is pertinent to remind that the establishment of this principle of Separation in the field of education was not due to any decline in the religious beliefs of the people. Horace Mann was a devout Christian, and the deep religious feeling of James Madison is stamped upon the Remonstrance. The secular public school did not imply indifference to the basic role of religion in the life of the people, nor rejection of religious education as a means of fostering it. The claims of religion were not minimized by refusing to make the public schools agencies for their assertion. The nonsectarian or secular public school was the means of reconciling freedom in general with religious freedom. The sharp confinement of the public schools to secular education was a recognition of the need of a democratic society to educate its children, insofar as the State undertook to do so, in an atmosphere free from pressures in a realm in which pressures are most resisted and where conflicts are most easily and most bitterly engendered. Designed to serve as perhaps the most powerful agency for promoting cohesion among a heterogeneous democratic |217 people, the public school must keep scrupu⊥lously free from entanglement in the strife of sects. The preservation of the community from divisive conflicts, of Government from irreconcilable pressures by religious groups, of religion from censorship and coercion however subtly exercised, requires strict confinement of the State to instruction other than religious, leaving to the individual's church and home, indoctrination in the faith of his choice.

This development of the public school as a symbol of our secular unity was not a sudden achievement nor attained without violent conflict. While in small communities of comparatively homogeneous religious beliefs, the need for absolute separation presented no urgencies, elsewhere the growth of the secular school encountered the resistance of feeling strongly engaged against it. But the inevitability of such attempts is the very reason for Constitutional provisions primarily concerned with the protection of minority groups. And such sects are shifting groups, varying from time to time, and place to place, thus representing in their totality the common interest of the nation.

Enough has been said to indicate that we are dealing not with a full-blown principle, nor one having the definiteness of a surveyor's metes and bounds. But by 1875 the separation of public education from Church entanglements, of the State from the teaching of religion, was firmly established in the |218 consciousness of the nation. In ⊥that year President Grant made his famous remarks to the Convention of the Army of the Tennessee: "Encourage free schools, and resolve that not one dollar appropriated for their support shall be appropriated to the support of any sectarian schools. Resolve that neither the State nor nation, nor both combined, shall support institutions of learning other than those sufficient to afford every child growing up in the land the opportunity of a good common-school education, unmixed with sectarian, pagan, or atheistical dogmas. Leave the matter of religion to the family altar, the church, and the private school, supported entirely by private contributions. Keep the church and the state forever separate." "The President's Speech at Des Moines," 22 *Catholic World* 433, 434-35(1876).

So strong was this conviction, that rather than rest on the comprehensive prohibitions of the First and Fourteenth Amendments, President Grant urged that there be written into the United States Constitution particular elaborations, including a specific prohibition against the use of public funds for sectarian education, such as had ⊥been written into many |219 State constitutions. By 1894, in urging the adoption of such a provision in the New York Constitution, Elihu Root was able to summarize a century of the nation's history: "It is not a question of religion, or of creed, or of party; it is a question of declaring and maintaining the great American principle of eternal separation between Church and State." Root, Addresses on Government and Citizenship, 137, 140. The extent to which ⊥this principle was deemed a |220 presupposition of our Constitutional system is strikingly illustrated by the fact that every State admitted into the Union since 1876 was compelled by Congress to write into its constitution a requirement that it maintain a school system "free from sectarian control."

Prohibition of the commingling of sectarian and secular instruction in the public school is of course only half the story. A religious people was naturally concerned about the part of the child's education entrusted "to the family altar, the church, and the private school." The promotion of religious education took many forms. Laboring under financial difficulties and exercising only persuasive authority, various denominations felt handicapped in their task of religious education. Abortive ⊥attempts were |221 therefore frequently made to obtain public funds for religious schools. But the major efforts of religious inculcation were a recognition of the principle of Separation by the establishment of church schools privately supported. Parochial schools were maintained by various denominations. These, however, were often beset by serious handicaps, financial and otherwise, so that the religious aims which they represented found other directions. There were experiments with vacation schools, with Saturday as well as Sunday schools. They all fell short of their purpose. It was urged that by appearing to make religion a one-day-a-week matter, the ⊥Sunday school, |222 which acquired national acceptance, tended to relegate the child's religious education, and thereby his religion, to a minor role not unlike the enforced piano lesson.

Out of these inadequate efforts evolved the weekday church school, held on one or more afternoons a week after the close of the public school. But children continued to be children; they wanted to play when school was out, particularly when other children were free to do so. Church leaders decided that if the week-day church school was to succeed, a way had to be found to give the child his religious education during what the child conceived to be his "business hours."

The initiation of the movement may fairly be attributed to Dr. George U. Wenner. The underlying assumption of his proposal, made at the Interfaith Conference on Federation held in New York City in 1905, was that the public school unduly monopolized the child's time and that the churches were entitled to their share of it. This, the schools should "release." Accordingly, the Federation, citing the example of the Third Republic of France, urged that ⊥223 upon the request of their parents ⊥children be excused from public school on Wednesday afternoon, so that the churches could provide "Sunday school on Wednesday." This was to be carried out on church premises under church authority. Those not desiring to attend church schools would continue their normal classes. Lest these public school classes unfairly compete with the church education, it was requested that the school authorities refrain from scheduling courses or activities of compelling interest or importance.

The proposal aroused considerable opposition and it took another decade for a "released time" scheme to become part of a public school system. Gary, Indiana, inaugurated the movement. At a time when in-
⊥224 dustrial ⊥expansion strained the communal facilities of the city, Superintendent of Schools Wirt suggested a fuller use of the school buildings. Building on theories which had become more or less current, he also urged that education was more than instruction in a classroom. The school was only one of several educational agencies. The library, the playground, the home, the church, all have their function in the child's proper unfolding. Accordingly, Wirt's plan sought to rotate the schedules of the children during the school-day so that some were in class, others were in the library, still others in the playground. And some, he suggested to the leading ministers of the City, might be released to attend religious classes if the churches of the City cooperated and provided them. They did, in 1914, and thus was "released time" begun. The religious teaching was held on church premises and the public schools had no hand in the conduct of these church schools. They did not supervise the choice of instructors or the subject matter taught. Nor did they assume responsibility for the attendance, conduct or achievement of the child in a church school; and he received no credit for it. The period of attendance in the religious schools would otherwise have been a play period for the child, with the result that the arrangement did not cut into public school instruction or truly affect the activities or feelings of the children who did not attend the church schools.

From such a beginning "released time" has attained substantial proportions. In 1914-15, under the Gary program, 619 pupils left the public schools for the church schools during one period a week. According to responsible figures almost 2,000,000 in
⊥225 some 2,200 communities ⊥participated in "released time" programs during 1947. A movement of such

scope indicates the importance of the problem to which the "released time" programs are directed. But to the extent that aspects of these programs are open to Constitutional objection, the more extensively the movement operates, the more ominous the breaches in the wall of separation.

Of course, "released time" as a generalized conception, undefined by differentiating particularities, is not an issue for Constitutional adjudication. Local programs differ from each other in many and crucial respects. Some "released time" classes are under separate denominational auspices, others are conducted jointly by several denominations, often embracing all the religious affiliations of a community. Some classes in religion teach a limited sectarianism; others emphasize democracy, unity and spiritual values not anchored in a particular creed. Insofar as these are manifestations merely of the free exercise of religion, they are quite outside the scope of judicial concern, except insofar as the Court may be called upon to protect the right of religious freedom. It is only when challenge is made to the share that the public schools have in the execution of a particular "released time" program that close judicial scrutiny is demanded of the exact relation between the religious instruction and the public educational system in the specific situation before the Court.

⊥The substantial differences among arrangements ⊥226 lumped together as "released time" emphasize the importance of detailed analysis of the facts to which the Constitutional test of Separation is to be applied. How does "released time" operate in Champaign? Public school teachers distribute to their pupils cards supplied by church groups, so that the parents may indicate whether they desire religious instruction for their children. For those desiring it, religious classes are conducted in the regular classrooms of the public schools by teachers of religion paid by the churches and appointed by them, but, as the State court found, "subject to the approval and supervision of the superintendent." The courses do not profess to give secular instruction in subjects concerning religion. Their candid purpose is sectarian teaching. While a child can go to any of the religious classes offered, a particular sect wishing a teacher for its devotees requires the permission of the school superintendent "who in turn will determine whether or not it is practical for said group to teach in said school
⊥system." If no provision is made for religious in- ⊥227 struction in the particular faith of a child, or if for other reasons the child is not enrolled in any of the offered classes, he is required to attend a regular school class, or a study period during which he is often left to his own devices. Reports of attendance in the religious classes are submitted by the religious instructor to the school authorities, and the child who fails to attend is presumably deemed a truant.

Religious education so conducted on school time and property is patently woven into the working scheme of the school. The Champaign arrangement thus presents powerful elements of inherent pressure by the school system in the interest of religious sects. The fact that this power has not been used to discriminate is beside the point. Separation is a requirement to abstain from fusing functions of Government and of religious sects, not merely to treat them all equally. That a child is offered an alternative may reduce the constraint; it does not eliminate the operation of influence by the school in matters sacred to conscience and outside the school's domain. The law of imitation operates, and nonconformity is not an outstanding characteristic of children. The result is an obvious pressure upon children to attend. Again, while the Champaign school population represents only a fraction of the more than two hundred and fifty sects of the nation, not even all the practicing sects in Champaign are willing or able to provide religious instruction. The children belonging to these non-participating sects will thus have inculcated in them a feeling of separatism when the school should be the training ground for habits of community, or they will have religious ⊥228 instruction in a faith which is not that of ⊥their parents. As a result, the public school system of Champaign actively furthers inculcation in the religious tenets of some faiths, and in the process sharpens the consciousness of religious differences at least among some of the children committed to its care. These are consequences not amenable to statistics. But they are precisely the consequences against which the Constitution was directed when it prohibited the Government common to all from becoming embroiled, however innocently, in the destructive religious conflicts of which the history of even this country records some dark pages.

Mention should not be omitted that the integration of religious instruction within the school system as practiced in Champaign is supported by arguments drawn from educational theories as diverse as those derived from Catholic conceptions and from the writings of John Dewey. Movements like ⊥229 "released time" are seldom ⊥single in origin or aim. Nor can the intrusion of religious instruction into the public school system of Champaign be minimized by saying that it absorbs less than an hour a ⊥230 week; in fact, that affords evidence of ⊥a design constitutionally objectionable. If it were merely a question of enabling a child to obtain religious instruction with a receptive mind, the thirty or forty-five minutes could readily be found on Saturday or Sunday. If that were all, Champaign might have drawn upon the French system, known in its American manifestation as "dismissed time", whereby one school day is shortened to allow all children to go where they please, leaving those who so desire to go to a religious school. The momentum of the whole school atmosphere and school planning is presumably put behind religious instruction, as given in Champaign, precisely in order to secure for the reli-⊥231 gious ⊥instruction such momentum and planning.

To speak of "released time" as being only half or three quarters of an hour is to draw a thread from a fabric.

We do not consider, as indeed we could not, school programs not before us which, though colloquially characterized as "released time," present situations differing in aspects that may well be constitutionally crucial. Different forms which "released time" has taken during more than thirty years of growth include programs which, like that before us, could not withstand the test of the Constitution; others may be found unexceptional. We do not now attempt to weigh in the Constitutional scale every separate detail or various combination of factors which may establish a valid "released time" program. We find that the basic Constitutional principle of absolute Separation was violated when the State of Illinois, speaking through its Supreme Court, sustained the school authorities of Champaign in sponsoring and effectively furthering religious beliefs by its educational arrangement.

Separation means separation, not something less. Jefferson's metaphor in describing the relation between Church and State speaks of a "wall of separation," not of a fine line easily overstepped. The public school is at once the symbol of our democracy and the most pervasive means for promoting our common destiny. In no activity of the State is it more vital to keep out divisive forces than in its schools, to avoid confusing, not to say fusing, what the Constitution sought to keep strictly apart. "The great American principle of eternal separation"— Elihu Root's phrase bears repetition—is one of the vital reliances of our Constitutional system for assuring unities among our people stronger than our diversities. It is the Court's duty to enforce this principle in its full integrity.

⊥We renew our conviction that "we have staked ⊥232 the very existence of our country on the faith that complete separation between the state and religion is best for the state and best for religion." *Everson* v. *Board of Education* If nowhere else, in the relation between Church and State, "good fences make good neighbors."

Mr. Justice JACKSON, concurring.

I join the opinion of *Mr. Justice FRANK-FURTER*, and concur in the result reached by the Court, but with these reservations: I think it is doubtful whether the facts of this case establish jurisdiction in this Court, but in any event that we should place some bounds on the demands for interference with local schools that we are empowered or willing to entertain. I make these reservations a matter of record in view of the number of litigations likely to be started as a result of this decision.

A Federal Court may interfere with local school authorities only when they invade either a personal liberty or a property right protected by the Federal

Constitution. Ordinarily this will come about in either of two ways:

First. When a person is required to submit to some religious rite or instruction or is deprived or threatened with deprivation of his freedom for resisting such unconstitutional requirement. We may then set him free or enjoin his prosecution. Typical of such cases was *West Virginia State Board of Education* v. *Barnette.* There penalties were threatened against both parent and child for refusal of the latter to perform a compulsory ritual which offended his convictions. We intervened to shield them against the penalty. But here, complainant's son may join religious classes if he chooses and if his parents so request, or he may stay out of them. The complaint is that when others join and he does not, it sets him ⌐233 apart as a dissenter, which is humiliating. ⊥Even admitting this to be true, it may be doubted whether the Constitution which, of course, protects the right to dissent, can be construed also to protect one from the embarrassment that always attends nonconformity, whether in religion, politics, behavior or dress. Since no legal compulsion is applied to complainant's son himself and no penalty is imposed or threatened from which we may relieve him, we can hardly base jurisdiction on this ground.

Second. Where a complainant is deprived of property by being taxed for unconstitutional purposes, such as directly or indirectly to support a religious establishment. We can protect a taxpayer against such a levy. This was the *Everson Case,* as I saw it then and see it now. It was complained in that case that the school treasurer drew a check on public funds to reimburse parents for a child's bus fare if he went to a Catholic parochial school or a public school, but not if he went to any other private or denominational school. Reference to the record in that case will show that the School District was not operating busses, so it was not a question of allowing Catholic children to ride publicly owned busses along with others, in the interests of their safety, health or morals. The child had to travel to and from parochial school on commercial busses like other paying passengers and all other school children, and he was exposed to the same dangers. If it could, in fairness, have been said that the expenditure was a measure for the protection of the safety, health or morals of youngsters, it would not merely have been constitutional to grant it; it would have been unconstitutional to refuse it to any child merely because he was a Catholic. But in the *Everson Case* there was a direct, substantial and measurable burden on the complainant as a taxpayer to raise funds that were used to subsidize transportation to parochial schools. ⌐234 Hence, we ⊥had jurisdiction to examine the constitutionality of the levy and to protect against it if a majority had agreed that the subsidy for transportation was unconstitutional.

In this case, however, any cost of this plan to the taxpayers is incalculable and negligible. It can be argued, perhaps, that religious classes add some wear and tear on public buildings and that they should be charged with some expense for heat and light, even though the sessions devoted to religious instruction do not add to the length of the school day. But the cost is neither substantial nor measurable, and no one seriously can say that the complainant's tax bill has been proved to be increased because of this plan. I think it is doubtful whether the taxpayer in this case has shown any substantial property injury.

If, however, jurisdiction is found to exist, it is important that we circumscribe our decision with some care. What is asked is not a defensive use of judicial power to set aside a tax levy or reverse a conviction, or to enjoin threats of prosecution or taxation. The relief demanded in this case is the extraordinary writ of mandamus to tell the local Board of Education what it must do. The prayer for relief is that a writ issue against the Board of Education "ordering it to immediately adopt and enforce rules and regulations prohibiting all instruction in and teaching of religious education in all public schools . . . and in all public school houses and buildings in said district when occupied by public schools." The plaintiff, as she has every right to be, is an avowed atheist. What she has asked of the courts is that they not only end the "released time" plan but also ban every form of teaching which suggests or recognizes that there is a God. She would ban all teaching of the Scriptures. She especially mentions as an example of invasion of her rights "having pupils learn and recite such statements as, 'The Lord is my Shepherd, I shall not want.' " And she objects to teaching that the King James version of the Bible "is ⊥called the Christian's Guide Book, the Holy Writ and the Word of God," and many other similar matters. This Court is directing the Illinois courts generally to sustain plaintiff's complaint without exception of any of these grounds of complaint, without discriminating between them and without laying down any standards to define the limits of the effect of our decision.

To me, the sweep and detail of these complaints is a danger signal which warns of the kind of local controversy we will be required to arbitrate if we do not place appropriate limitation on our decision and exact strict compliance with jurisdictional requirements. Authorities list 256 separate and substantial religious bodies to exist in the continental United States. Each of them, through the suit of some discontented but unpenalized and untaxed representative, has as good a right as this plaintiff to demand that the courts compel the schools to sift out of their teaching everything inconsistent with its doctrines. If we are to eliminate everything that is objectionable to any of these warring sects or inconsistent with any of their doctrines, we will leave public education in shreds. Nothing but educational confusion and a discrediting of the public school system can result from subjecting it to constant law suits.

While we may and should end such formal and explicit instruction as the Champaign plan and can at all times prohibit teaching of creed and catechism and ceremonial and can forbid forthright proselyting in the schools, I think it remains to be demonstrated whether it is possible, even if desirable, to comply with such demands as plaintiff's completely to isolate and cast out of secular education all that some people may reasonably regard as religious instruction. Perhaps subjects such as mathematics, physics or chemistry are, or can be, completely secularized. But it would not seem practical to teach either practice or appreciation of the arts if we are to forbid exposure of youth to any religious influences. Music without sacred music, architecture minus the cathedral, or painting without the scriptural themes would be eccentric and incomplete, even from a secular point of view. Yet the inspirational appeal of religion in these guises is often stronger than in forthright sermon. Even such a "science" as biology raises the issue between evolution and creation as an explanation of our presence on this planet. Certainly a course in English literature that omitted the Bible and other powerful uses of our mother tongue for religious ends would be pretty barren. And I should suppose it is a proper, if not an indispensable, part of preparation for a worldly life to know the roles that religion and religions have played in the tragic story of mankind. The fact is that, for good or for ill, nearly everything in our culture worth transmitting, everything which gives meaning to life, is saturated with religious influences, derived from paganism, Judaism, Christianity—both Catholic and Protestant—and other faiths accepted by a large part of the world's peoples. One can hardly respect a system of education that would leave the student wholly ignorant of the currents of religious thought that move the world society for a part in which he is being prepared.

But how one can teach, with satisfaction or even with justice to all faiths, such subjects as the story of the Reformation, the Inquisition, or even the New England effort to found "a Church without a Bishop and a State without a King," is more than I know. It is too much to expect that mortals will teach subjects about which their contemporaries have passionate controversies with the detachment they may summon to teaching about remote subjects such as Confucius or Mohammed. When instruction turns to proselyting and imparting knowledge becomes evangelism is, except in the crudest cases, a subtle inquiry.

⊥The opinions in this case show that public educational authorities have evolved a considerable variety of practices in dealing with the religious problem. Neighborhoods differ in racial, religious and cultural compositions. It must be expected that they will adopt different customs which will give emphasis to different values and will induce different experiments. And it must be expected that, no mat-

ter what practice prevails, there will be many discontented and possibly belligerent minorities. We must leave some flexibility to meet local conditions, some chance to progress by trial and error. While I agree that the religious classes involved here go beyond permissible limits, I also think the complaint demands more than plaintiff is entitled to have granted. So far as I can see this Court does not tell the State court where it may stop, nor does it set up any standards by which the State court may determine that question for itself.

The task of separating the secular from the religious in education is one of magnitude, intricacy and delicacy. To lay down a sweeping constitutional doctrine as demanded by complainant and apparently approved by the Court, applicable alike to all school boards of the nation, "to immediately adopt and enforce rules and regulations prohibiting all instruction in and teaching of religious education in all public schools," is to decree a uniform, rigid and, if we are consistent, an unchanging standard for countless school boards representing and serving highly localized groups which not only differ from each other but which themselves from time to time change attitudes. It seems to me that to do so is to allow zeal for our own ideas of what is good in public instruction to induce us to accept the role of a super board of education for every school district in the nation.

It is idle to pretend that this task is one for which we can find in the Constitution one word to help us as judges to decide where the secular ends and the sectarian ⊥begins in education. Nor can we find guidance in any other legal source. It is a matter on which we can find no law but our own prepossessions. If with no surer legal guidance we are to take up and decide every variation of this controversy, raised by persons not subject to penalty or tax but who are dissatisfied with the way schools are dealing with the problem, we are likely to have much business of the sort. And, more importantly, we are likely to make the legal "wall of separation between church and state" as winding as the famous serpentine wall designed by Mr. Jefferson for the University he founded.

Mr. Justice REED, dissenting.

The decisions reversing the judgment of the Supreme Court of Illinois interpret the prohibition of the First Amendment against the establishment of religion, made effective as to the states by the Fourteenth Amendment, to forbid pupils of the public schools electing, with the approval of their parents, courses in religious education. The courses are given, under the school laws of Illinois as approved by the Supreme Court of that state, by lay or clerical teachers supplied and directed by an interdenominational, local council of religious education. The classes are held in the respective school buildings of the pupils at study or released time periods so as to

_|239 avoid conflict with recitations. The teachers and supplies are paid for by the interdenominational group. As I am ⊥convinced that this interpretation of the First Amendment is erroneous, I feel impelled to express the reasons for my disagreement. By directing attention to the many instances of close association of church and state in American society and by recalling that many of these relations are so much a part of our tradition and culture that they are accepted without more, this dissent may help in an appraisal of the meaning of the clause of the First Amendment concerning the establishment of religion and of the reasons which lead to the approval or disapproval of the judgment below.

The reasons for the reversal of the Illinois judgment, as they appear in the respective opinions, may be summarized by the following excerpts. The opinion of the Court, after stating the facts, says: "The foregoing facts, without reference to others that appear in the record, show the use of tax-supported property for religious instruction and the close cooperation between the school authorities and the religious council in promoting religious education. . . . And it falls squarely under the ban of the First Amendment (made applicable to the States by the Fourteenth) as we interpreted it in *Everson* v. *Board of Education.*" Another opinion phrases it thus: "We do not now attempt to weigh in the Constitutional scale every separate detail or various combination of factors which may establish a valid 'released time' program. We find that the basic Constitutional principle of absolute separation was violated when the State of Illinois, speaking through its Supreme Court, sustained the school authorities of Champaign in sponsoring and effectively furthering religious beliefs by its educational arrangement." These expressions in the decisions seem to _|240 ⊥leave open for further litigation variations from the Champaign plan. Actually, however, future cases must run the gantlet not only of the judgment entered but of the accompanying words of the opinions. I find it difficult to extract from the opinions any conclusion as to what it is in the Champaign plan that is unconstitutional. Is it the use of school buildings for religious instruction; the release of pupils by the schools for religious instruction during school hours; the so-called assistance by teachers in handing out the request cards to pupils, in keeping lists of them for release and records of their attendance; or the action of the principals in arranging an opportunity for the classes and the appearance of the Council's instructors? None of the reversing opinions say whether the purpose of the Champaign plan for religious instruction during school hours is unconstitutional or whether it is some ingredient used in or omitted from the formula that makes the plan unconstitutional.

From the tenor of the opinions I conclude that their teachings are that any use of a pupil's school time, whether that use is on or off the school grounds, with the necessary school regulations to facilitate attendance, falls under the ban. I reach this conclusion notwithstanding one sentence of indefinite meaning in the second opinion: "We do not consider, as indeed we could not, school programs not before us which, though colloquially characterized as 'released time', present situations differing in aspects that may well be constitutionally crucial." The use of the words "cooperation," "fusion," "complete hands-off," "integrate" and "integrated" to describe the relations between the school and the Council in the plan evidences this. So does the interpretation of the word "aid." The criticized "momentum of the whole school atmosphere," "feeling of separatism," engendered in the non-participat⊥ing sects, "obvious _|241 pressure . . . attend," and "divisiveness" lead to the stated conclusion. From the holding and the language of the opinions, I can only deduce that religious instruction of public school children during school hours is prohibited. The history of American education is against such an interpretation of the First Amendment.

The opinions do not say in words that the condemned practice of religious education is a law respecting an establishment of religion contrary to the First Amendment. The practice is accepted as a state law by all. I take it that when the opinion of the Court says that "The operation of the state's compulsory education system thus assists and is integrated with the program of religious instruction carried on by separate religious sects" and concludes "This is beyond all question a utilization of the tax-established and tax-supported public school system to aid religious groups to spread their faith," the intention of its author is to rule that this practice is a law "respecting an establishment of religion." That was the basis of *Everson* v. *Board of Education.* It seems obvious that the action of the School Board in permitting religious education in certain grades of the schools by all faiths did not prohibit the free exercise of religion. Even assuming that certain children who did not elect to take instruction are embarrassed to remain outside of the classes, one can hardly speak of that embarrassment as a prohibition against the free exercise of religion. As no issue of prohibition upon the free exercise of religion is before us, we need only examine the School Board's action to see if it constitutes an establishment of religion.

The facts, as stated in the reversing opinions, are adequately set out if we interpret the abstract words used in the light of the concrete incidents of the record. It is ⊥correct to say that the parents "consented" to the religious instruction of the children, if we understand "consent" to mean the signing of a card. It is correct to say that "instructors were subject to the approval and supervision of the superintendent of schools," if it is understood that there were no definitive written rules and that the practice was as is shown in the excerpts from the findings

⌐243 below. The substance of the ⊥religious education course is determined by the members of the various churches on the council, not by the superintendent. The evidence and findings set out in the two preceding notes convince me that the "approval and supervision" referred to above are not of the teachers and the course of studies but of the orderly presentation of the courses to those students who may elect the instruction. The teaching largely covered Biblical incidents. The religious teachers and their teachings, ⌐244 in every real sense, ⊥were financed and regulated by the Council of Religious Education, not the School Board.

The phrase "an establishment of religion" may have been intended by Congress to be aimed only at a state church. When the First Amendment was pending in Congress in substantially its present form, "Mr. Madison said, he apprehended the meaning of the words to be, that Congress should not establish a religion, and enforce the legal observation of it by law, nor compel men to worship God in any manner contrary to their conscience." Passing years, however, have brought about acceptance of a broader meaning, although never until today, I believe, has this Court widened its interpretation to any such degree as holding that recognition of the interest of our nation in religion, through the granting, to qualified representatives of the principal faiths, of opportunity to present religion as an optional, extracurricular subject during released school time in public school buildings, was equivalent to an establishment of religion. A reading of the general statements of eminent statesmen of former days, referred to in the opinions in this case and in *Everson* v. *Board of Education*, will show that circumstances such as those in this case were far from the minds of the authors. The words and spirit of those statements may be wholeheartedly accepted without in the least impugning the judgment of the State of Illinois.

⌐245 ⊥ Mr. Jefferson, as one of the founders of the University of Virginia, a school which from its establishment in 1819 has been wholly governed, managed and controlled by the State of Virginia, was faced with the same problem that is before this Court today: the question of the constitutional limitation upon religious education in public schools. In his annual report as Rector, to the President and Directors of the Literary Fund, dated October 7, 1822, approved by the Visitors of the University of whom Mr. Madison was one, Mr. Jefferson set forth his views at some length. These suggestions of Mr. Jef⌐246 ferson were ⊥adopted and ch. II, § 1, of the Regulations of the University of October 4, 1824, provided that: "Should the religious sects of this State, or any of them, according to the invitation held out to them, establish within, or adjacent to, the precincts of the University, schools for instruction in the religion of their sect, the students of the University will be free, and expected to attend religious worship at

the establishment of their respective sects, in the morning, and in time to meet their school in the University at its stated hour."

⊥Thus, the "wall of separation between church ⌐247 and State" that Mr. Jefferson built at the University which he founded did not exclude religious education from that school. The difference between the generality of his statements on the separation of church and state and the specificity of his conclusions on education are considerable. A rule of law should not be drawn from a figure of speech.

Mr. Madison's *Memorial and Remonstrance against Religious Assessments*, relied upon by the dissenting Justices in *Everson*, is not applicable here. Mr. Madison was one of the principal opponents in the Virginia General Assembly of *A Bill Establishing a Provision for Teachers of the Christian Religion*. The monies raised by the taxing section of that bill were to be appropriated "by the Vestries, Elders, or Directors of each religious society, . . . to a provision for a Minister or Teacher ⊥of the Gospel of their denomination, or the provid- ⌐248 ing places of divine worship, and to none other use whatsoever. . . ." The conclusive legislative struggle over this act took place in the fall of 1785, before the adoption of the Bill of Rights. The *Remonstrance* had been issued before the General Assembly convened and was instrumental in the final defeat of the act, which died in committee. Throughout the *Remonstrance* Mr. Madison speaks of the "establishment" sought to be effected by the act. It is clear from its historical setting and its language that the *Remonstrance* was a protest against an effort by Virginia to support Christian sects by taxation. Issues similar to those raised by the instant case were not discussed. Thus, Mr. Madison's approval of Mr. Jefferson's report as Rector gives, in my opinion, a clearer indication of his views on the constitutionality of religious education in public schools than his general statements on a different subject.

This Court summarized the amendment's accepted reach into the religious field, as I understand its scope, in *Everson* v. *Board of Education*. The court's opinion quotes the gist of the Court's reasoning in *Everson*. I agree, as there stated, that none of our governmental entities can "set up a church." I agree that they cannot "aid" all or any religions or prefer one "over another." But "aid" must be understood as a purposeful assistance directly to the church itself or to some religious group or organization doing religious work of such a character that it may fairly be said to be performing ecclesiastical functions. "Prefer" must give an advantage to one "over another". I agree that pupils cannot, "be released in part from their legal duty" of school attendance upon condition that they attend religious classes. But as Illinois has held that it is within the discretion of the School Board to permit absence from school for religious instruc⊥tion no legal duty of school atten- ⌐249 dance is violated. If the sentence in the Court's opinion, concerning the pupils' release from legal duty, is intended to mean that the Constitution forbids a school to excuse a pupil from secular control during school hours to attend voluntarily a class in religious education, whether in or out of school buildings, I disagree. Of course, no tax can be levied to support organizations intended "to teach or practice religion." I agree too that the state cannot influence one toward religion against his will or punish him for his beliefs. Champaign's religious education course does none of these things.

It seems clear to me that the "aid" referred to by the Court in the *Everson* case could not have been those incidental advantages that religous bodies, with other groups similarly situated, obtain as a by-product of organized society. This explains the well-known fact that all churches receive "aid" from government in the form of freedom from taxation. The *Everson* decision itself justified the transportation of children to church schools by New Jersey for safety reasons. It accords with *Cochran* v. *Louisiana State Board of Education*, where this Court upheld a free textbook statute of Louisiana against a charge that it aided private schools on the ground that the books were for the education of the children, not to aid religious schools. Likewise the National School Lunch Act aids all school children attending tax-exempt schools. In *Bradfield* v. *Roberts*, this Court held proper the payment of money by the Federal Government to build an addition to a hospital, chartered by individuals who were members of a Roman Catholic sisterhood, and operated under the auspices of the Roman Catholic Church. This was done over the ⌐250 objection that it aided the establish⊥ment of religion. While obviously in these instances the respective churches, in a certain sense, were aided, this Court has never held that such "aid" was in violation of the First and Fourteenth Amendment.

Well-recognized and long-established practices support the validity of the Illinois statute here in question. That statute, as construed in this case, is comparable to those in many states. All differ to some extent. New York may be taken as a fair ex-⌐251 ample. In many states the pro⊥gram is under the supervision of a religious council composed of delegates who are themselves communicants of various faiths. As is shown by *Bradfield* v. *Roberts*, the fact that the members of the council have religious affili-⌐252 ations is not significant. In some, instruc⊥tion is given outside of the school buildings; in others, within these buildings. Metropolitan centers like New York usually would have available quarters convenient to schools. Unless smaller cities and rural communities use the school building at times that do not interfere with recitations, they may be compelled to give up religious education. I understand that pupils not taking religious education usually are given other work of a secular nature within the schools. Since all these states use the facilities of the schools to aid the religious education to some extent, their

desire to permit religious education to school children is thwarted by this Court's judgment. Under it, as I understand its language, children cannot be released or dismissed from school to attend classes in religion while other children must remain to pursue secular education. Teachers cannot keep the records as to which pupils are to be dismissed and which retained. To do so is said to be an "aid" in establishing religion; the use of public money for religion.

Cases running into the scores have been in the state courts of last resort that involved religion and the schools. Except where the exercises with religious significance partook of the ceremonial practice of sects or groups, their ⊥constitutionality has been ⌐253 generally upheld. Illinois itself promptly struck down as violative of its own constitution required exercises partaking of a religious ceremony. *People ex rel. Ring* v. *Board of Education*. In that case compulsory religious exercises—a reading from the King James Bible, the Lord's Prayer and the singing of hymns— were forbidden as "worship services." In this case, the Supreme Court of Illinois pointed out that in the *Ring* case, the activities in the school were ceremonial and compulsory; in this, voluntary and educational.

The practices of the federal government offer many examples of this kind of "aid" by the state to religion. The Congress of the United States has a chaplain for each House who daily invokes divine blessings and guidance for ⊥the proceedings. The ⌐254 armed forces have commissioned chaplains from early days. They conduct the public services in accordance with the liturgical requirements of their respective faiths, ashore and afloat, employing for the purpose property belonging to the United States and dedicated to the services of religion. Under the Servicemen's Readjustment Act of 1944, eligible veterans may receive training at government expense for the ministry in denominational schools. The schools of the District of Columbia have opening exercises which "include a reading from the Bible without note or comment, and the Lord's prayer."

In the United States Naval Academy and the United States Military Academy, schools wholly supported and completely controlled by the federal government, there are a number of religious activities. Chaplains are attached to both schools. Attendance at church services on Sunday is compulsory at both the Military and Naval Academies. At West Point the Protestant services are ⊥held in the Cadet ⌐255 Chapel, the Catholic in the Catholic Chapel, and the Jewish in the Old Cadet Chapel; at Annapolis only Protestant services are held on the reservation, midshipmen of other religious persuasions attend the churches of the city of Annapolis. These facts indicate that both schools since their earliest beginnings have maintained and enforced a pattern of participation in formal worship.

With the general statements in the opinions concerning the constitutional requirement that the nation and the states, by virtue of the First and Fourteenth Amendments, may "make no law respecting an establishment of religion," I am in agreement. But, in the light of the meaning given to those words by the precedents, customs, and practices which I have detailed above, I cannot agree with the Court's conclusion that when pupils compelled by law to go to school for secular education are released from school so as to attend the religious classes, churches are unconstitutionally aided. Whatever may be the wisdom of the arrangement as to the use of the school buildings made with the Champaign Council of Religious Education, it is clear to me that past practice shows such cooperation between the schools and a nonecclesiastical body is not forbidden by the First Amendment. When actual church services have always been permitted on government property, the mere use of the school buildings by a non-sectarian group for religious education ought not to be condemned as an establishment of religion. For a non-sectarian organization to give the type of instruction here offered cannot be said to violate our rule as to the establishment of religion by the state. The prohibition of enactments respecting the estab- ⊥256 lishment of religion do ⊥not bar every friendly gesture between church and state. It is not an absolute prohibition against every conceivable situation where the two may work together, any more than the other provisions of the First Amendment—free speech, free press—are absolutes. If abuses occur, such as the use of the instruction hour for sectarian purposes, I have no doubt, in view of the *Ring* case, that Illinois will promptly correct them. If they are of a kind that tend to the establishment of a church or interfere with the free exercise of religion, this Court is open for a review of any erroneous decision. This Court cannot be too cautious in upsetting practices embedded in our society by many years of experience. A state is entitled to have great leeway in its legislation when dealing with the important social problems of its population. A definite violation of legislative limits must be established. The Constitution should not be stretched to forbid national customs in the way courts act to reach arrangements to avoid federal taxation. Devotion to the great principle of religious liberty should not lead us into a rigid interpretation of the constitutional guarantee that conflicts with accepted habits of our people. This is an instance where, for me, the history of past practices is determinative of the meaning of a constitutional clause, not a decorous introduction to the study of its text. The judgment should be affirmed.

ZORACH v. CLAUSON

343 U.S. 306
ON APPEAL FROM THE COURT OF APPEALS
OF NEW YORK
Argued January 31-February 1, 1952 — Decided
April 28, 1952

⊥ *Mr. Justice DOUGLAS* delivered the opinion of ⊥308 the Court.

New York City has a program which permits its public schools to release students during the school day so that they may leave the school buildings and school grounds and go to religious centers for religious instruction or devotional exercises. A student is released on written request of his parents. Those not released stay in the classrooms. The churches make weekly reports to the schools, sending a list of children who have been released from public school but who have not reported for religious instruction.

This "released time" program involves neither religious instruction in public school classrooms nor the expendi⊥ture of public funds. All costs, including ⊥309 the application blanks, are paid by the religious organizations. The case is therefore unlike *McCollum v. Board of Education*, which involved a "released time" program from Illinois. In that case the classrooms were turned over to religious instructors. We accordingly held that the program violated the First Amendment which (by reason of the Fourteenth Amendment) prohibits the states from establishing religion or prohibiting its free exercise.

Appellants, who are taxpayers and residents of New York City and whose children attend its public schools, challenge the present law, contending it is in essence not different from the one involved in the *McCollum* case. Their argument, stated elaborately in various ways, reduces itself to this: the weight and influence of the school is put behind a program for religious instruction; public school teachers police it, keeping tab on students who are released; the classroom activities come to a halt while the students who are released for religious instruction are on leave; the school is a crutch on which the churches are leaning for support in their religious training; without the cooperation of the schools this "released time" program, ⊥like the one in the *McCollum* case, ⊥310 would be futile and ineffective. The New York Court of Appeals sustained the law against this claim of unconstitutionality. The case is here on appeal. . . .

[O]ur problem reduces itself to whether New York by this system has either prohibited the "free exercise" of religion or has made a law "respecting an establishment of religion" within the meaning of the First Amendment.

⊥It takes obtuse reasoning to inject any issue of ⊥311 the "free exercise" of religion into the present case. No one is forced to go to the religious classroom and no religious exercise or instruction is brought to the classrooms of the public schools. A student need not take religious instruction. He is left to his own desires as to the manner or time of his religious devotions, if any.

There is a suggestion that the system involves the use of coercion to get public school students into religious classrooms. There is no evidence in the record before us that supports that conclusion. The present record indeed tells us that the school authorities are neutral in this regard and do no more than release students whose parents so request. . . . Hence we put aside that claim of coercion ⊥ both as respects the "free exercise" of religion and "an establishment of religion" within the meaning of the First Amendment.

⌐312

Moreover, apart from that claim of coercion, we do not see how New York by this type of "released time" program has made a law respecting an establishment of religion within the meaning of the First Amendment. There is much talk of the separation of Church and State in the history of the Bill of Rights and in the decisions clustering around the First Amendment. There cannot be the slightest doubt that the First Amendment reflects the philosophy that Church and State should be separated. And so far as interference with the "free exercise" of religion and an "establishment" of religion are concerned, the separation must be complete and unequivocal. The First Amendment within the scope of its coverage permits no exception; the prohibition is absolute. The First Amendment, however, does not say that in every and all respects there shall be a separation of Church and State. Rather, it studiously defines the manner, the specific ways, in which there shall be no concert or union or dependency one on the other. That is the common sense of the matter. Otherwise the state and religion would be aliens to each other—hostile, suspicious, and even unfriendly. Churches could not be required to pay even property taxes. Municipalities would not be permitted to render police or fire protection to religious groups. Policemen who helped parishioners into their places of worship would violate the Constitution. Prayers in our legislative halls; the ap⊥peals to the Almighty in the messages of the Chief Executive; the proclamations making Thanksgiving Day a holiday; "so help me God" in our courtroom oaths—these and all other references to the Almighty that run through our laws, our public rituals, our ceremonies would be flouting the First Amendment. A fastidious atheist or agnostic could even object to the supplication with which the Court opens each session: "God save the United States and this Honorable Court."

⌐313

We would have to press the concept of separation of Church and State to these extremes to condemn the present law on constitutional grounds. The nullification of this law would have wide and profound effects. A Catholic student applies to his teacher for permission to leave the school during hours on a Holy Day of Obligation to attend a mass. A Jewish student asks his teacher for permission to be excused for Yom Kippur. A Protestant wants the afternoon off for a family baptismal ceremony. In each case the teacher requires parental consent in writing. In each case the teacher, in order to make sure the student is not a truant, goes further and requires a report from the priest, the rabbi, or the minister. The teacher in other words cooperates in a religious program to the extent of making it possible for her students to participate in it. Whether she does it occasionally for a few students, regularly for one, or pursuant to a systematized program designed to further the religious needs of all the students does not alter the character of the act.

We are a religious people whose institutions presuppose a Supreme Being. We guarantee the freedom to worship as one chooses. We make room for as wide a variety of beliefs and creeds as the spiritual needs of man deem necessary. We sponsor an attitude on the part of government that shows no partiality to any one group and that lets each flourish according to the zeal of its adherents and the appeal of its dogma. When the state ⊥encourages religious instruction or cooperates with religious authorities by adjusting the schedule of public events to sectarian needs, it follows the best of our traditions. For it then respects the religious nature of our people and accommodates the public service to their spiritual needs. To hold that it may not would be to find in the Constitution a requirement that the government show a callous indifference to religious groups. That would be preferring those who believe in no religion over those who do believe. Government may not finance religious groups nor undertake religious instruction nor blend secular and sectarian education nor use secular institutions to force one or some religion on any person. But we find no constitutional requirement which makes it necessary for government to be hostile to religion and to throw its weight against efforts to widen the effective scope of religious influence. The government must be neutral when it comes to competition between sects. It may not thrust any sect on any person. It may not make a religious observance compulsory. It may not coerce anyone to attend church, to observe a religious holiday, or to take religious instruction. But it can close its doors or suspend its operations as to those who want to repair to their religious sanctuary for worship or instruction. No more than that is undertaken here. . . .

⌐314

⊥ In the *McCollum* case the classrooms were used for religious instruction and the force of the public school was used to promote that instruction. Here, as we have said, the public schools do no more than accommodate their schedules to a program of outside religious instruction. We follow the *McCollum* case. But we cannot expand it to cover the present released time program unless separation of Church and State means that public institutions can make no adjustments of their schedules to accommodate the religious needs of the people. We cannot read

⌐31

into the Bill of Rights such a philosophy of hostility to religion.

Affirmed.

Mr. Justice BLACK, dissenting.

Illinois ex rel. McCollum v. *Board of Education* held invalid as an "establishment of religion" an Illinois system under which school children, compelled by law to go to public schools, were freed from some hours of required school work on condition that they attend special religious classes held in the school buildings. Although the classes were taught by sec- ⊥316 tarian ⊥ teachers neither employed nor paid by the state, the state did use its power to further the program by releasing some of the children from regular class work, insisting that those released attend the religious classes, and requiring that those who remained behind do some kind of academic work while the others received their religious training. We said this about the Illinois system: "Pupils compelled by law to go to school for secular education are released in part from their legal duty upon the condition that they attend the religious classes. This is beyond all question a utilization of the tax-established and tax-supported public school system to aid religious groups to spread their faith. And it falls squarely under the ban of the First Amendment. . . ." *McCollum* v. *Board of Education.*

I see no significant difference between the invalid Illinois system and that of New York here sustained. Except for the use of the school buildings in Illinios, there is no difference between the systems which I consider even worthy of mention. In the New York program, as in that of Illinois, the school authorities release some of the children on the condition that they attend the religious classes, get reports on whether they attend, and hold the other children in the school building until the religious hour is over. As we attempted to make categorically clear, the *McCollum* decision would have been the same if the religious classes had not been held in the school buildings. We said: "Here *not only* are the State's tax-supported public school buildings used for the dissemination of religious doctrines. The State *also* affords sectarian groups an invaluable aid in that it helps to provide pupils for their religious classes through use of the State's compulsory public school ⊥317 machinery. *This* is ⊥ not separation of Church and State." (Emphasis supplied.)

McCollum thus held that Illinois could not constitutionally manipulate the compelled classroom hours of its compulsory school machinery so as to channel children into sectarian classes. Yet that is exactly what the Court holds New York can do. . . .

In dissenting today, I mean to do more than give routine approval to our *McCollum* decision. I mean ⊥318 also to reaffirm my faith in the ⊥ fundamental philosophy expressed in *McCollum* and *Everson* v. *Board of Education.* That reaffirmation can be brief

because of the exhaustive opinions in those recent cases.

Difficulty of decision in the hypothetical situations mentioned by the Court, but not now before us, should not confuse the issues in this case. Here the sole question is whether New York can use its compulsory education laws to help religious sects get attendants presumably too unenthusiastic to go unless moved to do so by the pressure of this state machinery. That this is the plan, purpose, design and consequence of the New York program cannot be denied. The state thus makes religious sects beneficiaries of its power to compel children to attend secular schools. Any use of such coercive power by the state to help or hinder some religious sects or to prefer all religious sects over nonbelievers or vice versa is just what I think the First Amendment forbids. In considering whether a state has entered this forbidden field the question is not whether it has entered too far but whether it has entered at all. New York is manipulating its compulsory education laws to help religious sects get pupils. This is not separation but combination of Church and State.

The Court's validation of the New York system rests in part on its statement that Americans are "a religious people whose institutions presuppose a Supreme Being." This was at least as true when the First Amendment was adopted; and it was just as true when eight Justices of this Court invalidated the released time system in *McCollum* on the premise that a state can no more "aid all religions" than it can aid one. It was precisely because Eighteenth ⊥ Century Americans were a religious people divided ⊥319 into many fighting sects that we were given the constitutional mandate to keep Church and State completely separate. Colonial history had already shown that, here as elsewhere zealous sectarians entrusted with governmental power to further their causes would sometimes torture, maim and kill those they branded "heretics," "atheists" or "agnostics." The First Amendment was therefore to insure that no one powerful sect or combination of sects could use political or governmental power to punish dissenters whom they could not convert to their faith. Now as then, it is only by wholly isolating the state from the religious sphere and compelling it to be completely neutral, that the freedom of each and every denomination and of all nonbelievers can be maintained. It is this neutrality the Court abandons today when it treats New York's coercive system as a program which *merely* "encourages religious instruction or cooperates with religious authorities." The abandonment is all the more dangerous to liberty because of the Court's legal exaltation of the orthodox and its derogation of unbelievers.

Under our system of religious freedom, people have gone to their religious sanctuaries not because they feared the law but because they loved their God. The choice of all has been as free as the choice of those who answered the call to worship moved only by the music of the old Sunday morning church bells. The spiritual mind of man has thus been free to believe, disbelieve, or doubt, without repression, great or small, by the heavy ⊥ hand of government. Statutes authorizing such repression have been stricken. Before today, our judicial opinions have refrained from drawing invidious distinctions between those who believe in no religion and those who do believe. The First Amendment has lost much if the religious follower and the atheist are no longer to be judicially regarded as entitled to equal justice under law.

State help to religion injects political and party prejudices into a holy field. It too often substitutes force for prayer, hate for love, and persecution for persuasion. Government should not be allowed, under cover of the soft euphemism of "co-operation," to steal into the sacred area of religious choice.

Mr. Justice FRANKFURTER, dissenting.

By way of emphasizing my agreement with *Mr. Justice JACKSON's* dissent, I add a few words.

The Court tells us that in the maintenance of its public schools, "[The State government] can close its doors or suspend its operations" so that its citizens may be free for religious devotions or instruction. If that were the issue, it would not rise to the dignity of a constitutional controversy. Of course, a State may provide that the classes in its schools shall be dismissed, for any reason, or no reason, on fixed days, or for special occasions. The essence of this case is that the school system did not "close its doors" and did not "suspend its operations." There is all the difference in the world between letting the children out of school and letting some of them out of school into religious classes. If every one is free to make what use he will of time wholly unconnected from schooling required by law—those who wish sectarian instruction devoting it to that purpose, those who have ethical instruction at home, to that, those who study music, to that—then of course there is no conflict with the Fourteenth Amendment.

⊥ The pith of the case is that formalized religious instruction is substituted for other school activity which those who do not participate in the released-time program are compelled to attend. The school system is very much in operation during this kind of released time. If its doors are closed, they are closed upon those students who do not attend the religious instruction, in order to keep them within the school. That is the very thing which raises the constitutional issue. It is not met by disregarding it. Failure to discuss this issue does not take it out of the case.

Again, the Court relies upon the absence from the record of evidence of coercion in the operation of the system. "If in fact coercion were used," according to the Court, "if it were established that any one or more teachers were using their office to persuade or force students to take the religious instruction, a wholly different case would be presented." Thus,

"coercion" in the abstract is acknowledged to be fatal. But the Court disregards the fact that as the case comes to us, there could be no proof of coercion, for the appellants were not allowed to make proof of it. . . .

⊥ The result in the *McCollum* case was based on principles that received unanimous acceptance by this Court, barring only a single vote. I agree with *Mr. Justice BLACK* that those principles are disregarded ⊥ in reaching the result in this case. Happily they are not disavowed by the Court. From this I draw the hope that in future variations of the problem which are bound to come here, these principles may again be honored in the observance.

The deeply divisive controversy aroused by the attempts to secure public school pupils for sectarian instruction would promptly end if the advocates of such instruction were content to have the school "close its doors or suspend its operations"—that is, dismiss classes in their entirety, without discrimination—instead of seeking to use the public schools as the instrument for securing attendance at denominational classes. The unwillingness of the promoters of this movement to dispense with such use of the public schools betrays a surprising want of confidence in the inherent power of the various faiths to draw children to outside sectarian classes—an attitude that hardly reflects the faith of the greatest religious spirits.

Mr. Justice JACKSON, dissenting.

This released time program is founded upon a use of the State's power of coercion, which, for me, determines its unconstitutionality. Stripped to its essentials, the plan has two stages: first, that the State compel each student to yield a large part of his time for public secu⊥lar education; and, second, that some of it be "released" to him on condition that he devote it to sectarian religious purposes.

No one suggests that the Constitution would permit the State directly to require this "released" time to be spent "under the control of a duly constituted religious body." This program accomplishes that forbidden result by indirection. If public education were taking so much of the pupils' time as to injure the public or the students' welfare by encroaching upon their religious opportunity, simply shortening everyone's school day would facilitate voluntary and optional attendance at Church classes. But that suggestion is rejected upon the ground that if they are made free many students will not go to the Church. Hence, they must be deprived of freedom for this period, with Church attendance put to them as one of the two permissible ways of using it.

The greater effectiveness of this system over voluntary attendance after school hours is due to the truant officer who, if the youngster fails to go to the Church school, dogs him back to the public schoolroom. Here schooling is more or less suspended during the "released time" so the nonreligious attendants will not forge ahead of the churchgoing absentees. But it serves as a temporary jail for a pupil who will not go to Church. It takes more subtlety of mind than I possess to deny that this is governmental constraint in support of religion. It is as unconstitutional, in my view, when exerted by indirection as when exercised forthrightly.

As one whose children, as a matter of free choice, have been sent to privately supported Church schools, I may challenge the Court's suggestion that opposition to this plan can only be antireligious, atheistic, or agnostic. My evangelistic brethren confuse an objection to compulsion with an objection to religion. It is possible to hold a faith with enough confidence to believe that what should be ⊥rendered to God does not need to be decided and collected by Caesar.

The day that this country ceases to be free for irreligion it will cease to be free for religion—except for the sect that can win political power. The same epithetical jurisprudence used by the Court today to beat down those who oppose pressuring children into some religion can devise as good epithets tomorrow against those who object to pressuring them into a favored religion. And, after all, if we concede to the State power and wisdom to single out "duly constituted religious" bodies as exclusive alternatives for compulsory secular instruction, it would be logical to also uphold the power and wisdom to choose the true faith among those "duly constituted." We start down a rough road when we begin to mix compulsory public education with compulsory godliness.

A number of Justices just short of a majority of the majority that promulgates today's passionate dialectics joined in answering them in *Illinois ex rel. McCollum* v. *Board of Education*. The distinction attempted between that case and this is trivial, almost to the point of cynicism, magnifying its nonessential details and disparaging compulsion which was the underlying reason for invalidity. A reading of the Court's opinion in that case along with its opinion in this case will show such difference of overtones and undertones as to make clear that the *McCollum* case has passed like a storm in a teacup. The wall which the Court was professing to erect between Church and State has become even more warped and twisted than I expected. Today's judgment will be more interesting to students of psychology and of the judicial processes than to students of constitutional law.

ENGEL v. VITALE

370 U.S. 421
ON CERTIORARI TO THE COURT OF
APPEALS OF NEW YORK
Argued April 3, 1962 — Decided June 25, 1962

⊥*Mr. Justice* BLACK delivered the opinion of the Court.

The respondent Board of Education of Union Free School District No. 9, New Hyde Park, New York, acting in its official capacity under state law, directed the School District's principal to cause the following prayer to be said aloud by each class in the presence of a teacher at the beginning of each school day: "Almighty God, we acknowledge our dependence upon Thee, and we beg Thy blessings upon us, our parents, our teachers and our Country."

This daily procedure was adopted on the recommendation of the State Board of Regents, a governmental agency created by the State Constitution to which the New York Legislature has granted broad supervisory, executive, and ⊥legislative powers over the State's public school system. These state officials composed the prayer which they recommended and published as a part of their "Statement on Moral and Spiritual Training in the Schools," saying: "We believe that this Statement will be subscribed to by all men and women of good will, and we call upon all of them to aid in giving life to our program."

Shortly after the practice of reciting the Regents' prayer was adopted by the School District, the parents of ten pupils brought this action in a New York State Court insisting that use of this official prayer in the public schools was contrary to the beliefs, religions, or religious practices of both themselves and their children. Among other things, these parents challenged the constitutionality of both the state law authorizing the School District to direct the use of prayer in public schools and the School District's regulation ordering the recitation of this particular prayer on the ground that these actions of official governmental agencies violate that part of the First Amendment of the Federal Constitution which commands that "Congress shall make no law respecting an establishment of religion"—a command which was "made applicable to the State of New York by the Fourteenth Amendment of the said Constitution." The New York Court of Appeals, over the dissents of Judges Dye and Fuld, sustained an order of the lower state courts which had upheld the power of New York to use the Regent's prayer as a part of the daily procedures of its public schools so long as the schools did not compel any pupil to join in the prayer over his or his parents' objection. ⊥We granted certiorari to review this important decision involving rights protected by the First and Fourteenth Amendments.

We think that by using its public school system to encourage recitation of the Regents' prayer, the State of New York has adopted a practice wholly inconsistent with the Establishment Clause. There can, of course, be no doubt that New York's program of daily classroom invocation of God's blessing as prescribed in the Regents' prayer is a religious activity. It is a solemn avowal of divine faith and supplication for the blessings of the Almighty. The nature of such a prayer has always been ⊥religious, none of the respondents has denied this and the trial court expressly so found: "The religious nature of prayer was recognized by Jefferson and has been concurred in by theological writers, the United States Supreme Court and State courts and administrative officials, including New York's Commissioner of Education. A committee of the New York Legislature has agreed.

"The Board of Regents as *amicus curiae*, the respondents and intervenors all concede the religious nature of prayer, but seek to distinguish this prayer because it is based on our spiritual heritage. . . ."

The petitioners contend among other things that the state laws requiring or permitting use of the Regents' prayer must be struck down as a violation of the Establishment Clause because that prayer was composed by governmental officials as a part of a governmental program to further religious beliefs. For this reason, petitioners argue, the State's use of the Regents' prayer in its public school system breaches the constitutional wall of separation between Church and State. We agree with that contention since we think that the constitutional prohibition against laws respecting an establishment of religion must at least mean that in this country it is no part of the business of government to compose official prayers for any group of the American people to recite as a part of a religious program carried on by government.

It is a matter of history that this very practice of establishing governmentally composed prayers for religious services was one of the reasons which caused many of our early colonists to leave England and seek religious freedom in America. The Book of
⌋426 Common Prayer, ⊥which was created under governmental direction and which was approved by Acts of Parliament in 1548 and 1549, set out in minute detail the accepted form and content of prayer and other religious ceremonies to be used in the established, tax-supported Church of England. The controversies over the Book and what should be its content repeatedly threatened to disrupt the peace of that country as the accepted forms of prayer in the established church changed with the views of the particular ruler that happened to be in control at the time. Powerful groups representing some of the varying religious views of the people struggled among themselves to impress their particular views upon
⌋427 the Government and ⊥obtain amendments of the Book more suitable to their respective notions of how religious services should be conducted in order that the official religious establishment would advance their particular religious beliefs. Other groups, lacking the necessary political power to influence the Government on the matter, decided to leave England and its established church and seek freedom in America from England's governmentally ordained and supported religion.

It is an unfortunate fact of history that when some of the very groups which had most strenuously op-

posed the established Church of England found themselves sufficiently in control of colonial governments in this country to write their own prayers into law, they passed laws making their own religion the official religion of their respective colonies. Indeed, as late as the time of the Revolu⊥tionary War, there ⌋42 were established churches in at least eight of the thirteen former colonies and established religions in at least four of the other five. But the successful Revolution against English political domination was shortly followed by intense opposition to the practice of establishing religion by law. This opposition crystallized rapidly into an effective political force in Virginia where the minority religious groups such as Presbyterians, Lutherans, Quakers and Baptists had gained such strength that the adherents to the established Episcopal Church were actually a minority themselves. In 1785-1786, those opposed to the established Church, led by James Madison and Thomas Jefferson, who, though themselves not members of any of these dissenting religious groups, opposed all religious establishments by law on grounds of principle, obtained the enactment of the famous "Virginia Bill for Religious Liberty" by which all religious groups were placed on an equal footing so far as the State was concerned. Similar though less far-reaching ⊥legislation was being considered and ⌋4² passed in other States.

By the time of the adoption of the Constitution, our history shows that there was a widespread awareness among many Americans of the dangers of a union of Church and State. These people knew, some of them from bitter personal experience, that one of the greatest dangers to the freedom of the individual to worship in his own way lay in the Government's placing its official stamp of approval upon one particular kind of prayer or one particular form of religious services. They knew the anguish, hardship and bitter strife that could come when zealous religious groups struggled with one another to obtain the Government's stamp of approval from each King, Queen, or Protector that came to temporary power. The Constitution was intended to avert a part of this danger by leaving the government of this country in the hands of the people rather than in the hands of any monarch. But this safeguard was not enough. Our Founders were no more willing to let the content of their prayers and their privilege of praying whenever they pleased be influenced by the ballot box than they were to let these vital matters of personal conscience depend upon the succession of monarchs. The First Amendment was added to the Constitution to stand as a guarantee that neither the power nor the prestige of Federal Government would be used to control, support or influence the kinds of prayer the American people can say—⊥that the peo- ⌋4 ple's religions must not be subjected to the pressures of government for change each time a new political administration is elected to office. Under that Amendment's prohibition against governmental establishment of religion, as reinforced by the provisions of the Fourteenth Amendment, government in this country, be it state or federal, is without power to prescribe by law any particular form of prayer which is to be used as an official prayer in carrying on any program of governmentally sponsored religious activity.

There can be no doubt that New York's state prayer program officially establishes the religious beliefs embodied in the Regents' prayer. The respondents, argument to the contrary, which is largely based upon the contention that the Regents' prayer is "non-denominational" and the fact that the program, as modified and approved by state courts, does not require all pupils to recite the prayer but permits those who wish to do so to remain silent or be excused from the room, ignores the essential nature of the program's constitutional defects. Neither the fact that the prayer may be denominationally neutral nor the fact that its observance on the part of the students is voluntary can serve to free it from the limitations of the Establishment Clause, as it might from the Free Exercise Clause, of the First Amendment, both of which are operative against the States by virtue of the Fourteenth Amendment. Although these two clauses may in certain instances overlap, they forbid two quite different kinds of governmental encroachment upon religious freedom. The Establishment Clause, unlike the Free Exercise Clause, does not depend upon any showing of direct governmental compulsion and is violated by the enactment of laws which establish an official religion whether those laws operate directly to coerce nonobserving individuals or not. This is not to say, of course, that ⊥432 ⊥ laws officially prescribing a particular form of religious worship do not involve coercion of such individuals. When the power, prestige and financial support of government is placed behind a particular religious belief, the indirect coercive pressure upon religious minorities to conform to the prevailing officially approved religion is plain. But the purposes underlying the Establishment Clause go much further than that. Its first and most immediate purpose rested on the belief that a union of government and religion tends to destroy government and to degrade religion. The history of governmentally established religion, both in England and in this country, showed that whenever government had allied itself with one particular form of religion, the inevitable result had been that it had incurred the hatred, disrespect and even contempt of those who held contrary beliefs. That same history showed that many people had lost their respect for any religion that had relied upon the support of government to spread ⊥432 its faith. The Establishment Clause ⊥ thus stands as an expression of principle on the part of the Founders of our Constitution that religion is too personal, too sacred, too holy, to permit its "unhallowed perversion" by a civil magistrate. Another purpose of the Establishment Clause rested upon an awareness

of the historical fact that governmentally established religions and religious persecutions go hand in hand. The Founders knew that only a few years after the Book of Common Prayer became the only accepted form of religious services in the established Church of England, an Act of Uniformity was passed to compel all Englishmen to attend those services and to make it a criminal offense to conduct or attend religious gatherings of any other kind—a law ⊥ which ⊥433 was consistently flouted by dissenting religious groups in England and which contributed to widespread persecutions of people like John Bunyan who persisted in holding "unlawful [religious] meetings . . . to the great disturbance and distraction of the good subjects of this kingdom. . . ." And they knew that similar persecutions had received the sanction of law in several of the colonies in this country soon after the establishment of official religions in those colonies. It was in large part to get completely away from this sort of systematic religious persecution that the Founders brought into being our Nation, our Constitution, and our Bill of Rights with its prohibition against any governmental establishment of religion. The New York laws officially prescribing the Regents' prayer are inconsistent both with the purposes of the Establishment Clause and with the Establishment Clause itself.

It has been argued that to apply the Constitution in such a way as to prohibit state laws respecting an ⊥ establishment of religious services in public ⊥434 schools is to indicate a hostility toward religion or toward prayer. Nothing, of course, could be more wrong. The history of man is inseparable from the history of religion. And perhaps it is not too much to say that since the beginning of that history many people have devoutly believed that "More things are wrought by prayer than this world dreams of." It was doubtless largely due to men who believed this that there grew up a sentiment that caused men to leave the cross-currents of officially established state religions and religious persecution in Europe and come to this country filled with the hope that they could find a place in which they could pray when they pleased to the God of their faith in the language they chose. And there were men of this same faith in the ⊥ power of prayer who led the fight for adoption of ⊥435 our Constitution and also for our Bill of Rights with the very guarantees of religious freedom that forbid the sort of governmental activity which New York has attempted here. These men knew that the First Amendment, which tried to put an end to governmental control of religion and of prayer, was not written to destroy either. They knew rather that it was written to quiet well-justified fears which nearly all of them felt arising out of an awareness that governments of the past had shackled men's tongues to make them speak only the religious thoughts that government wanted them to speak and to pray only to the God that government wanted them to pray to. It is neither sacrilegious nor anti-religious to say that each separate government in this country should stay out of the business of writing or sanctioning official prayers and leave that purely religious function to the people themselves and to those the people choose to look to for religious guidance.

⌐436   ⊥It is true that New York's establishment of its Regents' prayer as an officially approved religious doctrine of that State does not amount to a total establishment of one particular religious sect to the exclusion of all others—that, indeed, the governmental endorsement of that prayer seems relatively insignificant when compared to the governmental encroachments upon religion which were commonplace 200 years ago. To those who may subscribe to the view that because the Regents' official prayer is so brief and general there can be no danger to religious freedom in its governmental establishment, however, it may be appropriate to say in the words of James Madison, the author of the First Amendment: "[I]t is proper to take alarm at the first experiment on our liberties. . . . Who does not see that the same authority which can establish Christianity, in exclusion of all other Religions, may establish with the same ease any particular sect of Christians, in exclusion of all other Sects? That the same authority which can force a citizen to contribute three pence only of his property for the support of any one establishment, may force him to conform to any other establishment in all cases whatsoever?"

The judgment of the Court of Appeals of New York is reversed and the cause remanded for further proceedings not inconsistent with this opinion.

Reversed and remanded.

Mr. Justice FRANKFURTER took no part in the decision of this case.

Mr. Justice WHITE took no part in the consideration or decision of this case.

⌐437   ⊥*Mr. Justice DOUGLAS*, concurring.

It is customary in deciding a constitutional question to treat it in its narrowest form. Yet at times the setting of the question gives it a form and content which no abstract treatment could give. The point for decision is whether the Government can constitutionally finance a religious exercise. Our system at the federal and state levels is presently honeycombed with such financing. Nevertheless, I think it is an unconstitutional undertaking whatever form it takes.

First, a word as to what this case does not involve.

⌐438   ⊥Plainly, our Bill of Rights would not permit a State or Federal Government to adopt an official prayer and penalize anyone who would not utter it. This, however, is not the case, for there is no element of compulsion or coercion in New York's regulation requiring that public schools be opened each day with the following prayer: "Almighty God, we acknowledge our dependence upon Thee, and we beg Thy blessings upon us, our parents, our teachers and our Country."

The prayer is said upon the commencement of the school day, immediately following the pledge of allegiance to the flag. The prayer is said aloud in the presence of a teacher, who either leads the recitation or selects a student to do so. No student, however, is compelled to take part. The respondents have adopted a regulation which provides that "Neither teachers nor any school authority shall comment on participation or non-participation . . . nor suggest or request that any posture or language be used or dress be worn or be not used or not worn." Provision is also made for excusing children, upon written request of a parent or guardian, from the saying of the prayer or from the room in which the prayer is said. A letter implementing and explaining this regulation has been sent to each taxpayer and parent in the school district. As I read this regulation, a child is free to stand or not stand, to recite or not recite, without fear of reprisal or even comment by the teacher or any other school official.

In short, the only one who need utter the prayer is the teacher; and no teacher is complaining of it. Students can stand mute or even leave the classroom, if they desire.

⊥*McCollum* v. *Board of Education* does not de-   ⌐439 cide this case. It involved the use of public school facilities for religious education of students. Students either had to attend religious instruction or "go to some other place in the school building for pursuit of their secular studies. . . . Reports of their presence or absence were to be made to their secular teachers." The influence of the teaching staff was therefore brought to bear on the student body, to support the instilling of religious principles. In the present case, school facilities are used to say the prayer and the teaching staff is employed to lead the pupils in it. There is, however, no effort at indoctrination and no attempt at exposition. Prayers of course may be so long and of such a character as to amount to an attempt at the religious instruction that was denied the public schools by the *McCollum* case. But New York's prayer is of a character that does not involve any element of proselytizing as in the *McCollum* case.

The question presented by this case is therefore an extremely narrow one. It is whether New York oversteps the bounds when it finances a religious exercise.

What New York does on the opening of its public schools is what we do when we open court. Our Crier has from the beginning announced the convening of the Court and then added "God save the United States and this Honorable Court." That utterance is a supplication, a prayer in which we, the judges, are free to join, but which we need not recite any more than the students need recite the New York prayer.

What New York does on the opening of its public schools is what each House of Congress does at the open⊥ing of each day's business. . . .

⊥In New York the teacher who leads in prayer is on the public payroll; and the time she takes seems minuscule as compared with the salaries appropriated by state legislatures and Congress for chaplains to conduct prayers in the legislative halls. Only a bare fraction of the teacher's time is given to reciting this short 22-word prayer, about the same amount of time that our Crier spends announcing the opening of our sessions and offering a prayer for this Court. Yet for me the principle is the same, no matter how briefly the prayer is said, for in each of the instances given the person praying is a public official on the public payroll, performing a religious exercise in a governmental institution. It is said that the ⊥element of coercion is inherent in the giving of this prayer. If that is true here, it is also true of the prayer with which this Court is convened, and of those that open the Congress. Few adults, let alone children, would leave our courtroom or the Senate or the House while those prayers are being given. Every such audience is in a sense a "captive" audience.

At the same time I cannot say that to authorize this prayer is to establish a religion in the strictly historic meaning of those words. A religion is not established in the usual sense merely by letting those who choose to do so say the prayer that the public school teacher leads. Yet once government finances a religious exercise it inserts a divisive influence into our communities. The New York Court said that the prayer given does not conform to all of the tenets of the Jewish, Unitarian, and Ethical Culture groups. One of the petitioners is an agnostic.

"We are a religious people whose institutions presuppose a Supreme Being." *Zorach* v. *Clauson* Under our Bill of Rights free play is given for ⊥making religion an active force in our lives. But "if a religious leaven is to be worked into the affairs of our people, it is to be done by individuals and groups, not by the Government." *McGowan* v. *Maryland* By reason of the First Amendment government is commanded "to have no interest in theology or ritual," for on those matters "government must be neutral." The First Amendment leaves the Government in a position not of hostility to religion but of neutrality. The philosophy is that the atheist or agnostic—the nonbeliever—is entitled to go his own way. The philosophy is that if government interferes in matters spiritual, it will be a divisive force. The First Amendment teaches that a government neutral in the field of religion better serves all religious interests.

My problem today would be uncomplicated but for *Everson* v. *Board of Education*, which allowed taxpayers' money to be used to pay "the bus fares of parochial school pupils as a part of a general program under which" the fares of pupils attending public and other schools were also paid. The *Everson* case seems in retrospect to be out of line with the First Amendment. Its result is appealing, as it allows aid to be given to needy children. Yet by the same token, public funds could be used to satisfy other needs of children in parochial schools—lunches, books, and tuition being obvious examples. Mr. Justice Rutledge stated in dissent what I think is durable First Amendment philosophy: "The reasons underlying the Amendment's policy have not vanished with time or diminished in force. ⊥Now as when it was adopted the price of religious freedom is double. It is that the church and religion shall live both within and upon that freedom. There cannot be freedom of religion, safeguarded by the state, and intervention by t' church or its agencies in the state's domain or dependency on its largesse. The great condition of religious liberty is that it be maintained free from sustenanc as also from other interferences, by the state. For when it comes to rest upon that secular foundation it vanishes with the resting. Public money devoted to payment of religious costs, educational or other, brings the quest for more. It brings too the struggle of sect against sect for the larger share or for any. Here one by numbers alone will benefit most, there another. That is precisely the history of societies which have had an established religion and dissident groups. It is the very thing Jefferson and Madison experienced and sought to guard against, whether in its blunt or in its more screened forms. The end of such strife cannot be other than to destroy the cherished liberty. The dominating group will achieve the dominant benefit; or all will embroil the state in their dissensions."

What New York does with this prayer is a break with that tradition. I therefore join the Court in reversing the judgment below.

Mr. Justice STEWART, dissenting.

A local school board in New York has provided that those pupils who wish to do so may join in a brief prayer at the beginning of each school day, acknowledging their dependence upon God and asking His blessing upon them ⊥and upon their parents, their teachers, and their country. The Court today decides that in permitting this brief nondenominational prayer the school board has violated the Constitution of the United States. I think this decision is wrong.

The Court does not hold, nor could it, that New York has interfered with the free exercise of anybody's religion. For the state courts have made clear that those who object to reciting the prayer must be entirely free of any compulsion to do so, including any "embarrassments and pressures." But the Court says that in permitting school children to say this simple prayer, the New York authorities have established "an official religion."

With all respect, I think the Court has misapplied a great constitutional principle. I cannot see how an "official religion" is established by letting those who want to say a prayer say it. On the contrary, I think that to deny the wish of these school children to join in reciting this prayer is to deny them the opportunity of sharing in the spiritual heritage of our Nation.

The Court's historical review of the quarrels over the Book of Common Prayer in England throws no light for me on the issue before us in this case. England had then and has now an established church. Equally unenlightening, I think, is the history of the early establishment and later rejection of an official church in our own States. For we deal here not with the establishment of a state church, which would, of course, be constitutionally impermissible, but with whether school children who want to begin their day by joining in prayer must be prohibited from doing so. Moreover, I think that the Court's task, in this as in all areas of constitutional adjudication, is not responsibly aided by the uncritical invocation of metaphors like the "wall of separation," a phrase nowhere ⌐446 to ⊥ be found in the Constitution. What is relevant to the issue here is not the history of an established church in sixteenth century England or in eighteenth century America, but the history of the religious traditions of our people, reflected in countless practices of the institutions and officials of our government.

At the opening of each day's Session of this Court we stand, while one of our officials invokes the protection of God. Since the days of John Marshall our Crier has said, "God save the United States and this Honorable Court." Both the Senate and the House of Representatives open their daily Sessions with prayer. Each of our Presidents, from George Washington to John F. Kennedy, has upon assuming his Office asked the protection and help of God.

⌐449 ⊥ The Court today says that the state and federal governments are without constitutional power to prescribe any particular form of words to be recited by any group of the American people on any subject touching religion. One of the stanzas of "The Star-Spangled Banner," made our National Anthem by Act of Congress in 1931, contains these verses:

"Blest with victory and peace, may the heav'n rescued land

Praise the Pow'r that hath made and preserved us a nation!

Then conquer we must, when our cause it is just,
And this be our motto 'In God is our Trust.' "

In 1954 Congress added a phrase to the Pledge of Allegiance to the Flag so that it now contains the words "one Nation *under God*, indivisible, with liberty and justice for all." In 1952 Congress enacted legislation calling upon the President each year to proclaim a National Day of Prayer. Since 1865 the words "IN GOD WE TRUST" have been impressed on our coins.

⊥ Countless similar examples could be listed, but ⌐14 there is no need to belabor the obvious. It was all summed up by this Court just ten years ago in a single sentence: "We are a religious people whose institutions presuppose a Supreme Being." *Zorach* v. *Clauson*

I do not believe that this Court, or the Congress, or the President has by the actions and practices I have mentioned established an "official religion" in violation of the Constitution. And I do not believe the State of New York has done so in this case. What each has done has been to recognize and to follow the deeply entrenched and highly cherished spiritual traditions of our Nation—traditions which come down to us from those who almost two hundred years ago avowed their "firm Reliance on the Protection of divine Providence" when they proclaimed the freedom and independence of this brave new world.

I dissent.

ABINGTON TOWNSHIP SCHOOL DISTRICT v. SCHEMPP

374 U.S. 203
ON APPEAL FROM THE UNITED STATES
DISTRICT COURT FOR THE
EASTERN DISTRICT OF PENNSYLVANIA
Argued February 27-28, 1963 — Decided June 17, 1963

⊥ *Mr. Justice CLARK* delivered the opinion of the ⌐2 Court.

Once again we are called upon to consider the scope of the provision of the First Amendment to the United States Constitution which declares that "Congress shall make no law respecting an establishment of religion, or prohibiting the free exercise thereof. . . ." These companion cases present the issues in the context of state action requiring that schools begin each day with readings from the Bible. While raising the basic questions under slightly different factual situations, the cases permit of joint treatment. In light of the history of the First Amendment and of our cases interpreting and applying its requirements, we hold that the practices at issue and the laws requiring them are unconstitutional under the Establishment Clause, as applied to the States through the Fourteenth Amendment.

I

The Facts in Each Case: No. 142. The Commonwealth of Pennsylvania by law, requires that "At least ten verses from the Holy Bible shall be read, without comment, at the opening of each public school on each school day. Any child shall be excused from such Bible reading, or attending such Bible reading, upon the written request of his parent or guardian." The Schempp family, husband and wife and two of their three children, brought suit to enjoin enforcement of the statute, contending that their rights under the Fourteenth Amendment to the Constitution of the United States are, have been, and will continue to be violated unless this statute be declared unconstitutional as violative of these provisions of the First Amendment. They sought to enjoin the appellant school district, wherein the Schempp children attend school, and its officers and the ⊥206 ⊥Superintendent of Public Instruction of the Commonwealth from continuing to conduct such readings and recitation of the Lord's Prayer in the public schools of the district pursuant to the statute. A three-judge statutory District Court for the Eastern District of Pennsylvania held that the statute is violative of the Establishment Clause of the First Amendment as applied to the States by the Due Process Clause of the Fourteenth Amendment and directed that appropriate injunctive relief issue. On appeal by the District, its officials and the Superintendent, we noted probable jurisdiction.

The appellees Edward Lewis Schempp, his wife Sidney, and their children, Roger and Donna, are of the Unitarian faith and are members of the Unitarian Church in Germantown, Philadelphia, Pennsylvania, where they, as well as another son, Ellory, regularly attend religious services. The latter was originally a party but having graduated from the school system *pendente lite* was voluntarily dismissed from the action. The other children attend the Abington Senior High School, which is a public school operated by appellant district.

On each school day at the Abington Senior High School between 8:15 and 8:30 a.m., while the pupils are attending their home rooms or advisory sections, ⊥207 opening exer⊥cises are conducted pursuant to the statute. The exercises are broadcast into each room in the school building through an intercommunications system and are conducted under the supervision of a teacher by students attending the school's radio and television workshop. Selected students from this course gather each morning in the school's workshop studio for the exercises, which include readings by one of the students of 10 verses of the Holy Bible, broadcast to each room in the building. This is followed by the recitation of the Lord's Prayer, likewise over the intercommunications system, but also by the students in the various classrooms, who are asked to stand and join in repeating the prayer in unison. The exercises are closed with the flag salute and such pertinent announcements as are of interest to the students. Participation in the opening exercises, as directed by the statute, is voluntary. The student reading the verses from the Bible may select the passages and read from any version he chooses, although the only copies furnished by the school are the King James version, copies of which were circulated to each teacher by the school district. During the period in which the exercises have been conducted the King James, the Douay and

the Revised Standard versions of the Bible have been used, as well as the Jewish Holy Scriptures. There are no prefatory statements, no questions asked or solicited, no comments or explanations made and no interpretations given at or during the exercises. The students and parents are advised that the student may absent himself from the classroom or, should he elect to remain, not participate in the exercises.

It appears from the record that in schools not having an intercommunications system the Bible reading and the recitation of the Lord's Prayer were conducted by the ⊥home-room teacher, who chose ⊥208 the text of the verses and read them herself or had students read them in rotation or by volunteers. This was followed by a standing recitation of the Lord's Prayer, together with the Pledge of Allegiance to the Flag by the class in unison and a closing announcement of routine school items of interest.

At the first trial Edward Schempp and the children testified as to specific religious doctrines purveyed by a literal reading of the Bible "which were contrary to the religious beliefs which they held and to their familial teaching." The children testified that all of the doctrines to which they referred were read to them at various times as part of the exercises. Edward Schempp testified at the second trial that he had considered having Roger and Donna excused from attendance at the exercises but decided against it for several reasons, including his belief that the children's relationships with their teachers and classmates would be adversely affected.

⊥Expert testimony was introduced by both ap- ⊥209 pellants and appellees at the first trial, which testimony was summarized by the trial court as follows: "Dr. Solomon Grayzel testified that there were marked differences between the Jewish Holy Scriptures and the Christian Holy Bible, the most obvious of which was the absence of the New Testament in the Jewish Holy Scriptures. Dr. Grayzel testified that portions of the New Testament were offensive to Jewish tradition and that, from the standpoint of Jewish faith, the concept of Jesus Christ as the Son of God was 'practically blasphemous.' He cited instances in the New Testament which, assertedly, were not only sectarian in nature but tended to bring the Jews into ridicule or scorn. Dr. Grayzel gave as his expert opinion that such material from the New Testament could be explained to Jewish children in such a way as to do no harm to them. But if portions of the New Testament were read without explanation, they could be, and in his specific experience with children Dr. Grayzel observed, had been, psychologically harmful to the child and had caused a divisive force within the social media of the school.

"Dr. Grayzel also testified that there was significant difference in attitude with regard to the respective Books of the Jewish and Christian Religions in that Judaism attaches no special significance to the reading of the Bible *per se* and that the Jewish Holy Scriptures are source materials to be studied. But Dr. Grayzel did state that many ⌐210 portions of the New, ⊥as well as of the Old, Testament contained passages of great literary and moral value.

"Dr. Luther A. Weigle, an expert witness for the defense, testified in some detail as to the reasons for and the methods employed in developing the King James and the Revised Standard Versions of the Bible. On direct examination, Dr. Weigle stated that the Bible was non-sectarian. He later stated that the phrase 'non-sectarian' meant to him non-sectarian within the Christian faiths. Dr. Weigle stated that his definition of the Holy Bible would include the Jewish Holy Scriptures, but also stated that the 'Holy Bible' would not be complete without the New Testament. He stated that the New Testament 'conveyed the message of Christians.' In his opinion, reading of the Holy Scriptures to the exclusion of the New Testament would be a sectarian practice. Dr. Weigle stated that the Bible was of great moral, historical and literary value. This is conceded by all the parties and is also the view of the court."

The trial court, in striking down the practices and the statute requiring them, made specific findings of fact that the children's attendance at Abington Senior High School is compulsory and that the practice of reading 10 verses from the Bible is also compelled by law. It also found that: "The reading of the verses, even without comment, possesses a devotional and religious character and constitutes in effect a religious observance. The devotional and religious nature of the morning exercises is made all the more apparent by the fact that the Bible reading is followed immediately by a recital in unison by the pupils of the Lord's Prayer. The fact that some pupils, or theoretically all pupils, might be excused ⌐211 from attendance at the exercises ⊥does not mitigate the obligatory nature of the ceremony for . . . Section 1516 . . . unequivocally requires the exercises to be held every school day in every school in the Commonwealth. The exercises are held in the school buildings and perforce are conducted by and under the authority of the local school authorities and during school sessions. Since the statute requires the reading of the 'Holy Bible,' a Christian document, the practice . . . prefers the Christian religion. The record demonstrates that it was the intention of . . . the Commonwealth . . . to introduce a religious ceremony into the public schools of the Commonwealth."

No. 119. In 1905 the Board of School Commissioners of Baltimore City adopted a rule pursuant to Art. 77, § 202 of the Annotated Code of Maryland. The rule provided for the holding of opening exercises in the schools of the city, consisting primarily of the "reading, without comment, of a chapter in the Holy Bible and/or the use of the Lord's Prayer." The petitioners, Mrs. Madalyn Murray and her son, William J. Murray III, are both professed atheists.

Following unsuccessful attempts to have the respondent school board rescind the rule, this suit was filed for mandamus to compel its rescission and cancellation. It was alleged that William was a student in a public school of the city and Mrs. Murray, his mother, was a taxpayer therein; that it was the practice under the rule to have a reading on each school morning from the King James version of the Bible; that at petitioners' insistence the rule was amended to permit children to ⊥be excused from the exercise ⌐212 on request of the parent and that William had been excused pursuant thereto; that nevertheless the rule as amended was in violation of the petitioners' rights "to freedom of religion under the First and Fourteenth Amendments" and in violation of "the principle of separation between church and state, contained therein. . . ." The petition particularized the petitioners' atheistic beliefs and stated that the rule, as practiced, violated their rights "in that it threatens their religious liberty by placing a premium on belief as against non-belief and subjects their freedom of conscience to the rule of the majority; it pronounces belief in God as the source of all moral and spiritual values, equating these values with religious values, and thereby renders sinister, alien and suspect the beliefs and ideals of your Petitioners, promoting doubt and question of their morality, good citizenship and good faith."

The respondents demurred and the trial court, recognizing that the demurrer admitted all facts well pleaded, sustained it without leave to amend. The Maryland Court of Appeals affirmed, the majority of four justices holding the exercise not in violation of the First and Fourteenth Amendments, with three justices dissenting. We granted certiorari.

II

It is true that religion has been closely identified with our history and government. As we said in *Engel* v. *Vitale*, "The history of man is inseparable from the history of religion. And . . . since ⊥the ⌐213 beginning of that history many people have devoutly believed that "More things are wrought by prayer than this world dreams of." In *Zorach* v. *Clauson* we gave specific recognition to the proposition that "[w]e are a religious people whose institutions presuppose a Supreme Being." The fact that the Founding Fathers believed devotedly that there was a God and that the unalienable rights of man were rooted in Him is clearly evidenced in their writings, from the Mayflower Compact to the Constitution itself. This background is evidenced today in our public life through the continuance in our oaths of office from the Presidency to the Alderman of the final supplication, "So help me God." Likewise each House of the Congress provides through its Chaplain an opening prayer, and the sessions of this Court are declared open by the crier in a short ceremony, the final phrase of which invokes the grace of God. Again, there are such manifestations in our military forces, where those of our citizens who are under the restrictions of military service wish to engage in voluntary worship. Indeed, only last year an official survey of the country indicated that 64% of our people have church membership, while less than 3% profess no religion whatever. It can be truly said, therefore, that today, as in the beginning, our national life reflects a religious people who, in the words of Madison, are "earnestly praying, as . . . in duty bound, that the Supreme Lawgiver of the Universe . . . guide them into every measure which may be worthy of his [blessing. . . .]" Memorial and Remonstrance Against Religious Assessments.

⊥214 ⊥ This is not to say, however, that religion has been so identified with our history and government that religious freedom is not likewise as strongly imbedded in our public and private life. Nothing but the most telling of personal experiences in religious persecution suffered by our forebears, could have planted our belief in liberty of religious opinion any more deeply in our heritage. It is true that this liberty frequently was not realized by the colonists, but this is readily accountable by their close ties to the Mother Country. However, the views of Madison and Jefferson, preceded by Roger Williams, came to be incorporated not only in the Federal Constitution but likewise in those of most of our States. This freedom to worship was indispensable in a country whose people came from the four quarters of the earth and brought with them a diversity of religious opinion. Today authorities list 83 separate religious bodies, each with membership exceeding 50,000, existing among our people, as well as innumerable smaller groups.

III

Almost a hundred years ago in *Minor* v. *Board of Education of Cincinnati*, Judge Alphonso Taft, fa-
⊥215 ther ⊥ of the revered Chief Justice, in an unpublished opinion stated the ideal of our people as to religious freedom as one of "absolute equality before the law, of all religious opinions and sects. . . .

"The government is neutral, and, while protecting all, it prefers none, and it *disparages* none."

Before examining this "neutral" position in which the Establishment and Free Exercise Clauses of the First Amendment place our Government it is well that we discuss the reach of the Amendment under the cases of this Court.

First, this Court has decisively settled that the First Amendment's mandate that "Congress shall make no law respecting an establishment of religion, or prohibiting the free exercise thereof" has been made wholly applicable to the States by the Fourteenth Amendment. Twenty-three years ago in *Cantwell* v. *Connecticut*, this Court, through Mr. Justice Roberts, said: "The fundamental concept of liberty embodied in that [Fourteenth] Amendment embraces the liberties guaranteed by the First Amendment. The First Amendment declares that Congress shall

make no law respecting an establishment of religion or prohibiting the free exercise thereof. The Fourteenth Amend⊥ment has rendered the legislatures ⊥216 of the states as incompetent as Congress to enact such laws. . . ."

In a series of cases since *Cantwell* the Court has repeatedly reaffirmed that doctrine, and we do so now.

Second, this Court has rejected unequivocally the contention that the Establishment Clause forbids only governmental preference of one religion over another. Almost 20 years ago in *Everson*, the Court said that "[n]either a state nor the Federal Government can set up a church. Neither can pass laws which aid one religion, aid all religions, or prefer one religion over another." And Mr. Justice Jackson, dissenting, agreed: "There is no answer to the proposition . . . that the effect of the religious freedom Amendment to our Constitution was to take every form or propagation of religion out of the realm of things which could directly or indirectly be made public business and thereby be supported in whole or in part at taxpayers' expense. . . . This freedom was first in the Bill of Rights because it was first in the forefathers' minds; it was set forth in absolute terms, and its strength is its rigidity."

⊥ Further, Mr. Justice Rutledge, joined by Justices ⊥217 Frankfurter, Jackson and Burton, declared: "The [First] Amendment's purpose was not to strike merely at the official establishment of a single sect, creed or religion, outlawing only a formal relation such as had prevailed in England and some of the colonies. Necessarily it was to uproot all such relationships. But the object was broader than separating church and state in this narrow sense. It was to create a complete and permanent separation of the spheres of religious activity and civil authority by comprehensively forbidding every form of public aid or support for religion."

The same conclusion has been firmly maintained ever since that time and we reaffirm it now.

While none of the parties to either of these cases has questioned these basic conclusions of the Court, both of which have been long established, recognized and consistently reaffirmed, others continue to question their history, logic and efficacy. Such contentions, in the light of the consistent interpretation in cases of this Court, seem entirely untenable and of value only as academic exercises.

IV

The interrelationship of the Establishment and the Free Exercise Clauses was first touched upon by Mr. Justice Roberts for the Court in *Cantwell* v. *Connecticut*, where it was said that their "inhibition of legislation" had "a double aspect. On the one hand, it forestalls compulsion by law of the acceptance of any creed or the practice of any form of worship. Freedom of ⊥ conscience and freedom to ⊥218 adhere to such religious organization or form of worship as the individual may choose cannot be restricted by law. On the other hand, it safeguards the free exercise of the chosen form of religion. Thus the Amendment embraces two concepts,—freedom to believe and freedom to act. The first is absolute but, in the nature of things, the second cannot be."

A half dozen years later in *Everson* v. *Board of Education*, this Court, through *Mr. Justice BLACK*, stated that the "scope of the First Amendment . . . was designed forever to suppress" the establishment of religion or the prohibition of the free exercise thereof. In short, the Court held that the Amendment "requires the state to be a neutral in its relations with groups of religious believers and nonbelievers; it does not require the state to be their adversary. State power is no more to be used so as to handicap religions than it is to favor them."

And Mr. Justice Jackson, in dissent, declared that public schools are organized "on the premise that secular education can be isolated from all religious teaching so that the school can inculcate all needed temporal knowledge and also maintain a strict and lofty neutrality as to religion. The assumption is that after the individual has been instructed in worldly wisdom he will be better fitted to choose his religion."

Moreover, all of the four dissenters, speaking through Mr. Justice Rutledge, agreed that "Our constitutional policy . . . does not deny the value or the necessity for religious training, teaching or observance. Rather it secures their free exercise. But to that end it does deny that the state can undertake or sustain them in any form or degree. For this ⌊219 ⊥ reason the sphere of religious activity, as distinguished from the secular intellectual liberties, has been given the twofold protection and, as the state cannot forbid, neither can it perform or aid in performing the religious function. The dual prohibition makes that function altogether private."

Only one year later the Court was asked to reconsider and repudiate the doctrine of these cases in *McCollum* v. *Board of Education*. It was argued that "historically the First Amendment was intended to forbid only government preference of one religion over another. . . . In addition they ask that we distinguish or overrule our holding in the *Everson* case that the Fourteenth Amendment made the 'establishment of religion' clause of the First Amendment applicable as a prohibition against the States." The Court, with Mr. Justice Reed alone dissenting, was unable to "accept either of these contentions. Mr. Justice Frankfurter, joined by Justices Jackson, Rutledge and Burton, wrote a very comprehensive and scholarly concurrence in which he said that "[s]eparation is a requirement to abstain from fusing functions of Government and of religious sects, not merely to treat them all equally." Continuing, he stated that: "the Constitution . . . prohibited the Government common to all from becoming embroiled, however innocently, in the destructive reli-

gious conflicts of which the history of even this country records some dark pages."

In 1952 in *Zorach* v. *Clauson*, Mr. Justice DOUGLAS for the Court reiterated: "There cannot be the slightest doubt that the First Amendment reflects the philosophy that Church and State should be separated. And so far as interference with the 'free exercise' of religion and an ⊥ 'establishment' of religion ⌋220 are concerned, the separation must be complete and unequivocal. The First Amendment within the scope of its coverage permits no exception; the prohibition is absolute. The First Amendment, however, does not say that in every and all respects there shall be a separation of Church and State. Rather, it studiously defines the manner, the specific ways, in which there shall be no concert or union or dependency one on the other. That is the common sense of the matter."

And then in 1961 in *McGowan* v. *Maryland* and in *Torcaso* v. *Watkins* each of these cases was discussed and approved. *Chief Justice WARREN* in *McGowan*, for a unanimous Court on this point, said: "But, the First Amendment, in its final form, did not simply bar a congressional enactment *establishing a church*; it forbade all laws *respecting an establishment of religion*. Thus, this Court has given the Amendment a 'broad interpretation . . . in the light of its history and the evils it was designed forever to suppress. . . .' "

And *Mr. Justice BLACK* for the Court in *Torcaso*, without dissent but with Justices Frankfurter and *HARLAN* concurring in the result, used this language: "We repeat and again reaffirm that neither a State nor the Federal Government can constitutionally force a person 'to profess a belief or disbelief in any religion.' Neither can constitutionally pass laws or impose requirements which aid all religions as against nonbelievers, and neither can aid those religions based on a belief in the existence of God as against those religions founded on different beliefs."

Finally, in *Engel* v. *Vitale*, only last year, these principles were so universally recognized that the Court, with ⊥out the citation of a single case and ⌋221 over the sole dissent of *Mr. Justice STEWART*, reaffirmed them. The Court found the 22-word prayer used in "New York's program of daily classroom invocation of God's blessings as prescribed in the Regents' prayer . . . [to be] a religious activity." It held that "it is no part of the business of government to compose official prayers for any group of the American people to recite as a part of a religious program carried on by government." In discussing the reach of the Establishment and Free Exercise Clauses of the First Amendment the Court said: "Although these two clauses may in certain instances overlap, they forbid two quite different kinds of governmental encroachment upon religious freedom. The Establishment Clause, unlike the Free Exercise Clause, does not depend upon any showing of direct governmental compulsion and is violated by the enactment of laws which establish an official religion whether those laws operate directly to coerce non-observing individuals or not. This is not to say, of course, that laws officially prescribing a particular form of religious worship do not involve coercion of such individuals. When the power, prestige and financial support of government is placed behind a particular religious belief, the indirect coercive pressure upon religious minorities to conform to the prevailing officially approved religion is plain."

And in further elaboration the Court found that the "first and most immediate purpose [of the Establishment Clause] rested on the belief that a union of government and religion tends to destroy government and to degrade religion." When government, the Court said, allies itself with one particular form of religion, the ⊥ inevitable result is that it incurs "the hatred, disrespect and even contempt of those who held contrary beliefs."

⌊222

V

The wholesome "neutrality" of which this Court's cases speak thus stems from a recognition of the teachings of history that powerful sects or groups might bring about a fusion of governmental and religious functions or a concert or dependency of one upon the other to the end that official support of the State or Federal Government would be placed behind the tenets of one or of all orthodoxies. This the Establishment Clause prohibits. And a further reason for neutrality is found in the Free Exercise Clause, which recognizes the value of religious training, teaching and observance and, more particularly, the right of every person to freely choose his own course with reference thereto, free of any compulsion from the state. This the Free Exercise Clause guarantees. Thus, as we have seen, the two clauses may overlap. As we have indicated, the Establishment Clause has been directly considered by this Court eight times in the past score of years and, with only one Justice dissenting on the point, it has consistently held that the clause withdrew all legislative power respecting religious belief or the expression thereof. The test may be stated as follows: what are the purpose and the primary effect of the enactment? If either is the advancement or inhibition of religion then the enactment exceeds the scope of legislative power as circumscribed by the Constitution. That is to say that to withstand the strictures of the Establishment Clause there must be a secular legislative purpose and a primary effect that neither advances nor inhibits religion. The Free Exercise Clause, likewise considered many times here, withdraws from legislative power, state and federal, the exertion of any restraint on the free exer ⊥ cise of religion. Its purpose is to secure religious liberty in the individual by prohibiting any invasions thereof by civil authority, Hence it is necessary in a free exercise case for one to show the coercive effect of the enactment as it operates against him in the practice of his religion. The distinction between the two clauses is

⌊223

apparent—a violation of the Free Exercise Clause is predicated on coercion while the Establishment Clause violation need not be so attended.

Applying the Establishment Clause principles to the cases at bar we find that the States are requiring the selection and reading at the opening of the school day of verses from the Holy Bible and the recitation of the Lord's Prayer by the students in unison. These exercises are prescribed as part of the curricular activities of students who are required by law to attend school. They are held in the school buildings under the supervision and with the participation of teachers employed in those schools. None of these factors, other than compulsory school attendance, was present in the program upheld in *Zorach v. Clauson*. The trial court in No. 142 has found that such an opening exercise is a religious ceremony and was intended by the State to be so. We agree with the trial court's finding as to the religious character of the exercises. Given that finding, the exercises and the law requiring them are in violation of the Establishment Clause.

There is no such specific finding as to the religious character of the exercises in No. 119, and the State contends (as does the State in No. 142) that the program is an effort to extend its benefits to all public school children without regard to their religious belief. Included within its secular purposes, it says, are the promotion of moral values, the contradiction to the materialistic trends of our times, the perpetuation of our institutions and the teaching of literature. The case came up ⊥ on demurrer, of course, to a petition which alleged that the uniform practice under the rule had been to read from the King James version of the Bible and that the exercise was sectarian. The short answer, therefore, is that the religious character of the exercise was admitted by the State. But even if its purpose is not strictly religious, it is sought to be accomplished through readings, without comment, from the Bible. Surely the place of the Bible as an instrument of religion cannot be gainsaid, and the State's recognition of the pervading religious character of the ceremony is evident from the rule's specific permission of the alternative use of the Catholic Douay version as well as the recent amendment permitting nonattendance at the exercises. None of these factors is consistent with the contention that the Bible is here used either as an instrument for nonreligious moral inspiration or as a reference for the teaching of secular subjects.

⌊224

The conclusion follows that in both cases the laws require religious exercises and such exercises are being conducted in direct violation of the rights of the appellees and petitioners. Nor are these required exercises mitigated by the fact that individual students may absent ⊥ themselves upon a parental request, for that fact furnishes no defense to a claim of unconstitutionality under the Establishment Clause. Further, it is no defense to urge that the religious practices here may be relatively minor encroach-

⌊225

ments on the First Amendment. The breach of neutrality that is today a trickling stream may all too soon become a raging torrent and, in the words of Madison, "it is proper to take alarm at the first experiment on our liberties."

It is insisted that unless these religious exercises are permitted a "religion of secularism" is established in the schools. We agree of course that the State may not establish a "religion of secularism" in the sense of affirmatively opposing or showing hostility to religion, thus "preferring those who believe in no religion over those who do believe." *Zorach* v. *Clauson* We do not agree, however, that this decision in any sense has that effect. In addition, it might well be said that one's education is not complete without a study of comparative religion or the history of religion and its relationship to the advancement of civilization. It certainly may be said that the Bible is worthy of study for its literary and historic qualities. Nothing we have said here indicates that such study of the Bible or of religion, when presented objectively as part of a secular program of education, may not be effected consistently with the First Amendment. But the exercises here do not fall into those categories. They are religious exercises, required by the States in violation of the command of the First Amendment that the Government maintain strict neutrality, neither aiding nor opposing religion.

Finally, we cannot accept that the concept of neutrality, which does not permit a State to require a religious exercise even with the consent of the majority of those ⊥ affected, collides with the majority's right to free exercise of religion. While the Free Exercise Clause clearly prohibits the use of state action to deny the rights of free exercise to *anyone*, it has never meant that a majority could use the machinery of the State to practice its beliefs. Such a contention was effectively answered by Mr. Justice Jackson for the Court in *West Virginia Board of Education* v. *Barnette*: "The very purpose of a Bill of Rights was to withdraw certain subjects from the vicissitudes of political controversy, to place them beyond the reach of majorities and officials and to establish them as legal principles to be applied by the courts. One's right to . . . freedom of worship . . . and other fundamental rights may not be submitted to vote; they depend on the outcome of no elections."

The place of religion in our society is an exalted one, achieved through a long tradition of reliance on the home, the church and the inviolable citadel of the individual heart and mind. We have come to recognize through bitter experience that it is not within the power of government to invade that citadel, whether its purpose or effect be to aid or oppose, to advance or retard. In the relationship between man and religion, the State is firmly committed to a position of neutrality. Though the application of that rule requires interpretation of a delicate sort, the rule itself is clearly and concisely stated in the words of

⊥226

the First Amendment. Applying that rule to the facts of these cases, we affirm the judgment in No. 142. ⊥ In No. 119, the judgment is reversed and the cause remanded to the Maryland Court of Appeals for further proceedings consistent with this opinion.

It is so ordered.

Mr. Justice DOUGLAS, concurring. I join the opinion of the Court and add a few words in explanation.

While the Free Exercise Clause of the First Amendment is written in terms of what the State may not require of the individual, the Establishment Clause, serving the same goal of individual religious freedom, is written in different terms.

Establishment of a religion can be achieved in several ways. The church and state can be one; the church may control the state or the state may control the church; or the relationship may take one of several possible forms of a working arrangement between the two bodies. Under all of these arrangements the church typically has a place in the state's budget, and church law usually governs such matters as baptism, marriage, divorce and separation, at least for its members and sometimes for the entire body politic. Education, too, is usually high on the priority ⊥ list of church interests. In the past schools were often made the exclusive responsibility of the church. Today in some state-church countries the state runs the public schools, but compulsory religious exercises are often required of some or all students. . . .

The vice of all such arrangements under the Establishment Clause is that the state is lending its assistance to a church's efforts to gain and keep adherents. Under the First Amendment it is strictly a matter for the individual and his church as to what church he will belong to and how much support, in the way of belief, time, activity or money, he will give to it. "This pure Religious Liberty" "declared . . . [all forms of church-state relationships] and their fundamental idea to be oppressions of conscience and abridgments of that liberty which God and nature had conferred on every living soul."

In these cases we have no coercive religious exercise aimed at making the students conform. The prayers announced are not compulsory, though some may think they have that indirect effect because the nonconformist student may be induced to participate for fear of being called an "oddball." But that coercion, if it be present, ⊥ has not been shown; so the vices of the present regimes are different.

These regimes violate the Establishment Clause in two different ways. In each case the State is conducting a religious exercise; and, as the Court holds, that cannot be done without violating the "neutrality" required of the State by the balance of power between individual, church and state that has been struck by the First Amendment. But the Establishment Clause is not limited to precluding the State it-self from conducting religious exercises. It also forbids the State to employ its facilities or funds in a way that gives any church, or all churches, greater strength in our society than it would have by relying on its members alone. Thus, the present regimes must fall under that clause for the additional reason that public funds, though small in amount, are being used to promote a religious exercise. Through the mechanism of the State, all of the people are being required to finance a religious exercise that only some of the people want and that violates the sensibilities of others.

The most effective way to establish any institution is to finance it, and this truth is reflected in the appeals by church groups for public funds to finance their religious schools. Financing a church either in its strictly religious activities or in its other activities is equally unconstitutional, as I understand the Establishment Clause. Budgets for one activity may be technically separable from budgets for others. But the institution is an inseparable whole, a living organism, which is strengthened in proselytizing when it is strengthened in any department by contributions from other than its own members.

⊥230 ⊥ Such contributions may not be made by the State even in a minor degree without violating the Establishment Clause. It is not the amount of public funds expended; as this case illustrates, it is the use to which public funds are put that is controlling. For the First Amendment does not say that some forms of establishment are allowed; it says that "no law respecting an establishment of religion" shall be made. What may not be done directly may not be done indirectly lest the Establishment Clause become a mockery.

Mr. Justice BRENNAN, concurring.

Almost a century and a half ago, John Marshall, in *M'Culloch* v. *Maryland*, enjoined: ". . . we must never forget, that it is *a constitution* we are expounding." The Court's historic duty to expound the meaning of the Constitution has encountered few issues more intricate or more demanding than that of the relationship between religion and the public schools. Since undoubtedly we are "a religious people whose institutions presuppose a Supreme Being," *Zorach* v. *Clauson*, deep feelings are aroused when aspects of that relationship are claimed to violate the injunction of the First Amendment that government may make "no law respecting an establishment of religion, or prohibiting the free exercise thereof. . . ." Americans regard the public schools as a most vital civic institution for the preservation of a democratic system of government. It is therefore understandable that the constitutional prohibitions encounter their severest test when they are sought to be applied in the school classroom. Nevertheless it is this Court's inescapable duty to declare whether exercises in the

public schools of the States, such as those of Pennsylvania and Maryland questioned here, are involvements of religion in public institutions of a kind which offends the First and Fourteenth Amendments.

⊥ When John Locke ventured in 1689, "I esteem it ⊥231 above all things necessary to distinguish exactly the business of civil government from that of religion and to settle the just bounds that lie between the one and the other," he anticipated the necessity which would be thought by the Framers to require adoption of a First Amendment, but not the difficulty that would be experienced in defining those "just bounds." The fact is that the line which separates the secular from the sectarian in American life is elusive. The difficulty of defining the boundary with precision inheres in a paradox central to our scheme of liberty. While our institutions reflect a firm conviction that we are a religious people, those institutions by solemn constitutional injunction may not officially involve religion in such a way as to prefer, discriminate against, or oppress, a particular sect or religion. Equally the Constitution enjoins those involvements of religious with secular institutions which (a) serve the essentially religious activities of religious institutions; (b) employ the organs of government for essentially religious purposes; or (c) use essentially religious means to serve governmental ends where secular means would suffice. The constitutional mandate expresses a deliberate and considered judgment that such matters are to be left to the conscience of the citizen, and declares as a basic postulate of the relation between the citizen and his government that "the rights of conscience are, in their nature, of peculiar delicacy, and will little bear the gentlest touch of governmental hand. . . ."

I join fully in the opinion and the judgment of the Court. I see no escape from the conclusion that the exer⊥cises called in question in these two cases vio- ⊥232 late the constitutional mandate. The reasons we gave only last Term in *Engel* v. *Vitale* for finding in the New York Regents' prayer an impermissible establishment of religion, compel the same judgment of the practices at bar. The involvement of the secular with the religious is no less intimate here; and it is constitutionally irrelevant that the State has not composed the material for the inspirational exercises presently involved. It should be unnecessary to observe that our holding does not declare that the First Amendment manifests hostility to the practice or teaching of religion, but only applies prohibitions incorporated in the Bill of Rights in recognition of historic needs shared by Church and State alike. While it is my view that not every involvement of religion in public life is unconstitutional, I consider the exercises at bar a form of involvement which clearly violates the Establishment Clause.

The importance of the issue and the deep conviction with which views on both sides are held seem to me to justify detailing at some length my reasons for joining the Court's judgment and opinion.

I

The First Amendment forbids both the abridgment of the free exercise of religion and the enactment of laws "respecting an establishment of religion." The two clauses, although distinct in their objectives and their applicability, emerged together from a common panorama of history. The inclusion of both restraints upon the power of Congress to legislate concerning religious matters shows unmistakably that the Framers of the First Amendment were not content to rest the protection of religious liberty exclusively upon either clause. "In assuring the free exercise of religion," Mr. Justice Frankfurter ⌐233 has said, ⊥"the Framers of the First Amendment were sensitive to the then recent history of those persecutions and impositions of civil disability with which sectarian majorities in virtually all of the Colonies had visited deviation in the matter of conscience. This protection of unpopular creeds, however, was not to be the full extent of the Amendment's guarantee of freedom from governmental intrusion in matters of faith. The battle in Virginia, hardly four years won, where James Madison had led the forces of disestablishment in successful opposition to Patrick Henry's proposed Assessment Bill levying a general tax for the support of Christian teachers, was a vital and compelling memory in 1789." *McGowan* v. *Maryland*

It is true that the Framers' immediate concern was to prevent the setting up of an official federal church of the kind which England and some of the Colonies had long supported. But nothing in the text of the Establishment Clause supports the view that the prevention of the setting up of an official church was meant to be the full extent of the prohibitions against official involvements in religion. It has rightly been said: "If the framers of the Amendment meant to prohibit Congress merely from the establishment of a 'church,' one may properly wonder why they didn't so state. That the words *church* and *religion* were regarded as synonymous seems highly improbable, particularly in view of the fact that the contemporary state constitutional provisions dealing with the subject of establishment used definite phrases such as 'religious sect,' 'sect,' or 'denomination.' . . . With such specific wording in contemporary state constitutions, why was not a similar wording adopted for the First Amendment if its framers intended to prohibit nothing more than what ⌐234 the States were pro⊥hibiting?" Lardner, How Far Does the Constitution Separate Church and State? 45 Am. Pol. Sci. Rev. 110, 112 (1951).

Plainly, the Establishment Clause, in the contemplation of the Framers, "did not limit the constitutional proscription to any particular, dated form of state-supported theological venture." "What Virginia had long practiced, and what Madison, Jef-

ferson and others fought to end, was the extension of civil government's support to religion in a manner which made the two in some degree interdependent, and thus threatened the freedom of each. The purpose of the Establishment Clause was to assure that the national legislature would not exert its power in the service of any purely religious end; that it would not, as Virginia and virtually all of the Colonies had done, make of religion, as religion, an object of legislation. . . . The Establishment Clause withdrew from the sphere of legitimate legislative concern and competence a specific, but comprehensive, area of human conduct: man's belief or disbelief in the verity of some transcendental idea and man's expression in action of that belief or disbelief." *McGowan* v. *Maryland*

In sum, the history which our prior decisions have summoned to aid interpretation of the Establishment Clause permits little doubt that its prohibition was designed comprehensively to prevent those official involvements of religion which would tend to foster or discourage religious worship or belief.

But an awareness of history and an appreciation of the aims of the Founding Fathers do not always resolve concrete problems. The specific question before us has, for example, aroused vigorous dispute whether the architects of the First Amendment—James Madison and Thomas Jefferson particularly—understood the prohibition against any "law respecting an establishment of ⊥religion" to reach devotional exercises in the public schools. It may be that Jefferson and Madison would have held such exercises to be permissible—although even in Jefferson's case serious doubt is suggested by his admonition against "putting the Bible and Testament into the hands of the children at an age when their judgments are not sufficiently matured for religious inquiries. . . ." But ⊥I doubt that their view, even if perfectly clear one way or the other, would supply a dispositive answer to the question presented by these cases. A more fruitful inquiry, it seems to me, is whether the practices here challenged threaten those consequences which the Framers deeply feared; whether, in short, they tend to promote that type of interdependence between religion and state which the First Amendment was designed to prevent. Our task is to translate "the majestic generalities of the Bill of Rights, conceived as part of the pattern of liberal government in the eighteenth century, into concrete restraints on officials ⊥dealing with the problems of the twentieth century. . . ." *West Virginia State Board of Education* v. *Barnette*

A too literal quest for the advice of the Founding Fathers upon the issues of these cases seems to me futile and misdirected for several reasons: First, on our precise problem the historical record is at best ambiguous, and statements can readily be found to support either side of the proposition. The ambiguity of history is understandable if we recall the nature of the problems uppermost in the thinking of the statesmen who fashioned the religious guarantees; they were concerned with far more flagrant intrusions of government into the realm of religion than any that our century has witnessed. While it is clear to me that the Framers meant the Establishment Clause to prohibit more than the creation of an established federal church such as existed in England, I have no doubt that, in their preoccupation with the imminent question of established churches, they ⊥238 gave no dis⊥tinct consideration to the particular question whether the clause also forbade devotional exercises in public institutions.

Second, the structure of American education has greatly changed since the First Amendment was adopted. In the context of our modern emphasis upon public education available to all citizens, any views of the eighteenth century as to whether the exercises at bar are an "establishment" offer little aid to decision. Education, as the Framers knew it, was in the main confined to private schools more often than not under strictly sectarian supervision. Only gradually did control of education pass largely to ⊥239 public officials. It would, therefore, ⊥hardly be significant if the fact was that the nearly universal devotional exercises in the schools of the young Republic did not provoke criticism; even today religious ceremonies in church-supported private schools are constitutionally unobjectionable.

⊥240 ⊥Third, our religious composition makes us a vastly more diverse people than were our forefathers. They knew differences chiefly among Protestant sects. Today the Nation is far more heterogeneous religiously, including as it does substantial minorities not only of Catholics and Jews but as well of those who worship according to no version of the Bible ⊥241 and those who worship no God at all. ⊥In the face of such profound changes, practices which may have been objectionable to no one in the time of Jefferson and Madison may today be highly offensive to many persons, the deeply devout and the nonbelievers alike.

Whatever Jefferson or Madison would have thought of Bible reading or the recital of the Lord's Prayer in what few public schools existed in their day, our use of the history of their time must limit itself to broad purposes, not specific practices. By such a standard, I am persuaded, as is the Court, that the devotional exercises carried on in the Baltimore and Abington schools offend the First Amendment because they sufficiently threaten in our day those substantive evils the fear of which called forth the Establishment Clause of the First Amendment. It is "*a constitution* we are expounding," and our interpretation of the First Amendment must necessarily be responsive to the much more highly charged nature of religious questions in contemporary society.

Fourth, the American experiment in free public education available to all children has been guided in large measure by the dramatic evolution of the reli-

gious diversity among the population which our public schools serve. The interaction of these two important forces in our national life has placed in bold relief certain positive values in the consistent application to public institutions generally, and public schools particularly, of the constitutional decree against official involvements of religion which might produce the evils the Framers meant the Establishment Clause to forestall. The public schools are supported entirely, in most communities, by public funds—funds exacted not only from parents, nor alone from those who hold particular religious views, nor indeed from those who subscribe to any creed at all. It is implicit in the history and character of American public education that the public schools serve a uniquely ⊥*public* function: the training of ⊥242 American citizens in an atmosphere free of parochial, divisive, or separatist influences of any sort— an atmosphere in which children may assimilate a heritage common to all American groups and religions. This is a heritage neither theistic nor atheistic, but simply civic and patriotic.

Attendance at the public schools has never been compulsory; parents remain morally and constitutionally free to choose the academic environment in which they wish their children to be educated. The relationship of the Establishment Clause of the First Amendment to the public school system is preeminently that of reserving such a choice to the individual parent, rather than vesting it in the majority of voters of each State or school district. The choice which is thus preserved is between a public secular education with its uniquely democratic values, and some form of private or sectarian education, which offers values of its own. In my judgment the First Amendment forbids the State to inhibit that freedom of choice by diminishing the attractiveness of either alternative—either by restricting the liberty of the private schools to inculcate whatever values they wish, or by jeopardizing the freedom of the public schools from private or sectarian pressures. The choice between these very different forms of education is one—very much like the choice of whether or not to worship—which our Constitution leaves to the individual parent. It is no proper function of the state or local government to influence or restrict that election. The lesson of history—drawn more from the experiences of other countries than from its own—is that a system of free public education forfeits its unique contribution to the growth of democratic citizenship when that choice ceases to be freely available to each parent.

II

⊥The exposition by this Court of the religious ⊥243 guarantees of the First Amendment has consistently reflected and reaffirmed the concerns which impelled the Framers to write those guarantees into the Constitution. It would be neither possible nor appropriate to review here the entire course of our decisions on religious questions. There emerge from those decisions, however, three principles of particular relevance to the issue presented by the cases at bar, and some attention to those decisions is therefore appropriate.

First. One line of decisions derives from contests for control of a church property or other internal ecclesiastical disputes. This line has settled the proposition that in order to give effect to the First Amendment's purpose of requiring on the part of all organs of government a strict neutrality toward theological questions, courts should not undertake to decide such questions. These principles were first expounded in the case of *Watson* v. *Jones*, which declared that judicial intervention in such a controversy would open up "the whole subject of the doctrinal theology, the usages and customs, the written laws, and fundamental organization of every religious denomination. . . ." Courts above all must be neutral, for "[t]he law knows no heresy, and is committed to the support of no dogma, the establishment of no sect." This principle has re-
⊥244   ⊥cently been reaffirmed in *Kedroff* v. *St. Nicholas Cathedral*, and *Kreshik* v. *St. Nicholas Cathedral*.

The mandate of judicial neutrality in theological controversies met its severest test in *United States* v. *Ballard*. That decision put in sharp relief certain principles which bear directly upon the questions presented in these cases. Ballard was indicted for fraudulent use of the mails in the dissemination of religious literature. He requested that the trial court submit to the jury the question of the truthfulness of the religious views he championed. The requested charge was refused, and we upheld that refusal, reasoning that the First Amendment foreclosed any judicial inquiry into the truth or falsity of the defendant's religious beliefs. We said: "Man's relation to his God was made no concern of the state. He was granted the right to worship as he pleased and to answer to no man for the verity of his religious views." "Men may believe what they cannot
⊥245   ⊥prove. They may not be put to the proof of their religious doctrines or beliefs. . . . Many take their gospel from the New Testament. But it would hardly be supposed that they could be tried before a jury charged with the duty of determining whether those teachings contained false representations."

The dilemma presented by the case was severe. While the alleged truthfulness of *nonreligious* publications could ordinarily have been submitted to the jury, Ballard was deprived of that defense only because the First Amendment forbids governmental inquiry into the verity of *religious* beliefs. In dissent Mr. Justice Jackson expressed the concern that under this construction of the First Amendment "[p]rosecutions of this character easily could degenerate into religious persecution." The case shows how elusive is the line which enforces the Amendment's injunction of strict neutrality, while manifesting no official hostility toward religion—a

line which must be considered in the cases now before us. Some might view the result of the *Ballard* case as a manifestation of hostility—in that the conviction stood because the defense could not be raised. To others it ⊥might represent merely strict adher-   ⊥246
ence to the principle of neutrality already expounded in the cases involving doctrinal disputes. Inevitably, insistence upon neutrality, vital as it surely is for untrammeled religious liberty, may appear to border upon religious hostility. But in the long view the independence of both church and state in their respective spheres will be better served by close adherence to the neutrality principle. If the choice is often difficult, the difficulty is endemic to issues implicating the religious guarantees of the First Amendment. Freedom of religion will be seriously jeopardized if we admit exceptions for no better reason than the difficulty of delineating hostility from neutrality in the closest cases.

Second. It is only recently that our decisions have dealt with the question whether issues arising under the Establishment Clause may be isolated from problems implicating the Free Exercise Clause. *Everson* v. *Board of Education* is in my view the first of our decisions which treats a problem of asserted unconstitutional involvement as raising questions purely under the Establishment Clause. A scrutiny of several earlier decisions said by some to have etched the contours of the clause shows that such cases neither raised nor decided any constitutional issues under the First Amendment. *Bradfield* v. *Roberts*, for example, involved challenges to a federal grant to a hospital administered by a Roman Catholic order. The Court rejected the claim for lack of evidence that any sectarian influence changed its character as a secular institution chartered as such by the Congress. . . .

⊥[Another] case in this group is *Cochran* v.   ⊥248
Louisiana State Board, which involved a challenge to a state statute providing public funds to support a loan of free textbooks to pupils of both public and private schools. The constitutional issues in this Court extended no further than the claim that this program amounted to a taking of private property for nonpublic use. The Court rejected the claim on the ground that no private use of property was involved; ". . . we can not doubt that the taxing power of the State is exerted for a public purpose." The case therefore raised no issue under the First Amendment.

In *Pierce* v. *Society of Sisters*, a Catholic parochial school and a private but nonsectarian military academy challenged a state law requiring all children between certain ages to attend the public schools. This Court held the law invalid as an arbitrary and unreasonable interference both with the rights of the schools and with the liberty of the parents of the children who attended them. The due process guarantee of the Fourteenth Amendment "excludes any general power of the State to standardize its children by forcing them to accept instruction from public teachers only." While one of the plaintiffs was indeed a parochial school, the case obviously decided no First Amendment question but recognized only the constitutional right to establish and patronize private schools—including parochial schools—which meet the state's reasonable minimum curricular requirements.

249 ⊥ *Third.* It is true, as the Court says, that the "two clauses [Establishment and Free Exercise] may overlap." Because of the overlap, however, our decisions under the Free Exercise Clause bear considerable relevance to the problem now before us, and should be briefly reviewed. The early free exercise cases generally involved the objections of religious minorities to the application to them of general non-religious legislation governing conduct. *Reynolds* v. *United States* involved the claim that a belief in the sanctity of plural marriage precluded the conviction of members of a particular sect under nondiscriminatory legislation against such marriage. The Court rejected the claim, saying: "Laws are made for the government of actions, and while they cannot interfere with mere religious beliefs and opinions, they may with practices. . . . Can a man excuse his practices to the contrary because of his religious belief? To permit this would be to make the professed doctrines of religious belief superior to the law of the land, and in effect to permit every citizen to become a law unto himself. Government could exist only in name under such circumstances."

250 ⊥ *Davis* v. *Beason* similarly involved the claim that the First Amendment insulated from civil punishment certain practices inspired or motivated by religious beliefs. The claim was easily rejected: "It was never intended or supposed that the amendment could be invoked as a protection against legislation for the punishment of acts inimical to the peace, good order and morals of society."

But we must not confuse the issue of governmental power to regulate or prohibit conduct *motivated by religious beliefs* with the quite different problem of governmental authority to compel behavior *offensive to religious principles.* In *Hamilton* v. *Regents of the University of California,* the question was that of the power of a State to compel students at the State University to participate in military training instruction against their religious convictions. The validity of the statute was sustained against claims based upon the First Amendment. But the decision rested on a very narrow principle: since there was neither a constitutional right nor a legal obligation to attend the State University, the obligation to participate in

251 military training courses, ⊥reflecting a legitimate state interest, might properly be imposed upon those who chose to attend. Although the rights protected by the First and Fourteenth Amendments were presumed to include "the right to entertain the beliefs, to adhere to the principles and to teach the doctrines on which these students base their objections to the

order prescribing military training," those Amendments were construed not to free such students from the military training obligations if they chose to attend the University. Justices Brandeis, Cardozo and Stone, concurring separately, agreed that the requirement infringed no constitutionally protected liberties. They added, however, that the case presented no question under the Establishment Clause. The military instruction program was not an establishment since it in no way involved "instruction in the practice or tenets of a religion." Since the only question was one of free exercise, they concluded, like the majority, that the strong state interest in training a citizen militia justified the restraints imposed, at least so long as attendance at the University was voluntary.

Hamilton has not been overruled, although *United States* v. *Schwimmer* and *United States* v. *Macintosh,* upon which the Court in *Hamilton* relied, have since been overruled by *Girouard* v. *United States.* But if *Hamilton* retains any vitality with respect to higher education, we recognized its inapplicability to cognate questions in the public primary and secondary schools when we held in *West Virginia Board of Education* v. *Barnette* that a State had no power to expel from public schools students who refused on religious grounds to comply with a daily flag ⊥ salute 252 requirement. Of course, such a requirement was no more a law "respecting an establishment of religion" than the California law compelling the college students to take military training. The *Barnette* plaintiffs, moreover, did not ask that the whole exercise be enjoined, but only that an excuse or exemption be provided for those students whose religious beliefs forbade them to participate in the ceremony. The key to the holding that such a requirement abridged rights of free exercise lay in the fact that attendance at school was not voluntary but compulsory. The Court said: "This issue is not prejudiced by the Court's previous holding that where a State, without compelling attendance, extends college facilities to pupils who voluntarily enroll, it may prescribe military training as part of the course without offense to the Constitution. . . . *Hamilton* v. *Regents* In the present case attendance is not optional."

The *Barnette* decision made another significant point. The Court held that the State must make participation in the exercise voluntary for all students and not alone for those who found participation obnoxious on religious grounds. In short, there was simply no need to "inquire whether nonconformist beliefs will exempt from the duty to salute" because the Court found no state "power to make the salute a legal duty."

The distinctions between *Hamilton* and *Barnette* are, I think, crucial to the resolution of the cases before us. The different results of those cases are attributable only in part to a difference in the strength of the particular state interests which the respective statutes were designed to serve. Far more significant is the fact that *Hamilton* dealt with the voluntary attendance at college of young adults, while *Barnette* ⌐253 involved the compelled attendance ⊥of young children at elementary and secondary schools. This distinction warrants a difference in constitutional results. And it is with the involuntary attendance of young school children that we are exclusively concerned in the cases now before the Court.

III

No one questions that the Framers of the First Amendment intended to restrict exclusively the powers of the Federal Government. Whatever limitations that Amendment now imposes upon the States derive from the Fourteenth Amendment. The process of absorption of the religious guarantees of the First Amendment as protections against the States under the Fourteenth Amendment began with the Free Exercise Clause. In 1923 the Court held that the protections of the Fourteenth included at least a person's freedom "to worship God according to the dictates of his own conscience. . . ." *Meyer* v. *Nebraska Cantwell* v. *Connecticut* completed in 1940 ⌐254 the process of absorption ⊥of the Free Exercise Clause and recognized its dual aspect: the Court affirmed freedom of belief as an absolute liberty, but recognized that conduct, while it may also be comprehended by the Free Exercise Clause, "remains subject to regulation for the protection of society." This was a distinction already drawn by *Reynolds* v. *United States.* From the beginning this Court has recognized that while government may regulate the behavioral manifestations of religious beliefs, it may not interfere at all with the beliefs themselves.

The absorption of the Establishment Clause has, however, come later and by a route less easily charted. It has been suggested, with some support in history, that absorption of the First Amendment's ban against congressional legislation "respecting an establishment of religion" is conceptually impossible because the Framers meant the Establishment Clause also to foreclose any attempt by Congress to disestablish the existing official state churches. Whether or not such was the understanding of the Framers and whether such a purpose would have inhibited the absorption of the Establishment Clause at the threshold of the Nineteenth Century are questions not dispositive of our present inquiry. For it is ⌐255 ⊥clear on the record of history that the last of the formal state establishments was dissolved more than three decades before the Fourteenth Amendment was ratified, and thus the problem of protecting official state churches from federal encroachments could hardly have been any concern of those who framed the post-Civil War Amendments. Any such objective of the First Amendment, having become historical anachronism by 1868, cannot be thought to have deterred the absorption of the Establishment Clause to any greater degree than it would, for example, have deterred the absorption of the Free Exercise Clause.

That no organ of the Federal Government possessed in 1791 any power to restrain the interference of the States in religious matters is indisputable. It is equally plain, on the other hand, that the Fourteenth Amendment created a panoply of new federal rights for the protection of citizens of the various States. And among those rights was freedom from such state governmental involvement in the affairs of religion as the Establishment Clause had originally foreclosed on the part of Congress.

⊥It has also been suggested that the "liberty" ⌐256 guaranteed by the Fourteenth Amendment logically cannot absorb the Establishment Clause because that clause is not one of the provisions of the Bill of Rights which in terms protects a "freedom" of the individual. The fallacy in this contention, I think, is that it underestimates the role of the Establishment Clause as a co-guarantor, with the Free Exercise Clause, of religious liberty. The Framers did not entrust the liberty of religious beliefs to either clause alone. The Free Exercise Clause "was not to be the full extent of the Amendment's guarantee of freedom from governmental intrusion in matters of faith." *McGowan* v. *Maryland*

Finally, it has been contended that absorption of the Establishment Clause is precluded by the absence of any intention on the part of the Framers of the Fourteenth Amendment to circumscribe the residual powers of the States to aid religious activities and institutions in ways which fell short of formal establishments. That argument relies in part upon the express terms of the ⊥abortive Blaine Amend- ⌐257 ment—proposed several years after the adoption of the Fourteenth Amendment— which would have added to the First Amendment a provision that "[n]o State shall make any law respecting an establishment of religion. . . ." Such a restriction would have been superfluous, it is said, if the Fourteenth Amendment had already made the Establishment Clause binding upon the States.

The argument proves too much, for the Fourteenth Amendment's protection of the free exercise of religion can hardly be questioned; yet the Blaine Amendment would also have added an explicit protection against state laws abridging that liberty. Even if we assume that the draftsmen of the Fourteenth Amendment saw no immediate connection between its protections against state action infringing personal liberty and the guarantees of the First Amendment, it is certainly too late in the day to suggest that their assumed inattention to the question dilutes the force of these constitutional guarantees in their application to the States. It is enough to conclude ⊥that the religious liberty em- ⌐2 bodied in the Fourteenth Amendment would not be viable if the Constitution were interpreted to forbid only establishments ordained by Congress.

⊥The issue of what particular activities the Es- ⌐2 tablishment Clause forbids the States to undertake is our more immediate concern. In *Everson* v. *Board of*

Education, a careful study of the relevant history led the Court to the view, consistently recognized in decisions since *Everson*, that the Establishment Clause embodied the Framers' conclusion that government and religion have discrete interests which are mutually best served when each avoids too close a proximity to the other. It is not only the nonbeliever who fears the injection of sectarian doctrines and controversies into the civil polity, but in as high degree it is the devout believer who fears the secularization of a creed which becomes too deeply involved with and dependent upon the government. ⊥It has rightly been said of the history of the Establishment Clause that "our tradition of civil liberty rests not only on the secularism of a Thomas Jefferson but also on the fervent sectarianism. . . of a Roger Williams." Freund, The Supreme Court of the United States (1961), 84.

Our decisions on questions of religious education or exercises in the public schools have consistently reflected this dual aspect of the Establishment Clause. *Engel* v. *Vitale* unmistakably has its roots in three earlier cases which, on cognate issues, shaped the contours of the Establishment Clause. First, in *Everson* the Court held that reimbursement by the town of parents for the cost of transporting their children by public carrier to parochial (as well as public and private nonsectarian) schools did not offend the Establishment Clause. Such reimbursement, by easing the financial burden upon Catholic parents, may indirectly have fostered the operation of the Catholic schools, and may thereby indirectly have facilitated the teaching of Catholic principles, thus serving ultimately a religious goal. But this form of governmental assistance was difficult to distinguish from myriad other incidental if not insignificant government benefits enjoyed by religious institutions—fire and police protection, tax exemptions, and the pavement of streets and sidewalks, for example. "The State contributes no money to the schools. It does not support them. Its legislation, as applied, does no more than provide a general program to help parents get their children, regardless of their religion, safely and expeditiously to and from ⊥accredited schools." Yet even this form of assistance was thought by four Justices of the *Everson* Court to be barred by the Establishment Clause because too perilously close to that public support of religion forbidden by the First Amendment.

The other two cases, *Illinois ex rel. McCollum* v. *Board of Education* and *Zorach* v. *Clauson*, can best be considered together. Both involved programs of released time for religious instruction of public school students. I reject the suggestion that *Zorach* overruled *McCollum* in silence. The distinction which the Court drew in *Zorach* between the two cases is, in my view, faithful to the function of the Establishment Clause.

I should first note, however, that *McCollum* and *Zorach* do not seem to me distinguishable in terms of the free exercise claims advanced in both cases. The nonparticipant in the *McCollum* program was given secular instruction in a separate room during the times his classmates had religious lessons; the nonparticipant in any *Zorach* program also received secular instruction, while his classmates repaired to a place outside the school for religious instruction.

The crucial difference, I think, was that the *McCollum* program offended the Establishment Clause while the *Zorach* program did not. This was not, in my view, because of the difference in public expenditures involved. True, the *McCollum* program involved the regular use of school facilities, classrooms, heat and light and time from the regular school day—even though the actual ⊥incremental cost may have been negligible. All religious instruction under the *Zorach* program, by contrast, was carried on entirely off the school premises, and the teacher's part was simply to facilitate the children's release to the churches. The deeper difference was that the *McCollum* program placed the religious instructor in the public school classroom in precisely the position of authority held by the regular teachers of secular subjects, while the *Zorach* program did not. The *McCollum* pro⊥gram, in lending to the support of sectarian instruction all the authority of the governmentally operated public school system, brought government and religion into that proximity which the Establishment Clause forbids. To be sure, a religious teacher presumably commands substantial respect and merits attention in his own right. But the Constitution does not permit that prestige and capacity for influence to be augmented by investiture of all the symbols of authority at the command of the lay teacher for the enhancement of secular instruction.

More recent decisions have further etched the contours of Establishment. In the *Sunday Law Cases*, we found in state laws compelling a uniform day of rest from worldly labor no violation of the Establishment Clause. The basic ⊥ground of our decision was that, granted the Sunday Laws were first enacted for religious ends, they were continued in force for reasons wholly secular, namely, to provide a universal day of rest and ensure the health and tranquillity of the community. In other words, government may originally have decreed a Sunday day of rest for the impermissible purpose of supporting religion but abandoned that purpose and retained the laws for the permissible purpose of furthering overwhelmingly secular ends.

Such was the evolution of the contours of the Establishment Clause before *Engel* v. *Vitale*. There, a year ago, we held that the daily recital of the state-composed Regents' Prayer constituted an establishment of religion because, although the prayer itself revealed no *sectarian* content or purpose, its nature and meaning were quite clearly *religious*. New York, in authorizing its recitation, had not maintained that distance between the public and the religious sectors commanded by the Establishment Clause when it placed the "power, prestige and financial support of government" behind the prayer. In *Engel*, as in *McCollum*, it did not matter that the amount of time and expense allocated to the daily recitation was small so long as the exercise itself was manifestly religious. Nor did it matter that few children had complained of the practice, for the measure of the seriousness of a breach of the Establishment Clause has never been thought to be the number of people who complain of it.

We also held two Terms ago in *Torcaso* v. *Watkins*, that a State may not constitutionally require an applicant for the office of Notary Public to swear or affirm that he believes in God. The problem of that case was strikingly similar to the issue presented 18 years before in the flag salute case, *West Virginia Board of Education* v. *Barnette*. In neither case was there any claim of establishment of ⊥265 religion, but only of infringement of ⊥the individual's religious liberty—in the one case, that of the nonbeliever who could not attest to a belief in God; in the other, that of the child whose creed forbade him to salute the flag. But *Torcaso* added a new element not present in *Barnette*. The Maryland test oath involved an attempt to employ essentially religious (albeit nonsectarian) means to achieve a secular goal to which the means bore no reasonable relationship. No one doubted the State's interest in the integrity of its Notaries Public, but that interest did not warrant the screening of applicants by means of a religious test. The *Sunday Law Cases* were different in that respect. Even if Sunday Laws retain certain religious vestiges, they are enforced today for essentially secular objectives which cannot be effectively achieved in modern society except by designating Sunday as the universal day of rest. The Court's opinions cited very substantial problems in selecting or enforcing an alternative day of rest. But the teaching of both *Torcaso* and the *Sunday Law Cases* is that government may not employ religious means to serve secular interests, however legitimate they may be, at least without the clearest demonstration that nonreligious means will not suffice.

IV

⊥266   ⊥I turn now to the cases before us. The religious nature of the exercises here challenged seems plain. Unless *Engel* v. *Vitale* is to be overruled, or we are to engage in wholly disingenuous distinction, we cannot ⊥267 sus⊥tain these practices. Daily recital of the Lord's Prayer and the reading of passages of Scripture are quite as clearly breaches of the command of the Establishment Clause as was the daily use of the rather bland Regents' Prayer in the New York public schools. Indeed, I would suppose that, if anything, the Lord's Prayer and the Holy Bible are more clearly sectarian, and the present violations of the First Amendment consequently more serious. But the religious exercises challenged in these cases have

a long history. And almost from the beginning, Bible reading and daily prayer in the schools have been the subject of debate, criticism by educators and other public officials, and proscription by courts and legislative councils. At the outset, then, we must carefully canvass both aspects of this history.

The use of prayers and Bible readings at the opening of the school day long antedates the founding of our Republic. The Rules of the New Haven Hopkins Grammar School required in 1684 ⊥268 "[t]hat the Scholars being ⊥called together, the Mr. shall every morning begin his work with a short prayer for a blessing on his Laboures and their learning. . . ." More rigorous was the provision in a 1682 contract with a Dutch schoolmaster in Flatbush, New York: "When the school begins, one of the children shall read the morning prayer, as it stands in the catechism, and close with the prayer before dinner; in the afternoon it shall begin with the prayer after dinner, and end with the evening prayer. The evening school shall begin with the Lord's prayer, and close by singing a psalm."

After the Revolution, the new States uniformly continued these long-established practices in the private and the few public grammar schools. The school committee of Boston in 1789 for example, required the city's several schoolmasters "daily to commence the duties of their office by prayer and reading a portion of the Sacred Scriptures. . . ." That requirement was mirrored throughout the original States, and exemplified the universal practice well into the nineteenth century. As the free public schools gradually supplanted the private academies and sectarian schools between 1800 and 1850, morning devotional exercises were retained with few alterations. Indeed, public pressures upon school administrators in many parts of the country would hardly have condoned abandonment of practices to which a century or more of private religious education had accustomed the American people. The controversy centered, in ⊥269 ⊥fact, principally about the elimination of plainly sectarian practices and textbooks, and led to the eventual substitution of nonsectarian, though still religious, exercises and materials.

Statutory provision for daily religious exercises is, however, of quite recent origin. At the turn of this century, there was but one State—Massachusetts—which had a law making morning prayer or Bible reading obligatory. Statutes elsewhere either permitted such practices or simply left the question to local option. It was not until after 1910 that 11 more States, within a few years, joined Massachusetts in making one or both exercises compulsory. The Pennsylvania law with which we are ⊥270 ⊥concerned in the *Schempp* case, for example, took effect in 1913; and even the Rule of the Baltimore School Board involved in the *Murray* case dates only from 1905. In no State has there ever been a constitutional or statutory prohibition against the recital of prayers or the reading of Scripture, although a number of States have outlawed these practices by judicial decision or administrative order. What is noteworthy about the panoply of state and local regulations from which these cases emerge is the relative recency of the statutory codification of practices which have ancient roots, and the rather small number of States which have ever prescribed compulsory religious exercises in the public schools.

The purposes underlying the adoption and perpetuation of these practices are somewhat complex. It is beyond question that the religious benefits and values realized from daily prayer and Bible reading have usually been considered paramount, and sufficient to justify the continuation of such practices. To Horace Mann, embroiled in an intense controversy over the role of *sectarian* instruction and textbooks in the Boston public schools, there was little question that the regular use of the Bible—which he thought essentially nonsectarian—would bear fruit in the spiritual enlightenment of his pupils. A contemporary of Mann's, the Commissioner of Education of a neighboring State, expressed a view which many enlightened educators of that day shared: "As a textbook of morals the Bible is pre-eminent, and should have a prominent place in our schools, ⊥ either as a reading book or as a source of appeal and instruction. Sectarianism, indeed, should not be countenanced in the schools; but the Bible is not sectarian. . . . The Scriptures should at least be read at the opening of the school, if no more. Prayer may also be offered with the happiest effects."

⊥271

Wisconsin's Superintendent of Public Instruction, writing a few years later in 1858, reflected the attitude of his eastern colleagues, in that he regarded "with special favor the use of the Bible in public schools, as pre-eminently first in importance among text-books for teaching the noblest principles of virtue, morality, patriotism, and good order—love and reverence for God—charity and good will to man."

Such statements reveal the understanding of educators that the daily religious exercises in the schools served broader goals than compelling formal worship of God or fostering church attendance. The religious aims of the educators who adopted and retained such exercises were comprehensive, and in many cases quite devoid of sectarian bias—but the crucial fact is that they were nonetheless religious. While it has been suggested that daily prayer and reading of Scripture now serve secular goals as well, there can be no doubt that the origins of these practices were unambiguously religious, even where the educator's aim was not to win adherents to a particular creed or faith.

Almost from the beginning religious exercises in the public schools have been the subject of intense criticism, vigorous debate, and judicial or administrative prohibition. Significantly, educators and school boards ⊥ early entertained doubts about both the legality and the soundness of opening the school day with compulsory prayer or Bible reading. Partic-

⊥272

ularly in the large Eastern cities, where immigration had exposed the public schools to religious diversities and conflicts unknown to the homogeneous academies of the eighteenth century, local authorities found it necessary even before the Civil War to seek an accommodation. In 1843, the Philadelphia School Board adopted the following resolutions:

"RESOLVED, that no children be required to attend or unite in the reading of the Bible in the Public Schools, whose parents are conscientiously opposed thereto:

"RESOLVED, that those children whose parents conscientiously prefer and desire any particular version of the Bible, without note or comment, be furnished with same."

A decade later, the Superintendent of Schools of New York State issued an even bolder decree that prayers could no longer be required as part of public school activities, and that where the King James Bible was read, Catholic students could not be compelled to attend. This type of accommodation was not restricted to the East Coast; the Cincinnati Board of Education resolved in 1869 that "religious instruction and the reading of religious books, including the Holy Bible, are prohibited in the common schools of Cincinnati, it being the true object and intent of this rule to allow the children of the parents of all sects and opinions, in matters of faith and worship, ⊥ to enjoy alike the benefit of the common-school fund." The Board repealed at the same time an earlier regulation which had required the singing of hymns and psalms to accompany the Bible reading at the start of the school day. And in 1889, one commentator ventured the view that "[t]here is not enough to be gained from Bible reading to justify the quarrel that has been raised over it."

⊥273

Thus a great deal of controversy over religion in the public schools had preceded the debate over the Blaine Amendment, precipitated by President Grant's insistence that matters of religion should be left "to the family altar, the church, and the private school, supported entirely by private contributions." There was ample precedent, too, for Theodore Roosevelt's declaration that in the interest of "absolutely nonsectarian public schools" it was "not our business to have the Protestant Bible or the Catholic Vulgate or the Talmud read in those schools." The same principle appeared in the message of an Ohio Governor who vetoed a compulsory Bible-reading bill in 1925: "It is my belief that religious teaching in our homes, Sunday schools, churches, by the good ⊥ mothers, fathers, and ministers of Ohio is far preferable to compulsory teaching of religion by the state. The spirit of our federal and state constitutions from the beginning . . . [has] been to leave religious instruction to the discretion of parents."

⊥274

The same theme has recurred in the opinions of the Attorneys General of several States holding religious exercises or instruction to be in violation of the state or federal constitutional command of separation of church and state. Thus the basic principle upon which our decision last year in *Engel* v. *Vitale* necessarily rested, and which we reaffirm today, can hardly be thought to be radical or novel.

Particularly relevant for our purposes are the decisions of the state courts on questions of religion in the public schools. Those decisions, while not, of course, authoritative in this Court, serve nevertheless to define the problem before us and to guide our inquiry. With the growth of religious diversity and the rise of vigorous dissent it was inevitable that the courts would be called upon to enjoin religious practices in the public schools which offended certain sects and groups. The earliest of such decisions declined to review the propriety of actions taken by school authorities, so long as those actions were ⊥275 within ⊥ the purview of the administrators' powers. Thus, where the local school board *required* religious exercises, the courts would not enjoin them, and where, as in at least one case, the school officials *forbade* devotional practices, the court refused on similar grounds to overrule that decision. Thus, whichever way the early cases came up, the governing principle of nearly complete deference to administrative discretion effectively foreclosed any consideration of constitutional questions.

The last quarter of the nineteenth century found the courts beginning to question the constitutionality of public school religious exercises. The legal context was still, of course, that of the state constitutions, since the First Amendment had not yet been held applicable to state action. And the state constitutional prohibitions against church-state cooperation or governmental aid to religion were generally less rigorous than the Establishment Clause of the First Amendment. It is therefore remarkable that the courts of a half dozen States found compulsory religious exercises in the public schools in violation of their respective state constitutions. These ⊥276 ⊥ courts attributed much significance to the clearly religious origins and content of the challenged practices, and to the impossibility of avoiding sectarian controversy in their conduct. The Illinois Supreme Court expressed in 1910 the principles which characterized these decisions: "The public school is supported by the taxes which each citizen, regardless of his religion or his lack of it, is compelled to pay. The school, like the government, is simply a civil institution. It is secular, and not religious, in its purposes. The truths of the Bible are the truths of religion, which do not come within the province of the public school. . . . No one denies that they should be taught to the youth of the State. The constitution and the law do not interfere with such teaching, but they do banish theological polemics from the schools and the school districts. This is done, not from any hostility to religion, but because it is no part of the duty of the State to teach religion,—to take the money of all and apply it to teaching the children of

all the religion of a part, only. Instruction in religion must be voluntary." *Ring* v. *Board of Education*

The Supreme Court of South Dakota, in banning devotional exercises from the public schools of that State, also cautioned that "[t]he state as an educator must keep out of this field, and especially is this true in the common schools, where the child is immature, without fixed religious convictions. . . ." *Finger* v. *Weedman*

⊥ Even those state courts which have sustained ⊥27* devotional exercises under state law have usually recognized the primarily religious character of prayers and Bible readings. If such practices were not for that reason unconstitutional, it was necessarily because the state constitution forbade only public expenditures for *sectarian* instruction, or for activities which made the schoolhouse a "place of worship," but said nothing about the subtler question of laws "respecting an establishment of religion." Thus the panorama of history permits no ⊥ other conclusion ⊥27* than that daily prayers and Bible readings in the public schools have always been designed to be, and have been regarded as, essentially religious exercises. Unlike the Sunday closing laws, these exercises appear neither to have been divorced from their religious origins nor deprived of their centrally religious character by the passage of time. On this distinction alone we might well rest a constitutional decision. But three further contentions have been pressed in the argument of these cases. These contentions deserve careful consideration, for if the position of the school authorities were correct in respect to any of them, we would be misapplying the principles of *Engel* v. *Vitale*.

A

First, it is argued that however clearly religious may have been the origins and early nature of daily prayer and Bible reading, these practices today serve so clearly secular educational purposes that their religious attributes may be overlooked. I do not doubt, for example, that morning devotional exercises may foster better discipline in the classroom, and elevate the spiritual level on which the school day opens. The Pennsylvania Superintendent of Public Instruction, testifying by deposition in the *Schempp* case, offered his view that daily Bible reading "places upon the children or those hearing the reading of this, and the atmosphere which goes on in the reading . . . one of the last vestiges of moral value ⊥ that we have left in our school system." The ex- ⊥279 ercise thus affords, the Superintendent concluded, "a strong contradiction to the materialistic trends of our time." Baltimore's Superintendent of Schools expressed a similar view of the practices challenged in the *Murray* case, to the effect that "[t]he acknowledgement of the existence of God as symbolized in the opening exercises establishes a discipline tone which tends to cause each individual pupil to constrain his overt acts and to consequently conform to accepted standards of behavior during his attendance at school." These views are by no means novel.

It is not the business of this Court to gainsay the judgments of experts on matters of pedagogy. Such decisions must be left to the discretion of those administrators charged with the supervision of the Nation's public schools. The limited province of the courts is to determine whether the means which the educators have chosen to achieve legitimate pedagogical ends infringe the constitutional freedoms of the First Amendment. The secular purposes which devotional exercises are said to serve fall into two categories—those which depend upon an immediately religious experience shared by the participating children; and those which appear sufficiently divorced from the religious content of the devotional material that they can be served equally by nonreligious ⊥materials. With respect to the first objective, much has been written about the moral and spiritual values of infusing some religious influence or instruction into the public school classroom. To the extent that only *religious* materials will serve this purpose, it seems to me that the purpose as well as the means is so plainly religious that the exercise is necessarily forbidden by the Establishment Clause. The fact that purely secular benefits may eventually result does not seem to me to justify the exercises, for similar indirect nonreligious benefits could no doubt have been claimed for the released time program invalidated in *McCollum*.

The second justification assumes that religious exercises at the start of the school day may directly serve solely secular ends—for example, by fostering harmony and tolerance among the pupils, enhancing the authority of the teacher, and inspiring better discipline. To the extent that such benefits result not from the content of the readings and recitation, but simply from the holding of such a solemn exercise at the opening assembly or the first class of the day, it would seem that less sensitive materials might equally well serve the same purpose. I have previously suggested that *Torcaso* and the *Sunday Law Cases* forbid the use of religious means to achieve sec⊥ular ends where nonreligious means will suffice. That principle is readily applied to these cases. It has not been shown that readings from the speeches and messages of great Americans, for example, or from the documents of our heritage of liberty, daily recitation of the Pledge of Allegiance, or even the observance of a moment of reverent silence at the opening of class, may not adequately serve the solely secular purposes of the devotional activities without jeopardizing either the religious liberties of any members of the community or the proper degree of separation between the spheres of religion and government. Such substitutes would, I think, be unsatisfactory or inadequate only to the extent that the present activites do in fact serve religious goals. While I do not question the judgment of experienced educators that the challenged practices may well

achieve valuable secular ends, it seems to me that the State acts unconstitutionally if it either sets about to attain even indirectly religious ends by religious means, or if it uses religious means to serve secular ends where secular means would suffice.

B

Second, it is argued that the particular practices involved in the two cases before us are unobjectionable ⊥because they prefer no particular sect or sects at the expense of others. Both the Baltimore and Abington procedures permit, for example, the reading of any of several versions of the Bible, and this flexibility is said to ensure neutrality sufficiently to avoid the constitutional prohibition. One answer, which might be dispositive, is that any version of the Bible is inherently sectarian, else there would be no need to offer a system of rotation or alternation of versions in the first place, that is, to allow different sectarian versions to be used on different days. The sectarian character of the Holy Bible has been at the core of the whole controversy over religious practices in the public schools throughout its long and often bitter history. To ⊥vary the version as the Abington and Baltimore schools have done may well be less offensive than to read from the King James version every day, as once was the practice. But the result even of this relatively benign procedure is that majority sects are preferred in approximate proportion to their representation in the community and in the student body, while the smaller sects suffer commensurate discrimination. So long as the subject matter of the exercise is sectarian in character, these consequences cannot be avoided.

The argument contains, however, a more basic flaw. There are persons in every community—often deeply devout—to whom any version of the Judaeo-Christian Bible is offensive. There are others whose reverence for the Holy Scriptures demands private study or reflection and to whom public reading or recitation is sacrilegious, as one of the expert witnesses at the trial of the *Schempp* case explained. To such persons it is not the fact of using the Bible in the public schools, nor the content of any particular version, that is offensive, but only the *manner* in ⊥which it is used. For such persons, the anathema of public communion is even more pronounced when prayer is involved. Many deeply devout persons have always regarded prayer as a necessarily private experience. One Protestant group recently commented, for example: "When one thinks of prayer as sincere outreach of a ⊥human soul to the Creator, 'required prayer' becomes an absurdity." There is a similar problem with respect to comment upon the passages of Scripture which are to be read. Most present statutes forbid comment, and this practice accords with the views of many religious groups as to the manner in which the Bible should be read. However, as a recent survey discloses, scriptural passages read without comment frequently convey no message to the younger children in the school. Thus there has developed a practice in some schools of bridging the gap between faith and understanding by means of "definitions," even where "comment" is forbidden by statute. The present practice therefore poses a difficult dilemma: While Bible reading is almost universally required to be without comment, since only by such a prohibition can sectarian interpretation be excluded from the classroom, ⊥the rule breaks down at the point at which rudimentary definitions of Biblical terms are necessary for comprehension if the exercise is to be meaningful at all.

It has been suggested that a tentative solution to these problems may lie in the fashioning of a "common core" of theology tolerable to all creeds but preferential to none. But as one commentator has recently observed, "[h]istory is not encouraging to" those who hope to fashion a "common denominator of religion detached from its manifestation in any organized church." Sutherland, Establishment According to *Engel*, 76 Harv. L. Rev. 25, 51 (1962). Thus, the notion of a "common core" litany or supplication offends many deeply devout worshippers who do not find clearly sectarian practices objectionable. Father Gustave Weigel has recently expressed ⊥a widely shared view: "The moral code held by each separate religious community can reductively be unified, but the consistent particular believer wants no such reduction." And, as the American Council on Education warned several years ago, "The notion of a common core suggests a watering down of the several faiths to the point where common essentials appear. This might easily lead to a new sect—a public school sect—which would take its place alongside the existing faiths and compete with them." *Engel* is surely authority that nonsectarian religious practices, equally with sectarian exercises, violate the Establishment Clause. Moreover, even if the Establishment Clause were oblivious to nonsectarian religious practices, I think it quite likely that the "common core" approach would be sufficiently objectionable to many groups to be foreclosed by the prohibitions of the Free Exercise Clause.

C

A third element which is said to absolve the practices involved in these cases from the ban of the religious guarantees of the Constitution is the provision to excuse or exempt students who wish not to participate. Insofar as these practices are claimed to violate the Establishment ⊥Clause, I find the answer which the District Court gave after our remand of *Schempp* to be altogether dispositive: "The fact that some pupils, or theoretically all pupils, might be excused from attendance at the exercises does not mitigate the obligatory nature of the ceremony. . . . The exercises are held in the school buildings and perforce are conducted by and under the authority of the local school authorities and during school sessions. Since the statute requires the reading of the 'Holy Bible,' a Christian document, the practice, as we said in our first opinion, prefers the Christian religion. The record demonstrates that it was the intention of the General Assembly of the Commonwealth of Pennsylvania to introduce a religious ceremony into the public schools of the Commonwealth."

Thus the short, and to me sufficient, answer is that the availability of excusal or exemption simply has no relevance to the establishment question, if it is once found that these practices are essentially religious exercises designed at least in part to achieve religious aims through the use of public school facilities during the school day.

The more difficult question, however, is whether the availability of excusal for the dissenting child serves to refute challenges to these practices under the Free Exercise Clause. While it is enough to decide these cases to dispose of the establishment questions, questions of free exercise are so inextricably interwoven into the history and present status of these practices as to justify disposition of this second aspect of the excusal issue. The answer is that the excusal procedure itself necessarily operates in such a way as to infringe the rights of free exercise of those children who wish to be excused. We have held in *Barnette* and *Torcaso*, respectively, that a State may require neither public school students nor candidates ⊥for an office of public trust to profess beliefs offensive to religious principles. By the same token the State could not constitutionally require a student to profess publicly his disbelief as the prerequisite to the exercise of his constitutional right of abstention. And apart from *Torcaso* and *Barnette*, I think *Speiser* v. *Randall* suggests a further answer. We held there that a State may not condition the grant of a tax exemption upon the willingness of those entitled to the exemption to affirm their loyalty to the Government, even though the exemption was itself a matter of grace rather than of constitutional right. We concluded that to impose upon the eligible taxpayers the affirmative burden of proving their loyalty impermissibly jeopardized the freedom to engage in constitutionally protected activities close to the area to which the loyalty oath related. *Speiser* v. *Randall* seems to me to dispose of two aspects of the excusal or exemption procedure now before us. First, by requiring what is tantamount in the eyes of teachers and schoolmates to a profession of disbelief, or at least of nonconformity, the procedure may well deter those children who do not wish to participate for any reason based upon the dictates of conscience from exercising an indisputably constitutional right to be excused. Thus the excusal ⊥provision in its operation subjects them to a cruel dilemma. In consequence, even devout children may well avoid claiming their right and simply continue to participate in exercises distasteful to them because of an understandable reluctance to be stigmatized as atheists or nonconformists simply on the basis of their request.

Such reluctance to seek exemption seems all the more likely in view of the fact that children are disinclined at this age to step out of line or to flout "peer group norms." Such is the widely held view of experts who have studied the behaviors and attitudes of children. This is also ⊥the basis of Mr. Justice Frankfurter's answer to a similar contention made in the *McCollum* case: "That a child is offered an alternative may reduce the constraint; it does not eliminate the operation of influence by the school in matters sacred to conscience and outside the school's domain. The law of imitation operates, and nonconformity is not an ⊥outstanding characteristic of children. The result is an obvious pressure upon children to attend.". . .

⊥ *Speiser* v. *Randall* also suggests the answer to a further argument based on the excusal procedure. It has been suggested by the School Board, in *Schempp*, that we ought not pass upon the appellees' constitutional challenge at least until the children have availed themselves of the excusal procedure and found it inadequate to redress their grievances. Were the right to be excused not itself of constitutional stature, I might have some doubt about this issue. But we held in *Speiser* that the constitutional vice of the loyalty oath procedure discharged any obligation to seek the exemption before challenging the constitutionality of the conditions upon which it might have been denied. Similarly, we have held that one need not apply for a permit to distribute constitutionally protected literature, *Lovell* v. *Griffin*, or to deliver a speech, *Thomas* v. *Collins*, before he may attack the constitutionality of a licensing system of which the defect is patent. Insofar as these cases implicate only questions of establishment, it seems to me that the availability of an excuse is constitutionally irrelevant. Moreover, the excusal procedure seems to me to operate in such a way as to discourage the free exercise of religion on the part of those who might wish to utilize it, thereby rendering it unconstitutional in an additional and quite distinct respect.

To summarize my views concerning the merits of these two cases: The history, the purpose and the operation of the daily prayer recital and Bible reading leave no doubt that these practices standing by themselves constitute an impermissible breach of the Establishment Clause. Such devotional exercises may well serve legitimate nonreligious purposes. To the extent, however, that such pur⊥poses are really without religious significance, it has never been demonstrated that secular means would not suffice. Indeed, I would suggest that patriotic or other nonreligious materials might provide adequate substitutes—inadequate only to the extent that the purposes now served are indeed directly or indirectly religious. Under such circumstances, the States may not employ religious means to reach a secular goal unless secular means are wholly unavailing. I therefore agree with the Court that the judgment in *Schempp* must be affirmed, and that in *Murray* must be reversed.

V

These considerations bring me to a final contention of the school officials in these cases: that the invalidation of the exercises at bar permits this Court no alternative but to declare unconstitutional every vestige, however slight, of cooperation or accommodation between religion and government. I cannot accept that contention. While it is not, of course, appropriate for this Court to decide questions not presently before it, I venture to suggest that religious exercises in the public schools present a unique problem. For not every involvement of religion in public life violates the Establishment Clause. Our decision in these cases does not clearly forecast anything about the constitutionality of other types of interdependence between religious and other public institutions.

Specifically, I believe that the line we must draw between the permissible and the impermissible is one which accords with history and faithfully reflects the understanding of the Founding Fathers. It is a line which the Court has consistently sought to mark in its decisions expounding the religious guarantees of the First Amendment. What the Framers meant to foreclose, and what our decisions under the Establishment Clause have for ⊥bidden, are those involvements of religious with secular institutions which (a) serve the essentially religious activities of religious institutions; (b) employ the organs of government for essentially religious purposes; or (c) use essentially religious means to serve governmental ends, where secular means would suffice. When the secular and religious institutions become involved in such a manner, there inhere in the relationship precisely those dangers—as much to church as to state—which the Framers feared would subvert religious liberty and the strength of a system of secular government. On the other hand, there may be myriad forms of involvements of government with religion which do not import such dangers and therefore should not, in my judgment, be deemed to violate the Establishment Clause. Nothing in the Constitution compels the organs of government to be blind to what everyone else perceives—that religious differences among Americans have important and pervasive implications for our society. Likewise nothing in the Establishment Clause forbids the application of legislation having purely secular ends in such a way as to alleviate burdens upon the free exercise of an individual's religious beliefs. Surely the Framers would never have understood that such a construction sanctions that involvement which violates the Establishment Clause. Such a conclusion can be reached, I would suggest, only by using the words of the First Amendment to defeat its very purpose.

The line between permissible and impermissible forms of involvement between government and religion has already been considered by the lower federal and state courts. I think a brief survey of certain of these forms of accommodation will reveal that the First Amendment commands not official hostility toward religion, but only a strict neutrality in matters of religion. Moreover, it may serve to suggest that ⌊296 the scope of our holding today ⊥ is to be measured by the special circumstances under which these cases have arisen, and by the particular dangers to church and state which religious exercises in the public schools present. It may be helpful for purposes of analysis to group these other practices and forms of accommodation into several rough categories.

A. *The Conflict Between Establishment and Free Exercise.*—There are certain practices, conceivably violative of the Establishment Clause, the striking down of which might seriously interfere with certain religious liberties also protected by the First Amendment. Provisions for churches and chaplains at military establishments for those in the armed services ⌊297 may afford one such example. ⊥ The like provision by state and federal governments for chaplains in penal institutions may afford another example. It is argued that such provisions may be assumed to contravene the Establishment Clause, yet be sustained on constitutional grounds as necessary to secure to the members of the Armed Forces and prisoners those rights of worship guaranteed under the Free Exercise Clause. Since government has deprived ⌊298 such persons of the oppor⊥tunity to practice their faith at places of their choice, the argument runs, government may, in order to avoid infringing the free exercise guarantees, provide substitutes where it requires such persons to be. Such a principle might support, for example, the constitutionality of draft exemptions for ministers and divinity students; of the excusal of children from school on their respective religious holidays; and of the allowance by government of temporary use of public buildings by religious organizations when their own churches have become unavailable because of a disaster or emergency.

Such activities and practices seem distinguishable from the sponsorship of daily Bible reading and prayer recital. For one thing, there is no element of coercion present in the appointment of military or prison chaplains; the soldier or convict who declines the opportunities for worship would not ordinarily subject himself to the suspicion or obloquy of his peers. Of special significance to this distinction is ⌊299 the fact that we are here usually deal⊥ing with adults, not with impressionable children as in the public schools. Moreover, the school exercises are not designed to provide the pupils with general opportunities for worship denied them by the legal obligation to attend school. The student's compelled presence in school for five days a week in no way renders the regular religious facilities of the commu-

nity less accessible to him than they are to others. The situation of the school child is therefore plainly unlike that of the isolated soldier or the prisoner.

The State must be steadfastly neutral in all matters of faith, and neither favor nor inhibit religion. In my view, government cannot sponsor religious exercises in the public schools without jeopardizing that neutrality. On the other hand, hostility, not neutrality, would characterize the refusal to provide chaplains and places of worship for prisoners and soldiers cut off by the State from all civilian opportunities for public communion, the withholding of draft exemptions for ministers and conscientious objectors, or the denial of the temporary use of an empty public building to a congregation whose place of worship has been destroyed by fire or flood. I do not say that government *must* provide chaplains or draft exemptions, or that the courts should intercede if it fails to do so.

B. *Establishment and Exercises in Legislative Bodies.*—The saying of invocational prayers in legislative chambers, state or federal, and the appointment of legislative chaplains, might well represent no involvements of the kind prohibited by the Establishment Clause. Legislators, federal and state, are mature adults who may presumably absent themselves from such public and cere⊥monial exercises ⌊30 without incurring any penalty, direct or indirect. It may also be significant that, at least in the case of the Congress, Art. I, § 5, of the Constitution makes each House the monitor of the "Rules of its Proceedings" so that it is at least arguable whether such matters present "political questions" the resolution of which is exclusively confided to Congress. Finally, there is the difficult question of who may be heard to challenge such practices.

C. *Non-Devotional Use of the Bible in the Public Schools.*—The holding of the Court today plainly does not foreclose teaching *about* the Holy Scriptures or about the differences between religious sects in classes in literature or history. Indeed, whether or not the Bible is involved, it would be impossible to teach meaningfully many subjects in the social sciences or the humanities without some mention of religion. To what extent, and at what points in the curriculum, religious materials should be cited are matters which the courts ought to entrust very largely to the experienced officials who superintend our Nation's public schools. They are experts in such matters, and we are not. We should heed Mr. Justice Jackson's caveat that any attempt by this Court to announce curricular standards would be "to decree a uniform, rigid and, if we are consistent, an unchanging standard for countless school boards represent⊥ing and serving highly localized groups which ⌊30 not only differ from each other but which themselves from time to time change attitudes. *Illinois ex rel. McCollum* v. *Board of Education*

We do not, however, in my view usurp the jurisdiction of school administrators by holding as we do today that morning devotional exercises in any form are constitutionally invalid. But there is no occasion now to go further and anticipate problems we cannot judge with the material now before us. Any attempt to impose rigid limits upon the mention of God or references to the Bible in the classroom would be fraught with dangers. If it should sometime hereafter be shown that in fact religion can play no part in the teaching of a given subject without resurrecting the ghost of the practices we strike down today, it will then be time enough to consider questions we must now defer.

D. *Uniform Tax Exemptions Incidentally Available to Religious Institutions.*—Nothing we hold today questions the propriety of certain tax deductions or exemptions which incidentally benefit churches and religious institutions, along with many secular charities and nonprofit organizations. If religious institutions benefit, it is in spite of rather than because of their religious character. For religious institutions simply share benefits which government makes generally available to educational, charitable, and eleemosynary groups. There is no indication that taxing authorities have used such benefits in any way to subsidize worship or foster belief in God. And as ⊥among religious beneficiaries, the tax exemption or deduction can be truly nondiscriminatory, available on equal terms to small as well as large religious bodies, to popular and unpopular sects, and to those organizations which reject as well as those which accept a belief in God.

E. *Religious Considerations in Public Welfare Programs.*—Since government may not support or directly aid religious *activities* without violating the Establishment Clause, there might be some doubt whether nondiscriminatory programs of governmental aid may constitutionally include *individuals* who become eligible wholly or partially for religious reasons. For example, it might be suggested that where a State provides unemployment compensation generally to those who are unable to find suitable work, it may not extend such benefits to persons who are unemployed by reason of religious beliefs or practices without thereby establishing the religion to which those persons belong. Therefore, the argument runs, the State may avoid an establishment only by singling out and excluding such persons on the ground that religious beliefs or practices have made them potential beneficiaries. Such a construction would, it seems to me, require government to impose religious discriminations and disabilities, thereby jeopardizing the free exercise of religion, in order to avoid what is thought to constitute an establishment.

The inescapable flaw in the argument, I suggest, is its quite unrealistic view of the aims of the Establishment Clause. The Framers were not concerned with the effects of certain incidental aids to individual worshippers which come about as byproducts of general and nondiscriminatory welfare programs. If such benefits serve to make ⊥easier or less ex-

pensive the practice of a particular creed, or of all religions, it can hardly be said that the purpose of the program is in any way religious, or that the consequence of its nondiscriminatory application is to create the forbidden degree of interdependence between secular and sectarian institutions. I cannot therefore accept the suggestion, which seems to me implicit in the argument outlined here, that every judicial or administrative construction which is designed to prevent a public welfare program from abridging the free exercise of religious beliefs, is for that reason *ipso facto* an establishment of religion.

F. *Activities Which, Though Religious in Origin, Have Ceased to Have Religious Meaning.*—As we noted in our *Sunday Law* decisions, nearly every criminal law on the books can be traced to some religious principle or inspiration. But that does not make the present enforcement of the criminal law in any sense an establishment of religion, simply because it accords with widely held religious principles. As we said in *McGowan* v. *Maryland*, "the 'Establishment' Clause does not ban federal or state regulation of conduct whose reason or effect merely happens to coincide or harmonize with the tenets of some or all religions." This rationale suggests that the use of the motto "In God We Trust" on currency, on documents and public buildings and the like may not offend the clause. It is not that the use of those four words can be dismissed as "de minimis"— for I suspect there would be intense opposition to the abandonment of that motto. The truth is that we have simply interwoven the motto so deeply into the fabric of our civil polity that its present use may well not present that type of involvement which the First Amendment prohibits.

This general principle might also serve to insulate the various patriotic exercises and activities used in the public schools and elsewhere which, whatever may have been ⊥their origins, no longer have a religious purpose or meaning. The reference to divinity in the revised pledge of allegiance, for example, may merely recognize the historical fact that our Nation was believed to have been founded "under God." Thus reciting the pledge may be no more of a religious exercise than the reading aloud of Lincoln's Gettysburg Address, which contains an allusion to the same historical fact.

The principles which we reaffirm and apply today can hardly be thought novel or radical. They are, in truth, as old as the Republic itself, and have always been as integral a part of the First Amendment as the very words of that charter of religious liberty. No less applicable today than they were when first pronounced a century ago, one year after the very first court decision involving religious exercises in the public schools, are the words of a distinguished Chief Justice of the Commonwealth of Pennsylvania, Jeremiah S. Black: "The manifest object of the men who framed the institutions of this country, was to have a *State without religion*, and a *Church without poli-*

tics—that is to say, they meant that one should never be used as an engine for any purpose of the other, and that no man's rights in one should be tested by his opinions about the other. As the Church takes no note of men's political differences, so the State looks with equal eye on all the modes of religious faith. . . . Our fathers seem to have been perfectly sincere in their belief that the members of the Church would be more patriotic, and the citizens of the State more religious, by keeping their respective functions entirely separate." Essay on Religious Liberty, in Black, ed., Essays and Speeches of Jeremiah S. Black, (1886), 53.

⊥305   ⊥*Mr. Justice GOLDBERG*, with whom *Mr. Justice HARLAN* joins, concurring.

As is apparent from the opinions filed today, delineation of the constitutionally permissible relationship between religion and government is a most difficult and sensitive task, calling for the careful exercise of both judical and public judgment and restraint. The considerations which lead the Court today to interdict the clearly religious practices presented in these cases are to me wholly compelling; I have no doubt as to the propriety of the decision and therefore join the opinion and judgment of the Court. The singular sensitivity and concern which surround both the legal and practical judgments involved impel me, however, to add a few words in further explication, while at the same time avoiding repetition of the carefully and ably framed examination of history and authority by my Brethren.

The First Amendment's guarantees, as applied to the States through the Fourteenth Amendment, foreclose not only laws "respecting an establishment of religion" but also those "prohibiting the free exercise thereof." These two proscriptions are to be read together, and in light of the single end which they are designed to serve. The basic purpose of the religion clause of the First Amendment is to promote and assure the fullest possible scope of religious liberty and tolerance for all and to nurture the conditions which secure the best hope of attainment of that end.

The fullest realization of true religious liberty requires that government neither engage in nor compel religious practices, that it effect no favoritism among sects or between religion and nonreligion, and that it work deterrence of no religious belief. But devotion even to these simply stated objectives presents no easy course, for the unavoidable accommodations ⊥306 necessary to achieve the ⊥maximum enjoyment of each and all of them are often difficult of discernment. There is for me no simple and clear measure which by precise application can readily and invariably demark the permissible from the impermissible.

It is said, and I agree, that the attitude of government toward religion must be one of neutrality. But untutored devotion to the concept of neutrality can lead to invocation or approval of results which partake not simply of that noninterference and noninvolvement with the religious which the Constitution commands, but of a brooding and pervasive devotion to the secular and a passive, or even active, hostility to the religious. Such results are not only not compelled by the Constitution, but, it seems to me, are prohibited by it.

Neither government nor this Court can or should ignore the significance of the fact that a vast portion of our people believe in and worship God and that many of our legal, political and personal values derive historically from religious teachings. Government must inevitably take cognizance of the existence of religion and, indeed, under certain circumstances the First Amendment may require that it do so. And it seems clear to me from the opinions in the present and past cases that the Court would recognize the propriety of providing military chaplains and of the teaching *about* religion, as distinguished from the teaching *of* religion, in the public schools. The examples could readily be multiplied, for both the required and the permissible accommodations between state and church frame the relation as one free of hostility or favor and productive of religious and political harmony, but without undue involvement of one in the concerns or practices of the other. To be sure, the judgment in each case is a delicate one, but it must be made if we are to do loyal service as judges to the ultimate First Amendment objective of religious liberty.

⊥The practices here involved do not fall within ⊥307 any sensible or acceptable concept of compelled or permitted accommodation and involve the state so significantly and directly in the realm of the sectarian as to give rise to those very divisive influences and inhibitions of freedom which both religion clauses of the First Amendment preclude. The state has ordained and has utilized its facilities to engage in unmistakably religious exercises—the devotional reading and recitation of the Holy Bible—in a manner having substantial and significant import and impact. That it has selected, rather than written, a particular devotional liturgy seems to me without constitutional import. The pervasive religiosity and direct governmental involvement inhering in the prescription of prayer and Bible reading in the public schools, during and as part of the curricular day, involving young impressionable children whose school attendance is statutorily compelled, and utilizing the prestige, power, and influence of school administration, staff, and authority, cannot realistically be termed simply accommodation, and must fall within the interdiction of the First Amendment. I find nothing in the opinion of the Court which says more than this. And, of course, today's decision does not mean that all incidents of government which import of the religious are therefore and without more banned by the strictures of the Establishment

Clause. As the Court declared only last Term in *Engel* v. *Vitale*: "There is of course nothing in the decision reached here that is inconsistent with the fact that school children and others are officially encouraged to express love for our country by reciting historical documents such as the Declaration of Independence which contain references to the Deity or by singing officially espoused anthems which include the composer's professions of faith in a Supreme Being, or ⊥with the fact that there are many manifestations in our public life of belief in God. Such patriotic or ceremonial occasions bear no true resemblance to the unquestioned religious exercise that the State . . . has sponsored in this instance."

⌐308

The First Amendment does not prohibit practices which by any realistic measure create none of the dangers which it is designed to prevent and which do not so directly or substantially involve the state in religious exercises or in the favoring of religion as to have meaningful and practical impact. It is of course true that great consequences can grow from small beginnings, but the measure of constitutional adjudication is the ability and willingness to distinguish between real threat and mere shadow.

Mr. Justice STEWART, dissenting.

I think the records in the two cases before us are so fundamentally deficient as to make impossible an informed or responsible determination of the constitutional issues presented. Specifically, I cannot agree that on these records we can say that the Establishment Clause has necessarily been violated. But I think there exist serious questions under both that provision and the Free Exercise Clause—insofar as each is imbedded in the Fourteenth Amendment—which require the remand of these cases for the taking of additional evidence.

I

The First Amendment declares that "Congress shall make no law respecting an establishment of religion, or prohibiting the free exercise thereof. . . ."

⌐309

It is, I ⊥think, a fallacious oversimplification to regard these two provisions as establishing a single constitutional standard of "separation of church and state," which can be mechanically applied in every case to delineate the required boundaries between government and religion. We err in the first place if we do not recognize, as a matter of history and as a matter of the imperatives of our free society, that religion and government must necessarily interact in countless ways. Secondly, the fact is that while in many contexts the Establishment Clause and the Free Exercise Clause fully complement each other, there are areas in which a doctrinaire reading of the Establishment Clause leads to irreconcilable conflict with the Free Exercise Clause.

A single obvious example should suffice to make the point. Spending federal funds to employ chaplains for the armed forces might be said to violate the Establishment Clause. Yet a lonely soldier stationed at some faraway outpost could surely complain that a government which did *not* provide him the opportunity for pastoral guidance was affirmatively prohibiting the free exercise of his religion. And such examples could readily be multiplied. The short of the matter is simply that the two relevant clauses of the First Amendment cannot accurately be reflected in a sterile metaphor which by its very nature may distort rather than illumine the problems involved in a particular case.

II

As a matter of history, the First Amendment was adopted solely as a limitation upon the newly created National Government. The events leading to its adoption strongly suggest that the Establishment Clause was primarily an attempt to insure that Congress not only would be powerless to establish a national church, but ⊥would also be unable to interfere with existing state establishments. Each State was left free to go its own way and pursue its own policy with respect to religion. Thus Virginia from the beginning pursued a policy of disestablishmentarianism. Massachusetts, by contrast, had an established church until well into the nineteenth century.

⌐310

So matters stood until the adoption of the Fourteenth Amendment, or more accurately, until this Court's decision in *Cantwell* v. *Connecticut*, in 1940. In that case the Court said: "The First Amendment declares that Congress shall make no law respecting an establishment of religion or prohibiting the free exercise thereof. The Fourteenth Amendment has rendered the legislatures of the states as incompetent as Congress to enact such laws."

I accept without question that the liberty guaranteed by the Fourteenth Amendment against impairment by the States embraces in full the right of free exercise of religion protected by the First Amendment, and I yield to no one in my conception of the breadth of that freedom. I accept too the proposition that the Fourteenth Amendment has somehow absorbed the Establishment Clause, although it is not without irony that a constitutional provision evidently designed to leave the States free to go their own way should now have become a restriction upon their autonomy. But I cannot agree with what seems to me the insensitive definition of the Establishment Clause contained in the Court's opinion, nor with the different but, I think, equally mechanistic definitions contained in the separate opinions which have been filed.

III

⊥ Since the *Cantwell* pronouncement in 1940, this Court has only twice held invalid state laws on the ground that they were laws "respecting an establishment of religion" in violation of the Fourteenth Amendment: *McCollum* v. *Board of Education*; *En-*

⌐311

gel v. *Vitale*. On the other hand, the Court has upheld against such a challenge laws establishing Sunday as a compulsory day of rest, and a law authorizing reimbursement from public funds for the transportation of parochial school pupils.

Unlike other First Amendment guarantees, there is an inherent limitation upon the applicability of the Establishment Clause's ban on state support to religion. That limitation was succinctly put in *Everson* v. *Board of Education*. "State power is no more to be used so as to handicap religions than it is to favor them." And in a later case, this Court recognized that the limitation was one which was itself compelled by the free exercise guarantee. "To hold that a state cannot consistently with the First and Fourteenth Amendments utilize its public school system to aid any or all religious faiths or sects in the dissemination of their doctrines and ideals does not . . . manifest a governmental hostility to religion or religious teachings. A manifestation of such hostility would be at war with our national tradition as embodied in the First Amendment's guaranty of the ⌐312 free ⊥exercise of religion." *McCollum* v. *Board of Education*.

That the central value embodied in the First Amendment—and, more particularly, in the guarantee of "liberty" contained in the Fourteenth—is the safeguarding of an individual's right to free exercise of his religion has been consistently recognized. Thus, in the case of *Hamilton* v. *Regents*, Mr. Justice Cardozo, concurring, assumed that it was ". . . *the religious liberty* protected by the First Amendment against invasion by the nation [which] is protected by the Fourteenth Amendment against invasion by the states." And in *Cantwell* v. *Connecticut* the purpose of those guarantees was described in the following terms: "On the one hand, it forestalls compulsion by law of the acceptance of any creed or the practice of any form of worship. Freedom of conscience and freedom to adhere to such religious organization or form of worship as the individual may choose cannot be restricted by law. On the other hand, it safeguards the free exercise of the chosen form of religion."

It is this concept of constitutional protection embodied in our decisions which makes the cases before us such difficult ones for me. For there is involved in these cases a substantial free exercise claim on the part of those who affirmatively desire to have their children's school day open with the reading of passages from the Bible.

It has become accepted that the decision in *Pierce* v. *Society of Sisters*, upholding the right of parents to send their children to nonpublic schools, was ultimately based upon the recognition of the validity of the free exercise claim involved in that situation. It might be argued here that parents who wanted their children to be exposed to religious influences in school could, under *Pierce*, send their children to ⌐313 private or parochial ⊥schools. But the consideration

which renders this contention too facile to be determinative has already been recognized by the Court: "Freedom of speech, freedom of the press, freedom of religion are available to all, not merely to those who can pay their own way." *Murdock* v. *Pennsylvania*.

It might also be argued that parents who want their children exposed to religious influences can adequately fulfill that wish off school property and outside school time. With all its surface persuasiveness, however, this argument seriously misconceives the basic constitutional justification for permitting the exercises at issue in these cases. For a compulsory state educational system so structures a child's life that if religious exercises are held to be an impermissible activity in schools, religion is placed at an artificial and state-created disadvantage. Viewed in this light, permission of such exercises for those who want them is necessary if the schools are truly to be neutral in the matter of religion. And a refusal to permit religious exercises thus is seen, not as the realization of state neutrality, but rather as the establishment of a religion of secularism, or at the least, as government support of the beliefs of those who think that religious exercises should be conducted only in private.

What seems to me to be of paramount importance, then, is recognition of the fact that the claim advanced here in favor of Bible reading is sufficiently substantial to make simple reference to the constitutional phrase "establishment of religion" as inadequate an analysis of the cases before us as the ritualistic invocation of the nonconstitutional phrase "separation of church and state." What these cases compel, rather, is an analysis of just what the "neutrality" is which is required by the interplay of the Establishment and Free Exercise Clauses of the First Amendment, as imbedded in the Fourteenth.

IV

⊥ Our decisions make clear that there is no con-   ⌐314 stitutional bar to the use of government property for religious purposes. On the contrary, this Court has consistently held that the discriminatory barring of religious groups from public property is itself a violation of First and Fourteenth Amendment guarantees. A different standard has been applied to public school property, because of the coercive effect which the use by religious sects of a compulsory school system would necessarily have upon the children involved. But insofar as the *McCollum* decision rests on the Establishment rather than the Free Exercise Clause, it is clear that its effect is limited to religious instruction—to government support of proselytizing activities of religious sects by throwing the weight of secular authority behind the dissemination of religious tenets.

The dangers both to government and to religion inherent in official support of instruction in the tenets of various religious sects are absent in the present cases, which involve only a reading from the

Bible unaccompanied by comments which might otherwise constitute instruction. Indeed, since, from all that appears in either record, any teacher who does not wish to do so is free not to participate, it cannot even be contended that some ⊥infinitesimal part of the salaries paid by the State are made contingent upon the performance of a religious function.

In the absence of evidence that the legislature or school board intended to prohibit local schools from substituting a different set of readings where parents requested such a change, we should not assume that the provisions before us—as actually administered— may not be construed simply as authorizing religious exercises, nor that the designations may not be treated simply as indications of the promulgating body's view as to the community's preference. We are under a duty to interpret these provisions so as to render them constitutional if reasonably possible. In the *Schempp* case there is evidence which indicates that variations were in fact permitted by the very school there involved, and that further variations were not introduced only because of the absence of requests from parents. And in the *Murray* case the Baltimore rule itself contains a provision permitting another version of the Bible to be substituted for the King James version.

If the provisions are not so construed, I think that their validity under the Establishment Clause would be extremely doubtful, because of the designation of a particular religious book and a denominational prayer. But since, even if the provisions ·are construed as I believe they must be, I think that the cases before us must be remanded for further evidence on other issues—thus affording the plaintiffs an opportunity to prove that local variations are not in fact permitted—I shall for the bal⊥ance of this dissenting opinion treat the provisions before us as making the variety and content of the exercises, as well as a choice as to their implementation, matters which ultimately reflect the consensus of each local school community. In the absence of coercion upon those who do not wish to participate—because they hold less strong beliefs, or no beliefs at all—such provisions cannot, in my view, be held to represent the type of support of religion barred by the Establishment Clause. For the only support which such rules provide for religion is the withholding of state hostility—a simple acknowledgment on the part of secular authorities that the Constitution does not require extirpation of all expression of religious belief.

V

I have said that these provisions authorizing religious exercises are properly to be regarded as measures making possible the free exercise of religion. But it is important to stress that, strictly speaking, what is at issue here is a privilege rather than a right. In other words, the question presented is not whether exercises such as those at issue here are constitutionally compelled, but rather whether

they are constitutionally invalid. And that issue, in my view, turns on the question of coercion.

It is clear that the dangers of coercion involved in the holding of religious exercises in a schoolroom differ qualitatively from those presented by the use of similar exercises or affirmations in ceremonies attended by adults. Even as to children, however, the duty laid upon government in connection with religious exercises in the public schools is that of refraining from so structuring the school environment as to put any kind of pressure on a child to participate in those exercises; it is not that of providing an atmosphere in which children are kept scrupulously insulated from any awareness that some of their fellows ⊥may want to open the school day with prayer, or of the fact that there exist in our pluralistic society differences of religious belief.

These are not, it must be stressed, cases like *Brown* v. *Board of Education*, in which this Court held that, in the sphere of public education, the Fourteenth Amendment's guarantee of equal protection of the laws required that race not be treated as a relevant factor. A segregated school system is not invalid because its operation is coercive; it is invalid simply because our Constitution presupposes that men are created equal, and that therefore racial differences cannot provide a valid basis for governmental action. Accommodation of religious differences on the part of the State, however, is not only permitted but required by that same Constitution.

The governmental neutrality which the First and Fourteenth Amendments require in the cases before us, in other words, is the extension of evenhanded treatment to all who believe, doubt, or disbelieve—a refusal on the part of the State to weight the scales of private choice. In these cases, therefore, what is involved is not state action based on impermissible categories, but rather an attempt by the State to accommodate those differences which the existence in our society of a variety of religious beliefs makes inevitable. The Constitution requires that such efforts be struck down only if they are proven to entail the use of the secular authority of government to coerce a preference among such beliefs.

It may well be, as has been argued to us, that even the supposed benefits to be derived from noncoercive religious exercises in public schools are incommensurate with the administrative problems which they would create. The choice involved, however, is one for each local community and its school board, and not for this Court. For, as I have said, religious exercises are not constitutionally invalid if they simply reflect differences which exist in the ⊥society from which the school draws its pupils. They become constitutionally invalid only if their administration places the sanction of secular authority behind one or more particular religious or irreligious beliefs.

To be specific, it seems to me clear that certain types of exercises would present situations in which no possiblity of coercion on the part of secular officials could be claimed to exist. Thus, if such exercises were held either before or after the official school day, or if the school schedule were such that participation were merely one among a number of desirable alternatives, it could hardly be contended that the exercises did anything more than to provide an opportunity for the voluntary expression of religious belief. On the other hand, a law which provided for religious exercises during the school day and which contained no excusal provision would obviously be unconstitutionally coercive upon those who did not wish to participate. And even under a law containing an excusal provision, if the exercises were held during the school day, and no equally desirable alternative were provided by the school authorities, the likelihood that children might be under at least some psychological compulsion to participate would be great. In a case such as the latter, however, I think we would err if we *assumed* such coercion in the absence of any evidence.

VI

⊥319   ⊥ Viewed in this light, it seems to me clear that the records in both of the cases before us are wholly inadequate to support an informed or responsible decision. Both cases involve provisions which explicitly permit any student who wishes, to be excused from participation in the exercises. There is no evidence in either case as to whether there would exist any coercion of any kind upon a student who did not want to participate. No evidence at all was adduced in the *Murray* case, because it was decided upon a demurrer. All that we have in that case, therefore, is the conclusory language of a pleading. While such conclusory allegations are acceptable for procedural purposes, I think that the nature of the constitutional problem involved here clearly demands that no decision be made except upon evidence. In the *Schempp* case the record shows no more than a subjective prophecy by a parent of what he thought would happen if a request were made to be excused from participation in the exercises under the amended statute. No such request was ever made, and there is no evidence whatever as to what might or would actually happen, nor of what administrative arrangements the school actually might or could make to free from pressure of any kind those who do not want to participate in the exercises. There were no District Court findings on this issue, since the case under the amended statute was decided exclusively on Establishment Clause grounds.

What our Constitution indispensably protects is the freedom of each of us, be he Jew or Agnostic, ⊥320   Christian or ⊥ Atheist, Buddhist or Freethinker, to believe or disbelieve, to worship or not worship, to pray or keep silent, according to his own conscience, uncoerced and unrestrained by government. It is conceivable that these school boards, or even all school boards, might eventually find it impossible to administer a system of religious exercises during

school hours in such a way as to meet this constitutional standard—in such a way as completely to free from any kind of official coercion those who do not affirmatively want to participate. But I think we must not assume that school boards so lack the qualities of inventiveness and good will as to make impossible the achievement of that goal.

I would remand both cases for further hearings.

EPPERSON v. ARKANSAS

393 U.S. 97
ON APPEAL FROM THE SUPREME COURT OF ARKANSAS
Argued October 16, 1968 — Decided November 12, 1968

⊥ *Mr. Justice FORTAS* delivered the opinion of ⊥9█ the Court.

I

This appeal challenges the constitutionality of the "anti-evolution" statute which the State of Arkansas adopted in 1928 to prohibit the teaching in its public schools and universities of the theory that man evolved from other species of life. The statute was a product of the upsurge of "fundamentalist" religious fervor of the twenties. The Arkansas statute was an adaptation of the famous Tennessee "monkey law" which that State adopted in 1925. The constitutionality of the Tennessee law was upheld by the Tennessee Supreme Court in the celebrated *Scopes* case in 1927.

The Arkansas law makes it unlawful for a teacher in any state-supported school or university "to teach the ⊥ theory or doctrine that mankind ascended or ⊥9█ descended from a lower order of animals," or "to adopt or use in any such institution a textbook that teaches" this theory. Violation is a misdemeanor and subjects the violator to dismissal from his position.

The present case concerns the teaching of biology in a high school in Little Rock. According to the testimony, until the events here in litigation, the official textbook furnished for the high school biology course did not have a section on the Darwinian Theory. Then, for the academic year 1965-1966, the school administration, on recommendation of the teachers of biology in the school system, adopted and prescribed a textbook which contained a chapter setting forth "the theory about the origin . . . of man from a lower form of animal."

⊥ Susan Epperson, a young woman who graduated ⊥1C from Arkansas' school system and then obtained her master's degree in zoology at the University of Illinois, was employed by the Little Rock school system in the fall of 1964 to teach 10th grade biology at Central High School. At the start of the next academic year, 1965, she was confronted by the new textbook (which one surmises from the record was not unwelcome to her). She faced at least a literal dilemma because she was supposed to use the new textbook for classroom instruction and presumably to teach the statutorily condemned chapter; but to do so would be a criminal offense and subject her to dismissal.

She instituted the present action in the Chancery Court of the State, seeking a declaration that the Arkansas statute is void and enjoining the State and the defendant officials of the Little Rock school system from dismissing her for violation of the statute's provisions.

The Chancery Court held that the statute violated the Fourteenth Amendment to the United States Constitution. The court noted that this Amendment encompasses the prohibitions upon state interference with freedom of speech and thought which are contained in the First Amendment. Accordingly, it held that the challenged statute is unconstitutional because, in violation of the First Amendment, it "tends to hinder the quest for knowledge, restrict the freedom to learn, and restrain the freedom to teach." 01 In this perspective, the Act, ⊥it held, was an unconstitutional and void restraint upon the freedom of speech guaranteed by the Constitution.

On appeal, the Supreme Court of Arkansas reversed. Its two-sentence opinion is set forth in the margin.* It sustained the statute as an exercise of the State's power to specify the curriculum in public schools. It did not address itself to the competing constitutional considerations.

Appeal was duly prosecuted to this Court.. Only Arkansas and Mississippi have such "anti-evolution" or "monkey" laws on their books. There is no record 02 of any prosecutions in Arkan⊥sas under its statute. It is possible that the statute is presently more of a curiosity than a vital fact of life in these States. Nevertheless, the present case was brought, the appeal as of right is properly here, and it is our duty to decide the issues presented.

II

At the outset, it is urged upon us that the challenged statute is vague and uncertain and therefore within the condemnation of the Due Process Clause of the Fourteenth Amendment. The contention that the Act is vague and uncertain is supported by language in the brief opinion of Arkansas' Supreme Court. . . .

03 ⊥In any event, we do not rest our decision upon the asserted vagueness of the statute. On either interpretation of its language, Arkansas' statute cannot stand. It is of no moment whether the law is deemed

---

* "Per Curiam. Upon the principal issue, that of constitutionality, the court holds that Initiated Measure No. 1 of 1928 is a valid exercise of the state's power to specify the curriculum in its public schools. The court expresses no opinion on the question whether the Act prohibits any explanation of the theory of evolution or merely prohibits teaching that the theory is true; the answer not being necessary to a decision in the case, and the issue not having been raised.

"The decree is reversed and the cause dismissed."

to prohibit mention of Darwin's theory, or to forbid any or all of the infinite varieties of communication embraced within the term "teaching." Under either interpretation, the law must be stricken because of its conflict with the constitutional prohibition of state laws respecting an establishment of religion or prohibiting the free exercise thereof. The overriding fact is that Arkansas' law selects from the body of knowledge a particular segment which it proscribes for the sole reason that it is deemed to conflict with a particular religious doctrine; that is, with a particular interpretation of the Book of Genesis by a particular religious group.

III

The antecedents of today's decision are many and unmistakable. They are rooted in the foundation soil of our Nation. They are fundamental to freedom.

Government in our democracy, state and national, must be neutral in matters of religious theory, doctrine, ⊥and practice. It may not be hostile to any religion or to the advocacy of no-religion; and it may ⌐104 not aid, foster, or promote one religion or religious theory against another or even against the militant opposite. The First Amendment mandates governmental neutrality between religion and religion, and between religion and nonreligion.

As early as 1872, this Court said: "The law knows no heresy, and is committed to the support of no dogma, the establishment of no sect." *Watson* v. *Jones*. This has been the interpretation of the great First Amendment which this Court has applied in the many and subtle problems which the ferment of our national life has presented for decision within the Amendment's broad command.

Judicial interposition in the operation of the public school system of the Nation raises problems requiring care and restraint. Our courts, however, have not failed to apply the First Amendment's mandate in our educational system where essential to safeguard the fundamental values of freedom of speech and inquiry and of belief. By and large, public education in our Nation is committed to the control of state and local authorities. Courts do not and cannot intervene in the resolution of conflicts which arise in the daily operation of school systems and which do not directly and sharply implicate basic constitutional values. On the other hand, "[t]he vigilant protection of constitutional freedoms is nowhere more vital than in the community of American schools," *Shelton* v. *Tucker*. As this ⊥Court said in ⌐105 *Keyishian* v. *Board of Regents*, the First Amendment "does not tolerate laws that cast a pall of orthodoxy over the classroom. . . ."

⊥There is and can be no doubt that the First ⌐106 Amendment does not permit the State to require that teaching and learning must be tailored to the principles or prohibitions of any religious sect or dogma. In *Everson* v. *Board of Education*, this Court, in upholding a state law to provide free bus service to school children, including those attending parochial schools, said: "Neither [a State nor the Federal Government] can pass laws which aid one religion, aid all religions, or prefer one religion over another."

At the following Term of Court, in *McCollum* v. *Board of Education*, the Court held that Illinois could not release pupils from class to attend classes of instruction in the school buildings in the religion of their choice. This, it said, would involve the State in using tax-supported property for religious purposes, thereby breaching the "wall of separation" which, according to Jefferson, the First Amendment was intended to erect between church and state. While study of religions and of the Bible from a literary and historic viewpoint, presented objectively as part of a secular program of education, need not collide with the First Amendment's prohibition, the State may not adopt programs or practices in its public schools or colleges which "aid or oppose" any religion. This prohibition is absolute. It forbids alike the preference of a religious doctrine or the prohibi-
⌐107 tion ⊥of theory which is deemed antagonistic to a particular dogma. As Mr. Justice Clark stated in *Joseph Burstyn, Inc.* v. *Wilson*, "the state has no legitimate interest in protecting any or all religions from views distasteful to them. . . ." The test was stated as follows in *Abington School District* v. *Schempp*: "[W]hat are the purpose and the primary effect of the enactment? If either is the advancement or inhibition of religion then the enactment exceeds the scope of legislative power as circumscribed by the Constitution."

These precedents inevitably determine the result in the present case. The State's undoubted right to prescribe the curriculum for its public schools does not carry with it the right to prohibit, on pain of criminal penalty, the teaching of a scientific theory or doctrine where that prohibition is based upon reasons that violate the First Amendment. It is much too late to argue that the State may impose upon the teachers in its schools any conditions that it chooses, however restrictive they may be of constitutional guarantees.

In the present case, there can be no doubt that Arkansas has sought to prevent its teachers from discussing the theory of evolution because it is contrary to the belief of some that the Book of Genesis must be the exclusive source of doctrine as to the origin of man. No suggestion has been made that Arkansas' law may be justified by considerations of state policy other than the religious views of some of
⌐108 its citizens. It is clear ⊥that fundamentalist sectarian conviction was and is the law's reason for existence. Its antecedent, Tennessee's "monkey law," candidly stated its purpose: to make it unlawful "to teach any theory that denies the story of the Divine Creation of man as taught in the Bible, and to teach
⌐109 instead that man has descended from a ⊥lower order of animals." Perhaps the sensational publicity atten-

dant upon the *Scopes* trial induced Arkansas to adopt less explicit language. It eliminated Tennessee's reference to "the story of the Divine Creation of man" as taught in the Bible, but there is no doubt that the motivation for the law was the same: to suppress the teaching of a theory which, it was thought, "denied" the divine creation of man.

Arkansas' law cannot be defended as an act of religious neutrality. Arkansas did not seek to excise from the curricula of its schools and universities all discussion of the origin of man. The law's effort was confined to an attempt to blot out a particular theory because of its supposed conflict with the Biblical account, literally read. Plainly, the law is contrary to the mandate of the First, and in violation of the Fourteenth, Amendment to the Constitution.

The judgment of the Supreme Court of Arkansas is *Reversed*.

Mr. Justice BLACK, concurring.

I am by no means sure that this case presents a genuine justiciable case or controversy. Although Arkansas Initiated Act No. 1, the statute alleged to be unconstitutional, was passed by the voters of Arkansas in 1928, we are informed that there has never been even a single attempt by the State to enforce it. And the pallid, unenthusiastic, even apologetic defense of the Act presented by the State in this Court indicates that the State would make no attempt to enforce the law ⊥should it remain on the books for ⌐1 the next century. Now, nearly 40 years after the law has slumbered on the books as though dead, a teacher alleging fear that the state might arouse from its lethargy and try to punish her has asked for a declaratory judgment holding the law unconstitutional. She was subsequently joined by a parent who alleged his interest in seeing that his two then school-age sons "be informed of all scientific theories and hypotheses. . . ." But whether this Arkansas teacher is still a teacher, fearful of punishment under the Act, we do not know. It may be, as has been published in the daily press, that she has long since given up her job as a teacher and moved to a distant city, thereby escaping the dangers she had imagined might befall her under this lifeless Arkansas Act. And there is not one iota of concrete evidence to show that the parent-intervenor's sons have not been or will not be taught about evolution. The textbook adopted for use in biology classes in Little Rock includes an entire chapter dealing with evolution. There is no evidence that this chapter is not being freely taught in the schools that use the textbook and no evidence that the intervenor's sons, who were 15 and 17 years old when this suit was brought three years ago, are still in high school or yet to take biology. Unfortunately, however, the State's languid interest in the case has not prompted it to keep this Court informed concerning facts that might easily justify dismissal of this alleged lawsuit as moot or as lacking the qualities of a genuine case or controversy.

Notwithstanding my own doubts as to whether the case presents a justiciable controversy, the Court brushes aside these doubts and leaps headlong into the middle of the very broad problems involved in federal intrusion into state powers to decide what subjects and schoolbooks it may wish to use in teaching state pupils. While I hesitate to enter into the consideration and deci⊥sion of such sensitive state-federal relationships, I reluctantly acquiesce. But, agreeing to consider this as a genuine case or controversy, I cannot agree to thrust the Federal Government's long arm the least bit further into state school curriculums than decision of this particular case requires. And the Court, in order to invalidate the Arkansas law as a violation of the First Amendment, has been compelled to give the State's law a broader meaning than the State Supreme Court was willing to give it. . . .

⊥It seems to me that in this situation the statute is too vague for us to strike it down on any ground but that: vagueness. Under this statute as construed by the Arkansas Supreme Court, a teacher cannot know whether he is forbidden to mention Darwin's theory at all or only free to discuss it as long as he refrains from contending that it is true. It is an established rule that a statute which leaves an ordinary man so doubtful about its meaning that he cannot know when he has violated it denies him the first essential of due process. Holding the statute too vague to enforce would not only follow longstanding constitutional precedents but it would avoid having this Court take unto itself the duty of a State's highest court to interpret and mark the boundaries of the State's laws. And, more important, it would not place this Court in the unenviable position of violating the principle of leaving the States absolutely free to choose their own curriculums for their own schools so long as their action does not palpably conflict with a clear constitutional command.

The Court, not content to strike down this Arkansas Act on the unchallengeable ground of its plain vagueness, chooses rather to invalidate it as a violation of the Establishment of Religion Clause of the First Amendment. I would not decide this case on such a sweeping ground for the following reasons, among others.

1. In the first place I find it difficult to agree with the Court's statement that "there can be no doubt that Arkansas has sought to prevent its teachers from discussing the theory of evolution because it is contrary to the belief of some that the Book of Genesis must be the exclusive source of doctrine as to the origin of man." It may be instead that the people's motive was merely that it would be best to remove this contro⊥versial subject from its schools; there is no reason I can imagine why a State is without power to withdraw from its curriculum any subject deemed too emotional and controversial for

its public schools. And this Court has consistently held that it is not for us to invalidate a statute because of our views that the "motives" behind its passage were improper; it is simply too difficult to determine what those motives were.

2. A second question that arises for me is whether this Court's decision forbidding a State to exclude the subject of evolution from its schools infringes the religious freedom of those who consider evolution an anti-religious doctrine. If the theory is considered anti-religious, as the Court indicates, how can the State be bound by the Federal Constitution to permit its teachers to advocate such an "anti-religious" doctrine to schoolchildren? The very cases cited by the Court as supporting its conclusion hold that the State must be neutral, not favoring one religious or anti-religious view over another. The Darwinian theory is said to challenge the Bible's story of creation; so too have some of those who believe in the Bible, along with many others, challenged the Darwinian theory. Since there is no indication that the literal Biblical doctrine of the origin of man is included in the curriculum of Arkansas schools, does not the removal of the subject of evolution leave the State in a neutral position toward these supposedly competing religious and anti-religious doctrines? Unless this Court is prepared simply to write off as pure nonsense the views of those who consider evolution an anti-religious doctrine, then this issue presents problems under the Establishment Clause far more troublesome than are discussed in the Court's opinion.

3. I am also not ready to hold that a person hired to teach school children takes with him into the classroom a constitutional right to teach sociological, economic, ⊥political, or religious subjects that the school's managers do not want discussed. This Court has said that the rights of free speech "while fundamental in our democratic society, still do not mean that everyone with opinions or beliefs to express may address a group at any public place and at any time." I question whether it is absolutely certain, as the Court's opinion indicates, that "academic freedom" permits a teacher to breach his contractual agreement to teach only the subjects designated by the school authorities who hired him. Certainly the Darwinian theory, precisely like the Genesis story of the creation of man, is not above challenge. In fact the Darwinian theory has not merely been criticized by religionists but by scientists, and perhaps no scientist would be willing to take an oath and swear that everything announced in the Darwinian theory is unquestionably true. The Court, it seems to me, makes a serious mistake in bypassing the plain, unconstitutional vagueness of this statute in order to reach out and decide this troublesome, to me, First Amendment question. However wise this Court may be or may become hereafter, it is doubtful that, sitting in Washington, it can successfully supervise and censor the curriculum of every public school in every hamlet and city

in the United States. I doubt that our wisdom is so nearly infallible.

I would either strike down the Arkansas Act as too vague to enforce, or remand to the State Supreme Court for clarification of its holding and opinion.

Mr. Justice HARLAN, concurring.

I think it deplorable that this case should have come to us with such an opaque opinion by the State's highest court. With all respect, that court's ⌐115 handling of the ⊥ case savors of a studied effort to avoid coming to grips with this anachronistic statute and "to pass the buck" to this Court. This sort of temporizing does not make for healthy operations between the state and federal judiciaries. Despite these observations, I am in agreement with this Court's opinion that, the constitutional claims having been properly raised and necessarily decided below, resolution of the matter by us cannot properly be avoided.

I concur in so much of the Court's opinion as holds that the Arkansas statute constitutes an "establishment of religion" forbidden to the States by the Fourteenth Amendment. I do not understand, however, why the Court finds it necessary to explore at length appellants' contentions that the statute is unconstitutionally vague and that it interferes with free speech, only to conclude that these issues need not be decided in this case. In the process of *not* deciding them, the Court obscures its otherwise straightforward holding, and opens its opinion to possible implications from which I am constrained to disassociate myself.

Mr. Justice STEWART, concurring in the result.

The States are most assuredly free "to choose their own curriculums for their own schools." A State is ⌐116 en⊥tirely free, for example, to decide that the only foreign language to be taught in its public school system shall be Spanish. But would a State be constitutionally free to punish a teacher for letting his students know that other languages are also spoken in the world? I think not.

It is one thing for a State to determine that "the subject of higher mathematics, or astronomy, or biology" shall or shall not be included in its public school curriculum. It is quite another thing for a State to make it a criminal offense for a public school teacher so much as to mention the very existence of an entire system of respected human thought. That kind of criminal law, I think, would clearly impinge upon the guarantees of free communication contained in the First Amendment, and made applicable to the States by the Fourteenth.

The Arkansas Supreme Court has said that the statute before us may or may not be just such a law. The result, as *Mr. Justice BLACK* points out, is that "a teacher cannot know whether he is forbidden to

mention Darwin's theory at all." Since I believe that no State could constitutionally forbid a teacher "to mention Darwin's theory at all," and since Arkansas may, or may not, have done just that, I conclude that the statute before us is so vague as to be invalid under the Fourteenth Amendment.

STONE v. GRAHAM

449 U.S. 39
ON WRIT OF CERTIORARI TO THE SUPREME
COURT OF
THE STATE OF KENTUCKY
Without Argument Decided November 17, 1980

⊥*PER CURIAM.*   ⌐39

A Kentucky statute requires the posting of a copy of the Ten Commandments, purchased with private contributions, on the wall of each public classroom in the State. Peti⊥tioners, claiming that this statute   ⌐40 violates the Establishment and Free Exercise Clauses of the First Amendment, sought an injunction against its enforcement. The state trial court upheld the statute, finding that its "avowed purpose" was "secular and not religious," and that the statute would "neither advance nor inhibit any religion or religious group" nor involve the State excessively in religious matters. The Supreme Court of the Commonwealth of Kentucky affirmed by an equally divided court. *Stone* v. *Graham*. We reverse.

This Court has announced a three-part test for determining whether a challenged state statute is permissible under the Establishment Clause of the United States Constitution: "First, the statute must have a secular legislative purpose; second, its principal or primary effect must be one that neither advances nor inhibits religion . . .; finally the statute must not foster 'an excessive government entanglement with religion.'" *Lemon* v. *Kurtzman.*

If a statute violates any of these three principles, it must be ⊥struck down under the Establishment   ⌐41 Clause. We conclude that Kentucky's statute requiring the posting of the Ten Commandments in public schoolrooms had no secular legislative purpose, and is therefore unconstitutional.

The Commonwealth insists that the statute in question serves a secular legislative purpose, observing that the legislature required the following notation in small print at the bottom of each display of the Ten Commandments: "The secular application of the Ten Commandments is clearly seen in its adoption as the fundamental legal code of Western Civilization and the Common Law of the United States."

The trial court found the "avowed" purpose of the statute to be secular, even as it labeled the statutory declaration "self-serving." Under this Court's rulings, however, such an "avowed" secular purpose is not sufficient to avoid conflict with the First Amendment. In *Abington School District* v. *Shempp* this Court held unconstitutional the daily reading of

Bible verses and the Lord's Prayer in the public schools, despite the school district's assertion of such secular purposes as "the promotion of moral values, the contradiction to the materialistic trends of our times, the perpetuation of our institutions and the teaching of literature."

The pre-eminent purpose for posting the Ten Commandments on schoolroom walls is plainly religious in nature. The Ten Commandments is undeniably a sacred text in the Jewish and Christian faiths, and no legislative recitation of a supposed secular purpose can blind us to that fact. The Commandments do not confine themselves to arguably secular matters, such as honoring one's parents, ⌐42 killing or murder, ⊥adultery, stealing, false witness, and covetousness. Rather, the first part of the Commandments concerns the religious duties of believers: worshipping the Lord God alone, avoiding idolatry, not using the Lord's name in vain, and observing the sabbath day.

This is not a case in which the Ten Commandments are integrated into the school curriculum, where the Bible may constitutionally be used in an appropriate study of history, civilization, ethics, comparative religion, or the like. *Abington School District* v. *Schempp*. Posting of religious texts on the wall serves no such educational function. If the posted copies of the Ten Commandments are to have any effect at all, it will be to induce the school children to read, meditate upon, perhaps to venerate and obey, the Commandments. However desirable this might be as a matter of private devotion, it is not a permissible state objective under the Establishment Clause.

It does not matter that the posted copies of the Ten Commandments are financed by voluntary private contributions, for the mere posting of the copies under the auspices of the legislature provides the "official support of the State . . . Government" that the Establishment Clause prohibits. Nor is it significant that the Bible verses involved in this case are merely posted on the wall, rather than read aloud as in *Schempp* and *Engel*, for "it is no defense to urge that the religious practices here may be relatively minor encroachments on the First Amendment." *Abington School District* v. *Schempp*. We conclude ⌐43 that Ky. Rev. ⊥Stat. § 158.178 (1980) violates the first part of the *Lemon* v. *Kurtzman* test and thus the Establishment Clause of the Constitution.

The petition for a writ of certiorari is granted and the judgment below is reversed.

The *CHIEF JUSTICE* and *Justice BLACKMUN* dissent. They would grant certiorari and give this case plenary consideration.

Justice STEWART dissents from this summary reversal of the courts of Kentucky, which, so far as

appears, applied wholly correct constitutional criteria in reaching their decisions.

Justice REHNQUIST, dissenting.

With no support beyond its own *ipse dixit*, the Court concludes that the Kentucky statute involved in this case "has *no* secular legislative purpose," (emphasis supplied), and that "[t]he pre-eminent purpose for posting the Ten Commandments on schoolroom walls is plainly religious in nature." This even though, as the trial court found, "[t]he General Assembly thought the statute had a secular legislative purpose and specifically said so." The Court's summary rejection of a secular purpose articulated by the legislature and confirmed by the state court is without precedent in Establishment Clause jurisprudence. This Court regularly looks to legislative articulations of a statute's purpose in Establishment Clause cases ⊥and accords such pronouncements the ⌐44 deference they are due. See, *e.g., Committee for Public Education* v. *Nyquist*, ("we need touch only briefly on the requirement of a 'secular legislative purpose.' As the recitation of legislative purposes appended to New York's law indicates, each measure is adequately supported by legitimate, nonsectarian state interests."); *Lemon* v. *Kurtzman*, ("the statutes themselves clearly state they are intended to enhance the quality of the secular education"); *Sloan* v. *Lemon; Board of Education* v. *Allen*. See also *Florey* v. *Sioux Falls School District* (upholding rules permitting public school Christmas observances with religious elements as promoting the articulated secular purpose of "advanc[ing] the student's knowledge and appreciation of the role that our religious heritage has played in the social, cultural and historical development of civilization"). The fact that the asserted secular purpose may overlap with what some may see as a religious objective does not render it unconstitutional. As this Court stated in *McGowan* v. *Maryland*, in upholding the validity of Sunday closing laws, "the present purpose and effect of most of [these laws] is to provide a uniform day of rest for all citizens; the fact that this day is Sunday, a day of particular significance for the dominant Christian sects, does not bar the state from achieving its secular goals."

Abington School District v. *Schempp*, repeatedly cited by the Court, is not to the contrary. No statutory findings of secular purpose supported the challenged enactments in that case. In one of the two cases considered in *Abington School District* the trial court had determined that the challenged exercises were intended by the State to be religious exercises. A contrary finding is presented here. In the other case no specific finding had been ⊥made, and ⌐45 "the religious character of the exercise was admitted by the State."

The Court rejects the secular purpose articulated by the State because the Decalogue "is undeniably a sacred text." It is equally undeniable, however, as the elected representatives of Kentucky determined, that the Ten Commandments have had a significant impact on the development of secular legal codes of the western world. The trial court concluded that evidence submitted substantiated this determination. See also *Anderson* v. *Salt Lake City Corp.* (upholding construction on public land of monument inscribed with Ten Commandments because they have "substantial secular attributes"). Certainly the State was permitted to conclude that a document with such secular significance should be placed before its students, with an appropriate statement of the document's secular import. ("It does not seem reasonable to require removal of a passive monument, involving no compulsion, because its accepted precepts, as a foundation for law, reflect the religious nature of an ancient era.") See also *Opinion of the Justices* (upholding placement of plaques with the motto "In God We Trust" in public schools).

⌐46 The Establishment Clause does not require that the public sector be insulated from all things which may have a religious ⊥significance or origin. This Court has recognized that "religion has been closely identified with our history and government," *Abington School District*, and that "[t]he history of man is inseparable from the history of religion," *Engel* v. *Vitale*. Kentucky has decided to make students aware of this fact by demonstrating the secular impact of the Ten Commandments. The words of Mr. Justice Jackson, concurring in *McCollum* v. *Board of Education*, merit quotation at length: "I think it remains to be demonstrated whether it is possible, even if desirable, to comply with such demands as plaintiff's completely to isolate and cast out of secular education all that some people may reasonably regard as religious instruction. Perhaps subjects such as mathematics, physics or chemistry are, or can be, completely secularized. But it would not seem practical to teach either practice or appreciation of the arts if we are to forbid exposure of youth to any religious influences. Music without sacred music, architecture minus the cathedral, or painting without the scriptural themes would be eccentric and incomplete, even from a secular point of view. . . . I should suppose it is a proper, if not an indispensable, part of preparation for a worldly life to know the roles that religion and religions have played in the tragic story of mankind. The fact is that, for good or for ill, nearly everything in our culture worth transmitting, everything which gives meaning to life, is saturated with religious influences, derived from paganism, Judaism, Christianity—both Catholic and Protestant—and other faiths accepted by a large part of the world's peoples. One can hardly respect the system of education that would leave the student wholly ignorant of the currents of religious thought that move the world society for a part in which he is being prepared."

⊥I therefore dissent from what I cannot refrain ⌐47 from describing as a cavalier summary reversal, without benefit of oral argument or briefs on the merits, of the highest court of Kentucky.

WALLACE v. JAFFREE

105 S.Ct. 2479
ON APPEAL FROM THE UNITED STATES
COURT OF APPEALS
FOR THE ELEVENTH CIRCUIT
Argued December 4, 1984 — Decided June 4, 1985

Justice STEVENS delivered the opinion of the Court.

At an early stage of this litigation, the constitutionality of three Alabama statutes was questioned: (1) § 16-1-20, enacted in 1978, which authorized a one-minute period of silence in all public schools "for meditation"; (2) § 16-1-20.1, enacted in 1981, which authorized a period of silence "for meditation or voluntary prayer"; and (3) § 16-1-20.2, enacted in 1982, which authorized teachers to lead "willing students" in a prescribed prayer to "Almighty God . . . the Creator and Supreme Judge of the world."

At the preliminary injunction stage of this case, the District Court distinguished § 16-1-20 from the other two statutes. It then held that there was "nothing wrong" with § 16-1-20, but that §§ 16-1-20.1 and 16-1-20.2 were both invalid because the sole purpose of both was "an effort on the part of the State of Alabama to encourage a religious activity." After the trial on the merits, the District Court did not change its interpretation of these two statutes, but held that they were constitutional because, in its opinion, Alabama has the power to establish a state religion if it chooses to do so.

The Court of Appeals agreed with the District Court's initial interpretation of the purpose of both §§ 16-1-20.1 and 16-1-20.2, and held them both unconstitutional. We have already affirmed the Court of Appeals' holding with respect to § 16-1-20.2. Moreover, appellees have not questioned the holding that § 16-1-20 is valid. Thus, the narrow question for decision is whether § 16-1-20.1, which authorizes a period of silence for "meditation or voluntary prayer," is a law respecting the establishment of religion within the meaning of the First Amendment.

I

Appellee Ishmael Jaffree is a resident of Mobile County, Alabama. On May 28, 1982, he filed a complaint on behalf of three of his minor children; two of them were second-grade students and the third was then in kindergarten. The complaint named members of the Mobile County School Board, various school officials, and the minor plaintiffs' three teachers as defendants. The complaint alleged that the appellees brought the action "seeking principally a declaratory judgment and an injunction restraining the Defendants and each of them from maintaining or allowing the maintenance of regular religious prayer services or other forms of religious observances in the Mobile County Public Schools in violation of the First Amendment as made applicable to states by the Fourteenth Amendment to the United States Constitution." The complaint further alleged that two of the children had been subjected to various acts of religious indoctrination "from the beginning of the school year in September, 1981"; that the defendant teachers had "on a daily basis" led their classes in saying certain prayers in unison; that the minor children were exposed to ostracism from their peer group class members if they did not participate; and that Ishmael Jaffree had repeatedly but unsuccessfully requested that the devotional services be stopped. The original complaint made no reference to any Alabama statute.

On June 4, 1982, appellees filed an amended complaint seeking class certification, and on June 30, 1982, they filed a second amended complaint naming the Governor of Alabama and various State officials as additional defendants. In that amendment the appellees challenged the constitutionality of three Alabama statutes: §§ 16-1-20, 16-1-20.1, 16-1-20.2.

On August 2, 1982, the District Court held an evidentiary hearing on appellees' motion for a preliminary injunction. At that hearing, State Senator Donald G. Holmes testified that he was the "prime sponsor" of the bill that was enacted in 1981 as § 16-1-20.1. He explained that the bill was an "effort to return voluntary prayer to our public schools . . . it is a beginning and a step in the right direction." Apart from the purpose to return voluntary prayer to public school, Senator Holmes unequivocally testified that he had "no other purpose in mind." A week after the hearing, the District Court entered a preliminary injunction. The court held that appellees were likely to prevail on the merits because the enactment of §§ 16-1-20.1 and 16-1-20.2 did not reflect a clearly secular purpose.

In November 1982, the District Court held a four-day trial on the merits. The evidence related primarily to the 1981-1982 academic year—the year after the enactment of § 16-1-20.1 and prior to the enactment of § 16-1-20.2. The District Court found that during that academic year each of the minor plaintiffs' teachers had led classes in prayer activities, even after being informed of appellees' objections to these activities.

In its lengthy conclusions of law, the District Court reviewed a number of opinions of this Court interpreting the Establishment Clause of the First Amendment, and then embarked on a fresh examination of the question whether the First Amendment imposes any barrier to the establishment of an official religion by the State of Alabama. After reviewing at length what it perceived to be newly discovered historical evidence, the District Court

concluded that "the establishment clause of the first amendment to the United States Constitution does not prohibit the state from establishing a religion." 554 F.Supp. 1104 at 1128 (1983) In a separate opinion, the District Court dismissed appellees' challenge to the three Alabama statutes because of a failure to state any claim for which relief could be granted. The court's dismissal of this challenge was also based on its conclusion that the Establishment Clause did not bar the States from establishing a religion. 554 F.Supp. 1130 (1983)

The Court of Appeals consolidated the two cases; not surprisingly, it reversed. The Court of Appeals noted that this Court had considered and had rejected the historical arguments that the District Court found persuasive, and that the District Court had misapplied the doctrine of *stare decisis.* The Court of Appeals then held that the teachers' religious activities violated the Establishment Clause of the First Amendment. With respect to § 16-1-20.1 and § 16-1-20.2, the Court of Appeals stated that "both statutes advance and encourage religious activities." The Court of Appeals then quoted with approval the District Court's finding that § 16-1-20.1, and § 16-1-20.2, were efforts " 'to encourage a religious activity. Even though these statutes are permissive in form, it is nevertheless state involvement respecting an establishment of religion.' " Thus, the Court of Appeals concluded that both statutes were "specifically the type which the Supreme Court addressed in *Engel* v. *Vitale.*" 705 F.Supp. 1526 at 1535 (1983)

A suggestion for rehearing *en banc* was denied over the dissent of four judges who expressed the opinion that the full court should reconsider the panel decision insofar as it held § 16-1-20.1 unconstitutional. When this Court noted probable jurisdiction, it limited argument to the question that those four judges thought worthy of reconsideration. The judgment of the Court of Appeals with respect to the other issues presented by the appeals was affirmed.

II

Our unanimous affirmance of the Court of Appeals' judgment concerning § 16-1-20.2 makes it unnecessary to comment at length on the District Court's remarkable conclusion that the Federal Constitution imposes no obstacle to Alabama's establishment of a state religion. Before analyzing the precise issue that is presented to us, it is nevertheless appropriate to recall how firmly embedded in our constitutional jurisprudence is the proposition that the several States have no greater power to restrain the individual freedoms protected by the First Amendment than does the Congress of the United States.

As is plain from its text, the First Amendment was adopted to curtail the power of Congress to interfere with the individual's freedom to believe, to worship, and to express himself in accordance with the dictates of his own conscience. Until the Fourteenth Amendment was added to the Constitution, the First Amendment's restraints on the exercise of federal power simply did not apply to the States. But when the Constitution was amended to prohibit any State from depriving any person of liberty without due process of law, that Amendment imposed the same substantive limitations on the States' power to legislate that the First Amendment had always imposed on the Congress' power. The Court has confirmed and endorsed this elementary proposition of law time and time again.

Writing for a unanimous Court in *Cantwell* v. *Connecticut, Justice* ROBERTS explained: " . . . We hold that the statute, as construed and applied to the appellants, deprives them of their liberty without due process of law in contravention of the Fourteenth Amendment. The fundamental concept of liberty embodied in that Amendment embraces the liberties guaranteed by the First Amendment. The First Amendment declares that Congress shall make no law respecting an establishment of religion or prohibiting the free exercise thereof. The Fourteenth Amendment has rendered the legislatures of the states as incompetent as Congress to enact such law. The constitutional inhibition of legislation on the subject of religion has a double aspect. On the one hand, it forestalls compulsion by law of the acceptance of any creed or the practice of any form of worship. Freedom of conscience and freedom to adhere to such religious organization or form of worship as the individual may choose cannot be restricted by law. On the other hand, it safeguards the free exercise of the chosen form of religion."

Cantwell, of course, is but one case in which the Court has identified the individual's freedom of conscience as the central liberty that unifies the various clauses in the First Amendment. Enlarging on this theme, *The CHIEF JUSTICE* recently wrote: "We begin with the proposition that the right of freedom of thought protected by the First Amendment against state action includes both the right to speak freely and the right to refrain from speaking at all. A system which secures the right to proselytize religious, political, and ideological causes must also guarantee the concomitant right to decline to foster such concepts. The right to speak and the right to refrain from speaking are complementary components of the broader concept of 'individual freedom of mind.'

"The Court in *Barnette* was faced with a state statute which required public school students to participate in daily ceremonies by honoring the flag both with words and traditional salute gestures. In overruling its prior decision in *Minersville District* v. *Gobitis,* the Court held that 'a ceremony so touching matters of opinion and political attitude may [not] be imposed upon the individual by official authority under powers committed to any political organization under our Constitution.' Compelling the affirm-

ative act of a flag salute involved a more serious infringement upon personal liberties than the passive act of carrying the state motto on a license plate, but the difference is essentially one of degree. Here, as in *Barnette,* we are faced with a state measure which forces an individual, as part of his daily life—indeed constantly while his automobile is in public view—to be an instrument for fostering public adherence to an ideological point of view he finds unacceptable. In doing so, the State 'invades the sphere of intellect and spirit which it is the purpose of the First Amendment to our Constitution to reserve from all official control.' " *Wooley* v. *Maynard*

Just as the right to speak and the right to refrain from speaking are complementary components of a broader concept of individual freedom of mind, so also the individual's freedom to choose his own creed is the counterpart of his right to refrain from accepting the creed established by the majority. At one time it was thought that this right merely proscribed the preference of one Christian sect over another, but would not require equal respect for the conscience of the infidel, the atheist, or the adherent of a non-Christian faith such as Mohammedism or Judaism. But when the underlying principle has been examined in the crucible of litigation, the Court has unambiguously concluded that the individual freedom of conscience protected by the First Amendment embraces the right to select any religious faith or none at all. This conclusion derives support not only from the interest in respecting the individual's freedom of conscience, but also from the conviction that religious beliefs worthy of respect are the product of free and voluntary choice by the faithful, and from recognition of the fact that the political interest in forestalling intolerance extends beyond intolerance among Christian sects—or even intolerance among "religions"—to encompass intolerance of the disbeliever and the uncertain. As *Justice JACKSON* eloquently stated in *Board of Education* v. *Barnette:* "If there is any fixed star in our constitutional constellation, it is that no official, high or petty, can prescribe what shall be orthodox in politics, nationalism, religion, or other matters of opinion or force citizens to confess by word or act their faith therein." The State of Alabama, no less than the Congress of the United States, must respect that basic truth.

III

When the Court has been called upon to construe the breadth of the Establishment Clause, it has examined the criteria developed over a period of many years. Thus, in *Lemon* v. *Kurtzman,* we wrote: "Every analysis in this area must begin with consideration of the cumulative criteria developed by the Court over many years. Three such tests may be gleaned from our cases. First, the statute must have a secular legislative purpose; second, its principal or primary effect must be one that neither advances nor inhibits religion; finally, the statute must not foster 'an excessive government entanglement with religion.'" It is the first of these three criteria that is most plainly implicated by this case. As the District Court correctly recognized, no consideration of the second or third criteria is necessary if a statute does not have a clearly secular purpose. For even though a statute that is motivated in part by a religious purpose may satisfy the first criterion, the First Amendment requires that a statute must be invalidated if it is entirely motivated by a purpose to advance religion.

In applying the purpose test, it is appropriate to ask "whether government's actual purpose is to endorse or disapprove of religion." *Lynch* v. *Donnelly* In this case, the answer to that question is dispositive. For the record not only provides us with an unambiguous affirmative answer, but it also reveals that the enactment of § 16-1-20.1 was not motivated by any clearly secular purpose—indeed, the statute had *no* secular purpose.

IV

The sponsor of the bill that became § 16-1-20.1, Senator Donald Holmes, inserted into the legislative record—apparently without dissent—a statement indicating that the legislation was an "effort to return voluntary prayer" to the public schools. Later Senator Holmes confirmed this purpose before the District Court. In response to the question whether he had any purpose for the legislation other than returning voluntary prayer to public schools, he stated, "No, I did not have no other purpose in mind." The State did not present evidence of *any* secular purpose.

The unrebutted evidence of legislative intent contained in the legislative record and in the testimony of the sponsor of § 16-1-20.1 is confirmed by a consideration of the relationship between this statute and the two other measures that were considered in this case. The District Court found that the 1981 statute and its 1982 sequel had a common, nonsecular purpose. The wholly religious character of the later enactment is plainly evident from its text. When the differences between § 16-1-20.1 and its 1978 predecessor, § 16-1-20, are examined, it is equally clear that the 1981 statute has the same wholly religious character.

There are only three textual differences between § 16-1-20.1 and § 16-1-20: (1) the earlier statute applies only to grades one through six, whereas § 16-1-20.1 applies to all grades; (2) the earlier statute uses the word "shall" whereas § 16-1-20.1 uses the word "may"; (3) the earlier statute refers only to "meditation" whereas § 16-1-20.1 refers to "meditation or voluntary prayer." The first difference is of no relevance in this litigation because the minor appellees were in kindergarten or second grade during the 1981-1982 academic year. The second difference would also have no impact on this litigation because

the mandatory language of § 16-1-20 continued to apply to grades one through six. Thus, the only significant textual difference is the addition of the words "or voluntary prayer."

The legislative intent to return prayer to the public schools is, of course, quite different from merely protecting every student's right to engage in voluntary prayer during an appropriate moment of silence during the school day. The 1978 statute already protected that right, containing nothing that prevented any student from engaging in voluntary prayer during a silent minute of meditation. Appellants have not identified any secular purpose that was not fully served by § 16-1-20 before the enactment of § 16-1-20.1. Thus, only two conclusions are consistent with the text of § 16-1-20.1: (1) the statute was enacted to convey a message of State endorsement and promotion of prayer; or (2) the statute was enacted for no purpose. No one suggests that the statute was nothing but a meaningless or irrational act.

We must, therefore, conclude that the Alabama Legislature intended to change existing law and that it was motivated by the same purpose that the Governor's Answer to the Second Amended Complaint expressly admitted; that the statement inserted in the legislative history revealed; and that Senator Holmes' testimony frankly described. The Legislature enacted § 16-1-20.1 despite the existence of § 16-1-20 for the sole purpose of expressing the State's endorsement of prayer activities for one minute at the beginning of each school day. The addition of "or voluntary prayer" indicates that the State intended to characterize prayer as a favored practice. Such an endorsement is not consistent with the established principle that the Government must pursue a course of complete neutrality toward religion.

The importance of that principle does not permit us to treat this as an inconsequential case involving nothing more than a few words of symbolic speech on behalf of the political majority. For whenever the State itself speaks on a religious subject, one of the questions that we must ask is "whether the Government intends to convey a message of endorsement or disapproval of religion." *Lynch* v. *Donnelly* The well-supported concurrent findings of the District Court and the Court of Appeals—that § 16-1-20.1 was intended to convey a message of State-approval of prayer activities in the public schools—make it unnecessary, and indeed inappropriate, to evaluate the practical significance of the addition of the words "or voluntary prayer" to the statute. Keeping in mind, as we must, "both the fundamental place held by the Establishment Clause in our constitutional scheme and the myriad, subtle ways in which Establishment Clause values can be eroded," *Id.* we conclude that § 16-1-20.1 violates the First Amendment.

The judgment of the Court of Appeals is affirmed.

It is so ordered.

Justice POWELL, concurring.

I concur in the Court's opinion and judgment that Ala. Code § 16-1-20.1 violates the Establishment Clause of the First Amendment. My concurrence is prompted by Alabama's persistence in attempting to institute state-sponsored prayer in the public schools by enacting three successive statutes. I agree fully with *Justice O'CONNOR's* assertion that some moment-of-silence statutes may be constitutional, a suggestion set forth in the Court's opinion as well.

I write separately to express additional views and to respond to criticism of the three-pronged *Lemon* test. *Lemon* v. *Kurtzman* identifies standards that have proven useful in analyzing case after case both in our decisions and in those of other courts. It is the only coherent test a majority of the Court has ever adopted. Only once since our decision in *Lemon,* have we addressed an Establishment Clause issue without resort to its three-pronged test. See *Marsh* v. *Chambers. Lemon* has not been overruled or its test modified. Yet, continued criticism of it could encourage other courts to feel free to decide Establishment Clause cases on an *ad hoc* basis.

The first inquiry under *Lemon* is whether the challenged statute has a "secular legislative purpose." As *Justice O'CONNOR* recognizes, this secular purpose must be "sincere"; a law will not pass constitutional muster if the secular purpose articulated by the legislature is merely a "sham." In *Stone* v. *Graham,* for example, we held that a statute requiring the posting of the Ten Commandments in public schools violated the Establishment Clause, even though the Kentucky legislature asserted that its goal was educational. We have not interpreted the first prong of *Lemon,* however, as requiring that a statute have "exclusively secular" objectives. If such a requirement existed, much conduct and legislation approved by this Court in the past would have been invalidated.

The record before us, however, makes clear that Alabama's purpose was solely religious in character. Senator Donald Holmes, the sponsor of the bill that became Alabama Code § 16-1-20.1, freely acknowledged that the purpose of this statute was "to return voluntary prayer" to the public schools. I agree with *Justice O'CONNOR* that a single legislator's statement, particularly if made following enactment, is not necessarily sufficient to establish purpose. But, as noted in the Court's opinion, the religious purpose of § 16-1-20.1 is manifested in other evidence, including the sequence and history of the three Alabama statutes.

I also consider it of critical importance that neither the District Court nor the Court of Appeals found a secular purpose, while both agreed that the purpose was to advance religion. In its first opinion (enjoining the enforcement of § 16-1-20.1 pending a hearing on the merits), the District Court said that the statute did "not reflect a clearly secular purpose." Instead, the District Court found that the en-

actment of the statute was an "effort on the part of the State of Alabama to encourage a religious activity." The Court of Appeals likewise applied the *Lemon* test and found "a lack of secular purpose on the part of the Alabama legislature." It held that the objective of § 16-1-20.1 was the "advancement of religion." When both courts below are unable to discern an arguably valid secular purpose, this Court normally should hesitate to find one.

I would vote to uphold the Alabama statute if it also had a clear secular purpose. Nothing in the record before us, however, identifies a clear secular purpose, and the State also has failed to identify any non-religious reason for the statute's enactment. Under these circumstances, the Court is required by our precedents to hold that the statute fails the first prong of the *Lemon* test and therefore violates the Establishment Clause.

Although we do not reach the other two prongs of the *Lemon* test, I note that the "effect" of a straightforward moment-of-silence statute is unlikely to "advance or inhibit religion." Nor would such a statute "foster 'an excessive government entanglement with religion.'" *Lemon* v. *Kurtzman.*

I join the opinion and judgment of the Court.

Justice O'CONNOR, concurring in the judgment.

Nothing in the United States Constitution as interpreted by this Court or in the laws of the State of Alabama prohibits public school students from voluntarily praying at any time before, during, or after the school day. Alabama has facilitated voluntary silent prayers of students who are so inclined by enacting Ala. Code § 16-1-20, which provides a moment of silence in appellees' schools each day. The parties to these proceedings concede the validity of this enactment. At issue in these appeals is the constitutional validity of an additional and subsequent Alabama statute, Ala. Code § 16-1-20.1, which both the District Court and the Court of Appeals concluded was enacted solely to officially encourage prayer during the moment of silence. I agree with the judgment of the Court that, in light of the findings of the Courts below and the history of its enactment, § 16-1-20.1 of the Alabama Code violates the Establishment Clause of the First Amendment. In my view, there can be little doubt that the purpose and likely effect of this subsequent enactment is to endorse and sponsor voluntary prayer in the public schools. I write separately to identify the peculiar features of the Alabama law that render it invalid, and to explain why moment of silence laws in other States do not necessarily manifest the same infirmity. I also write to explain why neither history nor the Free Exercise Clause of the First Amendment validate the Alabama law struck down by the Court today.

I

The religion clauses of the First Amendment, coupled with the Fourteenth Amendment's guaranty of ordered liberty, preclude both the Nation and the States from making any law respecting an establishment of religion or prohibiting the free exercise thereof. Although a distinct jurisprudence has enveloped each of these clauses, their common purpose is to secure religious liberty. On these principles the Court has been and remains unanimous.

As this case once again demonstrates, however, "it is far easier to agree on the purpose that underlies the First Amendment's Establishment and Free Exercise Clauses than to obtain agreement on the standards that should govern their application." *Walz* v. *Tax Comm'n*. It once appeared that the Court had developed a workable standard by which to identify impermissible government establishments of religion. Under the now familiar *Lemon* test, statutes must have both a secular legislative purpose and a principal or primary effect that neither advances nor inhibits religion, and in addition they must not foster excessive government entanglement with religion. Despite its initial promise, the *Lemon* test has proven problematic. The required inquiry into "entanglement" has been modified and questioned, see *Mueller* v. *Allen*, and in one case we have upheld state action against an Establishment Clause challenge without applying the *Lemon* test at all, *Marsh* v. *Chambers*. The author of *Lemon* himself apparently questions the test's general applicability. See *Lynch* v. *Donnelly*. Justice REHNQUIST today suggests that we abandon *Lemon* entirely, and in the process limit the reach of the Establishment Clause to state discrimination between sects and government designation of a particular church as a "state" or "national" one.

Perhaps because I am new to the struggle, I am not ready to abandon all aspects of the *Lemon* test. I do believe, however, that the standards announced in *Lemon* should be reexamined and refined in order to make them more useful in achieving the underlying purpose of the First Amendment. We must strive to do more than erect a constitutional "signpost," *Hunt* v. *McNair*, to be followed or ignored in a particular case as our predilections may dictate. Instead, our goal should be "to frame a principle for constitutional adjudication that is not only grounded in the history and language of the first amendment, but one that is also capable of consistent application to the relevant problems." Choper, Religion in the Public Schools: A Proposed Constitutional Standard, 47 Minn.L.Rev. 329, 332-333 (1963) (footnotes omitted). Last Term, I proposed a refinement of the *Lemon* test with this goal in mind, *Lynch* v. *Donnelly*.

The *Lynch* concurrence suggested that the religious liberty protected by the Establishment Clause is infringed when the government makes adherence

to religion relevant to a person's standing in the political community. Direct government action endorsing religion or a particular religious practice is invalid under this approach because it "sends a message to nonadherents that they are outsiders, not full members of the political community, and an accompanying message to adherents that they are insiders, favored members of the political community." Under this view, *Lemon*'s inquiry as to the purpose and effect of a statute requires courts to examine whether government's purpose is to endorse religion and whether the statute actually conveys a message of endorsement.

The endorsement test is useful because of the analytic content it gives to the *Lemon*-mandated inquiry into legislative purpose and effect. In this country, church and state must necessarily operate within the same community. Because of this coexistence, it is inevitable that the secular interests of Government and the religious interests of various sects and their adherents will frequently intersect, conflict, and combine. A statute that ostensibly promotes a secular interest often has an incidental or even a primary effect of helping or hindering a sectarian belief. Chaos would ensue if every such statute were invalid under the Establishment Clause. For example, the State could not criminalize murder for fear that it would thereby promote the Biblical command against killing. The task for the Court is to sort out those statutes and government practices whose purpose and effect go against the grain of religious liberty protected by the First Amendment.

The endorsement test does not preclude government from acknowledging religion or from taking religion into account in making law and policy. It does preclude government from conveying or attempting to convey a message that religion or a particular religious belief is favored or preferred. Such an endorsement infringes the religious liberty of the nonadherent, for "[w]hen the power, prestige and financial support of government is placed behind a particular religious belief, the indirect coercive pressure upon religious minorities to conform to the prevailing officially approved religion is plain." *Engel* v. *Vitale*. At issue today is whether state moment of silence statutes in general, and Alabama's moment of silence statute is particular, embody an impermissible endorsement of prayer in public schools.

A

Twenty-five states permit or require public school teachers to have students observe a moment of silence in their classrooms. A few statutes provide that the moment of silence is for the purpose of meditation alone. The typical statute however, calls for a moment of silence at the beginning of the school day during which students may meditate, pray, or reflect on the activities of the day. Federal trial courts have divided on the constitutionality of these moment of silence laws. Relying on this Court's decisions disapproving vocal prayer and Bible reading in the public schools, see *Abington School District* v. *Schempp*, *Engel* v. *Vitale*, the courts that have struck down the moment of silence statutes generally conclude that their purpose and effect is to encourage prayer in public schools.

The *Engel* and *Abington* decisions are not dispositive on the constitutionality of moment of silence laws. In those cases, public school teachers and students led their classes in devotional exercises. In *Engel*, a New York statute required teachers to lead their classes in a vocal prayer. The Court concluded that "it is no part of the business of government to compose official prayers for any group of the American people to recite as part of a religious program carried on by the government." In *Abington*, the Court addressed Pennsylvania and Maryland statues that authorized morning Bible readings in public schools. The Court reviewed the purpose and effect of the statutes, concluded that they required religious exercises, and therefore found them to violate the Establishment Clause. Under all of these statutes, a student who did not share the religious beliefs expressed in the course of the exercise was left with the choice of participating, thereby compromising the nonadherent's belief, or withdrawing, thereby calling attention to his or her non-conformity. The decisions acknowledged the coercion implicit under the statutory schemes, but they expressly turned only on the fact that the government was sponsoring a manifestly religious exercise.

A state sponsored moment of silence in the public schools is different from state sponsored vocal prayer or Bible reading. First, a moment of silence is not inherently religious. Silence, unlike prayer or Bible reading, need not be associated with a religious exercise. Second, a pupil who participates in a moment of silence need not compromise his or her beliefs. During a moment of silence, a student who objects to prayer is left to his or her own thoughts, and is not compelled to listen to the prayers or thoughts of others. For these simple reasons, a moment of silence statute does not stand or fall under the Establishment Clause according to how the Court regards vocal prayer or Bible reading. Scholars and at least one member of this Court have recognized the distinction and suggested that a moment of silence in public schools would be constitutional. See *Abington*, (BRENNAN, J., concurring) ("[T]he observance of a moment of reverent silence at the opening of class" may serve "the solely secular purposes of the devotional activities without jeopardizing either the religious liberties of any members of the community or the proper degree of separation between the spheres of religion and government"); L. Tribe, American Constitutional Law § 14-6, p. 829 (1978); P. Freund, The Legal Issue, in Religion and the Public Schools 23 (1965); Choper, 47 Minn.L.Rev. at 371; Kauper, Prayer, Public Schools, and the Supreme Court, 61 Mich.L.Rev. 1031, 1041 (1963). As a general matter,

I agree. It is difficult to discern a serious threat to religious liberty from a room of silent, thoughtful schoolchildren.

By mandating a moment of silence, a State does not necessarily endorse any activity that might occur during the period. Even if a statute specifies that a student may choose to pray silently during a quiet moment, the State has not thereby encouraged prayer over other specified alternatives. Nonetheless, it is also possible that a moment of silence statute, either as drafted or as actually implemented, could effectively favor the child who prays over the child who does not. For example, the message of endorsement would seem inescapable if the teacher exhorts children to use the designated time to pray. Similarly, the face of the statute or its legislative history may clearly establish that it seeks to encourage or promote voluntary prayer over other alternatives, rather than merely provide a quiet moment that may be dedicated to prayer by those so inclined. The crucial question is whether the State has conveyed or attempted to convey the message that children should use the moment of silence for prayer. This question cannot be answered in the abstract, but instead requires courts to examine the history, language, and administration of a particular statute to determine whether it operates as an endorsement of religion.

Before reviewing Alabama's moment of silence law to determine whether it endorses prayer, some general observations on the proper scope of the inquiry are in order. First, the inquiry into the purpose of the legislature in enacting a moment of silence law should be deferential and limited. In determining whether the government intends a moment of silence statute to convey a message of endorsement or disapproval of religion, a court has no license to psychoanalyze the legislators. If a legislature expresses a plausible secular purpose for a moment of silence statute in either the text or the legislative history, or if the statute disclaims an intent to encourage prayer over alternatives during a moment of silence, then courts should generally defer to that stated intent. It is particularly troublesome to denigrate an expressed secular purpose due to post-enactment testimony by particular legislators or by interested persons who witnessed the drafting of the statute. Even if the text and official history of a statute express no secular purpose, the statute should be held to have an improper purpose only if it is beyond purview that endorsement of religion or a religious belief "was and is the law's reason for existence." *Epperson* v. *Arkansas*. Since there is arguably a secular pedagogical value to a moment of silence in public schools, courts should find an improper purpose behind such a statute only if the statute on its face, in its official legislative history, or in its interpretation by a responsible administrative agency suggests it has the primary purpose of endorsing prayer.

Justice REHNQUIST suggests that this sort of deferential inquiry into legislative purpose "means little," because "it only requires the legislature to express any secular purpose and omit all sectarian references." It is not a trivial matter, however, to require that the legislature manifest a secular purpose and omit all sectarian endorsement from its laws. That requirement is precisely tailored to the Establishment Clause's purpose of assuring that Government not intentionally endorse religion or a religious practice. It is of course possible that a legislature will enunciate a sham secular purpose for a statute. I have little doubt that our courts are capable of distinguishing a sham secular purpose from a sincere one, or that the *Lemon* inquiry into the effect of an enactment would help decide those close cases where the validity of an expressed secular purpose is in doubt. While the secular purpose requirement alone may rarely be determinative in striking down a statute, it nevertheless serves an important function. It reminds government that when it acts it should do so without endorsing a particular religious belief or practice that all citizens do not share. In this sense the secular purpose requirement is squarely based in the text of the Establishment Clause it helps to enforce.

Second, the *Lynch* concurrence suggested that the effect of a moment of silence law is not entirely a question of fact: "[W]hether a government activity communicates endorsement of religion is not a question of simple historical fact. Although evidentiary submissions may help answer it, the question is, like the question whether racial or sex-based classifications communicate an invidious message, in large part a legal question to be answered on the basis of judicial interpretation of social facts." The relevant issue is whether an objective observer, acquainted with the text, legislative history, and implementation of the statute, would perceive it as a state endorsement of prayer in public schools. A moment of silence law that is clearly drafted and implemented so as to permit prayer, meditation, and reflection within the prescribed period, without endorsing one alternative over the others, should pass this test.

B

The analysis above suggests that moment of silence laws in many States should pass Establishment Clause scrutiny because they do not favor the child who chooses to pray during a moment of silence over the child who chooses to meditate or reflect. Alabama Code § 16-1-20.1 does not stand on the same footing. However deferentially one examines its text and legislative history, however objectively one views the message attempted to be conveyed to the public, the conclusion is unavoidable that the purpose of the statute is to endorse prayer in public schools. I accordingly agree with the Court of Appeals that the Alabama statute has a purpose which is in violation of the Establishment Clause, and cannot be upheld.

In finding that the purpose of Alabama Code § 16-1-20.1 is to endorse voluntary prayer during a moment of silence, the Court relies on testimony elicited from State Senator Donald G. Holmes during a preliminary injunction hearing. Senator Holmes testified that the sole purpose of the statute was to return voluntary prayer to the public schools. For the reasons expressed above, I would give little, if any, weight to this sort of evidence of legislative intent. Nevertheless, the text of the statute in light of its official legislative history leaves little doubt that the purpose of this statute corresponds to the purpose expressed by Senator Holmes at the preliminary injunction hearing.

First, it is notable that Alabama already had a moment of silence statute before it enacted § 16-1-20.1. Appellees do not challenge this statute—indeed, they concede its validity. The only significant addition made by Alabama Code § 16-6-20.1 is to specify expressly that voluntary prayer is one of the authorized activities during a moment of silence. Any doubt as to the legislative purpose of that addition is removed by the official legislative history. The sole purpose reflected in the official history is "to return voluntary prayer to our public schools." Nor does anything in the legislative history contradict an intent to encourage children to choose prayer over other alternatives during the moment of silence. Given this legislative history, it is not surprising that the State of Alabama conceded in the courts below that the purpose of the statute was to make prayer part of daily classroom activity, and that both the District Court and the Court of Appeals concluded that the law's purpose was to encourage religious activity. In light of the legislative history and the findings of the courts below, I agree with the Court that the State intended Alabama Code § 16-1-20.1 to convey a message that prayer was the endorsed activity during the state-prescribed moment of silence. While it is therefore unnecessary also to determine the effect of the statute, it also seems likely that the message actually conveyed to objective observers by Alabama Code § 16-1-20.1 is approval of the child who selects prayer over other alternatives during a moment of silence.

Given this evidence in the record, candor requires us to admit that this Alabama statute was intended to convey a message of state encouragement and endorsement of religion. In *Walz* v. *Tax Comm'n*, the Court stated that the religion clauses of the First Amendment are flexible enough to "permit religious exercise to exist without sponsorship and without interference." Alabama Code § 16-1-20.1 does more than permit prayer to occur during a moment of silence "without interference." It endorses the decision to pray during a moment of silence, and accordingly sponsors a religious exercise. For that reason, I concur in the judgment of the Court.

II

In his dissenting opinion, *Justice REHNQUIST* reviews the text and history of the First Amendment religion clauses. His opinion suggests that a long line of this Court's decisions are inconsistent with the intent of the drafters of the Bill of Rights. He urges the Court to correct the historical inaccuracies in its past decisions by embracing a far more restricted interpretation that presumably would permit vocal group prayer in public schools.

The United States, in an *amicus* brief, suggests a less sweeping modification of Establishment Clause principles. In the Federal Government's view, a state sponsored moment of silence is merely an "accommodation" of the desire of some public school children to practice their religion by praying silently. Such an accommodation is contemplated by the First Amendment's guaranty that the Government will not prohibit the free exercise of religion. Because the moment of silence implicates free exercise values, the United States suggests that the *Lemon* mandated inquiry into purpose and effect should be modified.

There is an element of truth and much helpful analysis in each of these suggestions. Particularly when we are interpreting the Constitution, "a page of history is worth a volume of logic." *New York Trust Co.* v. *Eisner.* Whatever the provision of the Constitution that is at issue, I continue to believe that "fidelity to the notion of *constitutional*—as opposed to purely judicial—limits on governmental action requires us to impose a heavy burden on those who claim that practices accepted when [the provision] was adopted are now constitutionally impermissible." *Tennessee* v. *Garner.* The Court properly looked to history in upholding legislative prayer, *Marsh* v. *Chambers,* property tax exemptions for houses of worship, *Walz* v. *Tax Comm'n,* and Sunday closing laws, *McGowan* v. *Maryland.* As *Justice HOLMES* once observed, "[i]f a thing has been practiced for two hundred years by common consent, it will need a strong case for the Fourteenth Amendment to affect it." *Jackman* v. *Rosenbaum Co.*

Justice REHNQUIST does not assert, however, that the drafters of the First Amendment expressed a preference for prayer in public schools, or that the practice of prayer in public schools enjoyed uninterrupted government endorsement from the time of enactment of the Bill of Rights to the present era. The simple truth is that free public education was virtually non-existent in the late eighteenth century. Since there then existed few government-run schools, it is unlikely that the persons who drafted the First Amendment, or the state legislators who ratified it, anticipated the problems of interaction of church and state in the public schools. Even at the time of adoption of the Fourteenth Amendment, education in Southern States was still primarily in private hands, and the movement toward free public schools supported by general taxation had not taken hold.

This uncertainty as to the intent of the Framers of the Bill of Rights does not mean we should ignore history for guidance on the role of religion in public education. The Court has not done so. When the intent of the Framers is unclear, I believe we must employ both history and reason in our analysis. The primary issue raised by *Justice REHNQUIST's* dissent is whether the historical fact that our Presidents have long called for public prayers of Thanks should be dispositive on the constitutionality of prayer in public schools. I think not. At the very least, Presidential proclamations are distinguishable from school prayer in that they are received in a non-coercive setting and are primarily directed at adults, who presumably are not readily susceptible to unwilling religious indoctrination. This Court's decisions have recognized a distinction when government sponsored religious exercises are directed at impressionable children who are required to attend school, for then government endorsement is much more likely to result in coerced religious beliefs. Although history provides a touchstone for constitutional problems, the Establishment Clause concern for religious liberty is dispositive here.

The element of truth in the United States' arguments, I believe, lies in the suggestion that Establishment Clause analysis must comport with the mandate of the Free Exercise Clause that government make no law prohibiting the free exercise of religion. Our cases have interpreted the Free Exercise Clause to compel the Government to exempt persons from some generally applicable government requirements so as to permit those persons to freely exercise their religion. Even where the Free Exercise Clause does not compel the Government to grant an exemption, the Court has suggested that the Government in some circumstances may voluntarily choose to exempt religious observers without violating the Establishment Clause. See, *e.g., Gillette* v. *United States; Braunfeld* v. *Brown.* The challenge posed by the United States' argument is how to define the proper Establishment Clause limits on voluntary government efforts to facilitate the free exercise of religion. On the one hand, a rigid application of the *Lemon* test would invalidate legislation exempting religious observers from generally applicable government obligations. By definition, such legislation has a religious purpose and effect in promoting the free exercise of religion. On the other hand, judicial deference to all legislation that purports to facilitate the free exercise of religion would completely vitiate the Establishment Clause. Any statute pertaining to religion can be viewed as an "accommodation" of free exercise rights. Indeed, the statute at issue in *Lemon,* which provided salary supplements, textbooks, and instructional materials to Pennsylvania parochial schools, can be viewed as an accommodation of the religious beliefs of parents who choose to send their children to religious schools.

It is obvious that the either of the two Religion Clauses, "if expanded to a logical extreme, would tend to clash with the other." *Walz* The Court has long exacerbated the conflict by calling for government "neutrality" toward religion. It is difficult to square any notion of "complete neutrality," with the mandate of the Free Exercise Clause that government must sometimes exempt a religious observer from an otherwise generally applicable obligation. A government that confers a benefit on an explicitly religious basis is not neutral toward religion.

The solution to the conflict between the religion clauses lies not in "neutrality," but rather in identifying workable limits to the Government's license to promote the free exercise of religion. The text of the Free Exercise Clause speaks of laws that prohibit the free exercise of religion. On its face, the Clause is directed at government interference with free exercise. Given that concern, one can plausibly assert that government pursues free exercise clause values when it lifts a government imposed burden on the free exercise of religion. If a statute falls within this category, then the standard Establishment Clause test should be modified accordingly. It is disingenuous to look for a purely secular purpose when the manifest objective of a statute is to facilitate the free exercise of religion by lifting a government-imposed burden. Instead, the Court should simply acknowledge that the religious purpose of such a statute is legitimated by the Free Exercise Clause. I would also go further. In assessing the effect of such a statute—that is, in determining whether the statute conveys the message of endorsement of religion or a particular religious belief—courts should assume that the "objective observer," is acquainted with the Free Exercise Clause and the values it promotes. Thus individual perceptions, or resentment that a religious observer is exempted from a particular government requirement, would be entitled to little weight if the Free Exercise Clause strongly supported the exemption.

While this "accommodation" analysis would help reconcile our Free Exercise and Establishment Clause standards, it would not save Alabama's moment of silence law. If we assume that the religious activity that Alabama seeks to protect is silent prayer, then it is difficult to discern any state-imposed burden on that activity that is lifted by Alabama Code § 16-1-20.1. No law prevents a student who is so inclined from praying silently in public schools. Moreover, state law already provided a moment of silence to these appellees irrespective of Alabama Code § 16-1-20.1. Of course, the State might argue that § 16-1-20.1 protects not silent prayer, but rather group silent prayer under State sponsorship. Phrased in these terms, the burden lifted by the statute is not one imposed by the State of Alabama, but by the Establishment Clause as interpreted in *Engel* and *Abington*. In my view, it is beyond the authority of the State of Alabama to remove burdens imposed by the Constitution itself. I conclude that the Alabama statute at issue today lifts no state-imposed burden on the free exercise of religion, and accordingly cannot properly be viewed as an accommodation statute.

III

The Court does not hold that the Establishment Clause is so hostile to religion that it precludes the States from affording schoolchildren an opportunity for voluntary silent prayer. To the contrary, the moment of silence statutes of many States should satisfy the Establishment Clause standard we have here applied. The Court holds only that Alabama has intentionally crossed the line between creating a quiet moment during which those so inclined may pray, and affirmatively endorsing the particular religious practice of prayer. This line may be a fine one, but our precedents and the principles of religious liberty require that we draw it. In my view, the judgment of the Court of Appeals must be affirmed.

Chief Justice BURGER, dissenting.

Some who trouble to read the opinions in this case will find it ironic—perhaps even bizarre—that on the very day we heard arguments in this case, the Court's session opened with an invocation for Divine protection. Across the park a few hundred yards away, the House of Representatives and the Senate regularly open each session with a prayer. These legislative prayers are not just one minute in duration, but are extended, thoughtful invocations and prayers for Divine guidance. They are given, as they have been since 1789, by clergy appointed as official Chaplains and paid from the Treasury of the United States. Congress has also provided chapels in the Capitol, at public expense, where Members and others may pause for prayer, meditation—or a moment of silence.

Inevitably some wag is bound to say that the Court's holding today reflects a belief that the historic practice of the Congress and this Court is justified because members of the Judiciary and Congress are more in need of Divine guidance than are schoolchildren. Still others will say that all this controversy is "much ado about nothing," since no power on earth—including this Court and Congress—can stop any teacher from opening the school day with a moment of silence for pupils to meditate, to plan their day—or to pray if they voluntarily elect to do so.

I make several points about today's curious holding.

(a) It makes no sense to say that Alabama has "endorsed prayer" by merely enacting a new statute "to specify expressly that voluntary prayer is *one* of the authorized activities during a moment of silence." (O'CONNOR,J., concurring in the judgment) (emphasis added). To suggest that a moment-of-silence statute that includes the word "prayer" unconstitutionally endorses religion, while one that simply provides for a moment of silence does not, manifests not neutrality but hostility toward religion. For decades our opinions have stated that hostility toward any religion or toward all religions is as much forbidden by the Constitution as is an official establishment of religion. The Alabama legislature has no more "endorsed" religion than a state or the Congress does when it provides for legislative chaplains, or than this Court does when it opens each session with an invocation to God. Today's decision recalls the observation of *Justice GOLDBERG*: "[U]ntutored devotion to the concept of neutrality can lead to invocation or approval of results which partake not simply of that noninterference and noninvolvement with the religious which the Constitution commands, but of a brooding and pervasive dedication to the secular and a passive, or even active, hostility to the religious. Such results are not only not compelled by the Constitution but, it seems to me, are prohibited by it." *School District* v. *Schempp*.

(b) The inexplicable aspect of the foregoing opinions, however, is what they advance as support for the holding concerning the purpose of the Alabama legislature. Rather than determining legislative purpose from the fact of the statute as a whole, the opinions rely on three factors in concluding that the Alabama legislature had a "wholly religious" purpose for enacting the statute under review, Ala. Code § 16-1-20.1: (i) statements of the statute's sponsor, (ii) admissions in Governor James' Answer to the Second Amended Complaint, and (iii) the difference between § 16-1-20.1 and its predecessor statute.

Curiously, the opinions do not mention that *all* of the sponsor's statements relied upon—including the statement "inserted" into the Senate Journal—were made *after* the legislature had passed the statute; indeed, the testimony that the Court finds critical was given well over a year after the statute was enacted. As even the appellees concede, there is not a shred of evidence that the legislature as a whole shared the sponsor's motive or that a majority in either house was even aware of the sponsor's view of the bill when it was passed. The sole relevance of the sponsor's statement, therefore, is that they reflect the personal, subjective motives of a single legislator. No case in the 195-year history of this Court supports the disconcerting idea that postenactment statements by individual legislators are relevant in determining the constitutionality of legislation.

Even if an individual legislator's after-the-fact statements could rationally be considered relevant, all of the opinions fail to mention that the sponsor also testified that one of his purposes in drafting and sponsoring the moment-of-silence bill was to clear up a widespread misunderstanding that a schoolchild is legally *prohibited* from engaging in silent, individual prayer once he steps inside a public school building. That testimony is at least as important as the statements the Court relies upon, and surely that testimony manifests a permissible purpose.

The Court also relies on the admissions of Governor James' Answer to the Second Amended Complaint. Strangely, however, the Court neglects to mention that there was no trial bearing on the constitutionality of the Alabama statutes; trial became unnecessary when the District Court held that the Establishment Clause does not apply to the states. The absence of a trial on the issue of the constitutionality of § 16-1-20.1 is significant because the Answer filed by the State Board and Superintendent of Education did not make the same admissions that the Governor's Answer made. The Court cannot know whether, if this case had been tried, those state officials would have offered evidence to contravene appellees' allegations concerning legislative purpose. Thus, it is completely inappropriate to accord any relevance to the admissions in the Governor's Answer.

The several preceding opinions conclude that the principal difference between § 16-1-20.1 and its predecessor statute proves that the sole purpose behind the inclusion of the phase "or voluntary prayer" in § 16-1-20.1 was to endorse and promote prayer. This reasoning is simply a subtle way of focusing exclusively on the religious component of the statute rather than examining the statute as a whole. Such logic—if it can be called that—would lead the Court to hold, for example, that a state may enact a statute that provides reimbursement for bus transportation to the parents of all schoolchildren, but may not *add* parents of parochial school students to an existing program providing reimbursement for parents of public school students. Congress amended the statutory Pledge of Allegiance 31 years ago to add the words "under God." Do the several opinions in support of the judgment today render the Pledge unconstitutional? That would be the consequence of their method of focusing on the the difference between § 16-1-20.1 and its predecessor statute rather than examining § 16-1-20.1 as a whole. Any such holding would of course make a mockery of our decisionmaking in Establishment Clause cases. And even were the Court's method correct, the inclusion of the words "or voluntary prayer" in § 16-1-20.1 is wholly consistent with the clearly permissible purpose of clarifying that silent, voluntary prayer is not *forbidden* in the public school building.

(c) The Court's extended treatment of the "test" of *Lemon* v. *Kurtzman* suggests a naive preoccupation with an easy, bright-line approach for addressing constitutional issues. We have repeatedly cautioned that *Lemon* did not establish a rigid caliper capable of resolving every Establishment Clause issue, but that it sought only to provide "signposts." "In each [Establishment Clause] case, the inquiry calls for line drawing; no fixed, *per se* rule can be framed." *Lynch* v. *Donnelly* In any event, our responsibility is not to apply tidy formulas by rote; our duty is to determine whether the statute or practice at issue is a step toward establishing a state religion. Given today's decision, however, perhaps it is understandable that the opinions in support of the judgment all but ignore the Establishment Clause itself and the concerns that underlie it.

(d) The notion that the Alabama statute is a step toward creating an established church borders on, if it does not trespass into, the ridiculous. The statute does not remotely threaten religious liberty; it affirmatively furthers the values of religious freedom and tolerance that the Establishment Clause was designed to protect. Without pressuring those who do not wish to pray, the statute simply creates an opportunity to think, to plan, or to pray if one wishes—as Congress does by providing chaplains and chapels. It accommodates the purely private, voluntary religious choices of the individual pupils who wish to pray while at the same time creating a time for nonreligious reflection for those who do not choose to pray. The statute also provides a meaningful opportunity for schoolchildren to appreciate the absolute constitutional right of each individual to worship and believe as the individual wishes. The statute "endorses" only the view that the religious observances of others should be tolerated and, where possible, accommodated. If the government may not accommodate religious needs when it does so in a wholly neutral and noncoercive manner, the "benevolent neutrality" that we have long considered the correct constitutional standard will quickly translate into the "callous indifference" that the Court has consistently held the Establishment Clause does not require.

The Court today has ignored the wise admonition of *Justice GOLDBERG* that "the measure of constitutional adjudication is the ability and willingness to distinguish between real threat and mere shadow." *School District* v. *Schempp* The innocuous statute that the Court strikes down does not even rise to the level of "mere shadow." *Justice O'CONNOR* paradoxically acknowledges, "It is difficult to discern a serious threat to religious liberty from a room of silent, thoughtful schoolchildren." I would add to that, "even if they choose to pray."

The mountains have labored and brought forth a mouse.

Justice WHITE, dissenting.

For the most part agreeing with the opinion of *The CHIEF JUSTICE*, I dissent from the Court's judgment invalidating Alabama Code § 16-1-20.1. Because I do, it is apparent that in my view the First Amendment does not proscribe either (1) statutes authorizing or requiring in so many words a moment of silence before classes begin or (2) a statute that provides, when it is initially passed, for a moment of silence for meditation or prayer. As I read the filed opinions, a majority of the Court would approve statutes that provide for a moment of silence but did not mention prayer. But if a student asked whether he could pray during that moment, it is difficult to believe that the teacher could not answer in the af-

firmative. If that is the case, I would not invalidate a statute that at the outset provided the legislative answer to the question "May I pray?" This is so even if the Alabama statute is infirm, which I do not believe it is, because of its peculiar legislative history.

I appreciate *Justice REHNQUIST's* explication of the history of the religion clauses of the First Amendment. Against that history, it would be quite understandable if we undertook to reassess our cases dealing with these clauses, particularly those dealing with the Establishment Clause. Of course, I have been out of step with many of the Court's decisions dealing with this subject matter, and it is thus not surprising that I would support a basic reconsideration of our precedents.

Justice REHNQUIST, dissenting.

Thirty-eight years ago this Court, in *Everson* v. *Board of Education*, summarized its exegesis of Establishment Clause doctrine thus: "In the words of Jefferson, the clause against establishment of religion by law was intended to erect 'a wall of separation between church and State.' *Reynolds* v. *United States.*" This language from *Reynolds*, a case involving the Free Exercise Clause of the First Amendment rather than the Establishment Clause, quoted from Thomas Jefferson's letter to the Danbury Baptist Association the phrase "I contemplate with sovereign reverence that act of the whole American people which declared that their legislature should 'make no law respecting an establishment of religion, or prohibiting the free exercise thereof,' thus building a wall of separation between church and State." 8 Writings of Thomas Jefferson 113 (H. Washington ed. 1861).

It is impossible to build sound constitutional doctrine upon a mistaken understanding of constitutional history, but unfortunately the Establishment Clause has been expressly freighted with Jefferson's misleading metaphor for nearly forty years. Thomas Jefferson was of course in France at the time the constitutional amendments known as the Bill of Rights were passed by Congress and ratified by the states. His letter to the Danbury Baptist Association was a short note of courtesy, written fourteen years after the amendments were passed by Congress. He would seem to any detached observer as a less than ideal source of contemporary history as to the meaning of the Religion Clauses of the First Amendment.

Jefferson's fellow Virginian James Madison, with whom he was joined in the battle for the enactment of the Virginia Statute of Religious Liberty of 1786, did play as large a part as anyone in the drafting of the Bill of Rights. He had two advantages over Jefferson in this regard: he was present in the United States, and he was a leading member of the First Congress. But when we turn to the record of the proceedings in the First Congress leading up to the adoption of the Establishment Clause of the Constitution, including Madison's significant contributions thereto, we see a far different picture of its purpose than the highly simplified "wall of separation between church and State."

During the debates in the thirteen colonies over ratification of the Constitution, one of the arguments frequently used by opponents of ratification was that without a Bill of Rights guaranteeing individual liberty the new general government carried with it a potential for tyranny. The typical response to this argument on the part of those who favored ratification was that the general government established by the Constitution had only delegated powers, and that these delegated powers were so limited that the government would have no occasion to violate individual liberties. This response satisfied some, but not others, and of the eleven colonies which ratified the Constitution by early 1789, five proposed one or another amendments guaranteeing individual liberty. Three—New Hampshire, New York, and Virginia—included in one form or another a declaration of religious freedom. Rhode Island and North Carolina flatly refused to ratify the Constitution in the absence of amendments in the nature of a Bill of Rights. Virginia and North Carolina proposed identical guarantees of religious freedom: "[A]ll men have an equal, natural and unalienable right to the free exercise of religion, according to the dictates of conscience, and that no particular religious sect or society ought to be favored or established, by law, in preference to others." J. Elliot, Debates on the Federal Constitution 1891; vol. 3 at 659; 4 at 244.

On June 8, 1789, James Madison rose in the House of Representatives and "reminded the House that this was the day that he had heretofore named for bringing forward amendments to the Constitution." 1 Annals of Cong. 424. Madison's subsequent remarks in urging the House to adopt his drafts of the proposed amendments were less those of a dedicated advocate of the wisdom of such measures than those of a prudent statesman seeking the enactment of measures sought by a number of his fellow citizens which could surely do no harm and might do a great deal of good. He said, *inter alia:* "It appears to me that this House is bound by every motive of prudence, not to let the first session pass over without proposing to the State Legislatures, some things to be incorporated into the Constitution, that will render it as acceptable to the whole people on the United States, as it has been found acceptable to a majority of them. I wish, among other reasons why something should be done, that those who had been friendly to the adoption of this Constitution may have the opportunity of proving to those who were opposed to it that they were as sincerely devoted to liberty and a Republican Government, as those who charged them with wishing the adoption of this Constitution in order to lay the foundation of an aristocracy or despotism. It will be a desirable thing to extinguish from the bosom of every member of the community, any apprehensions that there are those among his countrymen who wish to deprive them of the liberty for which they valiantly fought and honorably bled. And if there are amendments desired of such a nature as will not injure the Constitution, and they can be ingrafted so as to give satisfaction to the doubting part of our fellow-citizens, the friends of the Federal Government will evince that spirit of deference and concession for which they have hitherto been distinguished." *Id.* at 431-432.

The language Madison proposed for what ultimately became the Religion Clauses of the First Amendment was this: "The civil rights of none shall be abridged on account of religious belief or worship, nor shall any national religion be established, nor shall the full and equal rights of conscience be in any manner, or on any pretext, infringed." *Id.* at 434. On the same day that Madison proposed them, the amendments which formed the basis for the Bill of Rights were referred by the House to a committee of the whole, and after several weeks' delay were then referred to a Select Committee consisting of Madison and ten others. The Committee revised Madison's proposal regarding the establishment of religion to read: "[N]o religion shall be established by law, nor shall the equal rights of conscience be infringed." *Id.* at 729.

The Committee's proposed revisions were debated in the House on August 15, 1789. The entire debate on the Religion Clauses is contained in two full columns of the "Annals," and does not seem particularly illuminating. Representative Peter Sylvester of New York expressed his dislike for the revised version, because it might have a tendency "to abolish religion altogether." Representative John Vining suggested that the two parts of the sentence be transposed; Representative Elbridge Gerry thought the language should be changed to read "that no religious doctrine shall be established by law." Roger Sherman of Connecticut had the traditional reason for opposing provisions of a Bill of Rights—that Congress had no delegated authority to "make religious establishments"—and therefore he opposed the adoption of the amendment. Representative Daniel Carroll of Maryland thought it desirable to adopt the words proposed, saying "[h]e would not contend with gentlemen about the phraseology, his object was to secure the substance in such a manner as to satisfy the wishes of the honest part of the community."

Madison then spoke, and said that "he apprehended the meaning of the words to be, that Congress should not establish a religion, and enforce the legal observation of it by law, nor compel men to worship God in any manner contrary to their conscience." *Id.*, at 730. He said that some of the state conventions had thought that Congress might rely on the "necessary and proper" clause to infringe the rights of conscience or to establish a national religion, and "to prevent these effects he presumed the amendment was intended, and he thought it as well expressed as the nature of the language would admit." *Ibid.*

Representative Benjamin Huntington then expressed the view that the Committee's language might "be taken in such latitude as to be extremely hurtful to the cause of religion. He understood the amendment to mean what had been expressed by the gentleman from Virginia; but others might find it convenient to put another construction upon it." Huntington, from Connecticut, was concerned that in the New England states, where state established religions were the rule rather than the exception, the federal courts might not be able to entertain claims based upon an obligation under the bylaws of a religious organization to contribute to the support of a minister or the building of a place of worship. He hoped that "the amendment would be made in such a way as to secure the rights of conscience, and a free exercise of the rights of religion, but not to patronize those who professed no religion at all." *Id.*, at 730-731.

Madison responded that the insertion of the word "national" before the word "religion" in the Committee version should satisfy the minds of those who had criticized the language. "He believed that the people feared one sect might obtain a pre-eminence, or two combine together, and establish a religion to which they would compel others to conform. He thought that if the word 'national' was introduced, it would point the amendment directly to the object it was intended to prevent." *Id.*, at 731. Representative Samuel Livermore expressed himself as dissatisfied with Madison's proposed amendment, and thought it would be better if the Committee language were altered to read that "Congress shall make no laws touching religion, or infringing the rights of conscience." *Ibid.*

Representative Gerry spoke in opposition to the use of the word "national" because of strong feelings expressed during the ratification debates that a federal government, not a national government, was created by the Constitution. Madison thereby withdrew his proposal but insisted that his reference to a "national religion" only referred to a national establishment and did not mean that the government was a national one. The question was taken on Representative Livermore's motion, which passed by a vote of 31 for and 20 against. *Ibid.*

The following week, without any apparent debate, the House voted to alter the language of the Religion Clause to read "Congress shall make no law establishing religion, or to prevent the free exercise thereof, or to infringe the rights of conscience." *Id.* at 766. The floor debates in the Senate were secret, and therefore not reported in the Annals. The Senate on September 3, 1789 considered several different forms of the Religion Amendment, and reported this language back to the House: "Congress shall make no law establishing articles of faith or a mode of worship, or prohibiting the free exercise of religion." C. Antieau, A. Downey, & E. Roberts, Freedom From Federal Establishment 130 (1964).

The House refused to accept the Senate's changes in the Bill of Rights and asked for a conference; the version which emerged from the conference was that which ultimately found its way into the Constitution as a part of the First Amendment.

"Congress shall make no law respecting an establishment of religion, or prohibiting the free exercise thereof." The House and the Senate both accepted this language on successive days, and the amendment was proposed in this form.

On the basis of the record of these proceedings in the House of Representatives, James Madison was undoubtedly the most important architect among the members of the House of the amendments which became the Bill of Rights, but it was James Madison speaking as an advocate of sensible legislative compromise, not as an advocate of incorporating the Virginia Statute of Religious Liberty into the United States Constitution. During the ratification debate in the Virginia Convention, Madison had actually opposed the idea of any Bill of Rights. His sponsorship of the amendments in the House was obviously not that of a zealous believer in the necessity of the Religion Clauses, but of one who felt it might do some good, could do no harm, and would satisfy those who had ratified the Constitution on the condition that Congress propose a Bill of Rights. His original language "nor shall any national religion be established" obviously does not conform to the "wall of separation" between church and State idea which latter day commentators have ascribed to him. His explanation on the floor of the meaning of his language—"that Congress should not establish a religion, and enforce the legal observation of it by law" is of the same ilk. When he replied to Huntington in the debate over the proposal which came from the Select Committee of the House, he urged that the language "no religion shall be established by law" should be amended by inserting the word "national" in front of the word "religion".

It seems indisputable from these glimpses of Madison's thinking, as reflected by actions on the floor of the House in 1789, that he saw the amendment as designed to prohibit the establishment of a national religion, and perhaps to prevent discrimination among sects. He did not see it as requiring neutrality on the part of government between religion and irreligion. Thus the Court's opinion in *Everson*—while correct in bracketing Madison and Jefferson together in their exertions in their home state leading to the enactment of the Virginia Statute of Religious Liberty—is totally incorrect in suggesting that Madison carried these views onto the floor of the United States House of Representatives when he proposed the language which would ultimately become the Bill of Rights.

The repetition of this error in the Court's opinion in *McCollum* v. *Board of Education* and *Engel* v. *Vitale*, does not make it any sounder historically. Finally, in *Abington School District* v. *Schempp*, the Court made the truly remarkable statement that "the views of Madison and Jefferson preceded by Roger Williams came to be incorporated not only in the Federal Constitution but likewise in those of most of our States." On the basis of what evidence we have, this statement is demonstrably incorrect as a matter of history. And its repetition in varying forms in succeeding opinions of the Court can give it no more authority than it possesses as a matter of fact; *stare decisis* may bind courts as to matters of law, but it cannot bind them as to matters of history.

None of the other Members of Congress who spoke during the August 15th debate expressed the slightest indication that they thought the language before them from the Select Committee, or the evil to be aimed at, would require that the Government be absolutely neutral as between religion and irreligion. The evil to be aimed at, so far as those who spoke were concerned, appears to have been the establishment of a national church, and perhaps the preference of one religious sect over another, but it was definitely not concern about whether the Government might aid all religions evenhandedly. If one were to follow the advice of *Justice BRENNAN*, concurring in *Abington School District* v. *Schempp*, and construe the Amendment in the light of what particular "practices . . . challenged threaten those consequences which the Framers deeply feared; whether, in short, they tend to promote that type of interdependence between religion and state which the First Amendment was designed to prevent," one would have to say that the First Amendment Establishment Clause should be read no more broadly than to prevent the establishment of a national religion or the governmental preference of one religious sect over another.

The actions of the First Congress, which reenacted the Northwest Ordinance for the governance of the Northwest Territory in 1789, confirm the view that Congress did not mean that the Government should be neutral between religion and irreligion. The House of Representatives took up the Northwest Ordinance on the same day as Madison introduced his proposed amendments which became the Bill of Rights; while at that time the Federal Government was of course not bound by draft amendments to the Constitution which had not yet been proposed by Congress, say nothing of ratified by the States, it seems highly unlikely that the House of Representatives would simultaneously consider proposed amendments to the Constitution and enact an important piece of territorial legislation which conflicted with the intent of those proposals. The Northwest Ordinance reenacted the Northwest Ordinance of 1787 and provided that "[r]eligion, morality, and knowledge, being necessary to good gov-

ernment and the happiness of mankind, schools and the means of education shall forever be encouraged." Land grants for schools in the Northwest Territory were not limited to public schools. It was not until 1845 that Congress limited land grants in the new States and Territories to nonsectarian schools.

On the day after the House of Representatives voted to adopt the form of the First Amendment Religion Clause which was ultimately proposed and ratified, Representative Elias Boudinot proposed a resolution asking President George Washington to issue a Thanksgiving Day proclamation. Boudinot said he "could not think of letting the session pass over without offering an opportunity to all the citizens of the United States of joining with one voice, in returning to Almighty God their sincere thanks for the many blessings he had poured down upon them." 1 Annals of Cong. 914 (1789). Representative Aedanas Burke objected to the resolution because he did not like "this mimicking of European customs"; Representative Thomas Tucker objected that whether or not the people had reason to be satisfied with the Constitution was something that the states knew better than the Congress, and in any event "it is a religious matter, and, as such, is proscribed to us." *Id.*, at 915. Representative Sherman supported the resolution "not only as a laudable one in itself, but as warranted by a number of precedents in Holy Writ: for instance, the solemn thanksgivings and rejoicings which took place in the time of Solomon, after the building of the temple, was a case in point. This example, he thought, worthy of Christian imitation on the present occasion. . . ." *Ibid.*

Boudinot's resolution was carried in the affirmative on September 25, 1789. Boudinot and Sherman, who favored the Thanksgiving proclamation, voted in favor of the adoption of the proposed amendments to the Constitution, including the Religion Clause; Tucker, who opposed the Thanksgiving proclamation, voted against the adoption of the amendments which became the Bill of Rights.

Within two weeks of this action by the House, George Washington responded to the Joint Resolution which by now had been changed to include the language that the President "recommend to the people of the United States a day of public thanksgiving and prayer, to be observed by acknowledging with grateful hearts the many and signal favors of Almighty God, especially by affording them an opportunity peaceably to establish a form of government for their safety and happiness." 1 J. Richardson, Messages and Papers of the Presidents, 1789-1897, p. 64 (1897). The Presidential proclamation was couched in these words: "Now, therefore, I do recommend and assign Thursday, the 26th day of November next, to be devoted by the people of these States to the service of that great and glorious Being who is the beneficent author of all the good that was, that is, or that will be; that we may then all unite in rendering unto Him our sincere and humble thanks for His kind care and protection of the people of this country previous to their becoming a nation; for the signal and manifold mercies and the favorable interpositions of His providence in the course and conclusion of the late war; for the great degree of tranquility, union, and plenty which we have since enjoyed; for the peaceable and rational manner in which we have been enabled to establish constitutions of government for our safety and happiness, and particularly the national one now lately instituted; for the civil and religious liberty with which we are blessed, and the means we have of acquiring and diffusing useful knowledge; and in general, for all the great and various favors which He has been pleased to confer upon us.

"And also that we may then unite in most humbly offering our prayers and supplications to the great Lord and Ruler of Nations, and beseech Him to pardon our national and other transgressions; to enable us all, whether in public or private stations, to perform our several and relative duties properly and punctually; to render our National Government a blessing to all the people by constantly being a Government of wise, just, and constitutional laws, discreetly and faithfully executed and obeyed; to protect and guide all sovereigns and nations (especially such as have shown kindness to us), and to bless them with good governments, peace, and concord; to promote the knowledge and practice of true religion and virtue, and the increase of science among them and us; and, generally, to grant unto all mankind such a degree of temporal prosperity as He alone knows to be best." *Ibid.*

George Washington, John Adams, and James Madison all issued Thanksgiving proclamations; Thomas Jefferson did not, saying: " Fasting and prayer are religious exercises; the enjoining them an act of discipline. Every religious society has a right to determine for itself the times for these exercises, and the objects proper for them, according to their own particular tenets; and this right can never be safer than in their own hands, where the Constitution had deposited it." 11 Writings of Thomas Jefferson 429 (A. Lipscomb ed. 1904).

As the United States moved from the 18th into the 19th century, Congress appropriated time and again public moneys in support of sectarian Indian education carried on by religious organizations. Typical of these was Jefferson's treaty with the Kaskaskia Indians, which provided annual cash support for the Tribe's Roman Catholic priest and church. It was not until 1897, when aid to sectarian education for Indians had reached $500,000 annually, that Congress decided thereafter to cease appropriating money for education in sectarian schools. This history shows the fallacy of the notion found in *Everson* that "no tax in any amount" may be levied for religious activities in any form.

Joseph Story, a member of this Court from 1811 to 1845, and during much of that time a professor at the Harvard Law School, published by far the most comprehensive treatise on the United States Constitution that had then appeared. Volume 2 of Story's Commentaries on the Constitution of the United States 630-632 (5th ed. 1891) discussed the meaning of the Establishment Clause of the First Amendment this way: "Probably at the time of the adoption of the Constitution and of the amendment to it now under consideration [First Amendment], the general if not the universal sentiment in America was, that Christianity ought to receive encouragement from the State so far as was not incompatible with the private rights of conscience and the freedom of religious worship. An attempt to level all religions, and to make it a matter of state policy to hold all in utter indifference, would have created universal disapprobation, if not universal indignation.

.   .   .   .   .   .

"The real object of the [First] [A]mendment was not to countenance, much less to advance, Mahometanism, or Judaism, or infidelity, by prostrating Christianity; but to exclude all rivalry among Christian sects, and to prevent any national ecclesiastical establishment which should give to a hierarchy the exclusive patronage of the national government. It thus cut off the means of religious persecution (the vice and pest of former ages), and of the subversion of the rights of conscience in matters of religion, which had been trampled upon almost from the days of the Apostles to the present age. . . ."

Thomas Cooley's eminence as a legal authority rivaled that of Story. Cooley stated in his treatise entitled Constitutional Limitations that aid to a particular religious sect was prohibited by the United States Constitution, but he went on to say: "But while thus careful to establish, protect, and defend religious freedom and equality, the American constitutions contain no provisions which prohibit the authorities from such solemn recognition of a superintending Providence in public transactions and exercises as the general religious sentiment of mankind inspires, and as seems meet and proper in finite and dependent beings. Whatever may be the shades of religious belief, all must acknowledge the fitness of recognizing in important human affairs the superintending care and control of the Great Governor of the Universe, and of acknowledging with thanksgiving his boundless favors, or bowing in contrition when visited with the penalties of his broken laws. No principle of constitutional law is violated when thanksgiving or fast days are appointed; when chaplains are designated for the army and navy; when legislative sessions are opened with prayer or the reading of the Scriptures, or when religious teaching is encouraged by a general exemption of the houses of religious worship from taxation for the support of State government. Undoubtedly the spirit of the Constitution will require, in all these cases, that care be taken to avoid discrimination in favor of or against any one religious denomination or sect; but the power to do any of these things does not become unconstitutional simply because of its susceptibility to abuse. . . ." *Id.*, at 470-471. Cooley added that, "[t]his public recognition of religious worship, however, is not based entirely, perhaps not even mainly, upon a sense of what is due to the Supreme Being himself as the author of all good and of all law; but the same reasons of state policy which induce the government to aid institutions of charity and seminaries of instruction will incline it also to foster religious worship and religious institutions, as conservators of the public morals and valuable, if not indispensable, assistants to the preservation of the public order." *Id.*, at 470.

It would seem from this evidence that the Establishment Clause of the First Amendment had acquired a well-accepted meaning: it forbade establishment of a national religion, and forbade preference among religious sects or denominations. Indeed, the first American dictionary defined the word "establishment" as "the act of establishing, founding, ratifying or ordainin(g,") such as in "[t]he episcopal form of religion so called, in England." 1 N. Webster, American Dictionary of the English Language (1st ed. 1828). The Establishment Clause did not require government neutrality between religion and irreligion nor did it prohibit the federal government from providing non-discriminatory aid to religion. There is simply no historical foundation for the proposition that the Framers intended to build the "wall of separation" that was constitutionalized in *Everson*.

Notwithstanding the absence of an historical basis for this theory of rigid separation, the wall idea might well have served as a useful albeit misguided analytical concept, had it led this Court to unified and principled results in Establishment Clause cases. The opposite, unfortunately, has been true; in the 38 years since *Everson* our Establishment Clause cases have been neither principled nor unified. Our recent opinions, many of them hopelessly divided pluralities, have with embarrassing candor conceded that the "wall of separation" is merely a "blurred, indistinct, and variable barrier," which "is not wholly accurate" and can only be "dimly perceived." *Lemon* v. *Kurtzman*

Whether due to its lack of historical support or its practical unworkability, the *Everson* "wall" has proven all but useless as a guide to sound constitutional adjudication. It illustrates only too well the wisdom of Benjamin Cardozo's observation that "[m]etaphors in law are to be narrowly watched, for starting as devices to liberate thought, they end often by enslaving it." *Berkey* v. *Third Avenue R. Co.*

But the greatest injury of the "wall" notion is its mischievous diversion of judges from the actual intentions of the drafters of the Bill of Rights. The "crucible of litigation," is well adapted to adjudicating factual disputes on the basis of testimony presented in court, but no amount of repetition of historical errors in judicial opinions can make the errors true. The "wall of separation between church and State" is a metaphor based on bad history, a metaphor which has proved useless as a guide to judging. It should be frankly and explicitly abandoned.

The Court has more recently attempted to add some mortar to *Everson's* wall through the three-part test of *Lemon* v. *Kurtzman*, which served at first to offer a more useful test for purposes of the Establishment Clause than did the "wall" metaphor. Generally stated, the *Lemon* test proscribes state action that has a sectarian purpose or effect, or causes an impermissible governmental entanglement with religion.

Lemon cited *Board of Education* v. *Allen* as the source of the "purpose" and "effect" prongs of the three-part test. The *Allen* opinion explains, however, how it inherited the purpose and effect elements from *Schempp* and *Everson*, both of which contain the historical errors described above. Thus the purpose and effect prongs have the same historical deficiencies as the wall concept itself: they are in no way based on either the language or intent of the drafters.

The secular purpose prong has proven mercurial in application because it has never been fully defined, and we have never fully stated how the test is to operate. If the purpose prong is intended to void those aids to sectarian institutions accompanied by a stated legislative purpose to aid religion, the prong will condemn nothing so long as the legislature utters a secular purpose and says nothing about aiding religion. Thus the constitutionality of a statute may depend upon what the legislators put into the legislative history and, more importantly, what they leave out. The purpose prong means little if it only requires the legislature to express any secular purpose and omit all sectarian references, because legislators might do just that. Faced with a valid legislative secular purpose, we could not properly ignore that purpose without a factual basis for doing so.

However, if the purpose prong is aimed to void all statutes enacted with the intent to aid sectarian institutions, whether stated or not, then most statutes providing any aid, such as textbooks or bus rides for sectarian school children, will fail because one of the purposes behind every statute, whether stated or not, is to aid the target of its largesse. In other words, if the purpose prong requires an absence of *any* intent to aid sectarian institutions, whether or not expressed, few state laws in this area could pass the test, and we would be required to void some state aids to religion which we have already upheld.

The entanglement prong of the *Lemon* test came from *Walz* v. *Tax Commission*. *Walz* involved a constitutional challenge to New York's time-honored practice of providing state property tax exemptions to church property used in worship. The *Walz* opinion refused to "undermine the ultimate constitutional objective [of the Establishment Clause] as illuminated by history," and upheld the tax exemption. The Court examined the historical relationship between the state and church when church property was in issue, and determined that the challenged tax exemption did not so entangle New York with the Church as to cause an intrusion or interference with religion. Interferences with religion should arguably be dealt with under the Free Exercise Clause, but the entanglement inquiry in *Walz* was consistent with that case's broad survey of the relationship between state taxation and religious property.

We have not always followed *Walz's* reflexive inquiry into entanglement, however. One of the difficulties with the entanglement prong is that, when divorced from the logic of *Walz* it creates an "insoluble paradox" in school aid cases: we have required aid to parochial schools to be closely watched lest it be put to sectarian use, yet this close supervision itself will create an entanglement. For example, in *Wolman*, the Court in part struck the State's non-discriminatory provision of buses for parochial school field trips because the state supervision of sectarian officials in charge of field trips would be too onerous. This type of self-defeating result is certainly not required to ensure that States do not establish religion.

The entanglement test as applied in cases like *Wolman* also ignores the myriad state administrative regulations properly placed upon sectarian institutions such as curriculum, attendance, and certification requirements for sectarian schools, or fire and safety regulations for churches. Avoiding entanglement between church and State may be an important consideration in a case like *Walz*, but if the entanglement prong were applied to all state and church relations in the automatic manner in which it has been applied to school aid cases, the State could hardly require anything of church-related institutions as a condition for receipt of financial assistance.

These difficulties arise because the *Lemon* test has no more grounding in the history of the First Amendment than does the wall theory upon which it rests. The three-part test represents a determined effort to craft a workable rule from an historically faulty doctrine; but the rule can only be as sound as the doctrine it attempts to service. The three-part test has simply not provided adequate standards for deciding Establishment Clause cases, as this Court has slowly come to realize. Even worse, the *Lemon* test has caused this Court to fracture into unworkable plurality opinions, depending upon how each of the three factors applies to a certain state action. The results from our school services cases show the difficulty we have encountered in making the *Lemon* test yield principled results.

For example, a State may lend to parochial school children geography textbooks that contain maps of the United States, but the State may not lend maps of the United States for use in geography class. A State may lend textbooks on American colonial history, but it may not lend a film on George Washington, or a film projector to show it in history class. A State may lend classroom workbooks, but may not lend workbooks in which the parochial school children write, thus rendering them non-reusable. A State may pay for bus transportation to religious schools but may not pay for bus transportation from the parochial school to the public zoo or natural history museum for a field trip. A State may pay for diagnostic services conducted in the parochial school but therapeutic services must be given in a different building; speech and hearing "services" conducted by the State inside the sectarian school are forbidden, but the State may conduct speech and hearing diagnostic testing inside the sectarian school. Exceptional parochial school students may receive counseling, but it must take place outside of the parochial school, such as in a trailer parked down the street. A State may give cash to a parochial school to pay for the administration of State-written tests and state-ordered reporting services, but it may not provide funds for teacher-prepared tests on secular subjects. Religious instruction may not be given in public school, but the public school may release students during the day for religion classes elsewhere, and may enforce attendance at those classes with its truancy laws.

These results violate the historically sound principle "that the Establishment Clause does not forbid governments . . . to [provide] general welfare under which benefits are distributed to private individuals, even though many of those individuals may elect to use those benefits in ways that 'aid' religious instruction or worship." *Committee for Public Education* v. *Nyquist*. It is not surprising in the light of this record that our most recent opinions have expressed doubt on the usefulness of the *Lemon* test.

Although the test initially provided helpful assistance, e.g., *Tilton* v. *Richardson*, we soon began describing the test as only a "guideline," *Committee for Public Education* v. *Nyquist*, and lately we have described it as "no more than [a] useful signpos[t]." *Mueller* v. *Allen* We have noted that the *Lemon* test is "not easily applied," *Meek*, and as *Justice WHITE* noted in *Committee for Public Education* v. *Regan*, under the *Lemon* test we have "sacrifice[d] clarity and predictability for flexibility." In *Lynch* we reiterated that the *Lemon* test has never been binding on the Court, and we cited two cases where we had declined to apply it.

If a constitutional theory has no basis in the history of the amendment it seeks to interpret, is difficult to apply and yields unprincipled results, I see little use in it. The "crucible of litigation," has produced only consistent unpredictability, and today's effort is just a continuation of "the sisyphean task of trying to patch together the 'blurred, indistinct and variable barrier' described in *Lemon* v. *Kurtzman.*" *Regan* (STEVENS, J. dissenting). We have done much straining since 1947, but still we admit that we can only "dimly perceive" the *Everson* wall. Our perception has been clouded not by the Constitution but by the mists of an unnecessary metaphor.

The true meaning of the Establishment Clause can only be seen in its history. As drafters of our Bill of Rights, the Framers inscribed the principles that control today. Any deviation from their intentions frustrates the permanence of that Charter and will only lead to the type of unprincipled decisionmaking that has plagued our Establishment Clause cases since *Everson.*

The Framers intended the Establishment Clause to prohibit the designation of any church as a "national" one. The Clause was also designed to stop the Federal Government from asserting a preference for one religious denomination or sect over others. Given the "incorporation" of the Establishment Clause as against the States via the Fourteenth Amendment in *Everson*, States are prohibited as well from establishing a religion or discriminating between sects. As its history abundantly shows, however, nothing in the Establishment Clause requires government to be strictly neutral between religion and irreligion, nor does that Clause prohibit Congress or the States from pursuing legitimate secular ends through nondiscriminatory sectarian means.

The Court strikes down the Alabama statute in *Wallace* v. *Jaffree* because the State wished to "endorse prayer as a favored practice." It would come as much of a shock to those who drafted the Bill of Rights as it will to a large number of thoughtful Americans today to learn that the Constitution, as construed by the majority, prohibits the Alabama Legislature from "endorsing" prayer. George Washington himself, at the request of the very Congress which passed the Bill of Rights, proclaimed a day of "public thanksgiving and prayer, to be observed by acknowledging with grateful hearts the many and signal favors of Almighty God." History must judge whether it was the father of his country in 1789, or a majority of the Court today, which has strayed from the meaning of the Establishment Clause.

The State surely has a secular interest in regulating the manner in which public schools are conducted. Nothing in the Establishment Clause of the First Amendment, properly understood, prohibits any such generalized "endorsement" of prayer. I would therefore reverse the judgment of the Court of Appeals in *Wallace* v. *Jaffree.*

GOVERNMENT AID TO CHURCH-RELATED SCHOOLS

The development of parochial schools in this country is closely related to the history of immigration. Beginning about 1830 vast numbers of immigrants began to come to this country from northern and western Europe; later, particularly after 1865, they came from southern and eastern Europe. Many of these immigrants were Roman Catholics. In an attempt to incorporate these immigrants into the church and simultaneously to try to educate the children born to American Catholic parents, the Roman Catholic Church began a massive effort to create Catholic schools. In 1790 there were not any Catholic educational institutions in this country, but by 1840 there were more than two hundred schools, about half of them being west of the Allegheny Mountains. For several reasons the Catholics did not rely on the developing public school system to educate their children.

Traditionally, Catholics had insisted that the education of children should be performed by the home, the church, and the church school. They did not believe that education provided by a secular state would fit the Catholic philosophy of education. The bishop of Trenton went so far as to say that "the idea that the state has a right to teach . . . is not a Christian idea. It is a pagan one."[1] Most Catholics could not conceive of the state's replacing the home and the church as the principal educative agents.[2] They believed that education without religion was, at best, stilted and truncated and, at worst, dangerous. The leadership of the church contended that education must include religion in order to give a sense of morality to children.

As noted above (p. 378), public schools attempted to teach morality through the teaching of religion. Why did Catholics think that they had to have their own schools? Because they saw that the religion which was taught in the public schools was a kind of "religion in general" with Protestant overtones. Consequently, when the bishops of the American Catholic church met in 1884, they insisted that a school be built next to every Catholic church within two years of that date and that all Catholic parents send their children to one of those schools unless a bishop gave special permission to do otherwise. Although neither school building nor attendance ever reached those goals, Catholics have continued to be serious about their schools.

Catholics were not the only ones who established parochial schools. Many Jewish congregations did, too, for the obvious reason that they could not accept the religious content of the public schools. Some Protestant groups began parochial schools because the public schools were not Protestant enough for them.[3]

---

[1] Quoted in Neil G. McCluskey, *Catholic Education in America* (New York: Teachers College, Columbia University, 1964), p. 11.

[2] Throughout the history of the Catholic church in the United States, however, about one-half of the Catholic children have attended public schools, probably because of economic necessity.

[3] For a survey of the history of church-related schools in this country, as well as some of the contemporary problems confronting such schools, see James C. Carper and Thomas C. Hunt, eds., *Religious Schooling in America* (Birmingham, AL: Religious Education Press, 1984.)

The Catholic church's efforts to create parochial schools intensified the anti-Catholicism which was rampant in the nineteenth and early part of the twentieth centuries. Many viewed the public schools as a means to unify the American population. If children of immigrants would attend the public schools with the children of native Americans, then their differences would disappear, they would become Americanized, and American society would become more homogeneous. The fact that Catholics had their own schools showed that they wanted to be different, which was regarded as un-American. [4]

During and just after World War I, this anti-Catholicism was combined with nationalism to form a direct attack upon foreignness and non-public schools. Right after America entered the war, a number of states passed laws forbidding the teaching of foreign languages, especially German. Among these states was Nebraska, which, in 1919, passed a law providing that no foreign language could be taught in any school in the state unless the student had completed the eighth grade. In *Meyer* v. *Nebraska* (1923) the U.S. Supreme Court held that such laws violated the Due Process Clause of the Fourteenth Amendment because they withdrew from teachers the liberty to teach and from parents the liberty to employ teachers to instruct their children.

Oregon's legislature, in 1922, passed a similar but broader law that required all able-bodied and teachable students to attend public school. The law was challenged by a private military academy and by a school operated by the Society of the Sisters of the Holy Name of Jesus and Mary. Again, because the First Amendment had not yet been applied to the states, the basis of the challenge was the Fourteenth Amendment. In the 1925 decision of PIERCE v. SOCIETY OF SISTERS (p. 458), the Court, recalling the *Meyer* case, held that the Oregon law impermissibly denied private and parochial schools the right to do business and interfered with the liberty of parents to educate their children as they chose. This case is often called the "Magna Carta" of parochial schools.

Now that it was clear that parochial schools had the right to exist, the Catholic church continued its efforts to obtain state aid for its schools, an effort which had been started as early as 1840 by Bishop John Hughes of New York. Legal questions growing out of such aid first came to the Court in the 1930 case of COCHRAN v. LOUISIANA STATE BOARD OF EDUCATION (p. 460). Louisiana's legislature had enacted a statute providing for the purchase of secular textbooks for use by school children, including those enrolled in parochial schools. The law was challenged on the basis that the Fourteenth Amendment forbids states from depriving persons of their property without due process of law. The use of tax money to provide books for parochial schools, it was argued, amounted to the use of the money for a private, rather than public, purpose; thus, the statute was unconstitutional. The Court did not agree, arguing that the beneficiaries of the program were not the parochial schools but

the children of the state, some of whom happened to be enrolled in parochial schools. This case introduced the "child benefit theory" into consideration of whether and how to provide state aid to church-related schools. Supporters of parochial schools were greatly encouraged by the ruling, although the relation of this theory to the First Amendment was not clear.

Seventeen years passed before another case concerning aid to parochial schools came before the Court. In EVERSON v. BOARD OF EDUCATION (1947) (p. 461), Justice Black's separationist rhetoric notwithstanding, the Court approved of providing bus fares for children enrolled in church schools. The opinion stated that the state-supported bus rides were part of the state's public welfare program; even though the program helped children to attend church schools, aid to the schools themselves was indirect and thus permissible. This language had a "child benefit" ring; furthermore, it was based on the Court's interpretation of the Establishment Clause. The decision suggested to proponents of state aid to church-related schools that a wide range of aid programs could become a reality. At the time, however, these proponents did not know that the limit of permissible aid which the Court would allow would not be expanded for the next thirty years.

Still later, advocates of state aid to church-related schools, primarily Catholics, were given more cause for optimism with the passage of the Elementary and Secondary Education Act of 1965. This act of Congress included a section which allowed federal funds to be used for aiding schools populated by educationally deprived children from low-income families, even though the schools were church-related. This surely would be a great supplement to book lending and bus transportation programs.

In 1968 the Court decided BOARD OF EDUCATION v. ALLEN (p. 474). The case reaffirmed the constitutionality of loans of secular textbooks to children in parochial schools. This time the Court used "child benefit" language and affirmed that the program had a secular purpose and did nothing to advance or inhibit religion. Justice White, the author of the opinion, assumed that one could easily distinguish between secular and religious education imparted in a parochial school. He seemed to say that virtually any kind of state aid could be provided to the secular side of the school.

Also decided in 1968 was FLAST v. COHEN (p. 249), in which the Court allowed taxpayer suits on First Amendment questions to be filed in federal courts. Two years later WALZ v. TAX COMMISSION was decided, adding the "excessive entanglement" test to the "secular purpose" and "primary effect" tests for interpreting the Establishment Clause (p. 278). These decisions of 1968 and 1970 were to play a major role in reversing what seemed to be a pro-accommodationist trend in decisions concerning aid to church-related schools.

In 1968 the Pennsylvania legislature enacted a law authorizing action whereby the state "purchased educational services" from church-related schools. That is, Pennsylvania paid parochial schools for teaching specified secular subjects: mathematics, modern foreign languages, physical sciences, and physical education. To guarantee the secularity of the courses, all instructional

---

[4] An expression of this attitude toward the public schools, without the anti-Catholicism, may be seen in Mr. Justice Frankfurter's majority opinion in MINERSVILLE SCHOOL DISTRICT v. GOBITIS (p. 82) and his dissenting opinion in WEST VIRGINIA BOARD OF EDUCATION v. BARNETTE (p. 87).

material had to be approved by the state superintendent of public instruction.

A year later Rhode Island adopted a plan whereby teachers of secular subjects in parochial schools that served students from the lower end of the socioeconomic scale would receive from the state 15 percent of their annual salary. Taxpayers in both states filed suits in federal courts. In 1971 the Supreme Court considered the Rhode Island plan in *Early* v. *DiCenso* and the Pennsylvania law in LEMON v. KURTZMAN (p. 480). The two cases were decided together under the latter title. Writing for a majority of eight, Chief Justice Burger found both programs to be in violation of the Establishment Clause because they fostered excessive entanglement between church and state. In each case, state aid was to be given only to the secular side of the parochial school's program. Burger declared that continual government surveillance would be required to guarantee that teachers receiving salary supplements were not teaching religion and that services purchased were really free from religious content. Such interaction between church schools and civil authority was not the separation that the Establishment Clause was designed to guarantee.

Still, the issue of providing aid to parochial schools was far from settled. Even before the *Lemon* decision, New York had enacted legislation to provide aid of a different type, some of which might be called "parent benefit." Pennsylvania also enacted new legislation immediately after *Lemon*. Challenges to all these programs made their way to the Supreme Court by means of taxpayers' suits in federal courts. Several decisions were handed down on 25 June 1973, a disastrous day from the viewpoint of those who favor state aid to church-related schools.

In COMMITTEE FOR PUBLIC EDUCATION AND RELIGIOUS LIBERTY (PEARL) v. NYQUIST (p. 504), the Court considered a comprehensive New York plan to aid church-related schools. The first section of the law provided for direct money grants to nonpublic schools serving a high concentration of pupils from low-income families. State money was to be used for maintenance and repair of facilities and equipment in order to insure the students' health, welfare, and safety. The amount of money would depend on the age of the facility but could not be more than 50 percent of the cost for equivalent services in the public schools. The second section of the act provided for tuition reimbursement to parents who had children in nonpublic elementary or secondary schools, if the parents' annual taxable income was less than $5,000. The third section of the law provided aid for parents whose annual taxable income was between $5,000 and $25,000. In filing a state income tax return, a parent was allowed to deduct a stipulated sum from his/her adjusted gross income for each child attending a nonpublic school. The amount of the deduction was unrelated to the amount of tuition actually paid and decreased as the amount of taxable income increased.

In a decision written by Justice Powell, the Court found all three of the programs unconstitutional because they failed the "primary effect" test. In the maintenance and repair section of the act, no provision was made to restrict payments to expenditures for the upkeep of facilities used exclusively for secular purposes; thus, the effect of the plan was to subsidize and advance the religious mission of sectarian schools. The fact that tuition reimbursements were made directly to parents did not mitigate the fact that the effect of the aid was clearly to provide financial support for sectarian institutions. The Court was convinced that the state sought to relieve parents' financial burden sufficiently to assure that they would continue to have the option of sending their children to church-related schools. Although the method of the third section of the act was different from the second, it also provided the parent "the same form of encouragement and reward for sending his children to nonpublic schools." 413 U.S. 756, 791 (p. 511)

On the same day the Nyquist decision was announced, the Court also struck down a Pennsylvania plan of tuition reimbursement that was virtually identical with that in section two of the New York plan. In *Sloan* v. *Lemon* (1973) the Court said that tuition reimbursement in Pennsylvania suffered from the same infirmity as in New York: the primary effect was to advance religion.

On that fateful day the Court struck down still another New York attempt to aid church-related schools, the purchase of mandated services. New York required all accredited schools to give examinations to students and to keep records on both students and teachers. It was contended that if the state paid for such expenses in the public schools, it ought to do the same for nonpublic schools. But the program paid for teacher-prepared tests as well as state standardized tests, and therein lay a problem. In *Levitt* v. *Committee for Public Education and Religious Liberty* (PEARL) (1973), the Court argued that testing was a part of the teaching process, and, because the state had no way to determine if the teacher-prepared tests were entirely free from religious instruction, the program was an impermissible aid to religion.

In 1974, in *Wheeler* v. *Barrera*, the Court ruled that a state receiving funds under Title I of the Elementary and Secondary Education Act must provide "comparable but not identical" services to disadvantaged students attending both public and nonpublic schools. This must be done even though the state's constitution prohibits any aid to church-related schools, as in the case of Missouri. A state may refuse to make comparable services available to disadvantaged children in nonpublic schools, but by doing so, Title I funds would be forfeited.

In MEEK v. PITTENGER (1975) (p. 517), the Court struck down still other attempts by Pennsylvania to provide aid to its church-related schools. At issue was another comprehensive law which provided for the loan of textbooks to church school students and the loan of instructional equipment (projectors, recorders, laboratory apparatus) and materials (periodicals, photographs, maps, films) directly to the schools. In addition, Pennsylvania provided "auxiliary services:" remedial teaching, psychological and therapeutic services, guidance, counseling, and testing by state-paid personnel who came to the premises of parochial schools.

In an opinion written by Justice Stewart, the Court found the loan of the textbooks to be permissible under the doctrine of the *Allen* case. But all other aspects of the law were found to violate the Establishment Clause. The loan of instructional equipment and materials had the primary effect of advancing the religious mission of the schools. Provision of "auxiliary services," because it involved the activity of public school teachers, fostered excessive entanglement between state and church because of the continual surveillance required to insure that religion was not taught.

The cumulative effect of all the decisions from *Lemon* through *Meek* was to dash accommodationists' hopes of providing new means for aiding church-related schools. As each of these cases was decided, the number and intensity of the dissenters increased (e.g., Chief Justice Burger's reference to "the crabbed attitude" of the Court in *Meek*). At the same time, many Catholic responses escalated in criticism of the Court until, after the *Meek* decision, John T. Cicco, superintendent of Catholic schools in the Pittsburgh diocese, could say: "I don't believe the Court would give Catholics anything, no matter what they would come up with."[5]

Some will argue that the Court responded to such criticism in its decision in WOLMAN v. WALTER (p. 537) (1977). More likely, the Court was acknowledging that the Ohio statute which was the basis for the case had been carefully written to avoid the objections the Court had found in *Meek*. For whatever reason, *Wolman* approved of a number of ways states could financially aid church-related schools: the news media described the decision as an "instruction manual" for legislatures. In a decision written by Justice Blackmun, the Court again approved of textbook loans to parochial school students. Approval was given to state-financed academic testing of students, using standardized tests, thus avoiding the objection, raised in *Levitt*, to the possibility of religious content in teacher-prepared tests. The justices approved of state-subsidized speech, hearing, and psychological diagnostic services administered in parochial schools by public school employees. However, the sole purpose of the services must be to determine a student's deficiency or need for assistance. Therapeutic services such as guidance counseling, speech help, or remedial reading would be allowed, so long as the services were performed away from the "pervasively sectarian atmosphere of the church-related school," thus distinguishing the Ohio plan from that disallowed in *Meek*.

However, the Court did not give blanket approval to the Ohio plan. It declared unconstitutional the state's supplying of projectors, maps and globes, and other instructional equipment because they were not actually loaned to parents and pupils, despite Ohio's protestations to the contrary. Finally, the Court struck down state financing of instructional field trips because they would be under the direction of religious schools and could easily be transformed into religious education.

In arriving at its decision, the Court claimed that it applied its three-part test consistently with its previous opinions, although seven of the justices disagreed with that claim enough to write dissents on one or more of the parts of Ohio's school plan. Consequently, *Wolman* is a very complicated case.

Although the impulse to establish parochial schools was over a century old, the 1970s and 1980s saw a rapid increase in parochial educational activity. One reason was the alleged secularization and incompetence of the public

schools, already noted; another was a protest against judicially commanded desegregation of public schools, in most cases implemented by busing. Although the accusation that proliferating private and parochial schools in this time were "segregation academies" was perhaps too broadly made, nonetheless, there was some truth to it.

A major question for the sponsors of the new private and church-related schools was whether or not any state or federal money could be used to help finance them. Many believed that *Wolman* was a definitive case, i.e., that it had set the limits once and for all. However, because its strict separationism was not to the liking of many supporters of church-related schools, various governmental agencies continued to devise plans to try to give public aid to the schools. Because such plans were routinely challenged by separationists, the Court ruled on several cases. One of these, *New York* v. *Cathedral Academy*, goes back to a much earlier set of cases. In 1973 the Court handed down a decision in *Levitt* v. *Committee for Public Education and Religious Liberty* (PEARL) in which it invalidated state financing of the grading of teacher-prepared tests on the grounds that such tests might have religious content. In that case the Court affirmed an injunction of a federal district court forbidding payments to parochial schools in New York, including payments for expenses the schools had already incurred in the last one-half of the 1971-1972 school year. In 1972 the New York legislature had passed a law which allowed the state to pay the schools for expenses already incurred in the program banned by the district court.

There was some precedent for New York's action. When the Court invalidated some state payments to parochial schools in Rhode Island and Pennsylvania in *Lemon*, Pennsylvania had not yet paid all the money due to the parochial schools for services they had already performed. In a dispute over whether the state could fulfill the remainder of its contract with the schools, the Court ruled, in a case designated *Lemon II* that it could. That is, even though the program had been declared unconstitutional, the Court permitted the remaining payments under the concept of fairness and equity because the schools had been led to believe, while the program was still in effect, that they would be paid for those services.

When a dispute arose over whether New York could finish its contracted payments for testing services in the parochial schools, invalidated in *Levitt*, *Lemon II* was cited as precedent. In *Cathedral Academy*, however, payments were not allowed because the Court declared that the situation was different from *Lemon II*. According to this finding, when the district court imposed the original injunction it had specifically enjoined payments for amounts "heretofore or hereafter expended." Consequently, for New York to try to fulfill the remainder of its obligation to the parochial schools, under the concept of equity, it had to go against the express language of the district court. The Supreme Court held that to be impermissible.

Even as this litigation was in progress, the New York legislature drafted a new bill to pay for state-mandated services in the parochial schools. This time, however, the legislature restricted payments to grading of state-prepared examinations, which naturally concerned only secular subjects. (There were other parts to the plan,

[5] "Parochiaid Defeated Again," *Church and State* 28 (July-August 1975): 7.

such as reporting pupil attendance and other educational data, but preparation and grading of exams were at the heart of the case.) This law was attacked by a group of strict separationists who contended that it made no difference who prepared and graded the tests. As long as the new law still provided for state funds to go to parochial schools, the separationists argued, it was unconstitutional under the Establishment Clause. After some complex legal transactions, the case finally reached the Supreme Court under the title COMMITTEE FOR PUBLIC EDUCATION AND RELIGIOUS FREEDOM v. REGAN (p. 545).

While *Regan* was making its way to the Court, the *Wolman* case had been decided. Included in the array of programs for which Ohio had been willing to pay parochial schools was one which provided payment for the administration of state-prepared standardized tests (the same ones used in the public schools) and scoring of same by state employees. The Court had been convinced that, under such circumstances, no danger existed that the tests could be used to teach religion. Consequently, the program was upheld.

A majority of five saw enough similarity between the testing program in *Wolman* and the one being considered in *Regan* to find the latter constitutional. Only state-prepared standardized tests were paid for by state money; thus the law was constitutional. That the money was paid directly to the parochial schools or that the tests were graded by parochial school personnel rather than state personnel were not deemed to be significant problems by the majority. Dissenting justices would have invalidated the law under the Establishment Clause.

In MUELLER v. ALLEN (1983) (p. 552) the Court again addressed the question as to whether a state can provide financial aid through tax deductions to parents who send their children to parochial schools. A decade before, in *Nyqusit*, income tax deductions to partially pay a student's tuition to parochial school had been declared unconstitutional because they had the primary effect of advancing religion. That is, by providing the tax advantage, the state provided parents an incentive to send their children to church-related schools, thereby furthering the schools' religious mission. *Mueller* grew out of a challenge to a Minnesota law which provided financial assistance, through state income tax deductions, for "tuition, textbooks, and transportation" of dependents attending elementary or secondary schools. The deduction was available to all parents who had children in school, whether the school were private, church-related, *or public*. That factual difference from *Nyquist* made the decision come out differently. Justice Rehnquist, who had dissented in *Nyqyist*, wrote for the Court that because the exemption could finance educational expenses at either public or parochial schools showed that the plan had the secular purpose of providing for a well-educated citizenry, that it did not have the primary effect of advancing religion, since the aid did not flow to religious schools exclusively (which had the effect of leaving *Nyquist* intact: a law aiding only parochial schools would still be unconstitutional), and it did not create excessive entanglement between church and state, since the act which triggered the tax deduction to the parent was the decision of the parent without any interaction with a state

official. The law did provide that state officials would have to choose which textbooks could qualify for the deduction (the state could not pay for religion books). But this was not a problem since the Court had approved a virtually identical procedure many years before in BOARD OF EDUCATION v. ALLEN (p. 474).

Four dissenters argued that the across-the-board feature of the plan was a fiction, since only under the most unusual circumstances did public schools charge any tuition. It was clear that parents who send their children to church-related schools were the primary (almost the only) beneficiaries of the tax reduction plan, so that it was not materially different from that declared unconstitutional in *Nyquist*. The majority was not persuaded. For them, the law was neutral on its face and its constitutionality should not be set aside on the basis of annual statistical reports. Justice Powell, the author of *Nyquist*, joined the majority. Thus was the way opened for other states, and perhaps the federal government, to provide tuition assistance for parents to send their children to private and church-related schools.

In 1985 the Court decided on still other ways to provide government aid to religious schools in GRAND RAPIDS SCHOOL DISTRICT v. BALL (p. 567) and AGUILAR v. FELTON (p. 559), handed down the same day. These cases involved the employment of public school teachers to teach secular subjects in parochial schools on a part-time basis. The Court had dealt with a similar plan indirectly in 1974 when it had affirmed a district court's invalidation of a plan for public school teachers to teach remedial reading and mathematics for nonpublic school pupils in *Public Funds for Public Schools* v. *Marburger*. But it was not until these two cases that such plans were given full review.

Grand Rapids involved two programs, Shared Time and Community Education. The former offered classes intended to supplement "core curriculum" courses required by the state; art, music, physical education, and "remedial" and "enrichment" reading and mathematics. The Shared Time teachers were full-time public school employees, although some of them had taught in parochial schools. The Community Education program offered classes after the regular school day in voluntary courses including, but not limited to, arts and crafts, gymnastics, yearbook production, newspaper, chess, and nature appreciation. The teachers were generally parochial school teachers hired, on a part-time basis, by the public schools to teach these supplementary courses. The offerings of both programs were taught in parochial school rooms, which, during the times of these particular classes, had to be devoid of any religious symbols. In addition, a sign had to be posted designating the room as a public school classroom.

Felton involved a program virtually identical to the Shared Time dimension of *Grand Rapids*. The teachers were public school teachers hired to present traditional academic subjects in parochial school classrooms. They were directed to avoid teaching religion, to avoid involvement in religious activities normally occurring in the parochial school room, and to minimize contact with parochial school personnel. Supervision procedures were created to try to guarantee the requisite level of secularity. The program under consideration in *Felton* was aimed at educationally deprived children from low-income families and was federally financed under Title I of the Elementary and Secondary Education Act of 1965. The program in *Grand Rapids*, on the other hand, was state financed and aimed at students (and even adults, in the Community Education program) from all economic classes.

In each case, the Court declared the school aid program to be unconstitutional. The plan in *Grand Rapids* was found to have the primary effect of advancing religion in three ways: (1) the state-paid teachers, working in a sectarian environment, might indoctrinate students in religion, (2) the fact of state-paid teachers working in parochial schools symbolically conveys the message of state support of religion, and (3) the programs effectively subsidize religion by assuming a portion of the parochial school's responsibility for teaching secular subjects. In *Felton* the defect was excessive entanglement. To guarantee that no religion was taught required an impermissible amount of surveillance by state personnel. Furthermore, state and parochial school officials had to regularly meet together to plan and to solve problems. There was also frequent contact between the regular parochial school teachers and the state-paid teachers.

Both decisions were five-to-four (although Justices Burger and O'Connor did agree to the unconstitutionality of the Community Education part of *Grand Rapids*). The dissenters criticized the majority for impugning the integrity of teachers hired to work in the parochial schools, especially since the record of the programs showed no evidence of indoctrination. They faulted the zealous application of the "*Lemon* test," especially the "excessive entanglement" portion. Finally, in *Felton*, they called attention to the human cost of the decision, since the remedial and enrichment teaching denied was for educationally-deprived children from low-income families.

During the latter part of the period in which the Court was handing down its most separationist decisions on state aid to elementary and secondary church-related schools, it also heard some cases on state aid to church-related colleges. Because the conditions were somewhat different in institutions of higher education, so were the decisions.

Title I of the Higher Education Facilities Act of 1963 provided federal construction grants for college building and facilities, but it specified that funds were not to be used to construct any building in which sectarian instruction or religious worship took place. The government maintained an interest in the federally financed buildings for twenty years. After that period, colleges could use the building for any purpose; they no longer had to be used for only secular educational activities.

The law was implemented at four church-related colleges in Connecticut and was challenged in federal court by some taxpayers from that state who claimed that it was unconstitutional. The Court dealt with their complaint in TILTON v. RICHARDSON (1971) (p. 498). Chief Justice Burger wrote the opinion of the Court. He said that the provision whereby federally financed buildings could be used for religious purposes after twenty years was a violation of the Establishment Clause, but that, in general, building grants for church-related colleges were not unconstitutional. The key distinctions between colleges and secondary and elementary schools are that the former do not have as their primary goal the inculcation of the doc-

trine of the sponsoring church, that college students are less impressionable than younger students, and that college teachers are guided by their own internal scholarly disciplines and seek to stimulate critical thinking by their students. Consequently, the building grants do not have the effect of advancing religion. In addition, because colleges and their teachers are more "objective" in their approach to religion and because the federal monies are used to construct buildings, which are non-ideological by nature, it is not necessary for government to maintain a continual surveillance to guarantee that the funds are put to secular use. Consequently, the law does not have the effect of creating excessive entanglement between state and church.

There were four dissenters in *Tilton* who felt that the distinctions between colleges and lower level schools were oversimplified and that the college grants ought to be found unconstitutional on the precedent of *Lemon*.

Two years later, on that important 25 June 1973, when the Court announced so many decisions on government aid to church-related schools, it also handed down *Hunt* v. *McNair*, a college case similar to *Tilton*. The South Carolina legislature had created an agency to issue bonds, the proceeds of which were to be used to finance college facilities. Facilities so financed could not be used for religious worship or instruction. The bonds were to be paid off from tuition and other income of the college. Actually, no state money was involved in the program. The only state aid was the creation of an instrumentality through which institutions could borrow money at a lower rate of interest because of the tax-exempt nature of the state agency. A South Carolina taxpayer challenged the arrangement, as implemented at a Baptist college, as a violation of the Establishment Clause.

In a six-to-three decision, the Court held that the law was constitutional. Relying heavily on *Tilton's* description of a church-related college and the teaching done there, the Court found that the law had a secular purpose and that it did not advance the religious mission of the sponsoring church. In reference to the third test, because religious indoctrination was not a major goal of the college and since the form of aid (buildings) was not one that lent itself to abuse, only modest policing was necessary. In addition, it was clear that the state agency did not participate in a significant way in the management of the college's facilities. Consequently, the program did not foster excessive entanglement between church and state.

In the case of ROEMER v. BOARD OF PUBLIC WORKS (1976) (p. 528), the Court dealt with a program of aid to church-related colleges that was not limited to construction and maintenance of buildings. In 1971 a Maryland statute was enacted which authorized the payment of state funds to any accredited private college so long as it met certain academic criteria, refrained from awarding "only seminarian or theological degrees," and did not utilize the funds for sectarian purposes. Otherwise, the institutions could use the state funds as they chose. Each time a college applied to the Board of Public Works, the Maryland agency administering the program, the school's chief executive officer was required to file an affidavit stating that the funds would not be used in a sectarian way and describing the nonsectarian use to which they would be put. At the end of the year, the chief executive officer was required to file another affidavit stating that the funds had not been used for sectarian purposes. Four Maryland taxpayers filed suit in federal court, claiming that this virtually unrestricted use of state money by church-related colleges was a violation of the Establishment Clause.

Justice Blackmun, writing for the Court, found that the legislation clearly had a secular purpose. The program passed the primary effect test because the church-related colleges were not "pervasively sectarian;" and, because of the requirement placed upon the colleges of certifying that the funds had been used for secular purposes, it was clear that the aid went to the "secular side" of the college, rather than to support religious activity. The fact of such certification did not raise entanglement between church and state to an excessive level, since only rarely would on-campus inspections be required and, if conducted, they would be brief and no more extensive than those inspections already made to determine accreditation. Four dissenters were incredulous that the program was held not to advance the religious mission of the colleges. Justice Stevens also pointedly remarked that the existence of state funds caused church-related colleges to compromise the level of their religiosity in order to get the money.

In the decade 1976-1986 the Court decided only one church-state case at the college level, WIDMAR v. VINCENT (p. 210), which did not confront the issue of state aid to church-related colleges. But in that same decade the Court did pass judgment on a type of state aid which included church colleges. During the 1970s a number of states created plans to give financial assistance to college students. Tennessee was one of those states. Actually, Tennessee legislated two such plans. The first was challenged in court and declared unconstitutional on establishment grounds. Before appeal was considered, the state modified the statute and then repealed it in its entirety and replaced it with another law. The second law provided that a student desiring aid initiated the process by submitting an application along with a financial disclosure form. If the information showed a student had financial need and was indeed enrolled in a college or university, he or she was sent a certificate showing the amount of state money to which he or she was entitled. The money could be spent by the student at any type of institution of higher learning; public, private, or church-related. The maximum amount which could be allocated to each student at the time of the litigation was the total of tuition and fees at the college of the student's choice or $1,200, whichever was less. However, the money did not have to be spent on tuition and fees. It could be used, and sometimes was, for other educational expenses such as books, room rent, health care, and transportation. There was clear evidence that some students utilizing the state's aid attended schools which were church-related and sometimes pervasively religious.

The program was challenged in a federal district court as being in violation of the Establishment Clause: *Americans United for Separation of Church and State* v. *Blanton* (1977). The court ruled that the plan was constitutional. Because the money went to the student, who could spend the money at any accredited college or university in the state, it was clear that the state did not intend to aid any particular religion or religious school and, as the program was implemented, it did not, especially because the money did not have to go to the school for tuition and fees, but could be spent for related educational expenses. What was essentially a "child benefit" plan did not violate the Establishment Clause. That judgment was affirmed without a hearing by the Supreme Court.

In summary, decisions of the Supreme Court indicate that certain kinds of state aid may be made available to parochial schools; bus transportation, textbook loans, and services for the educational health and welfare of the student, so long as it is manifestly clear that the performance of these services is absolutely secular. This secularity requirement is easily seen by comparing *Meek* and *Wolman*. Because the parochial school is an arm of the church and its principal purpose is the instruction of children in the church's doctrine and the advancement of its religious mission, any other forms of aid which would contribute to this cause have been declared unconstitutional. As as result of *Mueller*, government aid may be given to church-related schools by means of tuition supplements through tax deductions for parents sending children to such schools, provided that the deductions are available to parents of children going to any kind of school, i.e., the tax deductions must be applicable to educational expenses across the board. On the other hand, when it comes to the financing of particular educational activities within parochial schools, the negative decisions in *Grand Rapids* and *Felton* mean that *Wolman* still sets the boundaries of what is permissible. However, the Court recognizes that a college or university may be church-related without being sectarian or having as its primary purpose the advancement of the religious mission of the sponsoring church. This is the case primarily because of the greater sophistication of college students and the more objective nature of college-level teaching in accordance with the canons of academic freedom. Even though both *Tilton* and *Roemer* were decided by the slimmest of margins, five-to-four, while *Hunt* was a six-to-three decision, that distinction between precollegiate schools and colleges persisted through the 1985 term of the Court.

PIERCE v. SOCIETY OF THE SISTERS OF THE HOLY NAMES OF JESUS AND MARY

268 U.S. 510
ON APPEAL FROM THE DISTRICT COURT OF THE
UNITED STATES FOR THE DISTRICT OF OREGON
Argued March 16 and 17, 1925 — Decided June 1, 1925

⊥ *Mr. Justice McREYNOLDS* delivered the opinion of the court.

These appeals are from decrees, based upon undenied allegations, which granted preliminary orders restraining ⊥ appellants from threatening or attempting to enforce the Compulsory Education Act adopted November 7, 1922, under the initiative provision of her Constitution by the voters of Oregon. They present the same points of law; there are no controverted questions of fact. Rights said to be guaranteed by the Federal Constitution were specially set up, and appropriate prayers asked for their protection.

The challenged act, effective September 1, 1926, requires every parent, guardian, or other person having control or charge or custody of a child between eight and sixteen years to send him "to a public school for the period of time a public school shall be held during the current year" in the district where the child resides; and failure so to do is declared a ⌐531 misdemeanor. There are ⊥exemptions—not specially important here—for children who are not normal, or who have completed the eighth grade, or whose parents or private teachers reside at considerable distances from any public school, or who hold special permits from the county superintendent. The manifest purpose is to compel general attendance at public schools by normal children, between eight and sixteen, who have not completed the eighth grade. And without doubt enforcement of the statute would seriously impair, perhaps destroy, the profitable features of appellees' business, and greatly diminish the value of their property.

Appellee the Society of Sisters is an Oregon corporation, organized in 1880, with power to care for orphans, educate and instruct the youth, establish and maintain academies or schools, and acquire nec- ⌐532 essary real and per⊥sonal property. It has long devoted its property and effort to the secular and religious education and care of children, and has acquired the valuable good will of many parents and guardians. It conducts interdependent primary and high schools and junior colleges, and maintains orphanages for the custody and control of children between eight and sixteen. In its primary schools many children between those ages are taught the subjects usually pursued in Oregon public schools during the first eight years. Systematic religious instruction and moral training according to the tenets of the Roman Catholic Church are also regularly provided. All courses of study, both temporal and religious, contemplate continuity of training under appellee's charge; the primary schools are essential to the system and the most profitable. It owns valuable buildings, especially constructed and equipped for school purposes. The business is remunerative,—the annual income from primary schools exceeds $30,000,—and the successful conduct of this requires long-time contracts with teachers and parents. The Compulsory Education Act of 1922 has already caused the withdrawal from its schools of children who would otherwise continue, and their income has steadily declined. The appellants, public officers, have proclaimed their purpose strictly to enforce the statute.

After setting out the above facts, the Society's bill alleges that the enactment conflicts with the right of parents to choose schools where their children will receive appropriate mental and religious training, the right of the child to influence the parents' choice of a school, the right of schools and teachers therein to engage in a useful business or profession, and is accordingly repugnant to the Constitution and void. And, further, that unless enforcement of the measure is enjoined, the corporation's business and property will suffer irreparable injury.

Appellee Hill Military Academy is a private corporation organized in 1908 under the laws of Oregon, engaged ⊥in owning, operating, and conducting for ⌐533 profit an elementary, college preparatory, and military training school for boys between the ages of five and twenty-one years. The average attendance is one hundred, and the annual fees received for each student amount to some $800. The elementary department is divided into eight grades, as in the public schools; the college preparatory department has four grades, similar to those of the public high schools; the courses of study conform to the requirements of the state board of education. Military instruction and training are also given, under the supervision of an Army officer. It owns considerable real and personal property, some useful only for school purposes. The business and incident good will are very valuable. In order to conduct its affairs longtime contracts must be made for supplies, equipment, teachers, and pupils. Appellants, law officers of the state and county, have publicly announced that the Act of November 7, 1922, is valid, and have declared their intention to enforce it. By reason of the statute and threat of enforcement, appellee's business is being destroyed and its property depreciated; parents and guardians are refusing to make contracts for the future instruction of their sons, and some are being withdrawn.

The Academy's bill states the foregoing facts and then alleges that the challenged act contravenes the corporation's rights guaranteed by the 14th Amendment, and that unless appellants are restrained from proclaiming its validity and threatening to enforce it, irreparable injury will result. The prayer is for an appropriate injunction.

No answer was interposed in either cause, and after proper notices they were heard by three judges on motions for preliminary injunctions upon the specifically alleged facts. The court ruled that the 14th Amendment guaranteed appellees against the ⊥de- ⌐534 privation of their property without due process of law consequent upon the unlawful interference by appellants with the free choice of patrons, present and prospective. It declared the right to conduct schools was property, and that parents and guardians, as a part of their liberty, might direct the education of children by selecting reputable teachers and places. Also, the appellees' schools were not unfit or harmful to the public, and that enforcement of the challenged statute would unlawfully deprive them of patronage, and thereby destroy appellee's business and property. Finally, that the threats to enforce the act would continue to cause irreparable injury; and the suits were not premature.

No question is raised concerning the power of the state reasonably to regulate all schools, to inspect, supervise, and examine them, their teachers and pupils; to require that all children of proper age attend some school, that teachers shall be of good moral character and patriotic disposition, that certain studies plainly essential to good citizenship must be taught, and that nothing be taught which is manifestly inimical to the public welfare.

The inevitable practical result of enforcing the act under consideration would be destruction of appellees' primary shools, and perhaps all other private primary schools for normal children within the state of Oregon. Appellees are engaged in a kind of undertaking not inherently harmful, but long regarded as useful and meritorious. Certainly there is nothing in the present records to indicate that they have failed to discharge their obligations to patrons, students, or the state. And there are no peculiar circumstances or present emergencies which demand extraordinary measures relative to primary education.

Under the doctrine of *Meyer* v. *Nebraska* we think it entirely plain that the Act of 1922 unreasonably interferes with the liberty of parents and guardians
⌐535 to direct the upbringing and education of chil⊥dren under their control. As often heretofore pointed out, rights guaranteed by the Constitution may not be abridged by legislation which has no reasonable relation to some purpose within the competency of the state. The fundamental theory of liberty upon which all governments in this Union repose excludes any general power of the state to standardize its children by forcing them to accept instruction from public teachers only. The child is not the mere creature of the state; those who nurture him and direct his destiny have the right, coupled with the high duty, to recognize and prepare him for additional obligations.

Appellees are corporations, and therefore, it is said, they cannot claim for themselves the liberty which the 14th Amendment guarantees. Accepted in the proper sense, this is true. But they have business and property for which they claim protection. These are threatened with destruction through the unwarranted compulsion which appellants are exercising over present and prospective patrons of their schools. And this court has gone very far to protect against loss threatened by such action.

The courts of the state have not construed the act, and we must determine its meaning for ourselves. Evidently it was expected to have general application, and cannot be construed as though merely intended to amend the charters of certain private corporations, as in *Berea College* v. *Kentucky*. No argument in favor of such view has been advanced.

Generally it is entirely true, as urged by counsel, that no person in any business has such an interest in possible customers as to enable him to restrain exercise of proper power of the state upon the ground that he will be de⊥prived of patronage. But the in-   ⌐536 junctions here sought are not against the exercise of any *proper* power. Appellees asked protection against arbitrary, unreasonable, and unlawful interference with their patrons, and the consequent destruction of their business and property. Their interest is clear and immediate, within the rule approved in *Truax* v. *Raich, Truax* v. *Corrigan*, and *Terrace* v. *Thompson* and many other cases where injunctions have issued to protect business enterprises against interference with the freedom of patrons or customers.

The suits were not premature. The injury to appellees was present and very real,—not a mere possibility in the remote future. If no relief had been possible prior to the effective date of the act, the injury would have become irreparable. Prevention of impending injury by unlawful action is a well-recognized function of courts of equity.

The decrees below are *affirmed*.

COCHRAN v. LOUISIANA STATE BOARD OF EDUCATION

281 U.S. 370
ON APPEAL FROM THE SUPREME COURT
OF THE STATE OF LOUISIANA
Argued April 15, 1930 — Decided April 28, 1930

⊥*Mr. Chief Justice HUGHES* delivered the opin-   ⌐373
ion of the Court.

The appellants, as citizens and taxpayers of the state of Louisiana, brought this suit to restrain the State Board of Education and other state officials from expending any part of the severance tax fund in purchasing school books and in supplying them free of cost to the school children of the state, under Acts No. 100 and No. 143 of 1928, upon the ground that the legislation violated specified provisions of the Constitution of the state and also section 4 of article 4 and the Fourteenth Amendment of the Federal Constitution. The Supreme Court of the state affirmed the judgment of the trial court which refused to issue an injunction.

⊥Act No. 100 of 1928 provided that the severance   ⌐374
tax fund of the state, after allowing funds and appropriations as required by the state Constitution, should be devoted "first, to supplying school books to the school children of the State." The Board of Education was directed to provide "school books for school children free of cost to such children." Act No. 143 of 1928 made appropriations in accordance with the above provisions.

The Supreme Court of the state, following its decision in *Borden* v. *Louisiana State Board of Education*, held that these acts were not repugnant to either the state or the Federal Constitution.

No substantial Federal question is presented under section 4 of article 4 of the Federal Constitution guaranteeing to every state a republican form of government, as questions arising under this provision are political, not judicial, in character.

The contention of the appellant under the Fourteenth Amendment is that taxation for the purchase of school books constituted a taking of private property for a private purpose. The purpose is said to be to aid private, religious, sectarian, and other schools not embraced in the public educational system of the state by furnishing textbooks free to the children attending such private schools. The operation and effect of the legislation in question were described by the Supreme Court of the state as follows: "One may scan the acts in vain to ascertain where any money is appropriated for the purchase of school books for the use of any church, private, sectarian, or even public school. The appropriations were made for the specific purpose of purchasing school books for the use of the school children of the state, free of cost to them. ⊥It was for their benefit and the resulting benefit to the state that the appropriations were made. True, these children attend some school, public or private, the latter, sectarian or nonsectarian, and that the books are to be furnished them for their use, free of cost, whichever they attend. The schools, however, are not the beneficiaries of these appropriations. They obtain nothing from them, nor are they relieved of a single obligation, because of them. The school children and the state alone are the beneficiaries. It is also true that the sectarian schools, which some of the children attend, instruct their pupils in religion, and books are used for that purpose, but one may search diligently the acts, though without result, in an effort to find anything to the effect that it is the purpose of the state to furnish religious books for the use of such children. . . . What the statutes contemplate is that the same books that are furnished children attending public schools shall be furnished children attending private schools. This is the only practical way of interpreting and executing the statutes, and this is what the state board of education is doing. Among these books, naturally, none is to be expected, adapted to religious instruction." The court also stated, although the point is not of importance in relation to the Federal question, that it was "only the use of the books that is granted to the children, or, in other words, the books are lent to them."

Viewing the statute as having the effect thus attributed to it, we cannot doubt that the taxing power of the state is exerted for a public purpose. The legislation does not segregate private schools, or their pupils, as its beneficiaries or attempt to interfere with any matters of exclusively private concern. Its interest is education, broadly; its method, comprehensive. Individual interests are aided only as the common interest is safeguarded.

Judgment *affirmed*.

EVERSON v. BOARD OF EDUCATION OF EWING TOWNSHIP

330 U.S. 1
ON APPEAL FROM THE COURT OF ERRORS
AND APPEALS OF NEW JERSEY
Argued November 20, 1946 — Decided February 10, 1947

⊥*Mr. Justice BLACK* delivered the opinion of the Court.

A New Jersey statute authorizes its local school districts to make rules and contracts for the transportation of children to and from schools. The appellee, a township board of education, acting pursuant to this statute, authorized reimbursement to parents of money expended by them for the bus transportation of their children on regular busses operated by the public transportation system. Part of this money was for the payment of transportation of some children in the community to Catholic parochial schools. These church schools give their students, in addition to secular education, regular religious instruction conforming to the religious tenets and modes of worship of the Catholic Faith. The superintendent of these schools is a Catholic priest.

The appellant, in his capacity as a district taxpayer, filed suit in a state court challenging the right of the Board to reimburse parents of parochial school students. He ⊥contended that the statute and the resolution passed pursuant to it violated both the State and the Federal Constitutions. That court held that the legislature was without power to authorize such payment under the state constitution. The New Jersey Court of Errors and Appeals reversed, holding that neither the statute nor the resolution passed pursuant to it was in conflict with the State constitution or the provisions of the Federal Constitution in issue. The case is here on appeal.

Since there has been no attack on the statute on the ground that a part of its language excludes children attending private schools operated for profit from enjoying State payment for their transportation, we need not consider this exclusionary language; it has no relevancy to any constitutional question here presented. Furthermore, if the exclusion clause had been properly challenged, we do not know whether New Jersey's highest court would construe its statutes as precluding payment of the school ⊥transportation of any group of pupils, even those of a private school run for profit. Consequently, we put to one side the question as to the validity of the statute against the claim that it does not authorize payment for the transportation generally of school children in New Jersey.

The only contention here is that the state statute and the resolution, insofar as they authorized reimbursement to parents of children attending parochial schools, violate the Federal Constitution in these two respects, which to some extent overlap. *First*. They authorize the State to take by taxation the private property of some and bestow it upon others, to be used for their own private ⊥purposes. This, it is alleged, violates the due process clause of the Fourteenth Amendment. *Second*. The statute and the resolution forced inhabitants to pay taxes to help support and maintain schools which are dedicated to, and which regularly teach, the Catholic Faith. This is alleged to be a use of state power to support church schools contrary to the prohibition of the First Amendment which the Fourteenth Amendment made applicable to the states.

First. The due process argument that the state law taxes some people to help others carry out their private purposes is framed in two phases. The first phase is that a state cannot tax A to reimburse B for the cost of transporting his children to church schools. This is said to violate the due process clause because the children are sent to these church schools to satisfy the personal desires of their parents, rather than the public's interest in the general education of all children. This argument, if valid, would apply equally to prohibit state payment for the transportation of children to any non-public school, whether operated by a church or any other non-government individual or group. But, the New Jersey legislature has decided that a public purpose will be served by using tax-raised funds to pay the bus fares of all school children, including those who attend parochial schools. The New Jersey Court of Errors and Appeals has reached the same conclusion. The fact that a state law, passed to satisfy a public need, coincides with the personal desires of the individuals most directly affected is certainly an inadequate reason for us to say that a legislature has erroneously appraised the public need.

It is true that this Court has, in rare instances, struck down state statutes on the ground that the purpose for which tax-raised funds were to be expended was not a public one. But the Court has also pointed out that this far-reaching authority must be exercised with the most extreme caution. Otherwise, a state's power to legislate for the public welfare might be seriously curtailed, a power which is a primary reason for the existence of states. Changing local conditions create new local problems which may lead a state's people and its local authorities to believe that laws authorizing new types of public services are necessary to promote the general well-being ⊥of the people. The Fourteenth Amendment did not strip the states of their power to meet problems previously left for individual solution.

It is much too late to argue that legislation intended to facilitate the opportunity of children to get a secular education serves no public purpose. The same thing is no less true of legislation to reimburse needy parents, or all parents, for payment of the fares of their children so that they can ride in public busses to and from schools rather than run the risk of traffic and other hazards incident to walking or "hitchhiking." Nor does it follow that a law has a private rather than a public purpose because it provides that tax-raised funds will be paid to reimburse individuals on account of money spent by them in a way which furthers a public program. Subsidies and loans to individuals such as farmers and homeowners, and to privately owned transportation systems, as well as many other kinds of businesses, have been commonplace practices in our state and national history.

Insofar as the second phase of the due process argument may differ from the first, it is by suggesting that taxation for transportation of children to church schools constitutes support of a religion by the State. But if the law is invalid for this reason, it is because it violates the First Amendment's prohibition against the establishment of religion ⊥by law. This is the exact question raised by appellant's second contention, to consideration of which we now turn.

Second. The New Jersey statute is challenged as a "law respecting an establishment of religion." The First Amendment, as made applicable to the states by the Fourteenth, commands that a "state shall make no law respecting an establishment of religion, or prohibiting the free exercise thereof. . . ." These words of the First Amendment reflected in the minds of early Americans a vivid mental picture of conditions and practices which they fervently wished to stamp out in order to preserve liberty for themselves and for their posterity. Doubtless their goal has not been entirely reached; but so far has the Nation moved toward it that the expression "law respecting an establishment of religion," probably does not so vividly remind present-day Americans of the evils, fears, and political problems that caused that expression to be written into our Bill of Rights. Whether this New Jersey law is one respecting an "establishment of religion" requires an understanding of the meaning of that language, particularly with respect to the imposition of taxes. Once again, therefore, it is not inappropriate briefly to review the background and environment of the period in which that constitutional language was fashioned and adopted.

A large proportion of the early settlers of this country came here from Europe to escape the bondage of laws which compelled them to support and attend government-favored churches. The centuries immediately before and contemporaneous with the colonization of America had been filled with turmoil, civil strife, and persecutions, generated in large part by established sects determined to ⊥maintain their absolute political and religious supremacy. With the power of government supporting them, at various times and places, Catholics had persecuted Protestants, Protestants had persecuted Catholics, Protestant sects had persecuted other Protestant sects, Catholics of one shade of belief had persecuted Catholics of another shade of belief, and all of these had from time to time persecuted Jews. In efforts to force loyalty to whatever religious group happened to be on top and in league with the government of a particular time and place, men and women had been fined, cast in jail, cruelly tortured, and killed. Among the offenses for which these punishments had been inflicted were such things as speaking disrespectfully of the views of ministers of government-established churches, non-attendance at those churches, expressions of non-belief in their doctrines, and failure to pay taxes and tithes to support them.

These practices of the old world were transplanted to and began to thrive in the soil of the new America. The very charters granted by the English Crown to the individuals and companies designated to make the laws which would control the destinies of the colonials authorized these individuals and companies to erect religious establishments which all, whether believers or nonbelievers, would be required to support and attend. An exercise of ⊥ this authority was ⊥10 accompanied by a repetition of many of the old-world practices and persecutions. Catholics found themselves hounded and proscribed because of their faith; Quakers who followed their conscience went to jail; Baptists were peculiarly obnoxious to certain dominant Protestant sects; men and women of varied faiths who happened to be in a minority in a particular locality were persecuted because they steadfastly persisted in worshipping God only as their own consciences dictated. And all of these dissenters were compelled to pay tithes and taxes to support government-sponsored churches whose ministers preached inflammatory sermons designed to strengthen and consolidate the established faith by generating a burning hatred against dissenters.

⊥11   ⊥These practices became so commonplace as to shock the freedom-loving colonials into a feeling of abhorrence. The imposition of taxes to pay ministers' salaries and to build and maintain churches and church property aroused their indignation. It was these feelings which found expression in the First Amendment. No one locality and no one group throughout the Colonies can rightly be given entire credit for having aroused the sentiment that culminated in adoption of the Bill of Rights' provisions embracing religious liberty. But Virginia, where the established church had achieved a dominant influence in political affairs and where many excesses attracted wide public attention, provided a great stimulus and able leadership for the movement. The people there, as elsewhere, reached the conviction that individual religious liberty could be achieved best under a government which was stripped of all power to tax, to support, or otherwise to assist any or all religions, or to interfere with the beliefs of any religious individual or group.

The movement toward this end reached its dramatic climax in Virginia in 1785-86 when the Virginia legislative body was about to renew Virginia's tax levy for the support of the established church. Thomas Jeffer⊥son and James Madison led ⊥12 the fight against this tax. Madison wrote his great Memorial and Remonstrance against the law. In it, he eloquently argued that a true religion did not need the support of law; that no person, either believer or non-believer, should be taxed to support a religious institution of any kind; that the best interest of a society required that the minds of men always be wholly free; and that cruel persecutions were the inevitable result of government-established religions. Madison's Remonstrance received strong support throughout Virginia, and the Assembly postponed consideration of the proposed tax measure until its next session. When the proposal came up for consideration at that session, it not only died in committee, but the Assembly enacted the famous "Virginia Bill for Religious Liberty" originally written by Thomas Jefferson. The preamble to that Bill stated among other things that "Almighty God hath created the mind free; that all attempts to influence it by temporal punishments or burthens, or by civil incapacitations, tend only to beget habits of hypocrisy and meanness, and are ⊥a departure from the ⊥13 plan of the Holy author of our religion, who being Lord both of body and mind, yet chose not to propagate it by coercions on either . . . ; that to compel a man to furnish contributions of money for the propagation of opinions which he disbelieves, is sinful and tyrannical; that even the forcing him to support this or that teacher of his own religious persuasion, is depriving him of the comfortable liberty of giving his contributions to the particular pastor, whose morals he would make his pattern. . . ."

And the statute itself enacted "That no man shall be compelled to frequent or support any religious worship, place, or ministry whatsoever, nor shall be enforced, restrained, molested, or burthened in his body or goods, nor shall otherwise suffer on account of his religious opinions or belief. . . ."

This Court has previously recognized that the provisions of the First Amendment, in the drafting and adoption of which Madison and Jefferson played such leading roles, had the same objective and were intended to provide the same protection against governmental intrusion on religious liberty as the Virginia statute. Prior to the adoption of the Fourteenth Amendment, the First Amendment did not apply as a restraint against the states. Most of them did soon provide similar constitutional protections ⊥for religious liberty. But some states persisted for ⊥14 about half a century in imposing restraints upon the free exercise of religion and in discriminating against particular religious groups. In recent years, so far as the provision against the establishment of a religion is concerned, the question has most frequently arisen in connection with proposed state aid to church schools and efforts to carry on religious teachings in the public schools in accordance with the tenets of a particular sect. Some churches have either sought or accepted state financial support for their schools. Here again the efforts to obtain state aid or acceptance of it have not been limited to any one particular faith. The state courts, in the main, have remained faithful to the language of their own constitutional provisions designed to protect religious freedom and to separate religions and governments. Their decisions, however, show the difficulty in drawing the line between tax legislation which provides funds for the welfare of the general public and that which is designed to support institutions which teach religion.

⊥15 The meaning and scope of the First Amendment, preventing establishment of religion or prohibiting the free exercise thereof, in the light of its history and the evils it ⊥was designed forever to suppress, have been several times elaborated by the decisions of this Court prior to the application of the First Amendment to the states by the Fourteenth. The broad meaning given the Amendment by these earlier cases has been accepted by this Court in its decisions concerning an individual's religious freedom rendered since the Fourteenth Amendment was interpreted to make the prohibitions of the First applicable to state action abridging religious freedom. There is every reason to give the same application and broad interpretation to the "establishment of religion" clause. The interrelation of these complementary clauses was well summarized in a statement of the Court of Appeals of South Carolina, quoted with approval by this Court in *Watson* v. *Jones*: "The structure of our government has, for the preservation of civil liberty, rescued the temporal institutions from religious interference. On the other hand, it has secured religious liberty from the invasion of the civil authority."

The "establishment of religion" clause of the First Amendment means at least this: Neither a state nor the Federal Government can set up a church. Neither can pass laws which aid one religion, aid all religions, or prefer one religion over another. Neither can force nor influence a person to go to or to remain away from church against his will or force him to profess a belief or disbelief in any religion. No ⊥16 person can be punished for entertain⊥ing or professing religious beliefs or disbeliefs, for church attendance or non-attendance. No tax in any amount, large or small, can be levied to support any religious activities or institutions, whatever they may be called, or whatever form they may adopt to teach or practice religion. Neither a state nor the Federal Government can, openly or secretly, participate in the affairs of any religious organizations or groups and *vice versa*. In the words of Jefferson, the clause against establishment of religion by law was intended to erect "a wall of separation between church and State."

We must consider the New Jersey statute in accordance with the foregoing limitations imposed by the First Amendment. But we must not strike that state statute down if it is within the State's constitutional power even though it approaches the verge of that power. New Jersey cannot consistently with the "establishment of religion" clause of the First Amendment contribute tax-raised funds to the support of an institution which teaches the tenets and faith of any church. On the other hand, other language of the amendment commands that New Jersey cannot hamper its citizens in the free exercise of their own religion. Consequently, it cannot exclude individual Catholics, Lutherans, Mohammedans, Baptists, Jews, Methodists, Nonbelievers, Presbyterians, or the members of any other faith, *because of their faith, or lack of it*, from receiving the benefits of public welfare legislation. While we do not mean to intimate that a state could not provide transportation only to children attending public schools, we must be careful, in protecting the citizens of New Jersey against state-established churches, to be sure that we do not inadvertently prohibit New Jersey from extending its general state law benefits to all its citizens without regard to their religious belief.

⊥17 ⊥Measured by these standards, we cannot say that the First Amendment prohibits New Jersey from spending tax-raised funds to pay the bus fares of parochial school pupils as a part of a general program under which it pays the fares of pupils attending public and other schools. It is undoubtedly true that children are helped to get to church schools. There is even a possibility that some of the children might not be sent to the church schools if the parents were compelled to pay their children's bus fares out of their own pockets when transportation to a public school would have been paid for by the State. The same possibility exists where the state requires a local transit company to provide reduced fares to school children including those attending parochial schools, or where a municipally owned transportation system undertakes to carry all school children free of charge. Moreover, state-paid policemen, detailed to protect children going to and from church schools from the very real hazards of traffic, would serve much the same purpose and accomplish much the same result as state provisions intended to guarantee free transportation of a kind which the state deems to be best for the school children's welfare. And parents might refuse to risk their children to the serious danger of traffic accidents going to and from parochial schools, the approaches to which were not protected by policemen. Similarly, parents might be reluctant to permit their children to attend schools which the state had cut off from such general government services as ordinary police and fire protection, connections for sewage disposal, public ⊥highways and sidewalks. Of course, cutting ⊥18 off church schools from these services, so separate and so indisputably marked off from the religious function, would make it far more difficult for the schools to operate. But such is obviously not the purpose of the First Amendment. That Amendment requires the state to be a neutral in its relations with groups of religious believers and non-believers; it does not require the state to be their adversary. State power is no more to be used so as to handicap religions than it is to favor them.

This Court has said that parents may, in the discharge of their duty under state compulsory education laws, send their children to a religious rather than a public school if the school meets the secular educational requirements which the state has power to impose. It appears that these parochial schools meet New Jersey's requirements. The State contributes no money to the schools. It does not support them. Its legislation, as applied, does no more than provide a general program to help parents get their children, regardless of their religion, safely and expeditiously to and from accredited schools.

The First Amendment has erected a wall between church and state. That wall must be kept high and impregnable. We could not approve the slightest breach. New Jersey has not breached it here.

Affirmed.

Mr. Justice JACKSON, dissenting.

I find myself, contrary to first impressions, unable to join in this decision. I have a sympathy, though it is not ideological, with Catholic citizens who are compelled by law to pay taxes for public schools, and also feel constrained by conscience and discipline to support other schools for their own children. Such ⊥19 relief to them as ⊥ this case involves is not in itself a serious burden to taxpayers and I had assumed it to be as little serious in principle. Study of this case convinces me otherwise. The Court's opinion marshals every argument in favor of state aid and puts the case in its most favorable light, but much of its reasoning confirms my conclusions that there are no good grounds upon which to support the present legislation. In fact, the undertones of the opinion, advocating complete and uncompromising separation of Church from State, seem utterly discordant with its conclusion yielding support to their commingling in educational matters. The case which irresistibly comes to mind as the most fitting precedent is that of Julia who, according to Byron's reports, "whispering 'I will ne'er consent,'—consented."

I

The Court sustains this legislation by assuming two deviations from the facts of this particular case; first, it assumes a state of facts the record does not support, and secondly, it refuses to consider facts which are inescapable on the record.

The Court concludes that this "legislation, as applied, does no more than provide a general program to help parents get their children, regardless of their religion, safely and expeditiously to and from accredited schools," and it draws a comparison between "state provisions intended to guarantee free transportation" for school children with services such as police and fire protection, and implies that we are here dealing with "laws authorizing new types of public services. . . ." This hypothesis permeates the opinion. The facts will not bear that construction.

The Township of Ewing is not furnishing transportation to the children in any form; it is not operating school busses itself or contracting for their operation; and it is not performing any public service of any kind with this ⊥ taxpayer's money. All school ⊥20 children are left to ride as ordinary paying passengers on the regular busses operated by the public transportation system. What the Township does, and what the taxpayer complains of, is at stated intervals to reimburse parents for the fares paid, provided the children attend either public schools or Catholic Church schools. This expenditure of tax funds has no possible effect on the child's safety or expedition in transit. As passengers on the public busses they travel as fast and no faster, and are as safe and no safer, since their parents are reimbursed as before.

In addition to thus assuming a type of service that does not exist, the Court also insists that we must close our eyes to a discrimination which does exist. The resolution which authorizes disbursement of this taxpayer's money limits reimbursement to those who attend public schools and Catholic schools. That is the way the Act is applied to this taxpayer.

The New Jersey Act in question makes the character of the school, not the needs of the children, determine the eligibility of parents to reimbursement. The Act permits payment for transportation to parochial schools or public schools but prohibits it to private schools operated in whole or in part for profit. Children often are sent to private schools because their parents feel that they require more individual instruction than public schools can provide, or because they are backward or defective and need special attention. If all children of the state were objects of impartial solicitude, no reason is obvious for denying transportation reimbursement to students of this class, for these often are as needy and as worthy as those who go to public or parochial schools. Refusal to reimburse those who attend such schools is understandable only in the light of a purpose to aid the schools, because the state might well abstain from aiding a profit-making private enterprise. Thus, under the Act ⊥ and resolution brought to us by this ⊥21 case, children are classified according to the schools they attend and are to be aided if they attend the public schools or private Catholic schools, and they are not allowed to be aided if they attend private secular schools or private religious schools of other faiths.

Of course, this case is not one of a Baptist or a Jew or an Episcopalian or a pupil of a private school complaining of discrimination. It is one of a taxpayer urging that he is being taxed for an unconstitutional purpose. I think he is entitled to have us consider the Act just as it is written. The statement by the New Jersey court that it holds the Legislature may authorize use of local funds "for the transportation of pupils to any school," in view of the other constitutional views expressed, is not a holding that this Act authorizes transportation of *all* pupils to *all* schools. As applied to this taxpayer by the action he complains of, certainly the Act does not authorize reimbursement to those who choose any alternative to the public school except Catholic Church schools.

If we are to decide this case on the facts before us, our question is simply this: Is it constitutional to tax this complainant to pay the cost of carrying pupils to Church schools of one specified denomination?

II

Whether the taxpayer constitutionally can be made to contribute aid to parents of students because of their attendance at parochial schools depends upon the nature of those schools and their relation to the Church. The Constitution says nothing of education. It lays no obligation on the states to provide schools and does not undertake to regulate state systems of education if they see fit to maintain them. But they cannot, through school policy any more than through other means, invade ⊥ rights secured ⊥ to citizens by the Constitution of the United States. One of our basic rights is to be free of taxation to support a transgression of the constitutional command that the authorities "shall make no law respecting an establishment of religion, or prohibiting the free exercise thereof. . . ."

The function of the Church school is a subject on which this record is meager. It shows only that the schools are under superintendence of a priest and that "religion is taught as part of the curriculum." But we know that such schools are parochial only in name—they, in fact, represent a world-wide and age-old policy of the Roman Catholic Church. . . .

⊥ It is no exaggeration to say that the whole historic conflict in temporal policy between the Catholic Church and non-Catholics comes to a focus in their respective school policies. The Roman Catholic Church, counseled by experience in many ages and many lands and with all sorts and conditions of men, takes what, from the viewpoint of its own progress and the success of its mission, is a wise estimate of the importance of education to religion. It does not leave the individual to pick up religion by chance. It relies on early and indelible indoctrination in the faith and order of the Church by the word and example of persons consecrated to the task.

Our public school, if not a product of Protestantism, at least is more consistent with it than with the Catholic culture and scheme of values. It is a relatively recent development dating from about 1840. It is organized on ⊥ the premise that secular education can be isolated from all religious teaching so that the school can inculcate all needed temporal knowledge and also maintain a strict and lofty neutrality as to religion. The assumption is that after the individual has been instructed in worldly wisdom he will be better fitted to choose his religion. Whether such a disjunction is possible, and if possible whether it is wise, are questions I need not try to answer.

I should be surprised if any Catholic would deny that the parochial school is a vital, if not the most vital, part of the Roman Catholic Church. If put to the choice, that venerable institution, I should expect, would forego its whole service for mature persons before it would give up education of the young, and it would be a wise choice. Its growth and cohesion, discipline and loyalty, spring from its schools. Catholic education is the rock on which the whole structure rests, and to render tax aid to its Church school is indistinguishable to me from rendering the same aid to the Church itself.

III

It is of no importance in this situation whether the beneficiary of this expenditure of tax-raised funds is primarily the parochial school and incidentally the pupil, or whether the aid is directly bestowed on the pupil with indirect benefits to the school. The state cannot maintain a Church and it can no more tax its citizens to furnish free carriage to those who attend a Church. The prohibition against establishment of religion cannot be circumvented by a subsidy, bonus or reimbursement of expense to individuals for receiving religious instruction and indoctrination.

The Court, however, compares this to other subsidies and loans to individuals and says, "Nor does it follow that a law has a private rather than a public purpose because ⊥ it provides that tax-raised funds will be paid to reimburse individuals on account of money spent by them in a way which furthers a public program." Of course, the state may pay out tax-raised funds to relieve pauperism, but it may not under our Constitution do so to induce or reward piety. It may spend funds to secure old age against want, but it may not spend funds to secure religion against skepticism. It may compensate individuals for loss of employment, but it cannot compensate them for adherence to a creed.

It seems to me that the basic fallacy in the Court's reasoning, which accounts for its failure to apply the principles it avows, is in ignoring the essentially religious test by which beneficiaries of this expenditure are selected. A policeman protects a Catholic, of course—but not because he is a Catholic; it is because he is a man and a member of our society. The fireman protects the Church school—but not because it is a Church school; it is because it is property, part of the assets of our society. Neither the fireman nor the policeman has to ask before he renders aid "Is this man or building identified with the Catholic Church?" But before these school authorities draw a check to reimburse for a student's fare they must ask just that question, and if the school is a Catholic one they may render aid because it is such, while if it is of any other faith or is run for profit, the help must be withheld. To consider the converse of the Court's reasoning will best disclose its fallacy. That there is no parallel between police and fire protection and this plan of reimbursement is apparent from the incongruity of the limitation of this Act if applied to police and fire service. Could we sustain an Act that said the police shall protect pupils on the way to or from public schools and ⌐26 Catholic schools but not ⊥while going to and coming from other schools, and firemen shall extinguish a blaze in public or Catholic school buildings but shall not put out a blaze in Protestant Church schools or private schools operated for profit? That is the true analogy to the case we have before us and I should think it pretty plain that such a scheme would not be valid.

The Court's holding is that this taxpayer has no grievance because the state has decided to make the reimbursement a public purpose and therefore we are bound to regard it as such. I agree that this Court has left, and always should leave to each state, great latitude in deciding for itself, in the light of its own conditions, what shall be public purposes in its scheme of things. It may socialize utilities and economic enterprises and make taxpayers' business out of what conventionally had been private business. It may make public business of individual welfare, health, education, entertainment or security. But it cannot make public business of religious worship or instruction, or of attendance at religious institutions of any character. There is no answer to the proposition, more fully expounded by *Mr. Justice RUTLEDGE*, that the effect of the religious freedom Amendment to our Constitution was to take every form of propagation of religion out of the realm of things which could directly or indirectly be made public business and thereby be supported in whole or in part at taxpayers' expense. That is a difference which the Constitution sets up between religion and almost every other subject matter of legislation, a difference which goes to the very root of religious freedom and which the Court is overlooking today. This freedom was first in the Bill of Rights because it was first in the forefathers' minds; it was set forth in absolute terms, and its strength is its rigidity. It was intended not only to keep the states' hands out ⌐27 of religion, but to ⊥keep religion's hands off the state, and, above all, to keep bitter religious controversy out of public life by denying to every denomination any advantage from getting control of public policy or the public purse. Those great ends I cannot but think are immeasurably compromised by today's decision.

This policy of our Federal Constitution has never been wholly pleasing to most religious groups. They all are quick to invoke its protections; they all are irked when they feel its restraints. This Court has

gone a long way, if not an unreasonable way, to hold that public business of such paramount importance as maintenance of public order, protection of the privacy of the home, and taxation may not be pursued by a state in a way that even indirectly will interfere with religious proselyting.

But we cannot have it both ways. Religious teaching cannot be a private affair when the state seeks to impose regulations which infringe on it indirectly, and a public affair when it comes to taxing citizens of one faith to aid another, or those of no faith to aid all. If these principles seem harsh in prohibiting aid to Catholic education, it must not be forgotten that it is the same Constitution that alone assures Catholics the right to maintain these schools at all when predominant local sentiment would forbid them. Nor should I think that those who have done so well without this aid would want to see this separation between Church and State broken down. If the state may aid these religious schools, it may therefore regulate them. Many groups have sought aid from tax funds only to find that it carried political controls with it. Indeed this Court has ⊥declared ⌐28 that "It is hardly lack of due process for the Government to regulate that which it subsidizes." *Wickard v. Filburn.*

But in any event, the great purposes of the Constitution do not depend on the approval or convenience of those they restrain. I cannot read the history of the struggle to separate political from ecclesiastical affairs, well summarized in the opinion of *Mr. Justice RUTLEDGE* in which I generally concur, without a conviction that the Court today is unconsciously giving the clock's hands a backward turn.

Mr. Justice FRANKFURTER joins in this opinion.

Mr. Justice RUTLEDGE, with whom *Mr. Justice FRANKFURTER*, *Mr. Justice JACKSON* and *Mr. Justice BURTON* agree, dissenting. . . .

⊥This case forces us to determine squarely for the ⌐29 first time what was "an establishment of religion" in the First Amendment's conception; and by that measure to decide whether New Jersey's action violates its command. The facts may be stated shortly, to give setting and color to the constitutional problem.

By statute New Jersey has authorized local boards of education to provide for the transportation of children "to and from school other than a public school" except one ⊥operated for profit wholly or in ⌐30 part, over established public school routes, or by other means when the child lives "remote from any school." The school board of Ewing Township has provided by resolution for "the transportation of pupils of Ewing to the Trenton and Pennington High Schools and Catholic Schools by way of public carrier. . . ."

Named parents have paid the cost of public conveyance of their children from their homes in Ewing to three public high schools and four parochial schools outside the district. Semiannually the Board has reimbursed the parents from public school funds raised by general taxation. Religion is taught as part of the curriculum in each ⊥of the four private schools, as appears affirmatively by the testimony of the superintendent of parochial schools in the Diocese of Trenton. |31

The Court of Errors and Appeals of New Jersey, reversing the Supreme Court's decision, has held the Ewing board's action not in contravention of the state constitution or statutes or of the Federal Constitution. We have to consider only whether this ruling accords with the prohibition of the First Amendment implied in the due process clause of the Fourteenth.

I

Not simply an established church, but any law respecting an establishment of religion is forbidden. The Amendment was broadly but not loosely phrased. It is the compact and exact summation of its author's views formed during his long struggle for religious freedom. In Madison's own words characterizing Jefferson's Bill for Establishing Religious Freedom, the guaranty he put in our national charter, like the bill he piloted through the Virginia Assembly, was "a Model of technical precision, and perspicuous brevity." Madison could not have confused "church" and "religion," or "an established church" and "an establishment of religion."

The Amendment's purpose was not to strike merely at the official establishment of a single sect, creed or religion, outlawing only a formal relation such as had prevailed in England and some of the colonies. Necessarily it was to uproot all such relationships. But the object was broader than separating church and state in this narrow sense. It was to create a complete and permanent separation of the ⊥spheres of religious activity and civil authority by comprehensively forbidding every form of public aid or support for religion. In proof the Amendment's wording and history unite with this Court's consistent utterances whenever attention has been fixed directly upon the question. |32

"Religion" appears only once in the Amendment. But the word governs two prohibitions and governs them alike. It does not have two meanings, one narrow to forbid "an establishment" and another, much broader, for securing "the free exercise thereof." "Thereof" brings down "religion" with its entire and exact content, no more and no less, from the first into the second guaranty, so that Congress and now the states are as broadly restricted concerning the one as they are regarding the other.

No one would claim today that the Amendment is constricted, in "prohibiting the free exercise" of religion, to securing the free exercise of some formal or creedal observance, of one sect or of many. It secures all forms of religious expression, creedal, sectarian or nonsectarian, wherever and however taking place, except conduct which trenches upon the like freedoms of others or clearly and presently endangers the community's good order and security. For the protective purposes of this phase of the basic freedom, street preaching, oral or by distribution of ⊥literature, has been given "the same high estate under the First Amendment as . . . worship in the churches and preaching from the pulpits." And on this basis parents have been held entitled to send their children to private, religious schools. Accordingly, daily religious education commingled with secular is "religion" within the guaranty's comprehensive scope. So are religious training and teaching in whatever form. The word connotes the broadest content, determined not by the form or formality of the teaching or where it occurs, but by its essential nature regardless of those details. "Religion" has the same broad significance in the twin prohibition concerning "an establishment." The Amendment was not duplicitous. "Religion" and "establishment" were not used in any formal or technical sense. The prohibition broadly forbids state support, financial or other, of religion in any guise, form or degree. It outlaws all use of public funds for religious purposes. |33

II

No provision of the Constitution is more closely tied to or given content by its generating history than the religious clause of the First Amendment. It is at once the refined product and the terse summation of that history. The history includes not only Madison's authorship and the proceedings before the First Congress, but also the long and intensive struggle for religious freedom in America, more especially in Virginia, of which the Amend⊥ment was the direct culmination. In the documents of the times, particularly of Madison, who was leader in the Virginia struggle before he became the Amendment's sponsor, but also in the writings of Jefferson and others and in the issues which engendered them is to be found irrefutable confirmation of the Amendment's sweeping content. |34

For Madison, as also for Jefferson, religious freedom was the crux of the struggle for freedom in general. Madison was coauthor with George Mason of the religious clause in Virginia's great Declaration of Rights of 1776. He is credited with changing it from a mere statement of the principle of tolerance to the first official legislative pronouncement that freedom of conscience and religion are inherent rights of the individual. He sought also to have the Declara⊥tion expressly condemn the existing Virginia establishment. But the forces supporting it were then too strong. |35

Accordingly Madison yielded on this phase but not for long. At once he resumed the fight, continuing it before succeeding legislative sessions. As a member of the General Assembly in 1779 he threw his full weight behind Jefferson's historic Bill for Establishing Religious Freedom. That bill was a prime phase of Jefferson's broad program of democratic reform undertaken on his return from the Continental Congress in 1776 and submitted for the General Assembly's consideration in 1779 as his proposed revised Virginia code. With Jefferson's departure for Europe in 1784, Madison ecame the Bill's prime

⊥sponsor. Enactment failed in successive legislatures from its introduction in June, 1779, until its adoption in January, 1786. But during all this time the fight for religious freedom moved forward in Virginia on various fronts with growing intensity. Madison led throughout, against Patrick Henry's powerful opposing leadership until Henry was elected governor in November, 1784.

The climax came in the legislative struggle of 1784-1785 over the Assessment Bill. This was nothing more nor less than a taxing measure for the support of religion, designed to revive the payment of tithes suspended since 1777. So long as it singled out a particular sect for preference it incurred the active and general hostility of dissentient groups. It was broadened to include them, with the result that some subsided temporarily in their opposition. As altered, the bill gave to each taxpayer the privilege of designating which church should receive his share of the tax. In default of designation the legislature applied it to pious uses. But what is of the utmost significance here, "in ⊥ its final form the bill left the taxpayer the option of giving his tax to education."

Madison was unyielding at all times, opposing with all his vigor the general and nondiscriminatory as he had the earlier particular and discriminatory assessments proposed. The modified Assessment Bill passed second reading in December, 1784, and was all but enacted. Madison and his followers, however, maneuvered deferment of final consideration until November, 1785. And before the Assembly reconvened in the fall he issued his historic Memorial and Remonstrance.

This is Madison's complete, though not his only, interpretation of religious liberty. It is a broadside attack upon all forms of "establishment" of religion, both general and particular, nondiscriminatory or selective. Reflecting not only the many legislative conflicts over the Assessment Bill and the Bill for Establishing Religious Freedom but also, for example, the struggles for religious incorporations and the continued maintenance of the glebes, the Remonstrance is at once the most concise and the most accurate statement of the views of the First Amendment's author concerning what is "an establishment of religion. . . ."

⊥ The Remonstrance, stirring up a storm of popular protest, killed the Assessment Bill. It collapsed in committee shortly before Christmas, 1785. With this, the way was cleared at last for enactment of

Jefferson's Bill for Establishing Religious Freedom. Madison promptly drove it through in January of 1786, seven years from the time it was first introduced. This dual victory substantially ended the fight over establishments, settling the issue against them.

The next year Madison became a member of the Constitutional Convention. Its work done, he fought valiantly to secure the ratification of its great product in Virginia as elsewhere, and nowhere else more effectively. Madison was certain in his own mind that under the Constitution "there is not a shadow of right in the general government to intermeddle with religion" and that "this subject is, for the honor of America, perfectly free and ⊥unshackled. The government has no jurisdiction over it. . . ." Nevertheless he pledged that he would work for a Bill of Rights, including a specific guaranty of religious freedom, and Virginia, with other states, ratified the Constitution on this assurance.

Ratification thus accomplished, Madison was sent to the first Congress. There he went at once about performing his pledge to establish freedom for the nation as he had done in Virginia. Within a little more than three years from his legislative victory at home he had proposed and secured the submission and ratification of the First Amendment as the first article of our Bill of Rights.

All the great instruments of the Virginia struggle for religious liberty thus became warp and woof of our constitutional tradition, not simply by the course of history, but by the common unifying force of Madison's life, thought and sponsorship. He epitomized the whole of that tradition in the Amendment's compact, but nonetheless comprehensive, phrasing.

As the Remonstrance discloses throughout, Madison opposed every form and degree of official relation between religion and civil authority. For him religion was a wholly private matter beyond the scope of civil power ⊥either to restrain or to support. Denial or abridgment of religious freedom was a violation of rights both of conscience and of natural equality. State aid was no less obnoxious or destructive to freedom and to religion itself than other forms of state interference. "Establishment" and "free exercise" were correlative and coextensive ideas, representing only different facets of the single great and fundamental freedom. The Remonstrance, following the Virginia statute's example, referred to the history of religious conflicts and the effects of all sorts of establishments, current and historical, to suppress religion's free exercise. With Jefferson, Madison believed that to tolerate any fragment of establishment would be by so much to perpetuate restraint upon that freedom. Hence he sought to tear out the institution not partially but root and branch, and to bar its return forever.

In no phase was he more unrelentingly absolute than in opposing state support or aid by taxation.

Not even "three pence" contribution was thus to be exacted from any citizen for such a purpose.

⊥41   ⊥ Tithes had been the lifeblood of establishment before and after other compulsions disappeared. Madison and his coworkers made no exceptions or abridgments to the complete separation they created. Their objection was not to small tithes. It was to any tithes whatsoever. "If it were lawful to impose a small tax for religion, the admission would pave the way for oppressive levies." Not the amount but "the principle of assessment was wrong." And the principle was as much to prevent "the interference of law in religion" as to restrain religious intervention in political matters. In this field the authors of our freedom would not tolerate "the first experiment on our liberties" or "wait till usurped power had strengthened itself by exercise, and entangled the question in precedents." Nor should we.

In view of this history no further proof is needed that the Amendment forbids any appropriation, large or small, from public funds to aid or support any and all religious exercises. But if more were called for, the debates in the First Congress and this Court's consistent expressions, whenever it has touched on the matter directly, supply it.

⊥42   ⊥ By contrast with the Virginia history, the congressional debates on consideration of the Amendment reveal only sparse discussion, reflecting the fact that the essential issues had been settled. Indeed the matter had become so well understood as to have been taken for granted in all but formal phrasing. Hence, the only enlightening reference shows concern, not to preserve any power to use public funds in aid of religion, but to prevent the Amendment from outlawing private gifts inadvertently by virtue of the breadth of its wording. . . .

III

⊥44   ⊥ Compulsory attendance upon religious exercises went out early in the process of separating church and state, together with forced observance of religious forms and ceremonies. Test oaths and religious qualification for office followed later. These things none devoted to our great tradition of religious liberty would think of bringing back. Hence today, apart from efforts to inject religious training or exercises and sectarian issues into the public schools, the only serious surviving threat to maintaining that complete and permanent separation of religion and civil power which the First Amendment commands is through use of the taxing power to support religion, religious establishments, or establishments having a religious foundation whatever their form or special religious function.

Does New Jersey's action furnish support for religion by use of the taxing power? Certainly it does, if the test remains undiluted as Jefferson and Madison made it, that money taken by taxation from one is not to be used or given to support another's religious training or belief, or indeed one's own. Today as

then the furnishing of "con⊥tributions of money for   ⊥45 the propagation of opinions which he disbelieves" is the forbidden exaction; and the prohibition is absolute for whatever measure brings that consequence and whatever amount may be sought or given to that end.

The funds used here were raised by taxation. The Court does not dispute, nor could it, that their use does in fact give aid and encouragement to religious instruction. It only concludes that this aid is not "support" in law. But Madison and Jefferson were concerned with aid and support in fact, not as a legal conclusion "entangled in precedents." Here parents pay money to send their children to parochial schools and funds raised by taxation are used to reimburse them. This not only helps the children get to school and the parents to send them. It aids them in a substantial way to get the very thing which they are sent to the particular school to secure, namely, religious training and teaching.

Believers of all faiths, and others who do not express their feeling toward ultimate issues of existence in any creedal form, pay the New Jersey tax. When the money so raised is used to pay for transportation to religious schools, the Catholic taxpayer to the extent of his proportionate share pays for the transportation of Lutheran, Jewish and otherwise religiously affiliated children to receive their non-Catholic religious instruction. Their parents likewise pay proportionately for the transportation of Catholic children to receive Catholic instruction. Each ⊥ thus   ⊥46 contributes to "the propagation of opinions which he disbelieves" in so far as their religions differ, as do others who accept no creed without regard to those differences. Each thus pays taxes also to support the teaching of his own religion, an exaction equally forbidden since it denies "the comfortable liberty" of giving one's contribution to the particular agency of instruction he approves.

New Jersey's action therefore exactly fits the type of exaction and the kind of evil at which Madison and Jefferson struck. Under the test they framed it cannot be said that the cost of transportation is no part of the cost of education or of the religious instruction given. That it is a substantial and a necessary element is shown most plainly by the continuing and increasing demand for the state to assume it. Nor is there pretense that it relates only to the secular instruction given in religious schools or that any attempt is or could be made toward allocating proportional shares as between the secular and the religious instruction. It is precisely because the instruction is religious and relates to a particular faith, whether one or another, that parents send their children to religious schools under the *Pierce* doctrine. And the very purpose of the state's contribution is to defray the cost of conveying the pupil to the place where he will receive not simply secular, but also and primarily religious, teaching and guidance.

Indeed the view is sincerely avowed by many of various faiths, that the basic purpose of all education is or should be religious, that the secular cannot be and should not be separated from the religious phase and emphasis. Hence, ⊥the inadequacy of public or secular education and the necessity for sending the child to a school where religion is taught. But whatever may be the philosophy or its justification, there is undeniably an admixture of religious with secular teaching in all such institutions. That is the very reason for their being. Certainly for purposes of constitutionality we cannot contradict the whole basis of the ethical and educational convictions of people who believe in religious schooling.

Yet this very admixture is what was disestablished when the First Amendment forbade "an establishment of religion." Commingling the religious with the secular teaching does not divest the whole of its religious permeation and emphasis or make them of minor part, if proportion were material. Indeed, on any other view, the constitutional prohibition always could be brought to naught by adding a modicum of the secular.

An appropriation from the public treasury to pay the cost of transportation to Sunday school, to weekday special classes at the church or parish house, or to the meetings of various young people's religious societies, such as the Y.M.C.A., the Y.W.C.A., the Y.M.H.A., the Epworth League, could not withstand the constitutional attack. This would be true, whether or not secular activities we're mixed with the religious. If such an appropriation could not stand, then it is hard to see how one becomes valid for the same things upon the more extended scale of daily instruction. Surely constitutionality does not turn on where or how often the mixed teaching occurs.

Finally, transportation, where it is needed, is as essential to education as any other element. Its cost is as much a part of the total expense, except at times in amount, as the cost of textbooks, of school lunches, of athletic equipment, of writing and other materials; indeed of all other ⊥items composing the total burden. Now as always the core of the educational process is the teacher-pupil relationship. Without this the richest equipment and facilities would go for naught. But the proverbial Mark Hopkins conception no longer suffices for the country's requirements. Without buildings, without equipment, without library, textbooks and other materials, and without transportation to bring teacher and pupil together in such an effective teaching environment, there can be not even the skeleton of what our times require. Hardly can it be maintained that transportation is the least essential of these items, or that it does not in fact aid, encourage, sustain and support, just as they do, the very process which is its purpose to accomplish. No less essential is it, or the payment of its cost, than the very teaching in the classroom or payment of the teacher's sustenance. Many types of equipment, now considered essential, better could be done without.

For me, therefore, the feat is impossible to select so indispensable an item from the composite of total costs, and characterize it as not aiding, contributing to, promoting or sustaining the propagation of beliefs which it is the very end of all to bring about. Unless this can be maintained, and the Court does not maintain it, the aid thus given is outlawed. Payment of transportation is no more, nor is it any the less essential to education, whether religious or secular, than payment for tuitions, for teachers' salaries, for buildings, equipment and necessary materials. Nor is it any the less directly related, in a school giving religious instruction, to the primary religious objective all those essential items of cost are intended to achieve. No rational line can be drawn between payment for such larger, but not more necessary, items and payment for transportation. The only line that can be drawn is one between more dollars and less. Certainly in this ⊥realm such a line can be no valid constitutional measure. Now, as in Madison's time, not the amount but the principle of assessment is wrong.

IV

But we are told that the New Jersey statute is valid in its present application because the appropriation is for a public, not a private purpose, namely, the promotion of education, and the majority accept this idea in the conclusion that all we have here is "public welfare legislation." If that is true and the Amendment's force can be thus destroyed, what has been said becomes all the more pertinent. For then there could be no possible objection to more extensive support of religious education by New Jersey.

If the fact alone be determinative that religious schools are engaged in education, thus promoting the general and individual welfare, together with the legislature's decision that the payment of public moneys for their aid makes their work a public function, then I can see no possible basis, except one of dubious legislative policy, for the state's refusal to make full appropriation for support of private, religious schools, just as is done for public ⊥instruction. There could not be, on that basis, valid constitutional objection.

Of course paying the cost of transportation promotes the general cause of education and the welfare of the individual. So does paying all other items of educational expense. And obviously, as the majority say, it is much too late to urge that legislation designed to facilitate the opportunities of children to secure a secular education serves no public purpose. Our nationwide system of public education rests on the contrary view, as do all grants in aid of education, public or private, which is not religious in character.

These things are beside the real question. They have no possible materiality except to obscure the all-pervading, inescapable issue. Stripped of its religious phase, the case presents no substantial federal question. The public function argument, by casting the issue in terms of promoting the general cause of education and the welfare of the individual, ignores the religious factor and its essential connection with the transportation, thereby leaving out the only vital element in the case. So of course do the "public welfare" and "social legislation" ideas, for they come to the same thing.

|51   ⊥We have here then one substantial issue, not two. To say that New Jersey's appropriation and her use of the power of taxation for raising the funds appropriated are not for public purposes but are for private ends, is to say that they are for the support of religion and religious teaching. Conversely, to say that they are for public purposes is to say that they are not for religious ones.

This is precisely for the reason that education which includes religious training and teaching, and its support, have been made matters of private right and function, not public, by the very terms of the First Amendment. That is the effect not only in its guaranty of religion's free exercise, but also in the prohibition of establishments. It was on this basis of the private character of the function of religious education that this Court held parents entitled to send their children to private, religious schools. Now it declares in effect that the appropriation of public funds to defray part of the cost of attending those schools is for a public purpose. If so, I do not understand why the state cannot go farther or why this case approaches the verge of its power.

In truth this view contradicts the whole purpose and effect of the First Amendment as heretofore conceived. The "public function"—"public welfare"—"social legislation" argument seeks, in Madison's words, to "employ Religion [that is, here, religious education] as an engine of Civil policy." It is of one piece with the Assessment Bill's preamble, although with the vital difference that it wholly ignores what that preamble explicitly states.

|52   ⊥Our constitutional policy is exactly the opposite. It does not deny the value or the necessity for religious training, teaching or observance. Rather it secures their free exercise. But to that end it does deny that the state can undertake or sustain them in any form or degree. For this reason the sphere of religious activity, as distinguished from the secular intellectual liberties, has been given the twofold protection and, as the state cannot forbid, neither can it perform or aid in performing the religious function. The dual prohibition makes that function altogether private. It cannot be made a public one by legislative act. This was the very heart of Madison's Remonstrance, as it is of the Amendment itself.

It is not because religious teaching does not promote the public or the individual's welfare, but because neither is furthered when the state promotes religious education, that the Constitution forbids it to do so. Both legislatures and courts are bound by that distinction. In failure to observe it lies the fallacy of the "public function"—"social legislation" argument, a fallacy facilitated by easy transference of the argument's basing from due process unrelated to any religious aspect to the First Amendment.

By no declaration that a gift of public money to religious uses will promote the general or individual welfare, or the cause of education generally, can legislative bodies overcome the Amendment's bar. Nor may the courts sustain their attempts to do so by finding such consequences for appropriations which in fact give aid to or promote religious uses. Legislatures are free to make, ⊥and courts to sustain, appropriations only when it can be found that in fact they do not aid, promote, encourage or sustain religious teaching or observances, be the amount large or small. No such finding has been or could be made in this case. The Amendment has removed this form of promoting the public welfare from legislative and judicial competence to make a public function. It is exclusively a private affair. |53

The reasons underlying the Amendment's policy have not vanished with time or diminished in force. Now as when it was adopted the price of religious freedom is double. It is that the church and religion shall live both within and upon that freedom. There cannot be freedom of religion, safeguarded by the state, and intervention by the church or its agencies in the state's domain or dependency on its largesse. The great condition of religious liberty is that it be maintained free from sustenance, as also from other interferences, by the state. For when it comes to rest upon that secular foundation it vanishes with the resting. Public money devoted to payment of religious costs, educational or other, brings the quest for more. It brings too the struggle of sect against sect for the larger share or for any. Here one by numbers alone will benefit most, there another. That is precisely the history of societies which have had an established religion and dissident ⊥groups. It is the very thing Jefferson and Madison experienced and sought to guard against, whether in its blunt or in its more screened forms. The end of such strife cannot be other than to destroy the cherished liberty. The dominating group will achieve the dominant benefit; or all will embroil the state in their dissensions. |54

Exactly such conflicts have centered of late around providing transportation to religious schools from public funds. The issue and the dissension work typically, in Madison's phrase, to "destroy that moderation and harmony which the forbearance of our laws to intermeddle with Religion, has produced amongst its several sects." This occurs, as he well knew, over measures ⊥at the very threshold of departure from the principle. |55

In these conflicts wherever success has been obtained it has been upon the contention that by providing the transportation the general cause of education, the general welfare, and the welfare of the individual will be forwarded; hence that the matter lies within the realm of public function, for legislative determination. State courts have divided upon the issue, some taking the view that only the individual, others that the institution receives the benefit. A few have recognized that this dichotomy is false, that both in fact are aided.

⊥156 ⊥The majority here does not accept in terms any of those views. But neither does it deny that the individual or the school, or indeed both, are benefited directly and substantially. To do so would cut the ground from under the public function—social legislation thesis. On the contrary, the opinion concedes that the children are aided by being helped to get to the religious schooling. By converse necessary implication as well as by the absence of express denial, it must be taken to concede also that the school is helped to reach the child with its religious teaching. The religious enterprise is common to both, as is the interest in having transportation for its religious purposes provided.

Notwithstanding the recognition that this two-way aid is given and the absence of any denial that religious teaching is thus furthered, the Court concludes that the aid so given is not "support" of religion. It is rather only support of education as such, without reference to its religious content, and thus becomes public welfare legislation. To this elision of the religious element from the case is added gloss in two respects, one that the aid extended partakes of the nature of a safety measure, the other that failure to provide it would make the state unneutral in religious matters, discriminating against or hampering such children concerning public benefits all others receive.

⊥157 ⊥As will be noted, the one gloss is contradicted by the facts of record and the other is of whole cloth with the "public function" argument's excision of the religious factor. But most important is that this approach, if valid, supplies a ready method for nullifying the Amendment's guaranty, not only for this case and others involving small grants in aid for religious education, but equally for larger ones. The only thing needed will be for the Court again to transplant the "public welfare—public function" view from its proper nonreligious due process bearing to First Amendment application, holding that religious education is not "supported" though it may be aided by the appropriation, and that the cause of education generally is furthered by helping the pupil to secure that type of training.

This is not therefore just a little case over bus fares. In paraphrase of Madison, distant as it may be in its present form from a complete establishment of religion, it differs from it only in degree; and is the first step in that direction. Today as in his time "the same authority which can force a citizen to contribute three pence only . . . for the support of any one

[religious] establishment, may force him" to pay more; or "to conform to any other establishment in all cases whatsoever." And now, as then, "either . . . we must say, that the will of the Legislature is the only measure of their authority; and that in the plenitude of this authority, they may sweep away all our fundamental rights; or, that they are bound to leave this particular right untouched and sacred."

The realm of religious training and belief remains, as the Amendment made it, the kingdom of the individual ⊥man and his God. It should be kept in- ⊥158 violately private, not "entangled . . . in precedents" or confounded with what legislatures legitimately may take over into the public domain.

V

No one conscious of religious values can be unsympathetic toward the burden which our constitutional separation puts on parents who desire religious instruction mixed with secular for their children. They pay taxes for others' children's education, at the same time the added cost of instruction for their own. Nor can one happily see benefits denied to children which others receive, because in conscience they or their parents for them desire a different kind of training others do not demand.

But if those feelings should prevail, there would be an end to our historic constitutional policy and command. No more unjust or discriminatory in fact is it to deny attendants at religious schools the cost of their transportation than it is to deny them tuitions, sustenance for their teachers, or any other educational expense which others receive at public cost. Hardship in fact there is which none can blink. But, for assuring to those who undergo it the greater, the most comprehensive freedom, it is one written by design and firm intent into our basic law.

Of course discrimination in the legal sense does not exist. The child attending the religious school has the same right as any other to attend the public school. But he foregoes exercising it because the same guaranty which assures this freedom forbids the public school or any agency of the ⊥state to give ⊥159 or aid him in securing the religious instruction he seeks.

Were he to accept the common school, he would be the first to protest the teaching there of any creed or faith not his own. And it is precisely for the reason that their atmosphere is wholly secular that children are not sent to public schools under the *Pierce* doctrine. But that is a constitutional necessity, because we have staked the very existence of our country on the faith that complete separation between the state and religion is best for the state and best for religion.

That policy necessarily entails hardship upon persons who forego the right to educational advantages the state can supply in order to secure others it is precluded from giving. Indeed this may hamper the parent and the child forced by conscience to that choice. But it does not make the state unneutral to withhold what the Constitution forbids it to give. On the contrary it is only by observing the prohibition rigidly that the state can maintain its neutrality and avoid partisanship in the dissensions inevitable when sect opposes sect over demands for public moneys to further religious education, teaching or training in any form or degree, directly or indirectly. Like St. Paul's freedom, religious liberty with a great price must be bought. And for those who exercise it most fully, by insisting upon religious education for their children mixed with secular, by the terms of our Constitution the price is greater than for others.

The problem then cannot be cast in terms of legal discrimination or its absence. This would be true, even though the state in giving aid should treat all religious instruction alike. Thus, if the present statute and its application were shown to apply equally ⊥60 to all religious schools ⊥of whatever faith, yet in the light of our tradition it could not stand. For then the adherent of one creed still would pay for the support of another, the childless taxpayer with others more fortunate. Then too there would seem to be no bar to making appropriations for transportation and other expenses of children attending public or other secular schools, after hours in separate places and classes for their exclusively religious instruction. The person who embraces no creed also would be forced to pay for teaching what he does not believe. Again, it was the furnishing of "contributions of money for the propagation of opinions which he disbelieves" that the fathers outlawed. That consequence and effect are not removed by multiplying to all-inclusiveness the sects for which support is exacted. The Constitution requires, not comprehensive identification of state with religion, but complete separation.

VI

Short treatment will dispose of what remains. Whatever might be said of some other application of New Jersey's statute, the one made here has no semblance of bearing as a safety measure or, indeed, for securing expeditious conveyance. The transportation supplied is by public conveyance, subject to all the hazards and delays of the highway and the streets incurred by the public generally in going about its multifarious business.

Nor is the case comparable to one of furnishing fire or police protection, or access to public highways. These things are matters of common right, ⊥61 part of the general ⊥need for safety. Certainly the fire department must not stand idly by while the church burns. Nor is this reason why the state should pay the expense of transportation or other items of the cost of religious education. . . .

I have chosen to place my dissent upon the broad ground I think decisive, though strictly speaking the case might be decided on narrower issues. The New Jersey statute might be held invalid on its face for ⊥62 the exclusion of chil⊥dren who attend private, profit-making schools. I cannot assume, as does the

majority, that the New Jersey courts would write off this explicit limitation from the statute. Moreover, the resolution by which the statute was applied expressly limits its benefits to students of public and Catholic schools. There is no showing that there are no other private or religious schools in this populous district. I do not think it can be assumed there were none. But in the view I have taken, it is unnecessary to limit grounding to these matters.

⊥Two great drives are constantly in motion to ⊥63 abridge, in the name of education, the complete division of religion and civil authority which our forefathers made. One is to introduce religious education and observances into the public schools. The other, to obtain public funds for the aid and support of various private religious schools. In my opinion both avenues were closed by the Constitution. Neither should be opened by this Court. The matter is not one of quantity, to be measured by the amount of money expended. Now as in Madison's day it is one of principle, to keep separate the separate spheres as the First Amendment drew them; to prevent the first experiment upon our liberties; and to keep the question from becoming entangled in corrosive precedents. We should not be less strict to keep strong and untarnished the one side of the shield of religious freedom than we have been of the other.

The judgment should be reversed.

BOARD OF EDUCATION v. ALLEN

392 U.S. 236
ON APPEAL FROM THE COURT OF APPEALS
OF NEW YORK
Argued April 22, 1968 — Decided June 10, 1968

⊥*Mr. Justice WHITE* delivered the opinion of the ⊥238 Court.

A law of the State of New York requires local public school authorities to lend textbooks free of charge to all students in grades seven through 12; students attending private schools are included. This case presents the question whether this statute is a "law respecting an establishment of religion, or prohibiting the free exercise thereof," and so in conflict with the First and Fourteenth Amendments to the Constitution, because it authorizes the loan of textbooks to students attending parochial schools. We hold that the law is not in violation of the Constitution. . . .

⊥The books now loaned are "textbooks which are ⊥239 designated for use in any public, elementary or secondary schools of the state or are approved by any boards of education," and which—according to a 1966 amendment—"a pupil is required to use as a text for a semester or more in a particular class in the school he legally attends."

⊥Appellant Board of Education of Central School ⊥240 District No. 1 in Rensselaer and Columbia Counties, brought suit in the New York courts against appellee James Allen. The complaint alleged that § 701 violated both the State and Federal Constitutions; that if appellants, in reliance on their interpretation of the Constitution, failed to lend books to parochial school students within their counties appellee Allen would remove appellants from office; and that to prevent this, appellants were complying with the law and submitting to their constituents a school budget including funds for books to be lent to parochial school pupils. Appellants therefore sought a declaration that § 701 was invalid, an order barring appellee Allen from removing appellants from office for failing to comply with it, and another order restraining him from apportioning state funds to school districts for the purchase of textbooks to be lent to parochial students. . . .

⌐241
⌐242 ⊥ *Everson* v. *Board of Education* is the case decided by this Court that is most nearly in ⊥ point for today's problem. New Jersey reimbursed parents for expenses incurred in busing their children to parochial schools. The Court stated that the Establishment Clause bars a State from passing "laws which aid one religion, aid all religions, or prefer one religion over another," and bars too any "tax in any amount, large or small . . . levied to support any religious activities or institutions, whatever they may be called, or whatever form they may adopt to teach or practice religion." Nevertheless, said the Court, the Establishment Clause does not prevent a State from extending the benefits of state laws to all citizens without regard for their religious affiliation and does not prohibit "New Jersey from spending tax-raised funds to pay the bus fares of parochial school pupils as a part of a general program under which it pays the fares of pupils attending public and other schools." The statute was held to be valid even though one of its results was that "children are helped to get to church schools" and "some of the children might not be sent to the church schools if the parents were compelled to pay their children's bus fares out of their own pockets." As with public provision of police and fire protection, sewage facilities, and streets and sidewalks, payment of bus fares was of some value to the religious school, but was nevertheless not such support of a religious institution as to be a prohibited establishment of religion within the meaning of the First Amendment.

Everson and later cases have shown that the line between state neutrality to religion and state support of religion is not easy to locate. "The constitutional standard is the separation of Church and State. The problem, like many problems in constitutional law, is
⌐243 one of degree." Based ⊥ on *Everson, Zorach, McGowan,* and other cases, *Abington School District* v. *Schempp* fashioned a test subscribed to by eight Justices for distinguishing between forbidden involvements of the State with religion and those contacts which the Establishment Clause permits: "The test may be stated as follows: what are the purpose and

the primary effect of the enactment? If either is the advancement or inhibition of religion then the enactment exceeds the scope of legislative power as circumscribed by the Constitution. That is to say that to withstand the strictures of the Establishment Clause there must be a secular legislative purpose and a primary effect that neither advances nor inhibits religion. *Everson* v. *Board of Education. . . .*"

This test is not easy to apply, but the citation of *Everson* by the *Schempp* Court to support its general standard made clear how the *Schempp* rule would be applied to the facts of *Everson*. The statute upheld in *Everson* would be considered a law having "a secular legislative purpose and a primary effect that neither advances nor inhibits religion." We reach the same result with respect to the New York law requiring school books to be loaned free of charge to all students in specified grades. The express purpose of § 701 was stated by the New York Legislature to be furtherance of the educational opportunities available to the young. Appellants have shown us nothing about the necessary effects of the statute that is contrary to its stated purpose. The law merely makes available to all children the benefits of a general program to lend school books free of charge. Books are fur⊥nished at the request of the pupil and owner-   ⌐244 ship remains, at least technically, in the State. Thus no funds or books are furnished to parochial schools, and the financial benefit is to parents and children, not to schools. Perhaps free books make it more likely that some children choose to attend a sectarian school, but that was true of the state-paid bus fares in *Everson* and does not alone demonstrate an unconstitutional degree of support for a religious institution.

Of course books are different from buses. Most bus rides have no inherent religious significance, while religious books are common. However, the language of § 701 does not authorize the loan of religious books, and the State claims no right to distribute religious literature. Although the books loaned are those required by the parochial school for use in specific courses, each book ⊥ loaned must be approved   ⌐245 by the public school authorities; only secular books may receive approval. The law was construed by the Court of Appeals of New York as "merely making available secular textbooks at the request of the individual student" and the record contains no suggestion that religious books have been loaned. Absent evidence, we cannot assume that school authorities, who constantly face the same problem in selecting textbooks for use in the public schools, are unable to distinguish between secular and religious books or that they will not honestly discharge their duties under the law. In judging the validity of the statute on this record we must proceed on the assumption that books loaned to students are books that are not unsuitable for use in the public schools because of religious content.

The major reason offered by appellants for distinguishing free textbooks from free bus fares is that books, but not buses, are critical to the teaching process, and in a sectarian school that process is employed to teach religion. However this Court has long recognized that religious schools pursue two goals, religious instruction and secular education. In the leading case of *Pierce* v. *Society of Sisters* the Court held that although it would not question Oregon's power to compel school attendance or require that the attendance be at an institution meeting State-imposed requirements as to quality and nature of curriculum, Oregon had not shown that its interest in secular education required that all children attend publicly operated schools. A premise of this holding was the view that the State's interest in education would be served sufficiently by reliance on the secular teaching that accompanied religious training in the schools maintained by the Society of Sisters. Since *Pierce*, a substantial body of case law has confirmed the power of the States to insist that attendance at private schools, if it is to satisfy state compulsory-attendance ⊥laws, be at institutions which provide minimum hours of instruction, employ teachers of specified training, and cover prescribed subjects of instruction. Indeed, the State's interest in assuring that these standards are being met has been considered a sufficient reason for refusing to accept instruction at home as compliance with com⊥pulsory education statutes. These cases were a sensible corollary of *Pierce* v. *Society of Sisters*: if the State must satisfy its interest in secular education through the instrument of private schools, it has a proper interest in the manner in which those schools perform their secular educational function. Another corollary was *Cochran* v. *Louisiana State Board of Education* where appellants said that a statute requiring school books to be furnished without charge to all students, whether they attended public or private schools, did not serve a "public purpose," and so offended the Fourteenth Amendment. Speaking through Chief Justice Hughes, the Court summarized as follows its conclusion that Louisiana's interest in the secular education being provided by private schools made provision of textbooks to students in those schools a properly public concern: "[The State's] interest is education, broadly; its method, comprehensive. Individual interests are aided only as the common interest is safeguarded."

Underlying these cases, and underlying also the legislative judgments that have preceded the court decisions, has been a recognition that private education has played and is playing a significant and valuable role in raising national levels of knowledge, competence, and experience. . . .

⊥Against this background of judgment and experience, unchallenged in the meager record before us in this case, we cannot agree with appellants either that all teaching in a sectarian school is religious or that the processes of secular and religious training are so intertwined that secular textbooks furnished to students by the public are in fact instrumental in the teaching of religion. This case comes to us after summary judgment entered on the pleadings. Nothing in this record supports the proposition that all textbooks, whether they deal with mathematics, physics, foreign languages, history, or literature, are used by the parochial schools to teach religion. No evidence has been offered about particular schools, particular courses, particular teachers, or particular books. We are unable to hold, based solely on judicial notice, that this statute results in unconstitutional involvement of the State with religious instruction or that § 701, for this or the other reasons urged, is a law respecting the establishment of religion within the meaning of the First Amendment.

Appellants also contend that § 701 offends the Free Exercise Clause of the First Amendment. However, "it is necessary in a free exercise case for one to show the ⊥coercive effect of the enactment as it operates against him in the practice of his religion," *Abington School District* v. *Schempp*, and appellants have not contended that the New York law in any way coerces them as individuals in the practice of their religion.

The judgment is affirmed.

Mr. Justice HARLAN, concurring.

Although I join the opinion and judgment of the Court, I wish to emphasize certain of the principles which I believe to be central to the determination of this case, and which I think are implicit in the Court's decision.

The attitude of government toward religion must, as this Court has frequently observed, be one of neutrality. Neutrality is, however, a coat of many colors. It requires that "government neither engage in nor compel religious practices, that it effect no favoritism among sects or between religion and nonreligion, and that it work deterrence of no religious belief." *Abington School District* v. *Schempp*. Realization of these objectives entails "no simple and clear measure," *id.*, by which this or any case may readily be decided, but these objectives do suggest the principles which I believe to be applicable in the present circumstances. I would hold that where the contested governmental activity is calculated to achieve nonreligious purposes otherwise within the competence of the State, and where the activity does not involve the State "so significantly and directly in the realm of the sectarian as to give rise to . . . divisive influences and inhibitions of freedom," *id.*, it is not forbidden by the religious clauses of the First Amendment.

⊥In my opinion, § 701 of the Education Law of New York does not employ religion as its standard for action or inaction, and is not otherwise inconsistent with these principles.

⌐246

⌐247

⌐248

⌐249

⌐250

Mr. Justice BLACK, dissenting.

The Court here affirms a judgment of the New York Court of Appeals which sustained the constitutionality of a New York law providing state tax-raised funds to supply school books for use by pupils in schools owned and operated by religious sects. I believe the New York law held valid is a flat, flagrant, open violation of the First and Fourteenth Amendments which together forbid Congress or state legislatures to enact any law "respecting an establishment of religion." For that reason I would reverse the New York Court of Appeals' judgment. . . .

⊥ The *Everson* and *McCollum* cases plainly interpret the First and Fourteenth Amendments as protecting the taxpayers of a State from being compelled to pay taxes to their government to support the agencies of private religious organizations the taxpayers oppose. To authorize a State to tax its residents for such church purposes is to put the State squarely in the religious activities of certain religious groups that happen to be strong enough politically to write their own religious preferences and prejudices into the laws. This links state and churches together in controlling the lives and destinies of our citizenship—a citizenship composed of people of myriad religious faiths, some of them bitterly hostile to and completely intolerant of the others. It was to escape laws precisely like this that a large part of the Nation's early immigrants fled to this country. It was also to escape such laws and such consequences that the First Amendment was written in language strong and clear barring passage of any law "respecting an establishment of religion."

It is true, of course, that the New York law does not as yet formally adopt or establish a state religion. But it takes a great stride in that direction and coming events cast their shadows before them. The same powerful sectarian religious propagandists who have succeeded in securing passage of the present law to help religious schools carry on their sectarian religious purposes can and doubtless will continue their propaganda, looking toward complete domination and supremacy of their particular brand of religion. And it nearly always is ⊥ by insidious approaches that the citadels of liberty are more successfully attacked.

I know of no prior opinion of this Court upon which the majority here can rightfully rely to support its holding this New York law constitutional. In saying this, I am not unmindful of the fact that the New York Court of Appeals purported to follow *Everson* v. *Board of Education,* in which this Court, in an opinion written by me, upheld a New Jersey law authorizing reimbursement to parents for the transportation of children attending sectarian schools. That law did not attempt to deny the benefit of its general terms to children of any faith going to any legally authorized school. Thus, it was treated in the same way as a general law paying the streetcar fare

of all school children, or a law providing midday lunches for all children or all school children, or a law to provide police protection for children going to and from school, or general laws to provide police and fire protection for buildings, including, of course, churches and church school buildings as well as others.

As my *Brother DOUGLAS* so forcefully shows, in an argument with which I fully agree, upholding a State's power to pay bus or streetcar fares for school children cannot provide support for the validity of a state law using tax-raised funds to buy school books for a religious school. The First Amendment's bar to establishment of religion must preclude a State from using funds levied from all of its citizens to purchase books for use by sectarian schools, which, although "secular," realistically will in some way inevitably tend to propagate the religious views of the favored sect. Books are the most essential tool of education since they contain the resources of knowledge which the educational process is designed to exploit. In this sense it is not difficult ⊥ to distinguish books, which are the heart of any school, from bus fares, which provide a convenient and helpful general public service. With respect to the former, state financial support actively and directly assists the teaching and propagation of sectarian religious viewpoints in clear conflict with the First Amendment's establishment bar; with respect to the latter, the State merely provides a general and nondiscriminatory service in no way related to substantive religious views and beliefs.

This New York law, it may be said by some, makes but a small inroad and does not amount to complete state establishment of religion. But that is no excuse for upholding it. It requires no prophet to foresee that on the argument used to support this law others could be upheld providing for state or federal government funds to buy property on which to erect religious school buildings or to erect the buildings themselves, to pay the salaries of the religious school teachers, and finally to have the sectarian religious groups cease to rely on voluntary contributions of members of their sects while waiting for the Government to pick up all the bills for the religious schools. Arguments made in favor of this New York law point squarely in this direction, namely, that the fact that government has not heretofore aided religious schools with tax-raised funds amounts to a discrimination against those schools and against religion. . . .

I still subscribe to the belief that tax-raised funds cannot constitutionally be used to support religious schools, buy their school books, erect their buildings, pay their ⊥ teachers, or pay any other of their maintenance expenses, even to the extent of one penny. The First Amendment's prohibition against governmental establishment of religion was written on the assumption that state aid to religion and religious schools generates discord, disharmony, hatred, and strife among our people, and that any government that supplies such aids is to that extent a tyranny. And I still believe that the only way to protect minority religious groups from majority groups in this country is to keep the wall of separation between church and state high and impregnable as the First and Fourteenth Amendments provide. The Court's affirmance here bodes nothing but evil to religious peace in this country.

Mr. Justice DOUGLAS, dissenting.

We have for review a statute which authorizes New York State to supply textbooks to students in parochial as well as in public schools. The New York Court of Appeals sustained the law on the grounds that it involves only "secular textbooks" and that that type of aid falls within *Everson* v. *Board of Education*, where a divided Court upheld a state law which made bus service available to students in parochial schools as well as to students in public schools.

The statute on its face empowers each parochial school to determine for itself which textbooks will be eligible for loans to its students, for the Act provides �255 that the ⊥only text which the State may provide is "a book which a pupil is required to use as a text for a semester or more in a particular class in the school he legally attends." This initial and crucial selection is undoubtedly made by the parochial school's principal or its individual instructors, who are, in the case of Roman Catholic schools, normally priests or nuns.

The next step under the Act is an "individual request" for an eligible textbook, but the State Education Department has ruled that a pupil may make his request to the local public board of education through a "private school official." Local boards have accordingly provided for those requests to be made by the individual or "by groups or classes." And forms for textbook requisitions to be filled out by the head of the private school are provided.

The role of the local public school board is to decide whether to veto the selection made by the parochial school. This is done by determining first whether the text has been or should be "approved" for use in public schools and second whether the text is "secular," "non-religious," or "nonsectarian." The ⏢App256 local boards ap⊥parently have broad discretion in exercising this veto power.

Thus the statutory system provides that the parochial school will ask for the books that it wants. Can there be the slightest doubt that the head of the parochial school will select the book or books that best promote its sectarian creed?

If the board of education supinely submits by approving and supplying the sectarian or sectarian-oriented textbooks, the struggle to keep church and state separate has been lost. If the board resists, then the battle line between church and state will have been drawn and the contest will be on to keep the

school board independent or to put it under church domination and control.

⊥Whatever may be said of *Everson*, there is nothing ideological about a bus. There is nothing ideological about a school lunch, or a public nurse, or a scholarship. The constitutionality of such public aid to students in parochial schools turns on considerations not present in this textbook case. The textbook goes to the very heart of education in a parochial school. It is the chief, although not solitary, instrumentality for propagating a particular religious creed or faith. How can we possibly approve such state aid to a religion? A parochial school textbook may contain many, many more seeds of creed and dogma than a prayer. Yet we struck down in *Engel* v. *Vitale* an official New York prayer for its public schools, even though it was not plainly denominational. For we emphasized the violence done the Establishment Clause when the power was given religious-political groups "to write their own prayers into law." That risk is compounded here by giving parochial schools the initiative in selecting the textbooks they desire to be furnished at public expense.

Judge Van Voorhis, joined by Chief Judge Fuld and Judge Breitel, dissenting below, said that the difficulty with the textbook ⊥loan program "is that there is no reliable standard by which secular and religious textbooks can be distinguished from each other." The New York Legislature felt that science was a non-sectarian subject. Does this mean that any general science textbook intended for use in grades 7-12 may be provided by the State to parochial school students? May John M. Scott's Adventures in Science (1963) be supplied under the textbook loan program? This book teaches embryology in the following manner: "To you an animal usually means a mammal, such as a cat, dog, squirrel, or guinea pig. The new animal or embryo develops inside the body of the mother until birth. The fertilized egg becomes an embryo or developing animal. Many cell divisions take place. In time some cells become muscle cells, others nerve cells or blood cells, and organs such as eyes, stomach, and intestine are formed.

"The body of a human being grows in the same way, but it is much more remarkable than that of any animal, for the embryo has a human soul infused into the body by God. Human parents are partners with God in creation. They have very great powers and great responsibilities, for through their cooperation with God souls are born for heaven." (At 618-619.)

Comparative economics would seem to be a non-sectarian subject. Will New York, then, provide Arthur J. Hughes' general history text, Man in Time (1964), to ⊥parochial school students? It treats that topic in this manner: "Capitalism is an economic system based on man's right to private property and on his freedom to use that property in producing goods which will earn him a just profit on his investment. Man's right to private property stems from the Natural Law implanted in him by God. It is as much a part of man's nature as the will to self-preservation." (At 560.)

"The broadest definition of socialism is government ownership of all the means of production and distribution in a country. . . . Many, but by no means all, Socialists in the nineteenth century believed that crime and vice existed because poverty existed, and if poverty were eliminated, then crime and vice would disappear. While it is true that poor surroundings are usually unhealthy climates for high moral training, still, man has the free will to check himself. Many Socialists, however, denied free will and said that man was a creation of his environment. . . . If Socialists do not deny Christ's message, they often ignore it. Christ showed us by His life that this earth is a testing ground to prepare man for eternal happiness. Man's interests should be in this direction at least part of the time and not always directed toward a futile quest for material goods." (At 561-564.)

Mr. Justice Jackson said, ". . . I should suppose it is a proper, if not an indispensable, part of preparation for a ⊥worldly life to know the roles that religion and religions have played in the tragic story of mankind." *McCollum* v. *Board of Education.* Yet, as he inquired, what emphasis should one give who teaches the Reformation, the Inquisition, or the early effort in New England to establish " 'a Church without a Bishop and a State without a King?' " What books should be chosen for those subjects?

Even where the treatment given to a particular topic in a school textbook is not blatantly sectarian, it will necessarily have certain shadings that will lead a parochial school to prefer one text over another.

The Crusades, for example, may be taught as a Christian undertaking to "save the Holy Land" from the Moslem Turks who "became a threat to Christianity and its holy places," which "they did not treat . . . with respect" ⊥(H. Wilson, F. Wilson, B. Erb & E. Clucas, Out of the Past 284 (1954)), or as essentially a series of wars born out of political and materialistic motives (see G. Leinwand, The Pageant of World History 136-137(1965)).

Is the dawn of man to be explained in the words, "God created man and made man master of the earth" (P. Furlong, The Old World and America 5 (1937)), or in the language of evolution (see T. Wallbank, Man's Story 32-35 (1961))?

Is the slaughter of the Aztecs by Cortes and his entourage to be lamented for its destruction of a New World culture (see J. Caughey, J. Franklin, & E. May, Land of the Free 27-28 (1965)), or forgiven because the Spaniards "carried the true Faith" to a barbaric people who practiced human sacrifice (see P. Furlong, Sr. Margaret, & D. Sharkey, America Yesterday 17, 34(1963))?

Is Franco's revolution in Spain to be taught as a crusade against anti-Catholic forces (see R. Hoffman, G. Vincitorio, & M. Swift, Man and His History 666-667 (1958)) or as an effort by reactionary elements to regain control of that country (see G. Leinwand, The Pageant of World History, *supra*, at 512)? Is the expansion of ⊥communism in select areas of the world a manifestation of the forces of Evil campaigning against the forces of Good? See A. Hughes, Man in Time, *supra*, at 565-568, 666-669, 735-748.

It will be often difficult, as Mr. Justice Jackson said, to say "where the secular ends and the sectarian begins in education." But certain it is that once the so-called "secular" textbook is the prize to be won by that religious faith which selects the book, the battle will be on for those positions of control. Judge Van Voorhis expressed the fear that in the end the state might dominate the church. Others fear that one sectarian group, gaining control of the state agencies which approve the "secular" textbooks, will use their control to disseminate ideas most congenial to their faith. It must be remembered that the very existence of the religious school—whether Catholic or Mormon, Presbyterian or Episcopalian—is to provide an education oriented to the dogma of the particular faith. . . .

⊥The challenged New York law leaves to the Board of Regents, local boards of education, trustees, and other school authorities the supervision of the textbook program.

⊥The Board of Regents (together with the Commissioner of Education) has powers of censorship over all textbooks that contain statements seditious in character, or evince disloyalty to the United States or are favorable to any nation with which we are at war. Those powers can cut a wide swath in many areas of education that involve the ideological element.

In general textbooks are approved for distribution by "boards of education, trustees or such body or officer as perform the functions of such boards. . . ." These school boards are generally elected, though in a few cities they are appointed. Where there are trustees, they are elected. And superintendents who advise on textbook selection are appointed by the board of education or the trustees.

The initiative to select and requisition "the books desired" is with the parochial school. Powerful religious-political pressures will therefore be on the state agencies to provide the books that are desired.

These then are the battlegrounds where control of textbook distribution will be won or lost. Now that "secular" textbooks will pour into religious schools, we can rest assured that a contest will be on to provide those books for religious schools which the dominant religious group concludes best reflect the theocentric or other philosophy of the particular church.

⊥266   ⊥ The stakes are now extremely high—just as they were in the school prayer cases—to obtain approval of what is "proper." For the "proper" books will radiate the "correct" religious view not only in the parochial school but in the public school as well.

Even if I am wrong in that basic premise, we still should not affirm the judgment below. Judge Van Voorhis, dissenting in the New York Court of Appeals, thought that the result of tying parochial school textbooks to public funds would be to put nonsectarian books into religious schools, which in the long view would tend towards state domination of the church. That would, indeed, be the result if the school boards did not succumb to "sectarian" pressure or control. So, however the case be viewed—whether sectarian groups win control of school boards or do not gain such control—the principle of separation of church and state, inherent in the Establishment Clause of the First Amendment, is violated by what we today approve.

What Madison wrote in his famous Memorial and Remonstrance against Religious Assessments is highly pertinent here: "Who does not see that the same authority which can establish Christianity, in exclusion of all other Religions, may establish with the same ease any particular sect of Christians, in exclusion of all other Sects? That the same authority which can force a citizen to contribute three pence only of his property for the support of any one establishment, may force him to conform to any other establishment in all cases whatsoever?"

. . . . .

⊥269   ⊥ *Mr. Justice FORTAS*, dissenting.

The majority opinion of the Court upholds the New York statute by ignoring a vital aspect of it. Public funds are used to buy, for students in sectarian schools, textbooks which are selected and pre-

⊥270   scribed by the sec⊥tarian schools themselves. As my *Brother DOUGLAS* points out, despite the transparent camouflage that the books are furnished to students, the reality is that they are selected and their use is prescribed by the sectarian authorities. The child must use the prescribed book. He cannot use a different book prescribed for use in the public schools. The State cannot choose the book to be used. It is true that the public school boards must "approve" the book selected by the sectarian authorities; but this has no real significance. The purpose of these provisions is to hold out promise that the books will be "secular," but the fact remains that the books are chosen by and for the sectarian schools.

It is misleading to say, as the majority opinion does, that the New York "law merely makes available to all children the benefits of a general program to lend school books free of charge." This is not a "general" program. It is a specific program to

⊥271   use state ⊥ funds to buy books prescribed by sectarian schools which, in New York, are primarily Catho-

lic, Jewish, and Lutheran sponsored schools. It could be called a "general" program only if the school books made available to all children were precisely the same—the books selected for and used in the public schools. But this program is not one in which all children are treated alike, regardless of where they go to school. This program, in its unconstitutional features, is hand-tailored to satisfy the specific needs of sectarian schools. Children attending such schools are given *special* books—books selected by the sectarian authorities. How can this be other than the use of public money to aid those sectarian establishments?

It is also beside the point, in my opinion, to "assume," as the majority opinion does, that "books loaned to students are books that are not unsuitable for use in the public schools because of religious content." The point is that the books furnished to students of sectarian schools are selected by the religious authorities and are prescribed by them.

This case is not within the principle of *Everson* v. *Board of Education*. Apart from the differences between textbooks and bus rides, the present statute does not call for extending to children attending sectarian schools the same service or facility extended to children in public schools. This statute calls for furnishing special, separate, and particular books, specially, separately, and particularly chosen by religious sects or their representatives for use in their sectarian schools. This is the infirmity, in my opinion. This is the feature that makes it impossible, in my view, to reach any conclusion other than that this statute is an unconstitutional use of public funds to support an establishment of religion.

This is the feature of the present statute that makes it totally inaccurate to suggest, as the majority does ⊥ here, that furnishing these specially   ⊥272 selected books for use in sectarian schools is like "public provision of police and fire protection, sewage facilities, and streets and sidewalks." These are furnished to all alike. They are not selected on the basis of specification by a religious sect. And patrons of any one sect do not receive services or facilities different from those accorded members of other religions or agnostics or even atheists.

I would reverse the judgment below.

LEMON v. KURTZMAN

403 U.S. 602

ON APPEAL FROM THE UNITED STATES
DISTRICT COURT FOR THE
EASTERN DISTRICT OF PENNSYLVANIA
Argued March 3, 1971 — Decided June 28, 1971

⊥ *Mr. Chief Justice BURGER* delivered the opin-   ⊥606 ion of the Court.

These two appeals raise questions as to Pennsylvania and Rhode Island statutes providing state aid to church-related elementary and secondary schools. Both statutes are challenged as violative of the Establishment and Free Exercise Clauses of the First Amendment and the Due Process Clause of the Fourteenth Amendment.

_|607 Pennsylvania has adopted a statutory program that provides financial support to nonpublic elementary and ⊥ secondary schools by way of reimbursement for the cost of teachers' salaries, textbooks, and instructional materials in specified secular subjects. Rhode Island has adopted a statute under which the State pays directly to teachers in nonpublic elementary schools a supplement of 15% of their annual salary. Under each statute state aid has been given to church- related educational institutions. We hold that both statutes are unconstitutional.

I

The Rhode Island Statute

The Rhode Island Salary Supplement Act was enacted in 1969. It rests on the legislative finding that the quality of education available in nonpublic elementary schools has been jeopardized by the rapidly rising salaries needed to attract competent and dedicated teachers. The Act authorizes state officials to supplement the salaries of teachers of secular subjects in nonpublic elementary schools by paying directly to a teacher an amount not in excess of 15% of his current annual salary. As supplemented, however, a nonpublic school teacher's salary cannot exceed the maximum paid to teachers in the State's public schools, and the recipient must be certified by the state board of education in substantially the same manner as public school teachers.

In order to be eligible for the Rhode Island salary supplement, the recipient must teach in a nonpublic school at which the average per-pupil expenditure on secular education is less than the average in the State's public schools during a specified period. Appellant State Commissioner of Education also requires eligible schools to submit financial data. If this information indicates a per-pupil expenditure in _|608 excess of the statutory limita⊥tion, the records of the school in question must be examined in order to assess how much of the expenditure is attributable to secular education and how much to religious activity.

The Act also requires that teachers eligible for salary supplements must teach only those subjects that are offered in the State's public schools. They must use "only teaching materials which are used in the public schools." Finally, any teacher applying for a salary supplement must first agree in writing "not to teach a course in religion for so long as or during such time as he or she receives any salary supplements" under the Act.

Appellees are citizens and taxpayers of Rhode Island. They brought this suit to have the Rhode Island Salary Supplement Act declared unconstitutional and its operation enjoined on the ground that it violates the Establishment and Free Exercise Clauses of the First Amendment. Appellants are

state officials charged with administration of the Act, teachers eligible for salary supplements under the Act, and parents of children in church-related elementary schools whose teachers would receive state salary assistance.

A three-judge federal court was convened. It found that Rhode Island's nonpublic elementary schools accommodated approximately 25% of the State's pupils. About 95% of these pupils attended schools affiliated with the Roman Catholic church. To date some 250 teachers have applied for benefits under the Act. All of them are employed by Roman Catholic schools.

⊥ The court held a hearing at which extensive _|609 evidence was introduced concerning the nature of the secular instruction offered in the Roman Catholic schools whose teachers would be eligible for salary assistance under the Act. Although the court found that concern for religious values does not necessarily affect the content of secular subjects, it also found that the parochial school system was "an integral part of the religious mission of the Catholic Church."

The District Court concluded that the Act violated the Establishment Clause, holding that it fostered "excessive entanglement" between government and religion. In addition two judges thought that the Act had the impermissible effect of giving "significant aid to a religious enterprise." We affirm.

The Pennsylvania Statute

Pennsylvania has adopted a program that has some but not all of the features of the Rhode Island program. The Pennsylvania Nonpublic Elementary and Secondary Education Act was passed in 1968 in response to a crisis that the Pennsylvania Legislature found existed in the State's nonpublic schools due to rapidly rising costs. The statute affirmatively reflects the legislative conclusion that the State's educational goals could appropriately be fulfilled by government support of "those purely secular educational objectives achieved through nonpublic education. . . ."

The statute authorizes appellee state Superintendent of Public Instruction to "purchase" specified "secular education services" from nonpublic schools. Under the "contracts" authorized by the statute, the State directly reimburses nonpublic schools solely for their actual expenditures for teachers' salaries, textbooks, and instructional materials. A school seeking reimbursement must ⊥ maintain prescribed ac- _|610 counting procedures that identify the "separate" cost of the "secular educational service." These accounts are subject to state audit. The funds for this program were originally derived from a new tax on horse and harness racing, but the Act is now financed by a portion of the state tax on cigarettes.

There are several significant statutory restrictions on state aid. Reimbursement is limited to courses "presented in the curricula of the public schools." It is further limited "solely" to courses in the following "secular" subjects: mathematics, modern foreign languages, physical science, and physical education. Textbooks and instructional materials included in the program must be approved by the state Superintendent of Public Instruction. Finally, the statute prohibits reimbursement for any course that contains "any subject matter expressing religious teaching, or the morals or forms of worship of any sect."

The Act went into effect on July 1, 1968, and the first reimbursement payments to schools were made on September 2, 1969. It appears that some $5 million has been expended annually under the Act. The State has now entered into contracts with some 1,181 nonpublic elementary and secondary schools with a student population of some 535,215 pupils—more than 20% of the total number of students in the State. More than 96% of these pupils attend church-related schools, and most of these schools are affiliated with the Roman Catholic church.

Appellants brought this action in the District Court to challenge the constitutionality of the Pennsylvania statute. The organizational plaintiffs-appellants are associations of persons resident in ⌊611 Pennsylvania declaring ⊥ belief in the separation of church and state; individual plaintiffs-appellants are citizens and taxpayers of Pennsylvania. Appellant Lemon, in addition to being a citizen and a taxpayer, is a parent of a child attending public school in Pennsylvania. Lemon also alleges that he purchased a ticket at a race track and thus had paid the specific tax that supports the expenditures under the Act. Appellees are state officials who have the responsibility for administering the Act. In addition seven church-related schools are defendants-appellees.

A three-judge federal court was convened. The District Court held that the individual plaintiffs-appellants had standing to challenge the Act. The organizational plaintiffs-appellants were denied standing under *Flast* v. *Cohen*.

The court granted appellees' motion to dismiss the complaint for failure to state a claim for relief. It held that the Act violated neither the Establishment nor the Free Exercise Clause, Chief Judge Hastie dissenting. We reverse.

II

In *Everson* v. *Board of Edutation* this Court upheld a state statute that reimbursed the parents of ⌊612 parochial school children for bus transportation ⊥ expenses. There *Mr. Justice BLACK*, writing for the majority, suggested that the decision carried to "the verge" of forbidden territory under the Religion Clauses. Candor compels acknowledgment, moreover, that we can only dimly perceive the lines of demarcation in this extraordinarily sensitive area of constitutional law.

The language of the Religion Clauses of the First Amendment is at best opaque, particularly when compared with other portions of the Amendment. Its authors did not simply prohibit the establishment of a state church or a state religion, an area history shows they regarded as very important and fraught with great dangers. Instead they commanded that there should be "no law *respecting* an establishment of religion." A law may be one "respecting" the forbidden objective while falling short of its total realization. A law "respecting" the proscribed result, that is, the establishment of religion, is not always easily identifiable as one violative of the Clause. A given law might not *establish* a state religion but nevertheless be one "respecting" that end in the sense of being a step that could lead to such establishment and hence offend the First Amendment.

In the absence of precisely stated constitutional prohibitions, we must draw lines with reference to the three main evils against which the Establishment Clause was intended to afford protection: "sponsorship, financial support, and active involvement of the sovereign in religious activity." *Walz v. Tax Commission.*

Every analysis in this area must begin with consideration of the cumulative criteria developed by the Court over many years. Three such tests may be gleaned from our cases. First, the statute must have a secular legislative purpose; second, its principal or primary effect must be one that neither advances nor inhibits religion; ⊥ finally, the statute must not ⌊6▮ foster "an excessive government entanglement with religion." *Walz.*

Inquiry into the legislative purposes of the Pennsylvania and Rhode Island statutes affords no basis for a conclusion that the legislative intent was to advance religion. On the contrary, the statutes themselves clearly state that they are intended to enhance the quality of the secular education in all schools covered by the compulsory attendance laws. There is no reason to believe the legislatures meant anything else. A State always has a legitimate concern for maintaining minimum standards in all schools it allows to operate. As in *Allen*, we find nothing here that undermines the stated legislative intent; it must therefore be accorded appropriate deference.

In *Allen* the Court acknowledged that secular and religious teaching were not necessarily so intertwined that secular textbooks furnished to students by the State were in fact instrumental in the teaching of religion. The legislatures of Rhode Island and Pennsylvania have concluded that secular and religious education are identifiable and separable. In the abstract we have no quarrel with this conclusion.

The two legislatures, however, have also recognized that church-related elementary and secondary schools have a significant religious mission and that a substantial portion of their activities is religiously oriented. They have therefore sought to create statutory restrictions designed to guarantee the separation between secular and religious educational functions and to ensure that State financial aid supports only the former. All these provisions are precautions taken in candid recognition that these programs approached, even if they did not intrude upon, the forbidden areas under the Religion Clauses. We need not decide whether these legislative precautions restrict the principal or primary effect of the programs to the point where they do not |614 offend the Religion ⊥ Clauses, for we conclude that the cumulative impact of the entire relationship arising under the statutes in each State involves excessive entanglement between government and religion.

III

In *Walz* v. *Tax Commission* the Court upheld state tax exemptions for real property owned by religious organizations and used for religious worship. That holding, however, tended to confine rather than enlarge the area of permissible state involvement with religious institutions by calling for close scrutiny of the degree of entanglement involved in the relationship. The objective is to prevent, as far as possible, the intrusion of either into the precincts of the other.

Our prior holdings do not call for total separation between church and state; total separation is not possible in an absolute sense. Some relationship between government and religious organizations is inevitable. Fire inspections, building and zoning regulations, and state requirements under compulsory school-attendance laws are examples of necessary and permissible contacts. Indeed, under the statutory exemption before us in *Walz*, the State had a continuing burden to ascertain that the exempt property was in fact being used for religious worship. Judicial caveats against entanglement must recognize that the line of separation, far from being a "wall," is a blurred, indistinct, and variable barrier depending on all the circumstances of a particular relationship.

This is not to suggest, however, that we are to engage in a legalistic minuet in which precise rules and forms must govern. A true minuet is a matter of pure form and style, the observance of which is itself the substantive end. Here we examine the form of the relationship for the light that it casts on the substance.

|615 ⊥ In order to determine whether the government entanglement with religion is excessive, we must examine the character and purposes of the institutions that are benefited, the nature of the aid that the State provides, and the resulting relationship between the government and the religious authority. *Mr. Justice HARLAN*, in a separate opinion in *Walz*, echoed the classic warning as to "programs, whose very nature is apt to entangle the state in details of administration. . . ." Here we find that both

statutes foster an impermissible degree of entanglement.

(a) *Rhode Island program*

The District Court made extensive findings on the grave potential for excessive entanglement that inheres in the religious character and purpose of the Roman Catholic elementary schools of Rhode Island, to date the sole beneficiaries of the Rhode Island Salary Supplement Act.

The church schools involved in the program are located close to parish churches. This understandably permits convenient access for religious exercises since instruction in faith and morals is part of the total educational process. The school buildings contain identifying religious symbols such as crosses on the exterior and crucifixes, and religious paintings and statues either in the classrooms or hallways. Although only approximately 30 minutes a day are devoted to direct religious instruction, there are religiously oriented extracurricular activities. Approximately two-thirds of the teachers in these schools are nuns of various religious orders. Their dedicated efforts provide an atmosphere in which religious instruction and religious vocations are natural and proper parts of life in such schools. Indeed, as the District Court found, the role of teaching nuns in enhancing the religious atmosphere has led the parochial school au⊥thorities to attempt to maintain a |616 one-to-one ratio between nuns and lay teachers in all schools rather than to permit some to be staffed almost entirely by lay teachers.

On the basis of these findings the District Court concluded that the parochial schools constituted "an integral part of the religious mission of the Catholic Church." The various characteristics of the schools make them "a powerful vehicle for transmitting the Catholic faith to the next generation." This process of inculcating religious doctrine is, of course, enhanced by the impressionable age of the pupils, in primary schools particularly. In short, parochial schools involve substantial religious activity and purpose.

The substantial religious character of these church-related schools gives rise to entangling church-state relationships of the kind the Religion Clauses sought to avoid. Although the District Court found that concern for religious values did not inevitably or necessarily intrude into the content of secular subjects, the considerable religious activities of these schools led the legislature to provide for careful governmental controls and surveillance by state authorities in order to ensure that state aid supports only secular education.

The dangers and corresponding entanglements are enhanced by the particular form of aid that the Rhode Island Act provides. Our decisions from *Everson* to *Allen* have permitted the States to provide church-related schools with secular, neutral, or nonideological services, facilities, or materials. Bus transportation, school lunches, public health services, and secular textbooks supplied in common to all students |617 were not ⊥ thought to offend the Establishment Clause. We note that the dissenters in *Allen* seemed chiefly concerned with the pragmatic difficulties involved in ensuring the truly secular content of the textbooks provided at state expense.

In *Allen* the Court refused to make assumptions, on a meager record, about the religious content of the textbooks that the State would be asked to provide. We cannot, however, refuse here to recognize that teachers have a substantially different ideological character from books. In terms of potential for involving some aspect of faith or morals in secular subjects, a textbook's content is ascertainable, but a teacher's handling of a subject is not. We cannot ignore the danger that a teacher under religious control and discipline poses to the separation of the religious from the purely secular aspects of precollege education. The conflict of functions inheres in the situation.

In our view the record shows these dangers are present to a substantial degree. The Rhode Island Roman Catholic elementary schools are under the general supervision of the Bishop of Providence and his appointed representative, the Diocesan Superintendent of Schools. In most cases, each individual parish, however, assumes the ultimate financial responsibility for the school, with the parish priest authorizing the allocation of parish funds. With only two exceptions, school principals are nuns appointed either by the Superintendent or the Mother Provincial of the order whose members staff the school. By 1969 lay teachers constituted more than a third of all teachers in the parochial elementary schools, and their number is growing. They are first interviewed by the superintendent's office and then by the school principal. The contracts are signed by the parish priest, and he retains some discretion in negotiating salary levels. Religious authority necessarily pervades the school system.

|618   ⊥ The schools are governed by the standards set forth in a "Handbook of School Regulations," which has the force of synodal law in the diocese. It emphasizes the role and importance of the teacher in public schools: "The prime factor for the success or the failure of the school is the spirit and personality, as well as the professional competency, of the teacher. . . ." The Handbook also states that: "Religious formation is not confined to formal courses; nor is it restricted to a single subject area." Finally, the Handbook advises teachers to stimulate interest in religious vocations and missionary work. Given the mission of the church school, these instructions are consistent and logical.

Several teachers testified, however, that they did not inject religion into their secular classes. And the District Court found that religious values did not necessarily affect the content of the secular instruction.

But what has been recounted suggests the potential if not actual hazards of this form of state aid. The teacher is employed by a religious organization, subject to the direction and discipline of religious authorities, and works in a system dedicated to rearing children in a particular faith. These controls are not lessened by the fact that most of the lay teachers are of the Catholic faith. Inevitably some of a teacher's responsibilities hover on the border between secular and religious orientation.

We need not and do not assume that teachers in parochial schools will be guilty of bad faith or any conscious design to evade the limitations imposed by the statute and the First Amendment. We simply recognize that a dedicated religious person, teaching in a school affiliated with his or her faith and operated to inculcate its tenets, will inevitably experience great difficulty in remaining religiously neutral. Doctrines and faith are not inculcated or advanced by neutrals. With the best of intentions such a teacher would find it hard to make ⊥ a total separation be- |619 tween secular teaching and religious doctrine. What would appear to some to be essential to good citizenship might well for others border on or constitute instruction in religion. Further difficulties are inherent in the combination of religious discipline and the possibility of disagreement between teacher and religious authorities over the meaning of the statutory restrictions.

We do not assume, however, that parochial school teachers will be unsuccessful in their attempts to segregate their religious beliefs from their secular educational responsibilities. But the potential for impermissible fostering of religion is present. The Rhode Island Legislature has not, and could not, provide state aid on the basis of a mere assumption that secular teachers under religious discipline can avoid conflicts. The State must be certain, given the Religion Clauses, that subsidized teachers do not inculcate religion—indeed the State here has undertaken to do so. To ensure that no trespass occurs, the State has therefore carefully conditioned its aid with pervasive restrictions. An eligible recipient must teach only those courses that are offered in the public schools and use only those texts and materials that are found in the public schools. In addition the teacher must not engage in teaching any course in religion.

A comprehensive, discriminating, and continuing state surveillance will inevitably be required to ensure that these restrictions are obeyed and the First Amendment otherwise respected. Unlike a book, a teacher cannot be inspected once so as to determine the extent and intent of his or her personal beliefs and subjective acceptance of the limitations imposed by the First Amendment. These prophylactic contacts will involve excessive and enduring entanglement between state and church.

⊥ There is another area of entanglement in the |620 Rhode Island program that gives concern. The statute excludes teachers employed by nonpublic schools whose average per-pupil expenditures on secular education equal or exceed the comparable figures for public schools. In the event that the total expenditures of an otherwise eligible school exceed this norm, the program requires the government to examine the school's records in order to determine how much of the total expenditures is attributable to secular education and how much to religious activity. This kind of state inspection and evaluation of the religious content of a religious organization is fraught with the sort of entanglement that the Constitution forbids. It is a relationship pregnant with dangers of excessive government direction of church schools and hence of churches. The Court noted "the hazards of government supporting churches" in *Walz v. Tax Commission* and we cannot ignore here the danger that pervasive modern governmental power will ultimately intrude on religion and thus conflict with the Religion Clauses.

(b) *Pennsylvania program*

The Pennsylvania statute also provides state aid to church-related schools for teachers' salaries. The complaint describes an educational system that is very similar to the one existing in Rhode Island. According to the allegations, the church-related elementary and secondary schools are controlled by religious organizations, have the purpose of propagating and promoting a particular religious faith, and conduct their operations to fulfill that purpose. Since this complaint was dismissed for failure to state a claim for relief, we must accept these allegations as true for purposes of our review.

As we noted earlier, the very restrictions and surveillance necessary to ensure that teachers play a strictly nonideological role give rise to entanglements between ⊥ church and state. The Pennsylvania statute, like that of Rhode Island, fosters this kind of relationship. Reimbursement is not only limited to courses offered in the public schools and materials approved by state officials, but the statute excludes "any subject matter expressing religious teaching, or the morals or forms of worship of any sect." In addition, schools seeking reimbursement must maintain accounting procedures that require the State to establish the cost of the secular as distinguished from the religious instruction.

The Pennsylvania statute, moreover, has the further defect of providing state financial aid directly to the church-related school. This factor distinguishes both *Everson* and *Allen*, for in both those cases the Court was careful to point out that state aid was provided to the student and his parents—not to the church-related school. In *Walz* v. *Tax Commission* the Court warned of the dangers of direct payments to religious organizations: "Obviously a direct money subsidy would be a relationship pregnant with involvement and, as with most governmental grant

⌐621

programs, could encompass sustained and detailed administrative relationships for enforcement of statutory or administrative standards. . . ."

The history of government grants of a continuing cash subsidy indicates that such programs have almost always been accompanied by varying measures of control and surveillance. The government cash grants before us now provide no basis for predicting that comprehensive measures of surveillance and controls will not follow. In particular the government's post-audit power to inspect and evaluate a church-related school's financial records and to determine which expenditures are religious and ⊥ which are secular creates an intimate and continuing relationship between church and state.

⌐622

IV

A broader base of entanglement of yet a different character is presented by the divisive political potential of these state programs. In a community where such a large number of pupils are served by church-related schools, it can be assumed that state assistance will entail considerable political activity. Partisans of parochial schools, understandably concerned with rising costs and sincerely dedicated to both the religious and secular educational missions of their schools, will inevitably champion this cause and promote political action to achieve their goals. Those who oppose state aid, whether for constitutional, religious, or fiscal reasons, will inevitably respond and employ all of the usual political campaign techniques to prevail. Candidates will be forced to declare and voters to choose. It would be unrealistic to ignore the fact that many people confronted with issues of this kind will find their votes aligned with their faith.

Ordinarily political debate and division, however vigorous or even partisan, are normal and healthy manifestations of our democratic system of government, but political division along religious lines was one of the principal evils against which the First Amendment was intended to protect. The potential divisiveness of such conflict is a threat to the normal political process. To have States or communities divide on the issues presented by state aid to parochial schools would tend to confuse ⊥ and obscure other issues of great urgency. We have an expanding array of vexing issues, local and national, domestic and international, to debate and divide on. It conflicts with our whole history and tradition to permit questions of the Religion Clauses to assume such importance in our legislatures and in our elections that they could divert attention from the myriad issues and problems that confront every level of government. The highways of church and state relationships are not likely to be one-way streets, and the Constitution's authors sought to protect religious worship from the pervasive power of government. The history of many countries attests to the hazards of religion's intruding into the political arena or of po-

⌐623

litical power intruding into the legitimate and free exercise of religious belief.

Of course, as the Court noted in *Walz*, "[a]dherents of particular faiths and individual churches frequently take strong positions on public issues." We could not expect otherwise, for religious values pervade the fabric of our national life. But in *Walz* we dealt with a status under state tax laws for the benefit of all religious groups. Here we are confronted with successive and very likely permanent annual appropriations that benefit relatively few religious groups. Political fragmentation and divisiveness on religious lines are thus likely to be intensified.

The potential for political divisiveness related to religious belief and practice is aggravated in these two statutory programs by the need for continuing annual appropriations and the likelihood of larger and larger demands as costs and populations grow. The Rhode Island District Court found that the parochial school system's "monumental and deepening financial crisis" would "inescapably" require larger annual appropriations subsidizing greater percentages of the salaries of lay teachers. Although no facts have been developed in this respect ⊥ in the Pennsylvania case, it appears that such pressures for expanding aid have already required the state legislature to include a portion of the state revenues from cigarette taxes in the program.

|624

V

In *Walz* it was argued that a tax exemption for places of religious worship would prove to be the first step in an inevitable progression leading to the establishment of state churches and state religion. That claim could not stand up against more than 200 years of virtually universal practice imbedded in our colonial experience and continuing into the present.

The progression argument, however, is more persuasive here. We have no long history of state aid to church-related educational institutions comparable to 200 years of tax exemption for churches. Indeed, the state programs before us today represent something of an innovation. We have already noted that modern governmental programs have self-perpetuating and self-expanding propensities. These internal pressures are only enhanced when the schemes involve institutions whose legitimate needs are growing and whose interests have substantial political support. Nor can we fail to see that in constitutional adjudication some steps, which when taken were thought to approach "the verge," have become the platform for yet further steps. A certain momentum develops in constitutional theory and it can be a "downhill thrust" easily set in motion but difficult to retard or stop. Development by momentum is not invariably bad; indeed, it is the way the common law has grown, but it is a force to be recognized and reckoned with. The dangers are increased by the difficulty of perceiving in advance exactly where the "verge" of the precipice lies. As well as constituting an independent evil against which the Religion Clauses were intended to protect, involve-⊥ment or entanglement between government and religion serves as a warning signal.

|625

Finally, nothing we have said can be construed to disparage the role of church-related elementary and secondary schools in our national life. Their contribution has been and is enormous. Nor do we ignore their economic plight in a period of rising costs and expanding need. Taxpayers generally have been spared vast sums by the maintenance of these educational institutions by religious organizations, largely by gifts of faithful adherents.

The merit and benefits of these schools, however, are not the issue before us in these cases. The sole question is whether state aid to these schools can be squared with the dictates of the Religion Clauses. Under our system the choice has been made that government is to be entirely excluded from the area of religious instruction and churches excluded from the affairs of government. The Constitution decrees that religion must be a private matter for the individual, the family, and the institutions of private choice, and that while some involvement and entanglement are inevitable, lines must be drawn.

The judgment of the Rhode Island District Court in No. 569 and No. 570 is affirmed. The judgment of the Pennsylvania District Court in No. 89 is reversed, and the case is remanded for further proceedings consistent with this opinion.

Mr. Justice MARSHALL took no part in the consideration or decision of [*Lemon* v. *Kurtzman*].

Mr. Justice DOUGLAS, whom *Mr. Justice BLACK* joins, concurring.

While I join the opinion of the Court, I have expressed at some length my views as to the rationale of today's decision in these three cases. . . .

⊥ In *Walz* v. *Tax Commission* the Court in approving a tax exemption for church property said: "Determining that the legislative purpose of tax exemption is not aimed at establishing, sponsoring, or supporting religion does not end the inquiry, however. We must also be sure that the end result—the effect—is not an excessive government entanglement with religion."

|627

There is in my view such an entanglement here. The surveillance or supervision of the States needed to police grants involved in these three cases, if performed, puts a public investigator into every classroom and entails a pervasive monitoring of these church agencies by the secular authorities. Yet if that surveillance or supervision does not occur the zeal of religious proselytizers promises to carry the day and make a shambles of the Establishment

⌐628 Clause. Moreover, when taxpayers of ⊥ many faiths are required to contribute money for the propagation of one faith, the Free Exercise Clause is infringed.

The analysis of the constitutional objections to these two state systems of grants to parochial or sectarian schools must start with the admitted and obvious fact that the *raison d'être* of parochial schools is the propagation of a religious faith. They also teach secular subjects; but they came into existence in this country because Protestant groups were perverting the public schools by using them to propagate their faith. The Catholics naturally rebelled. If schools were to be used to propagate a particular creed or religion, then Catholic ideals should also be served. Hence the advent of parochial schools.

By 1840 there were 200 Catholic parish schools in the United States. By 1964 there were 60 times as many. Today 57% of the 9,000 Catholic parishes in the country have their church schools. "[E]very diocesan chancery has its school department, and enjoys a primacy of status." The parish schools indeed consume 40% to 65% of the parish's total income. The parish is so "school centered" "[t]he school almost becomes the very reason for being."

Early in the 19th century the Protestants obtained control of the New York school system and used it to promote reading and teaching of the Scriptures as revealed in the King James version of the Bible. The
⌐629 contests ⊥ between Protestants and Catholics, often erupting into violence including the burning of Catholic churches, are a twice-told tale; the Know-Nothing Party, which included in its platform "daily Bible reading in the schools," carried three States in 1854—Massachusetts, Pennsylvania, and Delaware. Parochial schools grew, but not Catholic schools alone. Other dissenting sects established their own schools—Lutherans, Methodists, Presbyterians, and others. But the major force in shaping the pattern of education in this country was the conflict between Protestants and Catholics. The Catholics logically argued that a public school was sectarian when it taught the King James version of the Bible. They therefore wanted it removed from the public schools; and in time they tried to get public funds for their own parochial schools.

The constitutional right of dissenters to substitute their parochial schools for public schools was sustained by the Court in *Pierce* v. *Society of Sisters.*

The story of conflict and dissension is long and well known. The result was a state of so-called equilibrium where religious instruction was eliminated from public schools and the use of public funds to support religious schools was deemed to be banned.

But the hydraulic pressures created by political forces and by economic stress were great and they
⌐630 began to ⊥ change the situation. Laws were passed—state and federal—that dispensed public funds to sustain religious schools and the plea was always in the educational frame of reference: education in all sectors was needed, from languages to calculus to nuclear physics. And it was forcefully argued that a linguist or mathematician or physicist trained in religious schools was just as competent as one trained in secular schools.

And so we have gradually edged into a situation where vast amounts of public funds are supplied each year to sectarian schools.

And the argument is made that the private parochial school system takes about $9 billion a year off the back of government—as if that were enough to justify violating the Establishment Clause.

While the evolution of the public school system in this country marked an escape from denominational control and was therefore admirable as seen through the eyes of those who think like Madison and Jefferson, it has disadvantages. The main one is that a state system may attempt to mold all students alike according to the views of the dominant group and to discourage the emergence of individual idiosyncrasies.

Sectarian education, however, does not remedy that condition. The advantages of sectarian education relate solely to religious or doctrinal matters. They give the ⊥ church the opportunity to in- ⌐631 doctrinate its creed delicately and indirectly, or massively through doctrinal courses.

Many nations follow that course; Moslem nations teach the Koran in their schools; Sweden vests its elementary education in the parish; Newfoundland puts its school system under three superintendents—one from the Church of England, one from the Catholic church, one from the United Church. In Ireland the public schools are under denominational managership—Catholic, Episcopalian, Presbyterian, and Hebrew.

England puts sectarian schools under the umbrella of its school system. It finances sectarian education; it exerts control by prescribing standards; it requires some free scholarships; it provides nondenominational membership on the board of directors.

The British system is, in other words, one of surveillance over sectarian schools. We too have surveillance over sectarian schools but only to the extent of making sure that minimum educational standards are met, *viz.*, competent teachers, accreditation of the school for diplomas, the number of hours of work and credits allowed, and so on.

But we have never faced, until recently, the problem of policing sectarian schools. Any surveillance to date has been minor and has related only to the consistently unchallenged matters of accreditation of the sectarian school in the State's school system.

The Rhode Island Act allows a supplementary salary to a teacher in a sectarian school if he or she "does not teach a course in religion."

⊥ The Pennsylvania Act provides for state fi- ⌐632 nancing of instruction in mathematics, modern foreign languages, physical science, and physical education, provided that the instruction in those courses "shall not include any subject matter expressing religious teaching, or the morals or forms of worship of any sect."

Public financial support of parochial schools puts those schools under disabilities with which they were not previously burdened. For, as we held in *Cooper* v. *Aaron*, governmental activities relating to schools "must be exercised consistently with federal constitutional requirements." There we were concerned with equal protection; here we are faced with issues of Establishment of religion and its Free Exercise as those concepts are used in the First Amendment.

Where the governmental activity is the financing of the private school, the various limitations or restraints imposed by the Constitution on state governments come into play. Thus, Arkansas, as part of its attempt to avoid the consequences of *Brown* v. *Board of Education*, withdrew its financial support from some public schools and sent the funds instead to private schools. That state action was held to violate the Equal Protection Clause. Louisiana tried a like tactic and it too was invalidated. Whatever might be the result in case of grants to students, it is clear that once ⊥ one of the States finances a private school, it is duty-bound to make certain that the school stays within secular bounds and does not use the public funds to promote sectarian causes.

The government may, of course, finance a hospital though it is run by a religious order, provided it is open to people of all races and creeds. The government itself could enter the hospital business; and it would, of course, make no difference if its agents who ran its hospitals were Catholics, Methodists, agnostics, or whatnot. For the hospital is not indulging in religious instruction or guidance or indoctrination. As Mr. Justice Jackson said in *Everson* v. *Board of Education*: "[Each State has] great latitude in deciding for itself, in the light of its own conditions, what shall be public purposes in its scheme of things. It may socialize utilities and economic enterprises and make taxpayers' business out of what conventionally had been private business. It may make public business of individual welfare, health, education, entertainment or security. But it cannot make public business of religious worship or instruction, or of attendance at religious institutions of any character."

The reason is that given by Madison in his Remonstrance: "[T]he same authority which can force a citizen to contribute three pence only of his property for ⊥ the support of any one establishment, may force him to conform to any other establishment. . . ."

When Madison in his Remonstrance attacked a taxing measure to support religious activities, he advanced a series of reasons for opposing it. One that is extremely relevant here was phrased as follows: "[I]t will destroy that moderation and harmony which the forbearance of our laws to intermeddle with Religion, has produced amongst its several sects." Intermeddling, to use Madison's word, or "entanglement," to use what was said in *Walz*, has

two aspects. The intrusion of government into religious schools through grants, supervision, or surveillance may result in establishment of religion in the constitutional sense when what the State does enthrones a particular sect for overt or subtle propagation of its faith. Those activities of the State may also intrude on the Free Exercise Clause by depriving a teacher, under threats of reprisals, of the right to give sectarian construction or interpretation of, say, history and literature, or to use the teaching of such subjects to inculcate a religious creed or dogma.

Under these laws there will be vast governmental suppression, surveillance, or meddling in church affairs. As I indicated in *Tilton* v. *Richardson*, decided this day, school prayers, the daily routine of parochial schools, must go if our decision in *Engel* v. *Vitale* is honored. If it is not honored, then the state has established a religious sect. Elimination of prayers is only part of the problem. The curriculum presents subtle and difficult problems. The constitutional mandate can in part be carried out by censoring the curricula. What is palpably a sectarian course can be marked for ⊥ deletion. But the problem only starts there. Sectarian instruction, in which, of course, a State may not indulge, can take place in a course on Shakespeare or in one on mathematics. No matter what the curriculum offers, the question is, what is *taught*? We deal not with evil teachers but with zealous ones who may use any opportunity to indoctrinate a class.

It is well known that everything taught in most parochial schools is taught with the ultimate goal of religious education in mind. Rev. Joseph H. Fichter, S.J., stated in Parochial School: A Sociological Study: "It is a commonplace observation that in the parochial school religion permeates the whole curriculum, and is not confined to a single half-hour period of the day. Even arithmetic can be used as an instrument of pious thoughts, as in the case of the teacher who gave this problem to her class: 'If it takes forty thousand priests and a hundred and forty thousand sisters to care for forty million Catholics in the United States, how many more priests and sisters will be needed to convert and care for the hundred million non-Catholics in the United States?' "

One can imagine what a religious zealot, as contrasted to a civil libertarian, can do with the Ref⊥ormation or with the Inquisition. Much history can be given the gloss of a particular religion. I would think that policing these grants to detect sectarian instruction would be insufferable to religious partisans and would breed division and dissension between church and state.

This problem looms large where the church controls the hiring and firing of teachers: "[I]n the public school the selection of a faculty and the administration of the school usually rests with a school board which is subject to election and recall by the voters, but in the parochial school the selection of a faculty and the administration of the school is in the hands of the bishop alone, and usually is administered through the local priest. If a faculty member in the public school believes that he has been treated unjustly in being disciplined or dismissed, he can seek redress through the civil court and he is guaranteed a hearing. But if a faculty member in a parochial school is disciplined or dismissed he has no recourse whatsoever. The word of the bishop or priest is final, even without explanation if he so chooses. The tax payers have a voice in the way their money is used in the public school, but the people who support a parochial school have no voice at all in such affairs." L. Boettner, Roman Catholicism 375 (1962)

Board of Education v. *Allen* dealt only with textbooks. Even so, some had difficulty giving approval. Yet books can be easily examined independently of other aspects of the teaching process. In the present cases we deal with the totality of instruction destined to be sectarian, at least in part, if the religious character of the school is to be maintained. A school which operates to commingle religion with other instruction plainly cannot completely secularize its instruction. ⊥ Parochial schools, in large measure, do not accept the assumption that secular subjects should be unrelated to religious teaching.

Lemon involves a state statute that prescribes that courses in mathematics, modern foreign languages, physical science, and physical education "shall not include any subject matter expressing religious teaching, or the morals or forms of worship of any sect." The subtleties involved in applying this standard are obvious. It places the State astride a sectarian school and gives it power to dictate what is or is not secular, what is or is not religious. I can think of no more disrupting influence apt to promote rancor and ill-will between church and state than this kind of surveillance and control. They are the very opposite of the "moderation and harmony" between church and state which Madison thought was the aim and purpose of the Establishment Clause.

The *DiCenso* cases have all the vices which are in *Lemon*, because the supplementary salary payable to the teacher is conditioned on his or her not teaching "a course in religion."

Moreover, the *DiCenso* cases reveal another, but related, knotty problem presented when church and state launch one of these educational programs. The Bishop of Rhode Island has a Handbook of School Regulations for the Diocese of Providence.

The school board supervises "the education, both spiritual and secular, in the parochial schools and diocesan high schools."

The superintendent is an agent of the bishop and he interprets and makes "effective state and diocesan educational directives."

⊥ The pastors visit the schools and "give their assistance in promoting spiritual and intellectual discipline."

Community supervisors "assist the teacher in the problems of instruction" and these duties are:

"I. To become well enough acquainted with the teachers of their communities so as to be able to advise the community superiors on matters of placement and reassignment.

"II. To act as liaison between the provincialate and the religious teacher in the school.

"III. To cooperate with the superintendent by studying the diocesan school regulations and to encourage the teachers of their community to observe these regulations.

"IV. To avoid giving any orders or directions to the teachers of their community that may be in conflict with diocesan regulations or policy regarding curriculum, testing, textbooks, method, or administrative matters.

"V. To refer questions concerning school administration beyond the scope of their own authority to the proper diocesan school authorities, namely, the superintendent of schools or the pastor."

The length of the school day includes Mass: "A full day session for Catholic schools at the elementary level consists of five and one-half hours, exclusive of lunch and Mass, but inclusive of recess for pupils in grades 1-3."

A course of study or syllabus prescribed for an elementary or secondary school is "mandatory."

⊥ Religious instruction is provided as follows:

"A. Systematic religious instructions must be provided in all schools of the diocese.

"B. Modern catechetics requires a teacher with unusual aptitudes, specialized training, and such unction of the spirit that his words possess the force of a personal call. He should be so filled with his subject that he can freely improvize in discussion, dramatization, drawing, song, and prayer. A teacher so gifted and so permeated by the message of the Gospel is rare. Perhaps no teacher in a given school attains that ideal. But some teachers come nearer it than others. If our pupils are to hear the Good News so that their minds are enlightened and their hearts respond to the love of God and His Christ, if they are to be formed into vital, twentieth-century Christians, they should receive their religious instructions only from the very best teachers.

"C. Inasmuch as the textbooks employed in religious instruction above the fifth grade require a high degree of catechetical preparation, religion should be a departmentalized subject in grade six through twelve."

Religious activities are provided, through observance of specified holy days and participation in Mass.

"Religious formation" is not restricted to courses but is achieved "through the example of the faculty, the tone of the school . . . and religious activities."

No unauthorized priest may address the students.

"Retreats and days of recollection form an integral part of our religious program in the Catholic schools."

Religious factors are used in the selection of students: "Although wealth should never serve as a criterion for accepting a pupil into a Catholic school, |640 all other ⊥ things being equal, it would seem fair to give preference to a child whose parents support the parish. Regular use of the budget, rather than the size of the contributions, would appear equitable. It indicates whether parents regularly attend Mass."

These are only highlights of the handbook. But they indicate how pervasive is the religious control over the school and how remote this type of school is from the secular school. Public funds supporting that structure are used to perpetuate a doctrine and creed in innumerable and in pervasive ways. Those who man these schools are good people, zealous people, dedicated people. But they are dedicated to ideas that the Framers of our Constitution placed beyond the reach of government.

If the government closed its eyes to the manner in which these grants are actually used it would be allowing public funds to promote sectarian education. If it did not close its eyes but undertook the surveillance needed, it would, I fear, intermeddle in parochial affairs in a way that would breed only rancor and dissension.

We have announced over and over again that the use of taxpayers' money to support parochial schools violates the First Amendment, applicable to the States by virtue of the Fourteenth.

We said in unequivocal words in *Everson* v. *Board of Education*, "No tax in any amount, large or small, can be levied to support any religious activities or institutions, whatever they may be called, or whatever form they may adopt to teach or practice religion. We reiterated the same idea in *Zorach* v. *Clauson*, and in *McGowan* v. *Maryland*, and in *Torcaso* v. *Watkins*. We repeated the same idea in *McCollum* v. |641 *Board of Education* and added that a State's ⊥ tax-supported public schools could not be used "for the dissemination of religious doctrines" nor could a State provide the church "pupils for their religious classes through use of the State's compulsory public school machinery."

Yet in spite of this long and consistent history there are those who have the courage to announce that a State may nonetheless finance the *secular* part of a sectarian school's educational program. That, however, makes a grave constitutional decision turn merely on cost accounting and bookkeeping entries. A history class, a literature class, or a science class in a parochial school is not a separate institute; it is part of the organic whole which the State subsidizes. The funds are used in these cases to pay or help pay the salaries of teachers in parochial schools; and the presence of teachers is critical to the essential purpose of the parochial school, *viz.*, to advance the religious endeavors of the particular church. It matters not that the teacher receiving taxpayers' money only teaches religion a fraction of the time. Nor does it matter that he or she teaches no religion. The school is an organism living on one budget. What the taxpayers give for salaries of those who teach only the humanities or science without any trace of proselytizing enables the school to use all of its own funds for religious training. As Judge Coffin said, we would be blind to realities if we let "sophisticated bookkeeping" sanction "almost total subsidy of a religious institution by assigning the bulk of the institution's expenses to 'secular' activities." And sophisticated attempts to avoid the Constitution are just as invalid as simple-minded ones.

In my view the taxpayers' forced contribution to the parochial schools in the ⊥ present cases violates |642 the First Amendment.

Mr. Justice MARSHALL, who took no part in the consideration or decision of No. 89, while intimating no view as to the continuing vitality of *Everson* v. *Board of Education*, concurs in *Mr. Justice DOUGLAS'* opinion covering Nos. 569 and 570.

Mr. Justice BRENNAN. *

I agree that the judgments in Nos. 569 and 570 must be affirmed. In my view the judgment in No. 89 must be reversed outright. I dissent in No. 153 insofar as the plurality opinion and the opinion of my *Brother WHITE* sustain the constitutionality, as applied to sectarian institutions, of the Federal Higher Education Facilities Act of 1963. In my view that Act is unconstitutional insofar as it authorizes grants of federal tax monies to sectarian institutions, but is unconstitutional only to that extent. I therefore think that our remand of the case should be limited to the direction of a hearing to determine whether the four institutional appellees here are sectarian institutions.

I continue to adhere to the view that to give concrete meaning to the Establishment Clause "the line we must draw between the permissible and the impermissible is one which accords with history and faithfully reflects the understanding of the Founding Fathers. It is a line which the Court has consistently sought to mark in its decisions expounding the religious guarantees of the First ⊥ Amendment. What |643 the Framers meant to foreclose, and what our decisions under the Establishment Clause have forbidden, are those involvements of religious with secular institutions which (a) serve the essentially religious activities of religious institutions; (b) employ the organs of government for essentially religious purposes; or (c) use essentially religious means to serve governmental ends, where secular means

---

* This opinion also applies to No. 153, *Tilton v. Richardson.*

would suffice. When the secular and religious institutions become involved in such a manner, there inhere in the relationship precisely those dangers—as much to church as to state—which the Framers feared would subvert religious liberty and the strength of a system of secular government." *Abington School District* v. *Schempp.*

The common feature of all three statutes before us is the provision of a direct subsidy from public funds for activities carried on by sectarian educational institutions. We have sustained the reimbursement of parents for bus fares of students under a scheme applicable to both public and nonpublic schools, *Everson* v. *Board of Education.* We have also sustained the loan of textbooks in secular subjects to students of both public and nonpublic schools, *Board of Education* v. *Allen.*

The statutory schemes before us, however, have features not present in either the *Everson* or *Allen* schemes. For example, the reimbursement or the loan of books ended government involvement in *Everson* and *Allen.* In contrast each of the schemes here exacts a promise in some form that the subsidy will not be used to finance ⊥ courses in religious subjects—promises that must be and are policed to assure compliance. Again, although the federal subsidy, similar to the *Everson* and *Allen* subsidies, is available to both public and nonpublic colleges and universities, the Rhode Island and Pennsylvania subsidies are restricted to nonpublic schools, and for practical purposes to Roman Catholic parochial schools. These and other features I shall mention mean for me that *Everson* and *Allen* do not control these cases. Rather, the history of public subsidy of sectarian schools, and the purposes and operation of these particular statutes must be examined to determine whether the statutes breach the Establishment Clause.

⌐1644

I

⌐1645

⊥ In sharp contrast to the "undeviating acceptance given religious tax exemptions from our earliest days as a Nation," subsidy of sectarian educational institutions became embroiled in bitter controversies very soon after the Nation was formed. Public education was, of course, virtually nonexistent when the Constitution was adopted. Colonial Massachusetts in 1647 had directed towns to establish schools, Benjamin Franklin in 1749 proposed a Philadelphia Academy, and Jefferson labored to establish a public school system in Virginia. But these were the exceptions. Education in the Colonies was overwhelmingly a private enterprise, usually carried on as a denominational activity by the dominant Protestant sects. In point of fact, government generally looked to the church to provide education, and often contributed support through donations of land and money.

Nor was there substantial change in the years immediately following ratification of the Constitution and the Bill of Rights. Schools continued to be local

and, in the main, denominational institutions. But the demand for public education soon emerged. The evolution of the struggle in New York City is illustrative. In 1786, the first New York State Legislature ordered that one section in each township be set aside for the "gospel and schools." With no public schools, various private agencies and churches operated "charity schools" for the poor of New ⊥ York City and received money from the state common school fund. The forerunner of the city's public schools was organized in 1805 when DeWitt Clinton founded "The Society for Establishment of a Free School in the City of New York for the Education of such poor Children as do not belong to or are not provided for by any Religious Society." The State and city aided the society, and it built many schools. Gradually, however, competition and bickering among the Free School Society and the various church schools developed over the apportionment of state school funds. As a result, in 1825, the legislature transferred to the city council the responsibility for distributing New York City's share of the state funds. The council stopped funding religious societies which operated 16 sectarian schools but continued supporting schools connected with the Protestant Orphan Asylum Society. Thereafter, in 1831, the Catholic Orphan Asylum Society demanded and received public funds to operate its schools but a request of Methodists for funds for the same purpose was denied. Nine years later, the Catholics enlarged their request for public monies to include all parochial schools, contending that the council was subsidizing sectarian books and instruction of the Public School Society, which Clinton's Free School Society had become. The city's Scotch Presbyterian and Jewish communities immediately followed with requests for funds to finance their schools. Although the Public School Society undertook to revise its texts to meet the objections, in 1842, the state legislature closed the bitter controversy by enacting a law that established a City Board of Education to set up free public schools, prohibited the distribution of public funds to sectarian schools, and prohibited the teaching of sectarian doctrine in any public school.

⌐1646

The Nation's rapidly developing religious heterogeneity, the tide of Jacksonian democracy, and growing ⊥ urbanization soon led to widespread demands throughout the States for secular public education. At the same time strong opposition developed to use of the States' taxing powers to support private sectarian schools. Although the controversy over religious exercises in the public schools continued into this century, the opponents of subsidy to sectarian schools had largely won their fight by 1900. In fact, after 1840, no efforts of sectarian schools to obtain a share of public school funds succeeded. Between 1840 and 1875, 19 States added provisions to their constitutions prohibiting the use of public school funds to aid sectarian schools, and by 1900,

⌐1647

16 more States had added similar provisions. In fact, no State admitted to the Union after 1858, except West Virginia, omitted such provision from its first constitution. Today fewer than a half-dozen States ⌐648 omit such provisions from their constitutions. ⊥ And in 1897, Congress included in its appropriation act for the District of Columbia a statement declaring it "to be the policy of the Government of the United States to make no appropriation of money or property for the purpose of founding, maintaining, or aiding by payment for services, expenses, or otherwise, any church or religious denomination, or any institution or society which is under sectarian or ecclesiastical control."

Thus for more than a century, the consensus, enforced by legislatures and courts with substantial consistency, has been that public subsidy of sectarian schools constitutes an impermissible involvement ⌐649 of secular with ⊥ religious institutions. If this history is not itself compelling against the validity of the three subsidy statutes, in the sense we found in *Walz* that "undeviating acceptance" was highly significant in favor of the validity of religious tax exemption, other forms of governmental involvement that each of the three statutes requires tip the scales in my view against the validity of each of them. These are involvements that threaten "dangers—as much to church as to state—which the Framers feared would subvert religious liberty and the strength of a system of secular government."

Schempp. "[G]overnment and religion have discrete interests which are mutually best served when each avoids too close a proximity to the other. It is not only the nonbeliever who fears the injection of sectarian doctrines and controversies into the civil polity, but in as high degree it is the devout believer who fears the secularization of a creed which becomes too deeply involved with and dependent upon the government." All three of these statutes require "too close a proximity" of government to the subsidized sectarian institutions and in my view create real dangers of "the secularization of a creed."

II

⌐650   ⊥ The Rhode Island statute requires Roman Catholic teachers to surrender their right to teach religion courses and to promise not to "inject" religious teaching into their secular courses. This has led at least one teacher to stop praying with his classes, a concrete testimonial to the self-censorship that inevitably accompanies state regulation of delicate First Amendment freedoms. Both the Rhode Island and Pennsylvania statutes prescribe extensive standardization of the content of secular courses, and of the teaching materials and textbooks to be used in teaching the courses. And the regulations to implement those requirements necessarily require policing of instruction in the schools. The picture of state inspectors prowling the halls of parochial schools and auditing classroom instruction surely raises more

than an imagined specter of governmental "secularization of a creed."

The same dangers attend the federal subsidy even if less obviously. The Federal Government exacts a promise that no "sectarian instruction" or "religious worship" will take place in a subsidized building. The Office of Education polices the promise. In one instance federal ⊥ officials demanded that a college ⌐651 cease teaching a course entitled "The History of Methodism" in a federally assisted building, although the Establishment Clause "plainly does not foreclose teaching *about* the Holy Scriptures or about the differences between religious sects in classes in literature or history." *Schempp.* These examples illustrate the complete incompatibility of such surveillance with the restraints barring interference with religious freedom.

Policing the content of courses, the specific textbooks used, and indeed the words of teachers is far different from the legitimate policing carried on under state compulsory attendance laws or laws regulating minimum levels of educational achievement. Government's legitimate interest in ensuring certain minimum skill levels and the acquisition of certain knowledge does not carry with it power to prescribe what shall *not* be taught, or what methods of instruction shall be used, or what opinions the teacher may offer in the course of teaching.

Moreover, when a sectarian institution accepts state financial aid it becomes obligated under the Equal Protection Clause of the Fourteenth Amendment not to discriminate in admissions policies and faculty selection. ⊥ The District Court in the Rhode ⌐652 Island case pinpointed the dilemma: "Applying these standards to parochial schools might well restrict their ability to discriminate in admissions policies and in the hiring and firing of teachers. At some point the school becomes 'public' for more purposes than the Church could wish. At that point, the Church may justifiably feel that its victory on the Establishment Clause has meant abandonment of the Free Exercise Clause."

III

In any event, I do not believe that elimination of these aspects of "too close a proximity" would save these three statutes. I expressed the view in *Walz* that "[g]eneral subsidies of religious activities would, of course, constitute impermissible state involvement with religion." I do not think the subsidies under these statutes fall outside "[g]eneral subsidies of religious activities" merely because they are restricted to support of the teaching of secular subjects. In *Walz*, the passive aspect of the benefits conferred by a tax exemption, particularly since cessation of the exemptions might easily lead to impermissible involvements and conflicts, led me to conclude that exemptions were consistent with the First Amendment values. However, I contrasted direct government subsidies: "Tax exemptions and general subsidies, however, are qualitatively different. Though both provide economic assistance, they do so in fundamentally different ways. A subsidy involves the direct transfer of public monies to the subsidized enterprise and uses resources exacted from taxpayers as a whole. An exemption, on the other hand, involves no such ⊥ transfer. It assists the exempted enterprise only passively, by relieving a privately funded venture of the burden of paying taxes. In other words, '[i]n the case of direct subsidy, the state forcibly diverts the income of both believers and non-believers to churches,' while '[i]n the case of an exemption, the state merely refrains from diverting to its own uses income independently generated by the churches through voluntary contributions.' Thus, 'the symbolism of tax exemption is significant as a manifestation that organized religion is not expected to support the state; by the same token the state is not expected to support the church.'"

Pennsylvania, Rhode Island, and the Federal Government argue strenuously that the government monies in all these cases are not "[g]eneral subsidies of religious activities" because they are paid specifically and solely for the secular education that the sectarian institutions provide.

Before turning to the decisions of this Court on which this argument is based, it is important to recall again the history of subsidies to sectarian schools. ⊥ The universality of state constitutional provisions forbidding such grants, as well as the weight of judicial authority disapproving such aid as a violation of our tradition of separation of church and state, reflects a time-tested judgment that such grants do indeed constitute impermissible aid to religion. The recurrent argument, consistently rejected in the past, has been that government grants to sectarian schools ought not be viewed as impermissible subsidies "because [the schools] relieve the State of a burden, which it would otherwise be itself required to bear . . . . they will render a service to the state by performing for it its duty of educating the children of the people." *Cook County* v. *Chicago Industrial School.*

Nonetheless, it is argued once again in these cases that sectarian schools and universities perform two separable functions. First, they provide secular education, and second, they teach the tenets of a particular sect. Since the State has determined that the secular education provided in sectarian schools serves the legitimate state interest in the education of its citizens, it is contended that state aid solely to the secular education function does not involve the State in aid to religion. *Pierce* v. *Society of Sisters* and *Board of Education* v. *Allen* are relied on as support for the argument.

Our opinion in *Allen* recognized that sectarian schools provide both a secular and a sectarian education: "[T]his Court has long recognized that religious schools pursue two goals, religious instruction and secular education. In the leading case of *Pierce* v.

Society of Sisters, the Court held that . . . Oregon had not shown that its interest in secular education required that all children attend publicly operated schools. A premise of this ⊥ holding was the view that the State's interest in education would be served sufficiently by reliance on the secular teaching that accompanied religious training in the schools maintained by the Society of Sisters.

.   .   .   .   .

"[T]he continued willingness to rely on private school systems, including parochial systems, strongly suggests that a wide segment of informed opinion, legislative and otherwise, has found that those schools do an acceptable job of providing secular education to their students. This judgment is further evidence that parochial schools are performing, in addition to their sectarian function, the task of secular education." *Board of Education* v. *Allen.*

But I do not read *Pierce* or *Allen* as supporting the proposition that public subsidy of a sectarian institution's secular training is permissible state involvement. I read them as supporting the proposition that as an identifiable set of skills and an identifiable quantum of knowledge, secular education may be effectively provided either in the religious context of parochial schools, or outside the context of religion in public schools. The State's interest in secular education may be defined broadly as an interest in ensuring that all children within its boundaries acquire a minimum level of competency in certain skills, such as reading, writing, and arithmetic, as well as a minimum amount of information and knowledge in certain subjects such as history, geography, science, literature, and law. Without such skills and knowledge, an individual will be at a severe disadvantage both in participating in democratic self-government and in earning a living in a modern industrial economy. But the State has no proper interest in prescribing the precise forum in which such skills and knowlege are learned since acquisition of this ⊥ secular education is neither incompatible with religious learning, nor is it inconsistent with or inimical to religious precepts.

When the same secular educational process occurs in both public and sectarian schools, *Allen* held that the State could provide secular textbooks for use in that process to students in both public and sectarian schools. Of course, the State could not provide textbooks giving religious instruction. But since the textbooks involved in *Allen* would, at least in theory, be limited to secular education, no aid to sectarian instruction was involved.

More important, since the textbooks in *Allen* had been previously provided by the parents, and not the schools, no aid to the institution was involved. Rather, as in the case of the bus transportation in *Everson*, the general program of providing all children in the State with free secular textbooks assisted all parents in schooling their children. And as in *Ev-*

⊥653

⊥654

⊥655

⊥656

erson, there was undoubtedly the possibility that some parents might not have been able to exercise their constitutional right to send their children to parochial school if the parents were compelled themselves to pay for textbooks. However, as my *Brother BLACK* wrote for the Court in *Everson*, "[C]utting off church schools from these [general] services, so separate and so indisputably marked off from the religious function, would make it far more difficult for the schools to operate. But such is obviously not the purpose of the First Amendment. That Amendment requires the state to be a neutral in its relations with groups of religious believers and non-believers; it does not require the state to be their adversary. State power is no more to be used so as to handicap religions than it is to favor them."

|657   ⊥ *Allen*, in my view, simply sustained a statute in which the State was "neutral in its relations with groups of religious believers and non-believers." The only context in which the Court in *Allen* employed the distinction between secular and religious in a parochial school was to reach its conclusion that the textbooks that the State was providing could and would be secular. The present cases, however, involve direct subsidies of tax monies to the schools themselves and we cannot blink the fact that the secular education those schools provide goes hand in hand with the religious mission that is the only reason for the schools' existence. Within the institution, the two are inextricably intertwined.

The District Court in the *DiCenso* case found that all the varied aspects of the parochial school's program—the nature of its faculty, its supervision, decor, program, extra-curricular activities, assemblies, courses, etc.—produced an "intangible 'religious atmosphere,'" since the "diocesan school system is an integral part of the religious mission of the Catholic Church" and "a powerful vehicle for transmitting the Catholic faith to the next generation." Quality teaching in secular subjects is an integral part of this religious enterprise. "Good secular teaching is as essential to the religious mission of the parochial schools as a roof for the school or desks for the classrooms." That teaching cannot be separated from the environment in which it occurs, for its integration with the religious mission is both the theory and the strength of the religious school.

|658   The common ingredient of the three prongs of the test ⊥ set forth at the outset of this opinion is whether the statutes involve government in the "essentially religious activities" of religious institutions. My analysis of the operation, purposes, and effects of these statutes leads me inescapably to the conclusion that they do impermissibly involve the States and the Federal Government with the "essentially religious activities" of sectarian educational institutions. More specifically, for the reasons stated, I think each government uses "essentially religious means to serve governmental ends, where secular means would suffice." This Nation long ago committed itself to

primary reliance upon publicly supported public education to serve its important goals in secular education. Our religious diversity gave strong impetus to that commitment. . . .

|659   ⊥ I conclude that, in using sectarian institutions to further goals in secular education, the three statutes do violence to the principle that "government may not employ religious means to serve secular interests, however legitimate they may be, at least without the clearest demonstration that nonreligious means will not suffice." *Schempp*.

IV

The plurality's treatment of the issues in *Tilton*, No. 153, diverges so substantially from my own that I add these further comments. I believe that the Establishment Clause forbids the Federal Government to provide funds to sectarian universities in which the propagation and advancement of a particular religion are a function or purpose of the institution. Since the District Court made no findings whether the four institutional appellees here are sectarian, I would remand the case to the District Court with directions to determine whether the institutional appellees are "sectarian" institutions.

I reach this conclusion for the reasons I have stated: the necessarily deep involvement of government in the religious activities of such an institution through the policing of restrictions, and the fact that subsidies of tax monies directly to a sectarian institution necessarily aid the proselytizing function of the institution. The plurality argues that neither of these dangers is present.

At the risk of repetition, I emphasize that a sectarian university is the equivalent in the realm of higher education of the Catholic elementary schools in Rhode Island; it is an educational institution in which the propagation ⊥ and advancement of a particular religion are a primary function of the institution. I do not believe that construction grants to such a sectarian institution are permissible. The reason is not that religion "permeates" the secular education that is provided. Rather, it is that the secular education is provided within the environment of religion; the institution is dedicated to two goals, secular education *and* religious instruction. When aid flows directly to the institution, both functions benefit. The plurality would examine only the activities that occur within the federally assisted building and ignore the religious nature of the school of which it is a part. The "religious enterprise" aided by the construction grants involves the maintenance of an educational environment—which includes high-quality, purely secular educational courses—within which religious instruction occurs in a variety of ways.

The plurality also argues that no impermissible entanglement exists here. My *Brother WHITE* cogently comments upon that argument: "Why the federal program in the *Tilton* case is not embroiled in the same difficulties [as the Rhode Island program] is never adequately explained." I do not see any significant difference in the Federal Government's telling the sectarian university not to teach any nonsecular subjects in a certain building, and Rhode Island's telling the Catholic school teacher not to teach religion. The vice is the creation through subsidy of a relationship in which the government polices the teaching practices of a religious school or university. The plurality suggests that the facts that college students are less impressionable and that college courses are less susceptible to religious permeation may lessen the need for federal policing. But the record shows that such policing has occurred and occurred in a heavy-handed way. Given the dangers of self-censorship in such a situation, I cannot agree that the dangers of ⊥ entanglement are insubstantial. Finally, the plurality suggests that the "nonideological" nature of a building, as contrasted with a teacher, reduces the need for policing. But the Federal Government imposes restrictions on every class taught in the federally assisted building. It is therefore not the "nonideological" building that is policed; rather, it is the courses given there and the teachers who teach them. Thus, the policing is precisely the same as under the state statutes, and that is what offends the Constitution.

⌐661

V

I, therefore, agree that the two state statutes that focus primarily on providing public funds to sectarian schools are unconstitutional. However, the federal statute in No. 153 is a general program of construction grants to all colleges and universities, including sectarian institutions. Since I believe the statute's extension of eligibility to sectarian institutions is severable from the broad general program authorized, I would hold the Higher Education Facilities Act unconstitutional only insofar as it authorized grants of federal tax monies to sectarian institutions—institutions that have a purpose or function to propagate or advance a particular religion. Therefore, if the District Court determines that any of the four institutional appellees here are "sectarian," that court, in my view, should enjoin the other appellees from making grants to it.

Mr. Justice WHITE, concurring in the judgments in No. 153 and No. 89 and dissenting in Nos. 569 and 570.

It is our good fortune that the States of this country long ago recognized that instruction of the young and old ranks high on the scale of proper governmental func⊥tions and not only undertook secular education as a public responsibility but also required compulsory attendance at school by their young. Having recognized the value of educated citizens and assumed the task of educating them, the States now before us assert a right to provide for the secular ed-

⌐662

ucation of children whether they attend public schools or choose to enter private institutions, even when those institutions are church- related. The Federal Government also asserts that it is entitled, where requested, to contribute to the cost of secular education by furnishing buildings and facilities to all institutions of higher learning, public and private alike. Both the United States and the States urge that if parents choose to have their children receive instruction in the required secular subjects in a school where religion is also taught and a religious atmosphere may prevail, part or all of the cost of such secular instruction may be paid for by government grants to the religious institution conducting the school and seeking the grant. Those who challenge this position would bar official contributions to secular education where the family prefers the parochial to both the public and nonsectarian private school.

The issue is fairly joined. It is precisely the kind of issue the Constitution contemplates this Court must ultimately decide. This is true although neither affirmance nor reversal of any of these cases follows automatically from the spare language of the First Amendment, from its history, or from the cases of this Court construing it and even though reasonable men can very easily and sensibly differ over the import of that language.

But, while the decision of the Court is legitimate, it is surely quite wrong in overturning the Pennsylvania and Rhode Island statutes on the ground that they amount to an establishment of religion forbidden by the First Amendment.

⊥ No one in these cases questions the constitutional right of parents to satisfy their state-imposed obligation to educate their children by sending them to private schools, sectarian or otherwise, as long as those schools meet minimum standards established for secular instruction. The States are not only permitted, but required by the Constitution, to free students attending private schools from any public school attendance obligation. The States may also furnish transportation for students and books for teaching secular subjects to students attending parochial and other private as well as public schools; we have also upheld arrangements whereby students are released from public school classes so that they may attend religious instruction. Outside the field of education, we have upheld Sunday closing laws, state and federal laws exempting church property and church activity from taxation, and governmental grants to religious organizations for the purpose of financing improvements in the facilities of hospitals managed and controlled by religious orders.

⌐663

Our prior cases have recognized the dual role of parochial schools in American society: they perform both religious and secular functions. Our cases also recognize that legislation having a secular purpose and extending governmental assistance to sectarian schools in the performance of their secular functions does not constitute "law[s] respecting an establishment of religion" forbidden by the First Amendment merely because a secular program may incidentally

|664 benefit a church in fulfilling its religious mis⊥sion. That religion may indirectly benefit from governmental aid to the secular activities of churches does not convert that aid into an impermissible establishment of religion.

This much the Court squarely holds in the *Tilton* case, where it also expressly rejects the notion that payments made directly to a religious institution are, without more, forbidden by the First Amendment. In *Tilton*, the Court decides that the Federal Government may finance the separate function of secular education carried on in a parochial setting. It reaches this result although sectarian institutions undeniably will obtain substantial benefit from federal aid; without federal funding to provide adequate facilities for secular education, the student bodies of those institutions might remain stationary or even decrease in size and the institutions might ultimately have to close their doors.

It is enough for me that the States and the Federal Government are financing a separable secular function of overriding importance in order to sustain the legislation here challenged. That religion and private interests other than education may substantially benefit does not convert these laws into impermissible establishments of religion.

It is unnecessary, therefore, to urge that the Free Exercise Clause of the First Amendment at least permits government in some respects to modify and mold its secular programs out of express concerns for

|665 free-exercise values. . . . ⊥ The Establishment Clause, however, coexists in the First Amendment with the Free Exercise Clause and the latter is surely relevant in cases such as these. Where a state program seeks to ensure the proper education of its young, in private as well as public schools, free exercise considerations at least counsel against refusing support for students attending parochial schools simply because in that setting they are also being instructed in the tenets of the faith they are constitutionally free to practice.

I would sustain both the federal and the Rhode Island programs at issue in these cases, and I therefore concur in the judgment in No. 153 and dissent from the judgments in Nos. 569 and 570. Although I would also reject the facial challenge to the Pennsylvania statute, I concur in the judgment in No. 89 for the reasons given below.

The Court strikes down the Rhode Island statute on its face. No fault is found with the secular purpose of the program; there is no suggestion that the purpose of the program was aid to religion disguised in secular attire. Nor does the Court find that the primary effect of the program is to aid religion rather than to implement secular goals. The Court never-

|666 theless finds ⊥ that impermissible "entanglement" will result from administration of the program. The

reasoning is a curious and mystifying blend, but a critical factor appears to be an unwillingness to accept the District Court's express findings that on the evidence before it none of the teachers here involved mixed religious and secular instruction. Rather, the District Court struck down the Rhode Island statute because it concluded that activities outside the secular classroom would probably have a religious content and that support for religious education therefore necessarily resulted from the financial aid to the secular programs, since that aid generally strengthened the parochial schools and increased the number of their students.

In view of the decision in *Tilton*, however, where these same factors were found insufficient to invalidate the federal plan, the Court is forced to other considerations. Accepting the District Court's observation in *DiCenso* that education is an integral part of the religious mission of the Catholic church—an observation that should neither surprise nor alarm anyone, especially judges who have already approved substantial aid to parochial schools in various forms—the majority then interposes findings and conclusions that the District Court expressly abjured, namely, that nuns, clerics, and dedicated Catholic laymen unavoidably pose a grave risk in that they might not be able to put aside their religion in the secular classroom. Although stopping short of considering them untrustworthy, the Court concludes that for them the difficulties of avoiding teaching religion along with secular subjects would pose intolerable risks and would in any event entail an unacceptable enforcement regime. Thus, the potential for impermissible fostering of religion in secular classrooms—an untested assumption of the Court—paradoxically renders unacceptable the State's efforts at insuring that secular teachers under religious discipline successfully avoid conflicts between the religious mission ⊥ of the school and the |667 secular purpose of the State's education program.

The difficulty with this is twofold. In the first place, it is contrary to the evidence and the District Court's findings in *DiCenso*. The Court points to nothing in this record indicating that any participating teacher had inserted religion into his secular teaching or had had any difficulty in avoiding doing so. The testimony of the teachers was quite the contrary. The District Court expressly found that "[t]his concern for religious values does not necessarily affect the content of secular subjects in diocesan schools. On the contrary, several teachers testified at trial that they did not inject religion into their secular classes, and one teacher deposed that he taught exactly as he had while employed in a public school. This testimony gains added credibility from the fact that several of the teachers were non-Catholics. Moreover, because of the restrictions of Rhode Island's textbook loan law . . . and the explicit requirement of the Salary Supplement Act, teaching materials used by applicants for aid must be approved for use in the public schools." *DiCenso* v. *Robinson.* Elsewhere, the District Court reiterated that the defect of the Rhode Island statute was "not that religious doctrine overtly intrudes into all instruction," but factors aside from secular courses plus the fact that good secular teaching was itself essential for implementing the religious mission of the parochial school.

Secondly, the Court accepts the model for the Catholic elementary and secondary schools that was rejected for the Catholic universities or colleges in the *Tilton* case. There it was urged that the Catholic condition of higher learning was an integral part of the religious mission of the church and that these institutions did everything they could to foster the faith. The Court's response was that on the record before it none of ⊥ the involved institutions was shown to have complied with the model and that it would not purport to pass on cases not before it. Here, however, the Court strikes down this Rhode Island statute based primarily on its own model and its own suppositions and unsupported views of what is likely to happen in Rhode Island parochial school classrooms, although on this record there is no indication that entanglement difficulties will accompany the salary supplement program.

The Court thus creates an insoluble paradox for the State and the parochial schools. The State cannot finance secular instruction if it permits religion to be taught in the same classroom; but if it exacts a promise that religion not be so taught—a promise the school and its teachers are quite willing and on this record able to give—and enforces it, it is then entangled in the "no entanglement" aspect of the Court's Establishment Clause jurisprudence.

Why the federal program in the *Tilton* case is not embroiled in the same difficulties is never adequately explained. Surely the notion that college students are more mature and resistant to indoctrination is a make-weight, for in *Tilton* there is careful note of the federal condition on funding and the enforcement mechanism available. If religious teaching in federally financed buildings was permitted, the powers of resistance of college students would in no way save the federal scheme. Nor can I imagine the basis for finding college clerics more reliable in keeping promises than their counterparts in elementary and secondary schools—particularly those in the Rhode Island case, since within five years the majority of teachers in Rhode Island parochial schools will be lay persons, many of them non-Catholic.

Both the District Court and this Court in *DiCenso* have seized on the Rhode Island formula for supplementing ⊥ teachers' salaries since it requires the State to verify the amount of school money spent for secular as distinguished from religious purposes. Only teachers in those schools having per-pupil expenditures for secular subjects below the state average qualify under the system, an aspect of the state scheme which is said to provoke serious "entangle-

ment." But this is also a slender reed on which to strike down this law, for as the District Court found, only once since the inception of the program has it been necessary to segregate expenditures in this manner.

The District Court also focused on the recurring nature of payments by the State of Rhode Island; salaries must be supplemented and money appropriated every year and hence the opportunity for controversy and friction over state aid to religious schools will constantly remain before the State. The Court in *DiCenso* adopts this theme, and makes much of the fact that under the federal scheme the grant to a religious institution is a one-time matter. But this argument is without real force. It is apparent that federal interest in any grant will be a continuing one since the conditions attached to the grant must be enforced. More important, the federal grant program is an ongoing one. The same grant will not be repeated, but new ones to the same or different schools will be made year after year. Thus the same potential for recurring political controversy accompanies the federal program. Rhode Island may have the problem of appropriating money each year to supplement the salaries of teachers, but the United States must each year seek financing for the new grants it desires to make and must supervise the ones already on the record.

With respect to Pennsylvania, the Court, accepting as true the factual allegations of the complaint, as it must for purposes of a motion to dismiss, would reverse the dismissal of the complaint and invalidate the legislation. ⊥ The critical allegations, as paraphrased by the Court, are that "the church-related elementary and secondary schools are controlled by religious organizations, have the purpose of propagating and promoting a particular religious faith, and conduct their operations to fulfill that purpose." From these allegations the Court concludes that forbidden entanglements would follow from enforcing compliance with the secular purpose for which the state money is being paid.

I disagree. There is no specific allegation in the complaint that sectarian teaching does or would invade secular classes supported by state funds. That the schools are operated to promote a particular religion is quite consistent with the view that secular teaching devoid of religious instruction can successfully be maintained, for good secular instruction is, as Judge Coffin wrote for the District Court in the Rhode Island case, essential to the success of the religious mission of the parochial school. I would no more here than in the Rhode Island case substitute presumption for proof that religion is or would be taught in state-financed secular courses or assume that enforcement measures would be so extensive as to border on a free exercise violation. We should not forget that the Pennsylvania statute does not compel church schools to accept state funds. I cannot hold that the First Amendment forbids an agreement be-

⌐668

⌐669

⌐670

tween the school and the State that the state funds would be used only to teach secular subjects. . . .

TILTON v. RICHARDSON

403 U.S. 672
ON APPEAL FROM THE UNITED STATES DISTRICT COURT
FOR THE DISTRICT OF CONNECTICUT
Argued March 2-3, 1971 — Decided June 28, 1971

⌐674   ⊥ *Mr. Chief Justice BURGER* announced the judgment of the Court and an opinion in which *Mr. Justice HARLAN, Mr. Justice STEWART*, and *Mr. Justice BLACKMUN* join.

This appeal presents important constitutional questions as to federal aid for church-related colleges and universities under Title I of the Higher Education Facilities Act of 1963, which provides construc-
⌐675 tion grants for buildings and facilities used ⊥ exclusively for secular educational purposes. We must determine first whether the Act authorizes aid to such church-related institutions, and, if so, whether the Act violates either the Establishment or Free Exercise Clauses of the First Amendment.

I

The Higher Education Facilities Act was passed in 1963 in response to a strong nationwide demand for the expansion of college and university facilities to meet the sharply rising number of young people demanding higher education. The Act authorizes federal grants and loans to "institutions of higher education" for the construction of a wide variety of "academic facilities." But § 751 (a) (2) expressly excludes "any facility used or to be used for sectarian instruction or as a place for religious worship, or . . . any facility which . . . is used or to be used primarily in connection with any part of the program of a school or department of divinity. . . ."

The Act is administered by the United States Commissioner of Education. He advises colleges and universities applying for funds that under the Act no part of the project may be used for sectarian instruction, religious worship, or the programs of a divinity school. The Commissioner requires applicants to provide assurances thar these restrictions will be respected. The United States retains a 20-year interest in any facility constructed with Title I funds. If, during this period, the recipient violates the statutory conditions, the United States is entitled to recover an amount equal to the proportion of its present value that the federal grant bore to the original cost of the facility. During the 20-year period, the statutory restrictions are enforced by the Office of Education primarily by way of on-site inspections.

⌐676   ⊥ Appellants are citizens and taxpayers of the United States and residents of Connecticut. They brought this suit for injunctive relief against the officials who administer the Act. Four church-related colleges and universities in Connecticut receiving federal construction grants under Title I were also named as defendants. Federal funds were used for five projects at these four institutions: (1) a library building at Sacred Heart University; (2) a music, drama, and arts building at Annhurst College; (3) a science building at Fairfield University; (4) a library building at Fairfield; and (5) a language laboratory at Albertus Magnus College.

A three-judge federal court was convened. Appellants attempted to show that the four recipient institutions were "sectarian" by introducing evidence of their relations with religious authorities, the content of their curricula, and other indicia of their religious character. The sponsorship of these institutions by religious organizations is not disputed. Appellee colleges introduced testimony that they had fully complied with the statutory conditions and that their religious affiliation in no way interfered with the performance of their secular educational functions. The District Court ruled that Title I authorized grants to church-related colleges and universities. It also sustained the constitutionality of the Act, finding that it had neither the purpose nor the effect of promoting religion. We noted probable jurisdiction.

II

We are satisfied that Congress intended the Act to include all colleges and universities regardless of any affiliation with or sponsorship by a religious body. Congress defined "institutions of higher education," which are eligible to receive aid under the Act, in broad and ⊥ inclusive terms. Certain institutions,   ⌐677 for example, institutions that are neither public nor nonprofit, are expressly excluded, and the Act expressly prohibits use of the facilities for religious purposes. But the Act makes no reference to religious affiliation or nonaffiliation. Under these circumstances "institutions of higher education" must be taken to include church-related colleges and universities.

This interpretation is fully supported by the legislative history. Although there was extensive debate on the wisdom and constitutionality of aid to institutions affiliated with religious organizations, Congress clearly included them in the program. The sponsors of the Act so stated and amendments aimed at the exclusion of church-related institutions were defeated.

III

Numerous cases considered by the Court have noted the internal tension in the First Amendment between the Establishment Clause and the Free Exercise Clause. *Walz* v. *Tax Comm'n* is the most recent decision seeking to define the boundaries of the neutral area between these two provisions within which the legislature may legitimately act. There, as in other decisions, the Court treated the three main concerns against which the Establishment Clause sought to protect: "sponsorship, financial support, and active involvement of the sovereign in religious activity."

Every analysis must begin with the candid acknowledgment that there is no single constitutional caliper that can be used to measure the precise degree to which these three factors are present or absent. Instead, our ⊥ analysis in this area must begin with a consideration of the cumulative criteria developed over many years and applying to a wide range of governmental action challenged as violative of the Establishment Clause.

⌐678

There are always risks in treating criteria discussed by the Court from time to time as "tests" in any limiting sense of that term. Constitutional adjudication does not lend itself to the absolutes of the physical sciences or mathematics. The standards should rather be viewed as guidelines with which to identify instances in which the objectives of the Religion Clauses have been impaired. And, as we have noted in *Lemon* v. *Kurtzman* and *Earley* v. *DiCenso*, candor compels the acknowledgment that we can only dimly perceive the boundaries of permissible government activity in this sensitive area of constitutional adjudication.

Against this background we consider four questions: First, does the Act reflect a secular legislative purpose? Second, is the primary effect of the Act to advance or inhibit religion? Third, does the administration of the Act foster an excessive government entanglement with religion? Fourth, does the implementation of the Act inhibit the free exercise of religion?

(a)

The stated legislative purpose appears in the preamble where Congress found and declared that "the security and welfare of the United States require that this and future generations of American youth be assured ample opportunity for the fullest development of their intellectual capacities, and that this opportunity will be jeopardized unless the Nation's colleges and universities are encouraged and assisted in their efforts to accommodate rapidly growing numbers of youth who aspire to a higher education."

⌐679

⊥ This expresses a legitimate secular objective entirely appropriate for governmental action.

The simplistic argument that every form of financial aid to church-sponsored activity violates the Religion Clauses was rejected long ago in *Bradfield* v. *Roberts*. There a federal construction grant to a hospital operated by a religious order was upheld. Here the Act is challenged on the ground that its primary effect is to aid the religious purposes of church-related colleges and universities. Construction grants surely aid these institutions in the sense that the construction of buildings will assist them to perform their various functions. But bus transportation, textbooks, and tax exemptions all gave aid in

the sense that religious bodies would otherwise have been forced to find other sources from which to finance these services. Yet all of these forms of governmental assistance have been upheld. The crucial question is not whether some benefit accrues to a religious institution as a consequence of the legislative program, but whether its principal or primary effect advances religion.

A possibility always exists, of course, that the legitimate objectives of any law or legislative program may be subverted by conscious design or lax enforcement. There is nothing new in this argument. But judicial concern about these possibilities cannot, standing alone, warrant striking down a statute as unconstitutional.

The Act itself was carefully drafted to ensure that the federally subsidized facilities would be devoted to the secular and not the religious function of the recipient institutions. It authorizes grants and loans only for academic facilities that will be used for defined secular purposes and expressly prohibits their use for religious ⊥ instruction, training, or worship. These restrictions have been enforced in the Act's actual administration, and the record shows that some church-related institutions have been required to disgorge benefits for failure to obey them.

⌐680

Finally, this record fully supports the findings of the District Court that none of the four church-related institutions in this case has violated the statutory restrictions. The institutions presented evidence that there had been no religious services or worship in the federally financed facilities, that there are no religious symbols or plaques in or on them, and that they had been used solely for nonreligious purposes. On this record, therefore, these buildings are indistinguishable from a typical state university facility. Appellants presented no evidence to the contrary.

Appellants instead rely on the argument that government may not subsidize any activities of an institution of higher learning that in some of its programs teaches religious doctrines. This argument rests on *Everson* where the majority stated that the Establishment Clause barred any "tax . . . levied to support any religious . . . institutions . . . whatever form they may adopt to teach or practice religion." In *Allen*, however, it was recognized that the Court had fashioned criteria under which an analysis of a statute's purpose and effect was determinative as to whether religion was being advanced by government action.

Under this concept appellants' position depends on the validity of the proposition that religion so permeates the secular education provided by church-related colleges and universities that their religious and secular educational functions are in fact inseparable. The argument that government grants would thus inevitably advance ⊥ religion did not escape the notice of Congress. It was carefully and thoughtfully debated, but was found unpersuasive. It

⌐681

was also considered by this Court in *Allen*. There the Court refused to assume that religiosity in parochial elementary and secondary schools necessarily permeates the secular education that they provide.

This record, similarly, provides no basis for any such assumption here. Two of the five federally financed buildings involved in this case are libraries. The District Court found that no classes had been conducted in either of these facilities and that no restrictions were imposed by the institutions on the books that they acquired. There is no evidence to the contrary. The third building was a language laboratory at Albertus Magnus College. The evidence showed that this facility was used solely to assist students with their pronunciation in modern foreign languages—a use which would seem peculiarly unrelated and unadaptable to religious indoctrinarion. Federal grants were also used to build a science building at Fairfield University and a music, drama, and arts building at Annhurst College.

There is no evidence that religion seeps into the use of any of these facilities. Indeed, the parties stipulated in the District Court that courses at these institutions are taught according to the academic requirements intrinsic to the subject matter and the individual teacher's concept of professional standards. Although appellants introduced several institutional documents that stated certain religious restrictions on what could be taught, other evidence showed that these restrictions were not in fact enforced and that the schools were characterized by an atmosphere of academic freedom rather than religous indoctrination. All four institutions, for example, subscribe to the 1940 Statement of Principles on ⊥682 Aca⊥demic Freedom and Tenure endorsed by the American Association of University Professors and the Association of American Colleges.

Rather than focus on the four defendant colleges and universities involved in this case, however, appellants seek to shift our attention to a "composite profile" that they have constructed of the "typical sectarian" institution of higher education. We are told that such a "composite" institution imposes religious restrictions on admissions, requires attendance at religious activities, compels obedience to the doctrines and dogmas of the faith, requires instruction in theology and doctrine, and does everything it can to propagate a particular religion. Perhaps some church-related schools fit the pattern that appellants describe. Indeed, some colleges have been declared ineligible for aid by the authorities that administer the Act. But appellants do not contend that these four institutions fall within this category. Individual projects can be properly evaluated if and when challenges arise with respect to particular recipients and some evidence is then presented to show that the institution does in fact possess these characteristics. We cannot, however, strike down an Act of Congress on the basis of a hypothetical "profile."

(b)

Although we reject appellants' broad constitutional arguments we do perceive an aspect in which the statute's enforcement provisions are inadequate to ensure that the impact of the federal aid will not advance religion. If a recipient institution violates any of the statutory restrictions on the use of a federally financed facility, § 754 (b) (2) permits the Government to recover an amount equal to the proportion of the facility's present value that the federal grant bore to its original cost.

⊥ This remedy, however, is available to the Government only if the statutory conditions are violated "within twenty years after completion of construction." This 20-year period is termed by the statute as "the period of Federal interest" and reflects Congress' finding that after 20 years "the public benefit accruing to the United States" from the use of the federally financed facility "will equal or exceed in value" the amount of the federal grant.   ⊥683

Under § 754 (b) (2), therefore, a recipient institution's obligation not to use the facility for sectarian instruction or religious worship would appear to expire at the end of 20 years. We note, for example, that under § 718 (b) (7) (C), an institution applying for a federal grant is only required to provide assurances that the facility will not be used for sectarian instruction or religious worship "during at least the period of the Federal interest therein (as defined in section 754 of this title)."

Limiting the prohibition for religious use of the structure to 20 years obviously opens the facility to use for any purpose at the end of that period. It cannot be assumed that a substantial structure has no value after that period and hence the unrestricted use of a valuable property is in effect a contribution of some value to a religious body. Congress did not base the 20-year provision on any contrary conclusion. If, at the end of 20 years, the building is, for example, converted into a chapel or otherwise used to promote religious interests, the original federal grant will in part have the effect of advancing religion.

To this extent the Act therefore trespasses on the Religion Clauses. The restrictive obligations of a recipient institution under § 751 (a) (2) cannot, compatibly with the Religion Clauses, expire while the building has substantial value. This circumstance does not require us to ⊥ invalidate the entire Act, however. . . .   ⊥684

We have found nothing in the statute or its objectives intimating that Congress considered the 20-year provision essential to the statutory program as a whole. ln view of the broad and important goals that Congress intended this legislation to serve, there is no basis for assuming that the Act would have failed of passage without this provision; nor will its excision impair either the operation or administration of the Act in any significant respect.

IV

We next turn to the question of whether excessive entanglements characterize the relationship between government and church under the Act. Our decision today in ⊥ *Lemon* v. *Kurtzman* and *Robinson* v. *DiCenso* has discussed and applied this independent measure of constitutionality under the Religion Clauses. There we concluded that excessive entanglements between government and religion were fostered by Pennsylvania and Rhode Island statutory programs under which state aid was provided to parochial elementary and secondary schools. Here, however, three factors substantially diminish the extent and the potential danger of the entanglement.

In *DiCenso* the District Court found that the parochial schools in Rhode Island were "an integral part of the religious mission of the Catholic Church." There, the record fully supported the conclusion that the inculcation of religious values was a substantial if not the dominant purpose of the institutions. The Pennsylvania case was decided on the pleadings, and hence we accepted as true the allegations that the parochial schools in that State shared the same characteristics.

Appellants' complaint here contains similar allegations. But they were denied by the answers, and there was extensive evidence introduced on the subject. Although the District Court made no findings with respect to the religious character of the four institutions of higher learning, we are not required to accept the allegations as true under these circumstances, particularly where, as here, appellants themselves do not contend that these four institutions are "sectarian."

There are generally significant differences between the religious aspects of church-related institutions of higher learning and parochial elementary and secondary schools. The "affirmative if not dominant policy" of the instruction in pre-college church schools is "to assure future ⊥ adherents to a particular faith by having control of their total education at an early age." *Walz* v. *Tax Comm'n.* There is substance to the contention that college students are less impressionable and less susceptible to religious indoctrination. Common observation would seem to support that view, and Congress may well have entertained it. The skepticism of the college student is not an inconsiderable barrier to any attempt or tendency to subvert the congressional objectives and limitations. Furthermore, by their very nature, college and postgraduate courses tend to limit the opportunities for sectarian influence by virtue of their own internal disciplines. Many church-related colleges and universities are characterized by a high degree of academic freedom and seek to evoke free and critical responses from their students.

The record here would not support a conclusion that any of these four institutions departed from this general pattern. All four schools are governed by Catholic religious organizations, and the faculties and student bodies at each are predominantly Catholic. Nevertheless, the evidence shows that non-Catholics were admitted as students and given faculty appointments. Not one of these four institutions requires its students to attend religious services. Although all four schools require their students to take theology courses, the parties stipulated that these courses are taught according to the academic requirements of the subject matter and the teacher's concept of professional standards. The parties also stipulated that the courses covered a range of human religious ⊥ experiences and are not limited to courses about the Roman Catholic religion. The schools introduced evidence that they made no attempt to indoctrinate students or to proselytize. Indeed, some of the required theology courses at Albertus Magnus and Sacred Heart are taught by rabbis. Finally, as we have noted, these four schools subscribe to a well-established set of principles of academic freedom, and nothing in this record shows that these principles are not in fact followed. In short, the evidence shows institutions with admittedly religious functions but whose predominant higher education mission is to provide their students with a secular education.

Since religious indoctrination is not a substantial purpose or activity of these church-related colleges and universities, there is less likelihood than in primary and secondary schools that religion will permeate the area of secular education. This reduces the risk that government aid will in fact serve to support religious activities. Correspondingly, the necessity for intensive government surveillance is diminished and the resulting entanglements between government and religion lessened. Such inspection as may be necessary to ascertain that the facilities are devoted to secular education is minimal and indeed hardly more than the inspections that States impose over all private schools within the reach of compulsory education laws.

The entanglement between church and state is also lessened here by the nonideological character of the aid that the Government provides. Our cases from *Everson* to *Allen* have permitted church-related schools to receive government aid in the form of secular, neutral, or nonideological services, facilities, or materials that are supplied to all students regardless of the affiliation of the school that they attend. In *Lemon* and *DiCenso*, however, the state programs subsidized teachers, either directly or indirectly. Since teachers are not necessarily ⊥ religiously neutral, greater governmental surveillance would be required to guarantee that state salary aid would not in fact subsidize religious instruction. There we found the resulting entanglement excessive. Here, on the other hand, the Government provides facilities that are themselves religiously neutral. The risks of Government aid to religion and the corresponding need for surveillance are therefore reduced.

Finally, government entanglements with religion are reduced by the circumstance that, unlike the direct and continuing payments under the Pennsylvania program, and all the incidents of regulation and surveillance, the Government aid here is a one-time, single-purpose construction grant. There are no continuing financial relationships or dependencies, no annual audits, and no government analysis of an institution's expenditures on secular as distinguished from religious activities. Inspection as to use is a minimal contact.

No one of these three factors standing alone is necessarily controlling; cumulatively all of them shape a narrow and limited relationship with government which involves fewer and less significant contacts than the two state schemes before us in *Lemon* and *DiCenso*. The relationship therefore has less potential for realizing the substantive evils against which the Religion Clauses were intended to protect.

We think that cumulatively these three factors also substantially lessen the potential for divisive religious fragmentation in the political arena. This conclusion is admittedly difficult to document, but neither have appellants pointed to any continuing religious aggravation on this matter in the political processes. Possibly this can be explained by the character and diversity of the recipient colleges and universities and the absence of any intimate continuing relationship or dependency between government and religiously affiliated institutions. The ⊥ |689 potential for divisiveness inherent in the essentially local problems of primary and secondary schools is significantly less with respect to a college or university whose student constituency is not local but diverse and widely dispersed.

V

Finally, we must consider whether the implementation of the Act inhibits the free exercise of religion in violation of the First Amendment. Appellants claim that the Free Exercise Clause is violated because they are compelled to pay taxes, the proceeds of which in part finance grants under the Act. Appellants, however, are unable to identify any coercion directed at the practice or exercise of their religious beliefs. Their share of the cost of the grants under the Act is not fundamentally distinguishable from the impact of the tax exemption sustained in *Walz* or the provision of textbooks upheld in *Allen*.

We conclude that the Act does not violate the Religion Clauses of the First Amendment except that part of § 754 (b) (2) providing a 20-year limitation on the religious use restrictions contained in § 751 (a) (2). We remand to the District Court with directions to enter a judgment consistent with this opinion.

Vacated and remanded.

Mr. Justice DOUGLAS, with whom *Mr. Justice BLACK* and *Mr. Justice MARSHALL* concur, dissenting in part.

The correct constitutional principle for this case was stated by President Kennedy in 1961 when questioned as ⊥ to his policy respecting aid to private |690 and parochial schools: "[T]he Constitution clearly prohibits aid to the school, to parochial schools. I don't think there is any doubt of that.

"The Everson case, which is probably the most celebrated case, provided only by a 5 to 4 decision was it possible for a local community to provide bus rides to nonpublic school children. But all through the majority and minority statements on that particular question there was a very clear prohibition against aid to the school direct. The Supreme Court made its decision in the Everson case by determining that the aid was to the child, not to the school. Aid to the school is—there isn't any room for debate on that subject. It is prohibited by the Constitution, and the Supreme Court has made that very clear. And therefore there would be no possibility of our recommending it."

Taxpayer appellants brought this suit challenging the validity of certain expenditures, made by the Department of Health, Education, and Welfare, for the construction of (1) a library at Sacred Heart University, (2) a music, drama, and arts building at Annhurst College, (3) a library and a science building at Fairfield University, and (4) a laboratory at Albertus Magnus College. The complaint alleged that all of these institutions were controlled by religious orders and the Roman Catholic Diocese of Bridgeport, Conn., and that if the funds for construction were authorized by Title I of the Higher Education Facilities Act of 1963, then that statute was unconstitutional because it violated the ⊥ Establishment Clause. A three-judge District Court was |691 convened and rejected appellants' claims.

Title I of the Higher Education Facilities Act of 1963 authorizes grants and loans up to 50% of the cost for the construction of undergraduate academic facilities in both public and private colleges and universities. A project is eligible if construction will result "in an urgently needed substantial expansion of the institution's student enrollment capacity, capacity to provide needed health care to students or personnel of the institution, or capacity to carry out extension and continuing education programs on the campus of such institution." The Commissioner of Education is authorized to prescribe basic criteria and is instructed to "give special consideration to expansion of undergraduate enrollment capacity."

Academic facilities are "structures suitable for use as classrooms, laboratories, libraries, and related facilities necessary or appropriate for instruction of students, or for research . . . programs." Specifically excluded are facilities "used or to be used for sectarian instruction or as a place for religious worship" or any facilities used "primarily in connection with any part of the program of a school or department of divinity." The United States retains a 20-year interest in the facilities and should a facility be used other than as an academic facility then the United States is entitled to recover an amount equal to the proportion of present value which the federal grant bore to the original cost of the facility. According to a stipulation entered below, during the 20 years the Office of Education attempts to insure that facilities are used in the manner required by the Act primarily by on-site inspections. At the end of the 20-year period the federal interest in the facility ceases and ⊥ the college may use it as it pleases.

The public purpose in secular education is, to be sure, furthered by the program. Yet the sectarian purpose is aided by making the parochial school system viable. The purpose is to increase "student enrollment" and the students obviously aimed at are those of the particular faith now financed by taxpayers' money. Parochial schools are not beamed at agnostics, atheists, or those of a competing sect. The more sophisticated institutions may admit minorities; but the dominant religious character is not changed.

The reversion of the facility to the parochial school at the end of 20 years is an outright grant, measurable by the present discounted worth of the facility. A gift of taxpayers' funds in that amount would plainly be unconstitutional. The Court properly bars it even though disguised in the form of a reversionary interest.

But the invalidation of this one clause cannot cure the constitutional infirmities of the statute as a whole. The Federal Government is giving religious schools a block grant to build certain facilities. The fact that money is ⊥ given once at the beginning of a program rather than apportioned annually as in *Lemon* and *DiCenso* is without constitutional significance. The First Amendment bars establishment of a religion. And as I noted today in *Lemon* and *DiCenso*, this bar has been consistently interpreted from *Everson* v. *Board of Education*, through *Torcaso* v. *Watkins*, as meaning: "No tax in any amount, large or small, can be levied to support any religious activities or institutions, whatever they may be called, or whatever form they may adopt to teach or practice religion." Thus it is hardly impressive that rather than giving a smaller amount of money annually over a long period of years, Congress instead gives a large amount all at once. The plurality's distinction is in effect that small violations of the First Amendment over a period of years are unconstitutional while a huge violation occurring only once is *de minimis*. I cannot agree with such sophistry.

What I have said in *Lemon* and in the *DiCenso* cases decided today is relevant here. The facilities financed by taxpayers' funds are not to be used for "sectarian" purposes. Religious teaching and secular teaching are so enmeshed in parochial schools that only the strictest supervision and surveillance would insure compliance with the condition. Parochial schools may require religious exercises, even in the classroom. A parochial school operates on one budget. Money not spent for one purpose becomes available for other purposes. Thus the fact that there are no religious observances in federally financed facilities is not controlling because required religious observances will take place in other buildings. Our decision in *Engel* v. *Vitale* held that a requirement of a prayer in public schools violated the Establishment Clause. Once these schools become federally funded they become bound by federal standards ⊥ and accordingly adherence to *Engel* would require an end to required religious exercises. That kind of surveillance and control will certainly be obnoxious to the church authorities and if done will radically change the character of the parochial school. Yet if that surveillance is not searching and continuous, this federal financing is obnoxious under the Establishment and Free Exercise Clauses for the reasons stated in the companion cases.

In other words, surveillance creates an entanglement of government and religion which the First Amendment was designed to avoid. Yet after today's decision there will be a requirement of surveillance which will last for the useful life of the building and as we have previously noted, "[it] is hardly lack of due process for the Government to regulate that which it subsidizes." *Wickard* v. *Filburn*. The price of the subsidy under the Act is violation of the Free Exercise Clause. Could a course in the History of Methodism be taught in a federally financed building? Would a religiously slanted version of the Reformation or Quebec politics under Duplessis be permissible? How can the Government know what is taught in the federally financed building without a continuous auditing of classroom instruction? Yet both the Free Exercise Clause and academic freedom are violated when the Government agent must be present to determine whether the course content is satisfactory.

As I said in the *Lemon* and *DiCenso* cases, a parochial school is a unitary institution with subtle blending of sectarian and secular instruction. Thus the practices of religious schools are in no way affected by the minimal requirement that the government financed facility may ⊥ not "be used for sectarian instruction or as a place of religious worship." Money saved from one item in the budget is free to be used elsewhere. By conducting religious services in another building, the school has—rent free—a building for nonsectarian use. This is not called Establishment simply because the government retains a continuing interest in the building for its useful life, even though the religious schools need never pay a cent for the use of the building.

Much is made of the need for public aid to church schools in light of their pressing fiscal problems. Dr. Eugene C. Blake of the Presbyterian Church, however, wrote in 1959: "When one remembers that churches pay no inheritance tax (churches do not die), that churches may own and operate business and be exempt from the 52 percent corporate income tax, and that real property used for church purposes (which in some states are most generously construed) is tax exempt, it is not unreasonable to prophesy that with reasonably prudent management, the churches ought to be able to control the whole economy of the nation within the predictable future. That the growing wealth and property of the churches was partially responsible for revolutionary expropriations of church property in England in the sixteenth century, in France in the eighteenth century, in Italy in the nineteenth century, and in Mexico, Russia, Czechoslovakia and Hungary (to name a few examples) in the twentieth century, seems self-evident. A government with mounting tax problems cannot be expected to keep its hands off the wealth of a rich church forever. That such a revolution is always ⊥ accompanied by anticlericalism and atheism should not be surprising."

⌊696

The mounting wealth of the churches makes ironic their incessant demands on the public treasury. I said in my dissent in *Walz* v. *Tax Comm'n*: "The religiously used real estate of the churches today constitutes a vast domain. Their assets total over $141 billion and their annual income at least $22 billion. And the extent to which they are feeding from the public trough in a variety of forms is alarming."

It is almost unbelievable that we have made the radical departure from Madison's Remonstrance memorialized in today's decision.

⌊697

⊥ I dissent not because of any lack of respect for parochial schools but out of a feeling of despair that the respect which through history has been accorded the First Amendment is this day lost.

It should be remembered that in this case we deal with federal grants and with the command that "Congress shall make no law respecting an establishment of religion, or prohibiting the free exercise thereof." The million-dollar grants sustained today put Madison's miserable "three pence" to shame. But he even thought, as I do, that even a small amount coming out of the pocket of taxpayers and going into the coffers of a church was not in keeping with our constitutional idea.

I would reverse the judgment below.

COMMITTEE FOR PUBLIC EDUCATION & RELIGIOUS LIBERTY v. NYQUIST

413 U.S. 756
ON APPEAL FROM THE UNITED STATES DISTRICT COURT
FOR THE SOUTHERN DISTRICT OF NEW YORK
Argued April 16, 1973 — Decided June 25, 1973

⊥ *Mr. Justice* POWELL delivered the opinion of the Court.   ⌊759

This case raises a challenge under the Establishment Clause of the First Amendment to the constitutionality of a recently enacted New York law which provides financial assistance, in several ways, to nonpublic elementary and secondary schools in that State. The case involves an intertwining of societal and constitutional issues of the greatest importance.

⊥ James Madison, in his Memorial and Remonstrance Against Religious Assessments, admonished   ⌊760
that a "prudent jealousy" for religious freedoms required that they never become "entangled . . . in precedents." His strongly held convictions, coupled with those of Thomas Jefferson and others among the Founders, are reflected in the first Clauses of the First Amendment of the Bill of Rights, which state that "Congress shall make no law respecting an establishment of religion, or prohibiting the free exercise thereof." Yet, despite Madison's admonition and the "sweep of the absolute prohibition" of the Clauses, this Nation's history has not been one of entirely sanitized separation between Church and State. It has never been thought either possible or desirable to enforce a regime of total separation, and as a consequence cases arising under these Clauses have presented some of the most perplexing questions to come before this Court. Those cases have occasioned thorough and ⊥ thoughtful scholarship   ⌊761
by several of this Court's most respected former Justices, including Justices Black, Frankfurter, Harlan, Jackson, Rutledge, and Chief Justice Warren.

As a result of these decisions and opinions, it may no longer be said that the Religion Clauses are free of "entangling" precedents. Neither, however, may it be said that Jefferson's metaphoric "wall of separation" between Church and State has become "as winding as the famous serpentine wall" he designed for the University of Virginia. *McCollum* v. *Board of Education* (Jackson, J., separate opinion). Indeed, the controlling constitutional standards have become firmly rooted and the broad contours of our inquiry are now well defined. Our task, therefore, is to assess New York's several forms of aid in the light of principles already delineated.

I

In May 1972, the Governor of New York signed into law several amendments to the State's Education and Tax Laws. The first five sections of these amendments established three distinct financial aid programs for non⊥public elementary and secondary schools. Almost immediately after the signing of these measures a complaint was filed in the United States District Court for the Southern District of New York challenging each of the three forms of aid as violative of the Establishment Clause. The plaintiffs were an unincorporated association, known as the Committee for Public Education and Religious Liberty (PEARL), and several individuals who were residents and taxpayers in New York, some of whom had children attending public schools. Named as defendants were the State Commissioner of Education, the Comptroller, and the Commissioner of Taxation and Finance. Motions to intervene on behalf of defendants were granted to a group of parents with children enrolled in nonpublic schools, and to the Majority Leader and President pro tem of the New York State Senate. By consent of the parties, a three-judge court was convened pursuant to 28 U.S.C. § § 2281 and 2283, and the case was decided without an evidentiary hearing. Because the questions before the District Court were resolved on the basis of the pleadings, that court's decision turned on the constitutionality of each provision on its face.

The first section of the challenged enactment, entitled "Health and Safety Grants for Nonpublic School Children," provides for direct money grants from the State to "qualifying" nonpublic schools to be used for the "maintenance and repair of . . . school facilities and equipment to ensure the health, welfare and safety of enrolled pupils." A "qualifying" school is any non⊥public, nonprofit elementary or secondary school which "has been designated during the [immediately preceding] year as serving a high concentration of pupils from low-income families for purposes of Title IV of the Federal Higher Education Act of 1965. Such schools are entitled to receive a grant of $30 per pupil per year, or $40 per pupil per year if the facilities are more than 25 years old. Each school is required to submit to the Commissioner of Education an audited statement of its expenditures for maintenance and repair during the preceding year, and its grant may not exceed the total of such expenses. The Commissioner is also required to ascertain the average per-pupil cost for equivalent maintenance and repair services in the public schools, and in no event may the grant to nonpublic qualifying schools exceed 50% of that figure.

"Maintenance and repair" is defined by the statute to include "the provision of heat, light, water, ventilation and sanitary faciltes, cleaning, janitorial and custodial services; snow removal; necessary upkeep and renovation of buildings, grounds and equipment; fire and accident protection; and such other items as

the commissioner may deem necessary to ensure the health, welfare and safety of enrolled pupils." This section is prefaced by a series of legislative findings which shed light on the State's purpose in enacting the law. These findings conclude that the State "has a primary responsibility to ensure the health, welfare and safety of children attending . . . nonpublic schools"; that the "fiscal crisis in nonpublic education . . . has caused a diminution of proper maintenance and repair programs, threatening the health, welfare and safety of nonpublic school children" ⊥ in low-income urban areas; and that "a healthy and safe school environment" contributes "to the stability of urban neighborhoods." For these reasons, the statute declares that "the state has the right to make grants for maintenance and repair expenditures which are clearly secular, neutral and nonideological in nature."

The remainder of the challenged legislation—§ § 2 through 5—is a single package captioned the "Elementary and Secondary Education Opportunity Program." It is composed, essentially, of two parts, a tuition grant program and a tax benefit program. Section 2 establishes a limited plan providing tuition reimbursements to parents of children attending elementary or secondary nonpublic schools. To qualify under this section the parent must have an annual taxable income of less than $5,000. The amount of reimbursement is limited to $50 for each grade school child and $100 for each high school child. Each parent is required, however, to submit to the Commissioner of Education a verified statement containing a receipted tuition bill, and the amount of state reimbursement may not exceed 50% of that figure. No restrictions are imposed on the use of the funds by the reimbursed parents.

This section, like § 1, is prefaced by a series of legislative findings designed to explain the impetus for the State's action. Expressing a dedication to the "vitality of our pluralistic society," the findings state that a "healthy competitive and diverse alternative to public education is not only desirable but indeed vital to a state and nation that have continually reaffirmed the value of individual differences." The findings further emphasize that the ⊥ right to select among alternative educational systems "is diminished or even denied to children of lower- income families, whose parents, of all groups, have the least options in determining where their children are to be educated." Turning to the public schools, the findings state that any "precipitous decline in the number of nonpublic school pupils would cause a massive increase in public school enrollment and costs," an increase that would "aggravate an already serious fiscal crisis in public education" and would "seriously jeopardize the quality education for all children." Based on these premises, the statute asserts the State's right to relieve the financial burden of parents who send their children to nonpublic schools through this tuition reimbursement program. Repeating the declaration contained in § 1, the findings conclude that "such assistance is clearly secular, neutral and nonideological."

The remainder of the "Elementary and Secondary Education Opportunity Program," contained in § § 3, 4, and 5 of the challenged law, is designed to provide a form of tax relief to those who fail to qualify for tuition reimbursement. Under these sections parents may subtract from their adjusted gross income for state income tax purposes a designated amount for each dependent for whom they have paid at least $50 in nonpublic school tuition. If the taxpayer's adjusted gross income is less than $9,000 he may subtract $1000 for each of as many as three dependents. As the taxpayer's income rises, the amount he may subtract diminishes. Thus, if a taxpayer has adjusted gross income of $15,000, he may subtract only $400 per dependent, and if his income is ⊥$25,000 or more, no deduction is allowed. The amount of the deduction is not dependent upon how much the taxpayer actually paid for nonpublic school tuition, and is given in addition to any deductions to which the taxpayer may be entitled for other religious or charitable contributions. As indicated in the memorandum from the Majority Leader and President pro tem of the Senate, submitted to each New York legislator during consideration of the bill, the actual tax benefits under these provisions were carefully calculated in advance. Thus, comparable tax ⊥ benefits pick up at approximately the point at which tuition reimbursement benefits leave off.

While the scheme of the enactment indicates that the purposes underlying the promulgation of the tuition reimbursement program should be regarded as pertinent as well to these tax law sections, § 3 does contain an additional series of legislative findings. Those findings may be summarized as follows: (i) contributions to religious, charitable and educational institutions are already deductible from gross income; (ii) nonpublic educational institutions are accorded tax exempt status; (iii) such institutions provide educations for children attending them and also serve to relieve the public school systems of the burden of providing for their education; and, therefore, (iv) the "legislature . . . finds and determines that similar modifications . . . should also be provided to parents for tuition paid to nonpublic elementary and secondary schools on behalf of their dependents."

Although no record was developed in this case, a number of pertinent generalizations may be made about the nonpublic schools which would benefit from these enactments. The District Court, relying on findings in a similar case recently decided by the same court, adopted a profile of these sectarian, nonpublic schools similar to the one suggested in the plaintiffs' complaint. Qualifying institutions, under all three segments of the enactment, could be ones that: "(a) impose religious restrictions on admissions; (b) require attendance of pupils at religious activities; (c) require obedience by students to the doctrines and dogmas of a particular faith; (d) require pupils to attend instruction in the theology or doc⊥trine of a particular faith; (e) are an integral part of the religious mission of the church sponsoring it; (f) have as a substantial purpose the inculcation of religious values; (g) impose religious restrictions on faculty appointments; and (h) impose religious restrictions on what or how the faculty may teach." 350 F. Supp., at 663.

Of course, the characteristics of individual schools may vary widely from that profile. Some 700,000 to 800,000 students, constituting almost 20% of the State's entire elementary and secondary school population, attend over 2,000 nonpublic schools, approximately 85% of which are church-affiliated. And while "all or practically all" of the 280 schools entitled to receive "maintenance and repair" grants "are related to the Roman Catholic Church and teach Catholic religious doctrine to some degree," institutions qualifying under the remainder of the statute include a substantial number of Jewish, Lutheran, Episcopal, Seventh Day Adventist, and other church-affiliated schools.

Plaintiffs argued below that because of the substantially religious character of the intended beneficiaries, each of the State's three enactments offended the Establishment Clause. The District Court, in an opinion carefully canvassing this Court's recent precedents, held ⊥ unanimously that § 1 (maintenance and repair grants) and § 2 (tuition reimbursement grants) were invalid. As to the income tax provisions of § § 3, 4, and 5, however, a majority of the District Court, over the dissent of Circuit Judge Hays, held that the Establishment Clause had not been violated. Finding the provisions of the law severable, it enjoined permanently any further implementation of § § 1 and 2 but declared the remainder of the law independently enforceable. The plaintiffs appealed directly to this Court, challenging the District Court's adverse decision as to the third segment of the statute. The defendant state officials have appealed so much of the court's decision as invalidates the first and second portions of the 1972 law, the intervenor Majority Leader and President pro tem of the Senate also appeals from those aspects of the lower court's opinion, and the intervening parents of nonpublic school children have appealed only from the decision as to § 2. This Court noted probable jurisdiction over each appeal and ordered the cases consolidated for oral argument. Thus, the constitutionality of each of New York's recently promulgated aid provisions is squarely before us. We affirm the District Court insofar as it struck down § § 1 and 2 and reverse its determination regarding § § 3, 4, and 5.

II

⊥ The history of the Establishment Clause has been recounted frequently and need not be repeated here. See *Everson* v. *Board of Education* (Black, J., opinion of the Court), (Rutledge, J., dissenting); |771 *McCollum* v. *Board* ⊥ *of Education* (Frankfurter, J., separate opinion); *McGowan* v. *Maryland*; *Engel* v. *Vitale*. It is enough to note that it is now firmly established that a law may be one "respecting the establishment of religion" even though its consequence is not to promote a "state religion," *Lemon* v. *Kurtzman*, and even though it does not aid one religion more than another but merely benefits all religions alike. *Everson* v. *Board of Education*. It is equally well established, however, that not every law that confers an "indirect," "remote," or "incidental" benefit upon religious institutions is, for that reason |772 alone, constitutionally invalid. ⊥ What our cases require is careful examination of any law challenged on establishment grounds with a view to ascertaining whether it furthers any of the evils against which that Clause protects. Primary among those evils have been "sponsorship, financial support, and active involvement in the sovereign in religious activity." *Walz* v. *Tax Commission*.

Most of the cases coming to this Court raising Establishment Clause questions have involved the relationship between religion and education. Among these religion-education precedents, two general categories of cases may be identified: those dealing with religious activities within the public schools, and those involving public aid in varying forms to sectarian educational institutions. While the New York legislation places this case in the latter category, its resolution requires consideration not only of the several aid-to-sectarian-education cases but also of our other education precedents and of several important non-education cases. For the now well defined three-part test that has emerged from our decisions is a product of considerations derived from the full sweep of the Establishment Clause cases. |773 Taken together ⊥ these decisions dictate that to pass muster under the Establishment Clause the law in question, first, must reflect a clearly secular legislative purpose, *e.g.*, *Epperson* v. *Arkansas*; second, must have a primary effect that neither advances nor inhibits religion, *e.g.*, *McGowan* v. *Maryland*; *School District of Abington Township* v. *Schemp*; and, third, must avoid excessive government entanglement with religion, *e.g.*, *Walz* v. *Tax Comm'n*.

In applying these criteria to the three distinct forms of aid involved in this case, we need touch only briefly on the requirement of a "secular legislative purpose." As the recitation of legislative purposes appended to New York's law indicates, each measure is adequately supported by legitimate, nonsectarian state interests. We do not question the propriety, and fully secular content, of New York's interest in preserving a healthy and safe educational environment for all of its school children. And we do not doubt—indeed, we fully recognize—the validity of the State's interests in promoting pluralism and diversity among its public and nonpublic schools.

Nor do we hesitate to acknowledge the reality of its concern for an already overburdened public school system that might suffer in the event that a significant percentage of children presently attending nonpublic schools should abandon those schools in favor of the public schools.

⊥ But the propriety of a legislature's purposes |774 may not immunize from further scrutiny a law which either has a primary effect that advances religion, or which fosters excessive entanglements between Church and State. Accordingly, we must weigh each of the three aid provisions challenged here against these criteria of effect and entanglement.

A

The "maintenance and repair" provisions of § 1 authorize direct payments to nonpublic schools, virtually all of which are Roman Catholic schools in low income areas. The grants, totaling $30 or $40 per pupil depending on the age of the institution, are given largely without restriction on usage. So long as expenditures do not exceed 50% of comparable expenses in the public school system, it is possible for a sectarian elementary or secondary school to finance its entire "maintenance and repair" budget from state tax- raised funds. No attempt is made to restrict payments to those expenditures related to the upkeep of facilities used exclusively for secular purposes, nor do we think it possible within the context of these religion-oriented institutions to impose such restrictions. Nothing in the statute, for instance, bars a qualifying school from paying out of state funds the salary of employees who maintain the school chapel, or the cost of renovating classrooms in which religion is taught, or the cost of heating and lighting those same facilities. Absent appropriate restrictions on expenditures for these and similar purposes, it simply cannot be denied that this section has a primary effect that advances religion in that it subsidizes directly the religious activities of sectarian elementary and secondary schools.

The state officials nevertheless argue that these expenditures for "maintenance and repair" are similar to other financial expenditures approved by this Court. ⊥ Primarily they rely on *Everson* v. *Board of* |775 *Education*, *Board of Education* v. *Allen*, and *Tilton* v. *Richardson*. In each of those cases it is true that the Court approved a form of financial assistance which conferred undeniable benefits upon private, sectarian schools. But a close examination of those cases illuminates their distinguishing characteristics. In *Everson*, the Court, in a five-to-four decision, approved a program of reimbursements to parents of public as well as parochial school children for bus fares paid in connection with transportation to and from school, a program which the Court characterized as approaching the "verge" of impermissible state aid. In *Allen*, decided some 20 years later, the Court upheld a New York law authorizing the provision of *secular* textbooks for all children in grades seven through 12 attending public and nonpublic schools. Finally, in *Tilton*, the Court upheld federal grants of funds for the construction of facilities to be used for clearly *secular* purposes by public and non-public institutions of higher learning.

These cases simply recognize that sectarian schools perform secular, educative functions as well as religious functions, and that some forms of aid may be channeled to the secular without providing direct aid to the sectarian. But the channel is a narrow one, as the above cases illustrate. Of course, it is true in each case that the provision of such neutral, nonideological aid, assisting only the secular functions of sectarian schools, served indirectly and incidentally to promote the religious function by rendering it more likely that children would attend sectarian schools and by freeing the budgets of those schools for use in other non-secular areas. But an indirect and incidental effect beneficial to religious institutions has never been thought a sufficient defect to warrant the invalidation of a state law. In *McGowan* v. *Maryland*, ⊥ Sunday Closing Laws were sustained even though one of their undeniable effects was to render it somewhat more likely that citizens would respect religious institutions and even attend religious services. Also, in *Walz* v. *Tax Commission*, property tax exemptions for church property were held not violative of the Establishment Clause despite the fact that such exemptions relieved churches of a financial burden.

Tilton draws the line most clearly. While a bare majority was there persuaded, for the reasons stated in the plurality opinion and in *Mr. Justice WHITE's* concurrence, that carefully limited construction grants to colleges and universities could be sustained, the Court was unanimous in its rejection of one clause of the federal statute in question. Under that clause, the Government was entitled to recover a portion of its grant to a sectarian institution in the event that the constructed facility was used to advance religion by, for instance, converting the building to a chapel or otherwise allowing it to be used to promote religious interests. But because the statute provided that the condition would expire at the end of 20 years, the facilities would thereafter be available for use by the institution for any sectarian purpose. In striking down this provision, the plurality opinion emphasized that "[l]imiting the prohibition for religious use of the structure to 20 years obviously opens the facility to use for any purpose at the end of that period." And in that event, "the original federal grant will in part have the effect of advancing religion." If tax-raised funds may not be granted to institutions of higher learning where the possibility exists that those funds will be used to construct a facility utilized for sectarian activities 20 ⊥777 years hence, *a fortiori* they ⊥ may not be distributed to elementary and secondary sectarian schools for the maintenance and repair of facilities without any

limitations on their use. If the State may not erect buildings in which religious activities are to take place, it may not maintain such buildings or renovate them when they fall into disrepair.

It might be argued, however, that while the New York "maintenance and repair" grants lack specifically articulated secular restrictions, the statute does provide a sort of statistical guarantee of separation by limiting grants to 50% of the amount expended for comparable services in the public schools. The legislature's supposition might have been that at least 50% of the ordinary public school maintenance and repair budget would be devoted to purely secular facility upkeep in sectarian schools. The shortest answer to this argument is that the statute itself allows, as a ceiling, grants satisfying the entire "amount of expenditures for maintenance and repair of such school" providing only that it is neither more than $30 or $40 per pupil nor more than 50% of the comparable ⊥ public school expenditures. Quite   ⊥778 apart from the language of the statute, our cases make clear that a mere statistical judgment will not suffice as a guarantee that state funds will not be used to finance religious education. In *Earley* v. *DeCenso*, the companion case to *Lemon* v. *Kurtzman*, the Court struck down a Rhode Island law authorizing salary supplements to teachers of secular subjects. The grants were not to exceed 15% of any teacher's annual salary. Although the law was invalidated on entanglement grounds, the Court made clear that the State could not have avoided violating the Establishment Clause by merely assuming that its teachers would succeed in segregating "their religious beliefs from their secular educational responsibilities."

"The Rhode Island Legislature has not, *and could not*, provide state aid on the basis of a mere assumption that secular teachers under religious discipline ⊥ can avoid conflicts. The State *must be certain,*   ⊥779 *given the Religion Clauses*, that subsidized teachers do not inculcate religion. . . ." (Emphasis supplied.)

Nor could the State of Rhode Island have prevailed by simply relying on the assumption that, whatever a secular teacher's inabilities to refrain from mixing the religious with the secular, he would surely devote at least 15% of his efforts to purely secular education, thus exhausting the state grant. It takes little imagination to perceive the extent to which States might openly subsidize parochial schools under such a loose standard of scrutiny.

What we have said demonstrates that New York's maintenance and repair provisions violate the Establishment Clause because their effect, inevitably, is to subsidize and advance the religious mission of sectarian ⊥ schools. We have no occasion, therefore, to   ⊥780 consider the further question whether those provisions as presently written would also fail to survive scrutiny under the administrative entanglement aspect of the three-part test because assuring the secular use of all funds requires too intrusive and continuing a relationship between Church and State, *Lemon* v. *Kurtzman.*

B

New York's tuition reimbursement program also fails the "effect" test, for much the same reasons that govern its maintenance and repair grants. The state program is designed to allow direct, unrestricted grants of $50 to $100 per child (but no more than 50% of tuition actually paid) as reimbursement to parents in low-income brackets who send their children to nonpublic schools. To qualify, a parent must have earned less than $5,000 in taxable income and must present a receipted tuition bill from a nonpublic school, the bulk of which are concededly sectarian in orientation.

There can be no question that these grants could not, consistently with the Establishment Clause, be given directly to sectarian schools, since they would suffer from the same deficiency that renders invalid the grants for maintenance and repair. In the absence of an effective means of guaranteeing that the state aid derived from public funds will be used exclusively for secular, neutral, and nonideological purposes, it is clear from our cases that direct aid in whatever form is invalid. As Mr. Justice Black put it quite simply in *Everson*: "No tax in any amount, large or small, can be levied to support any religious activities or institutions, whatever they may be called, or whatever form they may adopt to teach or practice religion."

⊥781 ⊥ The controlling question here, then, is whether the fact that the grants are delivered to parents rather than schools is of such significance as to compel a contrary result. The State and intervenor-appellees rely on *Everson* and *Allen* for their claim that grants to parents, unlike grants to institutions, respect the "wall of separation" required by the Constitution. It is true that in those cases the Court upheld laws that provided benefits to children attending religious schools and to their parents: As noted above, in *Everson* parents were reimbursed for bus fares paid to send children to parochial schools, and in *Allen* textbooks were loaned directly to the children. But those decisions made clear that, far from providing a *per se* immunity from examination of the substance of the State's program, the fact that aid is disbursed to parents rather than to the schools is only one among many factors to be considered.

In *Everson*, the Court found the bus fare program analogous to the provision of services such as police and fire protection, sewage disposal, highways, and ⊥782 sidewalks for parochial schools. Such services, ⊥ provided in common to all citizens, are "so separate and so indisputably marked off from the religious function," that they may fairly be viewed as reflections of a neutral posture toward religious institutions. *Allen* is founded upon a similar principle. The Court there repeatedly emphasized that upon the re-

cord in that case there was no indication that textbooks would be provided for anything other than purely secular courses. "Of course books are different from buses. Most bus rides have no inherent religious significance, while religious books are common. However, the language of [the law under consideration] does not authorize the loan of religious books, and the State claims no right to distribute religious literature. . . . Absent evidence, we cannot assume that school authorities . . . are unable to distinguish between secular and religious books or that they will not honestly discharge their duties under the law."

⊥ The tuition grants here are subject to no such ⊥783 restrictions. There has been no endeavor "to guarantee the separation between secular and religious educational functions and to ensure that State financial aid supports only the former." *Lemon* v. *Kurtzman.* Indeed, it is precisely the function of New York's law to provide assistance to private schools, the great majority of which are sectarian. By reimbursing parents for a portion of their tuition bill, the State seeks to relieve their financial burdens sufficiently to assure that they continue to have the option to send their children to religion-oriented schools. And while the other purposes for that aid—to perpetuate a pluralistic educational environment and to protect the fiscal integrity of overburdened public schools— are certainly unexceptionable, the effect of the aid is unmistakably to provide desired financial support for nonpublic, sectarian institutions.

⊥ Mr. Justice Black, dissenting in *Allen*, warned ⊥784 that "[i]t requires no prophet to foresee that on the argument used to support this law others could be up ⊥held providing for state or federal government ⊥785 funds to buy property on which to erect religious school buildings or to erect the buildings themselves, to pay the salaries of the religious school teachers, and finally to have the sectarian religious groups cease to rely on voluntary contributions of members of their sects while waiting for the government to pick up all the bills for the religious schools."

His fears regarding religious buildings and religious teachers have not come to pass, *Tilton* v. *Richardson; Lemon* v. *Kurtzman*, and insofar as tuition grants constitute a means of "pick[ing] up . . . the bills for the religious schools," neither has his greatest fear materialized. But the ingenious plans for channeling state aid to sectarian schools that periodically reach this Court abundantly support the wisdom of Justice Black's prophecy.

Although we think it clear, for the reasons above stated, that New York's tuition grant program fares no better under the "effect" test than its maintenance and repair program, in view of the novelty of the question we will address briefly the subsidiary arguments made by the state officials and intervenors in its defense.

First, it has been suggested that it is of controlling significance that New York's program calls for *reimbursement* for tuition already paid rather than for direct contributions which are merely routed through the parents to the schools, in advance of or in lieu of payment ⊥ by the parents. The parent is not a mere conduit, we are told, but is absolutely free to spend the money he receives in any manner he wishes. There is no element of coercion attached to the reimbursement, and no assurance that the money will eventually end up in the hands of religious schools. The absence of any element of coercion, however, is irrelevant to questions arising under the Establishment Clause. In *School District of Abington Township* v. *Schempp* it was contended that Bible recitations in public schools did not violate the Establishment Clause because participation in such exercises was not coerced. The Court rejected that argument, noting that while proof of coercion might provide a basis for a claim under the Free Exercise Clause, it was not a necessary element of any claim under the Establishment Clause. *Mr. Justice BRENNAN*'s concurring views reiterated the Court's conclusion: "Thus the short, and for me sufficient, answer is that the availability of excusal or exemption simply has no relevance to the establishment question, if it is once found that these practices are essentially religious exercises designed at least in part to achieve religious aims. . . ." [*Abington* v. *Schempp*].

A similar inquiry governs here: if the grants are offered as an incentive to parents to send their children to sectarian schools by making unrestricted cash payments to them, the Establishment Clause is violated whether or not the actual dollars given eventually find their way into the sectarian institutions. Whether the grant is labeled a reimbursement, a reward or a subsidy, its substantive impact is still the same. In sum, we agree with ⊥ the conclusion of the District Court that "[w]hether he gets it during the current year, or as reimbursement for the past year, is of no constitutional importance."

Second, the the Majority Leader and President pro tem of the State Senate argues that it is significant here that the tuition reimbursement grants pay only a portion of the tuition bill, and an even smaller portion of the religious school's total expenses. The New York statute limits reimbursement to 50% of any parent's actual outlay. Additionally, intervenor estimates that only 30% of the total cost of nonpublic education is covered by tuition payments, with the remaining coming from "voluntary contributions, endowments and the like." On the basis of these two statistics, appellee reasons that the "maximum tuition reimbursement by the State is thus only 15% of the educational costs in the nonpublic schools." And, "since compulsory education laws of the State, by necessity require significantly more than 15% of school time to be devoted to teaching secular courses," the New York statute provides "a statistical guarantee of neutrality." It should readily be seen that this is simply another variant of the argument we have rejected as to maintenance and repair

costs and it can fare no better here. Obviously, if accepted, this argument would provide the foundation for massive, direct subsidization of sectarian elementary and secondary schools. Our cases, however, have long since foreclosed ⊥ the notion that mere statistical assurances will suffice to sail between the Scylla and Charybdis of "effect" and "entanglement."

Finally, the State argues that its program of tuition grants should survive scrutiny because it is designed to promote the free exercise of religion. The State notes that only "low-income parents" are aided by this law, and without state assistance their right to have their children educated in a religious environment "is diminished or even denied." It is true, of course, that this Court has long recognized and maintained the right to choose nonpublic over public education. *Pierce* v. *Society of Sisters*. It is also true that a state law interfering with a parent's right to have his child educated in a sectarian school would run afoul of the Free Exercise Clause. But this Court repeatedly has recognized that tension inevitably exists between the Free Exercise and the Establishment Clauses and that it may often not be possible to promote the former without offending the latter. As a result of this tension, our cases require the State to maintain an attitude of "neutrality," neither "advancing" nor "inhibiting" religion. In its attempt to enhance the opportunities of the poor to choose between public and nonpublic education, the State has taken a step which can only be regarded as one "advancing" religion. However great our sympathy, *Everson* v. *Board of Education* (Jackson, J., dissenting), for the burdens experienced by those who must pay public school taxes at the same time that they support other schools because ⊥ of the constraints of "conscience and discipline," and notwithstanding the "high social importance" of the State's purposes, *Wisconsin* v. *Yoder*, neither may justify an eroding of the limitations of the Establishment Clause now firmly emplanted.

C

Sections 3, 4, and 5 establish a system for providing income tax benefits to parents of children attending New York's nonpublic schools. In this Court, the parties have engaged in a considerable debate over what label best fits the New York law. Appellants insist that the law is, in effect, one establishing a system of tax "credits." The State and the intervenors reject that characterization and would label it, instead, a system of income tax "modifications." The Solicitor General, in an *amicus curiae* brief filed in this Court, has referred throughout to the New York law as one authorizing tax "deductions." The District Court majority found that the aid was "in effect a tax *credit*" (emphasis in original). Because of the peculiar nature of the benefit allowed, it is difficult to adopt any single traditional label lifted from the law of income taxation. It is, at least in its form, a tax deduction since it is an amount subtracted from adjusted gross income, prior to computation of the tax due. Its effect, as the District Court concluded, is more like that of a tax credit since the deduction is not related to the amount actually spent for tuition and is apparently designed to yield a predetermined amount of tax "forgiveness" in exchange for performing a specific act which the State desires to encourage—the usual attribute of a tax credit. We see no reason to select one label over the other, as the constitutionality of this hybrid benefit does not turn in any event on the label we accord it. As *Mr. Chief Justice BURGER*'s opinion for the Court in *Lemon* v. *Kurtzman* notes, constitu- ⊥tional analysis is not a "legalistic minuet in which precise rules and forms govern." Instead we must "examine the form of the relationship for the light that it casts on the substance."

⌐790

These sections allow parents of children attending nonpublic elementary and secondary schools to subtract from adjusted gross income a specified amount if they do not receive a tuition reimbursement under § 2, and if they have an adjusted gross income of less than $25,000. The amount of the deduction is unrelated to the amount of money actually expended by any parent on tuition, but is calculated on the basis of a formula contained in the statute. The formula is apparently the product of a legislative attempt to assure that each family would receive a carefully estimated net benefit, and that the tax benefit would be comparable to, and compatible with, the tuition grant for lower income families. Thus, a parent who earns less than $5,000 is entitled to a tuition reimbursement of $50 if he has one child attending an elementary, nonpublic school, while a parent who earns more (but less than $9,000) is entitled to have a precisely equal amount taken off his tax bill. Additionally, a taxpayer's benefit under these sections is unrelated to, and not reduced by, any deductions to which he may be entitled for charitable contributions to religious institutions.

In practical terms there would appear to be little difference, for purposes of determining whether such aid has the effect of advancing religion, between the tax ⊥ benefit allowed here and the tuition grant allowed under § 2. The qualifying parent under either program receives the same form of encouragement and reward for sending his children to nonpublic schools. The only difference is that one parent receives an actual cash payment while the other is allowed to reduce by an arbitrary amount the sum he would otherwise be obliged to pay over to the State. We see no answer to Judge Hays' dissenting statement below that "[i]n both instances the money involved represents a charge made upon the state for the purpose of religious education."

⌐791

Appellees defend the tax portion of New York's legislative package on two grounds. First, they contend that it is of controlling significance that the grants or credits are directed to the parents rather than to the schools. This is the same argument made in support of the tuition reimbursements and rests on the same reading of the same precedents of this Court, primarily *Everson* and *Allen*. Our treatment of this issue in Part IIB is applicable here and requires rejection of this claim. Second, appellees place their strongest reliance on *Walz* in which New York's property tax exemption for religious organizations was upheld. We think that *Walz* provides no support for appellees' position. Indeed, its rationale plainly compels the conclusion that New York's tax package violates the Establishment Clause.

⊥ Tax exemptions for church property enjoyed an apparently universal approval in this country both before and after the adoption of the First Amendment. The Court in *Walz* surveyed the history of tax exemptions and found that each of the 50 States has long provided for tax exemptions for places of worship, that Congress has exempted religious organizations from taxation for over three-quarters of a century, and that congressional enactments in 1802, 1813, and 1870 specifically exempted church property from taxation. In sum, the Court concluded that "[f]ew concepts are more deeply embedded in the fabric of our national life, beginning with pre-Revolutionary colonial times, than for the government to exercise at the very least this kind of benevolent neutrality toward churches and religious exercise generally." We know of no historical precedent for New York's recently promulgated tax relief program. Indeed, it seems clear that tax benefits for parents whose children attend parochial schools are a recent innovation, occasioned by the growing financial plight of such nonpublic institutions and designed, albeit unsuccessfully, to tailor state aid in a manner not incompatible with the recent decisions of this Court.

⌐792

But historical acceptance without more would not alone have sufficed, as "no one acquires a vested or protected right in violation of the Constitution by long use." *Walz* v. *Tax Commission*. It was the reason underlying that long history of tolerance of tax exemptions for religion that proved controlling. A proper respect for both the Free Exercise and the Establishment Clauses compels the State ⊥ to pursue a course of "neutrality" towards religion. Yet governments have not always pursued such a course, and oppression has taken many forms, one of which has been taxation of religion. Thus, if taxation was regarded as a form of "hostility" toward religion, "exemption constitute[d] a reasonable and balanced attempt to guard against those dangers." Special tax benefits, however, cannot be squared with the principle of neutrality established by the decisions of this Court. To the contrary, insofar as such benefits render assistance to parents who send their children to sectarian schools, their purpose and inevitable effect are to aid and advance those religious institutions.

⌐793

Apart from its historical foundations, *Walz* is a product of the same dilemma and inherent tension

found in most government-aid-to-religion controversies. To be sure, the exemption of church property from taxation conferred a benefit, albeit an
indirect and incidental one. Yet that "aid" was a
product not of any purpose to support or to subsidize, but of a fiscal relationship designed to minimize involvement and entanglement between Church
and State. "The exemption," the Court emphasized,
"tends to complement and reinforce the desired separation insulating each from the other." Furthermore, "[e]limination of the exemption would tend to
expand the involvement of government by giving rise
to tax valuation of church property, tax liens, tax
foreclosures, and the direct confrontations and conflicts that follow in the train of those legal processes." The granting of the tax benefits under the
New York statute, unlike the extension of an exemption, would tend to increase rather than limit the
involvement between Church and State.

⌐1794   One further difference between tax exemptions for
church property and tax benefits for parents should
be ⊥ noted. The exemption challenged in *Walz* was
not restricted to a class composed exclusively or even
predominantly of religious institutions. Instead the
exemption covered all property devoted to religious,
educational or charitable purposes. As the parties
here must concede, tax reductions authorized by this
law flow primarily to the parents of children attending sectarian, nonpublic schools. Without intimating whether this factor alone might have
controlling significance in another context in some
future case, it should be apparent that in terms of
the potential divisiveness of any legislative measure
the narrowness of the benefited class would be an
important factor.

In conclusion, we find the *Walz* analogy unpersuasive, and in light of the practical similarity
between New York's tax and tuition reimbursement
programs, we hold that neither form of aid is sufficiently restricted to assure that it will not have the
impermissible effect of advancing the sectarian activities of religious schools.

III

Because we have found that the challenged sections have the impermissible effect of advancing
religion, we need not consider whether such aid
would result in entanglement of the State with religion in the sense of "[a] comprehensive, discriminating, and continuing surveillance." *Lemon* v.
Kurtzman. But the importance of the competing societal interests implicated in this case prompts us to
make the further observation that, apart from any
specific entanglement of the State in particular religious programs, assistance of the sort here involved
carries grave potential for entanglement in the
broader sense of continuing political strife over aid
to religion.

⌐1795   ⊥ Few would question most of the legislative findings supporting this statute. We recognized in *Board*

of Education v. *Allen* that "private education has
played and is playing a significant and valuable role
in raising levels of knowledge, competency, and experience," and certainly private parochial schools have
contributed importantly to this role. Moreover, the
tailoring of the New York statute to channel the aid
provided primarily to afford low-income families the
option of determining where their children are to be
educated is most appealing. There is no doubt that
the private schools are confronted with increasingly
grave fiscal problems, that resolving these problems
by increasing tuition charges forces parents to turn
to the public schools, and that this in turn—as the
present legislation recognizes—exacerbates the problems of public education at the same time that it
weakens support for the parochial schools.

These, in briefest summary, are the underlying
reasons for the New York legislation and for similar
legislation in other States. They are substantial reasons. Yet they must be weighed against the relevant
provisions and purposes of the First Amendment,
which safeguard the separation of Church from State
and which have been regarded from the beginning as
among the most cherished features of our constitutional system.

One factor of recurring significance in this
weighing process is the potentially divisive political
effect of an aid program. As Mr. Justice Black's
opinion in *Everson* ⊥ v. *Board of Education* empha-   ⌐1796
sizes, competition among religious sects for political
and religious supremacy has occasioned considerable
civil strife, "generated in large part" by competing
efforts to gain or maintain the support of government. As Mr. Justice Harlan put it, "[w]hat is at
stake as a matter of policy in Establishment Clause
cases is preventing that kind and degree of government involvement in religious life that, as history
teaches us, is apt to lead to strife and frequently
strain a political system to the breaking point."
Walz v. *Tax Commission* (concurring opinion).

The Court recently addressed this issue specifically
and fully in *Lemon* v. *Kurtzman.* After describing
the political activity and bitter differences likely to
result from the state programs there involved, the
Court said: "The potential for political divisiveness
related to religious belief and practice is aggravated
in these two statutory programs by the need for continuing annual appropriations and the likelihood of
larger and larger demands as costs and population
grow."

The language of the Court applies with peculiar
force to the New York statute now before us. Section
1 (grants for maintenance) and § 2 (tuition grants)
will require continuing annual appropriations. Sections 3,4, and 5 (income tax relief) will not necessarily require ⊥ annual re-examination, but the   ⌐1797
pressure for frequent enlargement of the relief is predictable. All three of these programs start out at
modest levels: the maintenance grant is not to exceed $40 per pupil per year in approved schools; the

tuition grant provides parents not more than $50 a year for each child in the first eight grades and $100 for each child in the high school grades; and the tax benefit, though more difficult to compute, is equally modest. But we know from long experience with both Federal and State Governments that aid programs of any kind tend to become entrenched, to escalate in cost, and to generate their own aggressive constituencies. And the larger the class of recipients, the greater the pressure for accelerated increases. Moreover, the State itself, concededly anxious to avoid assuming the burden of educating children now in private and parochial schools, has a strong motivation for increasing this aid as public school costs rise and population increases. In this situation, where the underlying issue is the deeply emotional one of Church-State relationships, the potential for serious divisive political consequences needs no elaboration. And while the prospect of such divisive-⊥ness may not alone warrant the invalidation of state laws that otherwise survive the careful scrutiny required by the decisions of this Court, it is certainly a "warning signal" not to be ignored.

⌐798

Our examination of New York's aid provisions, in light of all relevant considerations, compels the judgment that each, as written, has a "primary effect that advances religion" and offends the constitutional prohibition against laws "respecting the establishment of religion." We therefore affirm the three-judge court's holding as to § § 1 and 2, and reverse as to § § 3, 4, and 5.

It is so ordered.

Mr. Chief Justice BURGER, joined in part by *Mr. Justice WHITE*, and joined by *Mr. Justice REHN-QUIST*, concurring in part and dissenting in part.

I join in that part of the Court's opinion in *Committee for Public Education and Religious Liberty* v. *Nyquist*, which holds the New York "maintenance and repair" provision unconstitutional under the Establishment Clause because it is a direct aid to religion. I disagree, however, with the Court's decisions in *Nyquist* and in *Sloan* v. *Lemon* to strike down the New York and Pennsylvania tuition grant programs and the New York tax relief provisions. I believe the Court's decisions on those statutory provisions ignore the teachings of *Everson* v. *Board of Education*

⌐799

⊥ and *Board of Education* v. *Allen* and fail to observe what I thought the Court had held in *Walz* v. *Tax Comm'n*. I therefore dissent as to those aspects of the two holdings.

While there is no straight line running through our decisions interpreting the Establishment and Free Exercise Clauses of the First Amendment, our cases do, it seems to me, lay down one solid, basic principle: that the Establishment Clause does not forbid governments, state or federal, from enacting a program of general welfare under which benefits are distributed to private individuals, even though many of

those individuals may elect to use those benefits in ways that "aid" religious instruction or worship. Thus, in *Everson* the Court held that a New Jersey township could reimburse *all* parents of school-age children for bus fares paid in transporting their children to school. Justice Black's opinion for the Court stated that the New Jersey "legislation, as applied, does no more than provide a general program to *help parents* get their children, regardless of their religion, safely and expeditiously to and from accredited schools." (Emphasis added).

Twenty-one years later, in *Board of Education* v. *Allen*, the Court again upheld a state program that provided for direct aid to the parents of all school children including those in private schools. The statute there required "local public school authorities to lend textbooks free of charge to all students in grades seven through 12; students attending private schools [were] included." Recognizing that *Everson* was the case "most nearly in point," the *Allen* Court interpreted *Everson* as holding that "the Establishment ⊥ Clause does not prevent a state from extending the benefits of state laws to all citizens without regard to their religious affiliation. . . ." Applying that principle to the statute before it, the *Allen* Court stated: ". . . Appellants have shown us nothing about the necessary effects of the statute that is contrary to its stated purpose. The law merely *makes available to all children* the benefits of a general program to lend school books free of charge. Books are furnished at the request of the pupil and ownership remains, at least technically, in the State. *Thus no funds or books are furnished to parochial schools, and the financial benefit is to the parents and children, not to schools.*" (Emphasis added).

⌐800

The Court's opinions in both *Everson* and *Allen* recognized that the statutory programs at issue there may well have facilitated the decision of many parents to send their children to religious schools. Indeed, the Court in both cases specifically acknowledged that some children might not obtain religious instruction but for the benefits provided by the State. Notwithstanding, the Court held that such an indirect or incidental "benefit" to the religious institutions that sponsored parochial schools was not conclusive indicia of a "law respecting an establishment of religion."

⊥ One other especially pertinent decision should be noted. In *Quick Bear* v. *Leupp*, the Court considered the question whether government aid to individuals who choose to use the benefits for sectarian purposes contravenes the Establishment Clause. There the Federal Government had set aside certain trust and treaty funds for the educational benefit of the members of the Sioux Indian Tribe. When some beneficiaries elected to attend religious schools, and the Government entered into payment contracts with the sectarian institutions, suit was brought to enjoin the disbursement of public money to those schools. Speaking of the constitutionality of such a

⌐801

program, the Court said: "But we cannot concede the proposition that Indians cannot be allowed to use their own money to educate their children in the schools of their own choice because the Government is necessarily undenominational, as it cannot make any law respecting an establishment of religion or prohibiting the free exercise thereof."

The essence of all these decisions, I suggest, is that government aid to individuals generally stands on an entirely different footing from direct aid to religious institutions. I say "generally" because it is obviously possible to conjure hypothetical statutes that constitute either a subterfuge for direct aid to religious institutions or a discriminatory enactment favoring religious over nonreligious activities. Thus, a State could not enact a statute providing for a $10 gratuity to everyone who attended religious services weekly. Such a law would plainly be governmental sponsorship of religious activities; no statutory preamble expressing purely sec⊥ular legislative motives would be persuasive. But at least where the state law is genuinely directed at enhancing the freedom of individuals to exercise a recognized right, even one involving both secular and religious consequences as is true of the right of parents to send their children to private schools, see *Pierce* v. *Society of Sisters*, then the Establishment Clause no longer has a prohibitive effect.

This fundamental principle which I see running through our prior decisions in this difficult and sensitive field of law, and which I believe governs the present cases, is premised more on experience and history than on logic. It is admittedly difficult to articulate the reasons why a State should be permitted to reimburse parents of private-school children—partially at least—to take into account the State's enormous savings in not having to provide schools for those children, when a State is not allowed to pay the same benefit directly to sectarian schools on a per-pupil basis. In either case, the private individual makes the ultimate decision that may indirectly benefit church sponsored schools; to that extent the state involvement with religion is substantially attenuated. The answer, I believe, lies in the experienced judgment of various members of this Court over the years that the balance between the policies of free exercise and establishment of religion tips in favor of the former when the legislation moves away from direct aid to religious institutions and takes on the character of general aid to individual families. This judgment reflects the caution with which we scrutinize any effort to give official support to religion and the tolerance with which we treat general welfare legislation. But, whatever its ⊥ basis, that principle is established in our cases, from the early case of *Quick Bear* to the more recent holdings in *Everson* and *Allen*, and it ought to be followed here.

The tuition grant and tax relief programs now before us are, in my view, indistinguishable in principle, purpose and effect from the statutes in *Ev-*

erson and *Allen*. In the instant cases as in *Everson* and *Allen* the States have merely attempted to equalize the costs incurred by parents in obtaining an education for their children. The only discernible difference between the programs in *Everson* and *Allen* and these cases is in the method of the distribution of benefits: here the particular benefits of the Pennsylvania and New York statutes are given only to parents of private school children, while in *Everson* and *Allen* the statutory benefits were made available to parents of both public and private school children. But to regard that difference as constitutionally meaningful is to exalt form over substance. It is beyond dispute that the parents of public school children in New York and Pennsylvania presently receive the "benefit" of having their children educated totally at state expense; the statutes enacted in those States and at issue here merely attempt to equalize that "benefit" by giving to parents of private school children, in the form of dollars or tax deductions, what the parents of public school children receive in kind. It is no more than simple equity to grant partial relief to parents who support the public schools they do not use.

The Court appears to distinguish the Pennsylvania and New York statutes from *Everson* and *Allen* on the ground that here the state aid is not apportioned between the religious and secular activities of the sectarian schools attended by some recipients, while in *Everson* and *Allen* the state aid was purely secular in nature. But that distinction has not been followed in the past, see *Quick Bear* v. *Leupp*, and is not likely to be considered ⊥ controlling in the future. There are at present many forms of government assistance to individuals that can be used to serve religious ends, such as social security benefits or "G.I. Bill" payments, which are not subject to nonreligious use restrictions. Yet, I certainly doubt that today's majority would hold those statutes unconstitutional under the Establishment Clause.

Since I am unable to discern in the Court's analysis of *Everson* and *Allen* any neutral principle to explain the result reached in these cases, I fear that the Court has in reality followed the unsupportable approach of measuring the "effect" of a law by the percentage of the recipients who choose to use the money for religious, rather than secular, education. Indeed, in discussing the New York tax credit provisions, the Court's opinion argues that "the tax reductions authorized by this law flow primarily to the parents of children attending sectarian, nonpublic schools." While the opinion refrains from "intimating whether this factor alone might have controlling significance in another context in some future case," similar references to this factor elsewhere in the Court's opinion suggest that it has been given considerable weight. Thus, the Court observes as to the New York tuition grant program: "Indeed, it is precisely the function of New York's law to provide assistance to private schools, *the great majority of which are sectarian.*" (Emphasis added).

With all due respect, I submit that such a consideration is irrelevant to a constitutional determination of the "effect" of a statute. For purposes of constitutional adjudication of that issue, it should make no difference whether 5%, 20%, or 80% of the beneficiaries of an educational program of general application elect to utilize their benefits for religious purposes. The "primary effect" branch of our three-pronged test was never, at least to my understanding, intended to vary with the ⊥ number of churches benefitted by a statute under which state aid is distributed to private citizens.

Such a consideration, it is true, might be relevant in ascertaining whether the *primary legislative purpose* was to advance the cause of religion. But the Court has, and I think correctly, summarily dismissed the contention that either New York or Pennsylvania had an improper purpose in enacting these laws. The Court fully recognizes that the legislatures of New York and Pennsylvania have a legitimate interest in "promoting pluralism and diversity among . . . public and nonpublic schools," in assisting those who reduce the State's expenses in providing public education, and in protecting the already overburdened public school system against a massive influx of private school children. And in light of this Court's recognition of these secular legislative purposes, I fail to see any acceptable resolution to these cases except one favoring constitutionality.

I would therefore uphold these New York and Pennsylvania statutes. However sincere our collective protestations of the debt owed by the public generally to the parochial school systems, the wholesome diversity they engender will not survive on expressions of good will.

Mr. Justice WHITE joins this opinion insofar as it relates to the New York and Pennsylvania tuition grant statutes and the New York tax relief statute.

.   .   .   .   .

⊥ *Mr. Justice WHITE* joined in part by *The Chief Justice* and *Mr. Justice REHNQUIST*, dissenting.

Each of the States regards the education of its young to be a critical matter, so much so that it compels school attendance and provides an educational system at public expense. Any otherwise qualified child is entitled to a free elementary and secondary school education, or at least an education that costs him very little as compared with its cost to the State.

This Court has held, however, that the Due Process Clause of the Constitution entitles parents to send their children to nonpublic schools, secular or sectarian, if those schools are sufficiently competent to educate the child in the necessary secular subjects. *Pierce* v. *Society of Sisters.* About 10% of the Nation's children, approximately 5.2 million students, now take this option and are not being educated in public schools at public expense. Under state law these children have a right to a free public education and it would not appear unreasonable if the State, relieved of the expense of educating a child in the public school, contributed to the expense of his education elsewhere. The parents of such children pay taxes, including school taxes. They could receive in return a free education in the public schools. They prefer to send their children, as they have the right to do, to nonpublic schools that furnish the satisfactory equivalent of a public school education but also offer subjects or other assumed advantages not available in public schools. Constitutional considerations aside, it would be understandable if a State gave such parents a call on the public treasury up to the amount it would have cost the State to educate the child in public school, or to put it another way, up to the amount the parents save the State by not sending their children to public school.

In light of the Free Exercise Clause of the First Amendment, this would seem particularly the case where the parent desires his child to attend a school that offers not only secular subjects but religious training as well. A State should put no unnecessary obstacles in the way of religious training for the young. "When the State encourages religious instruction . . . it follows the best of our traditions." *Zorach* v. *Clauson; Walz* v. *Tax Commission.* Positing an obligation on the State to educate its children, which every State acknowledges, it should be wholly acceptable for the State to contribute ⊥ to the secular education of children going to sectarian schools rather than to insist that if parents want to provide their children with religious as well as secular education, the State will refuse to contribute anything to their secular training.

Historically the States of the Union have not furnished public aid for education in private schools. But in the last few years, as private education, particularly the parochial school system, has encountered financial difficulties, with many schools being closed and many more apparently headed in that direction, there has developed a variety of programs seeking to extend at least some aid to private educational institutions. Some States have provided only fringe benefits or auxiliary services. Others attempted more extensive efforts to keep the private school system alive. Some made direct arrangements with private and parochial schools for the purchase of secular educational services furnished by those schools. Others provided tuition grants to parents sending their children to private schools, permitted dual enrollments or shared time arrangements or extended substantial tax benefits in some form.

⊥1816   ⊥ The dimensions of the situations are not difficult to outline. The 5.2 million private elementary and secondary school students in 1972 attended some 3,200 nonsectarian private schools and some 18,000 schools that are church related. Twelve thousand of the latter were Roman Catholic schools and enrolled 4.37 million pupils or 83% of the total non-

⊥1817   public school membership. Sixty-⊥two percent of nonpublic school students are concentrated in eight industrialized, urbanized States: New York, Pennsylvania, Illinois, California, Ohio, New Jersey, Michigan, and Massachusetts. Eighty-three percent of the nonpublic school enrollment is to be found in large metropolitan areas. Nearly one out of five students in each of the Nation's largest cities are enrolled in nonpublic schools.

Nonpublic school enrollment has dropped at the rate of 6% per year for the past five years. Since 1965 nonpublic school enrollment has dropped 23%; the public schools show an increase of 12%. Projected to 1980, it is estimated that seven States (the eight mentioned in the text less Massachusetts) will lose 1,416,122 nonpublic school students. Whatever the reasons, there has been, and there probably will be, a movement to the public schools, with the pros-

⊥1818   pect of substantial increases ⊥in public school budgets that are already under intense attack and with the States and cities that are primarily involved already facing severe financial crises. It is this prospect that has prompted some of these States to attempt, by a variety of devices, to save or slow the demise of the nonpublic school system, an educational resource that could deliver quality education at a cost to the public substantially below the per pupil cost of the public schools.

⊥1819   ⊥ There are, then, the most profound reasons, in addition to those normally attending the question of the constitutionality of a state statute, for this Court to proceed with the utmost care in deciding these cases. It should not, absent a clear mandate in the Constitution, invalidate these New York and Pennsylvania statutes and thereby not only scuttle state efforts to hold off serious financial problems in their

⊥1820   public schools but ⊥ also make it more difficult, if not impossible, for parents to follow the dictates of their conscience and seek a religious as well as secular education for their children.

I am quite unreconciled to the Court's decision in *Lemon* v. *Kurtzman.* I thought then, and I think now, that the Court's conclusion there was not required by the First Amendment and is contrary to the long range interests of the country. I therefore have little difficulty in accepting the New York maintenance grant, which does not and could not, by its terms, approach the actual repair and maintenance cost incurred in connection with the secular education services performed for the State in parochial schools. But accepting *Lemon* and the invalidation of the New York maintenance grant, I would, with *The CHIEF JUSTICE* and *Mr. Justice REHN-*

QUIST, sustain the New York and Pennsylvania tuition grant statutes and the New York tax credit provisions.

No one contends that he can discern from the sparse language of the Establishment Clause that a State is forbidden to aid religion in any manner whatsoever or, if it does not mean that, what kind of or how much aid is permissible. And one cannot seriously believe that the history of the First Amendment furnishes unequivocal answers to many of the fundamental issues of church-state relations. In the end the courts have fashioned answers to these questions as best they can, the language of the Constitution and its history having left them a wide range of choice among many alternatives. But decision has been unavoidable; and, in choosing, the courts necessarily have carved out what they deemed to be the most desirable national policy governing various aspects of church-state relationships.

The course of these decisions has made it clear that the First Amendment does not bar all state aid to religion, of whatever kind or extent. States do,

⊥1821   and ⊥ they may, furnish churches and parochial schools with police and fire protection as well as water and sewage facilities. Also, "all of the 50 States provide for tax exemption of places of worship, most of them doing so by constitutional guarantee." *Walz* v. *Tax Commission.* This is a multimillion-dollar benefit to religious institutions, but a benefit that this Court has held is wholly consistent with the First Amendment. Bus transportation may be furnished to students attending parochial schools as well as to those going to public schools. So too the State may furnish school books to such students, although in doing so they "relieve[d] those churches of an enormous aggregate cost for those books." *Walz.* A State may also become the owner of the propety of a church-sponsored college and lease it back to the college, all with the purpose and effect of permitting revenue bonds issued in connection with the college's operation to be tax exempt and working a lower rate of interest and substantial savings to the sectarian institution. *Hunt* v. *McNair*

The Court thus has not barred all aid to religion or to religious institutions. Rather, it has attempted to devise a formula that would help identify the kind and degree of aid that is permitted or forbidden by the Establishment Clause. Until 1970, the test for compliance with the Clause was whether there "was a secular legislative purpose and primary effect that neither advances nor inhibits religion . . ."; given a secular purpose, what is "the primary effect of the enactment?" *Abington School District* v. *Schempp; Board of Education* v. *Allen.* In 1970, a third ele-

⊥1822   ment surfaced—whether there is "an ⊥ excessive government entanglement with religion." *Walz* v. *Tax Commission.* That element was not fatal to real property tax exemptions for church property but proved to be the crucial element in *Lemon* v. *Kurtzman* where the Court struck down the efforts by the States of Pennsylvania and Rhode Island to stave off financial disaster for their parochial school systems, the saving of which each of these States deemed important to the public interest. In accordance with one formula or the other, the laws in question furnished part of the cost incurred by private schools in furnishing secular education to substantial segments of the children in those States. Conceding a valid secular purpose and not reaching the question of primary effect, the Court concluded that the laws excessively, and therefore fatally, entangled the State with religion. What appeared to be an insoluble dilemma for the States, however, proved no insuperable barrier to the Federal Government in aiding sectarian institutions of higher learning by direct grants for specified facilities, *Tilton* v. *Richardson*. And *Hunt* v. *McNair*, decided this day, evidences the difficulty in perceiving when the State's involvement with religion passes the peril point.

But whatever may be the weight and contours of entanglement as a separate constitutional criterion, it is of remote relevance in the case before us with respect to the validity of tuition grants or tax credits involving or requiring no relationships whatsoever between the State and any church or any church school. So also the Court concedes the State's genuine secular purpose underlying these statutes. It therefore necessarily arrives at the remaining consideration in the three-fold test which is apparently accepted from prior cases: Whether the law in question has "a primary effect that neither advances nor inhibits religion." *Abington School District* v. *Schempp*. While purporting to ⊥ accept the standard stated in this manner, the Court strikes down the New York maintenance law, and for the same reason invalidates the tuition grants, because its "effect, inevitably, is to subsidize and advance the religious mission of sectarian schools." But the test is one of "primary" effect, not *any* effect. The Court makes no attempt at that ultimate judgment necessarily entailed by the standard heretofore fashioned in our cases. Indeed, the Court merely invokes the statement in *Everson* v. *Board of Education* that no tax can be levied "to support any religious activities. . . ." But admittedly there was no tax levied here for the *purpose* of supporting religious activities; and the Court appears to accept those cases, including *Tilton*, that inevitably involved aid of some sort or in some amount to the religious activities of parochial schools. In those cases the judgment was that as long as the aid to the school could fairly be characterized as supporting the secular educational functions of the school, whatever support to religion resulted from this direct, *Tilton* v. *Richardson*, or indirect, *Everson* v. *School District*; *Board of Education* v. *Allen*; *Walz* v. *Tax Commission*; *Hunt* v. *McNair*, contribution to the school's overall budget was not violative of the primary effect test nor of the Establishment Clause.

There is no doubt here that Pennsylvania and New York have sought in the challenged laws to keep their parochial schools system alive and capable of providing adequate secular education to substantial numbers of students. This purpose satisfies the Court, even though to rescue schools that would otherwise fail will inevitably enable those schools to continue whatever religious functions they perform. By the same token, it seems to me, preserving the secular functions of these schools is the overriding consequence of these laws and the resulting, ⊥ but incidental, benefit to religion should not invalidate them.

At the very least I would not strike down these statutes on their face. The Court's opinion emphasizes a particular kind of parochial school, one restricted to students of particular religious beliefs and conditioning attendance on religious study. Concededly, there are many parochial schools that do not impose such restrictions. Where they do not, it is even more difficult for me to understand why the primary effect of these statutes is to advance religion. I do not think it is and therefore dissent from the Court's judgment invalidating the challenged New York and Pennsylvania statutes.

The CHIEF JUSTICE and *Mr. Justice REHNQUIST* join this opinion insofar as it relates to the New York and Pennsylvania tuition grant statutes and the New York tax credit statute.

[Mr. Justice Rehnquist wrote an opinion, in which the Chief Justice and Mr. Justice White concurred, dissenting in part.]

MEEK v. PITTENGER

421 U.S. 349
ON APPEAL FROM THE UNITED STATES
DISTRICT COURT FOR
THE EASTERN DISTRICT OF
PENNSYLVANIA
Argued February 19, 1975 — Decided May 19, 1975

⊥ *Mr. Justice STEWART* announced the judgment of the Court and delivered the opinion of the Court (Parts I, II, IV, and V), together with an opinion (Part III), in which *Mr. Justice BLACKMUN* and *Mr. Justice POWELL*, joined.

This case requires us to determine once again whether a state law providing assistance to nonpublic, church-related, elementary and secondary schools is constitutional under the Establishment Clause of the First Amendment, made applicable to the States by the Fourteenth Amendment.

I

With the stated purpose of assuring that every school child in the Commonwealth will equitably share in the benefits of auxiliary services, textbooks, and instructional ⊥ material provided free of charge to children attending public schools, the Pennsylvania General Assembly in 1972 added Acts 194 and 195 to the Pennsylvania Public School Code of 1949.

Act 194 authorizes the Commonwealth to provide "auxiliary services" to all children enrolled in nonpublic elementary and secondary schools meeting Pennsylvania's compulsory attendance requirements. "Auxiliary serv⊥ices" include counseling, testing, and psychological services, speech and hearing therapy, teaching and related services for exceptional children, for remedial students, and for the educationally disadvantaged, "and such other secular, neutral, nonideologlcal services as are of benefit to nonpublic school children and are presently or hereafter provided for public schoolchildren of the Commonwealth." Act 194 specifies that the teaching and services are to be provided in the nonpublic schools themselves by personnel drawn from the appropriate "intermediate unit," part of the public school system of the Commonwealth established to provide special services to local school districts.

Act 195 authorizes the State Secretary of Education, either directly or through the intermediate units, to lend textbooks without charge to children attending nonpublic elementary and secondary schools that meet the Common⊥wealth's compulsory attendance requirements. The books that may be lent are limited to those "which are acceptable for use in any public, elementary, or secondary school of the Commonwealth."

Act 195 also authorizes the Secretary of Education, pursuant to requests from the appropriate nonpublic school officials, to lend directly to the nonpublic schools "instructional materials and equipment, useful to the education" of nonpublic school children. "Instructional ⊥ materials" are defined to include periodicals, photographs, maps, charts, sound recordings, films, "or any other printed and published materials of a similar nature." "Instructional equipment," as defined by the Act, includes projection equipment, recording equipment, and laboratory equipment.

On February 7, 1973, three individuals and four organizations filed a complaint in the District Court for the ⊥ Eastern District of Pennsylvania challenging the constitutionality of Act 194 and Act 195, and requesting an injunction prohibiting the expenditure of any funds under either statute. The complaint alleged that each Act "is a law respecting an establishment of religion in violation of the First Amendment" because each Act "authorizes and directs payments to or use of books, materials and equipment in schools which (1) are controlled by churches or religious organizations, (2) have as their purpose the teaching, propagation and promotion of a particular religious faith, (3) conduct their operations, curriculums and programs to fulfill that pur-

pose, (4) impose religious restrictions on admissions, (5) require attendance at instruction in theology and religious doctrine, (6) require attendance at or participation in religious worship, (7) are an integral part of the religious mission of the sponsoring church, (8) have as a substantial or dominant purpose the inculcation of religious values, (9) impose religious restrictions on faculty appointments, and (10) impose religious restrictions on what the faculty may teach." The Secretary of Education and the Treasurer of the Commonwealth were named as the defendants.

⊥ A three-judge court was convened. After an evidentiary hearing, the court entered its final judgment. In that judgment the court unanimously upheld the constitutionality of the textbook loan program authorized by Act 195. By a divided vote the court also upheld the constitutionality of Act 194's provision of auxiliary services to children in nonpublic elementary and secondary schools and Act 195's authorization of loans of instructional material directly to nonpublic elementary and secondary schools. The court unanimously invalidated that portion of Act 195 authorizing the expenditure of Commonwealth funds for the purchase of instructional equipment for loan to nonpublic schools, but only to the extent that the provision allowed the loan of equipment "which from its nature can be diverted to religious purposes." The court gave as examples projection and recording equipment. By a vote of 2-1, the court upheld this provision of Act 195 insofar as it authorizes the loan of instructional equipment that cannot be readily diverted to religious uses.

Except with respect to that provision of Act 195 which permits loan of instructional equipment capable of diversion, therefore, the plaintiffs' request for preliminary and final injunctive relief was denied. The plaintiffs (hereinafter the appellants) appealed directly to this Court. We noted probable jurisdiction.

II

⊥ In judging the constitutionality of the various forms of assistance authorized by Acts 194 and 195, the District Court applied the three-part test that has been clearly stated, if not easily applied, by this Court in recent Establishment Clause cases. First, the statute must have a secular legislative purpose. Second, it must have a "primary effect" that neither advances nor inhibits religion. Third, the statute and its administration must avoid excessive government entanglement with religion.

These tests constitute a convenient, accurate distillation of this Court's efforts over the past decades to evaluate a wide range of governmental action challenged as violative of the constitutional prohibition against laws "respecting an establishment of religion," and thus provide the proper framework of analysis for the issues presented in the case before us. It is well to emphasize, ⊥ however, that the tests must not be viewed as setting the precise limits to the necessary constitutional inquiry, but serve only as guidelines with which to identify instances in which the objectives of the Establishment Clause have been impaired.

Primary among the evils against which the Establishment Clause protects "have been sponsorship, financial support, and active involvement of the sovereign in religious activities." The Court has broadly stated that "[n]o tax in any amount, large or small, can be levied to support any religious activities or institutions, whatever they may be called, or whatever form they may adopt to teach or practice religion." But it is clear that not all legislative programs that provide indirect or incidental benefit to a religious institution are prohibited by the Constitution. "The problem, like many problems in constitutional law, is one of degree."

III

The District Court held that the textbook loan provisions of Act 195 are constitutionally indistinguishable from the New York textbook loan program upheld in *Board of Education* v. *Allen*. We agree.

Approval of New York's textbook loan program in the *Allen* case was based primarily on this Court's earlier decision in *Everson* v. *Board of Education*, holding that the constitutional prohibition against ⌐360 laws "respect⊥ing an establishment of religion" did not prevent "New Jersey from spending tax-raised funds to pay the bus fares of parochial school pupils as a part of a general program under which it pays the fares of pupils attending public and other schools." Similarly, the Court in *Allen* found that the New York textbook law "merely makes available to all children the benefits of a general program to lend school books free of charge. Books are furnished at the request of the pupil and ownership remains, at least technically, in the State. Thus no funds or books are furnished to parochial schools, and the financial benefit is to parents and children, not to schools." The Court conceded that provision of free textbooks might make it "more likely that some children choose to attend a sectarian school, but that was true of the state-paid bus fares in *Everson* and does not alone demonstrate an unconstitutional degree of support for a religious institution."

Like the New York program, the textbook provisions of Act 195 extend to all schoolchildren the benefits of Pennsylvania's well-established policy of lending textbooks free of charge to elementary and ⌐361 secondary school students. ⊥ As in *Allen*, Act 195 provides that the textbooks are to be lent directly to the student, not to the nonpublic school itself although, again as in *Allen*, the administrative practice is to have student requests for the books filed initially with the nonpublic school and to have the school authorities prepare collective summaries of these requests which they forward to the appropriate public officials. Thus, the financial benefit of Pennsylvania's textbook program, like New York's, is to parents and children, not to the nonpublic schools.

Under New York law the books that could be lent were limited to textbooks "which are designated for use in any public, elementary or secondary schools of the state or are approved by any boards of education, trustees, or other school authorities." The law was construed by the New York Court of Appeals to apply solely to secular textbooks. Act 195 similarly limits the books that may be lent to "textbooks which are acceptable for use in any public, elementary, or secondary school of the Commonwealth." Moreover, the record in the case ⊥ before us, like ⌐362 the record in *Allen*, contains no suggestion that religious textbooks will be lent or that the books provided will be used for anything other than purely secular purposes.

In sum, the textbook loan provisions of Act 195 are in every material respect identical to the loan program approved in *Allen*. Pennsylvania, like New York, "merely makes available to all children the benefits of a general program to lend school books free of charge." As such, those provisions of Act 195 do not offend the constitutional prohibition against laws "respecting an establishment of religion."

IV

Although textbooks are lent only to students, Act 195 authorizes the loan of instructional material and equip⊥ment directly to qualifying nonpublic ele- ⌐363 mentary and secondary schools in the Commonwealth. The appellants assert that such direct aid to Pennsylvania's nonpublic schools, including church-related institutions, constitutes an impermissible establishment of religion.

Act 195 is accompanied by legislative findings that the welfare of the Commonwealth requires that present and future generations of schoolchildren be assured ample opportunity to develop their intellectual capacities. Act 195 is intended to further that objective by extending the benefits of free educational aids to every schoolchild in the Commonwealth, including nonpublic school students who comprise approximately one quarter of the schoolchildren in Pennsylvania. We accept the legitimacy of this secular legislative purpose. But we agree with the appellants that the direct loan of instructional material and equipment has the unconstitutional primary effect of advancing religion because of the predominantly religious character of the schools benefiting from the Act.

The only requirement imposed on nonpublic schools to qualify for loans of instructional material and equipment is that they satisfy the Commonwealth's compulsory attendance law by providing, in the English language, the subjects and activities prescribed by the standards of the State

Board of Education. Commonwealth officials, as a matter of ⊥ state policy, do not inquire into the religious characteristics, if any, of the nonpublic schools requesting aid pursuant to Act 195. The Coordinator of Nonpublic School Services, the chief administrator of Acts 194 and 195, testified that a school would not be barred from receiving loans of instructional material and equipment even though its dominant purpose was the inculcation of religious values, even if it imposed religious restrictions on admissions or on faculty appointments, and even if it required attendance at classes in theology or at religious services. In fact, of the 1,320 nonpublic schools in Pennsylvania that comply with the requirements of the compulsory attendance law and thus qualify for aid under Act 195, more than 75% are church-related or religiously affiliated educational institutions. Thus, the primary beneficiaries of Act 195's instructional material and equipment loan provisions, like the beneficiaries of the "secular educational services" reimbursement program considered in *Lemon* v. *Kurtzman*, and the parent tuition reimbursement plan considered in *Sloan* v. *Lemon*, are nonpublic schools with a predominant sectarian character.

It is, of course, true that as part of general legislation made available to all students, a State may include church-related schools in programs providing bus transportation, school lunches, and public health facilities—secular and nonideological services unrelated to the primary, religious-oriented educational function of the sectarian school. The indirect and incidental benefits to church-related schools from those programs do not offend the constitutional prohibition against establish⊥ment of religion. But the massive aid provided the church-related nonpublic schools of Pennsylvania by Act 195 is neither indirect nor incidental.

For the 1972-1973 school year the Commonwealth authorized just under $12 million of direct aid to the predominantly church-related nonpublic schools of Pennsylvania through the loan of instructional material and equipment pursuant to Act 195. To be sure, the material and equipment that are the subjects of the loan—maps, charts, and laboratory equipment, for example—are "self-polic[ing], in that starting as secular, nonideological and neutral, they will not change in use." But faced with the substantial amounts of direct support authorized by Act 195, it would simply ignore reality to attempt to separate secular educational functions from the predominantly religious role performed by many of Pennsylvania's church-related elementary and secondary schools and to then characterize Act 195 as channeling aid to the secular without providing direct aid to the sectarian. Even ⊥ though earmarked for secular purposes, "when it flows to an institution in which religion is so pervasive that a substantial portion of its functions are subsumed in the religious

mission," state aid has the impermissible primary effect of advancing religion. *Hunt* v. *McNair.*

The church-related elementary and secondary schools that are the primary beneficiaries of Act 195's instructional material and equipment loans typify such religion-pervasive institutions. The very purpose of many of those schools is to provide an integrated secular and religious education; the teaching process is, to a large extent, devoted to the inculcation of religious values and belief. Substantial aid to the educational function of such schools, accordingly, necessarily results in aid to the sectarian school enterprise as a whole. "[T]he secular education those schools provide goes hand in hand with the religious mission that is the only reason for the schools' existence. Within the institution, the two are inestricably intertwined." *Lemon* v. *Kurtzman.* For this reason, Act 195's direct aid to Pennsylvania's predominantly church-related, nonpublic elementary and secondary schools, even though ostensibly limited to wholly neutral, secular instructional material and equipment, inescapably results in the direct and substantial advancement of religious activity and thus constitutes an impermissible establishment of religion.

V

⊥ Unlike Act 195, which provides only for the loan of teaching material and equipment, Act 194 authorizes the Secretary of Education, through the intermediate units, to supply professional staff, as well as supportive materials, equipment, and personnel, to the nonpublic schools of the Commonwealth. The "auxiliary services" authorized by Act 194—remedial and accelerated instruction, guidance counseling and testing, speech and hearing services—are provided directly to nonpublic schoolchildren with the appropriate special need. But the services are provided only on the nonpublic school premises, and only when "requested by nonpublic school representatives."

The legislative findings accompanying Act 194 are virtually identical to those in Act 195: Act 194 is intended to assure full development of the intellectual capacities of the children of Pennsylvania by extending the bene⊥fits of free auxiliary services to all students in the Commonwealth. The appellants concede the validity of this secular legislative purpose. Nonetheless, they argue that Act 194 constitutes an impermissible establishment of religion because the auxiliary services are provided on the premises of predominantly church- related schools.

In rejecting the appellants' argument, the District Court emphasized that "auxiliary services" are provided directly to the children involved and are expressly limited to those services which are secular, neutral, and nonideologlcal. The court also noted that the instruction and counseling in question served only to supplement the basic, normal educational offerings of the qualifying nonpublic schools.

Any benefits to church-related schools that may result from the provision of such services, the District Court concluded, are merely incidental and indirect, and thus not impermissible. The court also held that no continuing supervision of the personnel providing auxiliary services would be necessary to establish that Act 194's secular limitations were observed or to guarantee that a member of the auxiliary services staff had not "succumb[ed] to sectarianization of his or her professional work."

⊥ We need not decide whether substantial state expenditures to enrich the curricula of church-related elementary and secondary schools, like the expenditure of state funds to support the basic educational program of those schools, necessarily results in the direct and substantial advancement of religious activity. For decisions of this Court make clear that the District Court erred in relying entirely on the good faith and professionalism of the secular teachers and counselors functioning in church-related schools to ensure that a strictly nonideological posture is maintained.

In *Earley* v. *DiCenso*, a companion case to *Lemon* v. *Kurtzman*, the Court invalidated a Rhode Island statute authorizing salary supplements for teachers of secular subjects in nonpublic schools. The Court expressly rejected the proposition, relied upon by the District Court in the case before us, that it was sufficient for the State to assume that teachers in church-related schools would succeed in segregating their religious beliefs from the secular educational duties. "We need not and do not assume that teachers in parochial schools will be guilty of bad faith or any conscious design to evade the limitations imposed by the statute and the First Amendment. . . .

"But the potential for impermissible fostering of religion is present. . . . The State must be certain, given the Religion Clauses, that subsidized teachers do not inculcate religion. . . .

⊥ "A comprehensive, discriminating, and continuing state surveillance will inevitably be required to ensure that these restrictions are obeyed and the First Amendment otherwise respected. . . ."

The prophylactic contacts required to ensure that teachers play a strictly nonideological role, the Court held, necessarily give rise to a constitutionally intolerable degree of entanglement between church and state. The same excessive entanglement would be required for Pennsylvania to be "certain," as it must be, that Act 194 personnel do not advance the religious mission of the church-related schools in which they serve.

That Act 194 authorizes state-funding of teachers only for remedial and exceptional students, and not for normal students participating in the core curriculum, does not distinguish this case from *Earley* v. *DiCenso* and *Lemon* v. *Kurtzman*. Whether the subject is "remedial reading," "advanced reading," or simply "reading," a teacher remains a teacher, and

the danger that religious doctrine will become intertwined with secular instruction persists. The likelihood of inadvertent fostering of re⊥ligion may be less in a remedial arithmetic class than in a medieval history seminar, but a diminished probability of impermissible conduct is not sufficient: "The State must be certain, given the Religion Clauses, that subsidized teachers do not inculcate religion." And a state-subsidized guidance counselor is surely as likely as a state-subsidized chemistry teacher to fail on occasion to separate religious instruction and the advancement of religious beliefs from his secular educational responsibilities.

The fact that the teachers and counselors providing auxiliary services are employees of the public intermediate unit, rather than of the church-related schools in which they work, does not substantially eliminate the need for continuing surveillance. To be sure, auxiliary services personnel, because not employed by the nonpublic schools, are not directly subject to the discipline of a religious authority. But they are performing important educational services in schools in which education is an integral part of the dominant sectarian mission and in which an atmosphere dedicated to the advancement of religious belief is constantly maintained. ⊥ The potential for impermissible fostering of religion under these circumstances, although somewhat reduced, is nonetheless present. To be certain that auxiliary teachers remain religiously neutral, as the Constitution demands, the State would have to impose limitations on the activities of auxiliary personnel and then engage in some form of continuing surveillance to ensure that those restrictions were being followed.

In addition, Act 194, like the statutes considered in *Lemon* v. *Kurtzman* and *Committee for Public Education & Religious Liberty* v. *Nyquist*, creates a serious potential for divisive conflict over the issue of aid to religion—"entanglement in the broader sense of continuing political strife." *Committee for Public Education & Religious Liberty* v. *Nyquist*. The recurrent nature of the appropriation process guarantees annual reconsideration of Act 194 and the prospect of repeated confrontation between proponents and opponents of the auxiliary services program. The Act thus provides successive opportunities for political fragmentation and division along religious lines, one of the principal evils against which the Establishment Clause was intended to protect. This potential for political entanglement, together with the administrative entanglement which would be necessary to ensure that auxiliary services personnel remain strictly neutral and nonideological when functioning in church-related schools, compels the conclusion that Act 194 violates the constitutional prohibition against laws "respecting an establishment of religion."

⊥ The judgment of the District Court as to Act 194 is reversed; its judgment as to the textbook provisions of Act 195 is affirmed, but as to that Act's other provisions now before us its judgment is reversed.

It is so ordered.

Mr. Justice BRENNAN, with whom *Mr. Justice DOUGLAS* and *Mr. Justice MARSHALL* join, concurring and dissenting.

I join in the reversal of the District Court's judgment insofar as that judgment upheld the constitutionality of Act 194 and the provisions of Act 195 respecting instructional materials and equipment, but dissent from Part III and the affirmance of the judgment upholding the constitutionality of the textbook provisions of Act 195.

A three-factor test by which to determine the compatibility with the Establishment Clause of state subsidies of sectarian educational institutions has evolved over 50 years of this Court's stewardship in the field. The law in question must, first, reflect a clearly secular legislative purpose, second, have a primary effect that neither ⊥ advances nor inhibits religion, and, third, avoid excessive government entanglement with religion. But four years ago, the Court, albeit without express recognition of the fact, added a significant fourth factor to the test: "A broader basis of entanglement of yet a different character is presented by the divisive political potential of these state programs." *Lemon* v. *Kurtzman.* The evaluation of this factor in determining compatibility of a state subsidy law with the Establishment Clause is essential, said the Court, because: "In a community where . . . a large number of pupils are served by church-related schools, it can be assumed that state assistance will entail considerable political activity. Partisans of parochial schools, understandably concerned with rising costs and sincerely dedicated to both the religious and secular educational missions of their schools, will inevitably champion this cause and promote political action to achieve their goals. Those who oppose state aid, whether for constitutional, religious, or fiscal reasons, will inevitably respond and employ all the usual political techniques to prevail. Candidates will be forced to declare and voters to choose. It would be unrealistic to ignore the fact that many people confronted with issues of this kind will find their votes aligned with their faith.

"Ordinary political debate and division, however vigorous or even partisan, are normal and healthy manifestations of our democratic system of government, *but political division along religious lines was one of the principal evils against which the First Amendment was intended to Protect.* . . . The potential divisiveness of such conflict is a threat to the normal political process. . . . It conflicts with our whole history and tradition to permit questions of ⊥ the Religion Clauses to assume such importance in our legislatures and in our elections that they could divert attention from the myriad issues and problems that confront every level of government. . . .

". . . *Here we are confronted with successive and very likely permanent annual appropriations that benefit relatively few religious groups. Political fragmentation and divisiveness on religious lines are thus likely to be intensified.*

"*The potential for political divisiveness related to religious belief and practice is aggravated . . . by the need for continuing annual appropriations and the likelihood of larger and larger demands as costs and populations grow. . . .*" (Emphasis added.)

This factor was key in *Kurtzman's* determination that Pennsylvania and Rhode Island statutes providing state aid to church-related elementary and secondary schools violated the Establishment Clause. The Pennsylvania statute provided financial support by way of reimbursement for the cost of teachers' salaries, textbooks, and instructional materials in specified secular subjects. The Rhode Island statute provided a program under which the State paid directly to teachers in nonpublic schools a supplement of 15% of their annual salary.

Committee for Public Education v. *Nyquist,* decided two years later, emphasized the importance to be attached by judges to this fourth factor: "One factor of recurring significance in this weighing process is the potentially divisive political effect of an aid program." The Court held that the factor applied "with peculiar force to the New York statute now before us." That statute created three aid programs. The first provided for direct money grants to be used for maintenance and ⊥ repair of facilities to ensure the students' welfare, health, and safety. The second established a tuition reimbursement plan for parents of children attending nonpublic elementary schools. The third provided tax relief for parents not qualifying for tuition reimbursements. Stating that "while the prospect of [political] divisiveness may not alone warrant the invalidation of state laws that otherwise survive the careful scrutiny required by the decisions of this Court, it is certainly a 'warning signal' not to be ignored," the Court held that "in light of all relevant considerations," each of the New York programs had a " 'primary effect that advances religion' and offends the constitutional prohibition against laws 'respecting an establishment of religion.' "

The Court today also relies on the factor of divisive political potential but only as support for its holding that Act 194 is an unconstitutional law "respecting an establishment of religion," stating: "In addition, Act 194, like the statutes considered in [*Kurtzman* and *Nyquist*] creates a serious potential for divisive conflict over the issue of aid to religion—'entanglement in the broader sense of political strife.' . . . The recurrent nature of the appropriation process guarantees annual reconsideration of Act 194 and the prospect of repeated confrontation between proponents and opponents of the auxiliary services program. The Act thus provides successive opportunities for political fragmentation and division along religious lines, one of the principal evils against which the Establishment Clause was intended to protect."

Contrary to the plain and explicit teaching of *Kurtzman* and *Nyquist*, however, and inconsistently with its own treatment of Act 194, the Court, in considering ⊥ the constitutionality of Act 195 says not ⌐377 a single word about the political divisiveness factor in Part III of the opinion upholding the textbook loan program created by that Act, and makes only a passing footnote reference to the factor, without evaluation of its bearing on the result, in holding that Act 195's program for loans of instructional materials and equipment constitutes Act 195 in that respect "direct aid to Pennsylvania's predominantly church-related, nonpublic elementary and secondary schools, even though ostensibly limited to wholly neutral, secular instructional material and equipment, [that] inescapably results in the direct and substantial advancement of religious activity . . . and thus constitutes an impermissible establishment of religion."

I recognize that the plurality was on the horns of a dilemma. The plurality notes that the total 1972-1973 appropriation under Act 195 was $16,660,000, of which $4,670,000 was appropriated to finance the textbook program. The plurality notes further that "aid programs like Act 195 . . . are dependent on continuing annual appropriations . . . which generate increasing demands as costs and population grow . . .," and, indeed, that the total Act 195 appropriation was increased $900,000 to $17,560,000 for the 1973-1974 school year. Plainly then, as in *Nyquist*, the political divisiveness factor applies "with peculiar force to the . . . statute now before us." But to comply with *Nyquist*, as is required, the plurality obviously must attach determinative weight to the factor as respects both the textbook loan and instructional materials and equipment loan provisions, since both are inextricably intertwined in Act 195. For in light of the massive appropriations in ⊥volved, the plurality would be ⌐378 hard put to explain how the factor weighs determinatively against the validity of the instructional materials loan provisions, and not also against the validity of the textbook loan provisions. The plurality therefore would extricate itself from the horns of the dilemma by simply ignoring the factor in the weighing process.

But however much this evasion may be tolerable in the case of the instructional materials loan provisions, since these are invalidated on other grounds, responsibility for evaluating the weight to be accorded the factor cannot be evaded, in the case of the textbook loan provisions, by reliance, as the plurality does, upon its greement with the District Court that the textbook loan program is indistinguishable from the New York textbook loan program upheld in *Board of Education* v. *Allen*. For

Allen, which I joined, was decided before *Kurtzman* ordained that the political divisiveness factor must be involved in the weighing process, and understandably neither the parties to *Allen* nor the Court addressed that factor in that case. But whether or not *Allen* can withstand overruling in light of *Kurtzman* and *Nyquist*, which I question, it is clear that *Kurtzman*—which, I repeat, applied the factor to a Pennsylvania program that included reimbursement for the cost of textbooks—requires that the Court weigh the factor in the instant case. Further, giving the factor the weight that *Kurtzman* and *Nyquist* require, compels, in my view ⊥ the conclu- ⌐379 sion that the textbook loan program of Act 195, equally with the program for loan of instructional materials and equipment, violates the Establishment Clause. The plurality's answer is that a difference in result is justified because Act 195 distinguishes between recipients of the loans: textbooks are lent to students, while instructional material and equipment are lent directly to the schools. That answer will not withstand analysis.

First, it is pure fantasy to treat the textbook program as a loan to students. It is true that, like the New York statute in *Allen*, Act 195 in terms talks of loans by the State of acceptable secular textbooks directly to students attending nonpublic schools. But even the plurality acknowledges that "the administrative practice is to have student requests for the books filed initially with the nonpublic school and to have the school authorities prepare collective summaries of these requests which they forward to the appropriate public officials. . . ." Further, "the nonpublic schools are permitted to store on their premises the textbooks being lent to students." Even if these practices were also followed under the New York statute, the regulations implementing Act 195 make clear, as the record in *Allen* did not, that the nonpublic school in Pennsylvania is something more than a conduit between the State and pupil. The Commonwealth has promulgated "Guidelines for the Administration of Acts 194 and 195" to implement the statutes. These regulations, unlike those upheld in *Allen*, constitute a much more intrusive and detailed involvement of the State and its processes into the administration of nonpublic schools. The whole business is handled by the schools and public authorities and neither parents nor students have a say. The guidelines make crystal clear that the nonpublic school, not its pupils, is the motivating force behind the textbook ⊥ loan, and that virtually the ⌐380 entire loan transaction is to be, and is in fact, conducted between officials of the nonpublic school, on the one hand, and officers of the state, on the other.

For example, § 4.3 of the Guidelines requires that on or before March 1 of each year, an official of each nonpublic school submit to the Pennsylvania Department of Education a loan request for the desired textbooks. The requests must be submitted on standardized forms "distributed by the Department of Education . . . to each nonpublic school or the appropriate chief administrator." Section 4.6 of the Guidelines provides that the "[t]extbooks requested will be shipped directly to the appropriate nonpublic school." Thus, although in terms the form provided by the Commonwealth for parents of nonpublic school students states that the parents of these pupils request the loan of textbooks directly from the State, the form is not returnable to the State, but to the nonpublic school, which tabulates the requests and submits its total to the State. Then, after the submission by the nonpublic school is approved by the appropriate state official, the books are transported not to the children whose parents ostensibly made the request, but directly to the nonpublic school, where they are physically retained when not in use in the classroom.

Indeed, the Guidelines make no attempt to mask the true nature of the loan transaction. In explicit words § 4.10 describes the transaction: "Textbooks *loaned to the nonpublic schools*: (a) shall be maintained on an inventory by the nonpublic school." (Emphasis added.) Section 4.11 provides: "It is presumed that textbooks on *loan to nonpublic schools* after a period of time will be lost, missing, obsolete or worn out. This information should be communicated to the Department of Education. After a peri-

⌐381 od of six years, textbooks shall be ⊥ declared unserviceable and the disposal of such shall be at the discretion of the Secretary of Education." (Emphasis added.) Thus, the loan of the texts is treated by the regulations as what it in fact is: a loan from the State directly to the nonpublic school. Finally, § 4.12 completely removes any possible doubt. It provides: "The nonpublic school or the agency which it is a member shall be responsible for maintaining files on future certificates of requests from parents of children for all textbook materials loaned to them under this Act. The file must be open to inspection for the appropriate authority. A letter certifying the certificates on file shall accompany all loan requests."

Plainly, then, whatever may have been the case under the New York statute sustained in *Allen*, the loan ostensibly to students is, under Act 195, a loan in fact to the schools. In this regard, it should be observed that sophisticated attempts to avoid the Constitution are just as invalid as simple-minded ones.

Second, in any event, *Allen* itself made clear that, far from providing a *per se* immunity from examination of the substance of the State's program, even if the fact were, and it is not, that textbooks are loaned to the children rather than to the schools, that is only one among the factors to be weighed in determining the compatibility of the program with the Establishment Clause. And, clearly, in the context of application of the factor of political divisiveness, it is wholly irrelevant whether the loan is to the children or to the school. A divisive political potential exists because aid programs, like Act 195, are dependent on continuing ⊥ annual appropriations, and Act 195's

⌐382

textbook loan program, even if we accepted it as a form of loans to students, involves increasingly massive sums now approaching $5,000,000 annually. It would blind reality to treat massive aid to nonpublic schools, under the guise of loans to the students, as not creating "a serious potential for divisive conflict over the issue of aid to religion." The focus of the textbook loan program in terms of massive financial support for religious schools that creates the potential divisiveness is no less real than it is in the case of Act 195's instructional materials provisions and Act 194's invalidated program for auxiliary services. Act 195 is intended solely as a financial aid program to relieve the desperate financial plight of nonpublic, primarily parochial, schools. The plurality suggests that it is immaterial that Act 195 has that cast, in contrast with New York's statute in *Allen* which authorized loans to students attending both public and nonpublic schools. On the contrary, Act 195's limitation of its financial support to aid to nonpublic school children exacerbates the potential for political divisive⊥ness. "In this situation, where the under-   ⌐383 lying issue is the deeply emotional one of Church-State relationships, the potential for seriously divisive political consequences needs no elaboration." *Committee for Public Education* v. *Nyquist.*

Finally, the textbook loan provisions of Act 195, even if ostensibly limiting loans to nonpublic school children, violate the Establishment Clause for reasons independent of the political divisiveness factor. As I have said, unlike the New York statute in *Allen* which extended assistance to all students, whether attending public or nonpublic schools, Act 195 extends textbook assistance only to a special class of students, children who attend nonpublic schools which are, as the plurality notes, primarily religiously oriented. The Act in that respect contains the same fatal defect as the New York statute held violative of the Establishment Clause in *Public Funds* v. *Marburger*. The statute there involved was N. J. Stat. Ann. § 18A:58-63 which furnished state aid, in amounts up to $10 for elementary school students and up to $20 for high school students, to the parents of nonpublic school students as reimbursement for the cost of ⊥ "secular, non-ideological text-   ⌐384 books, instructional materials and supplies." We affirmed the holding of the three-judge court that "because the language of [the statute] limits the assistance provided therein only to parents of children who attend nonpublic, predominately religiously-affiliated schools and not to parents of all school children, we are satisfied that its primary effect is to advance religion and that it is thereby unconstitutional." *Marburger* thus establishes that the plurality's reliance today upon *Allen* is clearly misplaced.

Indeed, that reliance is also misplaced in light of its own holding today invalidating the provisions of Act 195 respecting the loan of instructional materials and equipment. I have no doubt that such materials and equipment are tools that substantially enhance the quality of the secular education provided by the religiously oriented schools. But surely the hearttools of that education are the textbooks that are prescribed for use and kept at the schools, albeit formally at the request of the students. Thus, what the Court says of the instructional materials and equipment, may be said perhaps even more accurately of the textbooks: "But faced with the substantial amounts of direct support authorized by Act 195, it would simply ignore reality to attempt to separate secular educational functions from the predominantly religious role performed by many of Pennsylvania's church-related elementary and secondary schools and to then characterize Act 195 as channeling aid to the secular without providing direct aid to the sectarian. Even though earmarked for secular purposes, 'when it flows to an institution in which religion is so pervasive that a substantial portion of its functions are subsumed in the religious mission,' state aid has the impermissible primary effect of advancing religion."

⌐385 In sum, I join the Court's opinion as to Parts I, II, IV, ⊥ and V, except that I would go further in Part IV and rest the invalidation of the provisions of Act 195 for loans of instructional materials and equipment also upon the political divisiveness factor. I dissent from part III.

Mr. Chief Justice BURGER, concurring in the judgment in part and dissenting in part.

I agree with the Court only insofar as it affirms the judgment of the District Court. My limited agreement with the Court as to this action leads me, however, to agree generally with the views expressed by *Mr. Justice REHNQUIST* and *Mr. Justice WHITE* in regard to the other programs under review. I especially find it difficult to accept the Court's extravagant suggestion of potential entanglement which it finds in the "auxiliary services" program of Pa. Stat. 194. Here, the Court's holding, it seems to me, goes beyond any prior holdings of this Court and, indeed, conflicts with our holdings in *Board of Education* v. *Allen* and *Lemon* v. *Kurtzman*. There is absolutely no support in this record or, for that matter, in ordinary human experience to support the concern some see with respect to the "dangers" lurking in extending common, nonsectarian tools of the education process—especially remedial tools—to students in private schools. As I noted in my separate opinion in *Committee for Public Education* v. *Nyquist*, the "fundamental principle which I see running through our prior decisions in this difficult and sensitive field of law . . . is premised more on experience and history than on logic." Certainly, there is no basis in "experience and history" to conclude that a State's attempt to provide—through the services of its own state-selected professionals—the remedial assistance neces-

⌐386 sary for *all* its children poses the same potential for ⊥

unnecessary administrative entanglement or divisive political confrontation which concerned the Court in *Lemon* v. *Kurtzman*. Indeed, I see at least as much potential for divisive political debate in opposition to the crabbed attitude the Court shows in this case.

If the consequence of the Court's holding operated only to penalize *institutions* with a religious affiliation, the result would be grievous enough; nothing in the Religion Clauses of the First Amendment permits governmental power to discriminate *against* or affirmatively stifle religions or religious activity. But this holding does more: it penalizes *children*— children who have the misfortune to have to cope with the learning process under extraordinarily heavy physical and psychological burdens, for the most part congenital. This penalty strikes them not because of any act of theirs but because of their parents' choice of religious exercise. This, as *Mr. Justice REHNQUIST* effectively demonstrates, totally turns its back on what *Mr. Justice DOUGLAS* wrote for the Court in *Zorach* v. *Clauson*, particularly that: "When the state encourages religious instruction or cooperates with religious authorities by adjusting the schedule of public events to sectarian needs, it follows the best of our traditions. For it then respects the religious nature of our people and accommodates the public service to the spiritual needs."

To hold, as the Court now does, that the Constitution permits the States to give special assistance to some of its children whose handicaps prevent their deriving the benefit normally anticipated from the education required to become a productive member of society and, at the same time, to deny those benefits to other children *only because* they attend a Lutheran, Catholic or other church- ⊥ sponsored school ⌐387 does not simply tilt the Constitution against religion; it literally turns the Religion Clause on its head. As *Mr. Justice DOUGLAS* said for the Court in *Zorach*, this is ". . . to find in the Constitution a requirement that the government show a callous indifference to religious groups. That would be preferring those who believe in no religion over those who do believe."

The melancholy consequence of what the Court does today is to force the parent to choose between the "free exercise" of a religious belief by opting for a sectarian education for his child or to forego the opportunity for his child to learn to cope with—or overcome—serious congenital learning handicaps, through remedial assistance financed by his taxes. Affluent parents, by employing private teaching specialists, will be able to cope with this denial of equal protection, which is, for me, a gross violation of Fourteenth Amendment rights, but all others will be forced to make a choice between their judgment as to their children's spiritual needs and their temporal need for special remedial learning assistance. One can only hope that, at some future date, the Court will come to a more enlightened and tolerant view of the First Amendment's guarantee of free exercise of religion, thus eliminating the denial of equal protection to children in church-sponsored schools, and take a more realistic view that carefully limited aid to children is not a step toward establishing a state religion—at least while this Court sits.

Mr. Justice REHNQUIST, with whom *Mr. Justice* WHITE joins, concurring in the judgment in part and dissenting in part.

Substantially for the reasons set forth in my dissent and those of The CHIEF JUSTICE and *Mr. Justice* ⊥ WHITE in *Committee for Public Education & Religious Liberty* v. *Nyquist*, and *Sloan* v. *Lemon*, I would affirm the judgment of the District Court. |388

Two Acts of the Pennsylvania Legislature are under attack in this case. Act 195 includes a program that provides for the loan of textbooks free of charge to elementary and secondary school students attending nonpublic schools, just as other provisions of Pennsylvania law provide similar benefits to children attending public schools. I agree with the Court that this program is constitutionally indistinguishable from the New York textbook loan program upheld in *Board of Education* v. *Allen* and on the authority of that case I join the judgment of the Court insofar as it upholds the textbook loan program.

The Court strikes down other provisions of Act 195 dealing with instructional materials and equipment because it finds that they have "the unconstitutional primary effect of advancing religion because of the predominantly religious character of the schools benefiting from the Act." This apparently follows from the high percentage of nonpublic schools that are "church-related or religiously affiliated educational institutions." The Court ⊥ thus again appears to follow "the unsupportable approach of measuring the 'effect' of a law by the percentage of" sectarian schools benefited. I find that approach to the "primary effect" branch of our three-pronged test no more satisfactory in the context of this instructional materials and equipment program than it was in the context of the tuition reimbursement and tax relief programs involved in *Nyquist* and *Sloan*. |389

One need look no further than to the majority opinion for a demonstration of the arbitrariness of the percentage approach to primary effect. In determining the constitutionality of the textbook loan program established by Act 195, the Court views the program in the context of the State's "well-established policy of lending textbooks free of charge to elementary and secondary school students." But when it comes time to consider the same Act's instructional materials and equipment program, which is not alleged to make available to private schools any materials and equipment that are not provided to public schools, the majority strikes down this pro-

gram because more than 75% of the nonpublic schools are church-related or religiously affiliated.

If the number of sectarian schools were measured as a percentage of all schools, public and private, then no doubt the majority would conclude that the primary effect of the instructional materials and equipment program is not to advance religion. One looks in vain, ⊥ however, for an explanation of the |390 majority's selection of the number of private schools as the denominator in its instructional materials and equipment calculations. The only apparent explanation might be that Act 195 applies only to private schools while different legislation provides equipment and materials to public schools. But surely this is not a satisfactory explanation, for the plurality tells us, in connection with its discussion of the textbook loan program, which is administered to the public schools through the same statutory provision that provides equipment and materials to the public schools, that "it is of no constitutional significance whether the general program is codified in one statute or two." We are left then with no explanation for the arbitrary course chosen.

The failure of the majority to justify the differing approaches to textbooks and instructional materials and equipment in the above respect is symptomatic of its failure even to attempt to distinguish the Pennsylvania textbook loan program, which it upholds, from the Pennsylvania instructional materials and equipment loan program, which it finds unconstitutional. One might expect that the distinction lies either in the nature of the tangible items being loaned or in the manner in which the programs are operated. But the majority concedes that "the material and equipment that are the subjects of the loan—maps, charts, and laboratory equipment, for example—are 'self-polic[ing], in that starting as secular, nonideo ⊥ logical and neutral, they will not |39 change in use.'" Nor can the fact that the school is the bailee be regarded as constitutionally determinative. In the textbook loan program upheld in *Allen*, the private schools were responsible for transmitting the book requests to the Board of Education and were permitted to store the loaned books on their premises. I fail to see how the instructional materials and equipment program can be distinguished in any significant respect. Under both programs "ownership remains, at least technically, in the State." Once it is conceded that no danger of diversion exists, it is difficult to articulate any principled basis upon which to distinguish the two Act 195 programs.

The Court eschews its primary effect analysis in striking down Act 194, and relies instead upon the proposition that the Act "give[s] rise to a constitutionally intolerable degree of entanglement between church and state." Acknowledging that Act 194 authorizes state financing "of teachers only for remedial and exceptional students, and not for normal students participating in the core curriculum," the Court nonetheless finds this case indistinguishable from *Lemon* v. *Kurtzman* and companion cases, in which salary supplement programs for core curriculum teachers were found unconstitutional. "[A] state-subsidized guidance counselor is surely as likely as a state-subsidized chemistry teacher to fail on occasion to separate religious instruction and the advancement of religious bodies from his secular educational responsibilities."

I find this portion of the Court's opinion deficient as ⊥ a matter of process and insupportable as a matter of law. The burden of proof ordinarily rests upon the plaintiff, but the Court's conclusion that the dangers presented by a state-subsidized guidance counselor are the same as those presented by a state-subsidized chemistry teacher is apparently no more than an *ex cathedra* pronouncement on the part of the Court, if one may use that term in a case such as this, since the District Court found the facts to be exactly the opposite—after consideration of stipulations of fact and an evidentiary hearing: "The Commonwealth, recognizing the logistical realities, provided for traveling therapists rather than traveling pupils. There is no evidence whatsoever that the presence of the therapists in the schools will involve them in the religious missions of the schools. . . . The notion that by setting foot inside a sectarian school a professional therapist or counselor will succumb to sectarianization of his or her professional work is not supported by any evidence."

The propensity of the Court to disregard findings of fact by district courts in Establishment Clause cases is at variance with the established division of responsibilities between trial and appellate courts in the federal system.

As a matter of constitutional law, the holding by the majority that this case is controlled by *Lemon* v. *Kurtzman* marks a significant *sub silentio* extension of that 1971 decision. In that case the Court struck down the Rhode Island salary supplement program, under which teachers employed by nonpublic schools could qualify for additional salary payments from the State in order to bring their salaries ⊥ more closely in line with the prevailing scale in public schools, and a Pennsylvania program authorizing direct reimbursement to nonpublic schools; in order to qualify, the teachers could teach only subjects that were offered in the public schools. The premise supporting the Court's conclusion that these programs "involve[d] excessive entanglement between government and religion" is found at 403 U.S., at 617: "We cannot ignore the danger that a teacher *under religious control and discipline* poses to the separation of the religious from the purely secular aspects of precollege education. The conflict of functions inheres in the situation." (Emphasis added.)

The auxiliary services program established by Act 194 differs from the programs struck down in *Lemon* in two important respects. First the opportunities for religious instruction through the auxiliary services program are greatly reduced because of the considerably more limited reach of the Act. Unlike the core curriculum instruction provided in the *Lemon* programs, "auxiliary services" are defined in Act 194 to embrace a narrow range of services: " 'Auxiliary services' means guidance, counseling and testing services; psychological services; services for exceptional children; remedial and therapeutic services; speech and hearing services; services for the improvement of the educational disadvantaged (such as, but not limited to, teaching English as a second language), and such other secular, neutral, nonideological services as are of benefit to nonpublic school children and are presently or hereafter provided for public school children of the Commonwealth."

Even if the distinction between these services and core curricula is thought to be matter of degree, the sec⊥ond distinction between the programs involved in *Lemon* and Act 194 is a difference in kind. Act 194 provides that these auxiliary services shall be provided by personnel of the *public* school system. Since the danger of entanglement articulated in *Lemon* flowed from the susceptibility of parochial school teachers to "religious control and discipline," I would have assumed that exorcisation of that constitutional "evil" would lead to a different constitutional result. The Court does not contend that the public school employees who would administer the auxiliary services are subject to "religious control and discipline." In fact the Court concedes that "auxiliary services personnel, because not employed by the nonpublic schools, are not directly subject to the discipline of a religious authority." The decision of the Court that Act 194 is unconstitutional rests ultimately upon the unsubstantiated factual proposition that "[t]he potential for impermissible fostering of religion under these circumstances, although somewhat reduced, is nonetheless present." "The test [of entanglement] is inescapably one of degree," *Walz* v. *Tax Commission*, but if the Court is free to ignore the record, then appellees are left to wonder, with good reason, whether the possibility of meeting the entanglement test is now anything more than "a promise to the ear to be broken to the hope, a teasing illusion like a munificent bequest in a pauper's will." *Edwards* v. *California*.

I remain convinced of the correctness of *Mr. Justice* ⊥ *WHITE's* statement in his dissenting opinion in *Committee for Public Education & Religious Liberty* v. *Nyquist*: "Positing an obligation on the State to educate its children, which every State acknowledges, it should be wholly acceptable for the State to contribute to the secular education of children going to sectarian schools rather than to insist that if parents want to provide their children with religious as well as secular education, the State will refuse to contribute anything to their secular training."

I am disturbed as much by the overtones of the Court's opinion as by its actual holding. The Court apparently believes that the Establishment Clause of the First Amendment not only mandates religious neutrality on the part of government but also requires that this Court go further and throw its weight on the side of those who believe that our society as a whole should be a purely secular one. Nothing in the First Amendment or in the cases interpreting it requires such an extreme approach to this difficult question, and "[a]ny interpretation of [the Establishment Clause] and constitutional values it serves must also take account of the free exercise clause and the values it serves." As *Mr. Justice DOUGLAS* wrote for the Court in *Zorach* v. *Clauson*: "We are a religious people whose institutions presuppose a Supreme Being. We guarantee the freedom to worship as one chooses. We make room for as wide a variety of beliefs and creeds as the spiritual needs of man deem necessary. We sponsor an attitude on the part of government that shows no partiality to any one group and that lets each flourish according to the zeal of its adherents and ⊥ the appeal of its dogma. When the state encourages religious instruction or cooperates with religious authorities by adjusting the schedule of public events to sectarian needs, it follows the best of our traditions. For it then respects the religious nature of our people and accommodates the public service to their spiritual needs. To hold that it may not would be to find in the Constitution a requirement that the government show a callous indifference to religious groups. That would be preferring those who believe in no religion over those who do believe. Government may not finance religious groups nor undertake religious instruction nor blend secular and sectarian education nor use secular institutions to force one or some religion on any person. But we find no constitutional requirement which makes it necessary for government to be hostile to religion and to throw its weight against efforts to widen the effective scope of religious influence."

⌐396

Except insofar as the Court upholds the textbook loan program, I respectfully dissent.

ROEMER v. BOARD OF PUBLIC WORKS OF MARYLAND

426 U.S. 736
ON APPEAL FROM THE UNITED STATES
DISTRICT COURT
FOR THE DISTRICT OF MARYLAND
Argued February 23, 1976 — Decided June 21, 1976

⌐739   ⊥ *Mr. Justice BLACKMUN* announced the judgment of the Court and delivered an opinion in which *The CHIEF JUSTICE* and *Mr. Justice POWELL* joined.

We are asked once again to police the constitutional boundary between church and state. Maryland, this time, is the alleged trespasser. It has enacted a statute which, as amended, provides for annual noncategorical grants to private colleges, among them religiously affiliated institutions, subject only to the restrictions that the funds not be used for "sectarian purposes." A three-judge District Court, by a divided vote, refused to enjoin the operation of the statute, and a direct appeal has been taken to this Court.

I

⊥ The challenged grant program was instituted by Laws of 1971 and is now embodied in Md. Ann. Code, Art. 77A, § § 65-69 (1975). It provides fundings for "any private institution of higher learning within the State of Maryland," provided the institution is accredited by the State Department of Education, was established in Maryland prior to July 1, 1970, maintains one or more "associate of arts or baccalaureate degree" programs, and refrains from awarding "only seminarian or theologlcal degrees." The aid is in the form of an annual fiscal year subsidy to qualifying colleges and universities. The formula by which each institution's entitlement is computed has been changed several times and is not independently at issue here. It now provides for a qualifying institution to receive, for each full-time student (excluding students enrolled in seminarian or theologlcal academic programs), an amount equal to 15% of the State's per full-time pupil appropriation for a student in the state college system. As first enacted, the grants were completely unrestricted. They remain noncategorical in nature, and a recipient institution may put them to whatever use it prefers, with but one exception. In 1972, following this Court's decisions in *Lemon* v. *Kurtzman, (Lemon I),* and *Tilton* v. *Richardson,* § 68A was added to the statute by Laws of 1972. It provides: "None of the moneys payable under this subtitle ⊥ shall be utilized by the institutions for sectarian purposes."

⌐740

⌐741

The administration of the grant program is entrusted to the State's Board of Public Works "assisted by the Maryland Council for Higher Education." These bodies are to adopt "criteria and procedures . . . for the implementation and administration of the aid program." They are specifically authorized to adopt "criteria and procedures" governing the method of application for grants and of their disbursement, the verification of degrees conferred, and the "submission of reports or data concerning the utilization of these moneys by [the aided] institutions." Primary responsibility for the program rests with the Council for Higher Education, an appointed commission which antedates the aid program, which has numerous other responsibilities in the educational field, and which has derived from these a "considerable expertise as to the character and functions of the various private colleges and universities in the State."

The Council performs what the District Court described as a "two-step screening process" to insure compliance with the statutory restrictions on the grants. First, it determines whether an institution applying for aid is eligible at all, or is one "awarding primarily theo ⊥ logical or seminary degrees." Several

⌐742

applicants have been disqualified at this stage of the process. Second, the Council requires that those institutions that are eligible for funds not put them to any sectarian use. An application must be accompanied by an affidavit of the institution's chief executive officer stating that the funds will not be used for sectarian purposes, and by a description of the specific nonsectarian uses that are planned. These may be changed only after written notice to the Council. By the end of the fiscal year the institution must file a "Utilization of Funds Report" describing and itemizing the use of the funds. The chief executive officer must certify the report and also file his own "Post-expenditure Affidavit," stating that the funds have not been put to sectarian uses. The recipient institution is further required to segregate state funds in a "special revenue account" and to identify aided nonsectarian expenditures separately in its budget. It must retain "sufficient documentation of the State funds expended to permit verification by the Council that funds were not spent for sectarian ⌐743 purposes." Any question of sectarian ⊥ use that may arise is to be resolved by the Council, if possible, on the basis of information submitted to it by the institution and without actual examination of its books. Failing that, a "verification or audit" may be undertaken. The District Court found that the audit would be "quick and non-judgmental," taking one day or less.

In 1971, $1.7 million was disbursed to 17 private institutions in Maryland. The disbursements were under the statute as originally enacted, and were therefore not subject to § 68A's specific prohibition on sectarian use. Of the 17 institutions, five were church related, and these received $525,000 of the $1.7 million. A total of $1.8 million was to be awarded to 18 institutions in 1972, the second year of the grant program; of this amount, $603,000 was to go to church-related institutions. Before disbursement, however, this suit, challenging the grants as in violation of the Establishment Clause of the First Amendment, was filed. The $603,000 was placed in escrow and was so held until after the entry of the District Court's judgment on October 21, ⌐744 1974. These and subsequent awards, therefore, are ⊥ subject to § 68A and to the Council's procedures for insuring compliance therewith.

Plaintiffs in this suit, appellants here, are four individual Maryland citizens and taxpayers. Their complaint sought a declaration of the statute's invalidity, an order enjoining payments under it to church-affiliated institutions, and a declaration that the State was entitled to recover from such institutions any amounts already disbursed. In addition to the responsible state officials, plaintiff-appellants joined as defendants the five institutions they claimed were constitutionally ineligible for this form of aid: Western Maryland College, College of Notre Dame, Mount Saint Mary's College, Saint Joseph College, and Loyola College. Of these, the last four

are affiliated with the Roman Catholic Church; Western Maryland, was a Methodist affiliate. The District Court ruled with respect to all five. Western Maryland, however, has since been dismissed as a defendant-appellee. We are concerned, therefore, only with the four Roman Catholic affiliates.

After carefully assessing the role that the Catholic Church plays in the lives of these institutions, a matter to which we return in greater detail below, and applying the ⊥ three-part requirement of Lem-   ⌐745 on I, that state aid such as this have a secular purpose, a primary effect other than the advancement of religion, and no tendency to entangle the State excessively in church affairs, the District Court ruled that the amended statute was constitutional and was not to be enjoined. The court considered the original, unamended statute to have been unconstitutional under Lemon I, but it refused to order a refund of amounts theretofore paid out, reasoning that any refund was barred by the decision in Lemon v. Kurtzman (Lemon II). The District Court therefore denied all relief. This appeal followed. We noted probable jurisdiction.

II

A system of government that makes itself felt as pervasively as ours could hardly be expected never to cross paths with the church. In fact, our State and Federal Governments impose certain burdens upon, and impart certain benefits to, virtually all our activities, and religious activity is not an exception. The Court has enforced a scrupulous neutrality by the State, as ⊥ among religions, and also as between   ⌐746 religious and other activities, but a hermetic separation of the two is an impossibility it has never required. It long has been established, for example, that the State may send a cleric, indeed even a clerical order, to perform a wholly secular task. In Bradfield v. Roberts, the Court upheld the extension of public aid to a corporation which, although composed entirely of members of a Roman Catholic sisterhood acting "under the auspices of said church," was limited by its corporate charter to the secular purpose of operating a charitable hospital.

And religious institutions need not be quarantined from public benefits that are neutrally available to all. The Court has permitted the State to supply transportation for children to and from church-related as well as public schools. Everson v. Board of Education. It has done the same with respect to secular textbooks loaned by the State on equal terms to students attending both public and church-related elementary schools. Board of Education v. Allen. Since it had not been shown in Allen that the secular textbooks would be put to other than secular purposes, the Court concluded that, as in Everson, the State was merely "extending the benefits of state laws to all citizens." Just as Bradfield dispels any notion that a religious person can never be in the

⌐747 State's pay for a secular purpose, ⊥ *Everson* and *Allen* put to rest any argument that the State may never act in such a way that has the incidental effect of facilitating religious activity. The Court has not been blind to the fact that in aiding a religious institution to perform a secular task, the State frees the institution's resources to be put to sectarian ends. If this were impermissible, however, a church could not be protected by the police and fire departments, or have its public sidewalk kept in repair. The Court never has held that religious activities must be discriminated against in this way.

Neutrality is what is required. The State must confine itself to secular objectives, and neither advance nor impede religious activity. Of course, that principle is more easily stated than applied. The Court has taken the view that a secular purpose and a facial neutrality may not be enough, if in fact the State is lending direct support to a religious activity. The State may not, for example, pay for what is actually a religious education, even though it purports to be paying for a secular one, and even though it makes its aid available to secular and religious institutions alike. The Court also has taken the view that the State's efforts to perform a secular task, and at the same time avoid aiding in the performance of a religious one, may not lead it into such an intimate relationship with religious authority that it appears ⌐748 either to be sponsoring or to be exces⊥sively interfering with that authority. In *Lemon I* as noted above, the Court distilled these concerns into a three-prong test, resting in part on prior case law, for the constitutionality of statutes affording state aid to church-related schools: "First, the statute must have a secular legislative purpose; second, its principal or primary effect must be one that neither advances nor inhibits religion . . .; finally, the statute must not foster 'an excessive government entanglement with religion.' "

At issue in *Lemon I* were two state-aid plans, a Rhode Island program to grant a 15% supplement to the salaries of private, church-related school teachers teaching secular courses, and a Pennsylvania program to reimburse private church-related schools for the entire cost of secular courses also offered in public schools. Both failed the third part of the test, that of "excessive government entanglement." This part the Court held in turn required a consideration of three factors: (1) the character and purposes of the benefited institutions, (2) the nature of the aid provided, and (3) the resulting relationship between the State and the religious authority. As to the first of these, in reviewing the Rhode Island program, the Court found that the aided schools, elementary and secondary, were characterized by "substantial religious activity and purpose." They were located near parish churches. Religious instruction was consid-⌐749 ered "part of the total ⊥ educational process." Religious symbols and religious activities abounded. Two-thirds of the teachers were nuns, and their operation of the schools was regarded as an " 'integral part of the religious mission of the Catholic Church.' " The schooling came at an impressionable age. The form of aid also cut against the programs. Unlike the textbooks in *Allen* and the bus transportation in *Everson*, the services of the state-supported teachers could not be counted on to be purely secular. They were bound to mix religious teachings with secular ones, not by conscious design, perhaps, but because the mixture was inevitable when teachers (themselves usually Catholics) were "employed by a religious organization, subject to the direction and discipline of religious authorities, and work[ed] in a system dedicated to rearing children in a particular faith." The State's efforts to supervise and control the teaching of religion in supposedly secular classes would therefore inevitably entangle it excessively in religious affairs. The Pennsylvania program similarly foundered.

The Court also pointed to another kind of church-state entanglement threatened by the Rhode Island and Pennsylvania programs, namely, their "divisive political potential." They represented "successive and very likely permanent annual appropriations that benefit relatively few religious groups." Political factions, supporting and opposing the programs, were bound to divide along religious lines. This was "one of the principal evils against which the First Amendment was intended to protect." It was stressed that the political divisiveness of the programs was "aggravated . . . by the need for continuing annual appropriations."

⊥ In *Tilton* v. *Richardson*, a companion case to ⌐750 *Lemon I*, the Court reached the contrary result. The aid challenged in *Tilton* was in the form of federal grants for the construction of academic facilities at private colleges, some of them church related, with the restriction that the facilities not be used for any sectarian purpose. Applying *Lemon I's* three-part test, the Court found the purpose of the federal aid program there under consideration to be secular. Its primary effect was not the advancement of religion, for sectarian use of the facilities was prohibited. Enforcement of this prohibition was made possible by the fact that religion did not so permeate the defendant colleges that their religious and secular functions were inseparable. On the contrary, there was no evidence that religious activities took place in the funded facilities. Courses at the colleges were "taught according the academic requirements intrinsic to the subject matter," and "an atmosphere of academic freedom rather than religious indoctrination" was maintained.

Turning to the problem of excessive entanglement, the Court first stressed the character of the aided institutions. It pointed to several general differences between college and precollege education: college students are less susceptible to religious indoctrination; college courses tend to entail an internal discipline that inherently limits the opportunities for sectarian influence; and a high degree of academic freedom tends to prevail at the college level. It found no evidence that the col⊥leges in *Tilton* varied from this pattern. Though controlled and largely populated by Roman Catholics, the colleges were not restricted to adherents of that faith. No religious services were required to be attended. Theology courses were mandatory, but they were taught in academic fashion, and with treatment of beliefs other than Roman Catholicism. There were no attempts to proselytise among students, and principles of academic freedom prevailed. With colleges of this character, there was little risk that religion would seep into the teaching of secular subjects, and the state surveillance necessary to separate the two, therefore, was diminished. The Court next looked to the type of aid provided, and found it to be neutral or nonideological in nature. Like the textbooks and bus transportation in *Allen* and *Everson*, but unlike the teachers services in *Lemon I*, physical facilities were capable of being restricted to secular purposes. Moreover, the construction grant was a one-shot affair, not involving annual audits and appropriations.

As for political divisiveness, no "continuing religious aggravation" over the program had been shown, and the Court reasoned that this might be because of the lack of continuity in the church-state relationship, the character and diversity of the colleges, and the fact that they served a dispersed student constituency rather than a local one. "Cumulatively," all these considerations persuaded the Court that church-state entanglement was not excessive.

In *Hunt* v. *McNair* the challenged aid was also for the construction of secular college facilities, the state plan being one to finance the construction by revenue bonds issued through the medium of a state authority. In effect, the college serviced and repaid the bonds, but at the lower cost resulting from the tax-free status of the interest payments. The Court upheld the program on reasoning analogous to that in ⊥ *Tilton*. In applying the second of the *Lemon I* test's three parts, that concerning "primary effect," the following refinement was added: "Aid normally may be thought to have a primary effect of advancing religion when it flows to an institution in which religion is so pervasive that a substantial portion of its functions are subsumed in the religious mission or when it funds a specifically religious activity in an otherwise substantially secular setting."

Although the college which *Hunt* concerned was subject to substantial control by its sponsoring Baptist Church, it was found to be similar to the colleges in *Tilton* and not "pervasively sectarian." As in *Tilton*, state aid went to secular facilities only, and thus not to any "specifically religious activity."

Committee for Public Education & Religious Liberty v. *Nyquist* followed in *Lemon I's* wake much as *Hunt* followed in *Tilton's*. The aid in *Nyquist* was to elementary and secondary schools which, the District Court found, generally conformed to a "profile"

of a sectarian or substantially religious school. The state aid took three forms: direct subsidies for the maintenance and repair of buildings; reimbursement of parents for a percentage of tuition paid; and certain tax benefits for parents. All three forms of aid were found to have an impermissible primary effect. The mainte⊥nance and repair subsidies, being unrestricted, could be used for the upkeep of a chapel or classrooms used for religious instruction. The reimbursements and tax benefits to parents could likewise be used to support wholly religious activities.

In *Levitt* v. *Committee for Public Education* the Court also invalidated a program for public aid to church-affiliated schools. The grants, which were to elementary and secondary schools in New York, were in the form of reimbursements for the schools' testing and recordkeeping expenses. The schools met the same sectarian profile as did those in *Nyquist*, at least in some cases. There was therefore "substantial risk" that the state-funded tests would be "drafted with an eye, unconsciously or otherwise, to inculcate students in the religious precepts of the sponsoring church."

Last Term, in *Meek* v. *Pittenger*, the Court ruled yet again on a state-aid program for church-related elementary and secondary schools. On the authority of *Allen*, it upheld a Pennsylvania program for lending textbooks to private school students. It found, however, that *Lemon I* required the invalidation of two other forms of aid to the private schools. The first was the loan of instructional materials and equipment. Like the textbooks, these were secular and nonideological in nature. Unlike the textbooks, however, they were loaned directly to the schools. The schools, similar to those in *Lemon I*, were ones in which "the teaching process is, to a large extent, devoted to the inculcation of religious values and belief." Aid flowing directly to such "religion-pervasive institutions" had the primary effect of advancing religion. The other form of aid was the provision of "auxiliary" educational serv⊥ices: remedial instruction, counseling and testing, and speech and hearing therapy. These also were intended to be neutral and nonideological, and in fact were to be provided by public school teachers. Still, there was danger that the teachers, in such a sectarian setting would allow religion to seep into their instruction. To attempt to prevent this from happening would excessively entangle the State in church affairs. The Court referred again to the danger of political divisiveness, heightened, as it had been in *Lemon I* and *Nyquist*, by the necessity of annual legislative reconsideration of the aid appropriation.

So the slate we write on is anything but clean. Instead, there is little room for further refinement of the principles governing public aid to church-affiliated private schools. Our purpose is not to unsettle those principles, so recently reaffirmed, or to expand upon them substantially, but merely to insure that they are faithfully applied in this case.

III

The first part of *Lemon I's* three-part test is not in issue; appellants do not challenge the District Court's finding that the purpose of Maryland's aid program is the secular one of supporting private higher education generally, as an economic alternative to a wholly public system. The focus of the debate is on the second and third parts, those concerning the primary effect ⊥755 of ad⊥vancing religion, and excessive church-state entanglement. We consider them in the same order.

A

While entanglement is essentially a procedural problem, the primary effect question is the substantive one of what private educational activities, by whatever procedure, may be supported by state funds. *Hunt* requires (I) that no state aid at all go to institutions that are so "pervasively sectarian" that secular activities cannot be separated from sectarian ones, and (2) that if secular activities *can* be separated out, they alone may be funded.

(1) The District Court's finding in this case was that the appellee colleges are not "pervasively sectarian." This conclusion it supported with a number of subsidiary findings concerning the role of religion on these campuses:

(a) Despite their formal affiliation with the Roman Catholic Church, the colleges are "characterized by a high degree of institutional autonomy." None of the four receives funds from, or makes reports to, the Catholic Church. The Church is represented on their governing boards, but, as with Mount Saint Mary's, "no instance of entry of Church considerations into college decisions was shown."

(b) The colleges employ Roman Catholic chaplains and hold Roman Catholic religious exercises on campus. Attendance at such is not required; the encouragement of spiritual development is only "one secondary objective" of each college; and "at none of these institutions does this encouragement go beyond providing the opportunities or occasions for religious experience. "It was the District Court's general finding that "religious indoctrination is not a substantial purpose or activity of any of these defendants."

⊥756   (c) ⊥ Mandatory religion or theology courses are taught at each of the colleges, primarily by Roman Catholic clerics, but these only supplement a curriculum covering "the spectritum of a liberal arts program." Nontheology courses are taught in an "atmosphere of intellectual freedom" and without "religious pressures." Each college subscribes to, and abides by, the 1940 Statement of Principles on Academic Freedom of the American Association of University Professors.

(d) Some classes are begun with prayer. The percentage of classes in which this is done varies with the college, from a "miniscule" percentage at Loyola and Mount Saint Mary's, to a majority at Saint Jo-

seph. There is no "actual college policy" of encouraging the practice. "It is treated as a facet of the instructor's academic freedom." Classroom prayers were therefore regarded by the District Court as "peripheral to the subject of religious permeation," as were the facts that some instructors wear clerical garb and some classrooms have religious symbols. The court concluded: "None of these facts impairs the clear and con⊥vincing evidence that courses at   ⊥757 each defendant are taught 'according to the academic requirements intrinsic to the subject matter and the individual teacher's concept of professional standards.' [citing *Tilton* v. *Richardson*]."

In support of this finding the court relied on the fact that a Maryland education department group had monitored the teacher education program at Saint Joseph College, where classroom prayer is most prevelant, and had seen "no evidence of religion entering any elements of that program."

(e) The District Court found that, apart from the theology departments, faculty hiring decisions are not made on a religious basis. At two of the colleges, Notre Dame and Mount Saint Mary's, no inquiry at all is made into an applicant's religion. Religious preference is to be noted on Loyola's application form, but the purpose is to allow full appreciation of the applicant's background. Loyola also attempts to employ each year two members of a particular religious order which once staffed a college recently merged into Loyola. Budgetary considerations lead the colleges generally to favor members of religious orders, who often receive less than full salary. Still, the District Court found that "academic quality" was the principal hiring criterion, and that any "hiring bias," or "effort by any defendant to stock its faculty with members of a particular religious group," would have been noticed by other faculty members, who had never been heard to complain.

(f) The great majority of students at each of the colleges are Roman Catholic, but the District Court concluded from a "thorough analysis of the student ad⊥mission and recruiting criteria" that the student   ⊥758 bodies "are chosen without regard to religion."

We cannot say that the foregoing findings as to the role of religion in particular aspects of the colleges are clearly erroneous. Appellants ask us to set those findings aside in certain respects. Not surprisingly, they have gleaned from this record of thousands of pages, compiled during several weeks of trial, occasional evidence of a more sectarian character than the District Court ascribes to the colleges. It is not our place, however, to reappraise the evidence, unless it plainly fails to support the findings of the trier of facts. That is certainly not the case here, and it would make no difference even if we were to second-guess the District Court in certain particulars. To answer the question whether an institution is so "pervasively sectarian" that it may receive no direct state aid of any kind, it is necessary to paint a general picture of the institution, composed of many elements. The general picture that the District Court has painted of the appellee institutions is similar in almost all respects to that of the church-affiliated colleges considered in *Tilton* and *Hunt*. We ⊥ find no constitutionally significant distinction between them, at least for purposes of the "pervasive sectarianism" test.

(2) Having found that the appellee institutions are not, "so permeated by religion that the secular side cannot be separated from the sectarian," the District Court proceeded to the next question posed by *Hunt*: whether aid in fact was extended only to "the secular side." This requirement the court regarded as satisfied by the statutory prohibition against sectarian use, and by the administrative enforcement of that prohibition through the Council for Higher Education. We agree. *Hunt* requires only that state funds not be used to support "specifically religious activity." It is clear that fund uses exist that meet this require⊥ment. We have no occasion to elaborate further on what is and is not a "specifically religious activity," for no particular use of the state funds is set out in this statute. Funds are put to the use of the college's choice, provided it is not a sectarian use, of which the college must satisfy the Council. If the question is whether the statute sought to be enjoined authorizes state funds for "specifically religious activity," that question fairly answers itself. The statute in terms forbids the use of funds for "sectarian purposes," and this prohibition appears to be at least as broad as *Hunt's* prohibition of the public funding of "specifically religious activity." We must assume that the colleges, and the Council, will exercise their delegated control over use of the funds in compliance with the statutory, and therefore the constitutional, mandate. It is to be expected that they will give a wide berth to "specifically religious activity," and thus minimize constitutional questions. ⊥ Should such questions arise, the courts will consider them. It has not been the Court's practice, in considering facial challenges to statutes of this kind, to strike them down in anticipation that particular applications may result in unconstitutional use of funds.

B

If the foregoing answer to the "primary effect" ques⊥tion seems easy, it serves to make the "excessive entanglement" problem more difficult. The statute itself clearly denies the use of public funds for "sectarian purposes." It seeks to avert such use, however, through a process of annual interchange— proposal and approval, expenditure and review— between the colleges and the Council. In answering the question whether this will be an "excessively entangling" relationship, we must consider the several relevant factors identified in prior decisions:

(1) First is the character of the aided institutions. This has been fully described above. As the District

Court found, the colleges perform "essentially secular educational functions" that are distinct and separable from religious activity. This finding, which is a prerequisite under the "pervasive sectarianism" test to any state aid at all, is also important for purposes of the entanglement test because it means that secular activities, for the most, can be taken at face value. There is no danger, or at least only a substantially reduced danger, that an ostensibly secular activity—the study of biology, the learning of a foreign language, an athletic event—will actually be infused with religious content or significance. The need for close surveillance of purportedly secular activities is correspondingly reduced. Thus the District Court found that in this case "there is no necessity for state officials to investigate the conduct of particular classes of educational programs to determine whether a school is attempting to indoctrinate its students under the guise of secular education." We cannot say the District Court erred in this judgment or gave it undue significance. The Court took precisely the same view with respect to the aid extended to the very similar institutions in *Tilton*.

⊥ (2) As for the form of aid, we have already noted that no particular use of state funds is before us in this case. The *process* by which aid is disbursed, and a use for it chosen, are before us. We address this as a matter of the "resulting relationship" of secular and religious authority.

(3) As noted, the funding process is an annual one. The subsidies are paid out each year, and they can be put to annually varying uses. The colleges propose particular uses for the Council's approval, and, following expenditure, they report to the Council on the use to which the funds have been put.

The District Court's view was that in the light of the character of the aided institutions, and the resulting absence of any need "to investigate the conduct of particular classes," the annual nature of the subsidy was not fatal. In fact, an annual, ongoing relationship had existed in *Tilton*, where the Government retained the right to inspect subsidized buildings for sectarian use, and the ongoing church-state involvement had been even greater in *Hunt*, where the State was actually the lessor of the subsidized facilities, retaining extensive powers to regulate their use.

We agree with the District Court that "excessive entanglement" does not necessarily result from the fact that the subsidy is an annual one. It is true that the Court favored the "one-time, single purpose" construction grants in *Tilton* because they entailed "no continuing financial relationships or dependencies, no annual audits, and no government analysis of an institution's expenditures." The present aid program cannot claim these aspects. But if the question is whether this case is more like *Lemon I* or more like *Tilton*—and surely that is the ⊥ fundamental question before us—the answer must be that it is more like *Tilton*.

⊥759
⊥760
⊥761
⊥762
⊥763
⊥764

Tilton is distinguishable only by the form of aid. We cannot discount the distinction entirely, but neither can we regard it as decisive. As the District Court pointed out, ongoing, annual supervision of college facilities was explicitly foreseen in *Tilton*, and even more so in *Hunt*. *Tilton* and *Hunt* would be totally indistinguishable, at least in terms of annual supervision, if funds were used under the present statute to build or maintain physical facilities devoted to secular use. The present statute contemplates annual decisions by the Council as to what is a "sectarian purpose," but, as we have noted, the secular and sectarian activities of the colleges are easily separated. Occasional audits are possible here, but we must accept the District Court's finding that they would be "quick and non-judgmental." They and the other contacts between the Council and the colleges are not likely to be any more entangling than the inspections and audits incident to the normal process of the colleges' accreditations by the State.

While the form-of-aid distinctions of *Tilton* are thus of questionable importance, the character-of-institution distinctions of *Lemon I* are most impressive. To reiterate a few of the relevant points: the elementary and secondary schooling in *Lemon* came at an impressionable age; the aided schools were "under the general supervision" of the Roman Catholic diocese; each had a local Catholic parish that assumed "ultimate financial responsibility" for it; the principals of the schools were usually appointed by church authorities; religion "pervade[d] the school system"; teachers were specifically in-|765 structed by the "Handbook of School Regula⊥tions" that "[r]eligious formation is not confined to formal courses; nor is it restricted to a single subject area." These things made impossible what is crucial to a nonentangling aid program: the ability of the State to identify and subsidize separate secular functions caried out at the school, without on-the-site inspections being necessary to prevent diversion of the funds to sectarian purposes. The District Court gave primary importance to this consideration, and we cannot say it erred.

(4) As for political divisiveness, the District Court recognized that the annual nature of the subsidy, along with its promise of an increasing demand for state funds as the colleges' dependency grew, aggravated the danger of "[p]olitical fragmentation . . . on religious lines." *Lemon I* Nonetheless, the District Court found that the program "does not create a substantial danger of political entanglement." Several reasons were given. As was stated in *Tilton*, the danger of political divisiveness is "substantially less" when the aided institution is not an elementary or secondary school, but a college, "whose student constituency is not local but diverse and widely dispersed." Furthermore, political divisiveness is diminished by the fact that the aid is extended to private colleges generally, more than two thirds of which have no religious affiliation; this is in sharp contrast to *Nyquist*, for example, where 95% of the aided schools were Roman Catholic parochial schools. Finally, the substantial autonomy of the colleges was thought to mitigate political divisiveness, in that controversies surrounding the aid program are not likely to involve the Catholic Church itself, or even the religious character of the schools, but only their "fiscal responsi⊥bility and educational re-|766 quirements."

The District Court's reasoning seems to us entirely sound. Once again, appellants urge that this case is controlled by previous cases in which the form of aid was similar *(Lemon I; Nyquist; Levitt)*, rather than those in which the character of the aided institution was the same *(Tilton; Hunt)*. We disagree. Though indisputably relevant, the annual nature of the aid cannot be dispositive. On the one hand, the Court has *struck down* a "permanent," nonannual tax exemption, reasoning that "the pressure for frequent enlargement of the relief is predictable," as it always is. *Committee for Public Education & Religious Liberty* v. *Nyquist*. On the other hand, in *Tilton* it has *upheld* a program for "one-time, single- purpose" construction grants, despite the fact that such grants would, in fact, be "annual," at least insofar as new grants would be annually applied for. Our holdings are better reconciled in terms of the character of the aided institutions, found to be so dissimilar as between those considered in *Tilton* and *Hunt*, on the one hand, and those considered in *Lemon I, Nyquist,* and *Levitt*, on the other.

There is no exact science in gauging the entanglement of church and state. The wording of the test, which speaks of *"excessive* entanglement," itself makes that clear. The relevant factors we have identified are to be considered "cumulatively" in judging the degree of entanglement. They may cut different ways, as certainly they do here. In reaching the conclusion that it did, the District Court gave dominant importance to the character of the aided institutions and to its finding that they are capable of separating secular and religious functions. For the rea⊥sons |767 stated above, we cannot say that the emphasis was misplaced or the finding erroneous.

The judgment of the District Court is affirmed.

It is so ordered.

Mr. *Justice WHITE*, with whom *Mr. Justice REHNQUIST* joins, concurring in the judgment.

While I join in the judgment of the Court, I am unable to concur in the plurality opinion substantially for the reasons set forth in my opinions in *Lemon* v. ⊥ *Kurtzman (Lemon I),* and *Committee for Public Education* v. *Nyquist.* I am no more reconciled now to *Lemon I* than I was when it was decided. The threefold test of *Lemon I* imposes unnecessary, and, as I believe today's plurality opinion demonstrates, superfluous tests for establishing "when the State's involvement with religion passes the peril point" for First Amendment purposes. *Nyquist*

"It is enough for me that the [State is] financing a separable secular function of overriding importance in order to sustain the legislation here challenged." *Lemon I*. As long as there is a secular legislative purpose, and as long as the primary effect of the legislation is neither to advance nor inhibit religion, I see no reason—particularly in light of the "sparse language of the Establishment Clause," *Nyquist*—to take the constitutional inquiry further. However, since 1970, the Court has added a third element to the inquiry: whether there is "an excessive government entanglement with religion." *Walz v. Tax Commission*. I have never understood the constitutional foundation for this added element; it is at once both ⌊769 insolubly paradoxical, ⊥ and—as the Court has conceded from the outset—a "blurred, indistinct and variable barrier." *Lemon I*. It is not clear that the "weight and contours of entanglement as a separate constitutional criterion," *Nyquist*, are any more settled now than when they first surfaced. Today's plurality opinion leaves the impression that the criterion really may not be "separate" at all. In affirming the District Court's conclusion that the legislation here does not create an "excessive entanglement" of church and state, the plurality emphasizes with approval that "the District Court gave dominant importance to the character of the aided institutions and to its finding that they are capable of separating secular and religious functions." Yet these are the same factors upon which the plurality focus in concluding that the Maryland legislation satisfies the first part of the *Lemon I* test: that on the record the "appellee colleges are not 'pervasively sectarian,'" and that the aid at issue was capable of, and is in fact, extended only to "the secular side" of the appellee colleges' operations. It is unclear to me how the first and third parts of the *Lemon I* test are substantially different. The "excessive entanglement" test appears no less "curious and mystifying" than when it was first announced. *Lemon I*

I see no reason to indulge in the redundant exercise of evaluating the same facts and findings under a different label. No one in this case challenges the District ⊥ Court's finding that the purpose of the legislation here is secular. And I do not disagree with the plurality that the primary effect of the aid program is not advancement of religion. That is enough in my view to sustain the aid programs against constitutional challenge, and I would say no more.

Mr. *Justice BRENNAN*, with whom *Mr. Justice MARSHALL* joins, dissenting.

I agree with Judge Bryan, dissenting from the judgment under review, that the Maryland Act *"in*

these instances does in truth offend the Constitution by its provisions of funds, in that it exposes State money for use in advancing religion, no matter the vigilance to avoid it." Each of the institutions is a church-affiliated or church-related body. The subsidiary findings concerning the role of religion on each of the campuses, summarized by the plurality opinion, conclusively establish that fact. In that circumstance, I agree with Judge Bryan that "[o]f telling decisiveness here is the payment of the grants directly to the colleges unmarked in purpose. . . . Presently the Act is simply a blunderbuss discharge of public funds to a church-affiliated or church-related college." In other words, the Act provides for payment of general subsidies to religious institutions from public funds and I have heretofore expressed my view that "[g]eneral subsidies of religious activities would, of course, constitute impermissible state involvement with religion." *Walz v. Tax Commission*. This is because general subsidies "tend to promote that type of interdependence between religion and state which the First Amendment was designed to prevent." *Abington School District* v. ⊥ ⌊771 *Schempp*. "What the Framers meant to foreclose, and what our decisions under the Establishment Clause have forbidden, are those involvements of religions with secular institutions which . . . serve the essentially religious activities of religious institutions. *Id.*

The history of the bitter controversies over public subsidy of sectarian educational institutions that began soon after the Nation was formed is recited in my separate opinion in *Lemon v. Kurtzman (Lemon I)*. My reasons for concluding in *Lemon I* that all three statutes there before us impermissibly provided a direct subsidy from public funds for activities carried on by sectarian educational institutions also support my agreement with Judge Bryan in this case "than an injunction should issue as prayed in the complaint, stopping future payments under the Maryland Act to the [appellee] colleges." I said in *Lemon I*: "I believe that the Establishment Clause forbids . . . Government to provide funds to sectarian universities in which the propagation and advancement of a particular religion are a function or purpose of the institution. . . .

"I reach this conclusion for [these] reasons . . . : the necessarily deep involvement of government in the religious activities of such an institution through the policing of restrictions, and the fact that subsidies of tax monies directly to a sectarian institution necessarily aid the proselytizing function of the institution. . . .

"I do not believe that [direct] grants to such a sectarian institution are permissible. The reason is not that religion 'permeates' the secular education that is provided. Rather, it is that the secular edu ⊥ cation is ⌊772 provided within the environment of religion; the institution is dedicated to two goals, secular education *and* religious instruction. When aid flows directly to the institution, both functions benefit." (Emphasis in original.)

The discrete interests of government and religion are mutually best served when each avoids too close a proximity to the other. "It is not only the non-believer who fears the injection of sectarian doctrines and controversies into the civil polity, but in as high degree it is the devout believer who fears the secularization of a creed which becomes too deeply involved with and dependent upon the government." *Abington School Dist.* v. *Schempp.* The Maryland Act requires "too close a proximity" of government to the subsidized sectarian institutions and in my view creates real dangers of the "secularization of a creed." *Ibid.; Lemon I.*

Unlike Judge Bryan, I would also reverse the District Court's denial of appellants' motion that the appellee institutions be required to refund all payments made to them. I adhere to the views expressed in Mr. Justice Douglas' dissent, which I joined, in *Lemon* v. *Kurtzman (Lemon II)*: "There is as much a violation of the Establishment Clause of the First Amendment whether the payment from public funds to sectarian schools involves last year, the current year or next year. . . .

"Whether the grant is for . . . last year or at the present time, taxpayers are forced to contribute to sectarian schools a part of their tax dollars."

I would reverse the judgment of the District Court and remand with directions to enter a new judgment ⊥773 per ⊥ manently enjoining the Board of Public Works of the State of Maryland from implementing the Maryland Act, and requiring the appellee institutions to refund all payments made to them pursuant to the Act.

Mr. Justice STEWART, dissenting.

In my view, the decisive differences between this case and *Tilton* v. *Richardson* lie in the nature of the theology courses that are a compulsory part of the curriculum at each of the appellee institutions and the type of governmental assistance provided to these church-affiliated colleges. In *Tilton* the Court emphasized that the theology courses were taught as academic subjects. "Although all four schools require their students to take theology courses, the parties stipulated that these courses are taught according to academic requirements of the subject matter and the teacher's concept of professional standards. The parties also stipulated that the courses covered a range of human religious experiences and are not limited to courses about the Roman Catholic religion. The schools introduced evidence that they made no attempt to indoctrinate students or to proselytize. Indeed, some of the required theology courses at Albertus Magnus and Sacred Heart are taught by rabbis."

Here, by contrast, the District Court was unable to find that the compulsory religion courses were taught as an academic discipline.

"[T]he hiring patterns for religion or theology departments are a special case and present a unique problem. All five defendants staff their religion or theology departments chiefly with clerics of the affiliated church. At two defendants, Western ⊥ Maryland and Mt. St. Mary's, *all* members of the religion or theology faculty are clerics. The problem presented by the make-up of these departments is obvious. Recognition of the academic freedom of these instructors does not necessarily lead to a conclusion that courses in the religion or theology departments at the five defendants have no overtones of indoctrination."

.   .   .   .   .

"The theology and religion courses of each defendant must be viewed in the light of that shared objective [of encouraging spiritual development of the students]. While most of the defendants do not offer majors in religion or theology, each maintains a vigorous religion or theology department. The primary concern of these departments, either admittedly or by the obvious thrust of the courses, is Christianity. As already noted, the departments are staffed almost entirely with clergy of the affiliated church. At each of the defendants, certain of these courses are required.

". . . [A] department staffed mainly by clerics of the affiliated church and geared toward a limited array of the possible theology or religion courses affords a congenial means of furthering the secondary objective of fostering religious experience." (Emphasis in the original).

In the light of these findings, I cannot agree with the Court's assertion that there is "no constitutionally significant distinction" between the colleges in *Tilton* and those in the present case. The findings in *Tilton* clearly established that the federal building construction grants benefited academic institutions that made no attempt to inculcate the religious beliefs of the affiliated church. In the present case, by contrast, ⊥ the compulsory theology courses may be ⊥775 "devoted to deepening religious experiences in the particular faith rather than to teaching theology as an academic discipline." In view of this salient characteristic of the appellee institutions and the noncategorical grants provided to them by the State of Maryland, I agree with the conclusion of the dissenting member of the three-judge court that the challenged Act *"in these instances* does in truth offend the Constitution by its provisions of funds, in that it exposes State money for use in advancing religion, no matter the vigilance to avoid it." (emphasis in original).

For the reasons stated, and those expressed by *Mr. Justice BRENNAN* and *Mr. Justice STEVENS*, I

⊥774

dissent from the judgment and opinion of the Court and the plurality's opinion.

Mr. Justice STEVENS, dissenting.

My views are substantially those expressed by *Mr. Justice BRENNAN*. However, I would add emphasis to the pernicious tendency of a state subsidy to tempt religious schools to compromise their religious mission without wholly abandoning it. The disease of entanglement may infect a law discouraging wholesome religious activity as well as a law encouraging the propagation of a given faith.

WOLMAN v. WALTER

433 U.S. 229
ON APPEAL FROM THE UNITED STATES
DISTRICT COURT
FOR THE SOUTHERN DISTRICT OF OHIO
Argued April 25, 1977 — Decided June 24, 1977

⊥232   ⊥ *Mr. Justice BLACKMUN* delivered the opinion of the Court (Parts I, V, VI, VII, and VIII), together with an opinion (Parts II, III, and IV), in which *The CHIEF JUSTICE, Mr. Justice STEWART*, and *Mr. Justice POWELL* joined.

This is still another case presenting the recurrent issue of the limitations imposed by the Establishment Clause of the First Amendment, made applicable to the States by the Fourteenth Amendment, on state aid to pupils in church-related elementary and secondary schools. Appellants are citizens and taxpayers of Ohio. They challenge all but one of the
⊥233   provisions of Ohio ⊥ Rev. Code § 3317.06 (Supp. 1976) which authorize various forms of aid. The appellees are the State Superintendent of Public Instruction, the State Treasurer, the State Auditor, the Board of Education of the City School District of Columbus, Ohio, and, at their request, certain representative potential beneficiaries of the statutory program. A three-judge court was convened. It held the statute constitutional in all respects. We noted probable jurisdiction.

I

Section 3317.06 was enacted after this Court's May 1975 decision in *Meek* v. *Pittenger*, and obviously is an attempt to conform to the teachings of

that decision. * The state appellees so acknowledged at oral argument. In broad outline, the statute authorizes the State to provide nonpublic school pupils with books, instructional materials and equipment, standardized testing and scoring, diagnostic services, therapeutic services, and field trip transportation.

The initial biennial appropriation by the Ohio Legislature for implementation of the statute was the sum of $88,800,000. ⊥ Funds so appropriated are   ⊥234
paid to the State's public school districts and are then expended by them. All disbursements made with respect to nonpublic schools have their equivalents in disbursements for public schools, and the amount expended per pupil in nonpublic schools may not exceed the amount expended per pupil in the public schools.

The parties stipulated that during the 1974-75 school year there were 720 chartered nonpublic schools in Ohio. Of these, all but 29 were sectarian. More than 96% of the nonpublic enrollment attended sectarian schools, and more than 92% attended Catholic schools. It was also stipulated that, if they were called, officials of representative Catholic schools would testify that such schools operate under the general supervision of the Bishop of their Diocese; that most principals are members of a religious order within the Catholic Church; that a little less than one-third of the teachers are members of such religious orders; that "in all probability a majority of the teachers are members of the Catholic faith"; and that many of the rooms and hallways in these schools are decorated with a Christian symbol. All such schools teach the secular subjects required to meet the State's minimum standards. The state-mandated five hour day is expanded to include, usually, one-half hour of religious instruction. Pupils who are not members of the Catholic faith are not required to attend religious classes or to participate in religious exercises or activities, and no teacher is required to teach religious doctrine as a part of the secular courses taught in the schools.

The parties also stipulated that nonpublic school officials, if called, would testify that none of the schools covered by the statute discriminate in the admission of pupils or in the hiring ⊥ of teachers on   ⊥235
the basis of race, creed, color, or national origin.

The District Court concluded: "Although the stipulations of the parties evidence several significant

---

* At the time Meek was decided, an appeal was pending before us from a district court judgment holding constitutional the predecessor Ohio statute providing for aid to nonpublic schools. Wolman v. Essex. This Court vacated that judgment and remanded the case for further consideration in light of Meek.

On remand, the District Court entered a consent order, dated November 17, 1975, declaring the predecessor statute, which by then had been repealed, violative of the First and Fourteenth Amendments, but reserving decision on the constitutionality of the successor legislation. Appellants, who were plaintiffs in the original suit, then shifted their challenge to the present, successor statute.

points of distinction, the character of these schools is substantially comparable to that of the schools involved in *Lemon* v. *Kurtzman*."

II

The mode of analysis for Establishment Clause questions is defined by the three-part test that has emerged from the ⊥ Court's decisions. In order to pass muster, a statute must have a secular legislative purpose, must have a principal or primary effect that neither advances nor inhibits religion, and must not foster an excessive government entanglement with religion.

In the present case we have no difficulty with the first prong of this three-part test. We are satisfied that the challenged statute reflects Ohio's legitimate interest in protecting the health of its youth and in providing a fertile educational environment for all the school children of the State. As is usual in our cases, the analytical difficulty has to do with the effect and entanglement criteria.

We have acknowledged before, and we do so again here, that the wall of separation that must be maintained between church and state "is a blurred, indistinct, and variable barrier depending on all the circumstances of a particular relationship." *Lemon* Nonetheless, the Court's numerous precedents "have become firmly rooted," *Nyquist* and now provide substantial guidance. We therefore turn to the task of applying the rules derived from our decisions to the respective provisions of the statute at issue.

III
Textbooks

Section 3317.06 authorizes the expenditure of funds:

"(A) To purchase such secular textbooks as have been approved by the superintendent of public instruction for ⊥ use in public schools in the state and to loan such textbooks to pupils attending nonpublic schools within the district or to their parents. Such loans shall be based upon individual requests submitted by such nonpublic school pupils or parents. Such requests shall be submitted to the local public school district in which the nonpublic school is located. Such individual requests for the loan of textbooks shall, for administrative convenience, be submitted by the nonpublic school pupil or his parent to the nonpublic school which shall prepare and submit collective summaries of the individual requests to the local public school district. As used in this section, 'textbook' means any book or book substitute which a pupil uses as a text or text substitute in a particular class or program in the school he regularly attends."

The parties stipulations reflect operation of the textbook program in accord with the dictates of the statute. In addition, it was stipulated: "The secular textbooks used in nonpublic schools will be the same as the textbooks used in the public schools of the

state. Common suppliers will be used to supply books to both public and nonpublic school pupils.

"Textbooks, including book substitutes, provided under this Act shall be limited to books, reusable workbooks, or manuals, whether bound or in looseleaf form, intended for use as a principal source of study material for a given class or group of students, a copy of which is expected to be available for the individual use of each pupil in such class or group."

This system for the loan of textbooks to individual students bears a striking resemblance to the systems approved in *Board of Education* v. *Allen* and in ⊥ *Meek* v. *Pittenger*. Indeed, the only distinction offered by appellants is that the challenged statute defines "textbook" as "any book or book substitute." Appellants argue that a "book substitute" might include auxiliary equipment and materials that, they assert, may not constitutionally be loaned. See Part VII. We find this argument untenable in light of the statute's separate treatment of instructional materials and equipment in its subsections (B) and (C), and in light of the stipulation defining textbooks as "limited to books, reusable workbooks, or manuals." Appellants claim that the stipulation shows only the intent of the Department of Education, and that the statute is so vague as to fail to insure against sectarian abuse of the assistance programs, citing *Meek* and *Lemon*. We find no grounds, however, to doubt the Board of Education's reading of the statute, or to fear that the Board is using the stipulations as a subterfuge. As read, the statute provides the same protections against abuse as were provided in the textbook programs under consideration in *Allen* and in *Meek*.

In the alternative, appellants urge that we overrule *Allen* and *Meek*. This we decline to do. Accordingly, we conclude that § 3317.06 (A) is constitutional.

IV
Testing and Scoring

Section 3317.06 authorizes expenditure of funds:

"(J) To supply for use by pupils attending nonpublic schools within the district such standardized tests and ⊥ scoring services as are in use in the public schools of the state."

These tests "are used to measure the progress of students in secular subjects." Nonpublic school personnel are not involved in either the drafting or scoring of the tests. The statute does not authorize any payment to nonpublic school personnel for the costs of administering the tests.

In *Levitt* v. *Committee for Public Education* this Court invalidated a New York statutory scheme for reimbursement of church-sponsored schools for the expenses of teacher-prepared testing. The reason behind that decision was straightforward. The system was held unconstitutional because "no means are available, to assure that internally prepared tests are free of religious instruction."

⊥240 ⊥ There is no question that the State has a substantial and legitimate interest in insuring that its youth receive an adequate secular education. The State may require that schools that are utilized to fulfill the State's compulsory education requirement meet certain standards of instruction, and may examine both teachers and pupils to ensure that the State's legitimate interest is being fulfilled. Under the section at issue, the State provides both the schools and the school district with the means of ensuring that the minimum standards are met. The nonpublic school does not control the content of the test or its result. This serves to prevent the use of the test as a part of religious teaching, and thus avoids that kind of direct aid to religion found present in *Levitt.* Similarly, the inability of the

⊥241 school to control the test eliminates the need for the supervision that gives rise to ⊥ excessive entanglement. We therefore agree with the District Court's conclusion that § 3317.06 (J) is constitutional.

V
Diagnostic Services

Section 3317.06 authorizes expenditures of funds:

"(D) To provide speech and hearing diagnostic services to pupils attending nonpublic schools within the district. Such service shall be provided in the nonpublic school attended by the pupil receiving the service.

.   .   .   .   .

"(F) To provide diagnostic psychological services to pupils attending nonpublic schools within the district. Such services shall be provided in the school attended by the pupil receiving the service."

It will be observed that these speech and hearing and psychological diagnostic services are to be provided within the nonpublic school. It is stipulated, however, the personnel (with the exception of physicians) who perform the services are employees of the local board of education; that physicians may be hired on a contract basis; that the purpose of these services is to determine the pupil's deficiency or need of assistance; and that treatment of any defect so found would take place off the nonpublic school premises.

Appellants assert that the funding of these services is constitutionally impermissible. They argue that

⊥242 the speech and ⊥ hearing staff might engage in unrestricted conversation with the pupil and, on occasion, might fail to separate religious instruction from secular responsibilities. They further assert that the communication between the psychological diagnostician and the pupil will provide an impermissible opportunity for the intrusion of religious influence.

The District Court found these dangers so insubstantial as not to render the statute unconstitutional. We agree. This Court's decisions contain a common thread to the effect that the provision of health services to all school children—public and nonpublic— does not have the primary effect of aiding religion. In *Lemon* v. *Kurtzman,* the Court stated: Our decisions from *Everson* to *Allen* have permitted the States to provide church-related schools with secular, neutral, or nonideological services, facilities, or materials. Bus transportation, school lunches, *public health services,* and secular textbooks supplied in common to all students were not thought to offend the Establishment Clause." (emphasis added).

See also *Meek* v. *Pittenger.* Indeed, appellants recognize this fact in not challenging subsection (E) of the statute that authorizes publicly funded physician, nursing, dental, and optometric services in nonpublic schools. We perceive no basis for drawing a different conclusion with respect to diagnostic speech and hearing services and diagnostic psychological services.

In *Meek* the Court did hold unconstitutional a portion of a Pennsylvania statute at issue there that authorized certain ⊥ auxiliary services—"remedial ⊥243 and accelerated instruction, guidance counseling and testing, speech and hearing services—on nonpublic school premises. The Court noted that the teacher or guidance counselor might "fail on occasion to separate religious instruction and the advancement of religious beliefs from his secular educational responsibilities." The Court was of the view that the publicly employed teacher or guidance counselor might depart from religious neutrality because he was "performing important educational services in schools in which education is an integral part of the dominant sectarian mission and in which an atmosphere dedicated to the advancement of religious belief is constantly maintained." The statute was held unconstitutional on entanglement grounds, namely, that in order to insure that the auxiliary teachers and guidance counselors remained neutral, the State would have to engage in continuing surveillance on the school premises. See also *Public Funds for Public Schools* v. *Marburger.* The Court in *Meek* explicitly stated, however, that the provision of diagnostic speech and hearing services by Pennsylvania seemed "to fall within that class of general welfare services for children that may be provided by the State regardless of the incidental benefit that accrues to church-related schools." ⊥ The provision of such ⊥244 services was invalidated only because it was found unseverable from the unconstitutional portions of the statute.

The reason for considering diagnostic services to be different from teaching or counseling is readily apparent. First, diagnostic services, unlike teaching or counseling, have little or no educational content and are not closely associated with the educational mission of the nonpublic school. Accordingly, any pressure on the public diagnostician to allow the intrusion of sectarian views is greatly reduced. Second, the diagnostician has only limited contact with the child, and that contact involves chiefly the use of objective and professional testing methods to detect students in need of treatment. The nature of the relationship between the diagnostician and the pupil does not provide the same opportunity for the transmission of sectarian views as attends the relationship between teacher and student or that between counselor and student.

We conclude that providing diagnostic services on the nonpublic school premises will not create an impermissible risk of the fostering of ideological views. It follows that there is no need for excessive surveillance, and there will not be impermissible entanglement. We therefore hold that § § 3317.06 (D) and (F) are constitutional.

VI
Therapeutic Services

Sections 3317.06 (G), (H), (I), and (K) authorize expenditures of funds for certain therapeutic, guidance, and remedial services for students who have been identified as having a need for specialized attention. Personnel providing the serv⊥ices must be employees of the local board of education or under contract with the State Department of Health. The services are to be performed only in public schools, in public centers, or in mobile units located off the nonpublic school premises. The parties have stipulated: "The determination as to whether these programs would be offered in the public school, public center, or mobile unit will depend on the distance between the public and nonpublic school, the safety factors involved in travel, and the adequacy of accommodations in public schools and public centers."

⊥ Appellants concede that the provision of remedial, therapeutic, and guidance services in public schools, public centers, or mobile units is constitutional if both public and nonpublic school students are served simultaneously. Their challenge is limited to the situation where a facility is used to service only nonpublic school students. They argue that any program that isolates the sectarian pupils is impermissible because the public employee providing the service might tailor his approach to reflect and reinforce the ideological view of the sectarian school attended by the children. Such action by the employee, it is claimed, renders direct aid to the sectarian institution. Appellants express particular concern over mobile units because they perceive a danger that such a unit might operate merely as an annex of the school or schools it services.

At the outset, we note that in its present posture the case does not properly present any issue concerning the use of a public facility as an adjunct of a sectarian educational enterprise. The District Court construed the statute, as do we, to authorize services only on sites that are "neither physically ⊥ nor educationally involved with the functions of the nonpublic school." Thus, the services are to be offered under circumstances that reflect their religious neutrality.

We recognize that, unlike the diagnostician, the therapist may establish a relationship with the pupil in which there might be opportunities to transmit ideological views. In *Meek* the Court acknowledged the danger that publicly employed personnel who provide services analogous to those at issue here might transmit religious instruction and advance religious beliefs in their activities. But, as discussed in Part V, the Court emphasized that this danger arose from the fact that the services were performed in the pervasively sectarian atmosphere of the church-related school. The danger existed there not because the public employee was likely deliberately to subvert his task to the service of religion, but rather because the pressures of the environment might alter his behavior from its normal course. So long as these types of services are offered at truly religiously neutral locations, the danger perceived in *Meek* does not arise.

The fact that a unit on a neutral site on occasion may serve only sectarian pupils does not provoke the same concerns that troubled the Court in *Meek*. The influence on a therapist's behavior that is exerted by the fact that he serves a sectarian pupil is qualitatively different from the influence of the pervasive atmosphere of a religious institution. The dangers ⊥ perceived in *Meek* arose from the nature of the institution, not from the nature of the pupils.

Accordingly, we hold that providing therapeutic and remedial services at a neutral site off the premises of the nonpublic schools will not have the impermissible effect of advancing religion. Neither will there be any excessive entanglement arising from supervision of public employees to insure that they maintain a neutral stance. It can hardly be said that the supervision of public employees performing public functions on public property creates an excessive entanglement between church and state. Sections 3317.06 (G), (H), (I), and (K) are constitutional.

VII
Instructional Materials and Equipment

Sections 3317.06 (B) and (C) authorize expenditures of funds for the purchase and loan to pupils or their parents upon individual request of instructional materials and instructional equipment of the kind in use in the public schools within the district and which is "incapable of diversion to religious use." Section 3717.06 also provides that the materials and equipment may be stored on the premises of a nonpublic school and that publicly hired personnel who ⊥ administer the lending program may perform their services upon the nonpublic school premises when necessary "for efficient implementation of the lending program."

Although the exact nature of the material and equipment is not clearly revealed, the parties have stipulated: "It is expected that materials and equipment loaned to pupils or parents under the new law will be similar to such former materials and equipment except that to the extent that the law requires that materials and equipment capable of diversion to religious issues will not be supplied." Equipment provided under the predecessor statute, invalidated as set forth in n. 1, *supra*, included projectors, tape recorders, record players, maps and globes, science kits, weather forecasting charts, and the like. The District Court found the new statute, as now limited, constitutional because the Court could not distinguish the loan of material and equipment from the textbook provisions upheld in *Meek* and in *Allen.*

In *Meek*, however, the Court considered the constitutional validity of a direct loan to nonpublic schools of instructional material and equipment, and, despite the apparent secular nature of the goods, held the loan impermissible. *Mr. Justice STEWART*, in writing for the Court, stated: "The very purpose of many of those schools is to provide an integrated secular and religious education; the teach⊥ing process is, to a large extent, devoted to the inculcation of religious values and belief. See *Lemon* v. *Kurtman.* Substantial aid to the educational function of such schools, accordingly, necessarily results in aid to the sectarian school enterprise as a whole. '[T]he secular education those schools provide goes hand in hand with the religious mission that is the only reason for the schools' existence. Within the institution, the two are inextricably intertwined.'

Thus, even though the loan ostensibly was limited to neutral and secular instructional material and equipment, it inescapably had the primary effect of providing a direct and substantial advancement of the sectarian enterprise.

Appellees seek to avoid *Meek* by emphasizing that it involved a program of direct loans to nonpublic schools. In contrast, the material and equipment at issue under the Ohio statute are loaned to the pupil or his parent. In our view, however, it would exalt form over substance if this distinction were found to justify a result different from that in *Meek.* Before *Meek* was decided by this Court, Ohio authorized the loan of material and equipment directly to the nonpublic schools. Then, in light of *Meek*, the state legislature decided to channel the goods through the parents and pupils. Despite the technical change in legal bailee, the program in substance is the same as before: the equipment is substantially the same; it will receive the same use by the students; and it may still be stored and distributed on the nonpublic school premises. In view of the impossibility of separating the secular education function from the sectarian, the state aid inevitably flows in part in support of the religious role of the schools.

Indeed, this conclusion is compelled by the Court's prior consideration of an analogous issue in *Committee for Public Education* v. *Nyquist.* There the Court considered, among others, a tuition reimbursement program ⊥ whereby New York gave low income parents who sent their children to nonpublic schools a direct and unrestricted cash grant of $50 to $100 per child (but no more than 50% of tuition actually paid). The State attempted to justify the program, as Ohio does here, on the basis that the aid flowed to the parents rather than to the church-related schools. The Court observed, however, that, unlike the bus program in *Everson* v. *Board of Education* and the book program in *Allen*, there "has been no endeavor 'to guarantee the separation between secular and religious educational functions and to insure that State financial aid supports only the former,' " quoting *Lemon* v. *Kurtman.* The Court thus found that the grant program served to establish religion. If a grant in cash to parents is impermissible, we fail to see how a grant in kind of goods furthering the religious enterprise can fare any better. Accordingly, we hold § § 3316.06 (B) and (C) to be unconstitutional.

VIII
Field Trips

⊥ Section 3316.06 also authorizes expenditures of funds:

"(L) To provide such field trip transportation and services to nonpublic school students as are provided to public school students in the district. School districts may contract with commerical transportation companies for such transportation service if school district busses are unavailable."

There is no restriction on the timing of field trips; the only restriction on number lies in the parallel the statute draws to field trips provided to public school students in the district. The parties have stipulated that the trips "would consist of visits to governmental, industrial, cultural, and scientific centers designed to enrich the secular studies of students." ⊥The choice of destination, however, will be made by the nonpublic school teacher from a wide range of locations.

The District Court held this feature to be constitutionally indistinguishable from that with which the Court was concerned in *Everson* v. *Board of Education.* We do not agree. In *Everson* the Court approved a system under which a New Jersey board of education reimbursed parents for the cost of sending their children to and from school, public or parochial, by public carrier. The Court analogized the reimbursement to situations where a municipal common carrier is ordered to carry all school children at a reduced rate, or where the police force is ordered to protect all children on their way to and from school. The critical factors in these examples, as in the *Everson* reimbursement system, are that the school has no control over the expenditure of the funds and the effect of the expenditure is unrelated to the content of the education provided. Thus, the bus fare program in *Everson* passed constitutional muster because the school did not determine how often the pupil traveled between home and school—every child must make one round trip every day—and because the travel was unrelated to any aspect of the curriculum.

The Ohio situation is in sharp contrast. First, the nonpublic school controls the timing of the trips and, within a certain range, their frequency and destinations. Thus, the schools, rather than the children, truly are the recipients of the service and, as this Court has recognized, this fact alone may be sufficient to invalidate the program as impermissible direct aid. See *Lemon* v. *Kurtzman*. Second, although a trip may be to a location that would be of interest to those in public schools, it is the individual teacher who makes a field trip meaningful. The experience begins with the study and discussion of the place to be visited; it continues on location with the teacher pointing out items of interest and stimu-|254 lating the imagination; and it ends with a ⊥ discussion of the experience. The field trips are an integral part of the educational experience, and where the teacher works within and for a sectarian institution, an unacceptable risk of fostering of religion is an inevitable byproduct. In *Lemon* the Court stated: "We need not and do not assume that teachers in parochial schools will be guilty of bad faith or any conscious design to evade the limitations imposed by the statute and the First Amendment. We simply recognize that a dedicated religious person, teaching in a school affiliated with his or her faith and operated to inculcate its tenets, will inevitably experience great difficulty in remaining religiously neutral."

Funding of field trips, therefore, must be treated as was the funding of maps and charts in *Meek* v. *Pittenger*, the funding of buildings and tuition in *Committee for Public Education* v. *Nyquist*, and the funding of teacher-prepared tests in *Levitt* v. *Committee for Public Education*; it must be declared an impermissible direct aid to sectarian education.

Moreover, the public school authorities will be unable adequately to insure secular use of the field trip funds without close supervision of the nonpublic teachers. This would create excessive entanglement: "A comprehensive, discriminating, and continuing state surveillance will inevitably be required to insure that these restrictions are obeyed and the First Amendment otherwise respected. Unlike a book, a teacher cannot be inspected once so as to determine the extent and intent of his or her personal beliefs and subjective acceptance of the limitations imposed by the First Amendment. These prophylactic contacts will involve excessive and enduring entanglement between church and state." *Lemon* v. *Kurtzman*.

|255   ⊥ We hold § 3317.06 (L) to be unconstitutional.

IX

In summary, we hold constitutional those portions of the Ohio statute authorizing the State to provide nonpublic school pupils with books, standardized

testing and scoring, diagnostic services, and therapeutic and remedial services. We hold unconstitutional those portions relating to instructional materials and equipment and field trip services.

The judgment of the District Court is therefore affirmed in part and reversed in part.

It is so ordered.

The CHIEF JUSTICE dissents from Parts VII and VIII of the Court's opinion.

For the reasons stated in *Mr. Justice REHNQUIST's* separate opinion in *Meek* v. *Pittenger* and *Mr. Justice WHITE's* dissenting opinion in *Committee for Public Education* v. *Nyquist, Mr. Justice WHITE* and *Mr. Justice REHNQUIST* concur in the judgment with respect to textbooks, testing, and scoring, and diagnostic and therapeutic services (Parts III, IV, V and VI of the opinion) and dissent from the judgment with respect to instructional materials and equipment and field trips (Parts VII and VIII of the opinion).

Mr. Justice BRENNAN, concurring and dissenting

I join Parts I, VII, and VIII of the Court's opinion, and the reversal of the District Court's judgment insofar as that judgment upheld the constitutionality of § § 3317.06(B), (C), and (L).

I dissent however from Parts II, III, IV, V, and VI |256 of the opinion and the affirm⊥ance of the District Court's judgment insofar as it sustained the constitutionality of § § 3317.06 (A), (D), (F), (G), (H), (I), (J), and (K). The Court holds that Ohio has managed in these respects to fashion a statute that avoids an effect or entanglement condemned by the Establishment Clause. But "The [First] Amendment nullifies sophisticated as well as simple-minded . . ." attempts to avoid its prohibitions, *Lane* v. *Wilson*, and, in any event, ingenuity in draftsmanship cannot obscure the fact that this subsidy to sectarian schools amounts to $88,800,000 (less now the sums appropriated to finance § § 3317.06 (B) and (C) which today are invalidated) just for the initial biennium. The Court nowhere evaluates this factor in determining the compatibility of the statute with the Establishment Clause, as that Clause requires, *Everson* v. *Board of Education*. Its evaluation, even after deduction of the amount appropriated to finance § § 3317.06 (B) and (C), compels in my view the conclusion that a divisive political potential of unusual magnitude inheres in the Ohio program. This suffices without more to require the conclusion that the Ohio statute in its entirety offends the First Amendment's prohibition against laws "respecting an establishment of religion." *Meek* v. *Pittenger*, (BRENNAN, J., concurring); *Lemon* v. *Kurtzman*,

(*DOUGLAS, J.*, concurring); *Everson* v. *Board of Education.*

Mr. Justice MARSHALL, concurring and dissenting.

I join Parts I, V, VII, and VIII of the Court's opinion. For the reasons stated below, however, I am unable to join the remainder of the Court's opinion or its judgment upholding the constitutionality of §§ 3317.06 (A), (G), (H), (I), (J), and (K).

The Court upholds the textbook loan provision, § 3317.06 (A), on the precedent of *Board of Education* v. *Allen.* ⊥ It also recognizes, however, that there is "a tension" between *Allen* and the reasoning of the Court in *Meek* v. *Pittenger.* I would resolve that tension by overruling *Allen.* I am now convinced that *Allen* is largely responsible for reducing the "high and impregnable" wall between church and state erected by the First Amendment, *Everson* v. *Board of Education*, to "a blurred, indistinct, and variable barrier" incapable of performing its vital functions of protecting both church and state.

In *Allen*, we upheld a textbook loan program on the assumption that the sectarian school's twin functions of religious instruction and secular education were separable. In *Meek*, we flatly rejected that assumption as a basis for allowing a State to loan secular teaching materials and equipment to such schools: "The very purpose of many of those schools is to provide an integrated secular and religious education; the teaching process is, to a large extent, devoted to the inculcation of religious values and belief. . . . Substantial aid to the educational function of such schools, accordingly, necessarily results in aid to the sectarian school enterprise as a whole. '[T]he secular education those schools provide goes hand in hand with the religious mission that is the only reason for the schools' existence. Within the institution, the two are inextricably intertwined.' [*Lemon* v. *Kurtzman*] (opinion of *BRENNAN, J.*)."

Thus, although *Meek* upheld a textbook loan program on the strength of *Allen*, it left the rationale of *Allen* undamaged only if there is a constitutionally significant difference between a loan of pedagogical materials directly to a sectarian school and a loan of those materials to students for use in sectarian ⊥ schools. As the Court convincingly demonstrates, there is no such difference.

Allen has also been undercut by our recognition in *Lemon* that "the divisive political potential" of programs of aid to sectarian schools is one of the dangers of entanglement of church and state that the First Amendment was intended to forestall. We were concerned in *Lemon* with the danger that the need for annual appropriations of larger and larger sums would lead to "[p]olitical fragmentation and divisiveness on religious lines." This danger exists whether the appropriations are made to fund textbooks, other instructional supplies, or, as in *Lemon*, teachers' sal-

aries. As *Mr. Justice BRENNAN* has noted, *Allen* did not consider the significance of the potential for political divisiveness inherent in programs of aid to sectarian schools. *Meek* v. *Pittenger* (separate opinion).

It is, of course, unquestionable that textbooks are central to the educational process. Under the rationale of *Meek*, therefore, they should not be provided by the State to sectarian schools because "[s]ubstantial aid to the educational function of such schools . . . necessarily results in aid to the sectarian school enterprise as a whole." It is ⊥ also unquestionable that the cost of textbooks is certain to be substantial. Under the rationale of *Lemon*, therefore, they should not be provided because of the dangers of political "divisiveness on religious lines." I would, accordingly, overrule *Board of Education* v. *Allen* and hold unconstitutional § 3317.06(A).

By overruling *Allen*, we would free ourselves to draw a line between acceptable and unacceptable forms of aid that would be both capable of consistent application and responsive to the concerns discussed above. That line, I believe, should be placed between general welfare programs that serve children in sectarian schools because the schools happen to be a convenient place to reach the programs' target populations and programs of educational assistance. General welfare programs, in contrast to programs of educational assistance, do not provide "[s]ubstantial aid to the educational function" of schools, whether secular or sectarian, and therefore do not provide the kind of assistance to the religious ⊥ mission of sectarian schools we found impermissible in *Meek*. Moreover, because general welfare programs do not assist the sectarian functions of denominational schools, there is no reason to expect that political disputes over the merits of those programs will divide the public along religous lines.

In addition to § 3317.06 (A), which authorizes the textbook loan program, paragraphs (B), (C), and (L), held unconstitutional by the Court, clearly fall on the wrong side of the constitutional line I propose. Those paragraphs authorize, respectively, the loan of instructional materials and equipment and the provision of transportation for school field trips. There can be no contention that these programs provide anything other than educational assistance.

I also agree with the Court that the services authorized by paragraphs (D), (F) and (G) are constitutionally permissible. Those services are speech and hearing diagnosis, psychological diagnosis and psychological and speech and hearing therapy. Like the medical, nursing, dental, and optometric services authorized by paragraph (E) and not challenged by appellants, these services promote the children's health and well-being, and have only an indirect and remote impact on their educational progress.

The Court upholds paragraphs (H), (I), and (K), which it groups with paragraph (G), under the rubric of "therapeutic services." I cannot agree that the ser-

⊥261 vices ⊥ authorized by these three paragraphs should be treated like the psychological services provided by paragraph (G). Paragraph (H) authorizes the provision of guidance and counseling services. The parties stipulated that the functions to be performed by the guidance and counseling personnel would include assisting students in "developing meaningful educational and career goals," and "planning school programs of study." In addition, these personnel will discuss with parents "their children's a) educational progress and needs, b) course selections c) educational and vocational opportunities and plans, and d) study skills." The counselors will also collect and organize information for use by parents, teachers, and students. This description makes clear that paragraph (H) authorizes services that would directly support the educational programs of sectarian schools. It is, therefore, in violation of the First Amendment.

Paragraphs (I) and (K) provide remedial services and programs for disabled children. The stipulation of the parties indicates that these paragraphs will fund specialized teachers who will both provide instruction themselves and create instructional plans for use in the students' regular classrooms. These "therapeutic services" are clearly intended to aid the sectarian schools to improve the performance of their students in the classroom. I would not treat them as if they were programs of physical or psychological therapy.

Finally, the Court upholds paragraph (J), which provides standardized tests and scoring services, on the ground that these tests are clearly nonideological and that the State has an interest in assuring that the education received by sectarian school students meets minimum standards. I do not question the legitimacy of this interest, and if Ohio required students to obtain specified scores on certain tests before being promoted or graduated, I would agree that it could administer those tests to sectarian school students to ensure that its standards were being met. The record indicates, however, only that ⊥262 the tests ⊥ "are used to measure the progress of students in secular subjects." It contains no indication that the measurements are taken to assure compliance with state standards rather than for internal administrative purposes of the schools. To the extent that the testing is done to serve the purposes of the sectarian schools rather than the State, I would hold that its provision by the State violates the First Amendment.

Mr. Justice POWELL, concurring in part and dissenting in part.

Our decisions in this troubling area draw lines that often must seem arbitrary. No doubt we could achieve greater analytical tidiness if we were to accept the broadest implications of the observation in *Meek* v. *Pittenger*, that "[s]ubstantial aid to the edu-

cational function of [sectarian] schools . . . necessarily results in aid to the sectarian enterprise as a whole." If we took that course, it would become impossible to sustain state aid of any kind—even if the aid is wholly secular in character and is supplied to the pupils rather than the institutions. *Meek* itself would have to be overruled, along with *Board of Education* v. *Allen*, and even perhaps *Everson* v. *Board of Education*. The persistent desire of a number of States to find proper means of helping sectarian education to survive would be doomed. This Court has not yet thought that such a harsh result is required by the Establishment Clause. Certainly few would consider it in the public interest. Parochial schools, quite apart from their sectarian purpose, have provided an educational alternative for millions of young Americans; they often afford wholesome competition with our public schools; and in some States they relieve substantially the tax burden incident to the operation of public schools. The State has, moreover, a legitimate interest in facilitating education of the highest quality for all children within its boundaries, whatever school their parents have chosen for them.

⊥ It is important to keep these issues in perspec- ⊥263 tive. At this point in the 20th century we are quite far removed from the dangers that prompted the Framers to include the Establishment Clause in the Bill of Rights. The risk of significant religious or denominational control over our democratic processes—or even of deep political division along religious lines—is remote, and when viewed against the positive contributions of sectarian schools, any such risk seems entirely tolerable in light of the continuing oversight of this Court. Our decisions have sought to establish principles that preserve the cherished safeguard of the Establishment Clause without resort to blind absolutism. If this endeavor means a loss of some analytical tidiness, then that too is entirely tolerable. Most of the Court's decision today follows in this tradition, and I join Parts I through VI of its opinion.

With respect to Part VII, I concur only in the judgment. I am not persuaded, nor did *Meek* hold, that all loans of secular instructional material and equipment "inescapably [have] the primary effect of providing a direct and substantial advancement of the sectarian enterprise." If that were the case, then *Meek* surely would have overruled *Allen*. Instead the Court reaffirmed *Allen*, thereby necessarily holding that at least some such loans of materials helpful in the educational process are permissible—so long as the aid is incapable of diversion to religious uses, cf. *Committee for Public Education* v. *Nyquist*, and so long as the materials are lent to the individual students or their parents and not to the sectarian institutions. Here the statute is expressly limited to materials incapable of diversion. Therefore the relevant question is whether the materials are such that they are "furnished for the use of *individual* students and at their request." *Allen*, (emphasis added).

The Ohio statute includes some materials such as ⌐264 wall maps, ⊥ charts and other classroom paraphernalia for which the concept of a loan to individuals is a transparent fiction. A loan of these items is indistinguishable from forbidden "direct aid" to the sectarian institution itself, whoever the technical bailee. Since the provision makes no attempt to separate these instructional materials from others meaningfully lent to individuals, I agree with the Court that it cannot be sustained under our precedents. But I would find no constitutional defect in a properly limited provision lending to the individuals themselves only appropriate instructional materials and equipment similar to that customarily used in public schools.

I dissent as to Part VIII, concerning field trip transportation. The Court writes as though the statute funded the salary of the teacher who takes the students on the outing. In fact only the bus and driver are provided for the limited purpose of physical movement between the school and the secular destination of the field trip. As I find this aid indistinguishable in principle from that upheld in *Everson*, I would sustain the District Court's judgment approving this part of the Ohio statute.

Mr. Justice STEVENS, concurring in part and dissenting in part.

The distinction between the religious and secular is a fundamental one. To quote from Clarence Darrow's argument in the *Scopes* case: "The realm of religion . . . is where knowledge leaves off, and where faith begins, and it never has needed the arm of the State for support, and wherever it has received it, it has harmed both the public and the religion that it would pretend to serve."

⌐265 ⊥ The line drawn by the Establishment Clause of the First Amendment must also have a fundamental character. It should not differentiate between direct and indirect subsidies, or between instructional materials like globes and maps on the one hand and instructional materials like textbooks on the other. For that reason, rather than the three-part test described in Part II of the Court's opinion, I would adhere to the test enunciated for the Court by Mr. Justice Black: "No tax in any amount, large or small, can be levied to support any religious activities or institutions, whatever they may be called, or whatever form they may adopt to teach or practice religion." *Everson* v. *Board of Education*

Under that test, a state subsidy of sectarian schools is invalid regardless of the form it takes. The financing of buildings, field trips, instructional materials, educational tests, and school books are all equally invalid. For all give aid to the school's educational mission, which at heart is religious. On the other hand, I am not prepared to exclude the possibility ⊥ that some parts of the statute before us may ⌐266 be administered in a constitutional manner. The State can plainly provide public health services to children attending nonpublic schools. The diagnostic and therapeutic services described in Parts V and VI of the Court's opinion may fall into this category. Although I have some misgivings on this point, I am not prepared to hold this part of the statute invalid on its face.

This Court's efforts to improve on the *Everson* test have not proved successful. "Corrosive precedents" have left us without firm principles on which to decide these cases. As this case demonstrates, the States have been encouraged to search for new ways of achieving forbidden ends. See *Committee for Public Education* v. *Nyquist*. What should be a "high and impregnable" wall between church and state, has been reduced to a "blurred, indistinct, and variable barrier." The result has been, as Clarence Darrow predicted, harm to "both the public and the religion that [this aid] would pretend to serve."

Accordingly, I dissent from Parts II, III, and IV of the Court's opinion.

COMMITTEE FOR PUBLIC EDUCATION AND RELIGIOUS LIBERTY v. REGAN

444 U.S. 646
ON APPEAL FROM THE UNITED STATES
DISTRICT COURT
FOR THE SOUTHERN DISTRICT OF NEW
YORK
Argued November 27, 1979 — Decided February 20,
1980

⊥ *Mr. Justice WHITE* delivered the opinion of ⌐648 the Court.

The issue in this case is the constitutionality under the First and Fourteenth Amendments of the United States Constitution of a New York statute authorizing the use of public funds to reimburse church-sponsored and secular nonpublic schools for performing various testing and reporting services mandated by state law. The District Court sustained the statute. We noted probable jurisdiction and now affirm the District Courts judgment.

I

In 1970 the New York Legislature appropriated public funds to reimburse both church-sponsored and secular nonpublic schools for performing various services mandated by the State. The most expensive of these services was the "administration, grading and the compiling and reporting of the results of tests and examinations." Covered tests included both state-prepared examinations and the more common and traditional teacher-prepared tests. Although the legislature stipulated that "[n]othing contained in

⌊649 this act shall be construed to authorize the making of any payment under this act for religious ⊥ worship or instruction," the statute did not provide for any state audit of school financial records that would ensure that public funds were used only for secular purposes.

In *Levitt* v. *Committee for Public Education, (Levitt I)*, the Court struck down this enactment as violative of the Establishment Clause. The majority focused its concern on the statute's reimbursement of funds spent by schools on traditional teacher-prepared tests. The Court was troubled that, "despite the obviously integral role of such testing in the total teaching process, no attempt is made under the statute, and no means are available, to assure that internally prepared tests are free of religious instruction." It was not assumed that nonpublic school teachers would attempt in bad faith to evade constitutional requirements. Rather, the Court simply observed that "the potential for conflict 'inheres in the situation,' and because of that the State is constitutionally compelled to assure that the state-supported activity is not being used for religious indoctrination." *Lemon* v. *Kurtzman.* Because the State failed to provide the required assurance, the challenged statute was deemed to constitute an impermissible aid to religion.

The Court distinguished its earlier holdings in *Everson* v. *Board of Education* and *Board of Education* v. *Allen* on grounds that the state aid upheld in those cases, in the form of bus rides and loaned secular textbooks for sectarian schoolchildren, was "of a substantially different character" from that presented in *Levitt I.* Teacher-prepared tests were deemed by the Court to be an integral part of the teaching ⌊650 process. But so obviously are textbooks an integral part of the teaching ⊥ process. The crucial feature that distinguished tests, according to the Court, was that, " '[i]n terms of potential for involving some aspect of faith or morals in secular subjects, a textbook's content is ascertainable, but a teacher's handling of a subject is not.' " *Lemon* v. *Kurtzman.* Thus the inherent teacher discretion in devising, presenting, and grading traditional tests, together with the failure of the legislature to provide for a method of auditing to ensure that public funds would be spent exclusively on secular services, disabled the enactment from withstanding constitutional scrutiny.

Almost immediately the New York Legislature attempted to eliminate these defects from its statutory scheme. A new statute was enacted in 1974, and it ⌊651 directed New York's Com⊥missioner of Education to apportion and to pay to nonpublic schools the actual costs incurred as a result of compliance with certain state-mandated requirements, including "the requirements of the state's pupil evaluation program, ⌊652 ⊥ the basic educational data system, regents examinations, the statewide evaluation plan, the uniform procedure for public attendance reporting, and other similar state prepared examinations and reporting procedures." New York Laws 1974, ch. 507, § 3.

Of signal interest and importance in light of *Levitt I*, the new scheme does not reimburse nonpublic schools for the preparation, administration, or grading of teacher-prepared tests. Further, the 1974 statute, unlike the 1970 version struck down in *Levitt I*, provides a means by which payments of state funds are audited, thus ensuring that only the actual costs incurred in providing the covered secular services are reimbursed out of state funds.

Although the new statutory scheme was tailored to comport with the reasoning in *Levitt I*, the District Court invalidated the enactment with respect to both the tests and the reporting procedure, *Committee for Public Education and Religious Liberty* v. *Levitt, (Levitt II).* The District Court understood the decision in *Meek* v. *Pittenger* to require this result. In *Meek*, decided after *Levitt I*, this Court held unconstitutional two Pennsylvania statutes insofar as they provided auxiliary services and instructional material and equipment apart from textbooks to nonpublic schools in the State, most of which were sectarian. The Court ruled that in "religion-pervasive" institutions, secular and religious education are so "inextricably intertwined" that "[s]ubstantial aid to the educational function of such schools . . . necessarily results in aid for the sectarian school enterprise as a whole" and hence amounts to a forbidden establishment of religion.

Levitt II was appealed to this Court. We vacated the District Court's judgment and remanded the case in light of our decision in *Wolman* v. *Walter.* On ⊥ ⌊65⌋ remand the District Court ruled that under *Wolman* "state aid may be extended to [a sectarian] school's educational activities if it can be shown with a high degree of certainty that the aid will only have secular value of legitimate interest to the State and does not present any appreciable risk of being used to aid transmission of religious views." Applying this "more flexible concept," the District Court concluded that New York's statutory scheme of reimbursement did not violate the Establishment Clause.

Our jurisdiction to review the District Court's judgment lies under 28 U.S.C. § 1253.

II

Under the precedents of this Court a legislative enactment does not contravene the Establishment Clause if it has a secular legislative purpose, if its principal or primary effect neither advances nor inhibits religion, and if it does not foster an excessive government entanglement with religion.

In *Wolman* v. *Walter* this Court reviewed and sustained in relevant part an Ohio statutory scheme that authorized, *inter alia*, the expenditure of state funds "[to] supply for use by pupils attending nonpublic schools within the district such standardized tests and scoring services as are in use in the public schools of the state."

We held that this provision, which was aimed at providing the young with an adequate secular education, reflected a secular state purpose. As the opinion of Mr. Justice Blackmun stated, "[t]he State may require that schools that are utilized to fulfill the State's compulsory-education requirement meet certain standards of instruction, . . . and may examine both ⊥ teachers and pupils to ensure that the State's legitimate interest is being fulfilled." *Wolman* v. *Walter.* See *Levitt I; Lemon* v. *Kurtzman.* Mr. Justice Blackmun further explained that under the Ohio provision the nonpublic school did not control the content of the test or its result. This "serves to prevent the use of the test as a part of religious teaching, and thus avoids that kind of direct aid to religion found present in *Levitt [I]."* *Wolman* v. *Walter.* The provision of testing services hence did not have the primary effect of aiding religion. It was also decided that "the inability of the school to control the test eliminates the need for the supervision that gives rise to excessive entanglement." We thus concluded that the Ohio statute, insofar as it concerned examinations, passed our Establishment Clause tests.

III

We agree with the District Court that *Wolman* v. *Walter* controls this case. Although the Ohio statute under review in *Wolman* and the New York statute before us here are not identical, the differences are not of constitutional dimension. Addressing first the testing provisions, we note that here, as in *Wolman,* there is clearly a secular purpose behind the legislative enactment: "To provide educational opportunity of a quality which will prepare [New York] citizens for the challenges of American life in the last decades of the twentieth century." Also like the Ohio statute, the New York plan calls for tests that are prepared by the State and administered on the premises by nonpublic school personnel. The nonpublic school thus has no control whatsoever over the content of the tests. The Ohio tests, however, were graded by the State; here there are three types of tests involved, one graded by the State and the other two by nonpublic school personnel, with the costs of the grading service, as well as the cost of administering all three ⊥ tests, being reimbursed by the State. In view of the nature of the tests, the District Court found that the grading of the examinations by nonpublic school employees afforded no control to the school over the outcome of any of the tests.

The District Court explained that the State-prepared tests are primarily of three types: pupil evaluation program (PEP) tests, comprehensive ("end-of-the-course") achievement tests, and Regents Scholarship and College Qualifications Tests

(RSCQT). Each of the tests addresses a secular academic subject; none deals with religious subject matter. The RSCQT examinations are graded by State Education Department personnel, and the District Court correctly concluded that "the risk of [RSCQT examinations] being used for religious purposes through grading is non-existent." The PEP tests, administered universally in grades three and six and optionally in grade nine, are graded by nonpublic school employees, but they "consist entirely of objective, multiple-choice questions, which can be graded by machine and, even if graded by hand, afford the schools no more control over the results than if the tests were graded by the State." The comprehensive tests, based on state courses of study for use in grades nine through twelve, are also graded on the premises by school employees, but "consist ⊥ largely or entirely of objective questions with multiple- choice answers." Even though some of the comprehensive tests may include an essay question or two, the District Court found that the chance that grading the answers to state-drafted questions in secular subjects could or would be used to gauge a student's grasp of religious ideas was "minimal," especially in light of the "complete" state procedures designed to guard against serious inconsistencies in grading and any misuse of essay questions. These procedures include the submission of completed and graded comprehensive tests to the State Department of Education for review off the school premises.

We see no reason to differ with the factual or legal characterization of the testing procedure arrived at by the District Court. As in *Wolman* v. *Walter,* "[t]he nonpublic school does not control the content of the test or its result"; and here, as in *Wolman,* this factor "serves to prevent the use of the test as a part of religious teaching," thus avoiding the kind of direct aid forbidden by the Court's prior cases. The District Court was correct in concluding that there was no substantial risk that the examinations could be used for religious educational purposes.

The District Court was also correct in its characterization of the recordkeeping and reporting services for which the State reimburses the nonpublic school. Under the New York law, "[e]ach year, private schools must submit to the State a Basic Educational Data System (BEDS) report. This report contains information regarding the student body, faculty, support staff, physical facilities, and curriculum of each school. Schools are also required to submit annually a report showing the attendance record of each minor who is a student at the school." Although recordkeeping is related to the educational program, the District Court characterized it and the reporting function as "ministerial [and] lacking in ideological content or use." ⊥ These tasks are not part of the teaching process and cannot "be used to foster an ideological outlook." Reimbursement for the costs of so complying with state law, therefore, has primarily a secular, rather than a religious, purpose and effect.

IV

The New York statute, unlike the Ohio statute at issue in *Wolman*, provides for direct cash reimbursement to the nonpublic school for administering the state-prescribed examinations and for grading two of them. We agree with the District Court that such reimbursement does not invalidate the New York statute. If the State furnished state-prepared tests, thereby relieving the nonpublic schools of the expense of preparing their own examinations, but left the grading of the tests to the schools, and if the grading procedures could be used to further the religious mission of the school, serious Establishment Clause problems would be posed under the Court's cases, for by furnishing the tests it might be concluded that the State was directly aiding religious education. But as we have already concluded, grading the secular tests furnished by the State in this case is a function that has a secular purpose and primarily a secular effect. This conclusion is not changed simply because the State pays the school for perform⊥ing the grading function. As the District Court observed, "[p]utting aside the question of whether direct financial aid can be administered without excessive entanglement by the State in the affairs of a sectarian institution, there does not appear to be any reason why payments to sectarian schools to cover the cost of specified activities would have the impermissible effect of advancing religion if the same activities performed by sectarian school personnel without reimbursement but with State-furnished materials have no such effect."

A contrary view would insist on drawing a constitutional distinction between paying the nonpublic school to do the grading and paying state employees or some independent service to perform that task, even though the grading function is the same regardless of who performs it and would not have the primary effect of aiding religion whether or not performed by nonpublic school personnel. In either event, the nonpublic school is being relieved of the cost of grading state-required, state-furnished examinations. We decline to embrace a formalistic dichotomy that bears so little relationship either to common sense or to the realities of school finance. None of our cases requires us to invalidate these reimbursements simply because they involve payments in cash. The Court "has not accepted the recurrent argument that all aid is forbidden because aid to one aspect of an institution frees it to spend its other resources on religious ends." *Hunt* v. *McNair*. Because the recordkeeping and ⊥ reporting functions also have neither a religious purpose nor a primarily religious effect, we reach the same results with respect to the reimbursements for these services.

Of course, under the relevant cases the outcome would likely be different were there no effective means for insuring that the cash reimbursements would cover only secular services. See *Levitt I; Committee for Public Education* v. *Nyquist; Lemon* v. *Kurtzman*. But here, as we shall see, the New York law provides ample safeguards against excessive or misdirected reimbursement.

V

The District Court recognized that "[w]here a state is required in determining what aid, if any, may be extended to a sectarian school, to monitor the day-to-day activities of the teaching staff, to engage in onerous, direct oversight, or to make on-site judgments from time to time as to whether different school activities are religious in character, the risk of entanglement is too great to permit governmental involvement." After examining the New York statute and its operation, however, the District Court concluded that "[t]he activities subsidized under the Statute here at issue . . . do not pose any substantial risk of such entanglement."

The District Court described the process of reimbursement: "Schools which seek reimbursement must 'maintain a separate account or system of accounts for the expenses incurred in rendering' the reimbursable services, and they must submit to the N.Y. State Commissioner of Education an application for reimbursement with additional reports and documents prescribed by the Commissioner. . . . Reimbursable costs include proportionate shares of the teachers' salaries and fringe benefits attrib⊥utable to administration of the examinations and reporting of State-required data on pupil attendance and performance, plus the cost of supplies and other contractual expenditures such as data processing services. Applications for reimbursement cannot be approved until the Commissioner audits vouchers or other documents submitted by the schools to substantiate their claims. . . . The Statute further provides that the State Department of Audit and Control shall from time to time inspect the accounts of recipient schools in order to verify the cost to the schools of rendering the reimbursable services. If the audit reveals that a school has received an amount in excess of its actual costs, the excess must be returned to the State immediately. . . ."

We agree with the District Court that "[t]he services for which the private schools would be reimbursed are discrete and clearly identifiable." The reimbursement process, furthermore, is straightforward and susceptible to the routinization that characterizes most reimbursement schemes. On its face, therefore, the New York plan suggests no excessive entanglement, and we are not prepared to read into the plan as an inevitability the bad faith ⊥ upon which any future excessive entanglement would be predicated.

VI

It is urged that the District Court judgment is unsupportable under *Meek* v. *Pittenger*, which is said to have held that any aid to even secular educational functions of a sectarian school is forbidden, or more broadly still, that any aid to a sectarian school is suspect since its religious teaching is so pervasively intermixed with each and every one of its activities. The difficulty with this position is that a majority of the Court, including the author of *Meek* v. *Pittenger*, upheld in *Wolman* a state statute under which the State, by preparing and grading tests in secular subjects, relieved sectarian schools of the cost of these functions, functions that they otherwise would have had to perform themselves and that were intimately connected with the educational processes. Yet the *Wolman* opinion at no point suggested that this holding was inconsistent with the decision in *Meek*. Unless the majority in *Wolman* was silently disavowing *Meek*, in whole or in part, that case was simply not understood by this Court to stand for the broad proposition urged by appellants and espoused by the District Court in *Levitt II*.

That Meek was understood more narrowly was suggested by Mr. Justice Powell in his separate opinion in *Wolman*: "I am not persuaded," he said, "nor did *Meek* hold, that all loans ⊥ of secular instructional material and equipment" inescapably have the effect of direct advancement of religion. And obviously the testing services furnished by the State in *Wolman* were approved on the premise that those services did not and could not have the primary effect of advancing the sectarian aims of the nonpublic schools. With these indicators before it, the District Court properly put the two cases together and sustained the reimbursements involved here because it had been shown with sufficient clarity that they would serve the State's legitimate secular ends without any appreciable risk of being used to transmit or teach religious views.

⌐662

This is not to say that this case, any more than past cases, will furnish a litmus-paper test to distinguish permissible from impermissible aid to religiously oriented schools. But Establishment Clause cases are not easy; they stir deep feelings; and we are divided among ourselves, perhaps reflecting the different views on this subject of the people of this country. What is certain is that our decisions have tended to avoid categorical imperatives and absolutist approaches at either end of the range of possible outcomes. This course sacrifices clarity and predictability for flexibility, but this promises to be the case until the continuing interaction between the courts and the States—the former charged with interpreting and upholding the Constitution and the latter seeking to provide education for their youth—produces a single, more encompassing construction of the Establishment Clause.

The judgment of the District Court is

Affirmed.

Mr. Justice BLACKMUN, with whom *Mr. Justice BRENNAN* and *Mr. Justice MARSHALL* join, dissenting.

The Court in this case, I fear, takes a long step backwards in the inevitable controversy that emerges when a state legislature continues to insist on providing public aid to parochial schools.

⊥ I thought that the Court's judgments in *Meek* v. *Pittenger* and in *Wolman* v. *Walter* (which the Court concedes is the controlling authority here), at last had fixed the line between that which is constitutionally appropriate public aid and that which is not. The line necessarily was not a straight one. It could not be, when this Court, on the one hand, in *Everson* v. *Board of Education*, by a 5-4 vote, decided that there was no barrier under the First and Fourteenth Amendments to parental reimbursement of the cost of fares for the transportation of children attending parochial schools, and in *Board of Education* v. *Allen*, by a 6-3 vote, ruled that New York's lending of approved textbooks to students in private secondary schools was not violative of those Amendments, and yet, on the other hand, in *Lemon* v. *Kurtzman*, struck down, as violative of the Religion Clauses, statutes that, respectively, would have supplemented nonpublic school teachers' salaries and would have authorized the "purchase" of certain "secular educational services" from nonpublic schools, and also in *Levitt* v. *Committee for Public Education (Levitt I)*, struck down New York's previous attempt to reimburse nonpublic schools for the expenses of tests and examinations. See also *Committee for Public Education* v. *Nyquist*, where the Court nullified New York's financial aid programs for "maintenance and repair" of facilities and equipment, a tuition reimbursement plan, and tax relief for parents who did not qualify for tuition reimbursement, and *Sloan* v. *Lemon*, where the Court ruled invalid a state plan for parental reimbursement of a portion of nonpublic school tuition expenses. And see *Roemer* v. *Maryland Public Works Bd.*

⌐663

But, I repeat, the line, wavering though it may be, was indeed drawn in *Meek* and in *Wolman*, albeit with different ⊥ combinations of Justices, those who perceive no barrier under the First and Fourteenth Amendments and who would rule in favor of almost any aid a state legislature saw fit to provide, on the one hand, and those who perceive a broad barrier and would rule against aid of almost any kind, on the other hand, in turn joining Justices in the center on these issues to make order and a consensus out of the earlier decisions. Now, some of those who joined in *Lemon, Levitt I, Meek*, and *Wolman* in invalidating, depart and validate. I am able to attribute this defection only to a concern about the continuing and emotional controversy and

⌐664

to a persuasion that a good-faith attempt on the part of a state legislature is worth a nod of approval.

I

In order properly to analyze the amended school aid plan that the New York Legislature produced in response to its defeat in *Levitt*, it is imperative, it seems to me, to examine the statute's operational details with great precision and with fewer generalities than the Court does today. One should do more than give a passing glance at selected provisions of the statute, and one should not ignore the considerations that prompted the three-judge District Court initially and *unanimously* to hold New York's revised plan to be unconstitutional, *Committee for Public Education and Religious Liberty* v. *Levitt*, (*Levitt II*) and that prompted Judge Ward, in his persuasive dissent in *Levitt III, Committee for Public Education and Religious Liberty* v. *Levitt*, after our remand, to differ so vigorously with his two colleagues who meanwhile changed their minds, mistakenly in my view.

II

The Court and all three judges of the District Court are correct, of course, in recognizing that the |665 "mode of analysis for Establishment ⊥ Clause questions is defined by the three-part test that has emerged from the Court's decisions." *Wolman* v. *Walter* (plurality opinion). To pass constitutional muster under this test, the New York statute now challenged, Chapter 507, 1974 N.Y. Laws, as amended, "must have a secular legislative purpose, must have a principal or primary effect that neither advances nor inhibits religion, and must not foster excessive government entanglement with religion."

I have no trouble in agreeing with the Court that Chapter 507 manifests a clear secular purpose. I therefore would evaluate Chapter 507 under the two remaining inquiries of the three-part test.

In deciding whether Chapter 507 has an impermissible primary effect of advancing religion, or whether it fosters excessive government entanglement with sectarian affairs, one must keep in focus the nature of the assistance prescribed by the New York statute. The District Court found that $8-10 million annually would be expended under Chapter 507, with the great majority of these funds going to sectarian schools to pay for personnel costs associated with attendance reporting. The court found that such payments would amount to from 1% to 5.4% of the personnel budget of an individual religious school receiving assistance under Chapter 507. Moreover, Chapter 507 provides direct cash payments by the State of New York to religious schools, as opposed to providing services or providing cash payments to third parties who have rendered services. And the money paid sectarian schools under Chapter 507 is designated to reimburse costs that are incurred by religious schools in order to meet basic state testing

and reporting requirements, costs that would have been incurred regardless of the availability of reimbursement from the State.

This direct financial assistance provided by Chapter 507 differs significantly from the types of state aid to religious schools approved by the Court in *Wolman* v. *Walter*. For ⊥ example, in *Wolman* the |666 Court approved that portion of the Ohio statute that provided to religious schools the standardized tests and scoring services furnished to public schools. But, unlike New York's Chapter 507, Ohio's statute provided only the tests themselves and scoring by employees of neutral testing organizations. It did not authorize direct financial aid of any type to religious schools.

Similarly, the other forms of assistance upheld in *Wolman* did not involve direct cash assistance. Rather, the Court approved the State's providing sectarian school students therapeutic, remedial, and guidance programs administered by public employees on public property. It also approved certain public health services furnished by public employees to religious school pupils, even though administered in part on the sectarian premises, on the basis of its recognition in a number of cases, see, *e.g., Meek* v. *Pittenger*, that provision of health services to all school children does not advance religion so as to contravene the Establishment Clause. And it upheld the lending by Ohio of textbooks to pupils under the "unique presumption" created by *Board of Education* v. *Allen* and reaffirmed since that time. *E.g., Meek* v. *Pittenger*.

It is clear, however, that none of the programs upheld in *Wolman* provided direct financial support to sectarian schools. At the very least, then, the Court's holding today goes further in approving state assistance to sectarian schools than the Court had gone in past decisions. But beyond merely failing to approve the type of direct financial aid at issue in this case, *Wolman* reaffirmed the finding of the Court in *Meek* v. *Pittenger* that *direct* aid to the educational function of religious schools necessarily advances the sectarian enterprise as a whole. ⊥ Thus, the Court in |667 *Wolman* invalidated Ohio's practice of loaning instructional materials directly to sectarian schools, "even though the loan ostensibly was limited to neutral and secular instructional material and equipment, [because] it inescapably had the primary effect of providing a direct and substantial advancement of the sectarian enterprise." In the same vein, the Court disapproved Ohio's provision of field-trip transportation directly to religious schools as impermissible direct aid that, because of the pervasively religious nature of the schools involved, furthered the religious goals of the schools, and that also required government surveillance of expenditures to such a degree as to foster entanglement of the State in religion.

Wolman thus re-enforces the conclusion that substantial direct financial aid to a religious school, even though ostensibly for secular purposes, runs the great risk of furthering the religious mission of the school as a whole because that religious mission so pervades the functioning of the school. The Court specifically recognized this in *Meek*: "[F]aced with the substantial amounts of direct support authorized by [the statute at issue], it would simply ignore reality to attempt to separate secular educational functions from the predominantly religious role performed by many . . . church-related elementary and secondary schools and to then characterize [the statute] as channeling aid to the secular without providing direct aid to the sectarian. Even though earmarked for secular purposes, 'when it flows to an institution in which religion is so pervasive that a substantial portion of its functions are subsumed in the religious mission,' state aid has the impermissible primary effect of advancing religion. *Hunt* v. *McNair*."

⊥668   ⊥ Under the principles announced in these decided cases, I am compelled to conclude that Chapter 507, by providing substantial financial assistance directly to sectarian schools, has a primary effect of advancing religion. The vast majority of the schools aided under Chapter 507 typify the religious-pervasive institution the very purpose of which is to provide an integrated secular and sectarian education. The aid provided by Chapter 507 goes primarily to reimburse such schools for personnel costs incurred in complying with state reporting and testing requirements, costs that must be incurred if the school is to be accredited to provide a combined sectarian-secular education to school-age pupils. To continue to function as religious schools, sectarian schools thus are required to incur the costs outlined in § 3 of Chapter 507, or else lose accreditation by the State of New York. These reporting and testing requirements would be met by the schools whether reimbursement were available or not. As such, the attendance, informational, and testing expenses compensated by Chapter 507 are essential to the overall educational functioning of sectarian schools in New York in the same way instruction in secular subjects is essential. Therefore, just as direct aid for ostensibly secular purposes by provision of instructional materials or direct financial subsidy is forbidden by the Establishment Clause, so direct aid for the performance of recordkeeping and testing activities that are an essential part of the sectarian school's functioning also is interdicted. The Court stated in *Meek*, and reaffirmed in *Wolman*: "The very purpose of many [religious] schools is to provide an integrated secular and religious education; the teaching process is, to a large extent, devoted to the inculcation of religious values and belief. See *Lemon* v. *Kurtzman*. Substantial aid to the educational function of such schools, accordingly, necessarily results in aid to the sectarian school enterprise as ⊥ a

⊥669   whole. '[T]he secular education those schools provide goes hand in hand with the religious mission that is the only reason for the schools' existence. Within the institution, the two are inextricably intertwined.'"

It is also true that the keeping of pupil attendance records is essential to the religious mission of sectarian schools. To ensure that the school is fulfilling its religious mission properly, it is necessary to provide a way to determine whether pupils are attending the sectarian classes required of them. Accordingly, Chapter 507 not only advances religion by aiding the educational mission of the sectarian school as a whole; it also subsidizes directly the religious mission of such schools. Chapter 507 makes no attempt, and none is possible, to separate the portion of the overall expense of attendance-taking attributable to the desire to ensure that students are attending religious instruction from that portion attributable to the desire to ensure that state attendance laws are complied with. This type of direct aid the Establishment Clause does not permit.

I thus would hold that the aid provided by Chapter 507 constitutes a direct subsidy of the operating costs of the sectarian school that aids the school as a whole, and that the statute therefore directly advances religion in violation of the Establishment Clause of the First Amendment.

III

Beyond this, Chapter 507 also fosters government entanglement with religion to an impermissible extent. Unlike *Wolman*, under Chapter 507 sectarian employees are compensated by the State for grading examinations. In some cases, such grading requires the teacher to exercise subjective judgment. For the State properly to ensure that judgment is ⊥ not ex-   ⊥670 ercised to inculcate religion, a "comprehensive, discriminating, and continuing state surveillance will inevitably be required." *Lemon* v. *Kurtzman*.

Moreover, Chapter 507 provides for continuing reimbursement with regard to examinations in which the questions may vary from year to year, and for examinations that may be offered in the future. This will require the State continually to evaluate the examinations to ensure that reimbursement for expenses incurred in connection with their administration and grading will not offend the First Amendment. This, too, fosters impermissible government involvement in sectarian affairs, since it is likely to lead to continuing adjudication of disputes between the State and others as to whether certain questions or new examinations present such opportunities for the advancement of religion that reimbursement for administering and grading them should not be permitted. Cf. *New York* v. *Cathedral Academy*.

Finally, entanglement also is fostered by the system of reimbursement for personnel expenses. The State must make sure that it reimburses sectarian schools only for those personnel costs attributable to the sectarian employees' secular activities described in § 3 of Chapter 507. It is difficult to see how the State adequately may discover whether the time for which reimbursement is made available was devoted only to secular activities without some type of on-going surveillance of the sectarian employees and religious schools at issue. It is this type of extensive entanglement that the Establishment Clause forbids. I fail to see, and I am uncomfortable with, the so-called "ample safeguards" upon which the Court and the District Court's majority, *Levitt III*, are content to rest so assured.

I therefore conclude that Chapter 507 has a primary effect of advancing religion and also fosters excessive government entanglement with religion. The statute, consequently, is unconstitutional under the Establishment Clause, ⊥ at least to the extent it provides reimbursement directly to sectarian nonpublic schools.

⌐671

I would reverse the judgment of the District Court.

Mr. Justice STEVENS, dissenting.

Although I agree with Mr. Justice Blackmun's demonstration of why today's holding is not compelled by precedent, my vote also rests on a more fundamental disagreement with the Court. The Court's approval of a direct subsidy to sectarian schools to reimburse them for staff time spent in taking attendance and grading standardized tests is but another in a long line of cases making largely ad hoc decisions about what payments may or may not be constitutionally made to nonpublic schools. In groping for a rationale to support today's decision, the Court has taken a position that could equally be used to support a subsidy to pay for staff time attributable to conducting fire drills or even for constructing and maintaining fireproof premises in which to conduct classes. Though such subsidies might represent expedient fiscal policy, I firmly believe they would violate the Establishment Clause of the First Amendment.

The Court's adoption of such a position confirms my view, expressed in *Wolman* v. *Walter*, (Stevens, J., dissenting), and *Roemer* v. *Board of Public Works*, (Stevens, J., dissenting), that the entire enterprise of trying to justify various types of subsidies to nonpublic schools should be abandoned. Rather than continuing with the sisyphean task of trying to patch together the "blurred, indistinct, and variable barrier" described in *Lemon* v. *Kurtzman*, I would resurrect the "high and impregnable" wall between church and state constructed by the Framers of the First Amendment. See *Everson* v. *Board of Education.*

MUELLER v. ALLEN

463 U.S. 388
ON WRIT OF CERTIORARI TO THE UNITED STATES
COURT OF APPEALS FOR THE EIGHTH CIRCUIT

Argued April 18, 1983 — Decided June 29, 1983

⊥*Justice REHNQUIST* delivered the opinion of the Court.   ⌐390

Minnesota allows taxpayers, in computing their state income tax, to deduct certain expenses incurred in providing for the education of their children. The United States Court of Appeals for the Eighth Circuit held that the Establishment Clause of the First and Fourteenth Amendments was not offended by this arrangement. Because this question was reserved in *Committee for Public Education* v. *Nyquist*, and bec⊥ause of a conflict between the decision of the Court of Appeals for the Eighth Circuit and that of the Court of Appeals for the First Circuit in *Rhode Island Federation of Teachers* v. *Norberg*, we granted certiorari. We now affirm.   ⌐391

Minnesota, like very other state, provides its citizens with free elementary and secondary schooling. It seems to be agreed that about 820,000 students attended this school system in the most recent school year. During the same year, approximately 91,000 elementary and secondary students attended some 500 privately supported schools located in Minnesota, and about 95% of these students attended schools considering themselves to be sectarian.

Minnesota, by a law originally enacted in 1955 and revised in 1976 and again in 1978, permits state taxpayers to claim a deduction from gross income for certain expenses incurred in educating their children. The deduction is limited to actual expenses incurred for the "tuition, textbooks and transportation" of dependents attending elementary or secondary schools. A deduction may not exceed $500 per dependent in grades K through six and $700 per dependent in grades seven through twelve.

⊥ Petitioners—certain Minnesota taxpayers—sued in the United States District court for the District of Minnesota claiming that § 290.09(22) violated the Establishment Clause by providing financial assistance to sectarian institutions. They named as respondents the Commissioner of the Department of Revenue of Minnesota and several parents who took advantage of the tax deduction for expenses incurred in sending their children to parochial schools. The District Court granted respondent's motion for summary judgment, holding that the statute was "neutral on its face and in its application and does not have a primary effect of either advancing or inhibiting religion." 514 F. Supp. 998. On appeal, the Court of Appeals affirmed, concluding that the Minnesota statute substantially benefited a "broad class of Minnesota citizens."   ⌐392

Today's case is no exception to our oft-repeated statement that the Establishment Clause presents especially difficult questions of interpretation and application. It is easy enough to quote the few words comprising that clause—"Congress shall make no law respecting an establishment of ⊥ religion." It is not at all easy, however, to apply this Court's various decisions construing the Clause to governmental programs of financial assistance to sectarian schools and the parents of children attending those schools. Indeed, in many of these decisions "we have expressly or implicitly acknowledged that 'we can only dimly perceive the lines of demarcation in this extraordinarily sensitive area of constitutional law.'" *Lemon* v. *Kurtzman.*

One fixed principle in this field is our consistent rejection of the argument that "any program which in some manner aids an institution with a religious affiliation" violates the Establishment Clause. *Hunt* v. *McNair.* For example, it is now well-established that a state may reimburse parents for expenses incurred in transporting their children to school, *Everson* v. *Board of Education*, and that it may loan secular textbooks to all schoolchildren within the state, *Board of Education* v. *Allen.*

Notwithstanding the repeated approval given programs such as those in *Allen* and *Everson*, our decisions also have struck down arrangements resembling, in many respects, these forms of assistance. In this case we ⊥ are asked to decide whether Minnesota's tax deduction bears greater resemblance to those types of assistance to parochial schools we have approved, or to those we have struck down. Petitioners place particular reliance on our decision in *Committee for Public Education* v. *Nyquist*, where we held invalid a New York statute providing public funds for the maintenance and repair of the physical facilities of private schools and granting thinly disguised "tax benefits," actually amounting to tuition grants, to the parents of children attending private schools. As explained below, we conclude that § 290.09(22) bears less resemblance to the arrangement struck down in *Nyquist* than it does to assistance programs upheld in our prior decisions and those discussed with approval in *Nyquist.*

The general nature of our inquiry in this area has been guided, since the decision in *Lemon* v. *Kurtzman*, by the "three-part" test laid down in that case: "First, the statute must have a secular legislative purpose; second, its principal or primary effect must be one that neither advances nor inhibits religion . . . ; finally, the statute must not foster 'an excessive government entanglement with religion.'" *Id.* While this principle is well settled, our cases have also emphasized that it provides "no more than [a] helpful signpost" in dealing with Establishment Clause challenges. *Hunt* v. *McNair* With this *caveat* in mind, we turn to the specific challenges raised against § 290.09(22) under the *Lemon* framework.

Little time need be spent on the question of whether the Minnesota tax deduction has a secular purpose. Under our prior decisions, governmental assistance programs have consistently survived this inquiry even when they have run afoul of other aspects of the *Lemon* framework. This reflects, at least in part, our reluctance to attribute unconstitutional motives to the states, particularly when a plausible secular purpose ⊥ for the state's program may be discerned from the face of the statute.

A state's decision to defray the cost of educational expenses incurred by parents—regardless of the type of schools their children attend—evidences a purpose that is both secular and understandable. An educated populace is essential to the political and economic health of any community, and a state's efforts to assist parents in meeting the rising cost of educational expenses plainly serves this secular purpose of ensuring that the state's citizenry is well-educated. Similarly, Minnesota, like other states, could conclude that there is a strong public interest in assuring the continued financial health of private schools, both sectarian and non-sectarian. By educating a substantial number of students such schools relieve public schools of a correspondingly great burden—to the benefit of all taxpayers. In addition, private schools may serve as a benchmark for public schools, in a manner analogous to the "TVA yardstick" for private power companies. As *Justice POWELL* has remarked: "Parochial schools, quite apart from their sectarian purpose, have provided an educational alternative for millions of young Americans; they often afford wholesome competition with our public schools; and in some States they relieve substantially the tax burden incident to the operation of public schools. The State has, moreover, a legitimate interest in facilitating education of the highest quality for all children within its boundaries, whatever school their parents have chosen for them. *Wolman* v. *Walter.* All these justifications are readily available to support § 290.09(22), and each is sufficient to satisfy the secular purpose inquiry of *Lemon.*

⊥ We turn therefore to the more difficult but related question whether the Minnesota statute has "the primary effect of advancing the sectarian aims of the nonpublic schools." In concluding that it does not, we find several features of the Minnesota tax deduction particularly significant. First, an essential feature of Minnesota's arrangement is the fact that § 290.09(22) is only one among many deductions—such as those for medical expenses and charitable contributions— available under the Minnesota tax laws. Our decisions consistently have recognized that traditionally "[l]egislatures have especially broad latitude in creating classifications and distinctions in tax statutes," *Reagan* v. *Taxation with Representation*, in part because the "familiarity with local conditions" enjoyed by legislators especially enables them to "achieve an equitable distribution of the tax burden." *Madden* v. *Kentucky.* Under our prior decisions, the Minnesota legislature's judgment that a deduction for educational expenses fairly equalizes the tax burden of its citizens and encourages desirable expenditures for educational purposes is entitled to substantial deference.

⌐397 ⊥Other characteristics of § 290.09(22) argue equally strongly for the provision's constitutionality. Most importantly, the deduction is available for educational expenses incurred by *all* parents, including those whose children attend non-sectarian private schools or sectarian private schools. Just as in *Widmar* v. *Vincent,* where we concluded that the state's provision of a forum neutrally "open to a broad class of nonreligious as well as religious speakers" does not "confer any imprimatur of State approval," so here: "the provision of benefits to so broad a spectrum of groups is an important index of secular effect."

⌐398 ⊥In this respect, as well as others, this case is vitally different from the scheme struck down in *Nyquist.* There, public assistance amounting to tuition grants, was provided only to parents of children in *nonpublic* schools. This fact had considerable bearing on our decision striking down the New York statute at issue; we explicitly distinguished both *Allen* and *Everson* on the grounds that "In both cases the class of beneficiaries included *all* schoolchildren, those in public as well as those in private schools." Moreover, we intimated that "public assistance (e.g., scholarships) made available generally without regard to the sectarian-nonsectarian or public-nonpublic nature of the institution benefited," might not offend the Establishment Clause. We think the tax deduction adopted by Minnesota is more similar to this latter type of program than it is to the arrangement struck down in *Nyquist.* Unlike the assistance at issue in *Nyquist,* § 290.09(22) permits *all* parents—whether their children attend public school or private—to deduct their childrens' educational expenses. As *Widmar* and our other decisions indicate, a program, like § 290.09(22), that neutrally pro-

⌐399 ⊥vides state assistance to a broad spectrum of citizens is not readily subject to challenge under the Establishment Clause.

We also agree with the Court of Appeals that, by channeling whatever assistance it may provide to parochial schools through individual parents, Minnesota has reduced the Establishment Clause objections to which its action is subject. It is true, of course, that financial assistance provided to parents ultimately has an economic effect comparable to that of aid given directly to the schools attended by their children. It is also true, however, that under Minnesota's arrangement public funds become available only as a result of numerous, private choices of individual parents of school-age children. For these reasons, we recognized in *Nyquist* that the means by which state assistance flows to private schools is of some importance: we said that "the fact that aid is disbursed to parents rather than to . . . schools" is a

material consideration in Establishment Clause analysis, albeit "only one among many to be considered." *Nyquist* It is noteworthy that all but one of our recent cases invalidating state aid to parochial schools have involved the direct transmission of assistance from the state to the schools themselves. The exception, of course, was *Nyquist,* which, as discussed previously, is distinguishable from this case on other grounds. Where, as here, aid to parochial schools is available only as a result of decisions of individual parents no "imprimatur of State approval," *Widmar,* can be deemed to have been conferred on any particular religion, or on religion generally.

We find it useful, in the light of the foregoing characteristics of § 290.09(22), to compare the attenuated financial benefits flowing to parochial schools from the section to the evils against which the Establishment Clause was designed to protect. These dangers are well-described by our statement that "what is at stake as a matter of policy [in Establishment Clause cases] is preventing that kind and degree of government involvement in religious life that, as history ⊥ teaches us, is apt to lead to strife and ⌐400 frequently strain a political system to the breaking point." *Walz* v. *Tax Comm'n.* It is important, however, to "keep these issues in perspective": "At this point in the 20th century we are quite far removed from the dangers that prompted the Framers to include the Establishment Clause in the Bill of Rights. The risk of significant religious or denominational control over our democratic processes—or even of deep political division along religious lines—is remote, and when viewed against the positive contributions of sectarian schools, any such risk seems entirely tolerable in light of the continuing oversight of this Court." *Wolman* The Establishment Clause of course extends beyond prohibition of a state church or payment of state funds to one or more churches. We do not think, however, that its prohibition extends to the type of tax deduction established by Minnesota. The historic purposes of the clause simply do not encompass the sort of attenuated financial benefit, ultimately controlled by the private choices of individual parents, that eventually flows to parochial schools from the neutrally available tax benefit at issue in this case.

Petitioners argue that, notwithstanding the facial neutrality of § 290.09(22), in application the statute primarily benefits religious institutions. Petitioners rely, as they did ⊥ below, on a statistical analysis of ⌐401 the type of persons claiming the tax deduction. They contend that most parents of public school children incur no tuition expenses, and that other expenses deductible under § 290.09(22) are negligible in value; moreover, they claim that 96% of the children in private schools in 1978-1979 attended religiously-affiliated institutions. Because of all this, they reason, the bulk of deductions taken under § 290.09(22) will be claimed by parents of children in sectarian schools. Respondents reply that petitioners have failed to consider the impact of deductions for items such as transportation, summer school tuition, tuition paid by parents whose children attended schools outside the school districts in which they resided, rental or purchase costs for a variety of equipment, and tuition for certain types of instruction not ordinarily provided in public schools.

We need not consider these contentions in detail. We would be loath to adopt a rule grounding the constitutionality of a facially neutral law on annual reports reciting the extent to which various classes of private citizens claimed benefits under the law. Such an approach would scarcely provide the certainty that this field stands in need of, nor can we perceive principled standards by which such statistical evidence might be evaluated. Moreover, the fact that private persons fail in a particular year to claim the tax relief to which they are entitled—under a facially neutral statute—should be of little importance in determining the constitutionality of the statute permitting such relief.

Finally, private educational institutions, and parents paying for their children to attend these schools, make special contributions to the areas in ⊥402 which they operate. "Parochial ⊥ schools, quite apart from their sectarian purpose, have provided an educational alternative for millions of young Americans; they often afford wholesome competition with our public schools; and in some States they relieve substantially the tax burden incident to the operation of public schools." *Wolman* If parents of children in private schools choose to take especial advantage of the relief provided by § 290.09(22), it is no doubt due to the fact that they bear a particularly great financial burden in educating their children. More fundamentally, whatever unequal effect may be attributed to the statutory classification can fairly be regarded as a rough return for the benefits, discussed above, provided to the state and all taxpayers by parents sending their children to parochial schools. In the light of all this, we believe it wiser to decline to engage in the type of empirical inquiry into those persons benefited by state law which petitioners urge.

Thus, we hold that the Minnesota tax deduction for educational expenses satisfies the primary effect inquiry of our Establishment Clause cases.

⊥403 ⊥ Turning to the third part of the *Lemon* inquiry, we have no difficulty in concluding that the Minnesota statute does not "excessively entangle" the state in religion. The only plausible source of the "comprehensive, discriminating, and continuing state surveillance" necessary to run afoul of this standard would lie in the fact that state officials must determine whether particular textbooks qualify for a deduction. In making this decision, state officials must disallow deductions taken from "instructional books and materials used in the teaching of religious tenets, doctrines or worship, the purpose of

which is to inculcate such tenets, doctrines or worship." § 290.09(22) Making decisions such as this does not differ substantially from making the types of decisions approved in earlier opinions of this Court. In *Board of Education* v. *Allen*, for example, the Court upheld the loan of secular textbooks to parents or children attending nonpublic schools; though state officials were required to determine whether particular books were or were not secular, the system was held not to violate the Establishment Clause. The same result follows in this case.

⊥ For the foregoing reasons, the judgment of the   ⊥404
Court of Appeals is *Affirmed.*

Justice MARSHALL, with whom *Justice BRENNAN, Justice BLACKMUN* and *Justice STEVENS* join, dissenting.

The Establishment Clause of the First Amendment prohibits a State from subsidizing religious education, whether it does so directly or indirectly. In my view, this principle of neutrality forbids not only the tax benefits struck down in *Committee for Public Education* v. *Nyquist*, but any tax benefit, including the tax deduction at issue here, which subsidizes tuition payments to sectarian schools. I also believe that the Establishment Clause prohibits the tax deductions that Minnesota authorizes for the cost of books and other instructional materials used for sectarian purposes.

I

The majority today does not question the continuing vitality of this Court's decision in *Nyquist*. That decision established that a State may not support religious education either through direct grants to parochial schools or through financial aid to parents of parochial school students. *Nyquist* also established that financial aid to parents of students attending parochial schools is no more permissible if it is provided in the form of a tax credit than if provided in the form of cash payments. Notwithstanding these accepted prin⊥ciples, the Court today upholds   ⊥405
a statute that provides a tax deduction for the tuition charged by religious schools. The Court concludes that the Minnesota statute is "vitally different" from the New York statute at issue in *Nyquist*. As demonstrated below, there is no significant difference between the two schemes. The Minnesota tax statute violates the Establishment Clause for precisely **the same reason as the statute struck** down in *Nyquist*: it has a direct and immediate effect of advancing religion.

A

In calculating their net income for state income tax purposes, Minnesota residents are permitted to deduct the cost of their children's tuition, subject to a ceiling of $500 or $700 per child. By taking this deduction, a taxpayer reduces his tax bill by a sum equal to the amount of tuition multiplied by his rate of tax. Although this tax benefit is available to any parents whose children attend schools which charge tuition, the vast majority of the taxpayers who are eligible to receive the benefit are parents whose children attend religious schools. In the 1978-1979 school year, 90,000 students were enrolled in non-public schools charging tuition; over 95% of those students attended sectarian schools. Although the statute also allows a deduction for the tuition expenses of children attending public schools, Minnesota public schools are generally prohibited by law from charging tuition. Public schools may assess tuition charges only for students accepted from outside the district. In the 1978-1979 school year, only 79 public school students fell into this category. The parents of the remaining 815,000 students who attended public schools were ineligible to receive this tax benefit.

Like the law involved in *Nyquist,* the Minnesota law can be said to serve a secular purpose: promoting pluralism and diversity among the State's public and nonpublic schools. But the Establishment Clause requires more than that legislation have a secular purpose. "[T]he ⊥ propriety of a legislature's purposes may not immunize from further scrutiny a law which . . . has a primary effect that advances religion." *Nyquist* Moreover, even if one " 'primary' effect [is] to promote some legitimate end under the State's police power," the legislation is not "immune from further examination to ascertain whether it also has the direct and immediate effect of advancing religion." *Id.*

⊥406

As we recognized in *Nyquist,* direct government subsidization of parochial school tuition is impermissible because "the effect of the aid is unmistakably to provide desired financial support for nonpublic, sectarian institutions." *Id.,* "[A]id to the educational function of [parochial] schools . . . necessarily results in aid to the sectarian enterprise as a whole" because "[t]he very purpose of those schools is to provide an integrated secular and religious education." *Meek* v. *Pittenger* For this reason, aid to sectarian schools must be restricted to ensure that it may be not used to further the religious mission of those schools. While "services such as police and fire protection, sewage disposal, highways, and sidewalks," may be provided to parochial schools in common with other institutions, because this type of assistance is clearly " 'marked off from the religious function' " of those schools, *Everson* v. *Board of Education* unrestricted financial assistance, such as grants for the maintenance and construction of parochial schools, may not be ⊥ provided. *Nyquist.* "In the absence of an effective means of guaranteeing that the state aid derived from public funds will be used exclusively for secular, neutral, and nonideological purposes, it is clear from our cases that direct aid in whatever form is invalid." *Id.*

⊥407

Indirect assistance in the form of financial aid to parents for tuition payments is similarly impermissible because it is not "subject to . . . restrictions" which " 'guarantee the separation between secular and religious educational functions and . . . ensure that State financial aid supports only the former.' " *Id.* By ensuring that parents will be reimbursed for tuition payments they make, the Minnesota statute requires that taxpayers in general pay for the cost of parochial education and extends a financial "incentive to parents to send their children to sectarian schools." *Nyquist* As was true of the law struck down in *Nyquist,* "it is precisely the function of [Minnesota's] law to provide assistance to private schools, the great majority of which are sectarian. By reimbursing parents for a portion of their tuition bill, the State seeks to relieve their financial burdens sufficiently to assure that they continue to have the option to send their children to religion-oriented schools. And while the other purposes for that aid—to perpetuate a pluralistic educational environment and to protect the fiscal integrity of overburdened public schools—are certainly unexceptional, the effect of the aid is unmistakably to provide desired financial support for nonpublic, sectarian institutions." *Id.*

That parents receive a reduction of their tax liability, rather than a direct reimbursement, is of no greater significance here than it was in *Nyquist.* "[F]or purposes of determining whether such aid has the effect of advancing religion," ⊥ it makes no difference whether the qualifying "parent receives an actual cash payment [or] is allowed to reduce . . . the sum he would otherwise be obliged to pay over to the State." *Id.* It is equally irrelevant whether a reduction in taxes takes the form of a tax "credit," a tax "modification," or a tax "deduction." *Id.* What is of controlling significance is not the form but the "substantive impact" of the financial aid. *Id.* "[I]nsofar as such benefits render assistance to parents who send their children to *sectarian* schools, their purpose and inevitable effect are to aid and advance those religious institutions." *Nyquist.*

⊥408

B

The majority attempts to distinguish *Nyquist* by pointing to two differences between the Minnesota tuition-assistance program and the program struck down in *Nyquist.* Neither of these distinctions can withstand scrutiny.

1

The majority first attempts to distinguish *Nyquist* on the ground that Minnesota makes all parents eligible to deduct up to $500 or $700 for each dependent, whereas the New York law allowed a deduction only for parents whose children attended nonpublic schools. Although Minnesota taxpayers who send their children to local public schools may not deduct tuition expenses because they incur none, they may deduct other expenses, such as the cost of gym clothes, pencils, and notebooks, which are shared by all parents of school-age children. This, in the majority's view, distinguishes the Minnesota scheme from the law at issue in *Nyquist*.

That the Minnesota statute makes some small benefit available to all parents cannot alter the fact that the most substantial benefit provided by the statute is available only to those parents who send their children to schools that charge tuition. It is simply undeniable that the single largest expense that may be deducted under the Minnesota statute is tuition. The statute is little more than a subsidy of ⌐409 tuition mas⊥querading as a subsidy of general educational expenses. The other deductible expenses are *de minimis* in comparison to tuition expenses.

Contrary to the majority's suggestion, the bulk of the tax benefits afforded by the Minnesota scheme are enjoyed by parents of parochial school children not because parents of public school children fail to claim deductions to which they are entitled, but because the latter are simply *unable* to claim the largest tax deduction that Minnesota authorizes. Fewer than 100 of more than 900,000 school-age children in Minnesota attend public schools that charge a general tuition. Of the total number of taxpayers who are eligible for the tuition deduction, approximately 96% send their children to religious schools. Parents who send their children to free public schools are simply ineligible to obtain the full benefit of the deduction except in the unlikely event that they buy $700 worth of pencils, notebooks, and bus rides for their school-age children. Yet parents who pay at least $700 in tuition to nonpublic, sectarian schools can claim the full deduction even if they incur no other educational expenses.

That this deduction has a primary effect of promoting religion can easily be determined without any resort to the type of "statistical evidence" that the majority fears would lead to constitutional uncertainty. The only factual inquiry necessary is the ⌐410 same as that employed in *Nyquist* ⊥ and *Sloan* v. *Lemon*: whether the deduction permitted for tuition expenses primarily benefits those who send their children to religious schools. In *Nyquist* we unequivocally rejected any suggestion that, in determining the effect of the New York statute, we emphasized that "virtually all" of the schools receiving direct grants for maintenance and repair were Roman Catholic schools, that reimbursements were given to parents "who send their children to nonpublic schools, the bulk of which are concededly sectarian in orientation," *id.*, that "it is precisely the function of New York's law to provide assistance to private schools, the great majority of which are sectarian," *id.* and that "tax reductions authorized by this law flow primarily to the parents of children attending sectarian, nonpublic schools." *Id.* Similarly, in *Sloan* v. *Lemon*, we considered important to our

"consider[ation of] the new law's effect . . . [that] 'more than 90% of the children attending nonpublic schools in the Commonwealth of Pennsylvania are enrolled in schools that are controlled by religious institutions or that have the purpose of propagating and promoting religious faith.' "

⊥ In this case, it is undisputed that well over 90%   ⌐411 of the children attending tuition-charging schools in Minnesota are enrolled in sectarian schools. History and experience likewise instruct us that any generally available financial assistance for elementary and secondary school tuition expenses mainly will further religious education because the majority of the schools which charge tuition are sectarian. Because Minnesota, like every other State, is committed to providing free public education, tax assistance for tuition payments inevitably redounds to the benefit of nonpublic sectarian schools and parents who send their children to those schools.

2

The majority also asserts that the Minnesota statute is distinguishable from the statute struck down in *Nyquist* in another respect: the tax benefit available under Minnesota law is a "genuine tax deduction," whereas the New York law provided a benefit which, while nominally a deduction, also had features of a "tax credit." Under the Minnesota law, the amount of the tax benefit varies directly with the amount of the expenditure. Under the New York law, the amount of deduction was not dependent upon the amount actually paid for tuition but was a predetermined amount which depended on the tax bracket of each taxpayer. The deduction was designed to yield roughly the same amount of tax "forgiveness" for each taxpayer.

This is a distinction without a difference. Our prior decisions have rejected the relevance of the majority's formalistic distinction between tax deductions and the tax benefit at issue in *Nyquist*. ⊥ The   ⌐412 deduction afforded by Minnesota law was "designed to yield a [tax benefit] in exchange for performing a specific act which the State desires to encourage." *Nyquist* Like the tax benefit held impermissible in *Nyquist* the tax deduction at issue here concededly was designed to "encourag[e] desirable expenditures for educational purposes." Of equal importance, as the majority also concedes, the "economic consequence" of these programs is the same, for in each case the "financial assistance provided to parents ultimately has an economic effect comparable to that of aid given directly to the schools." It was precisely the substantive impact of the financial support, and not its particular form, that rendered the program in *Nyquist* and *Sloan* ⊥ v. *Lemon* unconstitutional.   ⌐413

C

The majority incorrectly asserts that Minnesota's tax deduction for tuition expenses "bears less resemblance to the arrangement struck down in *Nyquist* than it does to assistance programs upheld in our prior decisions and discussed with approval in *Nyquist*." One might as well say that a tangerine bears less resemblance to an orange than to an apple. The two cases relied on by the majority, *Board of Education* v. *Allen,* and *Everson* v. *Board of Education*, are inapposite today for precisely the same reasons that they were inapposite in *Nyquist*.

We distinguished these cases in *Nyquist* and again in *Sloan* v. *Lemon*. Financial assistance for tuition payments has a consequence that "is quite unlike the sort of 'indirect' and 'incidental' benefits that flowed to sectarian schools from programs aiding *all* parents by supplying bus transportation and secular textbooks for their children. *Such benefits were carefully restricted to the purely secular side of church-affiliated institutions* and provided no special aid for those who had chosen to support religious schools. Yet such aid approached the 'verge' of the constitutionally impermissible." *Sloan* v. *Lemon*. As previously noted, the Minnesota tuition tax deduction is not available to *all* parents, but only to parents whose children attend schools that charge tuition, which are comprised almost entirely of sectarian schools. More importantly, the assistance that flows to parochial schools as a result of the tax benefit is not restricted, and cannot be restricted, to the secular functions of those schools.

⊥414

⊥ II

In my view, Minnesota's tax deduction for the cost of textbooks and other instructional materials is also constitutionally infirm. The majority is simply mistaken in concluding that a tax deduction, unlike a tax credit or a direct grant to parents, promotes religious eduction in a manner that is only "attenuated." A tax deduction has a primary effect that advances religion if it is provided to offset expenditures which are not restricted to the secular activities of parochial schools.

The instructional materials which are subsidized by the Minnesota tax deduction plainly may be used to inculcate religious values and belief. In *Meek* v. *Pittenger*, we held that even the use of "wholly neutral, secular instructional material and equipment" by church-related schools contributes to religious instruction because " '[t]he secular education those schools provide goes hand in hand with the religious mission that is the only reason for the schools' existence.' " In *Wolman* v. *Walter*, we concluded that precisely the same impermissible effect results when the instructional materials are loaned to the pupil or his parent, rather than directly to the schools. We stated that "it would exalt form over substance if this distinction were found to justify a result different from that in *Meek*." It follows that a tax deduction to offset the cost of purchasing instructional materials for use in sectarian schools, like a loan of such materials to parents, "necessarily results in aid

to the sectarian school enterprise as a whole" and is therefore a "substantial advancement of religious activity" that "constitutes an impermissible establishment of religion." *Ibid.*

There is no reason to treat Minnesota's tax deduction for textbooks any differently. Secular textbooks, like other secular instructional materials, contribute to the religious mission of the parochial school that use those books. Although this Court upheld the loan of secular textbooks to religious ⊥ schools in *Board* ⊥415 *of Education* v. *Allen*, the Court believed at that time that it lacked sufficient experience to determine "based solely on judicial notice" that "the processes of secular and religious training are so intertwined that secular textbooks furnished to students by the public [will always be] instrumental in the teaching of religion." This basis for distinguishing secular instructional materials and secular textbooks is simply untenable, and is inconsistent with many of our more recent decisions concerning state aid to parochial schools.

In any event, the Court's assumption in *Allen* that the textbooks at issue there might be used only for secular education was based on the fact that those very books had been chosen by the State for use in the public schools. In contrast, the Minnesota statute does not limit the tax deduction to those books which the State has approved for use in public schools. Rather, it permits a deduction for books that are chosen by the parochial schools themselves. Indeed, under the Minnesota statutory scheme, textbooks chosen by parochial schools but not used by public schools are likely to be precisely the ones purchased by parents for their children's use. Like the law upheld in *Board of Education* v. *Allen*, Minn. Stat. §§ 123.932 and 123.933 authorize the state board of education to provide textbooks used in public schools to nonpublic school students. Parents have little reason to purchase textbooks that can be borrowed under this provision.

⊥ III   ⊥416

There can be little doubt that the State of Minnesota intended to provide, and has provided, "[s]ubstantial aid to the educational function of [church-related] schools," and that the tax deduction for tuition and other educational expenses "necessarily results in aid to the sectarian school enterprise as a whole." *Meek* v. *Pittenger* It is beside the point that the State may have legitimate secular reasons for providing such aid. In focusing upon the contributions made by church-related schools, the majority has lost sight of the issue before us in this case. "The sole question is whether state aid to these schools can be squared with the dictates of the Religion Clauses. Under our system the choice has been made that government is to be entirely excluded from the area of religious instruction. . . . The Constitution decrees that religion must be a private matter for the individual, the family, and the institutions of private choice, and that while some involvement and entanglement are inevitable, lines must be drawn." *Lemon* v. *Kurtzman*

In my view, the lines drawn in *Nyquist* were drawn on a reasoned basis with appropriate regard for the principles of neutrality embodied by the Establishment Clause. I do not believe that the same can be said of the lines drawn by the majority today. For the first time, the Court has upheld financial support for religious schools without any reason at all to assume that the support will be restricted to the secular functions of those schools and will not be _|417 used to support reli⊥gious instruction. This result is flatly at odds with the fundamental principle that a State may provide no financial support whatsoever to promote religion. As the Court stated in *Everson*, "No tax in any amount, large or small, can be levied to support any religious activities or institutions, whatever they may be called, or whatever form they may adopt to teach or practice religion."

I dissent.

AGUILAR v. FELTON

105 S.Ct. 3232
ON APPEAL FROM THE UNITED STATES
COURT OF APPEALS FOR THE SECOND
CIRCUIT
Argued December 5, 1984 — Decided July 1, 1985
Justice BRENNAN delivered the opinion of the Court.

The City of New York uses federal funds to pay the salaries of public employees who teach in parochial schools. In this companion case to *School District of Grand Rapids* v. *Ball,* we determine whether this practice violates the Establishment Clause of the First Amendment.

I
A

The program at issue in this case, originally enacted as Title I of the Elementary and Secondary Education Act of 1965, authorizes the Secretary of Education to distribute financial assistance to local educational institutions to meet the needs of educationally deprived children from low-income families. The funds are to be appropriated in accordance with programs proposed by local educational agencies and approved by state educational agencies. 20 U.S.C. § 3805(a). "To the extent consistent with the number of educationally deprived children in the school district of the local educational agency who are enrolled in private elementary and secondary schools, such agency shall make provisions for including special educational services and arrangements . . . in which such children can participate." § 3806(a). The proposed programs must also meet the following statutory requirements: the children involved in the program must be educationally deprived, § 3804(a), the children must reside in areas comprising a high concentration of low-income families, § 3805(b), and the programs must supplement, not supplant, programs that would exist absent funding under Title I. § 3807(b).

Since 1966, the City of New York has provided instructional services funded by Title I to parochial school students on the premises of parochial schools. Of those students eligible to receive funds in 1981-1982, 13.2% were enrolled in private schools. Of that group, 84% were enrolled in schools affiliated with the Roman Catholic Archdiocese of New York and the Diocese of Brooklyn and 8% were enrolled in Hebrew day schools. With respect to the religious atmosphere of these schools, the Court of Appeals concluded that "the picture that emerges is of a system in which religious considerations play a key role in the selection of students and teachers, and which has as its substantial purpose the inculcation of religious values."

The programs conducted at these schools include remedial reading, reading skills, remedial mathematics, English as a second language, and guidance services. These programs are carried out by regular employees of the public schools (teachers, guidance counselors, psychologists, psychiatrists and social workers) who have volunteered to teach in the parochial schools. The amount of time that each professional spends in the parochial school is determined by the number of students in the particular program and the needs of these students.

The City's Bureau of Nonpublic School Reimbursement makes teacher assignments, and the instructors are supervised by field personnel, who attempt to pay at least one unannounced visit per month. The field supervisors, in turn, report to program coordinators, who also pay occasional unannounced supervisory visits to monitor Title I classes in the parochial schools. The professionals involved in the program are directed to avoid involvement with religious activities that are conducted within the private schools and to bar religious materials in their classrooms. All material and equipment used in the programs funded under Title I are supplied by the Government and are used only in those programs. The professional personnel are solely responsible for the selection of the students. Additionally, the professionals are informed that contact with private school personnel should be kept to a minimum. Finally, the administrators of the parochial schools are required to clear the classrooms used by the public school personnel of all religious symbols.

B

In 1978, six taxpayers commenced this action in the District Court for the Eastern District of New York, alleging that the Title I program administered by the City of New York violates the Establishment Clause. These taxpayers, appellees in today's case, sought to enjoin the further distribution of funds to programs involving instruction on the premises of parochial schools. Initially the case was held for the outcome of *National Coalition for Public Education and Religious Liberty* v. *Harris,* ("PEARL"), which involed an identical challenge to the Title I program. When the District Court in PEARL affirmed the constitutionality of the Title I program, and this Court dismissed the appeal for want of jurisdiction, the challenge of the present appellees was renewed. The District Court granted the appellants' motion for summary judgment based upon the evidentiary record developed in PEARL.

A unanimous panel of the Court of Appeals for the Second Circuit reversed, holding that "[t]he Establishment Clause, as it has been interpreted by the Supreme Court in *Public Funds for Public Schools* v. *Marburger, Meek* v. *Pittenger,* and *Wolman* v. *Walter,* constitutes an insurmountable barrier to the use of federal funds to send public school teachers and other professionals into religious schools to carry on instruction, remedial or otherwise, or to provide clinical and guidance services of the sort at issue here." 739 F. 2d, at 49-50. We postponed probable jurisdiction. We conclude that jurisdiction by appeal does not properly lie. Treating the papers as a petition for a writ of certiorari, we grant the petition and now affirm the judgment below.

II

In *School District of the City of Grand Rapids* v. *Ball,* the Court has today held unconstitutional under the Establishment Clause two remedial and enhancement programs operated by the Grand Rapids Public School District, in which classes were provided to private school children at public expense in classrooms located in and leased from the local private schools. The New York programs challenged in this case are very similar to the programs we examined in *Ball.* In both cases, publicly funded instructors teach classes composed exclusively of private school students in private school buildings. In both cases, an overwhelming number of the participating private schools are religiously affiliated. In both cases, the publicly funded programs provide not only professional personnel, but also all materials and supplies necessary for the operation of the programs. Finally, the instructors in both cases are told that they are public school employees under the sole control of the public school system.

The appellants attempt to distinguish this case on the ground that the City of New York, unlike the Grand Rapids Public School District, has adopted a system for monitoring the religious content of publicly funded Title I classes in the religious schools. At best, the supervision in this case would assist in preventing the Title I program from being used, intentionally or unwittingly, to inculcate the religious beliefs of the surrounding parochial school. But appellants' argument fails in any event, because the supervisory system established by the City of New York inevitably results in the excessive entanglement of church and state, an Establishment Clause concern distinct from that addressed by the effects doctrine. Even where state aid to parochial institutions does not have the primary effect of advancing religion, the provision of such aid may nonetheless violate the Establishment Clause owing to the nature of the interaction of church and state in the administration of that aid.

The principle that the state should not become too closely entangled with the church in the administration of assistance is rooted in two concerns. When the state becomes enmeshed with a given denomination in matters of religious significance, the freedom of religious belief of those who are not adherents of that denomination suffers, even when the governmental purpose underlying the involvement is largely secular. In addition, the freedom of even the adherents of the denomination is limited by the governmental intrusion into sacred matters. "[T]he First Amendment rests upon the premise that both religion and government can best work to achieve their lofty aims if each is left free from the other within its respective sphere." *McCollum* v. *Board of Education*

In *Lemon* v. *Kurtzman,* the Court held that the supervision necessary to ensure that teachers in parochial schools were not conveying religious messages to their students would constitute the excessive entanglement of church and state: "A comprehensive, discriminating, and continuing state surveillance will inevitably be required to ensure that these restrictions are obeyed and the First Amendment otherwise respected. Unlike a book, a teacher cannot be inspected once so as to determine the extent and intent of his or her personal beliefs and subjective acceptance of the limitations imposed by the First Amendment. These prophylactic contacts will involve excessive and enduring entanglement between state and church." Similarly, in *Meek* v. *Pittenger,* we invalidated a state program that offered, *inter allia,* guidance, testing, remedial and therapeutic services performed by public employees on the premises of the parochial schools. As in *Lemon,* we observed that though a comprehensive system of supervision might conceivably prevent teachers from having the primary effect of advancing religion, such a system would inevitably lead to an unconstitutional administrative entanglement between church and state. "The prophylactic contacts required to ensure that teachers play a strictly nonideological role, the Court held [in *Lemon*], necessarily give rise to a constitutionally intolerable degree of entanglement between chuch and state. The same excessive entanglement would be required for Pennsylvania to be 'certain,' as it must be, that . . . personnel do not advance the religious mission of the church- related schools in which they serve."

In *Roemer* v. *Maryland Public Works Board,* the Court sustained state programs of aid to religiously affiliated institutions of higher learning. The state allowed the grants to be used for any nonsectarian purpose. The Court upheld the grants on the ground that the institutions were not " 'pervasively sectarian,' " and therefore a system of supervision was unnecessary to ensure that the grants were not being used to effect a religious end. In so holding, the Court identified "what is crucial to a nonentangling aid program: the ability of the State to identify and subsidize separate secular functions carried out at the school, without on-the-site inspections being necessary to prevent diversion of the funds to sectarian purposes." Similarly, in *Tilton* v. *Richardson,* the Court upheld one-time grants to sectarian institutions because ongoing supervision was not required. See also *Hunt* v. *McNair.*

As the Court of Appeals recognized, the elementary and secondary schools here are far different from the colleges at issue in *Roemer, Hunt,* and *Tilton.* Unlike the colleges, which were found not to be "pervasively sectarian," many of the schools involved in this case are the same sectarian schools which had " 'as a substantial purpose the inculcation of religious values' " in *Committee for Public Education* v. *Nyquist.* Moreover, our holding in *Meek* invalidating instructional services much like those at issue in this case rested on the ground that the publicly funded teachers were "performing important educational services in schools in which education is an integral part of the dominant sectarian mission and in which an atmosphere dedicated to the advancement of religious belief is constantly maintained." The court below found that the schools involved in this case were "well within this characterization." Unlike the schools in *Roemer,* many of the schools here receive funds and report back to their affiliated church, require attendance at church religious exercises, begin the school day or class period with prayer, and grant preference in admission to members of the sponsoring denominations. In addition, the Catholic schools at issue here, which constitute the vast majority of the aided schools, are under the general supervision and control of the local parish.

The critical elements of the entanglement proscribed in *Lemon* and *Meek* are thus present in this case. First, as noted above, the aid is provided in a pervasively sectarian environment. Second, because assistance is provided in the form of teachers, ongoing inspection is required to ensure the absence of a religious message. In short, the scope and duration of New York's Title I program would require a permanent and pervasive State presence in the sectarian schools receiving aid.

This pervasive monitoring by public authorities in the sectarian schools infringes precisely those Establishment Clause values at the root of the prohibition of excessive entanglement. Agents of the State must visit and inspect the religious school regularly, alert for the subtle or overt presence of religious matter in

Title I classes. Cf. *Lemon* v. *Kurtzman,* ("What would appear to some to be essential to good citizenship might well for others border on or constitute instruction in religion"). In addition, the religious school must obey these same agents when they make determinations as to what is and what is not a "religious symbol" and thus off limits in a Title I classroom. In short, the religious school, which has as a primary purpose the advancement and preservation of a particular religion must endure the ongoing presence of state personnel whose primary purpose is to monitor teachers and students in an attempt to guard against the infiltration of religious thought.

The administrative cooperation that is required to maintain the educational program at issue here entangles Church and State in still another way that infringes interests at the heart of the Establishment Clause. Administrative personnel of the public and parochial school systems must work together in resolving matters related to schedules, classroom assignments, problems that arise in the implementation of the program, requests for additional services, and the dissemination of information regarding the program. Furthermore, the program necessitates "frequent contacts between the regular and the remedial teachers (or other professionals), in which each side reports on individual student needs, problems encountered, and results achieved."

We have long recognized that underlying the Establishment Clause is "the objective . . . to prevent, as far as possible, the intrusion of either [Church or State] into the precincts of the other." *Lemon* v. *Kurtzman.* Although "[s]eparation in this context cannot mean absence of all contact," *Walz* v. *Tax Commission,* the detailed monitoring and close administrative contact required to maintain New York's Title I program can only produce "a kind of continuing day-to-day relationship which the policy of neutrality seeks to minimize." The numerous judgments that must be made by agents of the state concern matters that may be subtle and controversial, yet may be of deep religious significance to the controlling denominations. As government agents must make these judgments, the dangers of political divisiveness along religious lines increase. At the same time, "[t]he picture of state inspectors prowling the halls of parochial schools and auditing classroom instruction surely raised more than an imagined specter of governmental 'secularization of a creed.' " *Lemon* v. *Kurtzman.*

III

Despite the well-intentioned efforts taken by the City of New York, the program remains constitutionally flawed owing to the nature of the aid, to the institution receiving the aid, and to the constitutional principles that they implicate—that neither the State nor Federal Government shall promote or hinder a particular faith or faith generally through the advancement of benefits or through the excessive entanglement of church and state in the administration of those benefits.

Affirmed.

Justice POWELL, concurring.

I concur in the Court's opinions and judgments today in this case and in *Grand Rapids School District* v. *Ball,* holding that the aid to parochial schools involved in those cases violates the Establishment Clause of the First Amendment. I write to emphasize additional reasons why precedents of this Court require us to invalidate these two educational programs that concededly have "done so much good and little, if any, detectable harm." The Court has previously recognized the important role of parochial schools: "Parochial schools, quite apart from their sectarian purpose, have provided an educational alternative for millions of young Americans; they often afford wholesome competition with our public schools; and in some States they relieve substantially the tax burden incident to the operation of public schools. The State has, moreover, a legitimate interest in facilitating education of the highest quality for all children within its boundaries, whatever school their parents have chosen for them". *Mueller* v. *Allen,* (quoting *Wolman* v. *Walter*). Regrettably, however, the Title I and Grand Rapids programs do not survive the scrutiny required by our Establishment Clause cases.

I agree with the Court that in this case the Establishment Clause is violated because there is too great a risk of government entanglement in the administration of the religious schools; the same is true in *Ball.* As beneficial as the Title I program appears to be in accomplishing its secular goal of supplementing the education of deprived children, its elaborate structure, the participation of public school teachers, and the government surveillance required to ensure that public funds are used for secular purposes inevitably present a serious risk of excessive entanglement. Our cases have noted that " '[t]he State must be *certain,* given the Religion Clauses, that subsidized teachers do not inculcate religion.' " *Meek* v. *Pittenger,* (emphasis added) (quoting *Lemon* v. *Kurtzman*). This is true whether the subsidized teachers are religious school teachers, as in *Lemon,* or public school teachers teaching secular subjects to parochial school children at the parochial schools. Judge Friendly, writing for the unanimous Court of Appeals, agreed with this assessment of our cases. He correctly observed that the structure of the Title I program required the active and extensive surveillance that the City has provided, and, "under *Meek,* this very surveillance constitutes excessive entanglement even if it has succeeded in preventing the fostering of religion."

This risk of entanglement is compounded by the additional risk of political divisiveness stemming from the aid to religion at issue here. I do not suggest that at this point in our history the Title I program or similar parochial aid plans could result in the establishment of a state religion. There likewise is small chance that these programs would result in significant religious or denominational control over our democratic processes. Nonetheless, there remains a considerable risk of continuing political strife over the propriety of direct aid to religious schools and the proper allocation of limited governmental resources. As this Court has repeatedly recognized, there is a likelihood whenever direct governmental aid is extended to some groups that there will be competition and strife among them and others to gain, maintain, or increase the financial support of government. In states such as New York that have large and varied sectarian populations, one can be assured that politics will enter into any state decision to aid parochial schools. Public schools, as well as private schools, are under increasing financial pressure to meet real and perceived needs. Thus, any proposal to extend direct governmental aid to parochial schools alone is likely to spark political disagreement from taxpayers who support the public schools, as well as from non-recipient sectarian groups, who may fear that needed funds are being diverted from them. In short, aid to parochial schools of the sort at issue here potentially leads to "that kind and degree of government involvement in religious life that, as history teaches us, is apt to lead to strife and frequently strain a political system to the breaking point." *Walz* v. *Tax Commission.* Although the Court's opinion does not discuss it at length, the potential for such divisiveness is a strong additional reason for holding that the Title I and Grand Rapids programs are invalid on entanglement grounds.

The Title I program at issue in this case also would be invalid under the "effects" prong of the test adopted in *Lemon* v. *Kurtzman.* As has been discussed thoroughly in *Ball,* with respect to the Grand Rapids programs, the type of aid provided in New York by the Title I program amounts to a state subsidy of the parochial schools by relieving those schools of the duty to provide the remedial and supplemental education their children require. This is not the type of "indirect and incidental effect beneficial to [the] religious institutions" that we suggested in *Nyquist* would survive Establishment Clause scrutiny. Rather, by directly assuming part of the parochial schools' education function, the effect of the Title I aid is "inevitably . . . to subsidize and advance the religious mission of [the] sectarian schools," even though the program provides that only secular subjects will be taught. As in *Meek* v. *Pittenger,* the secular education these schools provide goes " 'hand in hand' " with the religious mission that is the reason for the schools' existence. Because of the predominantly religious nature of the schools, the substantial aid provided by the Title I program "inescapably results in the direct and substantial advancement of religious activity."

I recognize the difficult dilemma in which governments are placed by the interaction of the "effects" and entanglement prongs of the *Lemon* test. Our decisions require governments extending aid to parochial schools to tread an extremely narrow line between being certain that the "principal or primary effect" of the aid is not to advance religion, and avoiding excessive entanglment. Nonetheless, the Court has never foreclosed the possibility that some types of aid to parochial schools could be valid under the Establishment Clause. Our cases have upheld evenhanded secular assistance to both parochial and public school children in some areas. I do not read the Court's opinion as precluding these types of indirect aid to parochial schools. In the cases cited, the assistance programs made funds available equally to public and nonpublic schools without entanglement. The constitutional defect in the Title I program, as indicated above, is that it provides a direct financial subsidy to be administered in significant part by public school teachers within parochial schools—resulting in both the advancement of religion and forbidden entanglement. If, for example, Congress could fashion a program of evenhanded financial assistance to both public and private schools that could be administered, without governmental supervision in the private schools, so as to prevent the diversion of the aid from secular purposes, we would be presented with a different question.

I join the opinions and judgments of the Court.

Chief Justice BURGER, dissenting.

Under the guise of protecting Americans from the evils of an Established Church such as those of the Eighteenth Century and earlier times, today's decision will deny countless schoolchildren desperately needed remedial teaching services funded under Title I. The program at issue covers remedial reading, reading skills, remedial mathematics, English as a second language, and assistance for chidren needing special help in the learning process. The "remedial reading" portion of this program, for example, reaches children who suffer from dyslexia, a disease known to be difficult to diagnose and treat. Many of these children now will not receive the special training they need, simply because their parents desire that they attend religiously affiliated schools.

What is disconcerting about the result reached today is that, in the face of the human cost entailed by this decision, the Court does not even attempt to identify any threat to religious liberty posed by the operation of Title I. I share Justice WHITE'S concern that the Court's obsession with the criteria identified in *Lemon* v. *Kurtzman* has led to results that are "contrary to the long-range interests of the country." As I wrote in *Wallace* v. *Jaffree*, "our re-

sponsibility is not to apply tidy formulas by rote; our duty is to determine whether the statute or practice at issue is a step toward establishing a state religion." Federal programs designed to prevent a generation of children from growing up without being able to read effectively are not remotely steps in that direction. It borders on paranoia to perceive the Archbishop of Canterbury or the Bishop of Rome lurking behind programs that are just as vital to the nation's schoolchildren as textbooks, transportation to and from school, and school nursing services.

On the merits of this case, I dissent for the reasons stated in my separate opinion in *Meek* v. *Pittenger.* We have frequently recognized that some interaction between church and state is unavoidable, and that an attempt to eliminate all contact between the two would be both futile and undesirable. Justice Douglas, writing for the Court in *Zorach* v. *Clauson,* stated: "The First Amendment . . . does not say that in every and all respects there shall be a separation of Church and State . . . Otherwise the state and religion would be aliens to each other—hostile, suspicious, and even unfriendly." The Court today fails to demonstrate how the interaction occasioned by the program at issue presents any threat to the values underlying the Establishment Clause.

I cannot join in striking down a program that, in the words of the Court of Appeals, "has done so much good and little, if any, detectable harm." The notion that denying these services to students in religious schools is a neutral act to protect us from an Established Church has no support in logic, experience, or history. Rather than showing the neutrality the Court boasts of, it exhibits nothing less than hostility toward religion and the children who attend church-sponsored schools.

Justice REHNQUIST, dissenting.

I dissent for the reasons stated in my dissenting opinion in *Wallace* v. *Jaffree.* In *Aguilar* v. *Felton* the Court takes advantage of the "Catch-22" paradox of its own creation, whereby aid must be supervised to ensure no entanglement but the supervison itself is held to cause an entanglement. The Court in *Aguilar* strikes down nondiscriminatory nonsectarian aid to educationally deprived children from low-income families. The Establishment Clause does not prohibit such sorely needed assistance; we have indeed travelled far afield from the concerns which prompted the adoption of the First Amendment when we rely on gossamer abstractions to invalidate a law which obviously meets an entirely secular need. I would reverse.

Justice O'CONNOR, with whom Justice REHNQUIST joins as to Parts II and III, dissenting.

Today the Court affirms the holding of the Court of Appeals that public schoolteachers can offer remedial instruction to disadvantaged students who attend religious schools "only if such instruction . . . [is] afforded at a neutral site off the premises of the religious school." This holding rests on the theory, enunciated in Part V of the Court's opinion in *Meek* v. *Pittenger*, that public schoolteachers who set foot on parochial school premises are likely to bring religion into their classes, and that the supervision necessary to prevent religious teaching would unduly entangle church and state. Even if this theory were valid in the abstract, it cannot validly be applied to New York City's 19-year-old Title I program. The Court greatly exaggerates the degree of supervision necessary to prevent public school teachers from inculcating religion, and thereby demonstrates the flaws of a test that condemns benign cooperation between chuch and state. I would uphold Congress' efforts to afford remedial instruction to disadvantaged schoolchildren in both public and parochial schools.

I

As in *Wallace* v. *Jaffree* and *Thornton* v. *Caldor, Inc.,* the Court in this litigation adheres to the three-part Establishment Clause test enunciated in *Lemon* v. *Kurtzman*. To survive the *Lemon* test, a statute must have both a secular legislative purpose and a principal or primary effect that neither advances nor inhibits religion. Under *Lemon* and its progeny, direct state aid to parochial schools that has the purpose or effect of furthering the religious mission of the schools is unconstitutional. I agree with that principle. According to the Court, however, the New York Title I program is defective not because of any improper purpose or effect, but rather because it fails the third part of the *Lemon* test: the Title I program allegedly fosters excessive government entanglement with religion. I disagree with the court's analysis of entanglement and I question the utility of entanglement as a separate Establishment Clause standard in most cases. Before discussing entanglement, however, it is worthwhile to explore the purpose and effect of the New York Title I program in greater depth than does the majority opinion.

The purpose of Title I is to provide special educational assistance to disadvantaged children who would not otherwise receive it. Congress recognized that poor academic performance by disadvantaged children is part of the cycle of poverty. Congress sought to break the cycle by providing classes in remedial reading, mathematics, and English to disadvantaged children in parochial as well as public schools, for public schools enjoy no monopoly on education in low income areas. Congress permitted remedial instruction by public school teachers on parochial school premises only if such instruction is "not normally provided by the nonpublic school" and would "contribute particularly to meeting the special educational needs of educationally deprived children."

After reviewing the text of the statute and its legislative history, the District Court concluded that Title I serves a secular purpose of aiding needy children regardless of where they attend school. The Court of Appeals did not dispute this finding, and no party in this Court contends that the purpose of the statute or of the New York City Title I program is to advance or endorse religion. Indeed, the record demonstrates that New York City public schoolteachers offer Title I classes on the premises of parochial schools solely because alternative means to reach the disadvantaged parochial school students—such as instruction for parochial school students at the nearest public school, either after or during regular school hours—were unsuccessful. As the Court of Appeals acknowledged, New York City "could reasonably have regarded [Title I instruction on parochial school premises] as the most effective way to carry out the purposes of the Act." Whether one looks to the face of the statute or to its implementation, the Title I program is undeniably animated by a legitimate secular purpose.

The Court's discussion of the effect of the New York City Title I program is even more perfunctory than its analysis of the program's purpose. The Court's opinion today in *Grand Rapids School Dist.* v. *Ball,* which strikes down a Grand Rapids scheme that the Court asserts is very similar to the New York program, identifies three ways in which public instruction on parochial school premises may have the impermissible effect of advancing religion. First, "state-paid instructors, influenced by the pervasively sectarian nature of the religious schools in which they work, may subtly or overtly indoctrinate the students in particular religious tenets at public expense". Second, "state-provided instruction in the religious school buildings threatens to convey a message of state support for religion to students and to the general public." Third, "the programs in effect subsidize the religious functions of the parochial schools by taking over a substantial portion of their responsibility for teaching secular subjects." While addressing the effect of the Grand Rapids program at such length, the Court overlooks the effect of Title I in New York City.

One need not delve too deeply in the record to understand why the Court does not belabor the effect of the Title I program. The abstract theories explaining why on-premises instruction might possibly advance religion dissolve in the face of experience in New York. As the District Court found in 1980: "New York City has been providing Title I services in nonpublic schools for fourteen years. The evidence presented in this action includes: extensive background information on Title I; an in-depth description of New York City's program; a detailed review of Title I rules and regulations and the ways in which they are enforced; and the testimony and affidavits of federal officials, state officers, school administrators, Title I teachers and supervisors, and parents of children receiving Title I services. The evidence establishes that the result feared in other cases has not materialized in the City's Title I program. The presumption—that the 'religious mission' will be advanced by providing educational services on parochial school premises—is not supported by the facts of this case." *National Coalition for Public Education and Religious Liberty* v. *Harris* Indeed, in 19 years there has never been a single incident in which a Title I instructor "subtly or overtly" attempted to "indoctrinate the students in particular religious tenets at public expense."

Common sense suggests a plausible explanation for this unblemished record. New York City's public Title I instructors are professional educators who can and do follow instructions not to inculcate religion in their classes. They are unlikely to be influenced by the sectarian nature of the parochial schools where they teach, not only because they are carefully supervised by public officials, but also because the vast majority of them visit several different schools each week and are not of the same religion as their parochial students. In light of the ample record, an objective observer of the implementation of the Title I program in New York would hardly view it as endorsing the tenets of the participating parochial schools. To the contrary, the actual and perceived effect of the program is precisely the effect intended by Congress: impoverished school children are being helped to overcome learning deficits, improving their test scores, and receiving a significant boost in their struggle to obtain both a thorough education and the opportunities that flow from it.

The only type of impermissible effect that arguably could carry over from the *Grand Rapids* decision to this litigation, then, is the effect of subsidizing "the religious functions of the parochial schools by taking over a substantial portion of their responsibility for teaching secular subjects." That effect is tenuous, however, in light of the statutory directive that Title I funds may be used only to provide services that otherwise would not be available to the participating students. The Secretary of Education has vigorously enforced the requirement that Title I funds supplement rather than supplant the services of local education agencies.

Even if we were to assume that Title I remedial classes in New York may have duplicated to some extent instruction parochial schools would have offered in the absence of Title I, the Court's delineation of this third type of effect proscribed by the Establishment Clause would be seriously flawed. Our Establishment Clause decisions have not barred remedial assistance to parochial school children, but rather remedial assistance *on the premises of the parochial school.* Under *Wolman* v. *Walter*, the New

York City classes prohibited by the Court today would have survived Establishment Clause scrutiny if they had been offered in a neutral setting off the property of the private school. Yet it is difficult to understand why a remedial reading class offered on parochial school premises is any more likely to supplant the secular course offerings of the parochial school than the same class offered in a portable classroom next door to the school. Unless *Wolman* was wrongly decided, the defect in the Title I program cannot lie in the risk that it will supplant secular course offerings.

II

Recognizing the weakness of any claim of an improper purpose or effect, the Court today relies entirely on the entanglement prong of *Lemon* to invalidate the New York City Title I program. The Court holds that the occasional presence of peripatetic public schoolteachers on parochial school grounds threatens undue entanglement of church and state because (1) the remedial instruction is afforded in a pervasively sectarian environment; (2) ongoing supervision is required to assure that the public schoolteachers do not attempt to inculcate religion; (3) the administrative personnel of the parochial and public school systems must work together in resolving administrative and scheduling problems; and (4) the instruction is likely to result in political divisiveness over the propriety of direct aid.

This analysis of entanglement, I acknowledge, finds support in some of this Court's precedents. In *Meek* v. *Pittenger* the Court asserted that it could not rely "on the good faith and professionalism of the secular teachers and counselors functioning in church related schools to ensure that a strictly nonideological posture is maintained." Because "a teacher remains a teacher," the Court stated, there remains a risk that teachers will intertwine religious doctrine with secular instruction. The continuing state surveillance necessary to prevent this from occurring would produce undue entanglement of church and state. The Court's opinion in *Meek* further asserted that public instruction on parochial school premises creates a serious risk of divisive political conflict over the issue of aid to religion. *Meek*'s analysis of entanglement was reaffirmed in *Wolman* two Terms later.

I would accord these decisions the appropriate deference commanded by the doctrine of *stare decisis* if I could discern logical support for their analysis. But experience has demonstrated that the analysis in Part V of the *Meek* opinion is flawed. At the time *Meek* was decided, thoughtful dissents pointed out the absence of any record support for the notion that public school teachers would attempt to inculcate religion simply because they temporarily occupied a parochial school classroom, or that such instruction would produce political divisiveness. Experience has given greater force to the arguments of the dissenting opinions in *Meek*. It is not intuitively obvious that a dedicated public school teacher will tend to disobey instructions and commence proselytizing students at public expense merely because the classroom is within a parochial school. *Meek* is correct in asserting that a teacher of remedial reading "remains a teacher", but surely it is significant that the teacher involved is a professional, full-time public school employee who is unaccustomed to bringing religion into the classroom. Given that not a single incident of religious indoctrination has been identified as occurring in the thousands of classes offered in Grand Rapids and New York over the past two decades, it is time to acknowledge that the risk identified in *Meek* was greatly exaggerated.

Just as the risk that public schoolteachers in parochial classrooms will inculcate religion has been exaggerated, so has the degree of supervision required to manage that risk. In this respect the New York Title I program is instructive. What supervision has been necessary in New York to enable public school teachers to help disadvantaged children for 19 years without once proselytizing? Public officials have prepared careful instructions warning public schoolteachers of their exclusively secular mission, and have required Title I teachers to study and observe them. Under the rules, Title I teachers are not accountable to parochial or private school officials; they have sole responsibility for selecting the students who participate in their class, must administer their own tests for determining eligibility, cannot engage in team teaching or cooperative activities with parochial school teachers, must make sure that all materials and equipment they use are not otherwise used by the parochial school, and must not participate in religious activities in the schools or introduce any religious matter into their teaching. To ensure compliance with the rules, a field supervisor and a program coordinator, who are full-time public school employees, make unannounced visits to each teacher's classroom at least once a month.

The Court concludes that this degree of supervision of public school employees by other public school employees constitutes excessive entanglement of church and state. I cannot agree. The supervision that occurs in New York's Title I program does not differ significantly from the supervision any public schoolteacher receives, regardless of the location of the classroom. *Justice POWELL* suggests that the required supervision is extensive because the State must be *certain* that public schoolteachers do not inculcate religion. That reasoning would require us to close our public schools, for there is always some chance that a public schoolteacher will bring religion into the classroom, regardless of its location. Even if I remained confident of the usefulness of entanglement as an Establishment Clause test, I would conclude that New York's efforts to prevent religious indoctrination in Title I classes have been adequate

and have not caused excessive institutional entanglement of church and state.

The Court's reliance on the potential for political divisiveness as evidence of undue entanglement is also unpersuasive. There is little record support for the proposition that New York's admirable Title I program has ignited any controversy other than this litigation. In *Mueller* v. *Allen,* the Court cautioned that the "elusive inquiry" into political divisiveness should be confined to a narrow category of parochial aid cases. The concurring opinion in *Lynch* v. *Donnelly,* went further, suggesting that Establishment Clause analysis should focus solely on the character of the government activity that might cause political divisiveness, and that "the entanglement prong of the *Lemon* test is properly limited to institutional entanglement."

I adhere to the doubts about the entanglement test that were expressed in *Lynch*. It is curious indeed to base our interpretation of the Constitution on speculation as to the likelihood of a phenomenon which the parties may create merely by prosecuting a lawsuit. My reservations about the entanglement test, however, have come to encompass its institutional aspects as well. As *Justice REHNQUIST* has pointed out, many of the inconsistencies in our Establishment Clause decisions can be ascribed to our insistence that parochial aid programs with a valid purpose and effect may still be invalid by virtue of undue entanglement. For example, we permit a State to pay for bus transportation to a parochial school, but preclude States from providing buses for parochial school field trips, on the theory such trips involve excessive state supervision of the parochial officials who lead them. To a great extent, the anomalous results in our Establishment Clause cases are "attributable to [the] 'entanglement' prong." Choper, The Religion Clauses of the First Amendment: Reconciling the Conflict, 41 U. Pitt. L. Rev. 673, 681 (1980).

Pervasive institutional involvement of church and state may remain relevant in deciding the *effect* of a statute which is alleged to violate the Establishment Clause, but state efforts to ensure that public resources are used only for nonsectarian ends should not in themselves serve to invalidate an otherwise valid statute. The State requires sectarian organizations to cooperate on a whole range of matters without thereby advancing religion or giving the impression that the government endorses religion. If a statute lacks a purpose or effect of advancing or endorsing religion, I would not invalidate it merely because it requires some ongoing cooperation between church and state or some state supervision to ensure that state funds do not advance religion.

III

Today's ruling does not spell the end of the Title I program of remedial education for disadvantaged children. Children attending public schools may still obtain the benefits of the program. Impoverished children who attend parochial schools may also continue to benefit from Title I programs offered off the premises of their schools—possibly in portable classrooms just over the edge of school property. The only disadvantaged children who lose under the Court's holding are those in cities where it is not economically and logistically feasible to provide public facilities for remedial education adjacent to the parochial school. But this subset is significant, for it includes more than 20,000 New York City schoolchildren and uncounted others elsewhere in the country.

For these children, the Court's decision is tragic. The Court deprives them of a program that offers a meaningful chance at success in life, and it does so on the untenable theory that public schoolteachers (most of whom are of different faiths than their students) are likely to start teaching religion merely because they have walked across the threshold of a parochial school. I reject this theory and the analysis in *Meek* v. *Pittenger* on which it is based. I cannot close my eyes to the fact that, over almost two decades, New York's public schoolteachers have helped thousands of impoverished parochial schoolchildren to overcome educational disadvantages without once attempting to inculcate religion. Their praiseworthy efforts have not eroded and do not threaten the religious liberty assured by the Establishment Clause. The contrary judgment of the Court of Appeals should be reversed.

I respectfully dissent.

SCHOOL DISTRICT OF THE CITY OF GRAND RAPIDS v. BALL

105 S.Ct. 3216
ON WRIT OF CERTIORARI TO THE UNITED STATES COURT OF APPEALS FOR THE SIXTH CIRCUIT
Argued December 5, l984 — Decided July 1, 1985
Justice BRENNAN delivered the opinion of the court.

The School District of Grand Rapids, Michigan, adopted two programs in which classes for nonpublic school students are financed by the public school system, taught by teachers hired by the public school system, and conducted in "leased" classrooms in the nonpublic schools. Most of the nonpublic schools involved in the programs are sectarian religious schools. This case raises the question whether these programs impermissibly involve the government in the support of sectarian religious activities and thus violate the Establishment Clause of the First Amendment.

I

A

At issue in this case are the Community Education and Shared Time programs offered in the nonpublic schools of Grand Rapids, Michigan. These programs, first instituted in the 1976-1977 school year, provide classes to nonpublic school students at public expense in classrooms located in and leased from the local nonpublic schools.

The Shared Time program offers classes during the regular school day that are intended to be supplementary to the "core curriculum" courses that the State of Michigan requires as a part of an accredited school program. Among the subjects offered are "remedial" and "enrichment" mathematics, "remedial" and "enrichment" reading, art, music, and physical education. A typical nonpublic school student attends these classes for one or two class periods per week; approximately "ten percent of any given nonpublic school student's time during the academic year would consist of Shared Time instruction." Although Shared Time itself is a program offered only in the nonpublic schools, there was testimony that the courses included in that program are offered, albeit perhaps in a somewhat different form, in the public schools as well. All of the classes that are the subject of this case are taught in elementary schools, with the exception of Math Topics, a remedial math course taught in the secondary schools.

The Shared Time teachers are full-time employees of the public schools, who often move from classroom to classroom during the course of the school day. A "significant portion" of the teachers (approximately l0%) "previously taught in nonpublic schools, and many of those had been assigned to the same nonpublic school where they were previously employed." The School District of Grand Rapids hires Shared Time teachers in accordance with its ordinary hiring procedures. The public school system apparently provides all of the supplies, materials, and equipment used in connection with Shared Time instruction.

The Community Education Program is offered throughout the Grand Rapids community in schools and on other sites, for children as well as adults. The classes at issue here are taught in the nonpublic elementary schools and commence at the conclusion of the regular school day. Among the courses offered are Arts and Crafts, Home Economics, Spanish, Gymnastics, Yearbook Production, Christmas Arts and Crafts, Drama, Newspaper, Humanities, Chess, Model Building, and Nature Appreciation. The District Court found that "[a]lthough certain Community Education courses offered at nonpublic school sites are not offered at the public schools on a Community Education basis, all Community Education programs are otherwise available at the public schools, usually as a part of their more extensive regular curriculum."

Community Education teachers are part-time public school employees. Community Education courses are completely voluntary and are offered only if 12 or more students enroll. Because a well-known teacher is necessary to attract the requisite number of students, the School District accords a preference in hiring to instructors already teaching within the school. Thus, "virtually every Community Education course conducted on facilities leased from nonpublic schools has an instructor otherwise employed full time by the same nonpublic school."

Both programs are administered similarly. The Director of the program, a public school employee, sends packets of course listings to the participating nonpublic schools before the school year begins. The nonpublic school administrators then decide which courses they want to offer. The Director works out an academic schedule for each school, taking into account, *inter alia*, the varying religious holidays celebrated by the schools of different denominations.

Nonpublic school administrators decide which classrooms will be used for the programs, and the Director then inspects the facilities and consults with Shared Time teachers to make sure the facilities are satisfactory. The public school system pays the nonpublic schools for the use of the necessary classroom space by entering into "leases" at the rate of $6 per classroom per week. The "leases", however, contain no mention of the particular room, space, or facility leased and teachers' rooms, libraries, lavatories, and similar facilities are made available at no additional charge. Each room used in the programs has to be free of any crucifix, religious symbol, or artifact, although such religious symbols can be present in the adjoining hallways, corridors, and other facilities used in connection with the program. During the time that a given classroom is being used in the programs, the teacher is required to post a sign stating that it is a "public school classroom." The signs read as follows: "GRAND RAPIDS PUBLIC SCHOOLS' ROOM. THIS ROOM HAS BEEN LEASED BY THE GRAND RAPIDS PUBLIC SCHOOL DISTRICT, FOR THE PURPOSE OF CONDUCTING PUBLIC SCHOOL EDUCATIONAL PROGAMS. THE ACTIVITY IN THIS ROOM IS CONTROLLED SOLELY BY THE GRAND RAPIDS PUBLIC SCHOOL DISTRICT." However, there are no signs posted outside the school buildings indicating that public school courses are conducted inside or that the facilities are being used as a public school annex.

Although petitioners label the Shared Time and Community Education students as "part-time public school students," the students attending Shared Time and Community Education courses in facilities leased from a nonpublic school are the same students who attend that particular school otherwise. There is no evidence that any public school student has ever attended a Shared Time or Community Education class in a nonpublic school.

The District Court found that "[t]hough Defendants claim the Shared Time program is available to all students, the record is abundantly clear that only nonpublic school students wearing the cloak of a 'public school student' can enroll in it." The District Court noted that "[w]hereas public school students are assembled at the public facility nearest to their residence, students in religious schools are assembled on the basis of religion without any consideration of residence or school district boundaries." Thus, "beneficiaries are wholly designated on the basis of religion," and these "public school" classes, in contrast to ordinary public school classes which are largely neighborhood-based, are as segregated by religion as are the schools at which they are offered.

Forty of the forty-one schools at which the programs operate are sectarian in character. The schools of course vary from one another, but substantial evidence suggests that they share deep religious purposes. For instance, the Parent Handbook of one Catholic school states the goals of Catholic education as "[a] God oriented environment which *permeates* the total educational program," "[a] Christian atmosphere which guides and encourages participation in the church's commitment to social justice," and "[a] continuous development of knowledge of the Catholic faith, its traditions, teachings and theology." A policy statement of the Christian schools similarly proclaims that "it is not sufficient that the teachings of Christianity be a separate subject in the curriculum, but *the Word of God must be an all-pervading force in the educational program.*" These Christian schools require all parents seeking to enroll their children either to subscribe to a particular doctrinal statement or to agree to have their children taught according to the doctrinal statement. The District Court found that the schools are "pervasively sectarian," and concluded "without hesitation that the purposes of these schools is to advance their particular religions," and that "a substantial portion of their functions are subsumed in the religious mission."

B

Respondents are six taxpayers who filed suit against the School District of Grand Rapids and a number of state officials. They charged that the Shared Time and Community Education programs violated the Establishment Clause of the First Amendment of the Constitution, made applicable to the States through the Fourteenth Amendment. After an 8-day bench trial, the District Court entered a judgment on the merits on behalf of respondents and enjoined further operation of the programs.

Applying the familiar three-part purpose, effect, and entanglement test set out in *Lemon* v. *Kurtzman*, the court held that, although the purpose of the programs was secular, their effect was "distinctly impermissible." The court relied in particular on the fact that the programs at issue involved publicly provided instructional services that served nonpublic school students segregated largely by religion on nonpublic school premises. The court also noted that the programs conferred "direct benefits, both financial and otherwise, to the sectarian institutions." Finally, the court found that the programs necessarily entailed an unacceptable level of entanglement, both political and administrative, between the public school systems and the sectarian schools. Petitioners appealed the judgment of the District Court to the Court of Appeals for the Sixth Circuit. A divided panel of the Court of Appeals affirmed. We granted certiorari and now affirm.

II
A

The First Amendment's guarantee that "Congress shall make no law respecting an establishment of religion," as our cases demonstrate, is more than a pledge that no single religion will be designated as a state religion. It is also more than a mere injunction that governmental programs discriminating among religions are unconstitutional. The Establishment Clause instead primarily proscribes "sponsorship, financial support, and active involvement of the sovereign in religious activity." *Nyquist*. As Justice Black, writing for the Court in *Everson* v. *Board of Education*, stated: "Neither [a State nor the Federal Government] can pass laws which aid one religion, aid all religions, or prefer one religion over another . . . No tax in any amount, large or small, can be levied to support any religious activities or institutions, whatever they may be called, or whatever form they may adopt to teach or practice religion."

Since *Everson* made clear that the guarantees of the Establishment Clause apply to the States, we have often grappled with the problem of state aid to nonpublic, religious schools. In all of these cases, our goal has been to give meaning to the sparse language and broad purposes of the Clause, while not unduly infringing on the ability of the States to provide for the welfare of their people in accordance with their own particular circumstances. Providing for the education of schoolchildren is surely a praiseworthy purpose. But our cases have consistently recognized that even such a praiseworthy, secular purpose cannot validate government aid to parochial schools when the aid has the effect of promoting a single religion or religion generally or when the aid unduly entangles the government in matters religious. For just as religion throughout history has provided spiritual comfort, guidance, and inspiration to many, it can also serve powerfully to divide societies and to exclude those whose beliefs are not in accord with particular religions or sects that have from time to time achieved dominance. The solution to this problem adopted by the Framers and consistently recognized by this Court is jealously to guard the right of every individual to worship according to the dictates of conscience while requiring the government to maintain a course of neutrality among religions, and between religion and non-religion. Only in this way can we "make room for as wide a variety of beliefs and creeds as the spiritual needs of man deem necessary" and "sponsor an attitude on the part of government that shows no partiality to any one group and lets each flourish according to the zeal of its adherents and the appeal of its dogma." *Zorach* v. *Clauson*.

We have noted that the three-part test first articulated in *Lemon* v. *Kurtzman* guides "[t]he general nature of our inquiry in this area," *Mueller* v. *Allen*: "Every analysis in this area must begin with consideration of the cumulative criteria developed by the Court over many years. Three such tests may be gleaned from our cases. First, the statute must have a secular legislative purpose; second, its principal or primary effect must be one that neither advances nor inhibits religion, finally, the statute must not foster 'an excessive government entanglement with religion.'" *Lemon* v. *Kurtzman*. These tests "must not be viewed as setting the precise limits to the necessary constitutional inquiry, but serve only as guidelines with which to identify instances in which the objectives of the Establishment Clause have been impaired." *Meek* v. *Pittenger*. We have particularly relied on *Lemon* in every case involving the sensitive relationship between government and religion in the education of our children. The government's activities in this area can have a magnified impact on impressionable young minds, and the occasional rivalry of parallel public and private school systems offers an all-too-ready opportunity for divisive rifts along religious lines in the body politic. The *Lemon* test concentrates attention on the issues—purposes, effect, entanglement—that determine whether a particular state action is an improper "law respecting an establishment of religion." We therefore reaffirm that state action alleged to violate the Establishment Clause should be measured against the *Lemon* criteria.

As has often been true in school aid cases, there is no dispute as to the first test. Both the District Court and the Court of Appeals found that the purpose of the Community Education and Shared Time programs was "manifestly secular." We find no reason to disagree with this holding, and therefore go on to consider whether the primary or principal effect of the challenged programs is to advance or inhibit religion.

B

Our inquiry must begin with a consideration of the nature of the institutions in which the programs operate. Of the 41 private schools where these "part-time public schools" have operated, 40 are identifiably religious schools. It is true that each school may not share all of the characteristics of religious schools as articulated, for example, in the complaint in *Meek* v. *Pittenger*. The district Court found, however that "[b]ased upon the massive testimony and exhibits, the conclusion is inescapable that the religious institutions receiving instructional services from the public schools are sectarian in the sense that a substantial portion of their functions are subsumed in the religious mission." At the religious schools here—as at the sectarian schools that have been the subject of our past cases—"the secular education those schools provide goes hand in hand with the religious mission that is the only reason for the schools' existence. Within that institution, the two are inextricably intertwined." *Lemon* v. *Kurtzman*.

Given that 40 of the 41 schools in this case are thus "pervasively sectarian," the challenged public-school programs operating in the religious schools may impermissibly advance religion in three different ways. First, the teachers participating in the programs may become involved in intentionally or inadvertently inculcating particular religious tenets or beliefs. Second, the programs may provide a crucial symbolic link between government and religion, thereby enlisting—at least in the eyes of impressionable youngsters—the powers of government to the support of the religious denomination operating the school. Third, the programs may have the effect of directly promoting religion by impermissibly providing a subsidy to the primary religious mission of the institutions affected.

(1)

Although Establishment Clause jurisprudence is characterized by few absolutes, the Clause does absolutely prohibit government-financed or government-sponsored indoctrination into the beliefs of a particular religious faith. Such indoctrination, if permitted to occur, would have devastating effects on the right of each individual voluntarily to determine what to believe (and what not to believe) free of any coercive pressures from the State, while at the same time tainting the resulting religious beliefs with a corrosive secularism.

In *Meek* v. *Pittenger*, the Court invalidated a statute providing for the loan of state-paid professional staff—including teachers—to nonpublic schools to provide remedial and accelerated instruction, guidance counseling and testing, and other services on the premises of the nonpublic schools. Such a program, if not subjected to a "comprehensive, discriminating, and continuing state surveillance," *Lemon* v. *Kurtzman*, would entail an unacceptable risk that the state-sponsored instructional personnel would "advance the religious mission of the church-related schools, in which they serve." *Meek*. Even though the teachers were paid by the State, "[t]he potential for impermissible fostering of religion under these circumstances, although somewhat reduced, is nonetheless present." The program in *Meek*, if not sufficiently monitored, would simply have entailed too great a risk of state-sponsored indoctrination.

The programs before us today share the defect that we identified in *Meek*. With respect to the Community Education Program, the District Court found that "virtually every Community Education course conducted on facilities leased from nonpublic schools has an instructor otherwise employed full time by the same nonpublic school." These instructors, many of whom no doubt teach in the religious schools precisely because they are adherents of the controlling denomination and want to serve their religious community zealously, are expected during the regular school day to inculcate their students with the tenets and beliefs of their particular religious faiths. Yet the premise of the program is that those instructors can put aside their religious convictions and engage in entirely secular Community Education instruction as soon as the school day is over. Moreover, they are expected to do so before the same religious-school students and in the same religious-school classrooms that they employed to advance religious purposes during the "official" school day. Nonetheless, as petitioners themselves asserted, Community Education classes are not specifically monitored for religious content.

We do not question that the dedicated and professional religious school teachers employed by the Community Education program will attempt in good faith to perform their secular mission conscientiously. Nonetheless, there is a substantial risk that, overtly or subtly, the religious message they are expected to convey during the regular school day will infuse the supposedly secular classes they teach after school. The danger arises "not because the public employee [is] likely deliberately to subvert his task to the service of religion, but rather because the pressures of the environment might alter his behavior from its normal course." *Wolman* v. *Walter*. "The conflict of functions inheres in the situation." *Lemon* v. *Kurtzman*.

The Shared Time program, though structured somewhat differently, nonetheless also poses a substantial risk of state-sponsored indoctrination. The most important difference between the programs is that most of the instructors in the Shared Time program are full-time teachers hired by the public schools. Moreover, although "virtually every" Community Education instructor is a full-time religious school teacher, only "[a] significant portion" of the Shared Time instructors previously worked in the religious schools. Nonetheless, as with the Community Education program, no attempt is made to monitor the Shared Time courses for religious content.

Thus despite these differences between the two programs, our holding in *Meek* controls the inquiry with respect to Shared Time, as well as Community Education. Shared Time instructors are teaching academic subjects in religious schools in courses virtually indistinguishable from the other courses offered during the regular religious-school day. The teachers in this program, even more than their Community Education colleagues, are "performing important educational services in schools in which education is an integral part of the dominant sectarian mission and in which an atmosphere dedicated to the advancement of religious belief is constantly maintained." *Meek* v. *Pittenger*. Teachers in such an atmosphere may well subtly (or overtly) conform their instruction to the environment in which they teach, while students will perceive the instruction provided in the context of the dominantly religious message of the institution, thus reinforcing the indoctrinating effect. As we stated in *Meek*, "[w]hether the subject is 'remedial reading,' 'advanced reading,' or simply 'reading,' a teacher remains a teacher, and the danger that religious doctrine will become intertwined with secular instruction persists." Unlike types of aid that the Court has upheld, such as state-created standardized tests, *Committee for Public Education* v. *Regan*, or diagnostic services, *Wolman* v. *Walter*, there is a "substantial risk" that programs operating in this environment would "be used for religious educational purposes." *Committee for Public Education* v. *Regan*.

The Court of Appeals of course recognized that respondents adduced no evidence of specific incidents of religious indoctrination in this case. But the absence of proof of specific incidents is not dispositive. When conducting a supposedly secular class in the pervasively sectarian environment of a religious school, a teacher may knowingly or unwillingly tailor the content of the course to fit the school's announced goals. If so, there is no reason to believe that this kind of ideological influence would be detected or reported by students, by their parents, or by the school system itself. The students are presumably attending religious schools precisely in order to receive religious instruction. After spending the balance of their school day in classes heavily influenced by a religious perspective, they would have little motivation or ability to discern improper ideological content that may creep into a Shared Time or Community Education course. Neither their parents nor the parochial schools would have cause to complain if the effect of the publicly-supported instruction were to advance the schools' sectarian mission. And the public school system itself has no incentive to detect or report any specific incidents or improper state- sponsored indoctrination. Thus, the lack of evidence of specific incidents of indoctrination is of little significance.

(2)

Our cases have recognized that the Establishment Clause guards against more than direct, state-funded efforts to indoctrinate youngsters in specific religious beliefs. Government promotes religion as effectively when it fosters a close identification of its powers and responsibilities with those of any—or all—religious denominations as when it attempts to in-

culcate specific religious doctrines. If this identification conveys a message of government endorsement or disapproval of religion, a core purpose of the Establishment Clause is violated. As we stated in *Larkin* v. *Grendel's Den, Inc.*: "[T]he mere appearance of a joint exercise of legislative authority by Church and State provides a significant symbolic benefit to religion in the minds of some by reason of the power conferred."

It follows that an important concern of the effects test is whether the symbolic union of church and state effected by the challenged governmental action is sufficiently likely to be perceived by adherents of the controlling denominations as an endorsement, and by the nonadherents as a disapproval, of their individual religious choices. The inquiry into this kind of effect must be conducted with particular care when many of the citizens perceiving the governmental message are children in their formative years. The symbolism of a union between church and state is most likely to influence children of tender years, whose experience is limited and whose beliefs consequently are the function of environment as much as of free and voluntary choice.

Our school-aid cases have recognized a sensitivity to the symbolic impact of the union of church and state. Grappling with problems in many ways parallel to those we face today, *McCollum* v. *Board of Education* held that a public school may not permit part-time religious instruction on its premises as a part of the school program, even if participation in that instruction is entirely voluntary and even if the instruction itself is conducted only by nonpublic-school personnel. Yet in *Zorach* v. *Clauson*, the Cout held that a similar program conducted off the premises of the public school passed constitutional muster. The difference in symbolic impact helps to explain the difference between the cases. The symbolic connection of church and state in the *McCollum* program presented the students with a graphic symbol of the "concert or union or dependency" of church and state. This very symbolic union was conspicuously absent in the *Zorach* program.

In the programs challenged in this case, the religious school students spend their typical school day moving between religious-school and "public-school" classes. Both types of classes take place in the same religious-school building and both are largely composed of students who are adherents of the same denomination. In this environment, the students would be unlikely to discern the crucial difference between the religious-school classes and the "public-school" classes, even if the latter were successfully kept free of religious indoctrination. As one commentator has written: "This pervasive [religious] atmosphere makes on the young student's mind a lasting imprint that the holy and transcendental should be central to all facets of life. It increases respect for the church as an institution to guide one's total life adjustments and undoubtedly helps stimulate interest in religious vocations. . . . In short, the parochial school's total operation serves to fulfill both secular and religious functions concurrently, and the two cannot be completely separated. Support of any part of its activity entails some support of the disqualifying religious function of molding the religious personality of the young student." Gianella, Religious Liberty, Nonestablishment and Doctrinal Development: Part II. The Nonestablishment Principle, 81 Harv. L. Rev. 513, 574 (l968). Consequently, even the student who notices the "public school" sign temporarily posted would have before him a powerful symbol of state endorsement and encouragement of the religious beliefs taught in the same class at some other time during the day.

As Judge Friendly, writing for the Second Circuit in the companion case to the case at bar, stated: "Under the City's plan public school teachers are, so far as appearance is concerned, a regular adjunct of the religious school. They pace the same halls, use classrooms in the same building, teach the same students, and confer with the teachers hired by the religious school, many of them members of religious orders. The religious school appears to the public as a joint enterprise staffed with some teachers paid by its religious sponsor and others by the public." *Felton* v. *Secretary, United States Dept. of Ed.* This effect—the symbolic union of government and religion in one sectarian enterprise—is an impermissible effect under the Establishment Clause.

(3)

In *Everson* v. *Board of Education*, the Court stated that "[no] tax in any amount, large or small, can be levied to support any religious activities or institutions, whatever they may be called, or whatever form they may adopt to teach or practice religion." With but one exception, our subsequent cases have struck down attempts by States to make payments out of public tax dollars directly to primary or secondary religious educational institutions.

Aside from cash payments, the Court has distinguished between two categories of programs in which public funds are used to finance secular activities that religious schools would otherwise fund from their own resources. In the first category, the Court has noted that it is "well established . . . that not every law that confers an 'indirect,' 'remote,' or 'incidental' benefit upon religious institutions is, for that reason alone, constitutionally invalid." *Committee for Public Education* v. *Nyquist*. In such "indirect" aid cases, the government has used primarily secular means to accomplish a primarily secular end, and no "primary effect" of advancing religion has thus been found. On this rationale, the Court has upheld programs providing for loans of secular textbooks to nonpublic school students, and programs providing bus transportation for nonpublic school children.

In the second category of cases, the Court has relied on the Establishment Clause prohibition of forms of aid that provide "direct and substantial advancement of the sectarian enterprise." *Wolman* v. *Walter*. In such "direct aid" cases, the government, although acting for a secular purpose, has done so by directly supporting a religious institution. Under this rationale, the Court has struck down state schemes providing for tuition grants and tax benefits for parents whose children attend religious school, and programs providing for "loan" of instructional materials to be used in religious schools. In *Sloan* and *Nyquist*, the aid was formally given to parents and not directly to the religious schools, while in *Wolman* and *Meek*, the aid was in-kind assistance rather than the direct contribution of public funds. Nonetheless, these differences in form were insufficient to save programs whose effect was indistinguishable from that of a direct subsidy to the religious school.

Thus, the Court has never accepted the mere possibility of subsidization, as the above cases demonstrate, as sufficient to invalidate an aid program. On the other hand, this effect is not wholly unimportant for Establishment Clause purposes. If it were, the public schools could gradually take on themselves the entire responsibility for teaching secular subjects on religious school premises. The question in each case must be whether the effect of the proffered aid is "direct and substantial," *Committee for Public Education* v. *Nyquist*, or indirect and incidental. "The problem, like many problems in constitutional law, is one of degree." *Zorach* v. *Clauson*.

We have noted in the past that the religious school has dual functions, providing its students with a secular education while it promotes a particular religious perspective. In *Meek* and *Wolman*, we held unconstitutional state programs providing for loans of instructional equipment and materials to religious schools, on the ground that the programs advanced the "primary, religion-oriented educational function of the sectarian school." *Meek*. The programs challenged here, which provide teachers in addition to the instructional equipment and materials, have a similar—and forbidden—effect of advancing religion. This kind of direct aid to the educational function of the religious school is indistinguishable from the provision of a direct cash subsidy to the religious school that is most clearly prohibited under the Establishment Clause.

Petitioners claim that the aid here, like the textbooks in *Allen*, flows primarily to the students, not to the religious schools. Of course, all aid to religious schools ultimately "flows to" the students, and petitioners' argument if accepted would validate all forms of nonideological aid to religious schools, including those explicitly rejected in our prior cases. Yet in *Meek*, we held unconstitutional the loan of instructional materials to religious schools and in *Wolman*, we rejected the fiction that a similar program could be saved by masking it as aid to individual students. It follows *a fortiori* that the aid here, which includes not only instructional materials but also the provision of instructional services by teachers in the parochial school building, "inescapably [has] the primary effect of providing a direct and substantial advancement of the sectarian enterprise." Where, as here, no meaningful distinction can be made between aid to the student and aid to the school, "the concept of a loan to individuals is a transparent fiction." *Wolman* v. *Walter.*

Petitioners also argue that this "subsidy" effect is not significant in this case, because the Community Education and Shared Time programs supplemented the curriculum with courses not previously offered in the religious schools and not required by school rule or state regulation. Of course, this fails to distinguish the programs here from those found unconstitutional in *Meek.* As in *Meek,* we do not find that this feature of the program is controlling. First, there is no way of knowing whether the religious schools would have offered some or all of these courses if the public school system had not offered them first. The distinction between courses that "supplement" and those that "supplant" the regular curriculum is therefore not nearly as clear as petitioners allege. Second, although the precise courses offered in these programs may have been new to the participating religious schools, their general subject matter— reading, math, etc.—was surely a part of the curriculum in the past, and the concerns of the Establishment Clause may thus be triggered despite the "supplemental" nature of the courses. Third, and most important, petitioners' argument would permit the public schools gradually to take over the entire secular curriculum of the religious school, for the latter could surely discontinue existing courses so that they might be replaced a year or two later by a Community Education or Shared Time course with the same content. The average religious school student, for instance, now spends 10 percent of the school day in Shared Time classes. But there is no principled basis on which this Court can impose a limit on the percentage of the religious-school day that can be subsidized by the public school. To let the genie out of the bottle in this case would be to permit ever larger segments of the religious school curriculum to be turned over to the public school system, thus violating the cardinal principle that the State may not in effect become the prime supporter of the religious school system.

III

We conclude that the challenged programs have the effect of promoting religion in three ways. The state-paid instructors, influenced by the pervasively sectarian nature of the religious school in which they work, may subtly or overtly indoctrinate the students in particular religious tenets at public expense. The symbolic union of church and state inherent in the provision of secular, state-provided instruction in the religious school buildings threatens to convey a message of state support for religion to students and to the general public. Finally, the programs in effect subsidize the religious functions of the parochial schools by taking over a substantial portion of their responsibility for teaching secular subjects. For these reasons, the conclusion is inescapable that the Community Education and Shared Time programs have the "primary or principal" effect of advancing religion, and therefore violate the dictates of the Establishment Clause of the First Amendment.

Nonpublic schools have played an important role in the development of American education, and we have long recognized that parents and their children have the right to choose between public schools and available sectarian alternatives. As The *Chief Justice* noted in *Lemon* v. *Kurtzman,* "nothing we have said can be construed to disparage the role of church-related elementary and secondary schools in our national life. Their contribution has been and is enormous." But the Establishment Clause "rest[s] on the belief that a union of government and religion tends to destroy government and to degrade religion." *Engel* v. *Vitale.* Therefore, "[t]he Constitution decrees that religion must be a private matter for the individual, the family, and the institutions of private choice, and that while some involvement and entanglement are inevitable, lines must be drawn." *Lemon* v. *Kurtzman.* Because "the controlling constitutional standards have become firmly rooted and the broad contours of our inquiry are now well defined," *Committee for Public Education* v. *Nyquist,* the position of those lines has now become quite clear and requires affirmance of the Court of Appeals. *It is so ordered.*

Chief Justice BURGER, concurring in the judgment in part and dissenting in part.

I agree with the Court that, under our decisions in *Lemon* v. *Kurtzman,* and *Earley* v. *DiCenso,* the Grand Rapids Community Education program violates the Establishment Clause. As to the Shared Time program, I dissent for the reasons stated in my dissenting opinion in *Aguilar* v. *Felton.*

Justice O'CONNOR, concurring in the judgment in part and dissenting in part.

For the reasons stated in my dissenting opinion in *Aguilar* v. *Felton,* I dissent from the Court's holding that the Grand Rapids Shared Time program impermissibly advances religion. Like the New York Title I program, the Grand Rapids Shared Time program employs full-time public school teachers who offer supplemental instruction to parochial school children on the premises of religious schools. Nothing in the record indicates that Shared-Time instructors have attempted to proselytize their students. I see no reason why public school teachers in Grand Rapids are any more likely than their counterparts in New York to disobey their instructions.

The Court relies on the District Court's finding that a "significant portion of the Shared Time instructors previously taught in nonpublic schools, and many of these had been assigned to the same non-public school where they were previously employed." In fact, only 13 Shared Time instructors have ever been employed by any parochial school, and only a fraction of those 13 now work in a parochial school where they were previously employed. The experience of these few teachers does not significantly increase the risk that the perceived or actual effect of the Shared Time program will be to inculcate religion at public expense. I would uphold the Shared Time program.

I agree with the Court, however, that the Community Education program violates the Establishment Clause. The record indicates that Community Education courses in the parochial schools are overwhelmingly taught by instructors who are current full-time employees of the parochial school. The teachers offer secular subjects to the same parochial school students who attend their regular parochial school classes. In addition, the supervisors of the Community Education program in the parochial schools are by and large the principals of the very schools where the classes are offered. When full-time parochial school teachers receive public funds to teach secular courses to their parochial school students under parochial school supervision, I agree that the program has the perceived and actual effect of advancing the religious aims of the church-related schools. This is particularly the case where, as here, religion pervades the curriculum and the teachers are accustomed to bring religion to play in everything they teach. I concur in the judgment of the Court that the Community Education program violates the Establishment Clause.

Justice WHITE, dissenting.

As evidenced by my dissenting opinions in *Lemon* v. *Kurtzman* and *Committee for Public Education* v. *Nyquist*, I have long disagreed with the Court's interpretation and application of the Establishment Clause in the context of state aid to private schools. For the reasons stated in those dissents, I am firmly of the belief that the Court's decisions in these cases, like its decisions in *Lemon* and *Nyquist*, are "not required by the First Amendment and [are] contrary to the long-range interests of the country." For those same reasons, I am satisfied that what the States have sought to do in these cases is well within their authority and is not forbidden by the Establishment Clause. Hence, I dissent and would reverse the judgment in each of these cases.

Justice REHNQUIST, dissenting.

I dissent for the reasons stated in my dissenting opinion in *Wallace* v. *Jaffree*. In *Grand Rapids*, the Court relies heavily on the principles of *Everson* and *McCollum*, but declines to discuss the faulty "wall" premise upon which those cases rest. In doing so the Court blinds itself to the first 150 years' history of the Establishment Clause.

The Court today attempts to give content to the "effects" prong of the *Lemon* test by holding that a "symbolic link between government and religion" creates an impermissible effect. But one wonders how the teaching of "Math Topics," "Spanish,"and "Gymnastics," which is struck down today, creates a greater "symbolic link" than the municipal crèche upheld in *Lynch* v. *Donnelly* or the legislative chaplain upheld in *Marsh* v. *Chambers*.

A most unfortunate result of *Grand Rapids* is that to support its holding the Court, despite its disclaimers, impugns the integrity of public school teachers. Contrary to the law and the teachers' promises, they are assumed to be eager inculcators of religious dogma requiring, in the Court's words, "ongoing supervison." Not one instance of attempted religious inculcation exists in the records of the school aid cases decided today, even though both the Grand Rapids and New York programs have been in operation for a number of years. I would reverse.

5 CONTINUING CHURCH-STATE CONTROVERSIES

The essays at the heads of chapters and subsections of this book not only trace the historical background of the various church-state controversies but also deal with their present status. However, there are other current issues which are not covered there. This chapter is designed to give an overview of several of the more important ones: they may some day receive attention from the United States Supreme Court.

▶One of the items which has stimulated recent interest in church-state relationships even in the general population has been the dramatic involvement of fundamentalist Christians in the political process. To be sure, there was some participation by this segment of the society in the 1976 presidential campaign, when Jimmy Carter's born-again style of religion was a topic of much interest. But it was in connection with the 1980 election and the candidacy of Ronald Reagan that the Moral Majority and similar groups seemed to burst upon public consciousness. As these Christians asserted themselves in congressional races as well as in the presidential campaign, journalists and others commented on the church-state implications of such political participation. Much of what was said and written missed the mark, because it assumed that church-state separation prohibited the Moral Majority and others of a like mind from the kind of political involvement in which they were engaging. What these commentators overlooked was the fact that the Free Exercise Clause guarantees religious groups the right to express their views on public issues and to vote accordingly. There was and is a dimension of danger, however, in that the "New Christian Right" has expressed the intention to "make America a Christian nation again." Aside from the dubious assumption that America was ever a Christian nation in any kind of narrow or confessional sense, which is the sense the Christian Right has in mind, the expressed goal is fraught with Establishment Clause prob-

lems, because it would be a violation for any particular group to impose its unique theology and ethical viewpoint upon the entire body politic. This issue is not likely to go away soon, because in February 1986, Jerry Falwell, the founder of the Moral Majority, subsumed that organization into a new structure called "Liberty Foundation." He said the purpose of the reorganization was to broaden the focus of the political activism; to speak out on issues that were previously not addressed. The Moral Majority/Liberty Foundation is singled out here because of its popular recognition, not because it is the only Christian activist group. There are others. One of the most visible is the American Coalition for Traditional Values (ACTV), founded and led by Rev. Tim LaHaye.

▶Related to and a part of the rise of the Christian Right was the increasing agitation over the issue of legalized abortions. Although that issue has been highly visible since the early 1970s, passions on both sides intensified with the rising tide of religious and political conservatism in the late 1970s and 1980s. Strong efforts were made to push through Congress a constitutional amendment that would nullify *Roe* v. *Wade* (1973) in which the Supreme Court held that a woman has a constitutional right to choose to terminate an unwanted pregnancy, particularly in the first trimester. Opponents of abortion were emboldened and advocates were enraged by the Court's decision in *Harris* v. *McRae* (1980). In this case the justices recognized that the right to choose an abortion is a constitutional right, but they held that a woman does not have a right to public funds to exercise that choice. The Court thus upheld the 1976 Hyde Amendment that severely restricted use of funds to reimburse cost of abortions under the Medicaid program. That decision stimulated activity both for and against a constitutional amendment forbidding abortion on demand.

Because the Roman Catholic Church is known to have strong theological objections to abortion, many call this a Catholic issue. It is not. Opponents of abortion include many Protestants and Jews and some with no religious belief. But the abortion controversy does raise again the issue of political participation by religious groups. As noted above, the Free Exercise Clause guarantees the right of groups and individuals to participate in political controversies. There is the danger, however, of using governmental means of imposing a particular theological belief on the entire population; this would raise strong establishment problems. In addition, there has been since 1972 the sword of *Christian Echoes National Ministry* v. *United States* hanging over the head of politically active religious groups; they run the risk of losing federal tax exemption by becoming substantially involved in the public arena.

▶That issue was raised to the level of great visibility in the early 1980s in *Abortion Rights Mobilization* v. *Baker*. The case was initiated by Abortion Rights Mobilization (ARM) and twenty other "pro-choice" groups and individuals challenging the tax-exempt status of the Roman Catholic Church. The controversy grew out of the election of 1980, when the Catholic Church became more aggressive in its recommending the election of candidates who opposed abortion. Among several instances of activism of that sort was a 1980 pastoral letter by Archbishop Humberto Medeiros of Boston written to 410 parishes throughout the state a few days before a primary election. Without mentioning any names, Archbishop Medeiros attacked pro-choice congressional candidates. The letter was read from many pulpits and published in the archdiocesan newspaper.

The suit filed by ARM named as defendants the Secretary of the Treasury, the Commissioner of Internal Revenue, the National Conference of Catholic Bishops, and the United States Catholic Conference. The plaintiffs challenged the enforcement of § 501(c)(3) of the Internal Revenue Code, the section which grants tax exemption to charitable organizations but also requires that they not endorse political candidates or spend a substantial part of their resources in political campaigns. Plaintiffs claimed that the Catholic Church's political activities disqualified it for continued exemption and that the government officials were guilty of not revoking the exemption, as the statute required them to do. Those speaking for ARM said that their aim was small; to sensitize religious groups about the illegality of supporting electoral candidates. This was to be done by insisting that the IRS enforce the law, in this case in reference to the Roman Catholic Church. They recognized that religious groups have the right to speak out on matters of public and political importance. Thus there was just one issue, obeying § 501(c)(3), specifically its prohibiting tax-exempt organizations from endorsing candidates. Because the suit was really about the enforcement of the statute, the Catholic bodies were early removed as defendants from the suit.

Spokespersons for the Catholic Church were not convinced that the attack was that narrow. They believed that the case raised the much broader issue of whether religious groups have the right to speak and act on behalf of their conscientious convictions regarding public issues. That their attitude was not just ecclesiastical paranoia was

borne out by the fact that in its suit, ARM not only asked that the statute be enforced, but also argued that the tax exemption violates the Establishment Clause. Furthermore, individual plaintiffs complained because they are unable to deduct from their income taxes contributions they make to organizations promoting abortions, whereas taxpayers who oppose abortion can make deductible contributions to the Catholic Church. Organizational plaintiffs complained because they are denied tax-exempt status for advocating abortion, whereas the Catholic Church enjoys exempt status while opposing abortion.

Even though the Catholic bodies were removed as defendants, for the case to go forward it was necessary to gain documents from them in order to determine whether or not the Church had endorsed candidates (in order to see whether or not the government agencies had, indeed, failed to enforce the law, since the Church still had its tax exemption). The Church, which throughout the legal proceedings had steadfastly denied that it had illegally supported candidates, was opposed to giving up the documents, considering that a government invasion into Church affairs. So, lawyers for the Church delayed the process in a variety of ways. In early May, 1986, the latest development in the case at the time of this writing, the federal judge found the National Conference of Catholic Bishops and the United States Catholic Conference in contempt of court and ordered them each to pay $50,000 for each day they withheld the documents, beginning after appeals to various legal issues were exhausted. At that point an array of religious groups from across the theological spectrum joined to file an *amicus curiae* brief on behalf of the Catholic Church's appeal of the contempt citation. Many felt that this was a tremendously important case, not only because of the disclosure/contempt dimensions, but on the broader issue of the latitude churches have to be involved in the political arena. The speculation was that this case might provide the Supreme Court interpretation of the applicability of § 501(c)(3) to churches that never materialized in *Christian Echoes*.

▶On 19 March 1981 the governor of Arkansas signed the "Balanced Treatment for Creation-Science and Evolution-Science Act." (Arkansas Act 590 of 1981.) The bill specified that creation-science should be taught equally with evolution-science, but without reference to any religious teaching. Instruction was to be limited to the scientific evidence for each model for understanding the origin of biological organisms, including human beings. It was specified that implementation of this act would promote academic freedom by providing students a choice between concepts and that it would ensure religious freedom and prevent the establishment of religion by avoiding the presentation of only one concept of origins, that one favored by theological liberalism or atheism.

The Arkansas statute was challenged by a variety of plaintiffs: ministers, education associations, and advocacy groups such as the American Jewish Congress and the American Civil Liberties Union. Challengers charged that the law was impermissibly vague and constituted an abridgment of the academic freedom of both teachers and students. The establishment argument (the creation-science disclaimer aside) insisted that creation-science cannot be taught without some reference to a creator, which is a religious concept. Furthermore, critics of creation-science declared that it is not science because any scientific statement must be subject to disproof. Because creation-science assumes the existence of a supernatural creator and supernatural processes, it is not subject to disproof.

In *McLean* v. *Arkansas*, Federal District Judge William Overton found in favor of the plaintiffs on 5 January 1982. He concluded that creation-science is based on religious assumptions, that it is the promotion of essentially fundamentalist perspectives, and thus is a violation of the Establishment Clause. The Arkansas Attorney General announced that the state would not appeal the decision, but advocates of creationism promised to continue the battle through legislation and litigation in other states.

The battle had actually been moved to another front before the *McLean* decision. In 1981 the Louisiana legislature added a provision to the state's general school law which required the public schools to give balanced treatment to creation-science and evolution-science. As in Arkansas, no school was required to give instruction in the origin of humankind, but if a school elected to cover the topic, both evolution-science *and* creation-science had to be covered. The statute prohibited discrimination against any teacher "who chooses to be a creation-scientist or to teach scientific data which points to creationism," although there was not a similar provision for those who taught evolution. The principal stated rationale for the statute was to promote academic freedom in the science classes of the public schools.

After the state supreme court decided that the act was consistent with the state constitution on the question of whether it was proper for the legislature to set curriculum policy for the public schools; the case went to federal court. The trial court granted the plaintiffs (consisting of Louisiana educators, religious leaders, and parents of school children) summary judgment, declaring the act unconstitutional and enjoining its implementation. The court of appeals affirmed that judgment: *Aguillard* v. *Edwards*.

The court began by recognizing that states have the right to prescribe the curricula of their public schools, but the right is limited by the Establishment Clause. This particular act is unconstitutional because it does not have a secular purpose. To require the teaching of creationism is to require the teaching of religion because "the theory of creation is a religious belief." Furthermore, the act does not promote academic freedom. Academic freedom means that instructors are free to teach what they, in their professional judgment, think is educationally appropriate.

> The Balanced Treatment Act is contrary to the very concept it avows; it requires, presumably upon risk of *sanction* or *dismissal* for failure to comply, the teaching of creation-science whenever evolution is taught. (765 F.2d. 1251, 1257, emphasis in original)

The act does not demonstrate that creation-science is a genuine academic discipline in that, if it were, it would be mandated for teaching in the public schools irrespective of whether evolution were taught. Finally, it is clear that the purpose of requiring creation-science to be taught alongside evolution "is to discredit evolution at every turn with the teaching of creationism, a religious belief." (Ibid.) For all these reasons, the court found the

statute to have a religious purpose and thus contrary to the Establishment Clause.

The United States Supreme Court agreed to hear this case in its 1986-87 term. One reason for this may be that when the plaintiffs requested that the Fifth Circuit Court of Appeals rehear the case *en banc,* the court voted eight-to-seven not to rehear. The seven dissenters wrote that they felt that the three-judge panel had wrongly decided the case. For whatever reason it agreed to hear the case, the Court's opinion will be of great interest to educators, students of church-state relationships, and those in the "Christian Right" who are convinced that the nation is becoming increasingly corrupt, a principal cause of which is the secularism of the public schools.

▶Another school-related issue in the 1980s has been the efforts of state departments of education to regulate curriculum content and teachers' qualifications in Christian schools. The dispute is over whether the state has the right to compel parochial schools to conform to its requirements on curriculum, training of teachers, use of textbooks, etc., when the entire teaching enterprise is permeated with religion. Traditionally, the view has been that states have the right, as well as the obligation, to insist on minimal standards in nonpublic, as well as public, schools in order to guarantee that students receive an education of such high quality that they can contribute to the economic, cultural, and political dimensions of society. For example, in PIERCE v. SOCIETY OF SISTERS (p. 458) one reads:

> No question is raised concerning the power of the state reasonably to regulate all schools, to inspect, supervise, and examine them, their teachers and pupils; to require that all children of proper age attend some school, that teachers shall be of good moral character and patriotic disposition, that certain studies plainly essential to good citizenship must be taught, and that nothing be taught which is manifestly inimical to the public welfare.

(The quote means that the case did not raise the issue of the right of states to impose minimal standards, but the context implies that the Court thought that there was no question but that the state did have that right.)

But in these latter years fundamentalist Christians have become increasingly convinced that the public schools do not provide students with a high quality education and, what is much worse, they teach "secular humanism," a religion void of the recognition of God and moral values. So, although schools run by conservative Christians have existed for years, in the late 1970s and throughout the first half of the 1980s such schools have been built at an impressive rate. But again, what about state accreditation requirements? Fundamentalist Christians have claimed that for the state to impose its regulations on their schools is to deny the schools' right to hire only born-again teachers, to teach every subject from a Christian perspective, to use fundamentalist-oriented curriculum materials, etc. In their view, that is wrong. They could quote, and probably have, another passage from that same *Pierce* case:

> The child is not the mere creature of the state; those who nurture him and direct his destiny [i.e., parents] have the right, coupled with the high duty,

to recognize and prepare him for additional obligation.

(The Court was referring to parents' right to send their children to private schools rather than public, not a right to send them to unaccredited schools, as the previous quotation suggests. But the meaning of this passage, removed from its context, certainly expresses the sentiments of many fundamentalist Christian parents and school operators.)

In the first half of the 1980s the most celebrated conflict of this sort was that which pitted Faith Baptist Church of Louisville, Nebraska, against the state. The issue was joined as just described. The church, which opened a school, refused to obey the requirement of a state-prescribed curriculum to be taught by state-licensed teachers. The church argued that when education is considered a church ministry it is outside state control. The state tried to force compliance by a lawsuit, *Douglas* v. *Faith Baptist Church*. Nebraska courts ruled that the Free Exercise Clause is not violated by requiring parents to send their children either to public schools or state-certified private schools. In 1981 the United States Supreme Court dismissed the appeal for lack of a substantial federal question.

Faith Baptist Church, and several sympathizing congregations, still refused to give in. Several pastors spent time in jail for continuing to operate their nonaccredited schools, as did some parents for failing to answer questions about the schools where they sent their children. Finally, the state legislature passed a compromise law which allowed parents to send their children to non-licensed private schools, provided they submitted to the state information: attendance reports, assurances that health and safety codes are met at the facility, and a statement indicating that the parents believe that teachers in the school are qualified to teach basic skills. In addition, children would periodically have to take state-formulated examinations to see that education is really taking place. While that compromise package was being worked out, another church filed suit against the state, again attempting to force the state to relax all standards: *North Platte Baptist Church* v. *Nebraska*. The result was the same: the state's standards do not have to give way to religious demands. The U.S. Supreme Court denied certiorari in 1984, although one could argue that the case had become moot by the time it got to the Court, in the light of the legislative leniency.

In litigation in other parts of the country, (*Ohio* v. *Whisner* and *Kentucky State Board of Education* v. *Rudasill*, courts have generally taken the position that states may not impose regulation on parochial schools beyond normal fire, health, and safety requirements. However, as now in Nebraska, it has generally been held that parochial schools must subject their students to standardized tests in basic subjects, and they must give their students a quality education, even if they do couch it in highly theological terminology and categories. "Reasonable" state regulations for the results of parochial school education are not improper.

▶A perennial problem which emerged again in the mid-1980s was the question of clergy confidentiality in relation to the law. The question, in its simplest form, is whether clergy may be required in a court of law to reveal in testi-

mony what had been said to them in confidence. A case in 1984 illustrated the dilemma. Rev. John Mellish, a minister of the Church of the Nazarene in Florida, had counseled with an individual who apparently confessed that he was guilty of child abuse. The minister persuaded the counselee to surrender to the police. When the man later came to trial, Rev. Mellish was commanded by the judge to testify about his conversation with the accused. Mellish refused, claiming the conversation was privileged as a confidential counseling session between a minister and a man who attended his church. The judge responded by reminding the minister that Florida had, in 1976, passed a law requiring all persons with knowledge of child abuse to report it to authorities. There were no exceptions, not even for ministers. Rev. Mellish continued to refuse to testify on the grounds of clergy privilege and was found in contempt of court and sentenced to jail for sixty days. He served only one night of the sentence before obtaining a temporary release while he filed an appeal to the contempt citation. Before the appeal was heard the Florida legislature passed an exception to the child abuse disclosure law for clergy, so the case became moot.

In this country, courts and legislatures have traditionally granted clergy exemptions from having to testify. This is because there is an assumption that clergy, lawyers, psychiatrists and therapists, to note the obvious examples, cannot function as helpers to their clients if the clients know that what they say in confidence may be disclosed in public. In particular reference to the clergy, there is a centuries-old tradition that the priest-penitent relationship is confidential. In the Roman Catholic, Eastern Orthodox, and Anglo-Catholic traditions confession is a sacrament, which means, among other things, that it has great spiritual significance and may touch on matters of the greatest sensitivity, since sin and grace are involved. The assumption in these traditions is that the priest will hold the confessions in confidence in all circumstances, both because it is the right thing to do and because disclosure could mean the priest's excommunication from the church.

For those traditions for which confession is not sacramental, the issue is somewhat cloudy. Yet, in this era when pastoral counseling is receiving ever more emphasis in ministerial training and practice, it is clear that confidentiality must be assumed for the counseling to be effective.

> There must be a genuine trust between the clergy and congregant or their relationship cannot proceed to the deep level of understanding necessary for good pastoral care. . . . Confidence must be complete if pastoral counseling is to be helpful. There must be no possibility of a disclosure of the shared confidences should a court of law call the pastor or rabbi as a witness. [1]

Generally the law recognizes this need, for both sacramental and nonsacramental traditions. All states except West Virginia have statutes which protect the confidentiality of clergy communication. However, a potential problem is the necessity of a court's determining, particularly in nonsacramental traditions, which

---

[1] William Harold Tieman and John C. Bush, *The Right to Silence: Privileged Clergy Communication and the Law* (Nashville: Abingdon Press, 2d ed., 1984), p. 23.

communication is counseling and thus privileged and which is just conversation and not privileged. Another problem, as the Mellish case illustrates, is that in this day of increasing concern about child abuse, thirty-five states have nullified the clergy privilege in child abuse situations. Only Kentucky, North Carolina, and Pennsylvania specifically exempt clergy from such disclosures. This issue is likely to become more volatile in the future.

▶Another clergy-related church-state issue is that of clergy malpractice. In this era of liability litigation for product failure and professional malpractice, the latter aimed primarily at the medical profession, it is not completely surprising that some should think of suing clergy for malpractice as well. The idea is that if the ministrations of the church, or particular clergy, should not turn out the way that those receiving the ministrations think they should, then the provider of the services is guilty of malpractice and liable for damages. It is obvious that pastoral counseling is most vulnerable to such attack.

The classic case in this area is *Nally* v. *Grace Community Church* (1985). Kenneth Nally was a young man who realized that he had some psychological and spiritual problems. He sought out people who might help him, including the staff of Grace Community Church, some of whom were lay counselors. He received counseling from various members of the ministerial staff periodically for about three years. He committed suicide in 1979. Thereafter Nally's parents sued the church and its various pastors for damages, claiming malpractice. Specifically, the charges were that Rev. John MacArthur, the senior minister, discouraged Nally from receiving professional help from any source other than the church, he failed to make himself and other pastors and lay counselors at the church available when Nally requested them, and that he failed to exercise the standard of care for a clergyman of his sect and training. A second count at trial was that MacArthur and the church were negligent in not requiring the proper level of psychological training and background on the part of lay counselors employed by the church. A third count charged outrageous conduct in that the clergy staff ridiculed the Catholic Church, in which Nally was raised, and thus instilled in him a disrespect for his parents, who had remained Catholics after their son had converted to Protestantism at Grace Church. The count further alleged outrageous conduct in that the ministerial staff knew Nally had suicidal tendencies and yet their behavior, noted above, exacerbated his feelings of guilt, anxiety, and depression and contributed to his suicide.

The court perceived that the case raised the question of whether pastoral counseling is a secular activity subject to state regulation, or is it clearly a religious activity protected from state standard-setting intervention by the First Amendment? The court answered the question rather eloquently:

> To attempt to regulate and impose standards upon pastoral counseling could open the courts to a flood of clergy malpractice suits that many established religions would be able to challenge. However, the effect upon these churches by the cost of defense of such lawsuits and upon a small church or the traditional itinerate preacher, as evidenced by the religious history in the United States, would have a chilling effect upon the exercise of the

freedom of religion. The guarantee of religious freedom requires the government to create an atmosphere of hospitality and accommodation to individual beliefs, and if there be, disbeliefs.

Ken Nally sought the counsel of various members and pastors of Grace Community Church, and he did this of his own free will. Men should have the liberty to seek counsel from the pastor whose teaching they choose to follow, and the state should not interfere in their choice of pastor or the teachings which they wish to accept from the pastor. There is no compelling state interest for this court to interfere in the pastoral counseling activities of Grace Community Church. Such interference would result in excessive entanglement of the state in church and religious beliefs and teachings. The court would by necessity, if it so interfered, have to set standards of competence and standards of training of counselors, determine who may or may not be counseled, determine if the problems counseled were moral or mental and monitor the counseling for all time to come. There is no compelling state interest to climb the wall of separation of church and state and plunge into the pit on the other side that certainly has no bottom.

Therefore, the court finds the defendants had no legally recognizable duty in law to (1) investigate Ken Nally's alleged suicidal manifestations, (2) inform other professionals and his family of his suicidal manifestations, (3) refer Ken Nally to a psychologist or psychiatrist or other professional, (4) train and employ competent counselors to secular standards, and (5) make counselors available to Ken Nally.

Even if these duties existed, the plaintiffs have failed to show the defendants breached these duties. . . .[2]

Many church leaders believe (and hope) that this strong opinion advocating noninterference by government may prevent the current trickle of clergy malpractice allegations from becoming a flood, at least in the important area of pastoral counseling.

▶From time to time the question of a United States ambassador to the Vatican has become an issue. To confine the discussion to this century, Franklin D. Roosevelt appointed a personal representative with the rank of ambassador who served 1939-49. President Truman nominated General Mark Clark to be ambassador to the Vatican (not just a personal representative), but before Senate confirmation hearings could begin there was such opposition that he withdrew the nomination and abandoned the idea. There the matter rested (John F. Kennedy, our first Catholic president, sent no representative) until Richard Nixon again appointed a personal representative of the President to the Vatican. Presidents Ford and Carter continued the practice.

The argument usually given for such an appointment is that because the Vatican is a sovereign state with a diplomatic corps, maintaining diplomatic relations with over

---

[2] The full text of the opinion is available in Samuel E. Ericsson, "Clergy Malpractice: An Illegal Legal Theory," *Focus #2* (published by the Christian Legal Society): 37-45.

seventy countries, it is a valuable "listening post" for the foreign policy of this country. Furthermore, if America had some sort of representative there, the Vatican might be able to use its good offices to facilitate communication with other countries or to mediate disputes between this country and others. The arguments made by strict separationists against such an appointment have been both practical and philosophical. Practically, it is not necessary to have a "listening post" at the Vatican because the United States has diplomatic contacts around the world, including an ambassador in Rome. Furthermore, although technically the Vatican is a sovereign power, it consists of only 108 acres and a population of around 1,000 and thus is not a sovereign power to which the United States needs to relate. Most importantly, such an appointment is a violation of the Establishment Clause in that it shows preferential treatment to a particular church (the United States has never had a diplomatic representative to any other religion or denomination) and that it creates excessive entanglement between government and religion.

All these arguments were resurrected when, in January 1984, President Reagan announced that the decision had been made to establish diplomatic ties with the Vatican at the ambassadorial level. Somewhat later the Senate confirmed William Wilson to be the ambassador. The Administration argued that this initiative was not a violation of First Amendment principles because the Vatican state is a political entity, separate from the Roman Catholic Church. But the position was regularly referred to as "Ambassador to the Holy See," which demonstrated some confusion, since the Holy See is clearly the administrative center of the Church. Opponents of the appointment called attention to the confusion in language and argued that it is impossible to separate the political dimension of the Vatican from the religious, and thus the appointment was unconstitutional.

The features which distinguished the 1980s argument from previous ones were Senate confirmation of the ambassadorship and a lawsuit filed challenging the appointment. The plaintiffs, twenty Protestant and Catholic groups and over eighty religious leaders and other individuals, sued in federal district court: *Americans United for Separation of Church and State* v. *Ronald Reagan.* Lawyers for the government asked the court to dismiss the suit because the plaintiffs lacked standing in that they were not directly injured by the appointment. In addition, the concept of separation of powers forbids the judiciary to interfere with the power of the executive branch to conduct foreign policy, including the appointment of ambassadors. Plaintiffs argued that they did have standing, because as taxpayers, they have an interest in how Congress appropriates their tax money, and, as citizens, they have an interest in seeing that the government obeys the Constitution. In reference to the separation of powers, they argued that the President, even in the conduct of foreign policy, cannot ignore the Constitution, in this case the Establishment Clause.

In May 1985, the federal district court agreed with the government and dismissed the suit, as did the court of appeals in March 1986. In July 1986, plaintiffs petitioned the Supreme Court for a writ of certiorari, but in October the Court held, as had the lower courts, that the plaintiffs did not have standing to sue.

▶Proliferation of "new" religious movements was a matter of great concern to a sizable portion of the population in the 1970s and the first half of the 1980s. Because many of the young people who joined these groups adopted lifestyles different from those of their parents, and because they were often intensely loyal to their group, the new "cults" were accused of brainwashing and mind control. That is, parents and other family members were frequently convinced that, because "nobody in their right mind" could believe that unconventional theology or would voluntarily give up the middle class lives to which they were accustomed in order to live in a commune or to solicit donations on the streets, it must be the case that the cult had bent the mind of their child. To the argument that the child had willingly joined the group, the rejoinder was usually "impossible." To the argument that the person had the constitutional right to join any religious group he or she wanted, the reply was usually an acknowledgment, followed by the protest that this did not fall under constitutional protection because this was obviously not an act of free will.

The argument against cults went on to claim that because the members were brainwashed, they could never leave. That is, because they did not voluntarily join the group, they could not voluntarily dissociate themselves from the group. Because of the mind-bending nature of cult conversion, those in the group were really captives (some people used the word "slaves"). These anxieties began to be expressed in the late 1960s, when cult groups began to make an impact on society. But they reached crisis proportions after the People's Temple massacre in November 1978, in which over 900 people took their lives, apparently many of them voluntarily, at the command of Jim Jones, the leader of the group. Thereafter anti-cultists were able to take an "I told you so" attitude: these new religious groups did make their devotees into mindless robots. Here was a ghastly illustration of the fact and of how dangerous such a condition could be.

Because all these things were true, at least in the view of concerned parents and anti-cultists, the question arose about how to get people out of the cults back into the mainstream of American life, so they could have freedom of mind and freedom of religion again. "Deprogramming" was the solution. Simply described, deprogramming is a kind of "counter brainwashing" in which the cult member is bombarded with ideas counter to the beliefs of the cult of which she or he is a member. Sometimes this takes the form of persuasive argument, sometimes ridiculing the cult founder and all the group stands for, sometimes forcing the devotee to become so sleepy, hungry, and fatigued that all resistance to a change of mind is removed. Usually a combination of these procedures is used. Of course, cult members who are happy in the group (or have been brainwashed to think they are happy), would not voluntarily subject themselves to deprogramming. Essentially two methods were devised to make cult members available for deprogramming. Apparently both of these methods were thought of before the Jonestown tragedy in 1978; they took on a new urgency after that time.

One method was the conservatorship. Conservatorship laws allow families of the aged and/or the mentally incompetent to take over the assets of the affected person in order to protect those assets and care for the person. Families began going to courts to use the conservatorship process to take control of children who had joined cults. Based on testimony of hurt and angry parents, a judge makes a judicial assessment that a particular religion is injurious. Many courts routinely granted parents and their lawyers the authority to take the young person (although some of these people were in their middle-to-late twenties or early thirties) from the religious group and to keep that person in their custody for a specified length of time for the purpose of persuading her or him to abandon faith in the cult. Many argued for the legality of this procedure, since it used a legal means to restore religious freedom to one who had been hoodwinked into a religion, i.e., had joined without informed consent. The argument against this procedure has been that, because it is virtually always an *ex parte* procedure, i.e., the cult member is not in the court to contest the granting of conservatorship, the order takes the person out of the cult without his or her prior knowledge or consent, it is a violation of his or her free exercise rights. In addition, it has been argued that for a judge to decide that a religion is injurious, based on testimony from only one side, is for the state to make an evaluation of the theology of a group, i.e., that it is bad; a violation of the Establishment Clause.

The procedure of conservatorships as a method of removing persons from cults was rather common until a California appeals court voided conservatorships granted by a lower court to the parents of five members of the Unification Church: *Katz* v. *Superior Court.* In its opinion the court said that only "gravely disabled" people could be confined for therapeutic reasons. The court also suggested that in trying to determine whether a person's religious commitment was a voluntary choice or the result of coercive persuasion, a court is inappropriately second-guessing the wisdom and validity of that faith. [3]

The other method of obtaining deprogramees has been abduction. There are numerous known instances of kidnappings in which cult members have been forcefully captured, usually by parents accompanied by professional deprogrammers (occasionally law enforcement personnel have participated), and have been physically restrained while the deprogrammers have tried to "counter brainwash" them. The arguments on either side of this method are the same as those concerning conservatorship. The cult member has been deceived, brainwashed, and detained, so the abduction and deprogramming is really an act of love and consistent with the law because it is designed to give the member freedom again. Opponents argue that this approach also infringes on the free exercise of religion and has the additional problem of kidnapping, which is certainly illegal.

A trend began in the late 1970s for cult members who had been removed from their chosen religion and confined for the purposes of deprogramming to sue parents and their accomplices. This process was greatly aided and given strong legal justification by *Ward* v. *Connor.* A member of the Unification Church was kidnapped by his parents and others, held captive, and subjected to physical abuse in an attempt to dissuade him from his religious beliefs. He later filed suit against his tormentors on several counts, among which was an 1871 civil rights law (42 U.S.C. § 1985(c)), an act which forbade conspiring to deprive an individual of civil rights on the basis of race. Among other things the statute provided that "the party so injured or deprived may have an action for the recovery of damages, occasioned by such injury or deprivation, against any one or more of the conspirators." A federal court of appeals ruled that "we think it reasonable to conclude that religious discrimination, being akin to invidious racial bias, falls within the ambit of § 1985(c), and that the plaintiff and other members of the Unification Church constitute a class which is entitled to invoke the statutory remedy." In short, they could sue their deprogrammers for conspiracy to deprive them of religious rights. In 1982 the United States Supreme Court allowed this ruling to stand. Civil libertarians hailed this as an effective means of deterring deprogramming.

Examples of two such suits with different results are *Peterson* v. *Sorlien* and *Eilers* v. *Coy.* The factual situations are essentially the same. A member of a religious group regarded by the member's parents to be unacceptable was captured and restrained for the purpose of deprogramming. That did not work and the member later filed suit against the parents and/or the professional deprogrammers. In *Peterson* the Minnesota Supreme Court ruled that a charge of false imprisonment cannot stand when parents or their agents are convinced that the judgment of an adult child is impaired, and when "at some juncture" the child consents to the deprogramming activity. This means that if, even after several days of deprogramming, the subject quits protesting and struggling to be free, acquiescence to the process can be inferred. Consequently, in a later court action, the cult member cannot win a charge of forced imprisonment. However, in *Eilers* a federal district court recognized that a cult member might well feign assent to the deprogramming in order to conclude it or to seek a means of escape. Consequently, referring specifically to *Peterson*, the judge ruled as a matter of law that apparent consent is not a defense to false imprisonment. Many civil libertarians believe that *Eilers*, along with *Ward*, have provided the means to slow the tendency to employ deprogramming as a means of returning children to the family fold, since they think it is an unconstitutional process.

▶An interesting issue of church-state relations, although one with wrenching implications for human suffering, emerged in the early 1980s: the "sanctuary" movement. The movement began when some few church people concerned with the well-being of refugees coming into this country across the Rio Grande came to realize that those from Central America, principally El Salvador and Guatamala, were not just economic refugees, as were most of those from Mexico, but were fleeing repressive and brutal governments. That is, economic refugees

[3] Thomas Robbins, "New Religious Movements, Brainwashing, and Deprogramming—The View from the Law Journals: A Review Essay and Survey," *Religious Studies Review* 11 (October 1985): 366. This is a useful article and some of the material in this section of this essay is drawn from it. See also, on the topic of deprogramming, William Shepherd, *To Secure the Blessings of Liberty: American Constitutional Law and the New Religious Movements.* (Chico, CA: Scholars Press, 1985).

are those who come to the United States to escape the grinding poverty of their homelands in order to make a new life for themselves and their families. But the Central American refugees who became the concern of sanctuary workers, although no less impoverished than the others, also were fleeing governments which, in the name of anticommunism and the preservation of law and order, regularly resort to political intimidation, land grabs, torture, and assassinations. The problem was that the United States Government, through the agency of the Immigration and Naturalization Service (INS), defined these people as economic refugees and routinely sent them back to their country of origin, to certain imprisonment or death, in the view of the sanctuary workers. The response of these concerned Americans was to try to help the refugees by giving them shelter, clothing, food, and refuge from the government, i.e., attempting to assist them to assimilate into the Hispanic communities in various cities so they would not be apprehended and deported.

Slowly a network of these concerned people grew. They were virtually all clergy or dedicated laypeople. They believed that they were performing a kind of religious ministry for these displaced persons. On 24 March 1982 they "went public," i.e., they held a press conference (which included the reading of an open letter to the United States Attorney General) and announced that some few churches in Arizona, New York, California, and Washington, D.C. would be sanctuary churches. The movement has grown. At the time of this writing some 300 local congregations have declared themselves to be sanctuaries, as have a Methodist seminary, eleven universities, nineteen cities, and the entire State of New Mexico. Some entire denominations have publicly affirmed the concept.

The church-state dimension of all this is that the government believes that this effort not only protects aliens who should be deported, but that it is a violation of the law. Under the Refugee Act of 1980, the President determines annually the number of refugees to be admitted into this country and the countries of their origin. For example, in 1984 the number of refugees authorized was 72,000: 50,000 from Indochina, 12,000 from the Soviet Union or other Eastern European countries, 6,000 from the Middle East and South Asia, 3,000 from Africa, and 1,000 from Latin America. Obviously, with such a small quota from Latin America, and with hordes of economic refugees crossing the border (the government prosecuted 18,000 alien smuggling cases in 1985), the government cannot allow any activity which gives incentive for any more to come. An irreconcilable difference between the government and the sanctuary workers is that the latter classify Central Americans as political refugees while the former classifies them as economic refugees, which makes sanctuary workers simple refugee smugglers. It was for that reason the government brought eleven sanctuary workers, both clergy and lay, to trial in 1985 (*United States* v. *Aguilar, et. al.*).

The Refugee Act of 1980, referred to above, has a bearing on that trial and the sanctuary movement generally. Sanctuary advocates argued that what they were doing was legal; that it was the government breaking the law! Government policy, against which sanctuary workers protested and from which they tried to save refugees,

was to capture Guatemalan and Salvadoran refugees and deport them to their native countries. However, the Refugee Act of 1980 forbade such practice, according to sanctuary interpretation. In 1968 the United States Senate ratified the United Nations Protocol Relating to the Status of Refugees. In that document, a refugee is defined as one who has a "well-founded fear of being persecuted for reasons of race, religion, nationality, political opinion or membership in a particular social group" and is outside one's country of nationality. Article 33 of the treaty speaks of the nonrefoulement of refugees. "Nonrefoulement" means that no party to the treaty shall expel or return a refugee to a country where she or he will be persecuted or threatened with death. Because Article VI, paragraph 2 of the United States Constitution clearly says that ratified treaties are the law of the land, this prohibition of refoulement has been the law since 1968. However, the very same concept is repeated in the Refugee Act of 1980. That law does not give anyone the *right* to enter this country, but it does give refugees the right to apply for political asylum (which does not guarantee that they will receive it) and protection against deportation to the country of persecution. (8 U.S.C. § 1253(h)) Sanctuary advocates argue that because of the refugee quotas, noted above, which are tilted in favor of those fleeing communist regimes rather than those fleeing "friendly" governments (because the latter are an embarrassment to the Administration), the government deports many Central Americans, particularly Guatemalans and Salvadorans, who have a "well-founded fear of being persecuted" if they return to their homelands. Such deportation is illegal under the Refugee Act of 1980. To be sure, 8 U.S.C. § 1324 prohibits knowingly giving aid to economically motivated migrants who are not also fleeing death and persecution. Sanctuary workers recognize that and have not argued that all refugees be accepted into the country or be given asylum. But they point to the conditional clause in the law and say that it should be interpreted in conformity with the Refugee Act of 1980, not in conflict with it, because there was some evidence that Guatemalan and Salvadoran refugees returned to their countries by the United States had been killed.

In the criminal trial of the sanctuary workers, the judge ruled that they could not mention conditions in Central America, American immigration policy, or international law in their defense. Furthermore, they were not allowed to speak of their religious motivations for aiding threatened refugees. In early July 1986, they were convicted and sentenced. While most of them were given suspended sentences, some were sent to prison. They planned to appeal their conviction on several grounds, not the least of which was their being forbidden to use their religious and humanitarian motivations as a defense.

In gathering evidence for this prosecution of sanctuary workers, the government employed at least two informants who had been recruited and paid to infiltrate the movement and spy on the participants. Because the participants were all active church workers (some were clergy), this meant that the spies had to infiltrate churches. These individuals, pretending to be sympathetic to the cause, established relationships with others and became regarded as trusted workers in the cause of political refugees. They participated regularly in religious services, prayer meetings, and Bible study groups. At many of these sessions they clandestinely made notes and tape recorded the proceedings. They took names and gained addresses under the pretext of making a Christmas card list.

When this activity was discovered (the principal infiltrator spent over twenty days on the witness stand) the defense asked that evidence gained in that method not be allowed. The judge would not suppress the evidence because the government argued that the meetings attended were not religious meetings, that the government was not interested in the religious beliefs of the sanctuary workers or the immigrants they helped, that it was all a part of a routine criminal investigation, in this case it just happened to take them into churches.

Religious leaders were appalled at what they considered to be an unconstitutional action by the government. On 13 January 1986 four congregations in Arizona (the criminal trial was in Tucson), The Presbyterian Church (U.S.A.), and The American Lutheran Church filed suit in federal district court in Phoenix, claiming that the government's action violated the freedom of religion, speech, and association provisions of the First Amendment, the prohibition against unreasonable searches provision of the Fourth Amendment, and the due process of law requirement of the Fifth Amendment. Defendants were the Immigration and Naturalization Service, particular employees of the INS, the infiltrators, the Department of Justice, and the United States. (*Presbyterian Church (U.S.A.)* v. *INS* CA #86-72, United States District Court, District of Arizona)

Finally, in early 1986, a federal suit was filed in San Francisco by a coalition of eighty national and local religious bodies: *American Baptist Church* v. *Meese*. This suit claimed that the federal government was breaking the law by ignoring the Refugee Act of 1980 and by violating the provisions of international treaties ratified by the United States Senate. It asked that all prosecutions of sanctuary work be halted because it is legal under those laws. These suits raise some fundamental issues about the relation of religion to government policy and activity. Many believe that the sanctuary movement may dominate the church-state arena for the last half of the 1980s.

APPENDIX A

A Bill for Establishing Religious Freedom *

[Jefferson presented this bill to the Virginia Assembly in June 1779. It was adopted by the Assembly in 1785 and became law 16 Janunry 1786.]

Well aware that the opinions and belief of men depend not on their own will, but follow involuntarily the evidence proposed to their own minds; that Almighty God hath created the mind free, and manifested his supreme will that free it shall remain by making it altogether insusceptible of restraint; that all attempts to influence it by temporal punishments, or burthens, or by civil incapacitations, tend only to beget habits of hypocrisy and meanness, and are a departure from the plan of the holy author of our religion, who being lord both of body and mind, yet chose not to propagate it by coercions on either, as was in his Almighty power to do, but to extend it by its influence on reason alone; that the impious presumption of legislators and rulers, civil as well as ecclesiastical, who, being themselves but fallible and uninspired men, have assumed dominion over the faith of others, setting up their own opinions and modes of thinking as the only true and infallible, and as such endeavoring to impose them on others, hath established and maintained false religions over the greatest part of the world and through all time: That to compel a man to furnish contributions of money for the propagation of opinions which he disbelieves and abhors, is sinful and tyrannical; that even the forcing him to support this or that teacher of his own religious persuasion, is depriving him of the comfortable liberty of giving his contributions to the particular pastor whose morals he would make his pattern, and whose powers he feels most persuasive to righteousness; and is withdrawing from the ministry those temporary rewards, which proceeding from an approbation of their personal conduct, are an additional incitement to earnest and unremitting labours for the instruction of mankind; that our civil rights have no dependance on our religious opinions, any more than our opinions in physics or geometry; that therefore the proscribing any citizen as unworthy the public confidence by laying upon him an incapacity of being called to offices of trust and emolument, unless he profess or renounce this or that religious opinion, is depriving him injuriously of those privileges and advantages to which, in common with his fellow citizens, he has a natural right; that it tends also to corrupt the principles of that very religion it is meant to encourage, by bribing, with a monopoly of worldly honours and emoluments, those who will externally profess and conform to it; that though indeed these are criminal who do not withstand such temptation, yet neither are those innocent who lay the bait in their way; that the opinions of men are not the object of civil government, nor under its jurisdiction; that to suffer the civil magistrate to intrude his powers into the field of opinion and to restrain the profession or propagation of principles on supposition of their ill tendency is a dangerous falacy, which at once destroys all religious liberty, because he being of course judge of that tendency will make his opinions the rule of judgment, and approve or condemn the sentiments of others only as they shall square with or differ from his own; that it is time enough for the rightful purposes of civil government for its officers to interfere when principles break out into overt acts against peace and good order; and finally, that truth is great and will prevail if left to herself; that she is the proper and sufficient antagonist to error, and has nothing to fear from the conflict unless by human interposition disarmed of her natural weapons, free argument and debate; errors ceasing to be dangerous when it is permitted freely to contradict them.

We the General Assembly of Virginia do enact that no man shall be compelled to frequent or support any religious worship, place, or ministry whatsoever, nor shall be enforced, restrained, molested, or burthened in his body or goods, nor shall otherwise suffer, on account of his religious opinions or belief; but that all men shall be free to profess, and by argument to maintain, their opinions in matters of religion, and that the same shall in no wise diminish, enlarge, or affect their civil capacities.

And though we well know that this Assembly, elected by the people for the ordinary purposes of legislation

---

* From *The Papers of Thomas Jefferson*, ed. Julian P. Boyd (Princeton, N.J.: Princeton University Press, 1950-) 2: 545-46. Reprinted by permission of Princeton University Press.

only, have no power to restrain the acts of succeeding Assemblies, constituted with powers equal to our own, and that therefore to declare this act irrevocable would be of no effect in law; yet we are free to declare, and do declare, that the rights hereby asserted are of the natural rights of mankind, and that if any act shall be hereafter passed to repeal the present or to narrow its operation, such act will be an infringement of natural right.

APPENDIX B

A Memorial and Remonstrance Against Religious Assessments *

1785

[This memorial, written by James Madison, was instrumental in the defeat of a proposal in the Virginia House of Delegates to provide assessments to be used for the teaching of religion.]

To the Honorable the General Assembly of the Commonwealth of Virginia
A Memorial and Remonstrance

We the subscribers, citizens of the said Commonwealth, having taken into serious consideration, a Bill printed by order of the last Session of General Assembly, entitled "A Bill establishing a provision for Teachers of the Christian Religion," and conceiving that the same if finally armed with the sanctions of a law, will be a dangerous abuse of power, are bound as faithful members of a free State to remonstrate against it, and to declare the reasons by which we are determined. We remonstrate against the said Bill,

1. Because we hold it for a fundamental and undeniable truth, "that Religion or the duty which we owe to our Creator and the manner of discharging it, can be directed only by reason and conviction, not by force or violence." The Religion then of every man must be left to the conviction and conscience of every man; and it is the right of every man to exercise it as these may dictate. This right is in its nature an unalienable right. It is unalienable, because the opinions of men, depending only on the evidence contemplated by their own minds cannot follow the dictates of other men: It is unalienable also, because what is here a right towards men, is a duty to-

wards the Creator. It is the duty of every man to render to the Creator such homage and such only as he believes to be acceptable to him. This duty is precedent, both in order of time and in degree of obligation, to the claims of Civil Society. Before any man can be considered as a member of Civil Society, he must be considered as a subject of the Governour of the Universe: And if a member of Civil Society, who enters into any subordinate Association, must always do it with a reservation of his duty to the General Authority; much more must every man who becomes a member of any particular Civil Society, do it with a saving of his allegiance to the Universal Sovereign. We maintain therefore that in matters of Religion, no mans right is abridged by the institution of Civil Society and that Religion is wholly exempt from its cognizance. True it is, that no other rule exists, by which any question which may divide a Society, can be ultimately determined, but the will of the majority; but it is also true that the majority may trespass on the rights of the minority.

2. Because if Religion be exempt from the authority of the Society at large, still less can it be subject to that of the Legislative Body. The latter are but the creatures and vicegerents of the former. Their jurisdiction is both derivative and limited: it is limited with regard to the co-ordinate departments, more necessarily is it limited with regard to the constituents. The preservation of a free Government requires not merely, that the metes and bounds which separate each department of power be invariably maintained; but more especially that neither of them be suffered to overleap the great Barrier which defends the rights of the people. The Rulers who are guilty of such an encroachment, exceed the commission from which they derive their authority, and are Tyrants. The People who submit to it are governed by laws made neither by themselves nor by an authority derived from them, and are slaves.

3. Because it is proper to take alarm at the first experiment on our liberties. We hold this prudent jealousy to be the first duty of Citizens, and one of the noblest characteristics of the late Revolution. The free men of America did not wait till usurped power had strengthened itself by exercise, and entangled the question in precedents. They saw all the consequences in the principle, and they avoided the consequences by denying the principle. We

revere this lesson too much soon to forget it. Who does not see that the same authority which can establish Christianity, in exclusion of all other Religions, may establish with the same ease any particular sect of Christians, in exclusion of all other Sects? that the same authority which can force a citizen to contribute three pence only of his property for the support of any one establishment, may force him to conform to any other establishment in all cases whatsoever?

4. Because the Bill violates that equality which ought to be the basis of every law, and which is more indispensible, in proportion as the validity or expediency of any law is more liable to be impeached. If "all men are by nature equally free and independent," all men are to be considered as entering into Society on equal conditions; as relinquishing no more, and therefore retaining no less, one than another, of their natural rights. Above all are they to be considered as retaining an "*equal* title to the free exercise of Religion according to the dictates of Conscience." Whilst we assert for ourselves a freedom to embrace, to profess and to observe the Religion which we believe to be of divine origin, we cannot deny an equal freedom to those whose minds have not yet yielded to the evidence which has convinced us. If this freedom be abused, it is an offence against God, not against man: To God, therefore, not to man, must an account of it be rendered. As the Bill violates equality by subjecting some to peculiar burdens, so it violates the same principle, by granting to others peculiar exemptions. Are the Quakers and Menonists the only sects who think a compulsive support of their Religions unnecessary and unwarrantable? Can their piety alone be entrusted with the care of public worship? Ought their Religions to be endowed above all others with extraordinary privileges by which proselytes may be enticed from all others? We think too favorably of the justice and good sense of these denominations to believe that they either covet pre-eminences over their fellow citizens or that they will be seduced by them from the common opposition to the measure.

5. Because the Bill implies either that the Civil Magistrate is a competent Judge of Religious Truth; or that he may employ Religion as an engine of Civil policy. The first is an arrogant pretension falsified by the contradictory opinions of Rulers in all ages, and throughout the world: the second an unhallowed perversion of the means of salvation.

6. Because the establishment proposed by the Bill is not requisite for the support of the Christian Religion. To say that it is, is a contradiction to the Christian Religion itself, for every page of it disavows a dependence on the powers of this world: it is a contradiction to fact; for it is known that this Religion both existed and flourished, not only without the support of human laws, but in spite of every opposition from them, and not only during the period of miraculous aid, but long after it had been left to its own evidence and the ordinary care of Providence. Nay, it is a contradiction in terms; for a Religion not invented by human policy, must have pre-existed and been supported, before it was established by human policy. It is moreover to weaken in those who profess this Religion a pious confidence in its innate excellence and the patronage of its Author; and to foster in those who still reject it,

a suspicion that its friends are too conscious of its fallacies to trust it to its own merits.

7. Because experience witnesseth that ecclesiastical establishments, instead of maintaining the purity and efficacy of Religion, have had a contrary operation. During almost fifteen centuries has the legal establishment of Christianity been on trial. What have been its fruits? More or less in all places, pride and indolence in the Clergy, ignorance and servility in the laity, in both, superstition, bigotry and persecution. Enquire of the Teachers of Christianity for the ages in which it appeared in its greatest lustre; those of every sect, point to the ages prior to its incorporation with Civil policy. Propose a restoration of this primitive State in which its Teachers depended on the voluntary rewards of their flocks, many of them predict its downfall. On which Side ought their testimony to have greatest weight, when for or when against their interest?

8. Because the establishment in question is not necessary for the support of the Civil Government. If it be urged as necessary for the support of Civil Government only as it is a means of supporting Religion, and it be not necessary for the latter purpose, it cannot be necessary for the former. If Religion be not within the cognizance of Civil Government how can its legal establishment be necessary to Civil Government? What influence in fact have ecclesiastical establishments had on Civil Society? In some instances they have been seen to erect a spiritual tyranny on the ruins of the Civil authority; in many instances they have been seen upholding the thrones of political tyranny: in no instance have they been seen the guardians of the liberties of the people. Rulers who wished to subvert the public liberty, may have found an established Clergy convenient auxiliaries. A just Government instituted to secure & perpetuate it needs them not. Such a Government will be best supported by protecting every Citizen in the enjoyment of his Religion with the same equal hand which protects his person and his property; by neither invading the equal rights of any Sect, nor suffering any Sect to invade those of another.

9. Because the proposed establishment is a departure from that generous policy, which, offering an Asylum to the persecuted and oppressed of every Nation and Religion, promised a lustre to our country, and an accession to the number of its citizens. What a melancholy mark is the Bill of sudden degeneracy? Instead of holding forth an Asylum to the persecuted, it is itself a signal of persecution. It degrades from the equal rank of Citizens all those whose opinions in Religion do not bend to those of the Legislative authority. Distant as it may be in its present form from the Inquisition, it differs from it only in degree. The one is the first step, the other the last in the career of intolerance. The magnanimous sufferer under this cruel scourge in foreign Regions, must view the Bill as a Beacon on our Coast, warning him to seek some other haven, where liberty and philanthrophy in their due extent, may offer a more certain repose from his Troubles.

10. Because it will have a like tendency to banish our Citizens. The allurements presented by other situations are every day thinning their number. To superadd a fresh motive to emigration by revoking the liberty which they now enjoy, would be the same species of folly which has dishonoured and depopulated flourishing kingdoms.

11. Because it will destroy that moderation and harmony which the forbearance of our laws to intermeddle with Religion has produced among its several sects. Torrents of blood have been spilt in the old world, by vain attempts of the secular arm, to extinguish Religious discord, by proscribing all difference in Religious opinion. Time has at length revealed the true remedy. Every relaxation of narrow and rigorous policy, wherever it has been tried, has been found to assuage the disease. The American Theatre has exhibited proofs that equal and compleat liberty, if it does not wholly eradicate it, sufficiently destroys its malignant influence on the health and prosperity of the State. If with the salutary effects of this system under our own eyes, we begin to contract the bounds of Religious freedom, we know no name that will too severely reproach our folly. At least let warning be taken at the first fruits of the threatened innovation. The very appearance of the Bill has transformed "that Christian forbearance, love and charity," which of late mutually prevailed, into animosities and jealousies, which may not soon be appeased. What mischiefs may not be dreaded, should this enemy to the public quiet be armed with the force of a law?

12. Because the policy of the Bill is adverse to the diffusion of the light of Christianity. The first wish of those who enjoy this precious gift ought to be that it may be imparted to the whole race of mankind. Compare the number of those who have as yet received it with the number still remaining under the dominion of false Religions; and how small is the former! Does the policy of the Bill tend to lessen the disproportion? No; it at once discourages those who are strangers to the light of revelation from coming into the Region of it; and countenances by example the nations who continue in darkness, in shutting out those who might convey it to them. Instead of Levelling as far as possible, every obstacle to the victorious progress of Truth, the Bill with an ignoble and unchristian timidity would circumscribe it with a wall of defence against the encroachments of error.

13. Because attempts to enforce by legal sanctions, acts obnoxious to so great a proportion of Citizens, tend to enervate the laws in general, and to slacken the bands of Society. If it be difficult to execute any law which is not generally deemed necessary or salutary, what must be the case, where it is deemed invalid and dangerous? And what may be the effect of so striking an example of impotency in the Government, on its general authority?

14. Because a measure of such singular magnitude and delicacy ought not to be imposed, without the clearest evidence that it is called for by a majority of citizens, and no satisfactory method is yet proposed by which the voice of the majority in this case may be determined, or its influence secured. "The people of the respective counties are indeed requested to signify their opinion respecting the adoption of the Bill to the next Session of Assembly." But the representation must be made equal, before the voice either of the Representatives or of the Counties will be that of the people. Our hope is that neither of the former will, after due consideration, espouse the dangerous principle of the Bill. Should the event disappoint us, it will still leave us in full confidence, that a fair appeal to the latter will reverse the sentence against our liberties.

15. Because finally, "the equal right of every citizen to the free exercise of his Religion according to the dictates of conscience" is held by the same tenure with all our other rights. If we recur to its origin, it is equally the gift of nature; if we weigh its importance, it cannot be less dear to us; if we consult the "Declaration of those rights which pertain to the good people of Virginia, as the basis and foundation of Government," it is enumerated with equal solemnity, or rather studied emphasis. Either then, we must say, that the Will of the Legislature is the only measure of their authority; and that in the plenitude of this authority, they may sweep away all our fundamental rights; or, that they are bound to leave this particular right untouched and sacred: Either we must say, that they may controul the freedom of the press, may abolish the Trial by jury, may swallow up the Executive and judiciary Powers of the State; nay that they may despoil us of our very right of suffrage, and erect themselves into an independent and hereditary Assembly or, we must say, that they have no authority to enact into law the Bill under consideration. We the Subscribers say, that the General Assembly of this Commonwealth have no such authority: And that no effort may be omitted on our part against so dangerous an usurpation, we oppose to it, this remonstrance; earnestly praying, as we are in duty bound, that the Supreme Lawgiver of the Universe, by illuminating those to whom it is addressed, may on the one hand, turn their Councils from every act which would affront his holy prerogative, or violate the trust committed to them: and on the other, guide them into every measure which may be worthy of his [blessing, may re]dound to their own praise, and may establish more firmly the liberties, the prosperity and the happiness of the Commonwealth.

BIBLIOGRAPHY

BOOKS

Abraham, Henry J. *Freedom and the Court: Civil Rights and Liberties in the United States.* 4th ed. New York: Oxford University Press, 1982.

_____. *The Judicial Process: An Introductory Analysis of the Courts of the United States, England, and France.* 5th ed. New York: Oxford University Press, 1986.

_____. *Justices and Presidents: A Political History of Appointments to the Supreme Court.* 2d ed. New York: Oxford University Press, 1985.

Adams, James L. *The Growing Church Lobby in Washington.* Grand Rapids, Mich.: William B. Eerdmans Publishing Co., 1970.

Ahlstrom, Sidney E. *A Religious History of the American People.* New Haven: Yale University Press, 1973.

Albanese, Catherine L. *Sons of the Fathers: The Civil Religion of the American Revolution.* Philadelphia: Temple University Press, 1976.

Alley, Robert S., ed. *James Madison on Religious Liberty.* New York: Prometheus Books, 1985.

_____. *So Help Me God: Religion and the Presidency, Wilson to Nixon.* Richmond, Va.: John Knox Press, 1972.

Allport, Gordon W. *The Individual and His Religion.* New York: The Macmillan Company, 1962.

American Association of School Administrators. *Religion in the Public Schools.* New York: Harper and Row, 1964.

Antieau, Chester J. *Freedom From Federal Establishment.* Milwaukee, Wis.: Bruce Publishing, 1964.

Arnold, O. Carroll. *Religious Freedom on Trial.* Valley Forge, Pa.: Judson Press, 1978.

Askew, Thomas A. and Peter W. Spellman. *The Churches and the American Experience: Ideals and Institutions.* Grand Rapids, Mich.: Baker Book House, 1984.

Atkins, Stanley and Theodore McConnell, eds. *Churches on the Wrong Road.* Lake Bluff, Ill.: Gateway Editions, 1986.

Baker, John W., ed. *Taxation and the Free Exercise of Religion: Papers and Proceedings of the Sixteenth Religious Liberty Conference, Washington, D.C., October 3-5, 1977.* Washington, D.C.: Baptist Joint Committee on Public Affairs, 1978.

Balk, Alfred. *The Religion Business.* Richmond, Va.: John Knox Press, 1968.

Barker, Sir Ernest. *Church, State and Education.* Ann Arbor: University of Michigan Press, 1957.

Barr, David L. and Nicholas Piediscalzi, eds. *The Bible in American Education: From Source Book to Textbook.* Philadelphia: Fortress Press, 1982.

Barrett, Patricia. *Religious Liberty and the American Presidency: A Study in Church-State Relations.* New York: Herder and Herder, 1963.

Barth, Karl. *Community, State, and Church.* Garden City, N.Y.: Doubleday & Co., 1960.

Becker, Theodore L. and Malcolm M. Feeley. *The Impact of Supreme Court Decisions.* New York: Oxford University Press, 1973.

Bellah, Robert N. *The Broken Covenant: American Civil Religion in Time of Trial.* New York: Seabury Press, 1975.

Bellah, Robert N. and Phillip E. Hammond. *Varieties of Civil Religion.* New York: Harper & Row, 1980.

Benson, Peter L. and Dorothy L. Williams. *Religion on Capitol Hill: Myths and Realities.* San Francisco: Harper and Row, 1982.

Berger, Peter L. *The Noise of Solemn Assemblies: Christian Commitment and the Religious Establishment in America.* Garden City, N.Y.: Doubleday & Co., 1961.

Berman, Harold J. *The Interaction of Law and Religion.* Nashville, Tn.: Abingdon Press, 1974.

Beth, Loren P. *The American Theory of Church and State.* Gainesville: University of Florida Press, 1958.

Blackwell, Victor V. *O'er the Ramparts They Watched.* New York: Carlton Press, 1976.

Blanchard, Paul. *Religion and the Schools: The Great Controversy.* Boston: Beacon Press, 1963.

Blau, Joseph L. *Cornerstones of Religious Freedom in America.* Rev. and enl. edition. New York: Harper and Brothers, 1964.

Blum, Virgil C. *Freedom in Education: Federal Aid for All Children.* Garden City, N.Y.: Doubleday & Co., 1965.

Boles, Donald E. *The Bible, Religion, and the Public Schools.* Ames: Iowa State University Press, 1961, 1964.

_____. *The Two Swords: Commentaries and Cases in Religion and Education.* Ames: Iowa State University Press, 1967.

Boyd, Julian P., ed. *The Papers of Thomas Jefferson.* 20 vols. Princeton: Princeton University Press, 1950-   .)

Brady, Joseph H. *Confusion Twice Confounded: The First Amendment and the Supreme Court.* South Orange, N.J.: Seton Hall University Press, 1954.

Brauer, Jerald C. *Religion and the American Revolution.* Philadelphia: Fortress Press, 1976.

Brickman, William and Stanley Lehrer, eds. *Religion, Government and Education.* New York: Society for the Advancement of Education, 1961.

Brock, Peter. *Pacifism in the United States: From the Colonial Era to the First World War.* Princeton: Princeton University Press, 1968.

Bromley, David G. and Anson Shupe, eds. *New Christian Politics.* Macon, Ga.: Mercer University Press, 1984.

Bromley, David G. and James T. Richardson, eds. *The Brainwashing/Deprogramming Controversy: Sociological, Psychological, Legal and Historical Perspectives.* Lewiston, N.Y.: The Edwin Mellen Press, 1983.

Bromley, David G. and Anson D. Shupe., Jr. *Strange Gods: The Great American Cult Scare.* Boston: Beacon Press, 1982.

Brown, Nicholas C., ed. *The Study of Religion in the Public Schools: An Appraisal.* Washington, D.C.: American Council on Education, 1958.

Brown, Robert McAfee. *Saying Yes and Saying No: On Rendering to God and Caesar.* Philadelphia: Westminster Press, 1986.

Burnstein, Abraham. *Law Concerning Religion in the United States.* 2d ed. Dobbs Ferry, N.Y.: Oceana Publications, 1966.

Butts, R. Freeman. *The American Tradition in Religion and Education.* Boston: Beacon Press, 1950.

Byrnes, Lawrence. *Religion and Public Education.* New York: Harper & Row, 1975.

Callahan, Daniel, ed. *Federal Aid and Catholic Schools.* Baltimore: Helicon Press, 1964.

Carey, George W. and James V. Shall, eds. *Essays on Christianity and Political Philosophy.* Lawham, Md.: University Press of America, 1984.

Carper, James C. and Thomas C. Hunt, eds. *Religious Schooling In America.* Birmingham, Ala.: Religious Education Press, 1984.

Catterall, James S. *Tuition Tax Credits: Fact and Fiction.* Bloomington, Ind.: Phi Delta Kappa Education Foundation, 1983.

Cherry, Conrad, ed. *God's New Israel: Religious Intepretations of American Destiny.* Englewood Cliffs, N.J.: Prentice-Hall, 1971.

Clayton, A. Stafford. *Religion and Schooling: A Comparative Study.* Waltham, Mass.: Blaisdell Publishing Co., 1969.

Cobb, Sanford H. *The Rise of Religious Liberty in America.* New York: Macmillan Co., 1902.

Cogdell, Gaston D. *What Price Parochiaid?* Washington, D.C.: Americans United for Separation of Church and State, 1970.

Cogley, John, ed. *Religion in America: Original Essays on Religion in a Free Society.* New York: Meridian Books, 1958.

Cohen, Richard. *Sunday in the Sixties.* New York: Public Affairs Committee, 1962.

Colombo, Furio. *God in America: Religion and Politics in the United States.* New York: Columbia University Press, 1984.

Conway, Flo and Jim Siegelman. *Holy Terror: The Fundamentalist War on America's Freedoms in Religion, Politics, and Our Private Lives.* Garden City, N.Y.: Doubleday and Co., 1982.

Cord, Robert L. *Separation of Church and State: Historical Fact and Current Fiction.* New York: Lambeth Press, 1982.

Cornell, Julian. *The Conscientious Objector and the Law.* New York: John Day Co., 1943.

Costanzo, Joseph T., S.J. *This Nation Under God: Church, State and Schools in America.* New York: Herder and Herder, 1964.

Cousins, Norman, ed., *'In God We Trust': The Religious Beliefs and Ideas of the American Founding Fathers.* New York: Harper and Row, 1958.

Cox, Archibald. *The Role of the Supreme Court in American Government.* New York: Oxford University Press, 1976.

Curry, Thomas J. *The First Freedoms: Church and State in America to the Passage of the First Amendment.* New York: Oxford University Press, 1985.

Dawson, Joseph M. *America's Way in Church, State, and Society.* New York: Macmillan Co., 1953.

——————. *Separate Church and State Now.* New York: Richard R. Smith, 1948.

Dierenfield, R.H. *Religion in American Public Schools.* Washington, D.C.: Public Affairs Press, 1962.

Dolbeare, Kenneth M. and Philip E. Hammond. *The School Prayer Decisions: From Court Policy to Local Practice.* Chicago: University of Chicago Press, 1971.

Dorsen, Norman, ed. *The Rights of Americans: What They Are—and What They Should Be.* New York: Pantheon, 1971. (See article by Leo Pfeffer, "The Right to Religious Liberty," pp. 326- 47.)

——————. *Religion, the Courts, and Public Policy.* New York: McGraw-Hill Book Co., 1963.

Douglas, William O. *The Bible and the Schools.* Boston: Little, Brown and Co., 1966.

Drinan, Robert F., S.J. *God and Caesar on the Potomac.* Wilmington, Del.: Michael Glazier, Inc., 1986.

——————. *Religion, the Courts, and Public Policy.* New York: McGraw-Hill Book Co., 1963.

Duker, Sam. *The Public Schools and Religion: The Legal Context.* New York: Harper & Row, 1966.

Dutile, Fernand N., and Edward McGlynn Gaffney, Jr. *State and Campus: State Regulation of Religiously Affiliated Higher Education.* Notre Dame, Ind.: University of Notre Dame Press, 1984.

Edwards, Newton. *The Courts and the Public Schools.* Chicago: University of Chicago Press, 1971.

Elliot, Jonathan, ed. *The Debates in the Several State Conventions on the Adoption of the Federal Constitution.* 2d ed., 5 vols. Philadelphia: J.P. Lippincott Company, 1891.

Engel, David E. *Religion in Public Education.* New York: Paulist Press, 1974.

Erickson, Donald A., ed. *Public Controls for Nonpublic Schools.* Chicago: University of Chicago Press, 1969.

Ervin, Sam J., Jr. *Preserving the Constitution.* Charlottesville, Va.: The Michie Co., 1985.

Fackre, Gabriel. *The Religious Right and Christian Faith.* Grand Rapids, Mich: William B. Eerdmans Publishing Company, 1982.

Fellman, David. *Religion in American Public Law.* Boston: Boston University Press, 1974.

Fellman, David, ed. *The Supreme Court and Education.* New York: Columbia University Press, 1969.

Finn, James D., ed. *A Conflict of Loyalties: The Case for Selective Conscientious Objection.* New York: Pegasus, 1968.

Fisher, Wallace E. *Politics, Poker and Piety: A Perspective on Cultural Religion in America.* Nashville: Abingdon Press, 1972.

Flowers, Ronald B. *Religion in Strange Times: The 1960's and 1970's.* Macon, Ga.: Mercer University Press, 1984.

Forell, George W. and William H. Lazareth. *God's Call to Public Responsibility.* Philadelphia: Fortress Press, 1978.

Fowler, Robert Booth. *A New Engagement: Evangelical Political Thought, 1966-1976.* Grand Rapids, Mich.: William B. Eerdmans Publishing Co., 1982.

——————. *Religion and Politics in America.* Metuchen, N.J.: Scarecrow Press, 1986.

Freund, Paul A. and Robert Ulich. *Religion and the Public Schools.* Cambridge, Mass.: Harvard Universiy Press, 1965.

Frommer, Arthur, ed. *The Bible and the Public Schools.* New York: Liberal Arts Press, 1963.

Gaffney, Edward McGlynn, Jr. *Private Schools and the Public Good: Policy Alternatives for the Eighties.* Notre Dame, Ind.: University of Notre Dame Press, 1981.

Gaffney, Edward McGlynn, Jr. and Philip R. Motts. *Government and Campus: Federal Regulation of Religiously Affiliated Higher Education.* Notre Dame, Ind.: University of Notre Dame Press, 1982.

Gaffney, Edward McGlynn, Jr. and Philip C. Sorensen. *Ascending Liability in Religious and Other Nonprofit Organizations.* Macon, Ga.: Mercer University Press, 1984.

Gaustad, Edwin Scott. *Dissent in American Religion.* Chicago: University of Chicago Press, 1973.

——————. *Religious Issues in American History.* New York: Harper & Row, 1968.

Geisler, Norman L., A.F. Brooke II, and Mark J. Keough. *The Creator in the Courtroom: "Scopes II."* Milford, Mich.: Mott Media, Inc., 1982.

Gellhorn, Walter and R. Kent Greenawalt. *The Sectarian College and the Public Press.* Dobbs Ferry, N.Y.: Oceana, 1970.

Giannella, Donald A., ed. *Religion and the Public Order, No. 5.* Ithaca, N.Y.: Cornell University Press, 1969.

Gilkey, Langdon. *Creationism on Trial: Evolution and God at Little Rock.* Minneapolis: Winston Press, 1985.

Goldberg, George. *Reconsecrating America.* Grand Rapids, Mich.: William B. Eerdmans Publishing Co., 1984.

Gordis, Robert. *Religion and the Schools.* New York: Fund for the Republic, 1959.

Grant, Daniel R. *The Christian and Politics.* Nashville: Broadman Press, 1968.

Greene, Evarts B. *Religion and the State: The Making and Testing of an American Tradition.* Ithaca, N.Y.: Cornell University Press, 1959.

Griffiths, William E. *Religion, the Courts, and the Public Schools: A Century of Litigation.* Cincinnati: W. H. Anderson Company, 1966.

Handy, Robert T. *A Christian America: Protestant Hopes and Historical Realities.* 2d ed. Oxford: Oxford University Press, 1984.

Hansen, Klaus J. *Mormonism and the American Experience.* Chicago: University of Chicago Press, 1981.

Hayes, Carlton J.H. *Nationalism: A Religion.* New York: Macmillan Co., 1960.

Healey, Robert M. *Jefferson on Religion in Public Education.* New Haven: Yale University Press, 1962.

Herberg, Will. *Protestant, Catholic, Jew: An Essay in American Religious Sociology.* Garden City, N.Y.: Doubleday & Co., 1955; rev. ed., 1960.

Hoekema, Anthony A. *The Four Major Cults: Christian Science, Jehovah's Witnesses, Mormonism, Seventh-Day Adventists.* Grand Rapids, Mich.: William B. Eerdmans Publishing Co., 1963.

Hogan, John C. *The Schools, the Courts, and the Public Interest.* Lexington, Mass.: Lexington Books, 1985.

Hook, Sidney. *Religion in a Free Society.* Lincoln: University of Nebraska Press. 1967.

Hostetler, John A. *Amish Society.* Rev. ed. Baltimore: Johns Hopkins University Press, 1968.

Howard, A.E. Dick. *State Aid to Private Higher Education.* Charlottesville, Va.: The Michie Co., 1977.

Howe, Mark DeWolfe, ed. *Cases on Church and State in the United States.* Cambridge, Mass.: Harvard University Press, 1952.

——————. *The Garden and the Wilderness: Religion and the Government in American Constitutional History.* Chicago: University of Chicago Press, 1965.

Hudson, Winthrop S. *The Great Tradition of The American Churches.* New York: Harper & Bros., 1953.

——————. *Religion in America.* New York: Scribner, 1965, 1973, 1981.

Jackson, Robert H. *The Supreme Court in the American System of Government.* New York: Harper and Row, 1955.

James, Thomas and Henry M. Levin, eds. *Public Dollars for Private Schools: The Case of Tuition Tax Credits.* Philadelphia: Temple University Press, 1983.

Johns, Warren L. *Dateline Sunday, U.S.A.* Mountain View, Ca.: Pacific Press Publishing Association, 1967.

Johnson, F. Ernest, ed. *American Education and Religion: The Problem of Religion in the Schools.* New York: Harper and Row, 1952.

Johnson, Alvin W. and Frank H. Yost. *Separation of Church and State in the United States.* Minneapolis: University of Minnesota Press, 1948.

Johnson, Richard M. *The Dynamics of Compliance: Supreme Court Decision-making from a New Perspective.* Evanston, Ill.: Northwestern University Press, 1967.

Jorstad, Erling. *The Politics of Moralism: The New Christian Right in American Life.* Minneapolis: Augsburg Publishing House, 1981.

Katz, Wilber G. *Religion and American Constitutions.* Evanston, Ill.: Northwestern University Press, 1963.

Kauper, Paul G. *Civil Liberties and the Constitution.* Ann Arbor: University of Michigan Press, 1962.

_____. *Religion and the Constitution.* Baton Rouge: Louisiana State University Press, 1964.

Keim, Albert N., ed. *Compulsory Education and the Amish: The Right Not to Be Modern.* Boston: Beacon Press, 1975.

Kelley, Dean M. *Why Churches Should Not Pay Taxes.* New York: Harper & Row, 1977.

_____, ed. *Government Intervention in Religious Affairs.* New York: Pilgrim Press, 1982.

_____, ed. *The Uneasy Boundary: Church and State.* Vol. 44 of *The Annals of the American Academy of Political and Social Science* (November 1979).

Kelly, George Armstrong. *Politics and Religious Consciousness in America.* New Brunswick, N.J.: Transaction Books, 1984.

Kliebard, Herbert M. *Religion and Education in America: A Documentary History.* Scranton, Pa.: International Textbook Co., 1969.

Kolbenschlag, Madonna, ed. *Between God and Caesar.* Rumsey, N.J.: Paulist Press, 1986.

Kommers, Donald P. and Michael J. Wahoske, eds. *Freedom and Education: Pierce v. Society of Sisters Reconsidered.* Notre Dame, Ind.: Center for Civil Rights, University of Notre Dame Law School, 1978.

Konvitz, Milton R. *Religious Liberty and Conscience: A Constitutional Inquiry.* New York: Viking Press, 1968.

Koob, C. Albert and Russell Shaw. *S.O.S. for Catholic Schools: A Strategy for Future Service to Church and Nation.* New York: Holt, Rinehart, and Winston, 1970.

Krason, Stephen M. *Abortion: Politics, Morality, and the Constitution: A Critical Study of Roe v. Wade and Doe v. Bolton and a Basis for Change.* Lanham, Md.: University Press of America, 1984.

Krinsky, Fred. *The Politics of Religion in America.* Beverly Hills: Glencoe Press, 1968.

Kurland, Philip B., ed. *Church and State: The Supreme Court and the First Amendment.* Chicago: University of Chicago Press, 1975.

_____. *Religion and the Law: Of Church and State and the Supreme Court.* Chicago: Aldine Publishing Co., 1962.

Kurland, Philip B., Gerhard Casper, and Dennis J. Hutchinson, eds. *The Supreme Court Review, 1983.* Chicago: University of Chicago Press, 1983.

La Noue, George R., ed. *Educational Vouchers: Concepts and Controversies.* New York: Teachers College, Columbia University Press, 1972.

Lannie, Vincent P. *Public Money for Parochial Education.* Cleveland: Case Western Reserve University Press, 1968.

Larson, Martin and C. Stanley Lowell. *Praise the Lord for Tax Exemption: How the Churches Grow Rich, While the Cities and You Grow Poor.* Washington, D.C.: Robert B. Luce, 1969.

_____. *The Religious Empire: The Growth and Danger of Tax-Exempt Property in the United States.* Washington, D.C.: Robert B. Luce Co., Inc., 1976.

Laubach, John H. *School Prayers: Congress, the Courts, and the Public.* Washington, D.C.: Public Affairs Press, 1969.

Liebman, Robert C. and Robert Wuthnow, eds. *The New Christian Right: Mobilization and Legitimation.* New York: Aldine Publishing Co., 1983.

Lincoln, C. Eric. *The Black Muslims in America.* Boston: Beacon Press, 1961, 1973.

Linder, Robert D. and Richard V. Pierard. *Politics: A Case for Christian Action.* Downers Grove, Ill.: Inter-Varsity Press, 1973.

Littell, Franklin Hamlin. *The Church and the Body Politic.* New York: Seabury Press, 1969.

_____. *From State Church to Pluralism: A Protestant Interpretation of Religion in American History.* New York: Macmillan Co., 1971.

_____. *The Origins of Sectarian Protestantism: A Study of the Anabaptist View of the Church.* New York: Macmillan Co., 1964.

Loder, James E. *Religion and the Public Schools.* New York: Association Press, 1965.

Malbin, Michael J. *Religion and Politics: The Intentions of the Authors of the First Amendment.* Washington, D.C.: American Enterprise Institute, 1978.

Manning, Leonard F. *The Law of Church-State Relations in a Nutshell.* St. Paul, Minn.: West Publishing Co., 1981.

Manwaring, David R. *Religion, Liberty and the State.* Indianapolis: Bobbs-Merrill, 1971.

_____. *Render Unto Caesar: The Flag Salute Controversy.* Chicago: University of Chicago Press, 1962.

Marnell, William H. *The First Amendment: The History of Religious Freedom in America.* Garden City, N.Y.: Doubleday & Co., 1964.

Marty, Martin E.. *The New Shape of American Religion.* New York: Harper & Row, 1958, 1959.

_____. *The Pro & Con Book of Religious America: A Bicentennial Argument.* Waco, Texas: Word Incorporated, 1975.

_____. *The Public Church: Mainline-Evangelical-Catholic.* New York: Crossroad Books, 1981.

McCarthy, Martha M. *A Delicate Balance: Church, State, and the Schools.* Bloomington: Indiana University Press, 1983.

McCluskey, Neil G. *Catholic Viewpoint on Education.* Rev. ed. Garden City, N.Y.: Image Books, 1962.

_____. *Catholic Education in America.* New York: Teachers College, Columbia University Press, 1964.

McCollum, Vashti C. *One Woman's Fight.* Boston: Beacon Press, 1951.

McGrath, Joseph H., ed. *Church and State in American Law.* Milwaukee, Wis.: Bruce Publishing Co., 1962.

McMillan, Richard C. *Religion in the Public Schools: An Introduction.* Macon, Ga.: Mercer University Press, 1984.

Mead, Sidney E. *The Lively Experiment: The Shaping of Christianity in America.* New York: Harper & Row, 1963.

_____. *The Nation With the Soul of a Church.* New York: Harper & Row, 1975.

_____. *The Old Religion in the Brave New World: Reflections on the Relation Between Christendom and the Republic.* Berkeley: University of California Press, 1977.

Mechling, Jay, ed. *Church, State and Public Policy: The New Shape of the Church-State Debate.* Washington, D.C.: American Enterprise Institute for Public Policy Research, 1978.

Melton, J. Gordon. *The Encyclopedia of American Religions,* 2 vols., Wilmington, N.C.: McGrath Publishing Co., 1978.

Menendez, Albert J. *Religious Conflict in America: A Bibliographic Guide.* New York: Garland Publishing, 1984.

_____. *Religion and the U.S. Presidency: A Bibliography.* New York: Garland Press, 1986.

_____. *School Prayer and Other Issues in American Public Education: An Annotated Bibliography.* New York: Garland Publishing, 1984.

Michaelson, Robert. *Piety in the Public School: Trends and Issues in Relationship between Religion and the Public Schools in the United States.* New York: Macmillan Co., 1970.

Miller, Glenn T. *Religious Liberty in America: History and Prospects.* Philadelphia: Westminster Press, 1976.

Miller, William Lee. *The First Liberty: Religion and the American Republic.* New York: Alfred A. Knopf, 1985.

Miller, William Lee. *The Protestant and Politics.* Philadelphia: Westminster Press, 1958.

Minear, Paul. *I Pledge Allegiance: Patriotism and the Bible.* Philadelphia: The Geneva Press, 1975.

Moehlman, Conrad H. *The Wall of Separation between Church and State: An Historical Study of Recent Criticism of the Religious Clause of the First Amendment.* Boston: Beacon Press, 1951.

Molnar, Thomas. *Politics and the State: The Catholic View.* Chicago: Franciscan Herald Press, 1980.

Moltmann, Jurgen, Herbert W. Richardson, Johann Baptist Metz, Willi Oelmuller, and M. Darrol Bryant. *Religion and Political Society.* New York: Harper & Row, 1974.

Moore, R. Laurence. *Religious Outsiders and the Making of Americans.* New York: Oxford University Press, 1985.

Moots, Philip R. and Edward M. Gaffney, Jr. *Church and Campus: Legal Issues in Religiously Affiliated Education.*

Notre Dame and London: University of Notre Dame Press, 1979.

Morgan, Edmund S. *Roger Williams: The Church and the State.* New York: Harcourt, Brace & World, 1967.

Morgan, Richard E. *The Politics of Religious Conflict: Church and State in America.* 2d ed. Washington, D.C.: University Press of America, 1980.

——————. *The Supreme Court and Religion.* New York: Free Press, 1972.

Muir, W.K. *Prayer in the Public Schools: Law and Attitude Change.* Chicago: University of Chicago Press, 1967.

Murray, John Courtney, S.J. *We Hold These Truths: Catholic Reflections on the American Proposition.* Garden City, N.Y.: Doubleday & Co., 1964.

Neuhaus, Richard J. *Christian Faith and Public Policy: Thinking and Acting in the Courage of Uncertainty.* Minneapolis: Augsburg Publishing House, 1977.

——————. *The Naked Public Square: Religion and Democracy in America.* Grand Rapids, Mich: William B. Eerdmans Publishing Co., 1984.

Noll, Mark A., Nathan O. Hatch, and George M. Marsden. *The Search for Christian America.* Westchester, Ill.: Crossway Books, 1983.

——————. *Christians in the American Revolution.* Washington D.C.: Christian University Press, 1977.

Oaks, Dallin H., ed. *The Wall between Church and State.* Chicago: University of Chicago Press, 1963.

——————. *Trust Doctrines in Church Controversies.* Macon, Ga.: Mercer University Press, 1984.

O'Brien, Francis W. *Justice Reed and the First Amendment: The Religion Clauses.* Washington: Georgetown University Press, 1958.

Odegard, Peter H. *Religion and Politics.* New York: Oceana Publications, 1960.

O'Hair, Madalyn Murray. *Freedom Under Siege: The Impact of Organized Religion on Your Liberty and Your Pocketbook.* Los Angeles: J. P. Tarcher, Inc., 1974.

O'Neill, James M. *Religion and Education under the Constitution.* New York: Harper & Bros, 1949.

Parsons, Wilfrid P. *The First Freedom: Considerations of Church and State in the United States.* McMullen, 1948.

Pattillo, Manning M., Jr., and Donald M. Mackenzie. *Church-Sponsored Higher Education in the United States.* Washington, D.C.: American Council on Education, 1966.

Pfeffer, Leo. *Church, State and Freedom.* Rev. and enl. ed. Boston: Beacon Press, 1967.

——————. *God, Caesar, and the Constitution: The Court as Referee of Church-State Confrontation.* Boston: Beacon Press, 1975.

——————. *The Liberties of an American: The Supreme Court Speaks.* Boston: Beacon Press, 1963.

——————. *Religion, State, and the Burger Court.* Buffalo, N.Y.: Prometheus Books, 1985.

——————. *Religious Freedom.* Skokie, Ill.: National Textbook Co. in conjunction with the American Civil Liberties Union, 1977.

Polishook, Irwin H. *Roger Williams, John Cotton and Religious Freedom.* Englewood Cliffs, N.J.: Prentice-Hall, 1967.

Poore, Benjamin P., ed. *The Federal and State Constitutions, Colonial Charters, and Other Organic Laws of the United States.* 2 vols. Washington: Government Printing Office, 1978.

Powell, Theodore. *The School Bus Law: A Case Study in Education, Religion and Politics.* Middleton, Conn.: Wesleyan University Press, 1960.

Power, M. Susan. *Before the Convention: Religion and the Founders.* New York: University Press of America, 1984.

Pritchett, C. Herman. *The American Constitution.* 3d ed. New York: McGraw-Hill Book Co., 1977.

Rader, Stanley R. *Against the Gates of Hell: The Threat to Religious Freedom in America.* New York: Everest House, 1980.

Regan, Richard J., S.J. *Private Conscience and Public Law: The American Experience.* New York: Fordham University Press, 1972.

Reichley, A. James. *Religion in American Public Life.* Washington, D.C.: The Brookings Institution, 1985.

Ribuffo, Leo P. *The Old Christian Right: The Protestant Far Right from the Great Depression to the Cold War.* Philadelphia: Temple University Press, 1983.

Rice, Charles E. *The Supreme Court and Public Prayer: The Need for Restraint.* New York: Fordham University Press, 1964.

Richey, Russell E. and Donald G. Jones, eds. *American Civil Religion.* New York: Harper & Row, 1974.

Richter, Edward J. and Dulce Berton. *Religion and the Presidency: A Recurring American Problem.* New York: Macmillan Co., 1962.

Robbins, Thomas and Roland Robertson, eds. *Church-State Relations: Tensions and Transitions.* New Brunswick, N.J.: Transaction Books, 1986.

Robbins, Thomas, William C. Shepherd and James McBride, eds. *Cults, Culture and the Law: Perspectives on New Religious Movements.* Chico, Ca.: Scholars Press, 1985.

Robertson, D.B. *Should Churches be Taxed?* Philadelphia: Westminster Press, 1968.

Rodgers, Harrell R., Jr. *Community Conflict, Public Opinion and the Law: The Amish Dispute in Iowa.* Columbus, Ohio: Charles E. Merrill Publishing Co., 1969.

Rohr, John A. *Prophets Without Honor: Public Policy an the Selective Conscientious Objector.* Nashville: Abingdon Press, 1971.

Rudin, James and Marcia. *Prison or Paradise: The New Religious Cults.* Philadelphia: Fortress Press, 1980.

Rutyna, Richard and John W. Kuehl, eds. *Conceived in Conscience: An Analysis of Contemporary Church-State Relations.* Norfolk, Va.: Donning Company, 1983.

Sandeen, Ernest R., ed. *The Bible and Social Reform.* Philadelphia: Fortress Press, 1982.

Sanders, Thomas G. *Protestant Concepts of Church and State: Historical Backgrounds and Approaches for the Future.* New York: Holt Rinehart and Winston, 1964.

Sanford, Charles B. *The Religious Life of Thomas Jefferson.* Charlottesville: University of Virginia Press, 1984.

Shepherd, David R. *Ronald Reagan: In God I Trust.* Wheaton, Ill.: Tyndale House Publishers, 1984.

Shepherd, William C. *To Secure the Blessings of Liberty: American Constitutional Law and the New Religious Movements.* Baltimore: Scholars Press, 1985.

Sibley, Mulford Q. *The Obligation to Disobey: Conscience and the Law.* New York: Council on Religion and International Affairs, 1970.

Sibley, Mulford Q. and Philip E. Jacob. *Conscription of Conscience: The American State and the Conscientious Objector, 1940-1947.* Ithaca, N.Y.: Cornell University Press, 1952.

Sizer, Theodore R., ed. *Religion and Public Education.* Boston: Houghton Mifflin Co., 1967; Lanham, Md.: University Press of America, 1982.

Smith, Elwyn A. *Church and State in Your Community.* Philadelphia: Westminster Press, 1963.

——————, ed. *The Religion of the Republic.* Philadelphia: Fortress Press, 1971, 1980.

——————. *Religious Liberty in the United States: The Development of Church-State Thought Since the Revolutionary Era.* Philadelphia: Fortress Press, 1972.

Smith, H. Shelton, Robert T. Handy and Lefferts A. Loetscher. *American Christianity: An Historical Interpretation with Representative Documents.* 2 vols. New York: Charles Scribner's Sons, 1960.

Sorauf, Frank. *The Wall of Separation: The Constitutional Politics of Church-State.* Princeton: Princeton University Press, 1976.

Spicer, George W. *The Supreme Court and Fundamental Freedom.* New York: Appleton-Century-Crofts, 1959.

Stedman, Murray S. *Religion and Politics in America.* New York: Harcourt, Brace & World, 1964.

Stokes, Anson Phelps. *Church and State in the United States.* 3 vols. New York: Harper & Bros., 1950.

Stokes, Anson Phelps and Leo Pfeffer. *Church and State in the United States.* Rev. one volume ed. New York: Harper and Row, 1964.

Stroup, Herbert H. *The Jehovah's Witnesses.* New York: Columbia University Press, 1945.

Strout, Cushing. *The New Heavens and New Earth: Political Religion in America.* New York: Harper & Row, 1974.

Sweet, William W., ed. *Religion in Colonial America.* New York: Charles Scribner's Sons, 1942.

Swomley, John M., Jr. *Religion, the State, and the Schools.* New York: Pegasus, 1968.

Tarr, B. Alan. *Judicial Impact and State Supreme Courts.* Lexington, Mass.: D.C. Heath and Co., 1977.

Tiemann, William Harold, and John C. Bush. *The Right to Silence: Privileged Clergy Communication and the Law.* Nashville: Abingdon Press, 1983.

Torpey, William G. *Judicial Doctrines of Religious Rights in America.* Chapel Hill: University of North Carolina Press, 1948.

Tribe, Laurence H. *The Constitutional Protection of Individual Rights: Limits on Government Authority.* Mineola, N.Y.: The Foundation Press, Inc., 1978.

_____. *God Save This Honorable Court: How the Choice of Supreme Court Justices Shapes our History.* New York: Random House, 1985.

Tussman, Joseph, ed. *The Supreme Court on Church and State.* New York: Oxford Press, 1962.

Twomley, Dale E. *Parochiaid and the Courts.* Perrier Springs, Mich.: Andrews University Press, 1981.

Walter, Erich A., ed. *Religion and the State University.* Ann Arbor: University of Michigan Press, 1964.

Ward, Hiley H. *Space-Age Sunday.* New York: Macmillan Co., 1960.

Whitehead, John W. *The Separation Illusion: A Lawyer Examines the First Amendment.* Milford, Mich.: Mott Media, 1977.

Wilson, John F. *Public Religion in American Culture.* Philadelphia: Temple University Press, 1979.

Weber, Paul J. and Dennis A. Gilbert. *Private Churches and Public Money: Church-Government Fiscal Relations.* Westport, Conn.: Greenwood Press, 1981.

Wilson, John F., ed. *Church and State in American History.* Boston: D.C. Heath and Co., 1965.

Wogaman, Philip. *Protestant Faith and Religious Liberty.* Nashville: Abingdon Press, 1967.

Wolf, Donald J., S.J. *Toward Consensus: Catholic-Protestant Interpretations of Church and State.* Garden City, N.Y.: Doubleday & Co., 1968.

Wood, James E., Jr. *Religion and Politics.* Waco, Tex.: Baylor University Press, 1983.

_____. ed. *Religion, the State, and Education.* Waco, Tex.: Baylor University Press, 1984.

Wood, James E., Jr., Robert T. Miller and E. Bruce Thompson. *Church and State in Scripture, History and Constitutional Law.* Waco, Tex.: Baylor University Press, 1958.

Worton, Stanley N. *Freedom of Religion.* Rochelle Park, N.J.: Hayden Book Co., 1975.

Zaretsky, I.I. and M.P. Leone, eds. *Religious Movements in Contemporary America.* Princeton: Princeton University Press, 1974.

Zetterbert, J. Peter, ed. *Evolution versus Creationism: The Public Education Controversy.* Phoenix: Oryz Press, 1983.

Zollman, Carl F. *American Church Law.* St. Paul, Minn.: West Publishing Co., 1933.

ARTICLES

Abraham, Henry J. "Religion, Medicine, and the State: Reflections on Some Contemporary Issues." *Journal of Church and State* 22 (Autumn 1980):423-46.

_____. "The Status of the First Amendment's Religion Clauses: Some Reflections on Lines and Limits." *Journal of Church and State* 22 (Spring 1980):215-31.

Adams, Arlin M. and William R. Hanlon. "*Jones* v. *Wolf*: Church Autonomy and the Religion Clauses of the First Amendment." *University of Pennsylvania Law Review* 128 (June 1980):409-26.

Ahlstrom, Sydney E. "Religion, Revolution and the Rise of Modern Nationalism: Reflections on the American Experience." *Church History* 44 (December 1975):492-504.

_____. "The Traumatic Years: American Religion and Culture in the '60s and '70s." *Theology Today* 36 (1980):504-22.

"Aid to Parochial Schools: A Free Exercise Perspective." *Santa Clara Law Review* 23 (Spring 1983):587-605.

"Another Brick in the Wall: Denominational Preferences and Strict Scrutiny Under the Establishment Clause." *Nebraska Law Review* 62 (1983):359-83.

Ayres, T.D. "*Widmar* v. *Vincent*: The Beginning of the End of the Establishment Clause." *Journal of College and University Law* 8 (No. 4, 1981-82):511-17.

Balitzer, Alfred. "Some Thoughts About Civil Religion." *Journal of Church and State* 16 (Winter 1974): 31- 50.

Becker, William H. "Creationism: New Dimensions of the Religion-Democracy Relation." *Journal of Church and State* 27 (Spring 1985): 315-33.

Bellah, Robert N. "Civil Religion in America." *Daedalus* 96 (Winter 1967):1-21.

Benjamin, Walter W. "Separation of Church and State: Myth and Reality." *Journal of Church and State* 11 (Winter 1969):93-110.

Berger, Raoul. "Standing to Sue in Public Actions: Is It a Constitutional Requirement?" *Yale Law Journal* 78 (April 1969):816-40.

Birkby, Robert "The Supreme Court and the Bible Belt: Tennessee Reaction to the Schempp Decision." *Midwest Journal of Political Science* 10 (August 1966):304-19.

"*Bob Jones University* v. *United States*: Paying the Price of Prejudice—Loss of Tax Exempt Status." *Mercer Law Review* 35 (Spring 1984): 937-63.

Boles, Donald E. "Church and State and the Burger Court: Recent Developments Affecting Parochial Schools." *Journal Of Church and State* 18 (Winter 1976):21-38.

_____. "Religion and the Public Schools in Judicial Review." *Journal of Church and State* 26 (Winter 1984):55-71.

Bolton, S. Charles and Cal Ledbetter, Jr. "Compulsory Bible Reading in Arkansas and the Culture of Southern Fundamentalism." *Social Science Quarterly* 64 (September 1983):670- 76.

Boothby, Lee and R.W. Nixon "Religious Accommodation: An Often Delicate Task." *The Notre Dame Lawyer* 57 (June 1982):797- 808.

Bowden, Henry Warner. "A Historian's Response to the Concept of American Civil Religion." *Journal of Church and State* 17 (Autumn 1975):495-505.

Brudney, Jeffrey L. and Gary W. Copeland. "Evangelicals as a Political Force: Reagan and the 1980 Religious Vote." *Social Science Quarterly* 65 (December 1984): 1072-79.

Buchanan, G.S. "Governmental Aid to Sectarian Schools: A Study in Corrosive Precedents." *Houston Law Rewiew* 15 (May 1978):783-838.

Burleson, Bruce "*E.E.O.C.* v. *Mississippi College*: The Applicability of Title VII to Sectarian Schools." *Baylor Law Review* 33 (Spring 1981):380-91.

Butler, William J. "The Effect of State Aid to Church Schools on Public Education." *Journal of Church and State* 6 (Winter 1964):74-84.

Cahn, Edmund. "On Government and Prayer." *New York Law Review* 37 (December 1962):981-1000.

Canavan, Francis, S.J. "The Impact of Recent Supreme Court Decisions on Religion in the United States." *Journal of Church and State* 16 (Spring 1974):217-36.

Capps, Kline and Carl H. Esbeck. "The Use of Government Funding and Taxing Power to Regulate Religious Schools." *Journal of Law and Education* 14 (October 1985): 553-74.

Carpenter, James G. "State Regulation of Religious Schools." *Journal of Law and Education* 14 (April 1985): 229-49.

Carroll, William A. "The Constitution, the Supreme Court, and Religion." *American Political Science Review* 61 (September 1967):657-74.

Chase, Jonathon B. "Litigating a Nativity Scene Case." *St. Louis University Law Journal* 24 (1980): 237-71.

Choper, J.H. "Religion in the Public Schools: A Proposed Constitutional Standard." *Minnesota Law Review* 47 (January 1963):329-416.

_____. "The Religion Clauses of the First Amendment: Reconciling the Conflict." *University of Pittsburgh Law Review* 41 (Summer 1980):673-701.

_____. "Defining 'Religion' in the First Amendment." *University of Illinois Law Review* 1982 (1982): 579-613.

Clark, J. Morris. "Guidelines for the Free Exercise Clause." *Harvard Law Review* 83 (December 1969):327-65.

"Constitutional Law—Legislative Prayer and the Establishment Clause: An Exception to the Traditional Analysis—*Marsh* v. *Chambers*" *Creighton Law Review* 17 (1983/1984): 157-85.

"Constitutional Law—the Clash Between the Free Exercise of Religion and the Military's Uniform Regulations—*Goldman* v. *Secretary of Defense.*" *Temple Law Quarterly* 58 (Spring 1985): 195-219.

"The Constitutional Dimensions of Student-Initiated Religious Activity in Public High Schools." *Yale Law Journal* 92 (December 1982):499-519.

"Constitutionality of Student-Initiated Religious Meetings on Public School Grounds." *University of Cincinnati Law Review* 50 (1981): 740- 85.

Cord, Robert L. "Church-State Separation: Restoring the 'No Preference' Doctrine of the First Amendment." *Harvard Journal of Law and Public Policy* 9 (Winter 1986): 129-72.

Cornelius, William J. "Church and State: The Mandate of the Establishment Clause: Wall of Separation or Benign Neutrality?" *St. Mary's Law Journal* 16 (1984): 1-39.

Corwin, E.S. "The Supreme Court as National School Board." *Law and Contemporary Problems* 14 (Winter 1949):3-22.

Cote, Denise. "Establishment Clause Analysis of Legislative and Administrative Aid to Religion." *Columbia Law Review* 74 (October 1974):1175-1202.

Crabb, Kelly C. "Religious Symbols, American Traditions and the Constitution." *Brigham Young University Law Review* 1984 (1984): 509-62.

Crockenberg, Vincent A. "An Argument for the Constitutionality of Direct Aid to Religious Schools." *Journal of Law and Education* 13 (January 1984): 1-18.

Curry, Particia E. "James Madison and the Burger Court: Converging Views of Church-State Separation." *Indiana Law Journal* 56 (Summer 1981):615-36.

"Daily Moments of Silence in Public Schools: A Constitutional Analysis." *New York University Law Review* 58 (May 1983):364-408.

"Defining the Limits of Free Exercise: The Religion Clause Defenses in *United States* v. *Moon.*" *Hastings Constitutional Law Quarterly* 12 (Spring 1985): 515-28.

Delgado, Richard. "Religious Totalism: Gentle and Ungentle Persuasion Under the First Amendment." *Southern California Law Review* 51 (November 1977): 1-98.

——————. "When Religious Exercise Is Not Free: Deprogramming and the Constitutional Status of Coercively Induced Belief." *Vanderbilt Law Review* 37 (October 1984): 1071-1115.

Devins, Neal. "Religious Symbols and the Establishment Clause." *Journal of Church and State* 27 (Winter 1985): 19-46.

——————. "State Regulation of Christian Schools." *Journal of Legislation* 10 (Summer 1983):351-81.

Dodge, Joseph M., II. "The Free Exercise of Religion: A Sociological Approach." *Michigan Law Review* 67 (February 1969):679-728.

"Does the Wall Still Stand?: Separation of Church and State in the United States." *Baylor Law Review* 37 (Summer 1985): 755-75.

Doyle, Denis P. "A Din of Inequity: Private Schools Reconsidered." *American Education* 18 (1982): 11-18.

Drakeman, Donald L. "Antidisestablishmentarianism: The Latest (and Longest) Word from the Supreme Court in *Marsh* v. *Chambers.*" *Cardozo Law Review* 5 (Fall 1983): 153-81.

——————. "Prayer in the Schools: Is New Jersey's Moment of Silence Constitutional?" *Rutgers Law Review* 35 (Winter 1983): 341-59.

——————. "Religion and the Republic: James Madison and the First Amendment." *Journal of Church and State* 25 (Autumn 1983): 427-45.

Drinan, Robert F., S.J. "State and Federal Aid to Parochial Schools." *Journal of Church and State* 7 (Winter 1965):67-77.

Dunsford, John E. "Prayer in the Well: Some Heretical Reflections on the Establishment Syndrome." *Utah Law Review* 1984 (1984): 1-44.

Durrant, Matthew B. "Accrediting Church-Related Schools: A First Amendment Analysis." *Journal of Law and Education* 14 (April 1985): 147-79

Ericsson, Samuel E. "Clergy Malpractice: Constitutional and Political Issues." *The Center for Law and Religious Freedom* (May 1981): 1-32.

Esbeck, Carl H. "The Establishment Clause and Liquor Sales: The Supreme Court Rushes In Where Angels Fear to Tread—*Larkin* v. *Grendel's Den.*" *Washington Law Review* 59 (1983-84):87-101.

——————. "Establishment Clause Limits on Governmental Interference With Religious Organizations." *Washington and Lee Law Review* 41 (Spring 1984): 347-420.

——————. "Religion and a Neutral State: Imperative or Impossibility?" *Cumberland Law Review* 15 (1984-1985): 67-88.

"Evolution and Creationism in the Public Schools." *Journal of Contemporary Law* 9 (1983): 81-126.

Fellman, David. "Religion, the State, and the Public University." *Journal of Church and State* 26 (Winter 1984): 73-90.

Flowers, Ronald B. "Can Churches Discipline Members and Win in Court?" *Journal of Church and State* 27 (Autumn 1985): 483-98.

——————. "The Supreme Court's Interpretation of the Free Exercise Clause." *Religion In Life* 49 (Fall 1980): 322-35.

——————. "The Supreme Court's Three Tests of the Establishment Clause." *Religion in Life* 45 (Spring 1976):41-52.

——————. "Withholding Medical Care for Religious Reasons." *Journal of Religion and Health* 23 (Winter 1984): 268-82.

Fordham, Jefferson B. "The Implications of the Supreme Court Decisions Dealing with Religious Practices in the Public Schools." *Journal of Church and State* 6 (Winter 1964):44-60.

Fox, Richard P. "Conscientious Objection to War: The Background and a Current Appraisal." *Cleveland State Law Review* 31 (Winter, 1982): 77-106.

Freund, Paul A. "Public Aid to Parochial Schools." *Harvard Law Review* 82 (June 1969):1680-92.

Fulbright, Linda. "The Great Revenue Forfeiture: Tax Exemption for Religious Property in Texas." In Eugene W. Jones et al. *Practicing Texas Politics*, 4th ed. Boston: Houghton Mifflin Co., 1980 pp. 540-45.

Gaffney, Edward M., Jr. "Political Divisiveness Along Religious Lines: Entanglement of the Court in Sloppy History and Bad Public Policy." *St. Louis University Law Journal* 24 (1980):205-36.

Galanter, Marc. "Religious Freedoms in the United States: A Turning Point?" *Wisconsin Law Review* 1966 (Spring 1966):217-96.

Galligan, Michael William. "Judicial Resolution of Intrachurch Disputes." *Columbia Law Review* 83 (December 1983): 2007-38.

Garrett, W. Barry. "IRS Proposal Scored." *Church and State* 29 (June 1976):10-11.

Garvey, John H. "Freedom and Equality in the Religion Clauses." *Supreme Court Review* 1981 (1981):193-221.

Gaustad, Edwin Scott. "A Disestablished Society: Origins of the First Amendment." *Journal of Church and State* 11 (Autumn 1969):409- 26.

Gavin, Charles O. and Neal Devins. "A Tax Policy Analysis of *Bob Jones University* v. *United States.*" *Vanderbilt Law Review* 36 (November 1983): 1353-82.

Gedicks, Frederick M. "Motivation, Rationality, and Secular Purpose in Establishment Clause Review." *Arizona State Law Journal* 1985 (1985): 677-726.

Giannella, Donald A. "Lemon and Tilton: The Bitter and Sweet of Church-State Entanglement." *Supreme Court Review* 147 (1971): 147- 200.

——————. "Religious Liberty, Nonestablishment, and Doctrinal Development. Part I. The Religious Liberty Guarantee." *Harvard Law Review* 80 (May 1967):1381-1431.

"Government Neutrality and Separation of Church and State: Tuition Tax Credits." *Harvard Law Review* 92 (January 1979):696-717.

Greenawalt, Kent. "Religion as a Concept in Constitutional Law." *California Law Review* 72 (September 1984): 753-816.

Griggs, Walter S., Jr. "The Selective Conscientious Objector: A Vietnam Legacy." *Journal of Church and State* 21 (Winter 1979):91-107.

Hall, Timothy L. "The Sacred and the Profane: A First Amendment Definition of Religion." *Texas Law Review* 61 (August 1982): 139-73.

Hammett, Harold D. "Separation of Church and State: By One Wall or Two?" *Journal of Church and State* 7 (Spring 1965):190-206.

Hanrahan, E.M. "Constitutionality of Legislation Denying Tax-Exempt Status to Racially Discriminatory Schools." *The Catholic Lawyer* 28 (Spring 1983):137- 43.

Horn, Carl III. "Secularism and Pluralism in Public Education." *Harvard Journal of Law and Public Policy* 7 (Winter 1984): 177-83.

Hostetler, John A. "The Amish and the Law: A Religious Minority and Its Legal Encounters." *Washington and Lee Law Review* 41 (Winter 1984):33-47.

Howarth, Don and William D. Connell. "Student Rights to Organize and Meet for Religious Purposes in the University Context." *Valparaiso Law Review* 16 (Fall 1981):103- 43.

Johnson, Phillip E. "Concepts and Compromise in First Amendment Religious Doctrine." *California Law Review* 72 (September 1984): 817-46.

Jones, Harry W. "The Constitutional Status of Public Funds for Church Related Schools." *Journal of Church and State* 6 (Winter 1964):61-73.

Katz, Wilber and Harold P. Southerland. "Religious Pluralism and the Supreme Court." *Daedalus* 96 (Winter 1967):180-92.

Kauper, Paul. "Church, State, and Freedom: A Review." *Michigan Law Review* 52 (April 1954):829-48.

——————. "*Everson v. Board of Education*: A Product of the Judicial Will." *Arizona Law Review* 15 (1973): 307-26.

——————. "Prayer, Public Schools, and the Supreme Court." *Michigan Law Review* 61 (April 1963): 1031-68.

——————. "Released Time and Religious Liberty: A Further Reply." *Michigan Law Review* 53 (November 1954):233-36.

Kelley, Dean M. "A Primer for Pastors: What to Do When the FBI Knocks." *Christianity and Crisis* 37 (2 May 1977):86-92.

——————. "When Religion Is Paid to be Silent." *Worldview* 16 (April 1973):32-7.

Killilea, Alfred G. "Privileging Conscientious Dissent: Another Look at *Sherbert v. Verner*." *Journal of Church and State* 16 (Spring 1974):194-216.

Kirby, James C., Jr. "Everson to Meek and Roemer: From Separation to Detente in Church-State Relations." *North Carolina Law Review* 55 (1977):563-75.

Knight, Barbara B. "Religion in Prison: Balancing the Free Exercise, No Establishment, and Equal Protection Clauses." *Journal of Church and State* 26 (Autumn 1984): 437-54.

Kurland, Philip B. "Of Church and State and the Supreme Court." *University of Chicago Law Review* 29 (Autumn 1961):1- 96.

——————. "The Irrelevance of the Constitution: The Religion Clauses of the First Amendment and the Supreme Court." *Villanova Law Review* 24 (November 1978): 3-27.

——————. "The Religion Clauses and the Burger Court." *Catholic University Law Review* 34 (Fall 1984): 1-19.

Lardner, Lynford A. "How Far Does the Constitution Separate Church and State?" *American Political Science Review* 45 (March 1951):110-32.

"Laws Respecting an Establishment of Religion: An Inquiry into Tuition Tax Benefits." *New York University Law Review* 58 (April 1983):207-37.

Laycock, Douglas. "Tax Exceptions for Racially Discriminatory Religious Schools." *Texas Law Review* 60 (Fall 1982):259-77.

Leavy, Edward N. and Eric A. Raps. "The Judicial Double Standard for State Aid to Church-Affiliated Educational Institutions." *Journal of Church and State* 21 (Spring 1979):209-22.

"The Legal Relationship of Conscience to Religion: Refusals to Bear Arms." *University of Chicago Law Review* 38 (Spring 1971):583-611.

Levit, Nancy. "Creationism, Evolution and the First Amendment: The Limits of Constitutionally Permissible Scientific Inquiry." *Journal of Law and Education* 14 (April 1985): 211-27.

Linder, Robert D. "Civil Religion in Historical Perspective: The Reality That Underlies the Concept." *Journal of Church and State* 17 (Autumn 1975):399-421.

Loewy, Arnold H. "School Prayer, Neutrality, and the Open Forum: Why We Don't Need a Constitutional Amendment." *North Carolina Law Review* 61 (October 1982):141-56.

Louisell, David W. and John H. Jackson. "Religion, Theology and Public Higher Education." *California Law Review* 50 (December 1962):751-99.

"*Lynch v. Donnelly*: Our Christmas Will Be Merry Still." *Mercer Law Review* 36 (Fall 1984): 409-20.

Mansfield, John H. "The Religion Clauses of the First Amendment and the Philosophy of the Constitution." *California Law Review* 72 (September 1984): 847- 907.

"*Marsh v. Chambers*: The Supreme Court Takes a New Look at the Establishment Clause." *Pepperdine Law Review* 11 (March 1984): 591-611.

Marshall, William P. "Solving the Free Exercise Dilemma: Free Exercise as Expression." *Minnesota Law Review* 67 (Fall 1983):545-94.

Mauney, Constance. "Religion and First Amendment Protections: An Analysis of Justice Black's Constitutional Interpretation." *Pepperdine Law Review* 10 (January 1983):377-420.

"*McLean v. Arkansas Board of Education*: Finding the Science in 'Creation Science.'" *Northwestern University Law Review* 77 (October 1982):374-402.

Mead, Sidney E. "The Nation with the Soul of a Church." *Church History* 36 (September 1967):262-83.

——————. "Neither Church nor State: Reflections on James Madison's 'Line of Separation.'" *Journal of Church and State* 10 (Autumn 1968):349-64.

——————. "The Post-Protestant Concept and America's Two Religions." *Religion in Life* 33 (Spring 1964):191-204.

——————. "Religion, Constitutional Federalism, Rights, and the Court." *Journal of Church and State* 14 (Spring 1972):191-210.

Meiklejohn, Donald. "Religion in the Burger Court: The Heritage of Mr. Justice Black." *Indiana Law Review* 10 (1977):645-74.

Michaelsen, Robert. "The Public Schools and 'America's Two Religions.'" *Journal of Church and State* 8 (Autumn 1966):380-400.

——————. "The Supreme Court and Religion in Public Higher Education." *Journal of Public Law* 13 (No. 2 1964):342-52.

Minker, Debra Gail. "Constitutional Law—First Amendment—State University's Policy of Equal Access to Campus Facilities for All Organizations Including Those of a Religious Character Does Not Violate the Establishment of Religion Clause of the First Amendment *Widmar v. Vincent*." *Emory Law Journal* 32 (Winter 1983): 319-48.

Moen, Matthew C. "School Prayer and the Politics of Life-Style Concern." *Social Science Quarterly* 65 (December 1984): 1072-79.

Mott, Kenneth F. "The Supreme Court and the Establishment Clause: From Separation to Accommodation and Beyond." *Journal of Law and Education* 14 (April 1985): 111-45.

Moynihan, Daniel P. "What Do You Do When the Supreme Court Is Wrong?" *The Public Interest* 57 (Fall 1979):3-24.

"*Mueller v. Allen*: A Constitutional Crosswalk to Federal Tuition Tax Credits." *Journal of Legislation* 11 (Winter 1984):163-74.

"*Mueller v. Allen*: The Continued Weakening of the Separation Between Church and State." *New England Law Review* 19 (1983/1984): 459-85.

"*Mueller v. Allen*: Tuition Tax Relief and the Original Intent." *Harvard Journal of Law and Public Policy* 7 (Fall 1984): 551-79.

Munich, John R. "Religious Activity in Public Schools: A Proposed Standard." *St. Louis University Law Journal* 24 (September 1980): 379-405.

Murray, John Courtney, S.J. "Law and Prepossessions?" *Law and Contemporary Problems* 14 (Winter 1949):23-43.

Nagel, Stuart and Robert Erickson. "Editorial Reaction to Supreme Court Decisions on Church and State." *Public Opinion Quarterly* 30 (Winter 1966-67):647-55.

Nathan, Richard. "Reflections on Pragmatic Jurisprudence: A Case Study of *Bob Jones University* v. *United States.*" *American Business Law Journal* 22 (Summer 1984): 227-48.

Newell, Lisa M. "Use of Campus Facilities for First Amendment Activity." *Journal of College and University Law* 9 (No. 1, 1982-83):27-39.

"A Non-Conflict Approach to the First Amendment Religion Clause." *University of Pennsylvania Law Review* 131 (April 1983): 1175-1208.

Nowak, John E. "The Supreme Court, the Religion Clauses and the Nationalization of Education." *Northwestern University Law Review* 70 (January-February 1976):883-909.

O'Hara, Julie U. "State Aid to Sectarian Higher Education." *Journal of Law and Education* 14 (April 1985): 181-209.

Patric, Gordon. "The Impact of a Court Decision: Aftermath of the McCollum Case." *Journal of Public Law* 6 (Fall 1967):455-65.

Pavis, John J. "Compulsory Medical Treatment and Religious Freedom: Whose Law Shall Prevail?" *University of San Francisco Law Review* 10 (Summer 1975):1-35.

Pepper, Stephen L. "The Conundrum of the Free Exercise Clause—Some Reflections on Recent Cases." *Northern Kentucky Law Review* 9 (1982):265-303.

Peterson, Walfred H. "The Thwarted Opportunity for Judicial Activism in Church-State Relations: Separation and Accommodation in Precarious Balance." *Journal of Church and State* 22 (Autumn 1980):437-58.

Pfeffer, Leo. "Court, Constitution, and Prayer." *Rutgers Law Review* 16 (Summer 1962):735-52.

_____. "Freedom and Separation: America's Contribution to Civilization." *Journal of Church and State* 2 (November 1960):100-11.

_____. "Freedom and/or Separation: The Constitutional Dilemma of the First Amendment." *Minnesota Law Review* 64 (March 1980): 561-84.

_____. "What Hath God Wrought to Caesar: The Church as Self-Interest Interest Group." *Journal of Church and State* 13 (Winter 1971):97-112.

_____. "Workers' Sabbath: Religious Belief and Employment." *Civil Liberties Review* 4 (November-December 1977):52-6.

Phenix, Philip H. "Religion in Public Education: Principles and Issues." *Journal of Church and State* 14 (Autumn 1972):415-30.

Piele, Philip K. and Stephen M. Pitt. "The Use of School Facilities by Student Groups for Religious Activities." *Journal of Legal Education* 13 (April 1984): 197-207.

"Political Entanglement as an Independent Test of Constitutionality Under the Establishment Clause." *Fordham Law Review* 52 (May 1984): 1209-41.

Pollak, Louis H. "Public Prayers in Public Schools." *Harvard Law Review* 77 (November 1963):62-78.

"Protecting Religious Exercise: The First Amendment and Legislative Responses to Religious Vandalism." *Harvard Law Review* 97 (December 1983): 547-63.

"Public School Prayer and the First Amendment: Reconciling Constitutional Claims." *Duquesne Law Review* 22 (Winter 1984): 465-78.

Redlich, Norman. "Separation of Church and State: The Burger Court's Tortuous Journey." *Notre Dame Law Review* 60 (1985): 1094-1149.

"The 'Released Time' Cases Revisited: A Study of Group Decision Making by the Supreme Court." *Yale Law Journal* 83 (May 1974):1202-36.

Reinertsen, Gail and Ken Vinson. "Florida's School Prayer Statute: *Wallace* v. *Jaffree* and a Crumbling Wall of Separation." *Florida Bar Journal* 60 (March 1986): 9-14.

"Reinterpreting the Religion Clauses: Constitutional Construction and Conceptions of the Self." *Harvard Law Review* 97 (April 1984): 1468-86.

"Religion and the Law." *Hastings Law Journal* 26 (1978). (The entire volume is devoted to this topic.)

"Religious Expression in the Public School Forum: The High School Student's Right to Free Speech." *Georgia Law Journal* 72 (October 1983):135-60.

"Religious Liberty in the Public High School: Bible Study Clubs." *The John Marshall Law Review* 17 (Summer 1981): 933-67.

"Restoring School Prayer by Eliminating Judicial Review: An Examination of Congressional Power to Limit Federal Court Jurisdiction." *North Carolina Law Review* 60 (April 1982):831-52.

Riggs, Robert E. "Judicial Doublethink and the Establishment Clause: The Fallacy of Establishment by Inhibition." *Valparaiso University Law Review* 18 (Winter 1984): 285-330.

"The Rights of Student Religious Groups Under the First Amendment to Hold Religious Meetings in the Public University Campus." *Rutgers Law Review* 33 (Summer 1981):1008-53.

Ripple, Kenneth F. "The Entanglement Test of the Religion Clauses—A Ten Year Assessment." *UCLA Law Review* 27 (August 1980):1195-1239.

Robbins, Thomas. "New Religious Movements, Brainwashing, and Deprogramming—The View From the Law Journals: A Review Essay and Survey." *Religious Studies Review* 11 (October 1985): 361-70.

Rudd, Myron S. "Toward an Understanding of the Landmark Federal Decisions Affecting Relations between Church and State." *University of Cincinnati Law Review* 36 (Summer 1967):413- 32.

Sauser, Robert W. "State Aid to Nonpublic Sectarian Colleges." *Tennessee Law Review* 44 (Winter 1977):377-88.

Schwarz, Alan. "No Imposition of Religion: The Establishment Clause Value." *Yale Law Review* 77 (March 1968):692-737.

Schwartz, David F. "*Larkin* V. *Grendel's Den, Inc.*: The Burger Court and the Establishment Clause Problem." *Houston Law Review* 21 (January 1984): 179-208.

Sciarrino, Alfred J. " 'Free Exercise' Footsteps in the Defamation Forest: Are 'New Religions' Lost?" *The American Journal of Trial Advocacy* 7 (Fall 1983): 57-121.

Scott, Kenneth E. "Standing in the Supreme Court—A Functional Analysis." *Harvard Law Review* 86 (February 1973):645-92.

"Sectarian Books, the Supreme Court, and the Establishment Clause." *Yale Law Journal* 79 (November 1969):111- 41.

Seeburger, Richard H. "Public Policy Against Religion: Doubting Thomas." *Pepperdine Law Review* 11 (January 1984): 311-30.

Sendor, Benjamin B. "*Congress* v. *The Courts*: Extracurricular Student Religious Groups." *School Law Bulletin* 166 (Spring 1985): 1-5.

Shaman, Jeffrey M. "The Constitution, the Supreme Court, and Creativity." *Hastings Constitutional Law Quarterly* 9 (Winter 1982):257-78.

Shapiro, Robert N. " 'Mind Control' or Intensity of Faith: The Constitutional Protection of Religious Beliefs." *Harvard Civil Rights—Civil Liberties Law Review* 13 (1978):751-797.

_____. "Of Robots, Persons, and the Protection of Religious Beliefs." *Southern California Law Review* 56 (Spring 1983): 1277-1318.

Sheffer, Martin S. "The Free Exercise of Religion and Selective Conscientious Objection: A Judicial Response to a Moral Problem." *Capital University Law Review* 9 (1979):7-29.

Shortt, Bruce Nevin. "The Establishment Clause and Religion—Based Categories: Taking Entanglement Seriously." *Hastings Constitutional Law Quarterly* 10 (Fall 1982):145-185.

Singleton, Marvin K. "Colonial Virginia as First Amendment Matrix: Henry, Madison, and the Establishment Clause." *Journal of Church and State* 8 (Autumn 1966):344-64.

Sirico, Louis J., Jr. "The Secular Contribution of Religion to the Political Process: The First Amendment and School Aid." *Missouri Law Review* 50 (Spring 1985): 321-76.

Slye, Terry L. "Rendering Unto Caesar: Defining 'Religion' for Purposes of Administering Religion-Based Tax Exemptions." *Harvard Journal of Law and Public Policy* 6 (Summer 1983): 219-94.

Smart, James M. "*Widmar* v. *Vincent* and the Purposes of the Establishment Clause." *Journal of College and University Law* 9 (1982-83): 469-83.

Smith, Michael R. "Emerging Consequences of Financing Private Colleges with Public Funds." *Valparaiso University Law Review* 9 (Summer 1973): 561- 610.

_____. "The Special Place of Religion in the Constitution." *1983 Supreme Court Review* (1983): 83-123.

Smith, Rodney K. "Getting Off on the Wrong Foot and Back On Again: A Reexamination of the History of the Framing of the Religion Clauses of the First Amendment and a Critique of the *Reynolds* and *Everson* Decisions." *Wake Forest Law Review* 20 (Fall 1984): 569-642.

——————. "Justice Potter Stewart: A Contemporary Jurist's View of Religious Liberty." *North Dakota Law Review* 59 (1983):183-210.

Smith, W. F. "Some Observations on the Establishment Clause." *Pepperdine Law Review* 11 (March 1984): 457-71.

Sorauf, Frank J. "*Zorach* v. *Clauson*: The Impact of a Supreme Court Decision." *American Political Science Review* 53 (September 1959):777-91.

Stevens, John V., Sr. and John G. Tulio. "Casenote *United States* v. *Lee*, A Second Look." *Journal of Church and State* 26 (Autumn 1984): 455-72.

Stewart, D.O. "Taking Christ Out of Christmas?" *American Bar Association Journal* 69 (December 1983): 1832-37.

Stone, Geoffrey R. "In Opposition to the School Prayer Amendment." *University of Chicago Law Review* 50 (Spring 1983): 823-48.

"Their Life Is in the Blood: Jehovah's Witnesses, Blood Transfusions, and the Courts." *Northern Kentucky Law Review* 10 (1983):281-304.

"The Supreme Court, Effect Inquiry, and Aid to Parochial Education." *Stanford Law Review* 37 (Fall 1984): 219-51.

"Title VII and Sectarian Institutions of Higher Education: Congress Shall Make No Law Prohibiting Free Exercise of Religion." *Cumberland Law Review* 14 (1983/1984): 597-641.

"Toward a Constitutional Definition of Religion." *Harvard Law Review* 91 (March 1978):1056-89.

Treiman, David. "Religion In the Public Schools." *Northern Kentucky Law Review* 9 (1982):229-63.

"*United States* v. *Lee*: Has the Retreat Been Sounded for Free Exercise?" *Stetson Law Review* 12 (Spring 1983): 852-64.

"The Unconstitutionality of State Statutes Authorizing Moments of Silence in the Public Schools." *Harvard Law Review* 96 (June 1983): 1874-93.

"The United States Military Chaplaincy Program: Another Seam in the Fabric of our Society?" *Notre Dame Law Review* 59 (1983): 181-223.

"The Unseen Regulator: The Role of Characterization in First Amendment Free Exercise Cases." *Notre Dame Law Review* 59 (1984): 978-1004.

Van Alstyne, William W. "Constitutional Separation of Church and State: The Quest for a Coherent Position." *American Political Science Review* 57 (December 1963):865-82.

Van Patten, Jonathan. "In the End Is the Beginning: An Inquiry Into the Meaning of the Religion Clauses." *St. Louis University Law Journal* 27 (Fall 1983): 1-93.

Walker, Robert S. "What Constitutes a Religious Use for Zoning Purposes?" *The Catholic Lawyer* 27 (Spring 1982):129-83.

"*Wallace* v. *Jaffree*: The Lemon Test Sweetened." *Houston Law Review* 22 (October 1985): 1273-92.

Warner, Carolyn. "Where There is No Vision: The Death of Public and Private Education in America." *Vital Speeches of the Day* 49 (1983): 215.

Way, Frank and Barbara J. Burt. "Religious Marginality and the Free Exercise Clause." *American Political Science Review* 77 (September 1983):652-65.

Way, H. Frank, Jr. "Survey Research on Judicial Decisions: The Prayer and Bible Reading Cases." *Western Political Quarterly* 12 (June 1968):189-205.

Weber, Francis J. "American Church-State Relations: A Catholic View." *Journal of Church and State* 7 (Winter 1965):30-4.

Weber, T.J. "Constitutional Law—Establishment Clause—Supreme Court Upholds Direct Noncategorical Grants to Church- Affiliated Colleges." *Fordham Law Review* 45 (March 1977):979-92.

Weiss, Jonathon. "Privilege, Posture and Protection: 'Religion' in the Law." *Yale Law Journal* 73 (March 1964):593-623.

Whitehair, J. Greg. "Teaching the Theories of Evolution and Scientific Creationism in the Public Schools: The First Amendment Religion Clauses and Permissible Relief." *Journal of Law Reform* 15 (Winter 1982):421-63.

Williams, J.D. "The Separation of Church and State in Mormon Theory and Practice." *Journal of Church and State* 9 (Spring 1967):238-62.

Wood, James E., Jr. "Equal Access: A New Direction in American Public Education." *Journal of Church and State* 27 (Winter 1985): 5-17.

——————. "Religion and America's Public Schools." *Journal of Church and State* 9 (Winter 1967):5-16.

——————. "Religion and Education in American Church-State Relations." *Journal of Church and State* 26 (Winter 1982): 421- 63.

——————. "Editorial: Religious Pluralism and American Society." *Journal of Church and State* 27 (Autumn 1985): 393-401.

——————. "Tax Exemption and the Churches." *Report from the Capital* 31 (April 1976): 2, 4.

Worthing, Sharon L. "The Internal Revenue Service As a Monitor of Church Institutions: The Excessive Entanglement Problem." *Fordham Law Review* 45 (March 1977):929-48.

——————. " 'Religion' and 'Religious Institutions' Under the First Amendment." *Pepperdine Law Review* 7 (1980): 313-53.

——————. "The State and the Church School: The Conflict Over Social Policy." *Journal of Church and State* 26 (Winter 1984): 91-104.

"Zoning Ordinances Affecting Churches: A Proposal for Expanded Free Exercise Protection." *University of Pennsylvania Law Review* 132 (June 1984): 1113-62.

There are eight regularly published periodicals completely devoted to church-state concerns: *Church and State*, published every month except August by Americans United for Separation of Church and State, 8120 Fenton Street, Silver Spring, Maryland 20910.

Focus, published monthly by the Christian Legal Society, P.O. Box 1492, Merrifield, Virginia 22116. Each issue is devoted to a particular topic in the church-state field.

Journal of Church and State, published three times a year by the J.M. Dawson Institute of Church-State Studies, Baylor University, Waco, Texas 76798.

The Journal of Law and Religion, published twice a year at the Hamline University School of Law, 1536 Hewitt Avenue, St. Paul, Minnesota 55104.

LIBERTY: A Magazine of Religious Freedom, published bimonthly by the Review and Herald Publishing Association, 6856 Eastern Avenue, N.W., Washington, D.C. 20012.

Religion and Public Education, published quarterly by the National Council on Religion and Public Education, 1300 Oread, Lawrence, Kansas 66045.

Religious Freedom Reporter, published monthly by the Christian Legal Society, P.O. Box 1492, Merrifield, Virginia 22116, is a compilation of up-to-date information on current litigation and periodical articles in the field.

Report from the Capital, published ten months per year by the Baptist Joint Committee on Public Affairs, 200 Maryland Avenue, N.E., Washington, D.C. 20002.

GLOSSARY OF LEGAL
TERMS AND PHRASES

ADVISORY OPINION. An opinion given by a court as to the constitutionality or legal effect of a law although no actual case or controversy is before it. In several states the highest court is authorized to give such opinions at the request of the governor or the legislature, but federal judges do not render advisory opinions.

AMICUS CURIAE. "Friend of the court." A person or group that, while not directly involved in the litigation, is granted permission by the court to enter into judicial proceedings before it in order to present information which will aid the court in its decision.

APPEAL. The procedure by which the losing party takes a case to a higher court for review. A superior court is called on to correct error or injustice on the part of a lower court in interpreting or applying a law. Cases brought to the Supreme Court on appeal are a matter of right. Statutes designate the specific grounds for appeal.

APPELLANT. The party that takes an appeal from a lower to a higher court.

APPELLEE. The party in a litigation against which an appeal is taken.

BRIEF. A document prepared by counsel to serve as the basis for argument before a court. It contains the points of law, arguments, and precedents the counsel desires to present in a case before the court.

CERTIORARI, WRIT OF. "To be informed of"; "to be certain in regard to." A writ issued at the discretion of an appellate court ordering a lower court to send up the record of a case for review so that the higher court can make certain that the court correctly applied the law. Issuance of the writ is completely discretionary, and four members of the Supreme Court must agree before the writ will be issued.

CLASS ACTION. A suit brought by one or more persons on behalf of themselves and all other persons similarly situated.

COMMON LAW. That body of Anglo-Saxon law which originated and developed in England. It is to be distinguished from the Roman, or code, law. It is also distinguished from statutory law in that it is judge-made law based on customary law in different parts of England which over the years became common to all England. There is no federal common law, but federal judges apply the state common law in cases involving citizens of different states if there is no applicable federal statutory provision.

DECLARATORY JUDGMENT. A judicial declaration by means of which, in an actual controversy, the legal rights of parties under a law, contract, or other legal document can be determined before a wrong has been committed or is immediately threatened. No declaratory process or specific order follows the determination of the court.

DEFENDANT. The party against which relief or recovery is sought in a case.

DIVERSITY OF CITIZENSHIP. Cases between citizens of different states. By statute, Congress has given state courts exclusive jurisdiction in such cases if less than $10,000 is involved. State and federal courts have concurrent jurisdiction if more than $10,000 is involved in the litigation.

EQUITY. A branch of law which is intended to provide a just remedy when the common law or statute law will not. It includes such remedies as prevention of threatened damage by means of an injunction or the assurance of an action by means of a writ of specific performance.

ERROR, WRIT OF. A writ issued by an appellate court to an inferior court directing that the records of a case in which that court has made final judgment be sent to the higher court for review. This was a frequently used procedure for seeking review by the Supreme Court prior to 1925, but it has not been used since then.

EX REL. "Upon relation or information." Used in the title of a case to indicate the person at whose instigation and on the basis of whose information the appropriate public official is acting.

FEDERAL QUESTION. A case which contains an issue involving the United States Constitution, an act of Congress, or a United States treaty.

INDICTMENT. A formal written accusation drawn by the prosecutor and brought by a grand jury charging one or more persons with the commission of a crime.

INJUNCTION. An equity writ ordering a person or group to refrain from performing some specific act.

IN RE. "In the matter of"; "concerning." A judicial proceeding may be thus entitled when there are no adversary parties but rather a thing or object concerning which judicial action is to be taken, such as an estate which is to be probated.

INTER ALIA. "Among other things."

MANDAMUS, WRIT OF. "We command." A court order directing a designated public official, lower court, corporation, or individual to perform a specific act.

OBITER DICTUM. A statement made in a court opinion that is not necessary or pertinent to the decision of the case at hand. In theory, it is not binding on courts in future cases.

PER CURIAM. "By the court." The term is used to distinguish an unsigned opinion of the whole court from an opinion written by a particular member of the court. It is usually very brief.

PETITIONER. The party that brings an action. The party that appeals to a court on a writ of certiorari.

PLAINTIFF. The party that brings an action; the complainant.

PLURALITY OPINION. An opinion that is referred to as the opinion of the court in a case but is actually not the opinion of a majority of the members participating in the decision. Any justice is free to write a separate concurring opinion in which he agrees with the result reached but takes issue with the line of reasoning applied or seeks to clarify the majority holding.

POLITICAL QUESTION. A question which a court refuses to decide because it is held to involve constitutional issues that can be resolved more effectively by the legislative or executive branches. The doctrine is most often advanced when a court decision might result in conflict with the other branches or when it would be difficult to enforce. It may be used to avoid a particularly controversial issue.

RESPONDENT. In appellate jurisdiction, the party that contends against an appeal. The party against which a writ of certiorari is sought.

STANDING TO SUE. In order to be able to bring an action in federal court against a government officer, the plaintiff must show that the interest he presents is personal, substantial, and legally protected, and that his interest has been injured or is in direct danger of injury from government.

TABLE OF
SUPREME COURT OPINIONS

This table lists Supreme Court justices who have written opinions printed in this volume. Justices have been listed alphabetically, and cases have been arranged by categories for quick reference. Years in parentheses indicate each justice's period of service on the Court. All opinions listed, except those that have been specifically identified as either concurring or dissenting, were the majority opinions of the Court.

For all justices except those most recently appointed, a reference has been given to biographical information in *The Justices of the United States Supreme Court: Their Lives and Major Opinions*, ed. Leon Friedman and Fred L. Israel, 5 vols. (New York: Chelsea House Publishers, 1969-1978). This source is abbreviated *J.U.S.S.C.* in the table. Brief biographical sketches of each justice also are found in *CQ Guide to Current American Government, Spring 1985* (New York: Congressional Quarterly, Inc., 1985), pp. 126-131. For information concerning new appointments to the Court, the reader should consult this semi-annually published source.

Church Exercising a Government Function
  Larkin v. *Grendel's Den*
Church Taxation
  Walz v. *Tax Commission*
Compulsory Education
  Wisconsin v. *Yoder*
Devotional Exercises in Public Schools
  Wallace v. *Jaffree* (dissenting)
Government Financed Nativity Scene
  Lynch v. *Donnelly*
Labor Relations (including sabbatarian concerns)
  Thomas v. *Review Board of the Indiana Employment Security Commission*
  Thornton v. *Caldor*
Prohibition of Ministers in Politics
  McDaniel v. *Paty*
Religious Test for Public Benefits
  Bowen v. *Roy*
Standing
  Bender v. *Williamsport* (dissenting)
State Supported Chaplains
  Marsh v. *Chambers*
Tax Exemption
  Bob Jones University v. *United States*
  United States v. *Lee*
BUTLER, PIERCE (1922-1939): *J.U.S.S.C.*, vol. 3, pp. 2183-2191.
  Conscientious Objection
  Hamilton v. *Regents of the University of California*
  United States v. *Schwimmer*
CARDOZO, BENJAMIN (1932-1938): *J.U.S.S.C.*, vol. 3, pp. 2287-2307.
  Conscientious Objection
  Hamilton v. *Regents of the University of California* (concurring)
CLARK, TOM C. (1949-1967): *J.U.S.S.C.*, vol. 4, pp. 2665-2676.
  Conscientious Objection
  United States v. *Seeger*
Devotional Exercises in Public Schools
  Abington School District v. *Schempp*
CLIFFORD, NATHAN (1858-1881): *J.U.S.S.C.*, vol. 2, pp. 963-975.
  Church Property
  Watson v. *Jones* (dissenting)
DOUGLAS, WILLIAM O. (1939-1975): *J.U.S.S.C.*, vol. 4, pp. 2447-2470, vol. 5, pp. 201-204.
  Aid to Parochial Schools
  Lemon v. *Kurtzman* (concurring)
  Tilton v. *Richardson* (dissenting in part)
  Church Taxation
  Walz v. *Tax Commission* (dissenting)
  Compulsory Education
  Wisconsin v. *Yoder* (dissenting in part)
  Conscientious Objection
  Gillette v. *United States* (dissenting)
  Girouard v. *United States*
  United States v. *Seeger* (concurring)

Devotional Exercises in Public Schools
  Abington School District v. *Schempp* (concurring)
  Engel v. *Vitale* (concurring)
Labor Relations (including sabbatarian concerns)
  Sherbert v. *Verner* (concurring)
Proselytizing on Public Property
  Murdock v. *Pennsylvania*
Released Time
  Zorach v. *Clauson*
Standing
  Flast v. *Cohen* (concurring)
Sunday Closing Laws
  McGowan v. *Maryland* (dissenting)
Test of Faith
  United States v. *Ballard*
Textbook Loan
  Board of Education v. *Allen* (dissenting)
FIELD, STEPHEN J. (1863-1897): *J.U.S.S.C.*, vol. 2, pp. 1069-1089.
  Mormon Polygamy
  Davis v. *Beason*
FORTAS, ABE (1965-1969): *J.U.S.S.C.*, vol. 4, pp. 3015-3027.
  Standing
  Flast v. *Cohen* (concurring)
  Teaching Evolution in Schools
  Epperson v. *Arkansas*
  Textbook Loan
  Board of Education v. *Allen* (dissenting)
FRANKFURTER, FELIX (1939- 1962): *J.U.S.S.C.*, vol. 3, pp. 2401-2419.
  Church Property
  Kedroff v. *St. Nicholas Cathedral* (concurring)
  Flag Salute
  Minersville School District v. *Gobitis*
  West Virginia Board of Education v. *Barnette* (dissenting)
  Proselytizing on Public Property
  Murdock v. *Pennsylvania* (dissenting)
  Released Time
  McCollum v. *Board of Education* (separate opinion)
  Zorach v. *Clauson* (dissenting)
  Sunday Closing Laws
  McGowan v. *Maryland* (separate opinion)
GOLDBERG, ARTHUR J. (1962-1965): *J.U.S.S.C.*, vol. 4, pp. 2977-3090.
  Devotional Exercises in Public Schools
  Abington School District v. *Schempp* (concurring)
HARLAN, JOHN M. (1955-1971): *J.U.S.S.C.*, vol. 4, pp. 2801-2820, vol. 5, pp. 215-224.
  Taxation
  Walz v. *Tax Commission* (concurring)
  Conscientious Objection
  Welsh v. *United States* (concurring)
  Employment on the Sabbath
  Sherbert v. *Verner* (dissenting)

Larkin v. *Grendel's Den* (dissenting)
Church Property
  Serbian Eastern Orthodox Diocese v. *Milivojevich* (dissenting)
Devotional Exercises in Public Schools
  Stone v. *Graham* (dissenting)
  Wallace v. *Jaffree* (dissenting)
Labor Relations (including sabbatarian concerns)
  Ohio Civil Rights Commission v. *Dayton Christian Schools*
  Thomas v. *Review Board of the Indiana Employment Security Division* (dissenting)
  Thornton v. *Caldor* (dissenting without opinion)
Religion in the Military
  Goldman v. *Weinberger*
Standing
  Valley Forge Christian College v. *Americans*
United State Regulation of Church Solicitation
  Larson v. *Valente* (dissenting)
Tax Exemption
  Bob Jones University v. *United States* (dissenting)
ROBERTS, OWEN J. (1930-1945): *J.U.S.S.C.*, vol. 4, pp. 2253- 2263.
  Proselytizing on Public Property
    Cantwell v. *Connecticut*
RUTLEDGE, WILEY (1943-1949): *J.U.S.S.C.*, vol. 4, pp. 2593-2601.
  Aid to Parochial Schools
    Everson v. *Board of Education* (dissenting)
  Proselytizing on Public Property
    Prince v. *Massachusetts*
STEVENS, JOHN PAUL (1975-): *J.U.S.S.C.*, vol.5, pp. 149-162.
  Aid to Parochial Schools
    Committee for Public Education and Religious Liberty v. *Regan* (dissenting)
    Roemer v. *Board of Public Works of Maryland* (dissenting)
    Wolman v. *Walter* (concurring and dissenting)
  Devotional Exercises in Public Schools
    Wallace v. *Jaffree*
  Devotional Exercises in Public Universities
    Widmar v. *Vincent* (concurring)
  Labor Relations (including sabbatarian concerns)
    Ohio Civil Rights Commission v. *Dayton Christian Schools* (concurring)
  Religion in the Military
    Goldman v. *Weinberger* (concurring)
  Religious Tests for Public Benefits
    Bowen v. *Roy* (concurring)
  Standing
    Valley Forge Christian College v. *Americans United* (dissenting)
  State Regulation of Church Solicitation
    Larson v. *Valente* (concurring)
  State Supported Chaplains

Marsh v. *Chambers* (dissenting)
Tax Exemption
  United States v. *Lee* (concurring)
STEWART, POTTER (1958-1981): *J.U.S.S.C.*, vol. 4, pp. 2921- 2938.
  Aid to Parochial Schools
    Meek v. *Pittenger*
    Roemer v. *Board of Public Works of Maryland* (dissenting)
  Compulsory Education
    Wisconsin v. *Yoder* (concurring)
  Devotional Exercises in Public Schools
    Abington School District v. *Schempp* (dissenting)
    Engel v. *Vitale* (dissenting)
  Employment on the Sabbath
    Sherbert v. *Verner* (concurring)
  Prohibition of Ministers in Politics
    McDaniel v. *Paty* (concurring)
  Sunday Closing Laws
    Braunfeld v. *Brown* (dissenting)
  Teaching Evolution in Schools
    Epperson v. *Arkansas* (concurring)
STONE, HARLAN F. (Assoc. Justice, 1925-1941; Chief Justice, 1941-1946): *J.U.S.S.C.*, Vol. 3, pp. 2221-2237.
  Flag Salute
    Minersville School District v. *Gobitis* (dissenting)
  Proselytizing on Public Property
    Jones v. *Opelika* (dissenting)
  Test of Faith
    United States v. *Ballard* (dissenting)
SUTHERLAND, GEORGE (1922-1938): *J.U.S.S.C.*, vol. 3, pp. 2133-2143.
  Conscientious Objection
    United States v. *Macintosh*
WAITE, MORRISON R. (Chief Justice, 1874-1888): *J.U.S.S.C.*, vol. 2, pp. 1243-1257).
  Mormon Polygamy
    Reynolds v. *United States*
WARREN, EARL (Chief Justice, 1953-1969): *J.U.S.S.C.*, vol.4, pp.2721-2746.
  Standing
    Flast v. *Cohen*
  Sunday Closing Laws
    Braunfeld v. *Brown*
    McGowan v. *Maryland*
WHITE, BYRON R. (1962-): *J.U.S.S.C.*, vol. 4, pp. 2951-2961.
  Aid to Religious Vocations
    Witters v. *Washington Department of Services for the Blind* (concurring)
  Aid to Parochial Schools
    Aguilar v. *Felton* (dissenting)
    Committee for Public Education and Religious Liberty v. *Nyquist* (dissenting)
    Committee for Public Education and Religious Liberty v. *Regan*
    Grand Rapids School District v. *Ball* (dissenting)

604

TABLES OF CASES

Listed in the following tables are Supreme Court cases printed in this volume (titles in capital letters) and many, but not all, of the Supreme Court and lower court cases cited by the Court in its church-state decisions. The tables provide readers with the full citations of these legal sources, with the locations of references to these cases and with the location of the first page of a printed opinion. Page numbers in regular print indicate where cases are referred to in the essay portions or in the cases themselves. A page number in **boldface** indicates the beginning page of each opinion printed herein.

Supreme Court Cases

A

ABINGTON TOWNSHIP SCHOOL DISTRICT v. SCHEMPP, 374 U.S. 203 (1963), 27, 143, 148, 149, 163, 164, 177, 190, 214, 243, 244, 247, 282, 285, 288, 291, 334, 341, 350, 351, 354, 356, 357, 362, 369, 371, 372, 380, 381, **402**, 430, 432-434, 440, 443-445, 448, 450, 475, 476, 491, 492, 494, 507, 510, 516, 517, 535, 536

AGUILAR v. FELTON, 105 S.Ct. 3237 (1985), 245, 246, 456-458, **559**, 573

Alamo Foundation v. *Secretary of Labor*, 471 U.S. 290 (1985), 324

Allen v. *Wright*, 104 S.Ct. 3315, rehearing desired 105 S.Ct. 51 (1984), 248

Arver v. *United States (Selective Draft Law Cases)*, 245 U.S. 366 (1918), 105

Ashwander v. *TVA*, 297 U.S. 288 (1936), 347

Associated Press v. *National Labor Relations Board*, 301 U.S. 103 (1937), 329, 330

B

Bain Peanut Co. v. *Pinson*, 282 U.S. 499 (1931), 309

Baker v. *Carr*, 369 U.S. 186 (1962), 262-264, 339

Barlow v. *Collins*, 397 U.S. 159 (1970), 269

Barron v. *Baltimore*, 7 Peters 243 (1833), 4, 162

BENDER v. WILLIAMSPORT AREA SCHOOL DISTRICT, 106 S.Ct. 1326 (1986), 199, 248, **270**, 381, 382

Benz v. *Compania Naviera Hidalgo*, 353 U.S. 138 (1957), 327

Berea College v. *Kentucky*, 211 U.S. 45 (1908), 460

Berman v. *United States*, 329 U.S. 795 (1946), 128

BOARD OF EDUCATION v. ALLEN, 392 U.S. 236 (1968), 214, 280, 342, 362, 433, 450, 453, 454, 456, **474**, 482-485, 489, 491, 493, 494, 499, 500, 502, 507, 509, 511-514, 516, 517, 519, 523-526, 529-531, 538, 539, 541, 543-546, 549, 550, 553-555, 558, 572

BOB JONES UNIVERSITY v. UNITED STATES, 461 U.S. 574 (1983), 190, 196, 217, **222**

Bond v. *Floyd*, 385 U.S. 116 (1966), 177

Bouldin v. *Alexander*, 82 U.S. 131 (1872), 37, 38, 42

BOWEN v. ROY, 106 S.Ct. 2147 (1986), 170, **187**

Bradfield v. *Roberts*, 175 U.S. 291 (1899), 265, 392, 412, 499, 529

Brandon v. *Holt*, 469 U.S. 464 (1985), 272

BRAUNFELD v. BROWN, 366 U.S. 599 (1961), 59, 142, 143, 146-151, 157, 162, 164, 192, 199, 205, 208, 220, 221, 291, 299, 302, 306, 307, 312, **316**, 442

Brown v. *Board of Education*, 347 U.S. 483 (1954), 197, 208, 225, 226, 427, 488

Brown v. *Glines*, 444 U.S. 348 (1980), 168

Brown v. *Hotel Employees*, 468 U.S. 491 (1984), 165

Bullock v. *Carter*, 405 U.S. 134 (1972), 178

C

California v. *LaRue*, 409 U.S. 109 (1972), 333

CANTWELL v. CONNECTICUT, 310 U.S. 296 (1940), 4, 18, 56, 57, **60**, 66, 70, 98, 136, 148, 162, 171, 174, 176, 177, 236, 243, 286, 351, 405, 414, 425, 426, 436

Carlson v. *California*, 310 U.S. 106 (1940), 98

Carey v. *Brown*, 447 U.S. 455 (1980), 211, 212

Cassius Marsellus Clay, Jr. also known as Muhammad Ali v. *United States*, 404 U.S. 698 (1971), 59

Chaplinsky v. *New Hampshire*, 315 U.S. 568 (1942), 58, 76

Chappell v. *Wallace*, 462 U.S. 296 (1983), 180, 182, 187

Chicago and Grand Trunk Railway Co. v. *Wellman*, 143 U.S. 339 (1892), 259, 260

Chicago, B. & Q. Rail Co. v. *Chicago*, 166 U.S. 226 (1897), 286

Christian Echoes National Ministry v. *United States*, 414 U.S. 864 (1973), 216

Church of Jesus Christ of Latter-Day Saints v. *United States*, 136 U.S. 1 (1890), 49

Church of the Holy Trinity v. *United States*, 143 U.S. 457 (1892), 372

City of Madison Joint School District v. *Wisconsin Public Employment Relations Commission*, 429 U.S. 167 (1976), 211

Cleveland v. *United States*, 329 U.S. 14 (1946), 49

COCHRAN v. LOUISIANA STATE BOARD OF EDUCATION, 281 U.S. 370 (1930), 242, 247, 392, 412, 453, **460**, 476

Coleman v. *Griffen*, 302 U.S. 636 (1937), 56

Commissioner v. *"Americans United," Inc.*, 416 U.S. 752 (1974), 230

COMMITTEE FOR PUBLIC EDUCATION AND RELIGIOUS LIBERTY v. NYQUIST, 413 U.S.

Lower Court Cases